TEXT-SUPPORTING WEB SITES

✱ THOMSON ONE—BUSINESS SCHOOL EDITION

Use the Thomson ONE academic online database to solve Get Real with Thomson ONE problems.

Thomson ONE BSE is a product developed for Thomson Financial's Investment Banking Group, combining a full range of fundamental financials, earnings estimates, market data and source documents for 500 domestic and international companies.

Most of these reports can be easily downloaded to Excel. Some statements and reports span 10 years.

This is an opportunity for students to access the tool and apply data that brokers and analysts use every day to do research!

✱ BESLEY SUPPORT WEB SITE

The Besley Web site, HTTP://BESLEY.SWLEARNING.COM, provides students with:

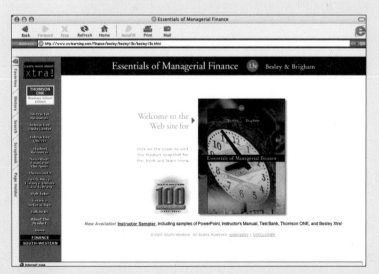

- Open access to online quizzes with immediate scoring feedback;

- Direct links to text Internet addresses and activities;

- Downloadable learning support tools and spreadsheet models, and

- Much more.

Essentials of
Managerial Finance

THIRTEENTH EDITION

SCOTT BESLEY
University of South Florida

EUGENE F. BRIGHAM
University of Florida

THOMSON
SOUTH-WESTERN

Australia • Canada • Mexico • Singapore • Spain • United Kingdom • United States

THOMSON
SOUTH-WESTERN

Essentials of Managerial Finance
Thirteenth Edition
Scott Besley
Eugene F. Brigham

VP/Editorial Director:
Jack W. Calhoun

VP/Editor-in-Chief:
Mike Roche

Executive Editor:
Mike Reynolds

Senior Developmental Editor:
Trish Taylor

Marketing Manager:
Heather MacMaster

Production Editor:
Cliff Kallemeyn

Manager of Technology, Editorial:
Vicky True

Technology Project Editor
John Barans

Manufacturing Coordinator:
Doug Wilke

Production House:
Shepherd Inc.

Printer:
RR Donnelley & Sons
Willard OH

Design Project Manager:
Rik Moore

Cover Design:
John Robb
JWR Design Interaction, LLC

Cover Photos:
© PhotoDisc, Inc.

For permission to use material from this text or product, submit a request online at http://www.thomsonrights.com.

For more information
contact South-Western,
5191 Natorp Boulevard,
Mason, Ohio 45040.
Or you can visit our Internet site at:
http://www.swlearning.com

✳ BRIEF CONTENTS

✳ CONTENTS

Essentials of Managerial Finance is intended for use in introductory finance courses. The book begins with a discussion of basic concepts, including security markets, interest rates, time value of money, risk analysis, and the basics of security valuation. Subsequent chapters explain how financial managers can help maximize their firms' values by improving decisions in such areas as capital budgeting, choice of capital structure, and working capital management. This organization has three important advantages:

1. Early in the book we explain how financial markets operate and how security prices are determined. This shows students how managerial finance can affect the value of the firm. Also, early coverage of such key concepts as time value, risk analysis, and valuation techniques permits their use and reinforcement throughout the remainder of the book.
2. The book is structured around markets and valuation, which helps students see how the various topics relate to one another.
3. Most students—even those who do not plan to major in finance—are interested in stock and bond valuation, rates of return, and other similar topics. Because learning is a function of interest and motivation, and because *Essentials* begins by showing the relationships between security markets, stock values, and managerial finance, this organization works well from a pedagogic standpoint.

Now in its thirteenth edition, *Essentials* has grown over the course of time, especially with respect to the long list of practical and theoretical developments it covers. On the recommendations of reviewers, we have restructured the discussion of a few topics that have been melded into *Essentials* that, because of level or simply the primary objectives of an introductory course in managerial finance, might be considered more appropriate for a more advanced book. We did not categorically omit these topics; rather, we placed some of them—such as modified internal rate of return and using interest tables to solve time value of money problems—in appendices to offer instructors the option of covering the topics in the course.

RELATIONSHIP WITH OUR OTHER BOOKS

As the field of finance has expanded, it first became difficult, then impossible, to provide everything one needs to know about managerial finance in one text, especially an introductory text. This recognition has led us to limit the scope of this book and also to write other texts to deal with the materials that cannot be included in *Essentials*. *Principles of Finance* provides a more general coverage of the subject of finance than *Essentials*. *Principles of Finance* gives a survey of finance as a field of study by covering three major subject areas: (1) financial markets and institutions; (2) investments; and (3) managerial finance. Also, Eugene Brigham and Phillip Daves have coauthored an intermediate undergraduate text (*Intermediate Financial Management*, Eighth Edition), and Eugene Brigham and Michael Ehrhardt have coauthored a comprehensive book aimed primarily at MBAs (*Financial Management: Theory and Practice*, Tenth Edition).

The relationship between *Essentials* and the more advanced books deserves special comment. First, we recognize that the advanced books are often used by students who have also used *Essentials* in the introductory finance course, so we have avoided excessive overlap while exposing students to alternative points of view on controversial subjects.

We should note, though, that students in advanced courses invariably tell us that they find it helpful to have the more difficult materials repeated—they need the review. Students also find that the style and notation used in our upper-level books are consistent with those in the introductory text—this makes learning easier. Regarding alternative points of view, we take a moderate, middle-of-the-road approach, and where serious controversy exists, we present the alternative points of view. Reviewers were asked to consider this point, and their comments have helped us eliminate potential biases.

INTENDED MARKET AND USE

As noted previously, *Essentials* is intended for use as an introductory textbook. The key chapters can be covered in a one-term course; or supplemented with cases and some outside readings, the book can also be used in a two-term course. If it is used in a one-term course, the instructor probably will cover only selected chapters, leaving the others for students either to examine on their own or to use as references in conjunction with work in later courses. Also, we wrote the chapters in a flexible, modular format to help instructors cover the material in a different sequence should they choose to do so.

MAJOR CHANGES IN THE THIRTEENTH EDITION

The theory and practice of finance are dynamic, and as new developments occur, they should be incorporated into a textbook such as this one. Also, working with a team of reviewers, we are constantly looking for ways to improve the book in terms of clarity and student understanding. As a result, some important changes appear in this edition, the most important of which are discussed here.

Time Value of Money, Risk, and Valuation Concepts

The coverage of these important topics now occurs much earlier in the book. Part II of the book ("Essential Concepts of Managerial Finance") includes chapters relating to time value of money (Chapter 3), risk and rates of return (Chapter 4), and general valuation concepts (Chapter 5). Moving these chapters to the front of the book allows us to emphasize the concept of valuation and the financial manager's goal of value maximization throughout the book. Because this is one of the most important concepts of finance, covering these concepts early is essential.

Capital Budgeting, Cost of Capital, and Capital Structure

The coverage of these topics now occurs earlier in the book. Capital budgeting is discussed immediately following Part II, "Essential Concepts of Managerial Finance." Positioning capital budgeting at this point in the book adds to the continuity of the general thread that is emphasized throughout the book—valuation.

Multinational Finance Coverage

Our reviewers suggested that we meld coverage of multinational finance into the chapters where the specific topics are covered rather than have a separate chapter devoted to multinational managerial finance. Thus, we have included updated coverage of multinational finance throughout the book where appropriate.

A Managerial Perspective and Industry Practice

Although boxed business anecdotes are not new to this edition of *Essentials*, we want to draw attention to them because each is either new to this edition or updated since the previous edition. Each chapter leads off with "A Managerial Perspective," which can be used for student reading, for class lecture, or for both. The "Industry Practice" boxes show the application of the concepts in real-world situations. Where possible, we have included in the "Industry Practice" boxes an indication of to what extent the methods discussed in the chapters are actually used by businesses in the "real world." In addition, the "Ethical Dilemmas" expose students to the relationship between ethics and business, promote critical thinking and decision-making skills, and provide interesting vehicles for class discussion.

Thomson ONE

Each chapter includes a problem from Thomson ONE, a powerful interactive database of financial information developed by Thomson Financial. These problems require students to apply the concepts discussed in the chapter using real-world data, which helps them to develop real-world critical thinking skills.

ANCILLARY MATERIALS

A number of items are available free of charge to adopting instructors:

1. Instructor's Manual. The comprehensive manual contains answers to all text questions and problems, detailed solutions to integrative problems, sample exam questions, and suggested course outlines.
2. Lecture Presentation Software. To facilitate classroom presentations, computer graphics slide shows written in Microsoft PowerPoint are available. One set of slides features the essential topics presented in each chapter and the other set includes more detailed lecture notes.
3. Test Bank. The Test Bank contains more than 1,000 class-tested questions and problems. True/false questions, multiple choice conceptual questions, multiple choice problems (which can be easily modified to short-answer problems by removing the answer choices), and financial calculator problems are included for every chapter. The Test Bank is available in computerized format, featuring the computerized test bank program ExamView. ExamView has many features that allow the instructor to modify test questions, select items by key words, scramble tests for multiple sections, and test completely on the computer.
4. Problem Diskette. A diskette containing models for the computer-related end-of-chapter problems is also available.
5. Web Site. A book-designated Web site with numerous resources for instructors and students can be accessed through http://besley.swlearning.com.
6. WebTutor Toolbox and WebTutor Advantage: WebTutor Toolbox provides instructors with text-specific content that interacts in the two leading Course Management Systems available in Higher Education—WebCT and Blackboard. WebTutor Advantage delivers innovative learning aids that actively engage students. Benefits include automatic and immediate feedback from quizzes; multimedia-rich concept review tutorials; streaming video applications; online exercises; and greater interaction and involvement through online discussion

forums. Powerful Instructor tools are also provided to assist communication and collaboration between students and faculty.

A number of additional items are available for purchase by students:

1. **Study Guide.** This supplement outlines the key sections of each chapter, provides students with self-test questions, and also provides a set of problems and solutions similar to those in the text and in the Test Bank. Because many instructors use multiple-choice exams, we include coverage of exam-type questions and problems in the Study Guide.
2. **Cases.** *Cases in Financial Management*, TextChoice by Thomson Custom Publishing, by Eugene F. Brigham and Lin Klein, is well suited for use with *Essentials*. The cases provide real-world applications of the methodologies and concepts developed in this book. In addition, all of the cases are available in a customized format, so your students pay only for the cases you decide to use.
3. **Spreadsheet Analysis Book.** *Financial Analysis with Microsoft Excel*, by Timothy Mayes and Todd Shank, fully integrates the teaching of spreadsheet analysis with the basic finance concepts. This book makes a good companion to *Essentials* in courses in which computer work is highly emphasized.
4. **Blueprints.** This supplement consists of the Lecture Presentation Software slides in a printed format in order to facilitate note taking in the classroom.
5. **Besley Xtra!.** Xtra! is our interactive study assistant especially developed for the Besley/Brigham text. It includes E-Lectures, Ask the Author Video, The Problem Bank, CNN Video, Xtra! Quizzing and more with a new book purchase. If an Instructor has elected to have an Xtra! Passport packaged with the text, see more at http://besleyxtra.swlearning.com.

ACKNOWLEDGMENTS

This book reflects the efforts of a great many people over a number of years. For the thirteenth edition, we are indebted to the following professors who provided their input for improving the book: George Y Andrea, University of Baltimore; Dean Balm, Pepperdine University; Bruce Costa, University of Montana, Missoula; Robert, M. Hull, Washburn University School of Business; Keith Jokob, University of Montana; Gregory Koutmous, Dolan School of Business, Fairfield University; Iihan Meric, Rider University; William E. O'Connell, Jr., College of William and Mary; Rakash Sah, Montana State University, Billings; Hersh Shefrin, Santa Clara University; Andrew Spieler, Hofstra University; David Suk, Rider University; David Zalewaki, Providence College.

Next, we would like to thank the following professors, whose reviews and comments have helped prior editions and our companion books: Mike Adler, Syed Ahmad, Ed Altman, Bruce Anderson, Ron Anderson, Bob Angell, Vince Apilado, Henry Arnold, Bob Aubey, Gil Babcock, Peter Bacon, Kent Baker, William Baker, Robert Balik, Tom Bankston, Les Barenbaum, Charles Barngrover, Bill Beedles, Yvett M. Bendeck, Moshe Ben-Horim, Bill Beranek, Tom Berry, Will Bertin, Dan Best, Roger Bey, Douglas Bible, Dalton Bigbee, John Bildersee, Russ Boisjoly, Keith Boles, Geof Booth, Jerry Boswell, Kenneth Boudreaux, Helen Bowers, Oswald Bowlin, Don Boyd, G. Michael Boyd, Pat Boyer, Joe Brandt, Elizabeth Brannigan, Greg Brauer, Mary Broske, Dave Brown, Kate Brown, Bill Brueggeman, Stephen G. Buell, Ted Byrley

Bill Campsey, Stephen Caples, Bob Carlson, Severin Carlson, David Cary, Steve Celec, Don Chance, Antony Chang, Susan Chaplinsky, Jay Choi, S. K. Choudhary, Shin-

Herng Michelle Chu, Lal Chugh, Maclyn Clouse, Margaret Considine, Paul F. Conway, Phil Cooley, Joe Copeland, David Cordell, Marcia Cornett, M. P. Corrigan, John Cotner, Charles Cox, David Crary, John Crockett, Jr., Roy Crum, Ed Daley, Brent Dalrymple, Bodie Dickerson, Bernard Dill, J. David Diltz, Gregg Dimkoff, Les Dlabay, Mark Dorfman, Gene Drzycimski, Dean Dudley, David Durst, Ed Dyl, Richard Edelman, Charles Edwards, John Ellis, Dave Ewert, John Ezell, Michael Ferri, Jim Filkins, John Finnerty, Susan Fischer, Steven Flint, Russ Fogler, Gordon Foster, Dan French

Michael Garlington, David Garraty, Jim Garven, Adam Gehr, Jr., Jim Gentry, Philip Glasgo, Rudyard Goode, Walt Goulet, Bernie Grablowsky, Theoharry Grammatikos, Reynold Griffith, Ed Grossnickle, John Groth, Alan Grunewald, Manak Gupta, Sam Hadaway, Don Hakala, Paul Halpern, Gerald Hamsmith, William Hardin, John Harris, Paul Hastings, Bob Haugen, Steve Hawke, Del Hawley, Robert Hehre, George Hettenhouse, Hans Heymann, Kendall Hill, Roger Hill, Tom Hindelang, Linda Hittle, Ralph Hocking, J. Ronald Hoffmeister, Robert Hollinger, Jim Horrigan, John Houston, John Howe, Keith Howe

Steve Isberg, Jim Jackson, Kose John, Craig Johnson, Keith Johnson, Ramon Johnson, Ray Jones, Frank Jordan, Manual Jose, Alfred Kahl, Gus Kalogeras, Mike Keenan, Bill Kennedy, James Keys, Carol Kiefer, Joe Kiernan, Rick Kish, Don Knight, Dorothy Koehl, Jaroslaw Komarynsky, Duncan Kretovich, V. Sivarama Krishnan, Harold Krogh, Charles Kroncke, Don Kummer, Joan Lamm, Larry Lang, P. Lange, Howard Lanser, John Lasik, Edward Lawrence, Martin Lawrence, Judy Maese, Bob Magee, Douglas Leary, Ileen Malitz, Phil Malone, Lewis Mandell, Terry Maness, Chris Manning, S. K. Mansinghka, Iqbal Mansur, Terry Martell, D. J. Masson, John Mathys, John McAlhany, Andy McCollough, Ambrose McCoy, Thomas McCue, Bill McDaniel, John McDowell, Charles McKinney, Robyn McLaughlin, Jamshid Mehran, Larry Merville, Massoud Metghalchi, Rick Meyer, Jim Millar, Ed Miller, John Mitchell, Carol Moerdyk, Bob Moore, Barry Morris, Gene Morris, Fred Morrissey, Chris Muscarella, David Nachman, Tim Nantell, Charlie Narron, Don Nast, Bill Nelson, Bob Nelson, Bob Niendorf, Gladson Nwanna Wayne Lee, Jim LePage, Jules Levine, John Lewis, Jason Lin, Chuck Linke, Bill Lloyd, Susan Long

Tom O'Brien, Dennis O'Connor, John O'Donnell, Jim Olsen, Robert Olsen, Jim Pappas, Stephen Parrish, Phil Pennell, Glenn Petry , Jim Pettijohn, Rich Pettit, Dick Pettway, Hugo Phillips, H. R. Pickett, John Pinkerton, Gerald Pogue, Eugene Poindexter, Ralph Pope, R. Potter, Franklin Potts, R. Powell, Chris Prestopino, Jerry Prock, Howard Puckett, Herbert Quigley, George Racette, Bob Radcliffe, Murli Rajan, Jim Reinemann, Bill Rentz, Ken Riener, Charles Rini, John Ritchie, Robert Ritzcovan, Pietra Rivoli, Antonio Rodriguez, James Rosenfeld, E. N. Roussakis, Dexter Rowell

Jim Sachlis, Abdul Sadik, Thomas Scampini, Kevin Scanlon, Frederick Schadler, John D. Schatzberg, Mary Jane Scheuer, Carl Schweser, David Scott, John Settle, Alan Severn, Ramesh Shah, Sol Shalit, Frederic Shipley, Dilip Shome, Ron Shrieves, Neil Sicherman, J. B. Silvers, Clay Singleton, Joe Sinkey, Stacy Sirmans, Jaye Smith, Patricia Smith, Steve Smith, Don Sorensen, David Speairs, Ken Stanly, Ed Stendardi, Alan Stephens, Don Stevens, Jerry Stevens, Glen Strasburg, Philip Swensen, Ernest Swift, Paul Swink, Gary Tallman, Dular Talukdar, Dennis Tanner, Craig Tapley, Russ Taussig, John Teall, Richard Teweles, Ted Teweles, Francis C. Thomas, Andrew Thompson, John Thompson, Dogan Tirtiroglu, Marco Tonietti, William Tozer, George Trivoli, Randy Trostle, George Tsetsekos, Ricardo Ulivi, David Upton, Howard Van Auken, Pretorious Van den Dool, Pieter Vandenberg, Paul Vanderheiden, JoAnn Vaughan, Jim Verbrugge, Patrick Vincent, Steve Vinson, Susan

Visscher, Gautam Vora, John Wachowicz, Mike Walker, Sam Weaver, Kuo-Chiang Wei, Bill Welch, Robert J. Wiley, Norm Williams, Tony Wingler, Ed Wolfe, Don Woods, Sally Jo Wright, Michael Yonan, Dennis Zocco, and Kent Zumwalt.

Special thanks are due to Dana Aberwald Clark, who worked closely with us in developing the Study Guide, and Rosemary Carlson, Morehead State University, who developed the Thomson ONE problems that are included at the ends of the chapters. Also, Louis Gapenski helped develop the integrative problems and offered advice on many other parts of the book.

ERRORS IN THE TEXT

At this point, most authors make a statement like this: "We appreciate all the help we received from the people listed above, but any remaining errors are, of course, our own responsibility." And generally there are more than enough remaining errors! Having experienced difficulty with errors ourselves, both as students and as instructors, we resolved to avoid this problem in *Essentials*. As a result of our error-detection procedures, we are convinced that it is relatively free of significant mistakes that either confuse or distract readers.

Partly due to our confidence that there are few errors in this book, but primarily because we want to correct any errors that might exist in this printing of the book, we offer a reward of $10 per error to the first person who reports it to us. For purposes of this reward, errors are defined as misspelled words, computation errors (not including rounding differences), errors in finance content and facts, and other errors that inhibit comprehension. Typesetting errors, such as spacing, or differences in opinion concerning grammatical or punctuation convention do not qualify for the reward. Also, because Internet addresses sometimes change, changes in Web addresses do not qualify as errors. However, we would like to know about such changes; so please send them to us. Updated Web addresses are regularly posted to the book's Web site at http://besley.swlearning.com. Finally, any qualifying error that has a follow-through effect is counted as two errors only. Errors should be reported to Scott Besley either via e-mail at sbesley@coba.usf.edu or by regular mail at the address given below.

CONCLUSION

Finance is, in a real sense, the cornerstone of the enterprise system—good financial management is vitally important to the economic health of business firms, and hence to the nation and the world. Because of its importance, finance should be widely and thoroughly understood, but this is easier said than done. The field is relatively complex, and it is undergoing constant change in response to shifts in economic conditions. All of this makes finance stimulating and exciting but also challenging and sometimes perplexing. We sincerely hope that *Essentials* will meet its own challenge by contributing to a better understanding of our financial system.

Scott Besley
College of Business Administration, BSN3403
University of South Florida
4202 E. Fowler Avenue
Tampa, FL 33620-5500

Eugene F. Brigham
College of Business
University of Florida
Gainesville, FL 32611-7160

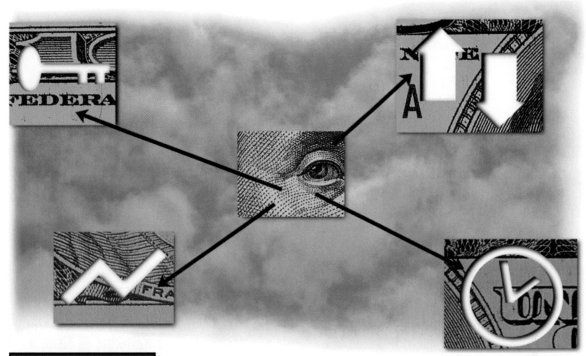

PART I

Introduction to Managerial Finance

CHAPTER 1

An Overview of Managerial Finance

Top executive shares salary bonus with management. What a novel idea! That's exactly what IBM's chief executive officer (CEO), Sam Palmisano, did. At the beginning of 2003, Mr. Palmisano asked the board of directors to use a large portion of the bonus he expected to earn that year to reward managers for their efforts to maximize IBM's value. Mr. Palmisano might not have used the words "maximize value," but you can bet that is what he meant. According to estimates, Mr. Palmisano was giving up between $3 million and $5 million. The plan was to share the "bonus money" with approximately 20 top executives based on their performance as part of a new three-team group that was formed to merge people and their ideas from throughout the company in an effort to return IBM to the top of its game and the prominence it enjoyed as the industry leader prior to the 1990s.

In 2003, Mr. Palmisano shook up IBM's bureaucratic structure by replacing the existing elitist, 12-person Corporate Executive Committee with three teams representing all employees. The purpose of the three-team group was to develop strategies and advise the CEO to help map IBM's future. The three teams—operating, strategy, and technology—could bring ideas from all areas of the company. In addition to top management, the teams included lower-level managers, engineers, and other employees who were most knowledgeable about company operations. Mr. Palmisano insisted that the company should operate as a team that strived to achieve a common goal. He defined success as a product of unity and the cooperative efforts of persons working in concert rather than pursuing individual agendas. Mr. Palmisano's attitude was that bureaucracy and red tape are roadblocks on the path to greatness.

To be a leader in any industry, a company must have foresight and flexibility to adapt as conditions change. Because the technology industry is dynamic, IBM tries to stay at least one step ahead of its competitors in research and development and the introduction of new technology. Mr. Palmisano hopes that IBM will redefine the current revolution in information technology with its innovative e-business on demand, or "utility computing." The plan is to offer computing power to businesses just as electric power is offered to businesses and individuals and thus improve the efficiency of the information technologies used by companies in various industries. The general premise is that companies have different needs, both in terms of software and computing capacity, than is available on most computers or information systems. E-business on demand could be used to customize the information technology to the needs of each company, thereby eliminating much of the waste that currently exists with the more standardized technology. Customers who subscribe to e-business on demand would simply connect to IBM's system, much as we do to access the Internet, and use whatever computing power they need for a fee. IBM's goal is to develop a network that can be used by companies in various industries to complete computing tasks, such as product research and sales forecasting. According to company forecasts, the improved efficiency that e-business on demand is expected to produce will decrease costs associated with providing information technology services significantly, perhaps by 50 percent. For this venture to succeed, IBM must function as a team; employees in operations, technology, finance, sales, research and development, and all other areas must work together to operate as one.

Although this book deals with managerial finance, keep in mind that no one area of a company can operate on its own. A company consists of many functional areas, such as operations, information technology, and sales and marketing, and these various areas must strive for a common goal. As you read this chapter, keep in mind that, as Mr. Palmisano hopes to prove to his constituents at IBM, excellence in any company requires teamwork, not individuality. Toward that end, regardless of your major in business, you should have some knowledge of other majors so that you can understand the blueprint of the company team. ∎

Sources: Spencer E. Ante, "The New Blue," *BusinessWeek*, March 17, 2003, 80–88, and Steve Hamm, "Utility Computing: Just Turn on the Data," *BusinessWeek*, August 25, 2003, 96–98.

"Why should I study finance?" As a student, you might be asking yourself this question right now. To answer this question, let's consider two other questions: (1) What is finance? and (2) What role does finance play in the successful operation of a firm?

In simple terms, finance is concerned with decisions about money, or more appropriately, cash flows. Finance decisions deal with how businesses, governments, and individuals raise and use money. As we will see in this chapter and in the chapters that follow, proper financial management helps any business provide better products to its customers at lower prices, pay higher salaries to its employees, and still deliver greater returns to investors who put up the funds needed to form and operate the business. Because the economy—both national and worldwide—consists of customers, employees, and investors, sound financial management contributes to the well-being of both individuals and the general population.

This chapter provides an overview of managerial finance. After you finish it, you should have a reasonably good idea of how knowledge of finance is used in the business world. You should also have a better understanding of some of the forces that affect managerial finance, both currently and in the future.

The Importance of Finance in Nonfinance Areas

The primary reason you must have some knowledge of finance is that you will be exposed to finance concepts almost every day, even in your personal life. When you borrow to buy a car or house, finance concepts are used to determine the monthly payments you are required to make. When you retire, finance concepts are used to determine the amount of the payments you receive from your retirement plan. If you want to start your own business, an understanding of finance concepts is essential for survival. Thus, even if you do not intend to pursue a career in a finance-related profession, it is important that you have some basic understanding of finance concepts.

If you pursue a career in finance, it is important that you have an understanding of marketing, accounting, and related fields to make more informed decisions about whether to replace or expand plant and equipment and how best to finance the firm. If you pursue a career in a nonfinance profession, however, consider how you will be exposed to finance concepts on the job.

Management

When we think of management, we often think of personnel decisions and employee relations, strategic planning, and the general operations of the firm. In each of these areas, finance concepts are important. For example, such personnel decisions as setting salary, hiring new staff, and paying bonuses must be coordinated with financial decisions to ensure any needed funds are available. Strategic planning, which is one of the most important activities of management, cannot be accomplished without considering how such plans impact the overall financial well-being of the firm. For these reasons, managers must have at least a general understanding of financial management concepts to make informed decisions in their areas.

Marketing

If you have taken a basic marketing course, probably one of the first things you learned was that the *four Ps of marketing*—product, price, place, and promotion—determine whether the products that are manufactured and sold by companies are successful. Clearly, the price that should be charged for a product and the amount of advertising a firm can afford for the product must be determined in conjunction with financial managers, because the firm will lose money if the price of the product is too low or too much is spent on advertising. Coordination of the finance function and the marketing function is critical to corporate success, especially for small, newly formed firms, because it is necessary to ensure firms generate sufficient cash to survive. For these reasons, people in marketing must understand how marketing decisions affect and are affected by such issues as funds availability, inventory levels, and excess plant capacity.

Information Systems

Businesses thrive on many forms of information, which must be reliable and available when needed for making decisions. The process by which the delivery of such information is planned, developed, and implemented is costly, but so are problems caused by the lack of timely, accurate information. Without appropriate information, decisions relating to finance, management, marketing, and accounting could prove disastrous. Information system specialists work with financial managers to determine what information is needed, how information should be stored, how information should be delivered, and what impact information management has on the firm's financial position.

Accounting

In many firms, especially small ones, it is difficult to differentiate between the finance function and the accounting function. Often, accountants make financial decisions, and vice versa, because the two disciplines are closely related. In fact, you might recognize some of the material covered in this book from accounting courses you have already taken. As you will discover, financial managers rely heavily on accounting information because decisions about the future require information about the past. As a result, it is important that accountants understand how financial managers use accounting information in planning and decision making so they can provide this data in an accurate and timely fashion. Similarly, accountants must understand how accounting data are viewed by investors, creditors, and other outsiders who are interested in the firm's operations. As we progress through this text, you will see distinctive differences between accounting and finance. The primary difference is that we emphasize cash flows in finance whereas accounting generally emphasizes profits, which are based on the matching of revenues and expenses. Because profits are determined using the *matching principle*, or **accrual accounting methods,** the cash flows associated with profits are not necessarily "recognized" at the same time as the profits are earned. In finance, however, we are concerned with how decisions about the firm's future affect its value, which, as you will discover, is based on the timing of the cash flows the firm is expected to generate in the future.

ACCRUAL ACCOUNTING METHODS
Accounting procedures used to match revenues earned in a particular period with appropriate expenses.

Economics

Finance and economics are so similar that some universities and colleges offer courses related to these areas in the same department or functional area. Many tools used to make financial decisions evolved from theories or models developed by economists. Perhaps the most noticeable difference between finance and economics is that financial managers evaluate information and make decisions about cash flows associated with a particular firm or a small group of firms, whereas economists analyze information and forecast changes in activities associated with entire industries and the economy as a whole. It is important that financial managers understand economics and that economists understand finance—economic activity and policy impact financial decisions, and vice versa.

As you can tell, finance will be a part of your life no matter what career you choose. During your life, both in business and in a personal capacity, you will make finance-related decisions. It is important, therefore, that you have some understanding of general finance concepts. *There are financial implications in virtually all business decisions, and nonfinancial executives simply must know enough finance to incorporate these implications into their own specialized analyses.* For this reason, every student of business, regardless of his or her major, should be concerned with finance.

Self-Test Question

Why do persons in areas outside financial management need to know something about managerial finance?

Career Opportunities in Finance

The study of finance consists of three interrelated areas: (1) *financial markets,* which deal with many of the topics covered in macroeconomics; (2) *investments,* which focus on the decisions of individuals and financial and other institutions as they choose securities for their investment portfolios; and (3) *managerial finance,* or "business finance," which involves the actual management of the firm. Although our concern in this text is primarily with managerial finance, these areas are interrelated, so an individual who works in any one area should have a good understanding of the other areas as well. The career opportunities within each field are many and varied. This section offers a general idea of the areas in which finance graduates can expect to work.

Financial Markets and Institutions

Many finance majors go to work for financial institutions. These organizations, which include banks, insurance companies, savings and loans, and credit unions, are an integral part of the financial services marketplace. To succeed in the financial services industry, one must understand the factors that cause interest rates to rise and fall, the regulations to which financial institutions are subject, and the various types of financial instruments, such as mortgages, auto loans, and certificates of deposit. One also needs a general knowledge of all aspects of business administration, because the management of a financial institution involves accounting, marketing, personnel, and computer systems as well as managerial finance.

Investments

Finance graduates who enter the investments field generally work for stock brokerage firms, financial institutions, investment companies, or insurance companies. The three main functions in the investments area are (1) selling, (2) analyzing individual securities, and (3) determining the optimal mix of securities for a given investor. As a finance graduate, you might get a job performing any one or some combination of these tasks. Even if you do not go into a career that has a direct link to finance, a basic understanding of the subject is necessary to evaluate the performance of your personal investments, such as retirement funds, in which you have a choice about where your contributions are invested.

The investments area fascinates most individuals, because we constantly hear about investors who started with little and turned their investments into fortunes. But, as you read this book, you will find that there is great risk in investments, which means investors can lose substantial amounts just as easily as they can gain. Basic knowledge of finance will help you understand how to (1) review companies and industries to determine their prospects for future growth and ability to maintain the safety of your investment, (2) determine how much risk you are willing to take with your investment position, and (3) evaluate how well your investments are performing so you can better ensure your funds are invested "appropriately."

Managerial Finance

Managerial finance, which is the broadest of the three areas and the one with the greatest number of job opportunities, deals with decisions that firms make concerning their cash flows. The types of tasks encountered in managerial finance jobs range from making decisions about plant expansions to choosing what types of securities to issue to finance expansion. Financial managers also have the responsibility for deciding under which credit terms customers can buy, how much inventory the firm should carry, how much cash to keep on hand, whether to acquire other firms (merger analysis), and how much of the firm's earnings to reinvest in the business and how much to pay out as dividends.

Regardless of which area you might enter, you will need some knowledge of the other areas. For example, a banker lending to businesses must have a good understanding of managerial finance to judge how well a business is operated. The same holds true for a securities analyst. Even stockbrokers must understand general financial principles if they are to give intelligent advice to their customers. At the same time, corporate financial managers need to know what their bankers are thinking about and how investors are likely to judge their corporations' performances and thus determine their stock prices.

Self-Test Questions

What are the three main areas of finance?

If you plan to work in one area of finance, why is it necessary that you know something about the other areas?

Financial Evolution during the Past Century[1]

When managerial finance emerged as a separate field of study in the early 1900s, the emphasis was on the legal aspects of mergers and acquisitions, the formation of new firms, and the various types of securities firms could issue to raise funds. This was a time when industrialization was sweeping the country; "big" was equated to power, so many takeovers and mergers were used to create large corporations. To illustrate the sentiment of the times, consider the fact that almost 4,300 companies were merged into 300 corporations from 1890 to 1905. The most famous merger was the combination of eight large steel companies to form U.S. Steel Corporation. The deal was worth $1.4 billion, which was equivalent to 7 percent of the country's gross national product at the time. In today's economy, a comparable merger would be valued at more than $730 billion.

Another wave of mergers occurred during the 1920s, fueled primarily by consolidations within the utilities industry. During the depression era of the 1930s, however, an unprecedented number of business failures caused the emphasis in managerial finance to shift to bankruptcy and reorganization, to corporate liquidity, and to regulation of securities markets. During this period, new rules were enacted that required firms to maintain and publicly disclose certain financial information.

Even with the frenzy of mergers in the early 1900s and the 1920s and the large numbers of bankruptcies that followed the Great Depression in the 1930s, finance was mostly a descriptive discipline that emphasized organizational relationships of firms and legal matters. For the most part, finance theory consisted of anecdotes and "rules of thumb." During the 1940s and early 1950s, finance continued to be taught as a descriptive, institutional subject, viewed more from the standpoint of an outsider than from that of management. Financial managers emphasized liquidity—cash budgeting and management of short-term assets and liabilities were stressed. At the same time, the scope of financial management began to widen somewhat, primarily because the responsibilities associated with proper liquidity management included

---

[1]For an excellent discussion of the evolution of finance in the 20th century, see J. Fred Weston, "A (Relatively) Brief History of Finance Ideas," *Financial Practice and Education* (Spring/Summer 1994), 7–26.

knowledge of accounts receivable activities, manufacturing operations, and short-term financing alternatives.

In the late 1950s and the 1960s, increased competition in established industries reduced the profit opportunities available to corporations. Financial managers shifted their focus toward techniques used to evaluate investment opportunities. Emphasis was given to finding investments that would improve the firm's ability to generate future profits. During the same period, the computer was introduced as a tool for general business use. The focus of managerial finance began to shift more toward the insider's point of view and the importance of financial decision making to the firm. A movement toward theoretical analysis began during the 1960s, and the emphasis of managerial finance shifted to decisions regarding the choice of assets and liabilities necessary to maximize the firm's value. This era is considered the birth of modern finance, from which many of the decision-making techniques we use today evolved.

The 1970s was a period of increased international competition, fast-paced innovation and technological changes, and, perhaps most important, persistent inflation and economic uncertainty fueled by deficits in government spending and in international trade. Changes in the business arena saw the beginning of a financial revolution of sorts in the late 1970s. Firms discovered innovative ways to manage financial risk and finance their operations. Stockholders became more concerned with how firms were managed and how managers' actions affected the firm's value.

The focus on valuation increased during the 1980s and 1990s. At the same time, financial analysis was expanded to include (1) inflation and its effects on business decisions; (2) deregulation of financial institutions and the resulting trend toward large, broadly diversified financial services companies; (3) the dramatic increase in the use of computers for both analysis and the electronic transfer of information; (4) the increased importance of global markets and business operations; and (5) innovations in the financial products offered to investors.

In today's fast-paced, technologically driven world, the area of managerial finance continues to evolve. The most important trends from the 1990s that have continued into the new millennium include (1) the continued globalization of business, (2) a further increase in the use of electronic technology, and (3) the regulatory attitude of the government.

The Globalization of Business

Four factors have made the trend toward globalization mandatory for most large businesses:

1. Improvements in transportation and communications have lowered shipping costs and made international trade more feasible.
2. The political clout of consumers who desire low-cost, high-quality products has helped lower trade barriers designed to protect inefficient, high-cost domestic manufacturers.
3. As technology advances, the cost of developing new products increases, and, as development costs rise, so must unit sales if the firm is to be competitive.
4. In a world populated with multinational firms able to shift production to wherever costs are lowest, a firm whose manufacturing operations are restricted to one country cannot compete unless costs in its home country happen to be low, a condition that does not necessarily exist for many U.S. corporations.

As a result of these four factors, survival requires that most manufacturers produce and sell globally. Later in this chapter we discuss international business and multinational financial management in greater detail.

Service companies, including banks, advertising agencies, and accounting firms, also are being forced to "go global," because such firms can better serve their multinational clients if they have worldwide operations. The most dynamic growth and the best opportunities are often with companies that operate worldwide. Some purely domestic companies will continue to operate in a single country. Even these companies, however, are affected by global events because of the interrelationships among the world's marketplaces. For example, as we saw in the late 1990s, economic catastrophes in Asia caused American investors to become skittish and the U.S. financial markets to become much more uncertain than before these events. Also, as funds flow among countries, interest rates are affected, which in turn affects the rates at which you and I can borrow and invest. As a result, knowledge of business conditions around the world is required to make informed decisions, even in businesses that only operate domestically.

Information Technology

Since the late 1970s, when the personal computer was introduced, an information technology revolution has been evident. Companies have networks of personal computers linked to one another, to the firm's own central computers, and to their customers' and suppliers' computers. Many companies conduct much of their business online by (1) using video conferencing to meet with colleagues in distant places, (2) requiring suppliers to be linked electronically so that orders and payments can be made via the computer, and (3) providing customers with electronic access to account information, such as the status of orders. Clearly, we will see continued advances in the use of electronic technology in managerial finance, and this technology will revolutionize the way financial decisions are made, just as it has in the past.

One result of this "electronic revolution" that we have seen during the past couple decades is the increased use of quantitative analysis via computer models for financial decision making. As a result, it is clear that the next generation of financial managers will need stronger computer and quantitative skills than were required in the past. In addition, financial managers will need a greater understanding of the effects future technological changes will impose on the competitive arena in which their firms operate. Electronic commerce, for example, has allowed consumers to shop in faraway places from the comfort of their homes or to comparison-shop for the best deals. In essence, consumers can now shop in "virtual malls" all around the world. As a result, electronic commerce has compelled companies to sell their products at competitive prices, which often are lower than would exist in a less competitive market. At the same time, the cost of doing business generally is lower via electronic commerce. Thus, financial managers must understand how technological advancements affect their companies' financial positions.

Regulatory Attitude of the Government

During the past 20 years, the government has taken fairly friendly positions through legislative enactments and regulatory enforcements affecting businesses. Much of the legislation has focused on deregulation of highly regulated industries, including financial services, transportation, communications, and utilities. In addition, for the most part, the government has not discouraged mergers and acquisitions, since 1985, record numbers of mergers at historically high values have taken place. In the late 1980s and most of the 1990s, economic conditions generally were favorable, as evidenced by record levels posted by the stocks markets. Generally, the government is business friendly when the economy prospers and consumer/investor friendly when the economy sours. In the first couple years of the new millennium, the New York Stock Exchange declined because economic conditions were poor. During that period, legislation was introduced in Congress in an effort to better protect investors and provide future stability in the financial markets. When economic conditions cause significant losses of wealth in the securities markets, you can bet many will blame the deregulation that occurred during the last two decades of the 20th century, which will result in a movement toward reregulation. Historically, after the country has experienced economic tragedy, cries for new, tougher regulations have been abundant, and for the most part, Congress has obliged.

Self-Test Questions

How has managerial finance changed since the early 1900s?

How do you think managerial finance will change in the future?

Alternative Forms of Business Organization

There are three main forms of business organization: (1) proprietorships, (2) partnerships, and (3) corporations. In terms of numbers, approximately 71 percent of businesses are operated as proprietorships, nearly 9 percent are partnerships, and the remaining 20 percent are corporations. Based on the dollar value of sales, however, almost 85 percent of all business is conducted by corporations, while the remaining 15 percent is generated by both proprietorships and partnerships.[2] Because most business is conducted by corporations, we will focus on this form in this book. However, it is important to understand the differences among the three forms.

Proprietorship

PROPRIETORSHIP
An unincorporated business owned by one individual.

A **proprietorship** is an unincorporated business owned by one individual. Starting a proprietorship is fairly easy—just begin business operations. In many cases, however, even the smallest business must be licensed by the municipality (city, county, or state) in which it operates.

The proprietorship has three important advantages:

1. It is easily and inexpensively formed.
2. It is subject to few government regulations.
3. It is taxed like an individual, not a corporation; thus earnings are only taxed once.

---

[2]The statistics provided in this section are based on business tax filings reported by the Internal Revenue Service (IRS). Additional statistics can be found on the IRS Web site at http://www.irs.ustreas.gov/tax_stats.

The proprietorship also has four important limitations:

1. The proprietor has *unlimited personal liability* for business debts, which can result in losses that exceed the money he or she has invested in the company.
2. A proprietorship's life is limited to the time the individual who created it owns the business.
3. Transferring ownership is somewhat difficult; disposing of the business is similar to selling a house in that the proprietor must seek out and negotiate with a potential buyer.
4. It is difficult for a proprietorship to obtain large sums of capital, because the firm's financial strength generally is based on the financial strength of the sole owner.

For these reasons, individual proprietorships are confined primarily to small business operations. In fact, only about 1 percent of all proprietorships have assets that are valued at $1 million or greater; nearly 90 percent have assets valued at $100,000 or less. However, most large businesses start out as proprietorships and then convert to corporations when their growth causes the disadvantages of being a proprietorship to outweigh the advantages.

Partnership

PARTNERSHIP

An unincorporated business owned by two or more persons.

A **partnership** is the same as a proprietorship, except that it has two or more owners. Partnerships can operate under different degrees of formality, ranging from informal, oral understandings to formal agreements filed with the secretary of the state in which the partnership does business. Most legal experts would recommend that partnership agreements be put in writing.

The advantages of a partnership are the same as for a proprietorship:

1. Formation is easy and relatively inexpensive.
2. It is subject to few government regulations.
3. It is taxed like an individual, not a corporation.

The disadvantages are also similar to those associated with proprietorships:

1. Unlimited liability for the owners.
2. Limited life of the organization.
3. Difficulty of transferring ownership.
4. Difficulty of raising large amounts of capital.

Regarding liability, the partners can potentially lose all of their personal assets, even those assets not invested in the business. Under partnership law each partner is liable for the business's debts. Therefore, if any partner is unable to meet his or her pro rata claim in the event the partnership goes bankrupt, the remaining partners must make good on the unsatisfied claims, drawing on their personal assets if necessary. Thus, the business-related activities of any of the firm's partners can bring ruin to the other partners, even though those partners were not a direct party to such activities. For example, the partners of the national accounting firm Laventhol and Horwath, a huge partnership that went bankrupt at the end of 1992 as a result of suits filed by investors who relied on faulty audit statements, learned all about the perils of doing business as a partnership. They discovered that a Texas partner who audited a savings and loan that went under could bring ruin to a millionaire New York partner who never went near the S&L. Early in this decade, other national accounting firms were trying to avoid a similar demise as a result of auditing practices linked to the misreporting of financial information of Enron, Tyco International, and WorldCom MCI.[3]

The first three disadvantages—unlimited liability, impermanence of the organization, and difficulty of transferring ownership—lead to the fourth, the difficulty partnerships have in attracting substantial amounts of funds. This is not a major problem for a slow-growing business. But if a business's products really catch on and it needs to raise large amounts of funds to capitalize on its opportunities, the difficulty in attracting funds becomes a real drawback. For this reason, growth companies such as Microsoft and Dell Computer generally begin life as proprietorships or partnerships, but at some point they find it necessary to convert to corporations.

Corporation

CORPORATION
A legal entity created by a state, separate and distinct from its owners and managers, having unlimited life, easy transferability of ownership, and limited liability.

A **corporation** is a legal entity created by a state. It is separate and distinct from its owners and managers. This separateness gives the corporation four major advantages:

1. A corporation can continue after its original owners and managers no longer have a relationship with the business; thus it is said to have *unlimited life.*
2. Ownership interests can be divided into shares of stock, which in turn can be *transferred far more easily* than can proprietorship or partnership interests.
3. A corporation offers its owners *limited liability.* To illustrate the concept of limited liability, suppose you invested $10,000 to become a partner in a business that subsequently went bankrupt, owing creditors $1 million. Because the owners are liable for the debts of a partnership, you could be assessed for a share of the company's debt; you could even be held liable for the entire $1 million if your partners could not pay their shares. This is the danger of unlimited liability. On the other hand, if you invested $10,000 in the stock of a corporation that then went bankrupt, your potential loss on the investment would be limited to your $10,000 investment.[4]
4. The first three factors—unlimited life, easy transferability of ownership interest, and limited liability—make it much easier for corporations than for proprietorships or partnerships to raise money in the financial markets.

---

[3]It is possible to limit the liability faced by some of the partners by establishing a *limited partnership,* wherein one (or more) partner is designated the *general partner* and the others are *limited partners.* The general partner(s) remains fully personally liable for all business debts, whereas the limited partners are only liable for the amounts they have invested in the business. Limited partnerships are quite common in the area of real estate investment, but they do not work well with most other types of businesses, including accounting firms, because one partner rarely is willing to assume all of the business's risk. Not long ago, the national accounting firms reorganized themselves as limited liability partnerships (LLP), which are partnerships in which only the assets of the partnership and the "engagement" partner (partner in charge of the particular case) are at risk.

[4]In the case of small corporations, the limited liability feature is often a fiction, because bankers and credit managers frequently require personal guarantees from the stockholders of small, weak businesses.

Even though the corporate form of business offers significant advantages over proprietorships and partnerships, it does have two primary disadvantages:

1. Setting up a corporation and filing required state and federal reports is more complex and time consuming than for a proprietorship or a partnership.
2. Corporate earnings are subject to double taxation: The earnings of the corporation are taxed at the corporate level, and then any earnings paid out as dividends are again taxed as income to stockholders.[5]

When a corporation is created, a *corporate charter* and a set of *bylaws* must be created for the business. To ensure the necessary documents are prepared correctly, it is recommended that the incorporators hire a lawyer. The **corporate charter** includes the (1) name of the proposed corporation, (2) types of activities it will pursue, (3) amount of capital stock, (4) number of directors, and (5) names and addresses of directors. The charter is filed with the secretary of the state in which the firm plans to incorporate, and, when it is approved, the corporation is officially in existence.[6] After the corporation begins operations, quarterly and annual financial statements and tax reports must be filed with state and federal authorities.

The **bylaws** consist of a set of rules drawn up by the founders of the corporation to aid in governing the internal management of the company. Included are such points as (1) how directors are to be elected (all elected each year, or perhaps one-third each year for three-year terms); (2) whether the existing stockholders will have the first right to buy any new shares the firm issues; and (3) procedures for changing provisions in the bylaws, should conditions require it.

The value of any business, other than a very small concern, probably will be maximized if it is organized as a corporation for the following reasons:

1. Limited liability reduces the risks borne by investors. Other things held constant, *the lower the firm's risk, the higher its market value.*
2. *A firm's current value is related to its future growth opportunities*, and corporations can attract funds more easily than can unincorporated businesses to take advantage of growth opportunities.
3. Corporate ownership can be transferred more easily than ownership of either a proprietorship or a partnership. Therefore, all else equal, investors would be willing to pay more for a corporation than a proprietorship or partnership, which means that the corporate form of organization can *enhance the value* of a business.

As we will see later in the chapter, most firms are managed with value maximization in mind, and this, in turn, has caused most large businesses to be organized as corporations.

CORPORATE CHARTER

A document filed with the secretary of the state in which the firm is incorporated that provides information about the company, including its name, address, directors, and amount of capital stock.

BYLAWS

A set of rules drawn up by the founders of the corporation that indicate how the company is to be governed; includes procedures for electing directors, whether the common stock has a preemptive right, and how to change the bylaws when necessary.

---

[5]There was a push in Congress in 2003 to eliminate the double taxation of dividends by either treating dividends paid by corporations the same as interest—that is, making them a tax deductible expense—or allowing dividends to be tax exempt to stockholders. Congress passed neither; instead the tax on dividends received by investors was reduced from the ordinary tax rate to the capital gains rate. Taxes will be discussed briefly later in this book.

[6]More than 300,000 businesses are incorporated in Delaware, which has, over the years, provided a favorable legal environment for corporations. It is not necessary for a firm to be headquartered, or even to conduct operations, in its state of incorporation.

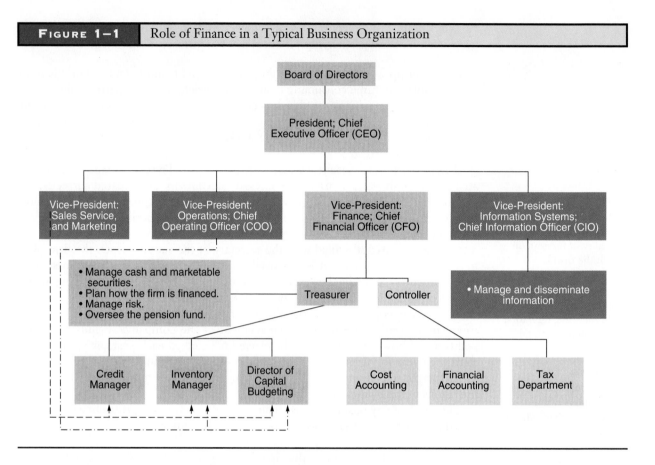

FIGURE 1–1 | Role of Finance in a Typical Business Organization

Self-Test Questions

What are the key differences among proprietorships, partnerships, and corporations?

Explain why the value of any business (other than a small firm) will be maximized if it is organized as a corporation.

Finance in the Organizational Structure of the Firm

Organizational structures vary from firm to firm. Figure 1–1 presents a fairly typical picture of the role of finance within a corporation. The chief financial officer (CFO), who may have the title of vice president of finance, reports to the president. The financial vice president's key subordinates are the treasurer and the controller. In most firms the treasurer has direct responsibility for managing the firm's cash and marketable securities, planning how the firm is financed and when funds are raised, managing risk, and overseeing the corporate pension fund. The treasurer also supervises the credit manager, the inventory manager, and the director of capital budgeting, who analyzes decisions related to investments in fixed assets. The controller is responsible for the activities of the accounting and tax departments.

Self-Test Question

Identify the two subordinates who report to the firm's chief financial officer and indicate the primary responsibilities of each.

Responsibilities of the Financial Management Area

The task of those involved in financial management is to make decisions concerning the acquisition and use of funds for the greatest benefit of the firm. Here are some specific activities involved in financial management:[7]

1. *Forecasting and planning.* The financial manager must interact with other executives as they look ahead and lay the plans that will shape the firm's future position.
2. *Major investment and financing decisions.* A successful firm generally has rapid growth in sales, which requires investments in plant, equipment, and inventory. The financial manager must help determine the optimal sales growth rate, and he or she must help decide on the specific assets to acquire and the best way to finance those assets. For example, should the firm raise funds by borrowing (debt) or by selling stock (equity)? If the firm uses debt (borrows), should it be long term or short term?
3. *Coordination and control.* The financial manager must interact with other executives to ensure that the firm is operated as efficiently as possible. All business decisions have financial implications, and all managers—financial and otherwise—must take these implications into account. For example, marketing decisions affect sales growth, which in turn influences investment requirements. Thus, marketing decision makers must consider how their actions affect (and are affected by) such factors as the availability of funds, inventory policies, and plant capacity utilization.
4. *Dealing with the financial markets.* The financial manager must deal with the money and capital markets. As we will see in Chapter 2, each firm affects and is affected by the general financial markets where funds are raised, the firm's securities are traded, and its investors are either rewarded or penalized.

In summary, financial managers make decisions regarding which assets their firms should acquire, how those assets should be financed, and how to manage their firms' existing resources. If these responsibilities are performed optimally, financial managers will help maximize the values of their firms, and this will also maximize the long-term welfare of those who buy from or work for the company as well as the community where the firm is located.

Self-Test Question

What are four specific activities with which financial managers are involved?

---

[7]Each of these reasons (topics) is discussed in more detail later in the book.

The Goals of the Corporation

Investors purchase the stock of a corporation because they expect to receive an acceptable return on their investment. If they are not involved in the day-to-day decisions, stockholders expect that managers run the business with the stockholders' best interests in mind. Because we know investors want to increase their wealth positions as much as possible, all else equal, then it follows that managers should behave in a manner that is consistent with enhancing the firm's value. For this reason, throughout this book we operate on the assumption that management's primary goal is **stockholder wealth maximization,** which, as we will see, translates into maximizing the value of the firm as measured by the price of the firm's common stock. Firms do, of course, have other objectives: In particular, managers who make the actual decisions are interested in their own personal satisfaction, in their employees' welfare, and in the good of the community and of society at large. Still, for the reasons set forth in the following sections, *stock price maximization is the most important goal of most corporations.*

STOCKHOLDER WEALTH MAXIMIZATION
The appropriate goal for management decisions; considers the risk and timing associated with expected cash flows to maximize the price of the firm's common stock.

Managerial Incentives to Maximize Shareholder Wealth

The stockholders own the firm and elect the board of directors, who then appoint the management team. Management, in turn, is supposed to operate in the best interests of the stockholders. As a stockholder of a company, you probably would want the managers to make decisions that would maximize the value of the stock you own, including dividends. We know, however, that because the stock of most large corporations is widely held, the managers of such organizations have a great deal of latitude in making business decisions. This being the case, might not managers pursue goals other than stock price maximization? For example, some have argued that the managers of a large, well-entrenched corporation could work just hard enough to keep stockholder returns at a "reasonable" level and then devote the remainder of their efforts and resources to public service activities, to employee benefits, to higher executive salaries, or to golf.

It is almost impossible to determine whether a particular management team is trying to maximize shareholder wealth or is merely attempting to keep stockholders satisfied while pursuing other goals. For example, how can we tell whether employee or community benefit programs are in the long-term best interests of stockholders? Similarly, are relatively high executive salaries really necessary to attract and retain excellent managers, or are they just another example of managers taking advantage of stockholders? Although it is extremely difficult to determine to what degree management decisions might deviate from the goal of wealth maximization, competitive forces generally require managers to make some attempt to maximize shareholder wealth. If they don't, then managers risk losing their jobs.

SOCIAL RESPONSIBILITY
The concept that businesses should be actively concerned with the welfare of society at large.

Social Responsibility

Another issue that deserves consideration is **social responsibility:** Should businesses operate strictly in their stockholders' best interests, or are firms also responsible for the welfare of their employees, customers, and the communities in which they operate? Certainly firms have an ethical responsibility to provide a safe working environment, to avoid polluting the air and water, and to produce safe products. However, socially responsible actions have costs, and it is questionable whether businesses would incur these costs voluntarily. If some firms act in a socially responsible manner while others do not, then the socially responsible firms will be at a disadvantage in attracting funds. To illustrate, suppose the firms in a given industry have **profits** and **rates of return on investment** that are close to **normal**—that is, close to the average for all firms and just sufficient to attract capital. If one company attempts to exercise social responsibility, it must raise prices to cover the added costs and maintain "normal" profits. If the other businesses in its industry do not follow suit, their costs and prices will be lower. The socially responsible firm will not be able to compete, and it will be forced to abandon its efforts. Thus, any voluntary socially responsible acts that raise costs will be difficult, if not impossible, in industries that are subject to keen competition.

NORMAL PROFITS/RATES OF RETURN
Those profits and rates of return that are close to the average for all firms and are just sufficient to attract capital.

What about oligopolistic firms with profits above normal levels? Cannot such firms devote resources to social projects? Undoubtedly they can, and many large, successful firms do engage in community projects, employee benefit programs, and the like, to a greater degree than would appear to be called for by pure profit or wealth maximization goals.[8] Still, publicly owned firms are constrained in such actions by capital market factors. To illustrate, suppose a saver who has funds to invest is considering two alternative firms. One firm devotes a substantial part of its resources to social actions, while the other concentrates on profits and stock prices. Most investors are likely to shun the socially oriented firm because its returns will be lower than other firms. Thus, the socially oriented firms will be at a disadvantage in the capital market. After all, why should the stockholders of one corporation subsidize society to a greater extent than those of other businesses? For this reason, even highly profitable firms (unless they are closely held rather than publicly owned) generally are constrained against taking unilateral cost-increasing social actions.

Does all this mean that firms should not exercise social responsibility? Not at all, but it does mean that most significant cost-increasing actions associated with social responsibility will have to be put on a *mandatory* rather than a voluntary basis, at least initially, to ensure that the burden falls uniformly on all businesses.

Stock Price Maximization and Social Welfare

If a firm attempts to maximize its stock price, is this good or bad for society? In general, it is good. Aside from such illegal actions as attempting to form monopolies, violating safety codes, and failing to meet pollution control requirements, *the same actions that maximize stock prices also benefit society.* First, note that stock price maximization requires efficient, low-cost plants that produce high-quality goods and services at the lowest possible cost. Second, stock price maximization requires the development of products that consumers want and need, so the profit motive leads to new technology, to new products, and to new jobs. Finally, stock price maximization necessitates efficient and courteous service, adequate stocks of merchandise, and well-located business establishments. These factors all are necessary to maintain a customer base that is necessary for producing sales and thus profits. Therefore, most actions that help a firm increase the price of its stock also are beneficial to society at

---

[8]Even firms like these often find it necessary to justify such projects at stockholder meetings by stating that these programs will contribute to long-term profit maximization.

large. This is why profit-motivated, free-enterprise economies have been so much more successful than socialistic and communistic economic systems. Because managerial finance plays a crucial role in the operation of successful firms, and because successful firms are absolutely necessary for a healthy, productive economy, it is easy to see why finance is important from a social standpoint.[9]

Self-Test Questions

What should be management's primary goal?

What would happen if one firm attempted to exercise costly social responsibility, while its competitors did not exercise social responsibility?

How does the goal of stock price maximization benefit society at large?

Managerial Actions to Maximize Shareholder Wealth

How do we measure value, and what types of actions can management take to maximize value? Although we will discuss valuation in much greater detail in Chapter 5, we introduce the concept of value here to give you an indication of how management can affect the price of the company's stock. First, the value of any investment, such as a stock, is based on the cash flows the asset is expected to generate during its life—both the amount and the timing of the cash flows. Second, investors generally are risk averse, which means that they are willing to pay more for investments with more certain future cash flows than investments with less certain, or riskier, cash flows, all else equal. For these reasons, we know that managers can increase the value of a firm by making decisions that increase the firm's expected future cash flows, generate the expected cash flows sooner, increase the certainty of the expected cash flows, or produce any combination of these actions.

CAPITAL STRUCTURE DECISIONS
Decisions about how much and what types of debt and equity should be used to finance the firm.

As we mentioned earlier, the financial manager makes decisions about the expected cash flows of the firm, which include decisions about how much and what types of debt and equity should be used to finance the firm (**capital structure decisions**), what types of assets should be purchased to help generate expected cash flows (**capital budgeting decisions**), and what to do with net cash flows generated by the firm—reinvest in the firm or pay dividends (**dividend policy decisions**). Each of these topics will be addressed in detail later in the book. But, at this point, it should be clear the decisions financial managers make can significantly affect the firm's value.

CAPITAL BUDGETING DECISIONS
Decisions as to what types of assets should be purchased to help generate future cash flows.

Although managerial actions affect the value of a firm's stock, external factors also influence stock prices. Included among these factors are legal constraints, the general

DIVIDEND POLICY DECISIONS
Decisions as to how much of current earnings to pay out as dividends rather than to retain for reinvestment in the firm.

---

[9]People sometimes argue that firms, in their efforts to raise profits and stock prices, increase product prices and gouge the public. In a reasonably competitive economy, which we have, prices are constrained by competition and consumer resistance. If a firm raises its prices beyond reasonable levels, it will simply lose its market share. Even giant firms like General Motors lose business to the Japanese and Germans, as well as to Ford and Chrysler, if they set prices above levels necessary to cover production costs and earn a "normal" profit. Of course, firms want to earn more, and they constantly try to cut costs or develop new products and thereby to earn above-normal profits. Note, though, that if they are indeed successful and do earn above-normal profits, those very profits will attract competition that will eventually drive prices down, so again the main long-term beneficiary is the consumer.

| FIGURE 1–2 | Value of the Firm |

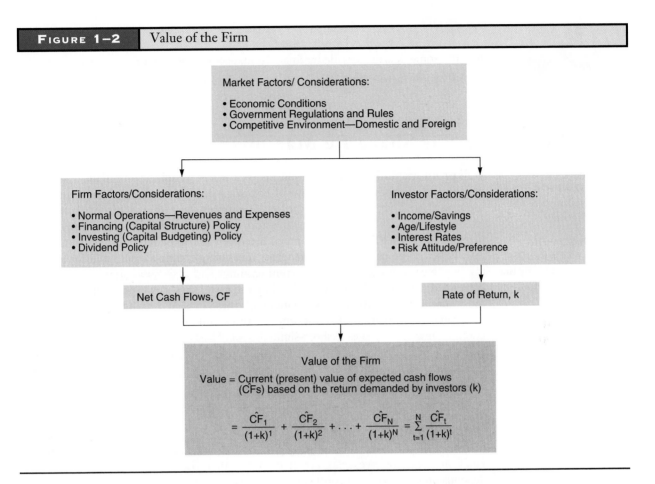

Market Factors/ Considerations:

• Economic Conditions
• Government Regulations and Rules
• Competitive Environment—Domestic and Foreign

Firm Factors/Considerations:

• Normal Operations—Revenues and Expenses
• Financing (Capital Structure) Policy
• Investing (Capital Budgeting) Policy
• Dividend Policy

Investor Factors/Considerations:

• Income/Savings
• Age/Lifestyle
• Interest Rates
• Risk Attitude/Preference

Net Cash Flows, CF

Rate of Return, k

Value of the Firm

Value = Current (present) value of expected cash flows
(ĈFs) based on the return demanded by investors (k)

$$= \frac{\hat{CF}_1}{(1+k)^1} + \frac{\hat{CF}_2}{(1+k)^2} + \ldots + \frac{\hat{CF}_N}{(1+k)^N} = \sum_{t=1}^{N} \frac{\hat{CF}_t}{(1+k)^t}$$

level of economic activity, tax laws, and conditions in the stock market. Working within the set of external constraints, management makes a set of long-run strategic policy decisions that chart a future course for the firm. These policy decisions, along with the general level of economic activity and government regulations and rules (for instance, tax payments), influence the firm's expected cash flows, the timing of these cash flows and their eventual transfer to stockholders in the form of dividends, and the degree of risk inherent in the expected cash flows.

Figure 1–2 diagrams the general relationships involved in the valuation process. As you can see, and we will discuss in much greater detail throughout the book, valuation is ultimately a function of the cash flows the firm is expected to generate in the future and the rate of return at which investors are willing to provide funds to the firm for the purposes of financing operations and growth. Many factors affect the determination of the expected cash flows and the rate people demand when investing their funds. Some of these factors are conditions in the economy and financial markets, the competitive environment, and the general operations of the firm, including operating efficiency and labor conditions. As we progress through the book, we will discuss these and other factors that affect a firm's value. When we refer to **value,** we mean the worth of the expected future cash flows stated in current dollars—that is, the present, or current, value of the cash flows.

VALUE

The present, or current, value of the cash flows an asset is expected to generate in the future.

Self-Test Questions

Identify some decisions made by financial managers that affect the firm's value.

Identify some factors beyond a firm's control that influence its stock price.

Should Earnings Per Share Be Maximized?

PROFIT MAXIMIZATION
The maximization of the firm's net income.

EARNINGS PER SHARE (EPS)
Net income divided by the number of shares of common stock outstanding.

Will **profit maximization** also result in stock price maximization? In answering this question, we introduce the concept of **earnings per share (EPS),** which equals net income (NI) divided by the number of outstanding shares of common stock (shares)—that is, NI/shares. Many investors use EPS to gauge the value of a stock. A primary reason EPS receives so much attention is the belief that net income, and thus EPS, can be used as a barometer for measuring the firm's potential for generating future cash flows. Although current earnings and cash flows are generally highly correlated, a firm's value is determined by the cash flows it is expected to generate in the future as well as the risk associated with these expected cash flows. Thus, financial managers who attempt to maximize earnings might not maximize value, because earnings maximization is a short-sighted goal. Most managers who focus solely on earnings generally do not consider the impact maximizing earnings in the current period has on either future earnings—that is, the timing of earnings maximization—or the firm's future risk position.

First, think about the *timing of the earnings.* Suppose Xerox has a project that will cause earnings per share to rise by $0.20 per year for five years, or $1 in total, whereas another project would have no effect on earnings for four years but would increase EPS by $1.25 in the fifth year. Which project is better—in other words, is $0.20 per year for five years better or worse than $1.25 in year five? The answer depends on which project contributes the most to the value of the firm, which in turn depends on the time value of money to investors. Thus, timing is an important reason to concentrate on wealth as measured by the price of the stock rather than on earnings alone.

Second, consider *risk.* Suppose one project is expected to increase EPS by $1, while another is expected to increase earnings by $1.20 per share. The first project is not very risky. If it is undertaken, earnings will almost certainly rise by approximately $1 per share. However, the other project is quite risky. Although our best guess is that earnings will rise by $1.20 per share, we must recognize the possibility that there might be no increase whatsoever, or the firm might even suffer a loss. Depending on how averse stockholders are to risk, the first project might be preferable to the second.

In many instances firms have taken actions that increased earnings per share, yet the stock price decreased because investors believed that either the higher earnings would not be sustained in the future or the riskiness of the firm would be increased substantially. Of course, the opposite effect has been observed as well. We see, then, that the firm's stock price, and thus its value, is dependent on (1) the cash flows the firm is expected to provide in the future, (2) when these cash flows are expected to occur, and (3) the risk associated with these cash flows. As you will discover as we proceed through the book, everything else equal, the firm's value increases if the cash flows the firm is expected to provide increase, they are received sooner, their risk is lowered, or some combination of these actions occurs. Every significant corporate decision should be analyzed in terms of its effect on the firm's value, and hence the price of its stock.

Self-Test Questions

Will profit maximization always result in stock price maximization?

Identify three factors that affect the value of the firm, and explain the effects of each.

Agency Relationships

In most large corporations, the owners—that is, the stockholders—are not involved in the day-to-day operations. As a result, stockholders "permit" the managers to make decisions as to how corporations are run. Of course, the stockholders want the managers to make decisions that are consistent with the goal of wealth maximization. However, managers' interests can potentially conflict with stockholders' interests.

An *agency relationship* exists when one or more individuals, who are called the *principals*, hire another person, the *agent*, to perform a service and delegate decision-making authority to that agent. In corporations, important agency relationships exist (1) between stockholders and managers and (2) between stockholders and creditors (debtholders).

Stockholders versus Managers

AGENCY PROBLEM

A potential conflict of interest between (1) the outside shareholders and the manager or (2) stockholders and creditors.

A potential **agency problem** arises whenever the manager of a firm *owns less than 100 percent* of the firm's common stock. If a firm is a proprietorship managed by the owner, the owner-manager will presumably operate the business in a fashion that will improve his or her own welfare, with welfare measured in the form of increased personal wealth, more leisure, or perquisites.[10] However, if the owner-manager incorporates and sells some of the firm's stock to outsiders, a potential conflict of interests immediately arises. For example, the owner-manager might now decide not to work as hard to maximize shareholder wealth because less of this wealth will go to him or her, or decide to take a higher salary or enjoy more perquisites because part of those costs will fall on the outside stockholders. This potential conflict between two parties—the principals (outside shareholders) and the agent (manager)—is an agency problem.

The potential for agency problems is greatest in large corporations with widely dispersed ownership, such as IBM and General Motors, because individual stockholders own very small proportions of the companies and managers have little, if any, of their own wealth tied up in the companies. For this reason, managers might be more concerned about pursuing their own agendas, such as increased job security, higher salary, or more power, than maximizing shareholder wealth. What can be done to ensure that management treats outside stockholders fairly? Several mechanisms are used to motivate managers to act in the shareholders' best interests. These

---

[10]Perquisites are executive fringe benefits, such as luxurious offices, use of corporate planes and yachts, personal assistants, and general use of business assets for personal purposes.

Are Top Executives Worth the Price?

If the bonuses awarded to top managers are performance-based, you would expect that such compensation should fall when the performances of companies decline relative to their benchmark measures, and vice versa. In general this does happen, but not to the extent that you might expect. Although the average executive compensation declined in 2002 (primarily because the compensation of some of the highest paid executives declined), the median compensation actually increased by 14 percent. Now consider the fact that during the same year the major stock market indexes declined by between 15 percent (Dow Jones Industrial Average) and 22 percent (S&P 500). Even as their companies' stock prices tumbled, many executives still earned tens of millions of dollars. For example, *Fortune* reported the compensation earned by 12 CEOs in 2002 along with the return earned by their respective shareholders. Most of the companies are recognizable—Abbott Laboratories, Alcoa, Apple Computer, Cisco Systems, Honeywell, Lucent Technologies, and Sun Microsystems, to name some. The average compensation the CEOs received was greater than $39 million, whereas the value of their companies' stock decreased by approximately 41 percent.

Even when companies report that they "do the right thing" by decreasing executive compensation when established benchmarks are not met, often executives receive alternative rewards. For example, the benchmark might be lowered so that it can more easily be met the following year, or the executives might be given another type of compensation that isn't "officially" recorded, or recognized, until some later period.[a] As a result, in most cases, the compensation paid to executives of large corporations continues to increase even when the value of their companies' stocks falters. The justification for the increases is that companies use compensation packages to retain top-quality executives. However, many stockholders and most "regular" employees believe that the general upward movement in executive pay is out of control, especially when compared to raises given to other employees over the years. Many people feel that executives of large corporations have created an elitist club that has produced an ever-widening chasm between top executives and the employees who work for them. In fact, it has been reported that the gap between executive pay and "regular" employee salary

continues

---

include (1) managerial compensation, (2) the threat of firing, (3) shareholder intervention, and (4) the threat of takeover.

1. **Managerial compensation (incentives).** A common method used to motivate managers to operate in a manner consistent with stock price maximization is to tie managers' compensation to the company's performance. Such compensation plans are also used to attract top managers to firms.

   One compensation plan that many firms use is to give managers **performance shares.** Under this plan, shares of stock are awarded on the basis of the firm's performance—as measured by earnings per share, return on assets, or return on equity, for example—and the executive's tenure with the firm. For example, Dell Computer Corporation uses performance targets based on growth in sales and profit margins relative to industry measures and such nonfinancial factors as customer satisfaction and product leadership. If the company achieves a targeted average growth in earnings per share, managers earn 100 percent of their shares. If the corporate performance is above the target,

PERFORMANCE SHARES

A type of incentive plan in which managers are awarded shares of stock on the basis of the firm's performance over given intervals with respect to earnings per share or other measures.

has increased from 42 to 1 in 1982 to nearly 411 to 1 in 2001, which is nearly a ten-fold increase.[b]

In June 2003, the Securities and Exchange Commission (SEC) approved proposals submitted by the New York Stock Exchange (NYSE) and the Nasdaq Stock Market (Nasdaq) that would require firms listed in these markets to get stockholder approval for all equity-based executive compensation plans.[c] The primary purpose of the proposals is to help ensure that these compensation plans serve the purposes for which they were created—that is, to better align the interests of managers and stockholders and retain quality management. The SEC approval is just the the "tip of the iceberg" regarding new corporate governance rules and regulations in light of recent reports of executive pay compared to both firm performance and employee pay and the continued existence of accounting irregularities in financial reporting.

What does all this mean for CFOs? Greater than 90 percent of the CFOs who responded to a recent survey believe their jobs will be more difficult as the result of increased regulations and reporting rules that are designed to improve the quality of information stockholders are provided by companies. Also, greater than 60 percent of the CFOs indicated that their job requires more time than it did prior to the movement to improve corporate governance, and, as a result, 45 percent find less satisfaction with their jobs.[d] CFOs aren't the only executives affected by the "corporate governance movement"—all senior management is. For this reason, you might expect that top executives will begin to earn their lavish compensation packages in the future. It is interesting to note, however, that the senior managers at most companies do not perceive there to be a problem with corporate governance or ethics in their respective organizations.[e] Perhaps the attitude is "this is not my problem."

[a]Jerry Useem, "Have They No Shame?" *Fortune*, April 28, 2003, 57–64.

[b]Scott Klinger, Sarah Anderson, and Holly Sklar, "Executive Excess 2002: CEOs Cook the Books, Skewer the Rest of Us," a research report published by Institute for Policy Studies and United for a Fair Economy (UFE), 2002. The report can be accessed at the UFE Web site at http://www.ufenet.org.

[c]Securities and Exchange Commission, Release No. 34-48108; Files Nos. SR-NYSE-2002-46 and SR-NASD-2002-140. The documentation can be found on the SEC Web site at http://www.sec.gov.

[d]"CFOs on the Hot Seat," *Business Week*, March 17, 2003, 66–70.

[e]"Increased Spending on Corporate Governance Expected as Part of Sustainability Focus," May 29, 2003, PricewaterhouseCoopers Barometer Report. The Barometer Reports provide the results of quarterly surveys conducted by PricewaterhouseCoopers. The results are available online at http://www.barometersurveys.com.

EXECUTIVE STOCK OPTION

A type of incentive plan that allows managers to purchase stock at some future time at a given price.

Dell's managers can earn even more shares. But if growth is below the target, they get less than 100 percent of the shares.

Many large corporations also offer **executive stock options,** which allow managers to purchase stock at some future time at a given price. Because the value of the options is tied directly to the price of the stock, it is assumed that granting options will provide an incentive for managers to take actions that will maximize the stock's price. This type of managerial incentive lost favor in the 1970s, however, because the general stock market declined, and stock prices did not necessarily reflect companies' earnings growth. Incentive plans should be based on those factors over which managers have control, and because they cannot control the general stock market, stock option plans that reward increases in stock prices regardless of economic conditions are not good incentive devices. Today, these plans are based on the performance of the firm's stock price relative to some standard, such as the performance of other stocks in the same industry or the market as a whole during a comparable time period.

There has been a recent movement to replace executive stock options with a fairly new compensation program, **restricted stock grants.** Firms that use this program grant what is termed *restrictive stock* to employees as an incentive for reaching certain financial and nonfinancial goals. The stock given to employees is restricted in the sense that an employee is not vested in the stock—that is, does not have the right to ownership—until some period in the future, say, five years. Once vested, the employee can trade the stock for its existing market value. Companies, especially those in technology industries, prefer restricted stock grants because, unless the price of the company's stock drops to zero, the stock that was granted to the employee will have value when he or she is vested. On the other hand, stock options would be worthless at the time they become exercisable if the market value of the stock is less than the exercise price (the price at which the stock can be purchased using the option—that is, exercising it).

All incentive compensation plans—executive stock options, performance shares, restricted stock grants, and other plans—are designed to accomplish two things: (1) provide inducements to executives to act on those factors under their control in a manner that will contribute to stock price maximization, and (2) attract and retain top-level executives. Well-designed plans can accomplish both goals.

2. **The threat of firing.** Not long ago, management teams of large firms felt secure in their positions, because the chances of being ousted by stockholders were so remote that managers rarely felt their jobs were in jeopardy. This situation existed because ownership of most firms was so widely distributed, and management's control over the voting mechanism was so strong, that it was almost impossible for dissident stockholders to gain enough votes to overthrow the managers. Today, however, in many cases, large blocks of the stock of an average large corporation are owned by a relatively few large institutions, such as pension funds and mutual funds, rather than by thousands of individual investors, and the institutional investors have the clout to influence a firm's operations. Examples of major corporations whose managements have been ousted in recent years include Coca-Cola, Lucent Technologies, United Airlines, and Xerox.

3. **Shareholder intervention.** Today more than 25 percent of the individuals in the United States invest *directly* in stocks. Along with such institutional stockholders as pension funds and mutual funds, individual stockholders are "flexing their muscles" to ensure that firms pursue goals that are in the best interests of shareholders rather than managers where conflicts might arise. Many institutional investors, especially pension funds such as TIAA-CREF and Laborers International Union of North America, routinely monitor top corporations to ensure that managers pursue the goal of wealth maximization. When it is determined that action is needed to "realign" management decisions with the interests of investors, these institutional investors exercise their influence by suggesting possible remedies to management or by sponsoring proposals that must be voted on by stockholders at the annual meeting. Stockholder-sponsored proposals are not binding, but the results of the votes are surely noticed by corporate management.

4. **The threat of takeover. Hostile takeovers,** instances in which management does not want the firm to be taken over, are most likely to occur when a firm's stock is undervalued relative to its potential, which often is caused by poor management. In a hostile takeover, the managers of the acquired firm generally

are fired, and those who do stay on typically lose the power they had prior to the acquisition. Thus, managers have a strong incentive to take actions that maximize stock prices. In the words of one company president, "If you want to keep control, don't let your company's stock sell at a bargain price."

Stockholders versus Creditors

Conflicts between stockholders and creditors (debtholders) can also exist. Creditors lend funds to the firm at rates that are based on (1) the riskiness of the firm's existing assets, (2) expectations concerning the riskiness of future asset additions, (3) the firm's existing capital structure (that is, the amount of debt financing it uses), and (4) expectations concerning future capital structure changes. These factors determine the riskiness of the firm's expected cash flows, so creditors (lenders) base the interest rate they charge on expectations regarding these factors.

Suppose that stockholders, acting through management, cause the firm to take on new ventures that have much greater risk than the creditors anticipated. This increased risk will cause the value of the outstanding debt to fall because new investors in the debt will demand a higher rate of return. If the risky ventures turn out to be successful, all benefits will go to the stockholders because the creditors only get a fixed return. However, if things go sour, the bondholders will have to share the losses. From the stockholders' point of view, this activity amounts to a game of "heads I win, tails you lose," which obviously is not a good game for the bondholders. Similarly, if the firm increases its use of debt in an effort to boost the return to stockholders, the value of the old debt will decrease because there will be a greater drain on cash flows that can be paid to stockholders due to the increased debt. Again, we have a "heads I win, tails you lose" situation. In both of these situations, stockholders can gain at the expense of debtholders.

Can and should stockholders, through their managers/agents, try to expropriate wealth from the firm's creditors? In general, the answer to this question is no. First, because such attempts have been made in the past, creditors today protect themselves reasonably well against stockholder actions through restrictions in credit agreements. Second, if potential creditors perceive that a firm will try to take advantage of them in unethical ways, they will either refuse to deal with the firm or require an interest rate that is much higher than normal to compensate for the risks of such "sneaky" actions. In the end, firms that try to deal unfairly with creditors either lose access to the debt markets or are saddled with higher interest rates and added restrictions, all of which decrease the long-run value of the stock.

STAKEHOLDERS
Individuals or entities that have an interest in the well-being of a firm, including stockholders, creditors, employees, customers, and suppliers.

In view of these constraints, it follows that the goal of maximizing shareholder wealth requires fair play with creditors: Stockholder wealth depends on continued access to capital markets, and access depends on fair play and abiding by both the letter and the spirit of credit agreements. Managers, as agents of both the creditors and the stockholders, must act in a manner that is fairly balanced between the interests of these two classes of securities holders. Similarly, because of other constraints and sanctions, management actions that would expropriate wealth from any of the firm's **stakeholders,** including employees, customers, and suppliers, will ultimately be to the detriment of shareholders. Therefore, maximizing shareholder wealth requires the fair treatment of all stakeholders.

Self-Test Questions

What is an agency relationship, and what two major agency relationships affect managerial finance?

Give some examples of potential agency problems between stockholders and managers.

List several factors that motivate managers to act in the shareholders' interests.

Why should managers act fairly with all stakeholders?

Business Ethics

BUSINESS ETHICS
A company's attitude and conduct toward its employees, customers, community, and stockholders.

The word *ethics* is defined in Webster's dictionary as "standards of conduct or moral behavior." **Business ethics** can be thought of as a company's attitude and conduct toward its employees, customers, community, and stockholders. High standards of ethical behavior demand that a firm treat each party it deals with in a fair and honest manner. A firm's commitment to business ethics can be measured by the tendency of the firm and its employees to adhere to laws and regulations relating to such factors as product safety and quality, fair employment practices, fair marketing and selling practices, the use of confidential information for personal gain, community involvement, bribery, and illegal payments to foreign governments to obtain business.

Unfortunately, there are many instances of firms that have engaged in unethical behavior. For example, companies, such as Arthur Andersen, Enron, and WorldCom MCI have fallen or been changed significantly as the result of unethical, and sometimes illegal, practices. In some cases, employees (generally top management) have been sentenced to prison for illegal actions that resulted from unethical behavior. In recent years, the number of high-profile instances in which unethical behavior has resulted in substantial gains to executives at the expense of stockholders' positions has increased to the point where public outcry resulted in legislation aimed at arresting the apparent tide of unethical behavior in the corporate world. As a result of the large number of scandals disclosed by major corporations at the end of the 20th century and the beginning of the 21st century, Congress passed the Sarbanes-Oxley Act of 2002. A major reason for the legislation was that accounting scandals caused the public to be skeptical of financial information reported by large U.S. corporations. Simply put, the public no longer trusted what managers said. Investors felt that executives were pursuing interests that too often resulted in large losses for stockholders.

The 11 "titles" in the Sarbanes-Oxley Act of 2002 establish standards for accountability and responsibility of reporting financial information for major corporations. The act provides that a corporation must (1) have a committee that consists of outside directors to oversee the firm's audits, (2) hire an external auditor that will render an unbiased (independent) opinion concerning the firm's financial statements, and (3) provide additional information about the procedures used to construct and report financial statements. In addition, the firm's CEO and CFO must certify financial reports submitted to the Securities and Exchange Commission. The act also stiffens the criminal penalties that can be imposed for producing fraudulent financial information and provides regulatory bodies with greater authority to enact prosecution for such actions.

Despite the recent decline in investor trust of financial reporting by corporations, the executives of most major firms in the United States believe their firms should, and do, try to maintain high ethical standards in all of their business dealings. Further, most executives believe that there is a positive correlation between ethics and long-run profitability because ethical behavior (1) avoids fines and legal expenses, (2) builds public trust, (3) attracts business from customers who appreciate and support ethical policies, (4) attracts and keeps employees of the highest caliber, and

(5) supports the economic viability of the communities where these firms operate. Surely some of the executives of Arthur Andersen, Enron, and WorldCom MCI would agree.

Today most firms have in place strong codes of ethical behavior, and they conduct training programs designed to ensure that all employees understand the correct behavior in different business situations. However, it is imperative that top management—the chairman, president, and vice presidents—be openly committed to ethical behavior and that they communicate this commitment through their own personal actions and through company policies, directives, and punishment/reward systems. Clearly, investors expect nothing less.

Self-Test Questions

How would you define *business ethics?*

Is "being ethical" good for profits in the long run? In the short run?

Forms of Businesses in Other Countries

Large U.S. corporations can best be described as "open" companies because they are publicly traded organizations that, for the most part, are independent of each other and of the government. As we described earlier, such companies offer limited liability to owners who usually do not participate in the day-to-day operations and who can easily transfer ownership by trading stock in the financial markets. While most developed countries with free economies have business organizations that are similar to U.S. corporations, some differences exist relating to ownership structure and management of operations. Although a comprehensive discussion is beyond the scope of this book, this section provides some examples of differences between U.S. companies and non-U.S. companies.

Firms in most developed economies, such as corporations in the United States, offer equities with limited liability to stockholders that can be traded in domestic financial markets. Such firms are not always called corporations, though. For instance, a comparable firm in England is called a "public limited company," or PLC, while in Germany it is known as an *Aktiengesellschaft,* or AG. In Mexico, Spain, and Latin America such as company is called a *Sociedad Anónima,* or SA. Some of these firms are publicly traded, whereas others are privately held.

Like corporations in the United States, most large companies in England and Canada are "open," and their stock is widely dispersed among a number of different investors. Of note, however, is that two-thirds of the traded stocks of English companies are owned by institutional investors rather than individuals. On the other hand, in much of continental Europe, stock ownership is more concentrated; major investor groups include families, banks, and other corporations. In Germany and France, for instance, corporations represent the primary group of shareholders, followed by families. Although banks do not hold a large number of shares of stock, they can greatly influence companies because many shareholders assign banks their proxy votes for the directors of the companies. Also, often the family unit has concentrated ownership and thus is a major influence in many large companies in developed countries such as these. The ownership structures of these firms and many other non-U.S. companies, including very large organizations, often are concentrated in the hands of a relatively few investors or investment groups. Such firms are considered "closed" because shares of stock are not publicly traded, relatively few individuals or groups own the stock, and major stockholders often are involved in the firms' daily operations.

The primary reason non-U.S. firms are likely to be more closed, and thus have more concentrated ownership, than U.S. firms results from the "universal" banking relationships that exist outside the United States. Financial institutions in other countries generally are less regulated than in the United States, which means foreign banks, for instance, can provide businesses a greater variety of services, including short-term loans, long-term financing, and even stock ownership. These services are available at many locations, or branches, throughout the country. As a result, non-U.S. firms tend to have close relationships with individual banking organizations, which also might take ownership positions in the companies. What this means is that banks in countries like Germany can meet the financing needs of family-owned businesses, even if they are very large. Therefore, such companies need not "go public," and thus relinquish some control, to finance additional growth. Consider the fact that in both France and Germany approximately 75 percent of the gross domestic product (GDP) comes from firms not publicly traded—that is, closed businesses. The opposite is true in the United States, where large firms do not have "one-stop" financing outlets; hence their growth generally must be financed by bringing in outside owners, which results in more widely dispersed ownership.

INDUSTRIAL GROUPS
Organizations comprised of companies in different industries with common ownership interests, which include firms necessary to manufacture and sell products—a network of manufacturers, suppliers, marketing organizations, distributors, retailers, and creditors.

In some parts of the world, firms belong to **industrial groups,** which are organizations comprised of companies in different industries with common ownership interests and, in some instances, shared management. Firms in the industrial group are "tied" by a major lender, typically a bank, which often also has a significant ownership interest along with other firms in the group. The objective of an industrial group is to include firms that provide materials and services required to manufacture and sell products—that is, to create an organization that ties together all the functions of production and sales from start to finish. Thus, an industrial group encompasses firms involved in manufacturing, financing, marketing, and distribution of products, which includes suppliers of raw materials, production organizations, retail stores, and creditors. A portion of the stocks of firms that are members of an industrial group might be traded publicly, but the "lead" company, which is typically a major creditor, controls the management of the entire group. Industrial groups are most prominent in Asian countries. In Japan, an industrial group is called a *keiretsu*, and it is called a *chaebol* in Korea. Well-known *keiretsu* groups include Mitsubishi, Toshiba, and Toyota, while the best-known *chaebol* probably is Hyundai. The success of industrial groups in Japan and Korea has inspired the formation of similar organizations in developing countries in Latin America and Africa as well as other parts of Asia.

The differences in ownership concentration of non-U.S. firms might cause the behavior of managers, and thus the goals they pursue, to differ. For instance, often it is argued that the greater concentration of ownership of non-U.S. firms permits managers to focus more on long-term objectives, especially wealth maximization, than short-term earnings, because firms have easier access to credit in times of financial difficulty. In other words, creditors who also are owners generally have greater interest in supporting short-term survival. On the other hand, it also has been argued that the ownership structures of non-U.S. firms create an environment where it is difficult to change managers, especially if they are significant stockholders. Such entrenchment could be detrimental to firms if management is extremely inefficient. Consider, for example, firms in

Japan that generally are reluctant to fire employees, because losing one's job is a disgrace in the Japanese culture. Whether the ownership structure of non-U.S. firms is an advantage or a disadvantage is debatable. But we do know that the greater concentration of ownership in non-U.S. firms permits greater monitoring and control by individuals or groups than the more dispersed ownership structures of U.S. firms.

Self-Test Questions

What is the primary difference between U.S. corporations and non-U.S. firms?

What is an industrial group?

What are some of the names given to firms in other countries?

Multinational Corporations

MULTINATIONAL CORPORATION

A firm that operates in two or more countries.

Large firms, both in the United States and in other countries, generally do not operate in a single country; rather they conduct business throughout the world. In fact, the largest firms in the world truly are multinational rather than domestic operations. Managers of such multinational companies face a wide range of issues that are not present when a company operates in a single country. This section highlights the key differences between multinational and domestic corporations and the impact these differences have on managerial finance for U.S. businesses.

The term **multinational corporation** is used to describe a firm that operates in two or more countries. Since World War II, a new and fundamentally different form of international commercial activity has developed, and it has greatly increased worldwide economic and political interdependence. Rather than merely buying resources from foreign concerns, multinational firms now make direct investments in fully integrated operations, with worldwide entities controlling all phases of the production process, from extraction of raw materials, through the manufacturing process, to distribution to consumers throughout the world. Today, multinational corporate networks control a large and growing share of the world's technological, marketing, and productive resources.

U.S. and foreign companies "go international" for the following major reasons:

1. **To seek new markets.** After a company has saturated its home market, growth opportunities often are better in foreign markets. As a result, such homegrown firms as Coca-Cola and McDonald's have aggressively expanded into overseas markets, and foreign firms such as Sony and Toshiba are major competitors in the U.S. consumer electronics market.

2. **To seek raw materials.** Many U.S. oil companies, such as ExxonMobil, have major subsidiaries around the world to ensure they have continued access to the basic resources needed to sustain their primary lines of business.

3. **To seek new technology.** No single nation holds a commanding advantage in all technologies, so companies scour the globe for leading scientific and design ideas. For example, Xerox has introduced more than 80 different office copiers in the United States that were engineered and built by its Japanese joint venture, Fuji Xerox.

4. **To seek production efficiency.** Companies in countries where production costs are high tend to shift production to low-cost countries. For example, General

Motors has production and assembly plants in Mexico and Brazil, and even Japanese manufacturers have shifted some of their production to lower-cost countries in the Pacific Rim. The ability to shift production from country to country has important implications for labor costs in all countries. For example, when Xerox threatened to move its copier rebuilding work to Mexico, its union in Rochester, New York, agreed to work rule and productivity improvements that kept the operation in the United States.

5. **To avoid political and regulatory hurdles.** Many years ago Japanese auto companies moved production to the United States to get around U.S. import quotas. Now, Honda, Nissan, and Toyota all assemble automobiles or trucks in the United States. Similarly, one of the factors that prompted U.S. pharmaceutical maker SmithKline and U.K. drug company Beecham to merge in 1989 was the desire to avoid licensing and regulatory delays in their largest markets, Western Europe and the United States. Now, GlaxoSmithKline, as the company is known today, can identify itself as an inside player in both Europe and the United States.

Since the 1980s, investments in the United States by foreign corporations have increased significantly. This "reverse" investment has created concerns for U.S. government officials, who contend it could erode the doctrine of independence and self-reliance that has traditionally been a hallmark of U.S. policy. Just as U.S. corporations with extensive overseas operations are said to use their economic power to exert substantial economic and political influence over host governments around the world, it is feared that foreign corporations might gain similar influence over U.S. policy. These developments also suggest an increasing degree of mutual influence and interdependence among business enterprises and nations, to which the United States is not immune.

During the past few decades, dramatic international changes have taken place, including the breakup, both politically and economically, of the former Soviet Union, the collapse of communism in most Eastern European countries, the reunification of Germany, the political revolution in South Africa, and economic disasters in Japan and Southeast Asia. Future events will include the continued development of the European Economic Community and the determination of how to help the cash-starved Eastern bloc nations. The 2003 U.S. Military incursion in Iraq and continuing turbulence in the Middle East and Eastern Europe will fuel ongoing economic upheaval in these regions. These events are examples of political and social developments that continually influence the world economy.

Self-Test Questions

What is a multinational corporation?

Why do companies "go international"?

Multinational versus Domestic Managerial Finance

In theory, the concepts and procedures discussed in the remaining chapters of this book are valid for both domestic and multinational operations. However, several problems uniquely associated with the international environment increase the complexity of the manager's task in a multinational corporation, and they often force the manager to alter the way alternative courses of action are evaluated and compared. Six major factors distinguish managerial finance as practiced by firms operating entirely within a single country from management by firms that operate in several different countries:

1. **Different currency denominations.** Cash flows in various parts of a multinational corporate system generally are denominated in different currencies. Hence, an analysis of **exchange rates** and the effects of fluctuating currency values must be included in all financial analyses.

2. **Economic and legal ramifications.** Each country in which the firm operates has its own unique political and economic institutions, and institutional differences among countries can cause significant problems when a firm tries to coordinate and control the worldwide operations of its subsidiaries. For example, differences in tax laws among countries can cause a particular transaction to have strikingly dissimilar after-tax consequences, depending on where it occurred. Also, differences in legal systems of host nations complicate many matters, from the simple recording of a business transaction to the role played by the judiciary in resolving conflicts. Such differences can restrict multinational corporations' flexibility to deploy resources as they wish and can even make procedures illegal in one part of the company that are required in another part. These differences also make it difficult for executives trained in one country to operate effectively in another.

3. **Language differences.** The ability to communicate is critical in all business transactions. Persons born and educated in the United States often are at a disadvantage because they generally are fluent only in English, whereas European and Japanese businesspeople usually are fluent in several languages, including English. As a result, it is often easier for international companies to invade U.S. markets than it is for Americans to penetrate international markets.

4. **Cultural differences.** Even within geographic regions long considered fairly homogeneous, different countries have unique cultural heritages that shape values and influence the role of business in the society. Multinational corporations find that such matters as defining the appropriate goals of the firm, attitudes toward risk taking, dealing with employees, and the ability to curtail unprofitable operations can vary dramatically from one country to the next.

5. **Role of governments.** Most traditional models in finance assume the existence of a competitive marketplace in which the terms of trade are determined by the participants. The government, through its power to establish basic ground rules, is involved in this process, but its participation is minimal. Thus, the market provides both the primary barometer of success and the indicator of the actions that must be taken to remain competitive. This view of the process is reasonably correct for the United States and a few other major industrialized nations, but it does not accurately describe the situation in most of the world. Frequently, the terms under which companies compete, the actions that must be taken or avoided, and the terms of trade on various transactions are determined not in the marketplace but by direct negotiation between the host government and the multinational corporation. This is essentially a political process, and it must be treated as such.

6. **Political risk.** The distinguishing characteristic that differentiates a nation from a multinational corporation is that the nation exercises sovereignty over the people and property in its territory. Hence, a nation is free to place constraints on the transfer of corporate resources and even to *expropriate*—that is, take for public use—the assets of a firm without compensation. This is political risk, and

EXCHANGE RATES
The prices at which the currency from one country can be converted into the currency of another country.

Chances Are What They Don't Know Won't Hurt Them!

Futuristic Electronic Technologies (FET) recently released a new advanced electronic micro system to be used by financial institutions, large corporations, and governments to process and store financial data, such as taxes and automatic payroll payments. Even though FET developed the technology used in the creation of the product, FET's competitors are expected to possess similar technology soon. To beat the competition to the market, FET introduced its new micro system a little earlier than originally planned. In fact, laboratory testing had not been fully completed before the product reached the market. The tests are complete now, and the final results suggest the micro system might be flawed with respect to how some data are retrieved and processed. The tests are not conclusive, though, and even if additional testing proves a flaw does exist, according to FET, it is of minuscule importance because the problem seems to occur for only one out of 100 million retrieval and processing attempts. The financial ramifications associated with the flaw are unknown at this time.

Assume you are one of FET's senior executives whose annual salary is based on the performance of the firm's common stock. You realize that if FET recalls the affected micro system, the stock price will suffer; thus your salary for the year will be less than you expected. To complicate matters, you just purchased an expensive house based on your salary expectations for the next few years—expectations that will not be realized unless the new micro system is a success for FET. As one of the senior executives, you will help determine what course of action FET will follow with respect to the micro system. What should you do? Should you encourage FET to recall the micro system until further testing is completed? Or can you suggest another course of action?

it tends to be largely a given rather than a variable that can be changed by negotiation. Political risk varies from country to country, and it must be addressed explicitly in any financial analysis. Another aspect of political risk is terrorism against U.S. firms or executives abroad. For example, in the past, U.S. executives have been captured and held for ransom in several South American and Middle Eastern countries.

These six factors complicate managerial finance within multinational firms, and they increase the risks these firms faced. However, prospects for high profits often make it worthwhile for firms to accept these risks and to learn how to minimize or at least live with them.

Self-Test Question

Identify and briefly explain the six major factors that complicate managerial finance within multinational firms.

Summary

This chapter provides an overview of managerial finance. The key concepts covered are listed here:

- It is important that persons who pursue careers in nonfinance professions have some understanding of finance concepts because there are **financial implications in nearly every business-related decision.**

■ Finance consists of three interrelated areas: (1) **financial markets and institutions,** (2) **investments,** and (3) **managerial finance.**

■ Managerial finance has undergone significant changes over time, but three issues have received the most emphasis in recent years: (1) the increased importance of **global financial markets and business operations,** (2) a dramatic increase in **information technology,** and (3) **deregulation** of financial institutions, utilities, transportation, and other industries.

■ The three main forms of business organization are the **proprietorship,** the **partnership,** and the **corporation.**

■ Although each form of organization offers some advantages and disadvantages, **most business is conducted by corporations** because this organizational form maximizes most firms' values.

■ **Financial managers** are responsible for obtaining and using funds in a way that will **maximize the value of their firms.**

■ The primary goal of management should be to **maximize stockholders' wealth,** which in turn means **maximizing the price of the firm's stock.** Further, actions that maximize stock prices also increase social welfare.

■ The price of the firm's stock depends on the firm's **projected cash flows,** the **timing of these cash flows,** and the **riskiness of the projected cash flows.**

■ An **agency problem** is a potential conflict of interests that can arise between (1) the owners of the firm and its management or (2) the stockholders and the creditors (debtholders).

■ Corporations can motivate managers to act in the best interests of stockholders in several ways, including (1) properly structured **managerial incentives,** (2) the **threat of firing,** (3) **shareholder intervention,** and (4) the **threat of takeovers.**

■ Many firms have established strict **codes of conduct,** or guidelines, that managers must follow to ensure that the firm behaves ethically when dealing with stakeholders.

■ **Non-U.S. firms** generally have more concentrated ownership than U.S. firms. In some cases, firms in other countries are part of an **industrial group,** which is a network of firms with common ownership ties that provides the different functions required to manufacture and sell a product from start to finish.

■ **International operations** have become increasingly important to individual firms and to the national economy. A **multinational corporation** is a firm that operates in two or more nations.

■ Companies go "international" for five primary reasons: (1) to **seek new markets,** (2) to **seek raw materials,** (3) to **seek new technology,** (4) to **seek production efficiency,** and (5) to **avoid trade barriers.**

■ Six major factors distinguish managerial finance as practiced by domestic firms from that of multinational corporations: (1) **different currency denominations,** (2) **economic and legal ramifications,** (3) **languages,** (4) **cultural differences,** (5) **role of governments,** and (6) **political risk.**

Questions

1–1 What are the three principal forms of business organization? What are the advantages and disadvantages of each?

1–2 Would the *normal* rate of return on investment be the same in all industries? Would *normal* rates of return change over time? Explain.

1–3 Would the role of the financial manager be likely to increase or decrease in importance relative to other executives if the rate of inflation increased? Explain.

1–4 Should stockholder wealth maximization be thought of as a long-term or a short-term goal? For example, if one action would probably increase the firm's stock price from a current level of $20 to $25 in six months and then to $30 in five years, but another action would probably keep the stock at $20 for several years but then increase it to $40 in five years, which action would be better? Can you think of some specific corporate actions that might have these general tendencies?

1–5 Drawing on your background in accounting, can you think of any accounting procedure differences that might make it difficult to compare the relative performance of different firms?

1–6 Would the management of a firm in an oligopolistic or in a competitive industry be more likely to engage in what might be called "socially conscious" practices? Explain your reasoning.

1–7 What is the difference between stock price maximization and profit maximization? Under what conditions might profit maximization not lead to stock price maximization?

1–8 If you were the president of a large, publicly owned corporation, would you make decisions to maximize stockholders' welfare or your own personal interests? What are some actions stockholders could take to ensure that management's interests and those of stockholders coincided? What are some other factors that might influence management's actions?

1–9 The president of United Semiconductor Corporation made this statement in the company's annual report: "United's primary goal is to increase the value of the common stockholders' equity over time." Later on in the report, the following announcements were made:

  a. The company contributed $1.5 million to the symphony orchestra in San Francisco, where it is headquartered.

  b. The company is spending $500 million to open a new plant in Mexico. No revenues will be produced by the plant for four years, so earnings will be depressed during this period in comparison to earnings had the decision not been made to open the new plant.

  c. The company is increasing its relative use of debt. Whereas assets were formerly financed with 35 percent debt and 65 percent equity, henceforth the financing mix will be 50-50.

  d. The company uses a great deal of electricity in its manufacturing operations, and it generates most of this power itself. Plans are to use nuclear fuel rather than coal to produce electricity in the future.

  e. The company has been paying out half of its earnings as dividends and retaining the other half. Henceforth, it will pay out only 30 percent as dividends.

Discuss how United's stockholders, customers, and labor force will react to each of these actions and then how each action might affect United's stock price.

1–10 Why do U.S. corporations build manufacturing plants abroad when they could build them at home?

1–11 Compared to the ownership structure of U.S. firms, which are "open" companies, what are some advantages of the ownership structure of non-U.S. firms, many of which are "closed" companies? Can you think of any disadvantages?

1–12 Compared to purely domestic firms, what are some factors that make financial decision making more complicated for firms that operate in foreign countries?

Self-Test Problem

Solution appears in Appendix B

ST-1 Define each of the following terms:
   a. Proprietorship; partnership; corporation
   b. Stockholder wealth maximization
   c. Hostile takeover
   d. Social responsibility; business ethics
   e. Normal profits; normal rate of return
   f. Agency problem; agency costs
   g. Performance shares; executive stock option
   h. Profit maximization
   i. Earnings per share
   j. Dividend policy decision; capital structure decision; capital budgeting decision
   k. Multinational corporation
   l. Political risk; exchange rate
   m. Industrial group; *chaebol; keiretsu*

GET REAL with Thomson ONE

1–1 Adobe Systems, Inc. [NASNM:ADBE] makes the popular Adobe Acrobat software for creating pdf-formatted files. Symantec Corporation [NASNM:SYMC] produces the popular Norton Security software for computer virus protection. These firms are peers, operating in the same industry—the technology industry—as well as the same market sector—software sector. Using the Thomson One database, answer the following questions:
   a. According to the Overview section, who are the key executives, based on their titles, in each firm?
   b. You can access the firms' websites from their Overview section. Go to their corporate websites and find the corporate executive structure. Create an organizational chart for each firm.
   c. Point out the similarities and differences for these firms, which are in the same market sector and industry, with regard to their organizational structure.
   d. Where does the Chief Financial Officer fit on the organizational charts of these two firms?

1–2 Using the Thomson One database, find a multinational firm that is based in the United States. Answer these questions:
   a. What is the name and ticker symbol of the company you selected?
   b. What is the industry and market sector in which the firm is classified?
   c. What is the firm's major line of business?
   d. In what countries does the firm operate?
   e. Why, in your opinion, do overseas operations help the firm you selected to maximize shareholder wealth? Be specific in your answer.

CHAPTER 2

The Financial Environment: Markets, Institutions, and Interest Rates

A MANAGERIAL PERSPECTIVE

During the 1990s, the performance of the stock market was quite impressive, earning investors record returns. After reaching record highs during 1999—the Dow Jones Industrial Average (DJIA) reached nearly 11500 at the end of the year—however, the stock market has been anything but stellar. According to the DJIA, investors who purchased stock on the first trading day of 1999, which was January 4, and held it until August 1, 2003, would have received approximately the same amount as they originally invested; thus, they earned a return equal to approximately 0 percent. The value of the DJIA on January 4, 1999, was 9184.26, and it was 9153.97 on August 1, 2003. The path that the DJIA took during this period can best be described as extremely precarious: The market lunged forward, then just as quickly pulled back. For example, except for a significant downward "adjustment," the market trended upward during 1999 and the DJIA was nearly 11500 at the end of the year. By March 2000, however, the DJIA had dropped by nearly 15 percent to approximately 9800. During 2000, the DJIA went up and then went down, much like a roller coaster, closing at approximately 10800 at the end of the year. As a result, investors who purchased stocks similar to those contained in the DJIA saw their investments decrease by 6 percent in 2000.

Investors didn't fare much better during 2001 and 2002. In late September 2001 the DJIA was less than 8240, which means that investors who entered the market at the beginning of the year had lost nearly 23 percent of their investments. Although the market rebounded some during the following few months—the DJIA reached nearly 10650 in February 2002—it just as quickly started moving downward. At the beginning of October 2002, the DJIA was at 7286, which was the lowest level since before the index first broke the 10000 barrier in March 1999. Although the stock market has continued its fickle ways, in 2003 the general trend was upward. Investors who purchased stock at the beginning of 2003 and then sold it on December 31 of the same year would have earned an equivalent annual return greater than 28 percent.

Forecasters blamed the roller-coaster ride that the market took at the beginning of the 21st century on the fact that technology stocks lost favor with investors, which resulted in huge losses for those who owned such stocks. Other factors were uncertainty generated by news that a global economic crisis was eminent, the recessionary economy in the United States during most of 2001, and disclosures that the executives of some large U.S. firms approved the use of, or ignored, unethical accounting practices their firms were using to "cook the books." These factors resulted in investors losing confidence in the financial markets, and thus withdrawing their funds to what they considered safer havens, such as certificates of deposit and savings accounts at banks and savings and loan associations.

As the economy slipped into a recession and financial markets faltered, companies slowed expansion and borrowed less. To encourage a reversal of this trend and attempt to prop up a declining economy, the Federal Reserve started to cut interest rates. To stimulate the economy the Fed cut interest rates several times during the period from the beginning of 2000 through 2002 (in 2001, cuts were made nearly every month). The effect was to lower the rates at which companies, individuals, and governments could borrow. The actions of the Fed and the investors decreased interest rates to their lowest levels in 45 years. For example, in June 2003, interest rates on Treasury bills that matured in one year dropped to less than 1 percent, and the rates on Treasury bonds that matured in 20 years were not much higher than 4 percent. With interest rates so low, the Fed still was poised to cut rates even further if it was necessary to support the liquidity of the financial markets and to help prop up a U.S. economy that was struggling to recover from a recession that had ended nearly four years earlier. If investors reached similar conclusions, they certainly would act on their expectations and begin reentering the financial markets and start buying bonds, which would further decrease interest rates and encourage businesses to borrow to replace worn-out assets. In fact, many experts believed that businesses would soon return to the financial markets to borrow funds because most companies had delayed replacement of deteriorating assets until they felt the economy had started its recovery, which would result in increased consumer buying, and thus increased demand for their products. Clearly, the behavior of participants in the financial markets—that is, businesses and individuals—is based on expectations about future interest rates. When rates are low, investors have little incentive to purchase stocks and bonds, but borrowers demand more loans, and vice versa.

Whether as a business or an individual, when we borrow, we would like interest rates to be low. When rates are low, as they were in 2003 and the beginning of 2004, many firms and individuals refinance to replace higher interest debt with lower interest debt. But, when interest rates are low, those who depend on the income from their investments suffer. Clearly, interest rates affect us all. Thus, as you read this chapter, think about (1) all the factors the Fed must consider before attempting to change interest rates and (2) the effects of interest rate changes on inflation, on the financial markets, on you as an individual, and on the economy as a whole. ∎

Financial markets are extremely important to the economic well-being of our country. For this reason, it is important that both investors and financial managers understand the environment and markets within which securities are traded and businesses operate. This chapter examines the markets in which firms raise funds, securities are traded, and the prices for stocks and bonds are established. In the process, we will explore the principal factors that determine money costs in the economy.

What Are Financial Markets?

Businesses, individuals, and government units often need to raise capital to fund investments. For example, suppose Progress Energy forecasts an increase in the demand for electricity in Florida, and the company decides to build a new power plant. Because Progress Energy almost certainly will not have the hundreds of millions of dollars needed to pay for the plant, the company will need to raise these funds in the financial markets. Similarly, if you want to buy a home that costs $100,000, but you only have $20,000 in savings, how can you raise the additional $80,000? Whereas some individuals and firms need funds, others have incomes that are greater than their current expenditures; thus they have funds available to invest, or save. For example, Derek Butler has an income of $60,000, but his annual expenses are only $45,000.

People and organizations that need money are brought together with those that have surplus funds in the *financial markets*. Note that "markets" is plural; there are a great many different financial markets, each one consisting of many institutions, in a developed economy such as ours. Unlike *physical (real) asset markets*, which are those for such products as wheat, autos, real estate, computers, and machinery, *financial asset markets* deal with stocks, bonds, mortgages, and other *claims on real assets* with respect to the distribution of future cash flows.

FINANCIAL MARKETS
"Mechanisms" by which borrowers and lenders get together.

In a general sense, the term *financial market* refers to a conceptual "mechanism" rather than a physical location or a specific type of organization or structure. We usually describe the **financial markets** as being a system comprised of individuals and institutions, instruments, and procedures that bring together borrowers and savers, no matter the location. Different types of financial markets involve a variety of investments and participants. Each market deals with a somewhat different type of instrument in terms of the instrument's maturity and the assets backing it. Also, different markets serve different types of customers or operate in different parts of the country.

Importance of Financial Markets

The primary role of financial markets is to help bring together *borrowers* and savers *(lenders)* by facilitating the flow of funds from individuals and businesses that have surplus funds to individuals, businesses, and governments that have needs for funds in excess of their incomes.[1] In developed economies, financial markets help efficiently allocate excess funds of savers to individuals and organizations in need of funds for investment or consumption. The more efficient the process of funds flow, the more productive the economy, both in terms of manufacturing and financing.

By providing *mechanisms* by which borrowers and lenders get together to transfer funds, the financial markets allow us to consume amounts different than our current

---

[1]We often refer to the parties involved in financial market transactions as *borrowers* and *lenders*, which implies that only loans are traded in the financial markets. But stocks, options, and many other financial assets also are traded in the financial markets. In our general discussions, we will use the term *borrowers* to refer to such parties as individuals and government units that raise needed funds using various types of loans, as well as corporations that use both loans and stock issues to raise needed funds. Further, we will use the term *lenders* to refer to those parties that provide funds, whether the medium is a loan or a stock.

incomes. Thus, financial markets provide us with the ability to transfer income through time. When we borrow, for example, we sacrifice future income to increase current income; when we save, or invest, we sacrifice current income in exchange for greater expected income in the future. For example, young adults borrow funds to go to college or to buy such high-priced items as houses or cars, so they tend to save little or nothing. Older adults, when they become established in their careers and reach or are near their peak income years, generally save (invest) greater percentages of their incomes. Finally, retirees rely on funds accumulated from prior years' savings to provide their retirement income. Consequently, as adults, we go through three general phases that would not be possible without financial markets:

1. Young adults desire to consume more than their incomes, so they must borrow.
2. Older working adults earn more than their consumption needs, so they save.
3. Retired adults use the funds accumulated in earlier years to at least partially replace income lost due to retirement.

Without financial markets, consumption would be restricted to income earned each year plus any amounts put aside (perhaps in a coffee can) in previous years. As a result, our standard of living would be much lower than is possible with financial markets.

Types of Financial Markets

We generally differentiate among financial markets according to the types of investments, maturities of investments, types of borrowers and lenders, locations of the markets, and types of transactions. There are too many different types of financial markets to discuss here; rather, we describe the more common market classifications.

DEBT MARKETS
Markets where loans are traded.

EQUITY MARKETS
Markets where stocks of corporations are traded.

MONEY MARKETS
The financial markets in which funds are borrowed or loaned for short periods (generally one year or less).

CAPITAL MARKETS
The financial markets for stocks and long-term debt (generally longer than one year).

1. **Debt versus equity markets. Debt markets** are the markets where loans are traded, whereas **equity markets** are the markets where stocks of corporations are traded. A debt instrument is a contract that specifies the amounts and schedule of when a borrower must repay funds provided by a lender. On the other hand, equity represents "ownership" in a corporation and entitles stockholders to share in any cash distribution generated from income (dividends) and from liquidation of the firm.

2. **Money versus capital markets. Money markets** are the markets for debt securities with maturities of *one year or less*, whereas **capital markets** are the markets for intermediate- and long-term debt and corporate stocks. The primary function of the money markets is to provide liquidity to businesses, governments, and individuals to meet short-term needs for cash, because, in most cases, the timings of cash inflows and cash outflows do not coincide exactly. For example, if you have funds that you do not need for tuition payments until six months from now, you can invest those funds in a money market security and earn a greater return than if the funds were left in a checking account. The primary function of the capital market is to provide the opportunity to transfer cash surpluses or deficits to future years. For example, without the availability of mortgages, most individuals could not afford to buy houses when they are young and just starting their careers.

   The debt market can be divided into more detailed, smaller markets. For example, *mortgage markets* deal with loans on residential, commercial, and

PRIMARY MARKETS
Markets in which
corporations raise funds
by issuing new securities.

**SECONDARY
MARKETS**
The markets for "used,"
or previously issued,
securities.

**INITIAL PUBLIC
OFFERING (IPO)
MARKET**
Market for corporations
that go public.

PRIVATE MARKETS
Markets in which stocks,
bonds, or other types of
debt are traded among
sophisticated investors
who generally are familiar
with each other.

PUBLIC MARKETS
Markets where
standardized transactions
take place.

SPOT MARKETS
Markets where assets that
are bought or sold for "on
the spot" delivery
(immediately or within a
few days) are traded.

FUTURES MARKETS
Markets for delivery of
assets at some later date.

industrial real estate and on farmland, whereas *consumer credit markets* involve loans on autos, appliances, education, vacations, and so forth.

3. **Primary versus secondary markets. Primary markets** are markets in which corporations (and governments) raise *new funds (capital)*. If Progress Energy were to sell a new issue of common stock to raise capital, this would be a primary market transaction. The corporation selling the newly created stock receives the proceeds from the sale in a primary market transaction. **Secondary markets** are markets in which existing, previously issued (already outstanding) securities are traded among investors. Thus, if Sally Anderson decided to buy 1,000 shares of IBM stock, the purchase would occur in the secondary market. The New York Stock Exchange is a secondary market, because it deals in outstanding, as opposed to newly issued stocks and bonds. Secondary markets also exist for mortgages, various other types of loans, and other financial assets. The corporation (or government) whose securities are traded is not involved in a secondary market transaction and thus does not receive any funds from such a sale.

  Whenever stock in a privately held corporation is offered to the public for the first time, the company is said to be "going public." The market for corporations that go public is called the **initial public offering (IPO) market.** For example, Microsoft went public March 13, 1986, with an IPO that sold for $21 per share.[2]

4. **Public versus private markets.** In **private market** transactions, stocks, bonds, or other types of debt are traded among sophisticated investors who generally are familiar with each other. As a result, the deals can be structured to fit both parties' (buyer and seller) needs. On the other hand, transactions in the **public markets** are standardized because securities traded in the public markets are traded among large numbers of investors who do not know each other and cannot devote (or afford) the time, effort, and cost necessary to ensure the validity of specialized, or nonstandardized, transactions such as those that occur in the private markets. Having standardized trades increases the liquidity and reduces the costs associated with transactions.

5. **Spot versus futures markets.** In **spot markets** the assets traded are bought or sold for "on the spot" delivery (immediately or within a few days), whereas **futures markets** are markets for delivery of assets at some later date. For example, a farmer in Nebraska might contract with General Mills to deliver 10,000 bushels of wheat in three months at a price of $3.20 cents per bushel. This futures contract requires the Nebraska farmer to deliver 10,000 bushels of wheat to General Mills in three months, and General Mills will pay the farmer $32,000 when the wheat is delivered.

6. **World, national, regional, and local markets.** Depending on an organization's size and scope of operations, it might be able to borrow all around the world, or it might be confined to a strictly local, even neighborhood, market. For this reason, some stocks and bonds are sold worldwide in markets such as the New York Stock Exchange, whereas others are sold in markets that are regional, such as the Chicago Stock Exchange.

---

[2]As of March 2004, Microsoft's stock sold for approximately $27 per share, which makes it appear that the value of the company's stock has increased little since the IPO in 1986. However, Microsoft has "split" its stock nine times since it first went public. One share of the stock that was issued in the IPO is equal to 288 shares of the current stock. At $27 per share, the value of one original share of Microsoft stock is worth $7,776 today. We will discuss stock splits in Chapter 10.

Other classifications could be made, but this breakdown is sufficient to show that there are many different types of financial markets.

A healthy economy depends on efficient transfers of funds from people who are net savers to firms, governments, and individuals who need funds. Without efficient transfers, the economy simply could not function: Progress Energy could not raise capital to provide electricity to all of its customers, you would not be able to buy the house you want, and Derek Butler would have no place to invest his savings. Clearly, without financial markets, the level of employment and productivity, and hence our standard of living, would be much lower.

Table 2–1 lists some of the instruments traded in the various financial markets. The instruments are arranged from those with the shortest maturities (money market instruments) to those with the longest maturities (capital market instruments). As we go through the book, many of these instruments will be discussed in much greater detail, and you will see that many different types of debt and equity have many different characteristics. Still, the table provides an idea of the characteristics and returns on the instruments traded in the major financial markets.

Self-Test Questions

Distinguish between debt and equity markets.

Distinguish between money and capital markets.

What is the difference between primary and secondary markets?

What is the difference between spot and futures markets?

Why are financial markets essential for a healthy economy?

Financial Institutions

Funds are transferred between those who have funds to invest (savers) and those who need the funds (borrowers) by the three different processes diagrammed in Figure 2–1:

1. A *direct transfer* of money and securities, as shown in the top section, occurs when a business sells its stocks or bonds directly to investors (savers), without going through any type of intermediary or financial institution. The business delivers its securities to investors, who in turn give the firm the money it needs.[3] Often direct transfers occur as a part of private market transactions.

2. As shown in the middle section, a transfer also can go through an *investment banking house*, which serves as a middleman and facilitates the issuance of securities. The company sells its stocks or bonds to the investment bank, which in turn sells these same securities to investors. The corporation's securities and the investors' money merely "pass through" the investment banking organization. However, the investment bank does buy and hold the securities for a period of time, so it is taking a chance—it might not be able to resell the securities to savers for as much as it paid.

---

[3]For simplicity, we assume that the entity needing capital is a business, specifically a corporation, but it is easy to visualize the demander of funds as a home purchaser or government unit, to cite two other examples.

TABLE 2–1	Summary of Major Financial Instruments, Market Participants, and Security Characteristics

INSTRUMENT	MARKET	MARKET PARTICIPANTS	RISKINESS	MATURITY	RATES ON 7/31/03[a]
Treasury bills	Money	Sold to institutional investors by the Treasury to finance the government	Default-free	91 days to 1 year	1.01%
Repurchase agreements	Money	Used by banks to adjust reserves—sell investments with a repurchase promise	Low degree of risk	Very short/ overnight	1.07%
Bankers' acceptances	Money	Firm's promise to pay; guaranteed by a bank	Low degree of risk if bank is strong	Up to 180 days	1.08%
Commercial paper	Money	Issued by large, financially secure firms to large investors	Low default risk	Up to 270 days	1.05%
Negotiable certificates of deposit (CDs)	Money	Issued by major money-center commercial banks to large investors	Riskier than Treasury bills	Up to 1 year	1.07%
Money market funds	Money	Invest in T-bills, CDs, and other short-term instruments; held by individuals and businesses	Low degree of risk	No specific maturity (instant liquidity): funds reinvested	0.75%
Eurodollar market time deposits	Money	Dollar denominated deposits in banks outside the United States	Risk depends on soundness of the issuing bank (foreign)	Up to 1 year	1.10%
U.S. Treasury notes and bonds	Capital	Issued by the U.S. government to finance expenditures	No default risk, but prices will change with changes in market interest rates	1 to 30 years	5.38%
State and local government bonds (municipals)	Capital	Issued by state and local governments to individuals and institutional investors	Riskier than Treasury bonds; exempt from federal taxes	Up to 30 years	5.32%
Mortgages	Capital	Loans from financial intermediates to individuals and businesses	Risk depends on the borrower; much riskier than government bonds	Up to 30 years	5.93%
Corporate bonds	Capital	Issued by corporations to individuals, institutional investors, and corporations	Risk depends on the company; riskier than government bonds, but not as risky as stock	Up to 40 years	6.09%
Preferred stock[b]	Capital	Issued by corporations to individuals, institutional investors, and corporations	Riskier than corporate bonds, but not as risky as common stock	None	7% to 11%
Common stock[b]	Capital	Issued by corporations to individuals and institutional investors	Risky	None	13% to 36%

[a]Interest rates are for the longest maturity securities of the type and for the strongest (safest) securities of a given type. Thus, the 6.09 percent interest rate shown for corporate bonds reflects that rate on 30-year, AAA bonds. Lower-rated bonds have higher interest rates.

[b]Common stocks are expected to provide a "return" in the form of dividends and capital gains rather than interest. The rates given for preferred and common stock represent the average returns investors would have earned during the previous one-year period—that is, August 2002 through July 2003, if market indexes were purchased. For example, the Nasdaq index increased nearly 36 percent, the Russell 2000, which includes relatively small firms, increased about 22 percent during the year, and the NYSE composite increased 13 percent.

FIGURE 2–1	Diagram of the Capital Formation Process

1. Direct Transfers

Business (Borrower)	Securities (Stocks or Bonds) ——→ Dollars ←——	Investors (Savers)

2. Indirect Transfers through an Investment Banker

Business (Borrower)	Securities ——→ Dollars ←——	Investment Banker	Securities ——→ Dollars ←——	Investors (Savers)

3. Indirect Transfers through a Financial Intermediary

Business (Borrower)	Business's Securities ——→ Dollars ←——	Financial Intermediary	Intermediary's Securities ——→ Dollars ←——	Investors (Savers)

INVESTMENT BANKER

An organization that underwrites and distributes new issues of securities; helps businesses and other entities obtain needed financing.

Direct transfers of funds from savers to businesses are possible and do occur on occasion, but it is generally more efficient for a business to enlist the services of an **investment banker.** Merrill Lynch, Morgan Stanley Dean Witter, and Goldman Sachs are examples of financial service corporations that offer investment banking services. Such organizations (1) help corporations design securities with the features that currently are most attractive to investors, (2) buy these securities from the corporation, and (3) then resell them to savers. Although the new securities are sold twice, this process really is one primary market transaction, with the investment banker acting as a middleman as funds are transferred from savers to businesses.

3. Transfers can also be made through a *financial intermediary* such as a bank or a mutual fund. In this case, the intermediary obtains funds from savers, issuing its own securities or liabilities in exchange, and then it uses the money to lend out or to purchase another business's securities. For example, when you deposit money in a savings account at your local bank, the bank takes those funds along with other depositors' funds and creates such loans as mortgages, business loans, and automobile loans. Thus, intermediaries literally create new forms of capital—in this case, savings accounts, which are both safer and more liquid than mortgages and thus are better securities for most savers to hold. The existence of intermediaries greatly increases the efficiency of the financial markets because, without them, savers would have to provide funds *directly* to borrowers, which would be a much costlier process.

FINANCIAL INTERMEDIARIES

Specialized financial firms that facilitate the transfer of funds from savers to borrowers.

The **financial intermediaries** referenced in the third section of Figure 2–1 do more than simply transfer money and securities between borrowers and savers—they literally create new financial products. Because the intermediaries generally are large, they gain economies of scale in analyzing the creditworthiness of potential borrowers, in processing and collecting loans, in pooling risks, and helping individual savers diversify—that is, not put all their financial eggs in one basket. Further, a system of specialized intermediaries can enable savings to do more than just draw interest. For example, individuals can put money into banks and get both interest income and a convenient way of making payments (checking), or put money into life insurance companies and get both interest income and financial protection for their beneficiaries.

In the United States and other developed nations, a large set of specialized, highly efficient financial intermediaries has evolved. However, competition and deregulation have created a rapidly changing arena in which different types of institutions currently perform services that formerly were reserved for others. This trend, which most certainly will continue into the future, has resulted in larger, more consolidated financial organizations and less distinctions among financial institutions. Still, there remains a degree of institutional identity. Here are the major classes of financial intermediaries:

1. *Commercial banks*, which are the traditional "department stores of finance," serve a wide variety of customers. Historically, commercial banks were the major institutions that handled checking accounts and through which the Federal Reserve System expanded or contracted the money supply. Today, however, other institutions also provide checking services and significantly influence the money supply. Conversely, commercial banking organizations provide an ever-widening range of services, including trust operations, stock brokerage services, and insurance.

   It is interesting to note that prior to 1933, commercial banks offered investment banking services, but the Glass-Steagall Act, which was passed in that year, prohibited commercial banks from engaging in investment banking activities. The act was passed because many believed that the Great Depression of the late 1920s and early 1930s was caused or compounded by the fact that banks were allowed to offer many financial services that some people believed presented serious conflicts of interest. As a result of the passage of the act, the Morgan Bank was divided into two separate organizations, now known as the JP Morgan Chase & Company, which is primarily a commercial bank, and Morgan Stanley, a major investment banking house, which is not considered a financial intermediary. In 1999, however, the Gramm-Leach-Bliley Act expanded the powers of banks by abolishing the major restrictions contained in the Glass-Steagall Act. The act permits qualified banks to engage in (1) investment banking and related activities, (2) insurance sales and underwriting, and (3) nonfinancial activities that do not substantially increase the risks of the institutions.

2. *Savings and loan associations (S&Ls)*, which have traditionally served individual savers and residential and commercial mortgage borrowers, take the funds of many small savers and lend this money to home buyers and other types of borrowers. Because the savers obtain a degree of liquidity that would be absent if they bought the mortgages or other securities directly, perhaps the most significant economic function of S&Ls is to "create liquidity" that otherwise would be lacking. Savers benefit by being able to invest their savings in more liquid, better managed, and less risky accounts (investments), whereas borrowers benefit from the economies of scale that allow them to obtain more capital at lower costs than would otherwise be possible.

3. *Credit unions* are cooperative associations whose members have a common bond, such as being employees of the same occupation or firm. Members' sav-

ings are loaned only to other members, generally for auto purchases, home improvements, and mortgages. Credit unions often are the cheapest source of funds available to individual borrowers.

4. *Pension funds* are retirement plans funded by corporations or government agencies for their workers and administered primarily by the trust departments of commercial banks or by life insurance companies. Pension funds invest primarily in long-term financial instruments, such as bonds, stocks, mortgages, and real estate.

5. *Life insurance companies* take savings in the form of annual premiums, then invest these funds in stocks, bonds, real estate, and mortgages, and ultimately make payments to the beneficiaries of the insured parties. Most life insurance companies also offer a variety of tax-deferred savings plans designed to provide benefits to participants when they retire.

6. *Mutual funds* are investment companies that accept money from savers and use these funds to buy various types of financial assets such as stocks, long-term bonds, and short-term debt instruments. These organizations pool funds and thus reduce risks through diversification. Different funds are designed to meet the objectives of different types of savers. For example, income funds are for those who prefer current income, growth funds are for savers who are willing to accept significant risks in the hopes of higher returns, and still other funds are used as interest-bearing checking accounts **(money market funds).** Literally hundreds of different types of mutual funds offer dozens of different goals and purposes.

MONEY MARKET FUND

A mutual fund that invests in short-term, low-risk securities and allows investors to write checks against their accounts.

With more than $7.4 trillion in assets at the beginning of 2004, mutual fund investment companies were approximately the same size as commercial banks, which represented the largest financial institutions in the United States. Today investment companies offer some 8,250 individual mutual funds. According to the Investment Company Institute (ICI), which monitors the performances of mutual funds, 75 percent of these mutual funds are owned by individuals. The primary reason that individuals invest in mutual funds is for retirement.[4]

Financial institutions historically have been heavily regulated in the United States, with the primary aim of ensuring the safety of the institutions and thus protecting depositors. These regulations have taken the form of prohibitions on nationwide branch banking, restrictions on the types of assets the institutions can buy and sell, ceilings on the interest rates they can pay, and limitations on the types of services they can provide. These restrictions have tended to impede the free flow of funds and thus have hurt the efficiency of our financial markets. Also, for the most part, U.S. financial institutions have been at a competitive disadvantage in the international financial markets because most foreign financial institutions, including banks, are not as restricted with respect to organizational structure, ability to branch, and nonbanking activities. Recognizing this fact, Congress has authorized some major changes recently, including the Gramm-Leach-Bliley Act of 1999, and more will be forthcoming.

The result of the ongoing regulatory changes has been a blurring of the distinctions among the different types of institutions. Indeed, the trend in the United States today is toward huge financial service organizations that own banks, S&Ls,

---

[4]Information concerning mutual funds can be found at the Mutual Fund Fact Book, which can be accessed on the Investment Company Institute (ICI) Web site at http://www.ici.org/.

investment banking houses, insurance companies, pension plan operations, and mutual funds, and that have branches across the country and even around the world. In recent years, for example, Citigroup was formed by combining (1) Travelers Group, which included an insurance company (Travelers) and an investment organization (Smith Barney); (2) Salomon Brothers, which was an investment organization that included an investment banking operation; and (3) Citicorp, which was one of the largest banking organizations in the United States. During the same period, BankAmerica Corporation and NationsBank Corporation combined forces to form the nation's largest bank at the time, Bank of America. In general, the direction of recent mergers and acquisitions in the financial services industry is to form larger, more diversified companies that can better compete internationally.

Self-Test Questions

Identify the three different ways capital is transferred between savers and borrowers.

What is the difference between an investment bank and a commercial bank?

List the major types of financial intermediaries and briefly describe the primary function of each.

What effect do you think regulatory changes and competitive pressures will have on financial institutions in the future?

Stock Markets

As noted earlier, secondary markets are those in which outstanding, previously issued securities are traded. By far the most active secondary market, and the most important one to financial managers, is the stock market. It is here that the prices of firms' stocks are established. Because the primary goal of managerial finance is to maximize the firm's stock price, a knowledge of this market is essential for anyone involved in managing a business.

When we differentiate stock markets, we have traditionally divided them into two basic types: (1) *organized exchanges*, which include the New York Stock Exchange (NYSE), the American Stock Exchange (AMEX), and several regional exchanges and (2) the less formal *over-the-counter market (OTC)*. The developments in information technology have created methods of trading securities that weren't available 20 years ago. For this reason, today it is more appropriate to classify stock markets as either (1) *physical stock exchanges*, which would include the NYSE and AMEX, and (2) *organized investment networks*, which would include the OTC, Nasdaq, and electronic communications networks (ECN).

PHYSICAL STOCK EXCHANGES
Formal organizations with physical locations where auction markets are conducted in designated ("listed") securities. The two major U.S. stock exchanges are the New York Stock Exchange (NYSE) and the American Stock Exchange (AMEX).

Physical Stock Exchanges

Physical security exchanges are tangible, "material" entities. Each of the larger exchanges occupies its own building, has specifically designated members, and has an elected governing body—its board of governors. Members are said to have "seats" on the exchange, although everybody stands up. These seats, which are bought and sold, give the holder the right to trade on the exchange. For example, there are 1,366 seats on the NYSE, and on March 1, 2004, a seat on the NYSE sold for $1.5 million, which was $500,000 lower than one year earlier.[5] Generally the price of a seat is high when the stock market is moving upward (a bull market) and low when the market is declining (a bear market).

Most of the larger investment banking houses operate *brokerage departments* that own seats on the exchanges and designate one or more of their officers as members. Exchange members meet in a large room equipped with computers, telephones, and other electronic equipment that enable each member to communicate with his or her firm's offices. Currently, U.S. exchanges are open during normal working hours, but there has been increased pressure for the exchanges to become globalized by expanding their trading hours because it is expected that within five years about one-third of all trades will be large multinational corporations.

Like other markets, security exchanges facilitate communication between buyers and sellers. For example, Merrill Lynch might receive an order in its Atlanta office from a customer who wants to buy 100 shares of IBM stock. Simultaneously, Morgan Stanley Dean Witter's Denver office might receive an order from a customer wishing to sell 100 shares of IBM. Each broker communicates electronically with the firm's representative on the NYSE. Other brokers throughout the country are also communicating with their own exchange members. The exchange members with *sell orders* offer the shares for sale, which in turn are bid for by the members with *buy orders*. Thus, the exchanges operate as *auction markets*.[6]

Organized Investment Networks—The Over-the-Counter (OTC) Market

If a security is not traded on a physical stock exchange, it has been customary to say it is traded in the **over-the-counter market,** which is an intangible trading system that consists of a network of brokers and dealers around the country. An explanation of the term *over-the-counter* will help clarify how the market got its name. As noted

OVER-THE-COUNTER MARKET
An intangible trading system that consists of a network of brokers and dealers around the country.

---

[5]NYSE stocks were not traded continuously until 1871. Prior to that time, stocks were traded sequentially according to their position on a stock roll, or roster, sheet. Members were assigned chairs, or "seats," to sit in while the roll call of stocks proceeded.

[6]The NYSE actually is a modified auction market, wherein people (through their brokers) bid for stocks. Originally—about 200 years ago—brokers would literally shout, "I have 100 shares of Union Pacific for sale; how much am I offered?" and then sell to the highest bidder. If a broker had a buy order, he or she would shout, "I want to buy 100 shares of Union Pacific; who'll sell at the best price?" The same general situation still exists, although the exchanges now have members known as *specialists* who facilitate the trading process by keeping an inventory of shares of the stocks in which they specialize. If a buy order comes in at a time when no sell order arrives, the specialist will sell off some inventory. Similarly, if a sell order comes in, the specialist will buy and add to inventory. The specialist sets a *bid price* (the price the specialist will pay for the stock) and an *asked price* (the price at which shares will be sold out of inventory). The bid and asked prices are set at levels designed to keep the inventory in balance. If many buy orders start coming in because of favorable developments or sell orders come in because of unfavorable events, the specialist will raise or lower prices to keep supply and demand in balance. Bid prices are somewhat lower than asked prices, with the difference, or spread, representing the specialist's profit margin.

Special facilities are available to help institutional investors such as mutual funds or pension funds sell large blocks of stock without depressing their prices. In essence, brokerage houses that cater to institutional clients purchase blocks (defined as 10,000 or more shares) and then resell the stock to other institutions or individuals. Also, when a firm has a major announcement that is likely to cause its stock price to change sharply, it will ask the exchanges to halt trading in its stock until the announcement has been made and digested by investors.

✳ INDUSTRY PRACTICE

Does Nasdaq Need CPR?

Has the Nasdaq market tripped over its ego? Or, is competition to blame? The popularity of the Nasdaq, which was an active stock market during the 1990s, appears to be waning. Much of the attraction to the Nasdaq was during a strong bull—that is, upward moving—market when technology stocks were considered the new "get-rich-quick" investments. During this period, Nasdaq thrived, and even implemented plans to grow the market globally. Business was good. More recently, however, Nasdaq opened its eyes and discovered that it was on life support, literally fighting to stay alive. So, what happened?

To some extent, Nasdaq ran into the same "buzz saw" as do many small, fast growing companies—its ego. The name Nasdaq is familiar to "techy" investors, because it has been the market where many hot technology stocks, including Microsoft, Intel, and Sun Microsystems, to name a few, are traded. During the 1990s, many investors were enamored with tech companies because their stocks provided annual returns between 40 percent and 60 percent, and, in some cases, greater than 100 percent. Life was very, very good! In fact, life was so good that Nasdaq executives encouraged expansion in an effort to become the premier stock market both in the United States and worldwide. To become more competitive with the New York Stock Exchange (NYSE), Nasdaq reorganized as a for-profit company in 1999. The plan at the time was that the newly converted organization would become an independent stock exchange and eventually go

public to raise capital needed for growth. But Nasdaq ran into a few unexpected roadblocks.

The initial efforts to capture a larger portion of the equity markets failed for the most part, primarily due to a lack of foresight, but also because the bull market turned into a bear—that is, declining—market and tech stocks lost their "investment luster." These events resulted in a sharp decline in Nasdaq trading activity worldwide. As a result, in 2003, Nasdaq's CEO, Robert Greifeld, reduced top management, closed foreign operations, which it had entered less than five years earlier, that were intended to grow the organization, and canceled plans for new growth. Although all stock markets were affected by an economic downturn, Nasdaq was especially harmed as a result of the sensitivity of the technology stocks that accounted for a large portion of its trading activity.

Even with poor market conditions, Nasdaq might not have been in the position it was in 2003 if it had better evaluated the competitive conditions in the stock markets at the time. Perhaps Nasdaq was a victim of its own hubris—that is, its bombastic confidence—in thinking that other stock markets could not compete in its backyard, especially in the technology area, whereas Nasdaq could freely enter the territory of other markets. Two major factors have kept Nasdaq from realizing its dream of transforming into the premier global stock market: its structure and competition from electronic communications networks (ECNs).

continues

earlier, the physical stock exchanges operate as auction markets, where buy and sell orders come in more or less simultaneously and exchange members match these orders. If a stock is traded less frequently, perhaps because it is the stock of a new or a small firm, few buy and sell orders come in, and matching them within a reasonable length of time would be difficult. To avoid this problem, some brokerage firms maintain inventories of such stocks. These firms buy when individual investors want to sell and sell when investors want to buy. At one time the inventory of securities was kept in a safe, and the stocks, when bought and sold, literally were passed over the counter.

Traditionally the OTC market has been defined to include all facilities that are needed to conduct security transactions not conducted on the physical stock

Although Nasdaq converted from a nonprofit organization to a for-profit corporation, it still was not a stand-alone stock exchange like the NYSE. And, in 2003, indications were that the Securities and Exchange Commission (SEC) would not approve the Nasdaq's request to operate as a stock exchange until changes were made so that Nasdaq trades were executed more like those on the NYSE. At the time, Nasdaq stock orders were not executed using an auction process—that is, a unified setting where traders fight for the best prices. Instead, trades often were executed by dealers who would make sure their own business did not suffer by matching buyers of particular stocks with sellers of those stocks "in house" rather than giving "outside" dealers a chance to provide better prices. This internalized trading system is not what the SEC prefers. The SEC prefers that stock markets offer "price-time priority" trading, which provides that those investors who offer the best prices first have their orders executed first. As a result, the SEC probably will not approve Nasdaq's request to become a stand-alone stock exchange until a price-time trading system is implemented.

Another factor that has restricted Nasdaq's growth is that much of its trading business has been captured by ECNs. (See the discussion about ECNs in this chapter.) It is estimated that ECNs accounted for approximately 50 percent of the trading activity in Nasdaq listed stocks in 2003, which was more than twice the dollar activity handled by Nasdaq itself. Although Nasdaq would like to increase the trading activity it handles, the organization finds itself in a catch 22. To increase trading activity, Nasdaq would take away business from the ECNs and its own dealers, both of which are customers who generate revenues

for the Nasdaq organization. In 2002, Nasdaq introduced the SuperMontage system, which is an electronic system that was supposed to consolidate and match stock orders better than the existing electronic network used by some 600 dealers. Unfortunately, SuperMontage was not as successful as expected because ECNs offered a better product at lower costs. For this reason, Nasdaq intends to overhaul Super-Montage to make it more competitive. Nasdaq wants to become more like ECNs, because ECNs have been very successful since they were introduced.

Another part of Nasdaq's survival plan is to try to convince NYSE-listed companies to become Nasdaq-listed. The success of this goal is extremely tenuous for two reasons. First, since the beginning of this millennium, greater than 100 companies have moved from Nasdaq to the NYSE, whereas only one company has ever moved the opposite direction since Nasdaq began operations in 1971. Second, Nasdaq lost more than 25 percent of its listed firms in 2001 and 2002, whereas NYSE lost less than 5 percent. This indicates that Nasdaq-list companies are on average riskier than NYSE-listed companies.

Will Nasdaq survive? Probably. But, its structure and the characteristics of its trading activities most likely will be significantly different than they were in 2003. Like "regular" corporations, Nasdaq must be aware of its competition and not become a victim of its own hubris, or ego, when planning for the future; otherwise, this stock market might find itself lamenting what might have been.

Source: Paula Dwyer and Amy Borrus, "NASDAQ: The Fight of Its Life," *BusinessWeek*, August 11, 2003, 64–71.

exchanges. These facilities consist of (1) the *dealers* who hold inventories of the less frequently traded securities and who are said to "make a market" in these securities, (2) the *brokers* who act as agents in bringing the dealers together with investors, and (3) the *electronic networks* that provide a communications link between dealers and brokers. The dealers who make a market in a particular stock continuously quote a price at which they are willing to buy the stock (the *bid price*) and a price at which they will sell shares (the *asked price*). Each dealer's prices, which are adjusted as supply and demand conditions change, can be read off computer screens all across the country. The spread between bid and asked prices represents the dealer's markup, or profit.

Brokers and dealers who make up the over-the-counter market are members of a self-regulating body known as the *National Association of Security Dealers* (NASD), which licenses brokers and oversees trading practices. The computerized trading network used by NASD is known as the NASD Automated Quotation System (Nasdaq). Although Nasdaq started as a medium to provide stock quotes, it has developed into a sophisticated market of its own, separate from the OTC. In fact, unlike the OTC, the Nasdaq has *market makers* who continuously monitor activities in various stocks to ensure they are available to traders who want to buy or sell. In an effort to become more competitive with the NYSE and with international markets, the Nasdaq, the AMEX, and the Philadelphia Stock Exchange merged in 1998 to form the Nasdaq-Amex Market Group, which might best be referred to as an **organized investment network.** Increased competition among global stock markets assuredly will result in similar alliances among various exchanges/markets in the future.

As information technology has evolved, so have the choices to investors as to how to trade securities. Today most stocks and bonds can be traded electronically using trading systems known as **electronic communications networks (ECN).** ECNs, which are registered with the Securities and Exchange Commission (SEC), are electronic systems that transfer information about securities transactions to facilitate the execution of the orders. ECNs automatically match the buy and sell orders by price for a large number of investors. Investors use ECNs through accounts they have at brokerage firms, such as Charles Schwab, that offer online trading services and subscribe to the ECNs. When an order (buy or sell) is placed electronically, the process is seamless in the sense that investors have no indication that an ECN is used to execute their transactions.

According to a study published by the SEC, nearly all the transactions executed by ECNs in 1999 involved Nasdaq stocks (93 percent). The study also reported that few of these transactions (4 percent) occurred after hours—that is, after the physical stock exchanges had closed.[7] Today approximately 50 percent of the total dollar volume of trades in Nasdaq stocks is executed using ECNs, whereas ECNs account for 3 percent of the dollar transactions of securities listed on the physical stock exchanges. As after-hour trading increases in the future, so will the use of ECNs.

In terms of numbers of issues, the majority of stocks are traded using organized investment networks, such as Nasdaq and the OTC. However, because the stocks of most of the largest companies in the United States are listed on the exchanges, about two-thirds of the dollar volume of stock trading takes place on the physical stock exchanges. It is interesting to note, however, that many of the companies that are "major players" in the information technology revolution, most notably Microsoft, Intel, and Sun Microsystems, trade on the Nasdaq even though they can be listed on the NYSE. Perhaps these companies choose to have their stocks Nasdaq-listed because transactions on the Nasdaq and other organized investment networks are primarily technology driven.

ORGANIZED INVESTMENT NETWORK
A system of stock markets, participants, and trading systems that are linked electronically.

ELECTRONIC COMMUNICATIONS NETWORKS (ECNS)
Electronic systems that transfer information about securities transactions to facilitate the execution of the orders by automatically matching buy and sell orders by price for a large number of investors.

Self-Test Questions

What are the two basic types of stock markets, and how do they differ?

Where are the greatest number of stocks traded, organized investment networks or physical stock exchanges?

Explain why the Nasdaq, AMEX, and Philadelphia merged. Do you expect that similar mergers will take place in the future? Why?

---

[7]Securities and Exchange Commission, "Special Study: Electronic Communication Networks and After-Hours Trading," June 2000. This study is available at the SEC Web site, which is located at http://www.sec.gov/.

The Cost of Money

Earlier in this chapter we stated that the primary role of the financial markets is to help bring together borrowers and lenders by facilitating the flow of funds from those who have surplus funds (investors/savers) to those who need funds in excess of their current incomes (borrowers). In a free economy such as that in the United States, the excess funds of lenders are allocated to borrowers in the financial markets through a pricing system that is based on the supply of, and the demand for, funds. The pricing system is represented by rates of return, such as interest rates, so that those who need additional funds and are willing to pay the rates that prevail in the financial markets are those who are able to use the excess funds provided by investors. This section describes the basic concepts associated with the cost of money—that is, returns paid to lenders, who receive interest, and paid to stockholders, who receive dividends and capital gains.

Four fundamental factors affect the cost of money: (1) **production opportunities,** (2) **time preferences for consumption,** (3) **risk,** and (4) **inflation.** To see how these factors operate, visualize an isolated island community where the people survive on fish. They have a stock of fishing gear that permits them to live reasonably well, but they would like to have more fish. Suppose one of the inhabitants, Mr. Crusoe, has a bright idea for a new type of fishnet that would enable him to double his daily catch. But, because it would take him a year to design and build his net and then learn how to use it efficiently, Mr. Crusoe most certainly would starve before he could put his new net into operation. Recognizing this, Mr. Crusoe might suggest to Ms. Robinson, Mr. Friday, and several others that if they would give him one fish each day for a year, he would return two fish a day during all of the following year. If Ms. Robinson accepted the offer, then the fish she gave to Mr. Crusoe would constitute *savings*, these savings would be *invested* in the fishnet, and the extra fish the net produced in the following year would constitute a *return* on the investment.

Obviously, the more *productive* Mr. Crusoe thought the new fishnet would be, the higher his expected return on the investment would be and the more he could afford to offer potential investors for their savings. In this example we assume that Mr. Crusoe thinks he will be able to pay, and thus he has offered, a 100 percent rate of return—he has offered to give back two fish for every one he receives. He might have tried to attract savings for less—say, only 1.5 fish a day next year for every one he receives this year, which would represent a 50 percent rate of return to Ms. Robinson.

How attractive Mr. Crusoe's offer appears to a potential saver would depend in large part on the saver's *time preference for consumption*. For example, Ms. Robinson might be thinking of retirement, and she might be willing to trade fish today for fish in the future on a one-for-one basis. On the other hand, Mr. Friday might be unwilling to "lend" a fish today for anything less than three fish next year, because he has a wife and several young children to feed with his current fish. Mr. Friday would be said to have a high time preference for consumption, whereas Ms. Robinson has a low time preference. Note also that if the entire population is living right at the subsistence level, time preferences for current consumption would necessarily be high, aggregate savings would be low, interest rates would be high, and capital formation would be difficult.

The *risk* inherent in the fishnet project, and thus in Mr. Crusoe's ability to repay the loan, also affects the return investors require: The higher the perceived risk, the higher the required rate of return. Also, in a more complex society there are many businesses like Mr. Crusoe's, many goods other than fish, and many savers like Ms. Robinson and

Mr. Friday. Further, people use money as a medium of exchange rather than barter with fish. When money is used, rather than fish, its value in the future, which is affected by inflation, comes into play: The higher the expected *rate of inflation*, the higher the required return.

Thus, we see that the interest rate paid to savers depends in a basic way on (1) the rate of return producers expect to earn on invested capital, (2) savers' time preferences for current versus future consumption, (3) the riskiness of the loan, and (4) the expected future rate of inflation. The returns borrowers expect to earn by investing the funds they borrow set an upper limit on how much they can pay for savings (demand). In turn, consumers' time preferences for consumption establish how much consumption they are willing to defer, and hence how much they will save at different levels of interest offered by borrowers (supply). Higher risk and higher inflation also lead to higher interest rates.

Self-Test Questions

What do we call the price paid to borrow (use) money?

What four fundamental factors affect the cost of money?

Interest Rate Levels[8]

Funds are allocated among borrowers by interest rates: Firms with the most profitable investment opportunities are willing and able to pay the most for capital, so they tend to attract it away from less efficient firms or from those whose products are not in demand. Of course, our economy is not completely free in the sense of being influenced only by market forces; the federal government has agencies that help designated individuals or groups obtain credit on favorable terms, including small businesses, certain minorities, and firms willing to build plants in areas with high unemployment. Still, most capital in the U.S. economy is allocated through the price system.

Figure 2–2 shows how supply and demand interact to determine interest rates in two financial markets. Markets A and B represent two of the many capital markets in existence. The going interest rate, which we designate as k, initially is 8 percent for the low-risk securities in Market A. Borrowers whose credit is strong enough to qualify for this market can obtain funds at a cost of 8 percent, and investors who want to put their money to work without much risk can earn an 8 percent return. The cost of funds for riskier borrowers is higher than 8 percent, as shown in Market B. Investors who are willing to take greater risks invest in Market B expecting to earn a 10 percent return but also realize that they might not earn 10 percent—that is, they might earn much less, or perhaps much more, than 10 percent.

If the demand for funds declines, as it typically does during business recessions, the demand curves in Figure 2–2 will shift to the left, as shown with line D_2 in Market A.

---

[8]Although the discussion in this section centers on interest rates, which we generally associate with the cost of debt in the financial markets, the concepts also apply to the returns associated with stocks. In general, we can say that the cost of using money provided by investors is based on the supply of, and the demand for, the available funds, regardless of whether those funds are in the form of debt or equity (stock).

FIGURE 2–2	Interest Rates as a Function of Supply and Demand

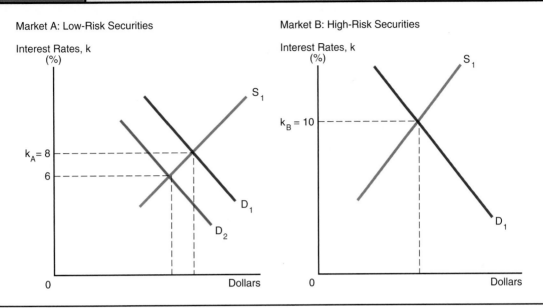

The market-clearing, or equilibrium, interest rate in this example then falls to 6 percent. Similarly, you should be able to visualize what would happen if the supply of funds tightens: The supply curve, S_1, would shift to the left, and this would raise interest rates and lower the level of (demand for) borrowing in the economy.

Financial markets are interdependent. For example, if Markets A and B were in equilibrium before the demand shift to D_2 in Market A, this means that investors were willing to accept the higher risk in Market B in exchange for a return that was 2 percent higher than can be earned in Market A. The 2 percent is called a **risk premium** because it is payment for the additional amount of risk investors take when purchasing the higher-risk securities. After the shift to D_2, the risk premium would initially increase to 4 percent—the existing 10 percent return in Market B less the new equilibrium return of 6 percent in Market A. In all likelihood, this much higher risk premium would induce some of the lenders in Market A to shift to Market B, which in turn would cause the supply curve in Market A to shift to the left (or up) and the supply curve in Market B to shift to the right. The transfer of capital between markets would raise the interest rate in Market A and lower it in Market B, thereby bringing the risk premium back closer to the original level of 2 percent. For example, when the rates on Treasury securities increase, the rates on corporate bonds and mortgages generally follow.

There are many financial markets in the United States and throughout the world. Examples of U.S. markets include home loans, farm loans, business loans, and government loans. For each type of loan, there is a price, and this price changes over time as shifts occur in supply and demand conditions. Figure 2–3 shows how long- and short-term interest rates to business borrowers have varied since 1970. Notice that short-term interest rates are especially prone to rise during booms and then fall during recessions. (The shaded areas of the chart indicate recessions.) When the economy is expanding, firms need capital, and this demand for capital pushes rates

RISK PREMIUM
Payment for the additional amount of risk investors take when purchasing risky securities.

FIGURE 2–3	Long- and Short-Term Interest Rates, 1970–2003

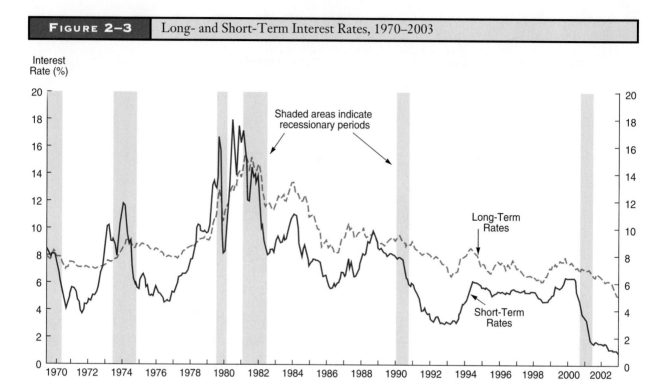

Notes:

a. Short-term interest rates are measured by three-month loans to large, strong corporations, and long-term rates are measured by AAA corporate bonds.

b. Tick marks on the X axis represent the middle of the year—i.e., June 15.

Sources: Interest rates are found at the Federal Reserve Web site at http://www.federalreserve.gov/; information about recessions can be found at the National Bureau of Economic Research Web site at http://www.nber.org/cycles.html/; and Consumer Price Index (CPI) data are found at the Web site of the U.S. Department of Labor, Bureau of Labor Statistics, http://www.bls.gov.

up. Also, inflationary pressures are strongest during business booms, and this also exerts upward pressure on rates. Conditions are reversed during recessions such as the one that occurred in 2001. Slack business reduces the demand for credit, the rate of inflation falls, and thus interest rates decline.

These tendencies do not hold exactly, and the period after 1984 is a case in point. Oil prices fell dramatically in 1985 and 1986, reducing inflationary pressures on other prices and easing fears of serious long-term inflation. Earlier, these fears had pushed interest rates to record levels. The economy from 1984 to 1987 was fairly strong, but the declining fears about inflation more than offset the normal tendency of interest rates to rise during good economic times, and the net result was lower interest rates.[9]

---

[9]Short-term rates are responsive to current economic conditions, whereas long-term rates primarily reflect long-run expectations for inflation. As a result, short-term rates are sometimes above and sometimes below long-term rates. The relationship between long-term and short-term rates is called the *term structure of interest rates*. This topic is discussed later in the chapter.

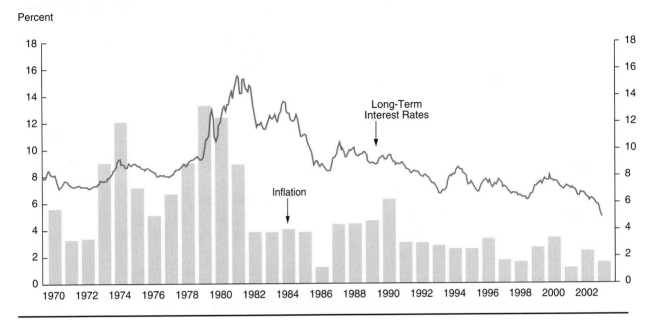

FIGURE 2–4   Relationship between Annual Inflation Rates and Long-Term Interest Rates, 1970–2003

Notes:

a. Interest rates are those for AAA long-term corporate bonds.

b. Inflation is measured as the annual rate of change in the Consumer Price Index (CPI).

Sources: Interest rates are found at the Federal Reserve Web site at http://www.federalreserve.gov/, and CPI data are found at the Web site of the U.S. Department of Labor, Bureau of Labor Statistics, http://www.bls.gov.

The relationship between inflation and long-term interest rates is highlighted in Figure 2–4, which plots rates of inflation along with long-term interest rates. Prior to the acceleration of the Vietnam conflict, when the average rate of inflation was relatively low, interest rates on the least risky bonds (AAA-rated) generally ranged from 4 percent to 5 percent. As the war in Vietnam accelerated in the late 1960s, the rate of inflation increased and interest rates began to rise. The rate of inflation dropped after 1970 and so did long-term interest rates. However, the 1973 Arab oil embargo was followed by a quadrupling of oil prices in 1974, which caused a spurt in inflation, which in turn drove interest rates to new record highs in 1974 and 1975. Inflationary pressures eased in late 1975 and 1976 but then rose again after 1976. In 1980, inflation rates were near 13 percent—the highest level on record—and fears of continued double-digit inflation pushed interest rates up to historic highs. From 1981 through 1986, the inflation rate dropped sharply, and in 1986 inflation was only 1.1 percent, the lowest level in 25 years. But interest rates remained relatively high until 1985 because investors were concerned that inflation would rise closer to the levels that had existed during the late 1970s and early 1980s. As you can see here and as we will discuss in the next section, investors "build in" an expectation for inflation when determining interest rates they believe to be appropriate for lending money—that is, purchasing debt securities such as bonds.

When inflation rates hit historically high levels in the early 1980s, the Federal Reserve developed a monetary policy that was aimed at keeping inflation in check. Once investors realized that the Fed was serious about following this policy in the long run, the fears about the return of runaway inflationary periods abated and interest rates began to decline. In fact, in 1993, interest rates dropped to historical lows at the time—the Treasury bill yield actually dropped below 3 percent. Since then, interest rates have remained relatively stable, at least until the economy entered a recession in 2001 when interest rates started to decline again. In 2003, there was a consensus among most economists, businesses, and consumers that the economy was in the midst of a recovery. Inflation was fairly low at 1.5 percent, Treasury bill rates were approximately 1 percent, and the interest rate on long-term debt to strong corporations was approximately 5.8 percent.

Self-Test Questions

How are interest rates used to allocate capital among firms?

What happens to market-clearing, or equilibrium, interest rates in a capital market when the demand for funds declines? What happens when inflation increases or decreases?

Why does the price of capital change during booms and recessions?

How does risk affect interest rates?

How does a change in rates in one financial market affect the rates in other financial markets?

The Determinants of Market Interest Rates

In general, the quoted (or nominal) interest rate on a *debt* security, k, is composed of a risk-free rate of interest plus a premium that reflects the riskiness of the security. This relationship can be expressed as follows:

2–1

$$\text{Rate of return (interest)} = k = \text{Risk-free rate} + \text{Risk premium}$$

This relationship is illustrated in Figure 2–5, which shows that investors require greater returns to invest in securities with greater risks. Although we discuss risk and return in detail in Chapter 4, the discussion in this section considers factors that affect interest rates on such debt securities as bonds.

The interest on debt can be expressed as follows:

2–2

$$\text{Quoted rate} = k = k_{RF} + RP = k_{RF} + [DRP + LP + MRP]$$

FIGURE 2–5	Rate of Return (Interest Rates)

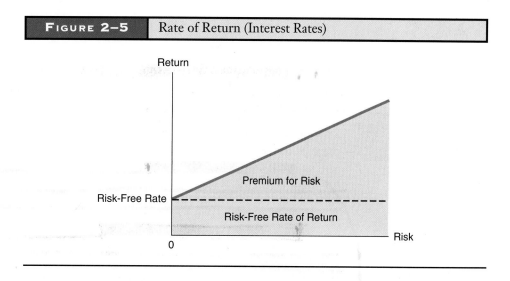

The variables in Equation 2–2 are defined as follows:

k = the quoted, or *nominal*, rate of interest on a given security.[10] There are many different securities, and hence many different quoted interest rates.

k_{RF} = the quoted risk-free rate of return. Theoretically this rate of return is the return associated with an investment that has a guaranteed outcome in the future—that is, it has no risk. We generally use the return on U.S. Treasury bills as the risk-free rate, because T-bills represent the short-term debt of the U.S. government that is liquid and free of most risks. In other words, the T-bills are considered close to pure risk-free assets.

RP = risk premium, which is the return that is greater than the risk-free rate of return, k_{RF}. $RP = DRP + LP + MRP$.

DRP = default risk premium, which reflects the chance that the borrower—that is, the issuer of the security—will not pay the debt's interest or principal on time.

LP = liquidity, or marketability, premium, which reflects the fact that some investments are more easily converted into cash on a short notice at a "reasonable price" than are other securities.

MRP = maturity risk premium, which accounts for the fact that longer-term bonds experience greater price reactions to interest rate changes than do short-term bonds.

We discuss the components whose sum makes up the quoted, or nominal, rate on a given security in the following sections.

---

[10]The term *nominal* as it is used here means the *stated* rate as opposed to the *real* rate, which is adjusted to remove the effects of inflation. If you bought a 10-year Treasury bond in July 2003, the quoted, or nominal, rate was 4.5 percent, but because inflation was expected to average 2 percent over the next 10 years, the real rate was 2.5% = 4.5%–2%.

The Nominal, or Quoted, Risk-Free Rate of Interest, k_{RF}

The **nominal, or quoted, risk-free rate, k_{RF},** is the interest rate on a security that has absolutely no risk at all—that is, one that has a guaranteed outcome in the future, regardless of the market conditions. No such security exists in the real world; hence there is no observable truly risk-free rate. However, there is one security that is free of most risks—a U.S. Treasury bill (T-bill), which is a short-term security issued by the U.S. government.

The nominal risk-free rate, k_{RF}, is comprised on two components: the *"real" risk-free rate*, which we designate k^*, and an adjustment for the average inflation that is expected during the life of the debt, which we designate IP, or the *inflation premium*. As a result, $k_{RF} = k^* + IP$ in Equation 2–2.

The **real risk-free rate of interest, k*,** is defined as the interest rate that would exist on a security with a *guaranteed* payoff—that is, a risk-free security—if inflation is expected to be zero during the investment period. It can be thought of as the rate of interest that would exist on short-term U.S. Treasury securities in an *inflation-free world*. The real risk-free rate changes over time depending on economic conditions, especially (1) on the rate of return corporations and other borrowers are willing to pay to borrow funds and (2) on people's time preferences for current versus future consumption. It is difficult to measure the real risk-free rate precisely, but most experts think that k^* fluctuates in the range of 2 to 4 percent in the United States.

No matter what investments they make, all investors are affected by inflation. For this reason, the minimum rate earned on any security, no matter its risk, must include compensation for the loss of purchasing power that is expected during the life of the investment due to inflation. Thus, k_{RF} must include a component for the average inflation, or purchasing power loss, investors expect in the future.

If the term *risk-free rate* is used without either the term "real" or the term "nominal," people generally mean the quoted (nominal) rate, and we will follow that convention in this book. Therefore, when we use the term *risk-free rate*, we mean the nominal risk-free rate, $k_{RF} = k^* + IP$. Also, we generally use the T-bill rate to approximate the short-term risk-free rate and the T-bond rate to approximate the long-term risk-free rate. Whenever you see the term *risk-free rate*, assume that we are referring either to the quoted T-bill rate or to the quoted T-bond rate.

$$K_{RF} = k^* + IP$$

"real" risk-free rate | inflation premium

Inflation Premium (IP)

Inflation has a major impact on interest rates because it erodes the purchasing power of the dollar and lowers the real rate of return on investments. To illustrate, suppose you saved $1,000 and invested it in a certificate of deposit that matures in one year and pays 4 percent interest. At the end of the year you will receive $1,040—your original $1,000 plus $40 in interest. Now suppose the inflation rate during the year is 5 percent, and it affects all items equally. If pizza had cost $1 per slice at the beginning of the year, it would cost $1.05 at the end of the year. Therefore, your $1,000 would have bought $1,000/$1 = 1,000 slices at the beginning of the year but only $1,040/$1.05 = 990 slices at year's end. *In real terms*, you would be worse off. You would receive $40 in interest, but it would not be sufficient to offset inflation. In this

The Determinants of Market Interest Rates   **59**

case, you would be better off buying 1,000 slices of frozen pizza (or some other storable asset such as land, timber, apartment buildings, wheat, or gold) than investing in the certificate of deposit.

Investors are well aware of all the effects of inflation. When they lend money, therefore, they build in an **inflation premium (IP)** equal to the average inflation rate expected over the life of the security. Thus, if the real risk-free rate of interest, k^*, is 3 percent, and if inflation is expected to be 2 percent (IP = 2%) during the next year, then the quoted rate of interest on one-year T-bills would be 3% + 2% = 5%.

It is important to note that the rate of inflation built into interest rates is the *rate of inflation expected in the future*, not the rate experienced in the past. Thus, although the rates reported by the government indicate that inflation is about 1.5 percent, if investors expect inflation to average 2 percent over the next few periods, then 2 percent would be built into current interest rates. Note also that the inflation rate reflected in the quoted interest rate of an investment is the *average inflation expected over the life of the investment*. Consequently, the inflation rate that is built into a one-year bond is the expected inflation rate for the next year, but the inflation rate built into a 30-year bond is the average rate of inflation expected over the next 30 years.

Generally, expectations for future inflation are closely correlated with rates experienced in the recent past. Thus, if the inflation rate reported for the month increased, people would tend to raise their expectations for future inflation and this change in expectations would cause an increase in interest rates.

Default Risk Premium (DRP)

The *risk* that a borrower will *default* on a loan, which means not to pay the interest or the principal, also affects the market interest rate on a security: The greater the default risk, the higher the interest rate lenders charge (demand). Treasury securities have no default risk, so they generally carry the lowest interest rates on taxable securities in the United States. For corporate bonds, the better the bond's overall credit rating, the lower its default risk, and, consequently, the lower its interest rate.[11] Following are some representative interest rates on long-term bonds (maturities of 10 years or longer) as of July 2003:

	RATE, k	DRP
U.S. Treasury, k_{RF}	4.4%	—
AAA	6.0	1.6%
AA	6.6	2.2
A	7.1	2.7

INFLATION PREMIUM (IP)

A premium for expected inflation that investors add to the real risk-free rate of return.

---

[11]Bond ratings, and bonds' riskiness in general, will be discussed in detail in Chapter 17. For now, merely note that bonds rated AAA are judged to have less default risk than bonds rated AA, AA bonds are less risky than A bonds, and so on. Ratings might also be designated AAA or Aaa, AA or Aa, and so forth, depending on the rating agency. In this book the designations are used interchangeably.

DEFAULT RISK PREMIUM (DRP)

The difference between the interest rate on a U.S. Treasury bond and a corporate bond of equal maturity and marketability.

The difference between the quoted interest rate on a T-bond and that on a corporate bond with similar maturity, liquidity, and other features is the **default risk premium (DRP)**. Therefore, if the bonds listed here were otherwise similar, the default risk premium would be DRP = k − k_{RF}. Default risk premiums vary somewhat over time. The DRPs shown here are relatively high compared with levels in more "normal" economic periods, because market confidence was somewhat shaky in the summer of 2003. At that time, because many investors had lost significant wealth in the stock markets during the prior two years, people were hesitant to put money into the financial markets until they were confident an upward trend could be sustained in the long run.

Liquidity Premium (LP)

LIQUIDITY PREMIUM (LP)

A premium added to the rate on a security if the security cannot be converted to cash on short notice and at close to the original cost.

Liquidity generally is defined as the ability to convert an asset into cash on short notice and reasonably recapture the amount initially invested. Because liquidity is important, investors evaluate and include **liquidity premiums (LP)** when interest rates are established. Although it is difficult to accurately measure liquidity premiums, a differential of at least 2 and probably 4 or 5 percentage points exists between the least liquid and the most liquid financial assets of similar default risk and maturity. Of course, the most liquid asset of all is cash, and the more easily an asset can be converted to cash at a price that substantially recovers the initial amount invested, the more liquid it is considered. Some investments, such as certificates of deposit, are not very liquid because they cannot be sold to other investors—that is, they do not have an active secondary market.

Maturity Risk Premium (MRP)

INTEREST RATE RISK

The risk of capital losses to which investors are exposed because of changing interest rates.

MATURITY RISK PREMIUM (MRP)

A premium that reflects interest rate risk; bonds with longer maturities have greater interest rate risk.

REINVESTMENT RATE RISK

The risk that a decline in interest rates will lead to lower income when bonds mature and funds are reinvested.

The prices of bonds change when interest rates change: Prices decline when interest rates rise, and vice versa. Because interest rates change daily, all bonds, even Treasury bonds, have an element of risk called **interest rate risk**. As a general rule, the longer the time to maturity of a bond, the greater its interest rate risk.[12] Therefore, a **maturity risk premium (MRP)**, which is higher the longer the years to maturity, must be included in the required interest rate. The effect of maturity risk premiums is to raise interest rates on long-term bonds relative to those on short-term bonds. This premium, like the others, is extremely difficult to measure, but (1) it seems to vary over time, rising when interest rates are more volatile and uncertain, then falling when interest rates are more stable, and (2) in recent years, the maturity risk premium on 30-year T-bonds appears to have generally been in the range of 1 or 2 percentage points.[13]

Although long-term bonds are heavily exposed to maturity risk, short-term investments are heavily exposed to **reinvestment rate risk.** When short-term investments

---

[12]For example, if someone bought a 20-year Treasury bond for $1,000 in January 1999, when the rate on such bonds was 5.4 percent, and held it until January 2004, when the rate was 4.3 percent, the value of the bond would have increased by $121. This demonstrates that long-term bonds, even U.S. Treasury bonds, are not riskless. However, had the investor purchased short-term T-bills and subsequently reinvested the principal each time the bills matured, he or she would still have had $1,000. This point will be discussed in detail in Chapter 5.

[13]The MRP has averaged 1.7 percentage points over the past 75 years. *See Stocks, Bonds, Bills, and Inflation: 2003 Yearbook* (Chicago: Ibbotson Associates, 2003).

mature and the proceeds are reinvested, or "rolled over," a decline in interest rates requires reinvestment at a lower rate and hence would lead to a decline in interest income. Thus, although "investing short" preserves one's principal, the interest income provided by short-term investments varies from year to year, depending on reinvestment rates.[14] For example, suppose a relative of yours invested $100,000 in one-year Treasury bills because he or she wanted to live on the income generated from this investment. In 1981, short-term rates were about 15 percent, so the income would have been about $15,000. However, because the $100,000 would have to be reinvested each year at the prevailing interest rate, by 1983 the income would have declined to about $9,000 and to about $1,000 by 2004. Had the money been invested in long-term, say, 30-year, Treasury bonds in 1981, your relative would have received a stable annual income of about $13,000. Thus, although "investing short" preserves one's principal, the interest income provided by short-term investments varies from year to year, depending on reinvestment rates.

Self-Test Questions

Write out an equation for the nominal interest rate on any debt security.

Distinguish between the real risk-free rate of interest, k*, and the nominal, or quoted, risk-free rate of interest, k_{RF}.

How is inflation included in interest rates? Explain.

Does the interest rate on a Treasury bond include a default risk premium? Explain.

Briefly explain the following statement: "Although long-term debt is heavily exposed to maturity rate risk, short-term debt is heavily exposed to reinvestment rate risk."

The Term Structure of Interest Rates

TERM STRUCTURE OF INTEREST RATES

The relationship between yields and maturities of securities.

The relationship between long- and short-term rates, which is known as the **term structure of interest rates,** is important to corporate treasurers, who must decide whether to borrow by issuing long- or short-term debt, and to investors, who must decide whether to buy long- or short-term bonds. Thus, it is important to understand (1) how long- and short-term rates are related to each other and (2) what causes shifts in their relative positions.

Interest rates for bonds with various maturities can be found in/on a large number of sources, including *The Wall Street Journal* (both in print and online), the *Federal Reserve Bulletin* (both in print and online), Bloomberg.com (online), and CNN Money (online). Using these sources, we can construct the term structure of interest

---

[14]Long-term bonds also have reinvestment rate risk. To actually earn the quoted rate on a long-term bond, the interest payments must be reinvested at the quoted rate. However, if interest rates fall, the interest payments would be reinvested at a lower rate; thus, the realized return would be less than the quoted rate. Note, however, that the reinvestment rate risk is lower on a long-term bond than on a short-term bond because only the interest payments (rather than interest plus principal) on the long-term bond are exposed to reinvestment rate risk. Only zero coupon bonds, discussed in Chapters 5 and 17, are completely free of reinvestment rate risk.

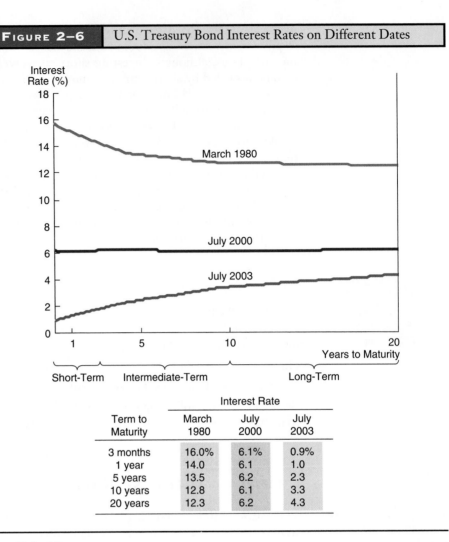

| FIGURE 2–6 | U.S. Treasury Bond Interest Rates on Different Dates |

		Interest Rate	
Term to Maturity	March 1980	July 2000	July 2003
3 months	16.0%	6.1%	0.9%
1 year	14.0	6.1	1.0
5 years	13.5	6.2	2.3
10 years	12.8	6.1	3.3
20 years	12.3	6.2	4.3

Source: Federal Reserve.

YIELD CURVE
A graph showing the relationship between yields and maturities of securities.

"NORMAL" YIELD CURVE
An upward-sloping yield curve.

INVERTED ("ABNORMAL") YIELD CURVE
A downward-sloping yield curve.

rates at a particular date. For example, the tabular section of Figure 2–6 includes interest rates for different maturities on three different dates. The set of data for a given date, when plotted on a graph such as that in Figure 2–6, is called the **yield curve** for that date. The yield curve changes both in position and in slope over time. In March 1980, all rates were relatively high, and short-term rates were higher than long-term rates, so the yield curve on that date was *downward sloping*. However, in July 2000, all rates were much lower, and long-term rates and short-term rates were approximately equal, so the yield curve was fairly *flat*, or *horizontal*. And, in July 2003, all rates were even lower than in 2000, and short-term rates were lower than long-term rates, so the yield curve at that time was *upward sloping*.

Historically, in most years, long-term rates have been above short-term rates, so usually the yield curve has been upward sloping. For this reason, people often call an upward-sloping yield curve a **"normal" yield curve** and a yield curve that slopes downward an **inverted,** or **"abnormal," yield curve.** Thus, in Figure 2–6, the yield curve for March 1980 was inverted, but the one for July 2003 was fairly normal.

Self-Test Questions

What is a yield curve, and what information would you need to draw this curve? How does a "normal" yield curve differ from a flat yield curve and an inverted yield curve?

Why Do Yield Curves Differ?

It is clear from Figure 2–6 that the shape of the yield curve at one point in time can be significantly different from the yield curve at another point in time. For example, interest rates were much higher in 1980 than in 2003, and the yield curve was downward sloping in 1980 whereas it was upward sloping in 2003. Remember that interest rates consist of a risk-free return, k_{RF}, which includes the real risk-free return (k^*), an adjustment for expected inflation (IP), and a risk premium that rewards investors for various risks, including default risk (DRP), liquidity risk (LP), and maturity risk (MRP). Although the real risk-free rate of return, k^*, does change at times, it generally is relatively stable from period to period. As a result, when interest rates shift to substantially different levels, it generally is because investors have changed their expectations concerning future inflation or their attitudes concerning risk. Because changes in investors' risk attitudes generally evolve over time, inflation expectations represent an important factor in the determination of current interest rates, and thus the shape of the yield curve.

To illustrate how inflation impacts the shape of the yield curve, let's examine interest rates on U.S. Treasury securities. First, the rate of return on these securities can be written as follows:

$$k = k_{RF} + MRP = [k^* + IP] + MRP$$

This equation is the same as Equation 2–2, except the default risk premium (DRP) and the liquidity premium (LP) are not included because we generally consider Treasury securities to be very liquid (marketable), default-free investments. As a result, DRP = 0 and LP = 0. The maturity risk premium (MRP) is included in the equation because Treasury securities vary in maturity from as little as a few days to as much as 30 years. All else equal, *investors generally prefer to hold short-term securities* because such securities are less sensitive to changes in interest rates and provide greater investment flexibility than longer-term securities. Investors will, therefore, generally accept lower yields on short-term securities, and this leads to relatively low short-term rates. *Borrowers, on the other hand, generally prefer long-term debt*, because short-term debt exposes them to the risk of having to refinance the debt under adverse conditions. Accordingly, borrowers want to "lock into" long-term funds, which means they are willing to pay a higher rate, other things held constant, for long-term funds than for short-term funds, which also leads to relatively low short-term rates. Taken together, these two sets of preferences imply that under normal conditions, a positive maturity risk premium (MRP) exists, and the MRP increases with years to maturity, causing the yield curve to be upward sloping. In economics, the general theory that supports this conclusion is referred to as the **liquidity preference theory,** which simply states that long-term bonds normally yield more than short-term bonds, all else equal, primarily because MRP > 0.

During the past few decades, we have observed three basic shapes to the yield curve associated with Treasury securities. Each of the three shapes is shown in

LIQUIDITY PREFERENCE THEORY
The theory that, all else equal, lenders prefer to make short-term loans rather than long-term loans; hence, they will lend short-term funds at lower rates than long-term funds.

Figure 2–6—that is, a normal, or upward sloping yield curve, an inverted, or downward sloping yield curve, and a flat yield curve. For this reason, it appears that the fact that MRP > 0, which supports the liquidity preference theory, does not fully explain the shape of the yield curve. Remember that the nominal risk-free rate of return consists of two components—the real risk-free rate of return, k*, which is considered to be relatively constant from one year to another, and an adjustment for the inflation expectations of investors, IP. Expectations about future inflation vary over time. But, the inflation premium, IP, that is included in interest rates is somewhat predictable because it is the average of the inflation rates that are expected to occur during the life of the investment (a Treasury security in this case). In fact, the yield curve is often used as an aid when forecasting future interest rates, because both investors and borrowers base their current decisions on expectations regarding which way interest rates will move in the future. For example, interest rates were at such low levels in 2003 (the lowest in 45 years) that most people believed that rates most certainly would have to increase in the future. The attitude was that rates could not possibly drop any lower. During this time, many homeowners refinanced their houses to take advantage of, and thus "lock in," the low rates, whereas most investors purchased short-term securities in hopes that rates would increase in the future, at which time they might choose to "lock in" the higher rates. Clearly, the expectations of the participants in the financial markets—that is, investors and borrowers—greatly impact interest rates. The **expectations theory** states that the yield curve depends on *expectations* concerning future inflation rates. We illustrate how expectations can be used to help forecast interest rates in the next section.

EXPECTATIONS THEORY

The theory that the shape of the yield curve depends on investors' expectations about future inflation rates.

Let's consider the impact of inflation expectations and maturity on the determination of interest rates with two simple examples: (1) inflation is expected to increase in the future, and (2) inflation is expected to decrease in the future. Assume the real risk-free rate, k*, is 2 percent and that investors demand a 0.1 percent premium for each year remaining until maturity for any debt with a term to maturity greater than one year, with a maximum value of 1 percent. For example, if a Treasury bill matures in one year, MRP = 0; but, if a Treasury bond matures in five years, MRP = 0.5%, and bonds that mature in 10 years or longer will have MRP = 1.0%. Also, assume that inflation expectations are as follows for the two situations:

YEAR	INCREASING INFLATION	DECREASING INFLATION
1	1.0%	5.0%
2	1.8	4.2
3	2.0	4.0
4	2.4	3.4
5	2.8	3.2
After Year 5	3.0	2.4

Note that these two situations are not related—that is, we are not assuming that the economic conditions in the first year in both cases are the same.

Using this information, we can compute the interest rates for Treasury securities with any term to maturity. To illustrate, consider a bond that matures in five years. For the case in which inflation is expected to increase, the interest rate, or yield, on this bond should be 4.5 percent: k* = 2%, IP = 2%, and MRP = 0.5%. Because IP is the average of the rate of inflation that is expected for each year during the life of the bond, IP = (1.0% + 1.8% + 2.0% + 2.4% + 2.8%)/5 = 2.0%. Also, MRP = 0.1% per

FIGURE 2–7	Illustrative Yield Curves for Treasury Securities

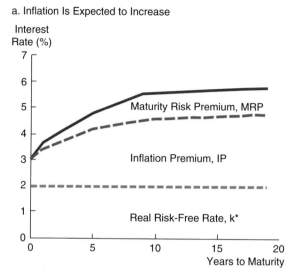

a. Inflation Is Expected to Increase

b. Inflation Is Expected to Decrease

	Inflation Is Expected to Increase			
Maturity	k*	IP	MRP	Yield
1 year	2.0%	1.0%	0.0%	3.0%
5 years	2.0	2.0	0.5	4.5
10 years	2.0	2.5	1.0	5.5
20 years	2.0	2.8	1.0	5.8

	Inflation Is Expected to Decrease			
Maturity	k*	IP	MRP	Yield
1 year	2.0%	5.0%	0.0%	7.0%
5 years	2.0	4.0	0.5	6.5
10 years	2.0	3.2	1.0	6.2
20 years	2.0	2.8	1.0	5.8

Note: The inflation premium is the average of the expected inflation rates during the life of the security. Therefore, in the case where inflation is expected to *increase*, IP_{10} is computed as follows:

$$IP_{10} = \frac{1.0\% + 1.8\% + 2.0\% + 2.4\% + 2.8\% + 3.0\% + 3.0\% + 3.0\% + 3.0\% + 3.0\%}{10} = \frac{25\%}{10} = 2.5\%$$

year for this bond because its term to maturity is greater than one year; thus, MRP = 0.1% × 5 years = 0.5%. As a result,

$$k = [k^* + IP] + MRP = [2\% + 2\%] + 0.5\% = 4.5\%$$

Figure 2–7 shows the yield curves for both inflationary situations. The yields are given in the tables below the graphs. As the graphs show, when inflation is expected to increase, the yield curve is upward sloping, and vice versa. In either case, economists often use the yield curve to form expectations about the future of the economy. For example, when inflation is high and expected to decline, as Panel b of Figure 2–7 indicates, the yield curve generally is downward sloping. In many cases a downward sloping yield curve suggests that the economy will weaken in the future. Consumers delay purchases because they expect prices to decline in the future, borrowers wait to borrow funds because they believe rates will be lower in the future, and investors provide more funds to the financial markets in an effort to capture higher current rates. All of these actions lead to lower long-term rates in the current period.

At times the yield curve is either humped or dips for bonds in a particular range of terms to maturity. In such cases, the supply/demand conditions within that range are significantly different than for shorter maturity ranges and longer maturity ranges.

This condition causes interest rates for bonds in that maturity range to be either substantially higher or substantially lower than rates in the maturity ranges on either side, and the resulting yield curve is not smooth or uniform; rather there will be a hump in the yield curve if rates are higher and a dip if rates are lower. The reason these humps and dips occur is because there are instances when investors and borrowers prefer bonds with specific maturity ranges. For example, a person borrowing to buy a long-term asset like a house, or an electric utility borrowing to build a power plant, would want a long-term loan. However, a retailer borrowing in September to build its inventories for Christmas would prefer a short-term loan. Similar differences exist among savers. For example, a person saving up to take a vacation next summer would want to lend in the short-term market, but someone saving for retirement 20 years hence would probably buy long-term securities.

MARKET SEGMENTATION THEORY
The theory that each borrower and lender has a preferred maturity and that the slope of the yield curve depends on the supply of and demand for funds in the long-term market relative to the short-term market.

According to the **market segmentation theory** that has been developed by economists, the slope of the yield curve depends on supply/demand conditions in the long- and short-term markets. Thus, the yield curve could at any given time be flat, upward sloping, or downward sloping and have humps or dips. Interest rates would be high in a particular segment compared to other segments when there was a low supply of funds in that segment relative to demand, and vice versa.

In this section, we used Treasury securities to illustrate concepts relating to the shape of the yield curve. The same concepts apply to corporate bonds. To include corporate bonds in the illustration, however, we would have to determine the default risk premium, DRP, and the liquidity premium, LP, associated with these bonds. In other words, the interest rates on corporate bonds would be determined using Equation 2–2:

$$k = k_{RF} + [DRP + LP + MRP] = [k^* + IP] + [MRP + DRP + LP]$$

For corporate bonds DRP > 0 and LP > 0, which means that interest rates on corporate bonds are greater than interest rates on Treasury securities. The risk-free rate of return for both types of securities is the same, $k_{RF} = k^* + IP$. But, because corporate bonds have default risk, liquidity risk, and maturity risk, whereas long-term Treasury securities only have maturity risk, the risk premiums on corporate bonds (MRP + DPR + LP) are greater than the risk premiums on Treasuries (MRP). As a result, if we plotted the yield curves for the bonds of a particular corporation, such as IBM or K-Mart, the curve would be higher than for Treasury securities, and it would be higher for riskier corporations. For instance, the yield curve for IBM's bonds would be below the yield curve for K-Mart's bonds, because K-Mart recently emerged from bankruptcy and is considered riskier than IBM. IBM's bonds are rated as investment grade, which means low default risk, whereas K-Mart's bonds are rated as "junk bonds," which means high default risk.

Self-Test Questions

Distinguish between the shapes of a "normal" yield curve and an "inverted" yield curve, and explain when each might exist.

How do the various risk premiums affect the yield curve?

Discuss the validity of each of the three theories mentioned in this section that have been proposed to explain the shape of the yield curve.

Does the Yield Curve Indicate Future Interest Rates?

As we noted earlier, the expectations theory states that the shape of the yield curve depends on expectations concerning future inflation rates. We also know that the *primary* reason interest rates change is because people who participate in the financial markets change their expectations concerning future inflation rates. If this is true, should we be able to use the yield curve to help forecast future interest rates? In this section, we examine Treasury securities to illustrate how interest rates might be forecasted using information provided by a yield curve. Because many, many factors affect interest rates in the real world, models that are used to forecast interest rates are complex and not always accurate. Therefore, the discussion in the section is greatly oversimplified: Significantly more analysis than examining a yield curve is needed to forecast interest rates.

Although we know that Treasury securities are exposed to maturity risk, to simplify the discussion here, we assume that MRP = 0 in the determination of interest rates for these securities. If MRP = 0, then all Treasury securities have the same risk, regardless of their terms to maturity, and neither investors nor borrowers should have a preference for securities with particular maturities because all securities are interchangeable. In other words, if a person wants to invest for a five-year period, he or she would not care whether the funds are invested in a Treasury bond that matures in five years or a Treasury bill that matures in one year and can be "turned over" for the next five years. The Treasury securities should be perfect substitutes for each other so that the investor earns the same return if the money is invested in the five-year Treasury bond or five one-year Treasury bills that mature one after the other. The reason for this is because the yield on the five-year T-bond is the average of the yields on the five one-year T-bills.

To illustrate, suppose that on January 1, 2005, the real risk-free rate of interest was $k^* = 3\%$ and expected inflation rates for the next three years were as follows:[15]

Year	Expected Annual (1-year) Inflation Rate	Expected Average Inflation Rate from January 1, 2005, to December 31 of Indicated Year, IP_t	
2005	2%	$IP_1 = (2\%)/1$	$= 2\%$
2006	4%	$IP_2 = (2\% + 4\%)/2$	$= 3\%$
2007	6%	$IP_3 = (2\% + 4\% + 6\%)/3$	$= 4\%$

Given these expectations, the following interest rate pattern should exist:

Bond Type	Real Risk-Free Rate(k^*)		Inflation Premium: Average Expected Inflation Rate (IP_t)		Nominal Treasury Bond Rate for Each Maturity ($k_{T\text{-}bond}$)
1-year bond	3%	+	2%	=	5%
2-year bond	3%	+	3%	=	6%
3-year bond	3%	+	4%	=	7%

---

[15]In this example we compute simple *arithmetic* averages. Technically, we should be using *geometric* averages, but the differences are not material in this example. For a discussion of this point, see Chapter 17 in Scott Besley and Eugene F. Brigham, *Principles of Finance*, 2nd ed. (Cincinnati, OH: South-Western, 2003).

If the yields on these hypothetical bonds were plotted, the yield curve would be upward sloping, similar to the July 2003 yield curve in Figure 2–6.

Had the pattern of expected inflation rates been reversed, with inflation expected to fall from 6 percent to 2 percent during the three-year period, the following situation would exist:

YEAR	EXPECTED ANNUAL (1-YEAR) INFLATION RATE	EXPECTED AVERAGE INFLATION RATE FROM JANUARY 1, 2005, TO DECEMBER 31 OF INDICATED YEAR, IP_t		
2005	6%	$IP_1 =$	$(6\%)/1$	$= 6\%$
2006	4%	$IP_2 =$	$(6\% + 4\%)/2$	$= 5\%$
2007	2%	$IP_3 =$	$(6\% + 4\% + 2\%)/3$	$= 4\%$

BOND TYPE	REAL RISK-FREE RATE (k*)		INFLATION PREMIUM: AVERAGE EXPECTED INFLATION RATE (IP_t)		NOMINAL TREASURY BOND RATE FOR EACH MATURITY ($k_{T\text{-BOND}}$)
1-year bond	3%	+	6%	=	9%
2-year bond	3%	+	5%	=	8%
3-year bond	3%	+	4%	=	7%

In this case, the pattern of interest rates would produce an inverted yield curve like the March 1980 yield curve in Figure 2–6. As you can see, whenever the annual rate of inflation is expected to decline, according to the expectations theory the yield curve must be downward sloping, or inverted, and vice versa.

We should also be able to forecast the interest rate each year by examining the yields that currently exist on bonds with various maturities. For example, if *The Wall Street Journal* reports that the yield on a one-year T-bill is 5 percent and the yield on a two-year T-bond is 6 percent, then, because the yield on any bond is the average of the annual interest rates during its life, we know the following relationship exists in this situation:

$$\text{Yield on a Two-Year Bond} = \frac{\left(\begin{array}{c}\text{Interest rate} \\ \text{in the first year}\end{array}\right) + \left(\begin{array}{c}\text{Interest rate} \\ \text{in the second year}\end{array}\right)}{2} = \frac{5\% + X\%}{2} = 6\%$$

Solving for X%, we have

$$5\% + X\% = 6\%(2) = 12\%, \text{ so } X\% = 12\% - 5\% = 7\%$$

This is the yield an investor who purchases a two-year bond would expect to earn during 2006. Therefore, according to this example, investors would expect the interest rate to equal 5 percent in 2005 and 7 percent in 2006. If this is true, then the average yield over the next two years is 6% = (5% + 7%)/2 which is the nominal rate, k, for the two-year bond in the first illustration. You can see that the yield curve is upward sloping whenever interest rates are expected to increase in future years, because the average yield increases as higher interest rates are included in the computation.

This information can also be used to determine the expected inflation rate. In the current example, the interest rate consists of the real risk-free rate, k*, which is constant, and an adjustment for inflation. Therefore, to determine the expected inflation rate each year, we simply subtract k* from the interest rate that is expected to occur during the year. Remember that we assumed the real risk-free rate, k*, is 3 percent each year. As a result, in the current example, investors expect inflation to be 2% = 5% − 3% in 2005 and 4% = 7% − 3% in 2006. These results are the same as the expected inflation rates that were reported earlier.

Self-Test Question

If interest rates are based solely on the expectations of investors and borrowers, how are long-term interest rates computed?

Other Factors That Influence Interest Rate Levels

Factors other than those discussed in the previous sections also influence both the general level of interest rates and the shape of the yield curve. The four most important factors are (1) Federal Reserve policy, (2) the level of the federal budget deficit, (3) the foreign trade balance, and (4) the level of business activity.

Federal Reserve Policy

As you probably learned in your economics courses, (1) the money supply has a major effect on both the level of economic activity and the rate of inflation, and (2) in the United States, the Federal Reserve controls the money supply. If the Fed wants to control growth in the economy, it slows growth in the money supply. The initial effect of such an action is to cause interest rates to increase and inflation to stabilize. The reverse holds if the Fed loosens the money supply.

To illustrate, to support market liquidity and to induce an economic recovery, the Federal Reserve took steps to reduce interest rates seven times in 2001. Because the Fed deals primarily in the short-term end of the market, these reductions had the direct effect of pushing short-term interest rates down. Long-run rates followed, but the fact that the Fed was taking action to control adverse economic pressures affected investors' expectations concerning inflation and, hence, interest rates.

During periods when the Fed is actively intervening in the markets, the yield curve is distorted. Short-term rates are temporarily "too low" if the Fed is easing credit and "too high" if it is tightening credit. Long-term rates are not affected as much by Fed intervention because they represent averages of short-term expectations.

Federal Deficits

If the federal government spends more than it takes in from tax revenues, it runs a deficit, and that deficit must be covered either by borrowing or by printing money. If the government borrows, this added demand for funds pushes up interest rates. If it prints money, this increases expectations for future inflation (more money to purchase the same amount of goods and services), which also drives up interest rates. Thus, the larger the federal deficit, other things held constant, the higher the level of interest rates. Whether long- or short-term rates are more affected depends on how the deficit is financed, so we cannot state, in general, how deficits will affect the slope of the yield curve.

Foreign Trade Balance

Businesses and individuals in the United States buy from and sell to people and firms in other countries. If we buy more than we sell—that is, if we import more than we export—we are said to be running a foreign trade deficit. When trade deficits occur, they must be financed, and the main source of financing is debt.[16] Therefore, the larger the trade deficit, the more we must borrow, and as we increase our borrowing, this drives up interest rates. Also, foreigners are willing to hold U.S. debt only if the interest rate on this debt is competitive with interest rates in other countries. Therefore, if the Federal Reserve attempts to lower interest rates in the United States, causing rates to fall below rates in other countries, foreigners will sell U.S. bonds, which will depress bond prices and cause U.S. interest rates to increase. As a result, the existence of a deficit trade balance hinders the Fed's ability to combat a recession by lowering interest rates.

The United States has run annual trade deficits since the mid-1970s, and the cumulative effect of these deficits is that the United States is by far the largest debtor nation of all time. As a result, our interest rates are very much influenced by interest rate trends in other countries around the world (higher rates abroad lead to higher U.S. rates). Because of all this, U.S. corporate treasurers—and anyone else who is affected by interest rates—must keep up with developments in the world economy.

Business Activity

Figures 2–3 and 2–4, presented earlier, can be examined to see how business conditions influence interest rates. Here are the key points revealed by the graphs:

1. Because inflation increased from the 1970s to 1981, the general tendency during this period was toward higher interest rates. However, since the 1981 peak, the trend has generally been downward.
2. Short-term rates have almost always been below long-term rates. Thus, the yield curve almost always is "normal" in the sense that it is upward sloping.
3. The shaded areas in Figure 2–3 represent recessions, during which both the demand for money and the rate of inflation tend to fall. At the same time, the Federal Reserve tends to increase the money supply in an effort to stimulate the economy. As a result, there is a tendency for interest rates to decline during recessions. During most of 2001 the economy was in a recession, so the Fed took actions to reduce interest rates to encourage a recovery. By mid-year 2003, the economy had recovered slightly, but consumers and investors were unsure of the future direction of the economy, so any actions taken by the Fed were to continue to promote recovery and to guard against an economic reversal.
4. During recessions, short-term rates decline more sharply than long-term rates. This occurs for two reasons. First, the Fed operates mainly in the short-term

---

[16]The deficit can also be financed by selling assets, including gold, corporate stocks, entire companies, and real estate. The United States has financed its massive trade deficits by all of these means at various times, but the primary method has been by borrowing.

sector, so its intervention has the strongest effect here. Second, long-term rates reflect the average expected inflation rate over the next 20 to 30 years, and this expectation generally does not change much, even when the current rate of inflation is low (or high).

Self-Test Questions

Other than inflationary expectations and normal supply/demand fluctuations, name four additional factors that influence interest rates. Explain their effects.

How does the Fed stimulate the economy? How does the Fed affect interest rates?

Interest Rate Levels and Stock Prices

Interest rates have two effects on corporate profits. First, because interest is a cost, the higher the rate of interest, the lower a firm's profits, other things held constant. Second, interest rates affect the level of economic activity, and economic activity affects corporate profits. Interest rates obviously affect stock prices because of their effects on profits, but, perhaps even more important, they have an effect due to competition in the marketplace between stocks and bonds. If interest rates rise sharply, investors can get higher returns in the bond market, which induces them to sell stocks and to transfer funds from the stock market to the bond market. A massive sale of stocks in response to rising interest rates obviously would depress stock prices. Of course, the reverse occurs if interest rates decline. Indeed, the bull market of December 1991, when the Dow Jones Industrial Index rose 10 percent in less than a month, was caused almost entirely by the sharp drop in long-term interest rates. On the other hand, the poor performance exhibited by the stock market in 1999 and 2000—common stocks declined in average by more than 10 percent—resulted from sharp increases in interest rates during that period. During 2002 and 2003, as interest rates declined to historically low levels, the stock market recovered somewhat. Given the significant decrease in interest rates, the stock market recovery probably was neither as rapid nor to the degree that might have been predicted according to the discussion in this chapter. Investors remained fairly skittish with respect to their investments because some large corporations disclosed that they had used unethical accounting practices to construct financial statements. As a result, investors' distrust of financial information kept them on the sidelines longer than would normally be expected—that is, when economic factors dominate general investing decisions.

Self-Test Question

In what two ways do changes in interest rates affect stock prices?

Interest Rates and Business Decisions

The yield curve for July 2003, shown earlier in Figure 2–6 indicates how much the U.S. government had to pay in 2003 to borrow money for one year, five years, 10 years, and 20 years. A business borrower would have had to pay somewhat more, but assume for the moment that we are back in 2003 and that the yield curve for that year also applies to your company. Now suppose your company has decided (1) to build a new plant that has a 20-year life and will cost $10 million and (2) to raise the necessary funds by selling an issue of debt (or borrowing) rather than by issuing stock. If the company borrows on a short-term basis—say, for one year—the rate on the loan would be only 1 percent, so the interest cost for the year would be $100,000, whereas, if the company used long-term (20-year) financing, the rate would be 4.3 percent, and the interest cost for the year would be $430,000. At first glance, it would seem that the company should use short-term debt to finance the plant.

However, this could prove to be a horrible mistake. If the company uses short-term debt, the loan would have to be renewed every year, and the rate charged on each new loan will reflect the then-current short-term rate. Interest rates could return to their March 1980 levels, so by 2004 the company could be paying 14 percent, or $1.4 million, per year. These high interest payments would cut into, and perhaps eliminate, the company's profits. The reduced profitability could easily increase your firm's risk to the point where its bond rating would be lowered, causing lenders to increase the risk premium built into the interest rates they charge, which in turn would force the company to pay even higher rates. These high interest rates would further reduce profitability, worrying lenders even more, and making them reluctant to renew the loan in the following year. If lenders refused to renew the loan and demanded payment, as they have every right to do, the company might have trouble raising the cash. If it had to make price cuts to convert physical assets to cash, heavy operating losses might be incurred, which could result in bankruptcy.

On the other hand, if the company used long-term financing, the interest costs would remain constant at $430,000 per year, so an increase in interest rates in the economy would not hurt the company. Your company might even be able to buy up some of your bankrupt competitors at bargain prices. Bankruptcies increase dramatically when interest rates rise, primarily because many firms use short-term debt.

Does all this suggest that firms should always avoid short-term debt? Not necessarily. If inflation falls, so will interest rates. If your company borrows on a long-term basis for 4.3 percent, then you would be at a major disadvantage if competitors who used short-term debt could borrow at a cost of only 3 percent in subsequent years. On the other hand, large federal deficits might drive inflation and interest rates up to new record levels. In that case, you would wish you had borrowed on a long-term basis.

Financing decisions would be easy if we could develop accurate forecasts of future interest rates. Unfortunately, predicting future interest rates with consistent accuracy is somewhere between difficult and impossible: People who make a living by selling interest rate forecasts say it is difficult, but many others say it is impossible. But, even if it is difficult to predict future interest rate levels, it is easy to predict that interest rates will fluctuate. They always have, and they always will. This being the case, sound financial policy calls for using a mix of long- and short-term debt, as well as equity, in such a manner that the firm can survive in most interest-rate environments. Further, the optimal financial policy depends in an important way on the nature of the firm's assets: The easier it is to sell off assets and thus to pay off debts, the more feasible it is to use large amounts of short-term debt. This makes it more feasible to finance current assets than fixed assets with short-term debt. We will return to this issue later in the book, when we discuss working capital policy.

Self-Test Question

If short-term interest rates are lower than long-term rates, why might a firm still choose to finance with long-term debt?

International Financial Markets

Financial markets have become much more global during the last few decades. As the economies of emerging countries in Asia and South America have developed and experienced enormous growth in their financial markets, greater numbers of investors were willing to provide funds to these regions. To illustrate, consider the fact that U.S. stocks accounted for nearly two-thirds of the value of worldwide stock markets in 1970. But, as Table 2–2 shows, U.S. stock markets now represent less than 50 percent of the total value worldwide. The areas of greatest growth are in the emerging markets in Asia, including Korea and China, and in South America, especially Brazil and Argentina.

Even with the expansion of stock markets internationally, exchanges in the United States still conduct the greatest numbers of trades, both with respect to volume and value. In 2001, stock trades in the United States exceeded $29 trillion, which was more than 15 times greater than the value of stocks traded in foreign countries with stock trades greater than $1 trillion: United Kingdom ($1.9 trillion), Japan ($1.8 trillion), Germany ($1.4 trillion), France ($1.1 trillion), and the Netherlands ($1.0 trillion). In fact, trading activity in the United States accounted for 69 percent of worldwide trading activity in 2001.[17]

The international market for bonds has experienced growth similar to the international stock markets. The value of the U.S. bond market is substantial, but the bond markets in such countries as the United Kingdom, Japan, and Germany have experienced substantial growth during the last decade. For example, from 1990 to 1999 the value of bond markets in the United States increased 132 percent, while the values of bond markets in the United Kingdom, Japan, and Germany increased by 166 percent, 120 percent, and 97 percent, respectively.

On January 1, 1999, the European Monetary Union (EMU) began. The EMU, often referred to as Euroland or Europa, which started with 11 countries, created a common currency, called the *euro*, and a common debt instrument that is denominated in the euro and is traded in a unified financial market called the Euro market.[18] The primary reason Euroland was created was to reduce or eliminate country boundaries with respect to member countries' economic and trading policies. In 2003, the Euroland bond market was nearly 40 percent of the size of the U.S. bond market. Today the bond markets in the United States and Euroland account for approximately 50 percent and 20 percent, respectively, of the total value of bonds outstanding worldwide.[19] As the EMU grows stronger during the next decade, so will the importance of the Euroland market. The financial markets truly are global in nature: Events that influence the markets in Asia and Europe also influence the markets in the United States.

While the globalization of financial markets continues and international markets offer investors greater frontiers of opportunities, investing overseas can be difficult due to restrictions or barriers erected by foreign countries. In many cases, individual investors find it difficult or unattractive to invest directly in foreign stocks because

---

[17]*Emerging Markets Factbook 2002* (New York: Standard & Poor's, 2002).

[18]In 1999, the 11 countries included in Euroland were Austria, Belgium, Finland, France, Germany, Ireland, Italy, Luxemburg, Netherlands, Portugal, and Spain. Greece has since joined the EMU.

[19]In May 2003, the total value of bonds traded in Euroland markets was $7.8 trillion, and the value was $20.6 trillion in the U.S. markets. Information sources: U.S. data came from The Bonds Market Association at http://www.bondmarket.com, and EMU data came from the European Central Bank Web site at http://www.ecb.int.

TABLE 2–2	Foreign Stock Market Values ($ billion)[a]

	YEAR-END 1992 MARKET VALUE	PERCENT OF TOTAL	YEAR-END 2001 MARKET VALUE	PERCENT OF TOTAL	10-YEAR GROWTH	DOMESTIC COMPANIES LISTED, 2001
I. Developed Stock Markets						
United States[b]	4,485.0	41.0	13,810.4	49.6	207.9	6,355
Japan[c]	2,399.0	21.9	2,251.8	8.1	–6.1	2,471
United Kingdom	927.1	8.5	2,217.3	8.0	139.2	1,923
France	350.9	3.2	1,174.4	4.2	234.7	791
Germany	348.1	3.2	1,071.7	3.9	207.9	988
Other developed markets	1,440.8	13.2	4,721.0	17.0	227.7	10,812
All developed markets (31 countries)	9,950.9	91.0	25,246.6	90.8	153.7	23,340
II. Emerging Stock Markets						
China	18.3	0.2	524.0	1.9	2,763.4	1,160
Taiwan, China	101.1	0.9	292.6	1.1	189.4	584
Korea	107.4	1.0	220.0	0.8	104.8	1,409
Argentina	18.6	0.2	192.5	0.7	934.9	111
Brazil	45.3	0.4	186.2	0.7	311.0	428
Other emerging markets	690.9	6.3	1,156.8	4.2	67.4	21,188
All emerging markets (78 countries)	981.6	9.0	2,572.1	9.2	162.0	24,880
All stock markets	10,932.5	100.0	27,818.7	100.0	154.5	48,220

[a]All market values are stated in U.S. dollars. Some of the changes in market values from 1992 to 2001 resulted from changes in the value of the dollar relative to foreign currencies (exchange rates).

[b]Based on the combined values of the New York Stock Exchange, the American Stock Exchange, Nasdaq, and the Chicago Stock Exchange.

[c]Based on the combined values of the Tokyo Stock Exchange and the Osaka Securities Exchange.

SOURCE: Emerging Stock Markets Factbook 2002 (New York: Standard & Poor's, 2002).

AMERICAN DEPOSITORY RECEIPTS (ADRs)
Certificates created by such organizations as banks that represent ownership in stocks of foreign companies.

many countries prohibit or severely limit the ability of foreigners to invest in their financial markets, or they make it extremely difficult to access reliable information concerning the companies that are traded in the stock markets. Therefore, most individuals interested in investing internationally do so indirectly by purchasing financial instruments that represent foreign stocks, bonds, and other investments but are offered by institutions in the United States. Investors can participate internationally by purchasing mutual funds that hold international stocks, foreign securities certificates issued in dollar denominations, or **American Depository Receipts (ADRs).** ADRs are not foreign stocks; rather they are "certificates" created by such organizations as banks that represent ownership in stocks of foreign companies. The values of the certificates, which are held in trust by a bank located in the country where the stock is traded, are closely related to the foreign stocks they represent.

Self-Test Questions

Why should investors in the United States be concerned with financial markets in other countries?

How do you think the European Monetary Union (EMU) affects the international financial markets?

International Banking

Two notable factors distinguish the banking system in the United States from banking structures in other countries. Both factors can be traced to the regulatory climate that has existed historically in the United States. Generally speaking, financial institutions in the United States have been much more heavily regulated and have faced greater limitations with regard to branching activity and nonbanking business relationships than their foreign counterparts. Such regulations have imposed an organizational structure and competitive environment that have historically curbed the ability of individual banking organizations in the United States to grow in size.

First, until recently, interstate branch banking was either prohibited or severely limited in the United States. As a result, the U.S. banking system traditionally has been characterized by a large number of independent banks of various sizes rather than a few large banks that might exist with unrestricted branch banking. For that reason, the country has more than 20,000 individual banks, credit unions, and thrift institutions. In contrast, the banking companies of nearly every other country in the world have been allowed to branch with few, if any, limitations; thus their banking systems include far fewer individual, or unit, institutions than exist in the United States. Japan, for example, has fewer than 170 such institutions; Australia has about 44 banks, four of which are considered large commercial banks; and Canada has only 53 chartered banks, seven of which operate nationally and internationally. Even India, which has a population nearly four times larger than the United States, has fewer than 300 individual banks, about 3.5 percent of the number in the United States. But, in India as well as other countries, each bank generally has many branches. For instance, the State Bank of India alone has more than 8,700 offices (branches).

The second major difference between U.S. banks and their foreign counterparts is that most foreign banks are allowed to engage in nonbanking business activities while the nonbanking activities of U.S. banks have been severely restricted until recently. Such developed countries as the United Kingdom, France, Germany, and Switzerland, to name a few, permit banking firms and commercial firms to interact without restriction; banking firms can own commercial firms, and vice versa. Other countries, including Canada, Japan, and Spain, allow the mixing of banking firms and commercial firms with some restrictions. In aggregate, banks in countries that permit banking and commerce to be combined account for about 75 percent of banking assets throughout the world. Thus, regulations that restrict the nonbanking activities of U.S. banks have positioned these institutions so that they have been at a competitive disadvantage internationally. But, as Congress has demonstrated recently, the legislative trend is to remove existing "competitive restraints" so U.S. institutions can better compete in the global financial arena.

Because foreign banks are less regulated and have fewer restrictions concerning the types of business activities they can pursue than their U.S. counterparts, such banks often engage in numerous aspects of multilayered financial deals. For example, a foreign bank might use its investment banking division to help a business raise funds through a new stock issue, even though the bank owns stock in the company and is its primary lender. Having the ability to act as a company's lender, owner, investment banker, and insurer permits foreign banking organizations to offer financial products that previously were not available to U.S. banking organizations. In addition, because such financial products can be packaged together by a single bank, it is possible to reduce the aggregate costs associated with financial services.

With less restrictive regulations and other limitations on banking activities than in the United States, foreign banking organizations have tended to develop huge, one-stop financial service institutions. And, it should not be surprising that foreign banks dominate international banking activities. Certainly, fewer restrictions have helped foreign banks attain such dominance. In addition, foreign banks have been involved in international banking much longer than U.S. banks. The worldwide presence of European banks can be documented as far back as the 12th century when banks from Italy dominated international trade. In fact, American banks were not permitted to have operations outside the United States until 1913, when the Federal Reserve Act was passed. Until about 40 years ago, not many U.S. banks even operated internationally.

Even with the restrictions on American banking operations overseas, the presence of U.S. banks in international banking has increased rapidly in recent years. At the same time, foreign banks face limitations in the United States, because they must abide by U.S. banking regulations. But these restrictions have not discouraged the presence of foreign banks, especially in California, where large Japanese banks have established significant market shares. As the world becomes more globally oriented, so will the banking industry. American banks will become more important internationally, while foreign banks will increase their presence in the United States.

Self-Test Questions

How do U.S. financial institutions differ from their counterparts in other countries?

What two factors distinguish the banking system in the United States from banking structures in other countries?

What changes are needed for U.S. financial institutions to become more competitive with financial institutions in other countries? Do you think such changes will occur in the near future?

Summary

In this chapter we discussed the nature of financial markets, the types of institutions that operate in these markets, the establishment of interest rates, and some of the ways in which interest rates affect business decisions. The key concepts covered are as follows:

- There are many different types of **financial markets.** Each market serves a different region or deals with a different type of security.
- Transfers of capital between borrowers and savers take place (1) by **direct transfers** of money and securities; (2) by transfers through **investment banking houses,** which act as middlemen; and (3) by transfers through **financial intermediaries,** which create new securities.
- The **stock market** is an especially important market because this is where stock prices, which are used to "grade" managers' performances are established.

- There are two basic types of stock markets: **physical stock exchanges** and **organized investment networks,** which include **Nasdaq,** the **over-the-counter market,** and **electronic communications networks (ECN).**

- Capital is allocated through the price system—a price must be paid to "rent" money. Lenders charge **interest** on funds they lend, while equity investors receive **dividends and capital gains** in return for letting firms use their money.

- Four fundamental factors affect the cost of money: (1) **production opportunities,** (2) **time preferences for consumption,** (3) **risk,** and (4) **inflation.**

- The **risk-free rate of interest, k_{RF},** is defined as the real risk-free rate, k^*, plus an inflation premium (IP): $k_{RF} = k^* + IP$.

- The **nominal (or quoted) interest rate** on a debt security, k, is composed of the real risk-free rate, k^*, plus premiums that reflect **inflation (IP), default risk (DRP), liquidity (LP),** and **maturity risk (MRP):** $k = [k^* + IP] + [DRP + LP + MRP]$.

- If the real risk-free rate of interest and the various premiums were constant over time, interest rates in the economy would be stable. However, both the real rate and the premiums, especially the premium for expected inflation, do change over time, causing market interest rates to change. Also, Federal Reserve intervention to increase or decrease the money supply (as well as international currency flows) leads to fluctuations in interest rates.

- The relationship between the yields on securities and the securities' maturities is known as the **term structure of interest rates,** and the **yield curve** is a graph of this relationship.

- The yield curve is normally **upward sloping**—this is called a **normal yield curve**—but the curve can **slope downward** (an **inverted yield curve**) if the demand for short-term funds is relatively strong or if the rate of inflation is expected to decline.

- The shape of a yield curve is influenced by investors' expectations as to future inflation rates **(expectations theory),** the fact that investors probably prefer shorter-term securities to longer-term securities **(liquidity preference theory),** all else equal, and the supply and demand relationship in various segments of the markets **(market segmentation theory).**

- Interest rate levels have a profound effect on stock prices. Higher interest rates (1) slow down the economy, (2) increase interest expenses and thus lower corporate profits, and (3) cause investors to sell stocks and transfer funds to the bond market. Each of these factors tends to depress stock prices.

- **International financial markets** have experienced significant growth during the past two decades, and the domination of the U.S. markets has decreased in recent years. Even so, the U.S. financial markets are much larger than the financial markets of any other country in the world. Generally, we invest in foreign companies indirectly through financial instruments sold in the United States.

- **Banking legislation** historically has restricted the ability of U.S. banks (1) to branch from one state to another and (2) to enter into nonbanking business activities. Recent legislation has removed many of these restrictions, and legislative actions to remove even more restrictions are expected in the future.

- As a result of previous regulatory restrictions, the number of banks in the United States is much greater than the number in most other countries. In addition, the average size of U.S. banks is much smaller than the average size of banks in other countries.

Questions

2-1 What are financial intermediaries, and what economic functions do they perform?

2-2 Suppose interest rates on residential mortgages of equal risk were 6 percent in California and 8 percent in New York. Could this differential persist? What forces might tend to equalize rates? Would differentials in borrowing costs for businesses of equal risk located in California and New York be more or less likely to exist than differentials in residential mortgage rates? Would differentials in the cost of money for New York and California firms be more likely to exist if the firms being compared were large or if they were small?

2-3 What would happen to the standard of living in the United States if people lost faith in the safety of our financial institutions? Why?

2-4 How does a cost-efficient capital market help to reduce the prices of goods and services?

2-5 Which fluctuate more, long- or short-term interest rates? Why?

2-6 Suppose you believe that the economy is just entering a recession. Your firm must raise capital immediately using debt (bonds). Should you borrow on a long-term or a short-term basis? Why?

2-7 Suppose a new process was developed that could be used to make oil out of seawater. The equipment required is quite expensive, but it would, in time, lead to low prices for gasoline, electricity, and other types of energy. What effect would this have on interest rates?

2-8 Suppose a new and much more liberal Congress and administration were elected, and their first order of business was to take away the independence of the Federal Reserve System and to force the Fed to expand greatly the money supply. What effect would this have:
   a. On the level and slope of the yield curve immediately after the announcement?
   b. On the level and slope of the yield curve that would exist two or three years in the future?

2-9 It is a fact that the federal government (1) encouraged the development of the savings and loan industry; (2) virtually forced the industry to make long-term, fixed-interest-rate mortgages; and (3) forced the savings and loans to obtain most of their capital as deposits that were withdrawable on demand. Would the savings and loan associations be better off in a world with a "normal" or an inverted yield curve?

2-10 Suppose interest rates on Treasury bonds rose from 5 to 8 percent as a result of higher interest rates in Europe. What effect would this have on the price of an average company's common stock?

2-11 How has deregulation of the financial services industry changed the makeup of financial intermediaries? How do you think intermediaries' characteristics will change in the future?

2-12 How do bank organizations in the United States differ from banking organizations in other countries? Why?

Self-Test Problems

(Solutions appear in Appendix B)

key terms   **ST-1** Define each of the following terms:
   a. Financial market
   b. Debt market; equity market
   c. Money market; capital market

d. Primary market; secondary market; initial public offering (IPO)
e. Private market; public market
f. Spot market; futures market
g. Investment banker; financial intermediary
h. Money market fund
i. Physical stock exchanges
j. Organized investment network; over-the-counter market; electronic communications network (ECN)
k. Production opportunities; time preferences for consumption
l. Risk; risk premium
m. Real risk-free rate of interest, k*; nominal risk-free rate of interest, k_{RF}
n. Inflation premium (IP); default risk premium (DRP); liquidity premium (LP)
o. Interest rate risk; maturity risk premium (MRP); reinvestment rate risk
p. Term structure of interest rates; yield curve
q. "Normal" yield curve; inverted ("abnormal") yield curve
r. Market segmentation theory; liquidity preference theory; expectations theory
s. American Depository Receipts (ADRs)

inflation rates **ST-2** Assume that it is now January 1, 2005. The rate of inflation is expected to be 2 percent throughout 2005. However, increased government deficits and renewed vigor in the economy are then expected to push inflation rates higher. Investors expect the inflation rate to be 3 percent in 2006, 5 percent in 2007, and 6 percent in 2008. The real risk-free rate, k*, currently is 3 percent. Assume that no maturity risk premiums are required on bonds with five years or less to maturity. The current interest rate on five-year T-bonds is 8 percent.

a. What is the average expected inflation rate over the next four years?
b. What should be the prevailing interest rate on four-year T-bonds?
c. What is the implied expected inflation rate in 2009, or Year 5, given that bonds that mature in that year yield 8 percent?

yields **ST-3** According to the results of a recent survey, investors expect the *annual* interest rates in each of the next three years to be:

YEAR	ONE-YEAR RATE
2005	5%
2006	9
2007	4

Given these expectations, what should be the yield to maturity for a three-year bond? To answer this question, assume today is January 1, 2005, and the three-year bond matures on December 31, 2007.

Problems

yield curve **2–1** Suppose you and most other investors expect the rate of inflation to be 7 percent next year, to fall to 5 percent during the following year, and then to remain at a rate of 3 percent thereafter. Assume that the real risk-free rate, k*, is 2 percent and that maturity risk premiums on Treasury securities rise from zero on very short-term bonds (those that mature in a few days) by 0.2 percentage points for each year to maturity, up to a limit of 1.0 percentage point on five-year or longer-term T-bonds.

a. Calculate the interest rate on one-, two-, three-, four-, five-, 10-, and 20-year Treasury securities, and plot the yield curve.

b. Now suppose IBM, a highly rated company, had bonds with the same maturities as the Treasury bonds. As an approximation, plot a yield curve for IBM on the same graph with the Treasury bond yield curve. (*Hint:* Think about the default risk premium on IBM's long-term versus its short-term bonds.)

c. Now plot the approximate yield curve of Long Island Lighting Company, a risky nuclear utility.

yield curves **2–2** The following yields on U.S. Treasury securities were taken from *The Wall Street Journal* on January 7, 2004:

TERM	RATE
6 months	1.0%
1 year	1.2
2 years	1.6
3 years	2.5
4 years	2.9
5 years	3.7
10 years	4.6
20 years	5.1
30 years	5.3

Plot a yield curve based on these data. Discuss how each term structure theory mentioned in the chapter can explain the shape of the yield curve you plot.

inflation and interest rates **2–3** Inflation currently is about 2 percent. Last year the Fed took actions to maintain inflation at this level. However, the economy is showing signs that it might be growing too quickly, and reports indicate that inflation is expected to increase during the next five years. Assume that *at the beginning of 2005*, the rate of inflation expected for the year is 4 percent; for 2006, it is *expected* to be 5 percent; for 2007, it is *expected* to be 7 percent; and, for 2008 and every year thereafter, it is *expected* to settle at 4 percent.

a. What is the average expected inflation rate over the five-year period 2005–2009?

b. What average nominal interest rate would, over the five-year period, be expected to produce a 2 percent real risk-free rate of return on five-year Treasury securities?

c. Assuming a real risk-free rate of 2 percent and a maturity risk premium that starts at 0.1 percent and increases by 0.1 percent *each year*, estimate the interest rate in January 2005 on bonds that mature in one, two, five, 10, and 20 years, and draw a yield curve based on these data.

d. Describe the general economic conditions that could be expected to produce an upward-sloping yield curve.

e. If the consensus among investors in early 2005 is that the expected rate of inflation for every future year is 5 percent (that is, $I_t = 5\%$ for t = 1 to ∞), what do you think the yield curve would look like? Consider all the factors that are likely to affect the curve. Does your answer here make you question the yield curve you drew in part c?

rate of interest **2–4** Assume that the real risk-free rate of return, k*, is 3 percent, and it will remain at that level far into the future. Also assume that maturity risk premiums on Treasury bonds increase from zero for bonds that mature in one year or less to a maximum of 2 percent, and MRP increases by 0.2 percent for each year to maturity that is greater than one year—that is, MRP equals 0.2 percent for a two-year bond, 0.4 percent for a three-year bond, and so forth. Following are the expected inflation rates for the next five years:

Year	Inflation Rate
2005	3%
2006	5
2007	4
2008	8
2009	3

a. What is the average expected inflation rate for a one-, two-, three-, four-, and five-year bond?

b. What should be the MRP for a one-, two-, three-, four-, and five-year bond?

c. Compute the interest rate for a one-, two-, three-, four-, and five-year bond.

d. If inflation is expected to equal 2 percent every year after 2009, what should be the interest rate for a 10- and 20-year bond?

e. Plot the yield curve for the interest rates you computed in parts c and d.

real risk-free rate, **2–5** Today's edition of *The Wall Street Journal* reports that the yield on Treasury
MRP, and DRP bills maturing in 30 days is 3.5 percent, the yield on Treasury bonds maturing in 10 years is 6.5 percent, and the yield on a bond issued by Nextel Communications that matures in six years is 7.5 percent. Also, today the Federal Reserve announced that inflation is expected to be 2 percent during the next 12 months. There is a maturity risk premium (MRP) associated with all bonds with maturities equal to one year or more.

a. Assume that the increase in the MRP each year is the same and the total MRP is the same for bonds with maturities equal to 10 years and greater—that is, MRP is at its maximum for bonds with maturities equal to 10 years and greater. What is the MRP per year?

b. What is the default risk premium associated with Nextel's bond?

c. What is the real risk-free rate of return?

Exam-Type Problems

The problems included in this section are set up in such a way that they could be used as multiple-choice exam problems.

expected inflation rate **2–6** According to *The Wall Street Journal*, the interest rate on one-year Treasury bonds is 2.2 percent, the rate on two-year Treasury bonds is 3.0 percent, and the rate on three-year Treasury bonds is 3.6 percent. These bonds are considered risk free, so the rates given here are risk-free rates (k_{RF}). The one-year bond matures one year from today, the two-year bond matures two years from today, and so forth. The *real* risk-free rate (k*) for each year is 2 percent. Using the expectations theory, compute the expected inflation rate for the next 12 months (Year 1) and Year 2.

expected rate of interest | **2–7** Suppose the annual yield on a two-year Treasury bond is 11.5 percent, while that on a one-year bond is 10 percent; k* is 3 percent, and the maturity risk premium is zero.
  a. Using the expectations theory, forecast the interest rate on a one-year bond during the second year. (Hint: Under the expectations theory, the yield on a two-year bond is equal to the average yield on one-year bonds in Years 1 and 2.)
  b. What is the expected inflation rate in Year 1? Year 2?

expected rate of interest | **2–8** Assume that the real risk-free rate is 4 percent and that the maturity risk premium is zero. If the nominal rate of interest on one-year bonds is 11 percent and that on comparable-risk two-year bonds is 13 percent, what is the one-year interest rate that is expected for Year 2? What inflation rate is expected during Year 2? Comment on why the average interest rate during the two-year period differs from the one-year interest rate expected for Year 2.

interest rates | **2–9** The rate of inflation for the coming year is expected to be 3 percent, and the rate of inflation in Year 2 and thereafter is expected to be constant at some level above 3 percent. Assume that the real risk-free rate, k*, is 2 percent for all maturities, and the expectations theory fully explains the yield curve, so there are no maturity premiums. If three-year Treasury bonds yield 2 percentage points more than one-year bonds, what rate of inflation is expected after Year 1?

interest rate | **2–10** Today is January 1, 2005, and according to the results of a recent survey, investors expect the *annual* interest rates for the years 2008–2010 to be:

YEAR	ONE-YEAR RATE
2008	5
2009	4
2010	3

The rates given here include the risk-free rate, k_{RF}, and appropriate risk premiums. Today a three-year bond—that is, a bond that matures on December 31, 2007—has an interest rate equal to 6 percent. What is the yield to maturity for bonds that mature at the end of 2008, 2009, and 2010?

expected interest rates | **2–11** Suppose current interest rates on Treasury securities are as follows:

MATURITY	YIELD
1 year	5.0
2 years	5.5
3 years	6.0
4 years	5.5

Using the expectations theory, compute the expected interest rates (yields) for each security one year from now. What will the rates be two years from today and three years from today?

Integrative Problem

financial markets | **2–12** Assume that you recently graduated with a degree in finance and have just reported to work as an investment advisor at the firm of Balik and Kiefer Inc. Your first assignment is to explain the nature of the U.S. financial markets and institutions to Michelle DeLatorre, a professional tennis player who has just come to the United States from Chile. DeLatorre is a highly ranked tennis player who expects to invest substantial amounts of money through Balik and

Kiefer. She is also very bright, and therefore she would like to understand in general terms what will happen to her money. Your boss has developed the following questions, which you must answer to explain the U.S. financial system to DeLatorre.

a. What is a *financial market?*

b. Differentiate between *debt markets* and *capital markets, money markets* and *capital markets, public market* and *private market.*

c. Differentiate between a *primary market* and a *secondary market.* If Microsoft decided to issue additional common stock, and DeLatorre purchased 100 shares of this stock from Merrill Lynch, the underwriter, would this transaction be a primary market transaction or a secondary market transaction? Would it make a difference if DeLatorre purchased previously outstanding Microsoft stock on the Nasdaq?

d. Describe the three primary ways in which capital is transferred between savers and borrowers.

e. Securities can be traded on *physical stock exchanges* or in stock markets that are *organized investment networks.* Define each of these markets, and describe how stocks are traded in each of them.

f. How do electronic communications networks (ECNs) help with the execution of orders in the stock markets?

g. What do we call the *price* that a borrower must pay for debt capital? What is the price of equity capital? What are the four most fundamental factors that affect the cost of money, or the general level of interest rates, in the economy?

h. What is the *real risk-free rate of interest* (k^*) and the *nominal risk-free rate* (k_{RF})? How are these two rates measured?

i. Define the terms *inflation premium (IP), default risk premium (DRP), liquidity premium (LP),* and *maturity risk premium (MRP).* Which of these premiums is included when determining the interest rate on (1) short-term U.S. Treasury securities, (2) long-term U.S. Treasury securities, (3) short-term corporate securities, and (4) long-term corporate securities? Explain how the premiums would vary over time and among the different securities listed earlier.

j. What is the term *structure* of interest rates? What is a *yield curve?*

k. Several theories have been advanced to explain the shape of the yield curve. The three major ones are (1) the *market segmentation theory,* (2) the *liquidity preference theory,* and (3) the *expectations theory.* Briefly describe each of these theories. Do you think economists regard one as being "true"?

l. Suppose most investors expect the rate of inflation to be 1 percent next year, 3 percent the following year, and 4 percent thereafter. The real risk-free rate is 3 percent. The maturity risk premium is zero for bonds that mature in one year or less, 0.1 percent for two-year bonds, and the MRP increases by 0.1 percent per year thereafter for 20 years, after which it is stable. What is the interest rate on one-, 10-, and 20-year Treasury bonds? Draw a yield curve with these data. Is your yield curve consistent with the three term-structure theories?

m. In relation to the yield curve in part l, where would the yield curves for the bonds of two corporations, one rated AAA and the other rated BB, be drawn? Explain. Draw the curves for the corporations on the curve that was previously constructed.

n. Suppose current interest rates on Treasury securities are as follows:

MATURITY	YIELD
1 year	4.4
2 years	4.8
3 years	5.0
4 years	5.4
5 years	6.0

Using the expectations theory, compute the expected interest rates (yields) for each security one year from now. What will the rates be three years from today?

Computer-Related Problem

Work the problem in this section only if you are using the computer problem diskette.

2–13 The problem requires you to use File C02 on the computer problem diskette.

a. Assume today is January 1, 2005, and the expected inflation rates for the next five years are as follows:

YEAR	INFLATION RATE
2005	8%
2006	6
2007	4
2008	3
2009	5

In 2010 and thereafter, inflation is expected to be 3 percent. The maturity risk premium is 0.1 percent per year to maturity for bonds with maturities greater than six months, with a maximum MRP equal to 2 percent. The real risk-free rate of return is currently 2.5 percent, and it is expected to remain at this level long into the future. Compute the interest rates on Treasury securities with maturities equal to one year, two years, three years, four years, five years, 10 years, 20 years, and 30 years. (The initial spreadsheet solution that you will see is for Problem 2–4.)

b. Discuss the yield curve that is constructed from the results in part a.

c. Rework part a assuming one year has passed—that is, today is January 1, 2006. All the other information given in part a is the same. Rework part a again assuming two, three, four, and five years have passed.

d. Assume that all the information given previously is the same and the default risk premium for corporate bonds rated AAA is 1.5 percent, whereas it is 4 percent for corporate bonds rated B. Compute the interest rates on AAA- and B-rated corporate bonds with maturities equal to one year, two years, three years, four years, five years, 10 years, 20 years, and 30 years.

GET REAL with Thomson ONE

2–14 The Dow Jones Industrial Index, a U.S.-based index including 30 blue-chip stocks, is one of the most quoted financial markets indexes in the world. Many investors use this index as a barometer of the performance of the U.S. financial markets, because it provides an indication as to how the U.S. economy is performing at any point in time.

As stated in this chapter, U.S. stock markets accounted for more than two-thirds of the value of world markets in 1970. Currently, however, U.S. markets account for less than 50 percent of the total value of worldwide markets, because emerging markets are quickly expanding. Some countries along the Pacific Rim, such as South Korea, as well as some South American countries, are responsible for continued growth in the world financial markets. Using the Thomson ONE database, compare the major market indexes of the following countries with regard to their change in value over the past 12 months:

Argentina [ARGMERV]
France [FRCAC40]
Germany [DAXINDX]
Japan [NIKI300]
South Korea [KORCOMP]
United States [DJIND]

Go to the Thomson ONE database and click on Indices in the upper left corner of the screen. Enter the ticker symbols one at a time and find the change in price for the last 12 months. Compare the change in value for each market index and write a paragraph about the growth in the markets in each country.

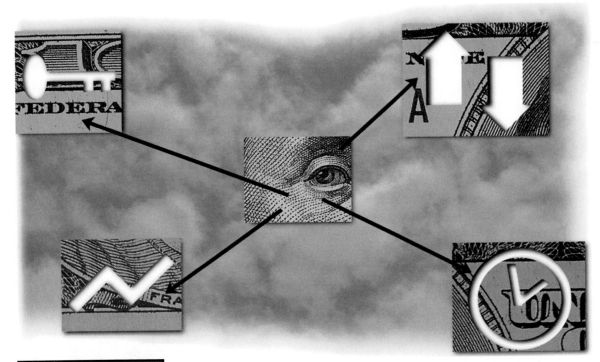

Essential Concepts in Managerial Finance

CHAPTER 3

The Time Value of Money

Even as a student, you should be thinking about retirement. Don't laugh—most experts would agree you should have some financial plan for achieving your retirement goals when you start your professional career, or soon afterward; otherwise you will find that achieving those goals is difficult, if not impossible. Chances are that unless you create a savings plan for retirement as soon as you start your career, either you will have to work longer than you had planned to attain the retirement lifestyle you desire or you will have to live below the standard of living you planned for your retirement years. According to the experts, it's never too soon to start saving for retirement. Unfortunately, most Americans are professional procrastinators when it comes to saving and investing for retirement. The savings rate in the United States is the lowest of any developed country. During the 1990s, individuals saved an average of approximately 4 percent of their income, down from 12 percent at its peak in the 1960s. In 1999, due to a poor economy, the savings rate actually dipped below zero, which meant that people borrowed more than they saved on average. Savings rates have been near zero since the beginning of the 21st century.

One reason many people give for their lack of savings is that they expect to receive Social Security benefits when they retire. But don't bet on it! The ratio of workers paying into Social Security to retirees receiving benefits, which was 16.5 in 1950, was down to 3.3 in 2002, and it is expected to be 2.2 by the year 2030 and then decline thereafter.

What does all this mean? Current projections are that the government retirement system will go bankrupt within the next 40 years. Several factors put the future of Social Security in doubt. First, the life expectancy of Americans has increased by more than 15 years, from 61 to over 76, since the inception of Social Security in 1935, and it is expected to increase further in the future. Second, the number of elderly as a percent of the American population has increased substantially. Consider the fact that the proportion of Americans 65 or older was only 4 percent in 1900, about 12.5 percent in 1998, and is expected to be 25 percent by the year 2040. Third, more than 77 million "baby boomers" born between 1946 and 1964 are beginning to retire, which will add a tremendous burden to the system. At some point in the future, there might be more retirees receiving social security benefits than workers making contributions to the plan, because birthrates since the mid-1960s have fallen sharply. From 1946 to 1964 the average family had three children; from 1970 to 1990 the average number of children dropped to two.

What does the retirement plight of the baby boomers (and their children) have to do with the time value of money? Actually, a great deal. According to a study published by the National Commission on Retirement Policy, Social Security currently is the primary source of retirement income for 65 percent of beneficiaries, and it represents the only income for 15 percent. An earlier study conducted by *Money* magazine and Oppenheimer Management Corporation indicated that

Americans do little more than talk about retirement plans until late in their professional careers; in many cases, they procrastinate too long for their retirement goals to be achievable. To retire comfortably, 10 to 20 percent of your income should be set aside each year. For example, it is estimated that a 35-year-old who is earning $55,000 would need at least $1 million to retire at the current standard of living in 30 years. To achieve this goal, the individual would have to save about $10,500 each year at 7 percent return, which represents nearly a 20 percent annual savings. The annual savings would have been less than one-half this amount if the individual had begun saving for retirement at age 25.

The techniques and procedures covered in this chapter are exactly the ones used by experts to forecast the boomers' retirement needs, their probable wealth at retirement, and the resulting shortfall. If you study this chapter carefully, perhaps you can avoid the trap into which many people seem to be falling—spending today rather than saving for the future. ■

Sources: "The 2003 Annual Report of the Board of Trustees of the Federal Old-Age and Survivors Insurance and Disability Insurance Trust Funds" and other reports that are available at Web site of the Social Security Administration, http://www.ssa.gov; "The 21st Century Retirement Security Plan" and "Can America Afford to Retire: The Retirement Security Challenge Facing You and the Nation," 1998, National Commission on Retirement Policy, Center for Strategic and International Studies, available on the Internet at http://csis.org/retire/index.html; Penelope Wang, "How to Retire with Twice as Much Money," *Money* (October 1994), 76(10).

TIME VALUE OF MONEY

The principles and computations used to revalue cash payoffs at different times so they are stated in dollars of the same time period; used to convert dollars from one time period to those of another time period.

Financial decision making, whether viewed from the perspective of firms or investors, is primarily concerned with determining how value will be affected by the expected outcomes (payoffs) associated with alternative choices. For example, if you have $5,500 to invest today, you must decide what to do with the money. If you have the opportunity to purchase an investment that will return $7,020 after five years or an investment that will return $8,126 after eight years, which should you choose? To answer this question, you must determine which investment alternative has greater value to you.

All else equal, a dollar received sooner is worth more than a dollar received at some later date, because *the sooner a dollar is received, the more quickly it can be invested to earn a positive return.* So does that mean the five-year investment is more valuable than the eight-year investment? Not necessarily, because the eight-year investment promises a higher dollar payoff than the five-year investment. To determine which investment is more valuable, we need to compare the dollar payoffs for the investments at the same point in time. Thus, for these two investments, we could determine the current values of both investments by restating, or revaluing, the payoffs expected at different times in the future—$7,020 in five years and $8,126 in eight years—in terms of current (today's) dollars. The concept used to revalue payoffs such as those associated with these investments is termed the **time value of money.** It is essential that both financial managers and investors have a clear understanding of the time value of money and its effect on the value of an asset. Time value of money concepts are discussed in this chapter, where we show how the timing of cash flows affects asset values and rates of return.

The principles of time value analysis that are developed in this chapter have many applications, ranging from setting up schedules for paying off loans to decisions about whether to acquire new equipment. In fact, of all the techniques used in finance, none is more important than the concept of the time value of money. Because this concept is used throughout the remainder of the book, it is vital that you understand the time value of money principles before you move on to other topics.

Cash Flow Time Lines

CASH FLOW TIME LINE
An important tool used in time value of money analysis; it is a graphical representation used to show the timing of cash flows.

One of the most important tools in time value of money analysis is the **cash flow time line,** which is used to help us visualize when the cash flows associated with a particular situation occur. Constructing a cash flow time line will help you to solve problems related to the time value of money, because illustrating what happens in a particular situation generally makes it easier to set up the problem for solution. To illustrate the time line concept, consider the following diagram:

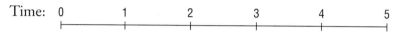

Here Time 0 is today; Time 1 is one period from today, or the end of Period 1; Time 2 is two periods from today, or the end of Period 2; and so on. Thus the values on top of the tick marks represent end-of-period values. Often the periods are years, but other time intervals, such as semiannual periods, quarters, months, or even days, are also used. If each period on the time line represents a year, the interval from the tick mark corresponding to 0 to the tick mark corresponding to 1 would be Year 1, the interval from the tick mark corresponding to 1 to the tick mark corresponding to 2 would be Year 2, and so on. Note that each tick mark corresponds to the end of one period as well as the beginning of the next period. In other words, the tick mark at Time 1 represents the end of Year 1; it also represents the beginning of Year 2 because Year 1 has just passed.[1]

Cash flows are placed directly below the tick marks, and interest rates are shown directly above the cash flow time line. Unknown cash flows, which we are trying to find in the analysis, are indicated by question marks. For example, consider the following time line:

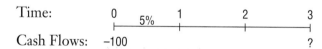

OUTFLOW
A payment, or disbursement, of cash for expenses, investments, and so forth.

INFLOW
A receipt of cash from an investment, an employer, or other sources.

Here the interest rate for each of the three periods is 5 percent; a single amount (or lump sum) cash **outflow** is made at Time 0; and the Time 3 value is an unknown **inflow.** Because the initial $100 is an outflow (an investment), it has a minus sign. Because the Period 3 amount is an inflow, it does not have a minus sign. Note that no cash flows occur at Time 1 and Time 2. Note also that we do not show dollar signs on time lines; this reduces clutter.

The cash flow time line is an essential tool for better understanding time value of money concepts—even experts use cash flow time lines to analyze complex problems. We will use cash flow time lines throughout the book, and you should get into the habit of using them when you work problems.

---

[1]For our discussions, the difference between the end of one period and the beginning of the next period is the same as one day ending and the next day beginning—it occurs in less than one second.

Self-Test Question

Draw a three-year cash flow time line to illustrate the following situation: (1) an outflow of $5,000 occurs at Time 0; (2) inflows of $2,000 occur at the end of Years 1, 2, and 3; and (3) the interest rate during the three years is 12 percent.

Future Value

A dollar in hand today is worth more than a dollar to be received in the future because, if you had the money now, you could invest it, earn interest, and end up with more than one dollar in the future. The process of converting today's values, which are termed present values (PV), to future values (FV) is called **compounding.** To illustrate, suppose you deposit $100 in a bank account that pays 5 percent interest each year. How much would you have at the end of one year? To begin, we define the following terms:

COMPOUNDING

The process of determining the value of a cash flow or series of cash flows some time in the future when compound interest is applied.

PV = Present value, or beginning amount, in your account. Here PV = $100.

k = Interest rate the bank pays on the account per year. The interest earned is based on the balance in the account at the beginning of each year, and we assume that it is paid at the end of the year. Here k = 5%, or, expressed as a decimal, k = 0.05.

INT = Dollars of interest you earn during the year = (Beginning-of-year-amount) $\times$ k. Here INT = $100 $\times$ 0.05 = $5 in the first year.

FV_n = Future value, or value of the account at the end of n periods (years in this case), after the interest earned has been added to the account.

n = Number of periods interest is earned. Here n = 1.

In our example, n = 1, so FV_n can be calculated as follows:

$$FV_n = FV_1 = PV + INT$$

$$= PV + PV(k)$$

$$= PV(1 + k)$$

$$= \$100(1 + 0.05) = \$100(1.05) = \$105.$$

FUTURE VALUE (FV)

The amount to which a cash flow or series of cash flows will grow over a given period of time when compounded at a given interest rate.

Thus the **future value (FV)** at the end of one year, FV_1, equals the present value multiplied by 1.0 plus the interest rate. You will have $105 in one year if you invest $100 today and 5 percent interest is paid at the end of the year.

How much money would you have if you left your $100 in the account for five years? Following is a cash flow time line that is set up to show the amount at the end of each year:

Time:	0	5%	1	2	3	4	5
Initial deposit:	−100		FV_1 = ?	FV_2 = ?	FV_3 = ?	FV_4 = ?	FV_5 = ?
Interest earned this year:			5.00	5.25	5.51	5.79	6.08
Interest from previous years:			0.00	5.00	10.25	15.76	21.55
Total amount at the end of each period:			105.00	110.25	115.76	121.55	**127.63**

Note the following points:

1. You start by depositing $100 in the account. This is shown as an outflow at time period 0.
2. You earn $100 × 0.05 = $5 of interest during the first year, so the amount at the end of Year 1 is $100 + $5 = $105.
3. You start the second year with $105. In the second year, you earn 5 percent interest both on the $100 you invested originally and on the $5 paid to you as interest in the first year—that is, $5.25 interest earned in the second year. As a result, at the end of the second year you have $110.25, which consists of the $105 you started with at the beginning of Year 2 and the $5.25 interest earned in the second year. The interest earned during Year 2, $5.25, is higher than the first year's interest of $5, because you earned $0.25 = $5 × 0.05 interest by leaving the $5 interest received in the first in the account to earn interest in Year 2.
4. This process continues. And because the beginning balance is higher in each succeeding year, the annual amount of interest earned increases.
5. The total interest earned, $27.63, is reflected in the final balance at the end of the fifth year, $127.63.

As you can see, the total interest earned ($27.63) is greater than $5 per year, which is 5 percent of the original $100 investment. Because the interest earned each year was left in the account to earn additional interest the following year, an *additional* $2.63 = $27.63 – $25.00 interest was earned during the life on the investment. When interest is reinvested, or left in the account, to earn additional interest, as in our example, the investment earns **compounded interest.**

COMPOUNDED INTEREST

Interest earned on interest that is reinvested.

The value at the end of Year 2, $110.25, is:

$$FV_2 = [\textbf{FV}_1](1 + k)$$

$$= [\textbf{PV}(1 + k)](1 + k)$$

$$= PV(1 + k)^2$$

$$= \$100(1.05)^2 = \$110.25$$

Continuing, the balance at the end of Year 3 is

$$FV_3 = [\textbf{FV}_2](1 + k)$$

$$= [\textbf{PV}(1 + k)^2](1 + k)$$

$$= PV(1 + k)^3$$

$$= \$100(1.05)^3 = \$115.76$$

and

$$FV_5 = \$100(1.05)^5 = \$127.63$$

In general, the future value of an initial sum at the end of n years can be found by applying Equation 3–1:

3–1
$$FV_n = PV(1 + k)^n$$

Equation 3–1 and most other time value of money (TVM) problems can be solved using either a calculator or a computer spreadsheet. Because it is easier to solve most TVM problems using a calculator, we will show the calculator solutions to the problems throughout the book. Appendix 3A at the end of this chapter gives some examples as to how to apply computer spreadsheets to solve the numerical examples given in the chapter.[2]

When solving the TVM problems in this chapter, we will show you the calculator solution in two forms. We will solve the problem using (1) the appropriate equation, such as Equation 3–1, which we refer to as the *numerical solution*, and (2) the time value of money functions that are programmed into a financial calculator, which we refer to as the *financial calculator solution*.

Numerical Solution

According to Equation 3–1, to compute the future value (FV) of an amount invested today (PV) we need to determine by what multiple the amount invested will increase in the future. As you can see, the multiple by which any amount will increase depends on both the interest rate and the length of time interest is earned—that is, $(1 + k)^n$.

The solution for $(1 + k)^n$ can be found using a regular calculator by using the exponential function to raise $(1 + k)$ to the nth power. To solve using the exponential function key on your calculator, which generally is labeled y^x, you would enter 1.05 into your calculator, press the ▮ y^x ▮ function key, enter 5, and then press the ▮ = ▮ key. The result that is displayed should be 1.27628, which you would multiply by $100 to get the final answer, $127.628, which rounds to $127.63.

Financial Calculator Solution

Equation 3–1 and most other TVM equations have been programmed directly into *financial calculators*, and such calculators can be used to find future values. These calculators have five keys that correspond to the five most commonly used TVM variables:

▮ N ▮   ▮ I/k ▮   ▮ PV ▮   ▮ PMT ▮   ▮ FV ▮

Here

       N = The number of periods; some calculators use n rather than N.

   I/k = Interest rate per period; some calculators use I, INT, or I/Y rather than I/k.

   PV = Present (today's) value.

 PMT = Annuity payment. This key is used only if the cash flows involve a series of equal, or constant, payments (an annuity). If there are no periodic payments in the particular problem, then PMT = 0. We will use this key later in the chapter.

   FV = Future (ending) value.

---

[2]Prior to the widespread use of modern calculators, interest tables were used to solve TVM problems. Interest tables provide the results for the interest factors—for example, $(1 + k)^n$—at various values of k, or interest rates, and n, or number of periods. Appendix 3B at the end of this chapter shows how interest tables are applied.

On some financial calculators, these "keys" actually are buttons on the face of the calculator, whereas on others they are shown on a screen after going into the TVM menu.

In this chapter, we will deal with equations that involve only four of the five variables at any one time—three of the variables will be known and the calculator will then solve for the fourth (unknown) variable. In the next chapter, when we deal with bonds, we will use all five variables in the bond valuation equation.[3]

To find the future value of $100 after five years at 5 percent interest using a financial calculator, note again that we are dealing with Equation 3–1:

$$FV_n = PV(1 + k)^n \tag{3-1}$$

The equation has four variables, FV_n, PV, k, and n. If we know any three, we can solve for the fourth. In our example, we can enter N = 5, I/k = 5, PV = –100, and PMT = 0. When we compute FV, we will get the answer, FV = 127.63 (rounded to two decimal places).[4] The inputs and the financial calculator results can be depicted as follows:

Inputs:	5	5	–100	0	?
	N	**I/k**	**PV**	**PMT**	**FV**
Output:					= 127.63

Financial calculators require that all cash flows be designated as either inflows or outflows, because the computations are based on the fact that we generally pay, which is a cash outflow, to receive a benefit, which is a cash inflow. As a result, you must enter cash outflows as negative numbers. In our illustration, you deposit, or put in, the initial amount, which is an outflow to you, and you take out, or receive, the ending amount, which is an inflow to you. Thus the PV should be entered as –100. If you forget the negative sign and enter 100, then the calculator would assume you receive $100 in the current period and that you must pay it back with interest in the future, so the FV would appear as –127.63, a cash outflow. Sometimes the convention of changing signs can be confusing, but, if you think about what you are doing, you should not have a problem with whether the calculator gives you a positive or a negative answer.

We also should note that financial calculators permit you to specify the number of decimal places that are displayed. For most calculators, at least 12 significant digits are used in the actual calculations. But, for the purposes of reporting the results of the computations, generally we use two places for answers when working with dollars or percentages and four or five places when working with decimals. *The nature of the problem dictates how many decimal places should be displayed.* To be safe, you might want to set your calculator so the floating decimal format is used and round the final results yourself.

---

[3]The equation that is programmed into the calculators actually has five variables, one for each key. In this chapter, the value of one of the variables is always zero. It is a good idea to develop the habit of clearing the calculator's memory. You can also input a zero for the unused variable; if you forget to clear your calculator, this procedure will help you avoid trouble.

[4]On some calculators you simply press the FV key to get the answer, whereas other calculators require you to press a "Compute" (sometimes labeled CPT or COMP) key before pressing the FV key to get the answer.

Problem Format

To help you understand the various types of time value problems, we generally use a standard format in the book. First, we state the problem in words. Next, we diagram the problem using a cash flow time line. Then, beneath the time line, we show the equation that must be solved and the result of solving the equation, which provides the numerical solution. Finally, we show how to solve the problem using a calculator.

To illustrate the format, we use the five-year, 5 percent example:

CASH FLOW TIME LINE:

EQUATION (NUMERICAL SOLUTION):

$$FV_n = PV(1 + k)^n$$

$$= \$100(1.05)^5 = \$100(1.27628) = \$127.63$$

FINANCIAL CALCULATOR SOLUTION:

Inputs:	5	5	–100	0	?
	N	**I/k**	**PV**	**PMT**	**FV**
Output:					= 127.63

The calculator diagram tells you to input N = 5, I/k = 5, PV = –100, and PMT = 0, and then compute FV = 127.63. In this particular problem the PMT key does not come into play, because no constant series of payments is involved.[5] Also, note that when using a financial calculator to solve TVM problems, the interest rate is input as a percentage—that is, 5.0—rather than as a decimal—that is. 0.05.

Graphic View of the Compounding Process: Growth

Figure 3–1 shows how $1 (or any other sum) grows over time at various interest rates. The data used to plot the curves could be obtained by solving Equation 3–1 for different values of k and n using either a calculator or a computer spreadsheet. We used a spreadsheet to generate values and draw the graph shown in Figure 3–1.

Figure 3–1 shows that the higher the rate of interest, the faster the rate of growth. *The interest rate is, in fact, a growth rate:* If a sum is deposited and earns 5 percent interest, then the funds on deposit will grow at a rate of 5 percent per period. Note also that TVM concepts can be applied to anything that is growing, such as sales, population, or earnings per share.

---

[5]We input PMT = 0, but if you cleared the calculator before you started, that already would have been done for you.

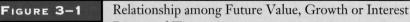

| **FIGURE 3–1** | Relationship among Future Value, Growth or Interest Rates, and Time |

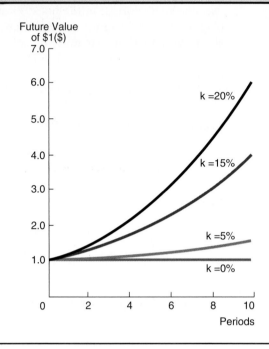

Self-Test Questions

Explain what the following statement means: "A dollar in hand today is worth more than a dollar to be received next year."

What is compounding? What is "interest on interest"?

Explain the following equation: $FV_1 = PV + INT$.

Present Value

OPPORTUNITY COST RATE

The rate of return on the best available alternative investment of equal risk.

PRESENT VALUE (PV)

The value today—that is, current value—of a future cash flow or series of cash flows.

Suppose you have some extra cash, and you have a chance to buy a low-risk security that will pay $127.63 at the end of five years. You consider this security to be as safe as the five-year certificates of deposit your local bank is currently offering, which earn 5 percent interest each year. The 5 percent rate is called your **opportunity cost rate,** or the rate of return you could earn on alternative investments of *similar risk.* How much should you be willing to pay for the security?

In the future value example presented in the previous section, we saw that an initial amount of $100 invested at 5 percent per year would be worth $127.63 at the end of five years. As we will see in a moment, you should be indifferent between the choice of receiving $100 today or $127.63 at the end of five years if you have the opportunity to earn 5 percent interest per year. The $100 that would be invested today is defined as the **present value,** or **PV,** of $127.63 due in five years when the opportunity cost rate is 5 percent. If the price of the security you are considering purchasing is anything less than $100, you should definitely buy it because it would cost you exactly $100 to produce the $127.63 in five years if you earned a 5 percent return. Therefore, if you could find another investment with the same risk that would produce the same future amount—that is, $127.63—but its cost is less than $100—say, $95—then you could earn a return higher than 5 percent by purchasing that investment. Similarly, if the price of the security is greater than $100, you should not buy it because it would cost you only $100 to produce the same future amount at the given rate of return. If the price is exactly $100, then you could either buy it or turn it down because $100 is the security's fair value if it has a 5 percent expected return. You would be indifferent between purchasing the security or putting the $100 in the bank and earning a 5 percent annual return.

In general, *the present value of a cash flow due n years in the future is the amount that, if it were on hand today, would grow to equal the future amount at a particular rate of return.* Because $100 would grow to $127.63 in five years at a 5 percent interest rate, $100 is the present value of $127.63 due five years in the future when the opportunity cost rate is 5 percent.

The process of finding present values is called **discounting**. Discounting simply is the reverse of compounding. In other words, if you know the PV, you can compound to find the FV; if you know the FV, you can discount to find the PV.

The cash flow time line and the solution to the current discounting problem are as follows:

DISCOUNTING
The process of determining the present value of a cash flow or a series of cash flows received (paid) in the future; the reverse of compounding.

CASH FLOW TIME LINE:

```
0       5%    1        2        3        4        5
|-------------|--------|--------|--------|--------|
PV = ?                                          127.63
```

EQUATION (NUMERICAL SOLUTION):

We begin with Equation 3–1:

$$FV_n = PV(1 + k)^n$$

When we solve for PV, we have:

3–2

$$PV = FV_n \left[\frac{1}{(1 + k)^n} \right]$$

Applying Equation 3–2 to the current situation gives the following numerical solution:

$$PV = 127.63 \left[\frac{1}{(1.05)^5} \right]$$

$$= 127.63(0.78353)$$

$$= 100.00$$

FIGURE 3–2	Relationship among Present Value, Growth or Interest Rates, and Time

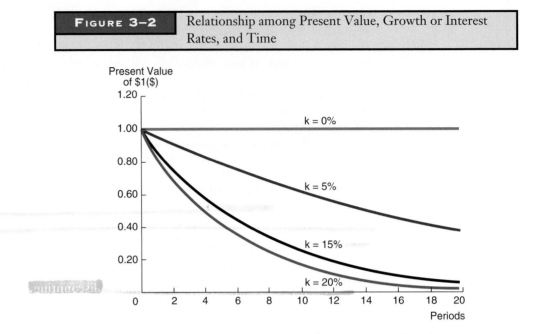

FINANCIAL CALCULATOR SOLUTION:

Inputs:	5	5	?	0	127.63
	N	**I/k**	**PV**	**PMT**	**FV**

Output: = –100.00

Enter N = 5, I/k = 5, PMT = 0, and FV = 127.63, and then compute PV = –100.

Graphic View of the Discounting Process

Figure 3–2 shows how the present value of $1 (or any other sum) to be received in the future diminishes as the time to receipt or the interest rate increases. Again, we used a spreadsheet to generate values and draw the graph shown in Figure 3–2. The graph shows that (1) the present value of a sum to be received at some future date decreases and approaches zero as the payment date is extended further into the future and (2) the rate of decrease is greater the higher the interest (discount) rate. At relatively high interest rates, funds due in the future are worth very little today, and even at a relatively low discount rate, the present value of a sum due in the very distant future is quite small. For example, at a 20 percent discount rate, $5 million due in 100 years is worth only about 6¢ today; conversely, 6¢ would grow to $5 million in 100 years at 20 percent.

Self-Test Questions

What is meant by the term *opportunity cost rate?*

What is discounting? How is discounting related to compounding?

How does the present value of an amount to be received in the future change as the time is extended and as the interest rate increases?

Solving for Time and Interest Rates

At this point, you should realize that the compounding and discounting processes are reciprocals, or inverses, of one another and that we have been dealing with one equation in two different forms:

FV FORM:

3-1

$$FV_n = PV(1 + k)^n$$

PV FORM:

3-2

$$PV = FV_n\left[\frac{1}{(1 + k)^n}\right]$$

These equations include four variables: PV, FV, k, and n. If you know the values of any three of the variables, you can find the value of the fourth. To this point, we have known the number of years, n, and the interest rate, k, plus either the PV or the FV. In many situations, however, you will need to solve for either k or n, as we discuss next.

Solving for k

Suppose you can buy a security at a price of $78.35 that will pay you $100 after five years. What rate of return will you earn if you purchase the security? Here we know PV, FV, and n, but we do not know k, the interest rate you will earn on your investment. We can solve this problem as follows:

CASH FLOW TIME LINE:

EQUATION (NUMERICAL SOLUTION):

$$FV_n = PV(1 + k)^n \qquad\qquad (3\text{--}1)$$

$$100.00 = 78.35(1 + k)^5$$

Solving for k, we find:

$$(1 + k)^5 = \frac{100.00}{78.35} = 1.27632$$

$$(1 + k) = (1.27632)^{1/5} = (1.27632)^{0.2} = 1.05$$

$$k = 1.05 - 1 = 0.05 = 5.0\%$$

FINANCIAL CALCULATOR SOLUTION:

Inputs: 5   ?   –78.35   0   100.00

| N | I/k | PV | PMT | FV |

Output: = 5.0

Enter N = 5, PV = –78.35, PMT = 0, and FV = 100, and then compute I/k = 5. You can use this procedure to calculate any interest rate, including fractional values.

Solving for n

Suppose you know that a security will provide a return of 10 percent per year, it will cost $68.30, and you will receive $100 at maturity. In how many years does the security mature? In this case, you know PV, FV, and k, but you do not know n, the number of periods. Here is the solution:

CASH FLOW TIME LINE:

```
0         1          2              n–1        n=?
├──10%──┼──────────┼──  • • •  ──────────┤
-68.30                                    100.00
```

EQUATION (NUMERICAL SOLUTION):

$$FV_n = PV(1 + k)^n$$ **(3–1)**

$$100.00 = 68.30(1.10)^n$$

One method of finding the value of n is to use a trial-and-error process in which you insert different values of n into Equation 3–1 until you find a value that "works" in the sense that the right side of the equation equals $100. You would eventually find that the solution n = 4. That is, it takes four years for $68.30 to grow to $100 if interest equal to 10 percent is paid each year. This trial-and-error procedure is extremely tedious and inefficient for most time value problems, so it is rarely used in the real world.[6]

---

[6]The value of n also can be found as follows:

$$100 = 68.30(1.10)^n$$

$$(1.10)^n = \frac{100}{68.30} = 1.46413$$

$$\ln[(1.10)^n] = n[\ln(1.10)] = \ln(1.46413)$$

$$n = \frac{\ln(1.46413)}{\ln(1.10)} = \frac{0.3813}{0.0953} = 4.0$$

You can use your calculator to find ln, which is the natural logarithm. For most calculators, you insert the number—say 1.46413—and then press the LN key (or its equivalent). The result in this case is 0.3813.

FINANCIAL CALCULATOR SOLUTION:

Inputs:	?	10	–68.30	0	100.00
	N	**I/k**	**PV**	**PMT**	**FV**
Output:	= 4.0				

Enter I/k = 10, PV = –68.30, PMT = 0, and FV = 100, and then compute N = 4.

Self-Test Questions

Assuming that you are given PV, FV, and the interest rate, k, write out an equation that can be used to determine the time period, n.

Assuming that you are given PV, FV, and the time period, n, write out an equation that can be used to determine the interest rate, k.

Explain how a financial calculator can be used to solve for k and for n.

Future Value of an Annuity

ANNUITY

A series of payments of an equal amount at fixed, equal intervals for a specified number of periods.

An **annuity** is a series of equal payments made at fixed equal-length intervals for a specified number of periods. For example, $100 at the end of each of the next three years is a three-year annuity. The payments are given the symbol PMT, and they can occur at either the beginning or the end of each period. If the payments occur at the end of each period, as they typically do in business transactions, the annuity is called an **ordinary,** or **deferred, annuity.** If payments are made at the *beginning* of each period, the annuity is an **annuity due.** Because ordinary annuities are more common in finance, when the term *annuity* is used in this book, you should assume that the payments occur at the end of each period unless otherwise noted.

ORDINARY (DEFERRED) ANNUITY

An annuity whose payments occur at the end of each period.

ANNUITY DUE

An annuity whose payments occur at the beginning of each period.

FVA$_n$

The future value of an ordinary annuity over n periods.

Ordinary Annuities

If you deposit $100 at the end of each year for three years in a savings account that pays 5 percent interest per year, how much will you have at the end of three years? To answer this question, we must find the future value of an ordinary annuity, **FVA$_n$.** Each payment is compounded out to the end of Period n, and the sum of the compounded payments is the future value of the annuity.

CASH FLOW TIME LINE:

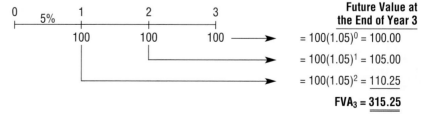

Here we show the regular cash flow time line as the top portion of the diagram, but we also show how each cash flow is processed to produce the value FVA$_3$ in the lower portion of the diagram.

The cash flow time line shows that we can compute the future value of the annuity simply by determining the future values of the individual payments and then summing the results. Thus, the equation for the future value of an ordinary annuity can be written as follows:

3–3

$$FVA_n = PMT(1+k)^0 + PMT(1+k)^1 + PMT(1+k)^2 + \cdots + PMT(1+k)^{n-1}$$

$$= PMT[(1+k)^0 + (1+k)^1 + (1+k)^2 + \cdots + (1+k)^{n-1}]$$

$$= PMT\left[\sum_{t=1}^{n}(1+k)^{n-t}\right] = PMT\left[\sum_{t=0}^{n-1}(1+k)^t\right]$$

The first line of Equation 3–3 presents the annuity payments in reverse order of payment, and the superscript in each term indicates the number of periods of interest each payment receives. In other words, because the first annuity payment was made at the end of Period 1, interest would be earned in Period 2 through Period n only, which means that compounding would be for n – 1 periods rather than n periods because interest is not earned in Period 1. Compounding for the second annuity payment would be for Period 3 through Period n, or n – 2 periods, and so on. The last annuity payment is made at the same time the computation is made, so there is no time for interest to be earned; thus, the superscript 0 represents the fact that no interest is earned. Because the payment, PMT, is the same—that is, $PMT_1 = PMT_2 = \ldots = PMT_n = PMT$—we can simplify the first line of Equation 3–3 to produce the next two lines.

NUMERICAL SOLUTION:

The lower section of the cash flow time line shows the numerical solution. The future value (FV) of each cash flow is found, and these FVs are summed to find the future value of the annuity (FVA). As a result, the solution for the three-period $100 annuity would be:

$$FVA_3 = 100(1.05)^0 + 100(1.05)^1 + 100(1.05)^2$$

$$= 100.00 + 105.00 + 110.25$$

$$= 315.25$$

This is a tedious process for long annuities. Therefore, we generally use the following equation, which is a simplified version of Equation 3–3, to solve for FVA_n:[7]

3–3a

$$FVA_n = PMT\left[\sum_{t=1}^{n}(1+k)^{n-t}\right] = PMT\left[\frac{(1+k)^n - 1}{k}\right]$$

---

[7]The simplification shown in Equation 3–3a is found by applying the algebra of geometric progressions.

Using Equation 3–3a, the future value of $100 deposited at the end of each year for three years in a savings account that earns 5 percent interest per year is:

$$FVA_n = 100\left[\frac{(1.05)^3 - 1}{0.05}\right]$$

$$= 100(3.15250)$$

$$= 315.25$$

FINANCIAL CALCULATOR SOLUTION:

Inputs: 3   5   0   −100   ?

           N   **I/k**   **PV**   **PMT**   **FV**

Output: =315.25

Enter N = 3, I/k = 5, PV = 0, and PMT = −100. Note that in annuity problems, the PMT key is used in conjunction with the N and I/k keys, plus either the PV or the FV key, depending on whether you are trying to find the present value or the future value of the annuity. In our example, you want the FV, so press the FV key to get the answer, 315.25. Because there is no initial payment, we input PV = 0.

Annuities Due

Had the three $100 payments in the previous example been made at the *beginning* of each year, the annuity would have been an *annuity due*. In the cash flow time line, each payment would be shifted to the left one year. Thus each payment would be *compounded for one extra year (period)*, which means each payment would earn interest for an additional year.

CASH FLOW TIME LINE:

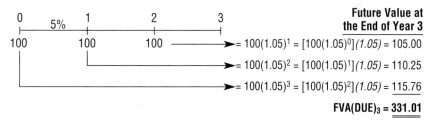

				Future Value at the End of Year 3
0	1	2	3	
	5%			
100	100	100	→	= 100(1.05)^1 = [100(1.05)^0](1.05) = 105.00
			→	= 100(1.05)^2 = [100(1.05)^1](1.05) = 110.25
			→	= 100(1.05)^3 = [100(1.05)^2](1.05) = 115.76

$FVA(DUE)_3 = \underline{\mathbf{331.01}}$

Again, the regular time line is shown at the top of the diagram, and the future value of each annuity payment at the end of Year 3 is shown in the column to the far right along with the actual computations.

FVA(DUE)$_n$
The future value of an annuity due over n periods.

NUMERICAL SOLUTION:

As shown in the lower section of the cash flow time line, we can find the FV of each cash flow and then sum the results to find the FV of the annuity due, **FVA(DUE)$_n$**. Note from the diagram that the difference between an ordinary annuity and an annuity due is that *each of the payments of the annuity due earns interest for one additional year (period)*. As a result, the solution for an annuity due can also be found by adjusting Equation 3–3a to account for the fact that each annuity payment is able to earn an additional period's interest when compared to an ordinary annuity. The solution for FVA(DUE)$_n$ is:

3–3b

$$FVA(DUE)_n = PMT\left[\sum_{t=1}^{n}(1+k)^t\right] = PMT\left\{\left[\frac{(1+k)^n - 1}{k}\right] \times (1+k)\right\}$$

The future value of the three $100 deposits made at the beginning of each year into a savings account that earns 5 percent annually is found as follows:

$$FVA(DUE)_3 = 100\left[\left\{\frac{(1.05)^3 - 1}{0.05}\right\} \times (1.05)\right]$$

$$= 100[3.15250 \times 1.05] = 100[3.31013]$$

$$= 331.01$$

FINANCIAL CALCULATOR SOLUTION:

Financial calculators have a switch, or key, generally marked DUE or BEG, that allows you to switch from end-of-period payments (ordinary annuity) to beginning-of-period payments (annuity due). When the beginning mode is activated, the display normally will show the word BEGIN, or the letters BGN. Thus, to deal with annuities due, switch your calculator to BEGIN and proceed as before:

BEGIN

Inputs:	3	5	0	–100	?
	N	**I/k**	**PV**	**PMT**	**FV**
Output:					= 331.01

Enter N = 3, I/k = 5, PV = 0, PMT = –100, and compute FV = 331.01. Because most problems specify end-of-period cash flows—that is, ordinary annuities—you should always switch your calculator back to END mode after you work an annuity due problem.

You should not be surprised that the future value of the annuity due, FVA(DUE)$_3$ = $331.01, is greater than the future value of the ordinary annuity, FVA$_3$ = $315.25, because each payment from the annuity due is received one year earlier than the corresponding payment from the ordinary annuity. As a result, the annuity due payments can be invested sooner, and thus earn greater total interest than the ordinary annuity. For this reason, everything else equal, FVA(DUE)$_n$ will always be greater than FVA$_n$.

Self-Test Questions

What is the difference between an ordinary annuity and an annuity due?

How do you modify the equation for determining the value of an ordinary annuity to compute the value of an annuity due?

Everything else equal, which annuity has the greater future value: an ordinary annuity or an annuity due? Why?

Explain how financial calculators can be used to solve future value of annuity problems.

Present Value of an Annuity

PVA$_n$
The present value of an ordinary annuity with n payments.

Suppose you were offered the following alternatives: (1) a three-year annuity with payments of $100 at the end of each year (an ordinary annuity) or (2) a lump-sum payment today. You have no need for the money during the next three years, so if you accept the annuity you would simply deposit the payments in a savings account that pays 5 percent interest per year. Similarly, the lump-sum payment would be deposited into the same account. How large must the lump-sum payment today be to make it equivalent to the annuity? To answer this question, we must find the present value of an ordinary annuity, **PVA$_n$**. In this case, we can compute the present value of each payment and then sum of the results to determine PVA$_n$. Here is the setup:

CASH FLOW TIME LINE:

$$\frac{100}{(1.05)^1} = 95.24$$

$$\frac{100}{(1.05)^2} = 90.70$$

$$\frac{100}{(1.05)^3} = 86.38$$

$$\mathbf{PVA_3 = \underline{272.32}}$$

The regular cash flow time line is shown at the top of the diagram, and the numerical solution is on the left. The present value of the annuity, PVA$_3$, is $272.32.

As you can see from the cash flow time line, the present value of an annuity can be determined by computing the PVs of the individual payments and summing the results. The general equation used to find the PV of an ordinary annuity is shown here:

3–4

$$PVA_n = PMT\left[\frac{1}{(1+k)^1}\right] + PMT\left[\frac{1}{(1+k)^2}\right] + \cdots + PMT\left[\frac{1}{(1+k)^n}\right]$$

$$= PMT\left\{\left[\frac{1}{(1+k)^1}\right] + \left[\frac{1}{(1+k)^2}\right] + \cdots + \left[\frac{1}{(1+k)^n}\right]\right\}$$

$$= PMT\left[\sum_{t=1}^{n}\frac{1}{(1+k)^t}\right]$$

NUMERICAL SOLUTION:

The lower section of the cash flow time line shows the numerical solution. Here the present value (PV) of each cash flow is found, and these PVs are summed to find the present value of the annuity (PVA). As was mentioned in the discussion of the future value of an annuity (FVA), this approach can be tedious if the number of annuity payments is large. Therefore, we generally use the following equation, which is a simplified version of Equation 3–4, to solve for PVA_n:[8]

3–4a

$$PVA_n = PMT\left[\sum_{t=1}^{n}\frac{1}{(1+k)^t}\right] = PMT\left[\frac{1-\dfrac{1}{(1+k)^n}}{k}\right] = PMT\left[\frac{1-(1+k)^{-n}}{k}\right]$$

Using Equation 3–4a, the PV of the three-year annuity with end-of-year payments of $100 and an opportunity cost of 5 percent is calculated as follows:

$$PVA_3 = 100\left[\frac{1-\dfrac{1}{(1.05)^3}}{0.05}\right] = 100\left[\frac{1-(1+0.05)^{-3}}{0.05}\right]$$

$$= 100(2.72325)$$

$$= 272.32$$

FINANCIAL CALCULATOR SOLUTION:

Inputs:	3	5	?	–100	0
	N	**I/k**	**PV**	**PMT**	**FV**
Output:			=272.32		

Enter N = 3, I/k = 5, PMT = –100, and FV = 0, and then compute PV = 272.32.

One especially important application of the annuity concept relates to loans with constant payments, such as mortgages and auto loans. With such loans, called amortized loans, *the amount borrowed is the present value of an ordinary annuity*, and the payments constitute the annuity stream. We will examine constant payment loans in more depth later in this chapter.

Annuities Due

Had the three $100 payments in our previous example been made at the *beginning* of each year, the annuity would have been an *annuity due*. On the cash flow time line, each payment would be shifted to the left one year, so each payment would be *discounted for one less year*. Here is the cash flow time line setup:

---

[8]Like Equation 3–3a, the simplification shown in Equation 3–4a is found by applying the algebra of geometric progressions.

CASH FLOW TIME LINE:

$$\frac{100}{(1.05)^1} \times (1.05) = \frac{100}{(1.05)^0} = 100.00$$

$$\frac{100}{(1.05)^2} \times (1.05) = \frac{100}{(1.05)^1} = 95.24$$

$$\frac{100}{(1.05)^3} \times (1.05) = \frac{100}{(1.05)^2} = \underline{90.70}$$

PVA(DUE)$_3$ = 285.94

PVA(DUE)$_n$
The present value of an annuity due over n periods.

NUMERICAL SOLUTION:

Again, we can find the PV of each cash flow and then sum the results to find the PV of the annuity due, **PVA(DUE)$_n$**. This procedure is illustrated in the lower section of the cash flow time line. Because the cash flows occur sooner, the PVA(DUE)$_3$ exceeds PVA$_3$—$285.94 versus $272.32.

The cash flow time line shows that the difference between the PV of an annuity due and the PV of an ordinary annuity is that *each of the payments of the annuity due is discounted one less year*. As a result, the numerical solution for an annuity due can also be found by adjusting Equation 3–4a to account for the fact each annuity payment will have the *opportunity* to earn an additional year's (period's) interest when compared with an ordinary annuity:

3–4b

$$PVA(DUE)_n = PMT\left[\sum_{t=0}^{n-1}\frac{1}{(1+k)^t}\right] = PMT\left[\left\{\frac{1-\dfrac{1}{(1+k)^n}}{k}\right\} \times (1+k)\right]$$

Therefore, if the three $100 payments were made at the beginning of the year, the PV of the annuity due would be:

$$PVA(DUE)_3 = 100\left[\left\{\frac{1-\dfrac{1}{(1.05)^3}}{0.05}\right\} \times (1.05)\right]$$

$$= 100\left[(2.72325)(1.05)\right]$$

$$= 100\left[2.85941\right]$$

$$= 285.94$$

FINANCIAL CALCULATOR SOLUTION:

				BEGIN	
Inputs:	3	5	?	–100	0
	N	**I/k**	**PV**	**PMT**	**FV**
Output:			= 285.94		

Switch to the beginning-of-period mode (BEGIN), then enter N = 3, I/k = 5, PMT = –100, and FV = 0, and then compute PV = 285.94. Again, *because most problems deal with end-of-period cash flows, don't forget to switch your calculator back to the END mode.*

Self-Test Questions

All else equal, which annuity has the greater present value: an ordinary annuity or an annuity due? Why?

Explain how financial calculators can be used to find present values of annuities.

Solving for Interest Rates with Annuities

The equations used to solve for either FVA or PVA contain four variables: Either FVA or PVA, depending on whether we are looking for the future value or the present value of an annuity, n, k, and PMT. As noted earlier, if we know the values of any three of these variables, we can find the value of the fourth. In this section, we show how to solve for k when we know the values for FVA or PVA, n, and PMT and how to solve for n when we know the values for FVA or PVA, k, and PMT.

Solving for k

Suppose you pay $846.80 for an investment that promises to pay you $250 per year for the next four years. If the payments are made at the end of each year, what interest rate (rate of return) will you earn on this investment? We can solve this problem as follows:

CASH FLOW TIME LINE:

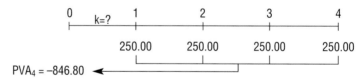

 EQUATION (NUMERICAL SOLUTION):

$$PVA_n = PMT\left[\frac{1 - \dfrac{1}{(1+k)^n}}{k}\right]$$

(3–4a)

$$846.80 = 100\left[\frac{1 - \dfrac{1}{(1+k)^4}}{k}\right]$$

To solve this problem numerically, you would have to use a trial-and-error process in which you plug different values for k into Equation 3–4a until you find the value for k where the present value of the four-year $250 annuity is equal to $846.80. The solution is k = 0.07, or 7 percent.

FINANCIAL CALCULATOR SOLUTION:

Inputs:	4	?	–846.80	250	0
	N	**I/k**	**PV**	**PMT**	**FV**
Output:		= 7.0			

Enter N = 4, PV = –846.80, PMT = 250, and FV = 0, and then solve for I/k = 7.0%.

In the problem we just solved, the information that was given included the amount of the annuity payment, the *present value* of the annuity, and the number of years the annuity payment is received. If the *future value* of the annuity was given instead of the present value, to find k, we would follow the same procedures outlined here, but Equation 3–3a would be used because it applies to future values. For example, let's assume a financial institution has an investment that requires you to make annual payments equal to $250 starting at the end of this year, and in four years the financial institution will pay you $1,110. In this case, we know the amount of the annuity ($250), the length of the annuity (four years), and the future value of the annuity ($1,110). What interest rate would you earn on this investment? The procedure to solve this problem is the same as just outlined, except you use the FVA$_n$ equation (Equation 3–3a) instead of the PVA$_n$ equation for the numerical solution and the FV key ($1,110) instead of the PV key for the financial calculator solution. Try it—you should get k = 7%.

Solving for n

Suppose you pay $1,685 for an investment that promises to pay you $400 per year. If the payments are made at the end of each year, how many payments must you receive to earn a 6 percent return? We can solve this problem as follows:

CASH FLOW TIME LINE:

$$\text{PVA}_n = -1,685$$

at times 0, 1(6%), 2, 3, ... n=? with payments of 400, 400, 400, 400

EQUATION (NUMERICAL SOLUTION):

$$\text{PVA} = \text{PMT}\left[\frac{1 - \dfrac{1}{(1+k)^n}}{k}\right] \tag{3–4a}$$

$$1,685 = 400\left[\frac{1 - \dfrac{1}{(1.06)^n}}{0.06}\right]$$

To solve this problem without a financial calculator, you would have to use a trial-and-error process in which you plug different values for n into Equation 3–4a until you find the value for n where the present value of the four-year $400 annuity is equal to $1,685 when the interest rate is 6 percent. The solution is n = 5.[9]

FINANCIAL CALCULATOR SOLUTION:

Inputs:	?	6	–1,685	400	0
	N	**I/k**	**PV**	**PMT**	**FV**
Output:	= 5.0				

Enter I/k = 6, PV = –1,685, PMT = 400, and FV = 0, and then compute N = 5.0.

In the problem we just solved, the information that was given included the amount of the annuity payment (PMT), the *present value* of the annuity (PVA), and the opportunity rate (k = interest). If we know the *future value* of the annuity (FVA) instead of the present value, to find n, we would follow the same procedures outlined previously, but Equation 3–3a would be used because it applies to future values.

Self-Test Question

How would you solve for interest rates or number of payments with annuities using the numerical solution method?

Perpetuities

PERPETUITY
A stream of equal payments expected to continue forever.

Most annuities call for payments to be made over some finite period of time—for example, $100 per year for three years. However, some annuities go on indefinitely, or perpetually. These perpetual annuities are called **perpetuities.** The present value of a perpetuity is found by applying the following equation:[10]

---

[9]The value for n can also be found as follows:

$$1,685 = 400 \left[\frac{1 - \dfrac{1}{(1.06)^n}}{0.06} \right]$$

$$1,685 = 6,666.67 \left[1 - \frac{1}{(1.06)^n} \right]$$

$$\frac{1,685}{6,666.67} = 1 - \frac{1}{(1.06)^n}$$

$$(1.06)^n = 1.33824$$

$$\ln[(1.06)^n] = n[\ln(1.06)] = \ln(1.332824)$$

$$n = \frac{\ln(1.33824)}{\ln(1.06)} = \frac{0.29136}{0.05827} = 5.0$$

You can use your calculator to find ln, which is the logarithm. For most calculators, you enter the number, say, 1.33824, and then press the LN key or its equivalent. The result is 0.29136.

[10]The derivation of Equation 3–5 is given in the Web/CD Extension to Chapter 5 in Eugene F. Brigham and Phillip R. Daves, *Intermediate Financial Management*, 8th ed. (Cincinnati, OH: South-Western College Publishing, 2004).

$$\boxed{\textbf{3-5} \qquad \text{PVP} = \frac{\text{Payment}}{\text{Interest rate}} = \frac{\text{PMT}}{k}}$$

CONSOL
A perpetual bond issued by the British government to consolidate past debts; in general, any perpetual bond.

Perpetuities can be illustrated by British securities that were issued after the Napoleonic Wars. In 1815, the British government sold a huge bond issue and used the proceeds to pay off many smaller bonds that were issued in prior years to pay for the wars. Because the purpose of the bonds was to consolidate past debts, the bonds were called **consols.** The consols paid constant interest, but did not have maturities—that is, the consols were perpetuities. Suppose each consol promised to pay $100 per year in perpetuity. (Actually, interest was stated in pounds.) What would each bond be worth if the opportunity cost rate, or discount rate, was 5 percent? The answer is $2,000:

$$\text{PVP} = \frac{100}{0.05} = 2,000$$

Suppose the interest rate rose to 10 percent; what would happen to the consol's value? The value would drop to $1,000:

$$\text{PVP} = \frac{100}{0.10} = 1,000$$

We see that the value of a perpetuity changes dramatically when interest rates change. This example shows that, all else equal, *when interest rates increase, the value of an investment decreases.* This is a fundamental valuation concept that we will discuss in greater detail in Chapter 5.

Self-Test Questions

What happens to the value of a perpetuity when interest rates increase? What happens when rates decrease?

Why does the value of a perpetuity change when interest rates change?

Uneven Cash Flow Streams

UNEVEN CASH FLOW STREAM
A series of cash flows in which the amount varies from one period to the next.

PAYMENT (PMT)
This term designates constant cash flows—that is, the amount of an annuity payment.

CASH FLOW (CF)
This term designates cash flows in general, including uneven cash flows.

The definition of an annuity includes the words *constant amount*—in other words, annuities involve payments that are the same for every period. Although many financial decisions involve constant payments, some important decisions involve uneven, or nonconstant, cash flows. For example, common stocks typically pay an increasing stream of dividends over time, and fixed asset investments such as new equipment normally do not generate constant cash flows. Consequently, it is necessary to extend our time value discussion to include **uneven cash flow streams.**

Throughout the book, we will follow convention and reserve the term **payment (PMT)** for annuity situations where the cash flows are constant, and we will use the term **cash flow (CF)** to denote cash flows in general, which includes uneven cash flows as well as annuities. Financial calculators are set up to follow this convention, so if you are using one and dealing with uneven cash flows, you will need to use the "cash flow register."

Present Value of an Uneven Cash Flow Stream

To find the present value (PV) of an uneven cash flow stream, we must sum the PVs of the individual cash flows included in the stream. For example, suppose we want to find the PV of the following cash flow stream, discounted at 6 percent:

The PV is found by applying this general present value equation:

3–6

$$PV = CF_1\left[\frac{1}{(1+k)^1}\right] + CF_2\left[\frac{1}{(1+k)^2}\right] + \cdots + CF_n\left[\frac{1}{(1+k)^n}\right]$$

$$= \sum_{t=1}^{n} CF_t\left[\frac{1}{(1+k)^t}\right]$$

We cannot simplify Equation 3–6 further because the cash flows, CFs, are not necessarily equal. In fact, in our example, $CF_1 \neq CF_2 \neq CF_3 = CF_4 \neq CF_5$, so we have an uneven cash flow stream. One way to find the present value of the cash flow stream in our example is to compute the PV of each individual cash flow and then sum these values. Here is what the process looks like:

	0	1	2	3	4	5
		6%					
		100	300	200	200	1,000

$$\frac{100}{(1.06)^1} = 94.34 \;\leftarrow$$

$$\frac{300}{(1.06)^2} = 267.00 \;\leftarrow$$

$$\frac{200}{(1.06)^3} = 167.92 \;\leftarrow$$

$$\frac{200}{(1.06)^4} = 158.42 \;\leftarrow$$

$$\frac{1,000}{(1.06)^5} = 747.26 \;\leftarrow$$

1,434.94 = PV

Here we apply Equation 3–6, show the individual PVs in the left column of the diagram, and then sum these individual PVs to find the present value of the entire stream. You can find the *present value of any cash flow stream by summing the present values of the individual cash flows* as shown here. When the cash flows are the same—that is, constant—we can simplify the computations by applying the annuity solutions discussed earlier. The annuity equations can only be used to compute the present value of cash flows that are all the same—that is, an annuity—whereas Equation 3–6 can be used to find the present value for any cash flow stream, constant or nonconstant.

Problems involving uneven cash flows can be solved in one step with most financial calculators. First, you input the individual cash flows in chronological order into the cash flow register. Cash flows usually are designated CF_0, CF_1, CF_2, CF_3, and so on. Next, you enter the interest rate. At this point, you have substituted in all the known values of Equation 3–6, so you only need to press the NPV key to find the present value of the cash flow stream. The calculator has been programmed to find the PV of each cash flow, including CF_0, and then to sum these values to find the PV of the entire stream. To input the cash flows for this problem, enter 0 (because $CF_0 = 0$), 100, 300, 200, 200, and 1,000 in that order into the cash flow register, enter I/k = 6, and then press NPV to get the answer, 1,434.94. Appendix 3D at the end of this chapter shows the steps to solve the current illustration using a BAII PLUS calculator.

Two points should be noted. First, when using the cash flow register, the calculator uses the term NPV rather than PV. The N stands for *net*, so NPV is the abbreviation for *net present value*, which is simply the net present value of a series of positive and negative cash flows, including CF_0, which in our example equals zero. Our example has no negative cash flows, but if it did, we simply would input them with negative signs.

The second point to note is that consecutive cash flows that are equal (annuities) can be entered into the cash flow register more efficiently by using the function that allows you to enter the number of times the cash flow occurs. The procedures for using the CF register vary somewhat on different calculators, so you should consult your calculator manual to determine the appropriate steps for your specific calculator. Also, note that amounts entered into the cash flow register remain in the register until they are cleared. Thus, if you had previously worked a problem with eight cash flows and then moved to a problem with only four cash flows, the calculator would assume that the last four cash flows from the first problem belonged to the second problem. Therefore, *you must be sure to clear the cash flow register before starting a new problem.*

Future Value of an Uneven Cash Flow Stream

TERMINAL VALUE
The future value of a cash flow stream.

The future value of an uneven cash flow stream, sometimes called the **terminal value**, is found by compounding each payment to the end of the stream and then summing the future values:[11]

The future value of our illustrative uneven cash flow stream is $1,920.27:

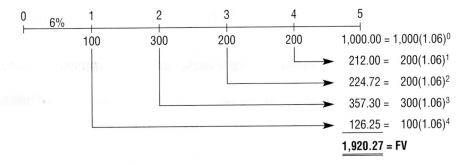

_____

[11]Some financial calculators have a net future value (NFV) key that, after the cash flows and interest rate have been entered into the calculator, can be used to compute the future value of an uneven cash flow stream. In any event, it is easy enough to compound the individual cash flows to the terminal year and then to sum them to find the FV of the stream.

Alternatively, because we already know the present value of the cash flows, we could have compounded this value to the future period (Year 5) to find the future value of the cash flows. The computation for our illustration would be as follows:

$$FV_n = PV(1 + k)^n$$

$$= \$1,434.94(1.06)^5$$

$$= \$1,434.94(1.338226)$$

$$= \$1,920.27$$

We generally are more interested in the present value of an asset's cash flow stream than in the future value because *the present value represents today's value,* which we can compare with the price of the asset.

Solving for k with Uneven Cash Flow Streams

To solve for k for an uneven cash flow stream without a financial calculator, you must go through tedious trial-and-error calculations. With a financial calculator, however, it is easy to find the value of k. Simply input the CF values into the cash flow register and then press the IRR key. IRR stands for *internal rate of return,* which is the return on an investment. We will defer further discussion of this calculation for now, but we will take it up later in our discussion of capital budgeting techniques in Chapter 6.

Self-Test Questions

Give two examples of financial decisions that would typically involve uneven flows of cash.

What is meant by the term *terminal value?*

Semiannual and Other Compounding Periods

ANNUAL COMPOUNDING
The arithmetic process of determining the final value of a cash flow or series of cash flows when interest is paid once per year.

In all of our examples to this point, we have assumed that interest is compounded once per year, or annually. This is called **annual compounding.** Suppose, however, that you put $100 into a bank that states it pays a 6 percent annual interest rate, but that interest is paid each six months. This is called **semiannual compounding.** How much would you accumulate at the end of one year, two years, or some other period under semiannual compounding?

To illustrate semiannual compounding, assume that $100 is invested at an interest rate of 6 percent for a period of three years. First, consider again what happens under *annual compounding:*

CASH FLOW TIME LINE AND NUMERICAL SOLUTION:

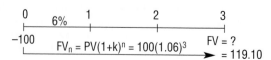

SEMIANNUAL COMPOUNDING
The arithmetic process of determining the final value of a cash flow or series of cash flows when interest is paid twice per year.

FINANCIAL CALCULATOR SOLUTION:

Input N = 3, I/k = 6, PV = −100, and PMT = 0, and then compute FV = 119.10.

How would the future value change if interest is paid twice each year—that is, semiannually? To find the future value, we must make two adjustments: (1) convert the annual interest rate to a rate per period, which is the *periodic rate*, and (2) convert the number of years to the total number of interest payments (compounding periods) during the life of the investment. These conversions are as follows:

$$\text{Periodic rate} = \frac{\text{Stated annual interest rate}}{\text{Number of interest payments per year}}$$

$$\text{Number of interest periods} = \text{Number of years} \times \text{Interest payments per year}$$

In our example, because interest is paid semiannually, we have n = 2 × 3 = 6 interest payments during the life of the investment, and interest is paid at a rate equal to I/k = 6%/2 = 3% every six months. Here is the value of the $100 at the end of three years at 6 percent with semiannual compounding:

CASH FLOW TIME LINE AND NUMERICAL SOLUTION:

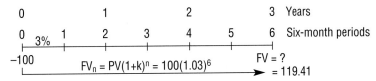

FINANCIAL CALCULATOR SOLUTION:

Input N = 3 × 2 = 6, I/k = 6%/2 = 3%, PV = −100, and PMT = 0, and then compute FV = 119.41.

The FV is larger under semiannual compounding because interest on interest is earned more frequently. As a result, interest is compounded—that is, previously paid interest earns interest—more often than annual compounding to provide greater total interest.

Throughout the world economy, different compounding periods are used for different types of investments. For example, bank accounts generally compute interest on a daily, or even continuous, basis; most bonds pay interest semiannually; and stocks generally pay dividends quarterly.[12] If we are to properly compare securities with different compounding periods, we need to put them on a common basis. This requires us to distinguish between the *simple (or quoted) interest rate* and the *effective annual rate (EAR)*:

SIMPLE (QUOTED) INTEREST RATE
The contracted, or quoted, interest rate that is used to determine the interest paid per period.

■ The **simple, or quoted, interest rate** in our example is 6 percent. On all types of contracts, interest is always quoted as an annual rate, and if compounding occurs more frequently than once a year, that fact is stated along with the rate. In our example, the quoted rate is *6 percent, compounded semiannually.* The

---

[12]For a discussion of continuous compounding, see the Web/CD Extension to Chapter 2 in Eugene F. Brigham and Michael Ehrhardt, *Financial Management: Theory and Practice with Thomson One*, 11th ed. (Fort Worth, TX: Harcourt College Publishers, 2005).

ANNUAL PERCENTAGE RATE (APR)

Another name for the simple interest rate; does not consider the effect of interest compounding.

EFFECTIVE ANNUAL RATE (EAR)

The annual rate of interest actually being earned, as opposed to the quoted rate, considering the compounding of interest.

simple rate is also called the **annual percentage rate, or APR.** This is the rate that is reported to you by banks, credit card companies, automobile dealerships, student loan officers, and other lenders when you borrow money. The APR is a noncompounded interest rate because it does not consider the effect compounding has when interest is paid more than once per year. In other words, you could have two loans (or investments) that have the same stated APR—say, 6 percent—but you could actually be paying different rates because the number of loan payments per year differs. As a result, to compare loans (or investments) where interest is paid at different times during the year, we must compare the loans' (investments') effective annual interest rates, not their APRs.

▪ The **effective annual rate (EAR)** is defined as the rate that would produce the same ending (future) value if annual compounding had been used. To find EAR, we adjust the APR to include the effect of interest compounding—that is, we convert the APR to its equivalent annual rate of return based on the number of interest payments (compounding periods) each year.

In our example, the effective annual rate is the rate that will grow a $100 investment to $119.41 at the end of three years. This is the rate at which you would need to invest $100 today to produce $119.41 at the end of Year 3 if interest is paid one time each year—that is, annual compounding. Here is a cash flow time line that shows this situation:

```
 0   EAR=?   1           2           3  Years
 |————————————|———————————|———————————|
-100                                119.41
```

We can find the EAR by solving for k in the following equation, just as we did earlier:

$$FV_n = PV(1 + k)^n$$

$$119.41 = 100(1 + EAR)^3$$

$$(1 + EAR)^3 = \frac{119.41}{100} = 1.1941$$

$$1 + EAR = (1.1941)^{1/3}$$

$$EAR = 1.06091 - 1$$

$$= 0.0609 = 6.09\%$$

We can also determine the effective annual rate, given the simple rate and the number of compounding periods per year, by solving the following equation:

3–8

$$\text{Effective annual rate (EAR)} = \left(1 + \frac{k_{SIMPLE}}{m}\right)^m - 1.0$$

Here k_{SIMPLE} is the simple, or quoted, interest rate—that is, APR—and m is the number of compounding periods (interest payments) per year. For example, to find the effective annual rate if the simple rate is 6 percent and interest is paid semiannually, we find the following result:

$$\text{Effective annual rate (EAR)} = \left(1 + \frac{0.06}{2}\right)^2 - 1.0$$

$$= (1.03)^2 - 1.0$$

$$= 1.0609 - 1.0$$

$$= 0.0609 = 6.09\%$$

This is the same result we found earlier.

Semiannual compounding (or any nonannual compounding) can be handled in either of two ways:

1. *State everything on a periodic basis rather than on an annual basis.* In other words, use the interest rate per period (periodic rate) and the total number of interest payments during the life of the investment, or loan, when finding the present value or future value. In our example, you would use $n = 3 \times 2 = 6$ periods rather than three years, and use $k = 6\%/2 = 3\%$ interest rate per period rather than 6 percent interest per year.

2. Find the effective annual rate (EAR) by applying Equation 3–8, and then use this rate as an annual rate over the given number of years. In our example, use $k = 6.09\%$ and $n = 3$ years.

Here are the cash flow time lines and numerical solutions for the two alternative procedures:

ALTERNATIVE 1: STATE EVERYTHING ON A PERIODIC BASIS

ALTERNATIVE 2: USE THE EFFECTIVE ANNUAL RATE (EAR)

Both procedures produce the same result, $119.41.

To illustrate the application of these alternatives to find the present value of an annuity, let's consider the case where we want to find the present value of an ordinary annuity that pays $100 every six months—that is, semiannually—for three years when the interest rate is 8 percent, compounded semiannually. On a cash flow time line, this situation can be depicted as follows:

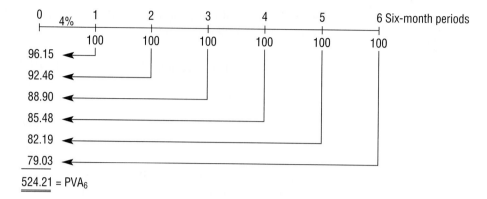

The cash flow time line shows that the present value of the annuity (PVA) is determined by computing the PV of each payment and then summing the resulting PVs. Thus, the numerical solution is:

$$PVA_3 = \frac{100}{(1.04)^1} + \frac{100}{(1.04)^2} + \frac{100}{(1.04)^3} + \frac{100}{(1.04)^4} + \frac{100}{(1.04)^5} + \frac{100}{(1.04)^6}$$

$$= 100(0.96154) + 100(0.92456) + 100(0.88900) + 100(0.85480)$$

$$+100(0.82193) + 100(0.79031)$$

$$= 96.15 + 92.46 + 88.90 + 85.48 + 82.19 + 79.03$$

$$= 100 \left[\frac{1 - \dfrac{1}{(1.04)^6}}{0.04} \right]$$

$$= 100\,[5.24214]$$

$$= 524.21$$

Because the interest rate for this investment is 8 percent compounded semiannually, or 4 percent is paid every six months, the effective annual rate (EAR) is:

$$EAR = (1.04)^2 - 1.0 = 0.0816 = 8.16\%$$

Using the EAR to compute PVA, the cash flow time line is as follows:

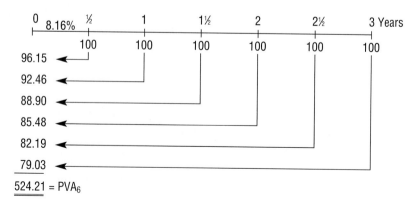

The numerical solution shown in the cash flow time line is computed as follows:

$$PVA_6 = \frac{100}{(1.0816)^{0.5}} + \frac{100}{(1.0816)^{1.0}} + \frac{100}{(1.0816)^{1.5}} + \frac{100}{(1.0816)^{2.0}}$$

$$+ \frac{100}{(1.0816)^{2.5}} + \frac{100}{(1.0816)^{3.0}}$$

$$= 100(0.96145) + 100(0.92456) + 100(0.88900) + 100(0.85480)$$

$$+ 100(0.82193) + 100(0.79031)$$

$$= 96.15 + 92.46 + 88.90 + 85.48 + 82.19 + 79.03$$

$$= 524.21$$

The solution given here illustrates the use of *fractional time periods* to compute the present value of a single payment, or lump-sum amount, using the effective annual rate (EAR). For example, according to the solution, the present value of $100 to be received (or paid) in six months is $96.15 if the effective interest rate is 8.16 percent per year. Previously, we showed that the present value of $100 to be received (or paid) in six months is also $96.15 if the simple annual interest rate is 8 percent and interest is paid semiannually. Stated differently, a simple interest rate equal to 8 percent compounded semiannually is the same as an effective rate of (1) 4 percent per six months—that is, a 4 percent interest payment twice per year—and (2) 8.16 percent per year—that is, an 8.16 percent interest payment once per year.

If you use a financial calculator to find PVA, you *must* convert the simple annual interest rate (APR) to the periodic interest rate that corresponds to each annuity payment. When computing PVA (or FVA), you must recognize all of the annuity payments; thus, the value of N must always equal the number of annuity payments. And, as a result, the interest rate, k, must equal the rate per annuity payment period. For our example, the financial calculator solution is as follows:

Inputs:	6	4	?	100	0
	N	**I/k**	**PV**	**PMT**	**FV**
Output:			= −524.21		

Enter N = 6 annuity payments, I/k = 8%/2 = 4%, PMT = 100, and FV = 0, and then compute PV = −524.21.

To solve for the present value (or future value) of any annuity when payments are made more than once per year, I/k should always equal the effective interest rate associated with each annuity payment period (periodic rate), not the effective *annual* rate (EAR). And, for this reason, N should equal the number of annuity payments, not the number of years the payments are made. For our example, therefore, I/k = 4% and N = 6 payments as shown in the financial calculator solution given previously.

A common mistake that many people make is to think that all the values that are entered into the financial calculator can be annualized when annuity payments are made more often than once per year. In other words, you might think that the required inputs to the calculator can be adjusted so they are stated on an annual basis. In our example, we know that the effective *annual* return, EAR, is 8.16 percent, so the tendency would be to set I/k = 8.16%. If we use the annual effective interest rate, then to be consistent it would make sense to annualize N and PMT. Because the life of the annuity is three years, let's make N = 3; and, because $100 is paid twice per year, let's make PMT = 100 × 2 = 200. If you enter these values into your financial calculator—that is, N = 3, I/k = 8.16, PMT = 200, and FV = 0—to find PVA, you will discover that PVA = $513.93. This is not the same result that we computed previously. The reason this answer differs is because the situation that was entered into the calculator differs from the original example. Here we solved for the present value of a $200 annuity paid once per year for three years when the interest rate is 8.16 percent compounded annually (or 8 percent compounded semiannually). We changed the situation by combining the $100 annuity payment that is made every six months to "create" a $200 annuity payment that is made every year. These are different annuities with respect to the timing of the payments, so their present values also are different.

For the two annuities we discussed here (the original situation and the modified situation just presented), the interest rate is 8 percent compounded semiannually, which equates to 8.16 percent compounded annually (the EAR). But the annuity payments differ as follows:

Annuity 1 (Original Situation):
$100 payment at the end of each six-month period for three years.

Annuity 2 (Modified Situation):
$200 payment at the end of each year for three years.

The total amount of the annuity payments during the three years is the same for both annuities—that is, $600. But because the *timing of the payments* differs for the annuities, the ability to earn interest during the three-year period also differs. The first payment from Annuity 1 is received six months after this investment is purchased, whereas the first payment from Annuity 2 is received 12 months (one year) after this investment is purchased. According to the earlier computations, the value of Annuity 1 is $524.21 and the value of Annuity 2 is $513.93. Consider what these values mean. The result of our computations indicate that, if the opportunity rate of interest is 8 percent compounded semiannually, you would need $524.21 today to generate the cash flows associated with Annuity 1, whereas you would need $513.93 to generate the cash flows associated with Annuity 2. First, let's consider whether these results make sense, both intuitively and mathematically.

To explain the logic of the values for the two annuities, let's examine the payments associated with each annuity in Year 1. To replicate Annuity 1, you would have to pay yourself $100 six months from today and another $100 payment six months later (12 months from today). To replicate Annuity 2, you would have to pay yourself $200 one year (12 months) from today. For which cash flow stream would you need to invest a greater amount today? You should answer Annuity 1. If you replicate Annuity 1, the first $100 payment to yourself will be in six months, which means that a portion of the total amount you invest today will earn interest for only six months—that is, the portion that, with interest, will make the first $100 payment—and a portion will earn interest for the entire year—that is, the portion that, with interest, will make the second $100 payment. On the other hand, if you replicate Annuity 2, the total amount you invest today will earn interest for the entire year, because the $200 payment is not needed until the end of the year. As a result, you need to invest less today to generate the single cash flow in the first year that is associated with Annuity 2 than to generate the two cash flows associ-

TABLE 3–1	Cash Flow Patterns for Comparative Annuities

	ANNUITY 1				ANNUITY 2			
YEAR	BEGINNING OF PERIOD BALANCE	INTEREST @4%	END OF PERIOD BALANCE	PAYMENT TO SELF	BEGINNING OF PERIOD BALANCE	INTEREST @8.16%	END OF PERIOD BALANCE	PAYMENT TO SELF
1	$524.21	$20.97	$545.18	$100	$513.93			
	445.18	17.81	462.99	100		$41.94	$555.87	$200
2	362.99	14.52	377.51	100	355.87			
	277.51	11.10	288.61	100		29.04	384.91	200
3	188.61	7.54	196.15	100	184.91			
	96.15	3.85	100.00	100		15.09	200.00	200

ated with Annuity 1. This is exactly what our computations show—the present value of Annuity 2 is less than the present value of Annuity 1.[13]

Table 3–1 shows how the cash flow patterns for both annuities are recreated. As you can see, if you invest $524.21 today at 8 percent compounded semiannually, you can pay yourself $100 every six months for three years. Assume you just won a contest and were offered (1) a single payment equal to $524.21, which you would receive today, or (2) annuity payments equal to $100 every six months for three years and you would receive the first payment six months from now. If your opportunity cost rate is 8 percent compounded semiannually and neither alternative has any risk, which should you choose? Table 3–1 shows that these two alternatives are the same—that is, you can create one alternative from the other. If you choose the single payment of $524.21 today, you can invest the money and pay yourself $100 every six months for the next three years. And, if you choose the $100 annuity, you can sell the annuity for $524.21 today.

Table 3–1 also shows that you only need to invest $513.93 today at 8 percent compounded semiannually to pay yourself $200 per year for three years. As we mentioned previously, although Annuity 1 and Annuity 2 both pay a total of $200 per year, $100 of the annual payments from Annuity 1 occurs six months earlier than the annual payments

---

[13]We can also view the annuities as investments that earn interest during their lifetimes. In this case, we know that both annuities will pay a total of $200 during the first year. But, because the first $100 payment from Annuity 1 is made six months after the investment is made, this $100 can be invested for the remaining six months of the year. As a result, the first payment from Annuity 1 will grow to $104 = $100(1.04) by the end of the first year; and, therefore, the value of Annuity 1 at the end of Year 1 will be $204, which equals the value of the first payment plus the interest it earns during the latter half of the year ($104) and the value of the second payment received at the end of the year ($100). On the other hand, the value of Annuity 2 at the end of Year 1 will be $200 because a single annuity payment is made at the end of the year, which means interest is not earned on this payment until Year 2. In this case, you should conclude that Annuity 1 is a more valuable investment than Annuity 2 because the payments from Annuity 1 are made sooner than the payments from Annuity 2, which permits Annuity 1 to earn more interest.

The Truth about "0% Financing" for Automobiles

Ask a group of your friends the following question: Which is better, the "special" 0 percent financing offered by many automobile manufacturers during the past few years or 6 percent financing (or any other rate) from a financial institution, such as a credit union? Most of your friends will be quick to say that the 0 percent financing alternative is better. But, is it really? Perhaps not. Remember the old adage: "There is no such thing as a free lunch." That adage applies to "0% financing" packages offered by automobile manufacturers as well.

Those who consider taking advantage of a financing deal that seems too good to be true should always look for hidden costs. If you choose the 0 percent financing (or any other "special" financing packages offered by automobile manufacturers), you generally forfeit any advertised rebates. For example, at various times during the year, many manufacturers offer rebates on in-stock, slower-selling models of automobiles, SUVs, and light trucks to try to move these inventories. The rebates normally range from $1,500 to $3,000 and are higher at the end of the model year when the new models start to appear in dealers' showrooms. In addition, a higher down payment is often required with special financing than with ordinary financing. But, perhaps the most restrictive factor associated with the dealer's special financing package is that you must have great credit to qualify. Reports indicate that approximately 10 percent of new car buyers qualify for such financing, which means 90 percent don't.

Let's assume that you are going to purchase a new car. You have already applied and been accepted for an automobile loan through your local credit union. The loan can be for an amount up to $25,000, depending on the final price of the car you choose. The terms of the loan call for monthly payments for a period of four years at a stated interest rate equal to 6 percent.

After selecting the car you want to purchase, you negotiate with the sales representative and agree on a price equal to $24,000, which does not include any rebates or incentives. The rebate on the car you chose is $3,000. The dealer offers "0% financing" for this car as well. But, if you take the dealer financing, you forfeit the $3,000 rebate. It is easy to compute the payments you will have to make with the 0% financing loan that has the same maturity as the credit union loan—simply divide $24,000 by 48 months. The monthly payments will be $500 if you use the dealer's loan to finance the car.

In this situation, should you use the dealer financing or the credit union loan to finance the car? When you finish reading this chapter, you should be able to answer this question. (You will find that the better loan alternative is the credit union financing. Solve the problem using the techniques given in the chapter to show why this is the case.)

from Annuity 2. As a result, the total amount invested today to create Annuity 1 does not earn interest for the entire year, which means that a greater amount needs to be invested to produce the cash flows for Annuity 1 than for Annuity 2.

The points made in this section can be generalized for other situations when compounding occurs more frequently than once per year. When finding either the future value or the present value of a lump-sum amount, either (1) convert the simple annual interest rate (APR) to the periodic interest rate and the number of years to the total number of compounding periods during the life of the investment (loan), or (2) convert the APR to the effective annual rate (EAR) and use the number of years. When dealing with annuities, follow the first alternative to find FVA or PVA—that is, n must equal the number of annuity payments, which means the APR must be converted to the periodic interest rate.

Self-Test Questions

What changes must you make in your calculations to determine the future value of an amount that is being compounded at 8 percent semiannually versus one being compounded annually at 8 percent?

Why is semiannual compounding better than annual compounding from a saver's standpoint?

What are meant by the terms *annual percentage rate*, *effective annual rate*, and *simple interest rate*?

Amortized Loans

AMORTIZED LOAN
A loan that requires equal payments over its life; the payments include both interest and repayment of the debt.

One of the most important applications of compound interest involves loans that are paid off in installments over time. Included in this category are automobile loans, home mortgages, student loans, and most business debt other than very short-term loans and corporate bonds. If a loan is to be repaid in equal periodic amounts (monthly, quarterly, or annually), it is said to be an **amortized loan.**[14]

To illustrate, suppose a firm borrows $15,000, and the loan is to be repaid in three equal payments at the end of each of the next three years. The lender will receive 8 percent interest on the loan balance that is outstanding at the beginning of each year. Our first task is to determine the amount the firm must repay each year, or the annual payment. To find this amount, recognize that the $15,000 represents the present value of an annuity (PVA) of PMT dollars per year for three years, discounted at 8 percent:

```
0        1         2          3 Years
|---8%---|---------|----------|
15,000  PMT       PMT        PMT
```

Plugging the known information into Equation 3–4a produces the following result:

$$PVA_n = PMT \left[\frac{1 - \frac{1}{(1+k)^n}}{k} \right] \tag{3-4a}$$

$$15,000 = PMT \left[\frac{1 - \frac{1}{(1.08)^3}}{0.08} \right]$$

$$15,000 = PMT\,[2.57710]$$

$$PMT = \frac{15,000}{2.57710} = 5,820.50$$

---

[14]The word *amortized* comes from the Latin *mors*, meaning "death," so an amortized loan is one that is "killed off" over time.

	TABLE 3–2	Loan Amortization Schedule, 8 Percent Interest Rate			
YEAR	**BEGINNING AMOUNT** (1)	**PAYMENT** (2)	**INTEREST**[a] (3)	**REPAYMENT OF PRINCIPAL**[b] (2) – (3) = (4)	**REMAINING BALANCE** (1) – (4) = (5)
1	$15,000.00	$5,820.50	$1,200.00	$4,620.50	$10,379.50
2	10,379.50	5,820.50	830.36	4,990.14	5,389.36
3	5,389.36	5,820.50	431.15	5,389.35	0.01[c]

NOTES:

[a]Interest is calculated by multiplying the loan balance at the beginning of the year by the interest rate. Therefore, interest in Year 1 is $15,000(0.08) = $1,200.00; in Year 2, it is $10,379.50(0.08) = $830.36; and in Year 3, it is $5,389.36(0.08) = $431.15 (rounded).

[b]Repayment of principal is equal to the payment of $5,820.50 minus the interest charge for each year.

[c]The $0.01 Remaining Balance at the end of Year 3 results from rounding differences.

As the numerical solution shows, we know everything except PMT. As a result, we can solve the equation for PMT. Using a financial calculator, the solution is:

Inputs:	3	8	15,000	?	0
	N	**I/k**	**PV**	**PMT**	**FV**
Output:				= –5,820.50	

Enter N = 3, I/k = 8, PV = 15,000 (the firm receives the cash), and FV = 0, and then compute PMT = –5,820.50.

Thus the firm must pay the lender $5,820.50 at the end of each of the next three years, in which case the percentage cost to the borrower, which is also the rate of return to the lender, is 8 percent. Each payment consists partly of interest and partly of repayment of the amount borrowed (principal). This breakdown is given in the **amortization schedule** shown in Table 3–2. The interest component is largest in the first year, and it declines as the outstanding balance of the loan decreases. For tax purposes, a business borrower reports the interest component shown in Column 3 as a deductible cost each year, whereas the lender reports this same amount as taxable income.

Column 5 in Table 3–2 shows the outstanding balance that is due for our illustrative loan at the end of each year. If you do not have an amortization schedule, such as the one shown in Table 3–2, you can still determine the outstanding balance of the loan by computing the present value of the remaining loan payments. For example, after the first payment equal to $5,820.49 (rounding) is made at the end of the first year, the loan agreement calls for two more payments equal to $5,820.50 each. If you compute the present value of the two remaining payments at 8 percent interest per year, you will find that PVA_2 = $10,379.50, which is the remaining balance at the end of Year 1 that is shown in Column 5 in Table 3–2. The same logic that is presented in Table 3–2 can be used to create amortization schedules for home mortgages.

Financial calculators are programmed to calculate amortization tables—you simply enter the input data, and then press one key to get each entry in Table 3–2. If you have a financial calculator, it is worthwhile to read the appropriate section of the

AMORTIZATION SCHEDULE
A schedule showing precisely how a loan will be repaid. It gives the required payment on each payment date and a breakdown of the payment, showing how much is interest and how much is repayment of principal.

manual and learn how to use its amortization feature. Appendix 3C at the end of this chapter shows the steps required to set up an amortization schedule using a financial calculator for the situation given in Table 3–2.

Self-Test Questions

To construct an amortization schedule, how do you determine the amount of the periodic payments?

How do you determine the amount of each payment that goes to interest and to repay the debt?

Comparison of Different Types of Interest Rates

To this point, we have discussed three different types of interest rates. It is useful to compare the three types to know when each should be used.

SIMPLE, OR QUOTED, RATE, k_{SIMPLE}
The rate quoted by borrowers and lenders that is used to determine the rate earned per compounding period (periodic rate).

1. **Simple, or quoted, rate, k_{SIMPLE}.** This is the rate that is quoted by borrowers and lenders, and it is used to determine the rate earned per compounding period (periodic rate). Practitioners in the stock, bond, lending, banking, and other markets generally express financial contracts in terms of simple rates. If you talk with a banker, broker, mortgage lender, auto finance company, or student loan officer about rates, the simple rate is the one he or she will normally mention. To be meaningful, however, the simple rate quotation must also include the number of compounding periods per year. For example, a bank might offer 6.5 percent, compounded annually, on CDs, or a mutual fund might offer 6 percent, compounded monthly, on its money market account.

   Simple rates can be compared with one another, *but only if the instruments being compared use the same number of compounding periods per year.* Thus, to compare a 6.5 percent annual payment CD with a 6 percent monthly payment money market fund, we would need to put both instruments on an effective annual rate (EAR) basis.

   The simple rate never is shown on a time line, and it is never used as an input in a financial calculator unless compounding occurs only once a year (in which case k_{SIMPLE} = periodic rate = EAR). If more frequent compounding occurs, you must use either the periodic rate or the effective annual rate as the following discussion indicates.[15]

PERIODIC RATE, k_{PER}
The rate charged by a lender or paid by a borrower each interest period (e.g., monthly, quarterly, annually, and so on).

2. **Periodic rate, k_{PER}.** This is the rate charged by a lender or paid by a borrower *each interest period.* It can be a rate per year, per six-month period, per quarter, per month, per day, or per any other time interval (usually one year or less). For example, a bank might charge 1 percent per month on its credit card loans, or a finance company might charge 3 percent per quarter on consumer loans. We find the periodic rate as follows:

---

[15]Some calculators have a switch that permits you to specify the number of payments per year. We find it less confusing to set this switch to "1" and then leave it there. We prefer to work with *periods* when more than one payment occurs each year because this maintains a consistency between number of periods and the periodic interest rate.

$$\boxed{3\text{–}9} \qquad \text{Periodic rate} = k_{PER} = \frac{k_{SIMPLE}}{m}$$

This equation implies that

$$\boxed{3\text{–}10} \qquad k_{SIMPLE} = k_{PER} \times m = APR$$

ANNUAL PERCENTAGE RATE, APR

The rate reported to borrowers—the periodic rate times the number of periods in the year; thus, interest compounding is not considered.

EFFECTIVE ANNUAL RATE, EAR

The annual rate earned or paid considering interest compounding during the year—that is, the annual rate that equates to a given periodic rate compounded for m periods during the year.

Here k_{SIMPLE} is the simple annual rate and m is the number of compounding periods per year. As discussed earlier, APR is the **annual percentage rate**, which represents the periodic rate stated on an annual basis without considering interest compounding. *The APR never is used in actual calculations; it is simply reported to borrowers.*

If there is one payment per year, or if interest is added only once a year, then m = 1 and the periodic rate is equal to the simple rate. *In all cases where interest is added or payments are made more frequently than annually, however, the periodic rate is less than the simple rate.*

The periodic rate is used for calculations in problems where two conditions hold: (a) payments occur on a regular basis more frequently than once per year, and (b) a payment is made on each compounding (or discounting) date. Thus, if you are dealing with an auto loan that requires monthly payments, with a semiannual payment bond, or with an education loan that calls for quarterly payments, then on your cash flow time line and in your calculations you would use k_{PER}, and the appropriate number of periods would be n × m.

3. **Effective annual rate, EAR.** The EAR represents the *annual* rate of return that provides the same result as if using a particular periodic rate with m compounding periods during the year. As stated earlier, the EAR is found as follows:

$$\boxed{3\text{–}8} \qquad \text{Effective annual rate (EAR)} = \left(1 + \frac{k_{SIMPLE}}{m}\right)^{m} - 1.0$$

To illustrate further, suppose you could borrow using either a credit card that charges 1 percent per month or a bank loan with a 12 percent quoted simple interest rate that is compounded quarterly. Which should you choose? To answer this question, the cost of each alternative must be expressed as an EAR:

$$\text{Credit card loan: EAR} = (1 + 0.01)^{12} - 1.0 = (1.01)^{12} - 1.0$$

$$= 1.12682 - 1.0 = 0.12683 = 12.68\%$$

$$\text{Bank loan: EAR} = (1 + 0.03)^{4} - 1.0 = (1.03)^{4} - 1.0$$

$$= 1.12551 - 1.0 = .012551 = 12.551\%$$

The credit card loan costs a little more than the bank loan. This result should have been intuitive to you—both loans have the same 12 percent simple rate, yet you would have to make monthly payments on the credit card versus quarterly payments under the bank loan.

| FIGURE 3–3 | Data for Chapter Summary |

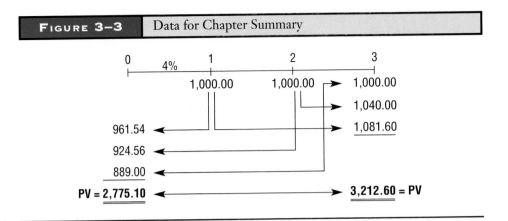

Self-Test Questions

Define the *simple (or quoted) rate*, the *periodic rate*, and the *effective annual rate*.

How are the simple rate, the periodic rate, and the effective annual rate related? Can you think of a situation where all three of these rates will be the same?

Summary

Financial decisions often involve situations in which someone pays money at one point in time and receives money at some other time. Dollars that are paid or received at two different points in time have different values, and this difference is recognized and accounted for by time value of money (TVM) analysis. Here we summarize the types of TVM analysis and the key concepts covered in this chapter, using the data shown in Figure 3–3 to illustrate the various points. Refer to the figure while reviewing the summary, and try to find in it an example of the points covered.

- **Compounding** is the process of determining the **future value (FV)** of a cash flow or a series of cash flows. The compounded amount, or future value, is equal to the beginning amount plus the interest earned.

  Future value (single payment): $FV_n = PV(1 + k)^n$

Example: $924.56 compounded for two years at 4 percent:

$$FV_2 = \$924.56(1.04)^2 = \$1,000$$

- **Discounting** is the process of finding the **present value (PV)** of a future cash flow or a series of cash flows; discounting is the reciprocal (inverse) of compounding.

  Present value (single payment): $PV = FV_n\left[\dfrac{1}{(1 + k)^n}\right]$

Example: $1,000 discounted back for two years at 4 percent:

$$PV = 1,000\left[\frac{1}{(1.04)^2}\right] = 1,000(0.92456) = 924.56$$

■ An **annuity** is defined as a series of equal periodic payments (PMT) for a specified number of periods.

Future value of an annuity:

$$FVA_n = PMT\left[\sum_{t=1}^{n}(1+k)^{n-t}\right] = PMT\left[\frac{(1+k)^n - 1}{k}\right]$$

Example: FVA of three payments of $1,000 when k = 4%:

$$FVA_n = 1,000\left[\frac{(1.04)^3}{0.04} - 1\right] = 1,000(3.12160) = 3,121.60$$

Present value of an annuity:

$$PVA_n = PMT\left[\sum_{t=1}^{n}\frac{1}{(1+k)^t}\right] = PMT\left[\frac{1 - \dfrac{1}{(1+k)^n}}{k}\right]$$

Example: PVA of three payments of $1,000 when k = 4%:

$$PVA_3 = 1,000\left[\frac{1 - \dfrac{1}{(1.04)^3}}{0.04}\right] = 1,000(2.77509) = 2,775.09$$

■ An annuity whose payments occur at the end of each period is called an **ordinary annuity.** The preceding formulas are for ordinary annuities.
■ If each payment occurs at the beginning of the period rather than at the end, then we have an **annuity due.** In Figure 3-3, the payments would be shown at Years 0, 1, and 2 rather than at Years 1, 2, and 3. The PV of each payment would be larger because each payment would be discounted back one year less; hence, the PV of the annuity would also be larger.

Similarly, the FV of the annuity due would be larger because each payment would be compounded for an extra year. The following formulas can be used to convert the PV and FV of an ordinary annuity to an annuity due:

$$PVA(DUE)_n = PMT\left[\sum_{t=0}^{n-1}\frac{1}{(1+k)^t}\right] = PMT\left[\left\{\frac{1 - \dfrac{1}{(1+k)^n}}{k}\right\} \times (1+k)\right]$$

Example: PVA of three beginning-of-year payments of $1,000 when k = 4%:

$$PVA(DUE)_3 = 1,000\left[\left\{\frac{1 - \dfrac{1}{(1.04)^3}}{0.04}\right\} \times (1.04)\right] = 1,000[(2.77509)(1.04) = 2,886.09$$

$$FVA(DUE)_n = PMT\left[\sum_{t=1}^{n}(1+k)^t\right] = PMT\left\{\left[\frac{(1+k)^n - 1}{k}\right] \times (1+k)\right\}$$

Example: FVA of three beginning-of-year payments of $1,000 when k = 4%:

$$FVA(DUE)_n = 1,000\left[\left\{\frac{(1.04)^3 - 1}{0.04}\right\} \times (1.04)\right]$$

$$= 1,000[(3.12160)(1.04)] = 3,246.46$$

- If the cash flow time line in Figure 3–3 was extended out forever so that the $1,000 payments went on forever, we would have a **perpetuity** whose value could be found as follows:

Value of a perpetuity:

$$PVP = \frac{Payment}{Interest\ rate} = \frac{PMT}{k} = \frac{1,000}{0.04} = 25,000$$

- If the cash flows in Figure 3–3 were unequal, we could not use the annuity formulas. To find the PV or FV of an **uneven cash flow series,** find the PV or FV of each individual cash flow and then sum them. However, if some of the cash flows constitute an annuity, then the annuity formula can be used to calculate the present value of that part of the cash flow stream.
- **Financial calculators** have built-in programs that perform all the operations discussed in this chapter. It would be useful for you to buy such a calculator and to learn how to use it. Even if you do, it is essential that you understand the logical processes involved.
- To this point in the summary we have assumed that payments are made and interest is earned at the end of each year, or annually. In the real world, many contracts call for more frequent payments. For example, mortgages and auto loans call for monthly payments, and most bonds pay interest semiannually. Similarly, most banks compute interest daily. When compounding occurs more frequently than once a year, this fact must be recognized. We can use the Figure 3–3 example to illustrate the procedures. First, the following formula is used to find an **effective annual rate (EAR):**

$$(EAR) = \left(1 + \frac{k_{SIMPLE}}{m}\right)^m - 1.0$$

For semiannual compounding, the effective annual rate is 4.04 percent:

$$EAR = \left(1 + \frac{0.04}{2}\right)^2 - 1.0 = 1.0404 - 1.0 = 0.0404 = 4.04\%$$

This rate could then be used (with a calculator) to find the PV or FV of each payment in Figure 3–3.

If the $1,000 per-year payments were actually payable as $500 each six months, you would simply redraw Figure 3–3 to show 6 payments of $500 each, but you would also need to use a periodic interest rate of 4% ÷ 2 = 2% for determining the PV or FV of the payments.

- The general equation for finding the future value of a single payment for any number of compounding periods per year is

$$FV_n = PV(1 + k_{PER})^{n \times m}$$

where k_{PER} is the periodic interest rate—in this case, $k_{PER} = 0.04/2 = 0.02$—m is the number of compounding periods per year, and n is the number of years.

■ An **amortized loan** is one that is paid off in equal payments over a specified period. An **amortization schedule** shows how much of each payment constitutes interest, how much is used to repay the debt, and the remaining balance of the loan at each point in time.

The concepts covered in this chapter will be used throughout the book. For example, in Chapter 5 we will apply present value concepts to determine the values of stocks and bonds, and we will see that the market prices of securities are established by determining the present values of the cash flows they are expected to provide. In later chapters, the same basic concepts are applied to corporate decisions involving both expenditures on capital assets and determining the types of capital that should be used to pay for such assets.

Questions

3–1 What is an *opportunity cost rate?* How is this rate used in time value analysis, and where is it shown on a cash flow time line? Is the opportunity rate a single number that is used in all situations?

3–2 An *annuity* is defined as a series of payments of a fixed amount for a specific number of periods. Thus, $100 a year for 10 years is an annuity, but $100 in Year 1, $200 in Year 2, and $400 in Years 3 through 10 does *not* constitute an annuity. However, the second series *contains* an annuity. Is this statement true or false? Explain.

3–3 If a firm's earnings per share grew from $1 to $2 over a 10-year period, the total *growth* would be 100 percent, but the *annual growth rate* would be *less than* 10 percent. True or false? Explain. Under what conditions would the annual growth rate *actually* be 10 percent per year?

3–4 Would you rather have a savings account that pays 5 percent interest compounded semiannually or one that pays 5 percent interest compounded daily? Explain.

3–5 To find the present value of an uneven series of cash flows, you must find the PVs of the individual cash flows and then sum them. Annuity procedures can never be of use, even if some of the cash flows constitute an annuity (for example, $100 each for Years 3, 4, 5, and 6), because the entire series is not an annuity. Is this statement true or false? Explain.

3–6 The present value of a perpetuity is equal to the payment on the annuity, PMT, divided by the interest rate, k: PVP = PMT/k. What is the *sum*, or *future value*, of a perpetuity of PMT dollars per year? (*Hint:* The answer is infinity, but explain why.)

3–7 Under what conditions would the simple interest rate, or APR (remember k_{SIMPLE} = APR) equal the effective annual rate, EAR?

Self-Test Problems *(Solutions appear in Appendix B)*

key terms **ST-1** Define each of the following terms:

   a. PV; k; INT; FV_n; n; PVA_n; FVA_n; PMT; m; k_{SIMPLE}
   b. Opportunity cost rate
   c. Annuity; lump-sum payment; cash flow; uneven cash flow stream
   d. Ordinary (deferred) annuity; annuity due
   e. Perpetuity; consol
   f. Outflow; inflow; cash flow time line
   g. Compounding; discounting

h. Annual, semiannual, quarterly, monthly, and daily compounding

i. Effective annual rate (EAR); simple (quoted) interest rate k_{SIMPLE}; APR; periodic rate

j. Amortization schedule; principal component versus interest component of a payment; amortized loan

k. Terminal value

rates of return **ST-2** In the introduction to this chapter we asked whether you would prefer to invest $5,500 today and receive either $7,020 in five years or $8,126 in eight years. You should now be able to determine which investment alternative is better.

a. Based only on the return you would earn from each investment, which is better?

b. Can you think of any factors other than the expected return that might be important to consider when choosing between the two investment alternatives?

future value **ST-3** Assume that it is now January 1, 2005. On January 1, 2006, you will deposit $1,000 into a savings account that pays 8 percent.

a. If the bank compounds interest annually, how much will you have in your account on January 1, 2009?

b. What would your January 1, 2009, balance be if the bank used quarterly compounding rather than annual compounding?

c. Suppose you deposited the $1,000 in four payments of $250 each on January 1 of 2006, 2007, 2008, and 2009. How much would you have in your account on January 1, 2009, based on 8 percent annual compounding?

d. Suppose you deposited four equal payments in your account on January 1 of 2006, 2007, 2008, and 2009. Assuming an 8 percent interest rate, how large would each of your payments have to be for you to obtain the same ending balance as you calculated in part a?

time value of money **ST-4** Assume that it is now January 1, 2005, and you will need $1,000 on January 1, 2009. Your bank compounds interest at an 8 percent annual rate.

a. How much must you deposit on January 1, 2006, to have a balance of $1,000 on January 1, 2009?

b. If you want to make equal payments on each January 1 from 2006 through 2009 to accumulate the $1,000, how large must each of the four payments be?

c. If your father were to offer either to make the payments calculated in part b ($221.92) or to give you a lump sum of $750 on January 1, 2006, which would you choose?

d. If you have only $750 on January 1, 2006, what interest rate, compounded annually, would you have to earn to have the necessary $1,000 on January 1, 2009?

e. Suppose you can deposit only $186.29 each January 1 from 2006 through 2009, but you still need $1,000 on January 1, 2009. What interest rate, with annual compounding, must you seek out to achieve your goal?

f. To help you reach your $1,000 goal, your father offers to give you $400 on January 1, 2006. You will get a part-time job and make six additional payments of equal amounts each six months thereafter. If all of this money is deposited in a bank that pays 8 percent, compounded semiannually, how large must each of the six payments be?

g. What is the effective annual rate being paid by the bank in part f?

effective annual rates **ST-5** Bank A pays 8 percent interest, compounded quarterly, on its money market account. The managers of Bank B want the rate on its money market account to equal Bank A's effective annual rate, but interest is to be compounded on a monthly basis. What simple, or quoted, rate must Bank B set?

Problems

present value | **3–1** If you invest $500 today in an account that pays 6 percent interest compounded annually, how much will be in your account after two years?

present value | **3–2** What is the present value of an investment that promises to pay you $1,000 in five years if you can earn 6 percent interest compounded annually?

present value | **3–3** What is the present value of $1,552.90 due in 10 years at (1) a 12 percent discount rate and (2) a 6 percent rate. Give a verbal definition of the term *present value*, and illustrate it using a cash flow time line with data from this problem. As a part of your answer, explain why present values are dependent on interest rates.

time to double a lump sum | **3–4** To the closest year, how long will it take $200 to double if it is deposited and earns 7 percent? How long will it take if the deposit earns 18 percent?

future value of an annuity | **3–5** Find the *future value* of the following annuities. The first payment in these annuities is made at the end of Year 1; that is, they are *ordinary annuities*.
a. $400 per year for ten years at 10 percent.
b. $200 per year for five years at 5 percent.
c. Now rework parts a and b assuming that payments are made at the beginning of each year; that is, they are *annuities due*.

present value of an annuity | **3–6** Find the present value of the following ordinary annuities:
a. $400 per year for ten years at 10 percent.
b. $200 per year for five years at 5 percent.
c. Now rework parts a and b assuming that payments are made at the beginning of each year; that is, they are *annuities due*.

uneven cash flow stream | **3–7** Find the *present values* of the following cash flow streams under the following conditions:

YEAR	CASH STREAM A	CASH STREAM B
1	$100	$300
2	400	400
3	400	400
4	400	400
5	300	100

a. The appropriate interest rate is 8 percent. (*Hint:* It is fairly easy to work this problem dealing with the individual cash flows. However, if you have a financial calculator, read the section of the manual that describes how to enter cash flows such as the ones in this problem. This will take a little time, but the investment will pay huge dividends throughout the course. Note, if you do work with the cash flow register, then you must enter $CF_0 = 0$.)
b. What is the value of each cash flow stream at a zero percent interest rate?

effective rate of interest | **3–8** Find the interest rates, or rates of return, on each of the following:
a. You *borrow* $700 and promise to pay back $749 at the end of one year.
b. You *lend* $700 and receive a promise to be paid $749 at the end of one year.
c. You borrow $85,000 and promise to pay back $201,229 at the end of 10 years.
d. You borrow $9,000 and promise to make payments of $2,684.80 per year for five years.

future value of various compounding periods | **3–9** Find the amount to which $500 will grow under each of the following conditions:
a. 12 percent compounded annually for five years.
b. 12 percent compounded semiannually for five years.

c. 12 percent compounded quarterly for five years.

d. 12 percent compounded monthly for five years.

present value of various **3–10** Find the present value of $500 due in the future under each of the following
compounding periods conditions:

  a. 12 percent simple rate, compounded annually, discounted back five years.

  b. 12 percent simple rate, semiannual compounding, discounted back five years.

  c. 12 percent simple rate, quarterly compounding, discounted back five years.

  d. 12 percent simple rate, monthly compounding, discounted back one year.

future value of an annuity **3–11** Find the future values of the following ordinary annuities:
for various compounding
periods
  a. FV of $400 each six months for five years at a simple rate of 12 percent, compounded semiannually.

  b. FV of $200 each three months for five years at a simple rate of 12 percent, compounded quarterly.

  c. The annuities described in parts a and b have the same amount of money paid into them during the five-year period and both earn interest at the same simple rate, yet the annuity in part b earns $101.75 more than the one in part a over the five years. Why does this occur?

EAR versus k_{SIMPLE} **3–12** The First City Bank pays 7 percent interest, compounded annually, on time deposits. The Second City Bank pays 6.5 percent interest, compounded quarterly.

  a. Based on effective interest rates, in which bank would you prefer to deposit your money?

  b. Could your choice of banks be influenced by the fact that you might want to withdraw your funds during the year as opposed to at the end of the year? In answering this question, assume that funds must be left on deposit during the entire compounding period in order for you to receive any interest.

amortization schedule **3–13** Lorkay Seidens Inc. just borrowed $25,000. The loan is to be repaid in equal installments at the end of each of the next five years, and the interest rate is 10 percent.

  a. Set up an amortization schedule for the loan.

  b. How large must each annual payment be if the loan is for $50,000? Assume that the interest rate remains at 10 percent and that the loan is paid off over five years.

  c. How large must each payment be if the loan is for $50,000, the interest rate is 10 percent, and the loan is paid off in equal installments at the end of each of the next 10 years? This loan is for the same amount as the loan in part b, but the payments are spread out over twice as many periods. Why are these payments not half as large as the payments on the loan in part b?

effective rates of return **3–14** Assume that AT&T's pension fund managers are considering two alternative securities as investments: (1) Security Z (for zero intermediate year cash flows), which costs $422.41 today, pays nothing during its 10-year life, and then pays $1,000 at the end of 10 years or (2) Security B, which has a cost today of $500 and pays $74.50 at the end of each of the next 10 years.

  a. What is the rate of return on each security?

  b. Assume that the interest rate AT&T's pension fund managers can earn on the fund's money falls to 6 percent immediately after the securities are purchased and is expected to remain at that level for the next 10 years. What would the price of each security change to, what would the fund's profit be on each security, and what would be the percentage profit (profit divided by cost) for each security?

c. Assuming that the cash flows for each security had to be reinvested at the new 6 percent market interest rate, (1) what would be the value attributable to each security at the end of ten years and (2) what "actual, after-the-fact" rate of return would the fund have earned on each security? (*Hint:* The "actual" rate of return is found as the interest rate that causes the PV of the compounded Year 10 amount to equal the original cost of the security.)

d. Now assume all the facts as given in parts b and c except assume that the interest rate rose to 12 percent rather than fell to 6 percent. What would happen to the profit figures as developed in part b and to the "actual" rates of return as determined in part c? Explain your results.

planning for college   **3–15** A father is planning a savings program to put his daughter through college. His daughter is now 13 years old. She plans to enroll at the university in five years, and it should take her four years to complete her education. Currently, the cost per year (for everything—food, clothing, tuition, books, transportation, and so forth) is $12,500, but these costs are expected to increase by 5 percent—the inflation rate—each year. The daughter recently received $7,500 from her grandfather's estate; this money, which is invested in a mutual fund paying 8 percent interest compounded annually, will be used to help meet the costs of the daughter's education. The rest of the costs will be met by money that the father will deposit in the savings account. He will make equal deposits to the account in each year from now until his daughter starts college, for a total of six deposits. These deposits, which will begin today, will also earn 8 percent interest.

a. What will be the present value of the cost of four years of education *at the time the daughter turns 18?* [*Hint:* Calculate the cost (at 5 percent inflation, or growth) for each year of her education, discount three of these costs back (at 8 percent) to the year in which she turns 18, then sum the four costs, which include the cost of the first year.]

b. What will be the value of the $7,500 that the daughter received from her grandfather's estate *when she starts college at age 18?* (*Hint:* Compound for five years at 8 percent.)

c. If the father is planning to make the first of six deposits today, how large must each deposit be for him to be able to put his daughter through college? (*Hint:* Be sure to draw a cash flow time line to depict the timing of the cash flows.)

future value of a retirement   **3–16** As soon as she graduated from college, Kay began planning for her retirement. **fund** Her plans were to deposit $500 semiannually into an IRA (a retirement fund) beginning six months after graduation and continuing until the day she retired, which she expected to be 30 years later. Today is the day Kay retires. She just made the last $500 deposit into her retirement fund, and now she wants to know how much she has accumulated for her retirement. The fund earned 10 percent compounded semiannually since it was established.

a. Compute the balance of the retirement fund assuming all the payments were made on time.

b. Although Kay was able to make all the $500 deposits she planned, 10 years ago she had to withdraw $10,000 from the fund to pay some medical bills incurred by her mother. Compute the balance in the retirement fund based on this information.

automobile loan   **3–17** Sarah is on her way to the local Chevrolet dealership to buy a new car. The list, **computation** or "sticker," price of the car is $13,000. Sarah has $3,000 in her checking account that she can use as a down payment toward the purchase of a new car. She has carefully evaluated her finances and determined that she can afford payments that *total* $2,400 per year on a loan to purchase the car. Sarah can borrow the money to purchase the car either through the dealer's "special financing package," which is advertised at 4.0 percent interest, or from a local bank, which has automobile loans at 12 percent interest. Each loan would be outstanding for a period of five years, and the payments would be made quarterly (every three months). Sarah knows the dealer's "special financing package" requires that she will have to pay the "sticker" price for the car. But if she uses the bank financing, she thinks she can negotiate with the dealer for a better price. Assume Sarah wants to pay $600 per payment, regardless of which loan she chooses, and the remainder of the purchase price will be a down payment that can be satisfied with any of the $3,000 in Sarah's checking account. Ignoring charges for taxes, tag, and title transfer, how much of a reduction in the sticker price must Sarah negotiate to make the bank financing more attractive than the dealer's "special financing package"?

required annuity payments **3–18** Janet just graduated from a women's college in Mississippi with a degree in business administration, and she is about to start a new job with a large financial services firm based in Tampa, Florida. From reading various business publications while she was in college, Janet has concluded it probably is a good idea to begin planning for her retirement now. Even though she is only 22 years old and just beginning her career, Janet is concerned that Social Security will not be able to meet her needs when she retires. Fortunately for Janet, the company that hired her has created a good retirement/investment plan that permits her to make contributions every year. So Janet is now evaluating the amount she needs to contribute to satisfy her financial requirements at retirement. She has decided that she would like to take a trip as soon as her retirement begins (a reward to herself for many years of excellent work). The estimated cost of the trip, including all expenses such as meals and souvenirs, will be $120,000, and it will last for one year (no other funds will be needed during the first year of retirement). After she returns from her trip, Janet plans to settle down to enjoy her retirement. She estimates she will need $70,000 each year to be able to live comfortably and enjoy her "twilight years." The retirement/investment plan available to employees where Janet is going to work pays 7 percent interest compounded annually, and it is expected this rate will continue as long as the company offers the opportunity to contribute to the fund. When she retires, Janet will have to move her retirement "nest egg" to another investment so she can withdraw money when she needs it. Her plans are to move the money to a fund that allows withdrawals at the beginning of each year; the fund is expected to pay 5 percent interest compounded annually. Janet expects to retire in 40 years, and, after looking at the life insurance actuarial tables, she has decided she will live another 20 years after she returns from her retirement trip around the world. If Janet's expectations are correct, how much must she contribute to the retirement fund to satisfy her retirement plans if she plans to make her first contribution to the fund one year from today, and the last contribution will be made on the day she retires?

Exam-Type Problems

The problems in this section are set up in such a way that they could be used as multiple-choice exam problems.

TVM comparisons **3–19** Which amount is worth more at 14 percent: $1,000 in hand today or $2,000 due in six years?

growth rates   **3–20** Martell Corporation's 2005 sales were $12 million. Sales were $6 million five years earlier.

    a. To the nearest percentage point, at what rate have sales grown?

    b. Suppose someone calculated the sales growth for Martell Corporation in part a as follows: "Sales doubled in five years. This represents a growth of 100 percent in five years, so, dividing 100 percent by five, we find the growth rate to be 20 percent per year." Explain what is wrong with this calculation.

rates of return   **3–21** Krystal Magee invested $150,000 18 months ago. Currently, the investment is worth $168,925. Krystal knows the investment has paid interest every three months (i.e., quarterly), but she doesn't know what the yield on her investment is. Help Krystal. Compute both the annual percentage rate (APR) *and* the effective annual rate (EAR) of interest.

effective rate of return   **3–22** Your broker offers to sell you a note for $13,250 that will pay $2,345.05 per year for 10 years. If you buy the note, what rate of interest (to the closest percent) will you be earning?

effective rate of return   **3–23** A mortgage company offers to lend you $85,000; the loan calls for payments of $8,273.59 per year for 30 years. What interest rate is the mortgage company charging you?

required lump-sum payment   **3–24** To complete your last year in business school and then go through law school, you will need $10,000 per year for four years, starting next year (that is, you will need to withdraw the first $10,000 one year from today). Your rich uncle offers to put you through school, and he will deposit in a bank paying 7 percent interest a sum of money that is sufficient to provide the four payments of $10,000 each. His deposit will be made today.

    a. How large must the deposit be?

    b. How much will be in the account immediately after you make the first withdrawal? After the last withdrawal?

loan payments   **3–25** Sue wants to buy a car that costs $12,000. She has arranged to borrow the total purchase price of the car from her credit union at a simple interest rate equal to 12 percent. The loan requires quarterly payments for a period of three years. If the first payment is due in three months (one quarter) after purchasing the car, what will be the amount of Sue's quarterly payments on the loan?

repaying a loan   **3–26** While Steve Bouchard was a student at the University of Florida, he borrowed $12,000 in student loans at an annual interest rate of 9 percent. If Steve repays $1,500 per year, how long, to the nearest year, will it take him to repay the loan?

reaching a financial goal   **3–27** You need to accumulate $10,000. To do so, you plan to make deposits of $1,750 per year, with the first payment being made one year from today, in a bank account that pays 6 percent annual interest. Your last deposit will be more than $1,750 if more is needed to round out to $10,000. How many years will it take you to reach your $10,000 goal, and how large will the last deposit be?

perpetuity   **3–28** What is the present value of a perpetuity of $100 per year if the appropriate discount rate is 7 percent? If interest rates in general were to double and the appropriate discount rate rose to 14 percent, what would happen to the present value of the perpetuity?

loan amortization   **3–29** Assume that your aunt sold her house on January 1 and that she took a mortgage in the amount of $10,000 as part of the payment. The mortgage has a quoted (or simple) interest rate of 10 percent, but it calls for payments every six months, beginning on June 30, and the mortgage is to be amortized over

10 years. Now, one year later, your aunt must file a Form 1099 with the IRS and with the person who bought the house, informing them of the interest that was included in the two payments made during the year. (This interest will be income to your aunt and a deduction to the buyer of the house.) To the closest dollar, what is the total amount of interest that was paid during the first year?

annuity amounts—ordinary annuity versus annuity due

3–30 Jason worked various jobs during his teenage years to save money for college. Now it is his 20th birthday, and he is about to begin his college studies at the University of South Florida. A few months ago, Jason received a scholarship that will cover all of his college tuition for a period not to exceed five years. The money he has saved will be used for living expenses while he is in college; in fact, Jason expects to use all of his savings while attending USF. The jobs he worked as a teenager allowed him to save a total of $10,000, which currently is invested at 12 percent in a financial asset that pays interest monthly. Because Jason will be a full-time student, he expects to graduate four years from today, on his 24th birthday.

    a. How much can Jason withdraw every month while he is in college if the first withdrawal occurs today?

    b. How much can Jason withdraw every month while he is in college if he waits until the end of this month to make the first withdrawal?

simple interest rate

3–31 Sue Sharpe, manager of Oaks Mall Jewelry, wants to sell on credit, giving customers three months in which to pay. However, Sue will have to borrow from her bank to carry the accounts payable. The bank will charge a simple 15 percent, but with monthly compounding. Sue wants to quote a simple rate to her customers (all of whom are expected to pay on time) that will exactly cover her financing costs. What simple annual rate should she quote to her credit customers?

selecting a financing alternative

3–32 Read the situation described in the Industry Practice box included in this chapter. Complete the appropriate computations to show that the credit union loan is better than the automobile dealer's "0% financing" loan.

Integrative Problem

time value of money analysis

3–33 Assume that you are nearing graduation and that you have applied for a job with a local bank. As part of the bank's evaluation process, you have been asked to take an examination that covers several financial analysis techniques. The first section of the test addresses time value of money analysis. See how you would do by answering the following questions:

    a. Draw cash flow time lines for (1) a $100 lump-sum cash flow at the end of Year 2, (2) an ordinary annuity of $100 per year for three years, (3) an uneven cash flow stream of –$50, $100, $75, and $50 at the end of Years 0 through 3.

    b. (1) What is the future value of an initial $100 after three years if it is invested in an account paying 10 percent annual interest?

    (2) What is the present value of $100 to be received in three years if the appropriate interest rate is 10 percent?

    c. We sometimes need to find how long it will take a sum of money (or anything else) to grow to some specified amount. For example, if a company's sales are growing at a rate of 20 percent per year, approximately how long will it take sales to triple?

d. What is the difference between an ordinary annuity and an annuity due? What type of annuity is shown in the following cash flow time line? How would you change it to the other type of annuity?

e. (1) What is the future value of a three-year ordinary annuity of $100 if the appropriate interest rate is 10 percent?
(2) What is the present value of the annuity?
(3) What would the future and present values be if the annuity were an annuity due?

f. What is the present value of the following uneven cash flow stream? The appropriate interest rate is 10 percent, compounded annually.

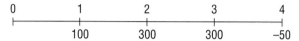

g. What annual interest rate will cause $100 to grow to $125.97 in three years?

h. (1) Will the future value be larger or smaller if we compound an initial amount more often than annually, for example, every six months, or *semiannually*, holding the stated interest rate constant? Why?
(2) Define (i) the stated, or quoted, or simple, rate (APR), (ii) the periodic rate, and (iii) the effective annual rate (EAR).
(3) What is the effective annual rate for a simple rate of 10 percent, compounded semiannually? Compounded quarterly? Compounded daily?
(4) What is the future value of $100 after three years under 10 percent semiannual compounding? Quarterly compounding?

i. Will the effective annual rate ever be equal to the simple (quoted) rate? Explain.

j. (1) What is the value at the end of Year 3 of the following cash flow stream if the quoted interest rate is 10 percent, compounded semiannually?

(2) What is the PV of the same stream?
(3) Is the stream an annuity?
(4) An important rule is that you should never show a simple rate on a time line or use it in calculations unless what condition holds? (*Hint:* Think of annual compounding, when k_{SIMPLE} = EAR = k_{PER}.) What would be wrong with your answers to parts (1) and (2) if you used the simple rate 10 percent rather than the periodic rate $k_{SIMPLE} \div 2$ = 10% ÷ 2 = 5%?

k. (1) Construct an amortization schedule for a $1,000 that has a 10 percent annual interest rate and is repaid in three equal installments.
(2) What is the annual interest expense for the borrower and the annual interest income for the lender during Year 2?

l. Suppose on January 1, 2005, you deposit $100 in an account that pays a simple, or quoted, interest rate of 11.33463 percent, with interest added (compounded) daily. How much will you have in your account on October 1, or after nine months?

m. Now suppose you leave your money in the bank for 21 months. Thus, on January 1, 2005, you deposit $100 in an account that pays a 12 percent effective annual interest rate. How much will be in your account on October 1, 2006?

n. Suppose someone offered to sell you a note calling for a $1,000 payment 15 months from today. The person offers to sell the note for $850. You have $850 in a bank time deposit (savings instrument) that pays a 6.76649 percent simple rate with daily compounding, which is a 7 percent effective annual interest rate; and you plan to leave this money in the bank unless you buy the note. The note is not risky—you are sure it will be paid on schedule. Should you buy the note? Check the decision in three ways: (1) by comparing your future value if you buy the note versus leaving your money in the bank, (2) by comparing the PV of the note with your current bank investment, and (3) by comparing the EAR on the note with that of the bank investment.

o. Suppose the note discussed in part n had a cost of $850, but called for five quarterly payments of $190 each, with the first payment due in three months rather than $1,000 at the end of 15 months. Would it be a good investment for you?

Computer-Related Problem

Work the problem in this section only if you are using the computer problem diskette.

amortization schedule   **3–34** Use the computerized model in the File C03 to solve this problem.

a. Set up an amortization schedule for a $30,000 loan to be repaid in equal installments at the end of each of the next 20 years at an interest rate of 10 percent. What is the annual payment?

b. Set up an amortization schedule for a $60,000 loan to be repaid in 20 equal annual installments at an interest rate of 10 percent. What is the annual payment?

c. Set up an amortization schedule for a $60,000 loan to be repaid in 20 equal annual installments at an interest rate of 20 percent. What is the annual payment?

GET REAL with Thomson ONE

3–35 Starbucks Corporation (SBUX) does much more than make a great latte. It purchases, roasts, and markets coffee beans, along with other related activities. The company also sells such products as premium teas and coffee-related accessories through its retail stores. Imagine that you are one of the shareholders of Starbucks and you would like to have an estimate of how much the stock will earn per share over the next three years. Using the Thomson One database, find the earnings estimates for Starbucks Corporation for the next three years and answer the following questions:

a. Calculate the present value of the mixed stream of cash flows if you own one share of Starbuck's common stock. In this case, the cash flows are the earnings per share (EPS) estimates. The interest rate is 3 percent. [*Hint:* Click on the Estimates tab for SBUX]

   b. What is the present value of the cash flows if you own 100 shares of Starbuck's stock?

   c. If you own 100 shares of Starbuck's stock and you want to hold the stock only if you can expect more than $3.00 in earnings over a three-year period, would you buy more of Starbuck's or sell the shares you already own?

   d. Calculate the present value of the cash flows if the interest rate rises to 5 percent.

   e. Why does the present value change when the interest rate rises?

APPENDIX 3A

Using Spreadsheets to Solve Time Value of Money Problems

Spreadsheets, such as Excel or Lotus 1-2-3, have preprogrammed functions that can be used to solve time value of money problems. In this appendix, we show the solutions to some of the examples given in the chapter using an Excel spreadsheet.

To access the time value of money functions, click on the "paste function," which is found in the Insert menu on the toolbar. The paste function is designated *fx*. When you click on *fx*, the following menu will appear:

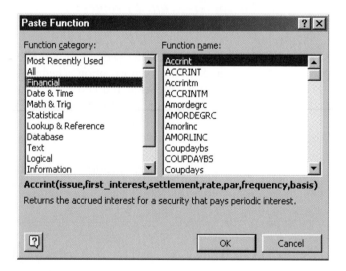

On the left side of the menu, click on "Financial" in the function category. This will give you access to the financial functions that are needed to solve the time value of money problems.

Solving for Future Value (FV): Lump-Sum Amount and Annuity

If you want to find the FV in five years of $100 invested today at 5 percent compounded annually, you might want to set up your spreadsheet as follows:

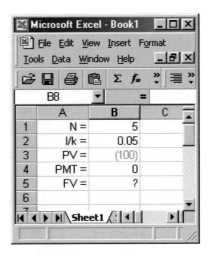

Note that the interest rate is entered as a decimal.

To solve for the future value, place the cursor in cell **B5,** click on the Paste function, and scroll down the list you see on the right side of the menu until you reach FV. When you click on FV, the following menu will appear:

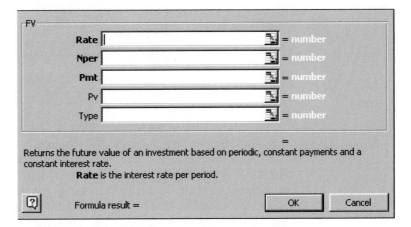

"Rate" represents the interest rate per period, "Nper" is the number of periods interest is earned, "Pmt" is the periodic payment (we will use this later), "Pv" is the present value of the amount, and "Type" refers to the type of annuity payment (0 = ordinary annuity; 1 = annuity due). To solve our problem, you need to refer to the appropriate cells in the spreadsheet that contain the information requested. As a result, you should insert **B2** in the first row of the table (Rate), **B1** in the second row (Nper), **B4** in the third row (Pmt), **B3** in the fourth row (Pv), and leave the last row blank. Click "OK" when you are finished and the answer, $127.63, will appear in cell **B5.** If you press the **F2** key, you will see the contents of **B5,** which should be "=FV(B2,B1,B4,B3)." Note that you can also insert the appropriate location for each row of the box shown above by clicking on ◤, placing the cursor in the cell that contains the data in the spreadsheet, and then pressing return. When enough information is entered, you will see the result of the computation at the bottom of the box. In our example, when you finish entering the cell locations, the box will look like the following:

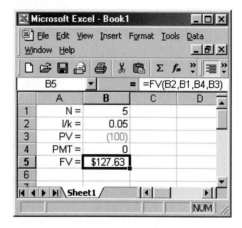

Once the locations of all the appropriate data are in the table, click "OK," and the answer will appear in cell **B5** in the spreadsheet. The spreadsheet will now be as follows:

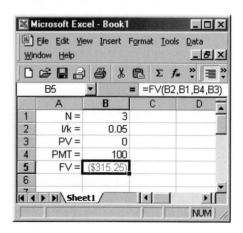

The future value amount we computed here, $127.63, is the same result as we found in the example we solved in the chapter.

To solve for the future value of an annuity, we use the same financial function—that is, FV. For example, in the chapter, we solved for a three-year $100 annuity with an opportunity cost equal to 5 percent. Using the same spreadsheet set up earlier, change the values so that N = 3, I/k = 0.05, PV = 0, and PMT = 100. You will see that the value for FV changes so that it is equal to –$315.25, which is the same result we found in the chapter—that is, FVA = $315.25.

The result given here is the future value of an ordinary annuity. To find the future value of an annuity due, place the cursor in cell **B5** and click on Paste function—that is, *fx*. When the menu appears, place a 1 in the last row so that the inputs are as follows:

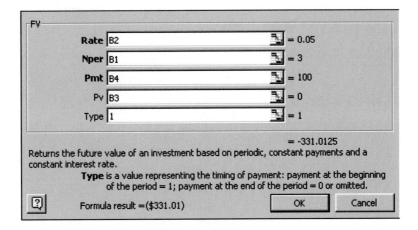

You will notice that the result shown in the menu changes to –331.01, and when you click on **OK** the result appears in cell **B5**. As you can see on the menu, when you enter 1 in the last row you change the timing of the cash flows from the end of the period to the beginning of the period for the purposes of the computation. The result found here is the same as we found earlier in the chapter.

Solving for Present Value (PV): Lump-Sum Amount and Annuity

To find the PV using a spreadsheet, you follow the same steps as described for solving for FV, except you use the PV financial function. The menus are the same as in the previous section, except the value for the future value (labeled "Fv" in the menu) is a required input rather than the present value (labeled "Pv") that was required previously.

Solving for k: Lump-Sum Amount and Annuity

Suppose you want to determine the rate of return that would be earned if you purchase an investment for $78.35 that will pay $100 after five years. To solve this problem using a spreadsheet, use the "RATE" function. The spreadsheet might be set up as follows:

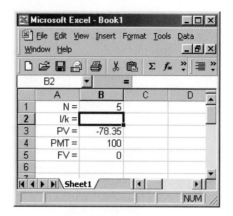

Once the appropriate cell locations are entered, the "RATE" function menu would be as follows:

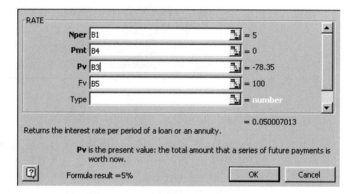

As you can see, the result of the computation is 5 percent, which will appear in cell **B2** when you press OK. You would use the same function to find the interest rate, k, for an annuity.

Solving for n: Lump-Sum Amount and Annuity

Suppose you want to determine how many years it will take to earn a 10 percent return if you invest $68.30 today and receive $100 at maturity. To solve this problem using a spreadsheet, use the "NPER" function. The spreadsheet might be set up as follows:

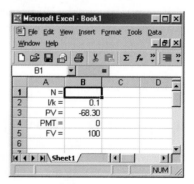

Once the appropriate cell locations are entered, the "NPER" function menu would be as follows:

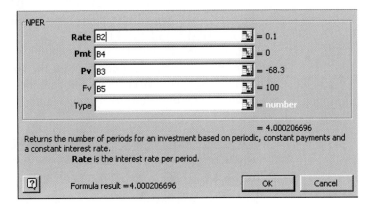

As you can see, the result of the computation is 4 years, which will appear in cell **B1** when you press OK. You would use the same function to solve for n, the number of periods, for an annuity.

Solving for Present Value and Future Value: Uneven Cash Flows

We will describe the steps to solve for the PV of an uneven cash flow stream in the appendix to Chapter 6.

Amortization Schedule

Let's take a look at the amortized loan that was described in the chapter. We assumed that a firm borrows $15,000, and the loan is to be repaid in equal payments at the end of each of the next three years. The interest on the loan is 8 percent. To set up an amortization schedule for the example given in the chapter, we first determined the amount of the payment the firm must make each year. The spreadsheet solution might be set up as follows:

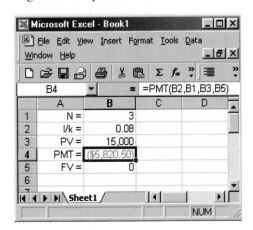

In this case, the financial function that is used is PMT. The locations of the cells that contain the appropriate values are shown in the window just above the columns labeled "C" and "D"—that is, "=PMT(B2,B1,B3,B5)."

To set up the amortization schedule for this loan, we would use two financial functions: IPMT and PPMT. IPMT gives the interest payment for a particular period, given the amount borrowed and the interest rate. PPMT gives the principal repayment for a particular period, given the amount borrowed and the interest rate. The following spreadsheet shows the content of each cell to construct an amortization schedule for our illustrative loan:

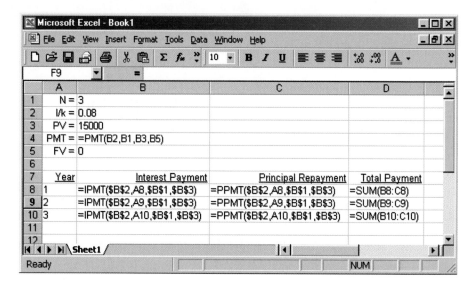

The $ sign is included to fix the locations of the cells that contain common values required for each computation so that you can use the Copy command to copy the relationships from row 8 to rows 9 and 10. The numerical results from these relationships would be as follows:

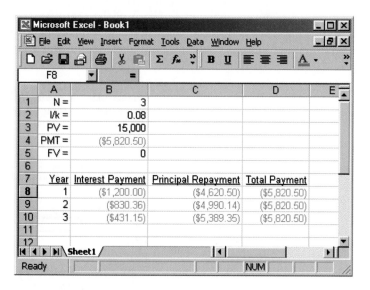

APPENDIX 3B

Using Interest Tables to Solve Time Value of Money Problems

Before modern technology became prevalent, tables that contain computations called *interest factors* were used to simplify time value of money computations. In this appendix, we show the solutions to the examples given in the chapter using the information provided by interest tables. The value of an interest factor is based on the interest rate, k, and the number of periods, n; thus, the values contained in the interest tables are simply the results of computing interest factors for different combinations of k and n.

Future Value of a Lump-Sum Amount

Applying Equation 3–1, we computed the future value of a lump-sum amount, FV_n, as follows:

3–1

$$FV_n = PV(1 + k)^n$$

The multiple by which the present value grows, $(1 + k)^n$, is called the *Future Value Interest Factor* for an amount that is invested at k interest for n periods, and it is designated $FVIF_{k,n}$. Using $FVIF_{k,n}$, Equation 3–1 is rewritten as follows:

$$FV_n = PV(1 + k)^n = PV(FVIF_{k,n})$$

Table A–3 in the appendix at the end of the book contains FVIFs for different values of k and n.

If we use the table to compute the future value of $100 invested at 5 percent for five years (the example given in the chapter), we have

$$FV_n = PV(FVIF_{k,n})$$
$$= \$100(FVIF_{5\%,5})$$
$$= \$100(1.2763)$$
$$= \$127.63$$

The value of the interest factor, $FVIF_{5\%,5} = 1.2763$, is found by looking in Table A–3 in the column labeled "5%" and the row labeled "5," which gives you the result of solving $(1 + k)^n = (1.05)^5 = 1.2763$. Each value in Table A–3 represents the solution to $(1 + k)^n$ for different combinations of k and n.

Present Value of a Lump-Sum Amount

Applying Equation 3–2, we computed the present value of a lump-sum amount, PV, as follows:

$$3\text{-}2$$

$$PV = FV_n\left[\frac{1}{(1 + k)^n}\right]$$

The factor by which the future value is discounted, $\left[\dfrac{1}{(1 + k)^n}\right]$, is called the *Present Value Interest Factor* for an amount that is invested at k interest for n periods, and it is designated $PVIF_{k,n}$. Using $PVIF_{k,n}$, Equation 3-2 is rewritten as follows:

$$PV = FV_n\left[\frac{1}{(1 + k)^n}\right] = FV_n(PVIF_{k,n})$$

Table A–1 in the appendix at the end of the book contains PVIFs for different values of k and n.

Let's use Table A–1 to solve the example given in the chapter. We want to determine the present value $127.63 to be received in five years if the opportunity cost rate is 5 percent.

$$PV_n = PV(PVIF_{k,n})$$
$$= \$127.63(PVIF_{5\%,5})$$
$$= \$127.63(0.7835)$$
$$= \$100.00$$

The value of the interest factor, $PVIF_{5\%,5} = 0.7835$, is found by looking in Table A–1 in the column labeled "5%" and the row labeled "5," which gives you the result of solving

$$PVIF_{5\%,5} = \left[\frac{1}{(1.05)^5}\right] = 0.7835$$

Each value in Table A–1 represents the solution to this equation for different combinations of k and n.

Future Value of an Annuity, FVA_n

Applying Equation 3–3a, we computed the future value of an annuity, FVA_n, as follows:

$$3\text{-}3a$$

$$FVA_n = PMT\left[\sum_{t=1}^{n}(1 + k)^{n-t}\right] = PMT\left[\frac{(1 + k)^n - 1}{k}\right]$$

The factor by which the payment is multiplied to determine FVA_n, $\left[\dfrac{(1 + k)^n - 1}{k}\right]$, is called the *Future Value Interest Factor for an Annuity* of n payments at k interest, and it is designated $FVIFA_{k,n}$. Using $FVIFA_{k,n}$, Equation 3–3a is rewritten as follows:

$$FVA_n = PMT\left[\sum_{t=1}^{n}(1+k)^{n-t}\right] = PMT\left[\frac{(1+k)^n - 1}{k}\right] = PMT(FVIFA_{k,n})$$

Table A–4 in the appendix at the end of the book contains FVIFAs for different values of k and n.

Using Table A–4 to solve the example given in the chapter, we find that if you invested $100 a year beginning at the end of the year for the next three years in an investment that returns 5 percent per year, the value of your investment in three years would be

$$FVA_3 = PMT(FVIFA_{k,n})$$
$$= \$100(FVIFA_{5\%,3})$$
$$= \$100(3.1525)$$
$$= \$315.25$$

The value of the interest factor, $FVIFA_{5\%,3} = 3.1525$, is found by looking in Table A–4 in the column labeled "5%" and the row labeled "3," which gives you the result of solving

$$FVIFA_{5\%,5} = \left[\frac{(1.05)^3 - 1}{0.05}\right] = 3.1525$$

Each value in Table A–4 represents the solution to this equation for different combinations of k and n.

Present Value of an Annuity, PVA_n

Applying Equation 3–4a, we computed the present value of an annuity, PVA_n, as follows:

3–4a

$$PVA_n = PMT\left[\sum_{t=1}^{n}\frac{1}{(1+k)^t}\right] = PMT\left[\frac{1 - \dfrac{1}{(1+k)^n}}{k}\right]$$

The factor by which the payment is multiplied to determine PVA_n, $\left[\dfrac{1 - \dfrac{1}{(1+k)^n}}{k}\right]$, is called the *Present Value Interest Factor for an Annuity* of n payments at k interest, and it is designated $PVIFA_{k,n}$. Using $PVIFA_{k,n}$, Equation 3–4a is rewritten as follows:

$$PVA_n = PMT\left[\sum_{t=1}^{n}\frac{1}{(1+k)^t}\right] = PMT\left[\frac{1 - \dfrac{1}{(1+k)^n}}{k}\right] = PMT(PVIFA_{k,n})$$

Table A–2 in the appendix at the end of the book contains PVIFAs for different values of k and n.

If we use Table A–2 to solve the example given in the chapter, we find that, if the opportunity cost rate is 5 percent, the present value of a three-year $100 ordinary annuity is

$$PVA_3 = PMT(PVIFA_{k,n})$$
$$= \$100(PVIFA_{5\%,3})$$
$$= \$100(2.7232)$$
$$= \$272.32$$

The value of the interest factor, $PVIFA_{5\%,3} = 2.7232$, is found by looking in Table A–2 in the column labeled "5%" and the row labeled "3," which gives you the result of solving

$$PVIFA_{5\%,3} = \left[\frac{1 - \dfrac{1}{(1.05)^3}}{0.05}\right] = 2.7232$$

Each value in Table A–2 represents the solution to this equation for different combinations of k and n.

As you can see, using the interest tables to work the examples given in the chapter give the same results as the earlier computations. The sole purpose of the interest tables is to provide the results of computing interest factors for different combinations of k and n. Because it is easy to perform the same computations with the calculators available today, interest tables are used much less now than 20 years ago.

APPENDIX 3C

Generating an Amortization Schedule for a Loan Using a Financial Calculator

The following steps show you how to generate an amortization schedule using a Texas Instruments BAII PLUS. For more information or if you have a different type of calculator, refer to the manual that came with the calculator. To illustrate the process of generating an amortization schedule, let's use the example given in the chapter: A firm borrows $15,000 at 8 percent, and the loan is to be repaid in three equal payments at the end of each of the next three years. In the chapter, we computed the annual payment necessary to repay the loan to be $5,820.50.

1. Enter the information for the amortized loan into the TVM registers as described in the chapter:

Inputs:	3	8	15,000	?	0
	N	**I/k**	**PV**	**PMT**	**FV**

   Output: = −5,820.50

2. Enter the amortization function by pressing **2nd** **PV**, which has "Amort" written above (a secondary function). P1 = 1 is displayed, which indicates that the starting point for the amortization schedule is the first period. Press **↓**,

and P2 = 1 is displayed, which indicates the ending point for the first set of computations is the first period.

3. **a.** Press ⬇, and BAL = 10,379.49729 is displayed. This result indicates that the remaining principal balance at the end of the first year is $10,379.50.

b. Press ⬇, and PRN = –4,620.502711 is displayed, which indicates that the amount of principal repaid in the first period is $4,620.50.

c. Press ⬇, and INT = –1,200 is displayed, which indicates that the amount of interest paid in the first period is $1,200.

4. Press ⬇ **CPT**, and P1 = 2 is displayed. Next, press ⬇, and P2 = 2 is displayed. This information indicates that the next series of computations relate to the second payment. Follow the procedures given above in Step 3:

a. Press ⬇; display shows BAL = 5,389.354362

b. Press ⬇; display shows PRN = –4,990.142928

c. Press ⬇; display shows INT = –830.3597831

These values represent the ending loan balance, the amount of principal repaid, and the amount of interest paid, respectively, for the second year.

5. Press ⬇ **CPT**, and P1 = 3 is displayed; then press ⬇, and P2 = 3 is displayed. This information indicates that the next series of computations relate to the third payment. Follow the procedures given in Step 3:

a. Press ⬇; display shows BAL = –0.000000

b. Press ⬇; display shows PRN = –5,389.354362

c. Press ⬇; display shows INT = –431.1483489

These values represent the ending loan balance, the amount of principal repaid, and the amount of interest paid, respectively, for the third, and final, year.

If you combine the results from Steps 3 through 5 in a table, you would find that it contains the same values given in Table 3–2. If you use a calculator to construct a complete amortization schedule, you must repeat Step 3 for each year the loan exists—that is, Step 3 must be repeated 10 times for a 10-year loan. If you would like to know either the balance, principal repayment, or interest paid in a particular year, you need only set P1 and P2 equal to that particular year to display the desired values.

APPENDIX 3D

Computing the PV of an Uneven Cash Flow Stream Using a Financial Calculator

To compute the PV of an uneven cash flow stream using your financial calculator, you need to use the cash flow (CF) function. You should refer to the manual that came with your calculator. The steps for computing the PV of the following cash flow stream using the Texas Instruments BAII PLUS are shown here:

YEAR	CASH FLOW
1	$100
2	300
3	200
4	200
5	1,000

1. Enter the cash flow function by pressing the **CF** key; $CF_0 = 0$ should be displayed. Press one of the arrow keys, either **↑** or **↓**, to see if the registers are clear. If there are numbers in any of the registers, you can clear them by pressing the 2nd key, **2nd**, and then pressing **CE/C**, which has "CLR Work" written above (this is a secondary function).

2. Enter CF_0 as follows: 0 **ENTER**.

3. Enter CF_1 as follows: **↓** 100 **ENTER**. Press **↓** again, and you will see F01 = 1 displayed on the screen—the calculator is telling you that it has assumed the 100 cash flow will occur (its frequency) only once. For problems where the same cash flow occurs more than once in consecutive periods, you can enter the frequency of the CFs, and then press **ENTER** to change the F01 value (the frequency for consecutive CFs received later in a project's life can be similarly changed).

4. Enter the *remaining* CFs using one of the following approaches:

I. ENTER EACH CASH FLOW INDIVIDUALLY—DO NOT RECOGNIZE ANNUITIES	II. ENTER EQUAL CONSECUTIVE CASH FLOWS ONCE— RECOGNIZE ANNUITIES
CF_2: **↓** 300 **ENTER** **↓**	CF_2: **↓** 300 **ENTER** **↓**
CF_3: **↓** 200 **ENTER** **↓**	CF_3: **↓** 200 **ENTER** **↓** 2 **ENTER**
CF_4: **↓** 200 **ENTER** **↓**	CF_4: **↓** 1,000 **ENTER**
CF_5: **↓** 1,000 **ENTER** **↓**	

5. Once all the CFs have been entered, press **NPV**. I = 0 will appear on the display. Enter 6 and press **ENTER** **↓** **CPT** to get the answer: NPV = 1,434.9393.

6. Before you exit the cash flow register, you should clear your work; otherwise, the values you entered for the CFs will remain in the registers until they either are cleared or another value is input into the same CF location (register). To clear your work, press **2nd** **CE/C**.

CHAPTER 4

Risk and Rates of Return

The performance of the major stock markets from 1995 through 1998 can best be described as remarkable—a period that investors would love to repeat again and again. During that four-year stretch, stocks traded on U.S. stock markets earned an average return greater than 20 percent per year. In 1998, for example, companies such as Microsoft and MCI WorldCom more than doubled in value. The value of some Internet companies, such as America Online, Amazon.com, and Yahoo!, increased by more than 500 percent. Consider the return that you would have earned in 1998 if you had purchased Amazon.com at the beginning of the year for $30.13 and then sold it at the end of the year for $321.25—a one-year return of 966 percent. On the other hand, if you waited until January 2000 to buy Amazon.com and then held it until the end of the year, you would have lost approximately 80 percent of your investment because the company's stock decreased significantly during 2000. In fact, during 2000, the values of most Internet company stocks experienced dramatic declines. Indeed, many Internet companies did not survive the "Internet skepticism" that existed during the year. By comparison, if you had purchased the stock of Enron Corporation at the beginning of 2000, your investment would have nearly doubled in value by the end of the year. But, in mid-2003 the value of Enron's stock was selling for $.05 per share, because the company was in bankruptcy at the time. If you purchased Amazon.com and held it during 2002 rather than 2000, you would have earned a positive 75 percent on your investment.

If you bet all your money on the stock of a single company, you essentially "put all your eggs in one basket" and thus face considerable risk. For example, you would have won big if you chose to invest in Amazon.com for one year either in 1998 or in 2002, or if you invested in Enron in 2000. But you would have lost big if you bought Amazon.com at the beginning of 2000 and sold it at the end of 2000, or held Enron from 2000 until 2003. Investors who diversified during these periods by spreading their investments among many stocks, perhaps through mutual funds, would have earned a return somewhere between the extraordinary increases posted by Amazon.com in 1998 and 2002 and the extraordinary decreases posted by Amazon.com and other Internet companies in 2000 and Enron from 2000 to 2003. Large "baskets" of such diversified investments would have earned returns fairly close to the average of the stock markets.

These examples show that *investing is risky*! Although the stock markets performed well from 1995 through 1998, they also go through periods characterized by decreasing prices or negative average returns. For instance, in 1990, 1994, and 2000–2002, the average stock listed on the New York Stock Exchange decreased in value by 7.5 percent, 3.1 percent, and between 2 percent and 25 percent, respectively. More recently, during the first half of 2003 the market was fickle: On the first trading day of the year, the Dow Jones Industrial Average decreased by 172 points (–2.0 percent), it increased by 178 (2.1 percent) points the next two trading days, and then decreased by 181 points (–2.1 percent) on the fourth trading day of the year. Even though this roller-coaster ride continued throughout the year, the overall change in the DJIA was an increase equal to approximately 28 percent. Some of the wealth lost during the three previous years—that is, 2000–2002—was regained during 2003. What risk!

Who knows what the stock market will be doing when you read this book. It could be an up market referred to as a *bull market*, or it could be a down market, referred to as a *bear market*. Whatever the case, as times change, investment strategies and portfolio mixes need to be changed to meet new conditions. For this reason, you need to understand the basic concepts of risk and return and to recognize how diversification affects investment decisions. As you will discover, investors can create portfolios of securities and significantly reduce risk without a dramatic reduction in the average return on their investments. After reading this chapter, you should have a better understanding of how risk affects investment returns and how to evaluate risk when selecting investments such as those described here. ∎

In this chapter we take an in-depth look at how investment risk should be measured and how it affects assets' values and rates of return. Recall that in Chapter 2, when we examined the determinants of interest rates, we defined the real risk-free rate, k*, to be the rate of interest on a risk-free security in the absence of inflation. The actual interest rate on a particular debt security was shown to be equal to the real risk-free rate plus several premiums that reflect both inflation and the riskiness of the security in question. In this chapter we define more precisely what the term *risk* means as it relates to investments, we examine procedures used to measure risk, and we discuss the relationship between risk and return. It is important that both investors and financial managers understand these concepts and use them when considering investment decisions, whether the decisions concern financial assets or real assets.

We will demonstrate in this chapter that each investment—each stock, bond, or physical asset—has two different types of risk: diversifiable risk and nondiversifiable risk. The sum of these two components is the investment's total risk. Diversifiable risk is not important to rational, informed investors because they can eliminate its effects by "diversifying" it away. *The significant risk is nondiversifiable risk*, which is bad in the sense that it cannot be eliminated, and if you invest in anything other than riskless (risk-free) assets, such as short-term Treasury bills, you will be exposed to it. Throughout the chapter we will explain these risk concepts and show you how risk enters into the investment decision process.

Defining and Measuring Risk

Webster's Dictionary defines *risk* as "a hazard; a peril; exposure to loss or injury." As this definition suggests, we generally use the term *risk* to refer to the chance that some unfavorable event will occur. For example, if you engage in skydiving, you are taking a chance with your life—skydiving is risky. If you bet on the horses, you are risking your money. If you invest in speculative stocks (or, really, *any* stock), you are taking a risk in the hope of receiving an appreciable return.

Most people view risk in the manner we just described—a chance of loss. But in reality, *risk occurs when we cannot be certain about the outcome of a particular activity or event*—that is, we are not sure what will happen in the future. Consequently, risk results from the fact that an action such as investing can produce more than one possible outcome in the future.

To illustrate the riskiness of financial assets, suppose you have a large amount of money to invest for one year. You could buy a Treasury security that has an expected return equal to 4 percent. The rate of return expected from this investment can be determined quite precisely because the chance of the government defaulting on Treasury securities is negligible; the outcome essentially is guaranteed, which means this is a risk-free investment. On the other hand, you could buy the common stock of a newly formed company that has developed technology that can be used to extract petroleum from the mountains in South America without defacing the landscape and without harming the ecology. The technology has yet to be proven economically feasible, so it is not known what returns the common stockholders will receive in the future. Experts who have analyzed the common stock of the company have determined that the *expected*, or average long-run, return for such an investment is 30 percent. Each year the investment could yield a positive return as high as 900 percent, but there also is the possibility the company will not survive, in which case, the entire investment will be lost and the return will be –100 percent. The return investors receive each year cannot be determined precisely because more than one outcome is possible—this is a risky investment. Because there is a significant danger of actually earning considerably less than the expected return—in this case, you could lose all your money— investors probably would consider the stock to be quite risky. But there also is a very good chance the actual return will be greater than expected, which, of course, is an outcome we gladly accept. *When we think of investment risk, along with the chance of actually receiving less than expected, we should consider the chance of actually receiving more than expected.* If we consider investment risk from this perspective, we can define **risk** as the chance of receiving an actual return other than expected, which simply means there is *variability in the returns,* or outcomes, from the investment. Therefore, investment risk can be measured by the variability of the investment's returns.

Investment risk, then, is related to the possibility of actually earning a return other than the expected one. *The greater the variability of the possible outcomes, the riskier the investment.* We will define risk more precisely in the next few sections.

RISK
The chance that an outcome other than expected will occur—that is, multiple future outcomes are possible.

Probability Distributions

PROBABILITY DISTRIBUTION
A listing of all possible outcomes, or events, with a probability (chance of occurrence) assigned to each outcome.

An event's *probability* is defined as the chance that the event will occur. For example, a weather forecaster might state, "There is a 40 percent chance of rain today," which also means there is a 60 percent chance that it will not rain. If all possible events, or outcomes, are listed, and if a probability is assigned to each event, the listing is called a **probability distribution.** For our weather forecast, we could set up the following probability distribution:

TABLE 4–1	Probability Distribution for Martin Products and U.S. Electric

STATE OF THE ECONOMY	PROBABILITY OF THIS STATE OCCURRING	MARTIN PRODUCTS	U.S. ELECTRIC
Boom	0.2	110%	20%
Normal	0.5	22	16
Recession	0.3	–60	10
	1.0		

OUTCOME (1)	PROBABILITY (2)	
Rain	0.40 =	40%
No rain	0.60 =	60
	1.00	100%

Here the possible outcomes are listed in column 1, and the probabilities of these outcomes, expressed both as decimals and as percentages, are given in column 2. Notice that the probabilities must sum to 1.0, or 100 percent, to account for all the possible outcomes.

Probabilities can also be assigned to the possible outcomes (or returns) from an investment. If you buy a bond, you expect to receive interest on the bond, and those interest payments will provide you with a rate of return on your investment. This investment has two possible outcomes: (1) the issuer makes the interest payments, or (2) the issuer fails to make the interest payments. The higher the probability of default on the interest payments, the riskier the bond; the higher the risk, the higher the rate of return you would require to invest in the bond. If, instead of buying a bond, you invest in a stock, you will again expect to earn a return on your money, which will come from dividends plus capital gains. Again, the riskier the stock—which means the greater the variability of the possible payoffs—the higher the stock's expected return must be to induce you to invest in it.

Keeping in mind what we have discussed to this point, consider the possible rates of return that you might earn next year on a $10,000 investment in the stock of either Martin Products Inc. or U.S. Electric. Martin manufactures and distributes computer terminals and equipment for the rapidly growing data transmission industry. Because its sales are cyclical, its profits rise and fall with the business cycle. Further, its market is extremely competitive, and some new company could develop better products that could literally bankrupt Martin. U.S. Electric, on the other hand, supplies electricity, which is an essential service, and because it has city franchises that protect it from competition, its sales and profits are relatively stable and predictable.

Table 4–1 shows the rate-of-return probability distributions for these two companies. Here we see that there is a 20 percent chance of a boom, in which case both companies will have high earnings, pay high dividends, and enjoy capital gains; there is a 50 percent probability of a normal economy and moderate returns; and there is a 30 percent probability of a recession, which will result in low earnings and dividends as well as capital losses. Notice, however, that Martin Products' rate of return could vary far more widely than that of U.S. Electric. There is a fairly high probability that the value of Martin's stock will vary substantially, possibility resulting in a loss of 60 percent or a gain of 110 percent, whereas there is no chance of a loss for U.S. Electric and its maximum gain is 20 percent.[1]

Self-Test Questions

What does *investment risk* mean?

Set up illustrative probability distributions for (1) a bond investment and (2) a stock investment.

Expected Rate of Return

EXPECTED RATE OF RETURN (VALUE)
The rate of return expected to be realized from an investment; the mean value of the probability distribution of possible results.

Table 4–1 provides the probability distributions showing the possible outcomes for investing in Martin Products and U.S. Electric. We can see that the most likely outcome is for the economy to be normal, in which case Martin will return 22 percent and U.S. Electric will return 16 percent. But other outcomes are also possible, so we need to somehow summarize the information contained in the probability distributions into a single measure that considers all these possible outcomes. That measure is the expected value, or *expected rate of return*, for the investments.

Simply stated, the **expected rate of return (value)** is the *weighted average* of the outcomes, where we use the outcomes' probabilities as the weights. Table 4–2 shows how we compute the expected rates of return for Martin Products and U.S. Electric. We multiply each possible outcome by the probability it will occur and then sum the results. Throughout the book we designate the expected rate of return as $\hat{k}$, which is termed "k hat."[2] We insert the "hat" over the k to indicate that this return is uncertain, because we do not know when each of the possible outcomes will occur in the future. For example, Martin Products will return its stockholders 110 percent when the economy is booming, but we do not know in which year the economy will be booming.

The expected rate of return can be calculated using the following equation:

4–1

$$\text{Expected rate of return} = \hat{k} = Pr_1k_1 + Pr_2k_2 + \cdots + Pr_nk_n$$

$$= \sum_{i=1}^{n} Pr_ik_i$$

---

[1]It is, of course, completely unrealistic to think that any stock has no chance of a loss. Only in hypothetical examples such as ours could this occur.

[2]In later chapters, we use k_d to signify the return on a debt instrument and k_s to signify the return on a stock. In this section, however, we discuss only returns on stocks; thus, the subscript s is unnecessary.

TABLE 4–2	Calculation of Expected Rates of Return: Martin Products and U.S. Electric				
		MARTIN PRODUCTS		**U.S. ELECTRIC**	
STATE OF THE ECONOMY (1)	**PROBABILITY OF THIS STATE OCCURRING** (2)	**RETURN IF THIS STATE OCCURS** (3)	**PRODUCT:** (2) x (3) = (4)	**RETURN IF THIS STATE OCCURS** (5)	**PRODUCT:** (2) x (5) = (6)
Boom	0.2	110%	22%	20%	4%
Normal	0.5	22	11	16	8
Recession	0.3	–60	–18	10	3
	1.0		$\hat{k}_{Martin} = 15\%$		$\hat{k}_{US} = 15\%$

Here k_i is the ith possible outcome, Pr_i is the probability the ith outcome will occur, and n is the number of possible outcomes. Using the data for Martin Products, we compute its expected rate of return as follows:

$$\hat{k}_{Martin} = Pr_1(k_1) + Pr_2(k_2) + Pr_3(k_3)$$

$$= 0.2(110\%) + 0.5(22\%) + 0.3(-60\%)$$

$$= 15.0\%$$

Notice that the expected rate of return does not equal any of the possible payoffs for Martin Products given in Table 4–2. Stated simply, the expected rate of return represents the average payoff investors will receive from Martin Products if the probability distribution given in Table 4–2 does not change over a long period of time. For example, if the probability distribution for Martin Products is correct, then 20 percent of the time in the future the economy will be booming and investors will earn a 110 percent rate of return; 50 percent of the time there will be a normal economy and the investment payoff will be 22 percent; and 30 percent of the time there will be a recession and the payoff will be a 60 percent loss. On average then, Martin Products' investors will earn 15 percent.

We can graph the rates of return to obtain a picture of the variability of possible outcomes, as shown in Figure 4–1. The height of each bar signifies the probability that a given outcome will occur. The range of probable returns for Martin Products is from +110 to –60 percent, with an expected return of 15 percent. The expected return for U.S. Electric also is 15 percent, but its range is much narrower.

Continuous versus Discrete Probability Distributions

DISCRETE PROBABILITY DISTRIBUTION
The number of possible outcomes is limited or finite.

So far, we have assumed that only three states of the economy can exist: recession, normal, and boom. As a result, the probability distributions given in Table 4–1 are called **discrete** because there is a finite, or limited, number of outcomes. In reality, of course, the state of the economy could range from a deep depression to a fantastic boom, with an unlimited number of possibilities in between. Suppose we had the time and patience to assign a probability to each possible state of the economy (with the sum of the probabilities still equaling 1.0) and to assign a rate of return to each stock for each state of the economy. We would have a table similar to Table 4–1, except that it would have

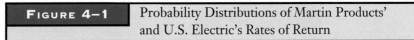

| **FIGURE 4–1** | Probability Distributions of Martin Products' and U.S. Electric's Rates of Return |

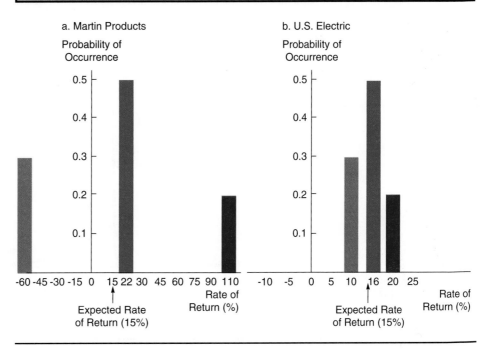

many more entries in each column. We could use this table to calculate the expected rates of return as described previously, and we could approximate the probabilities and outcomes by constructing continuous curves such as those presented in Figure 4–2. Here we have changed the assumptions so that there is essentially a zero probability that Martin Products' return will be less than –60 percent or more than 110 percent, or that U.S. Electric's return will be less than 10 percent or more than 20 percent. Virtually any return within these limits is possible. These probability distributions are **continuous** because, in each case, the number of possible outcomes is unlimited: U.S. Electric's return could be 10.01 percent, 10.001 percent, and so on.

    The *tighter the probability distribution*, the *less variability* there is and the more likely it is that the actual outcome will be close to the expected value; consequently, the less likely it is that the actual return will be much different from the expected return. Thus, *the tighter the probability distribution, the lower the risk assigned to a stock.* Because U.S. Electric has a relatively tight probability distribution, its *actual return* is likely to be closer to its 15 percent expected return than is that of Martin Products.

CONTINUOUS PROBABILITY DISTRIBUTION
The number of possible outcomes is unlimited or infinite.

Measuring Total (Stand-Alone) Risk: The Standard Deviation

Because we have defined risk as the variability of returns, we can measure total risk by examining the tightness of the probability distribution associated with the possible outcomes. In general, the width of a probability distribution indicates the amount of scatter, or variability, of the possible outcomes. To be most useful, any measure of risk

FIGURE 4–2	Continuous Probability Distributions of Martin Products' and U.S. Electric's Rates of Return

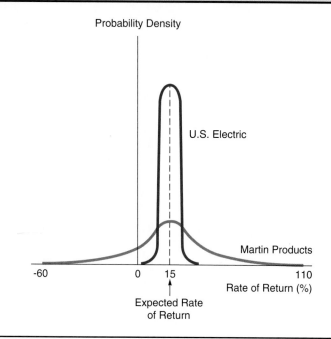

TABLE 4–3	Calculation of Martin Products' Standard Deviation (σ_{Martin})

PAYOFF k_i (1)		EXPECTED RETURN $\hat{k}$ (2)	DEVIATION $k_i - \hat{k} =$ (1) – (2) = (3)	$(k_i - \hat{k})^2$ (4)	PROBABILITY (5)	$(k_i - \hat{k})^2 Pr_i$ (4) × (5)	=	(6)
110%	–	15%	95	9,025	0.2	9,025 × 0.2	=	1,805.0
22	–	15	7	49	0.5	49 × 0.5	=	24.5
–60	–	15	–75	5,625	0.3	5,625 × 0.3	=	1,687.5
						Variance = σ^2 =		3,517.0
						Standard deviation = $\sigma = \sqrt{\sigma^2}$ =		59.3%

STANDARD DEVIATION, σ
A measure of the tightness, or variability, of a set of outcomes.

should have a definite value—we need a measure of the tightness of the probability distribution. The measure we use most often is the **standard deviation,** the symbol for which is σ, the Greek letter sigma. *The smaller the standard deviation, the tighter the probability distribution, and, accordingly, the lower the riskiness of the investment.* To calculate the standard deviation, we take the following steps, as shown in Table 4–3:

1. Calculate the expected rate of return using Equation 4–1. For Martin, we previously found $\hat{k}_{Martin} = 15\%$.
2. Subtract the expected rate of return, $\hat{k}$, from each possible outcome, k_i, to obtain a set of deviations from $\hat{k}$:

$$\text{Deviation}_i = (k_i - \hat{k})$$

The deviations are shown in Column 3 of Table 4–3.

3. Square each deviation (shown in Column 4), multiply the result by the probability of occurrence for its related outcome (Column 5), and then sum these products to get the **variance** of the probability distribution, which is shown in Column 6. The variance is computed as

VARIANCE, σ^2
The standard deviation squared.

4–2

$$\text{Variance} = \sigma^2 = \sum_{i=1}^{n} (k_i - \hat{k})^2 Pr_i$$

4. Take the square root of the variance to obtain the standard deviation shown at the bottom of Column 6:

4–3

$$\text{Standard deviation} = \sigma = \sqrt{\sigma^2} = \sqrt{\sum_{i=1}^{n} (k_i - \hat{k})^2 Pr_i}$$

As you can see, the standard deviation is the weighted average of all the deviations from the expected value, and it indicates how far above or below the expected value the actual value is likely to be. Martin's standard deviation is seen in Table 4–3 to be 59.3 percent. Using these same procedures, we find U.S. Electric's standard deviation to be 3.6 percent. The larger standard deviation of Martin Products indicates a greater variation of returns, thus a greater chance that the expected return will not be realized. Consequently, Martin Products would be considered a riskier investment than U.S. Electric, according to this measure of risk.[3]

---

[3]In the example we described the procedure for finding the mean and standard deviation when the data are in the form of a known probability distribution. If only sample returns data over some past period are available, the standard deviation of returns can be estimated using this formula:

$$\text{Estimated } \sigma = s = \sqrt{\frac{\sum_{t=1}^{n} (k_t - \bar{k})^2}{n - 1}}$$

Here k_t (italicized k) represents the past return observations, and $\bar{k}$ ("k bar") denotes the arithmetic average of the annual returns earned during the last n years. Here is a simple example:

Year	k
2004	15%
2003	−5
2002	20

$$\bar{k} = \frac{15 + (-5) + 20}{3} = 10\%$$

$$\text{Estimated } \sigma = s = \sqrt{\frac{(15 - 10)^2 + (-5 - 10)^2 + (20 - 10)^2}{3 - 1}} = \sqrt{\frac{350}{2}} = 13.2\%$$

The historical standard deviation often is used as an estimate of the future σ. Much less often, and generally incorrectly, $\bar{k}$ for some past period is used as an estimate of $\hat{k}$, the *expected* future return. Because past variability is likely to be repeated, s might be a good estimate of future risk. But it is much less reasonable to expect that the past *level* of return (which could have been as high as +20 percent or as low as −5 percent) is the best expectation of what investors think will happen in the future.

COEFFICIENT OF VARIATION (CV)

Standardized measure of the risk per unit of return; calculated as the standard deviation divided by the expected return.

Coefficient of Variation

Another useful measure to evaluate risky investments is the **coefficient of variation (CV),** which is the standard deviation divided by the expected return:

4–4

$$\text{Coefficient of variation} = \text{CV} = \frac{\text{Risk}}{\text{Return}} = \frac{\sigma}{\hat{k}}$$

The coefficient of variation shows the risk per unit of return, and it provides a more meaningful basis for comparison when the expected returns of two alternatives are not the same. Because U.S. Electric and Martin Products have the *same expected return, it is not necessary to compute the coefficient of variation* to compare the two investments. In this case, most people would prefer to invest in U.S. Electric because it offers the same expected return with lower risk than Martin Products. The firm with the larger standard deviation, Martin, must have the larger coefficient of variation; in fact, the coefficient of variation for Martin is 59.3% ÷ 15% = 3.95; for U.S. Electric it is 3.6% ÷ 15% = 0.24. Thus, when evaluating its total risk, we find that Martin is more than 16 times riskier than U.S. Electric using this criterion.

The coefficient of variation is more useful when we consider investments that have different expected rates of return *and* different levels of risk. For example, Biobotics Corporation is a biological research and development firm that, according to stock analysts, offers investors an expected rate of return equal to 35 percent with a standard deviation of 7.5 percent. Biobotics offers a higher expected return than U.S. Electric, but it also is riskier. So, with respect to both risk and return, which is a better investment? If we calculate the coefficient of variation for Biobotics, we find it equals 7.5% ÷ 35% = 0.21, which is slightly less than U.S. Electric's coefficient of variation of 0.24. Thus Biobotics actually has less risk per unit of return than U.S. Electric, even though its standard deviation is higher. In this case, the additional expected return offered by Biobotics is more than sufficient to compensate investors for the additional risk.

The probability distributions for U.S. Electric and Biobotics are graphed in Figure 4–3. U.S. Electric has the smaller standard deviation, and hence the more peaked probability distribution. As the graph clearly shows, however, the chances of a really high return are much better with Biobotics than with U.S. Electric, because Biobotics' expected return is so high. Because the coefficient of variation captures the effects of both risk and return, it is a better measure for evaluating risk in situations where investments differ with respect to both their amounts of total risk and their expected returns.[4]

---

[4]Different measures of risk will be described later in this chapter as well as later in the book. The risk measure used to compute the coefficient of variation should be the appropriate one for the specific situation. In this section of the chapter, we are discussing stand-alone risk, thus we used the measure for total risk, which is σ.

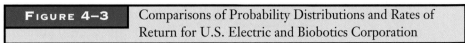

| FIGURE 4–3 | Comparisons of Probability Distributions and Rates of Return for U.S. Electric and Biobotics Corporation |

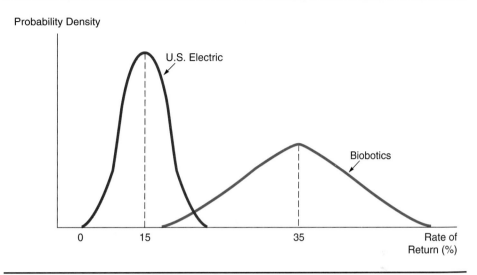

Risk Aversion and Required Returns

Suppose you have worked hard and saved $1 million, which you now plan to invest. You can buy a 10 percent U.S. Treasury note, and at the end of one year you will have a sure $1.1 million, which is your original investment plus $100,000 in interest. Alternatively, you can buy stock in R&D Enterprises. If R&D's research programs are successful, your stock will increase in value to $2.2 million; however, if the research fails, the value of your stock will go to zero, and you will be penniless. You regard R&D's chances of success or failure as being 50-50, so the expected value of the stock investment is 0.5($0) + 0.5 ($2,200,000) = $1,100,000. Subtracting the $1 million cost of the stock leaves an expected profit of $100,000, or an expected (but risky) 10 percent rate of return:

$$\begin{aligned} \frac{\text{Expected rate}}{\text{of return}} &= \frac{\text{Expected ending value} - \text{Beginning value}}{\text{Beginning value}} = \hat{k} \\ &= \frac{\$1,100,000 - \$1,000,000}{\$1,000,000} \\ &= \frac{\$100,000}{\$1,000,000} = 0.10 = 10.0\% \end{aligned}$$

In this case, you have a choice between a sure $100,000 profit (representing a 10 percent rate of return) on the Treasury note and a risky expected $100,000 profit (also representing a 10 percent expected rate of return) on the R&D Enterprises stock. Which one would you choose? *If you choose the less risky investment, you are risk averse.* Most investors are indeed risk averse. Certainly the average investor is risk averse, at least with regard to his or her "serious money." Because this is a well-documented fact, we shall assume **risk aversion** throughout the remainder of the book.

What are the implications of risk aversion for security prices and rates of return? The answer is that, other things held constant, the higher a security's risk, the higher the return investors demand, thus the less they are willing to pay for the investment. To see

RISK AVERSION
Risk-averse investors require higher rates of return to invest in higher-risk securities.

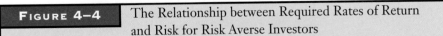

FIGURE 4–4	The Relationship between Required Rates of Return and Risk for Risk Averse Investors

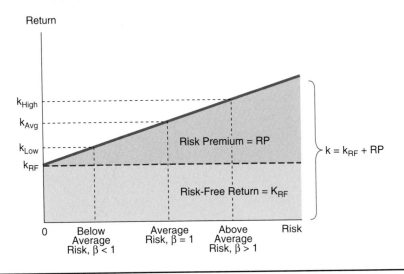

how risk aversion affects security prices, we can analyze the situation with the U.S. Electric and Martin Products stocks. Suppose each stock sells for $100 per share and each has an expected rate of return of 15 percent. Investors are averse to risk, so there is a general preference for U.S. Electric because there is less variability in its payoffs (less uncertainty), and thus less risk. People with money to invest will bid for U.S. Electric rather than Martin stock, and Martin's existing stockholders will start selling their stock and using the money to buy U.S. Electric stock. Buying pressure will drive up the price of U.S. Electric's stock, and selling pressure will simultaneously cause Martin's price to decline. These price changes, in turn, will cause changes in the expected rates of return on the two securities. Suppose, for example, that the price of U.S. Electric stock is bid up from $100 to $150, whereas the price of Martin's stock declines from $100 to $75. This will cause U.S. Electric's expected return to fall to 10 percent, whereas Martin's expected return will rise to 20 percent. The difference in returns, 20% – 10% = 10%, is a **risk premium, RP.** This risk premium represents the compensation investors require (demand) for assuming the *additional* risk associated with Martin's stock.

RISK PREMIUM, RP
The portion of the expected return that can be attributed to the additional risk of an investment; it is the difference between the expected rate of return on a given risky asset and that on a less risky asset.

This example demonstrates a very important principle: In a market dominated by risk-averse investors, *riskier securities must have higher expected returns*, as estimated by the average investor, than less risky securities. If this situation does not hold, investors will buy and sell investments and prices will continue to change until higher risk investments have higher expected returns than lower risk investments. Figure 4–4 illustrates this relationship. We will consider the question as to how much higher the returns on risky securities must be later in the chapter, after we see how diversification affects the way risk should be measured.

Self-Test Questions

Which of the two stocks graphed in Figure 4–2 is less risky? Why?

How do you calculate the standard deviation associated with an investment?

Why is the standard deviation used as a measure of total risk?

Which is a better measure of total risk: the standard deviation or the coefficient of variation? Explain.

What is meant by the following statement: "Most investors are risk averse"?

How does risk aversion affect relative rates of return?

Portfolio Risk—Holding Combinations of Assets

In the preceding section we considered the riskiness of investments held in isolation. For this reason, we examined the total risk associated with each investment. In this section we analyze the riskiness of investments held in portfolios.[5] As we shall see, holding an investment, whether a stock, bond, or other asset, as part of a portfolio generally is less risky than holding the same investment all by itself. In fact, most financial assets are not held in isolation; rather, they are held as parts of portfolios. Banks, pension funds, insurance companies, mutual funds, and other financial institutions are required by law to hold diversified portfolios. Even individual investors—at least those whose security holdings constitute a significant part of their total wealth—generally hold portfolios that contain multiple stocks, not the stock of only one firm. From an investor's standpoint, then, the fact that a particular stock goes up or down is not nearly as important as the return on his or her portfolio and the portfolio's risk. Logically, the risk and return characteristics of an investment should not be evaluated in isolation; rather, the risk and return of an individual security should be analyzed in terms of how that security affects the risk and return of the portfolio in which it is held.

To illustrate, consider Payco American, which is a collection agency company that operates several offices nationwide. The company is not well known, its stock is not very liquid, its earnings have fluctuated quite a bit in the past, and it doesn't even pay a dividend. This suggests that Payco is risky and that its required rate of return, k, should be relatively high. Even so, Payco's k always has been quite low in relation to those of most other companies. This indicates that investors regard Payco as being a low-risk company despite its uncertain profits and its nonexistent dividend stream. The reason for this somewhat counterintuitive fact relates to diversification and its effect on risk. Payco's stock price rises during recessions, whereas most other stocks tend to decline when the economy slumps. Therefore, holding Payco in a portfolio of "normal" stocks tends to stabilize the returns on the entire portfolio.

Portfolio Returns

EXPECTED RETURN ON A PORTFOLIO, $\hat{k}_P$
The weighted average expected return on the stocks held in the portfolio.

The **expected return on a portfolio, $\hat{k}_P$,** is simply the weighted average of the expected returns on the individual stocks in the portfolio, with the weights being the fraction of the total portfolio invested in each stock:

---

[5]A *portfolio* is a collection of investment securities or assets. If you own some General Motors stock, some Exxon-Mobil stock, and some IBM stock, you hold a three-stock portfolio. For the reasons set forth in this section, the majority of all stocks are held as parts of portfolios.

$$4\text{--}5$$

$$\hat{k}_P = w_1\hat{k}_1 + w_2\hat{k}_2 + \cdots + w_N\hat{k}_N$$

$$= \sum_{j=1}^{N} w_j\hat{k}_j$$

Here the $\hat{k}_j$ values are the expected returns on the individual stocks, the w_j values are the weights, and there are N stocks in the portfolio. Note that (1) w_j is the proportion of the portfolio's dollar value invested in Stock j—that is, the value of the investment in Stock j divided by the total value of the portfolio—and (2) the w_j values must sum to 1.0.

In January 2005, a security analyst estimates, the following returns might be expected on four large companies:

	Expected Return, $\hat{k}_J$
AT&T	8%
General Electric	19%
Microsoft	16%
Citigroup	13%

If we formed a $100,000 portfolio, investing $25,000 in each of these stocks, the expected portfolio return would be 14 percent:

$$\hat{k}_P = w_{ATT}\hat{k}_{ATT} + w_{Citi}\hat{k}_{Citi} + w_{GE}\hat{k}_{GE} + w_{Micro}\hat{k}_{Micro}$$

$$= 0.25(8\%) + 0.25(19\%) + 0.25(16\%) + 0.25(13\%)$$

$$= 14.0\%$$

Of course, after the fact and a year later, the actual realized rates of return on the individual stocks will almost certainly be different from their expected values, so the actual portfolio return will differ somewhat from $\hat{k}_p = 14\%$. For example, General Electric stock might double in price and provide a return of +100 percent, whereas Citigroup stock might have a terrible year, fall sharply, and have a return of –50 percent. Note, however, that those two events would be somewhat offsetting, so the portfolio's return might still be close to its expected return, even though the individual stocks' actual returns were far from their expected returns.

Portfolio Risk

As we just saw, the expected return of a portfolio is simply a weighted average of the expected returns of the individual stocks in the portfolio. Unlike returns, the riskiness of a portfolio (σ_P) generally is *not* a weighted average of the standard deviations of the individual securities in the portfolio. Instead, the portfolio's risk usually is *smaller* than the weighted average of the individual stocks' standard deviations. In fact, it is theoretically possible to combine two stocks that by themselves are quite risky as measured by their standard deviations and to form a portfolio that is completely riskless, or risk-free, with $\sigma_P = 0$.

FIGURE 4–5	Rate of Return Distributions for Two Perfectly Negatively Correlated Stock (r = –1.0) and for Portfolio WM

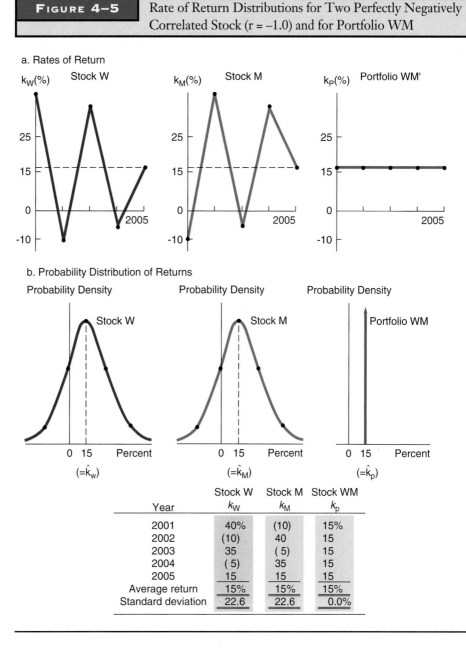

a. Rates of Return

b. Probability Distribution of Returns

	Stock W	Stock M	Stock WM
Year	k_W	k_M	k_p
2001	40%	(10)	15%
2002	(10)	40	15
2003	35	(5)	15
2004	(5)	35	15
2005	15	15	15
Average return	15%	15%	15%
Standard deviation	22.6	22.6	0.0%

To illustrate the effect of combining securities, consider the situation in Figure 4–5. The bottom section gives data on rates of return for Stocks W and M individually, and also for a portfolio invested 50 percent in each stock. The three top graphs show the actual historical returns for each investment from 2001 through 2005, and the lower graphs show the probability distributions of returns, assuming that the future is expected to be like the past. The two stocks would be quite risky if they were held in isolation. When these stocks are combined to form Portfolio WM, however, they are not risky at all. (*Note:* These stocks are called W and M because their returns graphs in Figure 4–5 resemble a W and an M.)

**CORRELATION
COEFFICIENT, r**
A measure of the degree
of relationship between
two variables.

The reason Stocks W and M can be combined to form a riskless portfolio is because their returns move opposite each other: When Stock W's returns fall, those of Stock M rise, and vice versa. The relationship between two variables is called *correlation*, and the **correlation coefficient, r,** measures the degree of the relationship between the variables.[6] In statistical terms, we say that the returns on Stocks W and M are perfectly negatively correlated, with r = –1.0.

The opposite of perfect negative correlation—that is, r = –1.0—is perfect positive correlation—that is, r = +1.0. Returns on two perfectly positively correlated stocks would move up and down together, and a portfolio consisting of two such stocks would be exactly as risky as the individual stocks. This point is illustrated in Figure 4–6, where we see that the portfolio's standard deviation is equal to that of the individual stocks. As you can see, there is no diversification effect in this case— that is, risk is not reduced if it contains perfectly positively correlated stocks.

Figure 4–5 and Figure 4–6 demonstrate that when stocks are perfectly negatively correlated (r = –1.0), all risk can be diversified away, but when stocks are perfectly positively correlated (r = +1.0), diversification is ineffective. In reality, most stocks are positively correlated, but not perfectly so. On average, the correlation coefficient for the returns on two randomly selected stocks would be about +0.4, and for most pairs of stocks, r would lie in the range of +0.3 to +0.6. *Under such conditions, combining stocks into portfolios reduces risk but does not eliminate it completely.* Figure 4–7 illustrates this point with two stocks whose correlation coefficient is r = +0.67. The portfolio's average return is 15 percent, which is exactly the same as the average return for each of the two stocks, but its standard deviation is 20.6 percent, which is less than the standard deviation of either stock. Thus, the portfolio's risk is *not* an average of the risks of its individual stocks. Diversification has reduced, but not eliminated, risk.

From these two-stock portfolio examples, we have seen that in one extreme case (r = –1.0), risk can be completely eliminated, whereas diversification is ineffective in the other extreme case (r = +1.0). In between these extremes, combining two stocks into a portfolio reduces, but does not eliminate, the riskiness inherent in the individual stocks.

What would happen if the portfolio includes more than two stocks? *As a rule, the riskiness of a portfolio is reduced as the number of stocks in the portfolio increases.* If we add enough stocks, can we completely eliminate risk? In general, the answer is no, but the extent to which adding stocks to a portfolio reduces its risk depends on the *degree of correlation* among the stocks: *The smaller the positive correlation coefficient, the greater the diversification effect of adding a stock to a portfolio.* If we can find a set of stocks whose correlations are negative, all risk can be eliminated. *In the typical case, where the correlations among the individual stocks are positive but less than +1.0, some, but not all, risk can be eliminated.*

To test your understanding of portfolio risk, consider the following question: Would you expect to find higher correlations between the returns on two companies in the same industry or in different industries? For example, would the correlation of returns on Ford's and General Motors' (GM) stocks be higher, or would the correla-

---

[6]The *correlation coefficient*, r, can range from +1.0, denoting that the two variables move in the same direction with exactly the same degree of synchronization every time movement occurs, to –1.0, denoting that the variables always move with the same degree of synchronization, but in opposite directions. A correlation coefficient of zero suggests that the two variables are not related to each other—that is, changes in one variable are *independent* of changes in the other.

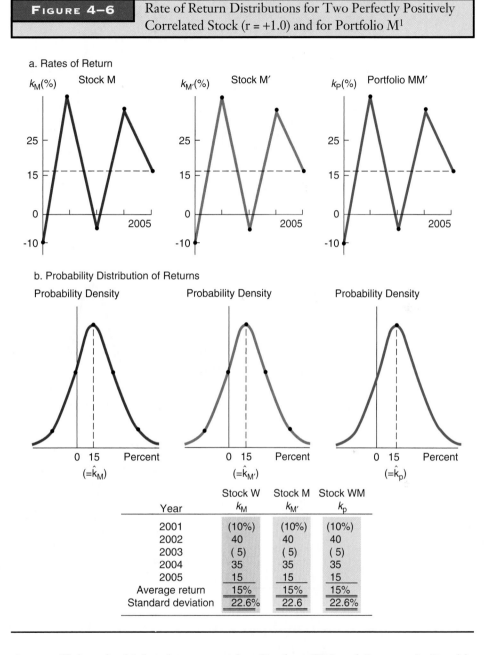

FIGURE 4-6   Rate of Return Distributions for Two Perfectly Positively Correlated Stock (r = +1.0) and for Portfolio M[1]

a. Rates of Return

b. Probability Distribution of Returns

Year	Stock W k_M	Stock M $k_{M'}$	Stock WM k_p
2001	(10%)	(10%)	(10%)
2002	40	40	40
2003	(5)	(5)	(5)
2004	35	35	35
2005	15	15	15
Average return	15%	15%	15%
Standard deviation	22.6%	22.6	22.6%

tion coefficient be higher between either Ford or GM and Procter & Gamble (P&G)? How would these correlations affect the risks of portfolios containing them?

Answer: Ford's and GM's returns should have a correlation coefficient of about 0.9 with one another because both are affected by auto sales. But, the correlation of Ford's and GM's returns with P&G's returns should be about 0.3.

Implications: A two-stock portfolio consisting of Ford and GM would be riskier than a two-stock portfolio consisting of Ford or GM plus P&G. Thus, to minimize risk, portfolios should be diversified *across* industries.

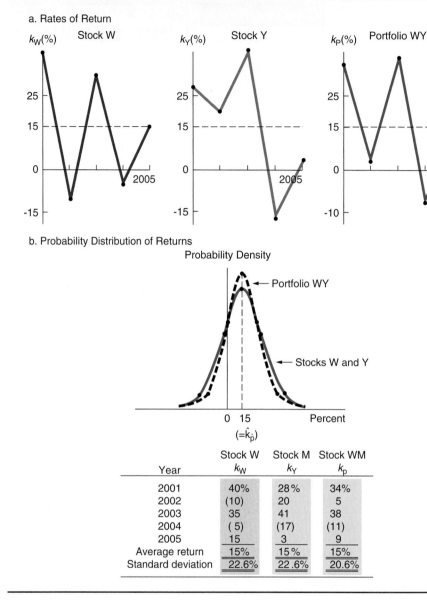

a. Rates of Return

b. Probability Distribution of Returns

Year	Stock W k_W	Stock M k_Y	Stock WM k_p
2001	40%	28%	34%
2002	(10)	20	5
2003	35	41	38
2004	(5)	(17)	(11)
2005	15	3	9
Average return	15%	15%	15%
Standard deviation	22.6%	22.6%	20.6%

Firm-Specific Risk versus Market Risk

As noted earlier, it is difficult—if not impossible—to find stocks with expected returns that are not positively correlated. Most stocks tend to do well when the economy is strong and do poorly when it is weak.[7] Thus, even very large portfolios end up with a substantial amount of risk, but the risk generally is less than if all of your money was invested in only one stock.

---

[7]It is not too hard to find a few stocks that happened to rise because of a particular set of circumstances in the past while most other stocks were declining; it is much harder to find stocks that could logically be *expected* to go up in the future when other stocks are falling. Payco American, the collection agency discussed earlier, is one of those rare exceptions.

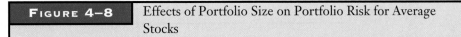

FIGURE 4–8 | Effects of Portfolio Size on Portfolio Risk for Average Stocks

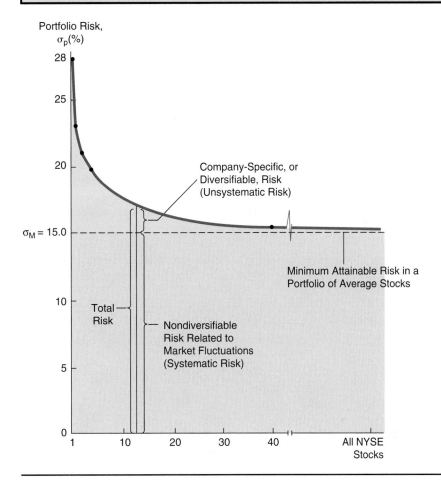

To see more precisely how portfolio size affects portfolio risk, consider Figure 4–8, which gives an indication as to how portfolio risk is affected by forming larger and larger portfolios of randomly selected stocks listed on the New York Stock Exchange (NYSE). Standard deviations are plotted for an average one-stock portfolio, for a two-stock portfolio, and so on, up to a portfolio consisting of all the common stocks listed on the NYSE. The graph illustrates that, in general, the riskiness of a portfolio consisting of average NYSE stocks tends to decline and to approach some minimum limit as the size of the portfolio increases. According to the data, σ_1, the standard deviation of a one-stock portfolio (or an average stock), is approximately 28 percent. A portfolio consisting of all of the stocks in the market, which is called the *market portfolio*, would have a standard deviation, σ_M, of approximately 15 percent (shown as the horizontal dashed line in Figure 4–8).

Figure 4–8 shows that almost half of the riskiness inherent in an average individual stock can be eliminated if the stock is held in a reasonably well-diversified portfolio—namely, a portfolio containing 40 or more stocks. Some risk always remains, however, so it is virtually impossible to diversify away the effects of broad stock market movements that affect almost all stocks.

That part of a stock's risk that can be eliminated is called *diversifiable risk, firm-specific risk,* or *unsystematic risk;* that part that cannot be eliminated is called *nondiversifiable risk, market risk,* or *systematic risk.* Although the name is not especially important, the fact that a large part of the riskiness of any individual stock can be eliminated through portfolio diversification is vitally important.

Firm-specific, or **diversifiable, risk** is caused by such things as lawsuits, strikes, successful and unsuccessful marketing programs, the winning and losing of major contracts, and other events that are unique to a particular firm. Because the actual outcomes of these events are essentially random (unpredictable), their effects on a portfolio can be eliminated by diversification—bad events in one firm will be offset by good events in another. **Market,** or **nondiversifiable, risk,** on the other hand, stems from factors that *systematically* affect most firms, such as war, inflation, recessions, and high interest rates. Because most stocks tend to be affected similarly (negatively in this case) by *market* conditions, systematic risk cannot be eliminated by portfolio diversification.

We know that investors demand a premium for bearing risk—that is, the higher the riskiness of a security, the higher the expected return required to induce investors to buy (or to hold) it. However, if investors are primarily concerned with *portfolio risk* rather than the risk of the individual securities in the portfolio, how should the riskiness of an individual stock be measured? The answer, as provided by a theoretical model called the **capital asset pricing model (CAPM),** is this: *The relevant riskiness of an individual stock is its contribution to the riskiness of a well-diversified portfolio.* In other words, the riskiness of General Electric's stock to a doctor who has a portfolio of 40 stocks or to a trust officer managing a 150-stock portfolio is the contribution that the GE stock makes to the portfolio's riskiness. The stock might be quite risky if held by itself, but if most of this total (stand-alone) risk can be eliminated by diversification, then its **relevant risk**—that is, its *contribution to the portfolio's risk*—is much smaller than its total, or stand-alone, risk.

A simple example will help clarify this point. Suppose you are offered the chance to flip a coin once. If a head comes up, you win $20,000; if a tail comes up, you lose $16,000. This is a good bet—the expected return is 0.5($20,000) + 0.5(–$16,000) = $2,000. However, it is a highly risky proposition because you have a 50 percent chance of losing $16,000. For this reason, you might well refuse to make the bet. Alternatively, suppose you were offered the chance to flip a coin 100 times, and you would win $200 for each head but lose $160 for each tail. It is possible that you would flip all heads and win $20,000, and it is also possible that you would flip all tails and lose $16,000, but the chances are very high that you would actually flip about 50 heads and 50 tails, winning a net of approximately $2,000. Although each individual flip is a risky bet, collectively you have a low-risk proposition because most of the risk has been diversified away. This is the idea behind holding portfolios of stocks rather than just one stock. With stock portfolios, however, all of the risk cannot be eliminated by diversification—those risks related to broad, systematic changes in the stock market remain.

Are all stocks equally risky in the sense that adding them to a well-diversified portfolio would have the same effect on the portfolio's riskiness? The answer is no. Different stocks will affect the portfolio differently, so different securities have different degrees of relevant risk. For example, automobile sales are affected more by rising interest rates than grocery sales. As a result, you would expect market conditions, and thus the relevant risk, to affect automobile manufactures more than grocery store chains. How can the relevant risk of an individual stock be measured? As we have

FIRM-SPECIFIC, OR DIVERSIFIABLE, RISK
That part of a security's risk associated with random outcomes generated by events, or behaviors, specific to the firm; it can be eliminated by proper diversification.

MARKET, OR NONDIVERSIFIABLE, RISK
That part of a security's risk that cannot be eliminated by diversification because it is associated with economic, or market, factors that systematically affect most firms.

CAPITAL ASSET PRICING MODEL (CAPM)
A model used to determine the required return on an asset, which is based on the proposition that any asset's return should be equal to the risk-free rate of return plus a risk premium that reflects the asset's nondiversifiable risk.

RELEVANT RISK
The risk of a security that cannot be diversified away, or its market (systematic) risk. This reflects a security's contribution to the risk of a portfolio.

seen, all risk except that related to broad market movements can, and presumably will, be diversified away. After all, why accept risk that can be easily eliminated? *The risk that remains after diversifying is market risk, or risk that is inherent in the market, and it can be measured by evaluating the degree to which a given stock tends to move up and down with the market.*

The Concept of Beta

BETA COEFFICIENT, β
A measure of the extent to which the returns on a given stock move with the stock market.

Recall that *the relevant risk associated with an individual stock is based on its systematic (market) risk,* which depends on how sensitive the firm's operations are to economic events such as interest rate changes and inflationary pressures. Because the general movements in the financial markets reflect movements in the economy, the market risk of a stock can be measured by observing its tendency to move with the market, or with an average stock that has the same characteristics as the market. The measure of a stock's sensitivity to market fluctuations is called its **beta coefficient,** and it generally is designated with the Greek symbol for beta, β. Beta is a key element of the CAPM.

An *average-risk stock* is defined as one that tends to move up and down in step with the general market as measured by some index, such as the Dow Jones Industrial Index (DJIA), the S&P 500 Index, or the New York Stock Exchange Composite Index. Such a stock will, *by definition,* have a beta (β) equal to 1.0, which indicates that, in general, if the market moves up by 10 percent, the stock will also move up by 10 percent, whereas if the market falls by 10 percent, the stock will fall by 10 percent. A portfolio of such $\beta = 1.0$ stocks will move up and down with the broad market averages, and it will be just as risky as the averages. If $\beta = 0.5$, the stock is only half as volatile as the market—it will rise and fall only half as much—and a portfolio of such stocks will be half as risky as a portfolio that includes only $\beta = 1.0$ stocks. On the other hand, if $\beta = 2.0$, the stock is twice as volatile as an average stock, so a portfolio of such stocks will be twice as risky as an average portfolio. The value of such a portfolio could double—or halve—in a short time.

Figure 4–9 graphs the relative volatility of three stocks. The data below the graph assume that in 2003 the "market," defined as a portfolio consisting of all stocks, had a total return (dividend yield plus capital gains yield) of $k_M = 14\%$, and Stocks H, A, and L (for High, Average, and Low risk) also had returns of 14 percent. In 2004, the market went up sharply, and the return on the market portfolio was $k_M = 28\%$. Returns on the three stocks also went up: the return on H soared to 42 percent; the return on A went up to 28 percent, the same as the market; and the return on L only went up to 21 percent. Now suppose that the market dropped in 2005, and the market return was $k_M = -14\%$. The three stocks' returns also fell, H plunging to –42 percent, A falling to –14 percent, and L going down only to 0 percent. As you can see, the three stocks all moved in the same direction as the market, but H was by far the most volatile; A was just as volatile as the market; and L was less volatile than the market.

The beta coefficient measures a stock's volatility relative to an average stock (or the market), which has $\beta = 1.0$. We can calculate a stock's beta by plotting a line like those in Figure 4–9. The slopes of the lines show how each stock moves in response to a movement in the general market. Indeed, *the slope coefficient of such a "regression line" is defined as a beta coefficient.* (Procedures for actually calculating betas are described in Appendix 4A at the end of this chapter.) Betas for literally thousands of companies are calculated and published by Merrill Lynch, *Value Line,* and numerous

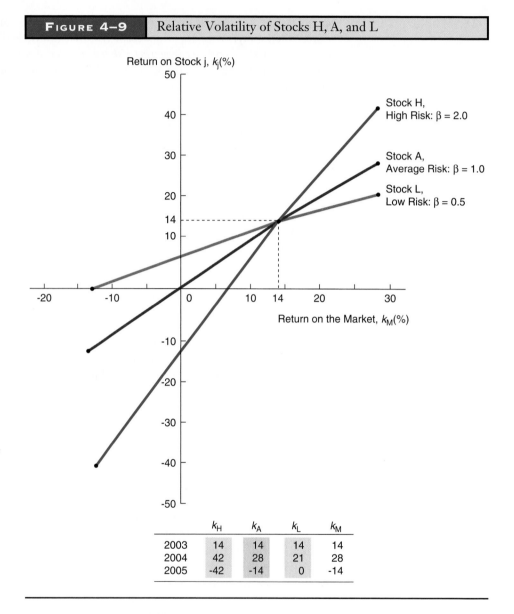

| **FIGURE 4–9** | Relative Volatility of Stocks H, A, and L |

	k_H	k_A	k_L	k_M
2003	14	14	14	14
2004	42	28	21	28
2005	-42	-14	0	-14

other organizations. The beta coefficients for some well-known companies are shown in Table 4–4. Most stocks have betas that range from 0.50 to 1.50, and the average for all stocks is 1.0 by definition.[8]

If a higher-than-average beta stock (β > 1.0) is added to an average beta (β = 1.0) portfolio, then the beta, and consequently the riskiness, of the portfolio will increase. Conversely, if a lower-than-average beta stock (β < 1.0) is added to an average-risk

---

[8]In theory, betas can be negative. In other words, if a stock's returns tend to rise when those of other stocks decline, and vice versa, then the regression line in a graph such as Figure 4–9 will have a downward slope, and the beta will be negative. Note, though, that *Value Line* follows nearly 1,800 stocks, and none has a negative beta. Payco American, the collection agency company, might have a negative beta, but it is too small to be followed by *Value Line* and most other services that calculate and report betas.

TABLE 4–4	Beta Coefficients for Selected Companies	

COMPANY	BETA	INDUSTRY/PRODUCT
I. **Above Average Market Risk: β > 1.0**		
Ariba Inc	4.07	Computer services
E*TRADE Group Inc.	3.45	Investment services/online financial services
Yahoo! Inc.	3.37	Computer services/global Internet communications
Nortel Networks Corporation	3.30	Communications equipment
eBay	2.63	Retail (specialty non-apparel)/ Web-based auction
II. **Average Market Risk: β ≈ 1.0**		
7-Eleven Inc.	1.00	Retail (grocery)/convenience stores
General Electric	1.06	Conglomerates/diversified industrial corporation
Walt Disney	1.01	Diversified entertainment/ broadcasting and cable TV
Toyota Motor Corporation	1.01	Auto and truck manufacturers
Progressive Corporation	1.01	Insurance (property and casualty)
K-Swiss Inc.	1.01	Footwear
III. **Below Average Market Risk: β < 1.0**		
PepsiCo Inc.	0.74	Beverages (nonalcoholic)
Walgreen Company	0.48	Retail (drugs)
Gillete Company	0.48	Personal and household products
General Mills	0.04	Food processing
Progress Energy	0.08	Electric utilities

SOURCE: American Association of Individual Investors, August 1, 2003.

portfolio, the portfolio's beta and risk will decline. *Thus, because a stock's beta measures its contribution to the riskiness of a portfolio and most stocks are held as part of a portfolio, theoretically beta is the correct measure of the stock's riskiness.*

The preceding analysis of risk in a portfolio setting is part of the CAPM. We can summarize our discussion to this point as follows:

1. A stock's risk consists of two components: *market risk* and *firm-specific risk.*
2. *Firm-specific risk* can be eliminated through diversification. Most investors do diversify, either by holding large portfolios or by purchasing shares in a mutual fund. We are left, then, with *market risk*, which is caused by general movements in the stock market and which reflects the fact that most stocks are systematically

affected by certain overall economic events like changes in interest rates and inflation. Market risk is the only relevant risk to a rational, diversified investor, because he or she should have already eliminated firm-specific risk by holding a large number of different stocks in a portfolio.

3. Investors must be compensated for bearing risk: *The greater the riskiness of a stock, the higher its required return.* However, compensation is required only for risk that cannot be eliminated by diversification. If risk premiums existed on stocks with high diversifiable risk, well-diversified investors would start buying these securities and bidding up their prices, and their final (equilibrium) expected returns would reflect only nondiversifiable market risk.

An example might help clarify this point. Suppose half of Stock A's risk is market risk and the other half of A's risk is diversifiable. You hold only Stock A, so you are exposed to all of its risk—that is, σ. As compensation for bearing so much risk, you demand a risk premium of 8 percent above the 5 percent Treasury bond rate. Thus, you demand a return equal to 13 percent (= 5% + 8%). But suppose other investors hold Stock A in their well-diversified portfolios so that they have eliminated its diversifiable risk and thus are exposed to only half as much risk as you are. Consequently, the diversified investors will demand a risk premium that is only half as large as yours, and they will require a return of only 9 percent (= 5% + 8%/2) to invest in the stock.

If the stock actually yielded more than 9 percent in the market, diversified investors would buy it. If it yielded the 13 percent you demand, you would be willing to buy the stock, but the well-diversified investors would compete with you to acquire it. They would bid its price up and its yield down, and this would keep you from getting the stock at the return you need to compensate you for taking on its *total risk*. In the end, you would have to accept a 9 percent return or else keep your money in the bank. Thus, risk premiums in a market populated with *rational* investors—that is, those who diversity—will reflect only market risk.

4. The market risk of a stock is measured by its *beta coefficient*, which is an index of the stock's relative volatility. Some benchmark values for beta are shown here:

$\beta = 0.5$: The stock is only half as volatile, or risky, as the average stock.

$\beta = 1.0$: The stock is of average risk, which is the same as the market.

$\beta = 2.0$: The stock is twice as risky as the average stock.

5. Because a stock's beta coefficient determines how the stock affects the riskiness of a diversified portfolio, beta is the most relevant measure of a stock's risk.

Portfolio Beta Coefficients

A portfolio consisting of low-beta securities will itself have a low beta because the beta of any set of securities is the weighted average of the individual securities' betas:

$$\boxed{\begin{array}{l} 4\text{-}6 \qquad\qquad \beta_P = w_1\beta_1 + w_2\beta_2 + \cdots + w_N\beta_N \\[2mm] \qquad\qquad\qquad = \sum_{j=1}^{N} w_j\beta_j \end{array}}$$

Here β_P, the beta of the portfolio, reflects how volatile the portfolio is in relation to the market; w_j is the fraction of the portfolio invested in the jth stock; and β_j is the beta coefficient of the jth stock. For example, if an investor holds a \$105,000 portfolio consisting of \$35,000 invested in each of three stocks, and each of the stocks has a beta of 0.7, then the portfolio's beta will be $\beta_{P1} = 0.7$:

$$\beta_{P1} = 0.333(0.7) + 0.333(0.7) + 0.333(0.7) = 0.7$$

Such a portfolio will be less risky than the market, which means it should experience relatively narrow price swings and have relatively small rate-of-return fluctuations. In terms of Figure 4–9, the slope of its regression line would be 0.7, which is less than that for a portfolio of average stocks.

Now suppose one of the existing stocks is sold and replaced by a stock with $\beta_j = 2.5$. This action will increase the riskiness of the portfolio from $\beta_{P1} = 0.7$ to $\beta_{P2} = 1.3$:

$$\beta_{P2} = 0.333(0.7) + 0.333(0.7) + 0.333(2.5) = 1.3$$

Had a stock with $\beta_j = 0.4$ been added, the portfolio beta would have declined from 0.7 to 0.6. Adding a low-beta stock, therefore, would reduce the riskiness of the portfolio.

Self-Test Questions

Explain the following statement: "A stock held as part of a portfolio is generally less risky than the same stock held in isolation."

What is meant by perfect positive correlation, by perfect negative correlation, and by zero correlation?

In general, can the riskiness of a portfolio be reduced to zero by increasing the number of stocks in the portfolio? Explain.

What is meant by diversifiable risk and nondiversifiable risk?

What is an average-risk stock?

Why is beta the theoretically correct measure of a stock's riskiness?

If you plotted the returns on a particular stock versus those on the Dow Jones Industrial Average index over the past five years, what would the slope of the line you obtained indicate about the stock's risk?

The Relationship between Risk and Rates of Return

In the preceding section we saw that under the CAPM theory, beta is the appropriate measure of a stock's relevant risk. Now we must specify the relationship between risk and return. For a given level of systematic risk, as measured by beta, what rate of return will investors require on a stock to compensate them for assuming the risk? To begin, let's define the following terms:

$\hat{k}_j$ = *Expected* rate of return on the jth stock; $\hat{k}_j$ is based on the probability distribution for the stock's returns.

k_j = *Required* rate of return on the jth stock; k_j is the rate that *investors demand* for investing in Stock j. If $\hat{k}_j < k_j$, you would not purchase this stock, or you would sell it if you owned it. If $\hat{k}_j > k_j$, you would want to buy the stock, and you would be indifferent if $\hat{k}_j = k_j$.

k_{RF} = Risk-free rate of return. In this context, k_{RF} is generally measured by the return on U.S. Treasury securities.

β_j = Beta coefficient of the jth stock. The beta of an average stock is $\beta_A = 1.0$.

k_M = Required rate of return on a portfolio consisting of all stocks, which is the market portfolio. k_M also is the required rate of return on an average, or $\beta_A = 1.0$, stock.

$RP_M = (k_M - k_{RF})$ = Market risk premium. This is the additional return above the risk-free rate required to compensate an average investor for assuming an average amount of risk ($\beta_A = 1.0$).

$RP_j = (k_M - k_{RF})\beta_j$ = Risk premium on the jth stock. The stock's risk premium is less than, equal to, or greater than the risk premium on an average stock, RP_M, depending on whether its beta is less than, equal to, or greater than 1.0. If $\beta_j = \beta_A = 1.0$, then $RP_j = RP_M$.

MARKET RISK PREMIUM, RP_M
The additional return over the risk-free rate needed to compensate investors for assuming risk associated with an average stock.

The **market risk premium (RP_M)** depends on the degree of aversion that investors on average have to risk.[9] Let's assume that at the current time, Treasury bonds yield $k_{RF} = 5\%$ and an average share of stock has a required return of $k_M = 13\%$. Therefore, the market risk premium is 8 percent:

$$RP_M = k_M - k_{RF} = 13\% - 5\% = 8\%$$

---

[9]This concept, as well as other aspects of CAPM, is discussed in more detail in Chapter 3 of Eugene F. Brigham and Phillip R. Daves, *Intermediate Financial Management*, 8th ed. (Cincinnati, OH: South-Western College Publishing, 2004). Note that the risk premium of an average stock, $RP_M = k_M - k_{RF}$, cannot be measured with great precision because it is impossible to obtain precise values for the expected future return on the market, $\hat{k}_M$. Empirical studies suggest that where long-term U.S. Treasury bonds are used to measure k_{RF} and where k_M is an estimate of the expected return on the S&P 400 Industrial Stocks, the market risk premium varies somewhat from year to year, and it has generally ranged from 4 to 8 percent during the past 20 years.

Chapter 3 of *Intermediate Financial Management* also discusses the assumptions embodied in the CAPM framework. Some of the assumptions of the CAPM theory are unrealistic. As a result, this theory does not hold exactly.

It follows that if one stock is twice as risky as another, its risk premium should be twice as high. Conversely, if a stock's risk is only half as much as that of another stock, its risk premium should be half as large. Furthermore, we can measure a stock's relative riskiness by its beta coefficient. Therefore, if we know the market risk premium, RP_M, and the stock's risk as measured by its beta coefficient, β_j, we can find its risk premium as the product $RP_M \times \beta_j$. For example, if $\beta_j = 0.5$ and $RP_M = 8\%$, then $RP_j = 4\%$:

4–7

$$\text{Risk premium for Stock j} = RP_j = RP_M \times \beta_j$$

$$= 8\% \times 0.5$$

$$= 4\%$$

As Figure 4-4 shows, the required return for any investment can be expressed in general terms as

$$\text{Required return} = \text{Risk-free return} + \text{Premium for risk}$$

$$k_j \qquad = \qquad k_{RF} \qquad + \qquad RP_j$$

Thus the required return for Stock j can be written as follows:

4–8

$$k_j = k_{RF} + (RP_M)\beta_j$$

$$= k_{RF} + (k_M - k_{RF})\beta_j$$

$$= 5\% + (13\% - 5\%)(0.5)$$

$$= 5\% + 8\%(0.5)$$

$$= 5\% + 4\%$$

$$= 9\%$$

SECURITY MARKET LINE (SML)

The line that shows the relationship between risk as measured by beta and the required rate of return for individual securities. SML = Equation 4–8.

Equation 4–8 is the equation for CAPM equilibrium pricing. It generally is called the **Security Market Line (SML).**

If some other stock was riskier than Stock j and had $\beta_{j2} = 2.0$, then its required rate of return would be 21 percent:

$$k_{j2} = 5\% + (8\%)2.0 = 21\%$$

An average stock, with $\beta_j = 1.0$, would have a required return of 13 percent, the same as the market return:

$$k_A = 5\% + (8\%)1.0 = 13\% = k_M$$

FIGURE 4–10	The Security Market Line (SML)

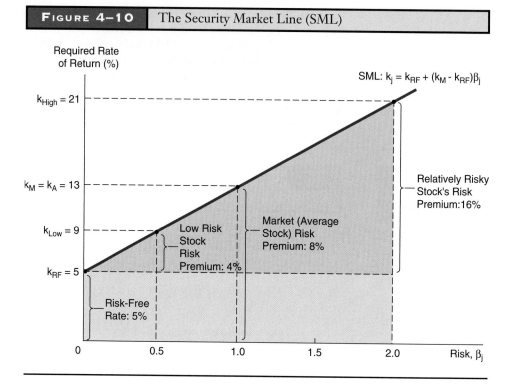

Equation 4–8, the SML equation, is often expressed in graph form. Figure 4–10, for example, shows the SML when $k_{RF} = 5\%$ and $k_M = 13\%$. Note the following points:

1. *Required rates of return* are shown on the vertical axis, and risk (as measured by beta) is shown on the horizontal axis. This graph is quite different from the one shown in Figure 4–9, where the returns on individual stocks were plotted on the vertical axis and returns on the market index were shown on the horizontal axis. The slopes of the three lines in Figure 4–9 represent the three stocks' betas. In Figure 4–10, these three betas are plotted as points on the horizontal axis.

2. Riskless securities have $\beta_j = 0$; therefore, k_{RF} appears as the vertical axis intercept in Figure 4–10.

3. The slope of the SML reflects the degree of risk aversion in the economy. The greater the average investor's aversion to risk, (a) the steeper the slope of the line, (b) the greater the risk premium for any stock, and (c) the higher the required rate of return on stocks.[10] These points are discussed further in a later section.

4. The values we worked out for stocks with $\beta_j = 0.5$, $\beta_j = 1.0$, and $\beta_j = 2.0$ agree with the values shown on the graph for k_{Low}, k_A, and k_{High}.

---

[10]Students sometime confuse beta with the slope of the SML. This is a mistake. The slope of any line is equal to the "rise" divided by the "run," or $(Y_1 - Y_0)/(X_1 - X_0)$. Consider Figure 4–10. If we let $Y = k$ and $X = \beta$, and we go from the origin to $\beta = 1.0$, we see that the slope is $(k_M - k_{RF})/(\beta_M - \beta_{RF}) = (13 - 5)/(1 - 0) = 8$. Thus, the slope of the SML is equal to $k_M - k_{RF}$, the market risk premium. In Figure 4–10, $k_j = 5\% + (8\%)\beta_j$, so a doubling of beta (for example, from 1.0 to 2.0) would produce an 8 percent increase in k_j. In this case, the total risk premium on Stock j would double—that is, $RP_j = (8\%)2.0 = 16\%$.

✳ **INDUSTRY PRACTICE**

The ~~Three~~ Four *P*s of Finance (Risk Management)

If you've taken a basic marketing course, you probably remember the four *P*s of marketing: product, price, promotion, and place. But have you heard about the three *P*s of finance?

In a recently published article, Andrew W. Lo describes how risk should be managed using the "3 P's of Total Risk Management": probabilities, prices, and preferences. Professor Lo proposes that, instead of relying entirely on statistical measures such as beta or standard deviation, risk management should include consideration of how much risk can be tolerated and how much diversification or hedging should be attempted. He contends this concept is based on the most basic of economic principle—that is, the law of supply and demand. In essence, the price of any commodity is based on demand relative to supply; demand is a function of average preferences of individuals relative to their needs and constraints; and, preferences, in turn, are affected by the chances, or probabilities, certain events will occur in the future.

In this chapter, we show how probabilities and various outcomes can be combined to determine the expected value (return) of an investment. We also introduce the capital asset pricing model (CAPM) and show that total risk is not the appropriate risk to consider when evaluating an investment if it is going to be added to a diversified portfolio. Applying the CAPM to determine the required rate of return of a stock seems straightforward. However, neither this model nor other risk management models does a good job of including preferences in risk evaluation, including the degree to which an individual is willing to take on additional risk and how the uncertainty of risk is viewed. To illustrate, consider two investments that have expected returns with the same standard deviation and the same beta. According to our discussion in the chapter, both investments should be considered equally risky; thus, investors should be indifferent when selecting between them. But, realistically, an investor might prefer one investment to the other because that investment has particular characteristics—generally intangible and not quantifiable—that he or she considers important. For example, perhaps the investment is also owned by investment guru Warren Buffett. Even though these differences should be captured by the measures we use to quantify risk, an investor might specifically act on such knowledge in the final investment decision. Clearly, then, if many other investors act similarly, the prices of the two investments in our example would differ.

The models and procedures that are currently available to evaluate investment risk do not adequately incorporate the three *P*s of risk. Thus, as Professor Lo notes, the "challenge" is to figure out how to include the three *P*s of risk into a single, functional model or technique that can be used to evaluate investment risk. As the development of this concept moves forward, we should see investment risk management evolve into a more comprehensive evaluation. Models that consider both quantitative and qualitative factors will be developed, and total risk management, or TRM, approach will emerge. As scholars search for the ideal model to evaluate risk, they probably should expand the "*P*s of risk" to include a fourth P—protection. As we discuss in this chapter, it is important for investors to understand that they can "self-manage" risk through proper diversification. When investing, diversification is synonymous with insurance, or "protection." Such protection is relatively inexpensive, especially when compared to the costs associated with insuring other similar-sized risks, such as catastrophes that affect your health or personal liability.

Source: Andrew W. Lo, "The Three P's of Total Risk Management," *Financial Analysts Journal*, January/Febuary 1999, 13–26.

Both the SML and a company's position on it change over time due to changes in interest rates, investors' risk aversion, and individual companies' betas. Such changes are discussed in the following sections.

The Impact of Inflation

As we learned in Chapter 2, interest, which amounts to "rent" on borrowed money, is the price of money. Therefore, k_{RF} is the price of money to a riskless borrower. We also learned that the risk-free rate as measured by the rate on U.S. Treasury securities is called the *nominal*, or *quoted*, rate, and it consists of two elements: (1) a *real inflation-free rate of return*, k^*, and (2) an *inflation premium*, IP, equal to the anticipated rate of inflation.[11] Thus, $k_{RF} = k^* + IP$.

If the expected rate of inflation increases by 2 percent, this would cause k_{RF} to increase 2 percent. Figure 4–11 illustrates the effects of such a change. Notice that under the CAPM, the increase in k_{RF} also causes an *equal* increase in the rate of return on all risky assets because the inflation premium is built into the required rate of return of both riskless and risky assets.[12] For example, the risk-free return increases from 5 percent to 7 percent, and the rate of return on an average stock, k_M, increases from 13 percent to 15 percent—all securities' returns increase by two percentage points.

Changes in Risk Aversion

The slope of the SML reflects the extent to which investors are averse to risk: The steeper the slope of the line, the greater the average investor's risk aversion. If investors are *indifferent* to risk, and if k_{RF} is 5 percent, then risky assets will also provide an expected return of 5 percent. If there is no risk aversion, there would be no risk premium, so the SML would be horizontal. *As risk aversion increases, so does the risk premium* and, thus, the slope of the SML.

Figure 4–12 illustrates an increase in risk aversion. The market risk premium rises from 8 percent to 10 percent, and k_M rises from $k_{M1} = 13\%$ to $k_{M2} = 15\%$. The returns on other risky assets also rise, with the effect of this shift in risk aversion being more pronounced on riskier securities. For example, the required return on a stock with $\beta_j = 0.5$ increases by only 1 percentage point, from 9 to 10 percent. By comparison, the required return on a stock with $\beta_j = 1.5$ increases by 3 percentage points, from 17 to 20 percent.

---

[11]Long-term Treasury bonds also contain a maturity risk premium, MRP. Here we include the MRP in k^* to simplify the discussion.

[12]Recall that the inflation premium for any asset is equal to the average expected rate of inflation over the life of the asset. In this analysis, therefore, we must assume either that all securities plotted on the SML graph have the same life or that the expected rate of future inflation is constant.

Also note that k_{RF} in a CAPM analysis can be proxied by either a long-term rate—the Treasury bond rate—or a short-term rate—the Treasury bill rate. Traditionally, the T-bill rate was used, but more recently there has been a movement toward the use of the T-bond rate because there is a closer relationship between T-bond yields and stocks than between T-bill yields and stocks. See *Stocks, Bonds, Bills, and Inflation; 2003 Yearbook* (Chicago: Ibbotson & Associates, 2003), for a discussion.

| FIGURE 4-11 | Shift in the SML Caused by an Increase in Inflation |

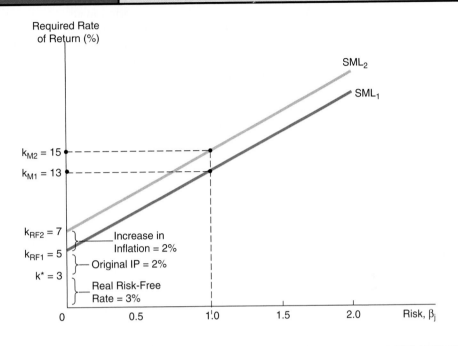

| FIGURE 4-12 | Shift in the SML Caused by Increased Risk Aversion |

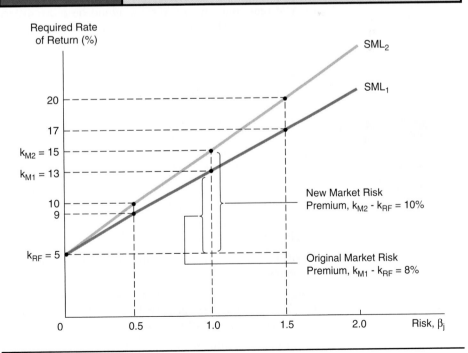

Changes in a Stock's Beta Coefficient

As we will see later in this book, a firm can affect its beta risk by changing the composition of its assets and the degree of debt financing it uses. A company's beta can also change as a result of external factors, such as increased competition in its industry or the expiration of basic patents. When such changes occur, the required rate of return also changes, and, as we will see in Chapter 5, this change affects the price of the firm's stock. For example, consider Argile Textiles, with a beta equal to 1.0. Now suppose some action occurred that caused Argile's beta to increase from 1.0 to 1.5. If the conditions depicted in Figure 4–10 held, Argile's required rate of return would increase from

$$k_1 = k_{RF} + (k_M - k_{RF})\beta_j$$
$$= 5\% + (13\% - 5\%)1.0$$
$$= 13\%$$

to

$$k_2 = 5\% + (13\% - 5\%)1.5$$
$$= 17\%$$

Any change that affects the required rate of return on a security, such as a change in its beta coefficient or in expected inflation, will affect the price of the security.

A Word of Caution

A word of caution about betas and the CAPM is in order. Although these concepts are logical, the entire theory is based on expected conditions, but we have available only past data. As a result, the betas we calculate show how volatile a stock has been in the *past*, but conditions might change. The stock's *future volatility*, which is the item of real concern to investors, could be quite different from its past volatility. Although the CAPM represents a significant step forward in security pricing theory, it does have some potentially serious deficiencies when applied in practice, so estimates of k_j found through use of the SML might be subject to considerable error. For this reason, investors and analysts use the CAPM and the concept of β to provide "ballpark" figures for further analysis.

Self-Test Questions

Differentiate between the expected rate of return ($\hat{k}$) and the required rate of return (k) on a stock. Which would have to be larger to get you to buy the stock?

What are the differences between the relative volatility graph (Figure 4–9), where "betas are made," and the SML graph (Figure 4–10), where "betas are used"? Consider both how the graphs are constructed and the purpose for which they were developed.

What happens to the SML graph (1) when inflation increases or (2) when inflation decreases?

What happens to the SML graph (1) when risk aversion increases or (2) when risk aversion decreases? What would the SML look like if investors were indifferent to risk—that is, had zero risk aversion?

How can a firm influence its market, or beta, risk?

Physical Assets versus Securities

Much of the discussion in this chapter relates to the riskiness of financial assets, especially stocks. It might seem that financial managers should be more concerned with the riskiness of such business (real) assets as plant and equipment. Why not examine the riskiness of real assets? The reason is that, for a financial manager whose goal is stock price maximization, the overriding consideration is the riskiness of the firm's stock, and the relevant risk of any physical asset must be measured in terms of its effect on the stock's risk. For example, suppose Goodyear Tire Company is considering a major investment in a new product, recapped tires. Sales of recaps and hence earnings on the new operation are highly uncertain, so it would appear that the new venture is quite risky. However, suppose returns on the recap business are negatively correlated with Goodyear's regular operations. That is, when times are good and people have plenty of money, they buy new tires, but when times are bad, they tend to buy more recaps. Therefore, returns would be high on regular operations and low on the recap division during good times, but the opposite situation would occur during recessions. The relationship between the sales of the tire division and the sales of the recap division might be a pattern like that shown earlier in Figure 4–5 for Stocks W and M. Thus, what appears to be a risky investment when viewed on a stand-alone basis might not be very risky when viewed within the context of the company as a whole.

We can extend this analysis to the corporation's owners—that is, the stockholders. Because the stock of Goodyear is owned by diversified stockholders, the real issue each time the company makes a major asset investment can be stated as follows: How does this investment affect the risk of the firm's stockholders? Again, the stand-alone risk of an individual project might look quite high, but it might be small when viewed in the context of the project's effect on stockholders' risk. We will address this subject again in Chapter 7, where we will examine the effects of capital budgeting projects on companies' beta coefficients and thus on their risk to stockholders.

Self-Test Questions

Explain the following statement: "The stand-alone risk of an individual project might look quite high, but viewed in the context of a project's effect on stockholders' risk, the project's risk might not be large."

How would the correlation between returns on the project and other assets' returns affect the preceding statement?

Different Types of Risk

In Chapter 2, we introduced the concept of risk in our discussion of interest rates, or the cost of money. At that point, we stated that the nominal, or quoted, rate of return, k, can be written as follows:

$$k = \text{Risk-free rate} + \quad \text{Risk premium} \qquad \textbf{2–1}$$

$$= \quad k_{RF} \quad + \quad RP$$

$$= \quad [k^* + IP] \quad + [DRP + LP + MRP] \qquad \textbf{2–2}$$

Remember that here

k = the quoted, or *nominal*, rate of interest on a given security required by investors. There are many different securities, and hence many different quoted interest rates.

k_{RF} = the nominal risk-free rate of return.

k^* = real risk-free rate of interest, which is the interest rate that would exist on a security with a *guaranteed* payoff if inflation is expected to be zero during the investment period.

IP = inflation premium, which equals the average inflation rate expected over the life of the security.

DRP = default risk premium, which reflects the chance that the borrower will not pay the debt's interest or principal on time.

LP = liquidity, or marketability, premium, which reflects the fact that some investments are more easily converted into cash on a short notice at a "reasonable price" than are other securities.

MRP = maturity risk premium, which accounts for the fact that longer-term bonds experience greater price reactions to interest rate changes than do short-term bonds.

The discussion in Chapter 2 presented an overall view of interest rates and general factors that affect these rates. But we did not discuss risk evaluation in detail; rather, we described some of the factors that determine the total risk associated with debt, such as default risk, liquidity risk, and maturity risk. In reality, these risks also affect other types of investments, including equity. Equity does not represent a legal contract that requires the firm to pay defined amounts of dividends at particular times or to "act" in specific ways. There is, however, an expectation that positive returns will be generated through future distributions of cash because dividends will be paid, capital gains provided through growth, or both. Investors also expect the firm to behave "appropriately." If these expectations are not met, investors generally consider the firm in "default" of their expectations. In such cases, as long as no laws have been broken, stockholders generally do not have legal recourse, as would be the case for a default on debt. As a result, investors penalize the firm by selling their stock, which causes the value of the firm's stock to decline.

In this chapter, we build on the general concept that was introduced in Chapter 2 by showing how the risk premium associated with any investment should be determined (at least in theory). The basis of our discussion is Equation 2–1, which we develop further as follows:

$$k_j = \text{Risk-free rate} + \text{Risk premium}$$

$$= k_{RF} + (k_M - k_{RF})\beta_j = \text{Capital Asset Pricing Model (CAPM)} \qquad \textbf{4–8}$$

According to the CAPM, investors should not expect to be rewarded for all of the risk associated with an investment—its total, or stand-alone, risk—because some risk can be eliminated through diversification. The relevant risk, and thus the risk for which investors should be compensated, is that portion of the total risk that cannot be "diversified away." Thus, in this chapter we show the following:

$$\text{Total risk} = \sigma = \text{Systematic risk} + \text{Unsystematic risk}$$

$$= \text{Market (economic) risk} + \text{Firm-specific risk}$$

$$= \text{Nondiversifiable risk} + \text{Diversifiable risk}$$

✳ ETHICAL DILEMMA

RIP—Retire in Peace

Retirement Investment Products (RIP) offers a full complement of retirement planning services and a diverse line of retirement investments that have varying degrees of risk. With the investment products available at RIP, investors could form retirement funds with any level of risk preferred, from risk-free to extremely risky. RIP's reputation in the investment community is impeccable because the service agents are required to fully inform their clients of the risk possibilities that exist for any investment position, whether it is recommended by an agent or requested by a client. Since 1950, RIP has built its investment portfolio of retirement funds to $60 billion, which makes it one of the largest providers of retirement funds in the United States.

You work for RIP as an investment analyst. One of your responsibilities is to help form recommendations for the retirement fund managers to evaluate when making investment decisions. Recently, Howard, a close friend from your college days who now works for SunCoast Investments, a large brokerage firm, called to tell you about a new investment that is expected to earn very high returns during the next few years. The investment is called a "piggyback asset investment device," PAID for short. Howard told you that he really does not know what this acronym means or how the investment is constructed, but all the reports he has read indicate PAIDs should be hot investments in the future; therefore, the returns should be handsome for those who get in now. The one piece of information he did provide you was that a PAID is a rather complex investment that consists of a combination of securities whose values are based on numerous debt instruments issued by government agencies, including the Federal National Mortgage Association and the Federal Home Loan Bank. Howard made it clear that he would like you to consider recommending to RIP that PAIDs be purchased through SunCoast Investments. The commissions from such a deal would bail him and his family out of a financial crisis that resulted because they had bad luck with their investments in the financial markets from 2000 through 2002. Howard indicated that somehow he would reward you if RIP invests in PAIDs through SunCoast because, in his words, "You would literally be saving my life." You told Howard you would think about it and call him back.

Further investigation into PAIDs has yielded little additional information beyond what Howard previously provided. The new investment is intriguing because its expected return is extremely high compared with similar investments. Earlier this morning, you called Howard to quiz him a little more about the return expectations and to try to get an idea concerning the riskiness of PAIDs. But Howard was unable to adequately explain the risk associated with the investment, although he reminded you that the debt of U.S. government agencies is involved. As he says, "How much risk is there with government agencies?"

The PAIDs are enticing because RIP can attract more clients if it can increase the return offered on its investments. If you recommend the new investment and the higher returns pan out, you will earn a sizable commission. In addition, you will be helping Howard out of his delicate financial situation, because his commissions will be substantial if the PAIDs are purchased through SunCoast Investments. Should you recommend the PAIDs as an investment?

= Cannot be eliminated + Can be eliminated

Relevant risk = Nondiversifiable risk + ~~Diversifiable risk~~ (eliminated)

= Systematic risk

Systematic risk is represented by an investment's beta coefficient, β, in Equation 4–8. The specific types and sources of risk to which a firm or an investor is exposed are numerous and vary considerably depending on the situation. A detailed discussion of all the different types of risks and the techniques used to evaluate risks is beyond the scope of this book. But, you should recognize that risk is an important factor in the determination of the required rate of return (k), which, according to the following equation, is one of the two variables we need to determine to find the value of an asset:

$$\text{Value} = \frac{\hat{CF}_1}{(1+k)^1} + \frac{\hat{CF}_2}{(1+k)^2} + \cdots + \frac{\hat{CF}_n}{(1+k)^n} = \sum_{t=1}^{n} \frac{\hat{CF}_t}{(1+k)^t}$$

This equation was first introduced in Chapter 1, and we will discuss it in more detail in the next chapter. What is important to understand here is that the value of an asset, which could be a stock or a bond, is based on the cash flows that the asset is expected to generate during its life ($\hat{CF}_t$) and the rate of return investors require to "put up" their money to purchase the investment (k). In this chapter, we provide you with an indication as to how the required rate of return, k, should be determined, and we show that investors demand higher rates of return to compensate them for taking greater amounts of "relevant" risks.

Because it is an important concept and has a direct affect on value, we will continue to discuss risk throughout the book. Although discussions focus on the risk to which investors are exposed, most of the discussions examine risks that affect corporations. Because we discuss different types of risk throughout the book, we thought it might be a good idea to summarize and describe these risks in brief terms. Table 4–5 shows the risks that are discussed in the book and whether each risk is considered a component of systematic (nondiversifiable) or unsystematic (diversifiable) risk. Note that (1) this table oversimplifies risk analysis, because some risks are not easily classified as either systematic or unsystematic, and (2) some of the risks included in the table will be discussed later in the book. Even so, this table should show the relationships among the different risks discussed in the book.

Self-Test Question

Classify default risk, maturity risk, and liquidity risk as either diversifiable or nondiversifiable risk.

Summary

The primary goals of this chapter were: (1) to show how risk is measured in financial analysis and (2) to explain how risk affects rates of return. The key concepts covered are listed here:

- **Risk** can be defined as the chance that some event other than expected will occur—that is, more than one possible outcome exists in the future.
- The **expected return** on an investment is the mean value of its probability distribution of possible returns.
- The **higher the probability** that the actual return will be *significantly different* from the expected return, the **greater the risk** associated with owning an asset.
- The average investor is **risk averse,** which means that he or she must be compensated for holding risky securities. For this reason, riskier securities must have higher expected returns than less risky securities.
- Risk can be **diversified** by holding portfolios of many different investments.

TABLE 4-5	Different Types (Sources) of Risk	
	TYPE OF RISK	**BRIEF DESCRIPTION**
I. **Systematic risks** (nondiversifiable risk; market risk; relevant risk)	Interest rate risk	When interest rates change, (1) the values of investments change (in opposite directions) and (2) the rate at which funds can be reinvested also changes (in the same direction).
	Inflation risk	The primary reason interest rates change is because investors change their expectations about future inflation.
	Maturity risk	Long-term investments experience greater price reactions to interest rate changes than do short-term bonds.
	Liquidity risk	Some investments are more easily converted into cash on a short notice at a "reasonable price" than are other securities.
	Exchange rate risk	Multinational firms deal with different currencies, and the rate at which these currencies can be exchanged into dollars changes as market conditions change.
	Political risk	Actions by a government might reduce the value of an investment.
II. **Unsystematic risks** (diversifiable risk; firm-specific risk)	Business risk	Risk that would be inherent in the firm's operations if it used no debt. Factors such as labor conditions, product safety, quality of management, and competitive conditions affect firm-specific risk.
	Financial risk	Risk associated with how the firm is financed (its credit risk).
	Default risk	This is a component of financial risk that reflects the chance that the firm will not be able to service its existing debt.
III. **Combined risks** (some systematic risk and some unsystematic risk)	Total risk	The combination of systematic risk and unsystematic risk is also referred to as stand-alone risk, because an investor takes this risk if he or she purchases only one investment, which is tantamount to "putting all your eggs into one basket."
	Corporate risk	The riskiness of the firm without considering the effect of stockholder diversification is based on the combination of assets held by the firm, such as inventory, accounts receivable, and plant and equipment. Some diversification is evident because the firm's assets represent a portfolio of investments in real assets.

- Most rational investors hold **portfolios of stocks,** and they are more concerned with the risks of their portfolios than with the risks of individual stocks.
- A stock's risk consists of (1) **company-specific risk,** which can be eliminated by diversification, plus (2) **market,** or **beta, risk,** which cannot be eliminated by diversification.
- The **relevant risk** of an individual security is its contribution to the riskiness of a well-diversified portfolio, which is the security's **market risk.** Because market risk cannot be eliminated by diversification, investors must be compensated for it.
- A stock's **beta coefficient,** β, is a measure of the stock's relevant risk. Beta measures the extent to which the stock's returns move with the market.

- A **high-beta stock** is more volatile than an average stock, whereas a **low-beta stock** is less volatile than an average stock. An **average stock** has β = 1.0.
- The **beta of a portfolio** is a **weighted average** of the betas of the individual securities in the portfolio.
- The **security market line (SML)** equation shows the relationship between a security's risk and its required rate of return. The return required for any security j is equal to the **risk-free rate** plus a **premium** that compensates investors for risk. The risk premium for the security is the **market risk premium** times the **security's beta.** Therefore, $k_j = k_{RF} + (k_M - k_{RF})\beta_j$.
- Even though the expected rate of return on a stock generally is equal to its required return, a number of things can happen to cause the required rate of return to change: (1) The **risk-free rate can change** because of changes in anticipated inflation, (2) a **stock's beta can change,** or (3) **investors' aversion to risk can change.**

In the next chapter, we will see how a security's rate of return affects its value. Then, in the remainder of the book, we will examine the ways in which a firm's management can influence a stock's riskiness and hence its price.

Questions

4-1 The probability distribution of a less risky expected return is more peaked than that of a riskier return. What shape would the probability distribution have for (a) completely certain returns and (b) completely uncertain returns?

4-2 Security A has an expected return of 7 percent, a standard deviation of expected returns of 35 percent, a correlation coefficient with the market of –0.3, and a beta coefficient of 20.5. Security B has an expected return of 12 percent, a standard deviation of returns of 10 percent, a correlation with the market of 0.7, and a beta coefficient of 1.0. Which security is riskier? Why?

4-3 Suppose you owned a portfolio consisting of $250,000 worth of long-term U.S. government bonds.

  a. Would your portfolio be riskless?

  b. Now suppose you hold a portfolio consisting of $250,000 worth of 30-day Treasury bills. Every 30 days your bills mature and you reinvest the principal ($250,000) in a new batch of bills. Assume that you live on the investment income from your portfolio and that you want to maintain a constant standard of living. Is your portfolio *truly* riskless?

  c. Can you think of any asset that would be completely riskless? Could someone develop such an asset? Explain.

4-4 A life insurance policy is a financial asset. The premiums paid represent the investment's cost.

  a. How would you calculate the expected return on a life insurance policy?

  b. Suppose the owner of a life insurance policy has no other financial assets. The person's only other asset is "human capital," or lifetime earnings capacity. What is the correlation coefficient between returns on the insurance policy and returns on the policyholder's human capital?

  c. Life insurance companies must pay administrative costs and sales representatives' commissions; hence, the expected rate of return on insurance premiums is generally low, or even negative. Use the portfolio concept to explain why people buy life insurance in spite of negative expected returns.

4-5 If investors' aversion to risk increases, would the risk premium on a high-beta stock increase more or less than that on a low-beta stock? Explain.

Self-Test Problems

(Solutions appear in Appendix B)

Key Terms   **ST-1** Define the following terms, using graphs or equations to illustrate your answers wherever feasible:

    a. Risk; probability distribution

    b. Expected rate of return, $\hat{k}$; required rate of return, k

    c. Continuous probability distribution

    d. Standard deviation, σ; variance, σ^2; coefficient of variation, CV

    e. Risk aversion; realized rate of return

    f. Risk premium for Stock j, RP_j; market risk premium, RP_M

    g. capital asset pricing model (CAPM)

    h. Expected return on a portfolio, $\hat{k}_p$

    i. Correlation coefficient, r

    j. Market risk; company-specific risk; relevant risk

    k. Beta coefficient, β; average stock's beta, β_A

    l. Security market line (SML); SML equation

    m. Slope of SML as a measure of risk aversion

expected rates of return   **ST-2** Stocks R and S have the following probability distributions of returns:

		RETURNS
PROBABILITY	**STOCK R**	**STOCK S**
0.5	–2%	20%
0.1	10	12
0.4	15	2

    a. Calculate expected return for each stock.

    b. Calculate the expected return of a portfolio consisting of 50 percent of each stock.

    c. Calculate the standard deviation of returns for each stock and for the portfolio. Which stock is considered riskier with respect to total risk?

    d. Compute the coefficient of variation for each stock. According to the coefficient of variation, which stock is considered riskier?

    e. Looking at the returns in the probability distributions of the two stocks, would you guess that the correlation coefficient between returns on the two stocks is closer to 0.9 or to –0.9?

    f. If you added more stocks at random to the portfolio, which of the following is the most accurate statement of what would happen to σ_P?

        (1) σ_P would remain constant, no matter how many stocks are added.

        (2) σ_P would approach 15 percent as more stocks are added.

        (3) σ_P would decline to zero if enough stocks were included.

Problems

expected returns   **4–1** Suppose you won the Florida lottery and are offered (1) $0.5 million or (2) a gamble in which you would get $1 million if a head is flipped but zero if a tail came up.

    a. What is the expected value of the gamble?

    b. Would you take the sure $0.5 million or the gamble?

    c. If you choose the sure $0.5 million, are you a risk averter or a risk seeker?

    d. Suppose you actually take the sure $0.5 million. You can invest it in either a U.S. Treasury bond that will return $537,500 at the end of one year or a common stock that has a 50-50 chance of being either worthless or worth $1,150,000 at the end of the year.

(1) What is the expected dollar profit on the stock investment? (The expected profit on the T-bond investment is $37,500.)

(2) What is the expected rate of return on the stock investment? (The expected rate of return on the T-bond investment is 7.5 percent.)

(3) Would you invest in the bond or the stock?

(4) Exactly how large would the expected profit (or the expected rate of return) have to be on the stock investment to make you invest in the stock, given the 7.5 percent return on the bond?

(5) How might your decision be affected if, rather than buying one stock for $0.5 million, you could construct a portfolio consisting of 100 stocks with $5,000 invested in each? Each of these stocks has the same return characteristics as the one stock—that is, a 50-50 chance of being worth either zero or $11,500 at year-end. Would the correlation between returns on these stocks matter?

security market line   **4–2** The McAlhany Investment Fund has total capital of $500 million invested in five stocks:

STOCK	INVESTMENT	STOCK'S BETA COEFFICIENT
A	$160 million	0.5
B	120 million	2.0
C	80 million	4.0
D	80 million	1.0
E	60 million	3.0

The current risk-free rate (k_{RF}) is 8 percent, whereas market returns have the following estimated probability distribution for the next period:

PROBABILITY	MARKET RETURN
0.1	10%
0.2	12
0.4	13
0.2	16
0.1	17

a. Compute the expected return for the market.

b. Compute the beta coefficient for the investment fund. (Remember, this is a portfolio.)

c. What is the estimated equation for the security market line (SML)?

d. Compute the fund's required rate of return for the next period.

e. Suppose John McAlhany, the president, receives a proposal for a new stock. The investment needed to take a position in the stock is $50 million, it will have an expected return of 18 percent, and its estimated beta coefficient is 2.0. Should the new stock be purchased? At what expected rate of return should McAlhany be indifferent to purchasing the stock?

expected rates of return   **4–3** Stocks A and B have the following probability distributions:

	RETURNS	
PROBABILITY	STOCK A	STOCK B
0.1	33%	60%
0.2	20	30
0.4	15	5
0.3	0	−20

a. Calculate expected return for each stock.
b. Calculate the expected return of a portfolio consisting of 50 percent of each stock.
c. Calculate the standard deviation of returns for each stock and for the portfolio. Which stock is considered riskier with respect to total risk?
d. Compute the coefficient of variation for each stock. According to the coefficient of variation, which stock is considered riskier?
e. Calculate the coefficient of variation for the portfolio.
f. If you are a risk-averse investor, would you prefer to hold Stock A, Stock B, or the portfolio? Why?

realized rates of return   4-4 Use the equations in Footnote 3 to perform computations required for this problem. Stocks A and B have the following *historical* returns:

YEAR	STOCK A'S RETURNS, k_A	STOCK B'S RETURNS, k_B
2000	−18.00%	−14.50%
2001	33.00	21.80
2002	15.00	30.50
2003	−0.50	−7.60
2004	27.00	26.30

a. Calculate the average rate of return ($\bar{k}$) for each stock during the period 2000 through 2004.
b. Assume that someone held a portfolio consisting of 50 percent of Stock A and 50 percent of Stock B. What would have been the realized rate of return on the portfolio in each year from 2000 through 2004? What would have been the average return on the portfolio during this period?
c. Calculate the standard deviation of returns for each stock and for the portfolio. (Use the equation to compute s, which is shown in Footnote 3.)
d. Calculate the coefficient of variation for each stock and for the portfolio.
e. If you are a risk-averse investor, would you prefer to hold Stock A, Stock B, or the portfolio? Why?

Exam-Type Problems

The problems included in this section are set up in such a way that they could be used as multiple-choice exam problems.

coefficient of variation   4-5 Based on the information given below, which investment has the greatest relative risk?

INVESTMENT	EXPECTED RETURN, $\hat{k}$	STANDARD DEVIATION, σ
Stock D	10.0%	8.0%
Stock E	36.0	24.0
Stock F	12.0	10.0

expected returns   4-6 The market and Stock S have the following probability distributions:

PROBABILITY	k_M	k_S
0.3	15%	20%
0.4	9	5
0.3	18	12

a. Calculate the expected rates of return for the market and Stock S.
b. Calculate the standard deviations for the market and Stock S.
c. Calculate the coefficients of variation for the market and Stock S.

expected returns **4–7** Stocks X and Y have the following probability distributions of expected future returns:

PROBABILITY	X	Y
0.1	–10%	–35%
0.2	2	0
0.4	12	20
0.2	20	25
0.1	38	45

a. Calculate the expected rate of return, $\hat{k}$, for Stock Y. ($\hat{k}_x$= 12%.)
b. Calculate the standard deviation of expected returns for Stock X. (σ_Y = 20.35%.) Now calculate the coefficient of variation for Stock Y. Is it possible that most investors might regard Stock Y as being less risky than Stock X? Explain.

required rate of return **4–8** Suppose k_{RF} = 8%, k_M = 11%, and k_B = 14%.
a. Calculate Stock B's beta.
b. If Stock B's beta were 1.5, what would be B's new required rate of return?

required rate of return **4–9** Suppose k_{RF} = 9%, k_M = 14%, and β_X = 1.3.
a. What is k_X, the required rate of return on Stock X?
b. Now suppose k_{RF} (1) increases to 10 percent or (2) decreases to 8 percent. The slope of the SML remains constant. How would this affect k_M and k_X?
c. Now assume k_{RF} remains at 9 percent, but k_M (1) increases to 16 percent or (2) falls to 13 percent. The slope of the SML does *not* remain constant. How would these changes affect k_X?

portfolio beta **4–10** Suppose you hold a diversified portfolio consisting of a $7,500 investment in each of 20 different common stocks. The total amount invested in the portfolio is $150,000 The portfolio beta is equal to 1.12. Now, suppose you have decided to sell one of the stocks in your portfolio with a beta equal to 1.0 for $7,500 and to use these proceeds to buy another stock for your portfolio. If the new stock's beta is equal to 1.75, what is your portfolio's new beta.

portfolio required return **4–11** Suppose you are the money manager of a $4 million investment fund. The fund consists of four stocks with the following investments and betas:

STOCK	INVESTMENT	BETA
A	$ 400,000	1.50
B	600,000	–0.50
C	1,000,000	1.25
D	2,000,000	0.75

If the market required rate of return is 14 percent and the risk-free rate is 6 percent, what is the fund's required rate of return?

required rate of return **4–12** Stock T has a beta of 1.5, Stock V has a beta of 0.75, the expected rate of return on an average stock is 15 percent, and the risk-free rate of return is 9 percent. By how much does the required return on the riskier stock exceed the required return on the less risky stock?

portfolio beta **4-13** Steve Brickson currently has an investment portfolio that contains four stocks with a total value equal to $200,000. The portfolio has a beta (β) equal to 1.5. Steve wants to invest an additional $50,000 in a stock that has β = 2.5. *After* Steve adds the new stock to his portfolio, what will be the portfolio's beta?

Integrative Problem

risk and return **4–14** Assume that you recently graduated with a major in finance, and you just landed a job in the trust department of a large regional bank. Your first assignment is to invest $100,000 from an estate for which the bank is trustee. Because the estate is expected to be distributed to the heirs in about one year, you have been instructed to plan for a one-year holding period. Further, your boss has restricted you to the following investment alternatives, shown with their probabilities and associated outcomes. (Disregard for now the items at the bottom of the table; you will fill in the blanks later.)

RETURNS ON ALTERNATIVE INVESTMENTS

STATE OF THE ECONOMY	PROB.	T-BILLS	HIGH TECH	COLLECTIONS	U.S. RUBBER	MARKET PORTFOLIO	2-STOCK PORTFOLIO
Recession	0.1	8.0%	−22.0%	28.0%	10.0%	−13.0%	
Below Average	0.2	8.0	−2.0	14.7	−10.0	1.0	
Average	0.4	8.0	20.0	0.0	7.0	15.0	
Above Average	0.2	8.0	35.0	−10.0	45.0	29.0	
Boom	0.1	8.0	50.0	−20.0	30.0	43.0	
$\hat{k}$							
σ							
CV							
β							

Table header: ESTIMATED RATE OF RETURN spans the columns T-Bills, High Tech, Collections, U.S. Rubber, Market Portfolio, 2-Stock Portfolio.

The bank's economic forecasting staff has developed probability estimates for the state of the economy, and the trust department has a sophisticated computer program that was used to estimate the rate of return on each alternative under each state of the economy. High Tech Inc. is an electronics firm; Collections Inc. collects past-due debts; and U.S. Rubber manufactures tires and various other rubber and plastics products. The bank also maintains an "index fund," which owns a market-weighted fraction of all publicly traded stocks; you can invest in that fund and thus obtain average stock market results. Given the situation as described, answer the following questions:

a. **(1)** Why is the T-bill's return independent of the state of the economy? Do T-bills promise a completely risk-free return?

(2) Why are High Tech's returns expected to move with the economy whereas Collections' are expected to move counter to the economy?

b. Calculate the expected rate of return on each alternative and fill in the row for $\hat{k}$ in the table.

c. You should recognize that basing a decision solely on expected returns is only appropriate for risk-neutral individuals. Because the beneficiaries of the trust, like virtually everyone, are risk averse, the riskiness of each alternative is an important aspect of the decision. One possible measure of risk is the *standard deviation* of returns, σ.

(1) Calculate σ for each alternative, and fill in the row for σ in the table.

(2) What type of risk is measured by the standard deviation?

(3) Draw a graph that shows *roughly* the shape of the probability distributions for High Tech, U.S. Rubber, and T-bills.

d. Suppose you suddenly remembered that the *coefficient of variation (CV)* is generally regarded as being a better measure of total risk than the standard deviation when the alternatives being considered have widely differing expected returns and risks. Calculate the CVs for the different securities, and fill in the row for CV in the table. Does the CV produce the same risk rankings as the standard deviation?

e. Suppose you create a two-stock portfolio by investing $50,000 in High Tech and $50,000 in Collections.

(1) Calculate the expected return ($\hat{k}_p$), the standard deviation (σ_P), and the coefficient of variation (CV_P) for this portfolio and fill in the appropriate rows in the table.

(2) How does the riskiness of this two-stock portfolio compare to the riskiness of the individual stocks if they are held in isolation?

f. Suppose an investor starts with a portfolio consisting of one randomly selected stock. What would happen to (1) the riskiness and (2) the expected return of the portfolio as more and more randomly selected stocks were added? What is the implication for investors? Draw two graphs to illustrate your answer.

g. **(1)** Should portfolio effects influence the way investors think about the riskiness of individual stocks?

(2) If you chose to hold a one-stock portfolio and consequently were exposed to more risk than diversified investors, could you expect to be compensated for all of your risk; that is, could you earn a risk premium on that part of your risk that you could have eliminated by diversifying?

h. The expected rates of return and the beta coefficients of the alternatives as supplied by the bank's computer program are as follows:

SECURITY	RETURN ($\hat{k}$)	RISK (β)
High Tech	17.4%	1.29
Market	15.0	1.00
U.S. Rubber	13.8	0.68
T-bills	8.0	0.00
Collections	1.7	(0.86)

(1) What is a *beta coefficient*, and how are betas used in risk analysis?

(2) Do the expected returns appear to be related to each alternative's market risk?

(3) Is it possible to choose among the alternatives on the basis of the information developed thus far?

(4) Use the data given at the start of the problem to construct a graph that shows how the T-bill's, High Tech's, and Collections' beta coefficients are calculated. Then discuss what betas measure and how they are used in risk analysis.

i. **(1)** Write out the security market line (SML) equation, use it to calculate the required rate of return on each alternative, and then graph the relationship between the expected and required rates of return.

(2) How do the expected rates of return ($\hat{k}_j$) compare with the required rates of return (k_j)?

(3) Does the fact that Collections has a negative beta make any sense? What is the implication of the negative beta?

(4) What would be the market risk and the required return of a 50-50 portfolio of High Tech and Collections? Of High Tech and U.S. Rubber?

j. **(1)** Suppose investors raise their inflation expectations by 3 percentage points over current estimates as reflected in the 8 percent T-bill rate.

What effect will higher inflation have on the SML and on the returns required on high- and low-risk securities?

(2) Suppose instead that investors' risk aversion increases enough to cause the market risk premium to increase by 3 percentage points. (Inflation remains constant.) What effect will this have on the SML and on returns of high- and low-risk securities?

Computer-Related Problem

Work the problem in this section only if you are using the computer problem diskette.

expected rates of return   **4–15** Using the computerized model in File C04, rework Problem 4–3, assuming that a third stock, Stock C, is available for inclusion in the portfolio. Stock C has the following probability distribution:

PROBABILITY	RETURNS FOR STOCK C
0.1	50%
0.2	10
0.4	25
0.3	–6

a. Calculate (or read from the computer screen) the expected return, standard deviation, and coefficient of variation for Stock C.

b. Assume that the portfolio now consists of 33.33 percent of Stock A, 33.33 percent of Stock B, and 33.33 percent of Stock C. How does this affect the portfolio return, standard deviation, and coefficient of variation versus when 50 percent was invested in A and in B?

c. Make some other changes in the portfolio, making sure that the percentages sum to 100 percent. For example, enter 25 percent for Stock A, 25 percent for Stock B, and 50 percent for Stock C. Notice that $\hat{k}_P$ remains constant and that σ_P changes. Why do these results occur?

d. Compare the standard deviations of the two-stock portfolio computed in Problem 4–3 and the three-stock portfolio computed in part (b) of this problem. What does this comparison suggest about the correlation between Stock C and Stocks A and B?

e. Would you prefer to hold the portfolio described in Problem 4–3 consisting only of Stocks A and B or a portfolio that also included Stock C? If others react similarly, how might this affect the stocks' prices and rates of return?

GET REAL with Thomson ONE

4–16 During the late 1990s, the U.S. stock market was volatile, just like the U.S. economy. As mentioned in the chapter, some stocks, including technology stocks, performed very well during the technology boom. However, stock market performance during the economic recession in the United States at the beginning of the 21st century was poor.

Using the Thomson ONE database, access the information for Yahoo!, Inc. [YHOO] and answer the following questions:

a. What is Yahoo!'s primary line of business?

b. Draw a price graph for Yahoo! for the last five years using daily data. What can you say about the general movement of the price of Yahoo! stock over the last five years? (Click on prices for Yahoo! and Interactive Chart.)

   c. Draw a price graph for Yahoo! for the last five years using daily data. What can you say about the general movement of the price of Yahoo! stock over the last five years? (Click on Prices for Yahoo! and Interactive Chart.)

   d. When did Yahoo! register its highest stock price over the last five years, and what was that price? (Click on Data for the chart.)

   e. When did Yahoo! register its lowest price during the five-year time period and what was that price?

   f. What percent changes in value did Yahoo!'s stock experience between the date of the highest price and the date of the lowest price?

   g. When did the stock price begin to recover?

   h. Compare the performance of Yahoo! during the past five years to the performance of General Electric [GE]. Write a paragraph on the riskiness of investing in stocks using Yahoo! and General Electric as examples.

APPENDIX 4A

Calculating Beta Coefficients

The CAPM is an *ex ante* model, which means that all of the variables represent before-the-fact, *expected* values. In particular, the beta coefficient used in the SML equation should reflect the expected volatility of a given stock's return versus the return on the market during some *future* period. Of course, people generally calculate betas using data from some *past* period and then assume that the stock's relative volatility will be the same in the future as it was in the past.

To illustrate how betas are calculated, consider Figure 4A–1. The data at the bottom of the figure show the historical realized returns for Stock J and for the market over a five-year period. The data points have been plotted on the scatter diagram, and a regression line has been drawn. If all of the data points had fallen on a straight line, as they did in Figure 4–9, it would be easy to draw an accurate line. If they do not, as in Figure 4A–1, then you must fit the line either "by eye" as an approximation or with a calculator or a computer.

Recall what the term *regression line*, or *regression equation*, means: The equation $Y = \alpha + \beta X + \varepsilon$ is the standard form of a simple linear regression. It states that the dependent variable, Y, is equal to a constant, α (the Y intercept), plus β times X, where β is the slope coefficient and X is the independent variable, plus an error term, ε. Thus the rate of return on the stock during a given time period (Y) depends on what happens to the general stock market, which is measured by $X = k_M$.

Once the data have been plotted and the regression line has been drawn on graph paper, we can estimate its intercept and slope, the α and β values in $Y = \alpha + \beta X$. The intercept, α is the point where the line cuts crosses the vertical axis. The slope coefficient, β, can be estimated by the "rise over run" method. This technique involves calculating the amount by which k_J increases for a given increase in k_M. For example, we observe in Figure 4A–1 that k_J increases from –8.9 to + 7.1 percent (the rise) when k_M increases from 0 to 10.0 percent (the run). Thus β, the beta coefficient, can be measured as follows:

$$\text{beta} = \beta = \frac{\text{Rise}}{\text{Run}} = \frac{\Delta Y}{\Delta X} = \frac{7.1 - (-8.9)}{10.0 - 0.0} = \frac{16.0}{10.0} = 1.6$$

Note that rise over run is a ratio. It would be the same if measured using any two arbitrarily selected points on the line.

FIGURE 4A-1	Calculating Beta Coefficients

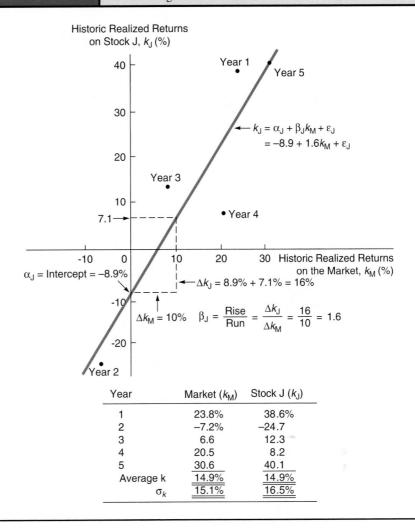

Year	Market (k_M)	Stock J (k_J)
1	23.8%	38.6%
2	–7.2%	–24.7
3	6.6	12.3
4	20.5	8.2
5	30.6	40.1
Average k	14.9%	14.9%
σ_k	15.1%	16.5%

The regression line equation enables us to predict a rate of return for Stock J, given a value of k_M. For example, if $k_M = 15\%$, we would predict $k_J = -8.9\% + 1.6(15\%) = 15.1\%$. The actual return probably would differ from the predicted return. This deviation is the error term, ε_J, for the year, and it varies randomly from year to year depending on company-specific factors. Note, however, that the higher the correlation coefficient, the closer the points lie to the regression line, and the smaller the errors.

If you have taken a statistics course that covered regression analysis, you are aware that five observations are not sufficient to attain valid results. In actual practice, monthly rather than annual returns are generally used for k_J and k_M, and five years of data are often employed. Thus the scatter diagram would include $5 \times 12 = 60$ data points. Also, in practice one would use the *least squares method* for finding the regression coefficients α and β. This procedure, which minimizes the squared values of the error terms, is discussed in statistics courses.

The least squares value of beta can be obtained quite easily with a financial calculator or a spreadsheet, such as Excel or Lotus 1-2-3.

CHAPTER 5

Valuation Concepts

A MANAGERIAL PERSPECTIVE

On January 14, 2000, 10-year Treasury bonds were selling at prices that promised investors an average return equal to 6.7 percent. As a result, a 10-year Treasury bond with a face, or par, value equal to $10,000 that paid $335 interest every six months had a market value equal to $10,000 on January 14, 2000. Nearly one year later, on January 5, 2001, the value of the same bond was approximately $11,220. Thus, if you had purchased the bond one year earlier, at least on paper, you would have incurred a capital gain equal to $1,220. Your "paper gains" would have been even higher if you still owned the bond on January 2, 2004, when its market value was approximately $12,000. During this three-year period you would have also received interest payments equal to $335 every six months ($670 during each year).

How could the market value of the Treasury bond gain so much value in 2000 and over the 2000–2003 period? The primary reason the value of this investment, as well as other debt instruments, increased was because the Fed cut interest rates several times during the period from the beginning of 2000 through 2002 to stimulate economic activity. In fact, interest rates were cut nearly every month in 2001. The cuts worked; the rates at which companies, individuals, and governments could borrow decreased dramatically during this period. But, the cuts also substantially reduced the returns that were promised to new investors. In the case of the 10-year Treasury bonds, rates dropped from 6.7 percent at

the beginning of 2000 to 4.3 percent at the beginning of 2004 (end of 2003). This decrease in rates caused the Treasury bonds issued in 2000 to increase above their par values—that is, they were selling at a premium.

An investor who purchased a 10-year Treasury bond on January 14, 2000, when interest rates were fairly high, and then sold the same bond on January 2, 2004, when interest rates were low, earned an average annual return equal to 12 percent. The return consisted of a capital gain equal to $2,000 and interest payments totaling $670 each year. If the investor continued to hold the bond until the end of March 2004, he or she would have found that the market price of the bond increased to $12,180, because market rates decreased from 3.5 percent to 3.2 percent during this period. In this case, the average annual return earned by investors who purchased the bonds on January 14, 2000 would have been greater than 12 percent.

Could investors have fared better in the stock market or in other types of investments? Probably not. According to the S&P 500 Index, the values of stocks decreased by a total of approximately 40 percent from January 2000 until January 2003. This decrease equates to an average annual rate equal to nearly –16 percent. Even after considering dividends paid by the companies, investors lost an average 13.5 percent during this period.

During the first nine months of 2003, both interest rates and the stock market rebounded. Interest rates on 10-year Treasury bonds increased from less than 4.0 percent to nearly 4.5 percent, and the S&P 500 rose from 880 to 1023. As market rates increase, investors who own bonds discover that the values of those bonds decrease. Should investors have sold their bonds? Not necessarily; rates declined again during the next six months.

As you read this chapter, think about why the value of the Treasury bonds increased during the period when interest rates decreased. What hap-pens to the value of financial assets when the returns demanded by investors change? Are bonds and stocks affected the same? Answering these questions will help you to get a basic under-standing of how stocks and bonds are valued in the financial markets. Such an understanding will help you make investment decisions, including those that are critical when establishing a retire-ment plan. ∎

In Chapter 3 we examined time value of money (TVM) analysis. Managers and investors use these TVM concepts to establish the worth of any asset whose value is derived from future cash flows, including such assets as real estate, factories, machin-ery, oil wells, stocks, and bonds. In this chapter, we use TVM techniques to explain how the values of assets are determined. The material covered in the chapter is important to investors who want to establish the values of their investments. But knowledge of valuation is equally important to financial managers because every important corporate decision should be analyzed in terms of how it will affect the firm's value. Remember that in Chapter 1 we noted the goal of managerial finance is to maximize the value of the firm. Thus, it is critical that we understand the valuation process so we can determine what affects that value.

Basic Valuation

After learning about the time value of money, you should realize that the *value* of anything, whether it is a financial asset like a stock or a bond or a real asset like a building or a piece of machinery, *is based on the present value of the cash flows the asset is expected to produce in the future.* On a cash flow time line, value can be depicted as follows:

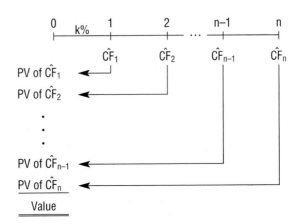

Therefore, the value of any asset can be expressed in general form as follows:

5–1

$$\text{Asset value} = V = \frac{\hat{CF}_1}{(1+k)^1} + \frac{\hat{CF}_2}{(1+k)^2} + \cdots + \frac{\hat{CF}_n}{(1+k)^n}$$

Here

$\hat{CF}_n$ = The cash flow expected to be generated by the asset in period t.

k = The return investors consider appropriate for holding such an asset. This return is termed the *required return*. As we showed in Chapters 2 and 4, k is based on both economic conditions and the riskiness of the asset.

According to Equation 5–1, the value of an asset is affected by the cash flows it is expected to generate, $\hat{CF}_n$, and the return required by investors, k. As you can see, everything else constant, *the higher the expected cash flows, the greater the asset's value; also, the lower the required return, the greater the asset's value.* In the remainder of this chapter, we discuss how this general valuation concept can be applied to determine the value of various types of assets. First, we examine the valuation process for financial assets, and then we apply the process to value real assets.

Self-Test Questions

Describe the general methodology used to value any asset.

All else equal, how would an increase in an asset's expected future cash flows affect its value? What would be the effect of an increase in the required rate of return?

Valuation of Financial Assets—Bonds

Corporations raise funds in two forms: debt and equity. Our first task in this chapter is to examine the valuation process for bonds, the principal type of long-term debt.

BOND

A long-term debt instrument.

A **bond** is a long-term promissory note issued by a business or governmental unit. The bond's conditions are contractually specified so that investors know how much is owed, the interest payments, maturity date, and any other features of the debt. For example, suppose on January 3, 2005, Unilate Textiles borrows $25 million by selling 25,000 individual bonds for $1,000 each. Unilate receives the $25 million, and it promises to pay the bondholders annual interest and to repay the $25 million on a specified date.[1] The lenders are willing to give Unilate $25 million, so the value of the bond issue is $25 million. But how do investors decide the issue is worth $25 million? As a first step in explaining how the values of this and other bonds are determined, we need to define some terms:

---

[1] Actually, Unilate would receive some amount less than $25 million because there are costs associated with issuing the bond, such as legal fees and investment banking fees. For our discussion here, however, we choose to ignore such costs to simplify the explanations. We address the topic of issuing securities and the investment banking process later in the book.

1. **Principal amount, face value, maturity value, and par value.** The **principal amount** of debt generally represents the amount of money the firm borrows and promises to repay at some future date. For much debt issued by corporations, including bonds, the principal amount is repaid at maturity, so we often refer to the principal value as the **maturity value.** In addition, the principal value generally is written on the "face" of the debt instrument, or certificate, so it is also called the **face value.** Further, when the market value of debt is the same as its face value, it is said to be selling at *par*; thus the principal amount is also referred to as the bond's **par value.** For most debt, then, the terms *principal amount, face value, maturity value,* and *par value* refer to the same value—the amount that must be repaid by the borrower. We use the terms interchangeably throughout the book.

    The face value of a corporate bond is usually set at $1,000, although multiples of $1,000 (for example, $5,000) are also used. The par value of each of Unilate bond is $1,000. Because Unilate issued 25,000 bonds, the total principal amount is $25 million.

2. **Coupon interest rate.** The bond requires the issuer to pay a specified number of dollars of interest each year (or, more typically, each six months). When this **coupon payment,** as it is called, is divided by the bond's par value, the result is the **coupon interest rate.** For example, Unilate's bonds have a $1,000 par value, and they pay $100 in interest each year. The bond's coupon interest is $100, so its coupon interest rate is $100/$1,000 = 10%. The $100 is the yearly "rent" on the $1,000 loan. This payment, which is fixed at the time the bond is issued, remains in force, by contract, during the life of the bond.[2]

3. **Maturity date.** Bonds generally have a specified **maturity date** on which the par value must be repaid. Unilate's bonds, which were issued on January 3, 2005, will mature on January 2, 2020; thus, they had a 15-year maturity at the time they were issued. Most bonds have **original maturities,** the maturities at the time the bonds are issued, of from 10 to 40 years, but any maturity is legally permissible. Of course, the effective maturity of a bond declines each year after its original issue. Thus, Unilate's bonds have a 15-year original maturity, but in 2006 they have a 14-year maturity, and so on.

4. **Call provisions.** Often, bonds have a provision whereby the issuer can pay them off prior to maturity by "calling them in" from the investors. This feature is known as a **call provision.** If a bond is callable, and if interest rates in the economy decline, then the company can sell a new issue of low-interest-rate bonds and use the proceeds to retire the old, high-interest-rate issue, just as a homeowner can refinance a home mortgage.

5. **New issues versus outstanding bonds.** As we will see, a bond's market price is determined primarily by the cash flows it generates, or the dollar interest it pays, which depends on the coupon interest rate. The higher the coupon, other

---

[2]The term *coupon payment* comes from the fact that some time ago, most bonds literally had a number of small (½- by 2-inch) dated coupons attached to them, and on the interest payment date, the owner would clip off the coupon for that date and either cash it at his or her bank or mail it to the company's paying agent, who then mailed back a check for the interest. A 30-year, semiannual bond would start with 60 coupons, whereas a five-year annual payment bond would start with only five coupons. Today most bonds are registered—no physical coupons are involved, and interest checks are mailed automatically to the registered owners of the bonds. Even so, people continue to use the terms *coupon* and *coupon interest rate* when discussing registered bonds.

things held constant, the higher the market price of the bond. At the time a bond is issued, the coupon generally is set at a level that will cause the market price of the bond to equal its par value. If a lower coupon were set, investors simply would not be willing to pay $1,000 for the bond, whereas if a higher coupon were set, investors would clamor for the bond and bid its price up over $1,000. Investment bankers can judge quite precisely the coupon rate that will cause a bond to sell at its $1,000 par value.

A bond that has just been issued is known as a *new issue*. (*The Wall Street Journal* classifies a bond as a new issue for about one month after it first has been issued.) Once the bond has been on the market for a while, it is classified as an *outstanding bond*, also called a *seasoned issue*. Newly issued bonds generally sell at close to par, but the prices of outstanding bonds can vary widely from par. Coupon interest payments are constant, so when economic conditions change, a bond with a $100 coupon that sold at par when it was issued can sell for more or less than $1,000 thereafter.

The Basic Bond Valuation Model[3]

Equation 5–1 shows that the value of a financial asset is based on the cash flows expected to be generated by the asset in the future. In the case of a bond, the cash flows consist of interest payments during the life of the bond plus a return of the principal amount when the bond matures. In a cash flow time line format, here is the situation:

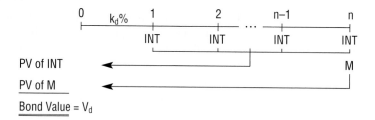

Here

k_d = The average rate of return investors require to invest in the bond. For the Unilate Textiles bond issue k_d = 10%.[4]

n = The number of years before the bond matures. For the Unilate bonds, n = 15. Note that n declines each year after the bond has been issued, so a bond that had a maturity of 15 years when it was issued (original maturity = 15) will have n = 14 after one year, n = 13 after two years, and so on. Note also that at this point we assume that the bond pays interest once a year, or annually, so n is measured in years. Later,

---

[3]In finance, the term *model* refers to an equation or set of equations designed to show how one or more variables affect some other variable. Thus, a bond valuation model shows the mathematical relationship between a bond's price and the set of variables that determine the price.

[4]The appropriate interest rate on debt securities was discussed in Chapter 2. The bond's riskiness, liquidity, and years to maturity, as well as supply and demand conditions in the capital markets, all influence the interest rates on bonds.

we will deal with semiannual payment bonds, which pay interest each six months.[5]

INT = Dollars of interest paid each period = Coupon rate × Par value. In our example, INT = 0.10 × $1,000 = $100.

M = The par, or face, value of the bond = $1,000. This amount must be paid off at maturity.

We can now redraw the cash flow time line to show the numerical values for Unilate's bonds for all variables except its value:

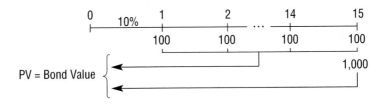

Now the following general equation can be solved to find the value of any bond:

$$
\begin{aligned}
\text{Bond value} = V_d &= \frac{\text{INT}}{(1+k_d)^1} + \frac{\text{INT}}{(1+k_d)^2} + \cdots + \frac{\text{INT}}{(1+k_d)^N} + \frac{M}{(1+k_d)^N} \\
&= \sum_{t=1}^{N} \frac{\text{INT}}{(1+k_d)^t} + \frac{M}{(1+k_d)^N}
\end{aligned}
$$

5–2

Figure 5–1 shows the cash flow time line and the result of computing the value of Unilate's bond using Equation 5–2. Notice, however, that the interest payments represent an annuity and repayment of the par value at maturity represents a single, or lump-sum, payment. Thus, Equation 5–2 can be rewritten as follows:

5–2a

$$
V_d = \text{INT} \left[\frac{1 - \dfrac{1}{(1+k_d)^N}}{k_d} \right] + M \left[\frac{1}{(1+k_d)^N} \right]
$$

---

[5]We should note that some bonds that have been issued either pay no interest during their lives (*zero* coupon bonds) or else pay very low coupon rates. Such bonds are sold at a discount below par, and hence they are called *original issue discount bonds.* The "interest" earned on a zero coupon bond comes at the end when the company pays off at par ($1,000) a bond that was purchased for, say, $321.97. The discount of $1,000 – $321.97 = $678.03 substitutes for interest.

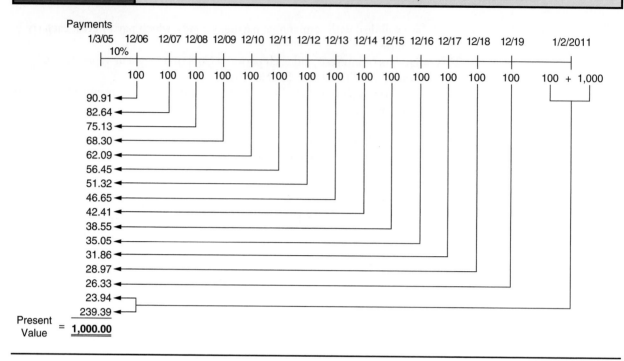

Note: The sum of the individual present Values recorded at two decimal places (as they are here) actually is 999.99 due to rounding.

Inserting values for our example provides the numerical solution (discussed in Chapter 3) for the value of the bond:

$$V_d = 100 \left[\frac{1 - \dfrac{1}{(1.10)^{15}}}{0.10} \right] + 1,000 \left[\frac{1}{(1.10)^{15}} \right]$$

$$= 100(7.60608) + 1,000(0.23939)$$

$$= 760.61 + 239.39 = 1,000$$

Using a financial calculator, the solution is set up as follows:

Inputs:	15	10	?	100	1,000
	N	I/k	PV	PMT	FV

Output: = −1,000

Input N = 15, I/k = k_d = 10, PMT = INT = 100, FV = M = 1,000, and then compute PV = V_d = −1,000. Because the PV is an outflow to the investor, it is shown with a negative sign on the calculator.[6]

Changes in Bond Values over Time

If k_d remained constant at 10 percent, what would be the value of the bond one year after it was issued? We can find this value using Equation 5–2a, but now the term to maturity is only 14 years, so n = 14. We see that V_d remains constant at $1,000:

---

[6]The solution will be the same if a spreadsheet is used to compute the bond's value. See Appendix 3A at the end of Chapter 3 for a discussion on how to use a spreadsheet to solve such problems.

$$V_d = 100 \left[\frac{1 - \frac{1}{(1.10)^{14}}}{0.10} \right] + 1,000 \left[\frac{1}{(1.10)^{14}} \right]$$

$$= 100(7.36669) + 1,000(0.26333)$$

$$= 736.67 + 263.33 = 1,000$$

With a financial calculator, simply override N = 15 with N = 14, and when you compute PV, you will get the same answer as before, –1,000. The value of the bond will remain at $1,000 as long as the appropriate interest rate, k_d, remains constant at 10 percent, and k_d equals the coupon interest rate. In other words, *if the market rate associated with a bond, k_d, equals the coupon rate of interest, the bond will sell at its par value.*[7]

Now suppose interest rates in the economy fall after the Unilate bonds are issued, and, as a result, k_d falls *below the coupon rate*, decreasing from 10 percent to 8 percent. *Both the coupon interest payments and the maturity value remain constant*, but now the required rate of return used in Equation 5–2a will equal 8 percent—that is, k_d = 8%. The value of the bond at the end of the first year (so, n = 14) would be $1,164.88:

$$V_d = 100 \left[\frac{1 - \frac{1}{(1.08)^{14}}}{0.08} \right] + 1,000 \left[\frac{1}{(1.08)^{14}} \right]$$

$$= 100(8.24424) + 1,000(0.34046)$$

$$= 824.42 + 340.46 = 1,164.88$$

The financial calculator solution is set up as follows:

Inputs:	14	8	?	100	1,000
	N	I/k	PV	PMT	FV
Output:			= –1,164.88		

If you did not clear your calculator after computing the value of the bond when N = 14 and I/k = 10, simply change I/k = k_d from 10 to 8, and compute PV = –1,164.88.

As you can see, when k_d falls below the coupon rate, the bond would sell above par, or at a *premium*. The arithmetic of the bond value increase should be clear, but what is the logic behind it? The fact that k_d has fallen to 8 percent means that if you had $1,000 to invest, you could buy new bonds like Unilate's (companies sell new bonds every day), except that these new bonds would pay $80 of interest each year rather than $100. Naturally, you would prefer $100 to $80, so you would be willing to pay

---

[7]The bond prices quoted by brokers are calculated as described. However, if you bought a bond between interest payment dates, you would have to pay the basic price plus accrued interest. Thus, if you purchased a Unilate bond six months after it was issued, your broker would send you an invoice stating that you must pay $1,000 as the basic price of the bond plus $50 interest, representing one-half the annual interest of $100. The seller of the bond would receive $1,050. If you bought the bond the day before its interest payment date, you would pay $1,000 + (364/365)($100) = $1,099.73. Of course, you would receive an interest payment of $100 at the end of the next day.

Throughout the chapter we assume that the bond is being evaluated immediately after an interest payment date. The more expensive financial calculators have a built-in calendar that permits the calculation of exact values between interest payment dates.

more than $1,000 for Unilate Textiles' bonds to obtain its higher interest payments. Because all investors would recognize this as well, the Unilate Textiles bonds would be bid up in price to $1,164.88. When the market value of Unilate's bonds equals $1,164.88, they would provide the same rate of return to a potential investor as the new bonds—that is, 8 percent.

Assuming that interest rates remain constant at 8 percent for the next 14 years, what would happen to the value of a Unilate Textiles bond? It would fall gradually from $1,164.88 at present to $1,000 at maturity (in 14 years), when Unilate Textiles will redeem each bond for $1,000. This point can be illustrated by calculating the value of the bond one year from now, when it has 13 years remaining to maturity. With a financial calculator, input the same values as previously—that is, I/k = 8, PMT = 100, and FV = 1,000, but now enter N = 13. You will find that the value of the bond when N = 13 is $1,158.08.

As you can see, the value of the bond will decrease from $1,164.88 to $1,158.08, or by $6.80. If you were to calculate the value of the bond at other future dates, the price would continue to fall as the maturity date is approached. At maturity, the value of the bond would have to equal $1,000 (as long as the firm does not go bankrupt).

Notice that if you purchased the bond at a price of $1,164.88 and then sold it one year later with k_d still at 8 percent, you would have a capital loss of $6.80, or a total return of $100.00 − $6.80 = $93.20. Your percentage rate of return would consist of an **interest yield** (also called a **current yield**) plus a **capital gains yield**. These yields are calculated as follows:

$$\frac{\text{Current}}{\text{yield}} = \frac{\text{INT}}{V_d}$$

$$\frac{\text{Capital}}{\text{gains yield}} = \frac{\left(\begin{array}{c}\text{Ending}\\ \text{bond value}\end{array}\right) - \left(\begin{array}{c}\text{Beginning}\\ \text{bond value}\end{array}\right)}{\left(\begin{array}{c}\text{Beginning}\\ \text{bond value}\end{array}\right)} = \frac{V_{d,End} - V_{d,Begin}}{V_{d,Begin}}$$

The yields for Unilate's bond after one year are as follows:

Current yield = $100.00/$1,164.88 = 0.0858 = 8.58%

Capital gains yield = −$6.80/$1,164.88 = −0.0058 = −0.58%

Total rate of return (yield) = $93.20/$1,164.88 = 0.0800 = 8.00% = 8.58% + (−0.58%)

Had interest rates risen from 10 to 12 percent rather than fallen during the first year after issue, the value of the bond would have declined to $867.44. With a financial calculator, input N = 14, I/k = 12, PMT = 100, and FV = 1,000, and compute the value of the bond, PV = −867.44.

In this case, the bond would sell at a *discount* equal to $132.56 below its par value:

Discount = Price − Par value

= $867.44 − $1,000.00 = −$132.56

The total expected future yield on the bond would again consist of a current yield and a capital gains yield, but now the capital gains yield would be positive, and the total yield would be 12 percent. To see this, calculate the price of the bond with 13 years left to maturity, assuming that interest rates remain at 12 percent. With a calculator, enter N = 13, I/k = 12, PMT = 100, and FV = 1,000, and then compute the bond's value, PV = −871.53.

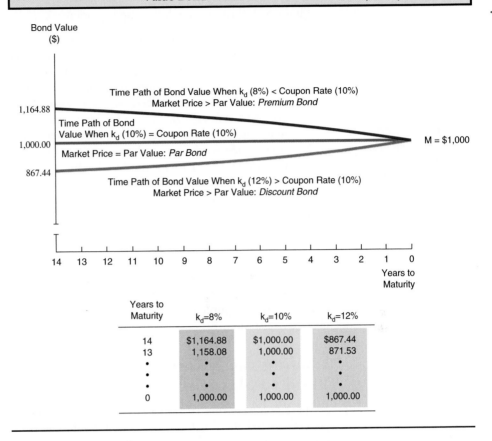

FIGURE 5-2 Time Path of the Value of a 10% Coupon, $1,000 Par Value Bond When Interest Rates Are 8%, 10%, and 12%

Years to Maturity	$k_d = 8\%$	$k_d = 10\%$	$k_d = 12\%$
14	$1,164.88	$1,000.00	$867.44
13	1,158.08	1,000.00	871.53
•	•	•	•
•	•	•	•
•	•	•	•
0	1,000.00	1,000.00	1,000.00

Notice that the capital gain for the year is the difference between the bond's value at n = 13 and the bond's value at n = 14, or $871.53 − $867.44 = $4.09. The current yield, capital gains yield, and total yield are calculated as follows:

$$\text{Current yield} = \$100.00/\$867.44 = 0.1153 = 11.53\%$$

$$\text{Capital gains yield} = \$4.09/\$867.44 = 0.0047 = \underline{0.47\%}$$

$$\text{Total rate of return (yield)} = \$104.09/\$867.44 = 0.1200 = \underline{12.00\%}$$

What would happen to the value of the bond if market interest rates remain constant at 12 percent until maturity? Because the value of the bond must equal the principal, or par, amount at maturity (as long as bankruptcy does not occur), its value will gradually increase from the current price of $871.53 to its maturity value of $1,000. For example, the value of the bond would increase to $876.11 at n = 12, its value would be $881.25 at n = 11, and so forth.

Figure 5–2 graphs the value of Unilate's bond over time, assuming that interest rates in the economy (1) remain constant at 10 percent, (2) fall to 8 percent and then remain constant at that level, or (3) rise to 12 percent and remain constant at that level. Of course, if interest rates do not remain constant, then the price of the bond will fluctuate over time. However, *regardless of how future interest rates change, the bond's price will approach $1,000 as it nears the maturity date* (barring bankruptcy, in which case the bond's value could drop to zero).

Figure 5–2 illustrates the following key points:

1. *Whenever the market rate of interest, k_d, is equal to the coupon rate, a bond will sell at its par value.* Normally, the coupon rate is set equal to the going interest rate when a bond is issued, so initially it sells at par.

2. Interest rates do change over time, but the coupon rate remains fixed after the bond has been issued. *Whenever the market rate of interest is greater than the coupon rate, a bond's price will fall below its par value.* Such a bond sells at a discount from its face value, so it is called a **discount bond.**

3. *Whenever the market rate of interest is less than the coupon rate, a bond's price will rise above its par value.* Such a bond sells at a premium compared to this face value, so it is called a **premium bond.**

4. *An increase in interest rates will cause the price of an outstanding bond to fall, whereas a decrease in rates will cause the price to rise.*

5. *The market value of a bond will always approach its par value as its maturity date approaches,* provided the firm does not go bankrupt (see Figure 5–2).

DISCOUNT BOND
A bond that sells below its par value; occurs whenever the going rate of interest rises above the coupon rate.

PREMIUM BOND
A bond that sells above its par value; occurs whenever the going rate of interest falls below the coupon rate.

These points are important because they show that bondholders can suffer capital losses or make capital gains, depending on whether interest rates rise or fall after the bond is purchased. And, as we saw in Chapter 2, interest rates do indeed change over time.

Finding the Interest Rate on a Bond: Yield to Maturity

YIELD TO MATURITY (YTM)
The average rate of return earned on a bond if it is held to maturity.

Suppose you were offered a 14-year, 10 percent coupon, $1,000 par value bond at a price of $1,164.88. What rate of interest would you earn on your investment if you bought the bond and held it to maturity? This rate is called the bond's **yield to maturity (YTM),** and it is the interest rate discussed by bond traders when they talk about rates of return. To find the yield to maturity, you could solve Equation 5–2a for k_d:

$$V_d = 1,164.88 = \frac{100}{(1+k_d)^1} + \cdots + \frac{100}{(1+k_d)^{14}} + \frac{1,000}{(1+k_d)^{14}}$$

$$= 100\left[\frac{1 - \dfrac{1}{(1+k_d)^{14}}}{k_d}\right] + 1,000\left[\frac{1}{(1+k_d)^{14}}\right]$$

$$= 100\left[\frac{1 - \dfrac{1}{(1+YTM)^{14}}}{YTM}\right] + 1,000\left[\frac{1}{(1+YTM)^{14}}\right]$$

It is easy to solve for k_d with a financial calculator. Here is the setup:

Inputs:	14	?	–1,164.88	100	1,000
	N	I/k	PV	PMT	FV
Output:		= 8%			

Input N = 14, PMT = 100, FV = 1,000, and PV = –1,164.88, and then compute I/k = 8.0.

If you do not have a financial calculator, you must use a trial-and-error approach to solve for k_d, which is the yield to maturity, in Equation 5–2. You would substitute values for k_d until you find a rate that "works" so that the present value of the interest payments combined with the present value of the repayment of the maturity value equals the current price of the bond. But what would be a good interest rate to use as a starting point? First, you know that the bond is selling at a premium over its par value ($1,164.88 versus $1,000), so the bond's yield to maturity must be below its 10 percent coupon rate. Therefore, you might start by trying rates below 10 percent. It could take you a while to "zero in" on the appropriate rate. It probably would be better to get an estimate of the rate by computing the *approximate* yield to maturity, which can be found with the following equation:[8]

$$5\text{-}3$$

$$\begin{aligned}
\text{Approximate} \atop \text{yield to maturity} &= \frac{\dfrac{\text{Annual}}{\text{interest}} + \dfrac{\text{Accrued}}{\text{capital gains}}}{\text{Average value of bond}} \\[2em]
&= \frac{\text{INT} + \left(\dfrac{M - V_d}{N}\right)}{\left[\dfrac{2(V_d) + M}{3}\right]}
\end{aligned}$$

Equation 5–3 is based on computations of approximate yields in the past and it does not consider the time value of money, so it *should be used only to approximate a bond's yield to maturity*. For the bond we are examining, the approximate yield to maturity is

$$\begin{aligned}
\text{Yield to} \atop \text{maturity} = k_d &\approx \frac{100 + \left(\dfrac{1,000 - 1,164.88}{14}\right)}{\left[\dfrac{2(1,164.88) + 1,000}{3}\right]} \\[2em]
&= \frac{100 + (-11.78)}{1,109.92} = \frac{88.22}{1,109.92} = 0.0795 = 7.95\% \approx 8.0\%
\end{aligned}$$

The result of this computation is close to the result we found using a financial calculator.

We determined that the yield to maturity for our bond is 8 percent. The yield to maturity (YTM) is identical to the total annual rate of return discussed in the preceding section. The YTM for a bond that sells at par consists entirely of an interest yield. But, if the bond sells at a price other than its par value, the YTM consists of the interest yield plus a positive or negative capital gains yield. Note also that a bond's yield to maturity changes whenever interest rates in the economy change—and such changes occur almost daily. An investor who purchases a bond and holds it until it matures will receive the YTM that existed on the purchase date, but the

[8]The form of Equation 5–3, which gives a "good" approximation for a bond's yield to maturity, is based on the work of Gabriel A. Hawawini and Ashok Vora, "Yield Approximations: A Historical Perspective," *Journal of Finance* (March 1982), 145–156.

bond's calculated YTM will change frequently between the purchase date and the maturity date.[9]

Bond Values with Semiannual Compounding

Although some bonds pay interest annually, *most* pay interest semiannually. To evaluate semiannual payment bonds, we modify the valuation equations just as we did in Chapter 3 when interest compounding occurs more than once per year. As a result, Equations 5-2 and 5-2a are modified as follows:

5–2b

$$V_d = \sum_{t=1}^{2N} \frac{\left(\dfrac{INT}{2}\right)}{\left(1 + \dfrac{k_d}{2}\right)^t} + \frac{m}{\left(1 + \dfrac{k_d}{2}\right)^{2N}}$$

$$= INT\left[\frac{1 - \dfrac{1}{\left(1 - \dfrac{k_d}{2}\right)^{2N}}}{\left(\dfrac{k_d}{2}\right)}\right] + m\left[\frac{1}{\left(1 + \dfrac{k_d}{2}\right)^{2N}}\right]$$

To illustrate, let's assume that Unilate's 14-year bonds pay $50 interest each six months rather than $100 at the end of each year. Now each interest payment is only half as large as before, but there are twice as many payments. When the market (sim-

---

[9]Bonds that contain call provisions (callable bonds) are often called by the firm prior to maturity. In cases where a bond issue is called, investors do not have the opportunity to earn the yield to maturity (YTM) because the bond issue is retired before the maturity date arrives. Thus, for callable bonds, we generally compute the yield to call (YTC) rather than the yield to maturity. The computation for the yield to call is the same as for the yield to maturity, except the call price of the bond is substituted for the maturity (par) value and the number of years until the bond can be called is substituted for the years to maturity. To calculate the yield to call (YTC), we modify Equation 5–2 and solve the following equation for k_d:

$$V_d = \frac{INT}{(1 + k_d)^1} + \cdots + \frac{INT}{(1 + k_d)^{n_c}} + \frac{Call\ price}{(1 + k_d)^{n_c}} = INT\left[\frac{1 - \dfrac{1}{(1 + k_d)^{n_c}}}{k_d}\right] + \left(\begin{matrix}Call \\ price\end{matrix}\right)\left[\frac{1}{(1 + k_d)^{n_c}}\right]$$

Here n_c is the number of years until the company can call the bond; call price is the price the company must pay in order to call the bond (it is often set equal to the par value plus one year's interest); and k_d is the yield to call (YTC). To solve for the YTC, proceed as you would to solve for the yield to maturity of a bond. For example, suppose Unilate's 10 percent coupon bonds, which have a current price of $1,164.88, are callable in nine years at $1,100. The setup for computing the YTC is:

$$1,164.88 = \frac{100}{(1 + k_d)^1} + \cdots + \frac{100}{(1 + k_d)^9} + \frac{1,100}{(1 + k_d)^9}$$

Using your calculator, you would find the solution for the yield to call is 8.14 percent.

ple) rate of interest is 8 percent with semiannual compounding, the value of this 14-year bond is found as follows:[10]

$$V_d = 50\left[\frac{1 - \frac{1}{(1.04)^{28}}}{0.04}\right] + 1,000\left[\frac{1}{(1.04)^{28}}\right]$$

$$= 50(16.66306) + 1,000(0.33348)$$

$$= 833.15 + 333.48 = 1,163.63$$

With a financial calculator, enter N = 28, I/k = k_d = 4, PMT = INT = 50, FV = 1,000, and then compute PV = –1,166.63.

The value with semiannual interest payments is slightly higher than $1,164.88, the value when interest is paid annually. This higher value occurs because interest payments are received, and therefore can be reinvested, somewhat faster under semiannual compounding.

Students sometimes want to discount the *maturity (par) value* at 8 percent over 14 years rather than at 4 percent over 28 six-month periods. This is incorrect. Logically, all cash flows in a given contract must be discounted at the same periodic rate—the 4 percent semiannual rate in this instance—because this is the opportunity rate for the investor. For consistency, bond traders must use the same discount rate for all cash flows, including the cash flow to be received at maturity.

Interest Rate Risk on a Bond

As we saw in Chapter 2, interest rates go up and down over time. Changes in interest rates affect bondholders in two ways. First, an increase in interest rates leads to a decline in the values of outstanding bonds. Because interest rates can rise, bondholders face the risk of losses in the values of their portfolios. This risk is called **interest rate price risk.** Second, many bondholders, including such institutional bondholders as pension funds and life insurance companies, buy bonds to build funds for some future use. These bondholders reinvest the cash flows, which include interest payments plus repayment of principal when the bonds mature or are called. If interest rates decline, the bondholders will earn a lower rate of return on reinvested cash flows, which will reduce the future value of their portfolios relative to the values they would have had if interest rates had not fallen. This is called **interest rate reinvestment risk.**

We see, then, that any given change in interest rates has two separate effects on bondholders: It changes the current values of their portfolios (price risk), and it also changes the rates of return at which the cash flows from their portfolios can be reinvested (reinvestment risk). These two risks tend to offset one another. For example, an increase in interest rates will lower the *current* value of a bond portfolio. But, because the future cash flows produced by the portfolio will then be reinvested at a

INTEREST RATE PRICE RISK

The risk of changes in bond prices to which investors are exposed due to changing interest rates.

INTEREST RATE REINVESTMENT RISK

The risk that income from a bond portfolio will vary because cash flows have to be reinvested at current market rates.

---

[10]We are also assuming a change in the effective annual interest rate, from 8 percent to EAR = $(1.04)^2 - 1 = 1.0816 - 1 = 0.0816 = 8.16\%$. Most bonds pay interest semiannually, and the rates quoted are simple rates compounded semiannually. Therefore, effective annual rates for most bonds are somewhat higher than the quoted rates, which, in effect, represent the APRs for the bonds.

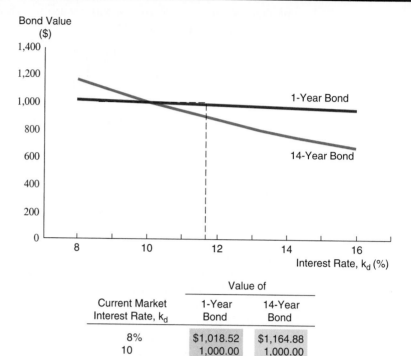

FIGURE 5-3 Value of Long- and Short-Term 10% Annual Coupon Rate Bonds at Different Market Interest Rates (k_d)

Current Market Interest Rate, k_d	Value of	
	1-Year Bond	14-Year Bond
8%	$1,018.52	$1,164.88
10	1,000.00	1,000.00
12	982.14	867.44
14	964.91	759.92
16	948.28	671.95

higher rate of return, the *future* value of the portfolio will be increased. In this section we will look at just how these two effects operate to affect bondholders' positions.[11]

Suppose you bought some of Unilate Textiles' 10 percent (annual payments), 14-year bonds at a price of $1,000, and interest rates subsequently rose to 12 percent. As we saw before, the price of the bonds would fall to $867.44, so you would have a loss equal to $132.56 per bond.[12] Interest rates can and do rise, and rising rates cause a loss of value for bondholders. Thus, people or firms who invest in bonds are exposed to risk from changing interest rates, known as *interest rate risk*.

An investor's exposure to interest rate price risk is higher on bonds with long maturities than on those maturing in the near future. We can demonstrate this fact by showing how the value of a one-year bond with a 10 percent coupon fluctuates with changes in k_d and then comparing these changes with Unilate's 14-year bond. Figure 5–3 shows the values for a one-year bond and Unilate's 14-year bond at several different market

[11]Actually, we will stop far short of a full examination of the effects of interest rate changes on bondholders' positions because such an examination would go well beyond the scope of the text. We can note, however, that a concept called *duration* has been developed to help fixed income investors deal with changing interest rates. With a properly structured portfolio (one that has the proper duration), most of the risks of changing interest rates can be eliminated because price risk and reinvestment risk can be made to exactly offset one another.

[12]You would have an *accounting* (and tax) loss only if you sold the bond; if you held it to maturity, you would not have such a loss. However, even if you did not sell, you would still have suffered a *real economic loss in an opportunity cost sense* because you would have lost the opportunity to invest at 12 percent and would be stuck with a 10 percent bond in a 12 percent market. Thus, in an economic sense "paper losses" are just as bad as realized accounting losses.

interest rates, k_d. The values for the bonds were computed assuming the coupon interest payments for the bonds occur annually. Notice how much more sensitive the price of the long-term bond is to changes in interest rates. At a 10 percent interest rate, both the long- and the short-term bonds are valued at $1,000. If rates rise to 12 percent, the long-term bond falls to $867.44, but the short-term bond falls only to $982.14.

For bonds with similar coupons, this differential sensitivity to changes in interest rates always holds true: *the longer the maturity of the bond, the greater its price changes in response to a given change in interest rates.* Thus, even if the risk of default on two bonds is exactly the same, the one with the longer maturity is typically exposed to more price risk from a change in interest rates.[13]

The logical explanation for this difference in interest rate price risk is simple. Suppose you bought a 14-year bond that yielded 10 percent, or $100 a year. Now suppose interest rates on comparable-risk bonds rose to 12 percent. You would be stuck with only $100 of interest for the next 14 years. On the other hand, had you bought a one-year bond, you would have had a low return for only one year. At the end of the year, you would get your $1,000 back, and you could then reinvest it and receive 12 percent, or $120 per year, for the next 13 years. Thus, interest rate price risk reflects the length of time one is committed to a given investment.

Although a one-year bond has less interest rate price risk than a 14-year bond, the one-year bond exposes the buyer to more interest rate reinvestment risk. Suppose you bought a one-year bond that yielded 10 percent, and then interest rates on comparable-risk bonds fell to 8 percent. After one year, when you got your $1,000 back, you would have to invest it at only 8 percent, so you would lose $100 − $80 = $20 in annual interest. Had you bought the 14-year bond, you would have continued to receive $100 in annual interest payments even if rates fell. If you reinvested those coupon payments, you would have to accept a lower rate of return, but you would still be much better off than if you had been holding the one-year bond.

Bond Prices in Recent Years

We know from Chapter 2 that interest rates fluctuate, and we have just seen that the prices of outstanding bonds rise and fall inversely with changes in interest rates. When interest rates fall, many firms "refinance" by issuing new, lower-cost debt and using the proceeds to repay higher-cost debt. In 1993, interest rates were low relative to the rates that existed during the previous 15 years. Not surprisingly, firms that had issued higher-cost debt in earlier years refinanced much of their debt at that time. Rates dropped even lower in 2002, to levels that had not been seen in more than 45 years. Again, corporations refinanced much of their debt, replacing it with much cheaper debt. As a result, many of the corporate bonds that exist today were issued in 2002 or later.[14]

Let's assume a company issued a 15-year bond on October 1, 1993, when the market average interest rate on AAA-rated bonds was 6.6 percent. Assume further that this bond still existed in late September 2003. Figure 5–4 shows what has happened to the price since it was issued in 1993, as well as what will happen to the price if interest rates remain constant from October 1, 2003, until the bond matures on September 30, 2008.

---

[13]If a 10-year bond were plotted in Figure 5–3, its curve would lie between those of the 14-year bond and the one-year bond. The curve of a one-month bond would be almost horizontal, indicating that its price would change little in response to an interest rate change, but a perpetuity would have a very steep slope.

[14]In some cases, corporate bonds could not be refinanced at lower rates due to restrictions that existed in the debt contracts or because the firms were not financially sound.

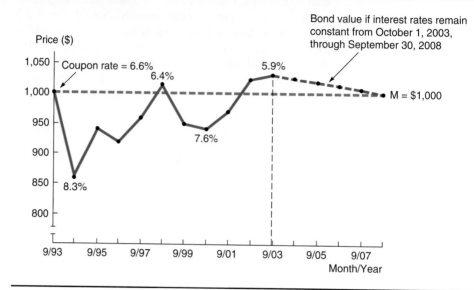

FIGURE 5–4 Value of a $1,000 Bond Issued September 30, 1993, That Matures on September 30, 2008

Because the interest rate on similar risk bonds was 6.6 percent when the bond was originally issued in 1993, the coupon rate of interest was set at 6.6 percent so that the bond was issued at its par value (that is, $1,000). But, as market interest rates changed, so did the value of the bond. Notice from Figure 5–4 that interest rates began to increase, and the value of the bond dropped to $859 (the bond was selling for a discount) one year after it was issued when the market yield on similar bonds was 8.3 percent. Although rates began to decrease in 1995, it wasn't until 1998 that the yield on similar bonds was below the coupon rate of this bond—that is, $k_d = 6.4\% <$ Coupon rate $= 6.6\%$. At this point, the bond was selling for a slight premium because its price was $1,014. In 1999 and 2000 interest rates increased again, before they began to decrease in 2001. The decrease in 2001 was one sign of the economic slowdown that continued through the mid-year 2003, when interest rates began to increase once again.

When you read this book, interest rates might be much higher or much lower than they were in September 2003. But, as Figure 5–4 shows, the value of the bond that was issued in 1993 will continue to approach its par value of $1,000 until the maturity date, at which time the bond's price should be exactly $1,000. This is the case for any corporate bond as long as the issuing firm is financially strong enough to pay both the interest when it is due and the face value of the debt on the maturity date. The prices of other bonds that existed during the period from 1993 through 2003 would have moved similar to the prices of the bond discussed in this example.

Self-Test Questions

What is meant by the terms *new issue* debt and *seasoned issue* debt?

Explain the meaning of the following equation:

$$V_d = \sum_{t=1}^{n} \frac{INT}{(1 + k_d)^t} + \frac{M}{(1 + k_d)^n}$$

Explain what happens to the price of a bond if (1) interest rates rise above the bond's coupon rate or (2) interest rates fall below the bond's coupon rate.

Write out a formula that can be used to calculate the discount or premium on a bond, and explain it.

Differentiate between interest rate price risk and interest rate reinvestment risk.

Differentiate between a bond's yield to maturity and its current yield.

How is the bond valuation formula shown previously changed to deal with bonds that have semiannual coupons rather than annual coupons?

Valuation of Financial Assets—Equity (Stock)

Each corporation issues at least one type of stock, or equity, called *common stock*. Some corporations issue more than one type of common stock, and some issue *preferred stock* in addition to common stock. As the names imply, most equity is in the form of common stock, and preferred shareholders have preference over common shareholders when a firm distributes funds to stockholders. Dividends, as well as liquidation proceeds resulting from bankruptcy, are paid to preferred stockholders before common stockholders. Preferred dividends are similar to interest payments on bonds, because they are fixed in amount and must be paid before common stock dividends can be paid. Common stock dividends, however, can vary and are often dependent on current and previous earnings levels and the future growth plans of the firm. We discuss the characteristics of both common stock and preferred stock in greater detail in later chapters. For the purposes of our discussion in this section, you need to be aware that the cash flows generated by investing in preferred stock are normally constant, whereas the cash flows generated by common stock can be constant but often vary from year to year.

In this section, we examine the process to value stock, both preferred and common. We begin by introducing a general stock valuation model. We then apply the model to three scenarios: (1) when there is no growth in dividends so the amount paid each year remains constant (the same as preferred dividends); (2) when dividends increase at a constant rate each year; and (3) when dividends grow at different rates.

Definitions of Terms Used in the Stock Valuation Models

Stocks provide an expected future cash flow stream, and a stock's value is found in the same manner as the values of other assets—namely, as the present value of the expected future cash flow stream. The expected cash flows consist of two elements: (1) the dividends expected in each year and (2) the price investors expect to receive when they sell the stock, which includes the return of the original investment plus a capital gain or loss. As you will see, when a stock is sold at some time in the future, the selling price is a function of the cash flows (dividends) that investors expect the corporation to distribute for the remainder of its life at that point in time.

Before we present the general stock valuation model, let's define some terms and notations we will use throughout this section.

$\hat{D}_t$ = Dividend the stockholder expects to receive at the end of Year t (pronounced "D hat t"). D_0 is the most recent dividend, which has already been paid; $\hat{D}_1$ is the next dividend expected to be paid, and it will be paid at the end of this year; $\hat{D}_2$ is the dividend expected at the end of Year 2; and so forth. $\hat{D}_1$ represents the first cash flow a new purchaser of the stock will receive. Note that D_0, the dividend that has just been paid, is known with certainty (which explains why there is no "hat" over the D). However, all future dividends are *expected* values, so the estimate of $\hat{D}_t$ might differ among investors for some stocks.[15]

MARKET PRICE, P_0

The price at which a stock sells in the market.

P_0 = Actual **market price** of the stock today.

INTRINSIC VALUE, $\hat{P}_0$

The value of an asset that in the mind of a particular investor is justified by the facts; $\hat{P}_0$ can be different from the asset's current market price, its book value, or both.

$\hat{P}_t$ = Expected price of the stock at the end of Year t. $\hat{P}_0$ is the **intrinsic,** or *theoretical,* **value** of the stock today as seen by the particular investor who is evaluating the stock; $\hat{P}_1$ is the price *expected* at the end of one year; and so on. Note that $\hat{P}_0$ is the intrinsic value of the stock today based on a particular investor's estimate of the stock's expected dividend stream and the riskiness of that stream. Whereas P_0 is fixed and is identical for all investors because it represents the price at which the stock currently can be purchased in the stock market, $\hat{P}_0$ could differ among investors depending on what they feel the firm actually is worth. The "hat" is used to indicate that $\hat{P}_t$ is an estimated value. $\hat{P}_0$, the individual investor's estimate of the intrinsic value today, could be above or below P_0, the current stock price, but an investor would buy the stock only if his or her estimate of $\hat{P}_0$ were equal to or greater than P_0.

Because there are many investors in the market, there can be many values for $\hat{P}_0$. However, we can think of a group of "average," or "marginal," investors whose actions actually determine the market price. For these marginal investors, P_0 must equal $\hat{P}_0$; otherwise, a disequilibrium would exist, and buying and selling in the market would change P_0 until $P_0 = \hat{P}_0$.

GROWTH RATE, g

The expected rate of change in dividends per share.

g = Expected **growth rate** in dividends as predicted by a marginal, or average, investor. (If we assume that dividends are expected to grow at a constant rate, g is also equal to the expected rate of growth in the stock's price.) Different investors might use different growth rates to evaluate a firm's stock, but the market price, P_0, reflects the g estimated by average investors.

REQUIRED RATE OF RETURN, k_s

The minimum rate of return on a stock that stockholders consider acceptable.

k_s = Minimum acceptable, or **required, rate of return** on the stock, considering both its riskiness and the returns available on other investments. Again, this term generally relates to average investors. The determinants of k_s were discussed in detail in Chapter 4.

DIVIDEND YIELD

The expected dividend divided by the current price of a share of stock.

$\dfrac{\hat{D}_1}{P_0}$ = Expected **dividend yield** on the stock during the coming year. If the stock is expected to pay a dividend of $1 during the next 12 months, and if its current price is $10, then the expected dividend yield is $1/$10 = 0.10 = 10%.

CAPITAL GAINS YIELD

The change in price (capital gain) during a given year divided by the price at the beginning of the year.

$\dfrac{\hat{P}_1 - P_0}{P_0}$ = Expected **capital gains yield** on the stock during the coming year. If the stock sells for $10 today, and if it is expected to rise to $10.50 at the end of one year, then the expected capital gain is

---

[15]Stocks generally pay dividends quarterly, so theoretically we should evaluate them on a quarterly basis. However, in stock valuation, most analysts work on an annual basis because the data generally are not precise enough to warrant refinement to a quarterly model.

$\hat{P}_1 - P_0 = \$10.50 - \$10.00 = \$0.50$, and the expected capital gains yield is $\$0.50/\$10 = 0.05 = 5\%$.

$\hat{k}_s$ = **Expected rate of return** that an investor who buys the stock anticipates, or expects to receive. The value of $\hat{k}_s$ could be above or below k_s (required rate of return), but one would buy the stock only if $\hat{k}_s$ was equal to or greater than k_s. $\hat{k}_s$ = expected dividend yield plus expected capital gains yield; in other words,

$$\hat{k}_s = \frac{\hat{D}_1}{P_0} + \frac{\hat{P}_1 - P_0}{P_0}$$

In our example, the expected total return = $\hat{k}_s$ = 10% + 5% = 15%.

k_s = **Actual,** or **realized,** *after the fact* **rate of return.** You might expect to obtain a return of $\hat{k}_s$ = 14 percent if you buy IBM stock today, but if the market goes down, next year you might end up with an actual realized return that is much lower—perhaps even negative. For example, k_s might actually turn out to be 8 percent.

Expected Dividends as the Basis for Stock Values

Remember that according to Equation 5–1 the value of any asset is the present value of the cash flows expected to be generated by the asset in the future. In our discussion of bonds, we found that the value of a bond is the present value of the interest payments over the life of the bond plus the present value of the bond's maturity (or par) value. Stock prices are likewise determined as the present value of a stream of cash flows, and the basic stock valuation equation is similar to the bond valuation equation (Equation 5–2).

What are the cash flows that corporations provide to their stockholders? First, think of yourself as an investor who buys a stock with the intention of holding it (in your family) forever. In this case, all that you (and your heirs) will receive is a stream of dividends, and the value of the stock today is calculated as the present value of an infinite stream of dividends, which is depicted on a cash flow time line as follows:

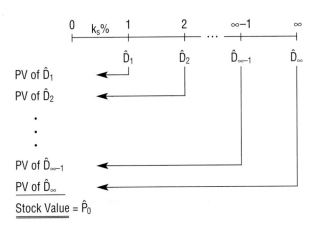

To compute the value of the stock, we must solve the following equation:

> **5–4**
>
> $$\text{Value of stock} = V_s = \hat{P}_0 = \text{PV of expected future dividends}$$
>
> $$= \frac{\hat{D}_1}{\left(1 + k_s\right)^1} + \frac{\hat{D}_2}{\left(1 + k_s\right)^2} + \cdots + \frac{\hat{D}_\infty}{\left(1 + k_s\right)^\infty}$$
>
> $$= \sum_{t=1}^{\infty} \frac{\hat{D}_t}{\left(1 + k_s\right)^t}$$

How do you determine the value of $\hat{P}_0$ when you expect to hold the stock for a specific (finite) period and then sell it, which is the more typical case? Unless the company is likely to be liquidated and thus to disappear, the value of the stock is still determined by Equation 5–4. To see why, recognize that for any individual investor, the expected cash flows consist of expected dividends plus the expected price of the stock when it is sold. However, the sale price the current investor receives will depend on the dividends the future investor expects. As a result, for all present and future investors in total, expected cash flows must be based on all of the expected future dividends. Put another way, unless a firm is liquidated or sold to another company, the cash flows it provides to its stockholders will consist only of a stream of dividends; therefore, the value of a share of its stock at any point in time must be established as the present value of the expected dividend stream that will be paid throughout the remaining life of the company.

The general validity of Equation 5–4 also can be confirmed by considering the following scenario: Suppose you buy a stock and expect to hold it for one year. You will receive dividends during the year plus the value $\hat{P}_1$ when you sell the stock at the end of the year. What will determine the value of $\hat{P}_1$? The answer is that it will be determined as the present value of the dividends during Year 2 plus the stock price at the end of that year, which in turn will be determined as the present value of another set of future dividends and an even more distant stock price. This process can be continued forever, with the ultimate result being Equation 5–4.[16]

Equation 5–4 is a generalized stock valuation model in the sense that over time the value of $\hat{D}_t$ can be anything: It can be rising, falling, constant, or even be fluctuating randomly, and Equation 5–4 will still hold. Often, however, the projected stream of dividends follows a systematic pattern, in which case we can develop a simplified version of the stock valuation model expressed in Equation 5–4. In the following sections we consider the cases of zero growth, constant growth, and nonconstant growth.

---

[16]We should note that investors periodically lose sight of the long-run nature of stocks as investments and forget that in order to sell a stock at a profit, one must find a buyer who will pay the higher price. If you analyzed a stock's value in accordance with Equation 5–4, concluded that the stock's market price exceeded a reasonable value, and then bought the stock anyway, then you would be following the "bigger fool" theory of investment: You think you may be a fool to buy the stock at its excessive price, but you also think that when you get ready to sell it, you can find someone who is an even bigger fool. The bigger fool theory was widely followed in the summer of 1987, just before the stock market lost over one-third of its value in the October 1987 crash. Some believe the bigger fool theory was followed more recently with the buying frenzy that occurred during the late 1990s in the Internet, or "dot.com," stocks.

Valuing Stocks with Zero Growth

ZERO-GROWTH STOCK

A common stock whose future dividends are not expected to grow at all; that is, $g = 0$, and $\hat{D}_1 = \hat{D}_2 = \cdots = \hat{D}_\infty = D_0$.

Suppose a firm's dividends are not expected to grow at all; instead they are expected to stay the same every year. In this case, we have a **zero-growth stock,** for which the dividends expected in future years are equal to some constant amount—the current dividend. That is, $\hat{D}_1 = \hat{D}_2 = \cdots = \hat{D}_\infty = D_0$. Therefore, we can drop the subscripts and the "hats" on D and rewrite Equation 5–4 as follows:

5–4a

$$\hat{P}_0 = \frac{D}{\left(1 + k_s\right)^1} + \frac{D}{\left(1 + k_s\right)^2} + \cdots + \frac{D}{\left(1 + k_s\right)^\infty}$$

As we noted in Chapter 3 in connection with the British consol bond, a security that is expected to pay a constant amount each year forever is called a *perpetuity*. A zero-growth stock is a perpetuity. Recall that the value of any perpetuity is simply the payment amount divided by the discount rate. As a result, the value of a zero-growth stock reduces to the following formula:

5–5

$$\text{Value of zero growth stock} = \hat{P}_0 = \frac{D}{k_s}$$

Suppose we have a stock that is expected to always pay a dividend equal to $1.20, and the required rate of return associated with such an investment is 12 percent. The stock's value should be:[17]

$$\hat{P}_0 = \frac{\$1.20}{0.12} = \$10.00$$

Generally, we can find the price of a stock and the most recent dividend paid to the stockholders by looking in a financial newspaper such as *The Wall Street Journal*. Therefore, if we have a stock with constant dividends, we can solve for the expected rate of return by rearranging Equation 5–5 as follows:

5–5a

$$\hat{k}_s = \frac{D}{P_0}$$

---

[17]If you think that having a stock pay dividends forever is unrealistic, then think of it as lasting only for 50 years. Here you would have an annuity of $1.20 per year for 50 years. The PV of a 50-year annuity of $1.20 with an opportunity rate of interest equal to 12 percent would be $1.20(8.30450) = $9.97, which would differ by only a few pennies from that of the perpetuity. Thus, the dividends from Years 51 to infinity contribute little to the stock's value.

Because we are dealing with an *expected rate of return*, we put a "hat" on the k value. Thus, if you buy a stock at a price of $10 and expected to receive a constant dividend of $1.20, your expected rate of return would be

$$\hat{k}_s = \frac{\$1.20}{\$10.00} = 0.12 = 12.0\%$$

By now, you probably have recognized that Equation 5–5 can be used to value preferred stock. Recall that preferred stocks entitle their owners to regular, or fixed, dividend payments. And, if the payments last forever, the issue is a *perpetuity* whose value is defined by Equation 5–5. We can use Equation 5–5 to value any asset, including common stock, with expected future cash flows that exhibit the properties of a perpetuity—that is, constant cash flows forever.

Valuing Stocks with Normal, or Constant, Growth

NORMAL (CONSTANT) GROWTH

Growth that is expected to continue into the foreseeable future at about the same rate as that of the economy as a whole; g is a constant such that $\hat{D}_t = D_0 (1 + g)^t$.

In general, investors expect the earnings and common stock dividends of most companies to increase each year. Even though expected growth rates vary from company to company, it is not uncommon for investors to expect dividend growth to continue in the foreseeable future at about the same rate as that of the nominal gross national product (real GNP plus inflation). On this basis, we might expect the dividend of an average, or "normal," company to grow at a rate of 3 to 5 percent a year. Thus, if the last dividend paid by a **normal, or constant, growth** company was D_0, the firm's dividend in any future Year t can be forecasted as $\hat{D}_t = D_0(1 + g)^t$, where g is the constant expected rate of growth. For example, if a firm just paid a dividend of $1.20 (that is, $D_0 = \$1.20$), and if investors expect a 5 percent growth rate, then the estimated dividend one year hence would be $\hat{D}_1 = \$1.20(1.05) = \$1.26$; $\hat{D}_2$ would be $\$1.323 = \$1.20(1.05)^2$; and the estimated dividend five years hence would be:

$$\hat{D}_5 = D_0(1 + g)^5 = \$1.20(1.05)^5 = \$1.532$$

Using this method for estimating future dividends, we can determine the current stock value, $\hat{P}_0$, using Equation 5–4. That is, we can find the expected future cash flow stream (the dividends), calculate the present value of each dividend payment, and sum these present values to find the stock's value. The intrinsic value of the stock is then equal to the present value of its expected future dividends.

If g is constant, we can rewrite Equation 5–4 as follows:[18]

5–6

$$\hat{P}_0 = \frac{D_0(1 + g)^1}{(1 + k_s)^1} + \frac{D_0(1 + g)^2}{(1 + k_s)^2} + \cdots + \frac{D_0(1 + g)^\infty}{(1 + k_s)^\infty}$$

$$= \frac{D_0(1 + g)}{k_s - g} = \frac{\hat{D}_1}{k_s - g}$$

[18]The last term in Equation 5–6 is derived in the Extensions section of Chapter 5 of Eugene F. Brigham and Phillip R. Daves, *Intermediate Financial Management*, 8th ed. (Cincinnati, OH: South-Western College Publishing, 2004). In essence, the full-blown version of Equation 5–6 is the sum of a geometric progression, and the last term is the solution value of the progression.

| **FIGURE 5–5** | Present Values of Dividends of a Constant Growth Stock: $D_0 = \$1.20$, $g = 5\%$, $k_s = 12\%$ |

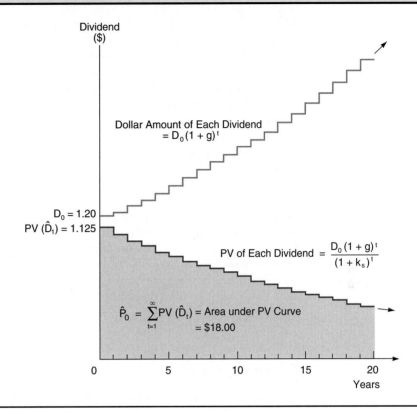

Inserting values into the last version of Equation 5–6, we find the value of our illustrative stock is $18.00:

$$\hat{P}_0 = \frac{\$1.20(1.05)}{0.12 - 0.05} = \frac{\$1.26}{0.07} = \$18.00$$

CONSTANT GROWTH DIVIDEND DISCOUNT MODEL
Also called the Gordon Model, it is used to find the value of a stock that is expected to experience constant growth.

The **constant growth dividend discount model** as set forth in the last term of Equation 5–6 is often called the Gordon Model, after Myron J. Gordon, who did much to develop and popularize it.

Note that Equation 5–6 can be used to value preferred stock. Because preferred stock dividends are constant, the growth (g) rate is zero. If growth is zero, this is simply a special case of constant growth, and Equation 5–6 becomes Equation 5–5. Note also that Equation 5–6 can be applied only if (1) dividends grow at a constant rate every period in the future, and (2) k_s is greater than g. If the equation is used in situations where g is not constant or k_s is not greater than g, the results will be meaningless. For example, when $k_s < g$, the numerator in Equation 5–6 will be negative, and the result of the computation will produce $\hat{P}_0 < 0$, which doesn't make sense in the world of finance.

Figure 5–5 illustrates the concept underlying the valuation process for a constant growth. Dividends are growing at the rate g = 5%. But because $k_s > g$, the present value of each future dividend is declining. For example, the dividend in Year 1 is

$\hat{D}_1 = D_0(1 + g)^1 = \$1.20(1.05) = \$1.26$. However, the present value of this dividend, discounted at 12 percent, is $PV(\hat{D}_1) = \$1.26/(1.12)^1 = \$1.125$. The dividend expected in Year 2 grows to $\$1.26(1.05) = \$1.323$, but the present value of this dividend falls to $\$1.055$. Continuing, $\hat{D}_3 = \$1.389$ and $PV(\hat{D}_3) = \$0.989$, and so on. Thus, the expected dividends are growing, but the present value of each successive dividend is declining because the dividend growth rate—5 percent—is less than the rate used for discounting the dividends to the present—12 percent.

If we sum the present values of each future dividend, this summation would be the value of the stock, $\hat{P}_0$. When g is a constant, this summation is equal to $\hat{D}_1 /(k_s - g)$, as shown in Equation 5–6. Therefore, if we extend the lower step function curve in Figure 5–5 on out to infinity and added up the present values of each future dividend, the summation would be identical to the value given by Equation 5–6—that is, $18.

Growth in dividends occurs primarily as a result of growth in *earnings per share (EPS)*. Earnings growth, in turn, results from a number of factors, including (1) inflation, (2) the amount of earnings the company retains and reinvests, and (3) the rate of return the company earns on its equity (ROE). Regarding inflation, if output (in units) is stable and if both sales prices and input costs rise at the inflation rate, then EPS will also grow at the inflation rate. EPS also will grow as a result of the reinvestment, or plowback, of earnings. If the firm's earnings are not all paid out as dividends (that is, if some fraction of earnings is retained), the dollars of investment behind each share will rise over time, which should lead to growth in future earnings and dividends.

Expected Rate of Return on a Constant Growth Stock

We can solve Equation 5–6 for $\hat{k}_s$, again using the hat to denote that we are dealing with an expected rate of return:[19]

5–7				
Expected rate of return	=	Expected dividend yield	+	Expected growth rate, or capital gains yield
$\hat{k}_s$	=	$\dfrac{\hat{D}_1}{P_0}$	+	g

For example, let's assume you buy a stock for a price $P_0 = \$18$, and you expect the stock to pay a dividend $\hat{D}_1 = \$1.26$ one year from now. The company is expected to grow at a constant rate g = 5% in the future. In this case, your expected rate of return will be 12 percent:

---

[19]The k_s value of Equation 5–6 is a *required* rate of return, but when we transform Equation 5–6 to obtain Equation 5–7, we are finding an *expected* rate of return. Obviously, the transformation requires that $k_s = \hat{k}_s$. This equality holds if the stock market is in equilibrium, a condition that will be discussed later in the chapter.

$$\hat{k}_s = \frac{\$1.26}{\$18.00} + 0.05 = 0.07 + 0.05 = 0.12 = 12.0\%$$

In this form, we see that $\hat{k}_s$ is the *expected total return* (12 percent), which consists of an *expected dividend yield*, $\hat{D}_1/P_0 = 7\%$, plus an *expected growth rate or capital gains yield*, $g = 5\%$.

Suppose we had conducted this analysis on January 1, 2005. That is, $P_0 = \$18$ is the January 1, 2005 stock price and $\hat{D}_1 = \$1.26$ is the dividend expected at the end of 2005 (December 31). What is the expected stock price at the end of 2005 (or the beginning of 2006)? We would again apply Equation 5–6, but this time we would use the expected 2006 dividend, $\hat{D}_{2006} = \hat{D}_2 = \hat{D}_1(1 + g) = \$1.26(1.05) = \$1.323$:

$$\hat{P}_{1/1/06} = \frac{\hat{D}_{2006}}{k_s - g} = \frac{\$1.323}{0.12 - 0.05} = \$18.90$$

Notice that $\$18.90$ is 5 percent greater than P_0, the $18 price on January 1, 2005:

$$P_{1/1/06} = \$18.00(1.05) = \$18.90$$

In this case, we would expect to make a capital gain of $\$18.90 - \$18.00 = \$0.90$ during the year, which is a capital gains yield of 5 percent:

$$\text{Capital gain yield }_{2005} = \frac{\text{Captial gain}}{\text{Beginning price}} = \frac{\text{Ending price} - \text{Beginning price}}{\text{Beginning price}}$$

$$= \frac{\$18.90 - \$18.00}{\$18.00} = \frac{\$0.90}{\$18.00} = 0.05 = 5.0\%$$

We could extend the analysis further, and in each future year the expected capital gains yield would equal $g = 5\%$, the expected dividend growth rate. Continuing, we could estimate the dividend yield in 2006 as follows:

$$\text{Dividend yield }_{2006} = \frac{\hat{D}_{2006}}{P_{1/1/06}} = \frac{\$1.323}{\$18.90} = 0.07 = 7.0\%$$

The dividend yield for 2007 could also be calculated, and again it would be 7 percent. Thus, for a constant growth stock, the following conditions must hold:

1. The dividend is expected to grow forever at a constant rate, g.
2. The stock price is expected to grow at this same rate, g. As a result, the expected capital gains yield is also a constant, and it is equal to g.
3. The expected dividend yield is a constant.
4. The expected total rate of return, $\hat{k}_s$, is equal to the expected dividend yield plus the expected growth rate: $\hat{k}_s = \text{dividend yield} + g$.

We should clarify the meaning of the term *expected*. It means expected in a probabilistic sense, as the statistically expected outcome. Thus, if we say the growth rate is expected to remain constant at 5 percent, we mean that the best prediction for the growth rate in any future year is 5 percent, not that we literally expect the growth rate to be exactly equal to 5 percent in each future year. In this sense, the constant growth assumption is a reasonable one for many large, mature companies.

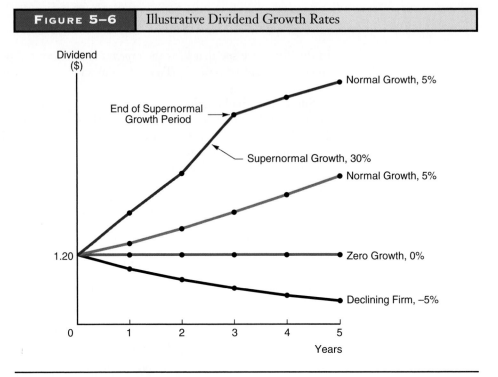

FIGURE 5-6 | Illustrative Dividend Growth Rates

Valuing Stocks with Nonconstant Growth

Firms typically go through life cycles. During the early part of their lives, their growth is much faster than that of the economy as a whole. Later, their growth matches the economy's growth. And, in the final stage of their lives, growth is slower than that of the economy.[20] Automobile manufacturers in the 1920s and computer software firms such as Microsoft in the 1990s are examples of firms in the early part of the cycle. Other firms, such as those in the tobacco industry or coal industry, are currently in the waning stages of their life cycles, so their growth is not keeping pace with the general economic growth (in some cases growth actually is negative). Firms with growth rates that do not match the economy's growth are called **nonconstant growth** firms. Figure 5–6 illustrates nonconstant growth and also compares it with normal, or constant, growth and zero growth.[21]

NONCONSTANT GROWTH

The part of the life cycle of a firm in which growth either is much faster or much slower than that of the economy as a whole.

---

[20]The concept of life cycles could be broadened to *product cycle*, which would include both small, start-up companies and large companies like IBM, which periodically introduce new products that give sales and earnings a boost. We should also mention *business cycles*, which alternately depress and boost sales and profits. The growth rate just after a major new product has been introduced, or just after a firm emerges from the depths of a recession, is likely to be much higher than the "expected long-run average growth rate," which is the proper value to use for evaluating the project.

[21]A negative growth rate indicates a declining company. A mining company whose profits are falling because of a declining ore body is an example. Someone buying such a company would expect its earnings, and consequently its dividends and stock price, to decline each year, and this would lead to capital losses rather than capital gains. Obviously, a declining company's stock price will be relatively low, and its dividend yield must be high enough to offset the expected capital loss and still produce a competitive total return. Investors sometimes argue that they would not be willing to buy a stock whose price was expected to decline. However, if the annual dividends are large enough to *more than offset* the falling stock price, the stock could still provide a good return.

In the figure, the dividends of the supernormal growth (growth much greater than the economy's growth) firm are expected to grow at a 30 percent rate for three years, after which the growth rate is expected to fall to 5 percent, the assumed average for the economy. The value of this firm, like any other, is the present value of its expected future dividends as determined by Equation 5–4. In the case in which $\hat{D}_t$ is growing at a constant rate, we simplified Equation 5–4 to $\hat{P}_0 = \hat{D}_1/(k_s - g)$. In the supernormal case, however, the expected growth rate is not a constant—it declines at the end of the period of supernormal growth. To find the value of such a stock, or of any nonconstant growth stock when the growth rate will eventually stabilize, we proceed in three steps:

1. Compute the value of the dividends affected by nonconstant growth, and then find the PV of these dividends.
2. Find the price of the stock *at the end of the nonconstant growth period, at which point it becomes a constant growth stock*. Equation 5–6 can be used at this point to calculate $\hat{P}_t$ because future dividends will grow at a constant rate. $\hat{P}_t$ would be computed as follows:

$$\hat{P}_t = \frac{\hat{D}_t\left(1 + g_{norm}\right)}{k_s - g_{norm}}$$

   Discount $\hat{P}_t$ back to the present.
3. Add these two components to find the intrinsic value of the stock, $\hat{P}_0$.

Figure 5–7 can be used to illustrate the process for valuing nonconstant growth stocks, assuming the following facts exist:

k_s = Stockholders' required rate of return = 12%. This rate is used to discount the cash flows.

n_{super} = Years of supernormal growth = 3.

g_{super} = Rate of growth in both earnings and dividends during the supernormal growth period = 30%. (*Note:* The growth rate during the supernormal growth period could vary from year to year. Also, there could be several different supernormal growth periods—for example, 30% for three years, 20% for two years, and then a constant rate.) This rate is shown directly on the time line.

g_{norm} = Rate of normal, constant growth after the supernormal period = 5%. This rate is also shown on the cash flow time line, after Year 3.

D_0 = Last (most recently paid) dividend the company paid = $1.20.

The valuation process as diagrammed in Figure 5–7 is explained in the steps set forth below the cash flow time line. The value of the supernormal growth stock is calculated to be $33.03.

Self-Test Questions

What are the two elements of a stock's expected return?

Write out and explain the valuation model for a zero growth stock.

Write out and explain the valuation model for a constant growth stock.

How does one calculate the capital gains yield and the dividend yield of a stock?

Explain how one would find the value of a stock with nonconstant growth.

FIGURE 5-7	Process for Finding the Value of a Nonconstant Growth Stock

$$
\begin{array}{c}
0 \quad g_s = 30\% \quad 1 \qquad\qquad 2 \qquad\qquad 3 \quad g_n = 5\% \quad 4 \qquad\qquad 20 \\
\hat{D}_1 = 1.5600 \quad \hat{D}_2 = 2.0280 \quad \hat{D}_3 = 2.6364 \quad \hat{D}_4 = 2.7682 \quad \hat{D}_{20} = 6.0427 \\
1.3929 \leftarrow \underline{12\%} \\
1.6167 \leftarrow \underline{12\%} \\
30.0244 \leftarrow \underline{12\%} \\
\underline{33.0340} \approx \mathbf{\$33.03} = \hat{P}_0 \\
\hat{P}_3 = \underline{39.5457} \\
42.1821
\end{array}
$$

Step 1. Calculate the dividends for each year during the nonconstant growth period—$\hat{D}_t = D_0(1 + g_s)^t$:

$$\hat{D}_1 = \hat{D}_3(1 + g_{norm})^1 = \$1.20(1.30)^1 = \$1.5600$$

$$\hat{D}_2 = \hat{D}_3(1 + g_{norm})^2 = \$1.20(1.30)^2 = \$2.0280$$

$$\hat{D}_3 = \hat{D}_3(1 + g_{norm})^3 = \$1.20(1.30)^3 = \$2.6364$$

Show these values on the cash flow time line as cash flows for Years 1 through 3.

Step 2. The price of the stock is the PV of dividends from Year 1 to infinity. So, in theory, we could continue projecting each future dividend beyond Year 3, when normal growth of 5 percent occurs. In other words, use $g_{norm} = 5\%$ to compute $\hat{D}_4$, $\hat{D}_5$, and so on with $\hat{D}_3$ as the base dividend for normal growth:

$$\hat{D}_4 = \$2.6364(1.05)^1 = \$2.7682$$

$$\hat{D}_5 = \$2.6364(1.05)^2 = \$2.9066$$

$$\cdot$$
$$\cdot$$
$$\cdot$$

$$\hat{D}_{20} = \$2.6364(1.05)^{17} = \$6.0427$$

We can continue this process and then find the PV of this stream of dividends. However, we know that after $\hat{D}_3$ has been paid in Year 3, the stock becomes a constant growth stock, so we can apply the constant growth formula at that point and find $\hat{P}_3$, which is the PV of the dividends from Year 4 through infinity as evaluated in Year 3. After the Year 3 dividend has been paid, all of the future dividends will grow at a constant rate equal to 5 percent, so

$$\hat{P}_3 = \frac{\hat{D}_4}{k_s - g_{norm}} = \frac{\$2.7682}{0.12 - 0.05} = \$39.5457$$

We show this $39.5457 on the cash flow time line as a second cash flow at Year 3. The $39.5457 is a Year 3 cash flow in the sense that the owner of the stock could sell it for $39.5457 at the end of Year 3, and also in the sense that $39.5457 is the present value equivalent of the dividend cash flows from Year 4 to infinity. Therefore, the *total cash flow* we recognize in Year 3 is the sum of $\hat{D}_3 + \hat{P}_3 = \$2.6364 + \$39.5457 = \$42.1821$.

Step 3. Now that the cash flows have been placed on the cash flow time line, we need to discount each cash flow at the required rate of return, $k_s = 12\%$. To find the present value, you either compute the PVs directly, or use the cash flow registers on your calculator. You can compute the PVs directly by dividing each cash flow by $(1.12)^t$. If you use the cash flow registers on your calculator, input $CF_0 = 0$, $CF_1 = 1.5600$, $CF_2 = 2.0280$, $CF_3 = 42.1821$, $I = 12$. The result, 33.0340, is shown to the left below the cash flow time line.

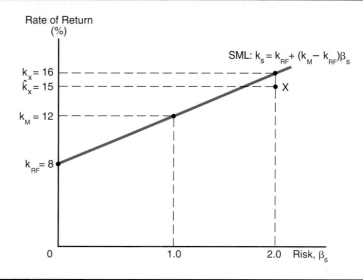

FIGURE 5–8   Expected and Required Returns on Stock X

Stock Market Equilibrium

Recall from Chapter 4 that the required return on a stock, k_s, can be found using the security market line (SML) equation as it was developed in our discussion of the capital asset pricing model (CAPM):

$$k_s = k_{RF} + (k_M - k_{RF})\beta_s$$

If the risk-free rate of return, k_{RF}, is 8 percent, the market risk premium, $k_m - k_{RF}$, is 4 percent, and Stock X has a beta coefficient of $\beta_x = 2$, then the marginal investor will require a return of 16 percent on Stock X, calculated as follows:

$$k_X = 8\% + (12\% - 8\%)2.0 = 16\%$$

This 16 percent required return is shown as a point on the SML in Figure 5–8.

The average investor will want to buy Stock X if the expected rate of return ($\hat{k}_X$) is more than 16 percent, will want to sell it if the expected rate of return is less than 16 percent, and will be indifferent, hence will hold but not buy or sell, if the expected rate of return is exactly 16 percent. Now suppose the investor's portfolio contains Stock X, and he or she analyzes the stock's prospects and concludes that its earnings, dividends, and price can be expected to grow at a constant rate of 5 percent per year. The last dividend was $D_0 = \$2.86$, so the next expected dividend is $\hat{D}_1 = \$2.86(1.05) = \$3.00$. Our average investor observes that the present price of the stock, P_0, is $30. Should he or she purchase more of Stock X, sell the present holdings, or maintain the present position?

The investor can calculate Stock X's *expected rate of return* as follows:

$$\hat{k}_X = \frac{\hat{D}_1}{P_0} + g = \frac{\$3.00}{\$30.00} + 0.05 = 0.15 = 15.0\%$$

This value is plotted on Figure 5–8 as Point X, which is below the SML. Because the expected rate of return ($\hat{k}_X = 15\%$) is less than the required return ($k_s = 16\%$), this marginal investor would want to sell the stock, as would other holders. However, few people would want to buy at the $30 price, so the present owners would be unable to find buyers unless they cut the price of the stock. Thus, the price would decline, and this decline would continue until the stock's price reached $27.27, at which point the market for this security would be in **equilibrium,** because the expected rate of return, 16 percent, would be equal to the required rate of return:

EQUILIBRIUM
The condition under which the expected return on a security is just equal to its required return, $\hat{k}_s$ = k_s, and the price is stable.

$$\hat{k}_X = \frac{\$3.00}{\$27.27} + 0.05 = 0.11 + 0.05 = 0.16 = 16.0\% = k_s$$

Had the stock initially sold for less than $27.27, say at $25, events would have been reversed. Investors would have wanted to buy the stock because its expected rate of return ($\hat{k}_X$ =17% if P_0 = $25) would have exceeded its required rate of return, and buy orders would have driven the stock's price up to $27.27.

To summarize, in equilibrium these two conditions must hold:

1. The expected rate of return as seen by the marginal investor must equal the required rate of return: $\hat{k}_X = k_X$.
2. The actual market price of the stock must equal its intrinsic value as estimated by the marginal investor: $P_0 = \hat{P}_0$.

Of course, some individual investors might believe that $\hat{k}_X > k_X$ and $P_0 < \hat{P}_0$, and hence they would invest most of their funds in the stock, while other investors might have an opposite view and would sell all of their shares. However, the marginal investor establishes the actual market price, and for this investor, $\hat{k}_X = k_X$ and $P_0 = \hat{P}_0$. If these conditions do not hold, trading—that is, buying or selling the stock—will occur until they do hold.

Changes in Equilibrium Stock Prices

Stock market prices are not constant—they undergo violent changes at times. For example, on October 19, 1987, the Dow Jones Industrial Average (DJIA) dropped 508 points, and the average stock lost about 23 percent of its value in just one day. Some stocks lost more than half of their value that day. More recently, from March 9, 2001, through March 22, 2001, the DJIA decreased by more than 1,255 points, which resulted in a decrease in the value of the average stock of nearly 12 percent. Not long after, during April 2001, the DJIA increased by almost 1,300 points, and the average stock increased by nearly 14 percent.

To see how such changes can occur, let's take another look at Stock X, which would sell at a price of $27.27 per share under the conditions presented earlier. Now consider what would happen to the price of Stock X if the value of any of the variables used to compute the current price changes. For instance, how would the price be affected if investors demand a higher rate of return—say, 20 percent rather than 16 percent? If we change the value of k_s to 20 percent in the previous computation, we find that the value of Stock X would be:

$$\hat{P}_0 = \frac{\hat{D}_1}{k_s - g} = \frac{\$2.86(1.05)}{0.20 - 0.05} = \frac{\$3.00}{0.15} = \$20.00$$

The new price is lower because investors demand a higher return for receiving the same future cash flows.

Great Expectations! But, What about the Results?

Do investors really value stocks based on the cash flows they expect to receive from owning stocks? To answer this question, consider what happens to stocks' values when companies report earnings that differ from what investors previously expected. Prices adjust accordingly—that is, if earnings are less than expected, prices fall, and vice versa. Although earnings are not fully representative of the cash flows generated by firms, investors rely on earnings forecasts to form their expectations of future dividend payments because dividends are paid from earnings.

Home Depot, Inc., the world's largest retail home improvement company, recently discovered how earnings expectations and stock value are related. In August 2003, Home Depot reported that earnings had increased 10 percent compared to the same period the previous year. Good news. Right? Then, why did the price of Home Depot's stock fall more than 5 percent on the same day? The primary reason was that Home Depot actually lost market share to its biggest rival, Lowe's. Although sales and profits increased, much of the growth in profits occurred because Home Depot decreased its profit margin. In addition, sales growth at Lowe's was three times greater than at Home Depot, which suggested that Home Depot was not "winning back" customers it had lost to Lowe's earlier. Further, at about the same time, Lowe's increased its earnings forecast for the remainder of the year, whereas Home Depot did not. As a result, on the same day the price of Home Depot's stock declined more than 5 percent, the price of Lowe's stock increased by nearly 1.5 percent. In the minds of the investors then, expectations about future earnings prospects were adjusted downward for Home Depot and upward for Lowe's. These expectations caused investors to modify their forecasts concerning the potential cash flows the companies would be able to generate in the future, and the stocks' values were adjusted accordingly.

If you are familiar with Home Depot and Lowe's, you know that the products offered by the two companies are nearly identical. But, Home Depot has been losing customers to Lowe's in recent years, which caused its stock price to decline dramatically from 1999 to 2003.* For this reason, Home Depot is trying to regain these lost customers by making some substantial changes in its business, including remodeling the stores, offering more conveniences to customers, centralizing its marketing efforts, and hiring more professional, full-time employees. The effect such a transformation will ultimately have on Home Depot's stock price is based on whether future earnings reported by the "new" Home Depot exceed (or fall short of) *investors' expectations.* Time will tell.

At the same time Home Depot announced higher earnings only to see its stock price decline, Staples Inc., a large office supply company, saw the price of its stock increase 11 percent when it announced that earnings had increased 47 percent compared to the same period one year earlier. The fact that the price of Staples stock increased 11 percent in one day indicates that the earnings report surprised investors. In this case, earnings were expected to grow, but not by as much as was announced in August 2003. As a result, investors viewed the announcement as good news and thus changed their expectations about future earnings. Earnings forecasts were adjusted upward because the existing earnings base had increased from where it was prior to the current announcement. And, because the revised expectations were more positive than previously, the stock price was adjusted upward.

As these examples illustrate, and as we discuss in this chapter, valuation should be based on the present value of the future cash flows generated by an asset. As a result, when cash flow expectations change, so does value. When valuing stock, the future cash flows are in the form of dividends, which are paid from earnings. Thus, when earnings forecasts (expectations) change, so do dividends expectations, which results in a change in the value of a firm's stock.

*The price of Home Depot's stock declined more than 50 percent during this period. However, some of this decline resulted from a poor economy.

How would the price change if the expected cash flows differ, but the required rate of return is the same as in the original situation—that is, $k_s = 16\%$? Consider the effect if the company's growth rate is 4 percent rather than 5 percent:

$$\hat{P}_0 = \frac{\hat{D}_1}{k_s - g} = \frac{\$2.86(1.04)}{0.16 - 0.04} = \frac{\$2.97}{0.12} = \$24.75$$

Again, the new price is lower. In this case, however, the price is lower because investors demand the same return as before, but the cash flows (dividends) that the stock is expected to provide are smaller than expected previously.

From this simple example, you should have concluded that changes in stock prices occur because (1) investors change the rates of return they require to invest in stocks or (2) expectations about the cash flows associated with stocks change. From this example, we can generalize how such changes affect stock prices: *Stock prices move opposite changes in rates of return, but they move the same as changes in future cash flows expected from the stock in the future.* Therefore, if investors demand higher (lower) returns to invest in stocks, prices or values should fall (increase). If investors expect their investments to generate lower (higher) future cash flows, prices also should fall (increase).

What do you think would happen to the price of Microsoft's stock if Bill Gates announced that the company's future growth opportunities looked to be better than previously expected? Because most investors would interpret such an announcement as "good news" concerning future cash flows—specifically that future cash flows should be higher than previously anticipated—you should expect the price of Microsoft to increase.

Evidence suggests that stocks, especially those of large companies like Microsoft, adjust rapidly to disequilibrium situations—that is, changes in expectations, such as required rates of return and future cash flows. Consequently, equilibrium ordinarily exists for any given stock, and, in general, required and expected returns are equal—that is $k_s = \hat{k}_s$. Stock prices certainly change, sometimes violently and rapidly, but this simply reflects changing conditions and expectations. There are, of course, times when a stock continues to react for several months to a favorable or unfavorable development, but this does not signify a long adjustment period; rather, it simply illustrates that as more new pieces of information about the situation become available, the market adjusts to them. The ability of the market to adjust to new information is discussed next.

The Efficient Markets Hypothesis (EMH)

INFORMATIONAL EFFICIENCY
Prices of investments reflect existing information.

The prices of investments bought and sold in the financial markets are based on available information. If the prices of investments reflect existing information and adjust quickly when new information becomes available, then the financial markets have achieved **informational efficiency.** When the financial markets have a large number of participants in search of the most profitable investments, informational efficiency generally exists. For instance, in the United States, millions of individual investors, along with more than 100,000 highly trained professionals, participate in the financial markets, so you would expect investment prices to adjust almost instantaneously to new information because a large number of the market participants will evaluate the new information as soon as possible in an effort to find more profitable investments.

EFFICIENT MARKETS HYPOTHESIS (EMH)
The hypothesis that securities are typically in equilibrium—that is, they are fairly priced in the sense that the price reflects all publicly available information on each security.

One body of theory, called the **efficient markets hypothesis (EMH),** holds (1) that stocks are always in equilibrium and (2) that it is impossible for an investor to *consistently* "beat the market." *Beat the market* means to earn a return that is greater than should be earned based on the risk associated with the investment. This return

ABNORMAL RETURN

A return that is greater than should be earned based on the riskiness of the investment.

generally is called an **abnormal return.** According to the EMH, there generally are three forms, or levels, of information efficiency in the market:

1. *Weak-form* efficiency states that all information contained in past price movements is fully reflected in current market prices. Therefore, information about recent, or past, trends in investment prices is of no use in selecting "winning" investments—the fact that an investment has risen for the past three days, for example, gives us no useful clues as to what it will do today or tomorrow.

2. *Semistrong-form* efficiency states that current market prices reflect all *publicly available* information. If this is true, it does no good to pore over such published data as a corporation's financial statements because market prices will have adjusted to any good or bad news contained in such reports as soon as they were made public. However, insiders—say, the presidents of companies—even under semistrong-form efficiency, can still make abnormal returns on their own companies' investments (stocks).

3. *Strong-form* efficiency states that current market prices reflect all pertinent information, whether publicly available or privately held. If this form of efficiency holds, even insiders would find it impossible to earn abnormal returns in the financial markets.[22]

The informational efficiency of the financial markets has received a great deal of attention. The results of most market efficiency studies suggest that the financial markets are highly efficient in the weak form and reasonably efficient in the semi-strong form, but strong-form efficiency does not hold.

Financial markets that are informationally efficient also tend to be economically efficient because investors can expect prices to reflect appropriate information and thus make intelligent choices about which investments are expected to provide the best returns. As a result, funds should be allocated to their optimal use at the lowest costs.

What bearing does the EMH have on financial decisions? Because stock prices do seem to reflect public information, most stocks appear to be fairly valued. This does not mean that new developments could not cause a stock's price to soar or to plummet, but it does mean that stocks, in general, are fairly priced, and the prices probably are in equilibrium—that is, it is safe to assume, $\hat{k}_s = k_s$ and $P_0 = \hat{P}_0$. However, there certainly are cases in which corporate insiders have information not known to outsiders.

Actual Stock Prices and Returns

Our discussion to this point has focused on expected stock prices and expected rates of return. Anyone who has ever invested in the stock market knows that there can be, and there generally are, large differences between expected and realized prices and returns.

Figure 5–9 shows how the price of an average share of stock (using the S&P 500 Index) has varied during the past few decades, and Figure 5–10 shows how total annual realized returns have varied. The market trend historically has been strongly up, but it has gone up in some years and down in others. Likewise, the stocks of individual companies have gone up and down. Theory tells us that expected returns as estimated by a marginal investor are always positive. In some years, however, as Figure 5–10 shows, negative returns have been realized. Of course, some individual

---

[22]Several cases of illegal insider trading have made the news headlines in the past.

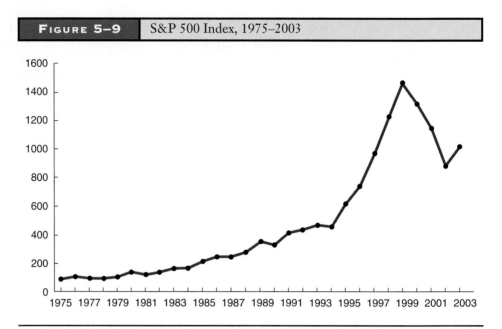

| FIGURE 5-9 | S&P 500 Index, 1975–2003 |

Note: Each data point represents the value of the S&P 500 Index on the last trading day of the year.

Source: Standard & Poor's; www.standardandpoors.com

companies do well even in bad years, such as the bear market that existed from 2000 through 2002, so the name of the game in securities analysis is to pick the winners. Financial managers attempt to take actions that will put their companies into the winners' column, but they don't always succeed. In subsequent chapters, we will examine the actions that managers can take to increase the odds of their firms doing relatively well in the marketplace.

Self-Test Questions

When a stock is in equilibrium, what two conditions must hold?

What is the major conclusion of the efficient markets hypothesis (EMH)?

What is the difference between the three forms of the EMH: (1) weak form, (2) semistrong form, and (3) strong form?

If a stock is not in equilibrium, explain how financial markets adjust to bring it into equilibrium.

Valuation of Real (Tangible) Assets

In the previous sections, we found that the values of financial assets—bonds and stocks—are based on the present value of the future cash flows expected from the assets. Valuing real assets is no different. We need to compute the present value of the expected cash flows associated with the asset. For example, suppose Unilate Tex-

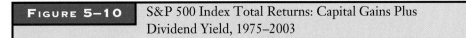

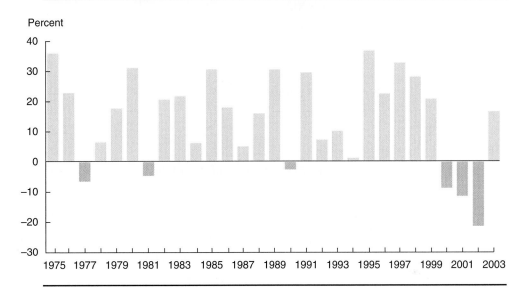

Note: S&P 500 data are from the last trading day of the year. Thus, total return is defined as the percent change in the S&P 500 Index from the beginning of the year to the end of the year plus the annual dividend yield.

Source: Standard & Poor's; www.standardandpoors.com

tiles is considering purchasing a machine so that it can manufacture a new line of products. After five years, the machine will be worthless because it will be used up. But during the five years Unilate uses the machine, the firm will be able to increase its net cash flows by the following amounts:

Year	Expected Cash Flow, $\hat{CF}_t$
1	$120,000
2	100,000
3	150,000
4	80,000
5	50,000

If Unilate wants to earn a 14 percent return on investments like this machine, what is the value of the machine to the company? To find the answer, we need to solve for the present value of the uneven cash flow stream produced by the machine. Thus, the value of this machine can be depicted as follows:

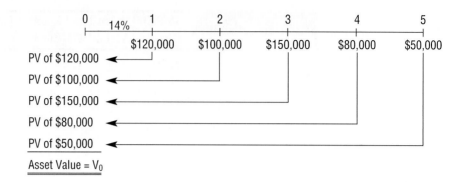

To compute the value of the machine, we apply Equation 5–1:

$$V_0 = \begin{array}{l}\text{Present value}\\ \text{of future CF}\end{array} = \frac{\$120,000}{(1.14)^1} + \frac{\$100,000}{(1.14)^2} + \frac{\$150,000}{(1.14)^3} + \frac{\$80,000}{(1.14)^4} + \frac{\$50,000}{(1.14)^5}$$

$$= \$105,263.16 + \$76,946.75 + \$101,245.73 + \$47,366.42$$

$$+ \$25,968.43$$

$$= \$356,790.49$$

To find the answer using your financial calculator, you must input the individual cash flows, in chronological order, into the cash flow register as we described in Chapter 3 (see Appendix 3D for instructions). According to the cash flow time line, the cash flows entered into the calculator are $CF_0 = 0$, $CF_1 = \$120,000$, $CF_2 = \$100,000$, $CF_3 = \$150,000$, $CF_4 = \$80,000$, and $CF_5 = \$50,000$. After entering these values, enter the required rate of return, $I/k = 14\%$. At this point, you have entered all the known information, so you only need to press the NPV key to find the present value of the cash flows. You should find the answer is $356,790.49.

Real asset valuation is a critical concern for financial managers because they need to know whether the plant (e.g., buildings) and equipment (e.g., machines) and other long-term assets they purchase will help achieve the goal of wealth maximization. To determine how investing in a particular asset will affect the value of the firm, the financial manager must be able to determine whether the asset is worth its purchase price and if the asset will increase the firm's wealth. Although the general valuation procedures we outlined in this section can be used to value real assets, other factors often need to be considered before a final purchasing decision can be made. The process of evaluating projects and deciding which projects should be purchased is called *capital budgeting*. The capital budgeting decision-making process is crucial to the firm's success, and it is especially important if the firm is to achieve the goal of wealth maximization. Therefore, in the next two chapters we will explain in great detail the procedures firms use to make capital budgeting decisions—procedures that you can apply to make decisions when purchasing personal assets.

Self-Test Question

How does the valuation of real assets differ from the valuation of financial assets?

Summary

Corporate decisions should be analyzed in terms of how alternative courses of action are likely to affect the value of a firm. However, it is necessary to know how bond and stock prices are established before attempting to measure how a given decision will affect a specific firm's value. Accordingly, this chapter showed how bond and stock values are determined as well as how investors go about estimating the rates of return they expect to earn. The key concepts covered in the chapter are summarized here:

- The **value** of any asset can be found by computing the **present value of the cash flows** the asset is expected to generate during its life.
- A **bond** is a long-term promissory note issued by a business or governmental unit. The firm receives the selling price of the bond in exchange for promising to make interest payments and to repay the principal on a specified future date.
- The **value of a bond** is found as the present value of an annuity (the **interest payments**) plus the present value of a lump sum (the **principal**). The bond is evaluated at the appropriate periodic interest rate over the number of periods for which interest payments are made.
- The equation used to find the value of a bond is

$$V_d = INT \left[\frac{1 - \dfrac{1}{\left(1 + \frac{k_d}{m}\right)^{N \times m}}}{\frac{k_d}{m}} \right] + M \left[\frac{1}{\left(1 + \frac{k_d}{m}\right)^{N \times m}} \right]$$

where INT is the dollar interest received each period, N represents the years to maturity, k_d is the required return on similar investments, and m equals the number of times interest is paid during the year.

- The return earned on a bond held to maturity is defined as the bond's **yield to maturity (YTM).**
- The longer the maturity of a bond, the more its price will change in response to a given change in interest rates; this is called **interest rate price risk.** Bonds with short maturities, however, expose the investor to high **interest rate reinvestment risk,** which is the risk that income will differ from what is expected because cash flows received from bonds must be reinvested at different interest rates.
- The **value of a share of stock** is calculated as the **present value of the stream of dividends** it is expected to provide in the future.
- A **zero-growth stock** is one whose future dividends are not expected to grow at all; a **constant growth stock** is one whose future dividends are expected to grow at a constant rate, g; and a **nonconstant growth stock** is one whose earnings and dividends are expected to grow at a rate different from the economy as a whole over some specified time period.
- Most **preferred stocks are perpetuities,** and thus are zero-growth stocks, and the value of a share of such stocks is found as the dividend divided by the required rate of return: $P_0 = D/k_s$.
- The equation used to find the **value of a constant,** or **normal, growth** stock is: $\hat{P}_0 = \hat{D}_1/(k_s - g)$.

■ The **expected total rate of return** from a stock consists of an **expected dividend yield** plus an **expected capital gains yield.** For a constant growth firm, both the expected dividend yield and the expected capital gains yield are constant.

■ The equation for $\hat{k}_s$, **the expected rate of return on a constant growth stock,** can be expressed as follows: $\hat{k}_s = \hat{D}_1/P_0 + g$.

■ To find the **present value of a nonconstant growth stock**, (1) find the dividends expected during the nonconstant growth period; (2) find the price of the stock at the end of the nonconstant growth period; (3) discount the dividends and the projected price back to the present; and (4) sum these PVs to find the current expected value of the stock, $\hat{P}_0$.

■ The **efficient markets hypothesis (EMH)** holds that (1) stocks are always in equilibrium and (2) it is impossible for an investor to consistently "beat the market." Therefore, according to the EMH, stocks always are fairly valued ($\hat{P}_0 = P_0$), the required return on a stock is equal to its expected return ($k_s = \hat{k}_s$), and all stocks' expected returns plot on the SML.

■ Differences can and do exist between expected and actual returns in the stock and bond markets—only for short-term, risk-free assets are expected and actual (or realized) returns equal.

■ Like a financial asset, the value of a **real asset** is computed as the present value of the cash flows the asset is expected to provide in the future.

Questions

5–1 Describe how you should determine the value of an asset, whether it is a real asset or a financial asset.

5–2 Two investors are evaluating IBM's stock for possible purchase. They agree on the expected value of $\hat{D}_1$ and also on the expected future dividend growth rate (g). Further, they agree on the riskiness of the stock. However, one investor normally holds stocks for two years, whereas the other normally holds stocks for 10 years. On the basis of the type of analysis done in this chapter, they should both be willing to pay the same price for IBM's stock. True or false? Explain.

5–3 A bond that pays interest forever and has no maturity date is a perpetual bond. In what respect is a perpetual bond similar to a no-growth common stock and to a share of preferred stock?

5–4 The rate of return you would get if you bought a bond and held it to its maturity date is called the bond's *yield to maturity*. If interest rates in the economy rise after a bond has been issued, what will happen to the bond's price and to its YTM? Does the length of time to maturity affect the extent to which a given change in interest rates will affect the bond's price?

5–5 If you buy a callable bond and interest rates decline, will the value of your bond rise by as much as it would have risen if the bond had not been callable? (Hint: Think about the "effective" terms to maturity of two bonds with identical characteristics, except one is callable.) Explain.

5–6 If you bought a share of common stock, you would typically expect to receive dividends plus capital gains. Would you expect the distribution between dividend yield and capital gains to be influenced by the firm's decision to pay more dividends rather than to retain and reinvest more of its earnings?

5–7 How do you think the price of Microsoft's stock will change if investors decide they want to earn a higher return for purchasing the stock? Assume all else remains constant. Do you think the price of Microsoft's stock would change if the CEO announced that the company was going to have to pay a 10-year, $10 million fine for unfair trade practices? Explain your rationale.

5–8 How do you think valuing a real asset, such as a building, differs from valuing a financial asset, such as a stock or a bond?

Self-Test Problems

(Solutions appear in Appendix B)

key terms   **ST–1** Define each of the following terms:
  a. Bond
  b. Par value; face value; maturity value
  c. Coupon payment; coupon interest rate
  d. Premium bond; discount bond
  e. Current yield (on a bond); yield to maturity (YTM)
  f. Interest rate price risk; interest rate reinvestment risk
  g. Intrinsic value ($\hat{P}_0$); market price (P_0)
  h. Required rate of return, k_s; expected rate of return, $\hat{k}_s$; actual, or realized, rate of return, k_s
  i. Capital gains yield; dividend yield; expected total return
  j. Zero-growth stock; normal, or constant, growth stock; nonconstant, growth stock
  k. Equilibrium
  l. Informational efficiency; abnormal retun
  m. Efficient markets hypothesis (EMH); forms (degrees) of EMH

stock growth rates and valuation   **ST–2** You are considering buying the stocks of two companies that operate in the same industry; they have similar characteristics except for their dividend payout policies. Both companies are expected to earn $6 per share this year. However, Company D (for "dividend") is expected to pay out all of its earnings as dividends, while Company G (for "growth") is expected to pay out only one-third of its earnings, or $2 per share. D's stock price is $40. G and D are equally risky. Which of the following is most likely to be true?
  a. Company G will have a faster growth rate than Company D. Therefore, G's stock price should be greater than $40.
  b. Although G's growth rate should exceed D's, D's current dividend exceeds that of G, and this should cause D's price to exceed G's.
  c. An investor in Stock D will get his or her money back faster because D pays out more of its earnings as dividends. Thus, in a sense, D is like a short-term bond, and G is like a long-term bond. Therefore, if economic shifts cause k_d and k_s to increase and if the expected streams of dividends from D and G remain constant, Stocks D and G will both decline, but D's price should decline more.
  d. D's expected and required rate of return is $\hat{k}_s = k_s = 15\%$. G's expected return will be higher because of its higher expected growth rate.
  e. On the basis of the available information, the best estimate of G's growth rate is 10 percent.

bond valuation   **ST–3** The Pennington Corporation issued a new series of bonds on January 1, 1985. The bonds were sold at par ($1,000), have a 12 percent coupon, and mature on December 31, 2014 (30 years after issue). Coupon payments are made semiannually (on June 30 and December 31).

   a. What was the YTM of Pennington's bonds on January 1, 1985?

   b. What was the price of the bond on January 1, 1990, five years later, assuming that the level of interest rates had fallen to 10 percent?

   c. Find the current yield and capital gains yield on the bond on January 1, 1990, given the price as determined in part b.

   d. On July 1, 2005, Pennington's bonds sold for $891.64. What was the YTM at that date?

   e. What were the current yield and capital gains yield on July 1, 2005?

constant growth stock valuation   **ST–4** Ewald Company's current stock price is $36, and its last dividend was $2.40. In view of Ewald's strong financial position and its consequent low risk, its required rate of return is only 12 percent. If dividends are expected to grow at a constant rate, g, in the future, and if k_s is expected to remain at 12 percent, what is Ewald's expected stock price five years from now?

nonconstant growth stock valuation   **ST–5** Snyder Computer Chips Inc. is experiencing a period of rapid growth. Earnings and dividends are expected to grow at a rate of 15 percent during the next two years, at 13 percent in the third year, and at a constant rate of 6 percent thereafter. Snyder's *last* dividend was $1.15, and the required rate of return on the stock is 12 percent.

   a. Calculate the value of the stock today.

   b. Calculate $\hat{P}_1$ and $\hat{P}_2$.

   c. Calculate the dividend yield and capital gains yield for Years 1, 2, and 3.

Problems

bond valuation   **5–1** Suppose Ford Motor Company sold an issue of bonds with a 10-year maturity, a $1,000 par value, a 10 percent coupon rate, and semiannual interest payments.

   a. Two years after the bonds were issued, the going rate of interest on bonds such as these fell to 6 percent. At what price would the bonds sell?

   b. Suppose that, two years after the initial offering, the going interest rate had risen to 12 percent. At what price would the bonds sell?

   c. Suppose that the conditions in part a existed—that is, interest rates fell to 6 percent two years after the issue date. Suppose further that the interest rate remained at 6 percent for the next eight years. Describe what would happen to the price of the Ford Motor Company bonds over time.

perpetual bond valuation   **5–2** The bonds of the Lange Corporation are perpetuities with a 10 percent coupon. Bonds of this type currently yield 8 percent, and their par value is $1,000.

   a. What is the price of the Lange bonds?

   b. Suppose interest rate levels rise to the point where such bonds now yield 12 percent. What would be the price of the Lange bonds?

   c. At what price would the Lange bonds sell if the yield on these bonds was 10 percent?

   d. How would your answers to parts a, b, and c change if the bonds were not perpetuities but had a maturity of 20 years?

constant growth stock valuation   **5–3** Your broker offers to sell you some shares of Wingler & Co. common stock that paid a dividend of $2 *yesterday*. You expect the dividend to grow at the rate of 5 percent per year for the next three years, and if you buy the stock, you plan to hold it for three years and then sell it.

   a. Find the expected dividend for each of the next three years; that is, calculate $\hat{D}_1$, $\hat{D}_2$, and $\hat{D}_3$. Note that $D_0 = \$2$.

b. Given that the appropriate discount rate is 12 percent and that the first of these dividend payments will occur one year from now, find the present value of the dividend stream; that is, calculate the PV of $\hat{D}_1$, $\hat{D}_2$, and $\hat{D}_3$, and then sum these PVs.

c. You expect the price of the stock three years from now to be $34.73; that is, you expect $\hat{P}_3$ to equal $34.73. Discounted at a 12 percent rate, what is the present value of this expected future stock price? In other words, calculate the PV of $34.73.

d. If you plan to buy the stock, hold it for three years, and then sell it for $34.73, what is the most you should pay for it?

e. Use Equation 5–6 to calculate the present value of this stock. Assume that g = 5%, and it is constant.

f. Is the value of this stock dependent upon how long you plan to hold it? In other words, if your planned holding period were two years or five years rather than three years, would this affect the value of the stock today, $\hat{P}_0$?

return on common stock   **5–4** You buy a share of Damanpour Corporation stock for $21.40. You expect it to pay dividends of $1.07, $1.1449, and $1.2250 in Years 1, 2, and 3, respectively, and you expect to sell it at a price of $26.22 at the end of three years.

     a. Calculate the growth rate in dividends.

     b. Calculate the expected dividend yield.

     c. Assuming that the calculated growth rate is expected to continue, you can add the dividend yield to the expected growth rate to get the expected total rate of return. What is this stock's expected total rate of return?

constant growth stock valuation   **5–5** Investors require a 15 percent rate of return on Goulet Company's stock ($k_s = 15\%$).

     a. What will be Goulet's stock value if the previous dividend was $D_0 = \$2$ and if investors expect dividends to grow at a constant compound annual rate of (1) –5 percent, (2) 0 percent, (3) 5 percent, and (4) 10 percent?

     b. Using data from part a and the constant growth model, what is the value for Goulet's stock if the required rate of return is 15 percent and the expected growth rate is (1) 15 percent or (2) 20 percent? Are these reasonable results? Explain.

     c. Is it reasonable to expect that a constant growth stock would have g > k_s? Explain.

nonconstant growth stock valuation   **5–6** Bayboro Sails is expected to pay dividends of $2.50, $3.00, and $4.00 in the next three years—$\hat{D}_1$, $\hat{D}_2$, and $\hat{D}_3$, respectively. After three years, the dividend is expected to grow at a constant rate equal to 4 percent per year indefinitely. Stockholders require a return of 14% to invest in the common stock of Bayboro Sails.

     a. Compute the present value of the dividends Bayboro is expected to pay over the next three years.

     b. For what price should investors expect to be able to sell the common stock of Bayboro at the end of three years? (*Hint:* The dividend will grow at a constant 4 percent in Year 4, Year 5, and every year thereafter, so Equation 5–6 can be used to find $\hat{P}_3$—the appropriate dividend to use in the numerator is $\hat{D}_4$.)

     c. Compute the value of Bayboro's common stock today, $\hat{P}_0$.

bond valuation   **5–7** In January 2004, the yield on AAA rated corporate bonds averaged about 5 percent; by the end of the year the yield on these same bonds was about 7 percent. Assume IBM issued a 10-year, 5 percent coupon bond on January 1, 2004. On the same date, General Motors issued a 20-year, 5 percent coupon bond. Both bonds pay interest *annually*. Also assume that the market rate on similar risk bonds was 5 percent at the time the bonds were issued.

a. Compute the market value of each bond at the time of issue.

b. Compute the market value of each bond one year after issue if the market yield for similar risk bonds was 7 percent on January 1, 2005.

c. Compute the 2004 capital gains yield for each bond.

d. Compute the current yield for each bond in 2004.

e. Compute the total return each bond would have generated for investors in 2004.

f. If you invested in bonds at the beginning of 2004, would you have been better off to have held long-term or short-term bonds? Explain why.

g. Assume interest rates stabilize at the January 2005 rate of 7.0 percent, and they stay at this level indefinitely. What would be the price of each bond on January 1, 2010, after six years from the date of issue have passed? Describe what should happen to the prices of these bonds as they approach their maturities.

nonconstant growth
stock valuation

5–8 It is now January 1, 2005. Swink Electric Inc. has just developed a solar panel capable of generating 200 percent more electricity than any solar panel currently on the market. As a result, Swink is expected to experience a 15 percent annual growth rate for the next five years. By the end of five years, other firms will have developed comparable technology, and Swink's growth rate will slow to 5 percent per year indefinitely. Stockholders require a return of 12 percent on Swink's stock. The most recent annual dividend (D_0), which was paid yesterday, was $1.75 per share.

a. Calculate Swink's expected dividends for 2005, 2006, 2007, 2008, and 2009.

b. Calculate the value of the stock today, $\hat{P}_0$. Proceed by finding the present value of the dividends expected at the end of 2005, 2006, 2007, 2008, and 2009, plus the present value of the stock price that should exist at the end of 2009. The year-end 2009 stock price can be found by using the constant growth equation (Equation 5–6). Notice that to find the December 31, 2009, price, you use the dividend expected in 2010, which is 5 percent greater than the 2009 dividend.

c. Calculate the expected dividend yield ($\hat{D}_1/P_0$), the capital gains yield expected in 2005, and the expected total return (dividend yield plus capital gains yield) for 2005. (Assume that $\hat{P}_0 = P_0$, and recognize that the capital gains yield is equal to the total return minus the dividend yield.) Also calculate these same three yields for 2009.

d. How might an investor's tax situation affect his or her decision to purchase stocks of companies in the early stages of their lives, when they are growing rapidly, versus stocks of older, more mature firms? When does Swink's stock become "mature" in this example?

e. Suppose your boss tells you she believes that Swink's annual growth rate will be only 12 percent during the next five years and that the firm's normal growth rate will be only 4 percent. Without doing any calculations, what general effect would these growth-rate changes have on the price of Swink's stock?

f. Suppose your boss also tells you that she regards Swink as being quite risky and that she believes the required rate of return should be 14 percent, not 12 percent. Again without doing any calculations, how would the higher required rate of return affect the price of the stock, its capital gains yield, and its dividend yield?

**supernormal growth
stock valuation**

5–9 Tanner Technologies Corporation (TTC) has been growing at a rate of 20 percent per year in recent years. This same growth rate is expected to last for another two years.

    a. If $D_0 = \$1.60$, $k = 10\%$, and $g_{norm} = 6\%$, what is TTC's stock worth today? What are its expected dividend yield and capital gains yield at this time?

    b. Now assume that TTC's period of supernormal growth is to last another five years rather than two years. How would this affect its price, dividend yield, and capital gains yield? Answer in words only.

    c. What will be TTC's dividend yield and capital gains yield once its period of supernormal growth ends? (*Hint:* These values will be the same regardless of whether you examine the case of two or five years of supernormal growth; the calculations are easy.)

    d. Of what interest to investors is the changing relationship between dividend yield and capital gains yield over time?

**constant growth
stock valuation**

5–10 The risk-free rate of return, k_{RF}, is 11 percent; the required rate of return on the market, k_M, is 14 percent; and Gerlunice Company's stock has a beta coefficient, β, of 1.5.

    a. Based on the capital asset pricing model (CAPM), what should be the required return for Gerlunice Company's stock?

    b. If the dividend expected during the coming year, $\hat{D}_1$, is $2.25, and $g = 5\%$ and is constant, at what price should Gerlunice's stock sell?

    c. Now suppose the Federal Reserve Board increases the money supply, causing the risk-free rate to drop to 9 percent and k_M to fall to 12 percent. What would this do to the price of the stock?

    d. In addition to the change in part c, suppose investors' risk aversion declines; this fact, combined with the decline in k_{RF}, causes k_M to fall to 11 percent. At what price would Gerlunice's stock sell?

    e. Now suppose Gerlunice has a change in management. The new group institutes policies that increase the expected constant growth rate to 6 percent. Also, the new management stabilizes sales and profits, which causes the beta coefficient to decline from 1.5 to 1.3. Assume that k_{RF} and k_M are equal to the values in part d. After all these changes, what is Gerlunice's new equilibrium price? (*Note:* $\hat{D}_1$ goes to $2.27.)

beta coefficients

5–11 Suppose Sartoris Chemical Company's management conducts a study and concludes that if Sartoris expanded its consumer products division (which is less risky than its primary business, industrial chemicals), the firm's beta would decline from 1.2 to 0.9. However, consumer products have a somewhat lower profit margin, and this would cause Sartoris's constant growth rate in earnings and dividends to fall from 7 to 5 percent.

    a. Should management make the change? Assume the following: $k_M = 12\%$; $k_{RF} = 9\%$; $D_0 = \$2$.

    b. Assume all the facts as given previously except the change in the beta coefficient. How low would the beta have to fall to cause the expansion to be a good one? (*Hint:* Set $\hat{P}_0$ under the new policy equal to $\hat{P}_0$ under the old one, and find the new beta that will produce this equality.)

Exam-Type Problems

The problems included in this section are set up in such a way that they could be used as multiple-choice exam problems.

bond valuation   **5-12** The Desreumaux Company has two bond issues outstanding. Both bonds pay $100 annual interest plus $1,000 at maturity. Bond L has a maturity of 15 years and Bond S a maturity of 1 year.

  a. What will be the value of each of these bonds when the going rate of interest is (1) 5 percent, (2) 8 percent, and (3) 12 percent? Assume that there is only one more interest payment to be made on Bond S.

  b. Why does the longer-term (15-year) bond fluctuate more when interest rates change than does the shorter-term (one-year) bond?

yield to maturity   **5-13** It is now January 1, 2005, and you are considering the purchase of an outstanding Puckett Corporation bond that was issued on January 1, 2003. The Puckett bond has a 9.5 percent annual coupon and a 30-year original maturity (it matures on December 31, 2032). Interest rates have declined since the bond was issued, and the bond now is selling at 116.575 percent of par, or $1,165.75. You want to determine the yield to maturity for this bond.

  a. Use Equation 5-3 to approximate the yield to maturity for the Puckett bond in 2005.

  b. What is the actual yield to maturity in 2005 for the Puckett bond?

yield to maturity   **5-14** The Severn Company's bonds have four years remaining to maturity. Interest is paid annually, the bonds have a $1,000 par value, and the coupon interest rate is 9 percent.

  a. Compute the *approximate* yield to maturity for the bonds if the current market price is either (1) $829 or (2) $1,104.

  b. Would you pay $829 for one of these bonds if you thought that the appropriate rate of interest was 12 percent—that is, if $k_d = 12\%$? Explain your answer.

rate of return for a perpetual bond   **5-15** What will be the rate of return on a perpetual bond with a $1,000 par value, an 8 percent coupon rate, and a current market price of (a) $600, (b) $800, (c) $1,000, and (d) $1,500? Assume interest is paid annually.

declining growth stock valuation   **5-16** McCue Mining Company's ore reserves are being depleted, so its sales are falling. Also, its pit is getting deeper each year, so its costs are rising. As a result, the company's earnings and dividends are *declining* at the constant rate of 5 percent per year. If $D_0 = \$5$ and $k_s = 15\%$, what is the value of McCue Mining's stock?

equilibrium rates of return   **5-17** The beta coefficient for Stock C is $\beta_C = 0.4$, whereas that for Stock D is $\beta_D = -0.5$. (Stock D's beta is negative, indicating that its rate of return rises whenever returns on most other stocks fall. There are very few negative beta stocks, although collection agency stocks are sometimes cited as an example.)

  a. If the risk-free rate is 9 percent and the expected rate of return on an average stock is 13 percent, what are the required rates of return on Stocks C and D?

  b. For Stock C, suppose the current price, P_0, is $25; the next expected dividend, $\hat{D}_1$, is $1.50; and the stock's expected constant growth rate is 4 percent. Is the stock in equilibrium? Explain, and describe what will happen if the stock is not in equilibrium.

supernormal growth stock valuation   **5-18** Assume that the average firm in your company's industry is expected to grow at a constant rate of 6 percent, and its dividend yield is 7 percent. Your company is about as risky as the average firm in the industry, but it has just successfully completed some R&D work that leads you to expect that earnings and dividends will grow at a rate of 50 percent $[\hat{D}_1 = D_0(1 + g) = D_0(1.50)]$ this year and 25 percent the following year, after which growth should match the 6 percent industry average rate. The last dividend paid (D_0) was $1. What is the value per share of your firm's stock?

effective annual rate **5–19** Assume that as investment manager of Florida Electric Company's pension plan (which is exempt from income taxes), you must choose between IBM bonds and AT&T preferred stock. The bonds have a $1,000 par value, they mature in 20 years, they pay $40 each six months, and they sell at a price of $897.40 per bond. The preferred stock is a perpetuity; it pays a dividend of $2 each quarter, and it sells for $95 per share. What is the effective annual rate of return (EAR) on the *higher* yielding security?

simple interest rate **5–20** Tapley Corporation's 14 percent coupon rate, semiannual payment, $1,000 par value bonds mature in 30 years. The bonds sell at a price of $1,353.54, and the yield curve is flat. Assuming that interest rates in the economy are expected to remain at their current level, what is the best estimate of Tapley's simple interest rate on *new* bonds?

nonconstant growth stock valuation **5–21** Microtech Corporation is expanding rapidly, and it currently needs to retain all of its earnings; hence, it does not pay any dividends. However, investors expect Microtech to begin paying dividends, with the first dividend of $1 coming three years from today. The dividend should grow rapidly—at a rate of 50 percent per year—during Years 4 and 5. After Year 5, the company should grow at a constant rate of 8 percent per year. If the required return on the stock is 15 percent, what is the value of the stock today?

valuation of real assets **5–22** Currently, there is so much demand for the Anderson Electric's products that the company cannot manufacture enough inventory to satisfy demand. Consequently, Anderson is considering purchasing a new machine that will increase inventory production. Anderson estimates that the new machine will generate the following net cash flows during its lifetime:

YEAR	NET CASH FLOW, $\hat{CF}_t$
1	$18,000
2	12,000
3	15,000
4	10,000
5	10,000
6	10,000

a. If Anderson normally requires a return equal to 12 percent for such projects, what is the *maximum* amount it should pay for the machine?

b. How would your answer to part a change if the appropriate rate of return is 15 percent?

Integrative Problem

valuation **5–23** Robert Campbell and Carol Morris are senior vice presidents of the Mutual of Chicago Insurance Company. They are codirectors of the company's pension fund management division, with Campbell having responsibility for fixed income securities (primarily bonds) and Morris being responsible for equity investments. A major new client, the California League of Cities, has requested that Mutual of Chicago present an investment seminar to the mayors of the represented cities, and Campbell and Morris, who will make the actual presentation, have asked you to help them by answering the following questions:

Section I: Bond valuation a. What are the key features of a bond?

b. How is the value of any asset whose value is based on expected future cash flows determined?

c. How is the value of a bond determined? What is the value of a one-year, $1,000 par value bond with a 10 percent annual coupon if its required rate of return is 10 percent? What is the value of a similar 10-year bond?

d. **(1)** What would be the value of the bond described in part c if, just after it had been issued, the expected inflation rate rose by 3 percentage points, causing investors to require a 13 percent return? Would we now have a discount or a premium bond?

   (2) What would happen to the bond's value if inflation fell, and k_d declined to 7 percent? Would we now have a premium or a discount bond?

   (3) What would happen to the value of the 10-year bond over time if the required rate of return remained at 13 percent or remained at 7 percent?

e. **(1)** What is the yield to maturity on a 10-year, 9 percent annual coupon, $1,000 par value bond that sells for $887.00? That sells for $1,134.20? What does the fact that a bond sells at a discount or at a premium tell you about the relationship between k_d and the bond's coupon rate?

   (2) What is the current yield, the capital gains yield, and the total return in each case?

f. What is interest rate price risk? Which bond in part c has more interest rate price risk, the one-year bond or the 10-year bond?

g. What is interest rate reinvestment risk? Which bond in part c has more interest rate reinvestment risk, assuming a 10-year investment horizon?

h. Redo parts c and d, assuming the bonds have semiannual rather than annual coupons.

i. Suppose you could buy, for $1,000, either a 10 percent, 10-year, annual payment bond or a 10 percent, 10-year, semiannual payment bond. They are equally risky. Which would you prefer? If $1,000 is the proper price for the semiannual bond, what is the proper price for the annual payment bond?

j. What is the value of a perpetual bond with an annual coupon of $100 if its required rate of return is 10 percent? 13 percent? 7 percent? Assess the following statement: "Because perpetual bonds match an infinite investment horizon, they have little interest rate price risk."

Section II: Stock valuation

To illustrate the common stock valuation process, Campbell and Morris have asked you to analyze the Bon Temps Company, an employment agency that supplies word processor operators and computer programmers to businesses with temporarily heavy workloads. You are to answer the following questions:

a. **(1)** Write out a formula that can be used to value any stock, regardless of its dividend pattern.

   (2) What is a constant growth stock? How are constant growth stocks valued?

   (3) What happens if the growth is constant, and $g > k_s$? Will many stocks have $g > k_s$?

b. Assume that Bon Temps has a beta coefficient of 1.2, that the risk-free rate (the yield on T-bonds) is 10 percent, and that the required rate of return on the market is 15 percent. What is the required rate of return on the firm's stock?

c. Assume that Bon Temps is a constant growth company whose last dividend (D_0, which was paid yesterday) was $2.00 and whose dividend is expected to grow indefinitely at a 6 percent rate.

   (1) What is the firm's expected dividend stream over the next three years?

   (2) What is the firm's current stock price?

(3) What is the stock's expected value one year from now?

(4) What are the expected dividend yield, the capital gains yield, and the total return during the first year?

d. Now assume that the stock is currently selling at $21.20. What is the expected rate of return on the stock?

e. What would the stock price be if its dividends were expected to have zero growth?

f. Now assume that Bon Temps is expected to experience supernormal growth of 30 percent for the next three years, then to return to its long-run constant growth rate of 6 percent. What is the stock's value under these conditions? What is its expected dividend yield and capital gains yield in Year 1? In Year 4?

g. Suppose Bon Temps is expected to experience zero growth during the first three years and then to resume its steady-state growth of 6 percent in the fourth year. What is the stock's value now? What is its expected dividend yield and its capital gains yield in Year 1? In Year 4?

h. Finally, assume that Bon Temps's earnings and dividends are expected to *decline* by a constant 6 percent per year, that is, $g = -6\%$. Why would anyone be willing to buy such a stock, and at what price should it sell? What would be the dividend yield and capital gains yield in each year?

Section III: Real asset valuation

Mutual of Chicago currently is examining the possibility of purchasing a piece of equipment that will scan data into its main computer. The new scanner will eliminate the need to hire part-time help to make sure information about clients is recorded accurately and in a timely manner. After evaluating all future costs and benefits, management has determined the new scanner will generate the following cash flows during its ten-year life:

YEAR/PERIOD	EXPECTED CASH FLOW, $\hat{CF}_t$
1–3	$30,000
4–6	15,000
7	–20,000
8–10	10,000

Campbell and Morris would like you to evaluate the value of the scanner.

a. If Mutual of Chicago believes the appropriate return for investments like the scanner is 15 percent, what is the value of the scanner to the company?

b. Would you recommend the machine be purchased if its current cost is $100,000? Explain your reasoning.

c. Would the scanner be more attractive if the appropriate return was 10 percent, rather than 15 percent? Explain your answer.

Computer-Related Problem

Work the problem in this section only if you are using the computer problem diskette.

5–24 Use the model on the computer problem diskette in the File C05 to solve this problem.

a. Refer back to Problem 5-8. Rework part e, using the computerized model to determine what Swink's expected dividends and stock price would be under the conditions given.

b. Suppose your boss tells you that she regards Swink as being quite risky and that she believes the required rate of return should be higher than the 12 percent originally specified. Rework the problem under the conditions given in part e, except change the required rate of return to (1) 13 percent, (2) 15 percent, and (3) 20 percent to determine the effects of the higher required rates of return on Swink's stock price.

GET REAL with Thomson ONE

5-25 Wachovia (WB) is a financial services company that is often held in the portfolios of investors who are interested in earning dividend income. These investors want to know the expected growth rate in dividends for such companies because they rely on dividends as part of their annual income. Answer the following questions:

a. Find the last dividend paid for Wachovia (WB). [*Hint:* Click on Overview/Full Reports/Thomson Reports/Stock Section]

b. Calculate the growth rate of the expected dividends for Wachovia using the forecasted figures for the next two years. [*Hint:* Click on Estimates and Consensus Estimates]

c. If you are a Wachovia stockholder and your required rate of return is 8 percent, what is the intrinsic value of the stock?

d. What does the term "intrinsic value" mean?

e. Bank of America (BAC) is another large banking organization. Calculate the growth rate of the expected dividends for Bank of America using the last dividend the company paid.

f. Would you rather own Wachovia or Bank of America if your primary concern is how much growth you can expect in your dividend payments? Explain.

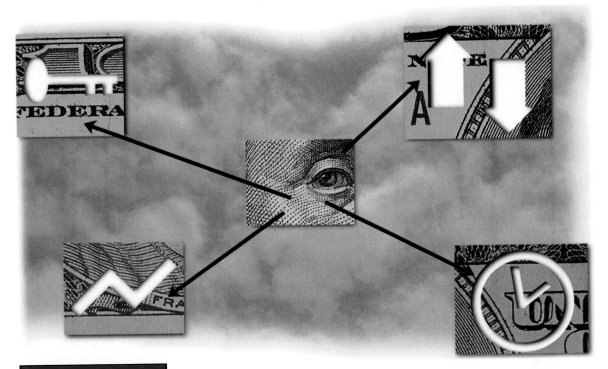

Capital Budgeting

CHAPTER 6

Capital Budgeting Techniques

A MANAGERIAL PERSPECTIVE

After five years of planning and $3.5 billion in costs for development and for new factories and equipment, in the summer of 1990 General Motors (GM) began production of a new compact car—the Saturn. Now, more than one decade later, it is safe to say that most people in the United States have heard of the Saturn car line. For it to have survived so long, you probably would expect that the Saturn has been a successful venture. Unfortunately for GM, however, the Saturn line has never really reached the sales necessary for the project to be considered a success. Even though consumers seem to like the Saturn concept and it has a good service reputation, annual sales of less than 100,000 in recent years have been well below the 500,000 needed for GM to begin to call the project a viable investment. Some believe GM has used the Saturn project as a loss leader to attract first-time new car buyers and as a means to satisfy federal regulations concerning the average fuel economy of the line of cars it offers. Even so, Saturn cannot survive if sales continue to decline. To try to reverse the trend, the Saturn Division of GM recently introduced a new sedan called the Ion, a sport utility vehicle called the Vue, and a convertible called the Saturn Sky. Unfortunately, these models have not shown the success GM expected, and the Saturn Division was expected to lose nearly $1 billion in 2003.

As GM tries to salvage its Saturn division, the company continues to develop new models that have the potential to generate large profits and search for ways to reduce the costs of producing cars. It was estimated that GM's capital budget exceeded $7 billion in 2003. At that time, the cost to get a new model in production was approximately $400 million. To justify such a large outlay, GM had to be confident that the investment would provide a sufficient return in the future. At the same time, GM was exploring new technologies that would cut in half the initial investment in developing and manufacturing new models. Because the capital outlays are so large, much planning and analysis goes into launching a new car model or changing manufacturing processes. The firm wants to ensure that such decisions, which have long-term, far-reaching effects, are in the best interest of shareholders—that is, they contribute to increasing the firm's value.

GM's Saturn project and changes in the manufacturing process are examples of massive capital budgeting ventures that required quite a bit of analysis and decision making before the hundreds of millions or billions of dollars required for development and implementation are spent. The principles set forth in this chapter and the next offer insights into how capital budgeting decisions such as these are made. ∎

Sources: Various articles available on Dow Jones Interactive® Publications Library located at http://www.wsj.com.

In the previous three chapters we showed how assets are valued and required rates of return are determined. Now we apply these concepts to investment decisions involving the fixed assets of a firm, or *capital budgeting*. Here the term *capital* refers to fixed assets used in production, while a *budget* is a plan that details projected inflows and outflows during some future period. Thus, the capital budget is an outline of planned expenditures on fixed assets, and **capital budgeting** is the process of analyzing projects and deciding which are acceptable investments and which actually should be purchased.

CAPITAL BUDGETING
The process of planning and evaluating expenditures on assets whose cash flows are expected to extend beyond one year.

Our treatment of capital budgeting is divided into two chapters. First, this chapter gives an overview and explains the basic techniques used in capital budgeting analysis. Chapter 7 shows how the cash flows associated with capital budgeting projects are estimated and how risk is considered in capital budgeting decisions.

Importance of Capital Budgeting

A number of factors combine to make capital budgeting decisions among the most important financial managers must make. First, the impact of capital budgeting is long-term; thus, the firm loses some decision-making flexibility when capital projects are purchased. For example, when a firm invests in an asset with a 10-year economic life, its operations are affected for 10 years. The firm is "locked in" by the capital budgeting decision. Further, because asset expansion is fundamentally related to expected future sales, a decision to buy a fixed asset that is expected to last 10 years involves an implicit 10-year sales forecast.

An error in the forecast of asset requirements can have serious consequences. If the firm invests too much in assets, it will incur unnecessarily heavy expenses. But if it does not spend enough on fixed assets, it might find that inefficient production and inadequate capacity lead to lost sales that are difficult, if not impossible, to recover.

Timing is also important in capital budgeting. Capital assets must be ready to come on line when they are needed; otherwise, opportunities might be lost. For example, consider what happened to Decopot, a decorative tile manufacturer with no formal capital budgeting process. Decopot attempted to operate at full capacity as often as possible. This was not a bad idea because demand for Decopot's product and services was relatively stable. A few years ago, however, Decopot began to experience intermittent spurts of additional demand for its products. Decopot could not satisfy the additional demand because it did not have the capacity to produce any more products, and customers had to be turned away. The spurts in demand continued, so senior management decided to add capacity to increase production so the additional orders could be filled. It took nine months to get the additional capacity ready. Finally, Decopot was ready for the increased demand the next time it arrived. Unfortunately, the "next time" never came because competitors had expanded their operations six months earlier, which allowed them to fill customers' orders when Decopot could not. Many of Decopot's customers are now its competitors' customers. If Decopot had properly forecasted demand and planned its capacity requirements, it would have been able to maintain or perhaps even increase its market share; instead, its market share decreased.

Effective capital budgeting can improve both the timing of asset acquisitions and the quality of assets purchased. A firm that forecasts its needs for capital assets in advance will have an opportunity to purchase and install the assets before they are needed. Unfortunately, like Decopot, many firms do not order capital goods until they approach full capacity or are forced to replace worn-out equipment. If many firms order capital goods at the same time, backlogs result, prices increase, and firms are forced to wait for the delivery of machinery; in general, the quality of the capital goods deteriorates. If a firm foresees its needs and purchases capital assets early, it can avoid these problems.

Finally, capital budgeting is important because the acquisition of fixed assets typically involves substantial expenditures, and before a firm can spend a large amount of money, it must have the funds available. Large amounts of money are not available automatically. Therefore, a firm contemplating a major capital expenditure program must arrange its financing well in advance to be sure the funds required are available.

Self-Test Questions

Why are capital budgeting decisions so important to a firm's success?

Why is the sales forecast a key element in a capital budgeting decision?

Generating Ideas for Capital Projects

The same general concepts that we developed for valuing financial assets are involved in capital budgeting. However, whereas a set of stocks and bonds already exists in the financial markets and investors select from this set, capital budgeting projects are created by the firm. For example, a sales representative might report that customers frequently ask for a particular product that the company does not currently produce. The sales manager then discusses the idea with the marketing research group to determine the size of the market for the proposed product. If it appears likely that a significant market does exist, cost accountants and engineers will be asked to estimate production costs. If those estimates show the product can be produced and sold at a sufficient profit, the project will be undertaken.

A firm's growth, and even its ability to remain competitive and to survive, depends on a constant flow of ideas for new products, ways to make existing products better, and ways to produce output at a lower cost. Accordingly, a well-managed firm will go to great lengths to develop good capital budgeting proposals. Some firms even provide incentives to employees to encourage suggestions that lead to beneficial investment proposals. If a firm has capable and imaginative executives and employees and its incentive system works properly, many ideas for capital investment will be advanced.

Because some capital investment ideas will be good and others will not, procedures must be established for evaluating the worth of such projects to the firm. Our topic in the remainder of this chapter is the evaluation of the acceptability of capital projects.

Self-Test Question

How does a firm generate ideas for capital projects?

Project Classifications

Capital budgeting decisions generally are termed either *replacement decisions* or *expansion decisions*. **Replacement decisions** involve determining whether capital projects should be purchased to take the place of existing assets that might be worn out, damaged, or obsolete. Usually the replacement projects are necessary to maintain or

REPLACEMENT DECISIONS
Whether to purchase capital assets to take the place of existing assets to maintain or improve existing operations.

EXPANSION DECISIONS
Whether to purchase capital projects and add them to existing assets to increase existing operations.

INDEPENDENT PROJECTS
Projects whose cash flows are not affected by decisions made about other projects.

MUTUALLY EXCLUSIVE PROJECTS
A set of projects in which the acceptance of one project means the others cannot be accepted.

improve profitable operations using the existing production levels. On the other hand, if a firm is considering whether to *increase* operations by adding capital projects to existing assets that will help produce either more of its existing products or entirely new products, **expansion decisions** are made.

Some of the capital budgeting decisions involve *independent projects*, while others will involve *mutually exclusive projects*. **Independent projects** are projects whose cash flows are not affected by one another, so the acceptance of one project does not affect the acceptance of the other project(s). *All independent projects can be purchased if they all are acceptable.* For example, if South-Western College Publishing, which publishes this book, decides to purchase the ABC television network, it still could publish a new textbook. Conversely, if a capital budgeting decision involves **mutually exclusive projects,** then when one project is taken on, the others must be rejected. *Only one mutually exclusive project can be purchased, even if they all are acceptable.* For example, Global Sports and Entertainment, Ltd., has a parcel of land on which it wants to build either a children's amusement park or a domed baseball stadium. The land is not large enough for both alternatives, so if Global chooses to build the amusement park, it cannot build the stadium, and vice versa.

In general, relatively simple calculations, and only a few supporting documents, are required for replacement decisions, especially maintenance-type investments in profitable plants. More detailed analysis is required for cost-reduction replacements, for expansion of existing product lines, and especially for investments in new products or areas. Also, within each category, projects are broken down by their dollar costs: Larger investments require both more detailed analysis and approval at a higher level within the firm. Thus, although a plant manager might be authorized to approve maintenance expenditures up to $10,000 on the basis of a relatively unsophisticated analysis, the full board of directors might have to approve decisions that involve either amounts greater than $1 million or expansions into new products or markets. Statistical data generally are lacking for new product decisions, so here judgments, as opposed to detailed cost data, are especially important.

Self-Test Question

Identify and briefly explain how capital project classification categories are used.

Similarities between Capital Budgeting and Asset Valuation

Capital budgeting decisions involve valuation of assets, or projects. Not surprisingly, then, capital budgeting involves exactly the same steps used in general asset valuation as described in the last few chapters:

1. Determine the cost, or purchase price, of the asset.
2. Estimate the cash flows expected to be generated by the asset during its life. This is similar to estimating the future dividend on a stock, along with the stock's expected selling price in the future.
3. Evaluate the riskiness of the projected cash flows to determine the appropriate rate of return to use for computing the present value of the estimated cash flows.

4. Compute the present value of the expected cash flows. This is equivalent to finding the present value of a stock's expected future dividends. In other words, solve the following:

$$\text{PV of CF} = \frac{\hat{CF}_1}{(1+k)^1} + \frac{\hat{CF}_2}{(1+k)^2} + \cdots + \frac{\hat{CF}_n}{(1+k)^n}$$

5. Compare the present value of the future expected cash flows with the initial investment, or cost, required to acquire the asset. Alternatively, the expected rate of return on the project can be calculated and compared with the rate of return considered appropriate for the project.

If a firm identifies (or creates) an investment opportunity with a present value greater than its cost, the value of the firm will increase if the investment is purchased. There is a direct link between capital budgeting and stock values: The more effective the firm's capital budgeting procedures, the higher the price of its stock.

Self-Test Questions

List the steps in the capital budgeting process, and compare them with the steps in general asset valuation.

Explain how capital budgeting is related to the wealth-maximization goal that should be pursued by the financial manager of a firm.

Capital Budgeting Evaluation Techniques

The three most popular methods businesses use to evaluate capital budgeting projects are: (1) payback period (PB), (2) net present value (NPV), and (3) internal rate of return (IRR).[1] As you will see, to determine a project's acceptability using any of these three techniques, its expected cash flows are needed. However, unlike the other two techniques, the payback method does not consider the time value of money, so we call payback a *nondiscounting technique* and NPV and IRR *discounting techniques.* We will explain how each evaluation criterion is calculated, and then we will determine how well each performs in terms of identifying those projects that will maximize the firm's stock price.

We use the cash flow data shown in Figure 6–1 for Project S and Project L to illustrate each method. Throughout this chapter we assume that the projects are equally risky. The expected cash flows, $\hat{CF}_t$, shown in Figure 6–1 are the "bottom line," after-tax cash flows, which we assume occur at the end of the designated year. Incidentally, the S stands for *short* and the L for *long:* Project S is a short-term project in the sense that its cash inflows tend to come in sooner than those for Project L. We use these two illustrative projects to simplify our presentations.

---

[1]For information about which methods firms use to make capital budgeting decisions, see the Industry Practice box in this chapter.

FIGURE 6–1	Net Cash Flows for Project S and Project L

	EXPECTED AFTER-TAX NET CASH FLOWS, $\hat{CF}_t$	
YEAR(t)	PROJECT S	PROJECT L
0[a]	$(3,000)	$(3,000)
1	1,500	400
2	1,200	900
3	800	1,300
4	300	1,500

Project S:

0	1	2	3	4
(3,000)	1,500	1,200	800	300

Project L:

0	1	2	3	4
(3,000)	1,500	1,200	800	300

[a]$\hat{CF}_0$ represents the initial investment, or net cost of the project

Payback Period

PAYBACK PERIOD
The length of time the original cost of an investment is recovered from the expected cash flows.

The **traditional payback period,** defined as the expected number of years required to recover the original investment (the cost of the asset), is the simplest and, as far as we know, the oldest *formal* method used to evaluate capital budgeting projects. To compute a project's payback period, simply add up the expected cash flows for each year until the cumulative value equals the amount that is initially invested. The total amount of time, including the fraction of a year if appropriate, that it takes to recapture the original amount invested is the payback period. Figure 6–2 shows the payback calculation process for both Project S and Project L.

The exact payback period can be found using the following formula:

6–1

$$\text{Payback} = \text{PB} = \left(\begin{array}{c} \text{Number of years} \\ \text{before full recovery} \\ \text{of initial investment} \end{array} \right) + \left(\dfrac{\begin{array}{c} \text{Amount of investment unrecovered} \\ \text{at start of the recovery year} \end{array}}{\begin{array}{c} \text{Total cash flow generated} \\ \text{during the recovery year} \end{array}} \right)$$

As Figure 6–2 shows, the payback period for Project S is between two years and three years. Using Equation 6–1, the exact payback period for Project S is computed as follows:

$$\text{PB}_S = 2 + \frac{300}{800} = 2.4 \text{ years}$$

| FIGURE 6–2 | Payback Period for Project S and Project L |

Project S:

	0	1	2	PB$_S$	3	4
Net cash flow	(3,000)	1,500	1,200		800	300
Cumulative net cash flow	(3,000)	(1,500)	(300)		500	800

Project L:

	0	1	2	3 PB$_L$	4
Net cash flow	(3,000)	400	900	1,300	1,500
Cumulative net cash flow	(3,000)	(2,600)	(1,700)	(400)	1,100

Applying the same procedure to Project L, we find PB$_L$ = 3.3 years.

Using payback to make capital budgeting decisions is based on the concept that it is better to recover the cost of (investment in) a project sooner rather than later. Therefore, Project S is considered better than Project L because it has a lower payback. *As a general rule, a project is considered acceptable if its payback is less than the maximum cost recovery time established by the firm.* For example, if the firm requires projects to have a payback of three years or less, Project S would be acceptable but Project L would not.

The payback method is simple, which explains why payback traditionally has been one of the most popular capital budgeting techniques. But, because payback ignores the time value of money, relying solely on this method could lead to incorrect decisions—at least if our goal is to maximize value. If a project has a payback of three years, we know how quickly the initial investment will be covered by the expected cash flows, but this information does not provide any indication of whether the return on the project is sufficient to cover the cost of the funds invested. In addition, when payback is used, the cash flows beyond the payback period are ignored. For example, even if Project L had a fifth year of cash flows equal to $50,000, its payback would remain 3.3 years, which is less desirable than the payback of 2.4 years for Project S. But, with the additional $50,000 cash flow, Project L most likely would be preferred.

DISCOUNTED CASH FLOW (DCF) TECHNIQUES
Methods of evaluating investment proposals that employ time value of money concepts; two of these are the net present value and the internal rate of return.

Net Present Value (NPV)

To correct for the fact that payback and other nondiscounting techniques ignore the time value of money, methods were developed to include consideration of the time value of money.[2] One such method is the *net present value (NPV) method,* which relies on **discounted cash flow (DCF) techniques.** To find a project's NPV, we compute

---

[2]Another capital budgeting technique that was once widely used is the *accounting rate of return (ARR),* which examines a project's contribution to the firm's net income. According to a study completed by Graham and Harvey, only about 12 percent of firms still calculate ARR as one of the techniques used to evaluate capital budgeting projects. See John R. Graham and Campbell R. Harvey, 2001, "The theory and practice of corporate finance: Evidence from the field," *Journal of Financial Economics* 60, 187–243.

the present value of all the future cash flows that the project is expected to generate and then subtract (add a negative cash flow) the project's initial investment (original cost). The result is the *net* benefit that the firm will realize from investing in the project. *If the net benefit computed on a present value basis—that is, NPV—is positive, then the project is considered an acceptable investment.* NPV is computed using the following equation:

6–2

$$NPV = \hat{CF}_0 + \frac{\hat{CF}_1}{(1+k)^1} + \frac{\hat{CF}_2}{(1+k)^2} + \cdots + \frac{\hat{CF}_n}{(1+k)^n}$$

$$= \sum_{t=0}^{n} \frac{\hat{CF}_t}{(1+k)^t}$$

Here $\hat{CF}_t$ is the expected net cash flow at Period t, and k is the rate of return required by the firm to invest in this project.[3] Cash outflows (expenditures on the project, such as the cost of buying equipment or building factories) are treated as negative cash flows. For Project S and Project L, only $\hat{CF}_0$ is negative, but for many large projects such as the Alaska Pipeline, an electric generating plant, or Chevrolet's Saturn project, outflows occur for several years before operations begin and cash flows turn positive.

At a 10 percent required rate of return, Project S's NPV is $161.33:

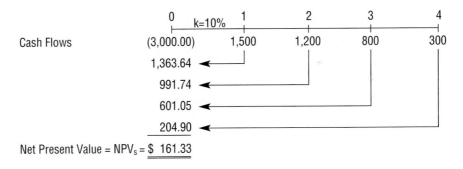

Because it is not widely used and because it relies on income rather than cash flows, we do not discuss ARR here. For those who are interested, the ARR is computed by dividing the average net income that is expected to be generated by the project over its life by its average value. In other words, the ARR is computed as follows:

$$ARR = \frac{\text{Average annual income}}{\text{Average book value of the investment}}$$

A project would be considered acceptable if its ARR was greater than a selected return, perhaps the firm's required rate of return. For a discussion of ARR, see Chapter 11 in Eugene F. Brigham and Phillip R. Daves, *Intermediate Financial Management*, 8th ed. (Cincinnati, OH: South-Western College Publishing, 2004).

[3]The rate of return required by the firm generally is termed the firm's *cost of capital*, because it is the average rate the firm must pay for the funds used to purchase capital projects. The concept of cost of capital is discussed in Chapter 8.

As the lower section of the cash flow time line shows, to find the NPV, we compute the present value of each cash flow and sum the results. Using Equation 6–2, the numerical solution for the NPV for Project S is:

$$NPV_s = (3,000) + \frac{1,500}{(1.10)^1} + \frac{1,200}{(1.10)^2} + \frac{800}{(1.10)^3} + \frac{300}{(1.10)^4}$$

$$= (3,000) + 1,363.64 + 991.74 + 601.05 + 204.90$$

$$= 161.33$$

It is not difficult to calculate the NPV using Equation 6–2 and a regular calculator as we did here. Nevertheless, the most efficient way to find the NPV is by using a financial calculator. Different calculators are set up somewhat differently, but they all have a section of memory called the "cash flow register" that is used for uneven cash flows such as those in Project S (as opposed to equal annuity cash flows). As we saw in Chapter 3, a solution process for Equation 6–2 is literally programmed into financial calculators. You simply input the cash flows (being sure to observe the signs) in the order they occur, along with the value of I/k = k. For Project S, you enter CF_0 = –3,000, CF_1 = 1,500, CF_2 = 1,200, CF_3 = 800, CF_4 = 300, and I/k = 10%. At this point you have (in your calculator) the following computation for Project S:

$$NPV_s = (3,000) + \frac{1,500}{(1.10)^1} + \frac{1,200}{(1.10)^2} + \frac{800}{(1.10)^3} + \frac{300}{(1.10)^4}$$

As you can see, the equation has one unknown—NPV. Now you just ask the calculator to solve the equation for you, which you do by pressing the NPV key (and, on some calculators, the "compute" key). The answer, 161.33, will appear on the screen.[4] Using this same process for Project L, we find NPV_L = \$108.67.[5] On this basis, both projects should be accepted if they are *independent*, but Project S should be the one chosen if they are *mutually exclusive*.

If you look at the cash flow time line that shows the NPV computation for Project S, you can see the reason it has a positive NPV is because the initial investment of \$3,000 is recovered on a present value basis prior to the end of the project's life. In fact, if we use the payback concept, we can easily compute how long it would take to recapture the initial outlay of \$3,000 using the discounted cash flows given in the cash flow time line. The sum of the present values of the cash flows for the first three years is \$2,956.43 = 1,363.64 + 991.74 + 601.05, so all of the \$3,000 cost is not recovered until 3.2 years = 3 years + [(\$3,000 – \$2,956.43)/\$204.90] years. Therefore, on a *present value basis*, it takes 3.2 years for Project S to recover, or pay back, its original cost. This is called the **discounted payback** of Project S, the length of time it takes for a project's *discounted* cash flows to repay the cost of the investment using this technique. The discounted payback for Project L is 3.90 years, so Project S is more acceptable. Figure 6–3 shows the discounted payback computations for Projects S and L.

Unlike the traditional payback computation, the discounted payback computation considers the time value of money. *Using the discounted payback method, a project should be accepted when its discounted payback is less than its expected life.* As Figure 6–3 shows,

DISCOUNTED PAYBACK
The length of time it takes for a project's discounted cash flows to repay the cost of the investment.

---

[4]Refer to the manual that came with your calculator to determine how the CF function is used.

[5]Appendix 6A at the end of this chapter shows how to compute the NPV for Project S using a spreadsheet. It also shows how to use a spreadsheet to compute the project's internal rate of return (IRR), which is discussed later in the chapter.

FIGURE 6-3	Discounted Payback Period for Project S and Project L

Project S:

	0	1	2	3 DPB$_S$	4
Actual net cash flow	(3,000)	1,500.00	1,200.00	800.00	300.00
Discounted cash flow, DCF	(3,000)	1,363.64	991.74	601.05	204.90
Cumulative DCF	(3,000)	(1,636.36)	(644.62)	(43.57)	161.33

$$\text{Discounted payback DPB}_S = 3 + \frac{\$43.57}{\$204.90} = 3.2 \text{ years} \qquad\qquad = \text{NPV}_S$$

Project L:

	0	1	2	3	DPB$_L$ 4
Actual net cash flow	(3,000)	400.00	900.00	1,300.00	1,500.00
Discounted cash flow, DCF	(3,000)	363.64	743.80	976.71	1,024.52
Cumulative DCF	(3,000)	(2,636.36)	(1,892.56)	(915.85)	108.67

$$\text{Discounted payback DPB}_L = 3 + \frac{\$915.85}{\$1,024.52} = 3.9 \text{ years} \qquad\qquad = \text{NPV}_L$$

when a project's discounted payback is less than its life, the present value of the future cash flows the project is expected to generate exceeds the initial cost of the asset (initial investment)—that is, NPV > 0.

Rationale for the NPV Method

The rationale for the NPV method is straightforward. An NPV of zero signifies that the project's cash flows are just sufficient to repay the invested capital and to provide the required rate of return on that capital. If a project has a positive NPV, then it generates a return that is greater than is needed to pay for funds provided by investors, and this excess return accrues solely to the firm's stockholders. Therefore, if a firm takes on a project with a positive NPV, the position of the stockholders is improved because the firm's value is greater. In our example, shareholders' wealth would increase by $161.33 if the firm takes on Project S but by only $108.67 if it takes on Project L. Viewed in this manner, it is easy to see why Project S is preferred to Project L, and it also is easy to see the logic of the NPV approach. If the two projects are independent, both should be accepted because shareholders wealth would increase by $270 = $161.33 + $108.67. *In general, a project is considered acceptable if its NPV is positive; it is not acceptable if its NPV is negative.*[6]

---

[6]This description of the process is somewhat oversimplified. Both analysts and investors anticipate that firms will identify and accept positive NPV projects, and current stock prices reflect these expectations. Thus, stock prices react to announcements of new capital projects only to the extent that such projects were not already expected. In this sense, we can think of a firm's value as consisting of two parts: (1) the value of its existing assets and (2) the value of its "growth opportunities," or projects with positive NPVs.

Internal Rate of Return (IRR)

In the previous chapter, we presented procedures for finding the yield to maturity (YTM), or rate of return, on a bond. Recall that if you invest in the bond and hold it to maturity, you can expect to earn the YTM on the money you invest. Exactly the same concepts are employed in capital budgeting to determine the **internal rate of return (IRR),** which is the rate of return the firm expects to earn if the project is purchased and held for its economic life. The IRR is defined as the discount rate that equates the present value of a project's expected cash flows to the initial amount invested. *As long as the project's IRR, which is its expected return, is greater than the rate of return required by the firm for such an investment, the project is acceptable.*

We can use the following equation to solve for a project's IRR:

INTERNAL RATE OF RETURN (IRR)
The discount rate that forces the PV of a project's expected cash flows to equal its initial cost. IRR is similar to the YTM on a bond.

6–3

$$\hat{CF}_0 + \frac{\hat{CF}_1}{(1 + IRR)^1} + \frac{\hat{CF}_2}{(1 + IRR)^2} + \cdots + \frac{\hat{CF}_n}{(1 + IRR)^n} = 0$$

$$= \sum_{t=0}^{n} \frac{\hat{CF}_t}{(1 + IRR)^t} = 0$$

For Project S, the cash flow time line for the IRR computation is as follows:

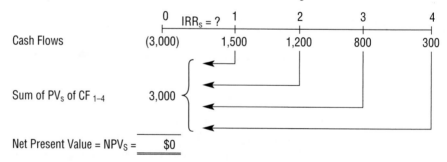

Using Equation 6–3, here is the setup for computing IRR_S:

$$(3,000) + \frac{1,500}{(1 + IRR)^1} + \frac{1,200}{(1 + IRR)^2} + \frac{800}{(1 + IRR)^3} + \frac{300}{(1 + IRR)^4} = 0$$

Although it is easy to find the NPV without a financial calculator, the same is *not* true of the IRR. Without a financial calculator, you must solve Equation 6–3 by trial and error—that is, you must try different discount rates until you find the one that forces NPV equal zero. This discount rate is the IRR. For a realistic project with a fairly long life, the trial and error approach is a tedious, time-consuming task. Fortunately, it is easy to find IRRs with a financial calculator.

To solve for IRR using a financial calculator, follow the steps used to find the NPV. First, enter the cash flows as shown on the preceding cash flow time line into the calculator's cash flow register. For Project S, enter $CF_0 = -3,000$, $CF_1 = 1,500$, $CF_2 = 1,200$, $CF_3 = 800$, and $CF_4 = 300$. In effect, you have entered the cash flows into the equation shown below the time line. You now have one unknown, IRR, or the discount rate that forces NPV to equal zero. The calculator has been programmed to solve for the IRR, and you activate this program by pressing the key labeled "IRR."

Following are the IRRs for Project S and Project L found using a financial calculator:

$$IRR_S = 13.1\%$$

$$IRR_L = 11.4\%.$$

REQUIRED RATE OF RETURN, OR HURDLE RATE

The discount rate (cost of funds) that the IRR must exceed for a project to be considered acceptable.

A project is acceptable if its IRR is greater than the firm's **required rate of return,** *or* **hurdle rate.** For example, if the hurdle rate required by the firm is 10 percent, then both Project S and Project L are acceptable. If they are mutually exclusive, Project S is more acceptable than Project L because $IRR_S > IRR_L$. On the other hand, if the firm's required rate of return is 15 percent, neither project is acceptable.

Notice from Equation 6–3 that you do not need to know the firm's required rate of return to solve for IRR. You need the required rate of return to make a decision as to whether a project is acceptable once its IRR is computed. Also, note that the *IRR is (1) the rate of return that will be earned by anyone who purchases the project, and (2) dependent on the project's cash flow characteristics—that is, the amounts and the timing of the cash flows—not the firm's required rate of return.* As a result, a project's IRR is the same for all firms, regardless of their particular required rates of return. A project might be acceptable to one firm (Project S would be acceptable to a firm that has a required rate of return equal to 10 percent), but not acceptable to another firm (Project S is not acceptable to a firm that has a required rate of return equal to 15 percent.)

Rationale for the IRR Method

If one is at the break even with present value of all in and out cash flow, at what rate money is growing?

Why is a project acceptable if its IRR is greater than its required rate of return? Because the IRR on a project is its expected rate of return, and if this return exceeds the cost of the funds used to finance the project, a surplus remains after paying for the funds. This surplus accrues to the firm's stockholders. Therefore, *taking on a project whose IRR exceeds its required rate of return, or cost of funds, increases shareholders' wealth.* On the other hand, if the IRR is less than the cost of funds, then taking on the project imposes a cost on current stockholders that decreases wealth.

Consider what would happen if you borrowed funds at a 10 percent interest rate to invest in the stock market. The 10 percent interest is your *cost of funds*, which is what you *require* your investments to earn to break even. You lose money if you earn less than 10 percent, and you gain money if you earn more than 10 percent. This break-even characteristic makes the IRR useful in evaluating capital projects.

Self-Test Questions

Discuss the capital budgeting techniques that were discussed in this section, and give the rationale for using each one.

How does the traditional payback differ from the discounted payback?

Comparison of the NPV and IRR Methods

We found the NPV for Project S is $161.33, which means that the firm's value will increase by $161.33 if the project is purchased. The IRR for Project S is 13.1 percent, which means that the firm will earn a 13.1 percent rate of return on its investment if it purchases Project S. We generally measure wealth in dollars, so the NPV method should be used to accomplish the goal of maximizing shareholders' wealth. In reality, using the IRR method could lead to investment decisions that increase, but do not maximize wealth. We choose to discuss the IRR method and compare it to the NPV method because many corporate executives are familiar with the meaning of IRR, it is entrenched in the corporate world, and it does have some virtues. For these reasons, it is important to understand the IRR method and be prepared to explain why a project with a lower IRR might sometimes be preferable to one with a higher IRR.

NPV Profiles

A graph that shows a project's NPV at various discount rates (required rates of return) is termed the project's **net present value (NPV) profile.** Figure 6–4 shows the NPV profiles for Project L and Project S. To construct the profiles, we calculate the projects' NPVs at various discount rates—say, 0, 5, 10, and 15—and then plot these values. The points plotted on our graph for each project are shown at the bottom of Figure 6–4.[7]

Because the IRR is defined as the discount rate at which a project's NPV equals zero, the point where its *NPV profile crosses the X axis indicates a project's internal rate of return.*

NPVs and the Required Rate of Return

Figure 6–4 shows that the NPV profiles for Project L and Project S decline as the discount rate increases. Notice, however, that Project L has the higher NPV at low discount rates, whereas Project S has the higher NPV at high discount rates. According to the graph, $NPV_S = NPV_L = \$268$ when the discount rate, k, equals 8.1 percent. We call this point the **crossover rate** because below this rate $NPV_S < NPV_L$, and above this rate, $NPV_S > NPV_L$—that is, the NPVs cross over at 8.1 percent.[8]

Figure 6–4 also indicates that Project L's NPV is "more sensitive" to changes in the discount rate than is NPV_S. That is, Project L's net present value profile has the steeper slope, indicating that a given change in k has a larger effect on NPV_L than on NPV_S. Project L is more sensitive to changes in k because the cash flows from Project S are received sooner than those from Project L. In a payback sense, S is a short-term project, whereas L is a long-term project. As a general rule, the impact of an increase in the discount rate is much greater on distant cash flows than on near-term cash flows.[9] Consequently, if a project has most of its cash flows coming in the early years, its NPV will not be lowered very much if the required rate of return increases.

---

[7]Note that the NPV profiles are curved—they are *not* straight lines. Also, the NPVs approach the cost of the project as the discount rate increases without limit. The reason is that, at an infinitely high discount rate, the PV of the future cash flows would be zero, so NPV at $k = \infty$ is CF_0, which in our example is –$3,000.

[8]The crossover rate is easy to calculate. Simply go back to Figure 6–1, where we first show the two projects' cash flows. Now calculate the difference in the cash flows for Project S and Project L in each year. The differences are $CF_S - CF_L = \$0$, +$1,100, +$300, –$500, and –$1,200, respectively. Enter these values into the cash flow register of a financial calculator, press the IRR key, and the crossover rate, 8.11, appears.

[9]To illustrate, consider the present value of $100 to be received in one year versus $100 to be received in 10 years. The present values of each $100 discounted at 10 percent and at 15 percent are as follows:

FUTURE VALUE	YEAR RECEIVED	PV AT 10%	PV AT 15%	PERCENT DIFFERENCE
$100	1	$90.91	$86.96	–4.3%
$100	10	38.55	24.72	–35.9

As you can see, the farther into the future the cash flows are, the greater their sensitivity to discount rate changes.

While NPV indicates total wealth builds over project life it does not tell anything about timing of cash flow. Higher NPV project L, can have lower IRR, than Projects which lower NPV at higher IRR, beccawse in project L, higher cash Flow occurs during has early phase of the project.

FIGURE 6-4   NPV Profiles for Project S and Project L

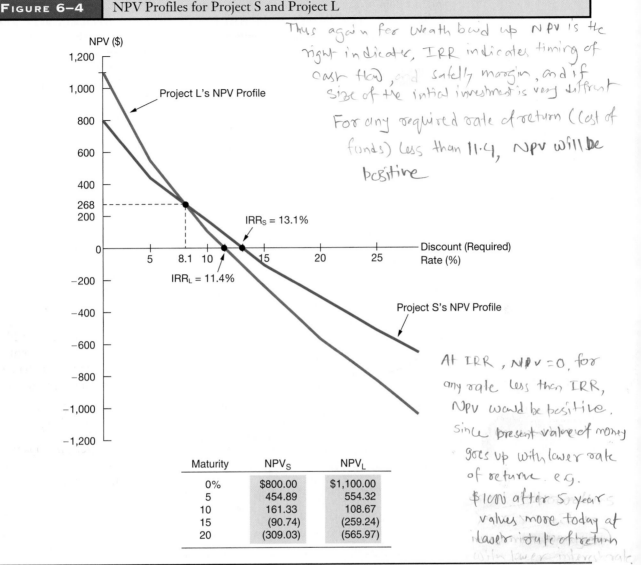

Thus again for wealth build up NPV is the right indicater, IRR indicates timing of cash flow, and safetly margin, and if size of the intial investmet is very different

For any required rate of return ((cost of funds) less than 11.4, NPV will be bositive

At IRR, NPV = 0, for any rate less than IRR, NPV would be bositive. Since present value of money goes up with lower rate of return. e.g. $1000 after 5 year values more today at lower rate of return with lower interest rate.

Maturity	NPV$_S$	NPV$_L$
0%	$800.00	$1,100.00
5	454.89	554.32
10	161.33	108.67
15	(90.74)	(259.24)
20	(309.03)	(565.97)

Conversely, a project whose cash flows come later will be severely penalized by high required rates of return. Accordingly, Project L, which has its largest cash flows in the later years, is hurt badly when the required rate of return is high, whereas Project S, which has relatively rapid cash flows, is affected less by high discount rates.

Independent Projects

Note that the internal rate of return formula, Equation 6–3, is simply the NPV formula, Equation 6–2, solved for the particular discount rate that forces the NPV to equal zero. Thus, the same basic equation is used for both methods. Mathematically, the NPV and IRR methods will always lead to the same accept/reject decisions for independent projects: *If a project's NPV is positive, its IRR will exceed k; if NPV is negative, k will exceed the IRR.* To see why this is so, look back at Figure 6–4, focus on Project L's profile, and note that (1) the IRR criterion for acceptance is that the required rate of return is less than (or to the left of) the IRR (11.4 percent) and (2) whenever the required rate of return is less than the IRR (11.4 percent), its NPV is positive. Thus, at any required rate of return less than 11.4 percent, Project L will be acceptable by both the NPV and the IRR criteria. Both methods reject the project if the required rate of return is greater than 11.4 percent. Project S—and all other independent projects under consideration—could be analyzed similarly, and *in every case, if a project is acceptable using the IRR method, then the NPV method also will show it is acceptable.*

Mutually Exclusive Projects

If Project S and Project L are *mutually exclusive* rather than independent, then only one project can be accepted. If you use IRR to make the decision as to which project is better, you would choose Project S because IRR$_S$ > IRR$_L$. If you use NPV to make the decision, you might reach a different conclusion depending on the firm's required rate of return. Note from Figure 6–4 that if the required rate of return is less than the crossover rate of 8.1 percent, NPV$_L$ > NPV$_S$, and NPV$_S$ > NPV$_L$ if the required rate of return is greater than 8.1 percent. As a result, Project L would be preferred if the firm's required rate of return is less than 8.1 percent, but Project S would be preferred if the firm's required rate of return is greater than 8.1 percent.

As long as the firm's required rate of return is greater than 8.1 percent, using either NPV or IRR will result in the same decision—that is, Project S should be purchased—because NPV$_S$ > NPV$_L$ and IRR$_S$ > IRR$_L$. On the other hand, if the firm's required rate of return is less than 8.1 percent, a person who uses NPV will reach a different conclusion as to which project should be purchased: He or she will choose Project L because NPV$_L$ > NPV$_S$. In this situation—that is, the required rate of return is less than 8.1 percent—*a conflict exists* because NPV says choose Project L over Project S, whereas IRR says just the opposite. Which answer is correct? Logic suggests that the NPV method is better because it selects the project that adds more to shareholder wealth.

Two basic conditions can cause NPV profiles to cross and thus lead to conflicts between NPV and IRR: (1) when *project size (or scale) differences* exist, meaning that the cost of one project is larger than that of the other, or (2) when *timing differences* exist, meaning that the timing of cash flows from the two projects differs such that most of the cash flows from one project come in the early years and most of the cash flows from the other project come in the later years, as occurs with Projects L and S.[10]

When either size or timing differences occur, the firm will have different amounts of funds to invest in the various years, depending on which of the two mutually exclusive projects it chooses. For example, if one project costs more than the other, then the firm will have more money at t = 0 to invest elsewhere if it

---

[10]Of course, it is possible for mutually exclusive projects to differ with respect to both scale and timing. Also, if mutually exclusive projects have different lives (as opposed to different cash flow patterns over a common life), this introduces further complications, and for meaningful comparisons, some mutually exclusive projects must be evaluated over a common life.

selects the smaller project. Similarly, for projects of equal size, the one with the larger early cash inflows provides more funds for reinvestment in the early years. Given this situation, the rate of return at which differential cash flows can be invested is an important consideration.

The critical issue in resolving conflicts between mutually exclusive projects is this: How useful is it to generate cash flows earlier rather than later? The value of early cash flows depends on the rate at which we can reinvest these cash flows. *The NPV method implicitly assumes that the rate at which cash flows can be reinvested is the required rate of return, whereas the IRR method implies that the firm has the opportunity to reinvest at the project's IRR.* These assumptions are inherent in the mathematics of the discounting process. The cash flows can actually be withdrawn as dividends by the stockholders and spent on pizza, but the NPV method still assumes that cash flows can be reinvested at the required rate of return, whereas the IRR method assumes reinvestment at the project's IRR.

Which is the better assumption—that cash flows can be reinvested at the required rate of return or that they can be reinvested at the project's IRR? To reinvest at the IRR associated with a capital project, the firm would have to be able to reinvest the project's cash flows in another project with an identical IRR. Such projects generally do not continue to exist, or it is not feasible to reinvest in such projects, because competition in the investment markets drives their prices up and their IRRs down. On the other hand, at the very least, a firm could repurchase the bonds and stock it has issued to raise capital budgeting funds and thus repay some of its investors, which would be the same as investing at its required rate of return. Thus, we conclude that the *more realistic* **reinvestment rate assumption** *is the required rate of return, which is implicit in the NPV method.* This, in turn, leads us to prefer the NPV method, at least for firms willing and able to obtain new funds at a cost reasonably close to their current cost of funds.

Cost of capital

REINVESTMENT RATE ASSUMPTION
The assumption that cash flows from a project can be reinvested (1) at the cost of capital, if using the NPV method, or (2) at the internal rate of return, if using the IRR method.

We should reiterate that when projects are independent, the NPV and IRR methods both provide exactly the same accept/reject decision. However, when evaluating mutually exclusive projects, especially those that differ in scale or timing, the NPV method should be used to determine which project should be purchased.

Multiple IRRs

There is one other situation in which the IRR approach might not be usable—this is when projects have unconventional cash flow patterns. A project has a *conventional* cash flow pattern if it has cash outflows (costs) in one or more periods at the beginning of its life followed by a series of cash inflows. If, however, a project has a large cash outflow either sometime during or at the end of its life, then it has an *unconventional* cash flow pattern. Projects with unconventional cash flow patterns present unique difficulties when the IRR method is used, including the possibility of **multiple IRRs.**[11]

MULTIPLE IRRS
The situation in which a project has two or more IRRs.

[11]Multiple IRRs result from the manner in which Equation 6–3 must be solved to arrive at a project's IRR. The mathematical rationale and the solution to multiple IRRs will not be discussed here. Instead, we want you to be aware that multiple IRRs can exist because this possibility complicates capital budgeting evaluation using the IRR method. Some financial calculators cannot compute the IRR for projects that have unconventional cash flows because there is not a single solution. In such cases, you would have to use NPV profiles, which essentially is a trial-and-error process.

Practice What We Preach (Teach)

The three capital budgeting techniques presented in this chapter traditionally have been considered the most popular by corporate financial managers. Just how popular are they? Do firms use methods that help to maximize value? Many surveys have been conducted over the years to determine which techniques firms rely on when making capital budgeting decisions. The results consistently show that firms rely on each of the methods discussed in this chapter to some extent to help to make final decisions about the acceptability of capital budgeting projects. As technology has advanced, firms have shifted to using the more sophisticated techniques, such as NPV and IRR. The following table shows to what extent this shift has occurred since the 1970s. The results given in the table were compiled from surveys conducted during each decade.* The numbers represent the average percentage of respondents who indicated that their firms use the particular capital budgeting technique "Always" or "Almost Always." In most cases, those who were surveyed were not asked to indicate the primary and secondary methods that were used.

PERIOD	PAYBACK	NPV	IRR
1970s	85%	65%	80%
1980s	78	75	88
1990s	60	80	79
2000s	53	85	77

As you can see, the use of the traditional payback period and IRR methods has declined, whereas the use of the NPV method has increased. Prior to the 1970s, many firms relied heavily on the payback period to make capital budgeting decisions. As technology and the understanding of the discounting techniques improved, both NPV and IRR became more popular. It appears that, for the most part, financial managers recognize these techniques provide correct decisions with respect to value maximization.

The results of the surveys also show that firms rarely rely on a single capital budgeting technique for evaluating projects; rather, decisions are based on information generated by more than one technique,

and often all three of the techniques listed in the table. Also, when asked whether using IRR presented any problems, especially with regard to multiple internal rates of return and ranking differences when compared to NPV, most financial managers indicated either that they had not heard of these problems or that such problems rarely occurred. In addition, it appears that most of the companies that face such problems choose to use NPV rather than IRR for their capital budgeting decisions.

For the most part, studies have shown that companies (1) use more sophisticated capital budgeting techniques today than in previous times, and (2) do not rely on a single evaluation method to make decisions about investing in capital projects. Clearly, firms still use payback period in their capital budgeting analyses. But even firms that previously relied on the traditional payback period seem to have switched to the discounted payback period. Thus, indications are that firms do use the methods we profess in finance courses.

*Studies that were examined include: Lawrence J. Gitman and John R. Forrester, Jr., 1977, "A Survey of Capital Budgeting Techniques Used by Major U.S. Firms," *Financial Management*, Fall, 66–71; David J. Oblak and Roy J. Helm, Jr., 1980, "Survey and Analysis of Capital Budgeting Methods Used by Multinationals," *Financial Management*, Winter, 37–41; Marjorie T. Stanley and Stanley B. Block, 1984, "A Survey of Multinational Capital Budgeting," *Financial Review*, March, 36–51; Glenn H. Petry and James Sprow, 1993, "The Theory of Finance in the 1990s," *The Quarterly Review of Economics and Finance*, Winter, 359–381; Erika Gilbert and Alan Reichert, 1995, "The Practice of Financial Management among Large United States Corporations," *Financial Practice and Education*, Spring/Summer, 16–23; Patricia Chadwell-Hatfield, Bernard Goitein, Philip Horvath, and Allen Webster, 1996/1997 "Financial Criteria, Capital Budgeting Techniques, and Risk Analysis of Manufacturing Firms," *Journal of Applied Business Research*, Winter, 95–104; John R. Graham and Campbell R. Harvey, 2001, "The Theory and Practice of Corporate Finance: Evidence from the Field," *Journal of Finance Economics*, Vol. 60, No 2–3, 197–243; and Patricia A. Ryan and Glenn P. Ryan, 2002, "Capital Budgeting Practices of the Fortune 1000: How Have Things Changed?" *Journal of Business and Management*, Fall, 335–364.

There exists an IRR solution for each time the *direction* of the cash flows associated with a project is interrupted—that is, inflows change to outflows. For example, a conventional cash flow pattern only has one net cash outflow at the beginning of the project's life, so the direction of the cash flows changes (is interrupted) once from negative (outflow) to positive (inflow), and there is only one IRR solution. A project with a 10-year life that has cash inflows every year except that $CF_0 < 0$ and $CF_5 < 0$ will have two IRR solutions because the cash flow pattern has two direction changes, or interruptions—one after the initial cost is paid and another five years later. Figure 6–5 illustrates the multiple IRR problem with a strip mining project that costs $1.6 million. The mine will produce a cash inflow of $10 million at the end of Year 1, but $10 million must be spent at the end of Year 2 to restore the land to its original condition. Two IRRs exist for this project—25 percent and 400 percent. The NPV profile for the mine shows that the project would have a positive NPV, and thus be acceptable, if the firm's required rate of return is between 25 percent and 400 percent.

Self-Test Questions

Describe how NPV profiles are constructed.

What is the crossover rate, and how does it affect the choice between mutually exclusive projects?

Why do the NPV and IRR methods always lead to the same accept/reject decisions for independent projects?

FIGURE 6–5	NVP Profile for Project M

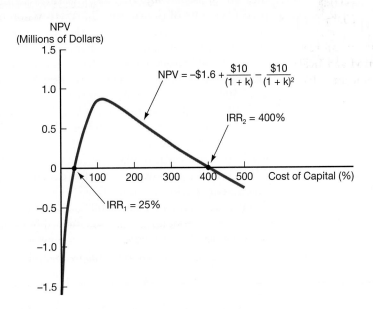

$$NPV = -\$1.6 + \frac{\$10}{(1 + k)} - \frac{\$10}{(1 + k)^2}$$

$IRR_2 = 400\%$

$IRR_1 = 25\%$

What two basic conditions can lead to conflicts between the NPV and IRR methods?

If a conflict exists, should the capital budgeting decision be made on the basis of the NPV or the IRR ranking? Why?

What is the multiple IRR problem, and what condition is necessary for its occurrence?

Conclusions on the Capital Budgeting Decision Methods

In the previous section, we compared the NPV and IRR methods to highlight their relative strengths and weaknesses for evaluating capital projects, and in the process we probably created the impression that "sophisticated" firms should use only one method in the decision process—NPV. However, virtually all capital budgeting decisions are analyzed by computer, so it is easy to calculate and list all the decision measures: traditional payback, discounted payback, NPV, and IRR. In making the accept/reject decision, most large, sophisticated firms such as IBM, General Electric, and General Motors calculate and consider multiple measures because each provides decision makers with a somewhat different piece of relevant information.

Payback and discounted payback provide information about both the risk and the *liquidity* of a project. A long payback means (1) that the investment dollars will be locked up for many years, hence the project is relatively illiquid, and (2) that the project's cash flows must be forecast far out into the future, hence the project is probably quite risky.[12] A good analogy for this is the bond valuation process. An investor should never compare the yields to maturity on two bonds without considering their terms to maturity because a bond's riskiness is significantly influenced by its maturity.

NPV is important because it gives a direct measure of the dollar benefit (on a present value basis) to the firm's shareholders, so we regard NPV as the best single measure of *profitability*. IRR also measures profitability, but here it is expressed as a percentage rate of return, which many decision makers, especially nonfinancial managers, seem to prefer. Further, IRR contains information concerning a project's "safety margin," which is not inherent in NPV. To illustrate, consider the following two projects: Project T costs $10,000 at t = 0 and is expected to return $16,500 at the end of one year, while Project B costs $100,000 and has an expected payoff of $115,500 after one year. At a 10 percent required rate of return, both projects have an NPV of $5,000, so by the NPV rule we should be indifferent between the two. However, Project T actually provides a much larger margin for error. Even if its realized cash inflow were almost 40 percent below the $16,500 forecast, the firm would still recover its $10,000 investment. On the other hand, if Project B's inflows fell by only 14 percent from the forecasted $115,500, the firm would not recover its investment. Further, if no inflows were generated at all, the firm would lose only $10,000 with Project T but $100,000 if it took on Project B.

The NPV contains no information about either the safety margin inherent in a project's cash flow forecasts or the amount of capital at risk, but the IRR does provide "safety margin" information: Project T's IRR is a whopping 65 percent, while Project

---

[12]We generally define liquidity as the ability to convert an asset into cash quickly while maintaining the original investment. Thus, in most cases, short-term assets are considered more liquid than long-term assets. We discuss liquidity in greater detail later in the book.

B's IRR is only 15.5 percent. As a result, the realized return could fall substantially for Project T, and it would still make money. Note, however, that the IRR method has a reinvestment assumption that probably is unrealistic, and it is possible for projects to have multiple IRRs. Both of these problems can be corrected using the modified IRR calculation, which is discussed in Appendix 6B at the end of this chapter.

In summary, the different methods provide different types of information to decision makers. Because it is easy to calculate them, all should be considered in the decision process. For any specific decision, more weight might be given to one method than another, but it would be foolish to ignore the information provided by any of the methods.

At this point, we should note that multinational corporations use essentially the same capital budgeting techniques described in this chapter. However, foreign governments, international regulatory environments, and financial and product markets in other countries pose certain challenges to U.S. firms that must make capital budgeting decisions for their foreign operations. We wait to discuss some of these challenges/differences until the next chapter.

Self-Test Questions

Describe the advantages and disadvantages of the capital budgeting methods discussed in this chapter.

Should capital budgeting decisions be made solely on the basis of a project's NPV?

The Post-Audit

POST-AUDIT
A comparison of the actual and expected results for a given capital project.

An important aspect of the capital budgeting process is the **post-audit,** which involves (1) comparing actual results with those predicted by the project's sponsors and (2) explaining why any differences occurred. For example, many firms require that the operating divisions send monthly reports for the first six months after a project goes into operation and quarterly reports thereafter, until the project's results are up to expectations. From then on, reports on the project are handled like those of other operations.

The post-audit has two main purposes:

1. **Improve forecasts.** When decision makers are forced to compare their projections to actual outcomes, there is a tendency for estimates to improve. Conscious or unconscious biases are observed and eliminated; new forecasting methods are sought as the need for them becomes apparent; and people simply tend to do everything better, including forecasting, if they know that their actions are being monitored.
2. **Improve operations.** Businesses are run by people, and people can perform at higher or lower levels of efficiency. When a divisional team has made a forecast about an investment, its members are, in a sense, putting their reputations on the line. If costs are above predicted levels, sales are below expectations, and so on, executives in production, marketing, and other areas will strive to improve operations and to bring results in line with forecasts. In a discussion related to this point, an IBM executive made this statement: "You academicians worry only about making good decisions. In business, we also worry about making decisions good."

✳ **ETHICAL DILEMMA**

This Is a Good Investment—Be Sure the Numbers Show That It Is!

Oliver Greene is the assistant to the financial manager at Cybercomp Inc., which is a company that develops software to drive network communications for personal computers. Oliver joined Cybercomp three years ago, following graduation from college. His primary responsibility has been to evaluate capital budgeting projects and make investment recommendations to the board of directors. Oliver enjoys his job very much: He often finds himself challenged with interesting tasks, and he is paid extremely well for what he does.

Last week, Oliver started evaluating the capital projects that have been proposed for investment this year. One of the proposals is to purchase NetWare Products, a company that manufactures circuit boards, called network cards, which are required to achieve communication connectivity between personal computers. Cybercomp packages network cards with the software it sells, but it currently purchases them from another manufacturer. The proposal, which was submitted by Nadine Wilson, Cybercomp's CEO, suggests the company can reduce costs and increase profit margins by producing the network cards in-house.

Oliver barely had time to scan the proposal when he was summoned to Ms. Wilson's office. The meeting was short and to the point. Ms. Wilson instructed Oliver to "make the numbers for NetWare Products look good because we want to buy that company." She also gave Oliver an evaluation of NetWare completed two years ago by an independent appraiser that suggests NetWare might not be worth the amount Cybercomp is willing to pay. Ms. Wilson instructed Oliver to find a way to rebut the report's findings.

Oliver was troubled by the meeting he had with Ms. Wilson. His gut feeling was that something was wrong. But he hadn't yet had time to examine the proposal carefully. His evaluation was cursory, and he was far from making a final decision concerning the acceptability of the capital budgeting project that Ms. Wilson proposed. Oliver felt that he needed much more information before forming a final recommendation.

Oliver has spent the entire day examining the appraisal report that Ms. Wilson provided and trying to gather additional information about the proposed investment. The report contains some background information concerning NetWare's operations, but crucial financial data are missing. Further investigation into NetWare Products has produced little information. Oliver has discovered that the company's stock is closely held by a small group of investors that owns numerous businesses and that generously contributes to the local university, which happens to be Ms. Wilson's alma mater. In addition, Oliver's secretary has informed him that the gossip around the water cooler at Cybercomp is that Ms. Wilson and the owners of NetWare are old college buddies, and she might even have a stake in NetWare.

This morning, Ms. Wilson called Oliver and repeated her feelings concerning the purchase of NetWare. This time she said: "We really want to purchase NetWare. Some people might not believe so, but this is a very good deal. It's your job to make the numbers work—that's why we pay you the big bucks!" As a result of the conversation, Oliver has the impression his job might be jeopardized if he doesn't make the "right" decision. This added pressure has made Oliver tense. What should he do? What would you do if you were Oliver? Would your answer change if you knew Ms. Wilson had recently sold much of her Cybercomp stock?

The post-audit is not a simple process—a number of factors can cause complications. First, we must recognize that each element of the cash flow forecast is subject to uncertainty, so a percentage of all projects undertaken by any reasonably venturesome firm will necessarily go awry. This fact must be considered when appraising the performances of the operating executives who submit capital expenditure requests. Second, projects sometimes fail to meet expectations for reasons beyond the control of the operating executives and for reasons that no one could realistically be expected to anticipate. For example, poor economic conditions in 2000–2002 adversely affected many projects. Third, it is often difficult to separate the operating results of one investment from those of a larger system. Although some projects stand alone and permit ready identification of costs and revenues, the actual cost savings that result from a new computer system, for example, might be hard to measure. Fourth, it is often hard to hand out blame or praise because the executives who were actually responsible for a given decision might have moved on by the time the results of a long-term investment are known.

Because of these difficulties, some firms tend to downplay the importance of the post-audit. However, observations of both businesses and governmental units suggest that the best-run and most successful organizations are the ones that put the greatest emphasis on post-audits. Accordingly, we regard the post-audit as being an extremely important element in a good capital budgeting system.

Self-Test Questions

What is done in the post-audit?

Identify several purposes of the post-audit.

What are some factors that can cause complications in the post-audit?

Summary

This chapter discussed the capital budgeting process, and the key concepts that were covered are listed here:

- **Capital budgeting** is the process of analyzing potential fixed asset investments. Capital budgeting decisions are probably the most important ones financial managers must make.
- The **payback period** is defined as the expected number of years required to recover a project's cost. The traditional payback method ignores cash flows beyond the payback period, and it does not consider the time value of money. The payback does, however, indicate a project's risk and liquidity because it shows how long the invested capital will be "at risk."
- The **discounted payback method** is similar to the traditional payback method except that it discounts cash flows at the project's required rate of return. Like the traditional payback, it ignores cash flows beyond the discounted payback period.
- The **net present value (NPV) method** discounts all cash flows at the project's required rate of return and then sums those cash flows. The project is acceptable if this sum, called the NPV, is positive.
- The **internal rate of return (IRR)** is defined as the discount rate that forces a project's NPV to equal zero. The project is acceptable if the IRR is greater than the project's required rate of return.
- The NPV and IRR methods make the same accept/reject decisions for **independent projects,** but if projects are **mutually exclusive,** then ranking conflicts can arise. If conflicts arise, the NPV method generally should be used. The NPV and IRR methods are both superior to the traditional payback, but NPV is generally the single best measure of a project's profitability.
- The NPV method assumes that cash flows can be reinvested at the firm's required rate of return, whereas the IRR method assumes reinvestment at the

project's IRR. Because **reinvestment at the required rate of return generally is a better (closer to the truth) assumption,** the NPV is superior to the IRR.

- **Multiple IRRs** exist if a project's cash flows do not follow a conventional pattern—that is, if cash outflows interrupt a series of cash inflows during the life of the project.
- Sophisticated managers consider several of the project evaluation measures because the **different measures provide different types of information.**
- The **post-audit** is a key element of capital budgeting. By comparing actual results with predicted results and then determining why differences occurred, decision makers can improve both their operations and their forecasts of project outcomes.

Although this chapter has presented the basic elements of the capital budgeting process, there are many other aspects of this crucial topic. Some of the more important ones are discussed in the next chapter.

Questions

6–1 How is a project classification scheme (for example, replacement, expansion into new markets, and so forth) used in the capital budgeting process?

6–2 Explain why the NPV of a relatively long-term project, defined as one for which a high percentage of its cash flows are expected in the distant future, is more sensitive to changes in the required rate of return than is the NPV of a short-term project.

6–3 Explain why, if two mutually exclusive projects are being compared, the project that generates most of its cash flows in the beginning of its life might have the higher ranking under the NPV criterion if the required rate of return is high, whereas the project that generates most of its cash flows toward the end of its life might be deemed better if the required rate of return is low. Would changes in the required rate of return ever cause a change in the IRR ranking of two such projects? Explain.

6–4 In what sense is a reinvestment rate assumption embodied in the NPV and IRR methods? What is the assumed reinvestment rate of each method?

6–5 "If a firm has no mutually exclusive projects, only independent ones, and it also has both a constant required rate of return and projects with conventional cash flow patterns, then the NPV and IRR methods will always lead to identical capital budgeting decisions." Discuss this statement. What does it imply about using the IRR method in lieu of the NPV method? If each of the assumptions made in the question were changed (one by one), how would these changes affect your answer?

6–6 Are there conditions under which a firm might be better off if it were to choose a machine with a rapid payback rather than one with a larger NPV? Explain.

6–7 A firm has $100 million available for capital expenditures. It is considering investing in one of two projects; each has a cost of $100 million. Project A has an IRR of 20 percent and an NPV of $9 million. It will be terminated at the end of one year at a profit of $20 million, resulting in an immediate increase in earnings per share (EPS). Project B, which cannot be postponed, has an IRR of 30 percent and an NPV of $50 million. However, the firm's short-run EPS will be reduced if it accepts Project B because no revenues will be generated for several years.

    a. Should the short-run effects on EPS influence the choice between the two projects?

    b. How might situations like the one described here influence a firm's decision to use payback as a part of the capital budgeting process?

Self-Test Problems

(Solutions appear in Appendix B)

key terms **ST-1** Define each of the following terms:

    a. Capital budget; capital budgeting

    b. Traditional payback period; discounted payback period

    c. Independent projects; mutually exclusive projects

    d. DCF techniques; net present value (NPV) method

    e. Internal rate of return (IRR) method; IRR

    f. NPV profile; crossover rate

    g. Unconventional cash flow patterns; multiple IRRs

    h. Hurdle rate; required rate of return

    i. Reinvestment rate assumption

    j. Post-audit

project analysis **ST-2** You are a financial analyst for Damon Electronics Company. The director of capital budgeting has asked you to analyze two proposed capital investments, Projects X and Y. Each project has a cost of $10,000, and the required rate of return for each project is 12 percent. The projects' expected net cash flows are as follows:

	Expected Net Cash Flows	
YEAR	**PROJECT X**	**PROJECT Y**
0	$(10,000)	$(10,000)
1	6,500	3,500
2	3,000	3,500
3	3,000	3,500
4	1,000	3,500

    a. Calculate each project's payback period (PB), net present value (NPV), and internal rate of return (IRR).

    b. Which project or projects should be accepted if they are independent?

    c. Which project should be accepted if they are mutually exclusive?

    d. How might a change in the required rate of return produce a conflict between the NPV and IRR rankings of these two projects? Would this conflict exist if k were 5 percent? (*Hint:* Plot the NPV profiles.)

    e. Why does the conflict exist?

Problems

payback, NPV, and IRR
calculations **6–1** Project K has a cost of $52,125, and its expected net cash inflows are $12,000 per year for eight years.

    a. What is the project's payback period (to the closest year)?

    b. The required rate of return for the project is 12 percent. What is the project's NPV?

c. What is the project's IRR?

d. What is the project's discounted payback period, assuming a 12 percent required rate of return?

NPR and IRR analysis   **6–2** Derek's Donuts is considering two mutually exclusive investments. The projects' expected net cash flows are as follows:

	EXPECTED NET CASH FLOWS	
YEAR	PROJECT A	PROJECT B
0	$(300)	$(405)
1	(387)	134
2	(193)	134
3	(100)	134
4	500	134
5	500	134
6	850	134
7	100	0

a. Construct NPV profiles for Projects A and B.

b. What is each project's IRR?

c. If you were told that each project's required rate of return was 12 percent, which project should be selected? If the required rate of return was 15 percent, what would be the proper choice?

d. Looking at the NPV profiles constructed in part a, what is the *approximate* crossover rate, and what is its significance?

timing differences   **6–3** The Southwestern Oil Exploration Company is considering two mutually exclusive plans for extracting oil on property for which it has mineral rights. Both plans call for the expenditure of $12 million to drill development wells. Under Plan A, all the oil will be extracted in one year, producing a cash flow at the end of Year 1 (t = 1) of $14.4 million. Under Plan B, cash flows will be $2.1 million per year for 20 years.

a. Construct NPV profiles for Plan A and Plan B, identify each project's IRR, and indicate the approximate crossover rate of return. (To compute the exact crossover rate, see footnote 8 in the chapter.)

b. Suppose a company has a required rate of return of 12 percent, and it can get unlimited funds at that cost. Is it logical to assume that it would take on all available independent projects (of average risk) with returns greater than 12 percent? Further, if all available projects with returns greater than 12 percent are purchased, would this mean that cash flows from past investments would have an opportunity cost of only 12 percent because all the firm could do with these cash flows would be to replace money that has a cost of 12 percent? Finally, does this imply that the required rate of return is the correct rate to assume for the reinvestment of a project's cash flows?

scale differences   **6–4** The Chaplinsky Publishing Company is considering two mutually exclusive expansion plans. Plan A calls for the expenditure of $40 million on a large-scale, integrated plant that will provide an expected cash flow stream of $6.4 million per year for 20 years. Plan B calls for the expenditure of $12 million to build a somewhat less efficient, more labor-intensive plant that has an expected cash flow stream of $2.72 million per year for 20 years. Chaplinsky's required rate of return is 10 percent.

a. Calculate each project's NPV and IRR.

b. Construct the NPV profiles for Plan A and Plan B. Using the NPV profiles, approximate the crossover rate.

c. Give a logical explanation, based on reinvestment rates and opportunity costs, as to why the NPV method is better than the IRR method when the firm's required rate of return is constant at some value such as 10 percent.

Exam-Type Problems

The problems included in this section are set up in such a way that they could be used as multiple-choice exam problems.

NPVs, IRRs, and payback for independent projects

6–5 Olsen Engineering is considering including two pieces of equipment—a truck and an overhead pulley system—in this year's capital budget. The projects are independent. The cash outlay for the truck is $22,430, and for the pulley system it is $17,100. Each piece of equipment has an estimated life of five years. The annual after-tax cash flow expected to be provided by the truck is $7,500, and for the pulley it is $5,100. The firm's required rate of return is 14 percent. Calculate the IRR, the NPV, and the traditional payback period for each project, and indicate which project(s) should be accepted.

NPVs and IRRs for mutually exclusive projects

6–6 Horrigan Industries must choose between a gas-powered and an electric-powered forklift truck for moving materials in its factory. Because both forklifts perform the same function, the firm will choose only one. (They are mutually exclusive investments.) The electric-powered truck will cost more, but it will be less expensive to operate; it will cost $22,000, whereas the gas-powered truck will cost $17,500. The required rate of return that applies to both investments is 12 percent. The life for both types of truck is estimated to be six years, during which time the net cash flows for the electric-powered truck will be $6,290 per year and those for the gas-powered truck will be $5,000 per year. Calculate the NPV and IRR for each type of truck, and decide which to recommend.

capital budgeting decisions

6–7 Project S costs $15,000 and is expected to produce benefits (cash flows) of $4,500 per year for five years. Project L costs $37,500 and is expected to produce cash flows of $11,100 per year for five years.

a. Calculate the NPV, IRR, and traditional payback period for each project, assuming a required rate of return of 14 percent.

b. If the projects are independent, which project(s) should be selected? If they are mutually exclusive projects, which project actually should be selected?

present value of costs

6–8 The Cordell Coffee Company is evaluating the within-plant distribution system for its new roasting, grinding, and packing plant. The two alternatives are (1) a conveyor system with a high initial cost but low annual operating costs and (2) several forklift trucks, which cost less but have considerably higher operating costs. The decision to construct the plant has already been made, and the choice here will have no effect on the overall revenues of the project. The required rate of return for the plant is 9 percent, and the projects' expected net costs are listed in the following table:

	EXPECTED NET CASH FLOWS	
YEAR	CONVEYOR	FORKLIFT
0	$(300,000)	$(120,000)
1	(66,000)	(96,000)
2	(66,000)	(96,000)
3	(66,000)	(96,000)
4	(66,000)	(96,000)
5	(66,000)	(96,000)

   a. What is the present value of costs of each alternative? Which method
   should be chosen? (*Hint:* Be careful—these cash flows are outflows.)
   b. What is the IRR of each alternative?

NPV and IRR analysis   **6-9** Your company is considering two mutually exclusive projects—C and R—
   whose costs and cash flows are shown in the following table:

YEAR	PROJECT C	PROJECT R
1	$(14,000)	$(22,840)
2	8,000	8,000
3	6,000	8,000
4	2,000	8,000
5	3,000	8,000

   The projects are equally risky, and their required rate of return is 12 percent.
   You must make a recommendation concerning which project should be purchased. To determine which is more appropriate, compute the NPV and IRR
   of each project.

NPV and IRR analysis   **6-10** The after-tax cash flows for two mutually exclusive projects have been estimated, and the following information has been provided:

YEAR	MACHINE D	MACHINE Q
0	$(2,500)	$(2,500)
1	2,000	0
2	900	1,800
3	100	1,000
4	100	900

   The company's required rate of return is 14 percent, and it can get unlimited
   funds at that cost. What is the IRR of the *better* project? (*Hint:* Note that the
   better project might not be the one with the higher IRR.)

NPV and IRR analysis   **6-11** Diamond Hill Jewelers is considering the following independent projects:

YEAR	PROJECT Y	PROJECT Z
0	$(25,000)	$(25,000)
1	10,000	0
2	9,000	0
3	7,000	0
4	6,000	36,000

   Which project(s) should be accepted if the required rate of return for the projects is 10 percent? Compute the NPVs and the IRRs for both projects.

Integrative Problem

basics of capital budgeting   **6-12** Your boss, the chief financial officer (CFO) for Southern Textiles, has just
   handed you the estimated cash flows for two proposed projects. Project L
   involves adding a new item to the firm's fabric line. It would take some time to
   build up the market for this product, so the cash inflows would increase over
   time. Project S involves an add-on to an existing line, and its cash flows would

decrease over time. Both projects have three-year lives because Southern is planning to introduce an entirely new fabric at that time.

Here are the net cash flow estimates (in thousands of dollars):

	EXPECTED NET CASH FLOWS	
YEAR	PROJECT L	PROJECT S
0	$(100)	$(100)
1	10	70
2	60	50
3	80	20

The CFO also made subjective risk assessments of each project, and he concluded that the projects both have risk characteristics that are similar to the firm's average project. Southern's required rate of return is 10 percent. You must now determine whether one or both of the projects should be accepted. Start by answering the following questions:

a. What is capital budgeting? Are there any similarities between a firm's capital budgeting decisions and an individual's investment decisions?

b. What is the difference between independent and mutually exclusive projects? Between projects with conventional cash flows and projects with unconventional cash flows?

c. (1) What is the payback period? Find the traditional paybacks for Project L and Project S.

   (2) What is the rationale for the payback measure? According to the payback criterion, which project or projects should be accepted if the firm's maximum acceptable payback is two years and Project L and Project S are independent? Mutually exclusive?

   (3) What is the difference between the traditional payback and the discounted payback? What is each project's discounted payback?

   (4) What are the main disadvantages of the traditional payback? Is the payback method of any real usefulness in capital budgeting decisions?

d. (1) Define the term *net present value (NPV)*. What is each project's NPV?

   (2) What is the rationale behind the NPV method? According to NPV, which project or projects should be accepted if they are independent? Mutually exclusive?

   (3) Would the NPVs change if the required rate of return changed?

e. (1) Define the term *internal rate of return (IRR)*. What is each project's IRR?

   (2) How is the IRR on a project related to the YTM on a bond?

   (3) What is the logic behind the IRR method? According to IRR, which projects should be accepted if they are independent? Mutually exclusive?

   (4) Would the projects' IRRs change if the required rate of return changed? Explain.

f. (1) Construct the NPV profiles for Project L and Project S. At what discount rate do the profiles cross?

   (2) Look at the NPV profile graph without referring to the actual NPVs and IRRs. Which project or projects should be accepted if they are independent? Mutually exclusive? Explain. Do your answers differ depending on the discount rate used? Explain.

g. (1) What is the underlying cause of ranking conflicts between NPV and IRR?

　　(2) What is the *reinvestment rate assumption*, and how does it affect the NPV versus IRR conflict?

　　(3) Which capital budgeting method should be used when NPV and IRR give conflicting rankings? Why?

Computer-Related Problem

Work the problem in this section only if you are using the computer problem diskette.

NPV and IRR analysis　　**6–13** Use the model in File C06 to solve this problem. West Coast Chemical Company (WCCC) is considering two mutually exclusive investments. The projects' expected net cash flows are as follows:

	EXPECTED NET CASH FLOWS	
YEAR	PROJECT A	PROJECT B
0	$(45,000)	$(50,000)
1	(20,000)	15,000
2	11,000	15,000
3	20,000	15,000
4	30,000	15,000
5	45,000	15,000

a. Construct NPV profiles for Projects A and B.

b. Calculate each project's IRR. Assume the required rate of return is 13 percent.

c. If the required rate of return for each project is 13 percent, which project should West Coast select? If the required rate of return is 9 percent, what would be the proper choice? If the required rate of return is 15 percent, what would be the proper choice?

d. At what rate do the NPV profiles of the two projects cross?

e. Project A has a large cash flow in Year 5 associated with ending the project. WCCC's management is confident of Project A's cash flows in Years 0 to 4 but is uncertain about what its Year 5 cash flow will be. (There is no uncertainty about Project B's cash flows.) Under a worst-case scenario, Project A's Year 5 cash flow will be $40,000, whereas under a best-case scenario, the cash flow will be $50,000. Redo parts a, b, and d for each scenario, assuming a 13 percent required rate of return. If the required rate of return for each project is 13 percent, which project should be selected under each scenario?

GET REAL with Thomson ONE

6-14 Cisco Systems, Inc. [CSCO], which is located in San Jose, California, manufactures and sells networking and communication products and provides related services. Cisco is a growing company that makes large capital outlays for plant and equipment to produce its inventory. Cisco's customer base includes corporations, telecommunication corporations, public institutions, and commercial enterprises.

Using the Thomson ONE database, analyze from a capital budgeting point of view Cisco's capital expenditures compared to its cash flows during the last three years. Answer the following questions:

a. What are Cisco's total cash flows for each of the last three years? (*Hint:* You can find this information by clicking on Price/Worldscope Market Data/Market Data Snapshot.)

b. How much did Cisco spend on capital expenditures in each of the last three years? (*Hint:* Click on Financials/Thomson Financial Annual Financial Statements.)

c. If you make the assumption that Cisco's cost of acquiring capital is 10 percent, determine the present value of the cash flows.

d. Calculate the net present value (NPV) of Cisco's capital expenditures.

e. Is the NPV positive or negative? What does this result mean for Cisco Systems, Inc. and its capital budgeting decisions during the past three years? Explain.

APPENDIX 6A

Using a Spreadsheet to Compute NPV and IRR

You can use a spreadsheet to compute the net present value (NPV) of a capital budgeting project, but you must be careful that you understand what the spreadsheet function actually computes. For example, if you want to compute the NPV for Project S (described in the chapter) using Excel, you could set up the spreadsheet as follows:

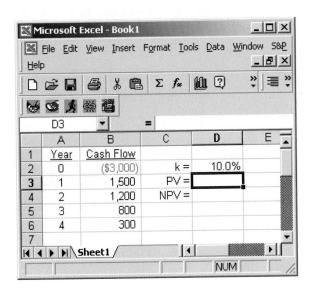

Place the cursor in cell **D3** as shown, click on the Paste Function, which is labeled f_x on the toolbar, and then select the NPV function from the financial function category. The following table should appear:

The description of this function indicates that the result of the computation is the present value of all the *future* cash flows—both inflows and outflows—associated with the investment. What this means is that the Excel function called "NPV" does not compute the net present value as described in this book; rather it computes the present value of all future cash flows. As a result, when you enter the cash flows or the locations for the cash flows the spreadsheet will assume the first cash flow is CF_1, the second cash flow is CF_2, and so on. The NPV function actually computes the discounted cash flows (DCF), from which you need to subtract—or add a negative value to—the initial cost to determine the net present value described in the chapter.

Click on the red arrow on the right side of the row labeled "Rate," place the cursor in the cell that contains the value for k (the required rate of return), and then press return. Then click on the arrow on the right side of the row labeled "Value1," use the cursor to highlight the *future cash flows only*—that is, the cash flows from Year 1 through Year 4—located in column B, and then press return. Now the table that originally appeared when you entered the NPV function menu will look as follows:

You can see the result of the computation at the bottom of the table; it is 3161.32778. If you click the "OK" button, this result will appear in cell **D3** of your spreadsheet. Now place the cursor in cell **D4** and enter the following relationship:

$$= D3 + B2$$

This computation will add the initial investment, which is stated as a negative amount, to the result that is shown in cell **D3.** Your spreadsheet should now look as follows:

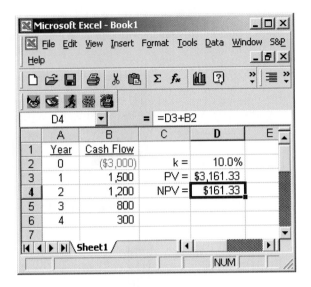

The result of the computation that is shown in cell **D4** is the same as the net present value we computed in the chapter.

To compute the internal rate of return (IRR) for the project using a spreadsheet, set up the problem as before, but type the label "IRR =" in cell **C5.** Place the cursor in cell **D5,** click on the Paste Function, and then select the IRR function from the financial function category. The following table should appear:

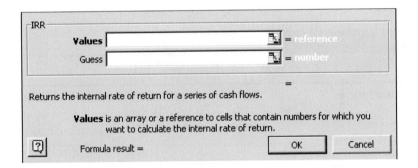

Click on the red arrow on the right side of the row labeled "Values," use the cursor to highlight *all* the cash flows (including CF_0) located in column B, and then press return. Now the IRR table will look as follows:

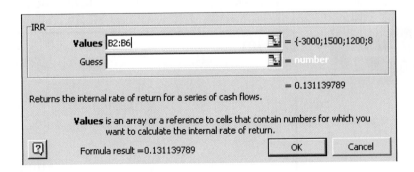

You can see the result of the computation; it is 0.131139789. If you click the "OK" button, this result will appear in cell **D5** of your spreadsheet, which will now look as follows:

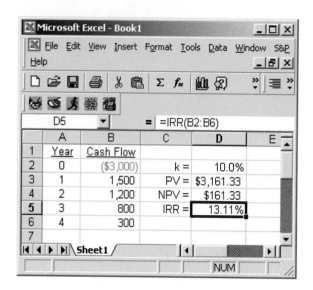

This is the same answer we computed in the chapter.

Now, use the same spreadsheet to compute the NPV and IRR for Project L; all you need to do is change the cash flows in column B. The answers should be the same as we computed in the chapter.

APPENDIX 6B

Modified Internal Rate of Return (MIRR)

MODIFIED IRR (MIRR)
The discount rate at which the present value of a project's cost is equal to the present value of its terminal value, in which the terminal value is found as the sum of the future values of the cash inflows, compounded at the firm's required rate of return (cost of capital).

Despite a strong academic preference for NPV, surveys indicate that many business executives prefer IRR over NPV. Apparently, managers find it intuitively more appealing to analyze investments in terms of percentage rates of return than dollars of NPV. But remember from the discussion in the chapter that the IRR method assumes the cash flows from the project are reinvested at a rate of return equal to the IRR, which we generally view as unrealistic. Given this fact, can we devise a percentage evaluator that is better than the regular IRR? The answer is yes—we can modify the IRR and make it a better indicator of relative profitability, hence better for use in capital budgeting. The new measure is called the **modified IRR,** or **MIRR,** and it is defined as follows:

6B–1

$$\text{PV costs} = \text{PV terminal value}$$

$$\sum_{t=0}^{n} \frac{COF_t}{(1+k)^t} = \frac{\displaystyle\sum_{t=0}^{n} CIF_t(1+k)^{n-t}}{(1+MIRR)^n}$$

$$\text{PV costs} = \frac{TV}{(1+MIRR)^n}$$

Here COF refers to cash outflows (negative numbers) and CIF refers to cash inflows (all positive numbers) associated with a project. The left term is simply the PV of the investment outlays when discounted at the project's required rate of return, k, and the numerator of the right term is the future value of the inflows, assuming that the cash inflows are reinvested at the project's required rate of return. The future value of the cash inflows is also called the *terminal value*, or TV. The discount rate that forces the PV of the TV to equal the PV of the costs is defined as the MIRR.[13]

If the investment costs are all incurred at t = 0, and if the first operating inflow occurs a t = 1, as is true for our illustrative Projects S and L (which we first presented in Figure 6-1), then this equation can be used:

6B–1a

$$\text{Cost} = \frac{TV}{(1 + \text{MIRR})^n} = \frac{\sum_{t=0}^{n} \text{CIF}_t (1 + k)^{n-t}}{(1 + \text{MIRR})^n}$$

We can illustrate the calculation with Project S:

CASH FLOW TIME LINE FOR PROJECT S:

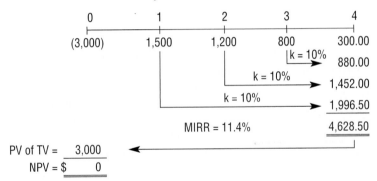

Using the cash flows as set out on the time line, first find the terminal value by compounding each cash inflow at the 10 percent required rate of return. Then, enter into your calculator PV = –3,000, FV = 4,628.5, and N = 4, and press the I key to find MIRR$_S$ = 11.4%. Similarly, we find MIRR$_L$ = 11.0%.

The modified IRR has a significant advantage over the traditional IRR measure. MIRR assumes that cash flows are reinvested at the required rate of return, whereas the traditional IRR measure assumes that cash flows are reinvested at the project's own IRR. Because reinvestment at the required rate of return (cost of funds) gener-

---

[13]There are several alternative definitions for the MIRR. The differences relate primarily to whether negative cash flows that occur after positive cash flows begin should be compounded and treated as part of the TV or discounted and treated as a cost. Our definition (which treats all negative cash flows as investments and thus discounts them) generally is the most appropriate procedure. For a complete discussion, see William R. McDaniel, Daniel E. McCarty, and Kenneth A. Jessell, "Discounted Cash Flow with Explicit Reinvestment Rates: Tutorial and Extension," *The Financial Review* (August 1988), 369–385.

ally is more correct, the MIRR is a better indicator of a project's true profitability. MIRR also solves the multiple IRR problem. To illustrate, with k = 10%, the strip mine project described in the chapter has MIRR = 5.6% versus the 10 percent required rate of return, so it should be rejected. This is consistent with the decision based on the NPV method because at k = 10%, NPV = –$0.77 million.

Is MIRR as good as NPV for choosing between mutually exclusive projects? If two projects are of equal size and have the same life, then NPV and MIRR will always lead to the same project selection decision. Thus, for any projects like our Projects S and L, if $NPV_S > NPV_L$, then $MIRR_S > MIRR_L$, and the kinds of conflicts we encountered between NPV and the traditional IRR will not occur. Also, if the projects are of equal size, but differ in lives, the MIRR will always lead to the same decision as the NPV if the MIRRs are both calculated using as the terminal year the life of the longer project. (Just fill in zeros for the shorter project's missing cash flows.) However, if the projects differ in size, then conflicts can still occur. For example, if we were choosing between a large project and a small mutually exclusive one, then we might find $NPV_L > NPV_S$, $MIRR_L < MIRR_S$.

Our conclusion is that the MIRR is superior to the regular IRR as an indicator of a project's "true" rate of return, or "expected long-term rate of return," but the NPV method is still better for choosing among competing projects that differ in size because it provides a better indicator of the extent to which each project will increase the value of the firm; thus, NPV is still the recommended approach.

Problem

MIRR and multiple rates of return

6B-1 The Upton Uranium Company is deciding whether it should open a strip mine, the net cost of which is $2 million. Net cash inflows are expected to be $13 million, all coming at the end of Year 1. The land must be returned to its natural state at a cost of $12 million, payable at the end of Year 2.

    a. Plot the project's NPV profile. (*Hint:* Calculate NPV at k = 0%, 10%, 80%, and 450%, and possibly at other k values.)

    b. Should the project be accepted if k = 10%? If k = 20%? Explain your reasoning.

    c. Can you think of some other capital budgeting situations in which negative cash flows during or at the other end of the project's life might lead to multiple IRRs?

    d. What is the project's MIRR at k = 10%? At k = 20%? Does the MIRR method lead to the same accept/reject decision as the NPV method?

CHAPTER 7

Project Cash Flows and Risk

When RJR Nabisco (now R.J. Reynolds Tobacco Holdings) canceled its smokeless cigarette project, called Premier, *The Wall Street Journal* called it "one of the most stunning new product disasters in recent history." RJR had spent more than $300 million on the product and had test marketed it for five months. The company had even built a new plant and was all set to produce smokeless cigarettes in huge quantities.

The new cigarette had two fatal flaws—it had to be lit with a special lighter and even then it was hard to light, and many, if not most, smokers didn't like the taste. In addition, it seems smokers didn't like the fact that there was no smoke to blow out or ashes to flick because Premier heated the tobacco rather than burning it. When the cigarette was introduced in 1988, these problems were well known early on, yet RJR still pumped money into the project.

What led RJR's top managers to downplay the flaws and to spend more than $300 million on a bad product? According to industry observers, many people inside the company were aware of the seriousness of the situation, but they were hesitant to voice their concerns because they did not want to offend top managers. The top managers, meantime, were so infatuated with their "new toy" that they assumed consumers would embrace the smokeless cigarette in spite of its obvious flaws. Interestingly, most of the top managers smoked, but none smoked the new smokeless cigarette!

At the time the Premier line was introduced, RJR was not a well-run company, even though it was entrenched in highly profitable markets and was generating billions of dollars of cash each year. The smokeless cigarette project didn't kill the company, but it did contribute to the downfall of the management team that backed the project.

Unfortunately, it seems RJR was intent on salvaging its investment in the first smokeless cigarette it introduced, so in 1996 it introduced a second smokeless cigarette called Eclipse. It invested an additional $150 million in the Eclipse brand, only to discover that it too was a flop.

Even so, in April 2000, RJR once again tested the potential market for Eclipse. But this time, the smokeless cigarette was touted as a smoking alternative that provided a lower chance of contracting some of the maladies that have been associated with traditional tobacco products. The fact that RJR was marketing Eclipse as a "safer" cigarette showed that the company still held hope for salvaging its investment in this project.

In 2003 the Eclipse brand was still alive and kicking. In an effort to make the smokeless cigarette more widely available, RJR began expanding distribution of the product by offering it in convenience stores nationwide, primarily in the 7-Eleven and Circle-K chains. At the same time, the company continued to test scientifically the merits of Eclipse as a safer alternative to the traditional cigarette. The thought was that as people became more health conscious, perhaps the Eclipse brand would find its niche, and finally start to pay off for RJR.

Had RJR's top managers followed the procedures set forth in this chapter, perhaps they would not have sunk as much money into the smokeless cigarette projects. Instead, they would have discovered their project should have been rejected originally because it was not expected to generate the cash flows necessary to make it a viable investment. Perhaps they would have discovered the project to be acceptable 15 years later however. ■

Sources: Various articles available on Dow Jones Interactive® Publications Library located at http://www.wsj.com.

The basic principles of capital budgeting were covered in Chapter 6. In this chapter we examine some additional issues, including cash flow estimation and incorporating risk into capital budgeting decisions. In addition, we present some of the challenges multinational firms face when applying the capital budgeting decision-making methods we describe in both Chapter 6 and this chapter.

Cash Flow Estimation

CASH FLOW

The actual cash, as opposed to accounting net income, that a firm receives or pays during some specified period.

The most important, but also the most difficult, step in the analysis of a capital project is estimating its **cash flows**—the investment outlays and the net cash flows expected after the project is purchased. Many variables are involved in cash flow estimation, and many individuals and departments participate in the process. For example, the forecasts of unit sales and sales prices normally are made by the marketing group based on its knowledge of advertising effects, the state of the economy, competitors' reactions, and trends in consumers' tastes. Similarly, the capital outlays associated with a new product generally are determined by the engineering and product development staffs, while operating costs are estimated by cost accountants, production experts, personnel specialists, purchasing agents, and so forth.

Because it is difficult to make accurate forecasts of the costs and revenues associated with a large, complex project, forecast errors can be quite large. For example, in the 1970s, when several major oil companies decided to build the Alaska Pipeline, the original cost estimates were in the neighborhood of $700 million, but the final cost was closer to $8 billion. Similar (or even worse) miscalculations are common in forecasts of product design costs. Further, as difficult as plant and equipment costs are to estimate, sales revenues and operating costs over the life of the project generally are even more uncertain. For example, several years ago Federal Express developed an electronic delivery service system (ZapMail). It used the correct capital budgeting technique—the net present value (NPV) method—but it incorrectly estimated the project's cash flows. Projected revenues were too high and projected costs were too low; thus, virtually no one was willing to pay the price required to cover the project's costs. As a result, cash flows failed to meet the forecasted levels, and Federal Express ended up losing about $200 million on the venture. This example demonstrates a basic truth: If cash flow estimates are not reasonably accurate, any analytical technique, no matter how sophisticated, can lead to poor decisions and hence to operating losses and lower stock prices. Because of its financial strength, Federal Express was able to absorb losses on the ZapMail venture with no problem, but a similar loss could have forced a weaker firm into bankruptcy.

The financial staff's role in the forecasting process includes (1) coordinating the efforts of the other departments, such as engineering and marketing, (2) ensuring that everyone involved with the forecast uses a consistent set of economic assumptions, and (3) making sure that no biases are inherent in the forecasts. This last point is extremely important, because division managers often become emotionally involved with pet projects or develop empire-building complexes, both of which can lead to cash flow forecasting biases that make bad projects look good on paper. The RJR smokeless cigarette project discussed in the Managerial Perspective is an example of this problem.

It is almost impossible to overstate the difficulties one can encounter with cash flow forecasts. Also, it is difficult to overstate the importance of these forecasts. In this chapter, we give you a sense of some of the inputs that are involved in forecasting the cash flows associated with a capital project and in minimizing forecasting errors.

Self-Test Questions

What is the most important step in the analysis of a capital project?

What is the financial staff's role in forecasting for capital projects?

Relevant Cash Flows

RELEVANT CASH FLOWS
The specific cash flows that should be considered in a capital budgeting decision.

One important element in cash flow estimation is the determination of **relevant cash flows,** which are defined as the specific set of cash flows that should be considered in the capital budgeting decision. This process can be rather difficult, but two cardinal rules can help financial analysts avoid mistakes: (1) Capital budgeting decisions must be based on *cash flows after taxes*, not accounting income, and (2) only *incremental cash flows* are relevant to the accept/reject decision. These two rules are discussed in detail in the following sections.

Cash Flow versus Accounting Income

In capital budgeting analysis, *after-tax cash flows, not accounting profits,* are used—it is cash that pays the bills and can be invested in capital projects, not profits. Cash flows and accounting profits can be very different. To illustrate, consider Table 7–1, which shows how accounting profits and cash flows are related. We assume that Unilate Textiles, a textile manufacturer based in North Carolina, is planning to start a new division at the end of 2005; that sales and all costs, except depreciation, represent actual cash flows and are projected to be constant over time; and that the division will use accelerated depreciation, which will cause its reported depreciation charges to decline over time.[1]

The top section of the table shows the situation in the first year of operations, 2006. Accounting profits are $7 million, but the division's net cash flow—money that is available to Unilate—is $22 million. The $7 million profit is the *return on the funds* originally invested, while the $15 million of depreciation is a *return of part of the funds*

---

[1]Depreciation procedures are discussed in detail in accounting courses, but we provide a summary and review in Appendix 7A at the end of this chapter. The tables provided in Appendix 7A are used to calculate depreciation charges used in the chapter examples. In some instances, we simplify the depreciation assumptions in order to reduce the arithmetic. Because Congress changes depreciation procedures fairly frequently, it is always necessary to consult the latest tax regulations before developing actual capital budgeting cash flows.

	ACCOUNTING PROFITS	CASH FLOWS
TABLE 7–1 Accounting Profits versus Net Cash Flow ($ thousands)		
I. 2006 Situation		
Sales	$ 50,000	$ 50,000
Costs except depreciation	(25,000)	(25,000)
Depreciation	(15,000)	—
Net operating income or cash flow	$ 10,000	$ 25,000
Taxes based on operating income (30%)	(3,000)	(3,000)
Net income or net cash flow	$7,000	$ 22,000
Net cash flow = Net income plus depreciation = $7,000 + $15,000 = $22,000		
II. 2011 Situation		
Sales	$ 50,000	$ 50,000
Costs except depreciation	(25,000)	(25,000)
Depreciation	(5,000)	—
Net operating income or cash flow	$ 20,000	$ 25,000
Taxes based on operating income (30%)	(6,000)	(6,000)
Net income or net cash flow	$ 14,000	$ 19,000
Net cash flow = Net income plus depreciation = $14,000 + $5,000 = $19,000		

originally invested, so the $22 million cash flow consists of both a return *on* and a return *of* part of the invested capital.

The bottom part of the table shows the situation projected for 2011. Here reported profits have doubled because of the decline in depreciation, but net cash flow is down sharply because taxes have doubled. The amount of money received by the firm is represented by the cash flow figure, not the net income figure. And although accounting profits are important for some purposes, cash flows are relevant for the purposes of setting a value on a project using discounted cash flow (DCF) techniques. Cash flows can be reinvested to create value, profits cannot. Therefore, in capital budgeting, we are interested in net cash flows, which, in most cases, we can define as

$$\text{Net cash flow} = \text{Net income} + \text{Depreciation}$$

$$= \text{Return } on \text{ capital} + \text{Return } of \text{ capital}$$

not in accounting profits per se.[2]

---

[2]Actually, net cash flow should be adjusted to reflect all noncash charges, not just depreciation. However, for most projects, depreciation is by far the largest noncash charge. Also, note that Table 7–1 ignores interest charges, which would be present if the firm uses debt. Most firms do use debt and hence finance part of their capital budgets with debt. Therefore, the question has been raised as to whether interest charges should be reflected in capital budgeting cash flow analysis. The consensus is that interest charges should not be dealt with explicitly in capital budgeting—rather, the effects of debt financing are reflected in the cost of funds, or required rate of return, which is used to discount the cash flows. If interest is subtracted and cash flows are then discounted, we would be double counting the cost of debt.

Incremental Cash Flows

In evaluating a capital project, we are concerned only with those cash flows that result directly from the decision to accept the project. These cash flows, called **incremental cash flows,** represent the changes in the firm's total cash flows that occur as a direct result of accepting the project. To determine if a specific cash flow is considered incremental, we need to determine whether it is affected by the purchase of the project. Cash flows that will change because the project is purchased are *incremental cash flows* that must be included in the capital budgeting evaluation. Cash flows that are not affected by the purchase of the project are not relevant to the capital budgeting decision. Unfortunately, identifying the relevant cash flows for a project is not always as simple as it seems. Some special problems in determining incremental cash flows are discussed next.

INCREMENTAL CASH FLOW

The change in a firm's net cash flow attributable to an investment project.

Sunk Costs   Sunk costs are not incremental costs, and they should not be included in the analysis. A **sunk cost** is an outlay that has already been committed or that has already occurred and hence is not affected by the accept/reject decision under consideration. To illustrate, in 2004 Unilate Textiles considered building a distribution center in New England in an effort to increase sales in that area of the country. To help with its evaluation, Unilate hired a consulting firm to perform a site analysis and provide a feasibility study for the project; the cost was $100,000, and this amount was expensed for tax purposes. This expenditure is *not* a relevant cost that should be included in the capital budgeting evaluation of the prospective distribution center because Unilate cannot recover this money, regardless of whether the new distribution center is built.

SUNK COST

A cash outlay that already has been incurred and that cannot be recovered regardless of whether the project is accepted or rejected.

Opportunity Costs   The second potential problem relates to **opportunity costs,** which are defined as the cash flows that could be generated from assets the firm already owns provided they are not used for the project in question. To illustrate, Unilate already owns a piece of land that is suitable for a distribution center. When evaluating the prospective center in New England, should the cost of the land be disregarded because no additional cash outlay would be required? The answer is no, because there is an opportunity cost inherent in the use of the property. In this case, the land could be sold to yield $150,000 after taxes. Use of the site for the distribution center would require forgoing this inflow, so the $150,000 must be charged as an opportunity cost against the project. Note that the proper land cost in this example is the $150,000 market-determined value, irrespective of whether Unilate originally paid $50,000 or $500,000 for the property. (What Unilate paid would, of course, have an effect on taxes and hence on the after-tax opportunity cost.)

OPPORTUNITY COST

The return on the best alternative use of an asset; the highest return that will not be earned if funds are invested in a particular project.

Externalities: Effects on Other Parts of the Firm   The third potential problem involves the effects of a project on other parts of the firm; economists call these effects **externalities.** For example, Unilate does have some existing customers in New England who would use the new distribution center because its location would be more convenient than the North Carolina distribution center they have been using. The sales, and hence profits, generated by these customers would not be new to Unilate; rather, they would represent a transfer from one distribution center to another. Thus, the net revenues produced by these customers should not be treated as incremental cash flows in the capital budgeting decision. Although they often are difficult to quantify, externalities such as these should be considered.

EXTERNALITIES

The effect accepting a project will have on the cash flows in other parts (areas) of the firm.

Shipping and Installation Costs When a firm acquires fixed assets, it often must incur substantial costs for shipping and installing the equipment. These charges are added to the invoice price of the equipment when the total cost of the project is being determined. Also, for depreciation purposes, the *depreciable basis* of an asset, which is the total amount that can be depreciated during the asset's life, includes the purchase price and any additional expenditures required to make the asset operational, including shipping and installation. Therefore, the full cost of the equipment, including shipping and installation costs, is used as the depreciable basis when depreciation charges are calculated. So if Unilate Textiles bought a computer with an invoice price of $100,000 and paid another $10,000 for shipping and installation, then the full cost of the computer, and its depreciable basis, would be $110,000.

Keep in mind that *depreciation is a noncash expense, so there is not a cash outflow associated with the recognition of depreciation expense each year.* But because depreciation is an expense, *it affects the taxable income of a firm, thus the amount of taxes paid by the firm, which is a cash flow.*

Inflation Inflation is a fact of life, and it should be recognized in capital budgeting decisions. If expected inflation is not built into the determination of expected cash flows, then the calculated net present value and internal rate of return will be incorrect—both will be artificially low. It is easy to avoid inflation bias—simply build inflationary expectations into the cash flows used in the capital budgeting analysis. Expected inflation should be reflected in the revenue and cost figures, and thus the annual net cash flow forecasts. The required rate of return does not have to be adjusted for inflation expectations because investors include such expectations when establishing the rate at which they are willing to permit the firm to use their funds. Investors decide at what rates a firm can raise funds in the capital markets, and they include an adjustment for inflation when determining the rate that is appropriate.

Self-Test Questions

Briefly explain the difference between accounting income and net cash flow. Which should be used in capital budgeting? Why?

Explain what these terms mean, and assess their relevance in capital budgeting: incremental cash flow, sunk cost, opportunity cost, externalities, shipping and installation costs, and depreciable basis.

Explain why incremental analysis is important in capital budgeting.

How should inflation expectations be included in analysis of capital projects?

Identifying Incremental Cash Flows

Generally, when we identify the incremental cash flows associated with a capital project, we separate them according to when they occur during the life of the project. In most cases, we can classify a project's incremental cash flows as (1) cash flows that occur *only at the start* of the project's life—that is, time period 0; (2) cash flows that *continue throughout* the project's life—that is, time periods 1 through n; and (3) cash flows that occur *only at the end*, or the termination, of the project—that is, time period n. We discuss these three incremental cash flow classifications and identify some of the relevant cash flows next. But keep in mind, when identifying the incremental cash flows for capital budgeting, the primary question is which cash flows will be affected by purchasing the project. If a cash flow does not change, it is not relevant for the capital budgeting analysis.

Initial Investment Outlay

INITIAL INVESTMENT OUTLAY
Includes the incremental cash flows associated with a project that will *occur only at the start of a project's life*, CF_0.

The **initial investment outlay** refers to the incremental cash flows that *occur only at the start of a project's life*, CF_0. It includes such cash flows as the purchase price of the new project and shipping and installation costs. If the capital budgeting decision is a *replacement decision*, then the initial investment must also take into account the cash flows associated with the disposal of the old, or replaced, asset; this amount includes any cash received or paid to scrap the old asset and any tax effects associated with the disposal.

In many cases, the addition or replacement of a capital asset also affects the firm's short-term assets and liabilities, which are known as the *working capital accounts*. For example, additional inventories might be required to support a new operation, and increased inventory purchases will increase accounts payable. The difference between the required increase in current assets and the spontaneous increase in current liabilities is the *change in net working capital*. If this change is positive, as it generally is for expansion projects, then additional financing, over and above the cost of the project, is needed to fund the increase.[3] *Thus, the change in net working capital that results from the acceptance of a project is an incremental cash flow that must be considered in the capital budgeting analysis.* Because the change in net working capital requirements occurs at the start of the project's life, this cash flow impact is an incremental cash flow included as a part of the initial investment outlay.

Incremental Operating Cash Flows

INCREMENTAL OPERATING CASH FLOWS
The changes in day-to-day cash flows that result from the purchase of a capital project and continue until the firm disposes of the asset.

Incremental operating cash flows are the changes in day-to-day operating cash flows that result from the purchase of a capital project. These changes occur throughout the life of the project; thus they continue to affect the firm's cash flows until the firm disposes of the asset.

In most cases, the *incremental operating cash flows* for each year can be computed directly by using the following equation:

7-1

$$
\begin{aligned}
\text{Incremental operating cash flow}_t &= \Delta\text{Cash revenues}_t - \Delta\text{Cash expenses}_t - \Delta\text{Taxes}_t \\
&= \Delta NOI_t \times (1 - T) + \Delta Depr_t \\
&= (\Delta S_t - \Delta OC_t - \Delta Depr_t) \times (1 - T) + \Delta Depr_t \\
&= (\Delta S_t - \Delta OC_t) \times (1 - T) + T(\Delta Depr_t)
\end{aligned}
$$

---

[3]We should note that there are instances in which the change in net working capital associated with a capital project actually results in a decrease in the firm's current funding requirements, which frees up cash flows for investment. Usually this occurs if the project being considered is much more efficient than the existing asset(s).

The symbols in Equation 7–1 are defined as follows:

Δ = The Greek letter delta, which indicates the change in something.

ΔNOI_t = $NOI_{t, accept} - NOI_{t, reject}$ = The change in net operating income in period t that results from accepting the capital project; the subscript *accept* indicates the firm's operations that would exist if the project is accepted, and the subscript *reject* indicates the level of operations that would exist if the project is rejected (the existing situation *without* the project).

$\Delta Depr_t$ = $Depr_{t,accept} - Depr_{t,reject}$ = The change in depreciation expense in period t that results from accepting the project.

ΔS_t = $S_{t,accept} - S_{t,reject}$ = The change in sales revenues in period t that results from accepting the project.

ΔOC_t = $OC_{t,accept} - OC_{t,reject}$ = The change in operating costs, excluding depreciation, in period t that results from accepting the project.

T = Marginal tax rate.

We have emphasized that depreciation is a *noncash* expense. So why is the change in depreciation expense included in the computation of incremental operating cash flow shown in Equation 7–1? The change in depreciation expense needs to be computed because, when depreciation changes, taxable income changes and so does the amount of income taxes paid; and the amount of taxes paid is a cash flow.

Terminal Cash Flow

The **terminal cash flow** occurs at the end of the life of the project. It is associated with (1) the final disposal of the project and (2) the return of the firm's operations to where they were before the project was accepted. Consequently, the terminal cash flow includes the salvage value, which could be either positive (selling the asset) or negative (paying for removal), and the tax impact of the disposition of the project. Because we assume the firm returns to the operating level that existed prior to the acceptance of the project, any changes in net working capital that occurred at the beginning of the project's life will be *reversed* at the end of its life. For example, as an expansion project's life approaches termination, inventories will be sold off and not replaced. The firm will therefore receive (invest) an end-of-project cash flow equal to the net working capital requirement, or cash outflow (inflow), that occurred when the project was begun.

Self-Test Questions

Identify the three classifications for the incremental cash flows associated with a project, and give examples of the cash flows that would be in each category.

Why are the changes in net working capital recognized as incremental cash flows both at the beginning and end of a project's life?

Capital Budgeting Project Evaluation

Up to this point, we have discussed several important aspects of cash flow analysis. Now we illustrate cash flow estimation for expansion projects and for replacement projects.

Expansion Projects

EXPANSION PROJECT
A project that is intended to increase sales.

Remember from Chapter 6 that an **expansion project** is one that calls for the firm to invest in new assets to *increase* sales. We illustrate an expansion project analysis with a project that is being considered by Household Energy Products (HEP), a Dallas-based technology company. HEP's research and development department has created a computerized home appliance control device that will increase a home's energy efficiency by simultaneously controlling all household appliances, large and small, the air-conditioning/heating system, the water heater, the security system, and the filtration and heating systems for pools and spas. At this point, HEP wants to decide whether it should proceed with full-scale production of the appliance control device.

HEP's marketing department plans to target sales of the appliance computer toward the owners of larger homes; the computer is cost-effective only in homes with 4,000 or more square feet of living space. The marketing vice president believes that annual sales would be 15,000 units if the units are priced at $2,000 each, so annual sales are estimated at $30 million. The engineering department has determined the firm would need no additional manufacturing or storage space; it would just need the equipment to manufacture the devices. The necessary equipment would be purchased and installed late in 2005, and it would cost $9.5 million, not including the $500,000 that would have to be paid for shipping and installation. The equipment would fall into the Modified Accelerated Cost Recovery System (MACRS) 5-year class for the purposes of depreciation (see Appendix 7A at the end of this chapter for depreciation rates and an explanation of MACRS).

The project would require an initial increase in net working capital equal to $4 million, primarily because the raw materials required to produce the devices will significantly increase the amount of inventory HEP currently holds. The investment necessary to increase net working capital will be made on December 31, 2005, when the decision to manufacture the appliance control occurs. The project's estimated economic life is four years. At the end of that time, the equipment would have a market value of $2 million and a book value of $1.7 million. The production department has estimated that variable manufacturing costs would total 60 percent of sales and fixed overhead costs, excluding depreciation, would be $5 million per year. Depreciation expenses would vary from year to year in accordance with the MACRS rates. HEP's marginal tax rate is 40 percent; its cost of funds, or required rate of return, is 15 percent; and, for capital budgeting purposes, the company's policy is to assume that operating cash flows occur at the end of each year. Because manufacture of the new product would begin on January 1, 2006, the first *operating cash flows* would occur on December 31, 2006.

Analysis of the Cash Flows   The first step in the analysis is to summarize the initial investment outlay required for the project; this is done in the 2005 column of Table 7–2. For HEP's appliance control device project, the initial cash flows consist of the purchase price of the needed equipment, the cost of shipping and installation, and the required investment in net working capital (NWC). Notice that these cash flows do not carry over in the years 2006 through 2009—they occur only at the start of the project. Thus, the *initial investment* outlay is $14 million.

Having estimated the investment requirements, we must now estimate the cash flows that will occur once production begins; these are set forth in the 2006 through 2009 columns of Table 7–2. The operating cash flow estimates are based on information provided by HEP's various departments. The depreciation amounts were obtained by multiplying the depreciable basis, $10 million ($9.5 million purchase price plus $0.5 million

TABLE 7–2	HEP Expansion Project Net Cash Flows, 2005–2009 ($ thousands)				
	2005	**2006**	**2007**	**2008**	**2009**
I. Initial Investment Outlay					
Cost of new asset	$(9,500)				
Shipping and installation	(500)				
Increase in net working capital	(4,000)				
Initial investment	$(14,000)				
II. Incremental Operating Cash Flow [a]					
Sales revenue		$ 30,000	$ 30,000	$ 30,000	$ 30,000
Variable costs (60% of sales)		(18,000)	(18,000)	(18,000)	(18,000)
Fixed costs		(5,000)	(5,000)	(5,000)	(5,000)
Depreciation on new equipment[b]		(2,000)	(3,200)	(1,900)	(1,200)
Earnings before taxes (EBT)		$ 5,000	$ 3,800	$ 5,100	$ 5,800
Taxes (40%)		(2,000)	(1,520)	(2,040)	(2,320)
Net income		$ 3,000	$ 2,280	$ 3,060	$ 3,480
Add back depreciation		2,000	3,200	1,900	1,200
Incremental operating cash flows		$ 5,000	$ 5,480	$ 4,960	$ 4,680
III. Terminal Cash Flow					
Return of net working capital					4,000
Net salvage value (see Table 7–3)					1,880
Terminal cash flow					$ 5,880
IV. Annual Net Cash Flow					
Total net cash flow each year	$(14,000)	$ 5,000	$ 5,480	$ 4,960	$ 10,560
Net present value (15%)	**$ 3,790**				

[a]Using Equation 7–1, the incremental operating cash flows can be computed as follows:

Year	**Incremental Operating Cash Flow Computation**
2006	$5,000 = ($30,000 − $18,000 − $5,000) (1 − 0.40) + $2,000 (0.40)
2007	5,480 = (30,000 − 18,000 − 5,000) (1 − 0.40) + 3,200 (0.40)
2008	4,960 = (30,000 − 18,000 − 5,000) (1 − 0.40) + 1,900 (0.40)
2009	4,680 = (30,000 − 18,000 − 5,000) (1 − 0.40) + 1,200 (0.40)

[b]Depreciation for the new equipment was calculated using MACRS (see Appendix 7A at the end of this chapter):

Year	**2006**	**2007**	**2008**	**2009**
Percent depreciated	20%	32%	19%	12%

These percentages were multiplied by the depreciable basis of $10,000 = $9,500 − $500 to get the depreciation expense each year.

TABLE 7–3	HEP Expansion Project Net Salvage Value, 2009 ($ thousands)

I. Book Value of HEP's Project in 2009

Cost of new asset in 2005	$ 9,500
Shipping and installation	500
Depreciable basis of asset	$ 10,000
Depreciation from 2006–2009	
= (0.20 + 0.32 + 0.19 + 0.12) × $10,000	(8,300)
Book value in 2009	$ 1,700

II. Tax Impact of the Sale of HEP's Project in 2009

Selling price of asset in	$ 2,000
Book value of asset in	(1,700)
Gain (loss) on sale of asset	$ 300
Taxes (40%)	$ 120

III. Net Salvage Value, CF, in 2009

Cash flow from sale of project	$ 2,000
Tax impact of sale	(120)
Net salvage value cash flow	$ 1,880

shipping and installaion), by the MACRS recovery allowance rates as set forth in the footnote to Table 7–2. As you can see, from the values given in footnote a in the table, the incremental operating cash flow differs each year only because the depreciation expense, and thus the impact depreciation has on taxes, differs each year.

The final cash flow component we need to compute is the terminal cash flow. For this computation, remember that the $4 million investment in net working capital will be recovered in 2009. Also, we need an estimate of the net cash flows from the disposal of the equipment in 2009. Table 7–3 shows the calculation of the net salvage value for the equipment. It is expected that the equipment will be sold for more than its book value, which means the company will have to pay taxes on the capital gain because, in essence, the equipment was depreciated too quickly, which allowed HEP to reduce its tax liability by too much in the years 2006–2009. The book value is calculated as the depreciable basis (purchase price plus shipping and installation) minus the accumulated depreciation. The net cash flow from salvage is merely the sum of the salvage value and the tax impact resulting from the sale of the equipment, $1.88 million in this case. Thus, the *terminal cash flow* totals $5.88 million—that is, the $1.88 million cash flow from salvage plus the $4 million cash flow from the return of the investment in net working capital.

Notice that the total net cash flow for the year 2009 is the sum of the incremental cash flow for the year and the terminal cash flow. In the final year of a project's economic life, the firm incurs two types of cash flows: the incremental operating cash flow attributed to the project's normal operation and the terminal cash flow associated with the disposal of the project. For the appliance control device project HEP is considering, the incremental operating cash flow in 2009 is $4.68 million and the terminal cash flow is $5.88 million, so the total expected net cash flow in 2009 is $10.56 million.

Making the Decision   A summary of the data and the computation of the project's NPV are provided with the cash flow time line that follows. The amounts are in thousands of dollars, just like in Table 7–2.

CASH FLOW TIME LINE FOR HEP'S APPLIANCE CONTROL DEVICE PROJECT (DOLLARS ARE IN THOUSANDS)

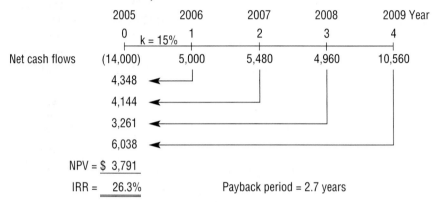

	2005	2006	2007	2008	2009 Year
	0	1	2	3	4
		k = 15%			
Net cash flows	(14,000)	5,000	5,480	4,960	10,560
	4,348				
	4,144				
	3,261				
	6,038				

NPV = $ 3,791

IRR =   26.3%   Payback period = 2.7 years

The project appears to be acceptable using the NPV and internal rate of return (IRR) methods, and it also would be acceptable if HEP required a maximum payback period of three years. Note, however, that the analysis thus far has been based on the assumption that the project has the same degree of risk as the company's average project. If the project was judged to be riskier than an average project, it would be necessary to increase the required rate of return used to compute the NPV. Later in this chapter, we will extend the evaluation of this project to include a risk analysis.

Replacement Analysis

All companies make replacement decisions. The analysis relating to replacements is the same as for expansion projects—that is, identify the relevant cash flows, and then find the net present value of the project. But, to some extent, identifying the *incremental* cash flows associated with a replacement project is more complicated than for an expansion project because the cash flows both from the new asset *and* from the old asset must be considered. **Replacement analysis** is illustrated with another HEP example.

REPLACEMENT ANALYSIS

An analysis involving the decision as to whether to replace an existing asset that is still productive with a new asset.

HEP has a lathe for trimming molded plastics that was purchased 10 years ago at a cost of $7,500. The machine had an expected life of 15 years at the time it was purchased, and management originally estimated, and still believes, that the salvage value will be zero at the end of the 15-year life. The machine has been depreciated on a straight line basis; therefore, its annual depreciation charge is $500, and its present book value is $2,500 = $7,500 – 10($500).

HEP is considering the purchase of a new special-purpose machine to replace the lathe. The new machine, which can be purchased for $12,000 (including shipping and installation), will reduce labor and raw materials usage sufficiently to cut annual operating costs from $8,000 to $4,500. This reduction in costs will cause before-tax profits to rise by $8,000 – $4,500 = $3,500 per year.

It is estimated that the new machine will have a useful life of five years, after which it can be sold for $2,000. The old machine's actual current market value is

$1,000, which is below its $2,500 book value. If the new machine is acquired, the old lathe will be sold to another company rather than exchanged for the new machine. Net working capital requirements will increase by $1,000 if the lathe is replaced by the new machine; this increase will occur at the time of replacement. By an IRS ruling, the new machine falls into the 3-year MACRS class, and because the risk associated with the new machine is considered average for HEP, the project's required rate of return is 15 percent. Should the replacement be made?

Table 7–4 shows the worksheet format HEP uses to analyze replacement projects. Determining the relevant cash flows for a replacement decision is more involved than for an expansion decision because we need to consider the fact that the cash flows associated with the replaced asset will not continue after the new asset is purchased— *the cash flows associated with the new asset will take the place of the cash flows associated with the old asset.* Because we want to evaluate how the acceptance of a capital budgeting project *changes* cash flows, we must compute the increase or decrease in cash flows that results from the replacement of the old asset with the new asset. Let's examine the cash flows computed in Table 7–4.

Analysis of Cash Flows   First, the initial investment outlay of $11,400 includes the cash flows associated with the cost of the new asset and the change in net working capital, which also is included in the initial investment computation for the expansion decision shown in Table 7–2. But when a replacement asset is purchased, the asset being replaced must be removed from operations. If the asset can be sold to another firm or to a scrap dealer, its disposal will generate a positive cash flow; but if the firm must pay to have the old asset removed, the cash flow will be negative. And if the firm disposes of the old asset at a value different from its book value (its purchase price less accumulated depreciation), there will be a tax effect. In our example, the old asset has a book value equal to $2,500, but it can be sold for only $1,000. So HEP will incur a capital loss equal to $(1,500) = $1,000 – $2,500 if it replaces the lathe with the new machine. This loss will result in a tax savings equal to Capital Loss × T = $1,500 × 0.4 = $600 to account for the fact that HEP did not adequately depreciate the old asset to reflect its market value. Consequently, the disposal of the old asset will generate a positive cash flow equal to $1,600—the $1,000 selling price plus the $600 tax savings, which effectively reduces the amount of cash required to purchase the new machine and thus the initial investment outlay. Any cash flows associated with disposing of the old asset must be included in the computation of the initial investment because they affect the net amount of cash required to purchase the asset.[4]

Next, we need to compute the incremental operating cash flow each year. Section II of Table 7–4 shows these computations. The procedure is the same as before— determine how operating cash flows will change if the new machine is purchased to replace the lathe. Remember, the lathe is expected to decrease operating costs from $8,000 to $4,500, and thus increase operating profits by $3,500—that is, less cash will have to be spent to operate the new machine. Had the replacement resulted in an increase in sales in addition to the reduction in costs (that is, if the new machine had been both larger and more efficient), then this amount would also be reported. Also, note that

---

[4]If you think about it, the computation of the initial investment outlay for replacement decisions is similar to determining the amount you would need to purchase a new automobile to replace your old one. If the purchase price of the new car is $20,000 and the dealer is willing to give you $5,000 for your car as a trade-in, then the amount you need is only $15,000. But, if you need to pay someone to take your old car out of the garage because that is where you are going to keep the new car at night, then the total amount you need to purchase the new car actually is greater than $20,000.

TABLE 7-4	HEP Replacement Project Net Cash Flows, 2005–2010

	2005	2006	2007	2008	2009	2010
I. Initial Investment Outlay						
Cost of new asset	$(12,000)					
Change in net working capital	(1,000)					
Net cash flow from sale of old asset[a]	1,600					
Initial investment	$(11,400)					
II. Incremental Operating Cash Flows						
Δ Operating costs		$3,500	$3,500	$3,500	$3,500	$3,500
Δ Depreciation[b]		(3,460)	(4,900)	(1,300)	(340)	500
Δ Earnings before taxes (EBT)		40	(1,400)	2,200	3,160	4,000
Δ Taxes (40%)		(16)	560	(880)	(1,264)	(1,600)
Δ Net income		24	(840)	1,320	1,896	2,400
Add back Δ depreciation		3,460	4,900	1,300	340	(500)
Incremental operating cash flows		$3,484	$4,060	$2,620	$2,236	$1,900
III. Terminal Cash Flow						
Return of net working capital						$1,000
Net salvage value of new asset[c]						1,200
Terminal cash flow						$2,200
IV. Annual Net Cash Flows						
Total net cash flow each year	$(11,400)	$3,484	$4,060	$2,620	$2,236	$4,100
Net present value (15%)	$(261)					

[a]The net present cash flow from the sale of the old (replaced) asset is computed as follows:

Selling price (market value)	$1,000
Subtract book value	(2,500)
Gain (loss) on sale of asset	(1,500)
Tax impact of sale of asset	(0.4) 600

Net cash flow from the sale of asset = $1,000 + $600 = $1,600

[b]The change in depreciation expense is computed by comparing the depreciation of the new asset with the depreciation that would have existed if the old asset was *not* replaced. The old asset has been depreciated on a straight-line basis, with five years of $500 depreciation remaining. The new asset will be depreciated using the rates for the three-year MACRS class (see Appendix 7A). So the change in annual depreciation would be as follows:

Year	New Asset Depreciation	Old Asset Depreciation		Change in Depreciation
2006	$12,000 × 0.33 = $ 3,960	– $500	=	$3,460
2007	12,000 × 0.45 = 5,400	– 500	=	4,900
2008	12,000 × 0.15 = 1,800	– 500	=	1,300
2009	12,000 × 0.07 = 840	– 500	=	340
2010	0	– 500	=	(500)
Accumulated depreciation	= $12,000			

[c]The book value of the new asset in 2010 will be zero because the entire $12,000 has been written off. So the net salvage value of the new asset in 2010 is computed as follows:

Selling price (market value)	$2,000
Subtract book value	(0)
Gain (loss) on sale of asset	2000
Tax impact on sale of asset	(800) = 2,000 × 0.40

Net salvage value of the new asset = $2,000 – $800 = $1,200

the $3,500 cost savings is constant over the years 2006–2010. Had the annual savings been expected to change over time, this fact would have to be built into the analysis.

The change in depreciation expense must be computed to determine the impact such a change will have on the taxes paid by the firm. If the new machine is purchased, the $500 depreciation expense of the lathe (old asset) no longer will be relevant for tax purposes; instead, the depreciation expense for the new machine will be used. For example, in 2006, the depreciation expense for the new machine will be $3,960 because, according to the 3-year MACRS classification, 33 percent of the cost of the new asset can be depreciated in the year it is purchased. Because HEP will dispose of the lathe if it buys the new machine, in 2006 it will replace the $500 depreciation expense associated with the lathe with the $3,960 depreciation expense associated with the new machine, and the depreciation expense will increase by $3,460 = $3,960 − $500. The computations for the remaining years are the same. Note that in 2010 the change in depreciation is negative. This results because the new machine will be fully depreciated at the end of 2009, so there is nothing left to write off in 2010; thus, if the lathe is replaced, its depreciation of $500 will be replaced by the new machine's depreciation of $0 in 2010, which is a change of $(500).

The terminal cash flow includes $1,000 for the return of net working capital, because a "normal" net working capital level will be restored at the end of the new machine's life. Any additional accounts receivable created by the purchase of the new machine will be collected and any additional inventories required by the new machine will be drawn down and not replaced. The net salvage value of the new machine is $1,200—it is expected that the new machine can be sold in 2010 for $2,000, but $800 in taxes will have to be paid on the sale because the new machine will be fully depreciated at the time of the sale.[5] Thus, the terminal cash flow is $2,200 = $1,000 + $1,200.

Making the Decision   A summary of the data and the computation of the project's NPV are provided with the following cash flow time line:

CASH FLOW TIME LINE FOR HEP'S REPLACEMENT PROJECT (DOLLARS ARE IN THOUSANDS)

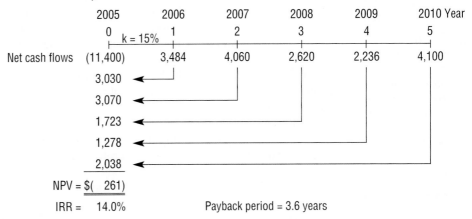

[5]In this analysis, the salvage value of the old machine is zero. However, if the old machine was expected to have a positive salvage value at the end of five years, replacing the old machine now would eliminate this cash flow. Thus, the after-tax salvage value of the machine would represent an opportunity cost to the firm, and it would be included as a Year 5 cash outflow in the terminal cash flow section of the worksheet.

According to the NPV and IRR methods, HEP should not replace the lathe with the new machine.

Before we leave our discussion of replacement decisions, we should note that a replacement decision involves comparing two mutually exclusive projects: retaining the old asset versus buying a new one. To simplify matters, in our replacement example we assumed that the new machine had a life equal to the remaining life of the old machine. If, however, we were choosing between two mutually exclusive alternatives with significantly different lives, an adjustment would be necessary to make the results of the capital budgeting analysis for the two projects comparable. To attain comparability, we can either (1) use a common life for the evaluation of the two projects or (2) compute the annual annuity that could be produced from the dollar amount of the NPV of each project. Both of these procedures are described in Appendix B at the end of this chapter. We mention the unequal life problem here to make you aware that the evaluation of mutually exclusive projects with significantly different lives requires a slightly different analysis to ensure a correct decision is made.

Self-Test Question

Explain and differentiate between the capital budgeting analyses required for expansion projects and for replacement projects.

Incorporating Risk in Capital Budgeting Analysis

STAND-ALONE RISK
The risk and asset would have if it were a firm's only asset; it is measured by the variability of the asset's expected returns.

CORPORATE (WITHIN-FIRM) RISK
Risk that does not take into consideration the effects of stockholders' diversification; it is measured by a project's effect on the firm's earnings variability.

BETA (MARKET) RISK
That part of a project's risk that cannot be eliminated by diversification; it is measured by the project's beta coefficient.

To this point, we have assumed the projects being evaluated have the same risk as the projects that the firm currently possesses. However, three separate and distinct types of project risk need to be examined to determine if the required rate of return used to evaluate a project should be different than the *average* required rate of the firm. The three risks are (1) the project's own **stand-alone risk,** or the risk it exhibits when evaluated alone rather than as part of a combination, or portfolio, of assets; (2) **corporate,** or **within-firm, risk,** which is the effect a project has on the total, or overall, riskiness of the company, without considering which risk component, systematic or unsystematic, is affected; and (3) **beta,** or **market, risk,** which is project risk assessed from the standpoint of a stockholder who holds a well-diversified portfolio. As we will see, a particular project might have high stand-alone risk, yet taking it on might not have much effect on either the firm's risk or that of its owners because of portfolio, or diversification, effects.

Although more difficult, evaluating the risk associated with a capital budgeting project is similar to evaluating the risk of a financial asset such as a stock. Therefore, much of our discussion in this section relies on the concepts introduced in Chapter 4.

As we will see shortly, a project's stand-alone risk is measured by the variability of the project's expected returns; its corporate risk is measured by the project's impact on the firm's earnings variability; and its beta risk is measured by the project's effect on the firm's beta coefficient. Taking on a project with a high degree of either stand-alone risk or corporate risk will not necessarily affect the firm's beta to any great extent. However, if the project has highly uncertain returns, and if those returns are highly correlated with returns on the firm's other assets and also with most other assets in the economy, the project will exhibit a high degree of all three types of risk. For example, suppose General Motors decides to undertake a major expansion to build solar-powered autos. GM is not sure how its technology will work on a mass production basis, so there are great risks in the venture—its stand-alone risk is high. Management also estimates that the project will have a higher probability of success if the economy is strong, because people will have more money to spend on the new autos. This means that the project will tend to do well if GM's other divisions also do well and to do badly if other divisions do badly. This being the case, the project will also have high corporate risk. Finally, because GM's profits are highly correlated with those of most other firms, the project's beta coefficient will also be high. Thus, this project will be risky under all three definitions of risk.

Self-Test Questions

What are the three types of project risk?

How is a project's stand-alone risk measured?

How is corporate risk measured?

How is beta risk measured?

Stand-Alone Risk

To what extent should a firm be concerned with stand-alone risk? In theory, stand-alone risk should be of little or no concern, because we know diversification can eliminate some of this type of risk. However, it is of great importance for the following reasons:

1. It is easier to estimate a project's stand-alone risk than its corporate risk, and it is far easier to measure stand-alone risk than beta risk.
2. In the vast majority of cases, all three types of risk are highly correlated. If the general economy does well, so will the firm, and if the firm does well, so will most of its projects. Thus, stand-alone risk generally is a good proxy for hard-to-measure corporate and beta risks.
3. Because of Points 1 and 2, if management wants a reasonably accurate assessment of a project's riskiness, it should spend considerable effort on determining the riskiness of the project's own cash flows—that is, its stand-alone risk.

The starting point for analyzing a project's stand-alone risk involves determining the uncertainty inherent in the project's cash flows. This analysis can be handled in a number of ways, ranging from informal judgments to complex economic and statistical analyses involving large-scale computer models. To illustrate what is involved, we shall refer to Household Energy Products' appliance control computer project that we discussed earlier. Many of the individual cash flows that were shown in Table 7–2 are subject to uncertainty. For example, sales for each year were projected at 15,000 units to be sold at a net price of $2,000 per unit, or $30 million in total. Actual unit sales almost certainly would be somewhat higher or lower than 15,000, however, and also the sales price might turn out to be different from the projected $2,000 per unit. In effect, the sales quantity and the sales price estimates are expected values taken from probability distributions, as are many of the other values that were shown in Table 7–2. The distributions could be relatively "tight," reflecting small standard deviations and low risk, or they could be "flat," denoting a

| **FIGURE 7–1** | Sensitivity Analysis ($ thousands) |

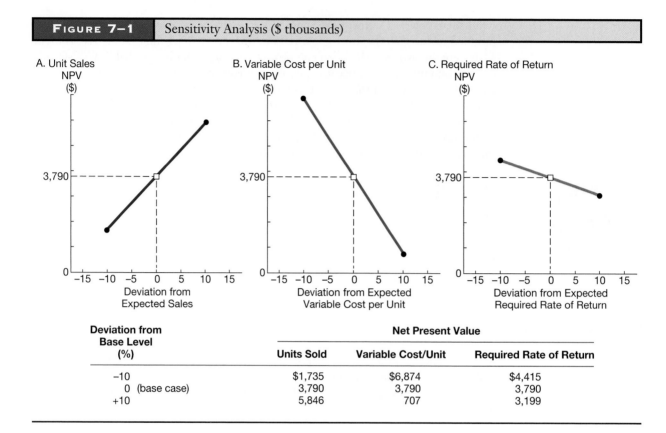

Deviation from Base Level (%)	**Net Present Value**		
	Units Sold	**Variable Cost/Unit**	**Required Rate of Return**
−10	$1,735	$6,874	$4,415
0 (base case)	3,790	3,790	3,790
+10	5,846	707	3,199

great deal of uncertainty about the final value of the variable in question and hence a high degree of stand-alone risk.

The nature of the individual cash flow distributions, and their correlations with one another, determine the nature of the NPV distribution and, thus, the project's stand-alone risk. We next discuss three techniques for assessing a project's stand-alone risk: (1) sensitivity analysis, (2) scenario analysis, and (3) Monte Carlo simulation.

Sensitivity Analysis

The cash flows used to determine the acceptability of a project result from forecasts of uncertain events, such as economic conditions in the future and expected demand for a product. Intuitively, then, we know the cash flow amounts used to determine the net present value of a project might be significantly different from what actually happens in the future. But those numbers represent our best, and most confident, prediction concerning the expected cash flows associated with a project. We also know that if a key input variable, such as units sold, changes, the project's NPV also will change. **Sensitivity analysis** is a technique that shows exactly how much the NPV will change in response to a given change in an input variable, other things held constant.

In a sensitivity analysis, we begin with the base case situation that was developed using the expected values for each input; next each variable is changed by specific percentage points above and below the expected value, holding other things constant; then a new NPV is calculated for each of these values; and, finally, the set of NPVs is plotted against the variable that was changed. Figure 7–1 shows sensitivity

SENSITIVITY ANALYSIS

A risk analysis technique in which key variables are changed and the resulting changes in the NPV and the IRR are observed.

graphs for HEP's computer project for three of the key input variables. The table below the graphs gives the NPVs that were used to construct the graphs. The slopes of the lines in the graphs show how sensitive NPV is to changes in each of the inputs: *the steeper the slope, the more sensitive the NPV is to a change in the variable.* In the figure we see that the project's NPV is very sensitive to changes in variable costs, less sensitive to changes in unit sales, and fairly insensitive to changes in the required rate of return. So when estimating these variables' values, HEP should take extra care to ensure the accuracy of the forecast for variable costs per unit.

If we were comparing two projects, the one with the steeper sensitivity lines would be regarded as riskier because for that project a relatively small error in estimating a variable such as variables costs per unit would produce a large error in the project's expected NPV. Thus, sensitivity analysis can provide useful insights into the riskiness of a project.

Scenario Analysis

Although sensitivity analysis probably is the most widely used risk analysis technique, it does have limitations. Consider, for example, a proposed coal mine project whose NPV is highly sensitive to changes in output, in variable costs, and in sales price. However, if a utility company has contracted to buy a fixed amount of coal at an inflation-adjusted price per ton, the mining venture might be quite safe despite its steep sensitivity lines. *In general, a project's stand-alone risk depends on both* (1) *the sensitivity of its NPV to changes in key variables and* (2) *the range of likely values of these variables as reflected in their probability distributions.* Because sensitivity analysis considers only the first factor, it is incomplete.

Scenario analysis is a risk analysis technique that considers both the sensitivity of NPV to changes in key variables and the likely range of variable values. In a scenario analysis, the financial analyst asks operating managers to pick a "bad" set of circumstances (low unit sales, low sales price, high variable cost per unit, high construction cost, and so on) and a "good" set. The NPVs under the bad and good conditions are then calculated and compared to the expected, or base case, NPV.

As an example, let us return to the appliance control computer project. Assume that HEP's managers are fairly confident of their estimates of all the project's cash flow variables except price and unit sales. Further, they regard a drop in sales below 10,000 units or a rise above 20,000 units as being extremely unlikely. Similarly, they expect the sales price as set in the marketplace to fall within the range of $1,500 to $2,500. Thus, 10,000 units at a price of $1,500 defines the lower bound, or the **worst-case scenario,** whereas 20,000 units at a price of $2,500 defines the upper bound, or the **best-case scenario.** Remember that the **base, or most likely, case** values are 15,000 units and a price of $2,000.

To carry out the scenario analysis, we use the worst-case variable values to obtain the worst-case NPV and the best-case variable values to obtain the best-case NPV.[6] We then use the result of the scenario analysis to determine the *expected* NPV, standard

---

SCENARIO ANALYSIS

A risk analysis technique in which "bad" and "good" sets of financial circumstances are compared with a most likely, or base case, situation.

WORST-CASE SCENARIO

An analysis in which all of the input variables are set at their worst reasonably forecasted values.

BEST-CASE SCENARIO

An analysis in which all of the input variables are set at their best reasonably forecasted values.

BASE, OR MOST LIKELY, CASE

An analysis in which all of the input variables are set at their most likely values.

---

[6]We could have included worst- and best-case values for fixed and variable costs, income tax rates, salvage values, and so on. For illustrative purposes, we limited the changes to only two variables. Also, note that we are treating sales price and quantity as independent variables; that is, a low sales price could occur when unit sales were low, and a high sales price could be coupled with high unit sales, or vice versa. As we discuss in the next section, it is relatively easy to vary these assumptions if the facts of the situation suggest a different set of conditions.

TABLE 7–5	Scenario Analysis (dollars are in thousands, except sales price)

SCENARIO	SALES VOLUME (UNITS)	SALES PRICE	NPV	PROBABILITY OF OUTCOME Pr_i	NPV × Pr_i
Best case	20,000	$2,500	$17,494	0.20	$3,499
Most likely case	15,000	2,000	3,790	0.60	2,274
Worst case	10,000	1,500	(6,487)	0.20	(1,297)
				1.00	Expected NPV = $4,475
					σ_{NPV} = $7,630
					CV_{NPV} = 1.7

$$\text{Expected NPV} = \sum_{i=1}^{n} Pr_i(NPV_i) = 0.20(\$17,494) + 0.60(\$3,790) + 0.20(-\$6,487) = \$4,475$$

$$\sigma_{NPV} = \sqrt{\sum_{i=1}^{n} Pr_i(NPV_i - \text{Expected NPV})^2}$$

$$= \sqrt{0.20(\$17,494 - \$4,475)^2 + 0.60(\$3,790 - \$4,475)^2 + 0.20(-\$6,487 - \$4,475)^2} = \$7,630$$

$$CV_{NPV} = \frac{\sigma_{NPV}}{\text{Expected NPV}} = \frac{\$7,630}{\$4,475} = 1.7$$

deviation of NPV, and the coefficient of variation. To complete these computations, we need an estimate of the probabilities of occurrence of the three scenarios, the Pr_i values. Suppose management estimates that there is a 20 percent probability of the worst-case scenario occurring, a 60 percent probability of the base case, and a 20 percent probability of the best case. Of course, it is *very difficult* to estimate scenario probabilities accurately. The scenario probabilities and NPVs constitute a probability distribution of returns just like those we dealt with in Chapter 4, except that the returns are measured in dollars instead of in percentages, or rates of return.

We performed the scenario analysis using a spreadsheet model, and Table 7–5 summarizes the results of this analysis. We see that the base case (or most likely case) forecasts a positive NPV result; the worst case produces a negative NPV; and the best case results in a large positive NPV. But the expected NPV for the project is $4.5 million and the project's coefficient of variation is 1.7. Now we can compare the project's coefficient of variation with the coefficient of variation of HEP's average project to get an idea of the relative riskiness of the appliance control computer project. HEP's existing projects, on average, have a coefficient of variation of about 1.0, so, on the basis of this stand-alone risk measure, HEP's managers would conclude that the appliance computer project is riskier than the firm's "average" project.

MONTE CARLO SIMULATION
A risk analysis technique in which probable future events are simulated on a computer, generating a probability distribution that indicates the most likely outcomes.

Monte Carlo Simulation

Scenario analysis provides useful information about a project's stand-alone risk. However, it is limited in that it only considers a few discrete outcomes (NPVs) for the project, even though there really are many more possibilities. **Monte Carlo simulation,** so named because this type of analysis grew out of work on the mathematics of casino gambling, ties together sensitivities and input variable probability distributions.

Greater Risk? Greater Return, Please.

Indications are that financial managers are quite concerned about risk when making capital budgeting decisions. A survey of financial managers by Glenn Petry and James Sprow[a] suggests that about 75 percent of companies use different required rates of return to account for risk differences when making capital budgeting decisions—only 25 percent use a single rate for all capital projects. Most of the financial managers indicated that they attempt to compute the cost of the funds used by their firms, and that rate is appropriate for determining the acceptability of projects with average risk only. For riskier projects, some of the companies adjust the expected cash flows, but most raise the rates of return required from such investments. In addition, some firms use a reduced minimum payback period to evaluate projects with above-average risk. While this approach is not common, it appears manufacturers and retailing firms are more likely to use an adjusted payback period to account for project risk than are financial service organizations, service companies, or utilities.

Other studies indicate similar results. For example, a couple of recent studies suggest that firms find risk to be an important consideration when making capital budgeting decisions; thus, the discount rate used to evaluate a project is often based on the risk of the project.[b] Further, in another study, Erika Gilbert and Alan Reichert found that more than 40 percent of the firms surveyed consider the impact of a capital project on the other assets of the firm (i.e., they consider the impact on the firm's portfolio of assets).[c]

It is interesting to note that firms generally do not attempt to use probability distributions to estimate cash flows for projects unless the outlay is extremely large. Perhaps the attitude is that it is not worth the effort to assign probabilities unless the project constitutes a major investment. When determining the terminal value of capital projects, most firms use either the expected market value or the book value of the asset at the anticipated liquidation date; in many cases, these values are expected to be the same.

In summary, it appears firms do make adjustments to the various techniques used for making capital budgeting decisions when the risks of the projects differ significantly from the average. And the most common approach for adjusting for project risk is to raise the discount rate (required rate of return) used to compute the project's net present value.

[a]Glenn H. Petry and James Sprow, "The Theory of Finance in the 1990s," *The Quarterly Review of Economics and Finance*, Winter 1993, 359–381.

[b]John R. Graham and Campbell R. Harvey, "The Theory and Practice of Corporate Finance: Evidence from the Field," *Journal of Financial Economics*, 60, No. 2–3, 2001, 187–243; Patricia Chadwell-Hatfield, Bernard Goitein, Philip Horvath, and Allen Webster, "Financial Criteria, Capital Budgeting Techniques, and Risk Analysis of Manufacturing Firms," *Journal of Applied Business Research*, Winter 1996/1997, 95–104; and James M. Poterba and Lawrence H. Summers, "A CEO Survey of U.S. Companies' Time Horizons and Hurdle Rates," *Sloan Management Review*, Fall 1995, 43–45.

[c]Erika Gilbert and Alan Reichert, "The Practice of Financial Management among Large United States Corporations," *Financial Practice and Education*, Spring/Summer 1995, 16–23.

Simulation is more complicated than scenario analysis because the probability distribution of each uncertain cash flow variable has to be specified. Once this has been done, a value from the probability distribution for each variable is randomly chosen to compute the project's cash flows, and then these values are used to determine the project's NPV. Simulation is usually completed using a computer because the process just described is repeated again and again, say, for 500 times, which results in 500 NPVs and a probability distribution for the project's NPV values. Thus, the output produced by simulation is a probability distribution that can be used to determine the most likely range of outcomes to be expected from a project. This provides the decision maker with a better idea of the various outcomes that are possible than is available from a point estimate of the NPV. In addition, simulation software packages can be used to estimate the probability of NPV > 0, of IRR > k, and so on. This additional information can be quite helpful in assessing the riskiness of a project.

Unfortunately, Monte Carlo simulation is not easy to apply because it is often difficult to specify the relationships, or correlations, among the uncertain cash flow variables. The problem is not insurmountable, but it is important not to underestimate the difficulty of obtaining valid estimates of probability distributions and correlations among variables. Such problems have been cited as reasons Monte Carlo simulation has not been widely used in industry.

Self-Test Questions

List three reasons why, in practice, a project's stand-alone risk is important.

Differentiate between sensitivity and scenario analyses. Why might scenario analysis be preferable to sensitivity analysis?

What is Monte Carlo simulation?

Identify some problems with (1) sensitivity analysis, (2) scenario analysis, and (3) Monte Carlo simulation.

Corporate (within-Firm) Risk

To measure corporate, or within-firm, risk, we need to determine how the capital budgeting project is related to the firm's existing assets. Remember from our discussion in Chapter 4 that two assets can be combined to reduce risk if their payoffs move in opposite directions—that is, when the payoff from one asset falls, the payoff from the other asset rises. In reality, it is not easy to find assets with payoffs that move opposite each other. But, as we discovered in Chapter 4, as long as assets are *not* perfectly positively related (r = +1.0), some diversification, or risk reduction, can still be achieved. Many firms use this principle to reduce the risk associated with their operations—adding new projects that are not highly related to existing assets can help reduce corporate risk and reduce fluctuations associated with sales.

Corporate risk is important for three primary reasons:

1. Undiversified stockholders, including the owners of small businesses, are more concerned about corporate risk than about beta risk.
2. Empirical studies of the determinants of required rates of return (k) generally find that both beta and corporate risk affect stock prices. This suggests that investors, even those who are well diversified, consider factors other than beta risk when they establish required returns.
3. The firm's stability is important to its managers, workers, customers, suppliers, and creditors, as well as to the community in which it operates. Firms that are in serious danger of bankruptcy, or even of suffering low profits and reduced output, have difficulty attracting and retaining good managers and workers. Also, both suppliers and customers are reluctant to depend on weak firms, and such firms have difficulty borrowing money at reasonable interest rates. These factors tend to reduce risky firms' prof-

itability and hence the prices of their stocks; thus they also make corporate risk significant.

Therefore, corporate risk is important even if a firm's stockholders are well diversified.

Self-Test Question

List three reasons why corporate risk is important.

Beta (Market) Risk

The types of risk analysis discussed thus far in the chapter provide insights into a project's risk and thus help managers make better accept/reject decisions. However, these risk measures do not take account of portfolio risk, and they do not specify whether a project should be accepted or rejected. In this section, we show how the capital asset pricing model (CAPM) can be used to help overcome those shortcomings. Of course, the CAPM has shortcomings of its own, but it nevertheless offers useful insights into risk analysis in capital budgeting.

Beta (or Market) Risk and Required Rate of Return for a Project

In Chapter 4 we developed the concept of beta, β, as a risk measure for individual stocks. From our discussion, we concluded systematic risk is the relevant risk of a stock because unsystematic, or firm-specific, risk can be reduced significantly or eliminated through diversification. This same concept can be applied to capital budgeting projects because the firm can be thought of as a composite of all the projects it has undertaken. Thus, the relevant risk of a project can be viewed as the impact it has on the firm's systematic risk. This line of reasoning leads to the conclusion that if the beta co-efficient for a project, β_{proj}, can be determined, then the **project required rate of return, k_{proj},** can be found using the following form of the CAPM equation:

PROJECT REQUIRED RATE OF RETURN, k_{proj}
The risk-adjusted required rate of return for an individual project.

$$k_{proj} = k_{RF} + (k_M - k_{RF})\beta_{proj}$$

As an example, consider the case of Erie Steel Company, an integrated steel producer operating in the Great Lakes region. For simplicity, let's assume that Erie is all equity financed, so the *average* required rate of return it needs to earn on capital budgeting projects is based solely on the average return demanded by stockholders—that is, there is no debt that might require a different return. Erie's existing beta = $\beta_{Existing}$ = 1.1; k_{RF} = 8%; and k_M = 12%. Thus, Erie's cost of equity is 12.4% = k_s = 8% + (12% – 8%)1.1, which suggests that investors should be willing to give Erie money to invest in *average risk* projects if the company expects to earn 12.4 percent or more on this money.[7] Here again, by average risk we mean projects having risk similar to the firm's existing assets.

---

[7]To simplify things somewhat, we assume at this point that the firm uses only equity capital. If debt is used, the cost of capital used must be a weighted average of the costs of debt and equity. This point is discussed at length in Chapter 8.

Suppose, however, that taking on a particular project will cause a change in Erie's beta coefficient and hence change the company's required rate of return. For example, suppose Erie is considering the construction of a fleet of barges to haul iron ore, and barge operations have betas of 1.5 rather than 1.1. Because the firm itself might be regarded as a "portfolio of assets," just like the beta of any portfolio, Erie's beta is a weighted average of the betas of its individual assets. Thus, taking on the barge project will cause the overall corporate beta to rise to somewhere between the original beta of 1.1 and the barge project's beta of 1.5. The exact value of the new beta will depend on the relative size of the investment in barge operations versus Erie's other assets. If 80 percent of Erie's total funds end up in basic steel operations with a beta of 1.1 and 20 percent in the barge operations with a beta of 1.5, the new corporate beta will increase to $1.18 = 0.8(1.1) + 0.2(1.5)$. This increase in Erie's beta coefficient will cause its stock price to decline unless the increased beta is offset by a higher expected rate of return. Note that taking on the new project will cause the *overall* corporate required rate of return to rise from the original 12.4 percent to 12.7 percent because the new beta will be 1.18. This higher average rate can be earned only if the new project generates a return higher than the existing assets are providing. Because Erie's overall return is based on its portfolio of assets, the return required from the barge project must be sufficiently high so that, in combination with returns of the other assets, the average return is 12.7 percent; only 20 percent of the average return will be provided by the barge project. Thus, the barge project, with $\beta_{Barge} = 1.5$, should be evaluated at a 14 percent required rate of return because $k_{Barge} = 8\% + (4\%)1.5 = 14\%$. On the other hand, a low-risk project such as a new steel distribution center with a beta of only 0.5 would have a required rate of return of 10 percent.

Figure 7–2 gives a graphic summary of these concepts as applied to Erie Steel. Note the following points:

1. The SML is a security market line like the one we developed in Chapter 4. It shows how investors are willing to make trade-offs between risk as measured by beta and expected returns. The higher the beta risk, the higher the rate of return needed to compensate investors for bearing this risk. The SML specifies the nature of this relationship.
2. Erie Steel initially had a beta of 1.1, so its required rate of return on average-risk investments was 12.4 percent.
3. High-risk investments such as the barge line require higher rates of return, whereas low-risk investments such as the distribution center require lower rates of return. If Erie concentrates its new investments in either high- or low-risk projects as opposed to average-risk ones, its corporate beta will either rise or fall from the current value of 1.1. Consequently, Erie's required rate of return on common stock would change from its current value of 12.4 percent.
4. If the expected rate of return on a given capital project lies *above* the SML, the expected rate of return on the project is more than enough to compensate for its risk, and the project should be accepted. Conversely, if the project's rate of return lies *below* the SML, it should be rejected. Thus, Project M in Figure 7–2 is acceptable, whereas Project N should be rejected. N has a higher expected return than M, but the differential is not enough to offset its much higher risk.

FIGURE 7–2	Using the Security Market Line Concept in Capital Budgeting

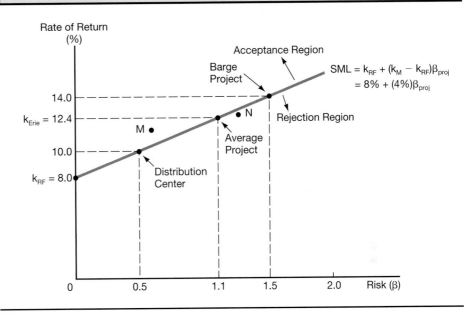

Measuring Beta Risk for a Project

In Chapter 4, we discussed the estimation of betas for stocks, and we indicated that it is difficult to estimate *true* future betas. The estimation of project betas is even more difficult and more fraught with uncertainty. One way a firm can try to measure the beta risk of a project is to find *single-product* companies in the same line of business as the project being evaluated and then use the betas of those companies to determine the required rate of return for the project being evaluated. This technique is termed the **pure play method,** and the single-product companies that are used for comparisons are called *pure play firms.* For example, if Erie could find three existing single-product firms that operate barges, it could use the average of the betas of those firms as a proxy for the barge project's beta.

The pure play approach can only be used for major assets such as whole divisions, and even then it is frequently difficult to implement because it is often impossible to find pure play proxy firms. However, when IBM was considering going into personal computers, it was able to obtain data on Apple Computer and several other essentially pure play personal computer companies. This is often the case when a firm considers a major investment outside its primary field.

PURE PLAY METHOD

An approach used for estimating the beta of a project in which a firm identifies companies whose only business is the product in question, determines the beta for each firm, and then averages the betas to find an approximation of its own project's beta.

Self-Test Questions

What is meant by the term *average-risk project?* How could you find the required rate of return for a project with average risk, low risk, and high risk?

Complete the following sentence: An increase in a company's beta coefficient would cause its stock price to decline unless . . .

Explain why a firm should accept a given capital project if its expected rate of return lies above the SML. What if the expected rate of return lies on or below the SML?

What is the pure play method, and how is it used to estimate a project's beta?

Project Risk Conclusions

We have discussed the three types of risk normally considered in capital budgeting analysis—stand-alone risk, within-firm (or corporate) risk, and beta (or market) risk—and we have discussed ways of assessing each. However, two important questions remain: (1) Should a firm be concerned with stand-alone and corporate risk in its capital budgeting decisions, and (2) what do we do when the stand-alone or within-firm risk assessments and the beta risk assessment lead to different conclusions?

These questions do not have easy answers. From a theoretical standpoint, well-diversified investors should be concerned only with beta risk, managers should be concerned only with stock price maximization, and these two factors should lead to the conclusion that beta risk should be given virtually all the weight in capital budgeting decisions. However, if investors are not well diversified, if the CAPM does not operate exactly as theory says it should, or if measurement problems keep managers from having confidence in the CAPM approach in capital budgeting, it might be appropriate to give stand-alone and corporate risk more weight than financial theorists suggest. Note also that the CAPM ignores bankruptcy costs, even though such costs can be substantial, and that the probability of bankruptcy depends on a firm's corporate risk, not on its beta risk. Therefore, one can easily conclude that even well-diversified investors should want a firm's management to give at least some consideration to a project's corporate risk instead of concentrating entirely on beta risk.

Although it would be desirable to reconcile these problems and to measure project risk on some absolute scale, the best we can do in practice is to determine project risk in a somewhat nebulous, relative sense. For example, we can generally say with a fair degree of confidence that a particular project has more or less stand-alone risk than the firm's average project. Then, assuming that stand-alone and corporate risk are highly correlated (which is typical), the project's stand-alone risk will be a good measure of its corporate risk. Finally, assuming that beta risk and corporate risk are highly correlated (as is true for most companies), a project with more corporate risk than average will also have more beta risk, and vice versa for projects with low corporate risk.

Self-Test Questions

In theory, is it correct for a firm to be concerned with stand-alone and corporate risk in its capital budgeting decisions? Should the firm be concerned with these risks in practice?

If a project's stand-alone, corporate, and beta risk are highly correlated, would this make the task of measuring risk easier or harder? Explain.

How Project Risk Is Considered in Capital Budgeting Decisions

RISK-ADJUSTED DISCOUNT RATE

The discount rate (required rate of return) that applies to a particular risky stream of income; it is equal to the risk-free rate of interest plus a risk premium appropriate to the level of risk associated with a particular project's income stream.

Thus far, we have seen that purchasing a capital project can affect a firm's beta risk, its corporate risk, or both. We also have seen that it is extremely difficult to quantify either type of risk. In other words, although it might be possible to reach the general conclusion that one project is riskier than another, it is difficult to develop a really good measure of project risk. This lack of precision in measuring project risk makes it difficult to incorporate differential risk into capital budgeting decisions.

In reality, most firms incorporate project risk in capital budgeting decisions using the **risk-adjusted discount rate** approach. With this approach, the required rate of return, which is the rate at which the expected cash flows are discounted, is adjusted if the project's risk is substantially different from the average risk associated with the firm's existing assets. Therefore, average-risk projects would be discounted at the rate of return required of projects that are considered "average," or normal for the firm; above-average risk projects would be discounted at a higher-than-average rate; and below-average risk projects would be discounted at a rate below the firm's average rate of return. Unfortunately, because risk cannot be measured precisely, there is no accurate way of specifying exactly how much higher or lower these discount rates should be; given the present state of the art, *risk adjustments are necessarily judgmental and somewhat arbitrary.*

Although the process is not exact, many companies use a two-step procedure to develop risk-adjusted discount rates for use in capital budgeting analysis. First, the overall required rate of return is established for the firm's existing assets. This process is completed on a division-by-division basis for very large firms, perhaps using the CAPM. Second, all projects generally are classified into three categories—high risk, average risk, and low risk. Then, the firm or division uses the average required rate of return as the discount rate for average-risk projects, reduces the average rate by 1 or 2 percentage points when evaluating low-risk projects, and raises the average rate by several percentage points for high-risk projects. For example, if a firm's basic required rate of return is estimated to be 12 percent, an 18 percent discount rate might be used for a high-risk project and a 9 percent rate for a low-risk project. Average-risk projects, which constitute about 80 percent of most capital budgets, would be evaluated at the 12 percent rate of return. Table 7–6 shows an example of the application of risk-adjusted discount rates for the evaluation of four projects. Each of the four projects has a five-year life, and each is expected to generate a constant cash flow stream during its life; therefore, each project's future cash flow pattern represents an annuity. The analysis shows that only Project A and Project C are acceptable when risk is considered. Note, however, that if the average required rate of return is used to evaluate all the projects, Project C and Project D would be considered acceptable because their IRRs are greater than 12 percent. Using the average required rate of return would lead to an incorrect decision. Thus, *if project risk is not considered in capital budgeting analysis, incorrect decisions are possible.*

Although the risk-adjusted discount rate approach is far from precise, it does at least recognize that different projects have different risks, and projects with different risks should be evaluated using different required rates of return.

TABLE 7–6	Capital Budgeting Decisions Using Risk-Adjusted Discount Rates

PROJECT	PROJECT RISK	REQUIRED RETURN	ESTIMATED LIFE	INITIAL INVESTMENT OUTLAY—CF_0	INCREMENTAL OPERATING CASH FLOWS— $CF_1 - CF_5$	NPV	IRR
A	Low	12%	5	$(10,000)	$2,850	$ 273.61	13.1%
B	Average	15	5	(11,000)	3,210	(239.58)	14.1
C	Average	15	5	(9,000)	2,750	218.43	16.0
D	High	20	5	(12,000)	3,825	(560.91)	17.9

PROJECT RISK CLASSIFICATION	REQUIRED RATE OF RETURN
Low	12%
Average	15
High	20

Self-Test Questions

How are risk-adjusted discount rates used to incorporate project risk into the capital budget decision process?

Briefly explain the two-step process many companies use to develop risk-adjusted discount rates for use in capital budgeting.

Capital Rationing

Capital budgeting decisions are typically made on the basis of the techniques presented in Chapter 6 and applied as described in this chapter: Independent projects are accepted if their NPVs are positive, and choices among mutually exclusive projects are made by selecting the one with the highest NPV. In this analysis, it is assumed that if in a particular year the firm has an especially large number of good projects, management simply will go into the financial markets and raise whatever funds are required to finance all of the acceptable projects. However, some firms do set limits on the amount of funds they are willing to raise, and, if this is done, the capital budget must also be limited. This situation is known as **capital rationing.**

CAPITAL RATIONING
A situation in which a constraint is placed on the total size of the firm's capital investment.

Elaborate and mathematically sophisticated models have been developed to help firms maximize their values when they are subject to capital rationing. However, a firm that subjects itself to capital rationing is deliberately forgoing profitable projects, and hence it is not truly maximizing its value. This point is well known, so few large, sophisticated firms ration capital today. Therefore, we shall not discuss it further, but you should know what the term *capital rationing* means.

Self-Test Questions

What is meant by the term *capital rationing?*

Why do few sophisticated firms ration capital today?

Multinational Capital Budgeting

Although the basic principles of capital budgeting analysis are the same for both domestic and foreign operations, some key differences need to be mentioned. First, cash flow estimation generally is much more complex for overseas investments. Most multinational firms set up a separate subsidiary in each foreign country in which they operate, and the relevant cash flows for these subsidiaries are the dividends and royalties **repatriated,** or returned, to the parent company. Second, these cash flows must be converted into the currency of the parent company, and thus are subject to future exchange rate changes. For example, General Motors' Brazilian subsidiary might make a profit of 150 million real in 2005, but the value of these profits to GM will depend on the dollar-to-real exchange rate. Third, dividends and royalties normally are taxed by both foreign and home-country governments. Furthermore, a foreign government might restrict the amount of cash that can be repatriated to the parent company, perhaps to force multinational firms to reinvest earnings in the host country or to prevent large currency outflows, which might affect the exchange rate. Whatever the host country's motivation, the result is that the parent corporation cannot use cash flows blocked in the foreign country to pay current dividends to its shareholders, nor does it have the flexibility to reinvest cash flows elsewhere in the world. Therefore, from the perspective of the parent organization, *the cash flows relevant for the analysis of a foreign investment are the cash flows that the subsidiary legally can send back to the parent.*

In addition to the complexities of the cash flow analysis, *the rate of return required for a foreign project might be different than for an equivalent domestic project because foreign projects might be more or less risky.* A higher risk could arise from two primary sources—(1) exchange rate risk and (2) political risk—while a lower risk might result from international diversification.

Exchange rate risk reflects the inherent uncertainty about the home currency value of cash flows sent back to the parent. In other words, foreign projects have an added risk element that relates to what the basic cash flows will be worth in the parent company's home currency. The foreign currency cash flows to be turned over to the parent must be converted into U.S. dollars by translating them at *expected* future exchange rates—actual exchange rates might differ substantially from expectations.

Political risk refers to any action (or the chance of such action) by a host government that reduces the value of a company's investment. It includes at one extreme the expropriation (seizure) without compensation of the subsidiary's assets; but it also includes less drastic actions that reduce the value of the parent firm's investment in the foreign subsidiary, such as higher taxes, tighter repatriation or currency controls, and restrictions on prices charged. The risk of expropriation of U.S. assets abroad is small in traditionally friendly and stable countries such as Great Britain or Switzerland. However, in Latin America and Africa, for example, the risk might be substantial. Past expropriations include those of ITT and Anaconda Copper in Chile, Gulf Oil in Bolivia, Occidental Petroleum in Libya, and the assets of many companies in Iraq, Iran, and Cuba.

Generally, political risk premiums are not added to the required rate of return to adjust for this risk. If a company's management has a serious concern that a given country might expropriate foreign assets, it simply will not make significant investments in that country. Expropriation is viewed as a catastrophic or ruinous event, and managers have been shown to be extraordinarily risk averse when faced

REPATRIATION OF EARNINGS
The process of sending cash flows from a foreign subsidiary back to the parent company.

EXCHANGE RATE RISK
The uncertainty associated with the price at which the currency from one country can be converted into the currency of another country.

POLITICAL RISK
The risk of expropriation (seizure) of a foreign subsidiary's assets by the host country or of unanticipated restrictions on cash flows to the parent company.

with ruinous loss possibilities. However, companies can take steps to reduce the potential loss from expropriation in three major ways: (1) by financing the subsidiary with capital raised in the country in which the asset is located, (2) by structuring operations so that the subsidiary has value only as a part of the integrated corporate system, and (3) by obtaining insurance against economic losses from expropriation from a source such as the Overseas Private Investment Corporation (OPIC). In the latter case, insurance premiums would have to be added to the project's cost.

Self-Test Questions

List some key differences in capital budgeting as applied to foreign versus domestic operations.

What are the relevant cash flows for an international investment?

Why might the required rate of return for a foreign project differ from that of an equivalent domestic project? Could it be lower?

Summary

This chapter presented two issues in capital budgeting: cash flow estimation and evaluation and risk analysis in capital budgeting. We also provided an indication of the capital budgeting decision-making process in multinational firms. The key concepts covered are listed here:

- The most important, but also the most difficult, step in analyzing a capital budgeting project is estimating the **incremental after-tax cash flows** the project will produce.
- **Net cash flows** consist of net income plus depreciation. In determining incremental cash flows, **opportunity costs** (the cash flow forgone by using an asset) must be included, but **sunk costs** (cash outlays that have been made and that cannot be recouped) should not be included. Any **externalities** (effects of a project on other parts of the firm) should also be reflected in the analysis. In addition, **inflation** effects must be considered in project analysis. The best procedure is to build inflation directly into the cash flow estimates.
- The **initial investment outlay** refers to the incremental cash flows that *occur only at the start of a project's life*. **Incremental operating cash flows** represent the *changes in day-to-day cash flows* that result from the purchase of a capital project that continue until the firm disposes of the asset. The **terminal cash flow** occurs at the end of the life of the project, and it is *associated with the final disposal of the project* and returning the firm's operations to where they were before the project was accepted.
- Capital projects often require an additional investment in **net working capital (NWC).** An *increase* (decrease) in NWC must be included in the Year 0 initial cash outlay and then shown as a cash inflow (outflow) in the project's final year.
- **Replacement analysis** is slightly different from that for **expansion projects** because the cash flows from the old asset must be considered in replacement decisions.

- A project's **stand-alone risk** is the risk the project would have if it were the firm's only asset and if the firm's stockholders held only that one stock. Stand-alone risk is measured by the variability of the asset's expected returns, and it is often used as a proxy for both beta and corporate risk because (1) beta and corporate risk are difficult to measure and (2) the three types of risk are usually highly correlated.

- **Within-firm,** or **corporate, risk** reflects the effects of a project on the firm's risk, and it is measured by the project's effect on the firm's earnings variability. Stockholder diversification is not taken into account.

- **Beta risk** reflects the effects of a project on the risks borne by stockholders, assuming stockholders hold diversified portfolios. In theory, beta risk should be the most relevant type of risk.

- **Corporate risk** is important because it influences the firm's ability to use low-cost debt, to maintain smooth operations over time, and to avoid crises that might consume management's energy and disrupt employees, customers, suppliers, and the community.

- **Sensitivity analysis** is a technique that shows how much an output variable such as NPV will change in response to a given change in an input variable such as sales, other things held constant.

- **Scenario analysis** is a risk analysis technique in which the best- and worst-case NPVs are compared with the project's expected, or base-case, NPV.

- **Monte Carlo simulation** is a risk-analysis technique in which a computer is used to simulate probable future events and thus to estimate the profitability distribution and riskiness of a project.

- The **pure play method** can be used to estimate betas for large projects or for divisions.

- The **risk-adjusted discount rate** is the rate used to evaluate a particular project. The discount rate is increased for projects that are riskier than the firm's average project but is decreased for less risky projects.

- **Capital rationing** occurs when management places a constraint on the size of the firm's capital budget during a particular period.

- Investments in **international capital projects** expose the investing firm to **exchange rate risk** and **political risk.** The relevant cash flows in international capital budgeting are the dollar cash flows that can be turned over to the parent company.

Both the measurement of risk and its incorporation into capital budgeting involve judgment. It is possible to use a quantitative technique such as simulation as an aid to judgment, but in the final analysis the assessment of risk in capital budgeting is a subjective process.

Questions

7–1 Cash flows rather than accounting profits are listed in Table 7–2. What is the basis for this emphasis on cash flows as opposed to net income?

7–2 Look at Table 7–4 and answer these questions:
   a. Why is the net salvage value shown in Section III reduced for taxes?
   b. How is the change in depreciation computed?

    c. What would happen if the new machine permitted a reduction in net working capital?

    d. Why are the cost savings shown as a positive amount?

7–3 Explain why sunk costs should not be included in a capital budgeting analysis but opportunity costs and externalities should be included.

7–4 Explain how net working capital is recovered at the end of a project's life and why it is included in a capital budgeting analysis.

7–5 In general, is an explicit recognition of incremental cash flows more important in new project analysis or replacement analysis? Why?

7–6 Why is it true, in general, that a failure to adjust expected cash flows for expected inflation biases the calculated NPV downward?

7–7 Define (a) simulation analysis, (b) scenario analysis, and (c) sensitivity analysis. If AT&T were considering two investments, one calling for the expenditure of $2 million to develop a satellite communications system and the other involving the expenditure of $30,000 for a new truck, on which one would the company be more likely to use simulation analysis?

7–8 Distinguish between beta (or market) risk, within-firm (or corporate) risk, and stand-alone risk for a project being considered for inclusion in the capital budget. Which type of risk do you believe should be given the greatest weight in capital budgeting decisions? Explain.

7–9 Suppose Reading Engine Company, which has a high beta as well as a great deal of corporate risk, merged with Simplicity Patterns Inc. Simplicity's sales rise during recessions, when people are more likely to make their own clothes, and, consequently, its beta is negative but its corporate risk is relatively high. What would the merger do to the costs of capital in the consolidated company's locomotive engine division and in its patterns division?

7–10 Suppose a firm estimates its required rate of return for the coming year to be 10 percent. What are reasonable required rates of return for evaluating average-risk projects, high-risk projects, and low-risk projects?

Self-Test Problems

(Solutions appear in Appendix B)

key terms   **ST-1** Define each of the following terms:

    a. Cash flow; accounting income; relevant cash flow

    b. Incremental cash flow; sunk cost; opportunity cost; externalities; inflation bias

    c. Initial investment outlay; incremental operating cash flow; terminal cash flow

    d. Change in net working capital; expansion project

    e. Salvage value

    f. Replacement analysis; expansion analysis

    g. Stand-alone risk; within-firm risk; beta (market) risk

    h. Corporate risk

    i. Sensitivity analysis

    j. Scenario analysis

    k. Monte Carlo simulation analysis

    l. Project beta versus corporate beta

    m. Pure play method of estimating project betas

    n. Risk-adjusted discount rate; project required rate of return

o. Capital rationing

p. Exchange rate risk; political risk

new project (expansion) analysis   **ST-2** You have been asked by the president of Ellis Construction Company, headquartered in Toledo, to evaluate the proposed acquisition of a new earthmover. The mover's basic price is $50,000, and it will cost another $10,000 to modify it for special use by Ellis Construction. Assume that the mover falls into the MACRS 3-year class. (See Table 7A–2 at the end of this chapter for MACRS recovery allowance percentages.) It will be sold after three years for $20,000, and it will require an increase in net working capital (spare parts inventory) of $2,000. The earthmover purchase will have no effect on revenues, but it is expected to save Ellis $20,000 per year in before-tax operating costs, mainly labor. Ellis's marginal tax rate is 40 percent.

a. What is the company's net initial investment outlay if it acquires the earthmover? (That is, what is the Year 0 net cash flow?)

b. What are the incremental operating cash flows in Years 1, 2, and 3?

c. What is the terminal cash flow in Year 3?

d. If the project's required rate of return is 10 percent, should the earthmover be purchased?

replacement analysis   **ST-3** The Dauten Toy Corporation currently uses an injection molding machine that was purchased two years ago. This machine is being depreciated on a straight line basis toward a $500 salvage value, and it has six years of remaining life. Its current book value is $2,600, and it can be sold for $3,000 at this time. Thus, the annual depreciation expense is ($2,600 – $500)/6 = $350 per year.

Dauten is offered a replacement machine that has a cost of $8,000, an estimated useful life of six years, and an estimated salvage value of $800. This machine falls into the MACRS 5-year class. (See Table 7A–2 at the end of this chapter for MACRS recovery allowance percentages.) The replacement machine would permit an output expansion, so sales would rise by $1,000 per year. In addition, the new machine's much greater efficiency would cause operating expenses to decline by $1,500 per year. The new machine would require that net working capital be increased by $1,500.

Dauten's marginal tax rate is 40 percent, and its required rate of return is 15 percent. Should the old machine be replaced?

corporate risk analysis   **ST-4** The staff of Heymann Manufacturing has estimated the following net cash flows and probabilities for a new manufacturing process:

	NET CASH FLOWS		
YEAR	$P_R = 0.2$	$P_R = 0.6$	$P_R = 0.2$
0	$(100,000)	$(100,000)	$(100,000)
1	20,000	30,000	40,000
2	20,000	30,000	40,000
3	20,000	30,000	40,000
4	20,000	30,000	40,000
5	20,000	30,000	40,000
5*	0	20,000	30,000

Line 0 gives the cost of the process, Lines 1 through 5 give operating cash flows, and Line 5* contains the estimated salvage values. Heymann's required rate of return for an average risk project is 10 percent.

a. Assume that the project has average risk. Find the project's expected NPV. (*Hint:* Use expected values for the net cash flow in each year.)

b. Find the best-case and worst-case NPVs. What is the probability of occurrence of the worst case if the cash flows are perfectly positively correlated over time? If they are independent over time?

c. Assume that all the cash flows are perfectly positively correlated; that is, there are only three possible cash flow streams over time: (1) the worst case, (2) the most likely, or base, case, and (3) the best case, with probabilities of 0.2, 0.6, and 0.2, respectively. These cases are represented by each of the columns in the table. Find the expected NPV, its standard deviation, and its coefficient of variation.

d. The coefficient of variation of Heymann's average project is in the range 0.8 to 1.0. If the coefficient of variation of a project being evaluated is greater than 1.0, 2 percentage points are added to the firm's required rate of return. Similarly, if the coefficient of variation is less than 0.8, 1 percentage point is deducted from the required rate of return. What is the project's required rate of return? Should Heymann accept or reject the project?

Problems

new project (expansion) analysis

7–1 You have been asked by the president of your company to evaluate the proposed acquisition of a spectrometer for the firm's R&D department. The equipment's base price is $140,000, and it would cost another $30,000 to modify it for special use by your firm. The spectrometer, which falls into the MACRS 3-year class, would be sold after three years for $60,000. (See Table 7A–2 at the end of this chapter for MACRS recovery allowance percentages.) Use of the equipment would require an increase in net working capital (spare parts inventory) of $8,000. The spectrometer would have no effect on revenues, but it is expected to save the firm $50,000 per year in before-tax operating costs, mainly labor. The firm's marginal tax rate is 40 percent.

a. What is the initial investment outlay associated with this project? (That is, what is the Year 0 net cash flow?)

b. What are the incremental operating cash flows in Years 1, 2, and 3?

c. What is the terminal cash flow in Year 3?

d. If the project's required rate of return is 12 percent, should the spectrometer be purchased?

new project (expansion) analysis

7–2 The Ewert Company is evaluating the proposed acquisition of a new milling machine. The machine's base price is $108,000, and it would cost another $12,500 to modify it for special use by the firm. The machine falls into the MACRS 3-year class, and it would be sold after three years for $65,000. (See Table 7A–2 at the end of this chapter for MACRS recovery allowance percentages.) The machine would require an increase in net working capital (inventory) of $5,500. The milling machine would have no effect on revenues, but it is expected to save the firm $44,000 per year in before-tax operating costs, mainly labor. Ewert's marginal tax rate is 34 percent.

a. What is the initial investment outlay of the machine for capital budgeting purposes? (That is, what is the Year 0 net cash flow?)

b. What are the incremental operating cash flows in Years 1, 2, and 3?

c. What is the terminal cash flow in Year 3?

d. If the project's required rate of return is 12 percent, should the machine be purchased?

replacement analysis   **7-3** Atlantic Control Company (ACC) purchased a machine two years ago at a cost of $70,000. At that time, the machine's expected economic life was six years and its salvage value at the end of its life was estimated to be $10,000. It is being depreciated using the straight line method so that its book value at the end of six years is $10,000. In four years, however, the old machine will have a market value of $0.

A new machine can be purchased for $80,000, including shipping and installation costs. The new machine has an economic life estimated to be four years. MACRS depreciation will be used, and the machine will be depreciated over its 3-year class life rather than its five-year economic life. (See Table 7A-2 at the end of this chapter for MACRS recovery allowance percentages.) During its four-year life, the new machine will reduce cash operating expenses by $20,000 per year. Sales are not expected to change. But the new machine will require net working capital to be increased by $4,000. At the end of its useful life, the machine is estimated to have a market value of $2,500.

The old machine can be sold today for $20,000. The firm's marginal tax rate is 40 percent. The appropriate required rate of return is 10 percent.

a. If the new machine is purchased, what is the amount of the initial investment outlay at Year 0?

b. What incremental operating cash flows will occur at the end of Years 1 through 4 as a result of replacing the old machine?

c. What is the terminal cash flow at the end of Year 4 if the new machine is purchased?

d. What is the NPV of this project? Should ACC replace the old machine?

replacement analysis   **7-4** The Boyd Bottling Company is contemplating the replacement of one of its bottling machines with a newer and more efficient one. The old machine has a book value of $600,000 and a remaining useful life of five years. The firm does not expect to realize any return from scrapping the old machine in five years, but it can sell it now to another firm in the industry for $265,000. The old machine is being depreciated toward a zero salvage value, or by $120,000 per year, using the straight line method.

The new machine has a purchase price of $1,175,000, an estimated useful life and MACRS class life of five years, and an estimated market value of $145,000 at the end of five years. (See Table 7A-2 at the end of this chapter for MACRS recovery allowance percentages.) It is expected to economize on electric power usage, labor, and repair costs, which will save Boyd $230,000 each year. In addition, the new machine is expected to reduce the number of defective bottles, which will save an additional $25,000 annually. The company's marginal tax rate is 40 percent and it has a 12 percent required rate of return.

a. What initial investment outlay is required for the new machine?

b. Calculate the annual depreciation allowances for both machines, and compute the change in the annual depreciation expense if the replacement is made.

c. What are the incremental operating cash flows in Years 1 through 5?

d. What is the terminal cash flow in Year 5?

e. Should the firm purchase the new machine? Support your answer.

f. In general, how would each of the following factors affect the investment decision, and how should each be treated?
   (1) The expected life of the existing machine decreases.
   (2) The required rate of return is not constant but is increasing as Boyd adds more projects into its capital budget for the year.

risky cash flows 7–5 The Singleton Company must decide between two mutually exclusive investment projects. Each project costs $6,750 and has an expected life of three years. Annual net cash flows from each project begin one year after the initial investment is made and have the following probability distributions:

PROJECT A		PROJECT B	
PROBABILITY	NET CASH FLOWS	PROBABILITY	NET CASH FLOWS
0.2	$6,000	0.2	$ 0
0.6	6,750	0.6	6,750
0.2	7,500	0.2	18,000

Singleton has decided to evaluate the riskier project at a 12 percent rate and the less risky project at a 10 percent rate.

a. What is the expected value of the annual net cash flows from each project? What is the coefficient of variation (CV_{NPV})? (*Hint:* Use Equation 4–3 from Chapter 4 to calculate the standard deviation of Project A. σ_B = $5,798 and CV_B = 0.76.)

b. What is the risk-adjusted NPV of each project?

c. If it were known that Project B was negatively correlated with other cash flows of the firm whereas Project A was positively correlated, how would this knowledge affect the decision? If Project B's cash flows were negatively correlated with the gross national product (GNP), would that influence your assessment of its risk?

CAPM approach 7–6 Goodtread Rubber Company has two divisions: the tire division, which manu-
to risk adjustments factures tires for new autos, and the recap division, which manufactures recapping materials that are sold to independent tire recapping shops throughout the United States. Because auto manufacturing fluctuates with the general economy, the tire division's earnings contribution to Goodtread's stock price is highly correlated with returns on most other stocks. If the tire division were operated as a separate company, its beta coefficient would be 1.5. The sales and profits of the recap division, on the other hand, tend to be countercyclical because recap sales boom when people cannot afford to buy new tires. The recap division's beta is estimated to be 0.5. Approximately 75 percent of Goodtread's corporate assets are invested in the tire division and 25 percent are invested in the recap division.

Currently, the rate of interest on Treasury securities is 6 percent, and the expected rate of return on an average share of stock is 10 percent. Goodtread uses only common equity capital, so it has no debt outstanding.

a. What is the required rate of return on Goodtread's stock?

b. What discount rate should be used to evaluate capital budgeting projects for each division? Explain your answer fully, and, in the process, illustrate your answer with a project that costs $160,000, has a 10-year life, and provides expected after-tax net cash flows of $30,000 per year.

scenario analysis 7–7 Your firm, Agrico Products, is considering the purchase of a tractor that will have a net cost of $36,000, will increase pretax operating cash flows before taking account of depreciation effects by $12,000 per year, and will be depreciated on a straight line basis to zero over five years at the rate of $7,200 per year, beginning the first year. (Annual cash flows will be $12,000 before taxes plus the tax savings that result from $7,200 of depreciation.) The board of directors is having a heated debate about whether the tractor actually will last five years. Specifically, Joan Lamm insists that she knows of some tractors have lasted only four years. Alan Grunewald agrees with Lamm, but he argues that most tractors do give five years of service. Judy Maese says she has known some to last for as long as eight years.

Given this discussion, the board asks you to prepare a scenario analysis to ascertain the importance of the uncertainty about the tractor's life span. Assume a 40 percent marginal tax rate, a zero salvage value, and a required rate of return of 10 percent. (*Hint:* Here straight line depreciation is based on the MACRS class life of the tractor and is not affected by the actual life. Also, ignore the half-year convention for this problem.)

Exam-Type Problems

The problems included in this section are set up in such a way that they could be used as multiple-choice exam problems.

replacement analysis   **7–8** The Gehr Company is considering the purchase of a new machine tool to replace an obsolete one. The machine being used for the operation has both a book value and a market value of zero; it is in good working order, however, and will last physically for at least another 10 years. The proposed replacement machine will perform the operation so much more efficiently that Gehr engineers estimate it will produce after-tax cash flows (labor savings and the effect of depreciation) of $9,000 per year. The new machine will cost $40,000 delivered and installed, and its economic life is estimated to be 10 years. Its expected salvage value is zero. The firm's required rate of return is 10 percent, and its marginal tax rate is 40 percent. Should Gehr buy the new machine?

replacement analysis   **7–9** Galveston Shipyards is considering the replacement of an eight-year-old riveting machine with a new one that will increase earnings before depreciation from $27,000 to $54,000 per year. The new machine will cost $82,500, and it will have an estimated life of eight years and no salvage value. The new machine will be depreciated over its 5-year MACRS recovery period. (See Table 7A–2 at the end of this chapter for MACRS recovery allowance percentages.) The firm's marginal tax rate is 40 percent, and the firm's required rate of return is 12 percent. The old machine has been fully depreciated and has no salvage value. Should the old riveting machine be replaced by the new one?

risk adjustment   **7–10** The risk-free rate of return is currently 5 percent and the market risk premium is 4 percent. The beta of the project under analysis is 1.4, with expected net cash flows estimated to be $1,500 per year for five years. The required investment outlay on the project is $4,500.
  a. What is the required risk-adjusted return on the project?
  b. Should the project be accepted?

beta risk   **7–11** Companioni Computer Corporation (CCC), a producer of office equipment, currently has assets of $15 million and a beta of 1.4. The risk-free rate is 8 percent and the market risk premium is 5 percent. CCC would like to expand into the risky home computer market. If the expansion is undertaken, CCC would create a new division with $3.75 million in assets. The new division would have a beta of 1.8.

a. What is CCC's current required rate of return?

b. If the expansion is undertaken, what would be the firm's new beta? What is the new overall required rate of return, and what rate of return must the home computer division produce to leave the new overall required rate of return unchanged?

Integrative Problems

capital budgeting and cash flow estimation

7–12 Unilate Textiles is evaluating a new product, a silk/wool blended fabric. Assume that you were recently hired as assistant to the director of capital budgeting, and you must evaluate the new project.

The fabric would be produced in an unused building adjacent to Unilate's Southern Pines, North Carolina, plant. Unilate owns the building, which is fully depreciated. The required equipment would cost $200,000, plus an additional $40,000 for shipping and installation. In addition, inventories would rise by $25,000, while accounts payable would go up by $5,000. All of these costs would be incurred at Year 0. By a special ruling, the machinery could be depreciated under the MACRS system as 3-year property.

The project is expected to operate for four years, at which time it will be terminated. The cash inflows are assumed to begin one year after the project is undertaken, or at t = 1, and to continue out to t = 4. At the end of the project's life (Year 4), the equipment is expected to have a salvage value of $25,000.

Unit sales are expected to total 100,000 five-yard rolls per year, and the expected sales price is $2.00 per roll. Cash operating costs for the project (total operating costs less depreciation) are expected to total 60 percent of dollar sales. Unilate's marginal tax rate is 40 percent, and its required rate of return is 10 percent. Tentatively, the silk/wool blend fabric project is assumed to be of equal risk to Unilate's other assets.

You have been asked to evaluate the project and to make a recommendation as to whether it should be accepted or rejected. To guide you in your analysis, your boss gave you the following set of tasks to complete:

a. Draw a cash flow time line that shows when the net cash inflows and outflows will occur, and explain how the time line can be used to help structure the analysis.

b. Unilate has a standard form that is used in the capital budgeting process; see Table IP7–1. Part of the table has been completed, but you must fill in the blanks. Complete the table in the following order:

(1) Complete the unit sales, sales price, total revenues, and operating costs excluding depreciation lines.

(2) Complete the depreciation line.

(3) Now complete the table down to net income and then down to net operating cash flows.

(4) Now fill in the blanks under Year 0 and Year 4 for the initial investment outlay and the terminal cash flows and complete the cash flow time line (net CF). Discuss working capital. What would have happened if the machinery were sold for less than its book value?

TABLE IP7-1	Unilate's Silk/Wool Blend Project ($ thousands)				

	END OF YEAR				
END OF YEAR:	0	1	2	3	4
Unit sales ($ thousands)			100		
Price/unit		$ 2.00	$ 2.00		
Total revenues				$200.0	
Costs excluding depreciation			$(120.0)		
Depreciation				(36.0)	(16.8)
Total operating costs		$(199.2)	$(228.0)		
Earnings before taxes (EBT)				$ 44.0	
Taxes		(0.3)			(25.3)
Net income				$ 26.4	
Depreciation		79.2		36.0	
Incremental operating CF		$ 79.7			$ 54.7
Equipment cost					
Installation					
Increase in inventory					
Increase in accounts payable					
Salvage value					
Tax on salvage value					
Return of net working capital					
Cash flow time line (Net CF)	$(260.0)				$ 89.7
Cumulative CF for payback	(260.0)	(180.3)			63.0
NPV =					
IRR =					
Payback =					

c. (1) Unilate uses debt in its capital structure, so some of the money used to finance the project will be debt. Given this fact, should the projected cash flows be revised to show projected interest charges? Explain.

(2) Suppose you learned that Unilate had spent $50,000 to renovate the building last year, expensing these costs. Should this cost be reflected in the analysis? Explain.

(3) Now suppose you learned that Unilate could lease its building to another party and earn $25,000 per year. Should this fact be reflected in the analysis? If so, how?

(4) Now assume that the silk/wool blend fabric project would take away profitable sales from Unilate's cotton/wool blend fabric business. Should this fact be reflected in your analysis? If so, how?

    d. Disregard all the assumptions made in part c, and assume there was no alternative use for the building over the next four years. Now calculate the project's NPV, IRR, and traditional payback. Do these indicators suggest that the project should be accepted?

    e. If this project had been a replacement project rather than an expansion project, how would the analysis have changed? No calculations are needed; just think about the changes that would have to occur in the cash flow table.

    f. Assume that inflation is expected to average 3 percent over the next four years, that this expectation is reflected in the required rate of return, and that inflation will increase variable costs and revenues by the same relative amount of 3 percent. Does it appear that inflation has been dealt with properly in the analysis? If not, what should be done, and how would the required adjustment affect the decision?

risk analysis   **7–13** Problem 7–12 contained the details of a new-project capital budgeting evaluation being conducted by Unilate Textiles. Although inflation was considered in the initial analysis, the riskiness of the project was not considered. The expected cash flows considering inflation as they were estimated in Problem 7–12 (in thousands of dollars) are given in Table IP7–2. Unilate's required rate of return is 10 percent.

    You have been asked to answer the following questions:

    a. (1) What are the three levels, or types, of project risk that are normally considered?

    (2) Which type is the most relevant?

    (3) Which type is the easiest to measure?

    (4) How are the three types of risk generally related?

    b. (1) What is sensitivity analysis?

    (2) Discuss how one would perform a sensitivity analysis on the unit sales, salvage value, and required rate of return for the project. Assume that each of these variables deviates from its base-case, or expected, value by plus and minus 10, 20, and 30 percent. How would you calculate the NPV, IRR, and the payback for each case?

    (3) What is the primary weakness of sensitivity analysis? What are its primary advantages?

    c. Assume that you are confident about the estimates of all the variables that affect the project's cash flows except unit sales. If product acceptance is poor, sales would be only 75,000 units a year, whereas a strong consumer response would produce sales of 125,000 units. In either case, cash costs would still amount to 60 percent of revenues. You believe that there is a 25 percent chance of poor acceptance, a 25 percent chance of excellent acceptance, and a 50 percent chance of average acceptance (the base case).

    (1) What is the worst-case NPV? The best-case NPV?

    (2) Use the worst-case, most likely (or base) case, and best-case NPVs and probabilities of occurrence to find the project's expected NPV, standard deviation (σ_{NPV}), and coefficient of variation (CV_{NPV}).

    d. (1) Assume that Unilate's average project has a coefficient of variation (CV_{NPV}) in the range of 1.25 to 1.75. Would the silk/wool blend fabric project be classified as high risk, average risk, or low risk? What type of risk is being measured here?

TABLE IP7–2					
			YEAR		
	0	**1**	**2**	**3**	**4**
Investment in:					
Fixed assets	$(240)				
Net working capital	(20)				
Unit sales (thousands)		100	100	100	100
Sales price (dollars)		$2.100	$ 2.205	$2.315	$2.431
Total revenues		$210.0	$ 220.5	$231.5	$243.1
Cash operating costs (60%)		(126.0)	(132.3)	(138.9)	(145.9)
Depreciation		(79.2)	(108.0)	(36.0)	(16.8)
Earnings before taxes (EBT)		$ 4.8	$(19.8)	$ 56.6	$ 80.4
Taxes (40%)		(1.9)	7.9	(22.6)	(32.2)
Net income		$ 2.9	$(11.9)	$ 34.0	$ 48.2
Plus depreciation		79.2	108.0	36.0	16.8
Net operating cash flow		$ 82.1	$ 96.1	$ 70.0	$ 65.0
Salvage value					25.0
Tax on SV (40%)					(10.0)
Recovery of NWC					20.0
Net cash flow	$(260)	$ 82.1	$ 96.1	$ 70.0	$100.0
Cumulative cash flow for payback:	(260.0)	(177.9)	(81.8)	(11.8)	88.2
NPV at 10% cost of capital = $15.0					
IRR = 12.6%					

    (2) Based on common sense, how highly correlated do you think the project would be to the firm's other assets? (Give a correlation coefficient, or range of coefficients, based on your judgment.)

    (3) How would this correlation coefficient and the previously calculated σ combine to affect the project's contribution to corporate, or within-firm, risk? Explain.

e. (1) Based on your judgment, what do you think the project's correlation coefficient would be with respect to the general economy and thus with returns on "the market"?

    (2) How would correlation with the economy affect the project's market risk?

f. (1) Unilate typically adds or subtracts 3 percentage points to the overall required rate of return to adjust for risk. Should the project be accepted?

    (2) What subjective risk factors should be considered before the final decision is made?

g. Define scenario analysis and simulation analysis, and discuss their principal advantages and disadvantages. (Note that you have already done scenario analysis in part c.)

h. (1) Assume that the risk-free rate is 10 percent, the market risk premium is 6 percent, and the new project's beta is 1.2. What is the project's required rate of return on equity based on the CAPM?

(2) How does the project's market risk compare with the firm's overall market risk?

(3) How does the project's stand-alone risk compare with that of the firm's average project?

(4) Briefly describe how you could estimate the project's beta. How feasible do you think that procedure actually would be in this case?

(5) What are the advantages and disadvantages of focusing on a project's market risk?

Computer-Related Problem

Work the problem in this section only if you are using the computer problem diskette.

expansion project

7–14 Use the computerized model in the File C07 to work this problem. Golden State Bakers Inc. (GSB) has an opportunity to invest in a new dough machine. GSB needs more productive capacity, so the new machine will not replace an existing machine. The new machine costs $260,000 and will require modifications costing $15,000. It has an expected useful life of 10 years, will be depreciated using the MACRS method over its 5-year class life, and has an expected salvage value of $12,500 at the end of Year 10. (See Table 7A–2 at the end of this chapter for MACRS recovery allowance percentages.) The machine will require a $22,500 investment in net working capital. It is expected to generate additional sales revenues of $125,000 per year, but its use will also increase annual cash operating expenses by $55,000. GSB's required rate of return is 10 percent and its marginal tax rate is 40 percent. The machine's book value at the end of Year 10 will be zero, so GSB will have to pay taxes on the $12,500 salvage value.

a. What is the NPV of this expansion project? Should GSB purchase the new machine?

b. Should GSB purchase the new machine if it is expected to be used for only five years and then sold for $31,250?

c. Would the machine be profitable if revenues increased by only $105,000 per year? Assume a 10-year project life and a salvage value of $12,500.

d. Suppose that revenues rose by $125,000 but that expenses rose by $65,000. Would the machine be acceptable under these conditions? Assume a 10-year project life and a salvage value of $12,500.

GET REAL with Thomson ONE

7–15 Imagine that you hold a portfolio of three stocks: Coca Cola Company [KO], a manufacturer and distributor of soft drinks; Dell, Inc. [DELL], a manufacturing of personal and enterprise computers, and Fifth Third Bank [FITB], a large, regional bank that offers commercial banking, retail banking, and investment advisory services. Each of these companies is preparing to launch a new project.

Coca Cola is launching a new version of Coca Cola with increased caffeine. Dell has produced a new, very low cost personal computer to deliver the basic functions of email, web browsing, and word processing for individuals who do not need all the "bells and whistles." Fifth Third Bank has shifted its investment in marketable securities so as to earn higher returns; this shift has increased the riskiness associated with the bank's investment portfolio.

The following betas were estimated by the companies for the *new projects:*

Company	Project Beta
Coca Cola	1.19
Dell	2.01
Fifth Third Bank	1.20

Using the Thomson ONE database, answer these questions:

a. What is the current beta of the three firms? (Click on Price/Interactive Charts.)
b. If the new project causes the corporate beta to rise, how will this impact the company's risk and the shareholder's required rate of return?
c. Can you use the pure play method to determine a more accurate project beta for any or all of these firms? Why or why not?

APPENDIX 7A

Depreciation

Suppose a firm buys a milling machine for $100,000 and uses it for five years, after which it is scrapped. The cost of the goods produced by the machine each year must include a charge for using the machine and reducing its value. This charge is called *depreciation.* In this appendix we review some of the depreciation concepts covered in your accounting courses.

Companies often calculate depreciation one way when figuring taxes and another way when reporting income to investors: many use the *straight line* method for stockholder reporting (or "book" purposes), but they use the fastest rate permitted by law for tax purposes.

According to the straight line method used for stockholder reporting, you normally would take the cost of the asset, subtract its estimated salvage value, and divide the net amount by the asset's useful economic life. For an asset with a five-year life that costs $100,000 and has a $12,500 salvage value, the annual straight line depreciation charge is ($100,000 – $12,500)/5 = $17,500. Note, however, as we discuss later in this appendix, that salvage value is not considered for tax depreciation purposes.

For tax purposes, Congress changes the permissible tax depreciation methods from time to time. Prior to 1954, the straight line method was required for tax purposes,

TABLE 7A–1	Major Classes and Asset Lives for MACRS

CLASS	TYPE OF PROPERTY
3-year	Certain special manufacturing tools; a race horse older than two years.
5-year	Automobiles, light-duty trucks, computers, office machinery, and certain special manufacturing equipment.
7-year	Most industrial equipment, office furniture, and fixtures.
10-year	Certain longer-lived equipment, and many water vessels.
15-year	Certain land improvement, such as shrubbery, fences, and roads; service station buildings.
20-year	Farm buildings
25-year	Property used in water treatment; municipal sewers.
27.5-year	Residential rental real property such as apartment buildings.
39-year	All nonresidential real property, including commercial and industrial buildings.

but in 1954 accelerated methods (double declining balance and sum-of-years'-digits) were permitted. Then, in 1981, the old accelerated methods were replaced by a simpler procedure known as the Accelerated Cost Recovery System (ACRS). The ACRS system was changed again in 1986 as a part of the Tax Reform Act, and it is now known as the Modified Accelerated Cost Recovery System (MACRS).

Tax Depreciation Life   For tax purposes, the *entire* cost of an asset is expensed over its depreciable life. Historically, an asset's depreciable life was determined by its estimated useful economic life; it was intended that an asset would be fully depreciated at approximately the same time that it reached the end of its useful economic life. However, MACRS totally abandoned that practice and set simple guidelines that created several classes of assets, each with a more-or-less arbitrarily prescribed life called a recovery period or class life. The MACRS class life bears only a rough relationship to the expected useful economic life.

A major effect of the MACRS system has been to shorten the depreciable lives of assets, thus giving businesses larger tax deductions and thereby increasing their cash flows available for reinvestment. Table 7A–1 describes the types of property that fit into the different class life groups, and Table 7A–2 sets forth the MACRS recovery allowances (depreciation rates) for selected classes of investment property.

Consider Table 7A–1 first. The first column gives the MACRS class life, while the second column describes the types of assets that fall into each category. Property classified with lives equal to or greater than 27.5 years (real estate) must be depreciated by the straight line method, but assets classified in the other categories can be depreciated either by the accelerated method using rates shown in Table 7A–2 or by an alternate straight line method.

As we saw earlier in the chapter, higher depreciation expenses result in lower taxes, hence higher cash flows. Therefore, because a firm has the choice of using the alternate straight line rates or the accelerated rates shown in Table 7A–2, most elect to use the accelerated rates. The yearly recovery allowance, or depreciation expense, is

TABLE 7A–2	Recovery Allowance Percentages for Personal Property			

	CLASS OF INVESTMENT			
OWNERSHIP YEAR	3-YEAR	5-YEAR	7-YEAR	10-YEAR
1	33%	20%	14%	10%
2	45	32	25	18
3	15	19	17	14
4	7	12	13	12
5		11	9	9
6		6	9	7
7			9	7
8			4	7
9				7
10				6
11				3
	100%	100%	100%	100%

NOTE: These recovery allowance percentages were taken from the Internal Revenue Service Web site, which is http://www.irs.gov. The percentages are based on the 200 percent declining balance method prescribed by MACRS, with a switch to straight line depreciation at some point in the asset's life. For example, consider the five-year recovery allowance percentages. The straight line percentage would be 20 percent per year, so the 200 percent declining balance multiplier is $2.0(20\%) = 40\% = 0.4$. However, because the half-year convention applies, the MACRS percentage for Year 1 is 20 percent. For Year 2, 80 percent of the depreciable basis remains to be depreciated, so the recovery allowance percentage is $0.40(80\%) = 32\%$, and so on. Although the tax tables carry the allowance percentages to two decimal places, we have rounded to the nearest whole number for ease of illustration.

determined by multiplying each asset's *depreciable basis* by the applicable recovery percentage shown in Table 7A–2. Calculations are discussed in the following sections.

Half-Year Convention   Under MACRS, the assumption generally is made that property is placed in service in the middle of the first year. Thus, for 3-year class life property, the recovery period begins in the middle of the year the asset is placed in service and ends three years later. The effect of the *half-year convention* is to extend the recovery period out one more year, so three-year class life property is depreciated over four calendar years, five-year property is depreciated over six calendar years, and so on. This convention is incorporated into Table 7A–2's recovery allowance percentages.[8]

[8]The half-year convention also applies if the straight line alternative is used, with half of one year's depreciation taken in the first year, a full year's depreciation taken in each of the remaining years of the asset's class life, and the remaining half-year's depreciation taken in the year following the end of the class life. You should recognize that virtually all companies have computerized depreciation systems. Each asset's depreciation pattern is programmed into the system at the time of its acquisition, and the computer aggregates the depreciation allowances for all assets when the accountants close the books and prepare the financial statements and tax returns.

Depreciable Basis The *depreciable basis* is a critical element of MACRS because each year's allowance (depreciation expense) depends jointly on the asset's depreciable basis and its MACRS class life. The depreciable basis under MACRS is equal to the purchase price of the asset plus any shipping and installation costs. The basis is not adjusted for salvage value.

Sale of a Depreciable Asset If a depreciable asset is sold, the sale price (salvage value) minus the then-existing undepreciated book value is added to operating income and taxed at the firm's marginal tax rate. For example, suppose a firm buys a 5-year class life asset for $100,000 and sells it at the end of the fourth year for $25,000. The asset's book value is equal to $100,000(0.11 + 0.06) = $17,000. Therefore, $25,000 − $17,000 = $8,000 is added to the firm's operating income and is taxed.

Depreciation Illustration Assume that Unilate Textiles buys a $150,000 machine that falls into the MACRS 5-year class life asset and places it into service on March 15, 2005. Unilate must pay an additional $30,000 for delivery and installation. Salvage value is not considered, so the machine's depreciable basis is $180,000. (Delivery and installation charges are included in the depreciable basis rather than expensed in the year incurred.) Each year's recovery allowance (tax depreciation expense) is determined by multiplying the depreciable basis by the applicable recovery allowance percentage. Thus, the depreciation expense for 2005 is 0.20($180,000) = $36,000, and for 2006 it is 0.32($180,000) = $57,600. Similarly, the depreciation expense is $34,200 for 2007, $21,600 for 2008, $19,800 for 2009, and $10,800 for 2010. The total depreciation expense over the six-year recovery period is $180,000, which is equal to the depreciable basis of the machine.

As noted previously, most firms use straight line depreciation for stockholder reporting purposes but MACRS for tax purposes. *For these firms, for capital budgeting, MACRS should be used* because in capital budgeting, we are concerned with cash flows, not reported income.

Problem

depreciation effects   **7A–1** Christina Manning, great granddaughter of the founder of Manning Tile Products and current president of the company, believes in simple, conservative accounting. In keeping with her philosophy, she has decreed that the company shall use straight line depreciation, based on the MACRS class lives, for all newly acquired assets. Your boss, the financial vice president and the only nonfamily officer, has asked you to develop an exhibit that shows how much this policy costs the company in terms of market value. Ms. Manning is interested in increasing the value of the firm's stock because she fears a family stockholder revolt that might remove her from office. For your exhibit, assume that the company spends $100 million each year on new capital projects, that the projects have on average a 10-year class life, that the company has a 9 percent cost of debt, and that its marginal tax rate is 34 percent. (*Hint:* Show how much the total NPV of the projects in an average year would increase if Manning used the standard MACRS recovery allowances.)

APPENDIX 7B

Comparing Projects with Unequal Lives

Two procedures used to compare capital projects with unequal lives are (1) the replacement chain (common life) method and (2) the equivalent annual annuity method.

Suppose the company we followed throughout the chapter, HEP, is planning to modernize its production facilities; and, as a part of the process, it is considering either a conveyor system (Project C) or some forklift trucks (Project F) for moving materials from the parts department to the main assembly line. Both the expected net cash flows and the NPVs for these two mutually exclusive alternatives are shown in Figure 7B–1.

We see that Project C, when discounted at a 15 percent required rate of return, has the higher NPV and thus appears to be the better project, in spite of the fact that Project F has the higher IRR.

Replacement Chain (Common Life) Approach   Although the analysis in Figure 7B–1 suggests that Project C should be selected, this analysis is incomplete, and the decision to choose Project C actually is incorrect. If we choose Project F, we will have the opportunity to make a similar investment in three years, and if cost and revenue conditions continue at the Figure 7B–1 levels, this second investment will also be profitable. However, if we choose Project C, we will not have this second investment opportunity. Therefore, to make a proper comparison of Projects C and F, we

---

FIGURE 7B–1   Expected Net Cash Flows for Project C and Project F

Project C:

	0	1	2	3	4	5	6
		$k = 15\%$					
Net $\hat{CF}_t$	(40,000)	13,000	8,000	14,000	12,000	11,000	15,000

NPV_C at 15% = $5,374
IRR_C = 19.7%

Project F:

	0	1	2	3
		$k = 15\%$		
Net $\hat{CF}_t$	(20,000)	7,000	13,000	12,000

NPV_F at 15% = $3,807
IRR_F = 25.2%

REPLACEMENT CHAIN (COMMON LIFE) APPROACH
A method of comparing projects of unequal lives that assumes each project can be replicated as many times as necessary to reach a common life span; the NPVs over this life span are then compared, and the project with the higher common life NPV is chosen.

could apply the **replacement chain (common life) approach;** that is, we could find the NPV of Project F over a six-year period and then compare this extended NPV with the NPV of Project C over the same six years.

The NPV for Project C as calculated in Figure 7B–1 is already over the six-year common life. For Project F, however, we must expand the analysis to include the replacement of F in Year 3, resulting in the following six-year cash flow time line[9]:

	0	1	2	3	4	5	6
k = 15%							
	(20,000)	7,000	13,000	12,000			
				(20,000)	7,000	13,000	12,000
Net $\hat{CF}_t$	(20,000)	7,000	13,000	(8,000)	7,000	13,000	12,000

Extended life NPV$_F$ at 15% = $6,310

Here we make the assumption that Project F's cost and annual cash inflows will not change if the project is repeated in three years, and that HEP's required rate of return will remain at 15 percent. Project F's extended NPV is $6,310. This is the value that should be compared with Project C's NPV, $5,374. Because Project F's "true" NPV is greater than that of Project C, Project F should be selected.

Equivalent Annual Annuity Approach   Although the preceding example illustrates why an extended analysis is necessary if we are comparing mutually exclusive projects with different lives, the arithmetic is generally more complex in practice. For example, one project might have a 6-year life versus a 10-year life for the other. This would require a replacement chain analysis over 30 years, the lowest common denominator of the two lives. In such a situation, it is often simpler to use a second procedure, the **equivalent annual annuity (EAA) method,** which involves three steps:

EQUIVALENT ANNUAL ANNUITY (EAA) METHOD
A method that calculates the annual payments a project would provide if it were an annuity. When comparing projects of unequal lives, the one with the higher equivalent annual annuity should be chosen.

1. Find each project's NPV over its initial life. In Figure 7B–1, we found NPV$_C$ = $5,374 and NPV$_F$ = $3,807.
2. Find the constant annuity cash flow—the equivalent annual annuity [EAA]— that has the same present value as each project's NPV. For Project F, here is the time line:

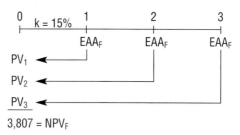

To find the value of EAA$_F$, with a financial calculator, enter –3,807 as the PV, I = k = 15, and N = 3, and solve for PMT. The answer, $1,667, represents

---

[9]We also could set up Project F's extended time line as follows:

1. The Stage 1 NPV is $3,807.
2. The Stage 2 NPV is also $3,807, but this value will not accrue until Year 3, so its value today, discounted at 15 percent, is $2,503.
3. The extended life NPV is thus $3,807 + $2,503 = $6,310.

the cash flow stream, which, when discounted back three years at 15 percent, has a present value equal to Project F's original NPV of $3,807. The payment figure we found, $1,667, is called the project's *equivalent annual annuity (EAA)*. The EAA for Project C was found similarly to be $1,420. Thus, Project C has an NPV that is equivalent to an annuity of $1,420 per year, while Project F's NPV is equivalent to an annuity of $1,667.

3. Assuming that continuous replacements can and will be made each time a project's life ends, these EAAs will continue on out to infinity; that is, they will constitute perpetuities. Recognizing that the value of a perpetuity is PVP = PMT/k, we can find the net present values of the infinite EAAs of Projects C and F as follows:

$$\text{Infinite horizon NPV}_C = \$1,420/0.15 = \$9,467.$$

$$\text{Infinite horizon NPV}_F = \$1,667/0.15 = \$11,113.$$

In effect, the EAA method assumes that each project, if taken on, will be replaced each time it wears out and will provide cash flows equivalent to the calculated annuity value. The PV of this infinite annuity is then the infinite horizon NPV for the project. Because the infinite horizon NPV of F exceeds that of C, Project F should be accepted. Therefore, the EAA method leads to the same decision rule as the replacement chain method—accept Project F.

The EAA method often is easier to apply than the replacement chain method, but the replacement chain method is easier to explain to decision makers. Still, the two methods always lead to the same decision if consistent assumptions are used. Also, note that Step 3 of the EAA method is not really necessary—we could have stopped after Step 2 because the project with the higher EAA will always have the higher NPV over any common life *if the same required rate of return is used to evaluate the projects.*

When should we worry about unequal life analysis? As a general rule, the unequal life issue (1) does not arise for independent projects, but (2) can arise if mutually exclusive projects with significantly different lives are being evaluated. However, even for mutually exclusive projects, it is not always appropriate to extend the analysis to a common life. This should only be done if there is a high probability that the projects will actually be replicated beyond their initial lives.

We should note several potentially serious weaknesses inherent in this type of unequal life analysis: (1) If inflation is expected, then replacement equipment will have a higher price, and both sales prices and operating costs will probably change. Thus, the static conditions built into the analysis would be invalid. (2) Replacements that occur down the road would probably employ new technology, which in turn might change the cash flows. This factor is not built into either replacement chain analysis or the EAA approach. (3) It is difficult enough to estimate the lives of most projects, so estimating the lives of a series of projects is often just speculation. (4) If reasonably strong competition is present, the profitability of projects will be eroded over time, and that would reduce the need to extend the analysis beyond the projects' initial lives.

In view of these problems, no experienced financial analyst would be too concerned about comparing mutually exclusive projects with lives of, say, eight years and 10 years. Given all the uncertainties in the estimation process, such projects, for all practical purposes, would be assumed to have the same life. Still, it is important to recognize that a problem does exist if mutually exclusive projects have substantially different lives. When we encounter such problems in practice, we build expected inflation or possible efficiency gains directly into the cash flow estimates and then use the replacement chain approach (but not the equivalent annual annuity method). The cash flow estimation is more complicated, but the concepts involved are exactly the same as in our example.

Problems

unequal lives **7B–1** Keenan Clothes Inc. is considering the replacement of its old, fully depreciated knitting machine. Two new models are available: Machine 190-3, which has a cost of $190,000, a 3-year expected life, and after-tax cash flows (labor savings and depreciation) of $87,000 per year; and Machine 360-6, which has a cost of $360,000, a six-year life, and after-tax cash flows of $98,300 per year. Knitting machine prices are not expected to rise because inflation will be offset by cheaper components (microprocessors) used in the machines. Assume that required rate of return appropriate for evaluating the machines is 14 percent.

    a. Should the firm replace its old knitting machine, and, if so, which new machine should it use?

    b. Suppose the firm's basic patents will expire in nine years, and the company expects to go out of business at that time. Assume further that the firm depreciates its assets using the straight line method, that its marginal tax rate is 40 percent, and that the used machines can be sold at their book values. Under these circumstances, should the company replace the old machine? Explain.

unequal lives **7B–2** Zappe Airlines is considering two alternative planes. Plane A has an expected life of five years, will cost $100, and will produce net cash flows of $30 per year. Plane B has a life of 10 years, will cost $132, and will produce net cash flows of $25 per year. Zappe plans to serve the route for 10 years. Inflation in operating costs, airplane costs, and fares is expected to be zero, and the company's required rate of return is 12 percent. By how much would the value of the company increase if it accepted the better project (plane)? Assume all costs and cash flows are in millions of dollars.

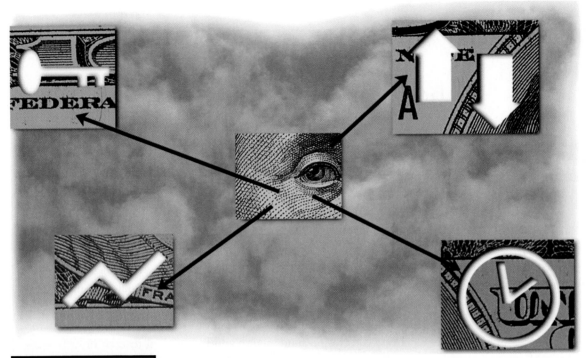

PART IV

Cost of Capital, Leverage, and Dividend Policy

CHAPTER 8

The Cost of Capital

A MANAGERIAL PERSPECTIVE

Not long ago, Boomtown Inc., a small Nevada gaming company, announced its intention to purchase National Gaming, a New Jersey casino developer. According to Boomtown's management, the purpose of the acquisition was to improve liquidity and strengthen the company's financial position. But the stockholders balked at the deal, primarily because they believed the transaction would boost Boomtown's cost of capital (funds) to more than 20 percent. With such a high cost of capital, Boomtown would have difficulty finding growth opportunities (acceptable capital budgeting projects) in the future, and, quite possibly, the burden of the high financing costs eventually could force the firm into bankruptcy. The company's stockholders wanted the deal blocked or restructured to reduce the effects on the company's cost of capital—they realized that a high cost of capital would be detrimental to their wealth position. And just as home buyers prefer to avoid high mortgage rates, companies should avoid using funds with high costs.

Firms raise capital in the financial markets, where interest rates and other yields change continuously. As interest rates change, so do the costs associated with the various types of capital. In 2000 and 2001, interest rates on corporate debt increased while stock prices dropped, which means that companies had to pay higher costs for using investors' funds. Many companies reduced their plans to expand or invest funds in other long-term projects because the price of the funds needed for such investments had risen so high. For example,

in 2001, Burlington Northern Santa Fe (BNSF) Corporation, a railroad company, estimated that the cost to the firm to raise funds to finance new investments would be as much as 12 percent. These same funds, however, could be invested to earn a return of less than 10 percent. Clearly, the firm would lose money if it paid 12 percent for funds that could be invested to earn only 10 percent. Would BNSF's stockholders be upset if the company raised new funds and knowingly invested those monies in projects that earned returns less than the cost of the funds? Absolutely! For that reason, BNSF postponed a large portion of its planned investments for 2001 until the cost of funds decreased. When interest rates on corporate debt declined in 2002 and 2003, the estimated cost of funds for BNSF had dropped to less than 7 percent. Before they began to creep upward again at the end of 2003, rates dropped to levels not seen during the previous 50 years. As a result, not only did the company resume its investment program, it also refinanced much of its older, more expensive debt (much like homeowners refinanced their homes during the same period).

As you read this chapter, keep in mind that firms need funds provided by investors to take advantage of acceptable capital budgeting projects. The financial marketplace, which consists of investors like you, determines the "price" that firms must pay for the funds they use. It is essential for us to be able to determine the "price," or the cost, of the capital used by a firm so that we know if the funds are being invested appropriately. ■

COST OF CAPITAL
The firm's average cost of funds, which is the average return required by the firm's investors—what must be paid to attract funds.

REQUIRED RATE OF RETURN
The return that must be earned on invested funds to cover the cost of financing such investments; also called the *opportunity cost rate*.

It is vitally important that a firm knows how much it pays for the funds used to purchase assets. The average return required by the firm's investors determines how much must be paid to attract funds. The firm's required rate of return is its average cost of funds, which more commonly is termed the **cost of capital.** The firm's cost of capital represents the minimum rate of return that must be earned from investments, such as capital budgeting projects, to ensure the value of the firm does not decrease. In other words the cost of capital is the firm's **required rate of return.** For example, if investors provide funds to a firm for an average cost of 15 percent, wealth will decrease if the funds are used to generate returns less than 15 percent, wealth will not change if exactly 15 percent is earned, and wealth will increase if the firm generates returns greater than 15 percent.

In this chapter, we discuss the concept of cost of capital, how the average cost of capital is determined, and how the cost of capital is used in financial decision making. Most of the models and formulas used in this chapter are the same ones we developed in Chapter 5, where we described how stocks and bonds are valued by investors. A firm's cost of funds is based on the return demanded by investors. If the return offered by the firm is not high enough, then investors will not provide sufficient funds. In other words, *the rate of return an investor earns on a corporate security effectively is a cost to the firm of using those funds*, so the same models are used by investors and by corporate treasurers to determine required rates of return.

The first topic in this chapter is the logic of the weighted average cost of capital. Next, we consider the costs of the major types of capital, after which we see how the costs of the individual components of the capital structure are brought together to form a weighted average cost of capital.

The Logic of the Weighted Average Cost of Capital

It is possible to finance a firm entirely with equity funds by issuing only stock. In that case, the cost of capital used to analyze capital budgeting decisions should be the company's required return on equity. However, most firms raise a substantial portion of their funds as long-term debt, and some also use preferred stock. For these firms, their cost of capital must reflect the average cost of the various sources of long-term funds used, not just the firms' costs of equity.

Assume that Unilate Textiles has a 10 percent cost of debt and a 13.5 percent cost of equity. Further, assume that Unilate has made the decision to finance next year's projects by selling debt only. The argument is sometimes made that the cost of capital for these projects is 10 percent because only debt will be used to finance them. However, this position is incorrect. If Unilate finances a particular set of projects with debt, the firm will be using up some of its potential for obtaining new debt in the future. As expansion occurs in subsequent years, Unilate will at some point find it necessary to raise additional equity to prevent the proportion of debt from becoming too large.

To illustrate, suppose Unilate borrows heavily at 10 percent during 2006, using up its debt capacity in the process, to finance projects yielding 11.5 percent. In 2007 it has new projects available that yield 13 percent, well above the return on 2006 projects, but it cannot accept them because they would have to be financed with 13.7 percent equity funds. To avoid this problem, Unilate should be viewed as an ongoing concern, and *the cost of capital used in capital budgeting should be calculated as a weighted average, or combination, of the various types of funds generally used, regardless of the specific financing used to fund a particular project.*

Self-Test Question

Why should the cost of capital used in capital budgeting be calculated as a weighted average of the various types of funds the firm generally uses, regardless of the specific financing used to fund a particular project?

Basic Definitions

CAPITAL COMPONENT

A particular type of capital used by a firm to raise money.

The items in the liability and equity section of a firm's balance sheet—various types of debt, preferred stock, and common equity—are its **capital components.** Any increase in total assets must be financed by an increase in one or more of these capital components.

Capital is a necessary factor of production, and, like any other factor, it has a cost. The cost of each component is called the *component cost* of that particular type of capital. For example, if Unilate can borrow money at 10 percent, its component cost of debt is 10 percent.[1] Throughout this chapter we concentrate on debt, preferred stock, retained earnings, and new issues of common stock, which are the four major capital structure components. We will use the following symbols to designate specific component costs of capital:

k_d = Interest rate on the firm's debt = before-tax component cost of debt. For Unilate, k_d = 10.0%.

k_{dT} = $k_d(1 - T)$ = After-tax component cost of debt, where T is the firm's marginal tax rate. k_{dT} is the debt cost used to calculate the weighted average cost of capital. For Unilate, T = 40%, so $k_{dT} = k_d(1 - T) =$ 10.0%(1 – 0.4) = 10.0%(0.6) = 6.0%.

k_{ps} = Component cost of preferred stock. Unilate has no preferred stock at this time, but, as new funds are raised, the company plans to issue preferred stock. The cost of preferred stock, k_{ps}, will be 11 percent.

k_s = Component cost of retained earnings (or internal equity). It is identical to the k_s developed in Chapters 4 and 5 and defined there as the required rate of return on common stock. As we will see shortly, for Unilate, k_s = 13.5%.

k_e = Component cost of external equity obtained by issuing new common stock as opposed to retaining earnings. As we shall see, it is necessary to distinguish between common equity needs that can be satisfied by retained earnings and the common equity needs that are satisfied by selling new stock. This is why we distinguish between internal and external equity, k_s and k_e. Further, k_e is always greater than k_s. For Unilate, k_e = 14.5%.

WACC = The weighted average cost of capital. In the future, when Unilate needs *new* capital to finance asset expansion, it will raise part of the new funds as debt, part as preferred stock, and part as common equity (with common equity coming either from retained earnings or from the issuance of new common stock).[2] We will calculate WACC for Unilate Textiles shortly.

[1]We will see shortly that there is both a before-tax and an after-tax cost of debt. For now it is sufficient to know that 10 percent is the before-tax component cost of debt.

[2]Firms try to keep their debt, preferred stock, and common equity in optimal proportions. We will learn how firms establish these proportions in the next chapter. However, firms do not try to maintain any proportional relationship between the common stock and retained earnings accounts as shown on the balance sheet—for capital structure purposes, common equity is common equity, whether it comes from selling new common stock or from retaining earnings.

CAPITAL STRUCTURE
The combination or mix of different types of capital used by a firm.

These definitions and concepts are explained in detail in the remainder of the chapter, where we develop a marginal cost of capital (MCC) schedule that can be used in capital budgeting. Later, in the next chapter, we will extend the analysis to determine the mix of types of capital, which is termed the **capital structure,** that will minimize the firm's cost of capital and thereby maximize its value.

Self-Test Question

Identify the firm's four major capital structure components, and give their respective component cost symbols.

Cost of Debt, k_{dT}

The **after-tax cost of debt, k_{dT},** is the interest rate on debt, k_d, less the tax saving that results because interest is deductible. This is the same as k_d multiplied by $(1 - T)$, where T is the firm's marginal tax rate:

8–1

$$\text{After-tax component cost of debt} = k_{dT} = \left(\begin{array}{c}\text{Bondholders' required}\\\text{rate of return}\end{array}\right) - \left(\begin{array}{c}\text{Tax}\\\text{savings}\end{array}\right)$$

$$= k_d - k_d \times T$$

$$= k_d(1 - T)$$

AFTER-TAX COST OF DEBT, k_{dT}
The relevant cost of new debt, taking into account the tax deductibility of interest.

In effect, the government pays part of the cost of debt because interest is deductible. Therefore, if Unilate can borrow at an interest rate of 10 percent, and if it has a marginal tax rate of 40 percent, then its after-tax cost of debt is 6 percent:

$$k_{dT} = k_d(1 - T) = 10.0\%(1.0 - 0.4)$$

$$= 10.0\%(0.6)$$

$$= 6.0\%$$

We use the after-tax cost of debt because the value of the firm's stock, which we want to maximize, depends on *after-tax* cash flows. Because interest is a deductible expense, it produces tax savings that reduce the net cost of borrowing, making the after-tax cost of debt less than the before-tax cost. We are concerned with after-tax cash flows, so after-tax rates of return are appropriate.[3]

Note that the cost of debt is the interest rate on *new* debt, not that on already outstanding debt; in other words, we are interested in the *marginal* cost of debt. Our primary concern with the cost of capital is to use it for capital budgeting decisions—for

---

[3]The tax rate is *zero* for a firm with losses. Therefore, for a company that does not pay taxes, the cost of debt is not reduced—that is, in Equation 8–1 the tax rate equals zero, so the after-tax cost of debt is equal to the before-tax interest rate.

example, a decision about whether to obtain the capital needed to acquire a new machine tool. The rate at which the firm has borrowed in the past is a sunk cost, and it is irrelevant for cost of capital purposes.

In Chapter 5, we solved the following equation to find k_d, the rate of return, or yield to maturity, for a bond:

$$P_0 = \text{Bond value} = \sum_{t=1}^{N} \frac{\text{INT}}{(1+k_d)^t} + \frac{M}{(1+k_d)^N}$$

where INT is the dollar coupon interest paid per period, M is the face value repaid at maturity, and N is the number of interest payments remaining until maturity.

Assume that Unilate issued a new bond a few years ago. The bond has face value of $1,000, 20 years left until it matures, and $90 interest is paid annually. Unilate is going to issue new bonds in a couple days that have the same general characteristics as this outstanding bond. If the market price of the outstanding bond is $915, what should the k_d be for the new bond? We would expect that the return investors demand for the new bond should be approximately the same as the outstanding bond because both bonds have the same characteristics. The solution for determining k_d is set up as follows:

$$\$915 = \frac{\$90}{(1+k_d)^1} + \frac{\$90}{(1+k_d)^2} + \cdots + \frac{\$1,090}{(1+k_d)^{20}}$$

Whether you use the trial-and-error method, the time value of money functions on your calculator, or the approximation equation given in Chapter 5, you should find k_d is 10 percent, which is the before-tax cost of debt for this bond.[4] Unilate's marginal tax rate is 40 percent, so the after-tax cost of debt, k_{dT}, is 6.0% = 10.0%(1 – 0.40).

Self-Test Questions

Why is the after-tax cost of debt rather than the before-tax cost used to calculate the weighted average cost of capital?

Is the relevant cost of debt the interest rate on already outstanding debt or that on new debt? Why?

---

[4]It should also be noted that we have ignored flotation costs (the costs incurred for new issuances) on debt because nearly all debt issued by small and medium-sized firms and by many large firms is privately placed and hence has no flotation costs. However, if bonds are publicly placed and do involve flotation costs, the solution value of k_d in the following formula is used as the before-tax cost of debt:

$$V_d(1-F) = \sum_{t=1}^{N} \frac{\text{INT}}{(1+k_d)^t} + \frac{M}{(1+k_d)^N}$$

Here F is the percentage amount (in decimal form) of the bond flotation, or issuing, cost; N is the number of periods to maturity; INT is the dollars of interest per period; M is the maturity value of the bond; and k_d is the cost of debt adjusted to reflect flotation costs. If we assume that the bond in the example calls for annual payments, that it has a 20-year maturity, and that F = 2%, then the flotation-adjusted, before-tax cost of debt is 10.23 percent versus 10 percent before the flotation adjustment.

Cost of Preferred Stock, k$_{ps}$

In Chapter 5, we found that the dividend associated with preferred stock, D$_{ps}$, is constant and that preferred stock has no stated maturity. Thus, D$_{ps}$ represents a perpetuity, and the component **cost of preferred stock, k$_{ps}$,** is the preferred dividend, D$_{ps}$, divided by the net issuing price, NP, or the price the firm receives after deducting the costs of issuing the stock, which are called *flotation costs:*

$$\text{Component cost of preferred stock} = k_{ps} = \frac{D_{ps}}{NP} = \frac{D_{ps}}{P_0 - \text{Flotation costs}} = \frac{D_{ps}}{P_0(1 - F)}$$

8–2

COST OF PREFERRED STOCK, k$_{ps}$
The rate of return investors require on the firm's preferred stock. k$_{ps}$ is calculated as the preferred dividend, D$_{ps}$, divided by the net issuing price, NP.

where F is the percentage (in decimal form) cost of issuing preferred stock and P$_0$ is the current market price of the stock.

To illustrate, in the future, Unilate plans to issue preferred stock that pays a $12.80 dividend per share and sells for $120 per share in the market. It will cost 3 percent, or $3.60 per share, to issue the new preferred stock, so Unilate will net $116.40 per share. Therefore, Unilate's cost of preferred stock is 11 percent:

$$k_{ps} = \frac{\$12.80}{\$120(1 - 0.03)} = \frac{\$12.80}{\$116.40}$$
$$= 0.11 = 11.0\%$$

No tax adjustments are made when calculating k$_{ps}$ because preferred dividends, unlike interest expense on debt, are not tax deductible, so there are no tax savings associated with the use of preferred stock.

Self-Test Questions

Does the component cost of preferred stock include or exclude flotation costs? Explain.

Is a tax adjustment made to the cost of preferred stock? Why or why not?

Cost of Retained Earnings, or Internal Equity, k$_s$

COST OF RETAINED EARNINGS, k$_s$
The rate of return required by stockholders on a firm's existing common stock.

The costs of debt and preferred stock are based on the returns investors require on these securities. Similarly, the **cost of retained earnings, k$_s$,** is the rate of return stockholders require on equity capital the firm obtains by retaining earnings that otherwise could be distributed to common stockholders as dividends.[5]

[5]The term *retained earnings* can be interpreted to mean either the balance sheet item "retained earnings," consisting of all the earnings retained in the business throughout its history, or the income statement item "additions to retained earnings." The income statement item is used in this chapter; for our purpose, *retained earnings* refers to that part of current earnings not paid out in dividends and hence available for reinvestment in the business this year.

The reason we must assign a cost of capital to retained earnings involves the *opportunity cost principle*. The firm's after-tax earnings literally belong to its stockholders. Bondholders are compensated by interest payments, and preferred stockholders by preferred dividends, but the earnings remaining after interest and preferred dividends belong to the common stockholders, and these earnings help compensate stockholders for the use of their capital. Management can either pay out the earnings in the form of dividends or retain earnings and reinvest them in the business. If management decides to retain earnings, there is an opportunity cost involved—stockholders could have received the earnings as dividends and invested this money for themselves in other stocks, in bonds, in real estate, or in anything else. Thus, the firm should earn a return on earnings it retains that is at least as great as the return stockholders themselves could earn on alternative investments of comparable risk.

What rate of return can stockholders expect to earn on equivalent-risk investments? First, recall from Chapter 5 that stocks normally are in equilibrium, with the expected and required rates of return being equal: $\hat{k}_s = k_s$. Therefore, we can assume that Unilate's stockholders expect to earn a return of k_s on their money. *If the firm cannot invest retained earnings and earn at least k_s, it should pay these funds to its stockholders and let them invest directly in other assets that do provide this return.*[6]

Whereas debt and preferred stocks are contractual obligations that have easily determined costs, it is not as easy to measure k_s. However, we can employ the principles developed in Chapters 4 and 5 to produce reasonably good cost of equity estimates. To begin, we know that if a stock is in equilibrium (which is the typical situation), then its required rate of return, k_s, is also equal to its expected rate of return, $\hat{k}_s$. Further, its required return is equal to a risk-free rate, k_{RF}, plus a risk premium, RP, whereas the expected return on a constant growth stock is equal to the stock's dividend yield, $\hat{D}_1/P_0$, plus its expected growth rate, g. That is:

> **8–3**
>
> Required rate of return = Expected rate of return
>
> $$k_s = \hat{k}_s$$
>
> $$k_{RF} + RP = \frac{\hat{D}_1}{P_0} + g$$

Because the two must be equal, we can estimate k_s using either the left side or the right side of Equation 8–3. Actually, three methods are commonly used for finding the cost of retained earnings: (1) the CAPM approach, (2) the discounted cash flow (DCF) approach, and (3) the bond-yield-plus-risk-premium approach. These three approaches are discussed next.

---

[6]Dividends and capital gains are taxed differently, with long-term gains being taxed at a lower rate than dividends for most stockholders. That makes it beneficial for companies to retain earnings rather than to pay them out as dividends, and that, in turn, results in a relatively low cost of capital for retained earnings. This point is discussed in Chapter 9.

The CAPM Approach

The capital asset pricing model (CAPM) we developed in Chapter 4 is as follows:

8–4

$$k_s = k_{RF} + (k_M - k_{RF})\beta_s$$

Equation 8–4 shows that the CAPM estimate of k_s begins with the risk-free rate, k_{RF}, to which is added a risk premium that is based on the stock's relation to the market as measured by its beta, β_s, and the magnitude of the market risk premium, which is the difference between the market return, k_M, and the risk-free rate, k_{RF}.

To illustrate the CAPM approach, assume that $k_{RF} = 6\%$, $k_M = 10.5\%$, and $\beta_s = 1.6$ for Unilate's common stock. Using the CAPM approach, Unilate's cost of retained earnings, k_s, is calculated as follows:

$$k_s = 6.0\% + (10.5\% - 6.0\%)(1.6)$$

$$= 6.0\% + 7.2\%$$

$$= 13.2\%$$

Although the CAPM approach appears to yield an accurate, precise estimate of k_s, there actually are several problems with it. First, as we saw in Chapter 4, if a firm's stockholders are not well diversified, they might be concerned with total risk rather than with market risk only (measured by β); in this case the firm's true investment risk will not be measured by its beta, and the CAPM procedure will understate the correct value of k_s. Further, even if the CAPM method is valid, it is difficult to obtain correct estimates of the inputs required to make it operational because: (1) there is controversy about whether to use long-term or short-term Treasury yields for k_{RF}; and (2) both β_s and k_M should be estimated values, which often are difficult to obtain.

Discounted Cash Flow (DCF) Approach

In Chapter 5 we learned that both the price and the expected rate of return on a share of common stock depend, ultimately, on the dividends expected on the stock, and the value of a share of stock can be written as follows:

8–5

$$P_0 = \frac{\hat{D}_1}{(1 + k_s)^1} + \frac{\hat{D}_2}{(1 + k_s)^2} + \cdots + \frac{\hat{D}_\infty}{(1 + k_s)^\infty}$$

$$= \sum_{t=1}^{\infty} \frac{\hat{D}_t}{(1 + k_s)^t}$$

Here P_0 is the current price of the stock; $\hat{D}_t$ is the dividend *expected* to be paid at the end of Year t; and k_s is the required rate of return. If dividends are expected to grow at a constant rate, then, as we saw in Chapter 5, Equation 8–5 reduces to

8–5a

$$P_0 = \frac{\hat{D}_1}{k_s - g}$$

We can solve Equation 8–5a for k_s to estimate the required rate of return on common equity, which for the marginal investor is also equal to the expected rate of return:

8–6

$$k_s = \hat{k}_s = \frac{\hat{D}_1}{P_0} + g$$

Thus, investors expect to receive a dividend yield, $\hat{D}_1/P_0$, plus a capital gain, g, for a total expected return of $\hat{k}_s$. In equilibrium, this expected return is also equal to the required return, k_s. From this point on, we will assume that equilibrium exists, and we will use the terms k_s and $\hat{k}_s$ interchangeably, so we will drop the "hat," ^, above k_s.

It is relatively easy to determine the dividend yield, but it is difficult to establish the proper growth rate. If past growth rates in earnings and dividends have been relatively stable, and if investors appear to be projecting a continuation of past trends, then g can be based on the firm's historical growth rate. However, if the company's past growth has been abnormally high or low, either because of its own unique situation or because of general economic fluctuations, then historical growth probably should not be used. Security analysts regularly make earnings and dividend growth forecasts, looking at such factors as projected sales, profit margins, and competitive factors. For example, *Value Line*, which is available in most libraries, provides growth rate forecasts for nearly 1,800 companies, and Merrill Lynch, Salomon Smith Barney, and other organizations make similar forecasts. Therefore, someone making a cost of capital estimate can obtain several analysts' forecasts, average them, and use the average as a proxy for the growth expectations, g.[7]

To illustrate the DCF approach, suppose Unilate's common stock sells for $15; the common stock dividend expected to be paid in 2006 is $1.40; and its expected

---

[7]Analysts' growth rate forecasts are usually for five years into the future, and the rates provided represent the average growth rate over that five-year horizon. Studies have shown that analysts' forecasts represent the best source of growth rate data for DCF cost of capital estimates. See Robert Harris, "Using Analysts' Growth Rate Forecasts to Estimate Shareholder Required Rates of Return," *Financial Management*, Spring 1986, 58–67.

long-term growth rate is 4 percent. Unilate's expected and required rate of return, and hence its cost of retained earnings, is 13.3 percent:

$$\hat{k}_s = k_s = \frac{\$1.40}{\$15.00} + 0.04$$
$$= 0.093 + 0.04$$
$$= 0.133 = 13.3\%$$

This 13.3 percent is the minimum rate of return that management must expect to earn to justify retaining earnings and plowing them back into the business rather than paying them out to stockholders as dividends.

Bond-Yield-Plus-Risk-Premium Approach

Although it is a subjective procedure, analysts often estimate a firm's cost of common equity by adding a risk premium of 3 to 5 percentage points to the before-tax interest rate on the firm's own long-term debt. It is logical to think that firms with risky, low-rated, and consequently high-interest-rate debt will also have risky, high-cost equity. Using this logic to estimate the cost of common stock is relatively easy—we simply add a risk premium to a readily observable debt cost. For example, Unilate's cost of equity might be estimated as follows:

$$k_s = \text{Bond yield} + \text{Risk premium}$$
$$= \quad 10.0\% \quad + \quad\quad 4.0\%$$
$$= \quad 14.0\%$$

Because the 4 percent risk premium is a judgmental estimate, the estimated value of k_s also is judgmental. Empirical work suggests that the risk premium over a firm's own bond yield generally has ranged from 3 to 5 percentage points, so this method is not likely to produce a precise cost of equity—about all it can do is get us into the right ballpark.

We have used three methods to estimate the cost of retained earnings, which actually is a single number. To summarize, we found the cost of common equity to be (1) 13.2 percent using the CAPM method; (3) 14.0 percent with the bond-yield-plus-risk-premium approach; and (2) 13.3 percent using the constant growth model, the DCF approach. It is not unusual to get different estimates, because each of the approaches is based on different assumptions. The CAPM assumes investors are well diversified, the bond-yield-plus-risk-premium approach assumes the cost of equity is closely related to the firm's cost of debt, and the constant growth model assumes the firm's dividends and earnings will grow at a constant rate far into the future. Which estimate should be used? Probably all of them. Many analysts use multiple approaches to estimate a single value, then average the results. For Unilate, then, the average of the estimates is 13.5% = (13.2% + 13.3% + 14.0%)/3.

People experienced in estimating equity capital costs recognize that both careful analysis and sound judgment are required. It would be nice to pretend that judgment is unnecessary and to specify an easy, precise way of determining the exact cost of equity capital. Unfortunately, this is not possible—finance is in large part a matter of judgment, and we simply must face that fact.

Self-Test Questions

Why must a cost be assigned to retained earnings?

What are the three approaches for estimating the cost of retained earnings?

Identify some problems with the CAPM approach.

What is the reasoning behind the bond-yield-plus-risk-premium approach? Which of the components of the constant growth DCF formula is most difficult to estimate? Why?

Cost of Newly Issued Common Stock, or External Equity, k_e

COST OF NEW COMMON EQUITY, k_e
The cost of external equity; based on the cost of retained earnings, but increased for flotation costs.

FLOTATION COSTS
The expenses incurred when selling new issues of securities.

The **cost of new common equity, k_e,** or external equity capital, is similar to the cost of retained earnings, k_s, except it is higher because the firm incurs *flotation costs* when it issues new common stock. The **flotation costs,** which are the expenses associated with issuing new securities (equity or debt), reduce the amount of funds the firm receives, and hence the amount that can be used for investments. Only the amount of funds that is left after paying flotation costs—that is, the *net* amount received by the firm—is available for investment. As a result, *the cost of issuing new common stock (external equity), k_e, is greater than the cost of retained earnings, k_s,* because there are no flotation costs associated with retained earnings (internal equity) financing.

In general, the cost of issuing new equity, k_e, can be found by modifying the DCF formula used to compute the cost of retained earnings, k_s, to obtain the following equation:

| 8–7 |

$$k_e = \frac{\hat{D}_1}{NP} + g = \frac{\hat{D}_1}{P_0(1 - F)} + g$$

Here F is the percentage flotation cost (in decimal form) incurred in selling the new stock issue, so $P_0(1 - F)$ is the net price per share received by the company.

If Unilate can issue new common stock at a flotation cost of 11 percent, k_e is computed as follows:

$$k_e = \frac{\$1.40}{\$15.00(1 - 0.11)} + 0.04$$

$$= \frac{\$1.40}{\$13.35} + 0.04$$

$$= 0.145 = 14.5\%$$

Using the DCF approach to estimate the cost of retained earnings, we found that investors require a return of $k_s = 13.3\%$ on the stock. However, because of flotation costs, the company must earn more than 13.3 percent on funds obtained by selling stock if it is to provide a 13.3 percent return. Specifically, if the firm earns 14.5 percent on funds obtained from new stock, then earnings per share will not fall below previously expected earnings, the firm's expected dividend can be maintained, and, as a result, the price per share will not decline. If the firm earns

Cost of Equity—How Do They Do It?

In this chapter, we describe three methods to estimate a firm's cost of internal equity: capital asset pricing model (CAPM), bond-yield-plus-risk-premium, and discounted cash flow (DCF). Which, if any, of these approaches is actually used by firms to compute the cost of equity capital?

The results of three recent surveys of large firms suggest that nearly every firm attempts to calculate the cost of equity capital. This is a stark contrast to the findings from 20 years ago, when about 60 percent of the firms indicated that they did *not* compute the cost of equity. According to these same studies, the method most commonly used to compute the cost of equity capital is the capital asset pricing model (CAPM), which is an interesting finding because the CAPM is considered the most theoretical in nature of the three techniques we described in the chapter. In their study, Glenn H. Petry and James Sprow surveyed financial executives from 151 firms listed in the 1990 *Business Week* 1000 and found that between 40 percent and 50 percent of the firms indicated they use the CAPM to determine the cost of equity. Many of the firms that did not use the CAPM indicated that they used the bond-yield-plus-risk-premium approach or some other method because either (1) they did not understand the application of the CAPM or (2) the CAPM approach was not considered appropriate for their situation. In more recent studies, Robert F. Bruner, Kenneth M. Eades, Robert S. Harris, and Robert C. Higgins and John R. Graham and Campbell R. Harvey found that 75–80 percent of the firms that were surveyed indicated they use the CAPM to estimate the cost of equity. From the results of these studies, therefore, we can conclude that many firms use the CAPM for estimating the cost of equity.

So how do firms apply the CAPM? More specifically, how are the values of the factors needed to apply the CAPM estimated? The results of the Bruner et al. study suggest that there is not a consensus as to how the variables—the risk-free rate (k_{RF}), the market risk premium (RP_M), and the firm's equity beta (β_s)—are computed. For example, when asked what rate they use for k_{RF}, one-third of the financial managers stated that they use the rate on 10-year Treasury securities, one-third indicated that they use the rate on Treasuries with maturities from 10 to 30 years, and 15 percent use rates on Treasuries with maturities shorter than 10 years. When asked what is used as the market risk

premium, nearly one-half of the financial managers indicated that they use a fixed rate between 4 and 6 percent, 15 percent use estimates provided by financial advisors, and relatively few either add a risk premium to a Treasury rate or use specific historical averages. When asked how they determine the beta for their companies, the financial managers showed greater agreement—more than 50 percent use betas from published sources, such as *Value Line*, and 30 percent compute the beta themselves.

The studies also gave an indication of how firms compute their weighted average costs of capital (WACC). First, the results of the studies suggest that most firms do *not* rely solely on book values to determine the weights used to compute their WACCs. In fact, according to the study by Bruner et al., nearly 60 percent of the firms use market values and only 15 percent use book values to determine the appropriate weights. The results of the study by Petry and Sprow indicate that more than 25 percent use book values to compute the weights for all capital components, between 17 and 20 percent use book values to determine the weights for debt but market values for equity, and about 21 percent use market values to determine all the weights. These results suggest that many firms attempt to use market values to determine the appropriate weights of the capital components used to compute the WACC. Second, the results of the Bruner et al. study indicate that fewer than 20 percent of the firms surveyed recompute their WACCs on an infrequent basis; rather 37 percent stated that they recompute their firms' WACCs annually, while 41 percent compute their WACCs more frequently (i.e., semiannually, quarterly, monthly, or for each investment).

In summary, indications are that firms actually do compute the cost of equity capital, as well as the WACC, and the methods used most often include those discussed in this chapter, including the model that is most theoretical in nature.

Sources: Glenn H. Petry and James Sprow, "The Theory and Practice of Finance in the 1990s," *The Quarterly Review of Economics and Finance*, Winter 1993, 381–395; Robert F. Bruner, Kenneth M. Eades, Robert S. Harris, and Robert C. Higgins, "Best Practices in Estimating the Cost of Capital: Survey and Synthesis," *Financial Practice and Education*, Spring/Summer 1998, 13–28; and John R. Graham and Campbell R. Harvey, "The Theory and Practice of Corporate Finance: Evidence from the Field," *Journal of Financial Economics*, vol. 60, 2001, No. 2–3, 187–243.

less than 14.5 percent, then earnings, dividends, and growth will fall below expectations, causing the price of the stock to decline. If it earns more than 14.5 percent, the price of the stock will rise.

The reason for the flotation adjustment can be made clear by a simple example. Suppose Weaver Realty Company has $100,000 of assets and no debt, it earns a 15 percent return (or $15,000) on its assets, and it pays all earnings out as dividends, so its growth rate is zero. The company has 1,000 shares of stock outstanding, so earnings per share (EPS) equals dividends per share (DPS)—DPS = $15 = $15,000/1,000—and P_0 = $100 = $100,000/1,000. Weaver's cost of equity is thus k_s = $15/$100 + 0 = 15.0%. Now suppose Weaver can get a return of 15 percent on new assets. Should it sell new stock to acquire new assets? If it sold 1,000 new shares of stock to the public for $100 per share, but it incurred a 10 percent flotation cost on the issue, it would net $100 − 0.10($100) = $90 per share, or $90,000 in total. It would then invest this $90,000 and earn 15 percent, or $13,500. Its new *total* earnings would be $28,500, which would consist of $15,000 generated from the old assets plus $13,500 from the new assets. But the $28,500 would have to be distributed equally to the 2,000 shares of stock that would now be outstanding. Therefore, Weaver's EPS and DPS would decline from $15 to $14.25 = $28,500/2,000. Because its EPS and DPS would fall, the price of the stock would also fall from P_0 = $100 to P_1 = $14.25/0.15 = $95.00. This result occurs because investors have put up $100 per share, but the company has received and invested only $90 per share. Thus, we see that the $90 must earn more than 15 percent to provide investors with a 15 percent return on the $100 they put up.

We can use Equation 8–7 to compute the return Weaver must earn on the $90,000 of new assets—that is, the amount raised with the new issue:

$$k_e = \frac{\$15}{\$100(1 - 0.10)} + 0.0$$

$$= 0.1667 = 16.67\%$$

If Weaver invests the funds from the new common stock issue at 16.67%, here is what would happen:

New total earnings = $15,000 + $90,000(0.16667) = $30,000

New EPS and DPS = $30,000/2,000 = $15

New price = $15/0.15 = $100 = Original price

Thus, if the return on the new assets is equal to k_e as calculated by Equation 8–7, then EPS, DPS, and the stock price will all remain constant. If the return on the new assets exceeds k_e, then EPS, DPS, and P_0 will rise. Because of flotation costs, the cost of external equity exceeds the cost of equity raised internally from retained earnings. If F = 0, however, then k_e = k_s.

Self-Test Questions

Why is the cost of external equity capital higher than the cost of retained earnings?

How can the DCF model be changed to account for flotation costs?

Weighted Average Cost of Capital, WACC

TARGET (OPTIMAL) CAPITAL STRUCTURE
The combination (percentages) of debt, preferred stock, and common equity that will maximize the price of the firm's stock.

WEIGHTED AVERAGE COST OF CAPITAL (WACC)
A weighted average of the component costs of debt, preferred stock, and common equity.

As we will see in the next chapter, each firm has an optimal capital structure, or mix of debt, preferred stock, and common equity, that causes its stock price to be maximized. Therefore, a rational, value-maximizing firm will establish a **target (optimal) capital structure** and then raise new capital in a manner that will keep the actual capital structure on target over time. In this chapter we assume that the firm has identified its optimal capital structure, it uses this optimum as the target, and it raises funds so it constantly remains on target. How the target is established will be examined in Chapter 9.[8]

The target proportions of debt, preferred stock, and common equity, along with the component costs of capital, are used to calculate the firm's **weighted average cost of capital (WACC)**. The WACC simply represents the average cost of each dollar of financing, no matter its source, that the firm uses to purchase assets. That is, WACC represents the minimum return the firm needs to earn on its investments (assets) to maintain its current level of wealth.

To illustrate, suppose Unilate Textiles has determined that in the future it will raise new capital according to the following proportions: 45 percent debt, 5 percent preferred stock, and 50 percent common equity (retained earnings plus new common stock). In the preceding sections, we found that its before-tax cost of debt, k_d, is 10 percent, so its *after-tax* cost of debt, k_{dT}, is 6 percent; its cost of preferred stock, k_{ps}, is 10.3 percent; and its cost of common equity, k_s, is 13.5 percent if all of its equity financing comes from retained earnings. Now we can calculate Unilate's weighted average cost of capital (WACC) as follows:

8–8

$$\text{WACC} = \left[\binom{\text{Proportion}}{\text{of debt}} \times \binom{\text{After - tax}}{\text{cost of debt}} \right] + \left[\binom{\text{Proportion}}{\text{of preferred stock}} \times \binom{\text{Cost of preferred stock}}{} \right] + \left[\binom{\text{Proportion}}{\text{of common equity}} \times \binom{\text{Cost of common equity}}{} \right]$$

$$= \quad w_d k_{dT} \quad + \quad w_{ps} k_{ps} \quad + \quad w_s k_s$$

$$= \quad 0.45(6.0\%) \quad + \quad 0.05(11.0\%) \quad + \quad 0.50(13.5\%)$$

$$= \quad 10.0\%$$

Here w_d, w_{ps}, and w_s are the weights used for debt, preferred stock, and common equity, respectively.

Every dollar of new capital that Unilate obtains consists of 45¢ of debt with an after-tax cost of 6 percent, 5¢ of preferred stock with a cost of 11 percent, and 50¢ of

---

[8]Notice that only long-term debt is included in the capital structure. Unilate uses its cost of capital in the capital budgeting process, which involves long-term assets, and it finances those assets with long-term capital. Thus, current liabilities do not enter the calculation. We will discuss this point in more detail in Chapter 9.

common equity (all from additions to retained earnings) with a cost of 13.5 percent. The average cost of each whole dollar, WACC, is 10 percent as long as these conditions continue. If the component costs of capital change when new funds are raised in the future, then WACC changes. We discuss changes in the component costs of capital in the next section.

Self-Test Question

How is the weighted average cost of capital calculated? Write out the equation.

The Marginal Cost of Capital, MCC

MARGINAL COST OF CAPITAL (MCC)

The cost of obtaining another dollar of new capital; the weighted average cost of the last dollar of new capital raised.

The marginal cost of any item is the cost of another unit of that item. For example, the marginal cost of labor is the cost of adding one additional worker. The marginal cost of labor might be $25 per person if 10 workers are added but $35 per person if the firm tries to hire 100 new workers because it will be harder to find that many people willing and able to do the work. The same concept applies to capital. As the firm tries to attract more new dollars, at some point, the cost of each dollar will increase. Thus, the **marginal cost of capital (MCC)** *is defined as the cost of the last dollar of new capital that the firm raises, and the marginal cost rises as more and more capital is raised during a given period.*

In the preceding section, we computed Unilate's WACC to be 10 percent. As long as Unilate keeps its capital structure on target, and as long as its debt has an after-tax cost of 6 percent, its preferred stock a cost of 11 percent, and its common equity a cost of 13.5 percent, then its weighted average cost of capital will be 10 percent. Each dollar the firm raises will consist of some long-term debt, some preferred stock, and some common equity, and the cost of the whole dollar will be 10 percent—its marginal cost of capital (MCC) will be 10 percent.

The MCC Schedule

MARGINAL COST OF CAPITAL (MCC) SCHEDULE

A graph that relates the firm's weighted average cost of each dollar of capital to the total amount of new capital raised.

A graph that shows how the WACC changes as more and more new capital is raised by the firm is called the **marginal cost of capital schedule.** Figure 8–1 shows Unilate's MCC schedule if the cost of debt, cost of preferred stock, and cost of common equity *never change.* Here the dots represent dollars raised, and because each dollar of new capital will have an average cost equal to 10 percent, the marginal cost of capital (MCC) for Unilate is constant at 10.0 percent under the assumptions we have used to this point.

Do you think Unilate actually could raise an unlimited amount of new capital at the 10 percent cost? Probably not. As a practical matter, as a company raises larger and larger amounts of funds during a given time period, the costs of those funds begin to rise, and as this occurs, the weighted average cost of each new dollar also rises. Thus, companies cannot raise unlimited amounts of capital at a constant cost. At some point, the cost of each new dollar will increase, no matter what its source (debt, preferred stock, or common equity).

How much can Unilate raise before the cost of its funds increases? As a first step to determining the point at which the MCC begins to rise, recognize that although

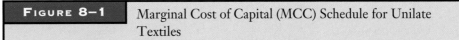

| FIGURE 8-1 | Marginal Cost of Capital (MCC) Schedule for Unilate Textiles |

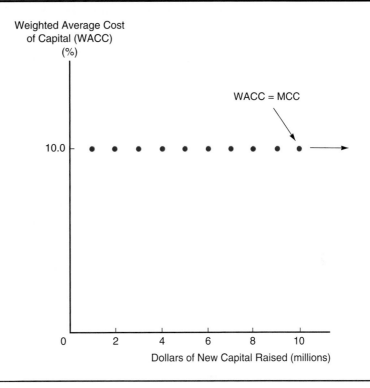

the company's balance sheet shows total long-term capital of $715 million at the end of 2005, all of this capital was raised in the past, and these funds have been invested in assets that are now being used in operations. If Unilate wants to raise any new (marginal) capital so that the total amount consists of 45 percent debt, 5 percent preferred stock, and 50 percent common equity, then to raise $1,000,000 in new capital, the company should issue $450,000 of new debt, $50,000 of new preferred stock, and $500,000 of additional common equity. The additional common equity could come from two sources: (1) retained earnings, defined as that part of this year's profits that management decides to retain in the business rather than pay out as dividends (but not earnings retained in the past, because these amounts have already been invested in existing assets); or (2) proceeds from the sale of new common stock.

We know that Unilate's WACC will be 10.0 percent as long as the after-tax cost of debt is 6 percent, the cost of preferred stock is 11 percent, and the funds needed from common equity can be satisfied by retained earnings with a cost of 13.5 percent ($k_s = 13.5\%$). But what happens if Unilate expands so rapidly that the retained earnings for the year are not sufficient to meet the common equity needs, forcing the firm to sell new common stock? Earlier, we determined that the cost of issuing new common stock, k_e, will be 14.5 percent, because the flotation costs associated with the new issue will be 11 percent. Because the cost of common equity increases when common stock has to be issued, the WACC also increases.

How much new capital can Unilate raise before it exhausts its retained earnings and is forced to sell new common stock? In other words, where will an increase in the MCC schedule occur?

Assume that Unilate's 2006 net income will be $61 million and that $30.5 million will be paid out as dividends so that $30.5 million will be added to retained earnings (the payout ratio is 50 percent). In this case, Unilate can invest in capital projects to the point where the common equity needs equal $30.5 million before new common stock has to be issued. Remember, though, that when Unilate needs new funds, the target capital structure indicates only 50 percent of the total should be common equity; the remainder of the funds should come from issues of bonds (45 percent) and preferred stock (5 percent). Thus, we know:

$$\text{Common equity} = 0.50(\text{Total new capital raised})$$

We can use this relationship to determine how much *total new capital*—that is, debt, preferred stock, and retained earnings—can be raised before the $30.5 million of retained earnings is exhausted and Unilate is forced to sell new common stock. Just set the common equity needs equal to the retained earnings amount, and solve for the total new capital amount:

$$\text{Common equity} = \text{Retained earnings} = \$30.5 \text{ million} = 0.50 \left(\begin{array}{c} \text{Total new} \\ \text{capital raised} \end{array} \right)$$

$$\left(\begin{array}{c} \text{Total new} \\ \text{capital raised} \end{array} \right) = \frac{\$30.5 \text{ million}}{0.50} = \$61.0 \text{ million}$$

Thus, Unilate can raise a total of $61 million before it has to sell new common stock to finance its capital projects.

If Unilate needs exactly $61 million in new capital, the breakdown of the amount that would come from each source of capital and the computation for the weighted average cost of capital (WACC) would be as follows:

Capital Source	Weight	Amount in Millions	After-Tax Component Cost	WACC
Debt	0.45	$27.45	6.0%	2.70%
Preferred stock	0.05	3.05	11.0	0.55
Common equity	0.50	30.50	13.5	6.75
	1.00	$61.00		$\text{WACC}_1 = 10.00\%$

Therefore, if Unilate needs *exactly* $61 million in new capital in 2006, retained earnings will be just enough to satisfy the common equity requirement, so the firm will not need to sell new common stock and its weighted average cost of capital (WACC) will be 10 percent. But what will happen if Unilate needs more than $61 million in new capital? If Unilate needs $64 million, for example, retained earnings will not be sufficient to cover the $32 million common equity requirements (50 percent of the total funds), so new common stock will have to be sold. The cost of issuing new common stock, k_e, is greater than the cost of retained earnings, k_s; hence, the WACC will be greater. If Unilate raises $64 million in new capital, the breakdown of the amount that would come from each source of capital and the computation for the weighted average cost of capital (WACC) would be as follows:

| FIGURE 8–2 | Marginal Cost of Capital Schedule for Unilate Textiles Using Both Retained Earnings and New Common Stock |

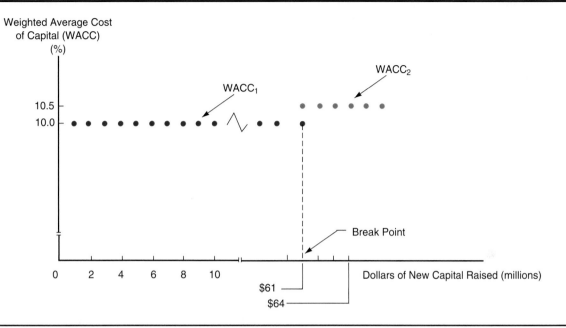

CAPITAL SOURCE	WEIGHT	AMOUNT IN MILLIONS	AFTER-TAX COMPONENT COST	WACC
Debt	0.45	$28.80	6.0%	2.70%
Preferred stock	0.05	3.20	11.0	0.55
Common equity	0.50	32.00	14.5	7.25
	1.00	$64.00		WACC$_2$ = 10.50%

The WACC will be greater because Unilate will have to sell new common stock, which has a higher component cost than retained earnings (14.5 percent versus 13.5 percent). Consequently, if Unilate's capital budgeting needs are greater than $61 million, new common stock will need to be sold, and its WACC will increase. The $61 million in total new capital is defined as the *retained earnings break point*, because above this amount of total capital, a break, or jump, in Unilate's MCC schedule occurs. In general, a **break point (BP)** is defined as the dollar of *new total capital* that can be raised before an increase in the firm's weighted average cost of capital occurs.

Figure 8–2 graphs Unilate's marginal cost of capital schedule with the retained earnings break point. Each dollar has a weighted average cost of 10.0 percent until the company raises a total of $61 million. This $61 million will consist of $27.45 million of new debt with an after-tax cost of 6 percent, $3.05 million of preferred stock with a cost of 11 percent, and $30.50 million of retained earnings with a cost of 13.5 percent. However, if Unilate raises one dollar over $61 million, each new dollar will contain 50¢ of equity *obtained by selling new common equity at a cost of 14.5 percent.* As a result, WACC jumps from 10.0 percent to 10.5 percent, as calculated previously and shown in Table 8–1.

BREAK POINT (BP)
The dollar value of new capital that can be raised before an increase in the firm's weighted average cost of capital occurs.

TABLE 8–1	WACC and Break Points for Unilate's MCC Schedule

I. Break Points

1. $BP_{Retained\ earnings} = \$30,500,000/0.50 = \$\ 61,000,000$

2. $BP_{Debt}\qquad = \$54,000,000/0.45 = \$120,000,000$

II. Weighted Average Cost of Capital (WACC)
1. New Capital Needs: $0–$61,000,000

	BREAKDOWN OF FUNDS AT $61,000,000	WEIGHT	×	AFTER-TAX COMPONENT COST	=	WACC
Debt (10%)	$27,450,000	0.45		6.0%		2.70%
Preferred stock	3,050,000	0.05		11.0		0.55
Common equity (Retained earnings)	30,500,000	0.50		13.5		6.75
	$61,000,000	1.00				$WACC_1 = 10.00\%$

2. New Capital Needs: $61,000,001–$120,000,000

	BREAKDOWN OF FUNDS AT $120,000,000	WEIGHT	×	AFTER-TAX COMPONENT COST	=	WACC
Debt (10%)	$ 54,000,000	0.45		6.0%		2.70%
Preferred stock	6,000,000	0.05		11.0		0.55
Common equity (New stock issue)	$ 60,000,000	0.50		14.5		7.25
	$120,000,000	1.00				$WACC_2 = 10.5\%$

3. New Capital Needs: Above $120,000,000

	BREAKDOWN OF FUNDS AT $130,000,000	WEIGHT	×	AFTER-TAX COMPONENT COST	=	WACC
Debt (12%)	$ 58,500,000	0.45		7.2%		3.24%
Preferred stock	6,500,000	0.05		11.0		0.55
Common equity (New stock issue)	65,000,000	0.50		14.5		7.25
	$130,000,000	1.00				$WACC_3 = 11.04\%$

Note that we really don't think the MCC jumps by precisely 0.5 percent when we raise $1 over $61 million. Thus, Figure 8–2 should be regarded as an approximation rather than as a precise representation of reality. We will return to this point later in the chapter.

Other Breaks in the MCC Schedule

There is a jump, or break, in Unilate's MCC schedule at $61 million of new capital because new common stock needs to be sold. Could there be other breaks in the schedule? Yes, there could. For example, suppose Unilate could obtain only $54 million of debt at a 10 percent interest rate, with any additional debt costing 12 percent.

This would result in a second break point in the MCC schedule, at the point where the $54 million of 10 percent debt is exhausted. At what amount of total financing would the 10 percent debt be used up? We know that this total financing will amount to $54 million of debt plus some amount of preferred stock and common equity. If we let BP_{Debt} represent the total financing at this second break point, then we know that 45 percent of BP_{Debt} will be debt, so

$$0.45(BP_{Debt}) = \$54 \text{ million}$$

Solving for BP_{Debt}, we have

$$BP_{debt} = \frac{\text{Maximum amount of 10\% debt}}{\text{Proportion of debt}}$$

$$= \frac{\$54 \text{ million}}{0.45} = \$120 \text{ million}$$

As you can see, there will be another break in the MCC schedule after Unilate has raised a total of $120 million, and this second break results from an increase in the cost of debt. The higher after-tax cost of debt (7.2 percent versus 6.0 percent) will result in a higher WACC. For example, if Unilate needs $130 million for capital budgeting projects, the WACC would be 11 percent:

CAPITAL SOURCE	WEIGHT	AMOUNT IN MILLIONS	AFTER-TAX COMPONENT COST	WACC
Debt	0.45	$ 58.50	7.2%	3.24%
Preferred stock	0.05	6.50	11.0	0.55
Common equity	0.50	65.00	14.5	7.25
	1.00	$130.00		WACC₃ = 11.04

In other words, the next dollar beyond $120 million will consist of 45¢ of 12 percent debt (7.2 percent after taxes), 5¢ of 11 percent preferred stock, and 50¢ of new common stock at a cost of 14.5 percent (retained earnings were used up much earlier), and this marginal dollar will have a cost of $WACC_3 = 11\%$.

The effect of this second WACC increase is shown in Figure 8–3. Now there are two break points, one caused by using up all the retained earnings and the other by using up all the 10 percent debt. With the two breaks, there are three different WACCs: $WACC_1 = 10.0\%$ for the first $61 million of new capital; $WACC_2 = 10.5\%$ in the interval between $61 million and $120 million; and $WACC_3 = 11.0\%$ for all new capital beyond $120 million.[9]

---

[9]When we use the term *weighted average cost of capital*, we are referring to the WACC, which is the cost of $1 raised partly as debt, partly as preferred stock, and partly as common equity. We could also calculate the average cost of all the capital the firm raised during a given year. For example, if Unilate raised $150 million, the first $61 million would have a cost of 10.0 percent, the next $59 million would cost 10.5 percent, and the last $30 million would cost 11.0 percent. The entire $150 million would have an average cost of

$$\left(\frac{\$61}{\$150}\right) \times (10.0\%) + \left(\frac{\$59}{\$150}\right) \times (10.5\%) + \left(\frac{\$30}{\$150}\right) \times (11.0\%) = 10.4\%$$

In general, this particular cost of capital should not be used for financial decisions—it usually has no relevance in finance. The only exception to this rule occurs when the firm is considering a very large asset that must be accepted in total or else rejected, and the capital required for it includes capital with different WACCs. For example, if Unilate were considering one $150 million project, that project should be evaluated with a 10.4 percent cost.

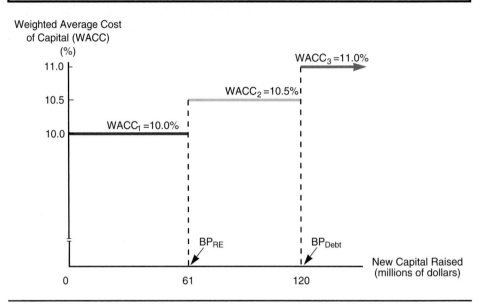

| FIGURE 8–3 | Marginal Cost of Capital Schedule for Unilate Textiles Using Retained Earnings, New Common Stock, and Higher-Cost Debt |

There could, of course, still be more break points; they would occur if the cost of debt continued to increase with more debt, if the cost of preferred stock increased at some level(s), or if the cost of common equity rose as more new common stock is sold.[10] In general, a break point will occur whenever the cost of one of the capital components increases, and the break point can be determined by the following equation:

| 8–9 | $$\text{Break point} = \frac{\text{Total amount of lower cost capital of a given type}}{\text{Proportion of this type of capital in the capital structure}}$$ |

As you can see, numerous break points are possible. At the extreme, an MCC schedule might have so many break points that it rises almost continuously beyond some given level of new financing. Such an MCC schedule is shown in Figure 8–4.

---

[10]The first break point is not necessarily the point at which retained earnings are used up; it is possible for low-cost debt to be exhausted *before* retained earnings have been used up. For example, if Unilate had available only $22.5 million of 10 percent debt, BP_{Debt} would occur at $50 million:

$$BP_{Debt} = \frac{\$22.5 \text{ million}}{0.45} = \$50 \text{ million}$$

Thus, the break point for debt would occur before the break point for retained earnings, which occurs at $61 million.

FIGURE 8–4	Smooth, or Continuous, Marginal Cost of Capital Schedule

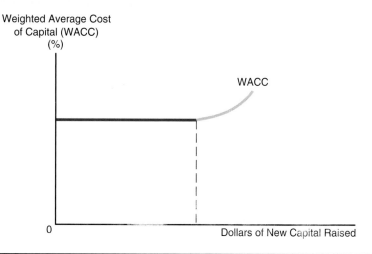

The easiest sequence for calculating MCC schedules is as follows:

1. Use Equation 8–9 to determine each point at which a break occurs. A break will occur any time the cost of one of the capital components rises. (It is possible, however, that two capital components could both increase at the same point.) After determining the exact break points, make a list of them.
2. Determine the cost of capital for each component in the intervals between breaks.
3. Calculate the weighted averages of these component costs to obtain the WACCs in each interval, as we did in Table 8–1. The WACC is constant within each interval, but it rises at each break point.

Notice that if there are n separate breaks, there will be n + 1 different WACCs. For example, in Figure 8–3 we see two breaks and three different WACCs. Also, we should note again that a different MCC schedule would result if a different capital structure is used.

Constructing an MCC Schedule—An Illustration

To further illustrate the construction of an MCC schedule, let's assume the following information is known about a firm's capital structure, the current market value of its debt and equity, and its financing opportunities:

	CAPITAL STRUCTURE	MARKET VALUE PER SHARE	DIVIDEND/INTEREST PAYMENT PER SHARE
Debt (10-year bond)	35.0%	$1,067.10	$90.00
Preferred stock	5.0%	$ 75.00	$ 7.20
Common equity	60.0%	$ 35.00	$ 3.00

The face value of the debt is $1,000, and interest is paid annually. The firm is expected to grow at a constant rate of 5 percent far into the future, and retained earnings are forecast to increase by $120 million in the coming year. The flotation costs associated with issuing new debt are negligible, but the costs associated with issuing new preferred stock equal 2 percent of the selling price as long as the amount issued is $15 million or less; amounts of preferred stock exceeding $15 million will have flotation costs of 4 percent. The cost to issue new common stock is 6 percent if $90 million or less is issued; this cost rises to 8 percent for amounts exceeding $90 million. The firm's investment banker estimates that the firm can issue new 10-year debt with the same characteristics as its existing debt up to a maximum of $105 million; any amount in excess of $105 million will have the same characteristics, except that the issue price will match the face value. Preferred stock and common stock can be issued at the current market values given in the preceding table. The firm's marginal tax rate is 40 percent.

Based on the information provided, we construct the MCC schedule as follows:

Step 1 Compute the break points. In this case, at most four break points are possible: (a) if the common equity financing needs exceed the $120 million expected retained earnings, because new common stock must be issued, and new equity has a higher cost than retained earnings; (b) if the debt financing needs exceed $105 million, because additional debt can be sold for the face value ($1,000), which is less than the current market value of the debt ($1,067.10); (c) if preferred stock financing needs exceed $15 million, because additional preferred stock will have higher flotation costs; and (d) if the firm needs to issue *new* common equity in excess of $90 million, because it will incur higher flotation costs than if lower amounts are issued. If the firm issues new common stock, then its common equity financing needs consist of the $120 million addition to retained earnings plus any new common stock that is issued.

Using Equation 8–9, we can calculate the four break points:

$$\text{BP}_{\text{Debt}} = \frac{\$105 \text{ million}}{0.35} = \$300 \text{ million}$$

$$\text{BP}_{\text{Preferred stock}} = \frac{\$15 \text{ million}}{0.05} = \$300 \text{ million}$$

$$\text{BP}_{\text{Retained earnings}} = \frac{\$120 \text{ million}}{0.60} = \$200 \text{ million}$$

$$\text{BP}_{\text{New common equity}} = \frac{\$120 \text{ million} + \$90 \text{ million}}{0.60} = \$350 \text{ million}$$

In this case, there are three *different* break points. The costs of both debt and preferred stock will increase at the same point, creating a break point at $300 million of total financing.

Step 2 Next, we compute the cost of capital for each component in the intervals between breaks.

1. *Debt*—$1,000 face; INT = $90, paid annually; N = 10 years; negligible flotation costs:
   a. If debt financing needs range from $1 to $105 million, the bond's market value will be $1,067.10. Thus k_d is

$$\$1,067.10 = \frac{\$90}{(1+k_d)^1} + \frac{\$90}{(1+k_d)^2} + \cdots + \frac{\$1,090}{(1+k_d)^{10}}$$

Using a financial calculator, we find that k_d = 8 percent:

Inputs:	10	?	−1,067.10	90	1,000
	N	I	PV	PMT	FV

Output: = 8.0

b. If debt financing needs are greater than $105 million, the market value of the bond will be $1,000. Thus k_d is

$$\$1,000 = \frac{\$90}{(1+k_d)^1} + \frac{\$90}{(1+k_d)^2} + \cdots + \frac{\$1,090}{(1+k_d)^{10}}$$

Using a financial calculator, we find that k_d = 9 percent:

Inputs:	10	?	−1000	90	1000
	N	I	PV	PMT	FV

Output: = 9.0

2. *Preferred Stock*—P_0 = $75; D_{ps} = $7.20:

a. If preferred stock financing needs range from $1 to $15 million, flotation costs are 2 percent. Using Equation 8–2, we find k_{ps} = 9.8 percent:

$$k_{ps} = \frac{D_{ps}}{P_0(1-F)} = \frac{\$7.20}{\$75.00(1-0.02)} = \frac{\$7.20}{\$73.50} = 0.098 = 9.8\%$$

b. If preferred stock financing needs are greater than $15 million, flotation costs increase to 4 percent. In this case, k_{ps} = 10.0 percent:

$$k_{ps} = \frac{\$7.20}{\$75.00(1-0.04)} = \frac{\$7.20}{\$72.00} = 0.10 = 10.0\%$$

3. *Common Equity*—P_0 = $35, D_0 = $3; g = 5%:

a. Expectations are that the addition to retained earnings this year will be $120 million, which represents the amount of internal financing that the firm has available for new investments. Using Equation 8–6, the cost of retained earning, k_s, is

$$k_s = \frac{\hat{D}_1}{P_0} + g = \frac{\$3.00(1.05)}{\$35.00} + 0.05$$

$$= \frac{\$3.15}{\$35.00} + 0.05 = 0.09 + 0.05 = 0.14 = 14.0\%$$

b. If common equity financing needs are greater than can be satisfied with retained earnings—that is, greater than $120 million—then the firm must sell new common stock to raise the additional amount. The flotation costs for new common stock in amounts from $1 to $90 million are 6 percent. Using Equation 8–7, the cost of new equity, k_e, is

$$k_e = \frac{\hat{D}_1}{P_0(1-F)} + g = \frac{\$3.00(1.05)}{\$35.00(1-0.06)} + 0.05$$

$$= \frac{\$3.15}{\$32.90} + 0.05 = 0.096 + 0.05 = 0.146 = 14.6\%$$

Thus, the cost of common equity is 14.6 percent if the common equity financing needs exceed the $120 million available from retained earnings but are less than or equal to $210 million, which includes the $120 million in retained earnings plus $90 million in new common stock.

c. If the amount of new common stock issued exceeds $90 million, the flotation costs are 8 percent. In this case, if common equity financing is greater than $210 million, the cost of equity is

$$k_e = \frac{\hat{D}_1}{P_0(1 - F)} + g = \frac{\$3.00(1.05)}{\$35.00(1 - 0.08)} + 0.05$$

$$= \frac{\$3.15}{\$32.20} + 0.05 = 0.098 + 0.05 = 0.148 = 14.8\%$$

Step 3   Calculate the weighted averages of these component costs to obtain the WACCs in each interval. Remember, there are three break points:

- At $200 million—the break results from a higher cost of common equity because all internal financing (retained earnings) will be used up at this point.
- At $300 million—the break occurs because cheaper debt *and* cheaper preferred stock will be used up at this point.
- At $350 million—the break occurs because greater amounts of new equity will have a higher cost.

With these break points, the WACC will be constant from $1 to $200 million financing. It will increase to a new level that will remain constant from $200 million plus $1 to $300 million, because the firm has exhausted its internal financing and must raise common equity funds by issuing new stock that has a higher cost. It will increase to a higher level that will remain constant from $300 million plus $1 to $350 million, because both debt and preferred stock financing are more expensive beyond $300 million. Finally, it will increase to a higher level at $350 million plus $1 because the cost of issuing new common equity is higher.

Table 8–2 shows the computations for the WACCs for each interval of new financing. If you compare the numbers in the column labeled "After-Tax Component Cost" for consecutive intervals, you will see which type of capital caused the WACC to increase from one interval to the next.

Self-Test Questions

What are break points, and why do they occur in MCC schedules? Write out and explain the equation for determining break points.

How is an MCC schedule constructed? If there are n breaks in the MCC schedule, how many different WACCs are there? Why?

Combining the MCC and Investment Opportunity Schedules

Now that we have calculated the MCC schedule, we can use it to develop a discount rate for use in the capital budgeting process—that is, *we can use the MCC schedule to find the cost of capital for determining projects' net present values (NPVs)* as discussed in Chapter 6.

TABLE 8–2	MCC Schedule Illustration ($ million)

1. New Capital Needs: Interval = $1 to $200

	BREAKDOWN OF FUNDS AT $200	WEIGHT	× AFTER-TAX COMPONENT COST	=	WACC
Debt (8%)	$70.0	0.35	4.8%		1.68%
Preferred stock	10.0	0.05	9.8		0.49
Common equity (retained earnings)	120.0	0.60	14.0		8.40
	$200.0	1.00			$WACC_1$ = 10.57%

2. New Capital Needs: Interval = $200+ to $300

	BREAKDOWN OF FUNDS AT $300	WEIGHT	× AFTER-TAX COMPONENT COST	=	WACC
Debt (8%)	$105.0	0.35	4.8%		1.68%
Preferred stock	15.0	0.05	9.8		0.49
Common equity (new issue)	180.0	0.60	14.6		8.76
	$300.0	1.00			$WACC_2$ = 10.93%

3. New Capital Needs: Interval = $300+ to $350

	BREAKDOWN OF FUNDS AT $350	WEIGHT	× AFTER-TAX COMPONENT COST	=	WACC
Debt (9%)	$122.5	0.35	5.4%		1.89%
Preferred stock	17.5	0.05	10.0		0.50
Common equity (new issue)	210.0	0.60	14.6		8.76
	$350.0	1.00			$WACC_3$ = 11.15%

4. New Capital Needs: Interval = Above $350

	BREAKDOWN OF FUNDS AT $360	WEIGHT	× AFTER-TAX COMPONENT COST	=	WACC
Debt (9%)	$126.0	0.35	5.4%		1.89%
Preferred stock	18.0	0.05	10.0		0.50
Common equity (new issue)	216.0	0.60	14.8		8.88
	$360.0	1.00			$WACC_4$ = 11.27%

To understand how the MCC schedule is used in capital budgeting, assume that Unilate Textiles has three financial executives: a financial vice president (VP), a treasurer, and a director of capital budgeting (DCB). The financial VP asks the treasurer to develop the firm's MCC schedule, and the treasurer produces the schedule shown earlier in Figure 8–3. At the same time, the financial VP asks the DCB to draw up a list of all projects that are potentially acceptable. The list shows each project's cost, projected annual net cash inflows, life, and internal rate of return (IRR). These data are presented at the bottom of Figure 8–5. For example, Project A has a cost of $39 million, it is expected to produce inflows of $9 million per year for six years, and,

FIGURE 8–5	Combining the MCC and IOS Schedules to Determine the Optimal Capital Budget

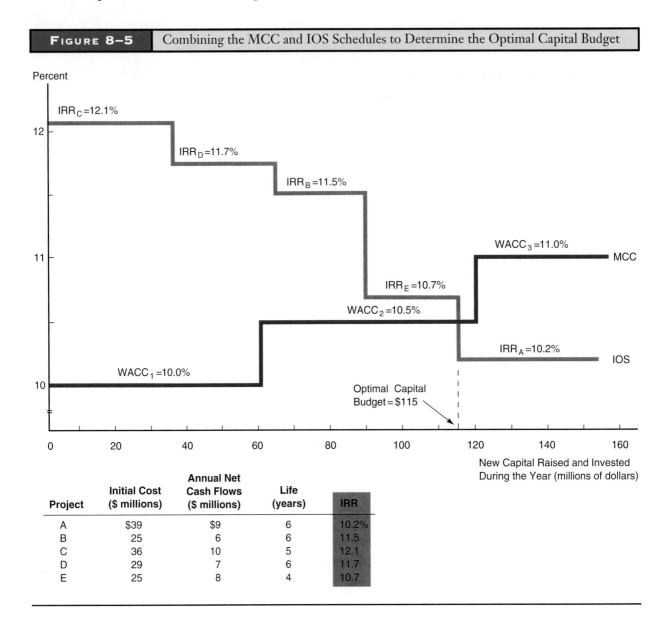

Project	Initial Cost ($ millions)	Annual Net Cash Flows ($ millions)	Life (years)	IRR
A	$39	$9	6	10.2%
B	25	6	6	11.5
C	36	10	5	12.1
D	29	7	6	11.7
E	25	8	4	10.7

INVESTMENT OPPORTUNITY SCHEDULE (IOS)

A graph of the firm's investment opportunities ranked in order of the projects' internal rates of return.

therefore, it has an IRR of 10.2 percent. Similarly, Project C has a cost of $36 million, it is expected to produce inflows of $10 million per year for five years, and thus it has an IRR of 12.1 percent. (NPVs cannot be shown yet because we do not yet know the marginal cost of capital.) For simplicity, we assume now that all projects are independent as opposed to mutually exclusive, that they are equally risky, and that their risks are all equal to those of the firm's average existing assets.

The DCB then plots the IRR data shown at the bottom of Figure 8–5 as the **investment opportunity schedule (IOS)** shown in the graph. The IOS schedule shows, in rank order, how much money Unilate can invest at different rates of return (IRRs). Figure 8–5 also shows Unilate's MCC schedule as it was developed by the treasurer and plotted in Figure 8–3. Now consider Project C: its IRR is 12.1 percent, and it can be financed with capital that costs only 10.0 percent; consequently, it should be accepted. Recall from Chapter 6 that if a project's IRR exceeds its cost of capital, its NPV also will be positive; therefore, Project C must also be acceptable by the NPV criterion. Projects B, D, and E can be analyzed similarly. They are all acceptable because IRR > MCC = WACC and hence NPV > 0. Project A, on the other hand, should be rejected because IRR_A < MCC; hence, NPV_A < 0.

People sometimes ask this question: "If we took Project A first, it would be acceptable because its 10.2 percent return would exceed the 10.0 percent cost of money used to finance it. Why couldn't we do this?" The answer is that we are seeking, in effect, to maximize the excess of *returns over costs*, or the area that is above the WACC but below the IOS. We accomplish this by graphing (and accepting) the most profitable projects first.

Another question that sometimes arises is this: What would happen if the MCC cut through one of the projects? For example, suppose the second break point in the MCC schedule had occurred at $100 million rather than at $120 million, causing the MCC schedule to cut through Project E. Should we then accept Project E? If Project E could be accepted in part, we would take on only part of it. Otherwise, the answer would be determined by (1) finding the average cost of the funds needed to finance Project E (some of the money would cost 10.5 percent and some 11.0 percent) and (2) comparing the average cost of this money with the 10.7 percent return on the project. We should accept Project E if its return exceeds the average cost of the $25 million needed to finance it.

The preceding analysis as summarized in Figure 8–5 reveals a very important point: *The cost of capital used in the capital budgeting process as discussed in Chapters 6 and 7 actually is determined at the intersection of the IOS and MCC schedules. If the cost of capital at the intersection ($WACC_2$ = 10.5% in Figure 8–5) is used, then the firm will make correct accept/reject decisions, and its level of financing and investment will be optimal. If it uses any other rate, its capital budget will not be optimal.*

The intersection WACC as determined in Figure 8–5 should be used to find the NPVs of new projects that are about as risky as the firm's existing assets, but this corporate cost of capital should be adjusted up or down to find NPVs for projects with higher or lower risk than the average project. This point was discussed in Chapter 7 in connection with the Home Energy Products appliance control computer example.

Self-Test Questions

Differentiate between the MCC and IOS schedules.

How is the corporate cost of capital, which is used to evaluate average risk projects to determine their NPVs, found?

As a general rule, do you think a firm's cost of capital as determined in this chapter should be used to evaluate all of its capital budgeting projects? Explain.

WACC versus Required Rate of Return of Investors

We introduced the concept of risk and rates of return in Chapter 4, and then in Chapter 5 we used this knowledge along with time value of money techniques to determine the values of financial assets, such as stocks and bonds. In these chapters we discovered that investors demand higher rates of return to be compensated for higher levels of risk. We also discovered that, everything else equal, an asset's value is inversely related to the rate of return investors require to invest in it. The following equation, with which you should be familiar by now, shows this relationship:

$$\text{Value} = \frac{\hat{CF}_1}{(1 + k)^1} + \frac{\hat{CF}_2}{(1 + k)^2} + \cdots + \frac{\hat{CF}_n}{(1 + k)^n} = \sum_{t=1}^{n} \frac{\hat{CF}_t}{(1 + k)^t}$$

This equation, which was first introduced in Chapter 1, shows that the value of any asset—real or financial—is based on (1) the cash flows that the asset is expected to generate during its life, $\hat{CF}_t$, and (2) the rate of return that investors require to "put up" their money to purchase the investment (asset), k. As a result, we know that investors purchase a firm's stocks and bonds—and thus provide funds to the firm—only if they expect to receive a return that sufficiently compensates them for the risk associated with those stocks and bonds. Consequently, the investors who purchase a firm's stocks and bonds determine the rates of return, or costs, the firm must pay to raise funds to invest in capital budgeting projects.

In Chapter 5, we discussed valuation from the standpoint of investors. For example, we described k_s as the required rate of return of investors—that is, the rate of return investors demand to purchase the firm's common stock and thus provide funds to the firm. In this chapter, we described k_s as the cost of internal common equity, which represents the return that the firm must earn to satisfy investors' demands. Which description is correct? They both are. This point can be illustrated with a simple analogy. Assume that Randy borrows money from his credit union to invest in common stocks. The loan agreement requires Randy to repay the amount borrowed and 10 percent interest at the end of one year. The 10 percent interest rate represents both Randy's cost of borrowing—that is, cost of debt—and his required rate of return. If he does not invest the borrowed funds in stocks that earn at least 10 percent return—that is, have internal rates of return greater than 10 percent— then Randy will lose wealth because he has to pay the credit union, and thus it costs him 10 percent interest to use the money. The 10 percent interest rate also represents the return the credit union demands to lend money to Randy, based on his credit risk—that is, 10 percent is the credit union's required rate, or the return it demands to lend money to (invest in) Randy. Although the situation is much more complex, this same relationship exists for firms that use funds provided by investors. Investors are similar to the credit union in the sense that they provide funds to the firms, whereas firms are similar to Randy in the sense that they use the funds provided by investors and must pay a return that is sufficient to attract such funds. And, much like the credit union determines the interest rate that Randy must pay for his loan, investors determine the rates that firms must pay to use their funds.

We first introduced and discussed rates of return in Chapter 4 and then further expanded this discussion in Chapter 5, where we showed how financial assets are valued. These discussions were developed primarily from the perspective of investors. In this chapter, we used the information introduced earlier in the book to explain the concept of cost of capital, which was discussed from the perspective of the firm. You should have noticed that the general concepts presented in this chapter are similar to the general concepts presented in Chapter 5—that is, determination of required rates of return and the impact on value. In reality, these two chapters present the same relationships from two perspectives—the investor (Chapter 5) and the firm (this chapter). The rates of return, or component costs of capital, discussed in this chapter, are the same rates that were introduced in Chapter 5. For this reason, we thought it might be a good idea to summarize these rates here. Table 8–3 shows the

TABLE 8-3   WACC Versus Required Rates of Return

Investor's Required Rate of Return/Firm's Cost of Capital:

$$\text{Investor's required rate of return} = k = k_{RF} + \left[\begin{array}{c}\text{Risk}\\\text{premium}\end{array}\right] = k_d,\ k_{ps},\ \text{or}\ k_s = \begin{array}{c}\text{Firm's component}\\\text{cost of capital}\end{array}$$

FINANCIAL ASSET	FINANCIAL ASSET'S MARKET VALUE	RETURN TO INVESTORS	COST TO FIRMS
Debt, k_d	$P_0 = \dfrac{INT}{(1+YTM)^1} + \cdots + \dfrac{INT+M}{(1+YTM)^N}$	$YTM = k_d$ = return investors require to purchase the firm's debt	$k_d = YTM$ = before-tax cost of debt $k_{dT} = k_d(1-T)$ = after-tax cost of debt
Preferred Stock, k_{ps}	$P_0 = \dfrac{D_{ps}}{k_{ps}}$	$k_{ps} = \dfrac{D_{ps}}{P_0}$ = return investors require to purchase the firm's preferred stock	$k_{ps} = \dfrac{D_{ps}}{P_0(1-F)}$ = cost of preferred stock
Common Equity, k_s *(internal) or* k_e *(external)*	$P_0 = \dfrac{\hat{D}_1}{k_s - g}$; (constant growth firm)	$k_s = \dfrac{\hat{D}_1}{P_0} + g$ = return investors require to purchase the firm's common stock	$k_s = \dfrac{\hat{D}_1}{P_0} + g$ = cost of retained earnings (internal) $k_e = \dfrac{\hat{D}_1}{P_0(1-F)} + g$ = cost of new common equity (external)

Variable Definitions:

k_{RF} = nominal risk-free rate of return

P_0 = market value of the financial asset

INT = dollar interest payment

M = maturity (face) value

N = number of remaining interest payments

g = constant growth rate of the firm

YTM = yield to maturity

T = the firm's marginal tax rate

D_{ps} = preferred stock dividend

$\hat{D}_1$ = next period's expected dividend

F = cost of issuing new stock (in decimal form)

rates of return discussed in Chapter 5 and compares them to the component costs of capital discussed in this chapter. Note that the equations shown in the column labeled "Return to Investors" are the same as those shown in the column labeled "Cost to Firms," except for adjustments for taxes and flotation costs.

Self-Test Questions

Who determines a firm's component costs of capital?

Why is k the required rate of return for both investors and the firm?

Summary

This chapter showed how (1) the weighted average cost of capital (WACC) is computed for a firm, and (2) the MCC schedule is developed for use in the capital budgeting process. The key concepts that were covered are listed here:

- The cost of capital to be used in capital budgeting decisions is the **weighted average** of the various types of capital the firm uses, typically debt, preferred stock, and common equity.
- The **component cost of debt** is the after-tax cost of new debt. It is found by multiplying the cost of new debt by $(1 - T)$, where T is the firm's marginal tax rate: $k_{dT} = k_d(1 - T)$.
- The **component cost of preferred stock** is calculated as the preferred dividend divided by the net issuing price, where the net issuing price is the price the firm receives after deducting flotation costs: $k_{ps} = D_{ps}/[P(1 - F)] = D_{ps}/NP$.
- The **cost of common equity** is the cost of retained earnings as long as the firm has retained earnings, but the cost of equity becomes the cost of new common stock once the firm has exhausted its retained earnings.
- The **cost of retained earnings** is the rate of return required by stockholders on the firm's common stock, and it can be estimated using one of three methods: (1) the **CAPM approach**, (2) the **discounted cash flow, DCF, approach,** and (3) the **bond-yield-plus-risk-premium approach.**
- To use the **CAPM approach**, (1) estimate the firm's beta, (2) multiply this beta by the market risk premium to determine the firm's risk premium, and (3) add the firm's risk premium to the risk-free rate to obtain the firm's cost of retained earnings: $k_s = k_{RF} + (k_M - k_{RF})\beta_s$.
- To use the **discounted cash flow (DCF) approach** when constant growth exists, add the firm's expected growth rate to its expected dividend yield: $k_s = \hat{D}_1/P_0 + g$.
- The **bond-yield-plus-risk-premium approach** calls for adding a risk premium of from 3 to 5 percentage points to the firm's interest rate on long-term debt: $k_s = k_d + RP$.
- The **cost of new common equity** is higher than the cost of retained earnings because the firm incurs **flotation expenses** to sell stock. To find the cost of new common equity, the stock price is first reduced by the flotation expense, then the dividend yield is calculated on the basis of the price the firm actually will receive, and finally the expected growth rate is added to this **adjusted dividend yield:** $k_e = \hat{D}_1/[P_0(1 - F)] + g$.

- Each firm has an **optimal capital structure,** defined as that mix of debt, preferred stock, and common equity that *minimizes* its **weighted average cost of capital (WACC):**

$$WACC = w_d k_{dT} + w_{ps} k_{ps} + w_e(k_s \text{ or } k_e)$$

- The **marginal cost of capital (MCC)** is defined as the cost of the last dollar of new capital that the firm raises. The MCC increases as the firm raises more and more capital during a given period. A graph of the MCC plotted against dollars raised is the **MCC schedule.**
- A **break point** occurs in the MCC schedule each time the cost of one of the capital components increases.
- The **investment opportunity schedule (IOS)** is a graph of the firm's investment opportunities, ranked in order of their internal rates of return (IRR).
- The MCC schedule is combined with the IOS schedule, and the intersection defines the **corporate cost of capital,** which is used to evaluate average-risk capital budgeting projects.

The concepts developed in this chapter are extended in Chapter 9, where we consider the effect of the capital structure on the cost of capital.

Questions

8–1 In what sense does the marginal cost of capital schedule represent a series of average costs?

8–2 The financial manager of a large national firm was overheard making the following statement: "We try to use as much retained earnings as possible for capital budgeting purposes because there is no *explicit* cost to these funds, and this allows us to invest in relatively low yielding projects that would not be feasible if we had to issue new common stock. We actually use retained earnings to invest in projects with yields below the coupon rate on our bonds." Comment on the validity of this statement.

8–3 How would each of the following affect a firm's after-tax cost of debt, k_{dT}; its cost of equity, k_s; and its weighted average cost of capital, WACC? Indicate by a plus (+), a minus (–), or a zero (0) if the factor would increase, decrease, or have an indeterminate effect on the item in question. Assume other things are held constant. Be prepared to justify your answer, but recognize that some of the parts probably have no single correct answer; these questions are designed to stimulate thought and discussion.

		EFFECT ON	
	K_{dT}	K_s	**WACC**
a. The corporate tax rate is lowered.	_____	_____	_____
b. The Federal Reserve tightens credit.	_____	_____	_____
c. The firm significantly increases the proportion of debt it uses.	_____	_____	_____
d. The dividend payout ratio (% of earnings paid as dividends) is increased.	_____	_____	_____
e. The firm doubles the amount of capital it raises during the year.	_____	_____	_____
f. The firm expands into riskier new areas.	_____	_____	_____

g. The firm merges with another firm whose earnings are countercyclical both to those of the first firm and to the stock market. _____ _____ _____

h. The stock market falls drastically, and the value of the firm's stock falls along with the rest. _____ _____ _____

i. Investors become more risk averse. _____ _____ _____

j. The firm is an electric utility with a large investment in nuclear plants. Several states propose a ban on nuclear power generation. _____ _____ _____

8–4 Suppose a firm estimates its MCC and IOS schedules for the coming year and finds that they intersect at the point 10 percent, $10 million. What cost of capital should be used to evaluate average projects, high-risk projects, and low-risk projects?

Self-Test Problems

(Solutions appear in Appendix B)

key terms **ST-1** Define each of the following terms:

a. After-tax cost of debt, k_{dT}; capital component cost
b. Cost of preferred stock, k_{ps}
c. Cost of retained earnings, k_s
d. Cost of new common equity, k_e
e. Flotation cost, F
f. Target capital structure; capital structure components
g. Weighted average cost of capital, WACC
h. Marginal cost of capital, MCC
i. Marginal cost of capital schedule; break point, BP
j. Investment opportunity schedule, IOS

optimal capital budget **ST-2** Lancaster Engineering Inc. (LEI) has the following capital structure, which it considers to be optimal:

Debt	25%
Preferred stock	15
Common equity	60
	100%

LEI's expected net income this year is $34,285.72; its established dividend payout ratio is 30 percent; its marginal tax rate is 40 percent; and investors expect earnings and dividends to grow at a constant rate of 9 percent in the future. LEI paid a dividend of $3.60 per share last year, and its stock currently sells at a price of $60 per share.

LEI can obtain new capital in the following ways:

Common: New common stock has a flotation cost of 10 percent for up to $12,000 of new stock and 20 percent for all common stock over $12,000.

Preferred: New preferred stock with a dividend of $11 can be sold to the public at a price of $100 per share. However, flotation costs of $5 per share will be incurred for up to $7,500 of preferred stock, and flotation costs will rise to $10 per share, or 10 percent, on all preferred stock over $7,500.

Debt: Up to $5,000 of debt can be sold at an interest rate of 12 percent; debt in the range of $5,001 to $10,000 must carry an interest rate of 14 percent; and all debt over $10,000 will have an interest rate of 16 percent.

LEI has the following independent investment opportunities:

Project	Cost at t = 0	Annual Net Cash Flow	Project Life	IRR
A	$10,000	$2,191.20	7 years	12.0%
B	10,000	3,154.42	5	17.4
C	10,000	2,170.18	8	14.2
D	20,000	3,789.48	10	13.7
E	20,000	5,427.84	6	?

a. Find the break points in the MCC schedule.
b. Determine the cost of each capital structure component.
c. Calculate the weighted average cost of capital in the interval between each break in the MCC schedule.
d. Calculate the IRR for Project E.
e. Construct a graph showing the MCC and IOS schedules.
f. Which projects should LEI accept?

Problems

cost of retained earnings   **8–1** The earnings, dividends, and stock price of Talukdar Technologies Inc. are expected to grow at 7 percent per year in the future. Talukdar's common stock sells for $23 per share, its last dividend was $2.00, and the company will pay a dividend of $2.14 at the end of the current year.
a. Using the discounted cash flow approach, what is its cost of retained earnings?
b. If the firm's beta is 1.6, the risk-free rate is 9 percent, and the average return on the market is 13 percent, what will be the firm's cost of equity using the CAPM approach?
c. If the firm's bonds earn a return of 12 percent, what will k_s be using the bond-yield-plus-risk-premium approach? (*Hint:* Use the midpoint of the risk premium range discussed in the chapter.)
d. Based on the results of parts a through c, what would you estimate Talukdar's cost of retained earnings to be?

cost of retained earnings   **8–2** The Shrieves Company's EPS was $6.50 in 2005 and $4.42 in 2000. The company pays out 40 percent of its earnings as dividends, and the stock sells for $36.
a. Calculate the past growth rate in earnings. (*Hint:* This is a five-year growth period.)
b. Calculate the *next* expected dividend per share, $\hat{D}_1$. [D_0 = 0.4($6.50) = $2.60.] Assume that the past growth rate will continue.
c. What is the cost of retained earnings, k_s, for the Shrieves Company?

break point calculations   **8–3** The Simmons Company expects earnings of $30 million next year. Its dividend payout ratio is 40 percent, and its proportion of debt (debt/assets ratio) is 60 percent. Simmons uses no preferred stock.
a. What amount of retained earnings does Simmons expect next year?
b. At what amount of financing will there be a break point in the MCC schedule?
c. If Simmons can borrow $12 million at an interest rate of 11 percent, another $12 million at a rate of 12 percent, and any additional debt at a rate of 13 percent, at what points will rising debt costs cause breaks in the MCC schedule?

calculation of g and EPS   **8-4** Rowell Products' stock is currently selling for $60 a share. The firm is expected to earn $5.40 per share this year and to pay a year-end dividend of $3.60.

    a. If investors require a 9 percent return, what rate of growth must be expected for Rowell?

    b. If Rowell reinvests retained earnings in projects whose average return is equal to the stock's expected rate of return, what will be next year's earnings per share.

weighted average   **8-5** On January 1, 2005, the total assets of the Dexter Company were $270 million.
cost of capital   The firm's present capital structure, which follows, is considered to be optimal. Assume that there is no short-term debt.

Long-term debt	$135,000,000
Common equity	135,000,000
Total liabilities and equity	$270,000,000

    New bonds will have a 10 percent coupon rate and will be sold at par. Common stock, currently selling at $60 a share, can be sold to net the company $54 a share. Stockholders' required rate of return is estimated to be 12 percent, consisting of a dividend yield of 4 percent and an expected growth rate of 8 percent. (The next expected dividend is $2.40, so $2.40/$60 = 4%.) Retained earnings are estimated to be $13.5 million. The marginal tax rate is 40 percent. Assuming that all asset expansion (gross expenditures for fixed assets plus related working capital) is included in the capital budget, the dollar amount of the capital budget, ignoring depreciation, is $135 million.

    a. To maintain the present capital structure, how much of the capital budget must Dexter finance by equity?

    b. How much of the new equity funds needed will be generated internally? Externally?

    c. Calculate the cost of each of the equity components.

    d. At what level of capital expenditure will there be a break in Dexter's MCC schedule?

    e. Calculate the WACC (1) below and (2) above the break in the MCC schedule.

    f. Plot the MCC schedule. Also, draw in an IOS schedule that is consistent with both the MCC schedule and the projected capital budget. (Any IOS schedule that is consistent will do.)

weighted average   **8-6** The following table gives earnings per share figures for the Brueggeman Com-
cost of capital   pany during the preceding 10 years. The firm's common stock, 7.8 million shares outstanding, is now (January 1, 2005) selling for $65 per share, and the expected dividend at the end of the current year (2005) is 55 percent of the EPS expected in 2005. Because investors expect past trends to continue, g can be based on the earnings growth rate. (Note that nine years of growth are reflected in the data.)

YEAR	EPS	YEAR	EPS
1995	$3.90	2000	$5.73
1996	4.21	2001	6.19
1997	4.55	2002	6.68
1998	4.91	2003	7.22
1999	5.31	2004	7.80

The current before-tax interest rate on new debt is 9 percent. The firm's marginal tax rate is 40 percent. Its capital structure, considered to be optimal, is as follows:

Debt	$104,000,000
Common equity	156,000,000
Total liabilities and equity	$260,000,000

a. Calculate Brueggeman's after-tax cost of new debt and of common equity, assuming that new equity comes only from retained earnings. Calculate the cost of equity as $k_s = D_1/P_0 + g$.

b. Find Brueggeman's weighted average cost of capital, again assuming that no new common stock is sold and that all debt costs 9 percent.

c. How much can be spent on capital investments before external equity must be sold? (Assume that retained earnings available for 2005 are 45 percent of 2005 earnings. Obtain 2005 earnings by multiplying the expected 2005 EPS by the shares outstanding.)

d. What is Brueggeman's weighted average cost of capital (cost of funds raised in excess of the amount calculated in part c) if new common stock can be sold to the public at $65 a share to net the firm $58.50 a share? The cost of debt is constant.

optimal capital budget **8–7** Ezzell Enterprises has the following capital structure, which it considers to be optimal under present and forecasted conditions:

Debt (long-term only)	45%
Common equity	55
Total liabilities and equity	100%

For the coming year, management expects after-tax earnings of $2.5 million. Ezzell's past dividend policy of paying out 60 percent of earnings will continue. Present commitments from its banker will allow Ezzell to borrow according to the following schedule:

LOAN AMOUNT	INTEREST RATE
$0 to $500,000	9% on this increment of debt
$500,001 to $900,000	11% on this increment of debt
$900,001 and above	13% on this increment of debt

The company's marginal tax rate is 40 percent, the current market price of its stock is $22 per share, its *last* dividend was $2.20 per share, and the expected growth rate is 5 percent. External equity (new common) can be sold at a flotation cost of 10 percent.

Ezzell has the following investment opportunities for the next year:

PROJECT	COST	ANNUAL CASH FLOWS	PROJECT LIFE	IRR
1	$675,000	$155,401	8 years	?
2	900,000	268,484	5	15.0%
3	375,000	161,524	3	?
4	562,500	185,194	4	12.0
5	750,000	127,351	10	11.0

Management asks you to help determine which projects (if any) should be undertaken. You proceed with this analysis by answering the following questions (or performing the tasks) as posed in a logical sequence:

a. How many breaks are there in the MCC schedule? At what dollar amounts do the breaks occur, and what causes them?

b. What is the weighted average cost of capital in each of the intervals between the breaks?

c. What are the IRR values for Projects 1 and 3?

d. Graph the IOS and MCC schedules.

e. Which projects should Ezzell's management accept?

f. What assumptions about project risk are implicit in this problem? If you learned that Projects 1, 2, and 3 were of above-average risk, yet Ezzell chose the projects that you indicated in part e, how would this affect the situation?

g. The problem stated that Ezzell pays out 60 percent of its earnings as dividends. How would the analysis change if the payout ratio was changed to zero, to 100 percent, or somewhere in between? (No calculations are necessary.)

Exam-Type Problems

The problems included in this section are set up in such a way that they could be used as multiple-choice exam problems.

after-tax cost of debt

8–8 Calculate the after-tax cost of debt, k_{dT}, under each of the following conditions:

a. Interest rate, 13 percent; tax rate, 0 percent.

b. Interest rate, 13 percent; tax rate, 20 percent.

c. Interest rate, 13 percent; tax rate, 34 percent.

after-tax cost of debt

8–9 The McDaniel Company's financing plans for next year include the sale of long-term bonds with a 10 percent coupon. The company believes it can sell the bonds at a price that will provide a yield to maturity of 12 percent. If the marginal tax rate is 34 percent, what is McDaniel's after-tax cost of debt?

cost of preferred stock

8–10 Maness Industries plans to issue some $100 par preferred stock with an 11 percent dividend. The stock is selling on the market for $97.00, and Maness must pay flotation costs of 5 percent of the market price. What is the cost of the preferred stock for Maness?

cost of new common stock

8–11 The Choi Company's next expected dividend, $\hat{D}_1$, is $3.18; its growth rate is 6 percent; and the stock now sells for $36. New stock can be sold to net the firm $32.40 per share.

a. What is Choi's percentage flotation cost, F?

b. What is Choi's cost of new common stock, k_e?

weighted average cost of capital

8–12 The Gupta Company's cost of equity is 16 percent. Its before-tax cost of debt is 13 percent, and its marginal tax rate is 40 percent. The stock sells at book value. Using the following balance sheet, calculate Gupta's after-tax weighted average cost of capital:

Assets		Liabilities and Equity	
Cash	$ 120	Long-term debt	$1,152
Accounts receivable	240	Equity	1,728
Inventories	360		
Net plant and equipment	2,160		
Total assets	$2,880	Total liabilities and equity	$2,880

optimal capital budget

8–13 The Mason Corporation's present capital structure, which is also its target capital structure, calls for 50 percent debt and 50 percent common equity. The firm has only one potential project, an expansion program with a 10.2 percent IRR and a cost of $20 million, which is completely divisible—that is, Mason can invest any amount up to $20 million. The firm expects to retain $3 million of earnings next year. It can raise up to $5 million in new debt at a before-tax cost of 8 percent, and all debt after the first $5 million will have a cost of 10 percent. The cost of retained earnings is 12 percent, and the firm can sell any amount of new common stock desired at a constant cost of new equity of 15 percent. The firm's marginal tax rate is 40 percent. What is the firm's optimal capital budget?

optimal capital budget   **8–14** The management of Ferri Phosphate Industries (FPI) is planning next year's capital budget. FPI projects its net income at $7,500, and its payout ratio is 40 percent. The company's earnings and dividends are growing at a constant rate of 5 percent, the last dividend, D_0, was $0.90, and the current stock price is $8.59. FPI's new debt will cost 14 percent. If FPI issues new common stock, flotation costs will be 20 percent. FPI is at its optimal capital structure, which is 40 percent debt and 60 percent equity, and the firm's marginal tax rate is 40 percent. FPI has the following independent, indivisible, and equally risky investment opportunities:

PROJECT	COST	IRR
A	$15,000	17%
B	20,000	14
C	15,000	16
D	12,000	15

What is FPI's optimal capital budget?

risk-adjusted optimal   **8–15** Refer to Problem 8-14. Management now decides to incorporate project risk
capital budget   differentials into the analysis. The new policy is to add 2 percentage points to the cost of capital of those projects significantly riskier than average and to subtract 2 percentage points from the cost of capital of those that are substantially less risky than average. Management judges Project A to be of high risk, Projects C and D to be of average risk, and Project B to be of low risk. None of the projects is divisible. What is the optimal capital budget after adjustment for project risk?

weighted average   **8–16** Florida Electric Company (FEC) uses only debt and equity. It can borrow
cost of capital   unlimited amounts at an interest rate of 10 percent as long as it finances at its target capital structure, which calls for 45 percent debt and 55 percent common equity. Its last dividend was $2, its expected constant growth rate is 4 percent, its stock sells at a price of $25, and new stock would net the company $20 per share after flotation costs. FEC's marginal tax rate is 40 percent, and it expects to have $100 million of retained earnings this year. Two projects are available: Project A has a cost of $200 million and an internal rate of return of 13 percent, while Project B has a cost of $125 million and an internal rate of return of 10 percent. All of the company's potential projects are equally risky.

    a. What is FEC's cost of equity from newly issued stock?

    b. What is FEC's marginal cost of capital—that is, what WACC cost rate should it use to evaluate capital budgeting projects (these two projects plus any others that might arise during the year, provided the cost of capital schedule remains as it is currently)?

after-tax cost of debt   **8–17** A company's 6 percent coupon rate, semiannual payment, $1,000 par value bond that matures in 30 years sells at a price of $515.16. The company's marginal tax rate is 40 percent. What is the firm's component cost of debt for purposes of calculating the WACC? (*Hint:* Base your answer on the simple rate, not the effective annual rate, EAR.)

marginal cost of equity   **8–18** Chicago Paints Corporation has a target capital structure of 40 percent debt and 60 percent common equity. The company expects to have $600 of after-tax income during the coming year, and it plans to retain 40 percent of its earnings. The current stock price is $P_0 = \$30$, the last dividend was $D_0 = \$2.00$, and the dividend is expected to grow at a constant rate of 7 percent. New stock can be sold at a flotation cost of $F = 25$ percent. What will Chicago Paints's marginal cost of *equity* capital (not the WACC) be if it raises a total of $500 of new capital?

Integrative Problem

cost of capital   **8–19** Assume that you were recently hired as assistant to Jerry Lehman, financial VP of Coleman Technologies. Your first task is to estimate Coleman's cost of capital. Lehman has provided you with the following data, which he believes is relevant to your task:

  (1) The firm's marginal tax rate is 40 percent.
  (2) The current price of Coleman's 12 percent coupon, semiannual payment, noncallable bonds with 15 years remaining to maturity is $1,153.72. Coleman does not use short-term interest-bearing debt on a permanent basis. New bonds would be privately placed with no flotation cost.
  (3) The current price of the firm's 10 percent, $100 par value, quarterly dividend, perpetual preferred stock is $113.10. Coleman would incur flotation costs of $2.00 per share on a new issue.
  (4) Coleman's common stock is currently selling at $50 per share. Its last dividend (D_0) was $4.19, and dividends are expected to grow at a constant rate of 5 percent in the foreseeable future. Coleman's beta is 1.2, the yield on Treasury bonds is 7 percent, and the market risk premium is estimated to be 6 percent. For the bond-yield-plus-risk-premium approach, the firm uses a 4 percentage point risk premium.
  (5) Up to $300,000 of new common stock can be sold at a flotation cost of 15 percent. Above $300,000, the flotation cost would rise to 25 percent.
  (6) Coleman's target capital structure is 30 percent long-term debt, 10 percent preferred stock, and 60 percent common equity.
  (7) The firm is forecasting retained earnings of $300,000 for the coming year.

To structure the task somewhat, Lehman has asked you to answer the following questions:

  a. (1) What sources of capital should be included when you estimate Coleman's weighted average cost of capital (WACC)?
  (2) Should the component costs be figured on a before-tax or an after-tax basis? Explain.
  (3) Should the costs be historical (embedded) costs or new (marginal) costs? Explain.
  b. What is the market interest rate on Coleman's debt and its component cost of debt?
  c. (1) What is the firm's cost of preferred stock?
  (2) Coleman's preferred stock is riskier to investors than its debt, yet the yield to investors is lower than the yield to maturity on the debt. Does this suggest that you have made a mistake? (*Hint:* Think about taxes.)
  d. (1) Why is there a cost associated with retained earnings?
  (2) What is Coleman's estimated cost of retained earnings using the CAPM approach?

e. What is the estimated cost of retained earnings using the discounted cash flow (DCF) approach?

f. What is the bond-yield-plus-risk-premium estimate for Coleman's cost of retained earnings?

g. What is your final estimate for k_s?

h. What is Coleman's cost for up to $300,000 of newly issued common stock, k_{e1}? What happens to the cost of equity if Coleman sells more than $300,000 of new common stock?

i. Explain in words why new common stock has a higher percentage cost than retained earnings.

j. **(1)** What is Coleman's overall, or weighted average, cost of capital (WACC) when retained earnings are used as the equity component?

  (2) What is the WACC after retained earnings have been exhausted and Coleman uses up to $300,000 of new common stock with a 15 percent flotation cost?

  (3) What is the WACC if more than $300,000 of new common equity is sold?

k. **(1)** At what amount of new investment would Coleman be forced to issue new common stock? To put it another way, what is the largest capital budget the company could support without issuing new common stock? Assume that the 30/10/60 target capital structure will be maintained.

  (2) At what amount of new investment would Coleman be forced to issue new common stock with a 25 percent flotation cost?

  (3) What is a marginal cost of capital (MCC) schedule? Construct a graph that shows Coleman's MCC schedule.

l. Coleman's director of capital budgeting has identified the following potential projects:

Project	Cost	Life	Cash Flow	IRR
A	$700,000	5 years	$218,795	17.0%
B	500,000	5	152,705	16.0
B*	500,000	20	79,881	15.0
C	800,000	5	219,185	11.5

Projects B and B* are mutually exclusive, whereas the other projects are independent. All of the projects are equally risky.

  (1) Plot the IOS schedule on the same graph that contains your MCC schedule. What is the firm's marginal cost of capital for capital budgeting purposes?

  (2) What are the dollar size and the included projects in Coleman's optimal capital budget? Explain your answer fully.

  (3) Would Coleman's MCC schedule remain constant at 12.8 percent beyond $2 million regardless of the amount of capital required?

  (4) If $WACC_3$ had been 18.5 percent rather than 12.8 percent, but the second WACC break point had still occurred at $1,000,000, how would that have affected the analysis?

m. Suppose you learned that Coleman could raise only $200,000 of new debt at a 10 percent interest rate and that new debt beyond $200,000 would have a yield to investors of 12 percent. Trace back through your work and explain how this new fact would change the situation.

Computer-Related Problem

Work the problem in this section only if you are using the computer problem diskette.

marginal cost of capital   **8–20** Use the model in the File C08 to work this problem.

    a. Refer back to Problem 8-7. Now assume that the debt ratio is increased to 65 percent, causing all interest rates to rise by 1 percentage point, to 10 percent, 12 percent, and 14 percent, and causing g to increase from 5 to 6 percent. What happens to the MCC schedule and the capital budget?

    b. Assume the facts as in part a, but suppose Ezzell's marginal tax rate falls (1) to 20 percent or (2) to 0 percent. How would this affect the MCC schedule and the capital budget?

    c. Ezzell's management would now like to know what the optimal capital budget would be if earnings were as high as $3.25 million or as low as $1 million. Assume a 40 percent marginal tax rate.

    d. Would it be reasonable to use the model to analyze the effects of a change in the payout ratio without changing other variables?

GET REAL with Thomson ONE

8–21 Compare the capital structures of the following firms and answer the questions below: General Motors Corporation [GM], an automobile manufacturing and financing firm; Walt Disney Company [DIS], an entertainment and information company; and Amazon Inc. [AMZN], an online retail sales firm.

    a. What is the percentage of long-term debt, common stock, retained earnings, and preferred stock in each firm's capital structure? Set up a table to illustrate your answer. (*Hint:* Click on Peers/Financial/Balance Sheet.)

    b. Which firm has the highest, and lowest, relative amount of long-term debt? Common equity? Retained earnings?

    c. In one paragraph describe how you would calculate the weighted average cost of capital for each firm.

    d. Where does each firm stand in relation to its industry peers with regard to the percentages of debt, common equity, preferred stock, and retained earnings in its capital structure? (Click on Peers and change the peer set to Industry.)

CHAPTER 9

Capital Structure

In September 1990, Unisys Corporation, a manufacturer of computers and related products for commercial and defense companies, took actions to substantially reduce the amount of debt it was using to finance the firm. At the time, the debt/assets ratio of Unisys was nearly 75 percent, which was much higher than the company felt was appropriate.

One step taken to change the mix of debt and equity in the firm (its capital structure) was to suspend the payment of future common stock dividends, which allowed Unisys to provide $162 million a year to repurchase, and thus reduce, debt. Unisys was able to reduce its amount of debt substantially in four years—the debt/assets ratio fell from nearly 75 percent in 1990 to just over 60 percent in 1993. The strategy to change its capital structure seemed to work, because Unisys increased its net income from a loss of a little more than $500 million in 1990 to a gain of $400 million in 1993. Unfortunately, in 1995 the company again increased its debt considerably, and its debt/assets ratio rose above 75 percent; then in 1996 and 1997, the debt/assets ratio was even higher, at about 78 percent.

Even though its actions seemed contradictory, Unisys did not abandon its goal to reduce debt. In September 1997, Lawrence A. Weinbach was appointed chairman, president, and CEO. One of his first actions was to announce that Unisys would decrease debt by $1 billion by the year 2000. True to his word, Weinbach decreased debt by more than $800 million in the first four months of his tenure. It was estimated that the debt reduction saved more than $58 million annually in interest and debt-related expenses. In 1998, debt reduction actions continued such that Unisys reached its goal of a $1 billion reduction in debt approximately 18 months ahead of schedule.

Further restructuring of the company's capital from 1999 through 2001 reduced the debt/assets ratio to nearly 62 percent. Unfortunately, a poor economy during the following two years resulted in losses that reduced retained earnings. In addition, Unisys incurred a substantial liability associated with its pension plan that exceeded $725 million. These two factors contributed to such a significant increase in the relative amount of debt in Unisys that its debt/assets ratio increased to greater than 80 percent in 2002, where it remained in 2003. In essence, the capital restructuring efforts that Unisys had undertaken during the previous decade were reversed as a result of the huge pension liability the company accrued in 2002. As a result, Unisys started a new restructuring plan to reduce the relative amount of debt in its capital structure.

Why does Unisys continue to make these capital structure changes? Primarily to improve the financial position of the firm and thus improve shareholder wealth. So how has the stock been affected by the capital structure changes made since 1990? When Unisys first announced its plan, which included the suspension of dividends, the price of its common stock dropped more than

continues

25 percent in one day and by about one-third of its value within one week. Trading at just under $5 per share, the value of Unisys common stock was 76 percent lower than its high during the previous 12-month period, and 90 percent lower than its high value during the previous five years. By 1994, however, Unisys stock was selling for $11 per share; in 1998, the price was nearly $26; and in September 1999, the stock was selling for more than $45. Thus, the stock's value rebounded substantially after the 1990 announcement. Apparently, the stockholders realized the capital structure changes benefited long-run stability and wealth maximization. Unfortunately, the combination of a poorly performing stock market from 1999 through 2002 and the increase of its debt/assets ratio to greater than 80 percent resulted in a significant decline in the value of Unisys stock. In September 2002, the stock sold for less than $7 per share. Efforts by Unisys to improve its capital structure, along with a rebounding stock market, resulted in an increase in the stock price to greater than $15 by the end of 2003.

As you can see from this example, a firm's capital structure can affect value. As you read this chapter, keep in mind the reasons Unisys wanted to decrease the proportion of debt in its capital structure, and consider the impact a particular capital structure can have on the value of a firm. ∎

In Chapter 8, when we calculated the weighted average cost of capital for use in capital budgeting, we took the capital structure weights, or the mix of securities the firm uses to finance its assets, as a given. However, if the weights are changed, the calculated cost of capital, and thus the set of acceptable projects, will also change. Further, changing the capital structure will affect the riskiness inherent in the firm's common stock, and this will affect the return demanded by stockholders, k_s, and the stock's price, P_0. Therefore, the choice of a capital structure is an important decision. In this chapter, we discuss concepts relating to capital structure decisions.

The Target Capital Structure

CAPITAL STRUCTURE

The combination of debt and equity used to finance a firm.

TARGET CAPITAL STRUCTURE

The mix of debt, preferred stock, and common equity with which the firm plans to finance its investments.

Firms can choose whatever mix of debt and equity they desire to finance their assets, subject to the willingness of investors to provide such funds. As we shall see, many different mixes of debt and equity, or **capital structures,** exist. In some firms, such as Chrysler Corporation, debt accounts for more than 80 percent of the financing, while other firms, like Microsoft, have little or no long-term debt. In the next few sections, we will discuss factors that affect a firm's capital structure, and we will conclude a firm should attempt to determine what its optimal, or best, mix of financing should be. It will become apparent that determining the exact optimal capital structure is not a science, so after analyzing a number of factors, a firm establishes a **target capital structure** it believes is optimal and which it uses as guidance for raising funds in the future. This target might change over time as conditions vary, but at any given moment the firm's management has a specific capital structure in mind, and individual financing decisions should be consistent with this target. If the actual proportion of debt is below the target level, new funds probably will be raised by issuing debt, whereas if the proportion of debt is above the target, stock probably will be sold to bring the firm back in line with the target ratio.

Capital structure policy involves a trade-off between risk and return. Using more debt raises the riskiness of the firm's earnings stream, but a higher proportion of debt generally leads to a higher expected rate of return. From the concepts we discussed in Chapter 4, we know that the higher risk associated with greater debt tends to lower the firm's stock price. At the same time, however, the higher expected rate of return makes the stock more attractive to investors, which, in turn, ultimately increases the stock's price. Therefore, *the optimal capital structure is the one that strikes a balance between risk and return to achieve the ultimate goal of maximizing the price of the stock.*

Four primary factors influence capital structure decisions.

1. The first is the firm's *business risk*, or the riskiness that would be inherent in the firm's operations if it used no debt. The greater the firm's business risk, the lower the amount of debt that is optimal.

2. The second key factor is the firm's *tax position*. A major reason for using debt is that interest is tax deductible, which lowers the effective cost of debt. However, if much of a firm's income is already sheltered from taxes by accelerated depreciation or tax loss carryovers, its tax rate will be low, and debt will not be as advantageous as it would be to a firm with a higher effective tax rate.

3. The third important consideration is *financial flexibility*, or the ability to raise capital on reasonable terms under adverse conditions. Corporate treasurers know that a steady supply of capital is necessary for stable operations, which in turn are vital for long-run success. They also know that when money is tight in the economy, or when a firm is experiencing operating difficulties, a strong balance sheet is needed to obtain funds from suppliers of capital. Thus, it might be advantageous to issue equity to strengthen the firm's capital base and financial stability.

4. The fourth debt-determining factor has to do with *managerial attitude (conservatism or aggressiveness)* with regard to borrowing. Some managers are more aggressive than others; hence, some firms are more inclined to use debt in an effort to boost profits. This factor does not affect the optimal, or value-maximizing, capital structure, but it does influence the target capital structure a firm actually establishes.

These four points largely determine the target capital structure, but, as we shall see, operating conditions can cause the actual capital structure to vary from the target at any given time. For example, the proportion of debt that Unisys uses clearly has been much higher than its target during most of the past decade, and the company has taken some significant corrective actions to improve its financial position. (See "A Managerial Perspective" at the beginning of this chapter.)

Self-Test Questions

What are the four factors that affect a firm's target capital structure?

In what sense does capital structure policy involve a trade-off between risk and return?

Business and Financial Risk

When we examined risk in Chapter 4, we distinguished between *market risk*, which is measured by the firm's beta coefficient, and *total risk*, which includes both beta risk and a type of risk that can be eliminated by diversification *(firm-specific risk)*. In Chapter 7 we considered how capital budgeting decisions affect the riskiness of the firm. There again we distinguished between beta risk (the effect of a project on the firm's beta) and corporate risk (the effect of the project on the firm's total risk).

Now we introduce two new dimensions of risk:

BUSINESS RISK
The risk associated with projections of a firm's future returns on assets (ROA) or returns on equity (ROE) if the firm uses no debt.

1. **Business risk** is defined as the uncertainty inherent in projections of future returns, either on assets (ROA) or on equity (ROE), if the firm uses no debt, or debt-like financing (i.e., preferred stock)—that is, it is the risk associated with the firm's operations, ignoring any financing effects.

FINANCIAL RISK
The portion of stockholders' risk, over and above basic business risk that results from the manner in which the firm is financed.

2. **Financial risk** is defined as the additional risk, over and above basic business risk, placed on common stockholders that results from using financing alternatives with fixed periodic payments, such as debt and preferred stock—that is, it is the risk associated with using debt or preferred stock.

Conceptually, the firm has a certain amount of risk inherent in its production and sales operations; this is its business risk. When it uses debt, it partitions this risk and concentrates most of it on one class of investors—the common stockholders—this is its financial risk.[1] Both business risk and financial risk affect the capital structure of a firm.

Business Risk

Business risk is the single most important determinant of capital structure. To illustrate the effects of business risk, consider Bigbee Electronics Company, a firm that currently uses 100 percent equity. Figure 9–1 shows the trend in ROE from 1995 through 2005, and it gives both security analysts and Bigbee's management an idea of the degree to which return on equity (ROE) has varied in the past and might vary in the future. Comparing the actual results to the trend line, you can see that Bigbee's ROE has fluctuated significantly since 1995. These fluctuations in ROE were caused by many factors: booms and recessions in the national economy, successful new products introduced both by Bigbee and its competitors, labor strikes, a fire in Bigbee's major plant, and so on. Similar events will doubtless occur in the future, and when they do, ROE will rise or fall. Further, there always is the possibility that a long-term disaster might strike, permanently depressing the company's earning power. For example, a competitor could introduce a new product that would permanently lower Bigbee's earnings.[2] This element of uncertainty about Bigbee's future ROE is the company's *basic business risk*.

Business risk varies from one industry to another and also among firms in a given industry. Further, business risk can change over time. For example, electric utilities were regarded for years as having little business risk, but a combination of events during the past couple of decades has altered their situation, producing sharp declines in ROE for some companies and greatly increasing the industry's business risk. Today, food processors and grocery retailers frequently are cited as examples of industries with low business risk, whereas cyclical manufacturing industries, such as steel and construction, are regarded as having especially high business risk. Smaller

---

[1]Using preferred stock also adds to financial risk. To simplify matters somewhat, in this chapter we shall consider only debt and common equity.

[2]Two examples of "safe" industries that turned out to be risky are the railroads just before automobiles, airplanes, and trucks took away most of their business and the telegraph business just before telephones came on the scene.

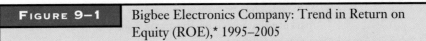

FIGURE 9–1	Bigbee Electronics Company: Trend in Return on Equity (ROE),* 1995–2005

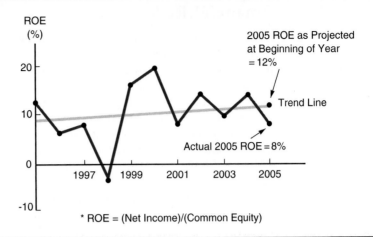

* ROE = (Net Income)/(Common Equity)

companies, especially single-product firms, also have a relatively high degree of business risk.[3]

Business risk depends on a number of factors, the more important of which include the following:

1. *Sales variability (volume and price).* The more stable the unit sales (volume) and prices of a firm's products, other things held constant, the lower its business risk.
2. *Input price variability.* A firm whose input prices—labor, product costs, and so forth—are highly uncertain is exposed to a high degree of business risk.
3. *Ability to adjust output prices for changes in input prices.* Some firms have little difficulty in raising the prices of their products when input costs rise; the greater the ability to adjust selling prices, the lower the degree of business risk. This factor is especially important during periods of high inflation.
4. *The extent to which costs are fixed: operating leverage.* If a high percentage of a firm's operating costs are fixed and hence do not decline when demand falls off, this increases the company's business risk. This factor is called *operating leverage*, which will be discussed in greater detail later in the chapter.

Each of these factors is determined partly by the firm's industry characteristics, but each also is controllable to some extent by management. For example, most firms can, through their marketing policies, take actions to stabilize both unit sales and sales prices. However, this stabilization might require either large expenditures on advertising or price concessions to induce customers to commit to purchasing fixed quantities at fixed prices in the future. Similarly, firms like Bigbee Electronics can reduce the volatility of future input costs by negotiating long-term labor and materials supply

---

[3]We have avoided any discussion of market versus company-specific risk in this section. We note now that (1) any action that increases business risk will generally increase a firm's beta coefficient, but (2) a part of business risk as we define it will generally be company-specific and hence subject to elimination through diversification by the firm's stockholders.

contracts, but they might have to agree to pay prices somewhat above the current market price to obtain these contracts.

Financial Risk

Financial risk results from using **financial leverage,** which exists when a firm uses fixed income securities, such as debt and preferred stock, to raise capital. When financial leverage is created, a firm intensifies the business risk borne by the common stockholders. To illustrate, suppose 10 people decide to form a corporation to produce operating systems for personal computers. There is a certain amount of business risk in the operation. If the firm is capitalized only with common equity, and if each person buys 10 percent of the stock, then each investor will bear an equal share of the business risk. However, suppose the firm is capitalized with 50 percent debt and 50 percent equity, with five of the investors putting up their capital as debt and the other five putting up their money as equity. In this case, the cash flows received by the debtholders are based on a contractual agreement, so the investors who put up the equity will have to bear essentially all of the business risk, and their position will be twice as risky as it would have been had the firm been financed only with equity. Thus, *the use of debt intensifies the firm's business risk borne by the common stockholders.*

In the next section, we will explain how financial leverage affects a firm's expected earnings per share, the riskiness of those earnings, and, consequently, the price of the firm's stock. As you will see, the value of a firm that has no debt first rises as it substitutes debt for equity, then hits a peak, and finally declines as the use of debt becomes excessive. The objective of our analysis is to determine the capital structure at which *value is maximized;* this point is then used as the target capital structure.[4]

Self-Test Questions

What is the difference between business risk and financial risk?

Identify and briefly explain some of the more important factors that affect business risk.

Why does business risk vary from one industry to another?

What creates financial risk?

Determining the Optimal Capital Structure

We can illustrate the effects of financial leverage using the data shown in Table 9–1 for a fictional company, which we will call OptiCap. As shown in the top section of the table, the company has no debt. Should it continue the policy of using no debt, or should it start using financial leverage? If it does decide to substitute debt for

---

[4]In this chapter we examine capital structures on a book value (or balance sheet) basis. An alternative approach is to calculate the market values of debt, preferred stock, and common equity and then to reconstruct the balance sheet on a market value basis. Although the market value approach is more consistent with financial theory, bond rating agencies and most financial executives focus their attention on book values. Moreover, the conversion from book to market values is a complicated process, and because market value capital structures change with stock market fluctuations, they are thought by many to be too unstable to serve as operationally useful targets. Finally, exactly the same insights are gained from the book value and market value analyses. For all these reasons, a market value analysis of capital structure is better suited for advanced finance courses.

TABLE 9-1	Financial Information for OptiCap, 2005 ($ thousands, except per-share values)

I. Balance Sheet on 12/31/05

Current assets	$100	Debt	$ 0
Net fixed assets	100	Common equity (10,000 shares)	200
Total assets	$200	Total liabilities and equity	$200

II. Income Statement for 2005

Sales	$200
Variable operating costs (60%)	(120)
Fixed operating costs	(40)
Earnings before interest and taxes (EBIT)	$ 40
Interest	0
Taxable income	$ 40
Taxes (40%)	(16)
Net income	$ 24

III. Per-Share Information

Earnings per share = EPS = $24,000/10,000 shares = $2.40.

Dividends per share = DPS = $24,000/10,000 shares = $2.40. Thus, OptiCap pays out all its earnings as dividends.

Book value per share = $200,000/10,000 shares = $20.

Market price per share = P_0 = $20. Thus, the stock sells at its book value, so (Market price)/(Book price) = M/B = 1.0.

---

equity, how far should it go? As in all such decisions, the correct answer is that it should *choose the combination of debt and equity, or a capital structure, that will maximize the price of the firm's stock.*

To answer the questions posed in the previous paragraph, we examine the effects of changing OptiCap's capital structure while keeping all other factors, such as the level of operations, constant. To keep all other factors constant, we assume that OptiCap changes its capital structure by *substituting* debt for equity—that is, new debt is issued and the proceeds are used to repurchase an equal amount of outstanding stock.

EPS Analysis of the Effects of Financial Leverage

If a firm changes the percentage of debt used to finance existing assets, we would expect the earnings per share and, consequently, the stock price to change as well. Remember that debt requires fixed payments, regardless of the firm's level of sales. To understand the relationship between financial leverage and earnings per share (EPS), we first examine how earnings per share are affected when our illustrative firm changes its capital structure to include greater relative amounts of debt.

TABLE 9–2	Cost of Debt, k_d, and Number of Common Shares Outstanding for OptiCap at Different Capital Structures ($ thousands)

TOTAL ASSETS	DEBT/ASSETS RATIO	AMOUNT BORROWED[a]	COMMON STOCK	SHARES OUTSTANDING[b]	COST OF DEBT, k_d
$200	0%	$ 0	$200	10,000	—
200	10	20	180	9,000	8.0%
200	20	40	160	8,000	8.3
200	30	60	140	7,000	9.0
200	40	80	120	6,000	10.0
200	50	100	100	5,000	12.0
200	60	120	80	4,000	15.0

[a]We assume the firm must borrow in increments of $20 thousand. We also assume that OptiCap cannot borrow more than $120 thousand, or 60 percent of assets, because of restrictions in its corporate charter.

[b]We assume that OptiCap uses the amount of funds raised by borrowing (issuing debt) to repurchase existing common stock at the current market value, which is $20 per share; thus, we assume there are no commissions or other transaction costs associated with repurchasing the stock. For example, if OptiCap's capital structure contains 40 percent debt, then $80 thousand of the $200 thousand total assets is financed with debt. We assume that if OptiCap borrows the $80 thousand, it would repurchase 4,000 shares = $80 million/$20 of its existing shares of common stock; hence 6,000 shares = 10,000 shares – 4,000 shares remain.

First, to simplify our example, we assume that OptiCap's level of operations—that is, production and sales—will not change if its capital structure changes.[5] Table 9–1 shows that OptiCap's level of sales was $200,000, which produced a net operating income (NOI), or earnings before interest and taxes (EBIT), equal to $40,000 in 2005. We expect that the firm's sales will remain at this level when economic conditions are "normal," but sales are expected to be $300,000 when the economy is booming and $100,000 when the economy is in a recession. The probabilities associated with each of these economic states are 0.6, 0.2, and 0.2, respectively. We give the different economic states so that we can see what happens to OptiCap's financial risk when its capital structure is changed.

OptiCap asked its investment banker to help determine what the cost of debt, k_d, will be at various levels of debt. The results are shown in Table 9–2. Naturally, we would expect that as a firm increases the percentage of debt it uses, the riskier

---

[5]In the real world, capital structure *does* at times affect EBIT. First, if debt levels are excessive, the firm probably will not be able to finance at all if its earnings are low at a time when interest rates are high. This could lead to stop-start construction and research and development programs, as well as to the necessity of passing up good investment opportunities. Second, a weak financial condition (i.e., too much debt) could cause a firm to lose sales. For example, prior to the time that its huge debt forced Eastern Airlines into bankrupcy, many people refused to buy Eastern tickets because they were afraid the company would go bankrupt and leave them holding unusable tickets. Third, financially strong companies can bargain hard with unions as well as with their suppliers, whereas weaker ones may have to give in simply because they do not have the financial resources to carry on the fight. Finally, a company with so much debt that bankruptcy is a serious threat will have difficulty attracting and retaining managers and employees, or it will have to pay premium salaries. For all these reasons, it is not totally correct to say that a firm's financial policy has no effect on its operating income.

lenders will perceive the debt to be, because the chance of financial distress is higher. As a result, lenders will charge higher interest rates to the firm as its percentage of debt increases, which is the pattern shown in the table.

We assume that OptiCap does not retain any earnings for reinvestment in the firm—that is, all earnings are paid to shareholders, which currently consist of stockholders only. In addition, we assume that the size of the firm remains at its current level. As long as the firm pays all earnings to shareholders and no additional funds are raised, growth will equal zero ($g = 0$), and future production and sales operations will continue as outlined previously. Thus any changes in EPS that we observe when the proportion of debt is changed will be a direct result of changing the firm's capital structure, not its level of operations.

Table 9–3 compares OptiCap's expected EPS at two levels of financial leverage: (1) zero debt, which is the existing capital structure; and (2) 50 percent debt. If OptiCap does not change its capital structure, all $200,000 of its assets will be financed with stock, so the interest expense will be zero because no debt exists. Section II of Table 9–3 shows that EPS is expected to be $2.40 with this capital structure—EPS will be as high as $4.80 and as low as $0, but, on average, it will be $2.40. We also calculate the standard deviation of EPS and the coefficient of variation as indicators of the firm's risk with this capital structure: $\sigma_{EPS} = \$1.52$, and $CV_{EPS} = 0.63$.[6]

Section III of Table 9–3 shows the effect on EPS of shifting OptiCap's capital structure so that the mix of financing is 50 percent debt and 50 percent equity; that is, when the $200,000 assets is financed with $100,000 debt and $100,000 equity. To accomplish this shift, OptiCap would issue $100,000 of debt and repurchase $100,000 of its existing equity. If we assume that stock can be repurchased at its current market price and transaction costs are negligible, then, using the information given in Table 9–1, we find that OptiCap can repurchase 5,000 shares = $100,000/$20 per share.[7] Thus the number of shares outstanding will decrease from 10,000 to 5,000. At the same time, because the firm now has debt, it will have to pay interest, which, according to the schedule given in Table 9–2, will equal $12,000 = $100,000 × 0.12 per year. The $12,000 interest expense is a fixed cost—it is the same regardless of the level of sales. With a debt/assets ratio of 50 percent, the expected EPS is $3.36, which is $0.96 higher than if the firm uses no debt. The EPS range is also greater; EPS can be as low as $(1.44) when the economy is poor or as high as $8.16 when the economy is booming. Thus, EPS has greater variability when the capital structure is 50 percent debt and 50 percent equity, which suggests that this capital structure is riskier than the capital structure of 100 percent equity financing. The standard deviation of EPS and the coefficient of variation computed

---

[6]See Chapter 4 for a review of procedures for calculating standard deviations and coefficients of variation. Recall that the advantage of the coefficient of variation is that it permits better comparisons when the expected values of EPS vary, as they do here for the two capital structures.

[7]We assume in this example that the firm could change its capital structure by repurchasing common stock at the current market value, which is $20 per share. However, if the firm attempts to purchase a large block of its stock, demand pressures might cause the market price to increase, in which case OptiCap would not be able to purchase 5,000 shares with the $100,000 that was raised with its debt issue. Also, we assume the flotation costs associated with the debt issue are negligible, so that OptiCap is able to use all $100,000 to repurchase stock. Clearly, the existence of flotation costs would mean OptiCap would have some amount less than $100,000 to repurchase stock. Neither of these assumptions affects the overall concept we are trying to provide through illustration—only the numbers change.

TABLE 9-3	OptiCap: EPS at Different Capital Structures ($ thousands, except per-share values)

I. Calculation of EBIT

Probability of indicated sales	0.2	0.6	0.2
Sales	$ 100.0	$ 200.0	$ 300.0
Variable costs (60% of sales)	(60.0)	(120.0)	(180.0)
Fixed costs	(40.0)	(40.0)	(40.0)
Total costs (except interest)	$(100.0)	$(160.0)	$(220.0)
Earnings before interest and taxes (EBIT)	$ 0.0	$ 40.0	$ 80.0

II. Situation If Debt/Assets (D/A) = 0%

EBIT (from Section I)	$ 0.0	$ 40.0	$ 80.0
Less interest	(0.0)	(0.0)	(0.0)
Earnings before taxes (EBT)	$ 0.0	$ 40.0	$ 80.0
Taxes (40%)	(0.0)	(16.0)	(32.0)
Net income	$ 0.0	$ 24.0	$ 48.0
Earnings per share (EPS) on 10,000 shares[a]	$ 0.0	$ 2.40	$ 4.80
Expected EPS		$ 2.40	
Standard deviation of EPS		$ 1.52	
Coefficient of variation		0.63	

III. Situation If Debt/Assets (D/A) = 50%

EBIT (from Section I)	$ 0.0	$ 40.0	$ 80.0
Less interest (0.12 × $100)	(12.0)	(12.0)	(12.0)
Earnings before taxes (EBT)	$(12.0)	$ 28.0	$ 68.0
Taxes (40%; tax credit on losses)	4.8	(11.2)	(27.2)
Net income	$(7.2)	$ 16.8	$ 40.8
Earnings per share (EPS) on 5,000 shares[a]	$(1.44)	$ 3.36	$ 8.16
Expected EPS		$ 3.36	
Standard deviation of EPS		$ 3.04	
Coefficient of variation		0.90	

[a]The EPS figures can be obtained using the following formula, in which the numerator amounts to an income statement at a given sales level laid out horizontally:

$$\text{EPS} = \frac{(\text{Sales} - \text{Fixed costs} - \text{Variable costs} - \text{Interest})(1 - \text{Tax rate})}{\text{Shares outstanding}} = \frac{(\text{EBIT} - \text{I})(1 - \text{T})}{\text{Shares outstanding}}$$

For example, with zero debt and Sales = $200,000, EPS is $2.40:

$$\text{EPS}_{\text{D/A}=0} = \frac{(\$200,000 - \$40,000 - \$120,000 - 0)(0.6)}{10,000} = \$2.40$$

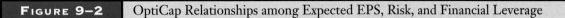

| FIGURE 9–2 | OptiCap Relationships among Expected EPS, Risk, and Financial Leverage |

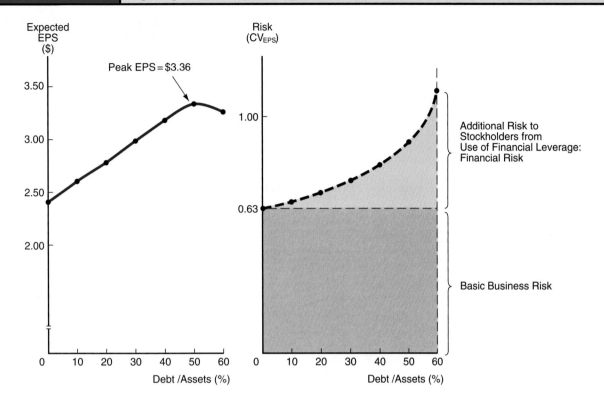

Debt/Assets Ratio	Expected EPS	Standard Deviation of EPS	Coefficient of Variation
0%[a]	$2.40[a]	$1.52[a]	0.63[a]
10	2.56	1.69	0.66
20	2.75	1.90	0.69
30	2.97	2.17	0.73
40	3.20	2.53	0.79
50[a]	3.36[a]	3.04[a]	0.90[a]
60	3.30	3.79	1.15

[a]Values for D/A = 0 and D/A = 50 percent are taken from Table 9–3. Values at other D/A ratios were calculated similarly.

for the capital structure with 50 percent debt are: σ_{EPS} = $3.04 and CV_{EPS} = 0.90. As you can see, these computations support our suspicion that this capital structure is riskier than the capital structure shown in Section II of Table 9–3.

Figure 9–2 shows the relationships among expected EPS, risk, and financial leverage for OptiCap for the all-equity capital structure and the various capital structures given in Table 9–2. The tabular data in the lower section were calculated in the manner set forth in Table 9–3, and the graph plots these data. Here we see that expected EPS rises until the firm is financed with 50 percent debt. Interest charges rise, but this effect is more than offset by the declining number of shares outstanding as debt is substituted for equity. EPS peaks at a debt/assets ratio of 50 percent. Beyond this amount, interest rates rise so rapidly that EPS declines despite the smaller number of shares outstanding.

The right panel of Figure 9–2 shows that risk, as measured by the coefficient of variation of EPS, rises continuously and at an increasing rate as debt is substituted for equity.

We see, then, that using leverage has both good and bad effects. Higher leverage increases expected earnings per share (in this example, until the firm is financed with 50 percent debt), but it also increases the firm's risk. Clearly, for OptiCap, the debt/assets ratio should not exceed 50 percent. But where in the range of 0 to 50 percent is the best debt/assets ratio for OptiCap? This issue is discussed in the following sections.

EBIT/EPS Examination of Financial Leverage

In the previous section, we assumed that OptiCap's EBIT had to be one of three possible values: $0, $40,000, or $80,000. Another way of evaluating alternative financing methods is to plot the EPS of each capital structure at many different levels of EBIT. Figure 9–3 shows such a graph for the two capital structures we considered for OptiCap in Table 9–3—that is, (1) 100 percent stock and (2) 50 percent stock and 50 percent debt. Notice that at low levels of EBIT, and hence low levels of sales, EPS is higher if OptiCap's capital structure includes only stock; at high levels of EBIT, however, EPS is higher with the capital structure that includes debt. Notice also that the "debt" line has a steeper slope, showing that earnings per share will increase more rapidly with increases in EBIT, and hence sales, if the firm uses debt. This relationship exists because the firm has a greater degree of financial leverage with the capital structure that includes 50 percent debt. In this case, the benefits of additional sales need not be shared with debtholders because debt payments are fixed; instead, any profits that remain after debtholders are paid "belong" to stockholders.

EPS INDIFFERENCE POINT

The level of sales at which EPS will be the same whether the firm uses debt or common stock financing.

The point on the graph where the two lines intersect is called the **EPS indifference point,** which is the level of sales where EPS is the same no matter which capital structure OptiCap uses. In Figure 9–3, the two lines cross where sales equal $160,000, which corresponds to EBIT equal to $24,000. If sales are below $160,000, EPS would be higher if the firm uses only common stock; above this level, the debt financing alternative would produce higher earnings per share.

If we were certain that sales would never again fall below $160,000, bonds would be the preferred method of financing any increases in assets. We cannot know this for certain, however. In fact, investors know that in a number of previous years, sales have fallen below this critical level, and if any of several detrimental events should occur in the future, sales again would fall below $160,000. On the other hand, if sales continue to expand, higher earnings per share would result from the use of bonds, and this is an advantage that no investor would want to forgo.

The Effect of Capital Structure on Stock Prices and the Cost of Capital

As we saw in Figure 9–2, OptiCap's expected EPS is maximized at a debt/assets ratio of 50 percent. Does this mean that OptiCap's optimal capital structure calls for 50 percent debt? The answer is a resounding "no." *The optimal capital structure is the one that maximizes the price of the firm's stock, and this always calls for a debt/assets ratio that is lower than the one that maximizes expected EPS.* As we shall discover shortly, the

| FIGURE 9-3 | Earnings per Share of Stock and Debt Financing for OptiCap |

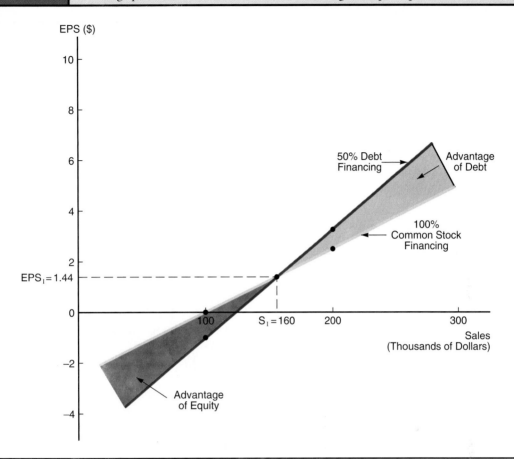

We can develop an equation to find the sales level at which EPS is the same under different degrees of financial leverage:

$$EPS_1 = \frac{S_I - F - VC - I_1}{Shares_1} = \frac{S_I - F - VC - I_2}{Shares_2} = EPS_2$$

Here, EPS_1 and EPS_2 are the EPSs at two debt levels; S_I is the sales indifference level at which $EPS_1 = EPS_2 = EPS_I$; I_1 and I_2 are interest charges at the two debt levels; $Shares_1$ and $Shares_2$ are shares outstanding at the two debt levels; F is the fixed costs; and VC = variable costs = Sales × v, where v is the variable cost percentage. Solving for S_I, we obtain this expression:

$$S_I = \left[\frac{(Shares_2)(I_1) - (Shares_1)(I_2)}{Shares_2 - Shares_1} + F\right]\left(\frac{1}{1 - v}\right)$$

In our example,

$$S_I = \left[\frac{(5,000)(0) - (10,000)(\$12,000)}{-5,000} + \$40,000\right]\left(\frac{1}{0.4}\right) = \$160,000$$

primary reason this relationship exists is because P_0 reflects changes in risk that accompany changes in capital structures and affect cash flows long into the future, whereas EPS generally measures only the expectations for the near term. That is, current EPS generally does not capture future risk, whereas P_0 should be indicative of all future expectations. Our analysis to this point has, therefore, indicated that OptiCap's optimal capital structure should contain something less than 50 percent

| TABLE 9–4 | | Stock Price and Cost of Capital Estimates for OptiCap with Different Debt/Assets Ratios | | | | |

DEBT/ ASSETS (1)	k_d (2)	EXPECTED EPS (AND DPS)[a] (3)	ESTIMATED BETA (4)	$k_s = [k_{RF} + (k_M - k_{RF})\beta_s]$[b] (5)	ESTIMATED PRICE[c] (6)	WEIGHTED AVERAGE COST OF CAPITAL, WACC[d] (7)
0%	—	$2.40	1.60	12.0%	$20.00	12.00%
10	8.0%	2.56	1.70	12.5	20.48	11.73
20	8.3	2.75	1.80	13.0	21.15	11.40
30	9.0	2.97	2.00	14.0	21.21	11.42
40	10.0	3.20	2.10	14.5	22.07	11.10
50	12.0	3.36	2.30	15.5	21.68	11.35
60	15.0	3.30	2.60	17.0	19.41	12.20

NOTES:

[a]OptiCap pays all of its earnings out as dividends, so EPS = DPS.

[b]We assume that $k_{RF} = 4\%$ and $k_M = 9\%$. Therefore, at debt/assets equal to zero, $k_s = 4\% + (9\% - 4\%)1.6 = 4\% + 8\% = 12\%$. Other values of k_s are calculated similarly.

[c]Because all earnings are paid out as dividends, no retained earnings will be plowed back into the business, and growth in EPS and DPS will be zero. Hence, the zero growth stock price model developed in Chapter 5 can be used to estimate the price of OptiCap's stock. For example, at debt/assets = 0,

$$\hat{P}_0 = \frac{\hat{D}_1}{k_s} = \frac{\$2.40}{0.12} = \$20$$

Other prices were calculated similarly.

[d]Column 7 is found by use of the weighted average cost of capital (WACC) equation developed in Chapter 8:

$$WACC = w_d k_d (1 - T) + w_s k_s$$
$$= (D/A)(k_{dT}) + (1 - D/A)k_s$$

For example, at D/A = 40%,

$$WACC = 0.4[(10\%)(0.06)] + 0.06(14.5\%) = 11.10\%$$

debt. The validity of this statement is demonstrated in Table 9–4, which develops OptiCap's estimated stock price and weighted average cost of capital at different debt/assets ratios. The debt cost and EPS data in Columns 2 and 3 were taken from Table 9–2 and Figure 9–2. The beta coefficients shown in Column 4 were estimated. Recall from Chapter 4 that a stock's beta measures its relative volatility compared with the volatility of an average stock. It has been demonstrated both theoretically and empirically that a firm's beta increases with its degree of financial leverage. The exact nature of this relationship for a given firm is difficult to estimate, but the values given in Column 4 do show the approximate nature of the relationship for OptiCap.

If we assume that the risk-free rate of return, k_{RF}, is 4 percent and that the required return on an average stock, k_M, is 9 percent, we can use the CAPM equation to develop estimates of the required rates of return, k_s, for OptiCap as shown in Column 5. Here we see that k_s is 12 percent if no financial leverage is used, but k_s rises to 17 percent if the company finances with 60 percent debt, the maximum permitted by its corporate charter.

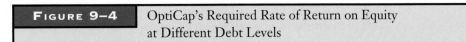

| FIGURE 9–4 | OptiCap's Required Rate of Return on Equity at Different Debt Levels |

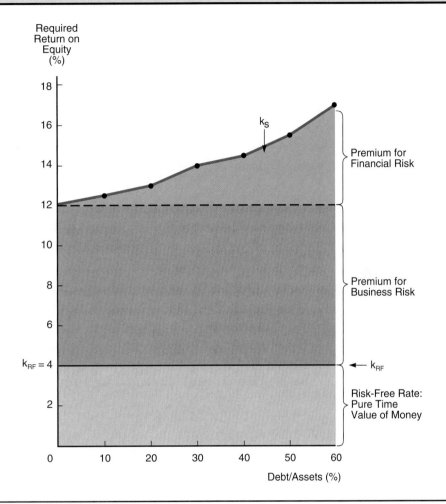

Figure 9–4 graphs OptiCap's required rate of return on equity at different debt levels. The figure also shows the composition of OptiCap's required return: the risk-free rate of 4 percent and the premiums for both business and financial risk, which were discussed earlier in this chapter. As you can see from the graph, the business risk premium does not depend on the debt level. Instead, it remains constant at 8 percent, which is the difference between the 12 percent WACC when the firm is financed with 100 percent equity and the risk-free rate of 4 percent (8% = 12% − 4%), at all debt levels. However, the financial risk premium varies depending on the debt level—the higher the debt level, the greater the premium for financial risk.

The zero growth stock valuation model developed in Chapter 5 is used in Table 9–4, along with the Column 3 values of dividends per share (DPS) and the Column 5 values of k_s, to develop the estimated stock prices shown in Column 6. Here we see that the expected stock price first rises with financial leverage, hits a peak of $22.07 at a debt/assets ratio of 40 percent, and then begins to decline. *Thus, OptiCap's optimal capital structure calls for 40 percent debt.*

Finally, Column 7 shows OptiCap's weighted average cost of capital (WACC), calculated as described in Chapter 8, at the different capital structures. If the company uses zero debt, its capital is all equity, so WACC = k_s = 12%. As the firm begins to use lower-cost debt, its weighted average cost of capital declines. However, as the debt/assets ratio increases, the costs of both debt and equity rise, and the increasing costs of the two components begin to offset the fact that larger amounts of the lower-cost component are being used. At 40 percent debt, WACC hits a minimum at 11.10 percent, then it begins rising as the debt/assets ratio is increased.

The EPS, cost of capital, and stock price data shown in Table 9–4 are plotted in Figure 9–5. As the graph shows, the debt/assets ratio that maximizes OptiCap's expected EPS is 50 percent. However, the expected stock price is maximized, and the cost of capital is minimized, at a 40 percent debt/assets ratio. Thus, *the optimal capital structure calls for 40 percent debt and 60 percent equity. Management should set its target capital structure at these ratios, and if the existing ratios are off target, it should move toward the target when new security offerings are made.*

Self-Test Questions

Explain the following statement: "Using leverage has both good and bad effects."

What does the EPS indifference point show? What occurs at sales below this point? What occurs at sales above this point?

Is the optimal capital structure the one that maximizes expected EPS? Explain.

Explain the following statement: "At the optimal capital structure, a firm has minimized its cost of capital." Do stockholders want the firm to minimize its cost of capital?

Degree of Leverage[8]

Leverage, whether operating or financial, is created when a firm has *fixed costs* associated either with its sales and production operations or with the types of financing it uses. These two types of leverage—operating and financial—are interrelated. Therefore, if OptiCap *reduced* its operating leverage, this probably would lead to an *increase* in its optimal use of financial leverage. On the other hand, if the firm decided to *increase* its operating leverage, its optimal capital structure probably would call for *less* debt.

The theory of finance has not been developed to the point where we can actually specify simultaneously the optimal levels of operating and financial leverage. However, we can see how operating and financial leverage interact through an analysis of the *degree of leverage concept.*

Degree of Operating Leverage (DOL)

DEGREE OF OPERATING LEVERAGE (DOL)
The percentage change in operating income (EBIT) associated with a given percentage change in sales.

The **degree of operating leverage (DOL)** is defined as the percentage change in operating income—that is, earnings before interest and taxes, or EBIT—associated with a given percentage change in sales. Thus, the degree of operating leverage is computed as

---

[8]A more detailed discussion of leverage is presented in Chapter 12, and the derivations of the equations contained in this section are included in the footnotes in that chapter.

FIGURE 9–5 Relationship between OptiCap's Capital Structure and Its EPS, Cost of Capital, and Stock Price

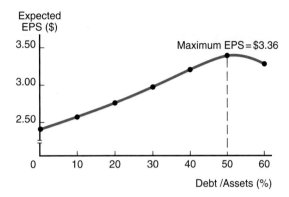

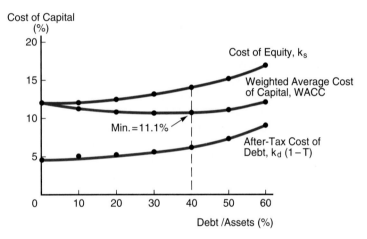

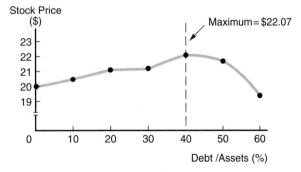

9–1

$$\text{DOL} = \frac{\%\text{ change in NOI}}{\%\text{ change in sales}} = \frac{\left(\dfrac{\Delta\text{EBIT}}{\text{EBIT}}\right)}{\left(\dfrac{\Delta\text{Sales}}{\text{Sales}}\right)} = \frac{\left(\dfrac{\Delta\text{EBIT}}{\text{EBIT}}\right)}{\left(\dfrac{\Delta Q}{Q}\right)}$$

According to Equation 9–1, the DOL is an index number that measures the effect of a change in sales on operating income, or EBIT.

DOL for a particular level of production and sales can be computed using the following equation:

9–2

$$DOL = \frac{Q(P - V)}{Q(P - V) - F} = \frac{S - VC}{S - VC - F} = \frac{\text{Gross Profit}}{\text{EBIT}}$$

Here, Q is the initial units of output, P is the average sales price per unit of output, V is the variable cost per unit, F is fixed operating costs, S is initial sales in dollars, and VC is total variable costs.

Applying Equation 9–2 to data for OptiCap at a sales level of $200,000 as shown back in Table 9–3, we find its degree of operating leverage to be 2.0:

$$DOL_{\$200,000} = \frac{\$200,000 - \$120,000}{\$200,000 - \$120,000 - \$40,000} = \frac{\$80,000}{\$40,000} = 2.0 \times$$

Thus, for every 1 percent change (increase or decrease) in sales there will be a 2 percent change (increase or decrease) in EBIT. This situation is confirmed by examining Section I of Table 9–3, where we see that a 50 percent increase in sales, from $200,000 to $300,000, causes EBIT to double. Note, however, that if sales decrease by 50 percent, then EBIT will decrease by 100 percent; according to Table 9–3, EBIT decreases to $0 if sales decrease to $100,000.

Note also that the DOL is specific to the initial sales level; thus, if we evaluated OptiCap from a sales base of $300,000, there would be a different DOL:

$$DOL_{\$300,000} = \frac{\$300,000 - \$180,000}{\$300,000 - \$180,000 - \$40,000} = \frac{\$120,000}{\$80,000} = 1.5$$

In general, if a firm is operating at close to its breakeven level, the degree of operating leverage will be high, but DOL declines the higher the base level of sales is above breakeven sales. All else equal, *a lower (higher) DOL suggests that lower (higher) risk is associated with the firm's normal operating activities.*

Degree of Financial Leverage (DFL)

DEGREE OF FINANCIAL LEVERAGE (DFL)
The percentage change in earnings per share (EPS) associated with a given percentage change in earnings before interest and taxes.

Operating leverage affects earnings before interest and taxes (EBIT), whereas financial leverage affects earnings after interest and taxes, or the earnings available to common stockholders. In terms of Table 9–3, operating leverage affects the top section (Section I), whereas financial leverage affects the lower sections (Sections II and III). *Financial leverage takes over where operating leverage leaves off, further magnifying the effects on earnings per share of changes in the level of sales.*

The **degree of financial leverage (DFL)** is defined as the percentage change in earnings per share (EPS) that results from a given percentage change in earnings before interest and taxes (EBIT), and it is calculated as follows:[9]

---

[9]This equation applies only if the firm has no preferred stock. See Chapter 12 for the equation that is appropriate when preferred stock exists.

$$9\text{-}3 \qquad \text{DFL} = \frac{\%\ \text{change in EPS}}{\%\ \text{change in EBIT}} = \frac{\left(\dfrac{\Delta EPS}{EPS}\right)}{\left(\dfrac{\Delta EBIT}{EBIT}\right)} = \frac{EBIT}{EBIT - I}$$

At sales of \$200,000 and an EBIT of \$40,000, the degree of financial leverage when OptiCap has a 50 percent debt/assets ratio (Section III in Table 9–3) is:

$$\text{DFL}_{S=\$200,000,\ \text{Debt}/TA\ =\ 50\%} = \frac{\$40,000}{\$40,000 - \$12,000} = 1.43\times$$

Therefore, a 100 percent change (increase or decrease) in EBIT would result in a $100(1.43) = 143$ percent change (increase or decrease) in earnings per share. This can be confirmed by referring Section III of Table 9–3, where we see that a 100 percent increase in EBIT, from \$40,000 to \$80,000, produces a 143 percent increase in EPS:

$$\%\Delta EPS = \frac{\Delta EPS}{EPS_0} = \frac{\$8.16 - \$3.36}{\$3.36} = \frac{\$4.80}{\$3.36} = 1.43 = 143\%$$

If no debt were used, the degree of financial leverage would by definition be 1.0, so a 100 percent increase in EBIT would produce exactly a 100 percent increase in EPS. This can be confirmed from the data in Section II of Table 9–3. All else equal, *a lower (higher) DFL suggests that lower (higher) risk is associated with the firm's financing—that is, the mix of debt and equity.*

Degree of Total Leverage (DTL)

**DEGREE OF TOTAL
LEVERAGE (DTL)**
The percentage change in
EPS that results from a
given percentage change
in sales; DTL shows the
effects of both operating
leverage and financial
leverage.

We have seen that (1) the greater the degree of operating leverage (or fixed operating costs), the more sensitive EBIT will be to changes in sales, and (2) the greater the degree of financial leverage (fixed financial costs), the more sensitive EPS will be to changes in EBIT. Therefore, if a firm uses a considerable amount of both operating and financial leverage, then even small changes in sales will lead to wide fluctuations in EPS.

Equation 9–2 for the degree of operating leverage can be combined with Equation 9–3 for the degree of financial leverage to produce the equation for the **degree of total leverage (DTL),** which shows how a given change in sales will affect earnings per share. Here are three equivalent equations for DTL:

$$9\text{-}4 \qquad \text{DTL} = \frac{\text{Percentage change in sales}}{\text{Percentage change in EPS}} = (\text{DOL}) \times (\text{DFL})$$

$$= \frac{Q(P - V)}{Q(P - V) - F - I}$$

$$= \frac{S - VC}{S - VC - F - I} = \frac{\text{Gross profit}}{EBIT - I}$$

For OptiCap at sales of $200,000, we can substitute data from Table 9–3 into Equation 9–4 to find the degree of total leverage if the debt ratio is 50 percent:

$$\text{DTL}_{S = \$200,000, \text{Debt/TA} = 50\%} = \frac{\$200,000 - \$120,000}{\$200,000 - \$120,000 - \$40,000 - \$12,000} = \frac{\$80,000}{\$28,000}$$

$$= 2.00 \times 1.43 = 2.86$$

We can use the degree of total leverage (DTL) to find the new earnings per share (EPS_1) for any given percentage increase in sales, proceeding as follows:

9–5	
	$\text{EPS}_1 = \text{EPS}_0 + \text{EPS}_0[(\text{DTL}) \times (\%\Delta\text{Sales})]$
	$= \text{EPS}_0[1.0 + (\text{DTL}) \times (\%\Delta\text{Sales})]$

For example, a 50 percent (or 0.5) increase in sales, from $200,000 to $300,000, would cause EPS_0 ($3.36 as shown in Section III of Table 9–3) to increase to $8.16:

$$\text{EPS}_1 = \$3.36[1.0 + (2.86)(0.5)] = \$3.36(2.43) = \$8.16.$$

This figure agrees with the one for EPS shown in Table 9–3. All else equal, *a lower (higher) DTL suggests that lower (higher) risk is associated with the firm*, both its business, risk and financial risk—that is, total risk.

The degree of leverage concept is useful primarily for the insights it provides regarding the joint effects of operating and financial leverage on earnings per share. The concept can be used to show management the effect of financing the firm with debt versus common stock. For example, management might find that the current capital structure is such that a 10 percent decline in sales would produce a 50 percent decline in earnings, whereas with a different financing package, thus a different degree of total leverage, a 10 percent sales decline would cause earnings to decline by perhaps only 20 percent. Having the alternatives stated in this manner gives decision makers a better idea of the ramifications of alternative financing plans, hence different capital structures.[10]

Self-Test Questions

Give the formula for calculating the degree of operating leverage (DOL), and explain what DOL is.

Why is the DOL different at various sales levels?

---

[10]The degree of leverage concept is also useful for investors. If firms in an industry are classified as to their degrees of total leverage, an investor who is optimistic about prospects for the industry might favor those firms with high leverage and vice versa if industry sales are expected to decline. However, it is very difficult to separate fixed from variable costs. Accounting statements generally do not contain this breakdown, so the analyst must make the separation in a judgmental manner. Note that costs really are fixed, variable, and "semivariable," for if times get tough enough, firms will sell off depreciable assets and thus reduce depreciation charges (a fixed cost), lay off "permanent" employees, reduce salaries of the remaining personnel, and so on. For this reason, the degree of leverage concept generally is more useful in explaining the general nature of the relationship than in developing precise numbers, and any numbers developed should be thought of as approximations rather than as exact specifications.

Give the formula for calculating the degree of financial leverage (DFL), and explain what this calculation means.

Give the formula for calculating the degree of total leverage (DTL), and explain what DTL is.

Why is the degree of leverage concept useful when making capital structure decisions?

Liquidity and Capital Structure

Some practical difficulties are associated with the type of analysis described in the previous section, including the following:

1. It is difficult to determine exactly how either P/E ratios or equity capitalization rates (k_s values) are affected by different degrees of financial leverage.
2. The managers might be more or less conservative than the average stockholder, so management might set a somewhat different target capital structure than the one that would maximize the stock price. The managers of a publicly owned firm never would admit this because, unless they owned voting control, they would be removed from office very quickly. However, in view of the uncertainties about what constitutes the value-maximizing capital structure, management could always say that the target capital structure employed is, in its judgment, the value-maximizing structure, and it would be difficult to prove otherwise. Still, if management is far off target, especially on the low side, then chances are very high that some other firm or management group will take over the company, increase its leverage, and thereby raise its value.
3. Managers of large firms, especially those that provide vital services such as electricity or telephones, have a responsibility to provide continuous service. Therefore, they must refrain from using leverage to the point where the firms' long-run survivals are endangered. Long-run viability might conflict with short-run stock price maximization and capital cost minimization.[11]

TIMES-INTEREST-EARNED (TIE) RATIO

A ratio that measures the firm's ability to meet its annual interest obligations; calculated by dividing earnings before interest and taxes by interest charges.

For all these reasons, managers are concerned about the effects of financial leverage on the risk of bankruptcy, and an analysis of this factor is therefore an important input in all capital structure decisions. Accordingly, managers give considerable weight to financial strength indicators such as the **times-interest-earned (TIE) ratio,** which is computed by dividing earnings before interest and taxes by interest expense. The TIE ratio provides an indication of how well the firm can cover its interest payments with operating income (EBIT)—the lower this ratio, the higher the probability that a firm will default on its debt and be forced into bankruptcy.

The tabular material in the lower section of Figure 9–6 shows OptiCap's expected TIE ratio at several different debt/assets ratios. If the debt/assets ratio was only

---

[11]Recognizing this fact, most public service commissions require utilities to obtain the commission's approval before issuing long-term securities, and Congress has empowered the SEC to supervise the capital structures of public utility holding companies. However, in addition to concern over the firms' safety, which suggests low debt ratios, both managers and regulators recognize a need to keep all costs as low as possible, including the cost of capital. Because a firm's capital structure affects its cost of capital, regulatory commissions and utility managers try to select capital structures that will minimize the cost of capital, subject to the constraint that the firm's financial flexibility not be endangered.

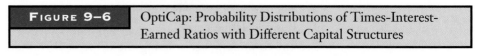

FIGURE 9–6   OptiCap: Probability Distributions of Times-Interest-Earned Ratios with Different Capital Structures

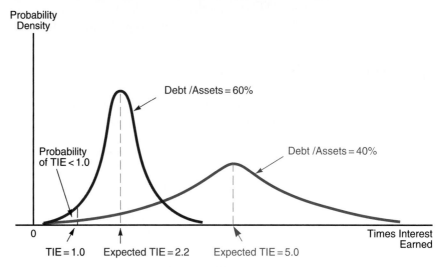

Debt/Assets	Expected TIE[a]
0%	Undefined
10	25.0
20	12.0
30	7.4
40	5.0
50	3.3
60	2.2

[a]TIE = EBIT/Interest. For example, when debt/assets = 50%, TIE = $40,000/$12,000 = 3.3. Data are from Tables 9–2 and 9–3.

10 percent, the expected TIE would be very high at 25 times, but the interest coverage ratio would decline rapidly if the debt/assets ratio was increased. Note, however, that these coverages are expected values at different debt/assets ratios; the actual TIE for any debt/assets ratio will be higher if sales exceed the expected $200,000 level, but lower if sales fall below $200,000.

The variability of the TIE ratio is highlighted in the graph in Figure 9–6, which shows the probability distributions of the TIEs at debt/assets ratios of 40 percent and 60 percent. The expected TIE is much higher if only 40 percent debt is used. In general, we know that with less debt, there is a much lower probability of a TIE of less than 1.0, the level at which the firm is not earning enough to meet its required interest payment and thus is seriously exposed to the threat of bankruptcy.[12]

---

[12]Note that cash flows can be sufficient to cover required interest payments even though the TIE is less than 1.0. Thus, at least for a while, a firm might be able to avoid bankruptcy even though its *operating income* is less than its interest charges. However, most debt contracts stipulate that firms must maintain the TIE ratio above some minimum level, say, 2.0 or 2.5, or else they cannot borrow any additional funds, which can severely constrain operations. Such potential constraints, as much as the threat of actual bankruptcy, limit the use of debt.

Self-Test Questions

Why do managers give considerable weight to the TIE ratio when they make capital structure decisions?

Why not just use the capital structure that maximizes the stock price?

Capital Structure Theory

Over the years, researchers have proposed numerous theories to explain what firms' capital structures should be and why firms have different capital structures. The general theories of capital structure have been developed along two main lines: (1) tax benefit/bankruptcy cost trade-off theory and (2) signaling theory. These two theories are discussed in this section.

Trade-Off Theory

Modern capital structure theory began in 1958, when Professors Franco Modigliani and Merton Miller (hereafter MM) published what is considered by many to be the most influential finance article ever written.[13] MM proved—under a very restrictive set of assumptions, including that there exist no personal income taxes, no brokerage costs, and no bankruptcy—that due to the tax deductibility of interest on corporate debt, a firm's value rises continuously as more debt is used, and hence its value will be maximized by financing almost entirely with debt.

Because several of the assumptions outlined by MM obviously were, and are, unrealistic, MM's position was only the beginning of capital structure research. Subsequent researchers, and MM themselves, extended the basic theory by relaxing the assumptions. Other researchers attempted to test the various theoretical models with actual data to see exactly how stock prices and capital costs are affected by capital structure. Both the theoretical and the empirical results have added to our understanding of capital structure, but none of these studies has produced results that can be used to precisely identify a firm's optimal capital structure. A summary of the theoretical and empirical research to date is expressed graphically in Figure 9–7. Here are the key points in the figure:

1. The fact that interest is a tax deductible expense makes corporate debt less expensive than common or preferred stock. In effect, the government pays, or subsidizes, part of the cost of debt capital; thus, using debt causes more of the firm's operating income (EBIT) to flow through to investors. So the more debt a company uses, the higher its value. Under the assumptions of the original MM paper, their analysis led to the conclusion that the firm's stock price will be maximized if it uses virtually 100 percent debt, and the line labeled "Pure MM Result" in Figure 9–7 expresses their relationship between stock prices and debt.

---

[13]Franco Modigliani and Merton H. Miller, "The Cost of Capital, Corporation Finance, and the Theory of Investment," *American Economic Review*, June 1958, 261–297, and "Corporate Income Taxes and the Cost of Capital," *American Economic Review*, June 1963, 433–443. Modigliani and Miller both won Nobel Prizes for their work.

FIGURE 9–7	Effect of Leverage on the Value of OptiCap's Stock

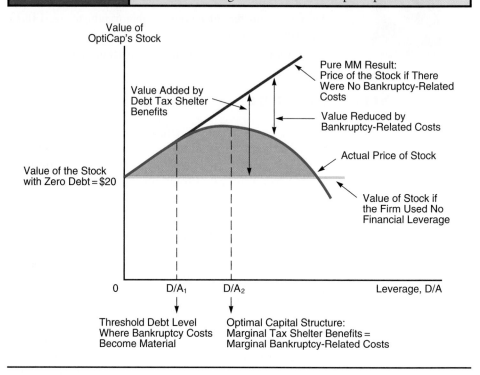

2. The MM assumptions do not hold in the real world. First, a firm pays higher interest rates as it uses greater amounts of debt. Second, expected tax rates fall at high debt levels, and this also reduces the expected value of the debt tax shelter. And, third, the probability of bankruptcy, which brings with it lawyers' fees and other costs, increases as the debt/assets ratio increases.

3. There is some threshold level of debt, labeled D/A_1 in Figure 9–7, below which the effects noted in Point 2 are immaterial. Beyond D/A_1, however, the bankruptcy-related costs, especially higher interest rates on new debt, become increasingly important, and they reduce the tax benefits of debt at an increasing rate. In the range from D/A_1 to D/A_2, bankruptcy-related costs reduce but do not completely offset the tax benefits of debt, so the firm's stock price rises (but at a decreasing rate) as the debt/assets ratio increases. However, beyond D/A_2 bankruptcy-related costs exceed the tax benefits, so from this point on increasing the debt/assets ratio lowers the value of the stock. Therefore, D/A_2 is the optimal capital structure.

4. Both theory and empirical evidence support the preceding discussion. However, researchers have not been able to identify points D/A_1 and D/A_2 precisely, so the graphs shown in Figures 9–5 and 9–7 must be taken as approximations, not as precisely defined functions.

5. Another disturbing aspect of capital structure theory as expressed in Figure 9–7 is the fact that many large, successful firms, such as Microsoft, use far less debt than the theory suggests. This point led to the development of signaling theory, which is discussed next.

Signaling Theory

SYMMETRIC
INFORMATION

The situation in which
investors and managers
have identical information
about the firm's prospects.

ASYMMETRIC
INFORMATION

The situation in which
managers have different
(better) information about
their firm's prospects than
do outside investors.

MM assumed that investors have the same information about a firm's prospects as its managers—this is called **symmetric information** because both those who are inside the firm (managers and employees) and those who are outside the firm (investors) have identical information. However, we know that in fact managers generally have better information about their firms than do outside investors. This is called **asymmetric information,** and it has an important effect on decisions to use either debt or equity to finance capital projects. To see why, consider two situations, one in which the company's managers know that its prospects are extremely favorable (Firm F) and one in which the managers know that the future looks very unfavorable (Firm U).

Suppose, for example, that Firm F's research and development labs have just discovered a cure for the common cold, but the product is not patentable. Firm F's managers want to keep the new product a secret for as long as possible to delay competitors' entry into the market. New plants and distribution facilities must be built to exploit the new product, so capital must be raised. How should Firm F's management raise the needed capital? If the firm sells stock, then when profits from the new product start flowing in, the price of the stock will rise sharply and the purchasers of the new stock will have made a bonanza. The current stockholders (including the managers) also will do well, but not as well as they would have if the company had not sold stock before the price increased, because then they would not have had to share the benefits of the new product with the new stockholders. *Therefore, one would expect a firm with very favorable prospects to try to avoid selling stock and, rather, to raise any required new capital by other means, including using debt beyond the normal target capital structure.*[14]

Now let's consider Firm U. Suppose its managers have information that new orders are off sharply because a competitor has installed new technology that has improved its products' quality. Firm U must upgrade its own facilities at a high cost, just to maintain its existing sales level. As a result, its return on investment will fall (but not by as much as if it took no action, which would lead to a 100 percent loss through bankruptcy). How should Firm U raise the needed capital? Here the situation is just the reverse of that facing Firm F, which did not want to sell stock so as to avoid having to share the benefits of future developments. *A firm with unfavorable prospects would want to sell stock, which would mean bringing in new investors to share the losses!*[15]

The conclusions from all this are that firms with extremely bright prospects prefer not to finance through new stock offerings, whereas firms with poor prospects do like to finance with outside equity. How would you, as an investor, react to these conclusions? You ought to say, "If I see that a company plans to issue new stock, this should worry me because I know that management would not want to issue stock if future prospects looked good, but it would want to issue stock if things looked bad. Therefore, I should lower my estimate of the firm's value, other things held constant, if I read an announcement of a new stock offering." Of course, the negative reaction would be stronger if the stock sale was by a large, established company such

---

[14]It would be illegal for Firm F's managers to purchase more shares on the basis of their inside knowledge of the new product. They could be sent to jail if they did.

[15]Of course, Firm U would have to make certain disclosures when it offered new shares to the public, but it might be able to meet the legal requirements without fully disclosing management's worst fears.

as GM or IBM, which surely would have many financing options, than if it was by a small company such as USR Industries. For USR, a stock sale might mean truly extraordinary investment opportunities that were so large that they just could not be financed without a stock sale.

If you gave the preceding answer, your views are completely consistent with those of many sophisticated portfolio managers of institutions such as Morgan Guaranty Trust. *So, simply stated, the announcement of a stock offering by a mature firm that seems to have multiple financing alternatives is taken as a* **signal** *that the firm's prospects as seen by its management are not bright.* This, in turn, suggests that when a mature firm announces a new stock offering, the price of its stock should decline. Empirical studies have shown that this situation does indeed exist.

What are the implications of all this for capital structure decisions? The answer is that firms should, in normal times, maintain a **reserve borrowing capacity** that can be used in the event that some especially good investment opportunities come along. *This means that firms should generally use less debt than would be suggested by the tax benefit/bankruptcy cost trade-off expressed in Figure 9–7.*

Signaling/asymmetric information concepts also have implications for the marginal cost of capital (MCC) curve as discussed in Chapter 8. There we saw that the weighted average cost of capital (WACC) jumped when retained earnings were exhausted and the firm was forced to sell new common stock to raise equity. The jump in the WACC, or the break in the MCC schedule, was attributed only to flotation costs. However, if the announcement of a stock sale causes a decline in the price of the stock, then k_e as measured by $k_e = \hat{D}_1/P_0(1 - F) + g$ will rise because of the decline in P_0. This factor reinforces the effects of flotation costs, and perhaps it is an even more important explanation for the jump in the MCC schedule at the point at which new stock must be issued. For example, assume that $P_0 = \$10$, $\hat{D}_1 = \$1$, $g = 5\%$, and $F = 10\%$. Therefore, $k_s = 10\% + 5\% = 15\%$, and k_e, the cost of external equity, is 16.1 percent:

$$k_e = \frac{\hat{D}_1}{P_0(1 - F)} + g = \frac{\$1}{\$10(1.0 - 0.10)} + 0.05 = 0.161 = 16.1\%$$

Suppose, however, that the announcement of a stock sale causes the current market price of the stock to fall from $10 to $8. This will produce an increase in the costs of both retained earnings (k_s) and external equity:

$$k_s = \frac{\hat{D}_1}{P_0} + g = \frac{\$1}{\$8} + 0.05 = 0.175 = 17.5\%$$

$$k_e = \frac{\hat{D}_1}{P_0(1 - F)} + g = \frac{\$1}{\$8(1.0 - 0.10)} + 0.05 = 0.189 = 18.9\%$$

This would, of course, have further implications for capital budgeting. Specifically, it would make it even more difficult for a marginal project to show a positive net present value (NPV) if the project required the firm to sell stock to raise capital.

If you find our discussion of capital structure theory somewhat inexact, you are not alone. In truth, no one knows how to identify precisely the optimal capital structure for a firm or how to measure precisely the effect of the firm's capital structure on either its value or its cost of capital. In real life, capital structure decisions must be made more on the basis of judgment than numerical analysis. Nevertheless, an understanding of the theoretical issues as presented here is essential to making sound judgments on capital structure issues.

SIGNAL

An action taken by a firm's management that provides clues to investors about how management views the firm's prospects.

RESERVE BORROWING CAPACITY

The ability to borrow money at a reasonable cost when good investment opportunities arise; firms often use less debt than specified by the MM optimal capital structure to ensure that they can obtain debt capital later if necessary.

Internal Equity First, External Equity Last

There has long been a debate concerning the relevance of financing decisions on the value of the firm. The controversy centers on the question of whether a change in the firm's capital structure has an impact on its value. According to empirical evidence, stock prices do change when firms alter capital structures. But a question remains as to the reason stock prices react to capital structure changes. The reactions could result because capital structure changes provide information to investors either about the firm's optimal capital structure, if one exists, or about investment opportunities, which affect the value of the firm.

A survey of *Fortune* 500 firms provides some insight into the attitudes of financial officers concerning capital structure financing decisions. According to the results, nearly 85 percent of firms reported that retained earnings was their first choice of financing long-term needs, about 15 percent indicated that debt was preferable, and none of the firms listed new equity, either common or preferred, as their first preference. Almost 40 percent of the firms said issuing new common stock would be their last choice of alternatives for raising capital. This is not surprising, considering the fact that the cost of new common equity is greater than the other sources of capital. In addition, more than 60 percent of the firms indicated that they prefer to use debt and preferred stock to avoid diluting the ownership position of common stockholders. Other important factors that were mentioned include restrictions contained in existing debt contracts, cash flows expected from the asset to be financed, and risk.

More than 85 percent of the firms indicated that financial flexibility and long-term survival are important factors to consider when making financial decisions. About 75 percent stated that firm value, stable cash flows, and financial independence significantly influence the capital structure of a company.[a]

Similar conclusions were produced from a more recent study conducted by John Graham and Campbell Harvey, two professors at Duke University. According to the results of their survey, 81 percent of the firms have a target range within which they try to maintain their capital structures. In addition, most firms (nearly 60 percent) indicated that it is important to maintain "financial flexibility" when making decisions to issue new debt.[b] In other words, it appears firms desire to maintain a reserve borrowing capacity that can be used to finance especially good investment opportunities when they come along unexpectedly.

The results of these surveys seem to suggest that firms have a particular capital structure in mind when deciding how to best finance capital budgeting projects. However, they prefer to maintain a flexible capital structure rather than to operate at what might be considered a more rigid optimal position. As a result, changes in capital structure probably should be perceived as an indication of management's desire to raise funds to acquire projects rather than an indication that management is consciously adjusting the financial makeup of the firm to maximize value.

[a]J. Michael Pinegar and Lisa Wilbricht, "What Managers Think of Capital Structure Theory: A Survey," *Financial Management*, Winter 1989, 82–89.

[b]John R. Graham and Campbell R. Harvey, 2001, "The Theory and Practice of Corporate Finance: Evidence from the Field," *Journal of Financial Economics*, vol. 26, no. 2–3, 187–243.

Self-Test Questions

What does it mean when one hears, "The MM capital structure theory involves a trade-off between the tax benefits of debt and costs associated with actual or potential bankruptcy"?

Explain how asymmetric information and signals affect capital structure decisions.

What is meant by reserve borrowing capacity, and why is it important for firms?

| | TABLE 9–5 | | Capital Structure Percentages, 2003: Selected Industries Ranked by Common Equity Ratios[a] | | | | | |

INDUSTRY	COMMON EQUITY (1)	PREFERRED STOCK (2)	TOTAL DEBT (3)	LONG-TERM DEBT (4)	SHORT-TERM DEBT (5)	TIMES-INTEREST-EARNED RATIO (6)	RETURN ON EQUITY[b] (7)
Biotechnology	69.0%	0.4%	30.6%	21.6%	9.0%	4.3×	9.1%
Drugs	58.2	0.3	41.5	19.6	21.9	5.2	8.7
Electronics	45.9	0.3	53.8	28.5	25.3	0.9	−5.4
Textiles	29.2	0.5	70.3	40.9	29.4	2.7	10.0
Utilities	23.8	0.7	75.5	55.3	20.2	2.2	5.8
Composite[c]	40.4	0.6	59.0	39.3	19.7	3.0	7.7

NOTES:

[a]These ratios are based on accounting, or book, values. Stated on a market value basis, the equity percentages would be higher because most stocks sell at prices that are much higher than their book values.

[b]A negative ROE results because poor economic conditions in 2002 resulted in operating losses for many firms in the industry.

[c]These composite ratios include all industries, not just those listed in this table, except financial and professional service industries.

SOURCE: *Standard & Poor's Research Insight*, 2003.

Variations in Capital Structures among Firms

As might be expected, wide variations in the use of financial leverage occur both across industries and among the individual firms in each industry. Table 9–5 illustrates differences for selected industries; the ranking is in descending order of common equity ratios, as shown in column 1.

Drug and biotechnology companies do not use much debt (their common equity ratios are high); the uncertainties inherent in industries that are cyclical, oriented toward research, or subject to huge product liability suits normally render the heavy use of debt unwise. On the other hand, utilities traditionally have used large amounts of debt, particularly long-term debt. Their fixed assets make good security for mortgage bonds, and their relatively stable sales make it safe for them to carry more debt than would be true for firms with more business risk.

Particular attention should be given to the times-interest-earned (TIE) ratio because it gives a measure of how safe the debt is and how vulnerable the company is to financial distress. The TIE ratio depends on three factors: (1) the percentage of debt, (2) the interest rate on the debt, and (3) the company's profitability. Generally, the least leveraged industries, such as the drug and biotechnology industries, have the highest coverage ratios, whereas the utility industry, which finances heavily with debt, has a low average coverage ratio. Table 9–5 shows that companies that manufacture drugs and biotechnology research have high average TIEs, whereas utilities have a very low TIE.

Wide variations in capital structures also exist among firms within given industries. For example, although the average common equity ratio in 2003 for the

TABLE 9-6	Capital Structure Percentages for Selected Countries Ranked by Common Equity Ratios, 1995			
COUNTRY	**EQUITY**	**TOTAL DEBT**	**LONG-TERM DEBT**	**SHORT-TERM DEBT**
United Kingdom	68.3%	31.7%	N/A	N/A
United States	48.4	51.6	26.8%	24.8%
Canada	47.5	52.5	30.2	22.3
Germany	39.7	60.3	15.6	44.7
Spain	39.7	60.3	22.1	38.2
France	38.8	61.2	23.5	37.7
Japan	33.7	66.3	23.3	43.0
Italy	23.5	76.5	24.2	52.3

NOTE: The percentages were computed from financial data that were stated in domestic currency. For example, the amount of total assets for French companies was stated in francs.
SOURCE: *OECD Financial Statistics, Part 3: Non-Financial Enterprises Financial Statements*, 1996.

biotechnology industry was 69 percent, Organogenesis Inc.'s equity ratio was greater than 100 percent (that is, owners' equity was negative), but Sangamo Biosciences Inc.'s equity ratio was approximately 4 percent. Thus, factors unique to individual firms, including managerial attitudes, play an important role in setting target capital structures.

Self-Test Question

Why do wide variations in the use of financial leverage occur both across industries and among the individual firms in each industry?

Capital Structures around the World

As you might expect, when we examine the capital structures of companies around the world, we find wide variations. Table 9–6 illustrates differences for selected countries; the ranking is in descending order of common equity ratios, as shown in column 1. As you can see, companies in Italy and Japan use much greater proportion of debt than companies in the United States or Canada, and companies in the United Kingdom use the lowest proportion of debt of all the countries listed. Of course, different countries use somewhat different accounting conventions, which make comparisons difficult. Still, even after adjusting for accounting differences, researchers find that Italian and Japanese firms use considerably more financial leverage than U.S. and Canadian companies. The gap among the countries has narrowed somewhat during the past several decades. In the early 1970s, companies in Canada and the United States had debt/assets ratios of about 40 percent, and companies in Japan and Italy had debt/assets ratios of more than 75 percent (Japanese companies averaged nearly 85 percent leverage).

Why do international differences in financial leverage exist? It seems logical to attribute the differences to dissimilar tax structures. Although the interest on corporate debt is deductible in each country, and individuals must pay taxes on interest received, both dividends and capital gains are taxed differently around the world. The tax codes in most developed countries encourage personal investing and savings more than the U.S. Tax Code. For example, Germany, Italy, and many other European countries do not tax capital gains, and in most other developed countries, including Japan, France, and Canada, capital gains are not taxed unless they exceed some minimum amount. Further, in Germany and Italy, dividends are not taxed as income, and in most other countries some amount of dividends is tax-exempt. Therefore, we can make the following general conclusions: (1) From a tax standpoint, corporations should be equally inclined to use debt in most developed countries. (2) In countries where capital gains are not taxed, investors should show a preference for stocks compared to countries that have capital gains taxes. (3) Investor preferences should lead to relatively low equity capital costs in those countries that do not tax capital gains, and this, in turn, should cause firms in those countries to use significantly more equity capital than their U.S. counterparts. But, for the most part, this is exactly the opposite of the actual capital structures we observe, so differential tax laws cannot explain the observed capital structure differences.

If tax rates cannot explain the different capital structures, what might be an appropriate explanation? Another possibility relates to risk, especially bankruptcy costs. Actual bankruptcy, and even the threat of potential bankruptcy, imposes a costly burden on firms with large amounts of debt. Note, however, that the threat of bankruptcy is dependent on the probability of bankruptcy. In the United States, *equity* monitoring costs are comparatively low because corporations produce quarterly reports and must comply with relatively stringent audit requirements. These conditions are less prevalent in other countries. On the other hand, *debt* monitoring costs probably are lower in such countries as Germany and Japan than in the United States because most of the corporate debt consists of bank loans as opposed to publicly issued bonds. More importantly, though, the banks in many European and developed Asian countries are closely linked to the corporations that borrow from them, often holding major equity positions in, and having substantial influence over, the management of the debtor firms. Given these close relationships, the banks are much more directly involved with the debtor firms' affairs, and as a result they also are more accommodating than U.S. bondholders in the event of financial distress. This, in turn, suggests that any given amount of debt gives rise to a lower threat of bankruptcy than for a U.S. firm with the same amount of business risk. Thus, an analysis of both bankruptcy costs and equity monitoring costs leads to the conclusion that U.S. firms should have more equity and less debt than firms in countries such as Japan and Germany, which is what we typically observe.

We cannot state that one financial system is better than another in the sense of making the firms in one country more efficient than those in another. However, as U.S. firms become increasingly involved in worldwide operations, they must become increasingly aware of worldwide conditions, and they must be prepared to adapt to conditions in the various countries in which they do business.

Self-Test Question

Why do international differences in financial leverage exist?

    d. EPS indifference point

    e. Degree of operating leverage; degree of financial leverage; degree of total leverage

    f. Times-interest-earned (TIE) ratio

    g. Symmetric information; asymmetric information

    h. Trade-off theory; signaling theory

    i. Reserve borrowing capacity

financial leverage   **ST-2** Gentry Motors Inc., a producer of turbine generators, is in this situation: EBIT = $4 million; tax rate = T = 35%; debt outstanding = $2 million; k_d = 10%; k_s = 15%; shares of stock outstanding = 600,000; and book value per share = $10. Because Gentry's product market is stable and the company expects no growth, all earnings are paid out as dividends. The debt consists of perpetual bonds.

    a. What are Gentry's earnings per share (EPS) and its price per share (P_0)?

    b. What is Gentry's weighted average cost of capital (WACC)?

    c. Gentry can increase its debt by $8 million, to a total of $10 million, using the new debt to buy back and retire some of its shares of common stock at the current price. Its interest rate on debt will be 12 percent (it will have to call and refund the old debt), and its cost of equity will rise from 15 percent to 17 percent. EBIT will remain constant. Should Gentry change its capital structure?

    d. If Gentry did not have to refund the $2 million of old debt, how would this affect things? Assume that the new and the still outstanding debt are equally risky, with k_d = 12%, but that the coupon rate on the old debt is 10 percent.

    e. What is Gentry's TIE coverage ratio under the original situation and under the conditions in part c of this question?

Problems

risk analysis   **9–1 a.** Given the following information, calculate the expected value for Firm C's EPS. E(EPS$_A$) = $5.10, and σ_A = $3.61; E(EPS$_B$) = $4.20, and σ_B = $2.96; and σ_C = $4.11.

	PROBABILITY				
	0.1	**0.2**	**0.4**	**0.2**	**0.1**
Firm A: EPS$_A$	($1.50)	$1.80	$5.10	$8.40	$11.70
Firm B: EPS$_B$	(1.20)	1.50	4.20	6.90	9.60
Firm C: EPS$_C$	(2.40)	1.35	5.10	8.85	12.60

    b. Discuss the relative riskiness of the three firms' (A, B, and C) earnings.

operating leverage effects   **9–2** Merville Corporation will begin operations next year to produce a single product at a price of $12 per unit. Merville has a choice of two methods of production: Method A, with variable costs of $6.75 per unit and fixed operating costs of $675,000; and Method B, with variable costs of $8.25 per unit and fixed operating costs of $401,250. To support operations under either production method, the firm requires $2,250,000 in assets, and it has established a debt-to-total-assets ratio of 40 percent. The cost of debt is k_d = 10 percent. The tax rate is irrelevant for the problem, and fixed operating costs do not include interest.

    a. The sales forecast for the coming year is 200,000 units. Under which method would EBIT be more adversely affected if sales did not reach the expected levels? (*Hint:* Compare DOLs under the two production methods.)

b. Given the firm's present debt, which method would produce the greater percentage increase in earnings per share for a given increase in EBIT? (*Hint:* Compare DFLs under the two methods.)

c. Calculate DTL under each method, and then evaluate the firm's total risk under each method.

d. Is there some debt ratio under Method A that would produce the same DTL_A as the DTL_B that you calculated in part c? (*Hint:* Let $DTL_A = DTL_B = 2.90$ as calculated in part c, solve for I, and then determine the amount of debt that is consistent with this level of I. Conceivably, debt could be negative, which implies holding liquid assets rather than borrowing.)

financing alternatives   9–3 Wired Communications Corporation (WCC) supplies headphones to airlines for use with movie and stereo programs. The headphones sell for $288 per set, and this year's sales are expected to be 45,000 units. Variable production costs for the expected sales under present production methods are estimated at $10,200,000, and fixed production (operating) costs at present are $1,560,000. WCC has $4,800,000 of debt outstanding at an interest rate of 8 percent. There are 240,000 shares of common stock outstanding, and there is no preferred stock. WCC pays out 70 percent of earnings and is in the 40 percent marginal tax bracket.

The company is considering investing $7,200,000 in new equipment. Sales would not increase, but variable costs per unit would decline by 20 percent. Also, fixed operating costs would increase from $1,560,000 to $1,800,000. WCC could raise the required capital by borrowing $7,200,000 at 10 percent or by selling 240,000 additional shares at $30 per share.

a. What would be WCC's EPS (1) under the old production process, (2) under the new process if it uses debt, and (3) under the new process if it uses common stock?

b. Calculate the DOL, DFL, and DTL under the existing setup and under the new setup with each type of financing. Assume that the expected sales level is 45,000 units, or $12,960,000.

c. At what unit sales level would WCC have the same EPS, assuming it undertakes the investment and finances it with debt or with stock? (*Hint:* V = variable cost per unit = $8,160,000/45,000, and EPS = $[(P \times Q - V \times Q - F - I)(1 - T)]$/Shares. Set $EPS_{Stock} = EPS_{Debt}$ and solve for Q.)

d. At what unit sales level would EPS = 0 under the three production/financing setups—that is, under the old plan, the new plan with debt financing, and the new plan with stock financing? (*Hint:* Note that $V_{Old} = $10,200,000/45,000$, and use the hints for part b, setting the EPS equation equal to zero.)

e. On the basis of the analysis in parts a through c, which plan is the riskiest, which has the highest expected EPS, and which would you recommend? Assume here that there is a fairly high probability of sales falling as low as 25,000 units, and determine EPS_{Debt} and EPS_{Stock} at that sales level to help assess the riskiness of the two financing plans.

financing alternatives   9–4 The Strasburg Company plans to raise a net amount of $270 million to finance new equipment and working capital in early 2006. Two alternatives are being considered: Common stock can be sold to net $60 per share, or bonds yielding

12 percent can be issued. The balance sheet and income statement of the Strasburg Company prior to financing are as follows:

THE STRASBURG COMPANY:
BALANCE SHEET AS OF DECEMBER 31, 2005
(MILLIONS OF DOLLARS)

Current assets	$ 900.00	Accounts payable	$ 172.50
Net fixed assets	450.00	Notes payable to bank	255.00
		Other current liabilities	225.00
		Total current liabilities	$ 652.50
		Long-term debt (10%)	300.00
		Common stock, $3 par	60.00
		Retained earnings	337.50
Total assets	$1,350.00	Total liabilities and equity	$1,350.00

THE STRASBURG COMPANY:
INCOME STATEMENT FOR YEAR ENDED DECEMBER 31, 2005
(MILLIONS OF DOLLARS)

Sales	$2,475.00
Operating costs	(2,227.50)
Earnings before interest and taxes (EBIT) (10%)	$ 247.50
Interest on short-term debt	(15.00)
Interest on long-term debt	(30.00)
Earnings before taxes (EBT)	$ 202.50
Taxes (40%)	(81.00)
Net income	$ 121.50

The probability distribution for annual sales is as follows:

PROBABILITY	ANNUAL SALES (MILLIONS OF DOLLARS)
0.30	$2,250
0.40	2,700
0.30	3,150

Assuming that EBIT is equal to 10 percent of sales, calculate earnings per share under both the debt financing and the stock financing alternatives at each possible level of sales. Then calculate expected earnings per share and σ_{EPS} under both debt and stock financing. Also, calculate the debt-to-total-assets ratio and the times-interest-earned (TIE) ratio at the expected sales level under each alternative. The old debt will remain outstanding. Which financing method do you recommend?

Exam-Type Problems

The problems included in this section are set up in such a way that they could be used as multiple-choice exam problems.

financial leverage effects **9–5** The firms HL and LL are identical except for their debt-to-total-assets ratios and interest rates on debt. Each has $20 million in assets, earned $4 million before interest and taxes in 2005, and has a 40 percent marginal tax rate. Firm HL, however, has a debt-to-total-assets ratio (D/TA) of 50 percent and pays 12 percent interest on its debt, whereas LL has a 30 percent debt-to-total-assets ratio and pays only 10 percent interest on debt.

a. Calculate the rate of return on equity (net income/equity) for each firm.

b. Observing that HL has a higher return on equity, LL's treasurer decides to raise the debt-to-total-assets ratio from 30 to 60 percent, which will increase LL's interest rate on all debt to 15 percent. Calculate the new rate of return on equity (ROE) for LL. ROE = (Net income)/(Common equity).

financial leverage effects   **9–6** The Damon Company wishes to calculate next year's return on equity (ROE) under different leverage ratios. Damon's total assets are $14 million, and its marginal tax rate is 40 percent. The company can estimate next year's earnings before interest and taxes for three possible states of the world: $4.2 million with a 0.2 probability, $2.8 million with a 0.5 probability, and $700,000 with a 0.3 probability. Calculate Damon's expected ROE, standard deviation, and coefficient of variation for each of the debt-to-total-assets ratios in the following list and evaluate the results.

ROE = (Net income)/(Common equity)

Leverage (Debt/Assets)	Interest Rate
0%	—
10	9%
50	11
60	14

Integrative Problem

optimal capital structure   **9–7** Assume that you have just been hired by Adams, Garitty, and Evans (AGE), a consulting firm that specializes in analyses of firms' capital structures. Your boss has asked you to examine the capital structure of Campus Deli and Sub Shop (CDSS), which is located adjacent to the campus. According to the owner, sales were $1,350,000 last year, variable costs were 60 percent of sales, and fixed costs were $40,000. As a result, EBIT totaled $500,000. Because the university's enrollment is capped, EBIT is expected to be constant over time. Because no expansion capital is required, CDSS pays out all earnings as dividends. The management group owns 50 percent of the stock, which is traded in the over-the-counter market.

CDSS currently has no debt—it is an all equity firm—and its 100,000 shares outstanding sell at a price of $20 per share. The firm's marginal tax rate is 40 percent. On the basis of statements made in your finance class, you believe that CDSS's shareholders would be better off if some debt financing were used. When you suggested this to your new boss, she encouraged you to pursue the idea, but to provide support for the suggestion.

You then obtained from a local investment banker the following estimates of the costs of debt and equity at different debt levels (in thousands of dollars):

Amount Borrowed	k_d	k_s
$ 0	—	15.0%
250	10.0%	15.5
500	11.0	16.5
750	13.0	18.0
1,000	16.0	20.0

If the firm were recapitalized, debt would be issued, and the borrowed funds would be used to repurchase stock. You plan to complete your report by asking and then answering the following questions:

a. (1) What is business risk? What factors influence a firm's business risk?
   (2) What is operating leverage, and how does it affect a firm's business risk?
b. (1) What is meant by the terms *financial leverage* and *financial risk?*
   (2) How does financial risk differ from business risk?
c. Now, develop an example that can be presented to CDSS's management. As an illustration, consider two hypothetical firms, Firm U, with zero debt financing, and Firm L, with $10,000 of 12 percent debt. Both firms have $20,000 in total assets and a 40 percent marginal tax rate, and they face the following EBIT probability distribution for next year:

PROBABILITY	EBIT
0.25	$2,000
0.50	3,000
0.25	4,000

(1) Complete the following partial income statements and the set of ratios for Firm L.

	FIRM U			FIRM L		
Assets	$20,000	$20,000	$20,000	$20,000	$20,000	$20,000
Equity	$20,000	$20,000	$20,000	$10,000	$10,000	$10,000
Probability	0.25	0.50	0.25	0.25	0.50	0.25
Sales	$ 6,000	$ 9,000	$12,000	$ 6,000	$ 9,000	$12,000
Operating costs	(4,000)	(6,000)	(8,000)	(4,000)	(6,000)	(8,000)
Earnings before interest and taxes	$ 2,000	$ 3,000	$ 4,000	$ 2,000	$ 3,000	$ 4,000
Interest (12%)	(0)	(0)	(0)	(1,200)		(1,200)
Earnings before taxes	$ 2,000	$ 3,000	$ 4,000	$ 800	$	$ 2,800
Taxes (40%)	(800)	(1,200)	(1,600)	(320)		(1,120)
Net income	$ 1,200	$ 1,800	$ 2,400	$ 480	$	$ 1,680
ROE = $\dfrac{\text{Net income}}{\text{Common equity}}$	6.0%	9.0%	12.0%	4.8%	%	16.8%
TIE = $\dfrac{\text{EBIT}}{\text{Interest}}$	∞	∞	∞	1.7×	×	3.3×
Expected ROE		9.0%			10.8%	
Expected TIE		∞			2.5×	
σ_{ROE}		2.1%			4.2%	
σ_{TIE}		0×			0.6×	

(2) What does this example illustrate concerning the impact of financial leverage on expected rate of return and risk?

d. With the preceding points in mind, now consider the optimal capital structure for CDSS.
   (1) To begin, define the term *optimal capital structure.*
   (2) Describe briefly, without using numbers, the sequence of events that would occur if CDSS decided to change its capital structure to include more debt.

(3) Assume that shares could be repurchased at the current market price of $20 per share. Calculate CDSS's expected EPS and TIE at debt levels of $0, $250,000, $500,000, $750,000, and $1,000,000. How many shares would remain after recapitalization under each scenario? [EPS = (Net income)/(outstanding shares)]

(4) What would be the new stock price if CDSS recapitalizes with $250,000 of debt? $500,000? $750,000? $1,000,000? Recall that the CDSS pays out all earnings as dividends, so g = 0.

(5) Considering only the levels of debt discussed, what is CDSS's optimal capital structure?

(6) Is EPS maximized at the debt level that maximizes share price? Why?

(7) What is the WACC at the optimal capital structure?

e. Suppose you discovered that CDSS had more business risk than you originally estimated. Describe how this would affect the analysis. What if the firm had less business risk than originally estimated?

f. What is meant by the terms *degree of operating leverage (DOL)*, *degree of financial leverage (DFL)*, and *degree of total leverage (DTL)?* If fixed costs total $40,000 and the company uses $500,000 of debt, what are CDSS's degrees of each type of leverage? Of what practical use is the degree of leverage concept?

g. What are some factors that should be considered when establishing a firm's target capital structure?

h. Put labels on the following graph, and then discuss the graph as you might use it to explain to your boss why CDSS might want to use some debt.

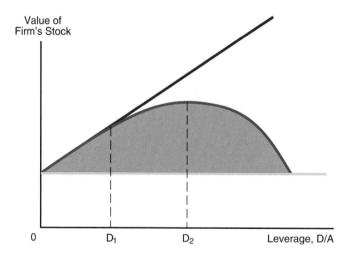

i. How does the existence of asymmetric information and signaling affect capital structure?

Computer-Related Problem

Work the problem in this section only if you are using the computer problem diskette.

effects of financial leverage   **9–8** Use the model in File C09 to work this problem.

a. Rework Problem 9–4, assuming that the old long-term debt will not remain outstanding but, rather, that it must be refinanced at the new long-term interest rate of 12 percent. What effect does this have on the decision to refinance?

b. What would be the effect on the refinancing decision if the rate on long-term debt fell to 5 percent or rose to 20 percent, assuming that all long-term debt must be refinanced?

c. Which financing method would be recommended if the stock price (1) rose to $105 or (2) fell to $30? (Assume that all debt will have an interest rate of 12 percent.)

d. With P_0 = $60 and k_d = 12%, change the sales probability distribution to the following:

ALTERNATIVE 1		ALTERNATIVE 2	
SALES	**PROBABILITY**	**SALES**	**PROBABILITY**
$2,250	0.0	$ 0	0.3
2,700	1.0	2,700	0.4
3,150	0.0	7,500	0.3

What are the implications of these changes?

GET REAL with Thomson ONE

9–9 Family Dollar Stores [FDO], a firm operating discount retail stores, has no long-term debt in its capital structure, even though the use of financial leverage in the form of long-term debt might increase the firm's earnings per share. Answer the following questions about Family Dollar:

a. What was the EBIT—that is, operating income—of Family Dollar for the past three years? [*Hint:* Click on Financials/Financial Statements]

b. Calculate the firm's net income and earnings per share for the past three years.

c. What was the average earnings per share during the past three years?

d. If the firm borrows $740 million in long-term debt at 10 percent to help finance its operations during the first year, what would be the earnings per share in each year?

e. Should Family Dollar start using long-term debt? Explain your answer.

f. Based on your findings, make an argument for and against using long-term debt in a firm's capital structure.

CHAPTER 10

Dividend Policy

A MANAGERIAL PERSPECTIVE

At the beginning of Chapter 9, we described the actions Unisys Corporation, a manufacturer of computers and related products for commercial and defense companies, has taken in recent years to reduce the relative amount of debt in its capital structure. One of the first actions taken to improve the financial position of the firm was to suspend the payment of common stock dividends. This policy, which directly affected stockholders' cash receipts, has been in effect since the board of directors made the decision in September 1990. Prior to that time, Unisys had paid a regular dividend to common stockholders for nearly 100 years. So why were dividend payments suspended? According to James Unruh, president and CEO at the time (he was replaced by Lawrence A. Weinbach in 1997), the dividend suspension was in the "best interests" of shareholders—the board felt Unisys needed to strengthen its financial condition to improve *shareholder wealth*.

Suspending the common stock dividend saved Unisys more than $162 million a year and allowed the company to use the funds to reduce debt. When Unisys announced the dividend suspension, the price of its common stock dropped more than 25 percent in one day and by about one-third of its pre-announcement value within one week.

Trading at just under $5 per share, the value of Unisys common stock was 76 percent lower than its high during the previous 12-month period, and 90 percent lower than its high value during the previous five years. Clearly, the dividend suspension was not greeted favorably by the stockholders. By 1994, Unisys stock was selling for $11 per share, and at the end of 1999 the price was nearly $32. During this five-year period, even though dividends were not being paid, the stock's value grew by nearly 24 percent per year. It seems the stockholders realized the dividend suspension in 1990 was beneficial for long-run stability and wealth maximization. Unfortunately, technology stocks, including Unisys, suffered substantial operating losses in 2000, and this trend continued into 2001. At the end of June 2001, Unisys stock had dropped to under $15 per share. The decline in share price was compounded by the fact that Unisys had difficulty meeting its earnings expectations. At the beginning of 2004, Unisys projected that its "normal" earnings would increase by 20 percent during the year. Unfortunately, this forecast did not consider the effects of the firm's substantial pension costs on earnings in 2004. As a result, the stock price remained fairly low, at approximately $15 per share, in January 2004. Investors appeared to be taking a "wait-and-see attitude" with regard to Unisys' earnings forecast.

As you can see from this example, a firm's dividend policy can have a significant impact on its market value. Also, from this Managerial Perspective as well as the one in Chapter 9, it should be clear that a firm's dividend policy affects its capital structure: A firm can use each dollar of earnings to finance projects internally or to pay dividends to stockholders, but not both. As you read this chapter, think about why Unisys suspended its common stock dividend. Consider the impact a particular dividend policy can have on the cash position of a firm and, more important, how a change in the policy can affect the value of a firm. ■

DIVIDENDS
Cash distributions made to stockholders from the firm's earnings, whether those earnings were generated in the current period or in previous periods.

We refer to the cash payments, or distributions, made to stockholders from the firm's earnings, whether those earnings were generated in the current period or in previous periods, as **dividends.** Consequently, a firm's *dividend policy* involves the decision to pay out earnings or to retain them for reinvestment in the firm. Remember that, according to the constant dividend growth model given in Chapter 5, the value of common stock can be computed as $P_0 = \hat{D}_1/(k_s - g)$. This equation shows that if the firm adopts a policy of paying out more cash dividends, $\hat{D}_1$ will rise, which will tend to increase the price of the stock. However, everything else equal, if cash dividends are increased, then less money will be available for reinvestment and the expected future growth rate, g, will be lowered, which will depress the price of the stock. Thus, changing the dividend has two opposing effects. *The* **optimal dividend policy** *for a firm strikes that balance between current dividends and future growth that maximizes the price of the stock.*

OPTIMAL DIVIDEND POLICY
The dividend policy that strikes a balance between current dividends and future growth and maximizes the firm's stock price.

In this chapter, we first examine factors that affect the optimal dividend policy and the types of dividend policies generally used by firms.

Dividend Policy and Stock Value

How do dividend policy decisions affect a firm's stock price? Academic researchers have studied this question extensively for many years, and they have yet to reach definitive conclusions. On the one hand, there are those who suggest that dividend policy is *irrelevant* because they argue a firm's value should be determined by the basic earning power and business risk of the firm, in which case value depends only on the income (cash) produced, not on how the income is split between dividends and retained earnings (and hence growth).

DIVIDEND IRRELEVANCE THEORY
The theory that a firm's dividend policy has no effect on either its value or its cost of capital.

Proponents of this line of reasoning, called the **dividend irrelevance theory,** would contend that investors care only about the *total returns* they receive, not whether they receive those returns in the form of dividends or capital gains. Thus, *if the dividend irrelevance theory is correct, there exists no optimal dividend policy because dividend policy does not affect the value of the firm.*[1]

---

[1]The principal proponents of the *dividend irrelevance theory* are Miller and Modigliani (MM), who outlined their theory in "Dividend Policy, Growth, and the Valuation of Shares," *Journal of Business,* October 1961, 411–433. The assumptions MM made to develop their dividend irrelevance theory are similar to those they introduced in their capital structure theory mentioned in the previous chapter, which include no personal taxes, no brokerage costs, no bankruptcy, and so forth. Such assumptions are made to afford them the ability to develop a manageable theory.

On the other hand, it is quite possible that investors prefer one dividend policy over another; if so, a firm's dividend policy is *relevant*. For example, it has been argued that investors prefer to receive dividends "today" because current dividend payments are more certain than the future capital gains that *might* result from investing retained earnings in growth opportunities, so k_s should decrease as the dividend payout is increased.[2]

Another factor that might cause investors to prefer a particular dividend policy is the tax effect of dividend receipts. Investors must pay taxes at the time dividends and capital gains are received. Thus, depending on his or her tax situation, an investor might prefer either a payout of current earnings as dividends, which would be taxed in the current period, or capital gains associated with growth in stock value, which would be taxed when the stock is sold, perhaps many years in the future. Investors who prefer to delay the impact of taxes would be willing to pay more for low payout companies than for otherwise similar high payout companies, and vice versa.

Those who believe the firm's dividend policy is relevant are proponents of the **dividend relevance theory,** which asserts dividend policy can affect the value of a firm through investors' preferences.

DIVIDEND RELEVANCE THEORY
The value of a firm is affected by its dividend policy—the optimal dividend policy is the one that maximizes the firm's value.

Self-Test Questions

Differentiate between the dividend irrelevance and dividend relevance theories.

How might taxes affect investors' preferences concerning the receipt of dividends and capital gains?

Investors and Dividend Policy

Although academic researchers have studied the dividend policy issue extensively, the issue remains unresolved; researchers at this time simply cannot tell corporate decision makers exactly how dividend policy affects stock prices and capital costs. But the research has provided some views concerning investors' reactions to dividend policy changes and why firms have particular dividend policies. Three of these views are discussed in this section.

Information Content, or Signaling

If investors expect a company's dividend to increase by 5 percent per year, and if, in fact, the dividend is increased by 5 percent, then the stock price generally will not change significantly on the day the dividend increase is announced. In Wall Street parlance, such a dividend increase would be "discounted," or *anticipated*, by the market. However, if investors expect a 5 percent increase, but the company actually increases the dividend by 25 percent—say from $2 to $2.50—this generally would be accompanied by an increase in the price of the stock. Conversely, a less-than-expected dividend increase, or an unexpected reduction, generally would result in a price decline.

---

[2]Myron J. Gordon, "Optimal Investment and Financing Policy," *Journal of Finance*, May 1963, 264–272, and John Lintner, "Dividends, Earnings, Leverage, Stock Prices, and the Supply of Capital to Corporations," *Review of Economics and Statistics*, August 1962, 243–269.

It is a well-known fact that corporations are extremely reluctant to cut dividends and, therefore, *managers do not raise dividends unless they anticipate higher, or at least stable, earnings in the future to sustain the higher dividends.* This means that a larger-than-expected dividend increase is taken by investors as a *signal* that the firm's management forecasts improved future earnings, whereas a dividend reduction signals a forecast of poor earnings. Thus, it can be argued investors' reactions to changes in dividend payments do not show that investors prefer dividends to retained earnings; rather, the stock price changes simply indicate that important information is contained in dividend announcements. In effect, dividend announcements provide investors with information previously known only to management. This theory is referred to as the **information content,** or **signaling, hypothesis.**

INFORMATION CONTENT (SIGNALING) HYPOTHESIS
The theory that investors regard dividend changes as signals of management's earnings forecasts.

Clientele Effect

It also has been shown that it is very possible that a firm sets a particular dividend payout policy, which then attracts a *clientele* consisting of those investors who like the firm's dividend policy. For example, some stockholders, such as retired individuals, prefer current income to future capital gains, so they want the firm to pay out a higher percentage of its earnings. Other stockholders have no need for current investment income, so they favor a low payout ratio. If investors could not invest in companies with different dividend policies, it might be very expensive for them to achieve their investment goals—investors who prefer capital gains could reinvest any dividends they receive, but they first would have to pay taxes on the income. In essence, then, a **clientele effect** might exist if stockholders are attracted to companies because they have particular dividend policies. Those investors who desire current investment income can purchase shares in high-dividend-payout firms, whereas those who do not need current cash income can invest in low-payout firms. Consequently, we would expect the stock price of a firm to change if the firm changes its dividend policy, because investors will adjust their portfolios to include firms with the desired dividend policy.

CLIENTELE EFFECT
The tendency of a firm to attract the type of investor who likes its dividend policy.

Free Cash Flow Hypothesis

If it is the intent of the financial manager to maximize the value of the firm, then investors should prefer that firms pay dividends only if acceptable capital budgeting opportunities do not exist. We know that acceptable capital budgeting projects increase the value of the firm. We also know that, because flotation costs are incurred when issuing new stock, it costs a firm more to raise funds using new common equity than it does using retained earnings. To maximize value, therefore, wherever possible a firm should use retained earnings rather than issue new common stock to finance capital budgeting projects. As a result, dividends should be paid only when *free cash flows* in excess of capital budgeting needs exist. If management does otherwise, the firm's value will not be maximized. According to the **free cash flow hypothesis,** the firm should distribute any earnings that cannot be reinvested at a rate at least as great as the investors' required rate of return, k_s—that is, payout, the free cash flows. Everything else equal, firms that retain *free cash flows* will have lower values than firms that distribute *free cash flows* because the firms that retain free cash flows actually decrease investors' wealth by investing in projects with IRR < k_s.

FREE CASH FLOW HYPOTHESIS
All else equal, firms that pay dividends from cash flows that cannot be reinvested in positive net present value projects, which are termed *free cash flows*, have higher values than firms that retain free cash flows.

The free cash flow hypothesis might help to explain why investors react differently to identical dividend changes made by similar firms. For example, a firm's stock price should not change dramatically if it reduces its dividend for the purposes of investing in capital budgeting projects with positive NPVs. On the other hand, a company that reduces its dividend simply to increase free cash flows should experience a significant decline in the market value of its stock because the dividend reduction is not in the best interests of the stockholders—in this case, an agency problem exists. Thus, the free cash flow hypothesis suggests that its dividend policy can provide information about the firm's behavior with respect to wealth maximization.

Self-Test Question

Define (1) information content, (2) the clientele effect, and (3) the free cash flow hypothesis, and explain how each affects dividend policy.

Dividend Policy in Practice

We have provided some insights concerning the relevance of dividend policy and how investors might view dividend payments from firms. However, no one has been able to develop a formula that can be used to tell management specifically how a given dividend policy will affect a firm's stock price. Even so, management still must establish a dividend policy. This section discusses several alternative policies and procedures that are used in practice.

Types of Dividend Payments

The dollar amounts of dividends paid by firms follow a variety of patterns. In general, though, firms pay dividends using one of the four payout policies discussed next.

RESIDUAL DIVIDEND POLICY
A policy in which the dividend paid is set equal to the actual earnings minus the amount of retained earnings necessary to finance the firm's optimal capital budget.

Residual Dividend Policy   In practice, dividend policy is very much influenced by investment opportunities and by the availability of funds with which to finance new investments. This fact has led to the development of a **residual dividend policy,** which states that a firm should follow these steps when deciding how much earnings should be paid out as dividends: (1) determine the optimal capital budget for the year, (2) determine the amount of capital needed to finance that budget, (3) use retained earnings to supply the equity component to the extent possible, and (4) pay dividends only if more earnings are available than are needed to support the optimal capital budget. The word *residual* means "left over," and the residual policy implies that dividends should be paid only out of "leftover" earnings.

The basis of the residual policy is the fact that *investors prefer to have the firm retain and reinvest earnings rather than pay them out in dividends if the rate of return the firm can earn on reinvested earnings exceeds the rate investors, on average, can themselves obtain on other investments of comparable risk.* For example, if the corporation can reinvest retained earnings at a 14 percent rate of return, whereas the best rate the average stockholder can obtain if the earnings are passed on in the form of dividends is 12 percent, then stockholders should prefer to have the firm retain the profits.

To continue, we saw in Chapter 8 that the cost of retained earnings is an *opportunity cost* that reflects rates of return available to equity investors. If a firm's stockholders can buy other stocks of equal risk and obtain a 12 percent dividend-plus-capital-gains yield, then 12 percent is the firm's cost of retained earnings. The cost of new outside equity raised by selling common stock will be higher than 12 percent because of the costs associated with issuing the new stock (flotation costs).

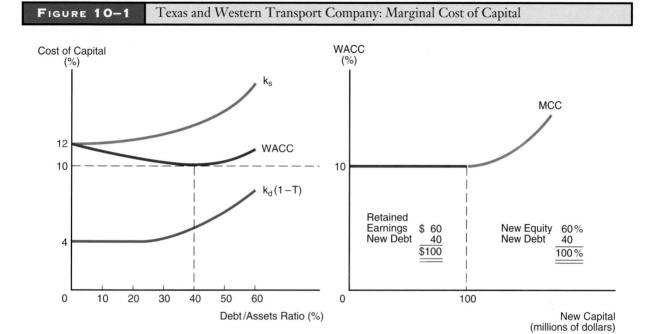

FIGURE 10–1   Texas and Western Transport Company: Marginal Cost of Capital

Most firms have a target capital structure that calls for at least some debt, so new financing is done partly with debt and partly with equity. As long as the firm finances with the optimal mix of debt and equity, and as long as it uses only internally generated equity (retained earnings), its marginal cost of each new dollar of capital will be minimized. Internally generated equity is available for financing a certain amount of new investment, but beyond that amount the firm must turn to more expensive new common stock. At the point where new stock must be sold, the cost of equity, and consequently the marginal cost of capital, rises.

These concepts, which were developed in Chapter 8, are illustrated in Figure 10–1 with data from the Texas and Western (T&W) Transport Company. T&W has a marginal cost of capital (MCC) of 10 percent. However, this cost rate assumes that all addition equity comes from retained earnings. Therefore, MCC = 10% as long as retained earnings are available, but MCC begins to rise at the point where new stock must be sold.

T&W has $60 million of net income and a 40 percent optimal debt ratio. Provided it does not pay cash dividends, T&W can make net investments (investments in addition to asset replacements financed from depreciation) of $100 million, consisting of $60 million from retained earnings plus $40 million of new debt supported by the retained earnings, at a 10 percent marginal cost of capital. Therefore, its MCC is constant at 10 percent up to $100 million of capital, beyond which it rises as the firm begins to use more expensive new common stock.

Suppose T&W's director of capital budgeting has determined that the optimal capital budget requires an investment equal to $70 million. The $70 million will be financed using $28 million debt ($70 million × 0.40) and $42 million in common equity ($70 million × 0.60). So the $60 million retained earnings will be more than sufficient to cover the common equity financing requirement, and the *residual* of $18 million ($60 million − $42 million) can be paid out as dividends to stockholders.

Now suppose T&W's optimal capital budget is $150 million. Should dividends be paid? Not if T&W follows the residual dividend policy. The $150 million capital budgeting needs will be financed with $60 million debt ($150 million × 0.40) and $90 million common equity ($150 million × 0.60). The common equity financing requirement of $90 million exceeds the $60 million retained earnings available, so $30 million of new common equity will have to be issued. The new, or external, common equity will have a higher cost than retained earnings, so the marginal cost of capital for T&W will be higher. Under these conditions, T&W should not pay dividends to its stockholders. If the company pays part of its earnings in dividends, the marginal cost of capital will be even higher because more common stock will have to be issued to account for the amount of retained earnings paid out as dividends. For example, if T&W pays stockholders $20 million in dividends, it still needs $90 million of common equity to satisfy the capital budgeting requirements. In this case, $50 million of external equity will be required, which means T&W's marginal cost of capital will increase sooner—new common equity will have to be issued when $40 million rather than $60 million of retained earnings are used. So to maximize value, T&W should retain all of its earnings for capital budgeting needs. Consequently, *according to the residual dividend policy, a firm that has to issue new common stock to finance capital budgeting needs does not have residual earnings, and dividends will be zero.*

Because both the earnings level and the capital budgeting needs of a firm vary from year to year, strict adherence to the residual dividend policy would result in dividend variability. One year the firm might declare zero dividends because investment opportunities are good, but the next year it might pay a large dividend because investment opportunities are poor. Similarly, fluctuating earnings would also lead to variable dividends even if investment opportunities were stable over time. Thus, following the residual dividend policy would be optimal only if investors were not bothered by fluctuating dividends. However, if investors prefer stable, dependable dividends, k_s would be higher, and the stock price lower, if the firm followed the residual theory in a strict sense rather than attempting to stabilize its dividends over time.

Stable, Predictable Dividends   In the past, many firms set a specific annual dollar dividend per share and then maintained it, increasing the annual dividend only if it seemed clear that future earnings would be sufficient to allow the new dividend to be maintained. A corollary of that policy was this rule: *Never reduce the annual dividend.*

When the economy expands quickly, inflationary pressures plus reinvested earnings generally tend to push earnings up, so many firms that would otherwise follow the stable dollar dividend payment policy switch to a "stable growth rate" policy. Here the firm sets a target growth rate for dividends (for example, 4 percent per year) and strives to increase dividends by this amount each year. Obviously, earnings must be growing at a reasonably steady rate for this policy to be feasible, but where it can be followed, such a policy provides investors with a stable real income.

A fairly typical dividend policy, that of Eastman Kodak, is illustrated in Figure 10–2. Prior to 1982, Kodak's earnings exhibited relatively stable growth, and so did the payout of dividends. But after 1982, more intense global competition, major litigation, and changing economic periods caused a great deal of volatility in Kodak's earnings. Management stopped increasing the dividend when earnings fell, but did not cut the dividend, even when earnings failed to cover it. Maintaining the dividend was Kodak's way of signaling to stockholders that management was confident that any declines in earnings were only temporary and that earnings would soon resume their upward trend. This was indeed the case—since 1992, earnings have fluctuated significantly, but Kodak maintained a nearly constant dividend until September 25, 2003, when the divi-

FIGURE 10-2	Eastman Kodak: Earnings per Share (EPS) and Dividends per Share (DPS), 1978–2010

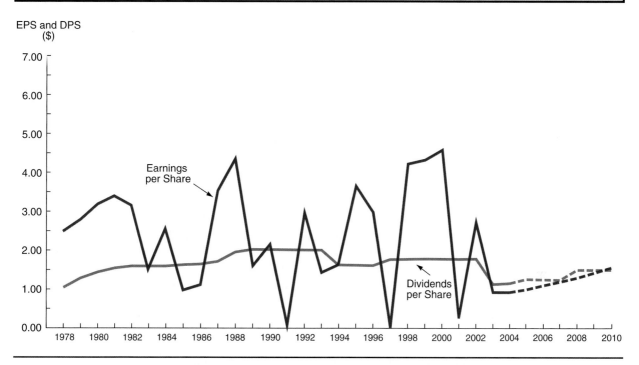

NOTE: Projected values, which are shown as dashed lines, are based on forecasts from sources available on the Internet, including Charles Schwab (located at http://www.schwab.com).

dend was cut by 72 percent. Kodak cut the dividend to help pay for the estimated $3 billion in capital budgeting investments that the company expected to make during the following three years when it planned to place greater emphasis on digital imaging products to generate future revenues. In addition, cutting the dividend helped Kodak to maintain what it considered to be an appropriate capital structure. On the day that the dividend cut was announced, the market price of Kodak's common stock dropped by nearly 20 percent. During the three months following the dividend cut, the stock price increased greater than 40 percent, however, because investors became convinced that the decision to cut the dividend was made to improve the company's wealth position, which was in the best interests of shareholders. As Kodak improves its competitive position, especially in digital imaging, it might again increase dividends.

STABLE, PREDICTABLE DIVIDENDS

Payment of a specific dollar dividend each year, or periodically increasing the dividend at a constant rate—the annual dollar dividend is relatively predictable by investors.

There are two good reasons for paying **stable, predictable dividends** rather than following the residual dividend policy. First, given the existence of the information content, or signaling, idea, a fluctuating payment policy would lead to greater uncertainty, hence to a higher k_s and a lower stock price, than would exist under a stable policy. Second, many stockholders use dividends for current consumption, and they would be put to trouble and expense if they had to sell part of their shares to obtain cash if the company cut the dividend.

As a rule, stable, predictable dividends imply more certainty than variable dividends, thus a lower k_s and a higher firm value. So it is this dividend policy that most firms favor. Even though the optimal dividend as prescribed by the residual policy might vary somewhat from year to year, a firm might delay some investment projects, depart from its target capital structure during a particular year, or even issue new common stock to avoid the problems associated with unstable dividends, and thus provide a lower k_s and a higher firm value.

Constant Payout Ratio It would be possible for a firm to pay out a constant *percentage* of earnings (dividends per share divided by earnings per share), but because earnings surely will fluctuate, this policy would mean that the dollar amount of dividends would vary. For example, if Eastman Kodak had followed the policy of paying a constant percentage of earnings per share, say 40 percent, the dividends per share paid since 1978 would have fluctuated exactly the same as earnings per share as shown in Figure 10–2, and thus the company would have had to cut its dividend in several different years. Therefore, with the **constant payout ratio** dividend policy, if earnings fluctuate, investors would have had much greater uncertainty concerning the expected dividends each year, and chances are k_s also would be greater; hence, its stock price would be lower. Although Kodak's stock price fluctuated somewhat from 1978 to 1997, it showed a general upward trend despite the substantial earnings fluctuations exhibited in Figure 10–2. In an effort to strengthen its financial position, in 1997 Kodak initiated a restructuring program to reduce annual costs by $1.5 billion. Part of the plan was to reduce payroll by laying off nearly 20,000 employees within three years. Because of these factors, Kodak's stock price fell approximately 25 percent in 1997. Since 2000, however, the stock's price has remained fairly constant. Had it cut the dividend to keep the payout ratio constant, Kodak's stock price would have "fallen out of bed" several times if investors interpreted the dividend reduction as a signal that management thought the earnings declines were permanent.

Low Regular Dividend Plus Extras A policy of paying a low regular dividend plus a year-end extra in good years is a compromise between a stable dividend (or stable growth rate) and a constant payout rate. Such a policy gives the firm flexibility, yet investors can count on receiving at least a minimum dividend. Therefore, if a firm's earnings and cash flows are quite volatile, this policy might be its best choice. The directors can set a relatively low regular dividend—low enough so that it can be maintained even in low-profit years or in years when a considerable amount of retained earnings is needed for investments—and then supplement it with an **extra dividend** in years when excess funds are available. Ford, General Motors, and other auto companies, whose earnings fluctuate widely from year to year, formerly followed such a policy, but in recent years they have joined the crowd and now follow a stable dividend policy.

Payment Procedures

Dividends normally are paid quarterly, and, when conditions permit, the dividend is increased. For example, on April 15, 2003, the board of directors of Eastman Kodak declared a $0.90 semiannual common stock dividend. Earlier in the year, Kodak's board indicated that it anticipated the annual dividend to be $1.80, which was the same as the dividend paid in 2002. So Kodak's stockholders were not surprised when the $0.90 semiannual dividend was announced; they would have been *shocked* if the dividend had been eliminated, because Kodak has paid a dividend for more than 40 years. As noted earlier, Kodak did cut its dividend by 72 percent in September 2003. Because this action was a surprise to shareholders, the price of Kodak's stock dropped sharply at the time.

CONSTANT PAYOUT RATIO
Payment of a constant *percentage* of earnings as dividends each year.

EXTRA DIVIDEND
A supplemental dividend paid in years when the firm does well, and excess funds are available for distribution.

Don't Touch That Dividend—Unless It Is Absolutely Necessary

Which dividend policy—residual dividends, stable, predictable dividends, constant payout ratio, or low regular dividend plus extras—do firms prefer? The many studies that have been conducted to find the answer to this question conclude that firms prefer to maintain relatively stable dividends and will go to great extremes to ensure dividends are not reduced. The studies show that more than 90 percent of financial managers believe that dividend stability suggests greater certainty to stockholders, thus higher stock prices than could be attained with other dividend policies. Financial managers state that dividends should be decreased only if income is significantly less than normal for extended periods of time. Similarly, dividends should be increased only if profits increase and future profitability is expected to continue. The suggestion, therefore, is that a change in dividend payments provides information about the management's expectations concerning the future profitability of the firm.

Consider the results of a survey of dividend policies of large firms commissioned by Spare, Kaplan, Bischel, & Associates, which is an investment firm located in San Francisco.* The results of the study were based on responses from senior financial managers of 110 of the Standard & Poor's 500 companies. The two major conclusions of the study were (1) companies use dividends as a signal of their future earnings and (2) companies are reluctant to cut dividends, regardless of the purpose for such a cut. More specifically, when asked whether dividends are used as informational signals, nearly 90 percent of the financial managers indicated that dividends provide information about expected earnings. Even when firms initiate stock buyback programs, they do not cut dividends to support the repurchases; rather, almost three-quarters of the firms actually increase their dividend payments. In addition, it was found that, among companies that pay dividends, the priority for the use of cash flows after current expenses have been paid is dividends. Further, firms are even reluctant to cut dividends when valuation models suggest such cuts would *theoretically* enhance value.

In summary, the results of the studies that have examined the dividend policies of firms have found that senior management believes dividends are important primarily because they provide information to investors. Thus payment of dividends is given a high priority with respect to how the operating cash flows generated by a firm should be used. *Dividend policy*, therefore, *does matter to financial managers*. And if dividends do actually provide information about the future earning ability of a firm, *dividend policy should matter to investors*.

*Shirley A. Lazo, "How Do Corporate Leaders See Payouts? As Important Signals, Survey Finds," *Barron's*, January 4, 1999, 40.

When Kodak declared the 2003 dividend, it issued the following statement:[3]

KODAK BOARD DECLARES SEMI-ANNUAL CASH DIVIDEND

ROCHESTER, N.Y., April 15—Eastman Kodak Company's board of directors today declared a semi-annual cash dividend of 90 cents per share on the outstanding common stock of the company.

The 90-cent per share dividend declared today will be payable July 16, 2003, to shareholders of record at the close of business on June 2, 2003. This payment represents the first dividend being distributed this year, consistent with a policy the board adopted in October 2001 to change the dividend disbursement to semi-annual from quarterly. The new schedule reflects an initiative by Kodak to align its cash disbursements with the seasonal cash flow pattern of the business.

---

[3]This statement was the announcement Kodak posted on the company's Web site, which was located at http://www.kodak.com/.

While solely the discretion of the board, Kodak also anticipates that dividends, when declared, will be paid on the company's 10th business day each July and December, to shareholders of record the first business day of the preceding month.

The three dates included in this announcement are important to current stockholders. These dates, as well as the ex-dividend date, are defined as follows:

1. **Declaration date.** On the *declaration date*, April 15, 2003 in Kodak's case, the board of directors meets and declares the regular dividend. For accounting purposes, the declared dividend becomes an actual liability on the declaration date, and if a balance sheet were constructed, the amount ($0.90 × Number of shares outstanding) would appear as a current liability, and retained earnings would be reduced by a like amount.

2. **Holder-of-record date.** At the close of business on the **holder-of-record date,** or **date of record,** the company closes its stock transfer books and produces a list of shareholders as of that date. Thus, if Kodak was notified of the sale and transfer of some stock before 5 P.M. on Monday, June 2, 2003, then the new owner received the dividend. However, if notification was received after June 2, the previous owner of the stock got the dividend check because his or her name appeared on the company's ownership records.

3. **Ex-dividend date.** The securities industry has set up a convention of declaring that the right to the dividend remains with the stock until two business days *prior to* the holder-of-record date. This is to ensure the company is notified of the transfer in time to record the new owner and thus pay the dividend to him or her. The date when the right to receive the next dividend payment no longer goes with the stock—that is, new purchasers will not receive the next dividend—is called the **ex-dividend date.** In the case of Kodak, the *ex-dividend* date was Thursday, May 29, 2003, which is two *business days* before the *holder-of-record* date, Monday, June 2, 2003. Therefore, any investor who purchased the stock on or after that date did not receive the next dividend payment associated with the stock. All else equal, then, we would expect that the price of Kodak's stock dropped on the ex-dividend date approximately by the amount of the dividend. Assuming no other price fluctuations, the price at which Kodak's stock opened on Thursday, May 29, should have been approximately $0.90 less than the close on Wednesday, May 28.[4] When the

HOLDER-OF-RECORD DATE (DATE OF RECORD)
The date the company opens the ownership books to determine who will receive the dividend; the stockholders of record on this date receive the dividend.

EX-DIVIDEND DATE
The date on which the right to the next dividend no longer accompanies a stock; it usually is two working days prior to the holder-of-record date.

---

[4]Tax effects cause the price decline on average to be less than the full amount of the dividend. Suppose you were an investor in the 40 percent tax bracket. If you bought Kodak's stock on May 28, you would receive the dividend, but you would have to pay 40 percent of it out in taxes within one year. Thus, you would want to wait until after May 28 to buy the stock if you thought you could get it for $0.90 less per share. Your reaction, and those of others, would influence stock prices around dividend payment dates. Here is what would happen:

1. Other things held constant, a stock's price should rise during the six-month period, with the daily price increase (for Kodak) equal to $0.90/180 = $0.005. Therefore, if the price started at $30 just after its last ex-dividend date, it would rise to $30.90 on May 28.
2. In the absence of taxes, the stock's price would fall to $30 on May 29 and then start up as the next dividend accrual period began. Thus, over time, if everything else were held constant, the stock's price would follow a sawtooth pattern if it were plotted on a graph.
3. Because of taxes, the stock's price would neither rise by the full amount of the dividend nor fall by the full dividend amount when it goes ex-dividend.
4. The amount of the rise and subsequent fall would depend on the average investor's marginal tax rate.

See Edwin J. Elton and Martin J. Gruber, "Marginal Stockholder Tax Rates and the Clientele Effect," *Review of Economics and Statistics,* February 1970, 68–74, for an interesting discussion of this concept.

PAYMENT DATE
The date on which a firm actually mails dividend checks.

market opened on Thursday, the price of the stock actually was about $1.00 lower than the closing price on Wednesday.

4. **Payment date.** Kodak paid the common stock dividends on July 16, 2003—this is the *payment date.* Recently, many firms have started paying dividends electronically.

Dividend Reinvestment Plans

DIVIDEND REINVESTMENT PLAN (DRIP)
A plan that enables a stockholder to automatically reinvest dividends received back into the stock of the paying firm.

Most larger companies offer **dividend reinvestment plans (DRIPs),** whereby stockholders can automatically reinvest dividends they receive in the stock of the paying corporation.[5] There are two types of DRIPs (referred to as "drips"): (1) plans that involve only "old" stock that already is outstanding and traded in the financial markets and (2) plans that involve newly issued stock. In either case, the stockholder must pay income taxes on the amount of the dividends even though stock rather than cash is received.

Under the "old-stock" type of plan, the stockholder chooses between receiving dividend checks or having the company use the dividends to buy more stock in the corporation. If the stockholder elects reinvestment, a bank, acting as trustee, takes the total funds available for reinvestment, purchases the corporation's stock on the open market, and allocates the shares purchased to the participating stockholders' accounts on a *pro rata* basis. The transactions costs of buying shares (brokerage costs) are low because of volume purchases, so these plans benefit small stockholders who do not need cash dividends for current consumption.

The "new-stock" type of DRIP provides for dividends to be invested in newly issued stock; hence, these plans raise new capital for the firm. AT&T, Florida Power & Light (now called Florida Progress), Union Carbide, and many other companies have had such plans in effect in recent years, using them to raise substantial amounts of new equity capital. No fees are charged to stockholders, and many companies offer stock at a discount of 5 percent below the actual market price. The companies absorb these costs as a trade-off against the flotation costs that would have been incurred had they sold stock through investment bankers rather than through the dividend reinvestment plans.[6]

Self-Test Questions

Explain the logic of the residual dividend policy, the steps a firm would take to implement it, and why it is more likely to be used to establish a long-run payout target than to set the actual year-by-year payout ratio.

Describe the stable, predictable dividend policy, and give two reasons why a firm might follow such a policy.

---

[5]See Richard H. Pettway and R. Phil Malone, "Automatic Dividend Reinvestment Plans," *Financial Management*, Winter 1973, 11–18, for an excellent discussion of this topic.

[6]One interesting aspect of DRIPs is that they are forcing corporations to reexamine their basic dividend policies. A high participation rate in a DRIP suggests that stockholders might be better off if the firm simply reduced cash dividends, as this would save stockholders some personal income taxes. Quite a few firms are surveying their stockholders to learn more about their preferences and to find out how they would react to a change in dividend policy. A more rational approach to basic dividend policy decisions might emerge from this research. Also, it should be noted that companies either use or stop using new-stock DRIPs depending on their need for equity capital.

Describe the constant payout ratio dividend policy. Why is this policy probably not as popular as a constant, or steadily increasing, dividend policy?

Explain what a low-regular-dividend-plus-extras policy is and why a firm might follow such a policy.

Why is the ex-dividend date important to investors?

Differentiate between the two types of dividend reinvestment plans.

Factors Influencing Dividend Policy

In addition to management's beliefs concerning which dividend theory is most correct, a number of other factors are considered when a particular dividend policy is chosen. The factors firms take into account can be grouped into these five broad categories:

1. **Constraints on dividend payments.** The amount of dividends a firm can pay might be limited due to (1) debt contract restrictions, which often stipulate that no dividends can be paid unless certain financial measures exceed stated minimums; (2) the fact that dividend payments cannot exceed the balance sheet item "retained earnings" (this is known as the *impairment of capital rule*, which is designed to protect creditors by prohibiting the company from distributing assets to stockholders before debt holders are paid); (3) cash availability, because cash dividends can be paid only with cash; and (4) restrictions imposed by the Internal Revenue Service (IRS) on improperly accumulated retained earnings. If the IRS can demonstrate that a firm's dividend payout ratio is being held down deliberately to help its stockholders avoid personal taxes, the firm is subject to heavy tax penalties. But this factor generally is relevant only to privately owned firms.

2. **Investment opportunities.** Firms that have large numbers of acceptable capital budgeting projects generally have low dividend payout ratios, and vice versa. But if a firm can accelerate or postpone projects (flexibility), then it can adhere more closely to a target dividend policy.

3. **Alternative sources of capital.** When a firm needs to finance a given level of investments and flotation costs are high, the cost of external equity, k_e, will be well above the cost of internal equity, k_s, making it better to set a low payout ratio and to finance by retaining earnings rather than through sale of new common stock. Also, if the firm can adjust its debt/assets ratio without raising capital costs sharply, it can maintain a stable dollar dividend, even if earnings fluctuate, by using a variable debt/assets ratio.

4. **Ownership dilution.** If management is concerned about maintaining control, it might be reluctant to sell new stock; hence, the company might retain more earnings than it otherwise would.

5. **Effects of dividend policy on k_s.** The effects of dividend policy on k_s might be considered in terms of four factors: (a) stockholders' desire for current versus future income; (b) the perceived riskiness of dividends versus capital gains; (c) the tax advantage of capital gains over dividends; and (d) the information content of dividends (signaling). Because we discussed each of these factors earlier, we need only note here that the importance of each factor in terms of its effect on k_s varies from firm to firm depending on the makeup of its current and possible future stockholders.

It should be apparent from our discussions that dividend policy decisions truly are exercises in informed judgment, not decisions that can be quantified precisely. Even so, to make rational dividend decisions, financial managers must consider all the points discussed in the preceding sections.

Self-Test Questions

Identify the five broad categories of factors that affect dividend policy.

What constraints affect dividend policy?

How do investment opportunities affect dividend policy?

How does the availability and cost of outside capital affect dividend policy?

Stock Dividends and Stock Splits

Stock dividends and stock splits are related to the firm's cash dividend policy. The rationale for stock dividends and splits can best be explained through an example. We will use Porter Electronic Controls Inc., a $700 million electronic components manufacturer, for this purpose. Since its inception, Porter's markets have been expanding, and the company has enjoyed growth in sales and earnings. Some of its earnings have been paid out in dividends, but some are also retained each year, causing earnings per share and market price per share to grow. The company began its life with only a few thousand shares outstanding, and, after some years of growth, each of Porter's shares had a very high earnings per share (EPS) and dividends per share (DPS). When a "normal" price/earnings (P/E) ratio was applied, the derived market price was so high that few people could afford to buy a "round lot" of 100 shares. This limited the demand for the stock and thus kept the total market value of the firm below what it would have been if more shares, at a lower price, had been outstanding. To correct this situation, Porter "split its stock," as described next.

Stock Splits

STOCK SPLIT

An action taken by a firm to increase the number of shares outstanding, and thus decrease the per-share price of the stock.

Although there is little empirical evidence to support the contention, a widespread belief in financial circles holds that an *optimal, or psychological, price range* exists for stocks. "Optimal" means that if the price is within this range, the P/E ratio, hence the value of the firm, will be maximized. Many observers, including Porter's management, believe that the best range for most stocks is from $20 to $80 per share. Accordingly, if the price of Porter's stock rose to $80, management probably would declare a two-for-one **stock split,** thus doubling the number of shares outstanding, halving the earnings and dividends per share, and thereby lowering the price of the stock. Each stockholder would have more shares, but each share would be worth less. If the post-split price were $40, Porter's stockholders would be exactly as well off as they were before the split because they would have twice as many shares at half the price as before the split. However, if the price of the stock were to stabilize above $40, stockholders would be better off. Stock splits can be of any size—for example, the stock could be split 2-for-1, 3-for-1, 1½-for-1, or in any other way.[7]

---

[7]Reverse splits, which reduce the shares outstanding, can also be used. For instance, a company whose stock sells for $5 might employ a 1-for-5 reverse split, exchanging one new share for five old ones and raising the value of the shares to about $25, which is within the optimal range. On June 16, 2003, for example, Priceline.com Incorporated initiated a 1-for-6 reverse split to avoid being delisted from NASDAQ.

Stock Dividends

Stock dividends are similar to stock splits in that they "divide the pie into smaller slices" without affecting the fundamental position of the current stockholders. On a 5 percent stock dividend, the holder of 100 shares would receive an additional five shares (without cost); on a 20 percent stock dividend, the same holder would receive 20 new shares; and so on. Again, the total number of shares is increased, so earnings, dividends, and price per share all decline.

If a firm wants to reduce the price of its stock, should it use a stock split or a stock dividend? Stock splits generally are used after a sharp price run-up to produce a large price reduction. Stock dividends typically are used on a regular annual basis to keep the stock price more or less constrained. For example, if a firm's earnings and dividends were growing at about 10 percent per year, its stock price would tend to go up at about that same rate, and it would soon be outside the desired trading range. A 10 percent annual stock dividend would maintain the stock price within the optimal trading range.

Balance Sheet Effects

Although the economic effects of stock splits and stock dividends are virtually identical, accountants treat them somewhat differently. On a 2-for-1 split, the shares outstanding are doubled, and the stock's par value is halved. This treatment is shown in Section II of Table 10–1 for Porter Electronic Controls, using a pro forma 2006 balance sheet.

Section III of Table 10–1 shows the effect of a 20 percent stock dividend. With a stock dividend, the par value is not reduced, but an accounting entry is made transferring funds from the retained earnings account to the common stock and paid-in capital accounts. The transfer from retained earnings is calculated as follows:

10–1

$$\text{Dollars transferred from retained earnings} = \left[\left(\begin{array}{c}\text{Number of shares}\\ \text{outstanding}\end{array}\right) \times \left(\begin{array}{c}\text{Percent stock dividend}\\ \text{as a decimal}\end{array}\right)\right] \times \left(\begin{array}{c}\text{Market price}\\ \text{of the stock}\end{array}\right)$$

Porter has 5 million shares outstanding, and they sell for $80 each, so a 20 percent stock dividend would require the transfer of $80 million:

$$\text{Dollars transferred} = [(5{,}000{,}000)(0.2)](\$80) = \$80{,}000{,}000$$

As shown in the table, $1 million of this $80 million is added to the common stock account and $79 million is added to the additional paid-in capital account. The retained earnings account is reduced from $285 million to $205 million.[8]

---

[8]Note that Porter could not pay a stock dividend that exceeded 71.25 percent; a stock dividend of that percentage would exhaust the retained earnings. Thus, a firm's ability to declare stock dividends is constrained by the amount of its retained earnings. Of course, if Porter had wanted to pay a 50 percent stock dividend, it could have just switched to a 1½-for-1 stock split and accomplished the same thing in terms of the number of shares owned by stockholders.

TABLE 10–1	Porter Electronic Controls Inc.: Stockholders' Equity Accounts, Pro Forma, December 31, 2006 ($ millions, except per share values)

I. Before a Stock Split or Stock Dividend

Common stock (5 million shares outstanding, $1 par)	$ 5.0
Additional paid-in capital	10.0
Retained earnings	285.0
Total common stockholders' equity	$300.0
Book value per share = $300/5	$ 60.0

II. After a Two-for-One Stock Split

Common stock (10 million shares outstanding, $0.50 par)	$ 5.0
Additional paid-in capital	10.0
Retained earnings	285.0
Total common stockholders' equity	$300.0
Book value per share = $300/10	$ 30.0

III. After a 20 Percent Stock Dividend

Common stock (6 million shares outstanding, $1 par)[a]	$ 6.0
Additional paid-in capital[b]	89.0
Retained earnings[b]	205.0
Total common stockholders' equity	$300.0
Book value per share = $300/6	$ 50.0

[a]Shares outstanding are increased by 20 percent, from 5 million to 6 million.

[b]A transfer equal to the market value of the new shares is made from the retained earnings account to the additional paid-in capital and common stock accounts:

$$\text{Transfer} = [(5,000,000 \text{ shares})(0.2)]($80) = $80,000,000.$$

Of this $80 million, ($1 par)(1,000,000 shares) = $1,000,000 goes to common stock and the remaining $79 million to paid-in capital.

Price Effects

Several empirical studies have examined the effects of stock splits and stock dividends on stock prices. These studies suggest that investors see stock splits and stock dividends for what they are—*simply additional pieces of paper*. If stock dividends and splits are accompanied by higher earnings and cash dividends, then investors will bid up the price of the stock. However, if stock dividends are not accompanied by increases in earnings and cash dividends, the dilution of earnings and dividends per share causes the price of the stock to drop by the same percentage as the stock dividend. Thus, the fundamental determinants of price are the underlying earnings and cash dividends per share, and stock splits and stock dividends merely cut the pie into thinner slices.

Self-Test Questions

What is the rationale for a stock split?

Differentiate between the accounting treatments for stock splits and stock dividends.

What is the effect of stock splits and dividends on stock prices?

Dividend Policies Around the World

The dividend policies of companies around the world vary considerably. A recent study found the dividend payout ratios of companies range from 10.5 percent in the Philippines to nearly 70 percent in Taiwan.[9] Table 10–2 shows some of the differences in payout ratios. As you can see, as a percent of earnings, the dividends paid out in Canada, France, and the United States range from about 20 percent to 25 percent, in Spain and the United Kingdom the range is from 30 percent to 40 percent, in Germany and Mexico the rate is between 40 percent and 50 percent, and it is more than 50 percent for companies in Japan and Southeast Asian countries. A study of firms in developing countries, such as Zimbabwe and Pakistan, shows that emerging market firms have average payout ratios that range from approximately 30 percent to 60 percent.[10]

Why do international differences in dividend policies exist? As we mentioned in Chapter 9, it seems logical to attribute the differences to dissimilar tax structures because both dividends and capital gains are taxed differently around the world. The tax codes in most developed countries encourage personal investing and savings more than the U.S. Tax Code. For example, Germany, Italy, and many other European countries do not tax capital gains, and in most other developed countries, including Japan, France, and Canada, capital gains are not taxed unless they exceed some minimum amount. Further, in Germany and Italy, dividends are not taxed as income, and in most other countries some amount of dividends is tax-exempt. The general conclusion we can make, then, is that in countries where capital gains are not taxed, investors should show a preference for companies that retain earnings rather than pay dividends. But it has been found that differences in taxes do not explain the differences in dividend payout ratios among the countries.

A study by Rafael La Porta, Florencio Lopez-de-Silanes, Andrei Shleifer, and Robert W. Vishny offers some insight into the dividend policy differences that exist around the world. They suggest that, all else equal, companies are more willing to pay out greater amounts of earnings as dividends in countries that have measures that help protect the rights of minority stockholders. In such countries, however, firms with many growth opportunities tend to pay lower dividends, which is to be expected because the funds are needed to finance the growth and shareholders are willing to forgo current income in hopes of greater future benefits. On the other hand, in countries where shareholders' rights are not well protected, investors want dividends to be paid because there is great uncertainty about whether management will use earnings for self-gratification rather than for the benefit of the firm. Investors in

---

[9]Rafael La Porta, Florencio Lopez-de-Silanes, Andrei Shleifer, and Robert W. Vishny, "Agency Problems and Dividend Policies Around the World," *Journal of Finance*, February 2000, 1–34.

[10]Varouj Aivazian, Laurence Booth, and Sean Cleary, "Do Emerging Market Firms Follow Different Dividend Policies from U.S. Firms?" *Journal of Financial Research*, Fall 2003, 371–387.

TABLE 10–2	Median Dividend Payout Ratios for Selected Countries

I. Dividend Payout Ratios Less Than 25 Percent

COUNTRY	PAYOUT RATIO
Philippines	10.5
Denmark	17.3
Canada	19.8
United States	22.1
France	23.6

II. Dividend Payout Ratios between 25 Percent and 40 Percent

COUNTRY	PAYOUT RATIO
Switzerland	25.3
Spain	30.5
South Africa	35.6
United Kingdom	36.9
Portugal	38.0

III. Dividend Payout Ratios above 40 Percent

COUNTRY	PAYOUT RATIO
Germany	42.9
Mexico	46.4
India	49.3
Japan	52.9
Taiwan	68.9

SOURCE: Rafael La Porta, Florencio Lopez-de-Silanes, Andrei Shleifer, and Robert W. Vishny, "Agency Problems and Dividend Policies Around the World," *Journal of Finance*, February 2000, 1–34.

these countries accept any dividends they can get—that is, they prefer a "bird in hand." Some countries, including Brazil, Chile, Colombia, Greece, and Venezuela, have regulations requiring firms to pay dividends. In these countries, minority shareholders have few, if any, legally protected rights.

In summary, it appears the most important factor that determines whether stockholders prefer earnings be retained or paid out as dividends is the level of risk associated with future expected dividends, which is mitigated to some degree by regulations that protect minority shareholders' rights.

Self-Test Question

Why do dividend payout ratios of companies differ among different countries?

Summary

Dividend policy involves the decision to pay out earnings versus retaining them for reinvestment in the firm, and dividend policy decisions can have either favorable or unfavorable effects on the price of a firm's stock. The key concepts covered in the chapter are listed here:

- The **optimal dividend policy** is that policy that strikes the balance between current dividends and future growth that maximizes the price of the firm's stock.
- Miller and Modigliani developed the **dividend irrelevance theory,** which holds that a firm's dividend policy has no effect either on the value of its stock or on its cost of capital.
- Those who believe in **dividend relevance** suggest that a particular dividend policy might be preferred because dividends are considered less risky than potential capital gains, taxes must be paid on dividends received in the current period, whereas taxes on capital gains can be deferred until the stock is sold, and so on.
- Because empirical tests of the theories have been inconclusive, *academicians simply cannot tell corporate managers precisely how a change in dividend policy will affect stock prices and capital costs.* Thus, actually determining the optimal dividend policy is often a matter of **judgment.**
- Dividend policy should reflect the existence of the **information content of dividends (signaling), the clientele effect,** and **the free cash flow effect.** The information content, or signaling, hypothesis states that investors regard a dividend change as a signal of management's forecast of future earnings. According to the clientele effect, a firm will attract investors who like the firm's dividend policy. And the free cash flow effect suggests that firms with few capital budgeting opportunities and great amounts of cash should have higher dividend payout ratios if the value maximization goal is pursued.
- In practice, most firms try to follow a policy of paying a **stable, predictable dividend.** This policy provides investors with a stable, dependable income, and it also gives investors information about management's expectations for earnings growth through signaling effects.
- Other dividend policies used include (1) the **residual dividend policy,** in which dividends are paid out of earnings left over after the capital budget has been financed; (2) the **constant payout ratio policy,** in which a constant *percentage* of earnings is targeted to be paid out; and (3) the **low-regular-dividend-plus-extras policy,** in which the firm pays a constant, low dividend that can be maintained even in bad years and then pays an extra dividend in good years.
- A **dividend reinvestment plan (DRIP)** allows stockholders to have the company automatically use their dividends to purchase additional shares of the firm's stock. DRIPs are popular with investors who do not need current income because the plans allow stockholders to acquire additional shares without incurring normal brokerage fees.
- Other factors, such as **legal constraints, investment opportunities, availability and cost of funds from other sources, dilution of ownership,** and **taxes,** are considered by managers when they establish dividend policies.
- A **stock split** is an action taken by a firm to increase the number of shares outstanding. Normally, splits reduce the price per share in proportion to the

increase in shares because splits merely *divide the pie into smaller slices*. A **stock dividend** is a dividend paid in additional shares of stock rather than in cash. Both stock dividends and splits are used to keep stock prices within an "optimal," or psychological, range.

■ Dividend polices differ substantially among companies in different countries. All else equal, firms are willing to pay out **greater relative amounts** of earnings as dividends **in countries that have measures that protect the rights of minority stockholders.**

Questions

10–1 As an investor, would you rather invest in a firm that has a policy of maintaining (a) a constant payout ratio, (b) a stable, predictable dividend per share with a target dividend growth rate, or (c) a constant regular quarterly dividend plus a year-end extra when earnings are sufficiently high or corporate investment needs sufficiently low? Explain your answer, stating how these policies would affect your required rate of return, k_s. Also, discuss how your answer might change if you were a student, a 50-year-old professional with peak earnings, or a retiree.

10–2 How would each of the following changes tend to affect the average dividend *payout ratios* for corporations, other things held constant? Explain your answers.
  a. An increase in the personal income tax rate.
  b. A liberalization of depreciation for federal income tax purposes—that is, faster tax write-offs.
  c. A rise in interest rates.
  d. An increase in corporate profits.
  e. A decline in corporate investment opportunities.
  f. Permission for corporations to deduct dividends for tax purposes as they now can do with interest charges.
  g. A change in the tax code so that both realized and unrealized capital gains in any year were taxed at the same rate as dividends.

10–3 Most firms would like to have their stock selling at a high P/E ratio, and they would also like to have a large number of different shareholders. Explain how stock dividends or stock splits might help achieve these goals.

10–4 What is the difference between a stock dividend and a stock split? As a stockholder, would you prefer to see your company declare a 100 percent stock dividend or a 2-for-1 split? Assume that either action is feasible.

10–5 "The cost of retained earnings is less than the cost of new outside equity capital. Consequently, it is totally irrational for a firm to sell a new issue of stock and to pay dividends during the same year." Discuss this statement.

10–6 Would it ever be rational for a firm to borrow money to pay dividends? Explain.

10–7 Give arguments to support both the relevance and the irrelevance of paying dividends.

10–8 One position expressed in the financial literature is that firms set their dividends as a residual after using income to support new investment.
  a. Explain what a residual dividend policy implies, illustrating your answer with a graph showing how different conditions could lead to different dividend payout ratios.

b. Could the residual dividend policy be consistent with (1) a stable, predictable dividend policy, (2) a constant payout ratio policy, or (3) a low-regular-dividend-plus-extras policy? Answer in terms of both short-run, year-to-year consistency, and longer-run consistency.

c. Think back to Chapter 9, where we considered the relationship between capital structure and the cost of capital. If the WACC-versus-debt-ratio plot was shaped like a sharp V, would this have a different implication for the importance of setting dividends according to the residual policy than if the plot was shaped like a shallow bowl (or a flattened U)?

Self-Test Problems

(Solutions appear in Appendix B)

key terms **ST-1** Define each of the following terms:

    a. Optimal dividend policy

    b. Dividend irrelevance theory; dividend relevance theory

    c. Information content, or signaling, hypothesis; clientele effect; free cash flow hypothesis

    d. Residual dividend policy; stable, predictable dividend policy; constant payout ratio policy; low-regular-dividend-plus-extra policy

    e. Declaration date; holder-of-record date; ex-dividend date; payment date

    f. Dividend reinvestment plan (DRIP)

    g. Stock split; stock dividend

alternative dividend policies **ST-2** Components Manufacturing Corporation (CMC) has an all-common-equity capital structure. It has 200,000 shares of $2 par value common stock outstanding. When CMC's founder, who was also its research director and most successful inventor, retired unexpectedly to the South Pacific in late 2005, CMC was left suddenly and permanently with materially lower growth expectations and relatively few attractive new investment opportunities. Unfortunately, there was no way to replace the founder's contributions to the firm. Previously, CMC found it necessary to plow back most of its earnings to finance growth, which averaged 12 percent per year. Future growth at a 5 percent rate is considered realistic, but that level would call for an increase in the dividend payout. Further, it now appears that new investment projects with at least the 14 percent rate of return required by CMC's stockholders ($k_s = 14\%$) would amount to only $800,000 for 2006 in comparison to a projected $2,000,000 of net income. If the existing 20 percent dividend payout were continued, retained earnings would be $1.6 million in 2006, but, as noted, investments that yield the 14 percent cost of capital would amount to only $800,000.

    The one encouraging factor is that the high earnings from existing assets are expected to continue, and net income of $2 million is still expected for 2006. Given the dramatically changed circumstances, CMC's management is reviewing the firm's dividend policy.

    a. Assuming that the acceptable 2006 investment projects would be financed entirely by earnings retained during the year, calculate DPS in 2006 if CMC follows the residual dividend policy.

    b. What *payout ratio* does your answer to part a imply for 2006?

    c. If a 60 percent payout ratio is maintained for the foreseeable future, what is your estimate of the present market price of the common stock? How does this compare with the market price that should have prevailed under the assumptions existing just before the news about the founder's retirement? If the two values of P_0 are different, comment on why.

  d. What would happen to the price of the stock if the old 20 percent payout were continued? Assume that if this payout is maintained, the average rate of return on the retained earnings will fall to 7.5 percent and the new growth rate will be 6 percent.

Problems

stock dividend   **10-1** The McLaughlin Corporation declared a 6 percent stock dividend. Construct a pro forma balance sheet showing the effect of this action. The stock was selling for $37.50 per share, and a condensed version of McLaughlin's balance sheet as of December 31, 2005, before the dividend, follows ($ millions):

Cash	$ 112.5	Debt	$1,500
Other assets	2,887.5	Common stock (75 million shares outstanding, $1 par)	75
		Paid-in capital	300
		Retained earnings	1,125
Total assets	$3,000.0	Total liabilities and equity	$3,000

alternative dividend policies   **10-2** In 2005 the Sirmans Company paid dividends totaling $3.6 million on net income of $10.8 million. Sirmans had a normal year in 2005, and for the past 10 years, earnings have grown at a constant rate of 10 percent. However, in 2006, earnings are expected to jump to $14.4 million, and the firm expects to have profitable investment opportunities of $8.4 million. It is predicted that Sirmans will not be able to maintain the 2006 level of earnings growth—the high 2006 earnings level is attributable to an exceptionally profitable new product line introduced that year—and the company will return to its previous 10 percent growth rate. Sirmans's target debt ratio is 40 percent.

  a. Calculate Sirmans's total dividends for 2006 if it follows each of the following policies:

   (1) Its 2006 dividend payment is set to force dividends to grow at the long-run growth rate in earnings.

   (2) It continues the 2005 dividend payout ratio.

   (3) It uses a pure residual dividend policy (40 percent of the $8.4 million investment is financed with debt).

   (4) It employs a regular-dividend-plus-extras policy, with the regular dividend being based on the long-run growth rate and the extra dividend being set according to the residual policy.

  b. Which of the preceding policies would you recommend? Restrict your choices to the ones listed, but justify your answer.

  c. Assume that investors expect Sirmans to pay total dividends of $9 million in 2006 and to have the dividend grow at 10 percent after 2006. The total market value of the stock is $180 million. What is the company's cost of equity?

  d. What is Sirmans's long-run average return on equity? [*Hint:* g = (Retention rate) × (ROE) = (1.0 – Payout rate) × (ROE).]

  e. Does a 2006 dividend of $9 million seem reasonable in view of your answers to parts c and d? If not, should the dividend be higher or lower?

dividend policy and capital structure   **10-3** Ybor City Tobacco Company has for many years enjoyed a moderate but stable growth in sales and earnings. However, cigar consumption and consequently

Ybor's sales have been falling recently, primarily because of an increasing awareness of the dangers of smoking to health. Anticipating further declines in tobacco sales for the future, Ybor's management hopes eventually to move almost entirely out of the tobacco business and into a newly developed, diversified product line in growth-oriented industries. The company is especially interested in the prospects for pollution-control devices because its research department has already done much work on the problems of filtering smoke. Right now the company estimates that an investment of $15 million is necessary to purchase new facilities and to begin operations on these products, but the investment could be earning a return of about 18 percent within a short time. The only other available investment opportunity totals $6 million and is expected to return about 10.4 percent.

The company is expected to pay a $3 dividend on its 3 million outstanding shares, the same as its dividend last year. The directors might, however, change the dividend if there are good reasons for doing so. Total earnings after taxes for the year are expected to be $14.25 million; the common stock is currently selling for $56.25; the firm's target debt ratio (debt/assets ratio) is 45 percent; and its marginal tax rate is 40 percent. The costs of various forms of financing are as follows:

New bonds, $k_d = 11\%$. This is a before-tax rate.

New common stock sold at $56.25 per share will net $51.25.

Required rate of return on retained earnings, $k_s = 14\%$.

a. Calculate Ybor's expected payout ratio, the break point at which the marginal cost of capital (MCC) rises, and its MCC above and below the point of exhaustion of retained earnings at the current payout. (*Hint:* k_s is given, and $\hat{D}_1/P_0$ can be found. Then, knowing k_s and $\hat{D}_1/P_0$, g can be determined.)
b. How large should Ybor's capital budget be for the year?
c. What is an appropriate dividend policy for Ybor? How should the capital budget be financed?
d. How might risk factors influence Ybor's cost of capital, capital structure, and dividend policy?
e. What assumptions, if any, do your answers to the preceding parts make about investors' preferences for dividends versus capital gains (in other words, what are investors' preferences regarding the $\hat{D}_1/P_0$ and g components of k_s)?

Exam-Type Problems

The problems included in this section are set up in such a way that they could be used as multiple-choice exam problems.

external equity financing **10–4** Northern California Heating and Cooling Inc. has a six-month backlog of orders for its patented solar heating system. To meet this demand, management plans to expand production capacity by 40 percent with a $10 million investment in plant and machinery. The firm wants to maintain a 40 percent debt/assets ratio in its capital structure; it also wants to maintain its past dividend policy of distributing 45 percent of last year's net income. In 2005, net income was $5 million. How much external equity must Northern California seek at the beginning of 2006 to expand capacity as desired?

dividend payout **10–5** The Garlington Corporation expects next year's net income to be $15 million. The firm's debt/assets ratio currently is 40 percent. Garlington has $12 million of profitable investment opportunities, and it wishes to maintain its existing debt ratio. According to the residual dividend policy, how large should Garlington's dividend payout ratio be next year?

stock split   **10–6** After a 5-for-1 stock split, the Swensen Company paid a dividend of $0.75 per new share, which represents a 9 percent increase over last year's presplit dividend. What was last year's dividend per share?

dividend payout   **10–7** The Scanlon Company's optimal capital structure calls for 50 percent debt and 50 percent common equity. The interest rate on its debt is a constant 10 percent; its cost of common equity from retained earnings is 14 percent; the cost of equity from new stock is 16 percent; and its marginal tax rate is 40 percent. Scanlon has the following investment opportunities:

Project A: Cost = $5 million; IRR = 20%

Project B: Cost = $5 million; IRR = 12%

Project C: Cost = $5 million; IRR = 9%

Scanlon expects to have net income of $7,287,500. If Scanlon bases its dividends on the residual policy, what will its payout ratio be?

Integrative Problem

dividend policy   **10–8** Information Systems Inc. (ISI), which develops software for the health care industry, was founded five years ago by Donald Brown and Margaret Clark, who are still its only stockholders. ISI has now reached the stage where outside equity capital is necessary if the firm is to achieve its growth targets yet still maintain its target capital structure of 60 percent equity and 40 percent debt. Therefore, Brown and Clark have decided to take the company public. Until now, Brown and Clark have paid themselves reasonable salaries but routinely reinvested all after-tax earnings in the firm, so dividend policy has not been an issue. However, before talking with potential outside investors, they must decide on a dividend policy.

Assume that you were recently hired by Andrew Adamson & Company (AA), a national consulting firm, which has been asked to help ISI prepare for its public offering. Martha Millon, the senior AA consultant in your group, has asked you to make a presentation to Brown and Clark in which you review the theory of dividend policy and discuss the following questions:

a. (1) What is meant by the term *dividend policy?*

   (2) The terms *irrelevance* and *relevance* have been used to describe theories regarding the way dividend policy affects a firm's value. Explain what these terms mean, and briefly discuss the relevance of dividend policy.

   (3) Explain the relationships between dividend policy and (i) stock price and (ii) the cost of equity under each dividend policy theory.

   (4) What results have empirical studies of the dividend theories produced? How does all this affect what we can tell managers about dividend policy?

b. Discuss (1) the information content, or signaling, hypothesis; (2) the clientele effect; (3) the free cash flow hypothesis; and (4) their effects on dividend policy.

c. (1) Assume that ISI has an $800,000 capital budget planned for the coming year. You have determined that its present capital structure (60 percent equity and 40 percent debt) is optimal, and its net income is forecasted at $600,000. Use the residual dividend policy approach to determine ISI's total dollar dividend and payout ratio. In the process, explain what the residual dividend policy is, and use a graph to illustrate your answer. Then explain what would happen if net income were forecasted at $400,000, or at $800,000.

(2) In general terms, how would a change in investment opportunities affect the payout ratio under the residual payment policy?

(3) What are the advantages and disadvantages of the residual policy? (*Hint:* Don't neglect signaling and clientele effects.)

d. What are some other commonly used dividend payment policies? What are their advantages and disadvantages? Which policy is most widely used in practice?

e. What are dividend reinvestment plans (DRIPs), and how do these plans work?

f. What are stock dividends and stock splits? What are the advantages and disadvantages of stock dividends and splits? When should a stock dividend as opposed to a stock split be used?

Computer-Related Problem

Work the problem in this section only if you are using the computer problem diskette.

dividend policy and capital structure

10–9 Use the model in the File C10 to work this problem. Refer back to Problem 10–3. Assume that Ybor's management is considering a change in the firm's capital structure to include more debt; thus, management would like to analyze the effects of an increase in the debt ratio to 60 percent. The treasurer believes that such a move would cause lenders to increase the required rate of return on new bonds to 12 percent and that k_s would rise to 14.5 percent.

a. How would this change affect the optimal capital budget?

b. If k_s rose to 16 percent, would the low-return project be acceptable?

c. Would the project selection be affected if the dividend was reduced to $1.88 from $3.00, still assuming $k_s = 16$ percent?

GET REAL with Thomson ONE

10-10 Compare the dividend payouts of McDonald's Corporation [MCD], a quick-service restaurant firm, and its peers, as denoted by SIC code. Answer the following questions:

a. What was the yearly dividend yield during the past five years for McDonald's? [Prices/Overviews/Thomsom Market Data/Stock Valuation Overviews]

b. How much did McDonald's pay out in dividends to shareholders in each of the five years? State your answer both in total dollars and on a per share basis. [Click on Financials/Thomson Financials/Cash Flow Statement/5 year Cash Flow Statement]

c. How did McDonald's average dividend compare to that of its peers? [*Hint:* Click on Peers/Overviews/Comparative Profiles]

d. If you analyze the total dividend paid and the dividend yield over the five-year period, would McDonald's or one of its peers be the best investment if you are concerned only with the dividend income generated by the investment? Explain your answer.

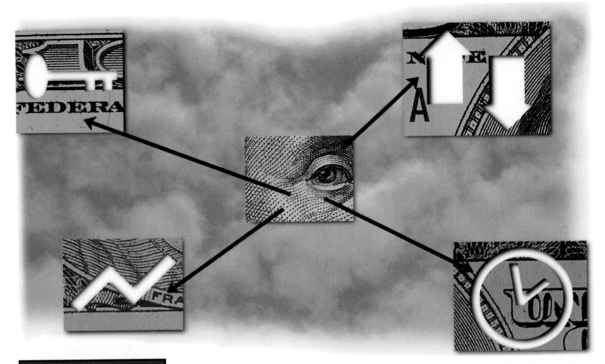

PART V

Forecasting, Planning, and Control

CHAPTER 11

Analysis of Financial Statements

A MANAGERIAL PERSPECTIVE

Corporations in the United States are required to make "full and fair" disclosure of their operations by publishing various financial statements and other reports required by the Securities and Exchange Commission (SEC), the Financial Accounting Standards Board (FASB), and the American Institute of Certified Public Accountants (AICPA). One such publication is the annual report, which is often used to convey more than financial results; in some cases, the annual report is viewed as an opportunity to showcase top management and sell the future of the company, without regard to the financial information. So it is not unusual for work on the annual report to begin as much as six months before its publication, and many firms hire professional designers and writers to ensure that the final product looks sharp and reads well. Some firms pride themselves in the unique packaging designs used. For example, since 1977, McCormick & Company has used one of the spices and seasonings it produces to scent the paper on which its annual report is printed—the scent for 2003 was from a cinnamon bun.

In most instances, the puffery contained in annual reports detracts from the primary purpose to provide objective financial information about the firm. Of course, some companies use the annual report as originally intended—to communicate the financial position of the firm. One such firm is Berkshire Hathaway, whose legendary chairman Warren Buffett says, "I assume I have a very intelligent partner who has been away for a year and needs to be filled in on all that's happened." Consequently, in his letters he often admits mistakes and emphasizes the negative along with the positive. Buffett also uses his letters to educate his shareholders and to help them interpret the data presented in the rest of the report. Berkshire Hathaway's annual reports contain little, if any, puffery, freeing readers to focus on the company's financial statements and Buffett's interpretation of them. Some CEOs might contend that such a bare-bones approach is too dull for the average stockholder and, further, that some readers might actually be intimidated by the information overload. But the manner in which Buffett presents financial information for Berkshire Hathaway seems to work, because the company's stockholders are considered more sophisticated than average investors. If you would like to examine some of the statements made by Warren Buffett, visit the Web site at http://berkshirehathaway.com.

More and more, firms are recognizing that the "slick" annual report has (1) lost its credibility with serious seekers of financial information and (2) become increasingly more expensive to produce. With the growth in electronic communications, the trend in recent years has been to post annual reports, devoid of the traditional "frills," on the company's Web site and refer stockholders to that location.

As you read this chapter, think about the kinds of information corporations provide their stockholders. Do you think the basic financial statements provide adequate data for investment decisions? What other information might be helpful? Also, consider the pros and cons of Warren Buffett's decision to include frank and frequently self-critical letters in his company's annual reports. Would you suggest that other companies follow suit? ■

Financial statement analysis involves a comparison of a firm's performance with that of other firms in the same line of business, which usually is identified by the firm's industry classification. Generally speaking, the analysis is used to determine the firm's financial position so as to identify its current strengths and weaknesses and to suggest actions the firm might pursue to take advantage of the strengths and correct any weaknesses.

Financial statement analysis is not only important for the firm's managers, but also for the firm's investors and creditors. Internally, financial managers use the information provided by financial analysis to help make financing and investment decisions to maximize the firm's value. Externally, stockholders and creditors use financial statement analysis to evaluate the attractiveness of the firm as an investment by examining its ability to meet its current and expected future financial obligations.

In this chapter, we discuss how to evaluate a firm's current financial position. For the most part, this chapter should be a review of what you learned in accounting. However, accounting focuses on how financial statements are made, whereas our focus is on how they are used by management to improve the firm's performance and by investors (either stockholders or creditors) to examine the firm's financial position when evaluating its attractiveness as an investment. In addition, because taxes are critically important in financial decisions, we discuss key features of the U.S. tax laws at the end of the chapter.

Financial Statements and Reports

ANNUAL REPORT
A report issued annually by a corporation to its stockholders, which contains basic financial statements, as well as management's opinion of the past year's operations and the firm's future prospects.

Of the various reports corporations issue to their stockholders, the **annual report** probably is the most important. Two types of information are provided in this report. First, the verbal section, often presented as a letter from the chairman, describes the firm's operating results during the past year and then discusses new developments that will affect future operations. Second, the annual report presents four basic financial statements: the *income statement*, the *balance sheet*, the *statement of retained earnings*, and the *statement of cash flows*. Together, these statements give an accounting picture of the firm's operations and financial position. Detailed data are provided for at least the two most recent years, along with historical summaries of key operating statistics for the past five or 10 years.[1]

---

[1]Firms also provide quarterly reports, but these are much less comprehensive than the annual reports. In addition, larger firms file even more detailed statements, giving breakdowns for each major division or subsidiary, with the Securities and Exchange Commission (SEC). These reports, called *10-K reports*, are made available to stockholders upon request to a company's corporate secretary. Finally, many larger firms also publish *statistical supplements*, which give financial statement data and key ratios going back 10 to 20 years.

TABLE 11-1	Unilate Textiles: Comparative Income Statements for Years Ending December 31 ($ millions, except per share data)

	2005	2004
Net sales	$ 1,500.0	$ 1,435.0
Cost of goods sold	(1,230.0)[a]	(1,176.7)
Gross profit	$ 270.0	$ 258.3
Fixed operating expenses except depreciation	(90.0)	(85.0)
Depreciation	(50.0)	(40.0)
Earnings before interest and taxes (EBIT)	$ 130.0	$ 133.3
Interest	(40.0)	(35.0)
Earnings before taxes (EBT)	$ 90.0	$ 98.3
Taxes (40%)	(36.0)	(39.3)
Net income	$ 54.0	$ 59.0
Preferred dividends	0.0	0.0
Earnings available to common stockholders (EAC)	$ 54.0	$ 59.0
Common dividends	(29.0)	(27.0)
Addition to retained earnings	$ 25.0	$ 32.0
Per Share Data:		
Shares outstanding	25.00	25.00
Common stock price	$ 23.00	$ 23.00
Earnings per share	$ 2.16	$ 2.36
Dividends per share	$ 1.16	$ 1.08

[a]Parentheses are used to denote negative numbers.

The quantitative and verbal information contained in the annual report are equally important. The financial statements report what actually has happened to the firm's financial position and to its earnings and dividends over the past few years, whereas the verbal statements attempt to explain why things turned out the way they did. To illustrate how annual reports can prove helpful, we will use data taken from Unilate Textiles, a textile manufacturer. Formed in 1980 in North Carolina, Unilate has experienced steady growth and has earned a reputation for selling quality products.

Table 11–1 shows that Unilate Textiles' earnings decreased by $5 million in 2005, to $54 million versus $59 million in 2004. In the annual report, management reported that the 8.5 percent earnings drop resulted from losses associated with a poor cotton crop and from increased costs due to a three-month strike and a retooling of the factory. Management then went on to paint a more optimistic picture for the future, stating that full operations had been resumed, that several unprofitable businesses had been eliminated, and that 2006 profits were expected to rise sharply. Of course, an increase in profitability might not occur, and analysts should compare management's past statements with subsequent results to determine if management's optimism is justified. In any event, *the information contained in an annual report is used by investors to form expectations about future earnings and dividends.* Clearly, investors are quite interested in the annual report.

The Income Statement

INCOME STATEMENT
A statement summarizing the firm's revenues and expenses over an accounting period, generally a quarter or a year.

The **income statement,** also called the profit and loss statement, presents the results of business operations during a specified period of time such as a quarter or a year. The statement summarizes the revenues generated and the expenses incurred by the firm during the accounting period. Table 11–1 gives the 2004 and 2005 income statements for Unilate Textiles. Net sales are shown at the top of each statement, after which various costs, including income taxes, are subtracted to obtain the net income available to common stockholders. A report on earnings and dividends per share is given at the bottom of the statement. In managerial finance, earnings per share (EPS) is called "the bottom line," denoting that of all the items on the income statement, EPS is the most important. Unilate earned $2.16 per share in 2005, down from $2.36 in 2004, but it still raised the per share dividend from $1.08 to $1.16.

Not all of the amounts shown on the income statement represent cash flows. Recall from what you learned in accounting that, for most corporations, the income statement is generated using the accrual method of accounting. This means revenues are recognized when they are earned, not when the cash is received, and expenses are realized when they are incurred, not when the cash is paid. This point will be addressed further later in the chapter.

The Balance Sheet

BALANCE SHEET
A statement of the firm's financial position at a specific point in time.

The **balance sheet** shows the financial position of a firm at a specific point in time. This financial statement indicates the investments made by the firm in the form of assets and the means by which the assets were financed—that is, whether the funds were raised by borrowing (liabilities) or by selling ownership shares (equity). Unilate's year-end 2004 and 2005 balance sheets are given in Table 11–2. The top portion of the balance sheet shows that on December 31, 2005, Unilate's assets totaled $845 million, while the bottom portion shows the liabilities and equity, or the claims against these assets. The assets are listed in order of their "liquidity," or the length of time it typically takes to convert them to cash. The claims are listed in the order in which they must be paid: Accounts payable generally must be paid within 30 to 45 days, accruals are payable within 60 to 90 days, and so on, down to the stockholders' equity accounts, which represent ownership and need never be "paid off."

Some additional points about the balance sheet are worth noting:

1. **Cash versus other assets.** Although the assets are all stated in terms of dollars, only cash represents actual money that can be spent. Receivables are bills others owe Unilate; inventories show the dollars the company has invested in raw materials, work-in-process, and finished goods available for sale; and net fixed assets reflect the amount of money Unilate paid for its plant and equipment when it acquired those assets less the amount that has been written off (depreciated) since the acquisition of those assets. Unilate can write checks at present for a total of $15 million (versus current liabilities of $130 million due within a year). The noncash assets should produce cash over time, but they do not represent cash in hand, and the amount of cash they would bring if they

TABLE 11–2	Unilate Textiles: December 31 Comparative Balance Sheets ($ millions)			

	2005		2004	
Assets				
Cash and marketable securities		$ 15.0		$ 40.0
Accounts receivable		180.0		160.0
Inventory		270.0		200.0
Total current assets		$465.0		$400.0
Gross plant and equipment	$680.0		$600.0	
Less: Accumulated depreciation	(300.0)		(250.0)	
Net plant and equipment		380.0		350.0
Total assets		$845.0		$750.0
Liabilities and Equity				
Accounts payable		$ 30.0		$ 15.0
Accruals		60.0		55.0
Notes payable		40.0		35.0
Total current liabilities		$130.0		$105.0
Long-term bonds		300.0		255.0
Total liabilities		$430.0		$360.0
Common stock		130.0		130.0
Retained earnings		285.0		260.0
Owners' equity		$415.0		$390.0
Total liabilities and equity		$845.0		$750.0

NOTE: Unilate has no preferred stock, so owners' equity includes common equity only.

were sold today could be higher or lower than the values at which they are carried on the books (their book values).

2. **Liabilities versus stockholders' equity.** The claims against assets—that is, the sources of financing—are of two types: liabilities (or money the company owes) and the stockholders' ownership position. The balance sheet must *balance*, so the **common stockholders' equity,** or **net worth,** is a residual that represents the amount stockholders would receive if all of the firm's assets could be sold at their book values and all of the liabilities could be paid at their book values. Unilate's 2005 net worth is

COMMON STOCKHOLDERS' EQUITY (NET WORTH)

The capital supplied by common stockholders— capital stock, paid-in capital, and retained earnings.

$$\text{Assets} - \text{Liabilities} = \text{Stockholders' equity}$$

$$\$845 \text{ million} - \$430 \text{ million} = \$415 \text{ million}$$

Suppose assets decline in value—for example, suppose some of the accounts receivable are written off as bad debts. If liabilities remain constant, the value of the stockholders' equity must decline. Therefore, the risk of asset value fluctuations is borne by the stockholders. Note, however, that if asset values rise (perhaps because of inflation), these benefits will accrue to the stockholders as well. The change in the firm's net worth is reflected by changes in the retained earnings account; if bad debts are written off in the asset section of the balance sheet, the retained earnings balance is reduced in the liabilities and equity section.

3. **Preferred versus common stock.** Chapter 18 includes a detailed discussion of preferred stock and its use as a source of financing. As we will see, preferred stock is a hybrid, or a cross between common stock and debt. In the event of bankruptcy, the payoff to preferred stock ranks below debt but above common stock. Common stockholders, who are the "true" owners of the firm, often view preferred stock as another form of debt because, like debt, the payment to preferred stockholders (dividend) is fixed, so preferred stockholders do not benefit if the company's earnings grow. Also, most financial analysts combine preferred stock with debt when evaluating the financial position of a firm because, even though it is not a liability, the preferred dividend is considered a fixed obligation of the firm. Therefore, when the term *equity* is used in finance, we generally mean *common equity*. Like most firms, Unilate Textiles does not currently use preferred stock financing.

4. **Breakdown of the common equity account.** A detailed discussion of the common equity accounts is given in Chapter 16. At this point, it is important to note that often the common equity section is divided into three accounts: common stock, paid-in capital, and retained earnings. The **retained earnings** account is built up over time as the firm "saves," or reinvests, a part of its earnings rather than paying the earnings out as dividends. The other two common equity accounts arise from the issuance of stock to raise new capital.

   The breakdown of the common equity accounts shows whether the company actually earned the funds reported in its equity accounts or whether the funds came mainly from selling stock. This information is important both to creditors and to stockholders. For instance, a potential creditor would be interested in the amount of money the owners put up, whereas stockholders would want to know the form in which the money was put up.

5. **Accounting alternatives.** Not every firm uses the same method to determine the account balances shown on the balance sheet. For instance, Unilate uses the FIFO (first-in, first-out) method to determine the inventory value shown on its balance sheet. It could have used the LIFO (last-in, first-out) method. During a period of rising prices, compared to LIFO, FIFO will produce a higher balance sheet inventory value but a lower cost of goods sold, thus a higher net income.

   In some cases, a company uses one accounting method to construct financial statements provided to stockholders and another accounting method for tax purposes, internal reports, and so forth. For example, a company will use the most accelerated method permissible to calculate depreciation for tax purposes because accelerated methods lower the taxable income. At the same time, the company might use straight line depreciation for constructing financial statements reported to stockholders, because a higher net income results. There is nothing illegal or unethical with this practice, but when evaluating firms, users of financial statements must be aware that more than one accounting alternative is available for constructing financial statements.

6. **The time dimension.** The balance sheet can be thought of as a snapshot of the firm's financial position *at a point in time*. For example, on December 31, 2004, Unilate had $40 million of cash and marketable securities, but this account had been reduced to $15 million by the end of 2005. The income statement, on the

RETAINED EARNINGS

That portion of the firm's earnings that has been retained (saved) rather than paid out as dividends.

TABLE 11–3	Unilate Textiles: Statement of Retained Earnings for the Year Ending December 31, 2005 ($ millions)

Balance of retained earnings, December 31, 2004	$260
Add: 2005 net income	54
Less: 2005 dividends to stockholders	(29)
Balance of retained earnings, December 31, 2005	$285

other hand, reports on operations *over a period of time*. For example, during the calendar year 2005. Unilate's 2005 sales amounted to $1.5 billion, and its net income available to common stockholders was $54 million. The balance sheet changes every day as inventories are increased or decreased, as fixed assets are added or retired, as bank loans are increased or decreased, and so forth. Companies whose businesses are seasonal have especially large changes in their balance sheets during the year. For example, most retailers have large inventories just before Christmas but low inventories and high accounts receivable just after Christmas. Therefore, firms' balance sheets will change over the year, depending on the date on which the statement is constructed.

Statement of Retained Earnings

STATEMENT OF RETAINED EARNINGS

A statement reporting the change in the firm's retained earnings as a result of the income generated and retained during the year. The balance sheet figure for retained earnings is the sum of the earnings retained for each year the firm has been in business.

Changes in the common equity accounts between balance sheet dates are reported in the **statement of retained earnings**. Unilate's statement is shown in Table 11–3. The company earned $54 million during 2005, it paid out $29 million in common dividends, and it retained $25 million for reinvestment in the business. Thus, the balance sheet item "Retained Earnings" increased from $260 million at the end of 2004 to $285 million reported at the end of 2005. Note that the balance sheet account "Retained Earnings" represents a claim *against assets*, not assets per se. Firms retain earnings primarily to expand the business, and this means investing in plant and equipment, in inventories, and so on, *not* necessarily in a bank account. Changes in retained earnings represent the recognition that income generated by the firm during the accounting period has been reinvested in assets rather than paid out as dividends to stockholders. In other words, changes in retained earnings result because common stockholders allow the firm to reinvest in itself funds that otherwise could be distributed as dividends. *As a result, retained earnings as reported on the balance sheet do not represent cash and are not "available" for the payment of dividends or anything else.*[2]

---

[2]The amount reported in the retained earnings account is *not* an indication of the amount of cash the firm has. Cash (as of the balance sheet date) is found in the cash account—an asset account. A positive number in the retained earnings account indicates only that in the past, according to generally accepted accounting principles, the firm has earned an income, but its dividends have been less than its reported income. Even though a company reports record earnings and shows an increase in the retained earnings account, it still might be short of cash.

The same situation holds for individuals. You might own a new BMW (no loan), lots of clothes, and an expensive stereo, and, hence, have a high net worth, but if you had only 23 cents in your pocket plus $5 in your checking account, you would still be short of cash.

Accounting Income versus Cash Flow

When you studied the construction of income statements in accounting, the emphasis probably was on determining the net income of the firm. In finance, however, we focus on *cash flows*. The value of an asset (or a whole firm) is determined by the cash flows it generates. The firm's net income is important, but cash flows are even more crucial, because cash is needed to continue normal business operations such as the payment of financial obligations, the purchase of assets, and the payment of dividends.

As we discussed in Chapter 1, the goal of the firm should be to maximize the price of its stock. Because the value of any asset, including a share of stock, depends on the cash flows produced by the asset, managers should strive to maximize cash flows available to investors over the long run. A business's **cash flows** include the cash receipts and the cash disbursements. The income statement contains revenues and expenses, some of which are cash items and some of which are noncash items. Generally the largest noncash item included on the income statement is depreciation, which is an operating cost. We need to understand the role of depreciation for the recognition of income, as well as the impact depreciation has on cash flows.

Depreciation results because we want to match revenues and expenses, not because we want to match cash inflows and cash outflows, to compute the income earned by the firm during a specific accounting period. When a firm purchases a long-term asset, it is intended to be used to produce revenues for multiple years in the future. The cash payment for the asset occurs on the date of purchase. But because the productive capacity of the asset is not used up in the year of purchase, its full cost is not recognized as an expense in that year. Rather, the value of the asset is expensed away over its lifetime, because, as it is used to generate revenues, the value of the asset declines. Depreciation is the means by which the reduction in the asset's value, which is an operating cost, is matched with the revenues the asset helps to produce. The bottom line is that *depreciation is a noncash charge used to compute net income, so if net income is used to obtain an estimate of the net cash flow from operations, the amount of depreciation must be added back to the income figure.*

To see how depreciation affects cash flows, consider the following simplified income statement (Column 1) and cash flow statement (Column 2). Here we assume that all sales revenues were received in cash during the year and that all costs except depreciation were paid in cash during the year. Cash flows are seen to equal net income plus depreciation:

CASH FLOWS
The cash receipts and the cash disbursements, as opposed to the revenues and expenses reported for the computation of net income, generated by a firm during some specified period.

	INCOME STATEMENT (1)		CASH FLOWS (2)	
Sales revenues		$750		$750
Cost, except depreciation	$(525)		$(525)	
Depreciation (DEP)	(75)		—	
Total operating costs		(600)		(525) (Cash costs)
Earnings before taxes		$150		$225 (Pretax cash flow)
Taxes (40%)		(60)		(60) (From Column 1)
Net income (NI)		$ 90		
Add back depreciation		75		
Net cash flow = NI + DEP		$165		$165

As we saw in Chapter 5, a stock's value is based on the cash flows that investors expect it to provide in the future. Although any individual investor could sell the stock and receive cash for it, the *cash flow* provided by the stock itself is the expected future dividend stream, and that expected dividend stream provides the fundamental basis for the stock's value.

Because dividends are paid in cash, a company's ability to pay dividends depends on its cash flows. Cash flows generally are related to the firm's **accounting profit,** which is simply the net income reported on its income statement. Although companies with relatively high accounting profits generally have relatively high cash flows, the relationship is not precise. Therefore, investors are concerned with cash flow projections as well as profit projections.

ACCOUNTING PROFIT

A firm's net income as reported on its income statement.

Firms can be thought of as having two separate but related bases of value: *existing assets,* which provide profits and cash flows, and *growth opportunities,* which represent opportunities to make new investments that will increase future profits and cash flows. The ability to take advantage of growth opportunities often depends on the availability of the cash needed to buy new assets, and the cash flows from existing assets are often the primary source of the funds used to make profitable new investments. This is another reason why both investors and managers are concerned with cash flows as well as profits.

For our purposes, it is useful to divide cash flows into two classes: (1) *operating cash flows* and (2) *other cash flows.* **Operating cash flows** are those that arise from normal operations, and they are, in essence, the difference between cash collections and cash expenses, including taxes paid. Other cash flows arise from borrowing, the sale of fixed assets, or the repurchase of common stock, for example. Our focus here is on operating cash flows.

OPERATING CASH FLOWS

Those cash flows that arise from normal operations; the difference between cash collections and cash expenses.

Operating cash flows can differ from accounting profits (or net income) for two primary reasons:

1. All the taxes reported on the income statement might not have to be paid during the current year, or, under certain circumstances, the actual cash payments for taxes might exceed the tax figure deducted from sales to calculate net income. The reasons for these tax cash flow differentials are discussed in detail in accounting courses.
2. Sales might be on credit, hence not represent cash, and some of the expenses (or costs) deducted from sales to determine profits might not be cash costs. Most important, depreciation is not a cash cost—that is, it is a noncash expense.

Thus, operating cash flows could be larger or smaller than accounting profits during any given year.

Statement of Cash Flows

STATEMENT OF CASH FLOWS

A statement reporting the impact of a firm's operating, investing, and financing activities on cash flows over an accounting period.

The **statement of cash flows** is designed to show how the firm's operations have affected its cash position by examining the investment (uses of cash) and financing decisions (sources of cash) of the firm. The information contained in the statement of cash flows can help answer questions such as: Is the firm generating the cash needed to purchase additional fixed assets for growth? Does the firm have excess cash flows that can be used to repay debt or to invest in new products? This information is useful both for financial managers and investors, so the statement of cash flows is an important part of the annual report.

Constructing a statement of cash flows is relatively easy. First, to some extent, the cash flow effects of a firm's operations are shown in its income statement. For example, Unilate reported its 2005 net income as $54 million, which we know includes a $50 million depreciation expense that is a noncash operating cost. So, if the $50 million depreciation expense is added back to the $54 million net income, we have an estimate of cash flows from normal operations equal to $104 million. For most firms, however, some of the reported revenues have not been collected and some of the reported expenses have not been paid at the time the income statement is constructed. To adjust the *estimate* of cash flows obtained from the income statement and to account for cash flows not reflected in the income statement, we need to examine the impact of changes in the balance sheet accounts during the year in question. Looking at the changes in the balance sheet accounts from the beginning to the end of the year, we want to identify which items provided cash (sources) and which items used cash (uses) during the year. To determine whether a change in a balance sheet account was a source or a use of cash, we can use the following simple rules:

SOURCES OF CASH	USES OF CASH
Increase in a Liability or Equity Account	***Decrease in a Liability or Equity Account***
Borrowing funds or selling stock provides the firm with cash.	Paying off a loan or buying back stock uses cash.
Decrease in an Asset Account	***Increase in an Asset Account***
Selling inventory or collecting receivables provides cash.	Buying fixed assets or buy more inventory uses cash.

Using these rules, we can identify which changes in Unilate's balance sheet accounts provided cash and which changes used cash during 2005. Table 11–4 shows the results of this identification. In addition, the table includes the cash flow information contained in Unilate's 2005 income statement.

The information contained in Table 11–4 can be used to construct the statement of cash flows shown in Table 11–5.[3] Each balance sheet change in Table 11–4 is classified as resulting from (1) operations, (2) long-term investments, or (3) financing activities. Operating cash flows are those associated with the production and sale of goods and services. The amount of net income plus depreciation is the primary operating cash flow, but changes in accounts payable, accounts receivable, inventories, and accruals are also classified as operating cash flows, because these accounts are directly affected by the firm's day-to-day operations. Investment cash flows arise from the purchase or sale of plant, property, and equipment. Financing cash inflows result from issuing debt or common stock, and financing outflows occur when the firm pays dividends or repays debt. The cash inflows and outflows from these three activities are summed to determine their impact on the firm's liquidity position, which is measured by the change in the cash and marketable securities accounts.

The top part of Table 11–5 shows cash flows generated by and used in operations—for Unilate, operations provided net cash flows of $34 million. The operating cash flows are generated principally from the day-to-day operations of the firm, and this

---

[3]There are two different formats for presenting the cash flow statement. The method we present here is called the *indirect method*. Cash flows from operations are calculated by starting with net income, adding back expenses not paid out of cash and subtracting revenues that do not provide cash. Using the *direct method*, operating cash flows are found by summing all revenues that provide cash and then subtracting all expenses that are paid in cash. Both formats produce the same result, and both are accepted by the Financial Accounting Standards Board.

TABLE 11–4	Unilate Textiles: Cash Sources and Uses during 2005 ($ millions)

			CHANGE	
	12/31/05	**12/31/04**	**SOURCES**	**USES**
Balance Sheet Changes				
Cash and marketable securities	$ 15.0	$ 40.0	$ 25.0	
Accounts receivable	180.0	160.0		$(20.0)
Inventory	270.0	200.0		(70.0)
Gross plant and equipment	680.0	600.0		(80.0)
Accounts payable	30.0	15.0	15.0	
Accruals	60.0	55.0	5.0	
Notes payable	40.0	35.0	5.0	
Long-term bonds	300.0	255.0	45.0	
Common stock (25 million shares)	130.0	130.0		
Income Statement Information				
Net income		$ 54.0		
Add: Depreciation		50.0		
Gross cash flow from operations		$104.0	104.0	
Dividend payment		29.0		(29.0)
Totals			$199.0	$(199.0)

amount can be determined by adjusting the net income figure to account for noncash items. The day-to-day operations of Unilate in 2005 provided $124 million of funds; however, the increases in inventories and investment in receivables during the year accounted for a combined use of funds equal to $90 million. The second section shows long-term investing activities. Unilate purchased fixed assets totaling $80 million; this was its only investment activity during 2005. Unilate's financing activities, shown in the lower section of Table 11–5, included borrowing from banks (notes payable), selling new bonds, and paying dividends to its common stockholders. Unilate raised $50 million by borrowing, but it paid $29 million in dividends, so its net inflow of funds from financing activities during 2005 was $21 million.

When all of these sources and uses of cash are totaled, we see that Unilate had a $25 million cash shortfall during 2005. It met that shortfall by drawing down its cash and marketable securities holdings by $25 million, as shown in Table 11–2, the firm's balance sheet, and in Table 11–4.

Unilate's statement of cash flows should be of some concern to the financial manager and to outside analysts. The company generated $34 million cash from operations, it spent an additional $80 million on new fixed assets, and it paid out another $29 million in dividends. It covered these cash outlays by borrowing heavily, by selling off marketable securities, and by drawing down its bank account. Obviously, this situation cannot continue year after year, so something will have to be done. We will consider some of the actions the financial manager might recommend, but first we must examine the financial statements in more depth.

TABLE 11-5	Unilate Textiles: Statement of Cash Flows for the Period Ending December 31, 2005 ($ millions)

Cash Flows from Operating Activities

Net income	$ 54.0	
Additions to net income		
Depreciation[a]	50.0	
Increase in accounts payable	15.0	
Increase in accruals	5.0	
Subtractions from net income		
Increase in accounts receivable	(20.0)	
Increase in inventory	(70.0)	
Net cash flow from operations		$ 34.0

Cash Flows from Long-Term Investing Activities

Acquisition of fixed assets		$(80.0)

Cash Flows from Financing Activities

Increase in notes payable	$ 5.0	
Increase in bonds	45.0	
Dividend payment	(29.0)	
Net cash flow from financing		$ 21.0
Net change in cash		$(25.0)
Cash at the beginning of the year		40.0
Cash at the end of the year		$ 15.0

[a]Depreciation is a noncash expense that was deducted when calculating net income. It must be added back to show the correct cash flow from operations.

Self-Test Questions

Identify the two types of information given in the annual report.

Describe these four basic financial statements: (1) the income statement, (2) the balance sheet, (3) the statement of retained earnings, and (4) the statement of cash flows.

Explain the following statement: "Retained earnings as reported on the balance sheet do not represent cash and are not 'available' for the payment of dividends or anything else."

Differentiate between operating cash flows and other cash flows.

List two reasons why operating cash flows can differ from net income.

In accounting, the emphasis is on the determination of net income. What is emphasized in finance, and why is this emphasis important?

Assuming that depreciation is the only noncash cost, how can someone calculate a business's cash flow?

Describe the general rules for identifying whether changes in balance sheet accounts represent sources or uses of cash.

Ratio Analysis

Financial statements provide information about a firm's position at a point in time as well as its operations over some past period. However, the real value of financial statements lies in the fact that they can be used to help predict a firm's financial position in the future and to determine expected earnings and dividends. From an investor's standpoint, *predicting the future is what financial statement analysis is all about*, and from management's standpoint, *financial statement analysis is useful both as a way to anticipate future conditions and, more important, as a starting point for planning actions that will influence the future course of events.*

An analysis of the firm's ratios generally is the first step in a financial analysis. The ratios are designed to show relationships between financial statement accounts *within* firms and *between* firms. Translating accounting numbers into relative values, or ratios, allows us to compare the financial position of one firm to another, even if their sizes are significantly different. For example, Firm A might have debt of $5,248,760 and interest charges of $419,900, while Firm B might have debt of $52,647,980 and interest charges of $3,948,600. Which company is stronger? The true burden of these debts, and the companies' ability to repay them, can be ascertained (1) by comparing each firm's debt to its assets and (2) by comparing the interest it must pay to the income it has available for payment of interest. Such comparisons are made by ratio analysis.

In the following sections, we calculate the 2005 financial ratios for Unilate Textiles and then evaluate those ratios in relation to the industry averages.[4] Note that all dollar amounts in the ratio calculations are in millions, except where per share values are used.

Liquidity Ratios

LIQUID ASSET
An asset that can be easily converted into cash without significant loss of its original value.

A **liquid asset** is one that can be easily converted to cash without significant loss of its original value. Converting assets, especially current assets such as inventory and receivables, to cash is the primary means by which a firm obtains the funds needed to pay its current bills. Therefore, a firm's "liquid position" deals with the question of how well the firm is able to meet its current obligations. Short-term, or current, assets are more easily converted to cash (more liquid) than long-term assets. So, in general, one firm would be considered more liquid than another firm if it has a greater proportion of its total assets in the form of current assets.

According to its balance sheet, Unilate has debts totaling $130 million that must be paid off within the coming year—that is, current liabilities equal $130 million. Will it have trouble satisfying those obligations? A full liquidity analysis requires the use of cash budgets (described later in the book), but, by relating the amount of cash and other current assets to the firm's current obligations, ratio analysis provides a quick, easy-to-use measure of liquidity. Two commonly used **liquidity ratios** are discussed in this section.

LIQUIDITY RATIOS
Ratios that show the relationship of a firm's cash and other current assets to its current liabilities.

---

[4]In addition to the ratios discussed in this section, financial analysts also employ a tool known as common size balance sheets and income statements. To form *a common size* balance sheet, one simply divides each asset, liability, and equity item by total assets and then expresses the result as a percentage. The resultant percentage statement can be compared with statements of larger or smaller firms, or with those of the same firm over time. To form a common size income statement, one simply divides each income statement item by sales.

CURRENT RATIO
This ratio is calculated by dividing current assets by current liabilities. It indicates the extent to which current liabilities are covered by assets expected to be converted into cash in the near future.

Current Ratio   The **current ratio** is calculated as follows:

$$\text{Current ratio} = \frac{\text{Current assets}}{\text{Current liabilities}}$$

$$= \frac{\$465.0}{\$130.0} = 3.6 \text{ times}$$

$$\text{Industry average} = 4.1 \text{ times}$$

Current assets normally include cash, marketable securities, accounts receivable, and inventories. Current liabilities consist of accounts payable, short-term notes payable, current maturities of long-term debt, accrued income taxes, and other accrued expenses (principally wages).

When a company is getting into financial difficulty, it begins paying its bills (accounts payable) more slowly, borrowing more from its bank, and so forth. If current liabilities are rising faster than current assets, the current ratio will fall, and this could spell trouble. Because the current ratio provides the best single indicator of the extent to which the claims of short-term creditors are covered by assets that are expected to be converted to cash fairly quickly, it is the most commonly used measure of short-term solvency. Care must be taken when examining the current ratio, just as it should be when examining any ratio individually. For example, just because a firm has a low current ratio, even one below 1.0, this does not mean the current obligations cannot be met. Consider a firm with a current ratio equal to 0.9, which suggests the current liabilities cannot be covered if existing current assets are liquidated at their book values. However, if the firm manufactures and sells a substantial amount of inventory for cash long before suppliers, employees, and short-term creditors need to be paid, then it really does not face a liquidity problem.

Unilate's current ratio of 3.6 is below the average for its industry, 4.1, so its liquidity position is somewhat weak. Still, because current assets are scheduled to be converted to cash in the near future, it is highly probable that they could be liquidated at close to their stated value. With a current ratio of 3.6, Unilate could liquidate current assets at only 28 percent of book value and still pay off current creditors in full.[5]

Although industry average figures are discussed later in some detail, it should be noted at this point that an industry average is not a magic number that all firms should strive to maintain. In fact, some well-managed firms will be above the average while other good firms will be below it. However, if a firm's ratios are far removed from the average for its industry, an analyst should be concerned about why this variance occurs. Thus, a significant deviation from the industry average should signal the analyst (or management) to *check further*, even if the deviation is considered to be in the "good" direction. For example, we know that Unilate's liquidity position currently is below average. But what would you conclude if Unilate's current ratio actually was nearly twice that of the industry, perhaps 8.0? Is this good? Maybe not. Because current assets, which are considered liquid, generally generate lower rates of return than long-term assets, it might be argued that firms with too much liquidity are not investing wisely.

---

[5] $1/3.6 = 0.28$, or 28 percent. Note that $0.28(\$465) = \$130$, which is the amount of current liabilities.

QUICK (ACID TEST) RATIO
This ratio is calculated by deducting inventories from current assets and dividing the result by current liabilities. The quick ratio is a variation of the current ratio.

Quick, or Acid Test, Ratio The **quick,** or **acid test, ratio** is calculated as follows:

$$\text{Quick, or acid test, ratio} = \frac{\text{Current assets} - \text{Inventories}}{\text{Current liabilities}}$$

$$= \frac{\$465.0 - \$270.0}{\$130.0} = \frac{\$195.0}{\$130.0} = 1.5 \text{ times}$$

$$\text{Industry average} = 2.1 \text{ times}$$

Inventories typically are the least liquid of a firm's current assets; hence, they are the assets on which losses are most likely to occur in the event of liquidation. Therefore, a measure of the firm's ability to pay off short-term obligations without relying on the sale of inventories is important.

The industry average quick ratio is 2.1, so Unilate's ratio value of 1.5 is low in comparison with the ratios of other firms in its industry. Still, if the accounts receivable can be collected, the company can pay off its current liabilities even without having to liquidate its inventory.

Our evaluation of the liquidity ratios suggests that Unilate's liquidity position currently is fairly poor. To get a better idea of why Unilate is in this situation, we must examine its asset management ratios.

Asset Management Ratios

ASSET MANAGEMENT RATIOS
A set of ratios that measures how effectively a firm is managing its assets.

The second group of ratios, the **asset management ratios,** measures how effectively the firm is managing its assets. These ratios are designed to answer this question: Does the total amount of each type of asset as reported on the balance sheet seem reasonable, too high, or too low in view of current and projected sales levels? Firms invest in assets to generate revenues both in the current period and in future periods. To purchase their assets, Unilate and other companies must borrow or obtain funds from other sources. If they have too many assets, their interest expenses will be too high; hence, their profits will be depressed. On the other hand, because production is affected by the capacity of assets, if assets are too low, profitable sales might be lost because the firm is unable to manufacture enough products.

INVENTORY TURNOVER RATIO
The ratio calculated by dividing cost of goods sold by inventories.

Inventory Turnover The **inventory turnover ratio** is defined as follows:[6]

$$\text{Inventory turnover ratio} = \frac{\text{Cost of goods sold}}{\text{Inventories}}$$

$$= \frac{\$1,230.0}{\$270.0} = 4.6 \text{ times}$$

$$\text{Industry average} = 7.4 \text{ times}$$

As a rough approximation, each item of Unilate's inventory is sold out and restocked, or "turned over," 4.6 times per year, which is considerably lower than the

---

[6]Some compilers of financial ratio statistics, such as Dun & Bradstreet, use the ratio of sales to inventories carried at cost to represent inventory turnover. If this form of the inventory turnover ratio is used, we must recognize that the true turnover will be overstated, because sales are stated at market prices while inventories are carried at cost.

industry average of 7.4 times.[7] This suggests that Unilate is holding excessive stocks of inventory; excess stocks are, of course, unproductive and represent an investment with a low or zero rate of return. Unilate's low inventory turnover ratio makes us question the current ratio. With such a low turnover, we must wonder whether the firm is holding damaged or obsolete goods (for example, textile types and patterns from previous years) not actually worth their stated value.

Care must be used when calculating and using the inventory turnover ratio because purchases of inventory, thus the cost of goods sold figure, occur over the entire year, whereas the inventory figure is for one point in time. For this reason, it is better to use an average inventory measure.[8] If the firm's business is highly seasonal, or if there has been a strong upward or downward sales trend during the year, it is essential to make such an adjustment. To maintain comparability with industry averages, however, we did not use the average inventory figure in our computations.

DAYS SALES OUTSTANDING (DSO)

The ratio calculated by dividing accounts receivable by average sales per day; indicates the average length of time it takes the firm to collect its credit sales.

Days Sales Outstanding   **Days sales outstanding (DSO),** also called the *average collection period* (ACP), is used to evaluate the firm's ability to collect its credit sales in a timely manner. DSO is calculated as follows:[9]

$$\text{DSO} = \frac{\text{Days sales}}{\text{outstanding}} = \frac{\text{Receivables}}{\text{Average sales per day}} = \frac{\text{Receivables}}{\left[\dfrac{\text{Annual sales}}{360}\right]}$$

$$= \frac{\$180.0}{\left[\dfrac{\$1,500.0}{360}\right]} = \frac{\$180.0}{\$4.167} = 43.2 \text{ days}$$

$$\text{Industry average} = 32.1 \text{ days}$$

The DSO represents the average length of time the firm must wait after making a sale before receiving cash, which is the average collection period. Unilate has about 43 days' sales outstanding, well above the 32-day industry average. The DSO can also be evaluated by comparison with the terms on which the firm sells its goods. For

---

[7]*Turnover* is a term that originated many years ago with the old Yankee peddler who would load up his wagon with goods and go off on his route to peddle his wares. The merchandise was his "working capital," because it was what he actually sold, or "turned over," to produce his profits, whereas his "turnover" was the number of trips he took each year. Annual sales divided by inventory equaled turnover, or trips per year.

[8]Preferably, the average inventory value should be calculated by summing the monthly figures during the year and dividing by 12. If monthly data are not available, one can add the beginning and ending figures and divide by two; this will adjust for growth but not for seasonal effects. Using this approach, Unilate's average inventory for 2005 would be $235 = ($200 + $270)/2, and its inventory turnover would be 5.2 = $1,230/$235, which is still well below the industry average.

[9]To compute DSO using this equation, we have to assume all of the firm's sales are credit. We usually compute DSO in this manner because information on credit sales generally is unavailable, so total sales must be used. Because all firms do not have the same percentage of credit sales, there is a chance that the days sales outstanding will be somewhat in error. Also, note that by convention the financial community generally uses 360 rather than 365 as the number of days in the year for purposes such as this. Finally, it would be better to use average receivables, either an average of the monthly figures or (beginning receivables + ending receivables)/2 = ($160 + $180)/2 = $170 in the formula. Had the annual average receivables been used, Unilate's DSO would have been $170/$4.17 = 40.8 days. The 40.8-day figure is the more accurate one, but because the industry average was based on year-end receivables, we used 43.2 days for our comparison. The DSO is discussed further in Chapter 14.

example, Unilate's sales terms call for payment within 30 days, so the fact that 43 days' sales, not 30 days', are outstanding indicates that customers, on the average, are not paying their bills on time. If the trend in DSO over the past few years has been rising, but the credit policy has not been changed, this would be even stronger evidence that steps should be taken to improve the time it takes to collect accounts receivable. This seems to be the case for Unilate because its 2004 DSO was about 40 days.

FIXED ASSETS TURNOVER RATIO
The ratio of sales to net fixed assets.

Fixed Assets Turnover   The **fixed assets turnover ratio** measures how effectively the firm uses its plant and equipment to help generate sales. It is computed as follows:

$$\text{Fixed assets turnover ratio} = \frac{\text{Sales}}{\text{Net fixed assets}}$$

$$= \frac{\$1,500.0}{\$380.0} = 3.9 \text{ times}$$

$$\text{Industry average} = 4.0 \text{ times}$$

Unilate's ratio of 3.9 times is almost equal to the industry average, indicating that the firm is using its fixed assets about as intensively (efficiently) as are the other firms in the industry. Unilate seems to have neither too much nor too few fixed assets in relation to other firms.

Care should be taken when using the fixed assets turnover ratio to compare different firms. Recall from accounting that most balance sheet accounts are stated in terms of historical costs. Inflation might cause the value of many assets that were purchased in the past to be seriously understated. Therefore, if we were comparing an old firm that acquired its fixed assets years ago at low prices with a new company that acquired its fixed assets only recently, we probably would find that the old firm had a higher fixed assets turnover. Because financial analysts typically do not have the data necessary to make inflation adjustments, they must simply recognize that a problem exists and deal with it judgmentally. In Unilate's case, the issue is not a serious one because all firms in the industry are about the same age and have been expanding at about the same rate; thus, the balance sheets of the comparison firms are indeed comparable.

TOTAL ASSETS TURNOVER RATIO
The ratio calculated by dividing sales by total assets.

Total Assets Turnover   The **total assets turnover ratio** measures the turnover of all of the firm's assets. It is calculated as follows:

$$\text{Total assets turnover ratio} = \frac{\text{Sales}}{\text{Total assets}}$$

$$= \frac{\$1,500.0}{\$845.0} = 1.8 \text{ times}$$

$$\text{Industry average} = 2.1 \text{ times}$$

Unilate's ratio is somewhat below the industry average, indicating that the company is not generating a sufficient volume of business given its investment in total assets. To become more efficient, sales should be increased, some assets should be disposed of, or a combination of these steps should be taken.

Our examination of Unilate's asset management ratios shows that its fixed assets turnover ratio is very close to the industry average, but its total assets turnover is below average. The fixed assets turnover ratio excludes current assets, while the total assets turnover ratio does not. Therefore, comparison of these ratios confirms our conclusion from the analysis of the liquidity ratios—Unilate seems to have a liquidity problem. The fact that the inventory turnover ratio and the average collection period are below average suggests, at least in part, the poor liquidity might be attributable to problems with inventory and receivables management. Slow sales and slow collections of credit sales suggest Unilate might rely more heavily on external funds, such as loans, than the industry to pay current obligations. Examining the debt management ratios will help us to determine if this actually is the case.

Debt Management Ratios

The extent to which a firm uses debt financing has three important implications: (1) By raising funds through debt, stockholder ownership is not diluted. (2) Creditors look to the equity, or owner-supplied funds, to provide a margin of safety; if the stockholders have provided only a small proportion of the total financing, the risks of the enterprise are borne mainly by its creditors. (3) If the firm earns more on investments financed with borrowed funds than it pays in interest, the return on the owners' capital is magnified, or "leveraged."

FINANCIAL LEVERAGE
The use of debt financing.

Financial leverage, or borrowing, affects the expected rate of return realized by stockholders for two reasons: (1) the interest on debt is tax deductible while dividend payments are not, so paying interest lowers the firm's tax bill, all else equal; and (2) usually the rate a firm earns from its investments in assets is different from the rate at which it borrows. If the firm has healthy operations, it generally invests the funds it raises at a rate of return that is greater than the interest rate on its debt. In combination with the tax advantage debt has compared to stock, the higher investment rate of return produces a magnified positive return to the stockholders. Under these conditions, leverage works to the advantage of the firm and its stockholders. Unfortunately, financial leverage is a double-edged sword. When the firm experiences poor business conditions, typically sales are lower and costs are higher than expected, but the cost of borrowing still must be paid. The *costs* (interest payments) associated with borrowing are contractual and do not vary with sales, and they must be paid to keep the firm from potential bankruptcy. Therefore, the required interest payments might be a very significant burden for a firm that has liquidity problems. In fact, if the interest payments are high enough, a firm with a positive operating income actually could end up with a negative return to stockholders. Under these conditions, leverage works to the detriment of the firm and its stockholders.

A detailed discussion of financial leverage is given in the next chapter. For the purposes of ratio analysis, we need to understand that firms with relatively high debt ratios have higher expected returns when the business is normal or good, but they are exposed to risk of loss when the business is poor. Thus, firms with low debt ratios are less risky, but they also forgo the opportunity to leverage up their return on equity. The prospects of high returns are desirable, but investors are averse to risk. Therefore, decisions about the use of debt require firms to balance higher expected returns against increased risk. Determining the optimal amount of debt for a given firm is a complicated process, which we discussed in Chapter 9. Here we will simply look at two procedures analysts use to examine the firm's debt in a financial statement analysis: (1) they check balance sheet ratios to determine the extent to which

What Do Corporate Controllers Really Think about Financial Reporting Requirements?

Recall from Chapter 1 that the Sarbanes-Oxley Act of 2002 establishes standards for accountability and responsibility of reporting financial information for major corporations. The act, which requires key executives and financial officers to "sign off" on certain financial reports filed with the Securities and Exchange Commission (SEC), was intended to discourage unethical and illegal financial reporting. Such legislation was warmly received by politicians in the wake of scandals at Enron, Tyco International, and WorldCom MCI, among others. How do you think the persons who construct financial statements feel about the new financial disclosure requirements?

First, a study conducted by *CFO* in 1996, a publication whose readership consists primarily of financial executives, gives some indication as to what it took to construct financial statements and how corporate controllers felt about the process prior to the passage of the Sarbanes-Oxley Act.[a] In the study, controllers from 500 large U.S. corporations were surveyed. According to the controllers, an average of 1,011 hours were spent preparing annual reports. In most cases, six or more employees were involved in the preparation of the reports. As a result, on average, it took one full-time employee about 126 days to construct annual reports, which means six employees needed 21 days to complete the same task. The costs of preparing these reports ranged from $85,000 to nearly $5 million.

The study produced two additional interesting results. First, about 86 percent of the controllers who responded said they believed their most important users, thus their intended audience, were either financial analysts (55 percent) or institutional investors (35 percent). Only 18 percent responded that they believed the intended audience was individual shareholders. Second, it seems controllers did not believe the required reports provided useful information. Fifty percent of the respondents indicated that they believed shareholders could not easily understand the information included in their financial reports.

It is interesting that at the time of the *CFO* study, regulatory and standard-setting organizations, such as the American Institute of Certified Public Accountants (AICPA), the Financial Accounting Standards Board (FASB), and the Securities and Exchange Commission (SEC), had proposed new financial reporting guidelines, including the disclosure of nonfinancial information, such as customer satisfaction, and forward-looking information, such as the strategies the firm intends to pursue in the future. When asked about the proposed changes, 84 percent of the controllers indicated that such information would not improve shareholders' understanding of their companies.

Since Congress passed the Sarbanes-Oxley Act, corporations have tried to produce more objective

continues

borrowed funds have been used to finance assets, and (2) they review income statement ratios to determine how well operating profits can cover fixed charges such as interest. These two sets of ratios are complementary, so analysts use both types.

DEBT RATIO
The ratio of total debt to total assets. It is a measure of the percentage of funds provided by creditors.

Debt Ratio   The **debt ratio** measures the percentage of the firm's assets financed by creditors (borrowing), and it is computed as follows:

$$\text{Debt ratio} = \frac{\text{Total debt}}{\text{Total assets}}$$

$$= \frac{\$130.0 + \$300.0}{\$845.0} = \frac{\$430.0}{\$845.0} = 0.509 = 50.9\%$$

$$\text{Industry average } = 45.0\%$$

financial reports by including more independent, outside members on their boards of directors who have financial expertise and by increasing their use of independent consultants to ensure the validity, and objectivity of financial statements. According to a recent study, however most executives—nearly 60 percent of those surveyed—think the act is too restrictive[b] Perhaps the reason for this response is that nearly 75 percent of those surveyed think they are at risk of greater liability as a result of the act. And, although nearly 34 percent of the respondents indicated that they believe the act made their boards of directors more effective, most did not think the act increased the confidence of investors in published financial reports. It is not surprising that nearly all the respondents believe that the costs associated with financial reporting will increase significantly because of the new reporting requirements. In fact, the results of another survey indicate that most executives believe that the act will increase the costs of financial reporting by as much as 20 percent.[c] The same study found that greater than 70 percent of the respondents indicated that their companies were not in full compliance with the act one year after it was enacted. However, 95 percent indicated that they would be in full compliance within the next year.

The primary reason given by Congress for passing legislation such as the Sarbanes-Oxley Act is to protect investors from such corporate scandals as Enron and Tyco that seem to have increased in recent years. There is talk that Congress and various regulators will require additional disclosure in the future. Are addi-

tional requirements necessary? Will they work as intended? Although the answers to these questions are debatable, most executives would answer "no." Very few executives believe that legislation or regulations similar to Sarbanes-Oxley can ensure that scandals in financial reporting will decrease in the future. Further, a recent survey of U.S. investors indicates that a majority believes that information provided by corporations is reliable, even more credible than information provided by outside analysts.[d]

In general, corporate executives believe financial reporting is an onerous, but necessary task. It appears, however, that they do not believe that information provided is as useful to shareholders as regulators and those who set reporting standards think. Clearly, then, changes should be made. But what should those changes be? The answer is not clear, primarily because there is debate concerning whether those who set the standards for financial reporting are more concerned with the needs of the reports' users or with trying to ensure that reporting systems are not abused either by inside management or outside investors.

[a]Lori Calabro, "The View from the Trenches," *CFO*, January 1997, 23; Randy Myers, "Indecent Disclosure," *CFO*, January 1997, 21–28.

[b]"Sarbanes-Oxley Act at One Year: A Report Card," *IOMA's Report on Financial Analysis, Planning & Reporting*, September 2003, 1–3.

[c]Jeffrey Marshall, "Today's Governance Codes: Demanding, Confusing and, Ultimately, How Effective?" *Financial Executive*, June 2003, 33–34.

[d]Howard Stock, "Majority of Investors Say U.S. Reporting Is Credible," *Investors Relations Business*, June 20, 2003, 1.

Total debt includes both current liabilities and long-term debt. Creditors prefer low debt ratios, because the lower the ratio, the greater the cushion against creditors' losses in the event of liquidation. The owners, on the other hand, can benefit from leverage because it magnifies earnings, and thus the return to stockholders. But too much debt often leads to financial difficulty, which eventually might cause bankruptcy.

Unilate's debt ratio is 50.9 percent; this means that its creditors have supplied about half the firm's total financing. Because the average debt ratio for this industry is 45 percent, Unilate might find it difficult to borrow additional funds without first raising more equity capital through a stock issue. Creditors might be reluctant to lend the firm more money, and management would be subjecting the firm to a greater chance of bankruptcy if it sought to increase the debt ratio much further by borrowing additional funds.[10]

TIMES-INTEREST-EARNED (TIE) RATIO

The TIE ratio is computed by dividing earnings before interest and taxes (EBIT) by interest charges; it measures the ability of the firm to meet its annual interest payments.

Times Interest Earned   The **times-interest-earned (TIE) ratio** is defined as follows:

$$\text{Times - interest - earned (TIE) ratio} = \frac{\text{EBIT}}{\text{Interest charges}}$$

$$= \frac{\$130.0}{\$40.0} = 3.3 \text{ times}$$

$$\text{Industry average} = 6.5 \text{ times}$$

The TIE ratio measures the extent to which earnings before interest and taxes (EBIT), also called *operating income*, can decline before the firm is unable to meet its annual interest costs. Failure to meet this obligation can bring legal action by the firm's creditors, possibly resulting in bankruptcy. Note that earnings before interest and taxes, rather than net income, is used in the numerator. Because interest is paid with pretax dollars, the firm's ability to pay current interest is not affected by taxes.

Unilate's interest is covered 3.3 times. Because the industry average is 6.5 times, compared to firms in the same business, Unilate is covering its interest charges by a low margin of safety. Thus, the TIE ratio reinforces our conclusion based on the debt ratio that Unilate would face difficulties if it attempted to borrow additional funds.

FIXED CHARGE COVERAGE RATIO

This ratio expands the TIE ratio to include the firm's annual long-term lease payments and sinking fund payments.

Fixed Charge Coverage   The **fixed charge coverage ratio** is similar to the times-interest-earned ratio, but it is more inclusive because it recognizes that many firms lease assets and also must make sinking fund payments.[11] Leasing has become widespread in certain industries, making this ratio preferable to the times-interest-earned ratio for many purposes. Unilate's annual long-term lease payments are $10 million, and it must make an annual $8 million sinking fund payment to help retire its debt. Because sinking fund payments must be paid with after-tax dollars, whereas interest and lease payments are paid with pretax dollars, the sinking fund payment must be divided by (1 – Tax rate) to find the before-tax income required to pay taxes and still have enough left to make the sinking fund payment.[12]

---

[10]The ratio of debt to equity is also used in financial analysis. The debt-to-assets (D/A) and debt-to-equity (D/E) ratios are simply transformations of each other, because total debt plus total equity must equal total assets:

$$D/E = \frac{D/A}{1 - D/A}, \text{ and } D/A = \frac{D/E}{1 - D/E}$$

[11]Generally, a long-term lease is defined as one that extends for more than one year. Thus, rent incurred under a six-month lease would not be included in the fixed charge coverage ratio, but rental payments under a one-year or longer lease would be defined as a fixed charge and would be included. A sinking fund is a required annual payment designed to reduce the balance of a bond or preferred stock issue. Sinking funds will be discussed in Chapter 17.

[12]Note that $8/(1 – 0.4) = $13.33. Therefore, if the company had pretax income of $13.33, it could pay taxes at a 40 percent rate and have exactly $8 left with which to make the sinking fund payment. Dividing by (1 – T) is called "grossing up" an after-tax value to find the corresponding pretax value.

Fixed charges include interest, annual long-term lease obligations, and sinking fund payments, and the fixed charge coverage ratio is defined as follows:

$$\text{Fixed charge coverage ratio } = \frac{\text{EBIT} + \text{Lease payments}}{\text{Interest charges} + \text{Lease payments} + \left[\dfrac{\text{Sinking fund payments}}{(1 - \text{Tax rate})}\right]}$$

$$= \frac{\$130.0 + \$10.0}{\$40.0 + \$10.0 + \left[\dfrac{\$8.0}{(1-0.4)}\right]} = \frac{\$140}{\$63.33} = 2.2 \text{ times}$$

$$\text{Industry average } = 5.8 \text{ times}$$

In the numerator of the fixed charge coverage ratio, the lease payments are added to EBIT because we want to determine the firm's ability to cover its fixed financing charges from the income generated before any of these fixed charges are deducted. Because the EBIT figure represents the firm's operating income net of lease payments, the lease payments must be added back.

Unilate's fixed charges are covered only 2.2 times, as opposed to an industry average of 5.8 times. Again, this indicates that the firm is weaker than average, and this points out the difficulties Unilate probably would encounter if it attempted to increase its debt.

Our examination of Unilate's debt management ratios indicates that the company has a debt ratio that is *above* the industry average, and it has coverage ratios that are significantly *below* the industry average. This suggests that Unilate is in a relatively dangerous position with respect to leverage (debt). In fact, Unilate might have great difficulty borrowing additional funds until its debt position improves. If Unilate cannot pay its current obligations as a result, it might be forced into bankruptcy. To see how Unilate's debt position has affected its profits, we next examine the profitability ratios.

PROFITABILITY RATIOS

A group of ratios showing the effect of liquidity, asset management, and debt management on operating results.

Profitability Ratios

Profitability is the net result of a number of policies and decisions. The ratios examined thus far provide some information about the way the firm is operating, but the **profitability ratios** show the combined effects of liquidity, asset management, and debt management on operating results.

NET PROFIT MARGIN ON SALES

This ratio measures net income per dollar of sales; it is calculated by dividing net income by sales.

Net Profit Margin on Sales The **net profit margin on sales,** which gives the profit per dollar of sales, is calculated as follows:

$$\text{Profit margin on sales } = \frac{\text{Net Income}}{\text{Sales}}$$

$$= \frac{\$54.0}{\$1,500} = 0.036 = 3.6\%$$

$$\text{Industry average } = 4.7\%$$

Unilate's profit margin is below the industry average of 4.7 percent, indicating that its sales are too low, its costs are too high, or both. Remember that, according to the debt ratio, Unilate has a greater proportion of debt than the industry average, and the times interest earned ratio shows that Unilate's interest payments on its debt are not covered as well as the rest of the industry. This is one of the reasons Unilate's profit margin is low. To see this, we can compute the ratio of EBIT (operating income) to sales, which is called the *operating profit margin*. Unilate's operating profit margin of 8.7 percent is about the same as the industry, so the cause of the low net profit margin is the relatively high interest attributable to the firm's above-average use of debt.

RETURN ON TOTAL ASSETS (ROA)

The ratio of net income to total assets; it provides an idea of the overall return on investment earned by the firm.

Return on Total Assets   The **return on total assets (ROA)** after interest and taxes is computed as follows:

$$\text{Return on total assets (ROA)} = \frac{\text{Net Income}}{\text{Total assets}}$$

$$= \frac{\$54.0}{\$845.0} = 0.064 = 6.4\%$$

$$\text{Industry average} = 12.6\%$$

Unilate's 6.4 percent return is well below the 12.6 percent average for the industry. This low return results from the company's above-average use of debt.

RETURN ON COMMON EQUITY (ROE)

The ratio of net income to common equity; it measures the rate of return on common stockholders' investment.

Return on Common Equity   The **return on common equity (ROE),** or the *rate of return on stockholders' investment* is measured as follows:

$$\text{Return on common equity (ROE)} = \frac{\text{Net income available to common stockholders}}{\text{Common equity}}$$

$$= \frac{\text{Net income} - \text{Preferred dividends}}{\text{Common equity}}$$

$$= \frac{\$54.0 - \$0}{\$415.0} = 0.130 = 13.0\%$$

$$\text{Industry average} = 17.2\%$$

Unilate's 13.0 percent return is below the 17.2 percent industry average. This result is due to the company's greater use of debt (leverage), a point that is analyzed further later in this chapter.

Our examination of Unilate's profitability ratios shows that its operating results have suffered due to its poor liquidity position, its poor asset management, and its above-average debt. In the final group of ratios, we will examine Unilate's market value ratios to get an indication of how investors feel about the company's current financial position.

MARKET VALUE RATIOS

A set of ratios that relate the firm's stock price to its earnings and book value per share.

Market Value Ratios

The **market value ratios** represent a group of ratios that relates the firm's stock price to its earnings and book value per share. These ratios give management an indication of what investors think of the company's past performance and future prospects. If the firm's liquidity, asset management, debt management, and profitability ratios are all good, then its market value ratios will be high, and its stock price will probably be as high as can be expected. Of course, the opposite also is true.

PRICE/EARNINGS (P/E) RATIO

The ratio of the price per share to earnings per share; it shows the dollar amount investors will pay for $1 of current earnings.

Price/Earnings Ratio   The **price/earnings (P/E) ratio** shows how much investors are willing to pay per dollar of reported profits. To compute the P/E ratio, we need to know the firm's earnings per share (EPS):

$$\text{Earnings per share} = \frac{\text{Net income available to common stockholders}}{\text{Number of common shares outstanding}}$$

$$= \frac{\$54.0}{25.0} = \$2.16$$

Unilate's stock sells for $23, so with an EPS of $2.16 its P/E ratio is 10.6:

$$\text{Price / earnings (PE) ratio} = \frac{\text{Market price per share}}{\text{Earnings per share}}$$

$$= \frac{\$23.00}{\$2.16} = 10.6 \text{ times}$$

$$\text{Industry average} = 13.0 \text{ times}$$

Other things held constant, P/E ratios are higher for firms with high growth prospects, but they are lower for riskier firms. Because Unilate's P/E ratio is below those of other textile manufacturers, this suggests that the company is regarded as being somewhat riskier than most, as having poorer growth prospects, or both. From our analysis of its debt management ratios, we know Unilate has above-average risk associated with leverage; but we do not know if its growth prospects are poor.

Market/Book Ratio   The ratio of a stock's market price to its book value gives another indication of how investors regard the company. Companies with relatively high rates of return on equity generally sell at higher multiples of book value than those with low returns. First, we find Unilate's book value per share:

$$\text{Book value per share} = \frac{\text{Common equity}}{\text{Number of common shares outstanding}}$$

$$= \frac{\$415.0}{25.0} = \$16.60$$

MARKET/BOOK (M/B) RATIO
The ratio of a stock's market price to its book value.

Now we divide the market value per share by the book value per share to get a **market/book (M/B) ratio** of 1.4 times for Unilate:

$$\text{Market / book ratio} = \frac{\text{Market price per share}}{\text{Book value per share}}$$

$$= \frac{\$23.00}{\$16.60} = 1.4 \text{ times}$$

$$\text{Industry average} = 2.0 \text{ times}$$

Investors are willing to pay less for Unilate's book value than for that of an average textile manufacturer. This should not be surprising, because, as we discovered previously, Unilate has generated below-average returns with respect to both total assets and common equity. Generally, the stocks of firms that earn high rates of return on their assets sell for prices well in excess of their book values. For very successful firms, the market/book ratio can be as much as 10 to 15 times.

Our examination of Unilate's market value ratios indicates that investors are not excited about the future prospects of its common stock as an investment. Perhaps investors believe Unilate is headed toward bankruptcy if actions are not taken to correct

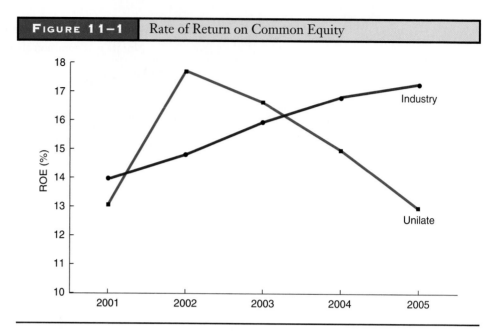

FIGURE 11–1 Rate of Return on Common Equity

its liquidity and asset management problems and to improve its leverage position. A method used to get an indication of the direction a firm is headed is to evaluate the trends of the ratios over the past few years to answer the question: Is the firm's position improving or deteriorating?

Trend Analysis

TREND ANALYSIS

An analysis of a firm's financial ratios over time that is used to determine the improvement or deterioration in its financial situation.

The analysis of its ratios indicates that Unilate's current financial position is poor when compared to the industry norm. But this analysis does not tell us whether Unilate's financial position is better or worse than previous years. To determine in which direction the firm is headed, it is important to analyze trends in ratios. By examining the paths taken in the past, **trend analysis** provides information about whether the firm's financial position is more likely to improve or deteriorate in the future. A simple approach to trend analysis is to construct graphs containing both the firm's ratios and the industry averages for the past five years. Using this approach, we can examine both the direction of the movement in, and the relationships between, the firm's ratios and the industry averages. Figure 11–1 shows that Unilate's return on equity has declined since 2002, even though the industry average has shown relatively stable growth. Other ratios could be analyzed similarly. If we were to compare Unilate's ratios from 2005 with those from 2004, we would discover Unilate's financial position has deteriorated, not strengthened. This is not a good trend.

Summary of Ratio Analysis: The DuPont Chart

DUPONT CHART

A chart designed to show the relationships among return on investment, asset turnover, profit margin, and leverage.

Table 11–6 summarizes Unilate's ratios. Figure 11–2, which is called a modified **DuPont chart** because that company's managers developed the general approach, shows the relationships among return on investment, asset turnover, profit margin, and leverage. The left side of the chart develops the *profit margin on sales*. The various expense items are listed and then summed to obtain Unilate's total costs, which

TABLE 11–6	Unilate Textiles: Summary of Financial Ratios ($ millions, except per share dollars)

RATIO	FORMULA FOR CALCULATION	CALCULATION	RATIO	INDUSTRY AVERAGE	COMMENT
Liquidity					
Current	$\dfrac{\text{Current assets}}{\text{Current liabilities}}$	$\dfrac{\$465.0}{\$130.0}$	= 3.6×	4.1×	Low
Quick, or acid test	$\dfrac{\text{Current assets} - \text{Inventories}}{\text{Current liabilities}}$	$\dfrac{\$195.0}{\$130.0}$	= 1.5×	2.1×	Low
Asset Management					
Inventory turnover	$\dfrac{\text{Cost of goods sold}}{\text{Inventories}}$	$\dfrac{\$1,230.0}{\$270.0}$	= 4.6×	7.4×	Low
Days sales outstanding (DSO)	$\dfrac{\text{Receivables}}{\left[\dfrac{\text{Annual sales}}{360}\right]}$	$\dfrac{\$180.0}{\$4.167}$	= 43.2 days	32.1 days	Poor
Fixed assets turnover	$\dfrac{\text{Sales}}{\text{Net fixed assets}}$	$\dfrac{\$1,500.0}{\$380.0}$	= 3.9×	4.0×	OK
Total assets turnover	$\dfrac{\text{Sales}}{\text{Total assets}}$	$\dfrac{\$1,500.0}{\$845.0}$	= 1.8×	2.1×	Low
Debt Management					
Debt ratio	$\dfrac{\text{Total debt}}{\text{Total assets}}$	$\dfrac{\$430.0}{\$845.0}$	= 50.9%	45.0%	Poor
Times interest earned (TIE)	$\dfrac{\text{EBIT}}{\text{Interest charges}}$	$\dfrac{\$130.0}{\$40.0}$	= 3.3×	6.5×	Low
Fixed charge coverage	$\dfrac{\text{EBIT} + \text{Lease payments}}{\text{Interest charges} + \text{Lease payments} + \left[\dfrac{\text{Sinking fund pmt}}{(1 - \text{Tax rate})}\right]}$	$\dfrac{\$140.0}{\$63.33}$	= 2.2×	5.8×	Low
Profitability					
Profit margin on sales	$\dfrac{\text{Net income}}{\text{Sales}}$	$\dfrac{\$54.0}{\$1,500.0}$	= 3.6%	4.7%	Poor
Return on total assets (ROA)	$\dfrac{\text{Net income}}{\text{Total assets}}$	$\dfrac{\$54.0}{\$845.0}$	= 6.4%	12.6%	Poor
Return on common equity (ROE)	$\dfrac{\text{Net income available to common stockholders}}{\text{Common equity}}$	$\dfrac{\$54.0}{\$415.0}$	= 13.0%	17.2%	Poor
Market Value					
Price/Earnings (P/E)	$\dfrac{\text{Market price per share}}{\text{Earnings per share}}$	$\dfrac{\$23.00}{\$2.16}$	= 10.6×	13.0×	Low
Market/Book	$\dfrac{\text{Market price per share}}{\text{Book value per share}}$	$\dfrac{\$23.00}{\$16.60}$	= 1.4×	2.0×	Low

FIGURE 11-2	DuPont Chart Applied to Unilate Textiles (millions of dollars)

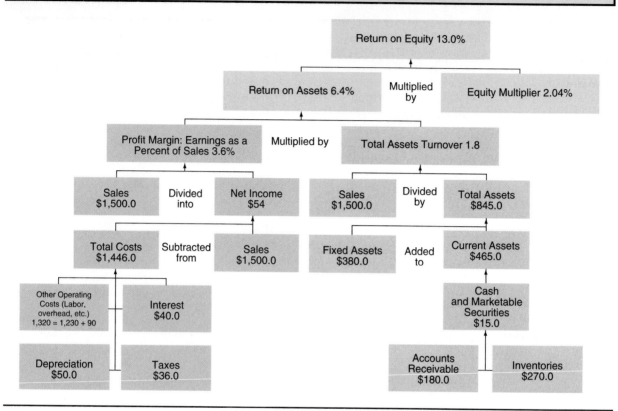

are subtracted from sales to obtain the company's net income. When we divide net income by sales, we find that 3.6 percent of each sales dollar is left over for stockholders. If the profit margin is low or trending down, one can examine the individual expense items to identify and then correct problems.

DUPONT EQUATION
A formula that gives the rate of return on assets by multiplying the profit margin by the total assets turnover.

The right side of Figure 11–2 lists the various categories of assets, totals them, and then divides sales by total assets to find the number of times Unilate "turns its assets over" each year. The company's total assets turnover ratio is 1.8 times.

The formula in which the profit margin is multiplied by the total assets turnover is called the **DuPont equation,** and it gives the rate of return on assets (ROA):[13]

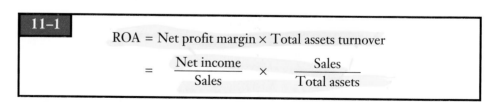

> **11–1**
>
> $$ROA = \text{Net profit margin} \times \text{Total assets turnover}$$
> $$= \frac{\text{Net income}}{\text{Sales}} \times \frac{\text{Sales}}{\text{Total assets}}$$

---

[13]The number reported here for the total assets turnover is rounded to the nearest decimal place, so the ROA does not equal 6.4 percent if the rounded result for the total assets turnover is used. If the ratios are carried to two decimal places, the DuPont computation would be ROA = 3.60% × 1.78 = 6.41%.

$$= \frac{\$54.0}{\$1,500.0} \times \frac{\$1,500.0}{\$845.0}$$

$$= \quad 3.6\% \quad \times \quad 1.8 \quad \approx 6.4\%$$

Unilate made 3.6 percent, or 3.6 cents, on each dollar of sales, and assets were "turned over" 1.8 times during the year. Thus, the company earned a return of 6.4 percent on its assets.

If the company were financed only with common equity—that is, there was no debt at all—the ROA and the ROE would be the same, because total assets would equal the amount of common equity. But, more than 50 percent of the capital for Unilate Textiles is debt, both long-term and short-term. Thus, as earlier computations show, the ROA and ROE are not equal. Instead, because ROA is defined as *net income available to common stockholders* divided by total assets, the ROA of 6.4 percent all goes to common stockholders. Because the common equity represents less than 100 percent of Unilate's capital, the return to the common stockholders, ROE, must be greater than the ROA of 6.4 percent. To translate the ROA into the ROE, we must multiply ROA by the *equity multiplier*, which is the ratio of assets to common equity, or the number of times the total assets exceed the amount of common equity (it is also the inverse of the percent of assets that is financed with equity). Using this approach, we can write ROE as follows:

11–2

$$\text{ROE} = \quad \text{ROA} \quad \times \text{Equity multiplier}$$

$$= \frac{\text{Net income}}{\text{Total assets}} \times \frac{\text{Total assets}}{\text{Common equity}}$$

$$= \quad 6.4\% \quad \times \quad \frac{\$845.0}{\$415.0}$$

$$= \quad 6.4\% \quad \times \quad 2.036$$

$$= \quad 13.0\%$$

We can combine Equations 11–1 and 11–2 to form the *extended* Du Pont equation, which is written as follows:

11–3

$$\text{ROE} = \left(\begin{array}{c} \text{Profit} \\ \text{margin} \end{array} \right) \times \left(\begin{array}{c} \text{Total assets} \\ \text{turnover} \end{array} \right) \times \left(\begin{array}{c} \text{Equity} \\ \text{multiplier} \end{array} \right)$$

$$= \frac{\text{Net income}}{\text{Sales}} \times \frac{\text{Sales}}{\text{Total assets}} \times \frac{\text{Total assets}}{\text{Common equity}}$$

For Unilate, we have

$$\text{ROE} = 3.6\% \times 1.8 \times 2.0 = 13.0\%$$

Unilate's management can use the DuPont system to analyze ways of improving the firm's performance. Focusing on the left, or "profit margin," side of its DuPont chart, Unilate's marketing people can study the effects of raising sales prices (or lowering them to increase volume), of moving into new products or markets with higher margins, and so on. The company's cost accountants can study various expense items and, working with engineers, purchasing agents, and other operating personnel, seek ways of holding down costs. On the "turnover" side, Unilate's financial analysts, working with both production and marketing people, can investigate ways of minimizing the investment in various types of assets. At the same time, its treasury staff can analyze the effects of alternative financing strategies, seeking to hold down interest expense and the risk of debt while still using leverage to increase the rate of return on equity.

As a result of such an analysis, Sarah Allen, Unilate's president, recently announced a series of moves designed to cut operating costs by more than 20 percent per year. Allen also announced that the company intends to concentrate its capital in markets where profit margins are reasonably high. If competition increases in certain of its product markets (such as the low-price end of the textiles market), Unilate will withdraw from those markets. The company is seeking a high return on equity, and Allen recognizes that if competition drives profit margins too low in a particular market, it then becomes impossible to earn high returns on the capital invested to serve that market. Therefore, if it is to achieve a high ROE, Unilate might have to develop new products and shift capital into new areas. The company's future depends on this type of analysis, and if the firm succeeds in the future, then the DuPont system will have helped Unilate achieve that success.

Self-Test Questions

Identify two ratios that are used to analyze a firm's liquidity position, and write out their equations.

Identify four ratios that are used to measure how effectively a firm is managing its assets, and write out their equations.

Identify three ratios that are used to measure the extent to which a firm uses debt financing, and write out their equations.

Identify three ratios that show the combined effects of liquidity, asset management, and debt management on profitability, and write out their equations.

Identify two ratios that relate a firm's stock price to its earnings and book value per share, and write out their equations.

Explain how the DuPont equation and chart combine several ratios to reveal the basic determinants of ROE.

Comparative Ratios (Benchmarking)

COMPARATIVE RATIO ANALYSIS
An analysis based on a comparison of a firm's ratios with those of other firms in the same industry.

The preceding analysis of Unilate Textiles involved a **comparative ratio analysis** because the ratios calculated for Unilate were compared with those of other firms in the same industry using the industry average. Comparative ratios for a large number of industries are available from several sources, including Dun & Bradstreet (D&B), Robert Morris Associates, and the U.S. Commerce Department. Trade associations and individual firms' credit departments also compile industry average financial ratios. Finally, financial statement data for thousands of publicly owned corporations are available from various databases; and because brokerage houses, banks, and other financial institutions have access to these data, security analysts can and do generate comparative ratios tailored to their specific needs. Table 11–7 provides a sample of the ratios provided by the *Almanac of Business and Industrial Financial Ratios* for selected industries.

TABLE 11-7 — Ratios for Selected Industries

SIC Code, Line of Business, (Number of Firms)	Type of Operations	Current Ratio (×)	Quick Ratio (×)	Debt Ratio (%)	TIE Ratio (×)	Days Sales Outstanding (Days)	Total Inventory Turnover (×)	Asset Turnover (×)	Profit Margin (%)	Return on Assets (%)	Return on Equity (%)
2830 Drugs (1,456)	Manufacturing	1.2	0.8	62.0	4.9	116.1	3.9	0.6	15.4	10.9	14.6
2840 Soaps, Cleansers, & Toilet Goods (1,969)	Manufacturing	0.4	0.2	76.6	3.7	47.4	8.4	0.7	7.8	10.8	22.9
3670 Electronic Components (12,173)	Manufacturing	1.9	1.2	48.3	8.7	61.0	6.2	1.1	8.7	14.9	17.9
5030 Lumber & Construction (9,118)	Wholesale	1.8	1.1	59.5	4.1	37.5	9.4	3.2	2.6	12.3	20.3
5170 Petroleum & Products (11,612)	Wholesale	1.2	0.9	55.6	1.2	56.3	4.2	3.3	0.8	18.9	6.6
5220 Building Materials Dealers (12,721)	Retail	2.1	0.8	43.3	6.2	25.5	5.7	2.4	3.6	13.7	14.7
5251 Hardware Stores (12,186)	Retail	2.3	0.7	66.0	1.5	28.7	3.2	2.2	0.3	2.1	4.2

SOURCE: *Almanac of Business and Industrial Financial Ratios, 2003 Edition*

SIC codes are "Standard Industrial Classification" codes used by the U.S. government to classify companies.

Each of the data-supplying organizations uses a somewhat different set of ratios designed for its own purposes. For example, D&B deals mainly with small firms, many of which are proprietorships, and it sells its services primarily to banks and other lenders. Therefore, D&B is concerned largely with the creditor's viewpoint, and its ratios emphasize current assets and liabilities, not market value ratios. Thus, when you select a comparative data source, you should be sure that your emphasis is similar to that of the agency whose ratios you plan to use. Additionally, there are often definitional differences in the ratios presented by different sources, so before using a source, be sure to verify the exact definitions of the ratios to ensure consistency with your work.

Self-Test Questions

Differentiate between trend analysis and comparative ratio analysis.

Why is it necessary to conduct both trend and comparative ratio analyses?

Uses and Limitations of Ratio Analysis

As noted earlier, ratio analysis is used by three main groups: (1) *managers*, who employ ratios to help analyze, control, and thus improve the firm's operations; (2) *credit analysts*, such as bank loan officers or bond rating analysts, who analyze ratios to help ascertain a company's ability to pay its debts; and (3) *security analysts*, including both stock analysts, who are interested in a company's efficiency and growth prospects, and bond analysts, who are concerned with a company's ability to pay interest on its bonds as well as with the liquidating value of the assets in the event the company fails.

While ratio analysis can provide useful information concerning a company's operations and financial condition, it does have inherent problems and limitations that necessitate care and judgment. Some potential problems are listed here:

1. Many large firms operate a number of different divisions in quite different industries, and in such cases it is difficult to develop a meaningful set of industry averages for comparative purposes. This tends to make ratio analysis more useful for small, narrowly focused firms than for large, multidivisional ones.

2. Most firms want to be better than average, so merely attaining average performance is not necessarily good. As a target for high-level performance, it is best to focus on the industry leaders' ratios.

3. Inflation might distort firms' balance sheets—if recorded values are historical, they could be substantially different from "true" values. Further, because inflation affects both depreciation charges and inventory costs, profits are also affected. Thus, a ratio analysis for one firm over time, or a comparative analysis of firms of different ages, must be interpreted with judgment.

4. Seasonal factors can also distort a ratio analysis. For example, the inventory turnover ratio for a textile firm will be radically different if the balance sheet figure used for inventory is the one just before versus the one just after the close of the fall fashion season. This problem can be minimized by using monthly averages for inventory (and receivables) when calculating ratios such as turnover.

5. Firms can employ **"window dressing" techniques** to make their financial statements look stronger. To illustrate, a Chicago builder borrowed on a two-year basis on December 28, 2005, held the proceeds of the loan as cash for a

"WINDOW DRESSING" TECHNIQUES

Techniques employed by firms to make their financial statements look better than they actually are.

few days, and then paid off the loan ahead of time on January 2, 2006. This improved the company's current and quick ratios, and made his year-end 2005 balance sheet look good. However, the improvement was strictly window dressing; a week later the balance sheet was back at the old level.

6. Different accounting practices can distort comparisons. As noted earlier, inventory valuation and depreciation methods can affect financial statements and thus make comparisons among firms difficult.

7. It is difficult to generalize about whether a particular ratio is "good" or "bad." For example, a high current ratio might indicate a strong liquidity position, which is good, or excessive cash, which is bad (because excess cash in the bank is a nonearning asset). Similarly, a high fixed assets turnover ratio might denote either a firm that uses its assets efficiently or one that is undercapitalized and cannot afford to buy enough assets.

8. A firm might have some ratios that look "good" and others that look "bad," making it difficult to tell whether the company is, on balance, strong or weak. However, statistical procedures can be used to analyze the net effects of a set of ratios. Many banks and other lending organizations use statistical procedures to analyze firms' financial ratios, and, on the basis of their analyses, classify companies according to their probability of getting into financial trouble.[14]

Ratio analysis is useful, but analysts should be aware of these problems and make adjustments as necessary. Ratio analysis conducted in a mechanical, unthinking manner is dangerous, but used intelligently and with good judgment, it can provide useful insights into a firm's operations. Probably *the most important and most difficult input to successful ratio analysis is the judgment used when interpreting the results to reach an overall conclusion about the firm's financial position.*

Self-Test Questions

Name three types of users of ratio analysis. What type of ratios does each group emphasize?

List several potential problems with ratio analysis.

The Federal Income Tax System

In earlier chapters, we discovered that the value of any asset, depends on the stream of cash flows produced by the asset. And, for the most part, cash flows from an asset consist of usable income plus depreciation, where usable income means income after taxes.

The Federal Tax Code is separated into two sections: (1) tax laws that are applicable to individuals, and (2) tax laws that are applicable to corporations.[15] As the names imply, the tax code for individuals applies to persons such as individuals and families,

---

[14]The technique used is discriminant analysis. For a discussion, see Edward T. Altman, "Financial Ratios, Discriminant Analysis, and the Prediction of Corporate Bankruptcy," *Journal of Finance*, September 1968, 589–609, or Eugene F. Brigham, and Phillip R. Daves, *Intermediate Financial Management*, 8th ed. (Cincinatti, OH: South-Western College Publishing, 2004), Chapter 24.

[15]Tax information is available at U.S. post offices and on the Internal Revenue Service Web site located at http://www.irs.ustreas.gov.

whereas the corporate tax code applies to businesses that are organized as corporations. For businesses that are not corporations, the corporate tax code is not applicable; so, proprietorships and partnerships are taxed according to the individual tax code. The income from partnerships and proprietorships is reported by the individual owners as personal income. Generally, the tax rates for corporations and the tax rates for proprietorships and partnerships differ. For example, in 2004, federal income tax rates for individuals went up to approximately 35 percent, and, when state and city income taxes were included, the marginal tax rate on an individual's income could have exceeded 40 percent. Corporate profits were subject to federal income tax rates of up to 39 percent, in addition to state income taxes. Because of the magnitude of the tax bite, taxes play an important role in many financial decisions.

The tax laws are very complicated. For this reason, we cover only a few highlights here. This really is enough, however, because business managers and investors should, and do, rely on tax specialists rather than trusting their own limited knowledge. Still, it is important to know the basic elements of the tax system to understand the impact taxes have on cash flows. Congress and the administration continuously debate the merits of different changes in the tax laws, so it is clear that the tax laws will change in coming years—they always do. In fact, Congress has enacted a major change, on average, every three to four years since 1913, when our federal tax system began; and in recent years some changes have occurred almost every year. Even in the unlikely event that Congress does not change the tax laws, changes still will occur because certain aspects of the tax calculation are tied to the rate of inflation. Thus, by the time you read this section, tax rates and other factors might be different from those provided here. Even so, this section should give you some understanding of the basics of our tax system.

Individual Income Taxes

Individuals pay taxes on wages and salaries, on investment income (dividends, interest, and profits from the sale of securities), and on the profits of *proprietorships and partnerships*. Our tax rates are **progressive**—that is, the higher one's income, the larger the percentage paid in taxes. The individual tax rates for 2004 are provided in the appendix at the end of this chapter, Table 11A–1. In this section, we discuss some of the general topics applicable to those who are affected by the individual tax code section.

PROGRESSIVE TAX
A tax that requires a higher percentage payment on higher incomes. The personal income tax in the U.S. is progressive.

TAXABLE INCOME
Gross income minus exemptions and allowable deductions as set forth in the tax code.

MARGINAL TAX RATE
The tax applicable to the last unit of income; the tax payer's tax bracket.

1. **Taxable income** is defined as gross income less a set of exemptions and deductions that are spelled out in the instructions to the tax forms individuals must file. When filing a tax return in 2005 for the tax year 2004, each taxpayer will receive an exemption of $3,100 for each dependent, including the taxpayer, which reduces taxable income. However, this exemption is indexed to rise with inflation, and the exemption is phased out for high-income taxpayers. Also, certain expenses, such as mortgage interest paid, state and local income taxes paid, and charitable contributions, can be deducted and thus can be used to reduce taxable income; but again, high-income taxpayers lose some of this benefit.

2. The **marginal tax rate** is defined as the tax on the last unit of income. The marginal tax rate is represented by the tax bracket you are in. For example, if you are single and your taxable income is $50,000, then your marginal tax rate is 25 percent. As Table 11A–1 shows, marginal rates begin at 10 percent, rise to 15, then to 25 percent, and so on.

AVERAGE TAX RATE
Taxes paid divided by taxable income.

3. One can calculate **average tax rates** from the data in Table 11A–1. The average tax rate equals the percent of taxable income that is paid in taxes. For example, if Jill Smith, a single individual, had taxable income of $35,000, her tax bill would be $4,000.00 + ($35,000 − $29,050)(0.25) = $5,487.50. Her average tax rate would be $5,487.50/$35,000 = 15.7% versus a marginal rate of 25 percent. If Jill received a raise of $1,000, bringing her income to $36,000, she would have to pay an additional $250 in taxes, so her after-tax raise would be $750. In addition, her Social Security taxes would increase.

Taxes on Interest Income   Interest income received by individuals from corporate securities or other investments is added to other income and thus is taxed at the rates shown in Table 11A–1. It should be noted that under U.S. tax laws, interest on most state and local government bonds, called *municipals* or *munis*, is not subject to federal income taxes. Thus, investors get to keep all of the interest received from most municipal bonds but only a fraction of the interest received from bonds issued by corporations or by the U.S. government. This means that a lower-yielding muni can provide the same after-tax return as a higher-yielding corporate bond. For example, a taxpayer in the 25 percent marginal tax bracket who could buy a muni that yields 6 percent would have to receive a before-tax yield of 8 percent on a corporate or U.S. Treasury bond to have the same after-tax income:

$$\text{Equivalent pretax yield on a taxable investment} = \frac{\text{Yield on tax-free investment}}{1 - \text{Marginal tax rate}}$$

$$= \frac{6\%}{1 - 0.25} = 8\%$$

If we know the yield on the taxable bond (investment), we can use the following equation to find the equivalent yield on a muni (tax-free investment):

$$\text{Yield on tax-free investment} = \left(\begin{array}{c} \text{Pretax yield on} \\ \text{taxable investment} \end{array} \right) \times (1 - \text{Marginal tax rate})$$

$$= 8\% \times (1 - 0.25) = 6\%$$

The exemption from federal taxes stems from the separation of federal and state powers, and its primary effect is to help state and local governments borrow at lower rates than otherwise would be available to them.

Taxes on Dividend Income   Prior to 2003, dividends received from corporations were taxed just like interest income. In 2003, however, Congress lowered the tax rates on dividends so that individuals pay a maximum of 5 percent or 15 percent. If an individual's marginal tax rate is below 25 percent, dividends he or she receives are taxed at 5 percent, whereas dividends are taxed at 15 percent if the individual's tax rate is 25 percent or higher. To qualify for these lower tax rates, you must hold the stock of the company that pays the dividend for at least 60 days.

Interest Paid by Individuals   For the most part, the interest paid by individuals on loans is *not* tax deductible. The principal exception to this is the interest paid on mortgage financing used to purchase a house for personal residence, which is tax deductible. The effect of tax deductible interest payments is to lower the actual cost of the mortgage to the taxpayer. For example, if Staci Jones has an 8 percent mortgage on her house and she has a marginal tax rate equal to 33 percent, the after-tax cost of her mortgage is as follows:

$$\text{After-tax rate} = 8\%(1 - 0.33) = 5.4\%$$

Capital Gains versus Ordinary Income   Assets such as stocks, bonds, and real estate are defined as *capital assets*. If you buy a capital asset and later sell it for more than your purchase price, the profit is called a **capital gain;** if you suffer a loss, it is called a **capital loss.** An asset sold within one year of the time it was purchased produces a *short-term gain or loss*, whereas one held for one year of longer produces a *long-term gain or loss*. If you sell a capital asset for exactly what you paid for it, you will have neither a gain nor a loss; you simply get back your original investment, and no tax is due.

CAPITAL GAIN (LOSS)

The profit (loss) from the sale of a capital asset for more (less) than its purchase price.

There has been a great deal of controversy over the proper tax rate for capital gains. It has been argued that lower tax rates on capital gains (1) stimulate the flow of venture capital to new, start-up businesses, which generally provide capital gains as opposed to dividend income, and (2) cause companies to retain and reinvest a high percentage of their earnings in an effort to provide their stockholders with lightly taxed capital gains as opposed to highly taxed dividend income. The proponents of preferential capital gains tax rates lost the argument in 1986, but in 1990 they did succeed in getting the rate for long-term capital gains capped at 28 percent. The cap was further lowered to 20 percent in 1998 and to 15 percent in 2003. In 2003, the tax rate applied to capital gains for assets held less than one year was the marginal tax rate of the taxpayer, and it was 15 percent for assets held for one year or longer (5 percent if the individual's regular tax rate is lower than 25 percent).

Business versus Personal Expenses   *Individuals* pay taxes on the income generated by proprietorships and partnerships they own—that is, the income *passes through* to the owners of these types of businesses. Therefore, we need to differentiate business expenses, which are tax deductible, from personal expenses, which are not tax deductible. Generally speaking, an allowable business expense is a cost incurred to generate business revenues. On the other hand, if the expense is incurred for personal benefit (use), it is considered a personal expense. For instance, Loretta Kay owns a house in which she lived until last month, at which time she moved and rented the house to a group of college students. Three months ago, the plumbing burst in the kitchen, and Loretta had to call the plumber for repairs. The repairs cost $1,000. Is this a tax deductible expense? No, because the house was Loretta's personal residence at the time. Last night, Loretta had to call the plumber again to fix pipes that had burst in the same house, which she now has rented to the students. The repairs cost $1,200. Is this a tax deductible expense? Yes, the expense was incurred for business purposes because the house now is rental property, which is considered a business operation.

Corporate Income Taxes

The corporate tax structure is shown in the appendix at the end of this chapter, Table 11A–2. The structure is similar to the individual rates. However, there are some areas where the corporate tax code and the individual tax code differ significantly. We discuss some of the differences in this section.

Interest and Dividend Income Received by a Corporation   Interest income received by a corporation is taxed as ordinary income at regular corporate tax rates. However, 70 percent of the dividends received by one corporation from another corporation is excluded from taxable income, while the remaining 30 percent is taxed at the ordinary tax rate.[16] Thus, a corporation earning $12 million with a 35 percent marginal tax rate would pay only $(1 - 0.70)(0.35) = 0.105 = 10.5\%$ of its dividend income as taxes, so its effective tax rate on intercorporate dividends would be 10.5 percent. If this firm receives $10,000 in dividends from another corporation, its after-tax dividend income would be $8,950:

$$\text{After-tax income} = \text{Before-tax income} - \text{Taxes}$$
$$= \$10,000 - [\$10,000(0.30)](0.35)$$
$$= \$10,000(1 - 0.105) = \$10,000(.895) = \$8,950$$

If the corporation pays out its own after-tax income to its stockholders as dividends, the income ultimately is subjected to triple taxation: (1) the original corporation is taxed first, (2) then the second corporation is taxed on the dividends it receives, and (3) the individuals who receive the final dividends are taxed again. This is the reason for the 70 percent exclusion on intercorporate dividends.

Interest and Dividends Paid by a Corporation   A firm's operations can be financed with either debt or equity capital. If it uses debt, it must pay interest on this debt (to banks and to bondholders), whereas if it uses equity, it will pay dividends to the stockholders. The *interest paid by a corporation is deducted* from its operating income to determine its taxable income, but the *dividends paid are not deductible*. Therefore, a firm needs $1 of pretax income to pay $1 of interest, but if it is in the 35 percent bracket, it needs $1.54 of pretax income to pay $1 of dividends:

$$\frac{\text{Pretax income needed}}{\text{to pay \$1 of dividends}} = \frac{\$1}{1 - \text{Tax rate}} = \frac{\$1}{1 - 0.35} = \$1.54$$

Of course, it generally is not possible to finance exclusively with debt capital, and the risk of doing so would offset the benefits of the higher expected income. Still, *the fact that interest is a deductible expense has a profound effect on the way businesses are financed—our tax system favors debt financing over equity financing.* This point was discussed in detail in Chapters 8 and 9.

Corporate Capital Gains   Before 1987, corporate long-term capital gains were taxed at lower rates than ordinary income, as was true for individuals. Under current law, however, corporations' capital gains are taxed at the same rates as their operating income.

---

[16]The size of the dividend exclusion actually depends on the degree of ownership. Corporations that own less than 20 percent of the stock of the dividend-paying company can exclude 70 percent of the dividends received; and firms that own over 20 percent but less than 80 percent can exclude 80 percent of the dividends; and firms that own over 80 percent can exclude the entire dividend payment. Because most companies own less than 20 percent of other companies, we will assume a 70 percent dividend exclusion.

TABLE 11–8	Apex Corporation: Partial Income Statements for 2002–2004 ($ millions)		

	2002	2003	2004
Original Statement:			
Taxable income	$260	$180	($700)
Taxes (35%)	(91)	(63)	245
Net income	$169	$117	($455)

			TOTAL EFFECT OF CARRY-BACK
Adjusted Statement:			
Original taxable income	$260	$180	
Carry-back credit	(260)	(180)	$440
Adjusted taxable income	0	0	
Taxes (35%)	0	0	0
Adjusted net income	$ 0	$ 0	
Taxes originally paid	91	63	$154 = Tax refund

Loss available to carry forward in 2005–2024 = $700 – $440 = $260

Corporate Loss Carryback and Carryover   Ordinary corporate operating losses can be carried back (**carryback**) to each of the preceding two years and carried over (**carryover**) for the next 20 years to offset taxable income in those years. For example, an operating loss reported in 2004 could be carried back and used to reduce taxable income in 2002 and 2003, and carried forward, if necessary, and used in 2005, 2006, and so on, to the year 2024 to offset future taxable income. The loss is applied first to the earliest year, then to the next earliest year, and so on, until losses have been used up or the 20-year carryover limit has been reached.

To illustrate, partial income statements for Apex Corporation are given in Table 11–8. In 2002 and 2003, Apex produced positive taxable income amounts, and it paid the appropriate taxes in each of these years, which totaled $154 million. However, in 2004, Apex incurred a taxable loss equal to $700 million. The carryback feature allows Apex to write off this taxable loss against positive taxable income beginning in 2002. Note, the loss is large enough that the *adjusted* taxable incomes for 2002 and 2003 equal zero. Apex can amend the tax forms it filed in 2002 and 2003, and, thus, it would receive a tax refund equal to $154 million. After adjusting the previous two years' tax forms, Apex still would have $260 million of unrecovered loss from 2004 to carry over through the year 2024, if necessary. The purpose of permitting firms to treat losses like this is to avoid penalizing corporations whose incomes fluctuate substantially from year to year.

Accumulated Earnings Tax   Corporations could refrain from paying dividends to permit their stockholders to avoid personal income taxes on dividends. To prevent this, the tax code contains an **improper accumulation** provision, which states that earnings accumulated by a corporation are subject to penalty rates *if the purpose of the*

TAX LOSS CARRYBACK AND CARRYOVER
Losses that can be carried backward or forward in time to offset taxable income in a given year.

IMPROPER ACCUMULATION
Retention of earnings by a business for the purpose of enabling stockholders to avoid personal income taxes.

accumulation is to enable stockholders to avoid personal income taxes. A cumulative total of $250,000 (the balance sheet item "retained earnings") is by law exempted from the accumulated earnings tax for most corporations. This is a benefit primarily to small corporations. But, the improper accumulation penalty applies only if the retained earnings in excess of $250,000 are shown to be *unnecessary to meet the reasonable needs of the business.* A great many companies do indeed have legitimate reasons for retaining more than $250,000 of earnings. For example, earnings might be retained and used to pay off debt, to finance growth, or to provide the corporation with a cushion against possible cash drains caused by losses. How much a firm should properly accumulate for uncertain contingencies is a matter of judgment.

Consolidated Corporate Tax Returns   If a corporation owns 80 percent or more of another corporation's stock, it can aggregate income and file one consolidated tax return; thus, the losses of one company can be used to offset the profits of another. (Similarly, one division's losses can be used to offset another division's profits.) No business ever wants to incur losses—you can go broke losing $1 to save 34¢ in taxes—but tax offsets do make it more feasible for large, multidivisional corporations to undertake risky new ventures or ventures that will suffer losses during a developmental period and profits thereafter.

Taxation of Small Businesses: S Corporations   The Internal Revenue Code provides that small businesses (fewer than 75 stockholders) that meet certain restrictions as spelled out in the tax code can be set up as corporations and thus receive the benefits of the corporate form of organization—especially limited liability—yet still be taxed as proprietorships or partnerships rather than as corporations.

These corporations are called **S corporations.** For a corporation that elects S corporation status for tax purposes, all of the income of the business is reported as personal income by the owners, and it is taxed at the rates that apply to individuals. This would be preferred by owners of small corporations in which all or most of the income earned each year is distributed as dividends because the income would be taxed only once at the individual level.

Depreciation   Depreciation plays an important role in income tax calculations. Congress specifies, in the tax code, the life over which assets can be depreciated for tax purposes and the methods of depreciation that can be used. Because these factors have a major influence on the amount of depreciation a firm can take in a given year, and thus on the firm's taxable income, depreciation has an important effect on taxes paid and cash flows from operations. We discussed how depreciation is calculated and how it affects income and cash flows when we discussed the subject of capital budgeting in Chapters 6 and 7.

S CORPORATION
A small corporation which, under Subchapter S of the Internal Revenue Code, elects to be taxed as a proprietorship or a partnership yet retains limited liability and other benefits of the corporate form of organization.

Self-Test Questions

Explain what is meant by the statement: "Our tax rates are progressive."

Are tax rates progressive for all income ranges?

Explain the difference between marginal tax rates and average tax rates.

What are capital gains and losses, and how are they differentiated from ordinary income?

How does the federal income tax system tax corporate dividends received by a corporation and those received by an individual? Why is this distinction made?

Briefly explain how tax loss carryback and carryover procedures work.

✳ **ETHICAL DILEMMA**

Hocus-Pocus—Look, An Increase in Sales!

Dynamic Energy Wares (DEW) manufactures and distributes products that are used to save energy and to help reduce and reverse the harmful environmental effects of atmospheric pollutants. DEW relies on a relatively complex distribution system to get the products to its customers—large companies, which account for nearly 30 percent of total sales, purchase directly from DEW, while smaller companies and retailers that sell to individuals are required to purchase from one of the 50 independent distributors that are contractually obligated to *exclusively* sell DEW's products.

DEW's accountants have just finished the financial statements for the third quarter of the fiscal year, which ended three weeks ago. The results are terrible—profits are down 30 percent from this time last year when a downturn in sales began. Profits are depressed primarily because DEW continues to lose market share to a competitor that started business nearly two years ago.

Senior management has decided it needs to take action that will boost sales in the fourth quarter so that year-end profits are "more acceptable." So, starting immediately, DEW will (1) eliminate all direct sales, which means large companies now must purchase from DEW's distributors like the smaller companies and retailers, (2) require distributors to maintain certain minimum inventory levels, which are much higher than previous levels, and (3) form a task force to study and propose ways the firm can recapture lost market share.

The financial manager, who is your boss, has asked you to attend a hastily called meeting of DEW's distributors to announce the implementation of the changes in operations. At the meeting, the distributors will be informed that they must increase inventory to the required minimum level before the end of DEW's current fiscal year or face losing the distributorship. According to your boss, the reason for this requirement is to ensure that distributors can meet the increased demand they will gain because the large companies no longer will be allowed to purchase directly from DEW. But the sales forecast you have been working on for the past couple of months indicates distributors' sales are expected to decline by almost 10 percent during the next year; thus the added inventories might be extremely burdensome to the distributors. When you approached your boss about this, she said: "Tell the distributors not to worry! We won't require payment for six months, and any of the additional inventory that remains unsold after nine months can be returned. But they *must* take delivery of the inventory within the next two months."

It appears the actions implemented by DEW will produce favorable year-end sales results for the current fiscal year. Do you agree with the decisions made by DEW's senior management? Will you be comfortable announcing the decisions to DEW's distributors? How would you respond to a distributor who says, "DEW doesn't care about us, the company just wants to look good, no matter who gets hurt—that's unethical"? What are you going to say to your boss? Are you going to the distributors' meeting?

Summary

The primary purposes of this chapter were (1) to describe the basic financial statements (2) to discuss techniques used by investors and managers to analyze the statements, and (3) to describe the key features of the U.S. tax laws. The key concepts covered are listed here.

■ The four basic statements contained in the annual report are the **balance sheet,** the **income statement,** the **statement of retained earnings,** and the **statement of cash flows.** Investors use the information provided in these statements to form expectations about the future levels of earnings and dividends, and about the firm's riskiness.

- **Operating cash flows** differ from reported **accounting income.** Investors should be more interested in a firm's projected cash flows than in reported earnings, because it is cash, not paper profits, that is paid out as dividends and plowed back into the business to produce growth.
- **Financial statement analysis** generally begins with the calculation of a set of **financial ratios** designed to reveal the relative strengths and weaknesses of a company as compared to other companies in the same industry and to show whether the firm's position has been improving or deteriorating over time.
- **Liquidity ratios** show the relationship of a firm's current assets to its current liabilities and thus indicate the firm's ability to meet its current obligations.
- **Asset management ratios** measure how effectively a firm is managing its assets.
- **Debt management ratios** reveal (1) the extent to which the firm is financed with debt and (2) its likelihood of defaulting on its debt obligations.
- **Profitability ratios** show the combined effects of liquidity, asset management, and debt management policies on operating results.
- **Market value ratios** relate the firm's stock price to its earnings and book value per share, providing an indication of how investors regard the firm's future prospects.
- **Trend analysis** is important because it reveals whether the firm's ratios are improving or deteriorating over time.
- The **DuPont chart** is designed to show how the profit margin on sales and the assets turnover ratio interact to determine the rate of return on equity.
- Ratio analysis has limitations, but used with care and judgment, it can be very helpful. The **interpretation of the computed ratio values is the most important ingredient** for reaching a conclusion regarding both the existing and the prospective financial position of a firm.
- The value of any asset depends on the stream of **after-tax cash flows** it produces. Tax rates and other aspects of our tax system are changed by Congress every year or so.
- In the United States, income tax rates are **progressive:** The higher one's income, the larger the percentage paid in taxes, up to a point.
- Assets such as stocks, bonds, and real estate are defined as **capital assets.** If a capital asset is sold for more than the purchase price, the profit is called a **capital gain.** If the capital asset is sold for a loss, it is called a **capital loss.**
- **Interest income** received by a corporation is taxed as ordinary income; however, **70 percent of the dividends received by one corporation from another is excluded from taxable income.**
- Because **interest paid by a corporation is a deductible expense** while dividends are not, our tax system favors debt financing over equity financing.
- Ordinary corporate operating losses can be **carried back** to each of the preceding two years and carried over for the next 20 years to offset taxable income in those years.
- **S corporations** are small businesses that have the limited-liability benefits of the corporate form of organization yet receive the benefits of being taxed as a partnership or a proprietorship.

Questions

11–1 What four statements are contained in most annual reports?

11–2 If a "typical" firm reports $20 million of retained earnings on its balance sheet, could its directors declare a $20 million cash dividend without any qualms whatsoever? Explain why or why not.

11–3 Describe the changes in balance sheet accounts that would constitute sources of funds. What changes would be considered uses of funds?

11–4 Financial ratio analysis is conducted by four groups of analysts: managers, equity investors, long-term creditors, and short-term creditors. What is the primary emphasis of each of these groups in evaluating ratios?

11–5 What are some cares that must be taken when using ratio analysis? What is the most important aspect of ratio analysis?

11–6 Profit margins and turnover ratios vary from one industry to another. What differences would you expect to find between a grocery chain like Safeway and a steel company? Think particularly about the turnover ratios and the profit margin, and think about the DuPont equation.

11–7 If a firm's ROE is low and management wants to improve it, explain how using more debt might help. Could using too much debt be a detriment?

11–8 How might (a) seasonal factors and (b) different growth rates distort a comparative ratio analysis? Give some examples. How might these problems be alleviated?

11–9 The following table shows the balance sheets for Batelan Corporation for the fiscal years 2004 and 2005. In the column to the right of the balance sheet amounts, indicate whether the change in the account balance represents a source or a use of cash for the firm. Place a (+) in the space provided to indicate a source of funds, a (–) to indicate a use of funds, and a (0) if it cannot be determined whether the change was a source or a use of cash.

	2005	2004	SOURCE (+) OR USE (–)?
Cash	$ 400	$ 500	_____
Accounts receivable	250	300	_____
Inventory	450	400	_____
Current assets	$1,100	$1,200	
Net property and equipment	1,000	950	_____
Total assets	$2,100	$2,150	
Accounts payable	$ 200	$ 400	_____
Accruals	300	250	_____
Notes payable	400	200	_____
Current liabilities	$ 900	$ 850	
Long-term debt	800	900	_____
Total liabilities	$1,700	$1,750	
Common stock	250	300	_____
Retained earnings	150	100	_____
Total equity	$ 400	$ 400	
Total liabilities and equity	$2,100	$2,150	

From these balance sheets, can you tell whether the Batelan Corporation generated a positive or negative net income during 2005? Can you tell if dividends were paid? Explain.

11–10 Indicate the effects of the transactions listed in the following table on total current assets, current ratio, and net income. Use (+) to indicate an increase, (–) to indicate a decrease, and (0) to indicate either no effect or an indeterminate effect. Be prepared to state any necessary assumptions, and assume an initial current ratio of greater than 1.0. (*Note:* A good accounting background is necessary to answer some of these questions; if yours is not strong, just answer the questions you can handle.)

	TOTAL CURRENT ASSETS	CURRENT RATIO	EFFECT ON NET INCOME
a. Cash is acquired through issuance of additional common stock.	____	____	____
b. Inventory is sold for cash.	____	____	____
c. Federal income tax due for the previous year is paid.	____	____	____
d. A fixed asset is sold for less than its book value.	____	____	____
e. A fixed asset is sold for more than its book value.	____	____	____
f. Inventory is sold on credit.	____	____	____
g. Payment is made to trade creditors for previous purchases.	____	____	____
h. A cash dividend is declared and paid.	____	____	____
i. Cash is obtained through short-term bank loans.	____	____	____
j. Marketable securities are sold below cost.	____	____	____
k. Advances are made to employees.	____	____	____
l. Current operating expenses are paid.	____	____	____
m. Short-term promissory notes are issued to trade creditors in exchange for past due accounts payable.	____	____	____
n. Ten-year notes are issued to pay accounts payable.	____	____	____
o. Accounts receivable are collected.	____	____	____
p. Equipment is purchased with short-term notes.	____	____	____
q. Inventory (raw materials) is purchased on credit.	____	____	____

11–11 Suppose you owned 100 shares of General Motors stock and the company earned $6 per share during the last reporting period. Suppose further that GM could either pay all its earnings out as dividends (in which case you would receive $600) or retain the earnings in the business, buy more assets, and cause the price of the stock to go by $6 per share (in which case the value of your stock would rise by $600).
   a. How would the tax laws influence what you, as a typical stockholder, would want the company to do?
   b. Would your choice be influenced by how much other income you had? Why might the desires of a 35-year-old doctor differ with respect to

corporate dividend policy from those of a pension fund manager or a retiree living on a small income?

c. How might the corporation's decision with regard to the dividends it pays influence the price of its stock?

11–12 What does *double taxation of corporate income* mean?

11–13 If you were starting a business, what tax considerations might cause you to prefer to set it up as a proprietorship or a partnership rather than as a corporation? Would you consider the average or the marginal tax rate more relevant?

11–14 Explain how the federal income tax structure affects the choice of financing (use of debt versus equity) of U.S. business firms.

Self-Test Problems

(Solutions appear in Appendix B)

key terms **ST-1** Define each of the following terms:

    a. Annual report; income statement; balance sheet

    b. Equity, or net worth; paid-in capital; retained earnings

    c. Cash flow cycle

    d. Statement of retained earnings; statement of cash flows

    e. Depreciation; inventory valuation methods

    f. Liquidity ratios: current ratios; quick, or acid test, ratio

    g. Asset management ratios: inventory turnover ratio; days sales outstanding (DSO); fixed assets turnover ratio; total assets turnover ratio

    h. Financial leverage; debt ratio; times-interest-earned (TIE) ratio; fixed charge coverage ratio

    i. Profitability ratios: profit margin on sales; return on total assets (ROA); return on common equity (ROE)

    j. Market value ratios: price/earnings (P/E) ratio; market/book (M/B) ratio; book value per share

    k. Trend analysis; comparative ratio analysis

    l. DuPont chart; DuPont equation

    m. "Window dressing"; seasonal effects on ratios

    n. Progressive tax

    o. Marginal and average tax rates

    p. Capital gain or loss

    q. Tax loss carryback and carryover

    r. S corporation

ratio analysis **ST-2** K. Billingsworth & Company had earnings per share of $4 last year, and it paid a $2 dividend. Total retained earnings increased by $12 million during the year, while book value per share at year-end was $40. Billingsworth has no preferred stock, and no new common stock was issued during the year. If Billingsworth's year-end debt (which equals its total liabilities) was $120 million, what was the company's year-end debt/assets ratio?

debt ratio **ST-3** The following data apply to A. L. Kaiser & Company ($ millions):

Cash and marketable securities	$ 100.00
Fixed assets	$ 283.50
Sales	$1,000.00
Net income	$ 50.00
Quick ratio	2.0×
Current ratio	3.0×
DSO	40.0 days
ROE	12.0%

Kaiser has no preferred stock—only common equity, current liabilities, and long-term debt.

    a. Find Kaiser's (1) accounts receivable (A/R), (2) current liabilities, (3) current assets, (4) total assets, (5) ROA, (6) common equity, and (7) long-term debt.

    b. In part a, you should have found Kaiser's accounts receivable (A/R) = $111.1 million. If Kaiser could reduce its DSO from 40 days to 30 days while holding other things constant, how much cash would it generate? If this cash were used to buy back common stock (at book value) and thus reduced the amount of common equity, how would this affect (1) the ROE, (2) the ROA, and (3) the total debt/total assets ratio?

form of business and taxes   **ST-4** John Thompson is planning to start a new business, JT Enterprises, and he must decide whether to incorporate or to do business as a sole proprietorship. Under either form, Thompson will initially own 100 percent of the firm, and tax considerations are important to him. He plans to finance the firm's expected growth by drawing a salary just sufficient for his family's living expenses, which he estimates will be about $40,000, and by retaining all other income in the business. Assume that as a married man with one child, Thompson has income tax exemptions of $3 \times 3,100 = 9,300$ and he estimates that his itemized deductions for each of the three years will be $11,000. He expects JT Enterprises to grow and to earn income of $60,000 in 2005, $90,000 in 2006, and $110,000 in 2007. Which form of business organization will allow Thompson to pay the lowest taxes (and retain the most income) during the period from 2005 to 2007? Assume that the tax rates given in the appendix at the end of this chapter are applicable for all future years. (Social Security taxes would also have to be paid, but ignore them.)

Problems

(Note: By the time this book is published, Congress might have changed rates or other provisions of current tax law; as noted in the chapter, such changes occur fairly often. Work all problems on the assumption that the information in the chapter is still current.)

ratio analysis   **11–1** Data for Unilate Textiles' 2004 financial statements are given in Table 11–1 and Table 11–2 in the chapter.

    a. Compute the 2004 values of the ratios indicated in the following table:

	2004 Values	
RATIO	**UNILATE**	**INDUSTRY**
Current ratio	_____	3.9×
Days sales outstanding	_____	33.5 days
Inventory turnover	_____	7.2×
Fixed asset turnover	_____	4.1×
Debt ratio	_____	45.0%
Net profit margin	_____	4.6%
Return on assets	_____	11.8%

    b. Briefly comment on Unilate's 2004 financial position. Can you see any obvious strengths or weaknesses?

    c. Compare Unilate's 2004 ratios with its 2005 ratios, which are presented in Table 11–6 in the chapter. Comment on whether you believe Unilate's financial position improved or deteriorated during 2005.

    d. What other information would be useful for projecting whether Unilate's financial position is expected to get better or worse in the future?

ratio analysis **11–2** Data for Campsey Computer Company and its industry averages follow.
   a. Calculate the indicated ratios for Campsey.
   b. Construct the DuPont equation for both Campsey and the industry.
   c. Outline Campsey's strengths and weaknesses as revealed by your analysis.
   d. Suppose Campsey had doubled its sales as well as its inventories, accounts receivable, and common equity during 2005. How would that information affect the validity of your ratio analysis? (*Hint:* Think about averages and the effects of rapid growth on ratios if averages are not used. No calculations are needed.)

CAMPSEY COMPUTER COMPANY:
Balance Sheet as of December 31, 2005

Cash	$ 77,500	Accounts payable	$129,000
Receivables	336,000	Notes payable	84,000
Inventories	241,500	Other current liabilities	117,000
Total current assets	$655,000	Total current liabilities	$330,000
Net fixed assets	292,500	Long-term debt	256,500
		Common equity	361,000
Total assets	$947,500	Total liabilities and equity	$947,500

CAMPSEY COMPUTER COMPANY:
Income Statement for Year Ended December 31, 2005

Sales	$ 1,607,500
Cost of goods sold	(1,353,000)
Gross profit	$ 254,500
Fixed operating expenses except depreciation	(143,000)
Depreciation	(41,500)
Earnings before interest and taxes	$ 70,000
Interest	(24,500)
Earnings before taxes	$ 45,500
Taxes (40%)	(18,200)
Net income	$ 27,300

RATIO	CAMPSEY	INDUSTRY AVERAGE
Current ratio	_____	2.0 ×
Days sales outstanding	_____	35 days
Inventory turnover	_____	5.6 ×
Total assets turnover	_____	3.0 ×
Profit margin on sales	_____	1.2%
Return on assets	_____	3.6%
Return on equity	_____	9.0%
Debt ratio	_____	60.0%

balance sheet analysis **11–3** Complete the balance sheet and sales information in the table that follows for Isberg Industries using the following financial data:

Debt ratio: 50%
Quick ratio: 0.80 ×
Total assets turnover: 1.5 ×
Days sales outstanding: 36 days
Gross profit margin on sales: (Sales – Cost of goods sold)/Sales = 25%
Inventory turnover ratio: 5 ×

BALANCE SHEET

Cash	_____	Accounts payable	_____
Accounts receivable	_____	Long-term debt	$ 60,000
Inventories	_____	Common stock	_____
Fixed assets	_____	Retained earnings	$ 97,500
Total assets	$300,000	Total liabilities and equity	=========
Sales	_____	Cost of goods sold	_____

DuPont analysis   **11–4** The Finnerty Furniture Company, a manufacturer and wholesaler of high-quality home furnishings, has experienced low profitability in recent years. As a result, the board of directors has replaced the president of the firm with a new president, Elizabeth Brannigan, who has asked you to make an analysis of the firm's financial position using the DuPont chart. The most recent industry average ratios and Finnerty's financial statements are as follows:

INDUSTRY AVERAGE RATIOS

Current ratio	2×	Fixed assets turnover	6×
Debt ratio	30%	Total assets turnover	3×
Times-interest-earned	7×	Profit margin on sales	3%
Inventory turnover	8.5×	Return on total assets	9%
Days sales outstanding	24 days	Return on common equity	12.9%

FINNERTY FURNITURE COMPANY:
BALANCE SHEET AS OF DECEMBER 31, 2005 ($ MILLIONS)

Cash	$ 45	Accounts payable	$ 45
Marketable securities	33	Notes payable	45
Net receivables	66	Other current liabilities	21
Inventories	159	Total current liabilities	$111
Total current assets	$303	Long-term debt	24
		Total liabilities	$135
Gross fixed assets	225	Common stock	114
Less depreciation	(78)	Retained earnings	201
Net fixed assets	$147	Total stockholders' equity	$315
Total assets	$450	Total liabilities and equity	$450

FINNERTY FURNITURE COMPANY:
INCOME STATEMENT FOR YEAR ENDED DECEMBER 31, 2005 ($ MILLIONS)

Net sales	$ 795.0
Cost of goods sold	(660.0)
Gross profit	$ 135.0
Selling expenses	(73.5)
Depreciation expense	(12.0)
Earnings before interest and taxes	$ 49.5
Interest expense	(4.5)
Earnings before taxes (EBT)	$ 45.0
Taxes (40%)	(18.0)
Net income	$ 27.0

a. Calculate those ratios that you think would be useful in this analysis.
b. Construct a DuPont equation for Finnerty, and compare the company's ratios to the industry average ratios.

c. Do the balance sheet accounts or the income statement figures seem to be primarily responsible for the low profit?

d. Which specific accounts seem to be most out of line in relation to other firms in the industry?

e. If Finnerty had a pronounced seasonal sales pattern, or if it grew rapidly during the year, how might that affect the validity of your ratio analysis? How might you correct for such potential problems?

ratio analysis **11–5** The Cary Corporation's forecasted 2006 financial statements follow, along with some industry average ratios.

a. Calculate Cary's 2006 forecasted ratios, compare them with the industry average data, and comment briefly on Cary's projected strengths and weaknesses.

b. What do you think would happen to Cary's ratios if the company initiated cost-cutting measures that allowed it to hold lower levels of inventory and substantially decrease the cost of goods sold? No calculations are necessary. Think about which ratios would be affected by changes in these two accounts.

CARY CORPORATION:
FORECASTED BALANCE SHEET AS OF DECEMBER 31, 2006

Cash	$ 72,000
Accounts receivable	439,000
Inventories	894,000
Total current assets	$1,405,000
Land and building	238,000
Machinery	132,000
Other fixed assets	61,000
Total assets	$1,836,000
Accounts and notes payable	$ 432,000
Accruals	170,000
Total current liabilities	$ 602,000
Long-term debt	404,290
Common stock	575,000
Retained earnings	254,710
Total liabilities and equity	$1,836,000

CARY CORPORATION FORECASTED INCOME STATEMENT FOR 2006

Sales	$ 4,290,000
Cost of goods sold	(3,580,000)
Gross operating profit	$ 710,000
General administrative and selling expenses	(236,320)
Depreciation	(159,000)
Miscellaneous	(134,000)
Earnings before taxes (EBT)	$ 180,680
Taxes (40%)	(72,272)
Net income	$ 108,408
Number of shares outstanding	23,000
Per-Share Data	
EPS	$ 4.71
Cash dividends	$ 0.95
P/E ratio	5×
Market price (average)	$23.57

INDUSTRY FINANCIAL RATIOS (2006)^A

Quick ratio	1.0×
Current ratio	2.7×
Inventory turnover[b]	5.8×
Days sales outstanding	32 days
Fixed assets turnover[b]	13.0×
Total assets turnover[b]	2.6×
Return on assets	9.1%
Return on equity	18.2%
Debt ratio	50.0%
Profit margin on sales	3.5%
P/E ratio	6.0×

[a]Industry average ratios have been constant for the past four years.

[b]Based on year-end balance sheet figures.

loss carryback, carryover **11–6** The Angell Company has made $150,000 before taxes during each of the past 15 years, and it expects to make $150,000 a year before taxes in the future. However, in 2005 the firm incurred a loss of $650,000. The firm will claim a tax credit at the time it files its 2005 income tax return, and it will receive a check from the U.S. Treasury. Show how it calculates this credit, and then indicate the firm's tax liability for each of the next five years. Assume a 30 percent tax rate on all income to ease the calculations.

loss carryback, carryover **11–7** The projected taxable income of the Glasgo Corporation, formed in 2004, is indicated in the following table. (Losses are shown in parentheses.) What is the corporate tax liability for each year? Use tax rates as shown in the appendix to this chapter.

YEAR	TAXABLE INCOME
2004	$ (95,000)
2005	70,000
2006	55,000
2007	80,000
2008	(150,000)

form of organization **11–8** Kate Brown has operated her small repair shop as a sole proprietorship for several years, but projected changes in her business's income have led her to consider incorporating. Brown is married and has two children. Her family's only income, an annual salary of $45,000, is from operating the business. (The business actually earns more than $45,000, but Kate reinvests the additional earnings in the business.) She itemizes deductions, and she is able to deduct $11,000. These deductions, combined with her four personal exemptions for 4 × $3,100 = $12,400, give her a taxable income of $45,000 – $11,000 – $12,400. (Assume the personal exemption remains at $3,100.) Of course, her actual taxable income, if she does not incorporate, would be higher by the amount of reinvested income. Brown estimates that her business earnings before salary and taxes for the period 2005 to 2007 will be as follows:

YEAR	EARNINGS BEFORE SALARY AND TAXES
2005	$65,000
2006	85,000
2007	95,000

a. What would her total taxes (corporate plus personal) be in each year under
   (1) A non-S corporate form of organization? (2005 tax = $5,525)
   (2) A proprietorship? (2005 tax = $5,525)

b. Should Brown incorporate? Discuss.

personal taxes **11–9** Margaret Considine has this situation for the year 2005: salary of $60,000; dividend income of $10,000; interest on IBM bonds of $5,000; interest on state of Florida municipal bonds of $10,000; proceeds of $22,000 from the sale of IBM stock purchased in 1990 at a cost of $9,000; and proceeds of $22,000 from the November 2005 sale of IBM stock purchased in October 2005 at a cost of $21,000. Margaret gets one exemption ($3,100), and she has allowable itemized deductions of $5,000; these amounts will be deducted from her gross income to determine her taxable income.

a. What is Margaret's federal tax liability for 2005?

b. What are her marginal and average tax rates?

c. If she had some money to invest and was offered a choice of either state of Florida bonds with a yield of 9 percent or more IBM bonds with a yield of 11 percent, which should she choose and why?

d. At what marginal tax rate would Margaret be indifferent in her choice between the Florida and IBM bonds?

tax liability **11–10** Donald Jefferson and his wife Maryanne live in a modest house located in a Los Angeles suburb. Donald has a job at Pittsford CastIron that pays him $50,000 annually. In addition, he and Maryanne receive $2,500 interest from bonds they purchased 10 years ago. To supplement his annual income, Donald bought rental property a few years ago. Every month he collects $3,500 rent from all the property he owns. Maryanne manages the rental property, and she is paid $15,000 annually for her work. During 2005, Donald had to have the plumbing fixed in the houses he rents and the house in which he and his wife live. The plumbing bill for the rented houses was $1,250, and it was $550 for the Jeffersons' personal residence. In 2005, Donald paid $18,000 for mortgage interest and property taxes—$12,650 was for the rental houses, and the remaining $5,350 was for the house occupied by him and his wife. Donald and Maryanne have three children who have graduated from medical college and now are working as physicians in other states.

a. What is the Jeffersons' tax liability for 2005?

b. What would the tax liability be if the Jeffersons did not have the rental property? (Assume Maryanne would not get another job if the Jeffersons did not own the rental property.)

c. Why is the plumbing expense a tax deduction for the rental property but not for the house in which the Jeffersons live?

Exam-Type Problems

The problems included in this section are set up in such a way that they could be used as multiple-choice exam problems.

ratio calculation **11–11** Assume you are given the following relationships for the Zumwalt Corporation:

Sales/total assets	1.5×
Return on assets (ROA)	3%
Return on equity (ROE)	5%

Calculate Zumwalt's profit margin and debt ratio.

liquidity ratio   **11–12** The Hindelang Corporation has $1,312,500 in current assets and $525,000 in current liabilities. Its initial inventory level is $375,000, and it will raise funds as additional notes payable and use them to increase inventory. How much can Hindelang's short-term debt (notes payable) increase without pushing its current ratio below 2.0? What will be the firm's quick ratio after Hindelang has raised the maximum amount of short-term funds?

ratio calculations   **11–13** The W. F. Bailey Company had a quick ratio of 1.4, a current ratio of 3.0, and inventory turnover of 5 times, total current assets of $810,000, and cash and marketable securities of $120,000 in 2005. If the cost of goods sold equaled 86 percent of sales, what were Bailey's annual sales and its DSO for 2005?

times-interest-earned ratio   **11–14** Wolken Corporation had $500,000 of debt outstanding, and it pays an interest rate of 10 percent annually. Wolken's annual sales are $2 million; its average tax rate is 20 percent; and its net profit margin on sales is 5 percent. If the company does not maintain a TIE ratio of at least five times, its bank will refuse to renew the loan, and bankruptcy will result. What is Wolken's TIE ratio?

return on equity   **11–15** Coastal Packaging's ROE last year was only 3 percent, but its management has developed a new operating plan designed to improve things. The new plan calls for a total debt ratio of 60 percent, which will result in interest charges of $300 per year. Management projects an EBIT of $1,000 on sales of $10,000, and it expects to have a total assets turnover ratio of 2.0. Under these conditions, the average tax rate will be 30 percent. If the changes are made, what return on equity will Coastal earn? What is the ROA?

return on equity   **11–16** Earth's Best Company has sales of $200,000, a net income of $15,000, and the following balance sheet:

Cash	$ 10,000	Accounts payable	$ 30,000
Receivables	50,000	Other current liabilities	20,000
Inventories	150,000	Long-term debt	50,000
Net fixed assets	90,000	Common equity	200,000
Total assets	$300,000	Total liabilities and equity	$300,000

a. The company's new owner thinks that inventories are excessive and can be lowered to the point where the current ratio is equal to the industry average, 2.5×, without affecting either sales or net income. If inventories are sold off and not replaced so as to reduce the current ratio to 2.5×, if the funds generated are used to reduce common equity (stock can be repurchased at book value), and if no other changes occur, by how much will the ROE change?

b. Now suppose we wanted to take this problem and modify it for use on an exam; that is, to create a new problem that you have not seen to test your knowledge of this type of problem. How would your answer change if (1)We doubled all of the dollar amounts? (2) We stated that the target current ratio was 3.0×? (3) We said that the company had 10,000 shares of stock outstanding, and we asked how much the change in part a would increase EPS? (4) What would your answer to (3) be if we changed the original problem to state that the stock was selling for twice book value, so common equity would not be reduced on a dollar-for-dollar basis?

c. Now explain how we could have set the problem up to have you focus on changing accounts receivable, or fixed assets, or using the funds generated to retire debt (we would give you the interest rate on outstanding debt), or how the original problem could have stated that the company needed *more* inventories and it would finance them with new common equity or with new debt.

11–17 The consolidated balance sheets for the Lloyd Lumber Company at the beginning and end of 2005 follow. The company bought $50 million worth of fixed assets. The charge for depreciation in 2005 was $10 million. Net income was $33 million, and the company paid out $5 million in dividends.

a. Fill in the amount of the source or use in the appropriate column.

LLOYD LUMBER COMPANY:
BALANCE SHEETS AT BEGINNING AND END OF 2005 ($ MILLIONS)

	JAN. 1	DEC. 31	CHANGE SOURCE	USE
Cash	$ 7	$ 15	8	
Marketable securities	0	11		11
Net receivables	30	22	8	
Inventories	53	75		22
Total current assets	$ 90	$123		
Gross fixed assets	75	125		50
Less accumulated depreciation	(25)	(35)		
Net fixed assets	$ 50	$ 90		
Total assets	$140	$213		
Accounts payable	$ 18	$ 15		3
Notes payable	3	15	12	
Other current liabilities	15	7		8
Long-term debt	8	24	16	
Common stock	29	57	28	
Retained earnings	67	95		28
Total liabilities and equity	$140	$213		

(handwritten margin notes: NI 33, Dep 10, 43, −433, Div 5)

(handwritten totals below columns: 115   127)

NOTE: Total sources must equal total uses.

b. Prepare a statement of cash flows.
c. Briefly summarize your findings.

11–18 The Montejo Corporation expects 2006 sales to be $12 million. Operating costs other than depreciation are expected to be 75 percent of sales, and depreciation is expected to be $1.5 million in 2006. All sales revenues will be collected in cash, and cost other than depreciation must be paid during the year. Montejo's interest expense is expected to be $1 million, and it is taxed at a 40 percent rate.

a. Set up an income statement and a cash flow statement (use two columns on one page) for Montejo. What is the expected cash flow from operations?
b. Suppose Congress changed the tax laws so that Montejo's depreciation expenses doubled in 2006, but no other changes occurred. What would happen to the net income and cash flow from operations expected in 2006?
c. Now suppose Congress, rather than increasing Montejo's 2006 depreciation, reduced it by 50 percent. How would the income and cash flows be affected?
d. If this company belonged to you, would you prefer Congress increase or decrease the depreciation expense allowed your company? Explain why.

11–19 The Zocco Corporation has a 2005 taxable income of $365,000 from operations after all operating costs, but before (1) interest charges of $50,000, (2) dividends received of $15,000, (3) dividends paid of $25,000, and (4) income taxes.

a. What is the firm's income tax liability and its after-tax income?

b. What are the company's marginal and average tax rates on taxable income?

capital gains tax liability   **11–20** Compute the capital gains tax liability for each of the following:

a. An individual sold a municipal bond for $1,150, two years after it was purchased for $950.

b. An individual sold 100 shares of a stock for $12 per share, two years after it was purchased at a price equal to $10 per share.

c. A corporation bought 100 shares of stock for another company for $55 per share, and then sold it for $57 per share two years later.

corporate tax liability   **11–21** In 2004, Ibis International had a taxable income of $150,000 from operations. During the year, Ibis paid $45,000 interest on its outstanding debt (e.g., bank loans and bonds), and it paid its common stockholders $22,000 dividends. The company received $18,000 interest because it invested in the debt of other companies, and it also received $8,000 dividends from its investments in other companies' common stocks. What was the company's tax liability and its after-tax income?

after-tax returns   **11–22** Carver Corporation has $10,000 that it plans to invest. It is thinking of putting the funds in either AT&T bonds that yield 11 percent, state of Florida municipal bonds that yield 8 percent, or AT&T preferred stock that has a dividend yield of 9 percent. Carver's corporate tax rate is 20 percent. Assuming that Carver chooses strictly on the basis of after-tax returns, which security should be selected? What is the after-tax return on the security that should be selected?

Integrative Problem

financial statement analysis   **11–23** Donna Jamison was recently hired as a financial analyst by Computron Industries, a manufacturer of electronic components. Her first task was to conduct a financial analysis of the firm covering the last two years. To begin, she gathered the following financial statements and other data.

BALANCE SHEETS	2005	2004
Assets		
Cash	$ 52,000	$ 57,600
Accounts receivable	402,000	351,200
Inventories	836,000	715,200
Total current assets	$1,290,000	$1,124,000
Gross fixed assets	527,000	491,000
Less accumulated depreciation	(166,200)	(146,200)
Net fixed assets	$ 360,800	$ 344,800
Total assets	$1,650,800	$1,468,800
Liabilities and Equity		
Accounts payable	$ 175,200	$ 145,600
Notes payable	225,000	200,000
Accruals	140,000	136,000
Total current liabilities	$ 540,200	481,600
Long-term debt	424,612	323,432
Common stock (100,000 shares)	460,000	460,000
Retained earnings	225,988	203,768
Total equity	$ 685,988	$ 663,768
Total liabilities and equity	$1,650,800	$1,468,800

INCOME STATEMENTS	2005	2004
Sales	$ 3,850,000	$ 3,432,000
Cost of goods sold	(3,250,000)	(2,864,000)
Other expenses	(430,300)	(340,000)
Depreciation	(20,000)	(18,900)
Total operating costs	$ 3,700,300	$ 3,222,900
EBIT	$ 149,700	$ 209,100
Interest expense	(76,000)	(62,500)
EBT	$ 73,700	$ 146,600
Taxes (40%)	(29,480)	(58,640)
Net income	$ 44,220	$ 87,960
EPS	$ 0.442	$ 0.880

STATEMENT OF CASH FLOWS (2005):

Operating Activities	
Net income	$ 44,220
Other additions (sources of cash):	
Depreciation	20,000
Increase in acccounts payable	29,600
Increase in accruals	4,000
Subtractions (uses of cash)	
Increases in accounts receivable	(50,800)
Increase in inventories	(120,800)
Net cash flow from operations	($ 73,780)
Long-Term Investing Activities	
Investment in fixed assets	($ 36,000)
Financing Activities	
Increase in notes payable	$ 25,000
Increase in long-term debt	101,180
Payment of cash dividends	(22,000)
Net cash flow from financing	104,180
Net reduction in cash account	($ 5,600)
Cash at beginning of year	57,600
Cash at end of year	$ 52,000

OTHER DATA	2005	2004
December 31 stock price	$ 6.00	$ 8.50
Number of shares	100,000	100,000
Dividends per share	$ 0.22	$ 0.22
Lease payments	$ 40,000	$ 40,000

Industry average data for 2005:

RATIO	INDUSTRY AVERAGE
Current	2.7×
Quick	1.0×
Inventory turnover	6.0×
Days sales outstanding (DSO)	32.0 days
Fixed assets turnover	10.7×
Total assets turnover	2.6×

Debt ratio	50.0%
TIE	2.5×
Fixed charge coverage	2.1×
Profit margin	3.5%
ROA	9.1%
ROE	18.2%
Price/earnings	14.2×
Market/book	1.4×

Assume that you are Donna Jamison's assistant and that she has asked you to help her prepare a report that evaluates the company's financial condition. Then answer the following questions:

a. What can you conclude about the company's financial condition from its statement of cash flows?

b. What is the purpose of financial ratio analysis, and what are the five major categories of ratios?

c. What are Computron's current and quick ratios? What do they tell you about the company's liquidity position?

d. What are Computron's inventory turnover, days sales outstanding, fixed assets turnover, and total assets turnover ratios? How does the firm's utilization of assets stack up against that of the industry?

e. What are the firm's debt, times-interest-earned, and fixed charge coverage ratios? How does Computron compare to the industry with respect to financial leverage? What conclusions can you draw from these ratios?

f. Calculate and discuss the firm's profitability ratios—that is, its profit margin, return on assets (ROA), and return on equity (ROE).

g. Calculate Computron's market value ratios—that is, its price/earnings ratio and its market/book ratio. What do these ratios tell you about investors' opinions of the company?

h. Use the DuPont equation to provide a summary and overview of Computron's financial condition. What are the firm's major strengths and weaknesses?

i. Use the following simplified 2005 balance sheet to show, in general terms, how an improvement in one of the ratios, say, the DSO, would affect the stock price. For example, if the company could improve its collection procedures and thereby lower the DSO from 37.6 days to 27.6 days, how would that change "ripple through" the financial statements (shown in thousands below) and influence the stock price?

Accounts receivable	$ 402	Debt	$ 965
Other current assets	888		
Net fixed assets	361	Equity	686
Total assets	$1,651	Total liabilities and equity	$1,651

j. Although financial statement analysis can provide useful information about a company's operations and its financial condition, this type of analysis does have some potential problems and limitations, and it must be used with care and judgment. What are some problems and limitations?

income taxes **11-24 a.** Working with Computron has required you to put in a lot of overtime, so you have had very little time to spend on your private finances. It's now April 1, and you have only two weeks left to file your income tax return.

You have managed to get all the information together that you will need to complete your return. Computron paid you a salary of $45,000, and you received $3,000 in dividends from common stock that you own. You are single, so your personal exemption is $3,100 and your itemized deductions are $5,500.

    (1) On the basis of the information above and the 2004 individual tax rate schedule, what is your tax liability?

    (2) What are your marginal and average tax rates?

b. Assume that a corporation has $100,000 of taxable income from operations plus $5,000 of interest income and $10,000 of dividend income. What is the company's tax liability?

c. Assume that after paying your personal income tax, as calculated in part a, you have $5,000 to invest. You have narrowed your investment choices down to California municipal bonds with a yield of 7 percent or IBM bonds with a yield of 10 percent. Which one should you choose, and why? At what marginal tax rate would you be indifferent to the choice between California and IBM bonds?

Computer-Related Problems

Work the problem in this section only if you are using the computer problem diskette.

ratio analysis **11–25** Use the computerized model in the File C11 to solve this problem.

a. Refer to Problem 11–5. Suppose Cary Corporation is considering installing a new computer system that would provide tighter control of inventories, accounts receivable, and accounts payable. If the new system is installed, the following data are projected (rather than the data given in Problem 11–5) for the indicated balance sheet and income statement accounts:

Accounts receivable	$ 395,000
Inventories	700,000
Other fixed assets	150,000
Accounts and notes payable	275,000
Accruals	120,000
Cost of goods sold	3,450,000
Administrative and selling expenses	248,775
P/E ratio	6×

How do these changes affect the projected ratios and the comparison with the industry averages? (Note that any changes to the income statement will change the amount of retained earnings; therefore, the model is set up to calculate 2006 retained earnings as 2005 retained earnings plus net income minus dividends paid. The model also adjusts the cash balance so that the balance sheet balances.)

b. If the new computer were even more efficient than Cary's management had estimated and thus caused the cost of goods sold to decrease by $125,000 from the projections in part a, what effect would that have on the company's financial position?

c. If the new computer were less efficient than Cary's management had estimated and caused the cost of goods sold to increase by $125,000 from the projections in part a, what effect would that have on the company's financial position?

effect of form of business on taxes

d. Change, one by one, the other items in part a to see how each change affects the ratio analysis. Then think about and write a paragraph describing how computer models like this one can be used to help make better decisions about the purchase of such things as a new computer system.

11–26 The problem requires you to rework Problem 11-8 using the following data. Use File C11 on the computer problem diskette.

   a. Suppose Brown decides to pay out (1) 50 percent or (2) 100 percent of the after-salary corporate income in each year as dividends. Would such dividend policy changes affect her decision about whether to incorporate?

   b. Suppose business improves so that actual earnings before salary and taxes in each year are twice the original estimate. Also assume that if Brown chooses to incorporate she will continue to receive a salary of $45,000 and to reinvest additional earnings in the business. (No dividends would be paid.) What would be the effect of this increase in business income on Brown's decision to incorporate?

GET REAL with Thomson ONE

11-27 Intel Corporation [INTC] designs, manufactures, and markets computer and communications products. Using the financial ratios discussed in the chapter, compare Intel to its peer firms, as designated by its industry group. Answer the following questions. [*Hint:* Click on Peers/Peer Sets/Peers by DJ Industry Group]

   a. How did Intel compare to its peers during the past three years with regard to liquidity, asset management, debt management, and profitability? [*Hint:* Click on Financials/Financial Ratios. You might have to calculate some of the ratios by clicking on Financial/Key Financials]

   b. Where did Intel rank among its peers with regard to liquidity, asset management, debt management, and profitability? Explain your answers.

   c. Based solely on your ratio analysis, if you had to recommend a firm in which to invest in this industry group, would you recommend Intel or another firm?

11-28 Nextel Communications, Inc. [NXTL] is a provider of digital wireless communication services. Using the information from the firm's cash flow statements, answer the following questions. [*Hint:* Click on Financials/Financial Statements/Thomson Financials/Cash Flow Statements]

   a. What conclusions can you make concerning the financial position of Nextel with regard to its operating, investing, and financing activities during the past five years?

   b. How has Nextel improved over the five-year period? What problems has the company experienced?

APPENDIX 11A

2004 Tax Rate Schedules

Table 11A–1 gives the 2004 tax rates for individuals and Table 11A–2 gives the 2004 tax rates for corporations. Even though these rates probably have changed, they should be used for all of the problems in this chapter that require the computation of tax liabilities.

| TABLE 11A-1 | Individual Tax Rates for 2004 |

UNMARRIED TAXPAYERS, NOT HEADS OF HOUSEHOLDS

TAXABLE INCOME BRACKET	BASE TAX AMOUNT	PLUS THIS PERCENT OF THE AMOUNT OVER		AVERAGE TAX RATE AT THE *Top* OF THE BRACKET
$ 1 – $7,150	$ 0.00	+ 10.0%	$ 0	10.0%
7,151 – 29,050	715.00	+ 15.0	7,150	13.8
29,051 – 70,350	4,000.00	+ 25.0	29,050	20.4
70,351 – 146,750	14,325.00	+ 28.0	70,350	24.3
146,751 – 319,100	35,717.00	+ 33.0	146,750	29.0
Above 319,100	92,592.50	+ 35.0	319,100	≈35.0

MARRIED TAXPAYERS FILING JOINT RETURNS

TAXABLE INCOME BRACKET	BASE TAX AMOUNT	PLUS THIS PERCENT OF THE AMOUNT OVER		AVERAGE TAX RATE AT THE *Top* OF THE BRACKET
$ 0 – $14,300	$ 0.00	+ 10.0%	$ 0	10.0%
14,300 – 58,100	1,430.00	+ 15.0%	14,300	13.8
58,101 – 117,250	8,000.00	+ 25.0	58,100	19.4
117,251 – 178,650	22,787.50	+ 28.0	117,250	22.4
178,651 – 319,100	39,979.50	+ 33.0	178,650	27.1
Above 319,100	86,328.00	+ 35.0	319,100	≈35.0

NOTES:

a. The personal exemption for 2004 was $3,100 per person or dependent. The total amount of this exemption can be deducted from income to compute taxable income. For example, for a family of four, the total personal exemption would be $12,400 = 4 × 3,100.

b. If the taxpayer does not want to itemize deductions such as interest payments made on mortgages, charitable contributions, and so on, the standard deduction can be taken. In 2004, the standard deduction for an unmarried taxpayer, not the head of a household, was $4,850, and it was $9,700 for married taxpayers filing joint returns.

c. The tax rate applied to capital gains for assets held less than 12 months (short term) was the marginal tax rate of the taxpayer, and 15 percent for assets held 12 months or more (long term).

| TABLE 11A–2 | Corporate Tax Rates for 2004 |

TAXABLE INCOME BRACKET	BASE TAX AMOUNT		PLUS THIS PERCENT OF THE AMOUNT OVER		AVERAGE TAX RATE AT THE *Top* OF THE BRACKET
$ 0 – $ 50,000	$ 0	+	15%	$ 0	15.0%
50,001 – 75,000	7,500	+	25	50,000	18.3
75,001 – 100,000	13,750	+	34	75,000	22.3
100,001 – 335,000	22,250	+	39	100,000	34.0
335,001 – 10,000,000	113,900	+	34	335,000	34.0
10,000,001 – 15,000,000	3,400,000	+	35	10,000,000	34.3
15,000,001 – 18,333,333	5,150,000	+	38	15,000,000	35.0
Above 18,333,333	6,416,667	+	35	18,333,333	35.0

NOTE:

For taxable income above $335,000, there is a surtax, which could increase the marginal tax rate to about 40 percent.

CHAPTER 12

Financial Planning and Control

A MANAGERIAL PERSPECTIVE

In November 1994, Sony Corporation, the Japanese consumer electronics firm, wrote off more than $3.2 billion in assets, causing the book value of its assets to immediately decrease by about 30 percent and the market value of its stock to decrease by 13 percent within a one-week period. The write-off was directly attributed to Sony Pictures, the motion picture business that had been formed five years earlier with the $5 billion purchase of Columbia Pictures and TriStar Pictures from Coca-Cola Company.

According to most analysts, the success of Sony's 1988 purchase of CBS Records, one of the world's largest record companies, teased the company into expanding its entertainment operations to the "Hollywood scene." Unfortunately, Sony did not follow the old adage "Look before you leap"—company executives seemingly did not have a formal financial plan or control mechanism for the movie business. Michael Schulhof, chairman of Sony Corporation of America, was put in charge of Sony Pictures, even though he was unknown in the motion picture industry. He hired two movie producers, neither of whom had previous experience running a movie studio, to head the production facilities. From 1989 to 1994 more than $1 billion was spent on refurbishing studio lots and on executive perquisites such as fresh flowers, antiques, private chefs, and lavish parties. But Sony Pictures' movie-production companies, Columbia and TriStar, were unable to consistently produce hit movies; in fact, most of the pictures were expensive flops, including *Last Action Hero*, *I'll Do Anything*, and *Mary Shelley's Frankenstein*.

Was Sony Pictures just unlucky? Not according to Chuck Goto, an analyst with Smith Barney at the time, who noted that "[i]f you look at it very objectively, it's clear the company mismanaged shareholders' money" by not planning adequately. It seems the only plan Sony had was to pour money into movies, and this strategy was destined to fail because there was not adequate forecasting and control to head off any problems that arose.

Even though it replaced the management and reorganized the operational structure of its motion picture business at the end of 1994, Sony had additional write-offs in 1995. Since that time, however, Sony Pictures Entertainment (SPE) has produced some hit motion pictures that have helped SPE weather the rocky financial storm it inherited from the previous managers. In fact, in 1997, the Columbia TriStar Motion Picture Group (the moniker that was born with the reorganization) broke revenue records in the motion picture industry by grossing nearly $1.3 billion in U.S. theaters and more than $2.3 billion internationally. Some of the movies that helped SPE achieve this success included *Men in Black*, *My Best Friend's Wedding*, and *Air Force One*.

Although Sony has achieved success at the box office with recent movies, including *Something's Got to Give*, which was the top movie when it debuted at the end of 2003, the company has not achieved the performance it wants. To cut costs, Sony Pictures announced that it would eliminate more than 500 jobs in 2004. In addition, top management was changed at the end of 2003; in December, Michael Lynton was named to head Sony Pictures. Lynton had limited experience in the entertainment industry in the mid-1990s, so it will be interesting to see how he handles the challenge at Sony Pictures.

Many of the problems Sony Pictures originally experienced could have been avoided or reduced substantially if Sony Corporation had a financial plan in place before it entered the movie industry. Most analysts agree that the value of Sony Pictures decreased by about 50 percent from 1989 to 1994 when Sony began "biting the bullet" and initiated efforts to turn around its motion picture business. At that time, Sony had to evaluate the effects on forecasted earnings and stock prices of cutting certain costs, writing off additional assets, and controlling the finances associated with the motion picture businesses. A *plan* was devised to salvage Sony Pictures, which provided encouragement to Sony Corporation's investors and potential investors and proved successful, at least so far. ∎

FINANCIAL PLANNING

The projection of sales, income, and assets as well as the determination of the resources needed to achieve these projections.

FINANCIAL CONTROL

The phase in which financial plans are implemented; control deals with the feedback and adjustment process required to ensure adherence to plans and modification of plans because of unforeseen changes.

In the previous chapter, we focused on how to use financial statement analysis to evaluate the existing financial position of a firm. In this chapter, we will see how a financial manager can use some of the information obtained through financial statement analysis for financial planning and control of the firm's future operations. Well-run companies generally base their operating plans on a set of forecasted financial statements. The **financial planning** process begins with a sales forecast for the next few years. Then the assets required to meet the sales targets are determined, and a decision is made concerning how to finance the required assets. At that point, income statements and balance sheets can be projected, and earnings and dividends per share, as well as the key ratios, can be forecasted.

Once the "base case" forecasted financial statements and ratios have been prepared, top managers want to know (1) how realistic the results are, (2) how to attain the results, and (3) what impact changes in operations would have on the forecasts. At this stage, which is the **financial control** phase, the firm is concerned with implementing the financial plans, or forecasts, and dealing with the feedback and adjustment process that is necessary to ensure the goals of the firm are pursued appropriately.

The first part of the chapter is devoted to financial planning using projected financial statements, or forecasts, and the second part of the chapter focuses on financial control using budgeting and the analysis of leverage to determine how changes in operations affect financial forecasts.

Sales Forecasts

Forecasting is an essential part of the planning process, and a **sales forecast** is the most important ingredient of financial forecasting. The sales forecast generally starts with a review of sales during the past five to 10 years, which can be expressed in a graph such as that in Figure 12–1. The first part of the graph shows five years of historical sales for Unilate Textiles, the textile and clothing manufacturer we analyzed

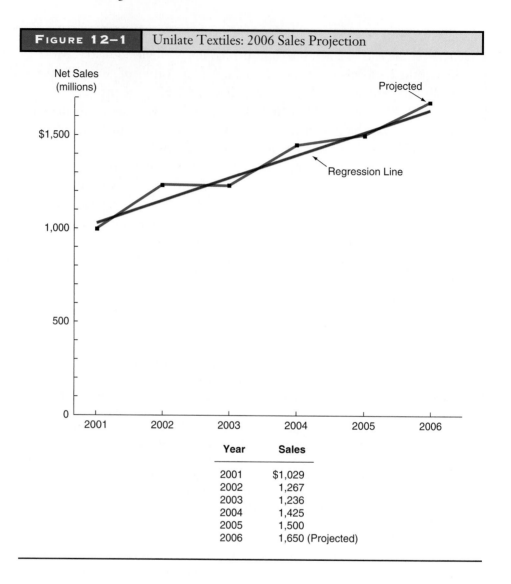

FIGURE 12–1	Unilate Textiles: 2006 Sales Projection

Year	Sales
2001	$1,029
2002	1,267
2003	1,236
2004	1,425
2005	1,500
2006	1,650 (Projected)

SALES FORECAST
A forecast of a firm's unit and dollar sales for some future period; generally based on recent sales trends plus forecasts of the economic prospects for the nation, region, industry, and so forth.

in the previous chapter. The graph could have contained 10 years of sales data, but Unilate typically focuses on sales figures for the latest five years because the firm's studies have shown that future growth is more closely related to the recent than to the distant past.

Unilate had its ups and downs from 2001 through 2005. In 2003, poor cotton production in the United States and diseased sheep in Australia resulted in low textile production, which caused sales to fall below the 2002 level. Then a significant increase in both the supply of cotton and the supply of wool in 2004 pushed sales up by 15 percent. Based on a regression analysis, Unilate's forecasters determined that the average annual growth rate in sales over the past five years was nearly 10 percent. To determine the forecasted sales growth for 2006, some of the factors that Unilate considered included projections of expected economic activity, competitive conditions, and product development and distribution both in the markets in which Unilate currently operates and in the markets it plans to enter into in the future. Often firms develop mathematical models such as regression equations to take into consideration such factors when forecasting future sales. Based on its historical sales trend, plans for new product and market introductions, and Unilate's forecast for the economy, the firm's planning committee has projected a 10 percent growth rate for sales during 2006. So 2006 sales are expected to be $1,650 million, which is 10 percent higher than 2005 sales of $1,500 million.

If the sales forecast is inaccurate, the consequences can be serious. First, if the market expands significantly *more* than Unilate has geared up for, the company probably will not be able to meet demand. Customers will buy competitors' products, and Unilate will lose market share, which will be hard to regain. On the other hand, if the projections are overly optimistic, Unilate could end up with too much plant, equipment, and inventory. This would mean low turnover ratios, high costs for depreciation and storage, and, possibly, write-offs of obsolete or unusable inventory. All of this would result in a low rate of return on equity, which in turn would depress the company's stock price. If Unilate had financed an unnecessary expansion with debt, its problems would, of course, be compounded. Remember from our analysis of its 2005 financial statements in the previous chapter that Unilate's current financial position is considered poor. Thus, an accurate sales forecast is critical to the well-being of the firm.[1]

Self-Test Questions

How do past trends affect a sales forecast?

Briefly explain why an accurate sales forecast is critical to profitability.

Projected (Pro Forma) Financial Statements

ADDITIONAL FUNDS NEEDED (AFN)
Funds that a firm must raise externally through new borrowing or by selling new stock.

Any forecast of financial requirements involves (1) determining how much money the firm will need during a given period, (2) determining how much money (funds) the firm will generate internally during the same period, and (3) subtracting the funds generated internally from the funds required to determine the external financial requirements. One method used to estimate external requirements is the *projected, or pro forma, balance sheet method*, which is discussed in this section.

The projected balance sheet method is straightforward. Simply project the asset requirements for the coming period, then project the liabilities and equity that will be generated under normal operations—that is, whithout additional external financing—and subtract the projected liabilities and equity from the required assets to estimate the **additional funds needed (AFN)** to support the level of forecasted operations. The steps in the procedure are explained next.

---

[1]A sales forecast is actually the *expected value of a probability distribution* with many possible levels of sales. Because any sales forecast is subject to a greater or lesser degree of uncertainty, for financial planning we are often just as interested in the degree of uncertainty inherent in the sales forecast (σ_{sales}) as we are in the expected value of sales. The concepts of probability distribution measures as they apply to corporate finance are discussed in Chapter 4.

TABLE 12–1	Unilate Textiles: Actual 2005 and Projected 2006 Income Statements ($ millions, except per share data)

	2005 RESULTS	2006 FORECAST BASIS[a]	INITIAL FORECAST
Net sales	$ 1,500.0	× 1.10	$ 1,650.0
Cost of goods sold	(1,230.0)	× 1.10	(1,353.0)
Gross profit	$ 270.0		$ 297.0
Fixed operating costs except depreciation	(90.0)	× 1.10	(99.0)
Depreciation	(50.0)	× 1.10	(55.0)
Earnings before interest and taxes (EBIT)	$ 130.0		143.0
Interest	(40.0)		(40.0)[b]
Earnings before taxes (EBT)	$ 90.0		$ 103.0
Taxes (40%)	(36.0)		(41.2)
Net Income	$ 54.0		$ 61.8
Common dividends	(29.0)		(29.0)[b]
Addition to retained earnings	$ 25.0		$ 32.8
Earnings per share	$ 2.16		$ 2.47
Dividends per share	$ 1.16		$ 1.16
Number of common shares (millions)	25.00		25.00

[a]× 1.10 indicates "times (1 + g)"; used for items that grow proportionally with sales.

[b]Indicates a 2005 figure carried over for the preliminary forecast.

Step 1. Forecast the 2006 Income Statement

PROJECTED (PRO FORMA) BALANCE SHEET METHOD
A method of forecasting financial requirements based on forecasted financial statements.

The **projected (pro forma) balance sheet method** begins with a forecast of sales. Next, the income statement for the coming year is forecasted to obtain an initial estimate of the amount of retained earnings (internal equity financing) the company will generate during the year. This requires assumptions about the operating cost ratio, the tax rate, interest charges, and the dividends paid. In the simplest case, the assumption is made that costs will increase at the same rate as sales; in more complicated situations, cost changes are forecasted separately. Still, the objective of this part of the analysis is to determine how much income the company will earn and then retain for reinvestment in the business during the forecasted year.

Table 12–1 shows Unilate's actual 2005 income statement and the initial forecast of the 2006 income statement if the firm's operating costs change at the same rate as sales. Thus, to create the 2006 income forecast, we assume that sales and variable operating costs will be 10 percent greater in 2006 than in 2005. In addition, it is assumed that Unilate currently *operates at full capacity*, which means it will need to expand its plant capacity in 2006 to handle the additional operations. Therefore, in Table 12–1, the 2006 forecasts of sales, *all* operating costs, and depreciation are 10 percent greater than their 2005 levels. The result is that earnings before interest and taxes (EBIT) is forecasted to be $143 million in 2006.

To complete the initial forecast of 2006 income, we assume no change in the financing of the firm because, at this point, it is not known if additional financing is needed. But it is apparent that the 2006 interest expense will change if the amount of debt (borrowing) the firm needs to support the forecasted increase in operations changes. To forecast the 2006 dividends, we simply assume the dividend per share will be the same as it was in 2005, $1.16; so the total common dividends forecasted for 2006 would be $29.0 million if no additional common stock is issued. Like the interest expense amount, however, the amount of total dividends used to create this initial forecast will increase if Unilate decides to sell new stock to raise any additional financing necessary to support the new operations or to raise the dividends per share paid to existing shareholders.

From the initial forecast of 2006 income we can see that $32.8 million dollars is expected to be added to retained earnings in 2006. As it turns out, this addition to retained earnings represents the amount Unilate is expected to invest in itself (internally generated funds) to support the increase in operations in 2006 if the conditions described here exist. So the next step is to determine what impact this level of investment will have on the Unilate's forecasted 2006 balance sheet.

Step 2. Forecast the 2006 Balance Sheet

If we assume the 2005 end-of-year asset levels were just sufficient to support 2005 operations, then in order for Unilate's sales to increase in 2006, its assets must also grow. Because the company was operating at full capacity in 2005, *each* asset account must increase if the higher sales level is to be attained: More cash will be needed for transactions, higher sales will lead to higher receivables, additional inventory will have to be stocked, and new plant and equipment must be added for production.

Further, if Unilate's assets are to increase, its liabilities and equity must also increase—the additional assets must be financed in some manner. Some liabilities will increase *spontaneously* due to normal business relationships. For example, as sales increase, so will Unilate's purchases of raw materials, and these larger purchases will spontaneously lead to higher levels of accounts payable. Similarly, a higher level of operations will require more labor, and higher sales will result in higher taxable income. Therefore, both accrued wages and accrued taxes will increase. In general, current liabilities that change naturally with sales changes provide **spontaneously generated funds,** which increase at the same rate as sales.

Notes payable, long-term bonds, and common stock will not rise spontaneously with sales. Rather, the projected levels of these accounts will depend on conscious financing decisions that will be made once it has been determined how much external financing is needed to support the projected operations. Therefore, for the initial forecast, it is assumed these account balances remain unchanged from their 2005 levels.

Table 12–2 contains Unilate's 2005 actual balance sheet and an initial forecast of its 2006 balance sheet. The mechanics of the balance sheet forecast are similar to those used to develop the forecasted income statement. First, those balance sheet accounts that are expected to increase directly with sales are multiplied by 1.10 to obtain the initial 2006 forecasts. Thus, 2006 cash is projected to be $15.0 × 1.10 = $16.5 million, accounts receivable are projected to be $180.0 × 1.10 = $198.0 million, and so on. In our example, all assets increase with sales, so once the individual assets have been forecasted, they can be summed to complete the asset section of the forecasted balance sheet.

SPONTANEOUSLY GENERATED FUNDS
Funds that are obtained from routine business transactions.

TABLE 12–2	Unilate Textiles: Actual 2005 and Projected 2006 Balance Sheets ($ millions)

	2005 BALANCES	FORECAST BASIS[a]	2006 INITIAL FORECAST
Cash	$ 15.0	× 1.10	$ 16.5
Accounts receivable	180.0	× 1.10	198.0
Inventories	270.0	× 1.10	297.0
Total current assets	$465.0		$511.5
Net plant and equipment	380.0	× 1.10	418.0
Total Assets	$845.0		$929.5
Accounts payable	$ 30.0	× 1.10	$ 33.0
Accruals	60.0	× 1.10	66.0
Notes payable	40.0		40.0[b]
Total current liabilities	$130.0		$139.0
Long-term bonds	300.0		300.0[b]
Total liabilities	$430.0		$439.0
Common stock	130.0		130.0[b]
Retained earnings	285.0	+$32.8[c]	317.8
Total owners' equity	$415.0		$447.8
Total Liabilities and Equity	$845.0		$886.8
Additional funds needed (AFN)			$ 42.7[d]

[a]× 1.10 indicates "times $(1 + g)$"; used for items which grow proportionally with sales.

[b]Indicates a 2005 figure carried over for the initial forecast.

[c]The $32.8 million represents the "addition to retained earnings" from the 2006 Projected Income Statement given in Table 12–1.

[d]The "additional funds needed (AFN)" is computed by subtracting the amount of total liabilities and equity from the amount of total assets.

Next, the spontaneously increasing liabilities (accounts payable and accruals) are forecasted. Then those liability and equity accounts whose values reflect conscious management decisions—notes payable, long-term bonds, and stock—*initially are not changed from* their 2005 levels. Thus, the amount of 2006 notes payable initially is set at $40.0 million, the long-term bond account is forecasted at $300.0 million, and so forth. The forecasted 2006 level of retained earnings will be the 2005 level plus the forecasted addition to retained earnings, which was computed as $32.8 million in the projected income statement we created in Step 1 (Table 12–1).

The forecast of total assets in Table 12–2 is $929.5 million, which indicates that Unilate must add $84.5 million of new assets (compared to 2005 assets) to support the higher sales level expected in 2006. However, according to the initial forecast of the 2006 balance sheet, the total liabilities and equity sum to only $886.8 million, which is an increase of only $41.8 million. So the amount of total assets exceeds the amount of total liabilities and equity by $42.7 million = $929.5 million − $886.8 million. This indicates $42.7 million of the forecasted increase in total assets will not be financed by liabilities that spontaneously increase with sales (accounts payable and accruals) or by an increase in retained earnings. Unilate can raise the additional $42.7 million, which we designate *additional funds needed (AFN)*, by borrowing from the bank as notes payable, by issuing long-term bonds, by selling new common stock, or by some combination of these actions.

The initial forecast of Unilate's financial statements has shown us that (1) higher sales must be supported by higher asset levels, (2) some of the asset increases can be financed by spontaneous increases in accounts payable and accruals and by retained earnings, and (3) any shortfall must be financed from external sources, either by borrowing or by selling new stock.

Step 3. Raising the Additional Funds Needed

Unilate's financial manager will base the decision of exactly how to raise the $42.7 million additional funds needed on several factors, including its ability to handle additional debt, conditions in the financial markets, and restrictions imposed by existing debt agreements. The decisions concerning how to best finance the firm are discussed in Chapter 9. Regardless of how Unilate raises the $42.7 million AFN, the initial forecasts of both the income statement and the balance sheet will be affected. If Unilate takes on new debt, its interest expenses will rise; and if additional shares of common stock are sold, *total* dividend payments will increase if the *same dividend per share* is paid to all common stockholders. Each of these changes, which we term *financing feedbacks*, will affect the amount of additional retained earnings originally forecasted, which in turn will affect the amount of additional funds needed.

Remember from our ratio analysis in the previous chapter that we concluded Unilate has a below-average debt position. Consequently, Unilate has decided any additional funds needed to support future operations will be raised mainly by issuing new common stock. Following this financing policy should help improve Unilate's debt position as well as its overall profitability.

Step 4. Financing Feedbacks

FINANCING FEEDBACKS

The effects on the income statement and balance sheet of actions taken to finance forecasted increases in assets.

As mentioned in Step 3, one complexity that arises in financial forecasting relates to **financing feedbacks.** The external funds raised to pay for new assets create additional financing expenses that must be reflected in the income statement and that lower the initially forecasted addition to retained earnings, which means more external funds than are initially forecasted are needed to make up for the lower amount added to retained earnings. In other words, if Unilate raised the $42.7 million AFN by issuing new debt and new common stock, it would find both the interest expense and the total dividend payments would be higher than the amounts contained in the forecasted income statement shown in Table 12–1. Consequently, after adjusting for the higher interest and dividend payments, the forecasted addition to retained earnings would be lower than the initial forecast of $32.8 million. Because the retained earnings will be lower than projected, a financing shortfall will exist even after the original AFN of $42.7 million is considered. So in reality, Unilate must raise more than $42.7 million to account for the financing feedbacks that affect the amount of internal financing expected to be generated from the increase in operations. To determine the amount of external financing actually needed, we have to adjust the initial forecasts of both the income statement (Step 1) and the balance sheet (Step 2) to reflect the impact of raising the additional external financing. This process has to be repeated until AFN = 0 in Table 12–2, which means Step 1 and Step 2 might have to be repeated several times to fully account for the financing feedbacks.

Table 12–3 contains the adjusted 2006 preliminary forecasts for the income statement and the balance sheet of Unilate Textiles after all of the financing effects are considered. To generate the adjusted forecasts, it is assumed that of the total external funds needed, 65 percent will be raised by selling new common stock at $23 per share, 15 percent will be borrowed from the bank at an interest rate of 7 percent, and 20 percent will be raised by selling long-term bonds with a coupon interest of 10 percent. Under these conditions, it can be seen from Table 12–3 that Unilate actually needs $45.0 million to support the forecasted increase in operations, not the $42.7 million contained in the initial forecast. The additional $2.3 million is needed because the added amounts of debt and common stock will cause interest and dividend payments to increase, which will decrease the contribution to retained earnings by $2.3 million.[2]

Analysis of the Forecast

The 2006 forecast as developed here represents a preliminary forecast, because we have completed only the first stage of the entire forecasting process. Next, the projected statements must be analyzed to determine whether the forecast meets the firm's financial targets. If the statements do not meet the targets, then elements of the forecast must be changed.

Table 12–4 shows Unilate's 2005 ratios as they were reported back in Table 11–6 in the previous chapter, plus the projected 2006 ratios based on the preliminary forecast and the industry average ratios. As we noted in Chapter 11, the firm's financial condition at the close of 2005 was weak, with many ratios being well below the industry averages. The preliminary final forecast for 2006 (after financing feedbacks are considered), which assumes that Unilate's past practices will continue into the future, shows an improved debt position. But the overall financial position still is somewhat weak, and this condition will persist unless management takes some actions to improve things.

Unilate's management actually plans to take steps to improve its financial condition. The plans are to (1) close down certain operations, (2) modify the credit policy to reduce the collection period for receivables, and (3) better manage inventory so that products are turned over more often. These proposed operational changes will affect both the income statement and the balance sheet, so the preliminary forecast will have to be revised again to reflect the impact of such changes. When this process is complete, management will have its final forecast. To keep things simple, we do not show the final forecast here; instead, for the remaining discussions we assume the preliminary forecast is not substantially different and use it as the final forecast for Unilate's 2006 operations.

As we have shown, forecasting is an iterative process, both in the way the financial statements are generated and in the way the financial plan is developed. For planning purposes, the financial staff develops a preliminary forecast based on a continuation of past policies and trends. This provides the executives with a starting point, or "straw man" forecast. Next, the model is modified to see what effects alternative operating plans would have on the firm's earnings and financial condition. This results in a revised forecast.

---

[2]Appendix 12A at the end of this chapter gives a more detailed description of the iterations required to generate the final forecasts.

What Is a "Good" Sales Forecast?

Managers know that sales forecasts are essential for effective planning and future survival of their businesses. In this chapter, we describe only one rather simple forecasting technique—pro forma forecasting.

Numerous forecasting techniques can be used to predict sales; some of the procedures are quantitative and sophisticated, while others are rather subjective in nature. Many of the quantitative methods are inexpensive to apply, and they provide more accurate forecasts than the judgmental, "seat-of-the-pants" forecasting approaches. Given the current understanding of the quantitative models, many of which are covered in the curricula offered by business schools, and the proliferation of computer technology in business, you would expect most managers to use the more sophisticated sales forecasting methods. But surveys of large companies in the United States indicate that managers primarily rely on judgmental methods, including the manager's opinion, to formulate sales forecasts, not the more sophisticated, quantitative techniques.[a, b] The managers surveyed indicated they possessed the knowledge and technology to apply the quantitative forecasting methods, but most preferred to trust their own or their colleagues' experiences when forecasting sales. Even those managers who use quantitative methods stated that they generally subjectively adjust the forecasts resulting from these models to incorporate qualitative factors, including knowledge of the operating environment, the product quality, and previous experience with the models. In fact, the results of the survey suggest that the primary reasons managers do not use sophisticated forecasting models is because they believe the data needed to use such models appropriately either are not relevant or are not available.

Consequently, for the most part, managers believe their judgments provide sales forecasts that are as "good" as sophisticated models. "Good" might not relate to forecast accuracy, however, because about 85 percent of the survey's respondents indicated that they would prefer to either underestimate or overestimate when forecasting sales. More than 70 percent said they "underforecast" sales because when the forecast is exceeded, an explanation is not needed and a reward might even be considered; but, when actual sales turn out to be less than forecasted, job security becomes tenuous. Interestingly, the respondents who said they "overforecast" indicated that the primary reason was because they could get more staff to support the higher amount of sales.

What are the methods used, and who generally develops forecasts for firms? According to one survey, "managerial judgment" is used by greater than 97 percent of wholesale companies; forecasts by the sales force are used by greater than 75 percent of the companies; and the previous year's sales is increased by a given percentage by greater than 67 percent of the firms (in most cases, multiple methods were employed). In nearly 50 percent of the companies, either the sales manager or the financial manager is responsible for developing the forecasts. The most common time periods for which the forecasts cover are one year (100 percent of the companies surveyed) and quarterly (67 percent of the companies surveyed).[b]

In summary, surveys of large companies indicate that, to most managers, forecasting sales is more of an art than a science.

[a]Nada R. Sanders and Karl B. Manrodt, "Forecasting Practices in U.S. Corporations: Survey Results," *Interfaces*, March–April 1994, 92(9).

[b]Robin T. Peterson and Jun Minjoon, "Forecasting Sales in Wholesale Industry," *The Journal of Business Forecasting Methods & Systems*, Summer 1999, 15–17.

be increased. In general, we can compute the sales capacity of the firm if it is known what percent of assets are used to produce a particular level of sales:

$$\text{Full capacity sales} = \frac{\text{Sales level}}{\left(\begin{array}{c}\text{Percent of capacity used} \\ \text{to generate sales level}\end{array}\right)}$$

If Unilate does not have to increase plant and equipment, fixed assets would remain at the 2005 level of $380 million, and the amount of AFN would actually be negative, which means that the amount of internally generated funds would be more than sufficient to support (finance) the forecasted 10 percent increase in sales in 2006. In fact, Unilate could increase the per share dividend it pays to stockholders in 2006 if it does not have to increase fixed assets.

In addition to the excess capacity of fixed assets, the firm could have excesses in other assets that can be used for increases in operations. For instance, in the previous chapter, we concluded that Unilate's inventory level at the end of 2005 probably was greater than it should have been. If true, some increase in 2006 forecasted sales can be absorbed by the above-normal inventory, and production would not have to be increased until inventory levels are reduced to normal. This requires no additional financing.

In general, excess capacity means less external financing is required to support increases in operations than would be needed if the firm previously operated at full capacity.

Economies of Scale

There are economies of scale in the use of many types of assets, and when such economies occur, a firm's variable cost of goods sold ratio is likely to change as the size of the firm changes (either increases or decreases) substantially. Currently, Unilate's variable cost ratio is 82 percent of sales; but the ratio might decrease to 80 percent of sales if operations increase significantly. If everything else is the same, changes in the variable cost ratio affect the addition to retained earnings, which in turn affects the amount of AFN.

Lumpy Assets

LUMPY ASSETS
Assets that cannot be acquired in small increments; instead, they must be obtained in large, discrete amounts.

In many industries, technological considerations dictate that if a firm is to be competitive, it must add fixed assets in large, discrete units; such assets often are referred to as **lumpy assets.** For example, in the paper industry, there are strong economies of scale in basic paper mill equipment, so when a paper company expands capacity, it must do so in large, lumpy increments. Lumpy assets primarily affect the turnover of fixed assets and, consequently, the financial requirements associated with expanding. For instance, if instead of $38 million Unilate needed an additional $50 million in fixed assets to increase operations 10 percent, the AFN would be much greater. With lumpy assets, it is possible that a small projected increase in sales would require a significant increase in plant and equipment, which would require a large financial requirement.

Self-Test Question

Discuss three factors that might cause "spontaneous" assets and liabilities to change at a different rate than sales.

Financial Control—Budgeting and Leverage

In the previous section, we focused on financial forecasting, emphasizing how growth in sales requires additional investment in assets, which in turn generally requires the firm to raise new funds externally. In the sections that follow, we consider the planning and control systems used by financial managers when implementing the forecasts. First, we look at the relationship between sales volume and profitability under different operating conditions. These relationships provide information that is used by managers to plan for changes in the firm's level of operations, financing needs, and profitability. Later, we examine the control phase of the planning and control process, because a good control system is essential both to ensure that plans are executed properly and to facilitate a timely modification of plans if the assumptions on which the initial plans were based turn out to be different than expected.

The planning process can be enhanced by examining the effects of changing operations on the firm's profitability, both from the standpoint of profits from operations and from the standpoint of profitability after financing effects are considered. In the next few sections, we look at some of the areas financial managers evaluate to provide information about the effects of changing GM's operations.

Self-Test Question

How can the planning process be enhanced with a good financial control system?

Operating Breakeven Analysis

OPERATING BREAKEVEN ANALYSIS
An analytical technique for studying the relationship between sales revenues, operating costs, and profits.

The relationship between sales volume and *operating profitability* is explored in cost-volume-profit planning, or operating breakeven analysis. **Operating breakeven analysis** is a method of determining the point at which sales will just cover operating costs—that is, the point at which the firm's operations will break even. It also shows the magnitude of the firm's operating profits or losses if sales exceed or fall below that point. Breakeven analysis is important in the planning and control process because the cost-volume-profit relationship can be influenced greatly by the proportion of the firm's investment in assets that are fixed. A sufficient volume of sales must be anticipated and achieved if fixed and variable costs are to be covered, or else the firm will incur losses from operations. In other words, if a firm is to avoid accounting losses, its sales must cover all costs—those that vary directly with production and those that remain constant even when production levels change. Costs that vary directly with the level of production generally include the labor and materials needed to produce and sell the product, whereas the fixed operating costs generally include costs such as depreciation, rent, and insurance expenses that are incurred regardless of the firm's production level.

Operating breakeven analysis deals only with the upper portion of the income statement—the portion from sales to net operating income (NOI), which is also termed earnings before interest and taxes (EBIT). This portion generally is referred to as the *operating section*, because it contains only the revenues and expenses associated with the *normal production and selling operations* of the firm. Table 12–5 gives the operating section of Unilate's forecasted 2006 income statement, which was shown in Table 12–3. For the discussion that follows, we have assumed that all of Unilate's products sell for $15.00 each and the variable cost of goods sold per unit is $12.30, which is 82 percent of the selling price.

TABLE 12–5	Unilate Textiles: 2006 Forecasted Operating Income ($ millions)

Sales (S)	$ 1,650.0
Variable cost of goods sold (VC)	(1,353.0)
Gross profit (GP)	$ 297.0
Fixed operating costs (F)	(154.0)
Net operating income (NOI-EBIT)	$ 143.0

NOTES:

Sales in units = 110 million units.

Selling price per unit = $15.00.

Variable costs per unit = $1,353/110 = $12.30

Fixed operating costs = $154 million, which includes $55 million depreciation and $99 million in other fixed costs such as rent, insurance, and general office expenses.

Breakeven Graph

Table 12–5 shows the net operating income for Unilate if 110 million products are produced and sold during the year. But what if Unilate doesn't sell 110 million products? Certainly, the firm's net operating income will be something other than $143 million. Figure 12–2 shows the total revenues and total operating costs for Unilate at various levels of sales, beginning with zero. According to the information given in Table 12–5, Unilate has fixed costs, which include depreciation, rent, insurance, and so on, equal to $154 million. This amount must be paid even if the firm produces and sells nothing, so the $154 million fixed cost is depicted by a horizontal line. If Unilate produces and sells nothing, its sales revenues will be zero; but *for each unit sold*, the firm's sales will increase by $15. Therefore, the total revenue line starts at the origin of the X and Y axes, and it has a slope equal to $15 to account for the dollar increase in sales for each additional unit sold. On the other hand, the line that represents the total operating costs intersects the Y axis at $154 million, which represents the fixed costs incurred even when no products are sold, and it has a slope equal to $12.30, which is the cost directly associated with the production of each additional unit sold. The point at which the total revenue line intersects the total operating cost line is the **operating breakeven point,** because this is where the revenues generated from sales just cover the *total operating costs* of the firm. Notice that prior to the breakeven point, the total cost line is above the total revenue line, which indicates that Unilate will suffer operating losses because the total costs cannot be covered by the sales revenues. But, after the breakeven point, the total revenue line is above the total cost line because revenues are more than sufficient to cover total operating costs, so Unilate will realize operating profits.[3]

OPERATING BREAKEVEN POINT

Represents the level of production and sales at which net operating income is zero; it is the point at which revenues from sales just equal total operating costs.

---

[3]In Figure 12–2, we assume the operating costs can be divided into two distinct groups—fixed costs and variable costs. It should be noted that some costs are considered semivariable (or semifixed). These costs are fixed for a certain range of operations but change if operations are either higher or lower. For the analysis that follows, we have assumed there are no semivariable costs, so that the operating costs can be separated into either a fixed component or a variable component.

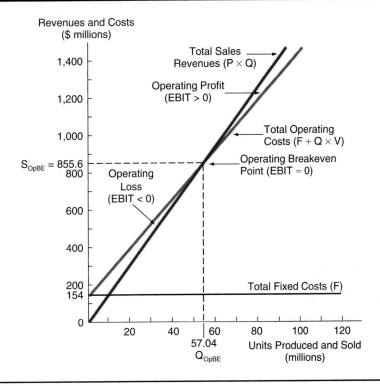

| FIGURE 12–2 | Unilate Textiles: Operating Breakeven Chart |

Notes:

S_{OpBE} = operating breakeven in dollars

Q = sales in units: Q_{OpBE} = operating breakeven in units

F = fixed costs = $154 million

V = variable costs per unit = $12.30

P = price per unit = $15.00

Breakeven Computation

Figure 12–2 shows that Unilate must sell 57.04 million units to be at the operating breakeven point. If Unilate sells 57.04 million products, it will generate $855 million in sales revenues, which will be just enough to cover the $855.6 million total operating costs—$154 million fixed costs and $701.6 million variable costs (57.04 million units at $12.30 per unit). If we do not have a graph like Figure 12–2, how can the operating breakeven point be computed? Actually, it is rather simple. Remember, the operating breakeven point is where the revenues generated from sales just cover the total operating costs, which include both the costs directly attributable to producing each unit and the fixed operating costs that remain constant regardless of the production level. As long as the selling price of each unit (the slope of the total revenue line) is greater than the variable operating cost of each unit (the slope of the total operating cost line), each unit sold will generate revenues that contribute to covering the fixed operating costs. For Unilate, this contribution (termed the *contribution margin*) is $2.70, which is the difference between the $15 selling price and the $12.30 variable cost of each unit. To compute the operating breakeven for Unilate then, we have to determine how many units need to be sold to cover the fixed operating cost of $154 million if each unit has a contribution margin equal to $2.70. Just divide the $154 million fixed cost by the $2.70 contribution margin and you will discover the breakeven point is 57.04 million units, which equates to $855.6 million in sales revenues.

More formally, the operating breakeven point can be found by setting the total revenues equal to the total operating costs so that net operating income (NOI) is zero. In equation form, NOI = 0 if

$$\frac{\text{Sales}}{\text{revenues}} = \frac{\text{Total operating}}{\text{costs}} = \frac{\text{Total}}{\text{variable costs}} + \frac{\text{Total}}{\text{fixed costs}}$$

$$(P \times Q) = \quad \text{TOC} \quad = \quad (V \times Q) \quad + \quad F$$

where P is the sales price per unit, Q is the number of units produced and sold, V is the variable operating cost per unit, and F is the total fixed operating costs. Solving for the quantity that needs to be sold, Q, produces a formula that can be used to find the number of units that needs to be sold to achieve operating breakeven.

12–1

$$Q_{\text{OpBE}} = \frac{F}{P - V} = \frac{F}{\text{Contribution margin}}$$

Thus, the operating breakeven point for Unilate is

$$Q_{\text{OpBE}} = \frac{\$154.0 \text{ million}}{\$15.00 - \$12.30} = \frac{\$154.0 \text{ million}}{\$2.70}$$

$$= 57.04 \text{ million units}$$

In the remainder of the chapter, we omit the word *million* in the computations and include it only in the final answer.

From Equation 12–1, we can see that the operating breakeven point is lower (higher) if the numerator is lower (higher) or if the denominator is higher (lower). Therefore, all else equal, one firm will have a lower operating breakeven point than another firm if its fixed costs are lower, if the selling price of its product is higher, if its variable operating cost per unit is lower, or if some combination of these exists. For instance, if Unilate could increase the sales price per unit from $15 to $15.38 without affecting either its fixed operating costs ($154 million) or its variable operating cost per unit ($12.30), then its operating breakeven point would fall to 50 million units.

The operating breakeven point also can be stated in terms of the total sales revenues needed to cover total operating costs. At this point, we just need to multiply the sales price per unit by the breakeven quantity we found using Equation 12–1, which yields $855.6 million (= 57.04 × $15.00) for Unilate. Or we can restate the contribution margin as a percent of the sales price per unit (this is called the *gross profit margin*) and then apply Equation 12–1. In other words,

12–2

$$S_{\text{OpBE}} = \frac{F}{1 - \left(\dfrac{V}{P}\right)} = \frac{F}{\text{Gross profit margin}}$$

Solving Equation 12–2 for Unilate, the operating breakeven based on dollar sales is

$$S_{OpBE} = \frac{\$154.0}{1 - \left(\dfrac{\$12.30}{\$15.00}\right)} = \frac{\$154.0}{1 - 0.82} = \frac{\$154.0}{0.18} = \$855.6 \text{ million}$$

Equation 12–2 shows that $0.18 of every $1 sales revenues goes to cover the fixed operating costs, so about $856 million worth of the product must be sold to break even.

Breakeven analysis based on dollar sales rather than on units of output is useful in determining the breakeven volume for a firm that sells many products at varying prices. This analysis requires only that total sales, total fixed costs, and total variable costs at a given level are known.

Using Operating Breakeven Analysis

Operating breakeven analysis can shed light on three important types of business decisions: (1) When making new product decisions, breakeven analysis can help determine how large the sales of a new product must be for the firm to achieve profitability. (2) Breakeven analysis can be used to study the effects of a general expansion in the level of the firm's operations; an expansion would cause the levels of both fixed and variable costs to rise, but it would also increase expected sales. (3) When considering modernization projects, where the fixed investment in equipment is increased to lower variable costs, particularly the cost of labor, breakeven analysis can help management analyze the consequences of purchasing these projects.

However, care must be taken when using operating breakeven analysis. To apply breakeven analysis as we have discussed here requires that the sales price *per unit*, the variable cost *per unit*, and the *total* fixed operating costs do not change with the level of the firm's production and sales. Within a narrow range of production and sales, this assumption probably is not a major issue. But if the firm expects either to produce a much greater (or fewer) number of products than normal or to expand (reduce) its plant and equipment significantly, these costs will change. Therefore, use of a single breakeven chart like the one presented in Figure 12–2 is impractical. Such a chart provides useful information, but the fact that it cannot deal with changes in the price of the product, with changing variable cost rates, and with changes in fixed cost levels suggests the need for a more flexible type of analysis. Today, such analysis is provided by computer simulation and other sophisticated models. Functions such as those expressed in Equations 12–1 and 12–2 (or more complicated versions of them) can be put into a spreadsheet or similarly modeled with other computer software, and then variables such as sales price, P, the variable cost per unit, V, and the level of fixed costs, F, can be changed. The model can instantaneously produce new versions of Figure 12–2, or a whole set of such graphs, to show what the operating breakeven point would be under different production setups and price-cost situations.

Self-Test Questions

Is interest paid considered in operating breakeven analysis? Why or why not?

Give the equations used to calculate the operating breakeven point in units and in dollar sales.

Give some examples of business decisions for which operating breakeven analysis might be useful.

Identify some limitations to the use of a single operating breakeven chart.

Operating Leverage

OPERATING LEVERAGE
The existence of fixed operating costs, such that a change in sales will produce a larger change in operating income (EBIT).

If a high percentage of a firm's total operating costs are fixed, the firm is said to have a high degree of **operating leverage.** In physics, leverage implies the use of a lever to raise a heavy object with a small amount of force. In politics, people who have leverage can accomplish a great deal with their smallest word or action. *In business terminology, a high degree of operating leverage, other things held constant, means that a relatively small change in sales will result in a large change in operating income.*

Operating leverage arises because the firm has *fixed operating costs* that must be covered no matter the level of production. The impact of the leverage, however, depends on the actual operating level of the firm. For example, Unilate has $154.0 million in fixed operating costs, which are covered rather easily because the firm currently sells 110 million products; thus, it is well above its operating breakeven point of 57.04 million units. But what would happen to the operating income if Unilate sold more or less than forecasted? To answer this question we need to determine the **degree of operating leverage (DOL)** associated with Unilate's forecasted 2006 operations.

DEGREE OF OPERATING LEVERAGE
The percentage change in NOI (or EBIT) associated with a given percentage change in sales.

Operating leverage can be defined more precisely in terms of the way a given change in sales volume affects operating income (NOI). To measure the effect of a change in sales volume on NOI, we calculate the degree of operating leverage, which is defined as the percentage change in NOI (or EBIT) associated with a given percentage change in sales:

12–3

$$DOL = \frac{\%\Delta \text{ in NOI}}{\%\Delta \text{ in sales}} = \frac{\left(\dfrac{\Delta NOI}{NOI}\right)}{\left(\dfrac{\Delta Sales}{Sales}\right)} = \frac{\left[\dfrac{NOI^* - NOI}{NOI}\right]}{\left[\dfrac{Sales^* - Sales}{Sales}\right]}$$

The symbol Δ (the Greek letter for "delta") means *change*. The term with the asterisk (*) indicates the actual outcome, whereas the term without the asterisk is the forecasted result. Thus, $NOI^* - NOI$ represents the actual NOI minus the forecasted NOI. In effect, the DOL is an index number that measures the effect of a change in sales on operating income or EBIT.

Table 12–5 shows that the NOI for Unilate is $143.0 million at production and sales equal to 110 million units. If the number of units produced and sold increases to 121 million, the operating income (in millions of dollars) would be

$$NOI = 121(\$15.00 - \$12.30) - \$154.0 = \$172.7$$

So the degree of operating leverage associated with this change is 2.08:

$$DOL = \frac{\left[\dfrac{\$172.7 - \$143.0}{\$143.0}\right]}{\left[\dfrac{\$15.00(121 - 110)}{\$15.00(110)}\right]} = \frac{\left(\dfrac{\$29.7}{\$143.0}\right)}{\left(\dfrac{11}{110}\right)} = \frac{0.208}{0.100} = \frac{20.8\%}{10.0\%} = 2.08\times$$

To interpret the meaning of the value of the degree of operating leverage, remember we computed the percent change in operating income and then divided the result by the percent change in sales. Taken literally then, Unilate's DOL of 2.08× indicates that the percent change in operating income will be 2.08 times the percent change in

	2006 FORECASTED OPERATIONS	**SALES INCREASE**	**UNIT CHANGE**	**PERCENT CHANGE**
	TABLE 12–6 Unilate Textiles: Operating Income at Sales Levels of 110 Million Units and 121 Million Units ($ millions)			

	2006 FORECASTED OPERATIONS	**SALES INCREASE**	**UNIT CHANGE**	**PERCENT CHANGE**
Sales in units (millions)	110	121	11	+10.0%
Sales revenues	$1,650.0	$1,815.0	$165.0	+10.0%
Variable cost of goods sold	(1,353.0)	(1,488.3)	(135.3)	+10.0%
Gross profit	$ 297.0	$ 326.7	$ 29.7	+10.0%
Fixed operating costs	(154.0)	(154.0)	(0.0)	0.0%
Net operating income (EBIT)	$ 143.0	$ 172.7	$ 29.7	+20.8%

sales from the current 110 million units ($1,650.0 million). So if the number of units sold increases from 110 million to 121 million, or by 10 percent, Unilate's operating income should increase by $2.08 \times 10\% = 20.8\%$. At 121 million units, *operating income* should be 20.8 percent greater than the $143.0 million generated at 110 million units of sales; the new operating income should be $172.7 million = $1.208 \times \$143$ million. Table 12–6 compares the operating incomes generated at the two different sales levels.

The results contained in Table 12–6 show that Unilate's *gross profit* would increase by $29.7 million, or by 10 percent, if sales increase 10 percent. The fixed operating costs remain constant at $154.0 million, so EBIT also increases by $29.7 million, and the total impact of a 10 percent increase in sales is a 20.8 percent increase in operating income. If the fixed operating costs were to increase in proportion to the increase in sales—that is, 10 percent—then the net operating income would also increase by 10 percent because all revenues and costs would have changed by the same proportion. In reality, fixed operating costs will not change (a zero percent increase); so, a 10 percent increase in Unilate's forecasted 2006 sales will result in an *additional* 10.8 percent increase in operating income. The total increase is 20.8 percent, which results because operating leverage exists.

Equation 12–3 can be simplified so that the degree of operating leverage at *a particular level of operations* can be calculated as follows:[4]

---

[4]Equation 12–4 can be derived by restating Equation 12–3 in terms of the variables we have defined previously, and then simplifying the result. Starting with Equation 12–3, we have

$$DOL = \frac{\%\Delta \text{ in NOI}}{\%\Delta \text{ in sales}} = \frac{\left(\dfrac{\Delta NOI}{NOI}\right)}{\left(\dfrac{\Delta Sales}{Sales}\right)}$$

NOI can be stated as the gross profit, $Q(P - V)$, minus the fixed operating costs, F. So, if we use Q to indicate the level of operations forecasted for 2006 and Q^* to indicate the level of operations that would exist if operations were different, the percent change in NOI is stated as

$$\%\Delta \, NOI = \frac{[Q^*(P - V) - F] - [Q(P - V) - F]}{Q(P - V) - F} = \frac{(Q^* - Q)(P - V)}{Q(P - V) - F}$$

Substituting into Equation 12–3, restating the denominator, and solving, yields

$$DOL = \frac{\left[\dfrac{(Q^* - Q)(P - V)}{Q(P - V) - F}\right]}{\left[\dfrac{P(Q^* - Q)}{P(Q)}\right]} = \frac{(Q^* - Q)(P - V)}{Q(P - V) - F} \times \left(\frac{Q}{Q^* - Q}\right) = \frac{Q(P - V)}{Q(P - V) - F}$$

12–4

$$DOL_Q = \frac{Q(P - V)}{Q(P - V) - F}$$

Or, rearranging the terms, DOL can be stated in terms of sales revenues as follows:

12–4a

$$DOL_s = \frac{(Q \times P) - (Q \times V)}{(Q \times P) - (Q \times V) - F} = \frac{S - VC}{S - VC - F} = \frac{Gross\ profit}{EBIT}$$

To compute DOL using Equation 12–4 or Equation 12–4a, we only need information from Unilate's forecasted operations; we do not need information about the possible change in forecasted operations. So Q represents the forecasted 2006 level of production and sales, and S and VC are the sales and variable operating costs, respectively, at that level of operations. For Unilate, the equation solution for DOL would be

$$DOL_{110} = \frac{110(\$15.00 - \$12.30)}{110(\$15.00 - \$12.30) - \$154} = \frac{\$1,650 - \$1,353}{\$1,650 - \$1,353 - \$154}$$

$$= \frac{\$297}{\$143} = 2.08 \times$$

Equation 12–4 normally is used to analyze a single product, such as GM's Chevrolet Cavalier, whereas Equation 12–4a is used to evaluate an entire firm with many types of products and, hence, for which "quantity in units" and "sales price" are not meaningful.

The DOL of 2.08× indicates that *each* 1 percent *change* in sales will result in a 2.08 percent *change* in operating income. What would happen if Unilate's sales decrease, say, by 10 percent? According to the interpretation of the DOL figure, Unilate's operating income would be expected to decrease by 20.8 percent. Table 12–7 shows that this actually would be the case. Therefore, *the DOL value indicates the* change *(increase or decrease) in operating income resulting from a* change *(increase or decrease) in the level of operations.* It should be apparent that the greater the DOL, the greater the impact of a change in operations on operating income, whether the change is an increase or a decrease.

The DOL value found by using Equation 12–4 is the degree of operating leverage only for a specific initial sales level. For Unilate, that sales level is 110 million units, or $1,650 million. The DOL value would differ if the initial (existing) level of operations differed. For example, if Unilate's operating cost structure was the same, but only 65 million units were produced and sold, the DOL would have been

$$DOL_{65} = \frac{(65)(\$15.00 - \$12.30)}{[(65)(\$15.00 - \$12.30)] - \$154.0} = \frac{\$175.5}{\$21.5} = 8.16 \times$$

The DOL at 65 million units produced and sold is nearly four times greater than the DOL at 110 million units. Thus, from a base sales of 65 million units, a 10 percent increase in sales, from 65 million units to 71.5 million units, would result in an 8.16 × 10% = 81.6% increase in operating income, from $21.5 million to $39.05 mil-

	TABLE 12–7	Unilate Textiles: Operating Income at Sales Levels of 110 Million Units and 99 Million Units ($ millions)		

	2006 FORECASTED OPERATIONS	**SALES DECREASE**	**UNIT CHANGE**	**PERCENT CHANGE**
Sales in units (millions)	110	99	(11)	–10.0%
Sales revenues	$1,650.0	$1,485.0	$(165.0)	–10.0%
Variable cost of goods sold	(1,353.0)	(1,217.7)	135.3	–10.0%
Gross profit	$ 297.0	$ 267.3	$(29.7)	–10.0%
Fixed operating costs	(154.0)	(154.0)	(0.0)	0.0%
Net operating income (EBIT)	$ 143.0	$ 113.3	$(29.7)	–20.8%

lion. This shows that when Unilate's operations are closer to its operating breakeven point of 57.04 million units, its degree of operating leverage is higher.

In general, given the same operating cost structure, if a firm's level of operations is decreased, its DOL increases; or, stated differently, the closer a firm is to its operating breakeven point, the greater is its degree of operating leverage. This occurs because, as Figure 12–2 indicates, the closer a firm is to its operating breakeven point, the more likely it is to incur an operating loss due to a decrease in sales. There is not a large buffer in operating income to absorb a decrease in sales and still be able to cover the fixed operating costs. Similarly, at the same level of production and sales, a firm's degree of operating leverage will be higher if the contribution margin for its products is lower. The lower the contribution margin, the less each product sold is able to help cover the fixed operating costs, and the closer the firm is to its operating breakeven point. Therefore, the higher the DOL for a particular firm, it generally can be concluded the closer the firm is to its operating breakeven point, and the more sensitive its operating income is to a change in sales volume. *Greater sensitivity generally implies greater risk; thus, it can be stated that firms with higher DOLs generally are considered to have riskier operations than firms with lower DOLs.*

Operating Leverage and Operating Breakeven

The relationship between operating leverage and the operating breakeven point is illustrated in Figure 12–3, where various levels of operations are compared for Unilate and two other textile manufacturers. One firm has a higher contribution margin than Unilate and the other firm has lower fixed operating costs, so we know the other two firms have operating breakeven points that are less than Unilate's. Allied Cloth has the lowest operating breakeven point, because it has the highest contribution margin relative to its fixed costs. Unilate has the highest operating breakeven point because it uses the greatest relative amount of operating leverage of the three firms. Consequently, all else equal, of the three textile manufacturers, Unilate's operating income would be magnified the most if actual sales turned out to be greater than forecasted; but it also would experience the greatest decrease in operating income if actual sales turned out to be less than expected.

Figure 12–3	Operating Leverage

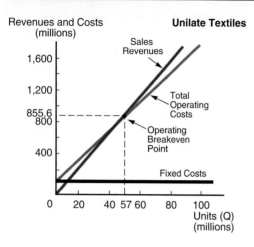

Selling price = $15.00

Variable cost per unit = $12.30

Fixed costs = $154 million

Operating breakeven = 57.04 million units

= $855.6 million

| SALES LEVEL | | TOTAL | OPERATING | |
| UNITS | REVENUES | OPERATING | PROFIT | |
(Q)	($)	COSTS	(EBIT)	DOL
30	$ 450	$ 523	$ (73)	
60	900	892	8	20.3
110	1,650	1,507	143	2.1
150	2,250	1,999	251	1.6

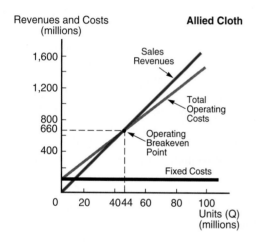

Selling price = $15.00

Variable cost per unit = $11.50

Fixed costs = $154 million

Operating breakeven = 44 million units

= $660 million

| SALES LEVEL | | TOTAL | OPERATING | |
| UNITS | REVENUES | OPERATING | PROFIT | |
(Q)	($)	COSTS	(EBIT)	DOL
30	$ 450	$ 499	$ (49)	
60	900	844	56	3.8
110	1,650	1,419	231	1.7
150	2,250	1,879	371	1.4

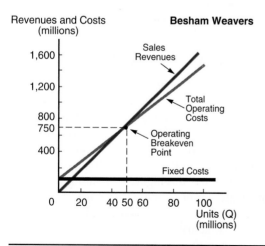

Selling price = $15.00

Variable cost per unit = $12.30

Fixed costs = $135 million

Operating breakeven = 50 million units

= $750 million

| SALES LEVEL | | TOTAL | OPERATING | |
| UNITS | REVENUES | OPERATING | PROFIT | |
(Q)	($)	COSTS	(EBIT)	DOL
30	$ 450	$ 504	$ (54)	
60	900	873	27	6.0
110	1,650	1,488	162	1.8
150	2,250	1,980	270	1.5

Self-Test Questions

What does the term "high degree of operating leverage" imply, and what are some implications of having a high degree of operating leverage?

What is the general equation used to calculate the degree of operating leverage?

What is the association between the concepts of operating breakeven and operating leverage?

Financial Breakeven Analysis

FINANCIAL BREAKEVEN ANALYSIS

Determining the operating income (EBIT) the firm needs to just cover all of its financing costs and produce earnings per share equal to zero.

Operating breakeven analysis deals with evaluation of production and sales to determine at what level the firm's sales revenues will just cover its operating costs; the point where the operating income is zero. **Financial breakeven analysis** is a method of determining the operating income, or EBIT, the firm needs to just cover all of its *financing costs* and produce earnings per share equal to zero. Typically, the financing costs involved in financial breakeven analysis consist of the interest payments to bondholders and the dividend payments to preferred stockholders. Usually these financing costs are fixed, and, in every case, they must be paid before dividends can be paid to common stockholders.

Financial breakeven analysis deals with the lower section of the income statement—the portion from operating income (EBIT) to earnings available to common stockholders. This portion of the income statement generally is referred to as the *financing section*, because it contains the expenses associated with the financing arrangements of the firm. The financing section of Unilate's forecasted 2006 income statement is contained in Table 12–8.

Breakeven Graph

FINANCIAL BREAKEVEN POINT

The level of EBIT at which EPS equals zero.

Figure 12–4 shows the earnings per share (EPS) for Unilate at various levels of EBIT. The point at which EPS equals zero is referred to as the **financial breakeven point.** As the graph indicates, the financial breakeven point for Unilate is where

TABLE 12–8	Unilate Textiles: 2006 Forecasted Earnings per Share ($ millions)
Earnings before interest and taxes (EBIT)	$ 143.0
Interest	(41.4)
Earnings before taxes (EBT)	$ 101.6
Taxes (40%)	(40.6)
Net income	$ 61.0
Preferred dividends	(0.0)
Earnings available to common stockholders	$ 61.0

NOTES:

$Shrs_C$ = Number of common shares = 26.3 million

EPS = Earnings per share = $61.0/26.3 = $2.32

| FIGURE 12–4 | Unilate Textiles: Financial Breakeven Chart |

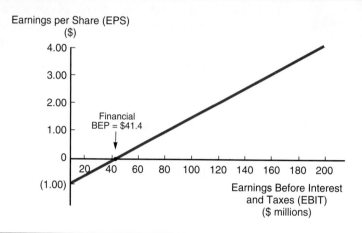

EBIT equals $41.4 million. At this EBIT level, the income generated from operations is just sufficient to cover the financing costs, including income taxes; thus, EPS equals zero. To see this, we can compute the EPS when EBIT is $41.4 million:

Earnings before interest and taxes (EBIT)	$41.4
Interest	(41.4)
Earnings before taxes (EBT)	0.0
Taxes (40%)	(0.0)
Net income	0.0
Earnings available to common stockholders (EAC)	$ 0.0

EPS = $0/26.3 = $0

Breakeven Computation

The results obtained from Figure 12–4 can be translated algebraically to produce a relatively simple equation that can be used to compute the financial breakeven point of any firm. First, remember the financial breakeven point is defined as the level of EBIT that generates EPS equal to zero. Therefore, at the financial breakeven point,

12–5

$$\text{EPS} = \frac{\text{Earnings available to common stockholders}}{\text{Number of common shares outstanding}} = 0$$

$$= \frac{(\text{EBIT} - \text{I})(1 - \text{T}) - \text{D}_{ps}}{\text{Shrs}_C} = 0$$

where EBIT is the earnings before interest and taxes, I represents the interest payments on debt, T is the marginal tax rate, D_{ps} is the amount of dividends paid to preferred stockholders, and Shrs_C is the number of common shares outstanding. Notice that EPS equals zero if the numerator in Equation 12–5, which is the earnings available to common stockholders, equals zero; so the financial breakeven point also can be stated as follows:

$$(EBIT - I)(1 - T) - D_{ps} = 0$$

Rearranging this equation to solve for EBIT gives the solution for the level of EBIT needed to produce EPS equal to zero. Therefore, the computation for a firm's financial breakeven point is

12–6	
	$$EBIT_{FinBE} = I + \frac{D_{ps}}{(1 - T)}$$

Using Equation 12–6, the financial breakeven point for Unilate Textiles in 2006 is

$$EBIT_{FinBE} = \$41.4 + \frac{\$0}{1 - 0.4} = \$41.4$$

which is the same result shown in Figure 12–4.

According to Equation 12–6, the amount of preferred stock dividends must be stated on a before-tax basis to determine the financial breakeven point. If a firm has no preferred stock though, the firm only needs to cover its interest payments, so the financial breakeven point simply equals the interest expense. This is the case for Unilate, because it has no preferred stock. Because most corporations in the United States do not have preferred stock outstanding, we will not include preferred dividends in the discussions that follow.

Using Financial Breakeven Analysis

Financial breakeven analysis can be used to help determine the impact of the firm's financing mix on the earnings available to common stockholders.[5] When the firm uses financing alternatives that require fixed financing costs such as interest, financial leverage exists. *Financial leverage affects the financing section* of the income statement like *operating leverage affects the operating section.* This point is discussed in the next section.

Self-Test Questions

Define the financial breakeven point. How does the financial breakeven point differ from the operating breakeven point?

Why is it important to carry out financial breakeven analysis?

Financial Leverage

FINANCIAL LEVERAGE
The existence of fixed financial costs such as interest and preferred dividends; when a change in EBIT results in a larger change in EPS.

While operating leverage considers how changing sales volume affects operating income, **financial leverage** considers how changing operating income affects earnings per share, or earnings available to common stockholders. Operating leverage affects the operating section of the income statement, whereas financial leverage affects the financing section of the income statement. *Financial leverage takes over*

---

[5]The effect of financing the firm with various proportions of debt and equity is discussed in greater detail in Chapter 9.

*where operating leverage leaves off, magnifying the effects on earnings per share of changes
in operating income.*

Like operating leverage, financial leverage arises because fixed costs exist; in this
case, the fixed costs are associated with how the firm is financed. The **degree of
financial leverage (DFL)** is defined as the percent change in earnings per share
(EPS) that results from a given percent change in earnings before interest and taxes
(EBIT). DFL is computed as follows:

12–7

$$DFL = \frac{\%\Delta \text{ in EPS}}{\%\Delta \text{ in EBIT}} = \frac{\left(\dfrac{\Delta EPS}{EPS}\right)}{\left(\dfrac{\Delta EBIT}{EBIT}\right)} = \frac{\left[\dfrac{EPS^* - EPS}{EPS}\right]}{\left[\dfrac{EBIT^* - EBIT}{EBIT}\right]}$$

The term with the asterisk (*) indicates the actual outcome, whereas term without
the asterisk is the forecasted result. Thus, EPS*–EPS represents the actual EPS
minus the forecasted EPS.

Table 12–9 shows the results of increasing Unilate's EBIT 20.8 percent. The
increase in EPS is 29.2 percent, which is 1.40 times the change in EBIT; so the DFL
for Unilate equals 1.41.

The degree of financial leverage at a particular level of EBIT can be computed
easily by using the following equation:[6]

---

[6]Equation 12–8 can be derived easily by expanding Equation 12–7, rearranging the terms, and then
simplifying the results. If we use EPS and EBIT to indicate the forecasted 2006 EPS and EBIT,
respectively, and EPS* and EBIT* to indicate the EPS and EBIT that would exist after a change in
sales volume, then

$$DFL = \frac{\left(\dfrac{\Delta EPS}{EPS}\right)}{\left(\dfrac{\Delta EBIT}{EBIT}\right)} = \frac{\left(\dfrac{EPS^* - EPS}{EPS}\right)}{\left(\dfrac{EBIT^* - EBIT}{EBIT}\right)}$$

The computation for 2006 forecasted earnings per share is

$$EPS = \frac{(EBIT - I)(1 - T)}{Shrs_C}$$

where $Shrs_C$ is the number of common shares outstanding. The percent change in EPS can be written and simplified as follows:

$$\Delta EPS = \frac{\left[\dfrac{(EBIT^* - I)(1 - T)}{Shrs_C}\right] - \left[\dfrac{(EBIT - I)(1 - T)}{Shrs_C}\right]}{\left[\dfrac{(EBIT - I)(1 - T)}{Shrs_C}\right]} = \frac{(EBIT^* - I)(1 - T) - (EBIT - I)(1 - T)}{(EBIT - I)(1 - T)}$$

$$= \frac{EBIT^* - EBIT}{(EBIT - I)}$$

TABLE 12–9	Unilate Textiles: Earnings per Share at Sales Levels of 110 Million Units and 121 Million Units ($ millions, except per share data)[a]

	2006 FORECASTED OPERATIONS	SALES INCREASE	DOLLAR CHANGE	PERCENT CHANGE
Sales in units (millions)	110	121		+10.0%
Earnings before interest and taxes (EBIT)	$ 143.0	$ 172.7	$ 29.7	+20.8%
Interest (I)	(41.4)	(41.4)	(0.0)	+ 0.0%
Earnings before taxes (EBT)	$ 101.6	$ 131.3	$ 29.7	+29.2%
Taxes (40%)	(40.6)	(52.5)	(11.9)	+29.2%
Net income	$ 61.0	$ 78.8	$ 17.8	+29.2%
Earning per share (26.3 million shares)	$ 2.32	$ 3.00	$ 0.68	+29.2%

NOTE:

[a]A spreadsheet was used to generate the results in this table. Only the final results are rounded; thus, there will be some rounding differences if you rely on some of the values in the table, which are rounded to one decimal place, to compute the other values.

12–8	$$DFL = \frac{EBIT}{EBIT - I} = \frac{EBIT}{EBIT - [\text{Financial BEP}]}$$

Using Equation 12–8, the DFL for Unilate Textiles at EBIT equal to $143.0 million (sales of 110 million units) is

$$DFL_{110} = \frac{\$143.0}{\$143.0 - \$41.4} = \frac{\$143.0}{\$101.6} = 1.41 \times$$

The interpretation of the DFL value is the same as for the degree of operating leverage, except the starting point for evaluating financial leverage is the earnings before interest and taxes (EBIT) and the ending point is earnings per share (EPS).

Substituting this relationship into the computation of DFL, we have

$$DFL = \frac{\left[\dfrac{(EBIT^* - EBIT)}{EBIT - I} \right]}{\left[\dfrac{(EBIT^* - EBIT)}{EBIT} \right]} = \frac{(EBIT^* - EBIT)}{(EBIT - I)} \times \frac{EBIT}{(EBIT^* - EBIT)}$$

$$= \frac{EBIT}{EBIT - I} = \frac{EBIT}{EBIT - [\text{Financial BEP}]}$$

If a firm has preferred stock, the relationship given in Equation 12–6 can be substituted in the previous equation for the financial breakeven point.

Because the DFL for Unilate is 1.41×, the company can expect a 1.41 percent change in EPS for every 1 percent change in EBIT; a 20.8 percent increase in EBIT results in approximately a 29.2 percent (20.8 percent × 1.41) increase in earnings available to common stockholders, thus the same percent increase in EPS (the number of common shares outstanding does not change). Unfortunately, the opposite also is true—if Unilate's 2006 EBIT is 20.8 percent below expectations, its EPS will be 29.2 percent below the forecast of $2.32, or $1.64. To prove this result is correct, construct the financing section of Unilate's income statement when EBIT equals $113.3 million = (1 − 0.208) × $143.0 million.

The value of the degree of financial leverage found using Equation 12–8 pertains to one specific initial EBIT level. If the level of sales changes, and thus the EBIT changes, so does the value computed for DFL. For example, at sales equal to 80 million units, Unilate's EBIT would be $62 million = [80 million ($15.00 − $12.30)] − $154.0 million, and the DFL value would be

$$DFL_{80} = \frac{\$62.0}{\$62.0 - \$41.4} = \frac{\$62.0}{\$20.6} = 3.01 \times$$

Compared to sales equal to 110 million units, at sales equal to 80 million units Unilate would have greater difficulty covering the fixed financing costs, so its DFL is much greater. At EBIT equal to $62.0 million, Unilate is close to its financial breakeven point—EBIT equal to $41.4 million—and its degree of financial leverage is high. So the more difficulty a firm has covering its fixed financing costs with operating income, the greater its degree of financial leverage. In general then, the higher the DFL for a particular firm, it generally can be concluded the closer the firm is to its financial breakeven point, and the more sensitive its earnings per share is to a change in operating income. *Greater sensitivity implies greater risk; thus it can be stated that firms with higher DFLs generally are considered to have greater financial risk than firms with lower DFLs.*

Self-Test Questions

What does the term "high degree of financial leverage" imply, and what are some implications of having a high degree of financial leverage?

Give the general equation used to calculate the degree of financial leverage. Compare the equation for DFL to the equation for times-interest-earned ratio given in Chapter 11.

Combining Operating and Financial Leverage (DTL)

Our analysis of operating leverage and financial leverage has shown that *(1) the greater the degree of operating leverage, or fixed operating costs for a particular level of operations, the more sensitive EBIT will be to changes in sales volume, and (2) the greater the degree of financial leverage, or fixed financial costs for a particular level of operations, the more sensitive EPS will be to changes in EBIT.* Therefore, if a firm has a considerable amount of both operating and financial leverage, then even small changes in sales will lead to wide fluctuations in EPS. Look at the impact leverage has on Unilate's forecasted 2006 operations. We found that if the sales volume increases by 10 percent, Unilate's EBIT would increase by 20.8 percent; and if EBIT increases by 20.8 percent, its EPS would increase by 29.2 percent. So in combination, a 10 percent increase in sales volume would result in a 29.2 percent increase in EPS. This shows the impact of total leverage, which is the combination of both operating leverage and financial leverage, with respect to Unilate's current operations.

The **degree of total leverage (DTL)** is defined as the percent change in EPS resulting from a 1 percent change in sales volume. This relationship can be written as follows:

DEGREE OF TOTAL LEVERAGE (DTL)
The percent change in EPS that results from a 1 percent change in sales.

$$\begin{array}{l} \text{Degree of} \\ \text{total leverage} \end{array} = \text{DTL} = \frac{\left(\dfrac{\Delta\text{EPS}}{\text{EPS}}\right)}{\left(\dfrac{\Delta\text{Sales}}{\text{Sales}}\right)} = \frac{\left(\dfrac{\Delta\text{EBIT}}{\text{EBIT}}\right)}{\left(\dfrac{\Delta\text{Sales}}{\text{Sales}}\right)} \times \frac{\left(\dfrac{\Delta\text{EPS}}{\text{EPS}}\right)}{\left(\dfrac{\Delta\text{EBIT}}{\text{EBIT}}\right)} = \text{DOL} \times \text{DFL}$$

12–9

Combining the equations for DOL (Equations 12–4 and 12–4a) and for DFL (Equation 12–8), Equation 12–9 can be restated as follows:

12–10

$$\text{DTL} = \frac{\text{Gross profit}}{\text{EBIT}} \times \frac{\text{EBIT}}{\text{EBIT} - [\text{Finanical BEP}]} = \frac{\text{Gross profit}}{\text{EBIT} - [\text{Finanical BEP}]}$$

$$= \frac{\text{S} - \text{VC}}{\text{EBIT} - \text{I}} = \frac{\text{Q}(\text{P} - \text{V})}{[\text{Q}(\text{P} - \text{V}) - \text{F}] - \text{I}}$$

Using Equation 12–10, the degree of total leverage for Unilate would be

$$\text{DTL}_{110} = \frac{110(\$15.00 - \$12.30)}{[110(\$15.00 - \$12.30) - \$154.0] - \$41.4}$$

$$= \frac{\$297.0}{\$143.0 - \$41.4} = \frac{\$297.0}{\$101.6} = 2.92 \times$$

$$= \text{DOL} \times \text{DFL}$$

$$= \frac{\$297.0}{\$297.0 - \$154.0} \times \frac{\$297.0 - \$154.0}{\$297.0 - \$154.0 - \$41.4}$$

$$= 2.077 \times 1.407 = 2.92 \times$$

This value indicates that for every 1 percent change in sales volume, Unilate's EPS will change by 2.92 percent; a 10 percent increase in sales will result in a 29.2 percent increase in EPS. This is exactly the impact expected.

The value of DTL can be used to compute the new earnings per share (EPS*) after a change in sales volume. We already know that Unilate's EPS will change by 2.92 percent for every 1 percent change in sales. So EPS* resulting from a 10 percent increase in sales can be computed as follows:

$$\text{EPS*} = \text{EPS}[1 + (.10)(2.92)] = \$2.32 \times (1 + 0.292) = \$3.00$$

which is the same result given in Table 12–9.

The degree of combined (total) leverage concept is useful primarily for the insights it provides regarding the joint effects of operating and financial leverage on earnings per share. The concept can be used to show management, for example, that a decision to finance new equipment with debt would result in a situation in which a 10 percent decline in sales would result in a nearly 50 percent decline in earnings, whereas with a different operating and financial package, a 10 percent sales decline would cause earnings to decline only by 15 percent. Having the alternatives stated in this manner gives decision makers a better idea of the ramifications of alternative actions with respect to the firm's level of operations and how those operations are financed.

Self-Test Questions

What information is provided by the degree of total (combined) leverage?

What does the term "high degree of total leverage" imply?

Using Leverage and Forecasting for Control

From the discussion in the previous sections, it should be clear what the impact on income would be if the 2006 sales forecast for Unilate Textiles is different than expected. If sales are greater than expected, both operating and financial leverage will magnify the "bottom line" effect on EPS (DTL = 2.92). But the opposite also holds. Consequently, if Unilate does not meet its forecasted sales level, leverage will result in a magnified loss in income compared to what is expected. This will occur because production facilities might have been expanded too greatly, inventories might be built up too quickly, and so on; the end result might be that the firm suffers a significant income loss. This loss will result in a lower than expected addition to retained earnings, which means the plans for additional external funds needed to support the firm's operations will be inadequate. Likewise, if the sales forecast is too low, then, if the firm is at full capacity, it will not be able to meet the additional demand, and sales opportunities will be lost—perhaps forever. In the previous sections, we showed only how changes in operations (2006 forecasts) affect the income generated by the firm; we did not continue the process to show the impact on the balance sheet and the financing needs of the firm. To determine the impact on the financial statements, the financial manager needs to repeat the steps discussed in the first part of this chapter. At this stage the financial manager needs to evaluate and act on the feedback received from the forecasting and budgeting processes. In effect, then, the forecasting (planning) and control of the firm is an ongoing activity, a vital function to the long-run survival of any firm.

The forecasting and control functions described in this chapter are important for several reasons. First, if the projected operating results are unsatisfactory, management can "go back to the drawing board," reformulate its plans, and develop more reasonable targets for the coming year. Second, it is possible that the funds required to meet the sales forecast simply cannot be obtained; if so, it obviously is better to know this in advance and to scale back the projected level of operations than to suddenly run out of cash and have operations grind to a halt. Third, even if the required funds can be raised, it is desirable to plan for their acquisition well in

✳ ETHICAL DILEMMA

Competition-Based Planning—Promotion or Payoff?

A few months ago, Kim Darby, financial manager of Republic Communications Corporation (RCC), contacted you about a job opening in the financial planning division of the company. RCC is a well-established firm that has offered long-distance phone service in the United States for more than three decades. But recent deregulation in the telecommunications industry has RCC concerned, because competition has increased significantly—today many more firms offer long-distance services than five years ago. In fact, RCC has seen its profits decline along with market share since deregulation began. Kim Darby indicated that RCC wants to reverse this trend by improving the company's planning function so that long-distance rates can be set to better attract and keep customers in the future. Kim says that is the reason she contacted you.

When she first called, Kim told you RCC would like to hire you because you are one of the "up-and-comers" in the telecommunications industry. You have worked at National Telecommunications, Inc. (NTI), one of RCC's fiercest competitors, since you graduated from college four years ago, helping to develop their rate-setting program, which many consider the best in the industry.

Taking the position at RCC would be comparable to a promotion with a $30,000 salary increase and provide greater chances for advancement than your current position at NTI. So, after interviewing with RCC and talking to friends and family, a couple of days ago you informally accepted the job at RCC. You have not yet notified NTI of your decision.

Earlier today, Kim called to see if you could start your new position in a couple of weeks. RCC would like you to start work as soon as possible because it wants to begin a redesign of its rate-setting plan in an effort to regain market share. During the conversation, Kim mentioned that it would be helpful if you could bring the rate-setting program and some rate-setting information with you to your new job—it will help RCC rewrite its rate-setting program. In an attempt to allay any reservations you might have, Kim told you that NTI sells its software to other companies and any rate setting information is available to the public through states' public service commissions, so everything you bring really is well known in the industry and should be considered in the public domain. And, according to Kim, RCC is not going to copy the rate-setting program; her attitude is "what is wrong with taking a look at it as long as we don't copy the program?" If you provide RCC with NTI's rate-setting program, you know it will help the company to plan better, and better planning will lead to increased market share and higher stock prices. An improved rate-setting plan might net RCC as much as $200 million each year, and RCC has a very generous bonus system to reward employees who help the company improve its market position. If you do not provide the software, you might start your new job "off on the wrong foot." What should you do?

advance. Finally, any deviation from the projections needs to be dealt with to improve future forecasts and the predictability of the firm's operations to ensure the goals of the firm are being pursued appropriately.

Self-Test Question

Why is it important that the forecasting and control of the firm be an ongoing activity?

Summary

The first part of this chapter described in broad outline how firms project their financial statements and determine their capital requirements. The second part of the chapter included a discussion of how we can evaluate the effects of changes in forecasts on the income of the firm. The key concepts covered in the chapter are listed here:

- **Financial planning** involves making projections of sales, income, and assets based on alternative production and marketing strategies and then deciding how to meet the forecasted financial requirements.
- **Financial control** deals with the feedback and adjustment process that is required (1) to ensure that plans are followed or (2) to modify existing plans in response to changes in the operating environment.
- Management establishes a **target balance sheet** on the basis of ratio analysis.
- The **projected, or pro forma, balance sheet method** is used to forecast financial requirements.
- A firm can determine the amount of **additional funds needed (AFN)** by estimating the amount of new assets necessary to support the forecasted level of sales and then subtracting from that amount the spontaneous funds that will be generated from operations. The firm can then plan to raise the AFN through bank borrowing, by issuing securities, or both.
- **Operating breakeven analysis** is a method of determining the point at which sales will just cover operating costs, and it shows the magnitude of the firm's operating profits or losses if sales exceed or fall below that point.
- The **operating breakeven point** is the sales volume at which total operating costs equal total revenues and operating income (EBIT) equals zero. The equation used to compute the operating breakeven point is

$$Q_{OpBE} = \frac{F}{P - V} = \frac{F}{\text{Contribution margin}}$$

- **Operating leverage** is a measure of the extent to which fixed operating costs are used in a firm's operations. A firm with a high percentage of fixed costs is said to have a **high** degree of operating leverage.
- The **degree of operating leverage (DOL)** shows how a change in sales will affect operating income. Whereas *breakeven analysis* emphasizes the volume of sales the firm needs to be profitable, the *degree of operating leverage* measures how sensitive the firm's profits are to changes in the volume of sales. The equation used to calculate the DOL is

$$DOL_Q = \frac{Q(P - V)}{Q(P - V) - F} = \frac{\text{Gross profit}}{\text{EBIT}}$$

- **Financial breakeven analysis** is a method of determining the point at which EBIT will just cover financing costs, and it shows the magnitude of the firm's earnings per share (EPS) if EBIT exceeds or falls below that point.
- The **financial breakeven point** is the level of EBIT that produces EPS = 0. The equation used to compute the financial breakeven point is

$$EBIT_{FinBE} = I + \frac{D_{ps}}{(1 - T)}$$

- **Financial leverage** is a measure of the extent to which fixed financial costs exist in a firm's operations. A firm with a high percentage of fixed financial costs is said to have a **high** degree of financial leverage.
- The **degree of financial leverage (DFL)** shows how a change in EBIT will affect EPS. The equation used to calculate the DFL for a firm that has no preferred stock is

$$DFL = \frac{EBIT}{EBIT - I} = \frac{EBIT}{EBIT - [\text{Financial BEP}]}$$

- **Total (combined) leverage** is a measure of the extent to which total fixed costs (operating and financial) exist in a firm's operations. A firm with a high percentage of total fixed costs is said to have a **high** degree of total leverage.
- The **degree of total leverage (DTL)** shows how a change in sales will affect EPS. The equation used to calculate the DTL is

$$DTL = \frac{S - VC}{EBIT - I} = \frac{Q(P - V)}{Q(P - V) - F - I}$$

The forecasting and control functions require continuous attention to ensure that the goals of the firm are being met. Forecasting and control provide the foresight needed to implement adjustments to future operations so the firm moves in the intended direction and wealth maximization is achieved.

Questions

12–1 Certain liability and net worth items generally increase spontaneously with increases in sales. Put a checkmark (✓) by those items that typically increase spontaneously:

Accounts payable	_____
Notes payable to banks	_____
Accrued wages	_____
Accrued taxes	_____
Mortgage bonds	_____
Common stock	_____
Retained earnings	_____

12–2 Suppose a firm makes the following policy changes. If the change means that external, nonspontaneous financial requirements (AFN) will increase, indicate this by a (+); indicate a decrease by a (–); and indicate indeterminate or no effect by a (0). Think in terms of the immediate, short-run effect on funds requirements.

a. The dividend payout ratio is increased.   _____

b. The firm contracts to buy, rather than make, certain components used in its products.   _____

c. The firm decides to pay all suppliers on delivery, rather than after a 30-day delay, to take advantage of discounts for rapid payment.   _____

d. The firm begins to sell on credit (previously all sales had been on a cash basis).   _____

    e. The firm's profit margin is eroded by increased
competition; sales are steady.

    f. Advertising expenditures are increased.   _____

    g. A decision is made to substitute long-term mortgage
bonds for short-term bank loans.   _____

    h. The firm begins to pay employees on a weekly basis
(previously it had paid at the end of each month).   _____

12–3 What benefits can be derived from breakeven analysis, both operating and financial? What are some problems with breakeven analysis?

12–4 Explain how profits or losses will be magnified for a firm with high operating leverage as opposed to a firm with lower operating leverage.

12–5 Explain how profits or losses will be magnified for a firm with high financial leverage as opposed to a firm with lower financial leverage.

12–6 What data are necessary to construct an operating breakeven chart?

12–7 What data are necessary to construct a financial breakeven chart?

12–8 What would be the effect of each of the following on a firm's operating and financial breakeven point? Indicate the effect in the space provided by placing a (+) for an increase, a (–) for a decrease, and a (0) for no effect. When answering this question, assume everything except the change indicated is held constant.

	OPERATING BREAKEVEN	FINANCIAL BREAKEVEN
a. An increase in the sales price	_____	_____
b. A reduction in the variable cost ratio	_____	_____
c. A decrease in fixed operating costs	_____	_____
d. Issuing new bonds	_____	_____
e. Issuing new preferred stock	_____	_____
f. Issuing new common stock	_____	_____

12–9 Assume that a firm is developing its long-run financial plan. What period should this plan cover—one month, six months, one year, three years, five years, or some other period? Justify your answer.

Self-Test Problems

(Solutions appear in Appendix B)

key terms   **ST-1** Define each of the following terms:

    a. Sales forecast

    b. Projected balance sheet method

    c. Spontaneously generated funds

    d. Dividend payout ratio

    e. Pro forma financial statement

    f. Additional funds needed (AFN)

    g. Financing feedback

    h. Financial planning; financial control

    i. Operating breakeven analysis; operating breakeven point, Q_{OpBE}

    j. Financial breakeven analysis; financial breakeven point ($EBIT_{FinBE}$)

    k. Operating leverage; degree of operating leverage (DOL)

    l. Financial leverage; degree of financial leverage (DFL)

    m. Combined (total) leverage; degree of total leverage (DTL)

operating leverage and
breakeven analysis

ST-2 Olinde Electronics Inc. produces stereo components that sell for P = $100. Olinde's fixed costs are $200,000; 5,000 components are produced and sold each year; EBIT is currently $50,000; and Olinde's assets (all equity financed) are $500,000. Olinde estimates that it can change its production process, adding $400,000 to investment and $50,000 to fixed operating costs. This change will (1) reduce variable costs per unit by $10 and (2) increase output by 2,000 units, but (3) the sales price on all units will have to be lowered to $95 to sell the 7,000 components. Olinde has tax loss carryovers, so its current tax rate equals zero. Olinde uses no debt, and its average cost of capital is 10 percent.

    a. Should Olinde make the change?

    b. Would Olinde's degree of operating leverage increase or decrease if it made the change? What about its operating breakeven point?

    c. Suppose Olinde was unable to raise additional equity financing and had to borrow the $400,000 to make the investment at an interest rate of 8 percent. Use the DuPont equation (see Chapter 11) to find the expected return on total assets (ROA) of the investment. Should Olinde make the change if debt financing must be used?

    d. What would Olinde's degree of financial leverage be if the $400,000 was borrowed at the 8 percent interest rate?

Problems

pro forma and ratios

12–1 Magee Computers makes bulk purchases of small computers, stocks them in conveniently located warehouses, and ships them to its chain of retail stores. Magee's balance sheet as of December 31, 2005, is shown here ($ millions):

Cash	$ 3.5	Accounts payable	$ 9.0
Receivables	26.0	Notes payable	18.0
Inventories	58.0	Accruals	8.5
Current assets	$ 87.5	Current liabilities	$ 35.5
Net fixed assets	35.0	Long-term bonds	6.0
		Common stock	15.0
		Retained earnings	66.0
Total assets	$122.5	Total liabilities and equity	$122.5

Sales for 2005 were $350 million, while net income for the year was $10.5 million. Magee paid dividends of $4.2 million to common stockholders. Sales are projected to increase by $70 million, or 20 percent, during 2006. The firm is operating at full capacity. Assume that the profit margin and dividend payout ratios remain constant.

    a. Construct Magee's pro forma balance sheet for December 31, 2006. Assume that all external capital requirements are met by bank loans and are reflected in notes payable. Do not consider any financing feedback effects.

    b. Now calculate the following ratios, based on your projected December 31, 2006, balance sheet. Magee's 2005 ratios and industry average ratios are shown here for comparison:

| | **Magee Computers** | | **Industry Average** |
	12/31/06	12/31/05	12/31/05
Current ratio	_____	2.5	3.0
Debt/total assets	_____	33.9%	30.0%
Return on equity	_____	13.0%	12.0%

c. (1) Now assume that Magee grows by the same $70 million but that the growth is spread over five years—that is, that sales grow by $14 million each year. Do not consider any financing feedback effects.

(2) Construct a pro forma balance sheet as of December 31, 2006, using notes payable as the balancing item.

(3) Calculate the current ratio, debt/assets ratio, and rate of return on equity as of December 31, 2010. [*Hint:* Be sure to use total sales, which amount to $1,960 million, to calculate retained earnings but 2010 profits to calculate the rate of return on equity—that is, return on equity = (2010 profits)/(12/31/10 equity).]

d. Do the plans outlined in parts a or c seem feasible to you? That is, do you think Magee could borrow the required capital, and would the company be raising the chance of its bankruptcy to an excessive level in the event of some temporary misfortune?

additional funds needed   **12–2** Noso Textile's 2005 financial statements are shown here:

NOSO TEXTILE:
BALANCE SHEET AS OF DECEMBER 31, 2005
($ THOUSANDS)

Cash	$ 1,080	Accounts payable	$ 4,320
Receivables	6,480	Accruals	2,880
Inventories	9,000	Notes payable	2,100
Current assets	$16,560	Current liabilities	$ 9,300
Net fixed assets	12,600	Long-term bonds	3,500
		Common stock	3,500
		Retained earnings	12,860
Total assets	$29,160	Total liabilities and equity	$29,160

NOSO TEXTILE:
INCOME STATEMENT FOR DECEMBER 31, 2005
($ THOUSANDS)

Sales	$36,000
Operating costs	(32,440)
Earnings before interest and taxes	$ 3,560
Interest	(560)
Earnings before taxes	$ 3,000
Taxes (40%)	(1,200)
Net Income	$ 1,800
Dividends (45%)	$ 810
Addition to retained earnings	$ 990

a. Suppose 2006 sales are projected to increase by 15 percent over 2005 sales. Determine the additional funds needed. Assume that the company was operating at *full capacity* in 2005, that it cannot sell off any of its fixed assets, and that any required financing will be borrowed as notes payable. Also, assume that assets, spontaneous liabilities, and operating costs are expected to increase by the same percentage as sales. Use the projected balance sheet method to develop a pro forma balance sheet and income statement for December 31, 2006. (Do not incorporate any financing feedback effects. Use the pro forma income statement to determine the addition to retained earnings.)

b. Use the financial statements developed in part a to incorporate the financing feedback as a result of the addition to notes payable. (That is, do the next financial statement iteration.) For the purpose of this part, assume that the notes payable interest rate is 10 percent. What is the AFN for this iteration?

degree of leverage   **12–3** Van Auken Lumber's 2005 income statement is shown here:

VAN AUKEN LUMBER:
INCOME STATEMENT FOR DECEMBER 31, 2005
($ THOUSANDS)

Sales	$36,000
Cost of goods sold	(25,200)
Gross profit	$10,800
Fixed operating costs	(6,480)
Earnings before interest and taxes	$ 4,320
Interest	(2,880)
Earnings before taxes	$ 1,440
Taxes (40%)	(576)
Net Income	$ 864
Dividends (50%)	$ 432

a. Compute the degree of operating leverage (DOL), degree of financial leverage (DFL), and degree of total leverage (DTL) for Van Auken Lumber.

b. Interpret the meaning of each of the numerical values you computed in part a.

c. Briefly discuss some ways Van Auken can reduce its degree of total leverage.

external financing   **12–4** The 2005 balance sheet and income statement for the Woods Company are
requirements   shown here:

WOODS COMPANY:
BALANCE SHEET AS OF DECEMBER 31, 2005
(THOUSANDS OF DOLLARS)

Cash	$ 80	Accounts payable	$ 160
Accounts receivable	240	Accruals	40
Inventories	720	Notes payable	252
Current assets	$1,040	Current liabilities	$ 452
Fixed assets	3,200	Long-term debt	1,244
		Common stock	1,605
		Retained earnings	939
Total assets	$4,240	Total liabilities and equity	$4,240

Woods Company:
Income Statement for the Year Ending December 31, 2005
($ thousands)

Sales	$8,000
Operating costs	(7,450)
Earnings before interest and taxes	$ 550
Interest	(150)
Earnings before taxes	$ 400
Taxes (40%)	(160)
Net income	$ 240

Per Share Data

Common stock price	$16.96
Earnings per share (EPS)	$ 1.60
Dividends per share (DPS)	$ 1.04

a. The firm operated at full capacity in 2005. It expects sales to increase by 20 percent during 2006 and expects 2006 dividends per share to increase to $1.10. Use the projected balance sheet method to determine how much outside financing is required, developing the firm's pro forma balance sheet and income statement, and use AFN as the balancing item.

b. If the firm must maintain a current ratio of 2.3 and a debt ratio of 40 percent, how much financing, after the first pass, will be obtained using notes payable, long-term debt, and common stock?

c. Make the second pass financial statements incorporating financing feedbacks, using the ratios in part b. Assume that the interest rate on debt averages 10 percent.

operating breakeven
analysis
12–5 The Weaver Watch Company manufactures a line of ladies' watches that is sold through discount houses. Each watch is sold for $25; the fixed costs are $140,000 for 30,000 watches or less; variable costs are $15 per watch.

a. What is the firm's gain or loss at sales of 8,000 watches? Of 18,000 watches?

b. What is the operating breakeven point? Illustrate by means of a chart.

c. What is Weaver's degree of operating leverage at sales of 8,000 units? Of 18,000 units? (*Hint:* Use Equation 12–4 to solve this problem.)

d. What happens to the operating breakeven point if the selling price rises to $31? What is the significance of the change to the financial manager?

e. What happens to the operating breakeven point if the selling price rises to $31 but variable costs rise to $23 a unit?

operating breakeven
analysis
12–6 The following relationships exist for Dellva Industries, a manufacturer of electronic components. Each unit of output is sold for $45; the fixed costs are $175,000, of which $110,000 are annual depreciation charges; and variable costs are $20 per unit.

a. What is the firm's gain or loss at sales of 5,000 units? Of 12,000 units?

b. What is the operating breakeven point?

c. Assume Dellva is operating at a level of 4,000 units. Are creditors likely to seek the liquidation of the company if it is slow in paying its bills?

financial leverage
12–7 Gordon's Plants has the following partial income statement for 2005:

Earnings before interest and taxes	$4,500
Interest	(2,000)
Earnings before taxes	$2,500
Taxes (40%)	(1,000)
Net income	$1,500
Number of common shares	1,000

a. If Gordon's has no preferred stock, what is its financial breakeven point? Show that the amount you come up with actually is the financial breakeven by recreating the portion of the income statement shown here for that amount.

b. What is the degree of financial leverage for Gordon's? What does this value mean?

c. If Gordon's actually has preferred stock that requires payment of dividends equal to $600, what would be the financial breakeven point? Show that the amount you compute is the financial breakeven by recreating the portion of the income statement shown here for that amount. What is the degree of financial leverage in this case?

Exam-Type Problems

The problems in this section are set up in such a way that they could be used as multiple-choice exam problems.

operating leverage

12-8 The Niendorf Corporation produces tea kettles, which it sells for $15 each. Fixed costs are $700,000 for up to 400,000 units of output. Variable costs are $10 per kettle.

a. What is the firm's gain or loss at sales of 125,000 units? Of 175,000 units?

b. What is the operating breakeven point? Illustrate by means of a chart.

c. What is Niendorf's degree of operating leverage at sales of 125,000 units? Of 150,000 units? Of 175,000 units?

degree of operating leverage

12-9 a. Given the following graphs on page 538, calculate the total fixed costs, variable costs per unit, and sales price for Firm A. Firm B's fixed costs are $120,000, its variable costs per unit are $4, and its sales price is $8 per unit.

b. Which firm has the higher degree of operating leverage? Explain.

c. At what sales level, in units, do both firms earn the same profit?

long-term financing needs

12-10 At year-end 2005, total assets for Shome Inc. were $1.2 million and accounts payable were $375,000. Sales, which in 2005 were $2.5 million, are expected to increase by 25 percent in 2006. Total assets and accounts payable are proportional to sales, and that relationship will be maintained. Shome typically uses no current liabilities other than accounts payable. Common stock amounted to $425,000 in 2005, and retained earnings were $295,000. Shome plans to sell new common stock in the amount of $75,000. The firm's profit margin on sales is 6 percent; and 40 percent of earnings will be paid out as dividends.

a. What was Shome's total debt in 2005?

b. How much new, long-term debt financing will be needed in 2006? (*Hint:* AFN – New stock = New long-term debt.) Do not consider any financing feedback effects.

Breakeven Charts for Problem 12–9

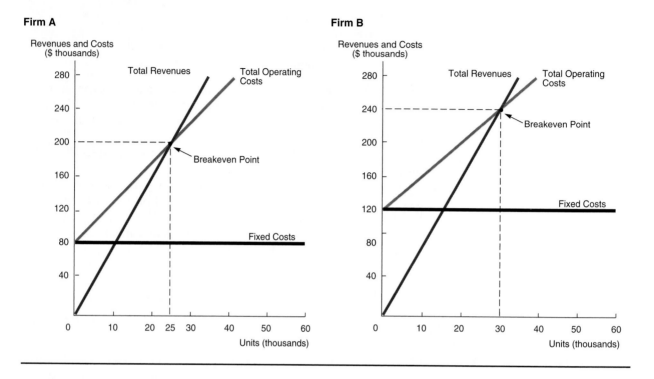

Firm A

Firm B

additional funds needed

12–11 The McGill Company's sales are forecasted to increase from $1,000 in 2005 to $2,000 in 2006. Here is the December 31, 2005, balance sheet:

Cash	$ 100	Accounts payable	$ 50
Accounts receivable	200	Notes payable	150
Inventories	200	Accruals	50
Current assets	$ 500	Current liabilities	$ 250
Net fixed assets	500	Long-term debt	400
		Common stock	100
		Retained earnings	250
Total assets	$1,000	Total liabilities and equity	$1,000

McGill's fixed *assets were used to only 50 percent of capacity* during 2005, but its current assets were at their proper levels. All assets except fixed assets increase at the same rate as sales, and fixed assets would also increase at the same rate if the current excess capacity did not exist. McGill's after-tax profit margin is forecasted to be 5 percent, and its payout ratio will be 60 percent. What is McGill's additional funds needed (AFN) for the coming year? Ignore financing feedback effects.

breakeven analysis and leverage

12–12 Straight Arrow Company manufactures golf balls. The following income statement information is relevant for Straight Arrow in 2006:

Selling price per sleeve of balls (P)	$ 5.00
Variable cost of goods sold (% of price, P)	75%
Fixed operating costs	$50,000

Interest expense	$10,000
Preferred dividends	$ 0.00
Marginal tax rate	40%
Number of common shares	20,000

a. What level of sales does Straight Arrow need to achieve in 2006 to breakeven with respect to *operating income?*

b. At its operating breakeven, what will be the EPS for Straight Arrow?

c. How many sleeves of golf balls (units) does Straight Arrow need to sell in 2006 to attain the financial breakeven point? (*Hint:* An easy way to look at this problem is to consider how many sleeves of balls [units] *beyond those needed for operating breakeven* Straight Arrow needs to sell to cover its fixed financial charges. Note that Straight Arrow has no preferred stock.)

d. If Straight Arrow expects its sales to be $300,000 in 2006, what is its degree of operating leverage, its degree of financial leverage, and its degree of total (combined) leverage? Based on the degree of total leverage, compute the earnings per share you would expect in 2006 if sales actually turn out to be $270,000.

Integrative Problem

forecasting, breakeven, and leverage

12–13 Sue Wilson is the new financial manager of Northwest Chemicals (NWC), an Oregon producer of specialized chemicals sold to farmers for use in fruit orchards. She is responsible for constructing financial forecasts and for evaluating the financial feasibility of new products.

Part I. Financial Forecasting

Sue must prepare a financial forecast for 2006 for Northwest. NWC's 2005 sales were $2 billion, and the marketing department is forecasting a 25 percent increase for 2006. Sue thinks the company was operating at full capacity in 2005, but she is not sure about this. The 2005 financial statements, plus some other data, are given in Table IP12–1.

Assume that you were recently hired as Sue's assistant, and your first major task is to help her develop the forecast. She asked you to begin by answering the following set of questions:

a. *Assume that NWC was operating at full capacity in 2005* with respect to all assets. Estimate the 2006 financing requirements using the projected financial statement approach, making an initial forecast plus one additional "pass" to determine the effects of "financing feedbacks." Assume that (1) each type of asset, as well as payables, accruals, and fixed and variable costs, grow at the same rate as sales; (2) the dividend payout ratio is held constant at 30 percent; (3) external funds needed are financed 50 percent by notes payable and 50 percent by long-term debt (no new common stock will be issued); and (4) all debt carries an interest rate of 8 percent.

b. Calculate NWC's forecasted ratios, and compare them with the company's 2005 ratios and with the industry averages. How does NWC compare with the average firm in its industry, and is the company expected to improve during the coming year?

c. Suppose you now learn that NWC's 2005 receivables and inventories were in line with required levels, given the firm's credit and inventory

TABLE IP12–1	Financial Statements and Other Data on NWC ($ millions)

A. 2005 Balance Sheet

Cash and securities	$ 20	Accounts payable and accruals	$ 100
Accounts receivable	240	Notes payable	100
Inventories	240	Total current liabilities	$ 200
Total current assets	$ 500	Long-term debt	100
Net fixed assets	500	Common stock	500
		Retained earnings	200
Total assets	$1,000	Total liabilities and equity	$1,000

B. 2005 Income Statement

Sales	$ 2,000.00
Less: Variable costs	(1,200.00)
Fixed costs	(700.00)
Earnings before interest and taxes	$ 100.00
Interest	(16.00)
Earnings before taxes	$ 84.00
Taxes (40%)	(33.60)
Net income	$ 50.40
Dividends (30%)	(15.12)
Addition to retained earnings	$ 35.28

C. Key Ratios

	NWC	INDUSTRY	COMMENT
Profit margin	2.52	4.00	
Return on equity	7.20	15.60	
Days sales outstanding (360 days)	43.20 days	34.00 days	
Inventory turnover	5.00×	8.00×	
Fixed assets turnover	4.00×	5.00×	
Total assets turnover	2.00×	2.50×	
Total debt ratio	30.00%	36.00%	
Times interest earned	6.25×	9.40×	
Current ratio	2.50×	3.00×	
Payout ratio	30.00%	30.00%	

policies, but that excess capacity existed with regard to fixed assets. Specifically, fixed assets were operated at only 75 percent of capacity.

   (1) What level of sales could have existed in 2005 with the available fixed assets? What would the fixed assets/sales ratio have been if NWC had been operating at full capacity?

   (2) How would the existence of excess capacity in fixed assets affect the additional funds needed during 2006?

   d. Without actually working out the numbers, how would you expect the ratios to change in the situation where excess capacity in fixed assets exists? Explain your reasoning.

   e. Based on comparisons between NWC's days sales outstanding (DSO) and inventory turnover ratios with the industry average figures, does it appear that NWC is operating efficiently with respect to its inventories and accounts receivable? If the company was able to bring these ratios into line with the industry averages, what effect would this have on its AFN and its financial ratios?

   f. How would changes in these items affect the AFN? (1) The dividend payout ratio, (2) the profit margin, (3) the plant capacity, and (4) NWC begins buying from its suppliers on terms that permit it to pay after 60 days rather than after 30 days. (Consider each item separately and hold all other things constant.)

Part II. Breakeven Analysis and Leverage

One of NWC's employees recently submitted a proposal that NWC should expand its operations and sell its chemicals in retail establishments such as Home Depot and Lowe's. To determine the feasibility of the idea, Sue needs to perform a breakeven analysis. The fixed costs associated with producing and selling the chemicals to retail stores would be $60 million, the selling price per unit is expected to be $10, and the variable cost ratio would be the same as it is currently.

   a. What is the operating breakeven point both in dollars and in number of units for the employee's proposal?

   b. Draw the operating breakeven chart for the proposal. Should the employee's proposal be adopted if NWC can produce and sell 20 million units of the chemical?

   c. If NWC can produce and sell 20 million units of its product to retail stores, what would be its degree of operating leverage? What would be NWC's percent increase in operating profits if sales actually were 10 percent higher than expected?

   d. Assume NWC has excess capacity, so it does not need to raise any additional external funds to implement the proposal—that is, its 2006 interest payments remain the same as 2005. What would be its degree of financial leverage and its degree of total leverage? If the actual sales turned out to be 10 percent greater than expected, as a percent, how much greater would the earnings per share be?

   e. Explain how breakeven analysis and leverage analysis can be used for planning the implementation of this proposal.

Computer-Related Problem

Work the problem in this section only if you are using the computer problem diskette.

forecasting **12–14** Use the model in File C12 to solve this problem. Stendardi Industries' 2005 financial statements are shown in the following table:

STENDARDI INDUSTRIES:
BALANCE SHEET AS OF DECEMBER 31, 2005
($ MILLIONS)

Cash	$ 4.0	Accounts payable	$ 8.0
Receivables	12.0	Notes payable	5.0
Inventories	16.0	Current liabilities	$13.0
Current assets	$32.0	Long-term debt	12.0
Net fixed assets	40.0	Common stock	20.0
		Retained earnings	27.0
Total assets	$72.0	Total liabilities and equity	$72.0

STENDARDI INDUSTRIES:
INCOME STATEMENT FOR DECEMBER 31, 2005
($ MILLIONS)

Sales	$80.0
Operating costs	(71.3)
Earnings before interest and taxes	$ 8.7
Interest	(2.0)
Earnings before taxes	$ 6.7
Taxes (40%)	(2.7)
Net income	$ 4.0
Dividends (40%)	$1.60
Addition to retained earnings	$2.40

Assume that the firm *has no excess capacity in fixed assets*, that the average interest rate for debt is 12 percent, and that the projected annual sales growth rate for the next five years is 15 percent.

a. Stendardi plans to finance its additional funds needed with 50 percent short-term debt and 50 percent long-term debt. Using the projected balance sheet method, prepare the pro forma financial statements for 2006 through 2010, and then determine (1) additional funds needed, (2) the current ratio, (3) the debt ratio, and (4) the return on equity.

b. Sales growth could be 5 percentage points above or below the projected 15 percent. Determine the effect of such variances on AFN and the key ratios.

c. Perform an analysis to determine the sensitivity of AFN and the key ratios for 2010 to changes in the dividend payout ratio as specified in the following, assuming sales grow at a constant 15 percent. What happens to AFN if the dividend payout ratio (1) is raised from 40 to 70 percent or (2) is lowered from 40 to 20 percent?

GET REAL with Thomson ONE

12–15 Gillette Company [G], a company that manufactures and sells consumer products, uses only debt and common stock to finance the firm. The firm's EBIT and interest expense have fluctuated during the past five years. Answer the following questions about Gillette:

  a. What is the degree of financial leverage (DFL) for Gillette in each of the past five years? [Click on Financials/Financial Statements]

  b. How has the change in EBIT from year to year affected Gillette's earnings per share in each of the past five years?

  c. Choose two of Gillette's industry peers that do not have preferred stock in their capital structures and compare these companies to Gillette with regard to their degree of financial leverage? Explain what your comparison means. [*Hint:* Click on Peers/Financials]

APPENDIX 12A

Projected Financial Statements, Including Financing Feedbacks

In the chapter, we discussed the procedure used to construct pro forma financial statements. The first step is to estimate the level of operations and then project the impact such operations will have on the financial statements of the firm. We found that when a firm needs additional external financing, its existing interest and dividend payments will change; thus, the values initially projected for the financial statements will be affected. Therefore, to recognize these *financing feedbacks*, the construction of projected financial statements needs to be an iterative process. In this appendix, we give an indication of the iterative process for constructing the pro forma statements for Unilate. Table 12A–1 contains the initial projected statements shown in Table 12–1 and Table 12–2 of the chapter, and some of the subsequent "passes" used to adjust the forecasted statements are given. According to the discussion given in the chapter, the forecasted statements first are constructed assuming only changes in retained earnings and spontaneous financing are available to support the forecasted operations. This "first pass" is necessary to provide an indication of the additional external funds that are needed. Unilate needs $42.7 million. But if Unilate raises this additional amount by borrowing from the bank and by issuing new bonds and new common stock, then its interest and dividend payments will increase. This can be seen by examining the income statement, which was constructed in the second pass to show the effects of raising the $42.7 million additional funds needed. Because Unilate would have additional debt, it would have to pay $1.30 million more interest; and because it has more shares of common stock outstanding, it would have to pay $1.40 million more dividends. Consequently, as the second pass balance sheet shows, if Unilate raises only the $42.7 million AFN (additional funds needed) initially computed, it would find there still would be a need for funds—the AFN would be $2.18 million—because the addition to retained earnings would be lower than expected originally. As it turns out, Unilate actually would need to raise $45.0 million to support the forecasted 2006 operations—$6.75 million from notes, $9.0 million from bonds, and $29.25 million from stock.

TABLE 12A–1	Unilate Textiles: 2006 Forecast of Financial Statements ($ millions)

INCOME STATEMENT

	INITIAL PASS	FEEDBACK	SECOND PASS		FINAL PASS
Earnings before interest and taxes (EBIT)	$143.00		$143.00		$143.00
Less interest	(40.00)	+ 1.30	(41.30)	+0.07	(41.37)
Earnings before taxes (EBT)	$103.00		$101.70		$101.63
Taxes (40%)	(41.20)	– 0.52	(40.68)	–0.03	(40.65)
Net Income	$ 61.80		$ 61.02		$ 60.98
Common dividends	(29.00)	+ 1.40	(30.40)	+0.08	(30.48)
Addition to retained earnings	$ 32.80	– 2.18	$ 30.62	–0.12	$ 30.50
Earnings per share	$ 2.47		$ 2.33		$ 2.32
Dividends per share	$ 1.16		$ 1.16		$ 1.16
Number of common shares (millions)	25.00		26.21		26.27

BALANCE SHEET

	INITIAL PASS	FEEDBACK	SECOND PASS		FINAL PASS
Cash	$ 16.50		$ 16.50		$ 16.50
Accounts receivable	198.00		198.00		198.00
Inventories	297.00		297.00		297.00
Total current assets	$511.50		$511.50		$511.50
Net plant and equipment	418.00		418.00		418.00
Total Assets	$929.50		$929.50		$929.50
Accounts payable	$ 33.00		$ 33.00		$ 33.00
Accruals	66.00		66.00		66.00
Notes payable	40.00	+ 6.41	46.41	+0.34	46.75
Total current liabilities	$139.00		$145.41		$145.75
Long-term bonds	300.00	+ 8.54	308.54	+0.46	309.00
Total liabilities	$439.00		$453.95		$454.75
Common stock	130.00	+27.76	157.76	+1.49	159.25
Retained earnings	317.80	– 2.18	315.62	–0.12	315.50
Total owners' equity	$447.80		$473.37		$474.75
Total Liabilities and Equity	$886.80	+40.52	$927.32	+2.18	$929.50
Additional Funds Needed (AFN)	$ 42.70		$ 2.18		$ 0.00

NOTE: The results in this table are carried to two decimal places to show some of the more subtle changes that occur. Even so, you will find some rounding differences when summing the feedback amounts.

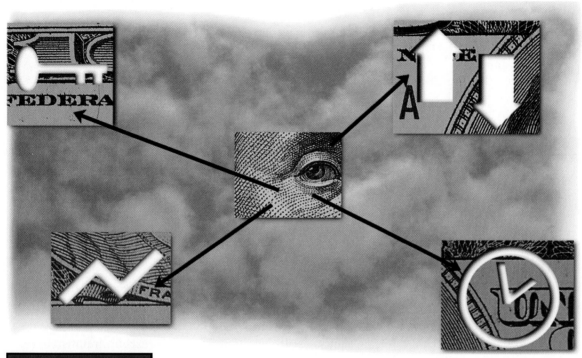

CHAPTER 13

Working Capital Policy

In December 1993, Trans World Airlines (TWA) was labeled the best domestic airline for long flights and the second best for short flights by American business travelers. TWA received this accolade just one month after emerging from bankruptcy court. The future seemed rosy: Employees had agreed to salary concessions in exchange for an equity position in the company, the airline had restructured its liabilities and lowered its cost structure, and the employees, with their new ownership position, appeared to possess a newfound motivation and concern for company success.

Unfortunately, the nation's seventh largest airlines discovered that its "new lease on life" was not a long-term contract. By the summer of 1994, TWA was struggling to find ways to cover a $135 million shortfall expected for the year. Many analysts believed the company was headed toward a second, and perhaps final, bankruptcy, primarily because it was in an extremely precarious position with respect to liquidity. The company's cash reserves were not sufficient to carry TWA through the lean sales that were expected during the coming months, and analysts were pessimistic that needed funds could be raised with a stock or bond issue or by selling off assets. Investors also recognized TWA's liquidity problems—the company's stock fell approximately 50 percent in less than four months. It was obvious that TWA needed to improve its liquidity position to ensure future survival. The

answer for TWA was to reduce costs by laying off employees, by eliminating some of its flights, and by replacing outdated airplanes with more fuel-efficient ones.

TWA emerged from its second bankruptcy and regained its status as the best domestic airline for long flights but its financial position was still very tenuous. Unforeseen circumstances, including a tragic crash and labor difficulties, resulted in large losses in the late 1990s. For instance, in 1996 TWA lost $285 million, and in 1997 and 1998 the losses were $110 million and $120 million, respectively. Nevertheless, TWA took actions to improve its liquidity position. In 1998 revenues began to increase at the same time that its operating expenses decreased, which helped boost its cash and other liquid assets by nearly 33 percent. Unfortunately, the benefits of these actions were short-lived. TWA filed for bankruptcy protection at the beginning of 2001. In April 2001, the company was acquired by American Airlines.

Firms strive to maintain a balance between current assets and current liabilities and between sales and each category of current assets in an effort to provide sufficient liquidity to survive—that is, to live to maximize value in the future. As long as a good balance is maintained, current liabilities can be paid on time, suppliers will continue to provide needed inventories, and companies will be able to meet sales demands. However, if the financial situation gets out of balance, liquidity problems surface and often multiply into more serious problems, and perhaps even bankruptcy. As you read this chapter, consider how important liquidity—thus proper management of working capital—is to the survival of a firm. Also consider the fact that many start-up firms never make it past the first few months of business, primarily because such firms do not have formal working capital policies in place. ∎

WORKING CAPITAL MANAGEMENT

The management of short-term assets (investments) and liabilities (financing sources).

Generally we divide financial management decisions into the management of assets (investments) and liabilities (sources of financing) in (1) the *long term* and (2) the *short term*. We discussed long-term decisions and analyses in previous chapters. In this and the next two chapters, we discuss *short-term financial management*, also termed **working capital management,** which involves management of the current assets and the current liabilities of a firm. As you read this chapter, you will realize that a firm's value cannot be maximized in the long run unless it survives the short run. In fact, the principal reason firms fail is because they are unable to meet their working capital needs. Thus, *sound working capital management is a requisite for firm survival.*

Much of a financial manager's time is devoted to working capital management, and many of you who get jobs in finance-related fields will find your first assignment on the job will involve working capital. For these reasons, working capital policy and management is an essential topic of study. In this chapter, we provide an overview of working capital policy, and the next two chapters discuss how current assets and current liabilities should be managed.

Working Capital Terminology[1]

It is useful to begin the discussion of working capital policy by reviewing some basic definitions and concepts:

WORKING CAPITAL

A firm's investment in short-term assets—cash, marketable securities, inventory, and accounts receivable.

NET WORKING CAPITAL

Current assets minus current liabilities—the amount of current assets financed by long-term liabilities.

1. The term **working capital,** sometimes called *gross working capital,* generally refers to current assets.
2. **Net working capital** is defined as current assets minus current liabilities.
3. The *current ratio,* which was discussed in Chapter 11, is calculated by dividing current assets by current liabilities, and it is intended to measure a firm's liquidity. However, a high current ratio does not insure that a firm will have the cash required to meet its needs. If inventories cannot be sold, or if receivables cannot be collected in a timely manner, then the apparent safety reflected in a high current ratio could be illusory.

---

[1]The term *working capital* originated with the old Yankee peddler, who would load up his wagon with goods and then go off on his route to peddle his wares. The merchandise was called *working capital* because it was what he actually sold, or "turned over," to produce his profits. The wagon and horse were his fixed assets. He generally owned the horse and wagon, so they were financed with "equity" capital. But to buy the merchandise, he borrowed funds, which were called *working capital* loans, that had to be repaid after each trip to demonstrate to the bank that the credit was sound. If the peddler was able to repay the loan, then the bank would make another loan, and banks that followed this procedure were said to be employing sound banking practices.

TABLE 13–1	Unilate Textiles: Historical and Projected Balance Sheets (millions of dollars)		
	12/31/05 (HISTORICAL)	**9/30/06** (PROJECTED)	**12/31/06** (PROJECTED)
Cash and marketable securities	$ 15.0	$ 30.0	$ 16.5
Accounts receivable	180.0	251.5	198.0
Inventories	270.0	410.0	297.0
Total current assets	$465.0	$ 691.5	$511.5
Net plant and equipment	380.0	408.5	418.0
Total assets	$845.0	$1,100.0	$929.5
Accounts payable	$ 30.0	$ 90.0	$ 33.0
Accruals	60.0	100.0	66.0
Notes payable	40.0	129.0	46.8
Total current liabilities	$130.0	$ 319.0	$145.8
Long-term bonds	300.0	309.0	309.0
Total liabilities	$430.0	$ 628.0	$454.8
Common stock	130.0	159.3	159.3
Retained earnings	285.0	312.7	315.5
Total owners' equity	$415.0	$ 472.0	$474.8
Total liabilities and equity	$845.0	$1,100.0	$929.5[a]
Net working capital	$335.0	$ 372.5	$365.7
Current ratio	3.6	2.2	3.5

[a]Rounding difference. These end-of-year forecasts were derived in Appendix 12A.

4. The best and most comprehensive picture of a firm's liquidity position is obtained by examining its *cash budget*. The cash budget, which forecasts cash inflows and outflows, focuses on what really counts, the firm's ability to generate sufficient cash inflows to meet its required cash outflows. Cash budgeting will be discussed in the next chapter.

5. **Working capital policy** refers to the firm's basic policies regarding (a) target levels for each category of current assets and (b) how current assets will be financed.

WORKING CAPITAL POLICY
Decisions regarding (1) the target levels for each current asset account and (2) how current assets will be financed.

We must distinguish between those current liabilities that are specifically used to finance current assets and those current liabilities that result from long-term decisions. Such current liabilities include (1) current maturities of long-term debt; (2) financing associated with a construction program that, after the project is completed, will be funded with the proceeds of a long-term security issue; or (3) the use of short-term debt to finance fixed assets.

Table 13–1 contains balance sheets for Unilate Textiles constructed at three different dates. According to the definitions given, Unilate's December 31, 2005, working capital—that is, current assets—was $465.0 million, and its net working capital was $335.0 million = $465.0 million – $130.0 million. Also, Unilate's year-end 2005 current ratio was 3.6.

What if the total current liabilities of $130 million at the end of 2005 included the current portion of long-term debt, say $10 million? This account is unaffected by changes in working capital policy because it is a function of past long-term debt financing decisions. Thus, even though we define long-term debt coming due in the next accounting period as a current liability, it is not a working capital decision variable in the current period. Similarly, if Unilate were building a new factory and initially financed the construction with a short-term loan that would be replaced later with mortgage bonds, the construction loan would not be considered part of working capital management. Although such accounts are not part of Unilate's working capital decision process, they cannot be ignored because they are *due* in the current period, and they must be taken into account when Unilate's managers construct the cash budget and assess the firm's ability to meet its current obligations (its liquidity position).

Self-Test Questions

Why is it important to properly manage short-term assets and liabilities?

The Requirement for External Working Capital Financing

Unilate's operations and the sale of textile products are seasonal, typically peaking in September and October. Thus, at the end of September Unilate's inventories are significantly higher than they are at the end of the calendar year. Unilate offers significant sales incentives to wholesalers during August and September in an effort to move inventories out of its warehouses and into those of its customers; otherwise, inventories would be even higher than shown in Table 13–1. Because of this sales surge, Unilate's receivables also are much higher at the end of September than at the end of December.

Consider what is expected to happen to Unilate's current assets and current liabilities from December 31, 2005, to September 30, 2006. Current assets are expected to increase from $465.0 million to $691.5 million, or by $226.5 million. Because increases on the asset side of the balance sheet must be financed by identical increases on the liabilities and equity side, the firm must raise $226.5 million to meet the expected increase in working capital over the period. However, the higher volume of purchases, plus labor expenditures associated with increased production, will cause accounts payable and accruals to increase *spontaneously* by only $100 million—from $90 million ($30 million in payables plus $60 million in accruals) to $190 million ($90 million in payables plus $100 million in accruals)—during the first nine months of 2006. This leaves a projected $126.5 million = $226.5 million – $100 million current asset financing requirement, which Unilate expects to finance primarily by an $89 million increase in notes payable. Therefore, for September 30, 2006, notes payable are projected to rise to $129 million. Notice that from December 2005 to September 2006, Unilate's net working capital is expected to increase from $335 million to $372.5 million, but its current ratio is expected to fall from 3.6 to 2.2. This occurs because most, but not all, of the funds invested in current assets are expected to come from current liabilities.[2]

The fluctuations in Unilate's working capital position shown in Table 13–1 result from seasonal variations. Similar fluctuations in working capital requirements, and hence in financing needs, also occur during business cycles—working capital needs typically decline during recessions but increase during booms. For some companies, such as those involved in agricultural products, seasonal fluctuations are much greater than business cycle fluctuations, but for other companies, such as appliance or automobile manufacturers, cyclical fluctuations are larger. In the following sections we look in more detail at the requirement for working capital financing, and we examine some alternative working capital policies.

Self-Test Question

Under normal circumstances, when does the working capital position of a firm change? Explain.

The Relationships Among Working Capital Accounts

It is important that you understand how the various working capital accounts are related. To illustrate the process of producing and selling inventory and the relationships between current assets and current liabilities, let's assume that you open a new textile manufacturing plant to compete with Unilate Textiles. Let's call the new business Global Cloth Products (GCP). Under normal conditions, the new plant is expected to produce and sell 50,000 units each day. Each unit, which will be sold for $14.00, has a direct production cost equal to $11.00. For simplicity, we will assume that the $11.00 unit cost can be broken into two components—the cost of raw materials purchased from suppliers (cotton, wool, etc.), which is $6.50, and the cost of labor, which is $4.50—and that there are no other costs associated with the manufacture and sale of the product. GCP will purchase materials from its suppliers for credit, with cash payment due 15 days after the purchase. Likewise, GCP will allow its customers to purchase for credit, and it will require cash payment 15 days after the sale. In our illustration, we assume all GCP customers will pay for their purchases 15 days after the sales, and that GCP will pay its suppliers 15 days after purchasing raw materials. In addition, employees will be paid every 15 days (twice a month).[3] Therefore, all the cash flows associated with the production and sales functions will occur 15 days after the purchase, manufacture, and sale of the products. To simplify the illustration, we assume all cash flows will occur at the beginning of the day, before daily purchasing, producing, and selling activities begin. Thus, at the beginning of day 16 (1) inventory purchases made on the first day of business will be paid, (2) collection for the products sold on the first day of business occur, and (3) the employees will be paid for their first 15 days of work.

---

[2]Mathematically, when both the numerator and the denominator of a ratio that has a value greater than 1.0 increase by the same amount (magnitude), the value of the ratio decreases. If the ratio's value is less than 1.0, its value will increase when both the numerator and denominator are increased by the same magnitude.

[3]The 15-day period is used for simplicity because there are two 15-day periods in a 30-day month and 24 15-day periods in a 360-day year. If a 14-day period was used, the illustration would become more cumbersome.

GCP will use $300,000 in common stock to finance the new processing plant facilities, and the raw materials purchases will be made daily and financed short term with accounts payable (owed to suppliers), wages payable (owed to employees), and short-term bank loans (notes payable). Each day, the raw materials that are purchased will be converted into finished goods and sold before the close of business.

On the first day of operations, just *prior to selling any products*, GCP will have 50,000 units in inventory at a cost of $11.00 per unit, so the inventory balance will be $550,000 = 50,000 × $11.00. The inventory cost consists of the raw materials, which amounts to $325,000 = 50,000 × $6.50 owed to suppliers, and the cost of labor, which is $225,000 = 50,000 × $4.50 owed to employees. At this point, then, the balance sheet for GCP's processing plant would be as follows:

Cash	$ 0	Accounts payable	$325,000
Accounts receivable	0	Accrued wages	225,000
Inventory	550,000	Notes payable	0
Current assets	550,000	Current liabilities	550,000
Fixed assets	300,000	Common equity	300,000
		Retained earnings	0
Total assets	$850,000	Total liabilities and equity	$850,000

On the first day, all of the 50,000 units in inventory will be sold for $14.00 each, so the first day's sales will be $700,000 = 50,000 × $14.00. And, after the first day's sales are complete, the balance sheet will be as follows:

Cash	$ 0	Accounts payable	$ 325,000
Accounts receivable	700,000	Accrued wages	225,000
Inventory	0	Notes payable	0
Current assets	700,000	Current liabilities	550,000
Fixed assets	300,000	Common equity	300,000
		Retained earnings	150,000
Total assets	$1,000,000	Total liabilities and equity	$1,000,000

Notice that the $150,000 profit on the first day's sales, which is the difference between the inventory cost of $550,000 and the first day's sales of $700,000, is recognized via retained earnings.[4] This shows that not all of the $700,000 in accounts receivable has to be financed because $150,000 represents the profit on the sales.

At the start of the second day, *after inventories are replenished but before daily sales begin*, the inventory balance again will be $550,000 and the balances in accounts payable and accrued wages will *increase* by $325,000 and $225,000, respectively. Thus, the balance sheet will be as follows:

Cash	$ 0	Accounts payable	$ 650,000
Accounts receivable	700,000	Accrued wages	450,000
Inventory	550,000	Notes payable	0
Current assets	1,250,000	Current liabilties	1,100,000
Fixed assets	300,000	Common equity	300,000
		Retained earnings	150,000
Total assets	$1,550,000	Total liabilities and equity	$1,550,000

---

[4]In reality, profits are not posted to retained earnings each day; rather, the recognition of profits (income) occurs at the end of the fiscal period via the income summary account. We recognize the daily profits in this manner for illustrative purposes only.

When the products are sold on the second day, accounts receivable again will increase by $700,000. In fact, the balances in accounts receivable, accounts payable, wages payable, and retained earnings will continue to increase (accumulate) until cash flows affect these accounts' balances. So the balances in receivables, payables, and accrued wages will increase for a total of 15 days, while the balance in retained earnings will continue to increase until dividends are paid or losses are incurred.

GCP neither receives nor disburses any cash until 15 days after the first day of business. At that time, GCP will have to *pay* for both the raw materials purchased on the first day of business and the wages owed to employees for the first 15 days of work. In addition, GCP will *receive* payment from those customers who purchased its products on the first day of business. So for the first 15 days of business, the balances in receivables, payables, accruals, and retained earnings continue to increase, reflecting the purchasing and selling activities of GCP prior to the receipt or payment of any cash flows. At the *end* of Day 15, therefore, the balance in each of these accounts would be as follows:

$$\text{Accounts receivable} = \$700,000 \times 15 \text{ days} = \$10,500,000$$

$$\text{Accounts payable} = \$325,000 \times 15 \text{ days} = \$4,875,000$$

$$\text{Accrued wages} = \$225,000 \times 15 \text{ days} = \$3,375,000$$

$$\text{Retained earnings} = \$150,000 \times 15 \text{ days} = \$2,250,000$$

And the balance sheet at the *end* of Day 15 would be as follows:

Cash	$ 0	Accounts payable	$ 4,875,000
Accounts receivable	10,500,000	Accrued wages	3,375,000
Inventory	0	Notes payable	0
Current assets	10,500,000	Current liabilities	8,250,000
Fixed assets	300,000	Common equity	300,000
		Retained earnings	2,250,000
Total assets	$10,800,000	Total liabilities and equity	$10,800,000

At the *beginning* of Day 16, GCP must pay its employees $3,375,000 for the first 15 days of work, and it also must pay $325,000 to the suppliers for the raw materials purchased on the first day of business. But, at the same time, GCP will be paid $700,000 for the products that were sold on the first day of business. This cash receipt can be used to pay the $325,000 now due to the suppliers, which leaves only $375,000 to help pay employees' salaries. This means GCP must borrow to meet its cash obligations. If GCP uses the entire $375,000 to help pay employees' salaries, the amount that needs to be borrowed to pay the remaining wages is

$$\text{Loan amount} = \left(\begin{array}{c} \text{Payment owed} \\ \text{to suppliers} \end{array} \right) + \left(\begin{array}{c} \text{Wages owed} \\ \text{employees} \end{array} \right) - \left(\begin{array}{c} \text{Cash} \\ \text{receipts} \end{array} \right)$$

$$= [\$325,000 + \$3,375,000] - (\$700,000)$$

$$= \$3,700,000 - \$700,000 = \$3,000,000$$

If GCP borrows the funds needed from a local bank, consider what the balance sheet would look like if all of the cash flow activity occurs at the very beginning of Day 16, *prior to the daily materials purchases, inventory production, and product sales.* At this point, GCP would have (1) paid *all* of the $3,375,000 wages owed its employees, so the balance of accrued wages would equal zero; (2) paid $325,000 to its suppliers, so the balance of accounts payable would decrease by $325,000; (3) received a $700,000 payment from its customers, so the balance of accounts receivable would decrease by $700,000; and (4) borrowed $3,000,000 from a local bank to pay employees, so the balance of notes payable would increase by $3,000,000. At this point, the balance sheet would be as follows:

Cash	$ 0	Accounts payable	$ 4,550,000
Accounts receivable	9,800,000	Accrued wages	0
Inventory	0	Notes payable	3,000,000
Current assets	9,800,000	Current liabilities	7,550,000
Fixed assets	300,000	Common equity	300,000
		Retained earnings	2,250,000
Total assets	$10,100,000	Total liabilities and equity	$10,100,000

But on Day 16, GCP must also conduct its normal daily business—raw materials must be purchased and finished goods must be manufactured and sold. Because no additional cash flows will occur on this day, the purchase of raw materials will increase accounts payable by $325,000, the use of employees to manufacture finished goods will increase accrued wages by $225,000, and credit sales will increase accounts receivable by $700,000. Consequently, at the *end of day 16*, the balance sheet will be as follows:

Cash	$ 0	Accounts payable	$ 4,875,000
Accounts receivable	10,500,000	Accrued wages	225,000
Inventory	0	Notes payable	3,000,000
Current assets	10,500,000	Current liabilities	8,100,000
Fixed assets	300,000	Common equity	300,000
		Retained earnings	2,400,000
Total assets	$10,800,000	Total liabilities and equity	$10,800,000

At this point, the accounts payable and accounts receivable balances reflect 15 days' worth of credit activities associated with the production and sales operations that took place from Day 2 through Day 16. On the other hand, because at the beginning of the day the employees were paid the wages due them for the first 15 days of business, accrued wages include only the amount owed to employees for their work to produce inventory on Day 16. And because there have not been any cash disbursements to stockholders, the balance in retained earnings represents the profits from the products sold for all 16 days GCP has been in business—$2,400,000 = $150,000 × 16 days.

At the beginning of Day 17, GCP will pay for the materials it purchased on Day 2. It will also receive payment for the products that were sold on Day 2. This process will continue as long as the purchasing and payment patterns of both GCP and its customers do not change. As a result GCP will pay out $325,000 every day to pay for materials purchased 15 days earlier (a decrease in payables), but the payables balance will remain the same from this point on because GCP will also purchase on credit raw materials valuing $325,000 (an increase in payables) every day to produce the product needed for that day's sales. Therefore, the accounts payable balance will remain constant at $4,875,000. Similarly, the balance in accounts receivable will remain at $10,500,000, because each day, once this steady state has been reached (after Day 15), GCP will receive cash payments from customers totaling $700,000 (a decrease in receivables) at the same time $700,000 worth of products are sold for credit (an increase in receivables).

At this point, consider the cash flow position of GCP. From Day 16 on, every day, GCP will receive cash payments from its customers that total $700,000, and it will make cash payments to its suppliers that total $325,000. But the employees are paid every 15 days, not every day. Therefore, GCP can accumulate $375,000 = $700,000 − $325,000 in cash each day until employees' salaries need to be paid again. The next time employees' salaries are paid is at the beginning of Day 31, so the cash account balance will increase by $375,000 for 15 days. Therefore, on Day 31, after all cash flows except accrued wages are recognized, GCP will have a cash balance equal to $5,625,000 = $375,000 × 15 days. Accrued wages will equal $3,375,000 = $225,000 × 15 days; so, after paying its employees, GCP will still have a cash balance equal to $2,250,000. This amount represents the *total cash profit* GCP has generated during the previous 15 days of business. This amount can be used to pay off a portion of the bank loan, or it could be used to expand operations. In any event, once the balances in receivables and payables have stabilized because the daily adjustments to those accounts are offsetting, GCP actually realizes a *cash* profit of $150,000 per day.

This illustration shows that, in general, once GCP's operations have stabilized so that the credit sales and credit purchasing patterns and the collection and payment activities stay the same day after day, the balances of accounts receivable and accounts payable will remain constant—the daily increase associated with each account will be offset by the daily decrease associated with the account. Therefore, once the firm's operations have stabilized and cash collections from credit sales and cash payments for credit purchases have begun, the balance in accounts receivable and accounts payable can be computed using the following equation:

13-1

$$\text{Account balance} = \left(\begin{array}{c}\text{Amount of} \\ \text{daily activity}\end{array}\right) \times \left(\begin{array}{c}\text{Average life} \\ \text{of the account}\end{array}\right)$$

For accounts receivable, the balance would be the daily credit sales times the length of time each account remains outstanding—$700,000 × 15 days = $10,500,000.

The preceding scenario will occur only if GCP's expectations, including forecasted sales, come true. But what happens if GCP's forecasts are too optimistic? If GCP finds it cannot sell 50,000 units each day, its cash collections will decrease, its inventory probably will build up, and perhaps notes payable also will increase. If this pattern continues, GCP eventually might find itself in financial difficulty.

Although the illustration we used here is oversimplified, it should give you an indication of the interrelationships among the working capital accounts. It should be apparent that a decision affecting one working capital account—for example, inventory—will have an impact on other working capital accounts—for example, receivables and payables).

Self-Test Questions

If a firm purchases raw materials on credit, which two working capital accounts are affected? What would happen if the purchase was for cash?

Write out the equation that gives the balance in accounts receivable once cash receipts for earlier credit sales begin (assume sales/collection patterns have stabilized).

The Cash Conversion Cycle

The concept of working capital management originated with the old Yankee peddler, who would borrow to buy inventory, sell the inventory to pay off the bank loan, and then repeat the cycle. The previous section illustrates the impact of such activity on the working capital accounts of the firm. That general concept has been applied to more complex businesses, and it is useful when analyzing the effectiveness of a firm's working capital management process.

The working capital management process that Unilate Textiles faces is similar to the process we described in the previous section for GCP, and it can be summarized as follows:

1. Unilate orders and then receives the materials it needs to produce the textile products its sells. Unilate purchases from its suppliers on credit, so an account payable is created for credit purchases. Such purchases have no immediate cash flow effect because payment is not made until some later date (perhaps 20 to 30 days after purchase).
2. Labor is used to convert the materials (cotton and wool) into finished goods (cloth products, thread, etc.). However, wages are not fully paid at the time the work is done, so accrued wages build up (maybe for a period of one or two weeks).
3. The finished products are sold, but on credit; so sales create receivables, not immediate cash inflows.
4. At some point during the cycle, Unilate must pay off its accounts payable and accrued wages. *If* these payments are made before Unilate has collected cash from its receivables, a net cash outflow occurs and this outflow must be financed.
5. The cycle is completed when Unilate's receivables are collected (perhaps in 30 to 40 days). At that time, the company is in a position to pay off the credit that was used to finance production of the product, and it can then repeat the cycle.

CASH CONVERSION CYCLE

The length of time from the payment for the purchase of raw materials to manufacture a product until the collection of accounts receivable associated with the sale of the product.

The preceding steps are formalized with the **cash conversion cycle** model, which focuses on the length of time between when the company makes payments, or invests in the manufacture of inventory, and when it receives cash inflows, or realizes a cash return from its investment in production.[5] The following terms are used in the model:

1. The *inventory conversion period* is the average length of time required to convert materials into finished goods and then to sell those goods; it is the amount of time the product remains in inventory in various stages of completion. The inventory conversion period is calculated by dividing inventory by the cost of goods sold per day. For example, we can compute the inventory conversion period for Unilate Textiles using the 2005 balance sheet figures shown in Table 13–1. In 2005, Unilate sold $1,500 million of its product with a cost of goods sold equal to $1,230 million, so the inventory conversion period would be

---

[5]See Verlyn Richards and Eugene Laughlin, "A Cash Conversion Cycle Approach to Liquidity Analysis," *Financial Management*, Spring 1980, 32–38.

13-2

$$\text{Inventory conversion period} = \frac{\text{Inventory}}{\text{Cost of goods sold per day}} = \frac{\text{Inventory}}{\left(\dfrac{\text{Cost of goods sold}}{360}\right)}$$

$$= \frac{\$270 \text{ million}}{\left(\dfrac{\$1,230 \text{ million}}{360}\right)} = \frac{\$270}{\$3.417}$$

$$= 79.0 \text{ days}$$

Thus, according to its 2005 operations, it takes Unilate 79.0 days to convert materials into finished goods and then to sell those goods.

2. The *receivables collection period* is the average length of time required to convert the firm's receivables into cash—that is, to collect cash following a sale. The receivables collection period also is called the days sales outstanding (DSO), and it is calculated by dividing accounts receivable by the average credit sales per day. Because sales in 2005 equaled $1,500 million, Unilate's receivables collection period (DSO) is:

13-3

$$\text{Receivables collection period} = \text{DSO} = \frac{\text{Receivables}}{\text{Daily credit sales}} = \frac{\text{Receivables}}{\left(\dfrac{\text{Credit sales}}{360}\right)}$$

$$= \frac{\$180 \text{ million}}{\left(\dfrac{\$1,500 \text{ million}}{360}\right)} = \frac{\$180}{\$4.167}$$

$$= 43.2 \text{ days}$$

Thus, the cash payments associated with credit sales are not collected until 43.2 days after the sales.

3. The *payables deferral period* is the average length of time between the purchase of raw materials and labor and the payment of cash for them. It is computed by dividing accounts payable by the daily credit purchases. Unilate's daily cost of goods sold is $3.417 million, so the payables deferral period for Unilate would be:

13-4

$$\begin{array}{l}\text{Payables}\\ \text{deferral period}\end{array} = \text{DPO} = \frac{\text{Accounts payable}}{\text{Credit purchases per day}} = \frac{\text{Accounts payable}}{\left(\dfrac{\text{Cost of goods sold}}{360}\right)}$$

FIGURE 13-1   The Cash Conversion Cycle

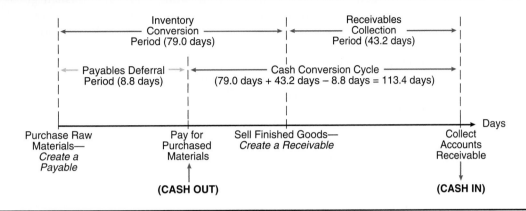

$$= \frac{\$30 \text{ million}}{\left(\dfrac{\$1,230 \text{ million}}{360} \right)} = \frac{\$30}{\$3.417}$$

$$= 8.8 \text{ days}$$

So Unilate pays its suppliers an average of 8.8 days after materials are purchased.[6]

4. The *cash conversion cycle* computation nets out the three periods just defined, resulting in a value that equals the length of time between the firm's actual cash expenditures to pay for (invest in) productive resources (materials and labor) and its own cash receipts from the sale of products (that is, the length of time between paying for labor and materials and collecting on receivables). The cash conversion cycle thus equals the average length of time a dollar is tied up, or invested, in current assets.

We can now use these definitions to analyze Unilate's cash conversion cycle. The concept is diagrammed in Figure 13–1. The cash conversion cycle can be expressed by this equation:

13-5

$$\begin{pmatrix} \text{Cash} \\ \text{conversion} \\ \text{cycle} \end{pmatrix} = \begin{pmatrix} \text{Inventory} \\ \text{conversion} \\ \text{period} \end{pmatrix} + \begin{pmatrix} \text{Receivables} \\ \text{collection} \\ \text{period} \end{pmatrix} - \begin{pmatrix} \text{Payables} \\ \text{deferral} \\ \text{period} \end{pmatrix}$$

$$= 79.0 \text{ days} \quad + \quad 43.2 \text{ days} \quad - \quad 8.8 \text{ days}$$

$$= 113.4 \text{ days}$$

---

[6]The computation for the payables deferral period shown here is the traditional method used to determine the value used in the calculation of the cash conversion cycle. However, if we recognize that the intent of the computation is to determine the length of time between the purchase of raw materials and the labor used to produce inventory and the payment for these inputs, the payables deferral period might more appropriately be written to include consideration of accrued wages.

To illustrate, according to Unilate's 2005 operations, it takes an average of 79.0 days to convert raw materials (cotton, wool, etc.) into finished goods (cloth, thread, etc.) and then sell these products, and then it takes another 43.2 days to collect on the sale (that is, receivables). However, 8.8 days normally elapse between the receipt of raw materials and payment for them. In this case, the cash conversion cycle is 113.4 days. The *receipt* of cash from manufacturing and selling the products will be delayed by approximately 122 days because (1) the product will be "tied up" in inventory for 79 days and (2) the cash from the sale will not be received until 43 days after the selling date. But the *disbursement* of cash for the raw materials purchased will be delayed by nearly 9 days because Unilate does not pay cash for the raw materials when they are purchased. So for Unilate, the net delay in cash receipts associated with an investment (cash disbursement) in inventory is 113.4 days. What does this mean to Unilate?

Given its cash conversion cycle, Unilate knows when it starts processing its textile products that it will have to finance the manufacturing and other operating costs for a 113-day period, which is nearly one-third of a year. The firm's goal should be to shorten its cash conversion cycle as much as possible without harming operations. This would improve profits because the longer the cash conversion cycle, the greater the need for external, or nonspontaneous, financing, and such financing has a cost.

The cash conversion cycle can be shortened (1) by reducing the inventory conversion period by processing and selling goods more quickly, (2) by reducing the receivables collection period by speeding up collections, or (3) by lengthening the payables deferral period by slowing down its own payments. To the extent that these actions can be taken *without harming the return* associated with the management of these accounts, they should be carried out. So when taking actions to reduce the inventory conversion period, a firm should be careful to *avoid inventory shortages* that could cause "good" customers to buy from competitors; when taking actions to speed up the collection of receivables, a firm should be careful to *maintain good relations with its "good" credit customers;* and when taking actions to lengthen the payables deferral period, a firm should be careful *not to harm its own credit reputation.*

We can illustrate the benefits of shortening the cash conversion cycle by looking again at Unilate Textiles. Unilate must spend an average of $12.30 on materials and labor to manufacture its products, which are sold for $15.00 per unit. To generate the $1,500 million sales realized in 2005, Unilate turned out 277,778 items per day. At this rate of production, it must invest $3.417 million = $12.30 × 277,778 units each day to support the manufacturing process. This investment must be financed for 113.4 days—the length of the cash conversion cycle—so the company's working capital financing needs will be $387.5 million = 113.4 × $3.417 million. If Unilate could reduce the cash conversion cycle to 93.4 days—say, by deferring payment of its accounts payable an additional 20 days or by speeding up either the production process or the collection of its receivables—it could reduce its working capital financing requirements by $68.3 million = 20 days × $3.417 million. We see, then, that actions that affect the inventory conversion period, the receivables collection period, and the payables deferral period all affect the cash conversion cycle; hence they influence the firm's need for current assets and current asset financing. You should keep the cash conversion cycle concept in mind as you go through the remainder of this chapter and the next two chapters.

Self-Test Questions

What steps are involved in estimating the cash conversion cycle?

What do the following terms mean?
    a. Inventory conversion period.
    b. Receivables collection period.
    c. Payables deferral period.

What is the cash conversion cycle model? How can it be used to improve current asset management?

Working Capital Investment and Financing Policies

Working capital policy involves two basic questions: (1) What is the appropriate level for current assets, both in total and by specific accounts, and (2) how should current assets be financed?

Alternative Current Asset Investment Policies

RELAXED CURRENT ASSET INVESTMENT POLICY
A policy under which relatively large amounts of cash and marketable securities and inventories are carried and under which sales are stimulated by a liberal credit policy that results in a high level of receivables.

RESTRICTED CURRENT ASSET INVESTMENT POLICY
A policy under which holdings of cash and marketable securities, inventories, and receivables are minimized.

MODERATE CURRENT ASSET INVESTMENT POLICY
A policy between the relaxed and restrictive policies.

Figure 13–2 shows three alternative policies regarding the total amount of current assets carried. Essentially, these policies differ in that different amounts of current assets are carried to support any given level of sales. The line with the steepest slope represents a **relaxed current asset investment** (or "fat cat") **policy,** where relatively large amounts of cash and marketable securities and inventories are carried and where sales are stimulated by the use of a credit policy that provides liberal financing to customers and a corresponding high level of receivables. Conversely, with the **restricted current asset investment** (or "lean-and-mean") **policy,** the holdings of cash and marketable securities, inventories, and receivables are minimized. The **moderate current asset investment policy** is between the two extremes.

Under conditions of certainty—when sales, costs, lead times, payment periods, and so on, are known for sure—all firms would hold only minimal levels of current assets. Any larger amounts would increase the need for external funding without a corresponding increase in profits, whereas any smaller holdings would involve late payments to labor and suppliers and lost sales due to inventory shortages and an overly restrictive credit policy.

However, the picture changes when uncertainty is introduced. Here the firm requires some minimum amount of cash and inventories based on expected payments, expected sales, expected order lead times, and so on, plus additional amounts, or *safety stocks*, that enable it to deal with departures from the expected values. Similarly, accounts receivable levels are determined by credit terms, and the tougher the credit terms, the lower the receivables for any given level of sales. With a restricted current asset investment policy, the firm would hold minimal levels of safety stocks for cash and inventories, and it would have a tight credit policy even though this would mean running the risk of losing sales. A restricted, lean-and-mean current asset investment policy generally provides the highest expected return on investment, but it entails the greatest risk, while the reverse is true under a relaxed policy. The moderate policy falls in between the two extremes in terms of both expected risk and return.

In terms of the cash conversion cycle, a restricted investment policy would tend to reduce the inventory conversion and receivables collection periods, which would

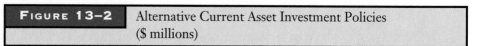

FIGURE 13–2   Alternative Current Asset Investment Policies ($ millions)

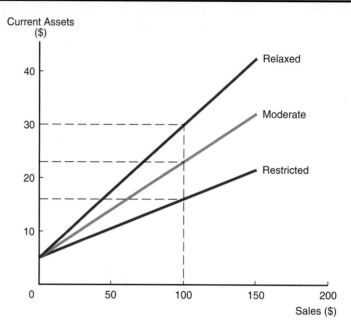

Policy	Current Assets to Support Sales of $100
Relaxed	$30
Moderate	23
Restricted	16

Note: The sales/current assets relationship is shown here as being linear, but the relationship is often curvilinear.

result in a relatively short cash conversion cycle. Conversely, a relaxed policy would create higher levels of inventories and receivables, longer inventory conversion and receivables collection periods, and a relatively long cash conversion cycle. A moderate policy would produce a cash conversion cycle somewhere between the two extremes.

Alternative Current Asset Financing Policies

PERMANENT CURRENT ASSETS
Current assets' balances that do not change due to seasonal or economic conditions; these balances exist even at the trough of a firm's business cycle.

Most businesses experience seasonal fluctuations, cyclical fluctuations, or both. For example, construction firms have peaks in the spring and summer, retailers peak around Christmas, and the manufacturers who supply both construction companies and retailers follow similar patterns. Similarly, virtually all businesses must build up current assets when the economy is strong, but they then sell off inventories and have net reductions of receivables when the economy slacks off. Still, current assets rarely drop to zero, and this realization has led to the development of the idea that some current assets should be considered **permanent current assets** because their levels remain stable no matter the seasonal or economic conditions. Applying this idea to Unilate Textiles, Table 13–1 (presented earlier) suggests that, at this stage in its life, Unilate's total assets are growing at a 10 percent rate, from $845.0 million at the end of 2005 to a projected $929.5 million by the end of 2006, but seasonal fluctuations are expected to push total assets up to $1,100.0 million during the firm's peak season in 2006. Assuming Unilate's permanent assets grow continuously, and at the *same rate*, throughout the year, then 9/12ths (75 percent) of the 10 percent growth in assets will accrue by the end of September and permanent assets would equal $908.4 million = $845.0 million + (9/12)($929.5 million − $845.0 million). But the actual level of assets is expected to be $1,100.0 million because this is Unilate's peak season. So at the end of September, Unilate's total assets of $1,100.0 million consist of $908.4 million of permanent assets and $191.6 million = $1,100.0 million − $908.4 million of seasonal, or **temporary, current assets.** Unilate's temporary current assets fluctuate from zero during the slow season in December to nearly $192 million during the peak season in September. Therefore, temporary current assets are those amounts of current assets that vary with respect to the seasonal or economic conditions of a firm. The manner in which the permanent and temporary current assets are financed is called the firm's *current asset financing policy*, which generally can be classified as one of the three approaches described next.

TEMPORARY CURRENT ASSETS
Current assets that fluctuate with seasonal or cyclical variations in a firm's business.

MATURITY MATCHING, OR "SELF-LIQUIDATING," APPROACH
A financing policy that matches asset and liability maturities. This would be considered a moderate current asset financing policy.

Maturity Matching, or "Self-Liquidating," Approach   The **maturity matching,** or **"self-liquidating," approach** calls for matching asset and liability maturities as shown in Panel a of Figure 13–3. This strategy minimizes the risk that the firm will be unable to pay off its maturing obligations *if* the liquidations of the assets can be controlled to occur on or before the maturities of the obligations. At the limit, a firm could attempt to match exactly the maturity structure of its assets and liabilities. Inventory expected to be sold in 30 days could be financed with a 30-day bank loan; a machine expected to last for five years could be financed by a five-year loan; a 20-year building could be financed by a 20-year mortgage bond; and so forth. Actually, of course, two factors prevent this exact maturity matching: (1) there is uncertainty about the lives of assets, and (2) some common equity must be used, and common equity has no maturity. To illustrate the uncertainty factor, Unilate might finance inventories with a 30-day loan, expecting to sell the inventories and to use the cash generated to retire the loan. But if sales were slow, the cash would not be forthcoming, and the use of short-term credit could end up causing a problem (e.g., look at the cash conversion cycle computed for Unilate in the previous section). Still, if Unilate makes an attempt to match asset and liability maturities, we would define this as a *moderate current asset financing policy*.

AGGRESSIVE APPROACH
A policy where all of the fixed assets of a firm are financed with long-term capital, but *some* of the firm's permanent current assets are financed with short-term nonspontaneous sources of funds.

Aggressive Approach   Panel b of Figure 13–3 illustrates the **aggressive approach,** used by a firm that (1) finances all of its temporary assets with short-term, nonspontaneous debt and (2) finances its fixed assets with long-term capital, but some of the remainder of its permanent current assets is financed with short-term, nonspontaneous credit. A look back at Table 13–1 shows that Unilate actually follows this strategy. Unilate has $499.9 million in permanent current assets ($908.4 million in permanent assets less $408.5 million fixed assets) projected for September 2006, so its temporary current assets must be $191.6 million = $691.5 million − $499.9 million. However, the firm is projected to have $129.0 million in notes payable as well as temporary financing equal to about $100.0 million from peak levels of accounts payable and accruals (payables are projected to be $60.0 million higher than at the end of 2005, and accruals are projected to be $40.0 million higher). Thus, Unilate's level of temporary financing, which is $229.0 million, exceeds its level of temporary current assets, which is $191.6 million; some part of its permanent assets is financed with temporary capital.

| FIGURE 13-3 | Alternative Current Asset Financing Policies |

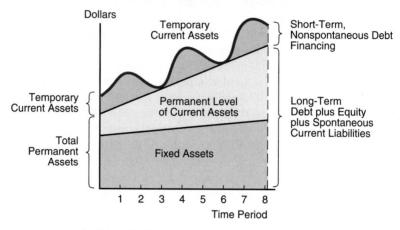

a. Moderate Approach (Maturity Matching)

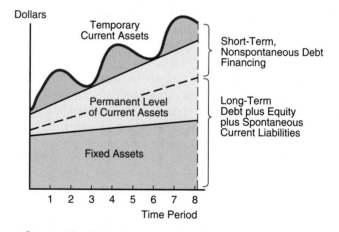

b. Relatively Aggressive Approach

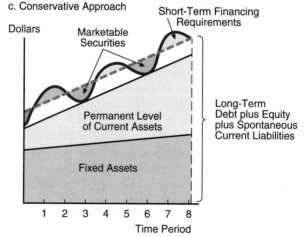

c. Conservative Approach

Working Capital Management—Conservative or Aggressive?

Unfortunately, not much is known about the actual working capital practices followed by firms. However, the results of a survey that was administered at different time periods (with some modifications) provide us with some indication of how firms manage working capital. The survey was administered to large U.S. industrial firms, first in 1978 and then again in 1988. The results indicate that the working capital policies of large firms in the United States, although varied, have become more formal over time. In 1978 fewer than 30 percent of the respondents indicated that they had formal working capital policies, while more than 70 percent said they had informal policies or none at all; in the 1988 survey, these results were about 37 percent and 63 percent, respectively.

The results of the 1978 and 1988 surveys also suggest that working capital policies have become more conservative over time. In 1978, 28 percent of the respondents indicated that their firms followed conservative, or "risk avoiding," policies; about 22 percent said they followed aggressive, or "risk accepting," policies; and greater than 50 percent indicated that their policies either depended on the situation or changed from time to time. Ten years later, the responses were significantly different—the firms that followed conservative working capital policies had increased to greater than 41 percent and those that followed aggressive policies had decreased to less than 7 percent (the percent indicating their policies were dependent on the situation or changed from time to time was about the same).

When the same survey was replicated in Australia in 1989, similar results were found concerning the formality of the working capital policy—about 38 percent of the respondents indicated that they followed a formal policy. The results relating the type of working capital management policies firms follow differed, however. Fewer than 3 percent of the respondents indicated that their firms followed aggressive policies, 25 percent followed conservative policies, and more than 72 percent indicated that their policies depended on the situation or change from time to time.

More recently (1994), a variation of the same survey was sent to small firms (sales between $500,000 and $5 million) in Canada. The results, which probably are indicative of small firms in other developed countries, proved interesting. First, it was not surprising that 93 percent of the firms in the study indicated they do not have formal working capital policies. When asked which type of working capital policy they followed, nearly 29 percent of the respondents indicated that their policies were conservative, about 10 percent indicated that they followed aggressive policies, and more than 61 percent indicated that their polices changed from time to time or were situational.

To summarize, it appears that most firms do not have formal working capital policies. Further, although firms are more likely to have conservative working capital management policies than aggressive policies, most firms' policies change over time or are situational in nature. It is interesting to note that the results of the surveys also show that most firms review their working capital policies "whenever necessary," which suggests that firms do not conduct regular formal reviews. The general conclusion we can reach from the results of the studies is that short-term financial management is based more on "seat-of-the-pants" methods than sophisticated models. But as firms attempt to improve the efficiency of their operations, the formality and rigor of firms' working capital policies should increase.

Source: Nabil T. Khoury, Keith V. Smith, and Peter I. MacKay, "Comparing Working Capital Practices in Canada, the United States, and Australia: A Note," *Canadian Journal of Administrative Sciences*, March 1999, 53–57.

Returning to Figure 13–3, note that we used the term *relatively* in the title for Panel b because there can be different *degrees* of aggressiveness. For example, the dashed line in Panel b could have been drawn *below* the line designating fixed assets, indicating that all of the permanent current assets and part of the fixed assets were financed with short-term credit; this would be a highly aggressive, extremely nonconservative position, and the firm would be very much subject to dangers from rising interest rates as well as to loan renewal problems. However, short-term debt often is cheaper than long-term debt, and some firms are willing to sacrifice safety for the chance of higher profits.

Conservative Approach   As shown in Panel c of Figure 13–3, the dashed line could also be drawn *above* the line designating permanent current assets, indicating that permanent capital is being used to finance all permanent asset requirements and also to meet some or all of the seasonal, temporary demands. In the situation depicted in our graph, the firm uses a small amount of short-term, nonspontaneous credit to meet its peak requirements, but it also meets a part of its seasonal needs by "storing liquidity" in the form of marketable securities during the off-season. The humps above the dashed line represent short-term financing; the troughs below the dashed line represent short-term security holdings. Panel c represents the **conservative approach,** which is a very safe current asset financing policy that generally is not as profitable as the other two approaches.

CONSERVATIVE APPROACH
A policy where all of the fixed assets, all of the permanent current assets, and some of the temporary current assets of a firm are financed with long-term capital.

Self-Test Questions

What two key issues does working capital policy involve?

What is meant by the term *current asset investment policy?*

What is meant by the term *current asset financing policy?*

What are three alternative current asset financing policies? Is one best?

What distinguishes *permanent current assets* from *temporary current assets?*

Which of the three alternative current asset financing policies uses the most short-term debt?

Advantages and Disadvantages of Short-Term Financing

The three possible financing policies described in the previous section were distinguished by the relative amounts of short-term debt used under each policy. The aggressive policy calls for the greatest use of short-term debt, whereas the conservative policy requires the least and maturity matching falls in between. Although using short-term credit generally is riskier than using long-term credit, short-term credit does have some significant advantages. The pros and cons of short-term financing are considered in this section.

Speed

A short-term loan can be obtained much faster than long-term credit. Lenders will insist on a more thorough financial examination before extending long-term credit, and the loan agreement will have to be spelled out in considerable detail because much can happen during the life of a 10- or 20-year loan. Therefore, if funds are needed in a hurry, a firm generally looks to short-term sources.

Flexibility

If the needs for funds are seasonal or cyclical, a firm might not want to commit itself to long-term debt for three reasons. First, the costs associated with issuing long-term debt are significantly greater than the costs of getting short-term credit. Second, some longterm debts carry expensive penalties for prepayments (paying prior to maturity). Accordingly, if a firm thinks its need for funds will diminish in the near future, it should choose short-term debt for the flexibility it provides. Third, long-term loan agreements always contain provisions, or covenants, that constrain the firm's future actions. Short-term credit agreements generally are much less onerous in this regard.

Cost of Long-Term versus Short-Term Debt

The yield curve normally is upward sloping, indicating that interest rates generally are lower on short-term than on long-term debt. Thus, under normal conditions, interest costs at the time the funds are obtained will be lower if the firm borrows on a short-term rather than on a long-term basis.

Risk of Long-Term versus Short-Term Debt

Even though short-term debt is often less expensive than long-term debt, short-term credit subjects the firm to more risk than does long-term financing. This occurs for two reasons: (1) If a firm borrows on a long-term basis, its interest costs will be relatively stable, perhaps even fixed, over time, but if it uses short-term credit, its interest expense will fluctuate widely, at times reaching quite high levels. For example, in 1994, because the Federal Reserve increased rates six times during the year, short-term rates increased by more than 3 percent, which created a significant burden for many firms. (2) If a firm borrows heavily on a short-term basis, it could find itself unable to repay this debt, and it might be in such a weak financial position that the lender will not extend the loan; this too could force the firm into bankruptcy. K-mart found itself in this position not long ago.

Self-Test Questions

What are some advantages of short-term debt over long-term debt as a source of capital?

What are some disadvantages of short-term debt?

Multinational Working Capital Management

For the most part, the techniques used to manage short-term assets and liabilities in multinational corporations are the same as those used in purely domestic corporations. But multinational corporations face a far more complex task because they operate in many different business cultures, political environments, economic conditions, and so forth. In Chapter 1, we described six factors that complicate managerial finance in general in the international business arena: (1) different currency denominations, (2) differences in economic and legal environments, (3) language differences, (4) cultural differences, (5) governmental role, and (6) political risk. Difficulties with each of these factors are more acute when managing working capital internationally because decisions made in the short run can have significant consequences on the long-run survival of the firm and such decisions are more difficult to adjust or reverse when rules and regulations and business cultures differ significantly from one business setting to another.

The results of one study provide some indication of how working capital policies of U.S. firms and European firms differ.[7] First, the average cash conversion cycle of European firms (about 263 days) was more than twice the average cash conversion cycle of U.S. firms (about 116 days). A possible explanation for this disparity is that European firms had much higher growth rates than their U.S. counterparts. Second, it appears from the results of the study that U.S. firms follow much more conservative working capital policies than European firms. The average current ratio and the average quick ratio proved to be significantly greater for U.S. firms than for European firms, which suggests that corporations in the United States use significantly more long-term financing alternatives than corporations in Europe (remember that when the current ratio equals 1.0, current assets equal current liabilities). Although a more in-depth study is needed to determine why U.S. firms seem to follow more conservative working capital policies than European firms, one possible explanation might be found in the differences that are apparent in the banking systems in Europe and in the United States. In Chapter 2 we mentioned that U.S. financial institutions generally are at a competitive disadvantage in the global arena because they are subject to more restrictions and regulations than banking organizations in other countries. Foreign banks generally can branch with little or no restrictions and are allowed, in many cases, to own corporations to which they also lend funds. For these reasons, European banks often have close relationships with their debtor corporations; thus, they tend be more willing to provide short-term, risky debt than we observe in U.S. banking organizations.

In the next chapter, we discuss some of the techniques used by U.S. firms to manage short-term assets and then we give some indication of how the factors just mentioned affect the methods used by multinational firms.

Self-Test Question

Which of the factors mentioned in this section do you think has the greatest impact on how working capital methods differ among countries?

Summary

In this chapter, we examined the relationship among working capital accounts, working capital policy, and alternative ways of financing current assets. The key concepts covered are listed here:

■ **Working capital** refers to current assets, and net **working capital** is defined as current assets minus current liabilities. **Working capital policy** refers to decisions relating to the level of current assets and the way they are financed.

■ Decisions affecting one **working capital** account will have an impact on other working capital accounts.

■ Once the firm's operations have stabilized so that the inflows and the outflows into working capital accounts are the same, the **account balance** can be **computed** using the following equation:

$$\text{Account balance} = \left(\begin{array}{c} \text{Amount of} \\ \text{daily activity} \end{array} \right) \times \left(\begin{array}{c} \text{Average life} \\ \text{of the account} \end{array} \right)$$

---

[7]Chun-Hao Chang, Krishnan Dandapani, and Arun J. Prakish, "Current Assets Policies of European Corporations: A Critical Examination," *Management International Review*, Special Issue 1995/2, 105–117.

- The **inventory conversion period** is the average length of time required to convert raw materials into finished goods and then to sell them.
- The **receivables collection period** is the average length of time required to convert the firm's receivables into cash, and it is equal to the days sales outstanding (DSO).
- The **payables deferral period** is the average length of time between the purchase of raw materials and labor and when payment for them is made.
- The **cash conversion cycle** is the length of time between paying for purchases and receiving cash from the sale of finished goods. The cash conversion cycle is calculated as follows:

$$\begin{pmatrix} \text{Cash} \\ \text{conversion} \\ \text{cycle} \end{pmatrix} = \begin{pmatrix} \text{Inventory} \\ \text{conversion} \\ \text{period} \end{pmatrix} + \begin{pmatrix} \text{Receivables} \\ \text{collection} \\ \text{period} \end{pmatrix} - \begin{pmatrix} \text{Payables} \\ \text{deferral} \\ \text{period} \end{pmatrix}$$

- Under a **relaxed current asset investment policy,** a firm holds relatively large amounts of each type of current asset. Under a **restricted current asset investment policy,** the firm holds minimal amounts of these items.
- **Permanent current assets** are those current assets that the firm holds even during slack times, whereas **temporary current assets** are the additional current assets that are needed during seasonal or cyclical peaks. The methods used to finance permanent and temporary current assets constitute the firm's **current asset financing policy.**
- A **moderate approach** to current asset financing involves **matching,** to the extent possible, the maturities of assets and liabilities so that temporary current assets are financed with short-term, spontaneous debt and permanent current assets and fixed assets are financed with long-term debt or equity plus nonspontaneous debt. Under an **aggressive approach,** some permanent current assets and perhaps even some fixed assets are financed with short-term debt. A **conservative approach** would be to use long-term capital to finance all permanent assets and some of the temporary current assets.
- The advantages of short-term credit are (1) the **speed** with which short-term loans can be arranged, (2) increased **flexibility,** and (3) the fact that short-term **interest rates** are generally **lower** than long-term rates. The principal disadvantage of short-term credit is the **extra risk** that the borrower must bear because (1) the lender can demand payment on short notice and (2) the cost of the loan will increase if interest rates rise.
- **Multinational firms** face a more complex task when managing working capital because business cultures, political environments, currencies, and so forth, differ among countries.

Questions

13-1 How does the seasonal nature of a firm's sales influence its decision regarding the amount of short-term credit to use in its financial structure?

13-2 Assuming the firm's sales volume remained constant, would you expect it to have a higher cash balance during a tight-money period or during an easy-money period? Why?

13-3 Describe the relationships between accounts payable, inventories, accounts receivable, and the cash account by tracing the impact on these accounts of a product manufactured and sold by a company. Start with the purchase of raw materials, and conclude with the collection for the sale of the product.

13–4 Describe the cash conversion cycle. How can a financial manager use knowledge of the cash conversion cycle to better manage the working capital of a firm?

13–5 What are the advantages of matching the maturities of assets and liabilities? What are the disadvantages?

13–6 From the standpoint of the borrower, is long-term or short-term credit riskier? Explain. Would it ever make sense to borrow on a short-term basis if short-term rates were above long-term rates?

13–7 If long-term credit exposes a borrower to less risk, why would people or firms ever borrow on a short-term basis?

Self-Test Problems

(Solutions appear in Appendix B)

key terms **ST-1** Define each of the following terms:

    a. Working capital; net working capital; working capital policy

    b. Permanent current assets; temporary current assets

    c. Cash conversion cycle; inventory conversion period; receivables collection period; payables deferral period

    d. Relaxed current asset investment policy; restricted current asset investment policy; moderate current asset investment policy

    e. Moderate, or maturity matching, current asset financing policy; aggressive current asset financing policy; conservative current asset financing policy

current asset financing **ST-2** Vanderheiden Press Inc. and the Herrenhouse Publishing Company had the following balance sheets as of December 31, 2005 ($ thousands):

	VANDERHEIDEN PRESS	HERRENHOUSE PUBLISHING
Current assets	$100,000	$ 80,000
Fixed assets (net)	100,000	120,000
Total assets	$200,000	$200,000
Current liabilities	$ 20,000	$ 80,000
Long-term debt	80,000	20,000
Common stock	50,000	50,000
Retained earnings	50,000	50,000
Total liabilities and equity	$200,000	$200,000

Earnings before interest and taxes (EBIT) for both firms are $30 million, and the marginal tax rate is 40 percent.

    a. What is the return on equity for each firm if the interest rate on current liabilities is 10 percent and the rate on long-term debt is 13 percent?

    b. Assume that the short-term rate rises to 20 percent. While the rate on new long-term debt rises to 16 percent, the rate on existing long-term debt remains unchanged. What would be the return on equity for Vanderheiden Press and Herrenhouse Publishing under these conditions?

    c. Which company is in a riskier position? Why?

working capital policy **ST-3** The Calgary Company is attempting to establish a current assets policy. Fixed assets are $600,000, and the firm plans to maintain a 50 percent debt-to-assets ratio. The interest rate is 10 percent on all debt. The three alternative current asset policies under consideration are to carry current assets that total 40, 50, and 60 percent of projected sales. The company expects to earn 15 percent before interest and taxes on sales of $3 million. Calgary's marginal tax rate is 40 percent. What is the expected return on equity under each alternative?

Problems

13-1 Go back to the GCP illustration at the beginning of the chapter. Assume the collection and payment patterns of both GCP and its customers do not change.

  a. Construct the balance sheet for GCP at the close of business on Day 31. Remember, the employees' salaries will have been paid at the *beginning* of the day for the *previous* 15 days they have worked, so accrued wages will include only one day of salaries (Day 31).

  b. How long will it take GCP to pay off the bank loan it took out on Day 16 if the *daily cash profits* are used to repay the loan (ignore any interest costs).

13-2 Look back in the chapter to Table 13–1, which showed the balance sheets for Unilate Textiles on three different dates. Unilate's sales fluctuate during the year due to the seasonal nature of its business; however, we can calculate its sales on an average day as total sales divided by 360, recognizing that daily sales will be much higher than this value during its peak selling season and much lower during its slack time. Unilate's projected sales for 2006 are $1,650 million, so daily sales are expected to average $4.583 million. The projected cost of goods sold for 2006 is $1,353 million, so daily credit costs associated with production are expected to average $3.76 million. Assume all sales and all purchases are made on credit.

  a. Calculate Unilate's inventory conversion period as of September 30, 2006, and December 31, 2006.

  b. Calculate Unilate's receivables collection period as of September 30, 2006, and December 31, 2006.

  c. Calculate the payables deferral period as of September 30, 2006, and December 31, 2006.

  d. Using the values calculated in parts a through c, calculate the length of Unilate's cash conversion cycle on the two balance sheet dates.

  e. In part d, you should have found that the cash conversion cycle was longer on September 30 than on December 31. Why did these results occur?

  f. Can you think of any reason why the cash conversion cycle of a firm with seasonal sales might be different during the slack selling season than during the peak selling season?

13-3 Verbrugge Corporation is a leading U.S. producer of automobile batteries. Verbrugge turns out 1,500 batteries a day at a cost of $6 per battery for materials and labor. It takes the firm 22 days to convert raw materials into a battery. Verbrugge allows its customers 40 days in which to pay for the batteries, and the firm generally pays its suppliers in 30 days.

  a. What is the length of Verbrugge's cash conversion cycle?

  b. If Verbrugge always produces and sells 1,500 batteries a day, what amount of working capital must it finance?

  c. By what amount could Verbrugge reduce its working capital financing needs if it was able to stretch its payables deferral period to 35 days?

  d. Verbrugge's management is trying to analyze the effect of a proposed new production process on the working capital investment. The new production process would allow Verbrugge to decrease its inventory conversion period to 20 days and to increase its daily production to 1,800 batteries. However, the new process would cause the cost of materials and labor to increase to $7. Assuming the change does not affect the receivables collection period (40 days) or the payables deferral period (30 days), what will be the length of the cash conversion cycle and the working capital financing requirement if the new production process is implemented?

working capital policy   **13–4** The Hawley Corporation is attempting to determine the optimal level of current assets for the coming year. Management expects sales to increase to approximately $2 million as a result of an asset expansion presently being undertaken. Fixed assets total $1 million, and the firm finances 60 percent of its total assets with debt and the rest with equity (common stock). Hawley's interest cost currently is 8 percent on both short-term and longer-term debt (which the firm uses in its permanent structure). Three alternatives regarding the projected current asset level are available to the firm: (1) a tight policy requiring current assets of only 45 percent of projected sales, (2) a moderate policy of 50 percent of sales in current assets, and (3) a relaxed policy requiring current assets of 60 percent of sales. The firm expects to generate earnings before interest and taxes (EBIT) at a rate of 12 percent on total sales.

   a. What is the expected return on equity under each current asset level? (Assume a 40 percent marginal tax rate.)
   b. In this problem we have assumed that the level of expected sales is independent of current asset policy. Is this a valid assumption?
   c. How would the overall riskiness of the firm vary under each policy?

Exam-Type Problems

The problems included in this section are set up in such a way that they could be used as multiple-choice exam problems.

cash conversion cycle   **13–5** The Saliford Corporation has an inventory conversion period of 60 days, a receivables collection period of 36 days, and a payables deferral period of 24 days.
   a. What is the length of the firm's cash conversion cycle?
   b. If Saliford's annual sales are $3,960,000 and all sales are on credit, what is the average balance in accounts receivable?
   c. How many times per year does Saliford turn over its inventory?
   d. What would happen to Saliford's cash conversion cycle if, on average, inventories could be turned over eight times a year?

cash conversion cycle and asset turnover   **13–6** The Flamingo Corporation is trying to determine the effect of its inventory turnover ratio and days sales outstanding (DSO) on its cash flow cycle. Flamingo's 2005 sales (all on credit) were $180,000, and it earned a net profit of 5 percent, or $9,000. The cost of goods sold equals 85 percent of sales. Inventory was turned over eight times during the year, and the DSO, or average collection period, was 36 days. The firm had fixed assets totaling $40,000. Flamingo's payables deferral period is 30 days.
   a. Calculate Flamingo's cash conversion cycle.
   b. Assuming Flamingo holds negligible amounts of cash and marketable securities, calculate its total assets turnover and return on assets (ROA).
   c. Suppose Flamingo's managers believe that the inventory turnover can be raised to 10×. What would Flamingo's cash conversion cycle, total assets turnover, and ROA have been if the inventory turnover had been 10× for 2005?

Integrative Problem

working capital policy and
working capital financing

13-7 Daniel Barnes, financial manager of New York Fuels (NYF), a heating oil distributor, is concerned about the company's working capital policy, and he is considering three alternative policies: (1) *a restrictive (lean and mean* or *tight)* policy, which calls for reducing receivables by $100,000 and inventories by $200,000; (2) *a relaxed (loose* or *fat cat)* policy, which calls for increasing receivables by $100,000 and inventories by $200,000; and (3) a *moderate* policy, which would mean leaving receivables and inventories at their current levels. NYF's 2005 financial statements and key ratios, plus some industry average data, are given in Table IP13-1.

The cost of long-term debt is 12 percent versus only 8 percent for short-term notes payable. Variable costs as a percentage of sales (74 percent) would not be affected by the firm's working capital policy, but fixed costs would be affected due to the storage, handling, and insurance costs associated with inventory. Here are the assumed fixed costs under the three policies:

POLICY	FIXED COSTS
Restrictive	$ 950,000
Moderate	1,000,000
Relaxed	1,100,000

Sales also would be affected by the policy chosen: Carrying larger inventories and using easier credit terms would stimulate sales, so sales would be highest under the relaxed policy and lowest under the restrictive policy. Also, these effects would vary depending on the strength of the economy. Here are the relationships Barnes assumes would have held in 2005:

	SALES ($ MILLIONS)		
STATE OF THE ECONOMY	RESTRICTIVE	MODERATE	RELAXED
Weak	$4.3	$4.5	$5.0
Average	4.7	5.0	5.5
Strong	5.3	5.5	6.0

Barnes considers the 2005 economy to be average.

You have been asked to answer the following questions to help determine NYF's optimal working capital policy:

a. How does NYF's current working capital policy as reflected in its financial statements compare with an average firm's policy? Do the differences suggest that NYF's policy is better or worse than that of the average firm in its industry?

b. Based on the 2005 ratios and financial statements, what were the company's inventory conversion period, its receivables collection period, and, assuming a 29-day payables deferral period, its cash conversion cycle? How could the cash conversion cycle concept be used to help improve the firm's working capital management?

c. Barnes has asked you to recast the 2005 financial statements, and calculate some key ratios, assuming an average economy and a restrictive (tight) working capital policy, and to check some calculations he has made. Construct these statements, and then calculate the new current ratio and return on equity (ROE). Assume that common stock is used to make the balance

TABLE IP13–1	Financial Statements and Other Data on NYF ($ thousands)

A. 2005 Balance Sheet

Cash and securities	$ 100	Accounts payable and accruals	$ 300
Accounts receivable	600	Notes payable (8%)	500
Inventories	1,000	Total current liabilities	$ 800
Total current assets	$1,700	Long-term debt (12%)	600
Net fixed assets	800	Common equity	1,100
Total assets	$2,500	Total liabilities and equity	$2,500

B. 2005 Income Statement

Sales	$ 5,000.00
Less: Variable costs	(3,700.00)
Fixed costs	(1,000.00)
EBIT	$ 300.00
Interest	(112.00)
Earnings before taxes	$ 188.00
Taxes (40%)	(75.20)
Net income	$ 112.80
Dividends (30% payout)	$ 33.84
Addition to retained earnings	$ 78.96

C. Key Ratios

	NYF	INDUSTRY
Profit margin	2.3%	3.0%
Return on equity	10.3%	15.0%
Days sales outstanding	43.2	30.0
Accounts receivable turnover	8.3×	12.0×
Inventory turnover	3.7	5.4
Fixed assets turnover	6.3	6.0
Total assets turnover	2.0	2.5
Debt/assets	56.0%	50.0%
Times interest earned	2.7×	4.8×
Current ratio	2.1	2.3
Quick ratio	0.9	1.3

sheet balance, but do not get into financing feedbacks. (*Hint:* You need to change sales, fixed costs, receivables, inventories, and common equity, plus items affected by those changes, and then calculate new ratios.)

d. Barnes himself has actually analyzed the situation for each of the policies under each economic scenario; the ROEs he has calculated are shown in Table IP13–2. What are the implications of these data for the working capital policy decision?

TABLE IP13-2	ROEs under the Alternative Policies		

	WORKING CAPITAL POLICY		
STATE OF THE ECONOMY	TIGHT	MODERATE	EASY
Weak	4.2%	3.2%	3.8%
Average	12.0	10.3	9.3
Strong	23.7	17.3	14.9
Average	13.3%	10.3%	9.3%

e. The working capital policy discussion thus far has focused entirely on current assets and not at all on the current asset financing policy. How would you bring financing policy into the analysis?

Computer-Related Problem

Work the problem in this section only if you are using the computer problem diskette.

working capital financing   **13-8** Three companies—Aggressive, Moderate, and Conservative—have different working capital management policies as implied by their names. For example, Aggressive employs only minimal current assets, and it finances almost entirely with current liabilities plus equity. This restricted approach has a dual effect. It keeps total assets low, which tends to increase return on assets; but because of stock-outs and credit rejections, total sales are reduced, and because inventory is ordered more frequently and in smaller quantities, variable costs are increased. Condensed balance sheets for the three companies follow:

	AGGRESSIVE	MODERATE	CONSERVATIVE
Current assets	$225,000	$300,000	$450,000
Fixed assets	300,000	300,000	300,000
Total assets	$525,000	$600,000	$750,000
Current liabilities (cost = 12%)	$300,000	$150,000	$ 75,000
Long-term debt (cost = 10%)	0	150,000	300,000
Total debt	$300,000	$300,000	$375,000
Equity	225,000	300,000	375,000
Total liabilities and equity	$525,000	$600,000	$750,000
Current ratio	0.75	2.0	6.0

The cost of goods sold functions for the three firms are as follows:

	COST OF GOODS SOLD	=	FIXED COSTS	+	VARIABLE COSTS
Aggressive:	Cost of goods sold	=	$300,000	+	0.70(Sales)
Moderate:	Cost of goods sold	=	$405,000	+	0.65(Sales)
Conservative:	Cost of goods sold	=	$577,500	+	0.60(Sales)

Because of the working capital differences, sales for the three firms under different economic conditions are expected to vary as follows:

	AGGRESSIVE	MODERATE	CONSERVATIVE
Strong economy	$1,800,000	$1,875,000	$1,950,000
Average economy	1,350,000	1,500,000	1,725,000
Weak economy	1,050,000	1,200,000	1,575,000

a. Construct income statements for each company for strong, average, and weak economies using the following format:

> Sales
> Less: Cost of goods sold
> Earnings before interest and taxes (EBIT)
> Less: Interest expense
> Earnings before taxes (EBT)
> Less: Taxes (at 40%)
> Net income (NI)

b. Compare the returns on equity for the companies. Which company is best in a strong economy? In an average economy? In a weak economy?

c. Suppose that, with sales at the average-economy level, short-term interest rates rose to 20 percent. How would this affect the three firms?

d. Suppose that because of production slowdowns caused by inventory shortages, the aggressive company's variable cost ratio rose to 80 percent. What would happen to its ROE? Assume a short-term interest rate of 12 percent.

e. What considerations for the management of working capital are indicated by this problem?

GET REAL with Thomson ONE

13–9 Office Depot, Inc. [ODP] and Staples, Inc. [SPLS] both sell office products, supplies, and services. Using the liquidity ratios and asset management ratios, in addition to the firms' financial statements, discuss the following questions:

a. Compare the firm's liquidity positions. [*Hint:* Click on Financials/Fundamental Ratios/Thomson Ratios for each firm]

b. Evaluate each firm with regard to the management of its current assets and current liabilities. [*Hint:* Click on Financials/Financial Statements and Financials/Fundamental Ratios for each firm]

c. Based on your analysis in questions a and b, which firm has the most aggressive working capital policy? How would you characterize each firm's working capital policy? Explain your answer.

Chapter 14

Managing Short-Term Assets

Cash is the oil that lubricates the wheels of business. Without adequate oil, machines grind to a halt, and a business with inadequate cash will do likewise. However, carrying cash is expensive because cash is a nonearning asset; a firm that holds cash beyond its minimum requirements lowers its earnings potential.

Cash management is a professional, highly refined activity. The following excerpt from SunTrust Bank's Web site (http://www.suntrust.com) describes its cash management services.

> Effective cash management is absolutely essential to your profitability. That's why SunTrust cash management professionals work with you and your Relationship Manager to develop customized solutions for your company.
>
> Through your banker, they keep you informed on the latest technology, industry trends and new ways to optimize your treasury management processes.
>
> - Online Treasury Manager puts the Internet to work for your business. It lets you perform balance reporting, check inquiries, ACH initiation, repetitive wire transfers and much more directly from your office's Internet-connected workstations.
> - Wholesale Lockbox collects, processes and deposits corporate-to-corporate payments, reducing your mail, processing and check-clearing times—and improving your access to deposited funds.
> - Lockbox Image Browser lets you retrieve and display digitized images of lockbox checks via your PC.

> - Cash Services processes and verifies large cash and coin deposits. It also facilitates currency orders in either a branch or high-security SunTrust vault facility.
> - Wire Transfer lets you use your PC or phone to quickly transfer funds from one bank to another.
> - Cash Concentration consolidates funds from multiple bank depository accounts to a master collection account on a periodic basis.
> - Direct Deposit Payroll Services frees your company from its most labor-intensive disbursement activity.
> - Controlled Payment is a tool for increasing your control over check payments. By enhancing controlled disbursement and positive pay, we've reengineered the payment process. We ensure that only your issued checks are paid, fraudulent activity is immediately identified and your account is reconciled daily.
> - Disbursement Image Services let you retrieve and display digitized check images of your disbursements using your PC. Access and store critical data instantly. Decrease handling costs and reengineer your disbursement workflow. Services include Online Check History, Online Disbursement Exceptions and CD-ROM Check Storage.
> - CD-ROM Services are a cost-effective alternative to storing paper checks or using microfilm. You can truncate the delivery of checks and retrieve paid check images for any disbursement account.

continues

- Zero Balance Accounts allow funds in multiple accounts to be maintained at zero by electronically transferring funds to or from a single master account.
- Account Reconcilement speedily reconciles your SunTrust depository or disbursement account transactions.
- Electronic Information Reporting allows you to initiate wire transfers, view summary and detailed balance information, place stop payment orders, request photocopies, and transmit data from a variety of SunTrust PC-based services.

For some companies, the arrangement offered by SunTrust makes good sense. However, firms sometimes go too far with their cash management systems. For example, the general practice in the securities brokerage business (until Merrill Lynch lost a major lawsuit and agreed to stop doing it) was to write checks to customers located east of the Mississippi on banks located on the West Coast, and vice versa. This slowed down payments on checks, deprived customers of the use of their money, and gave the brokerage firm use of billions of dollars of their customers' money for extended periods of time. According to the Securities and Exchange Commission, this practice, although it increased brokerage firms' profits by millions of dollars each year, was "inconsistent with a broker-dealer's obligation to deal fairly with its customers."

As you read this chapter, consider just how critical a firm's cash management practices really are, as well as how important it is to turn assets such as inventory and receivables into cash in a timely fashion. The lessons to be learned from this chapter apply to the cash management practices of individuals as well as to those of businesses. Maybe you will be able to take some of the ideas discussed here and apply them to your personal finances. ∎

As we discovered in the previous chapter, all else equal, the riskiness of the portfolio of assets held by a firm is based on the combination of short- and long-term investments (assets) the firm makes. The relative amount invested in short-term assets is a function of decisions that are made concerning the management of cash and marketable securities, accounts receivable, and inventories. Of these three assets, we generally consider cash and marketable securities to be least risky, or most *liquid*. But the degree of risk can vary for either accounts receivable or inventories, depending on the general characteristics of the firm's working capital policy. For example, we generally view receivables as relatively safe assets because they represent sales the firm expects to collect in the future. But a firm with an overly aggressive, or relaxed, credit policy might have many slow payers or bad-debt customers that make its receivables extremely risky, thus fairly *illiquid*.

In this chapter, we discuss working capital management policies with respect to the current (short-term) assets of the firm. As you read the chapter, keep in mind that, although short-term assets generally are safer than long-term assets, they earn a lower rate of return. Thus, all else equal, firms that hold greater amounts of short-term assets are considered less risky than firms that hold greater amounts of long-term assets; at the same time, firms with more short-term assets earn lower returns than firms with more long-term assets. Consequently, financial managers are faced with a dilemma of whether to forgo higher returns to attain lower risk or to forgo lower risk to achieve higher returns. In general, however, we will see that some amount of short-term assets is required to maintain normal operations.

Cash Management

In Chapter 5 we discovered that value, which we want to maximize, is based on cash flows. Thus, managing cash flows is an extremely important task for a financial manager. Part of this task is determining how much cash a firm should have on hand at any time to ensure normal business operations continue uninterrupted. In this section, we discuss some of the factors that affect the amount of cash firms hold, and we describe some of the cash management techniques currently used by businesses.

For the purposes of our discussion, the term *cash* refers to the funds a firm holds that can be used for immediate disbursement. This includes the amount a firm holds in its checking account as well as the amount of actual coin and currency it holds. Cash is a *nonearning, or idle, asset* that is required to pay bills. When possible, cash should be "put to work" by investing in assets that have positive expected returns. Thus, the goal of the cash manager is to minimize the amount of cash the firm must hold for use in conducting its normal business activities, yet, at the same time, to have sufficient cash to (1) pay suppliers, (2) maintain the firm's credit rating, and (3) meet unexpected cash needs.

Firms generally hold cash for the following reasons:

1. Cash balances are necessary in business operations because payments must be made in cash, and receipts are deposited in a cash account. Cash balances associated with routine payments and collections are known as **transactions balances.**
2. A bank often requires a firm to maintain a **compensating balance** on deposit to help offset the costs of providing services such as check clearing and cash management advice.
3. Because cash inflows and cash outflows are somewhat unpredictable, firms generally hold some cash in reserve for random, unforeseen fluctuations in cash flows. These *safety stocks* are called **precautionary balances**—the less predictable the firm's cash flows, the larger such balances should be. However, if the firm has easy access to borrowed funds—that is, if it can borrow on short notice (e.g., via a line of credit at the bank)—its need for precautionary balances is reduced.
4. Sometimes cash balances are held to enable the firm to take advantage of bargain purchases that might arise. These funds are called **speculative balances.** As with precautionary balances, though, firms that have easy access to borrowed funds are likely to rely on their ability to borrow quickly rather than to rely on cash balances for speculative purposes.

Although the cash accounts of most firms can be thought of as consisting of transactions, compensating, precautionary, and speculative balances, we cannot calculate the amount needed for each purpose, sum them, and produce a total desired cash balance because the same money often serves more than one purpose. For instance, precautionary and speculative balances can also be used to satisfy compensating balance requirements. Firms do, however, consider all four factors when establishing their target cash positions.

In addition to these four motives, a firm maintains cash balances to preserve its credit rating by keeping its liquidity position in line with those of other firms in the industry. A strong credit rating enables the firm both to purchase goods from suppliers on favorable terms and to maintain an ample line of credit with its bank.

TRANSACTIONS BALANCE
A cash balance necessary for day-to-day operations; the balance associated with routine payments and collections.

COMPENSATING BALANCE
A minimum checking account balance that a firm must maintain with a bank to help offset the costs of services such as check clearing and cash management advice.

PRECAUTIONARY BALANCES
A cash balance held in reserve for unforeseen fluctuations in cash flows.

SPECULATIVE BALANCE
A cash balance that is held to enable the firm to take advantage of any bargain purchases that might arise.

Self-Test Questions

Why is cash management important?

What are the motives for holding cash?

The Cash Budget

Perhaps the most critical ingredient to proper cash management is the ability to estimate the cash flows of the firm so the firm can make plans to borrow when cash is deficient or to invest when cash is in excess of what is needed. Without a doubt, financial managers will agree that the most important tool for managing cash is the cash budget (forecast). *The cash budget helps management plan investment and borrowing strategies,* and it also is used to provide feedback and control to improve the efficiency of cash management in the future.

The firm estimates its general needs for cash as a part of its overall budgeting, or forecasting, process. First, the firm forecasts its operating activities such as expenses and revenues for the period in question. Then, the financing and investment activities necessary to attain that level of operations must be forecasted. Such forecasts entail the construction of *pro forma* financial statements, which we discussed in Chapter 12. The information provided from the *pro forma* balance sheet and income statement is combined with projections about the delay in collecting accounts receivable, the delay in paying suppliers and employees, tax payment dates, dividend and interest payment dates, and so on. All of this information is summarized in the **cash budget,** which shows the firm's projected cash inflows and cash outflows over some specified period. Generally, firms use a monthly cash budget forecasted over the next year plus a more detailed daily or weekly cash budget for the coming month. The monthly cash budgets are used for planning purposes and the daily or weekly budgets are used for actual cash control.

CASH BUDGET

A schedule showing cash receipts, cash disbursements, and cash balances for a firm over a specified time period.

The cash budget provides much more detailed information concerning a firm's future cash flows than do the forecasted financial statements. Remember when we developed Unilate Textiles' 2006 forecasted financial statements in Chapter 12, we projected net sales to be $1,650 million and net income to be $61 million. Using the forecasted financial statements contained in Chapter 12, we find that the net cash flow (in millions of dollars) generated from operations in 2006 is expected to be as follows:

Net Income	$ 61.0
Add: Noncash expenses (depreciation)	55.0
Gross cash flow from operations	$116.0
Adjustments to gross cash flow:	
Increase in accounts receivable	(18.0)
Increase in inventories	(27.0)
Increase in accounts payable	3.0
Increase in accruals	6.0
Total adjustments to gross cash flow	($ 36.0)
Net cash flow from operations	$ 80.0

In 2006, Unilate expects to generate $80 million cash inflow through normal production and sales operations. Much of this $80 million will be used to satisfy the financing and investment activities of the firm. Even after these activities are considered,

Unilate's cash account is projected to increase by $1.5 million in 2006. Does this mean that Unilate will not have to worry about cash shortages during 2006? To answer this question, we must construct Unilate's cash budget for 2006.

To simplify the construction of Unilate's cash budget, we will only consider the last half of 2006 (July through December). Further, we will not list every cash flow that is expected to occur, but instead will focus on the operating flows. Remember that Unilate's sales peak is in September and October. All sales are made on credit with terms that allow a 2 percent cash discount for payments made within 10 days, and, if the discount is not taken, the full amount is due in 30 days. However, like most companies, Unilate finds that some of its customers delay payment for more than 90 days. Experience has shown that payment on 20 percent of Unilate's *dollar* sales is made during the month in which the sale is made—these are the discount sales. On 70 percent of sales, payment is made during the month immediately following the month of sale, and payment is made on 10 percent of sales two months or more after the initial sales. To simplify the cash budget, however, we will assume the last 10 percent of sales is collected in the second month following the sale.

The costs to Unilate of cotton, wool, and other cloth-related materials average 60 percent of the sales prices of the finished products. These purchases generally are made one month before the firm expects to sell the finished products. In 2006, Unilate's suppliers have agreed to allow payment for materials to be delayed for 30 days after the purchase. Accordingly, if July sales are forecasted at $150 million, then purchases during June will amount to $90 million, and this amount actually will be paid in July.

Other cash expenses such as wages and rent also are built into the cash budget, and Unilate must make estimated tax payments of $16 million on September 15 and $10 million on December 15, while a $20 million payment for a new plant must be made in October. Assuming that Unilate's **target, or minimum, cash balance** is $5 million and that it projects $8 million to be on hand on July 1, 2006, what will the firm's monthly cash surpluses or shortfalls be for the period from July through December?

Unilate's 2006 cash budget for July through December is presented in Table 14–1. The approach used to construct this cash budget generally is termed the **disbursements and receipts method** (also referred to as **scheduling**) because the cash disbursements and cash receipts are estimated to determine the net cash flow expected to be generated each month. The format used in Table 14–1 is quite simple—it is much like balancing a checkbook. The cash receipts are lumped into one category and the cash disbursements are lumped into another category to determine the net effect monthly cash flows have on the cash position of the firm. More detailed formats can be used, depending on how the firm prefers to present the cash budget information.

The first line of Table 14–1 gives the sales forecast for the period from May through December. These estimates are necessary to determine collections for July through December. Similarly, the second line of the table gives the credit purchases expected each month based on the sales forecasts so the monthly payments for credit purchases can be determined.

The *Cash Receipts* category shows cash collections based on credit sales originating in three months—in the current month and in the previous two months. Take a look at the collections expected in July. Remember that Unilate expects 20 percent of the dollar sales to be collected in the month of the sales, and thus to be affected by the 2 percent cash discount offered; 70 percent of the dollar sales will be collected one month after the sales; and the remaining 10 percent of the dollar sales will be collected two months after the sales (it is assumed there are no bad debts). So in July,

TARGET (MINIMUM) CASH BALANCE
The minimum cash balance a firm desires to maintain in order to conduct business.

DISBURSEMENTS AND RECEIPTS METHOD (SCHEDULING)
The net cash flow is determined by estimating the cash disbursements and the cash receipts expected to be generated each period.

TABLE 14–1 Unilate Textiles: 2006 Cash Budget ($ millions)

	MAY	JUNE	JULY	AUG.	SEPT.	OCT.	NOV.	DEC.
Credit sales	100.0	125.0	150.0	200.0	250.0	180.0	130.0	100.0
Credit purchases = 60% of next month's sales		90.0	120.0	150.0	108.0	78.0	60.0	
Cash Receipts								
Collections from this month's sales = 0.2 × 0.98 × (current sales)			29.4	39.2	49.0	35.3	25.5	19.6
Collections from previous month's sales = 0.7 × (previous month's sales)			87.5	105.0	140.0	175.0	126.0	91.0
Collect from sales two months previously = 0.1 × (sales 2 months earlier)			10.0	12.5	15.0	20.0	25.0	18.0
Total cash receipts			$126.9	$156.7	$204.0	$230.3	$176.5	$128.6
Cash Disbursements								
Payments made for credit purchases (1-month lag)			90.0	120.0	150.0	108.0	78.0	60.0
Wages and salaries (22% of monthly sales)			33.0	44.0	55.0	39.6	28.6	22.0
Rent			9.0	9.0	9.0	9.0	9.0	9.0
Other expenses			7.0	8.0	11.0	10.0	5.0	4.0
Taxes					16.0			10.0
Payment for plant construction						20.0		
Total cash disbursements			$139.0	$181.0	$241.0	$186.6	$120.6	$105.0
Net cash flow (Receipts – Disbursements)			($ 12.1)	($ 24.3)	($ 37.0)	$ 43.7	$ 55.9	$ 23.6
Beginning cash balance			$ 8.0	($ 4.1)	($ 28.4)	($ 65.4)	($ 21.7)	$ 34.2
Ending cash balance			(4.1)	(28.4)	(65.4)	(21.7)	34.2	57.8
Target (minimum) cash balance			5.0	5.0	5.0	5.0	5.0	5.0
Surplus (shortfall) cash			($ 9.1)	($ 33.4)	($ 70.4)	($ 26.7)	$ 29.2	$ 52.8

$29.4 million = 0.20 × (1 – 0.02) × $150 million collections will result from sales in July; $87.5 million = 0.70 × $125 million will be collected from sales that occurred in June; and, $10.0 million = 0.10 × $100 million will be collected from sales that occurred in May. Thus, the total collections received in July represent 20 percent of July sales (minus the discount) plus 70 percent of June sales plus 10 percent of May sales, or $126.9 million in total.

The *Cash Disbursements* category shows payments for raw materials, wages, rent, and so on. Raw materials are purchased on credit one month before the finished goods are expected to be sold, but payments for the materials are not made until one month later—that is the month of the expected sales. The cost of the raw materials is expected to be 60 percent of sales. July sales are forecasted at $150 million, so Unilate will purchase $90 million of materials in June and pay for these purchases in July. Similarly, Unilate will purchase $120 million of materials in July to meet August's forecasted sales of $200 million. Additional monthly cash disbursements include employees' salaries, which equal 22 percent of monthly sales; rent, which remains constant; and other operating expenses, which vary with respect to production levels. Cash disbursements that are not expected to occur monthly include taxes (September and December) and payment for the construction of additional facilities (October).

The line labeled *Net cash flow* shows whether Unilate's operations are expected to generate positive or negative net cash flows each month. But this is only the beginning of the story. We need to examine the firm's cash position based on the cash balance existing at the beginning of the month and based on the *Target (minimum) cash balance* desired by Unilate. The bottom line provides information as to whether Unilate can expect a monthly cash surplus that can be invested temporarily in marketable securities or a monthly cash shortfall that must be financed with external, nonspontaneous sources of funds.

At the beginning of July, Unilate will have cash equal to $8 million. During July, Unilate is expected to generate a negative $12.1 million net cash flow; thus, July cash disbursements are expected to exceed cash receipts by $12.1 million (that is, deficit spending is expected). Because Unilate only has $8 million cash to begin July, the cash balance at the end of July is expected to be overdrawn by $4.1 if the firm doesn't find additional funding. To make matters worse, Unilate has a target cash balance equal to $5 million, so without any additional financing its cash balance at the end of July is expected to be $9.1 million short of its target. As a result, Unilate must make arrangements to borrow $9.1 million in July to bring the cash account balance up to the target balance of $5 million. Assuming that this amount is indeed borrowed, loans outstanding will total $9.1 million at the end of July. (We assume that Unilate did not have any bank loans outstanding on July 1 because its beginning cash balance exceeded the target balance.)

The cash surplus or required loan balance (shortfall) is given on the bottom line of the cash budget. A positive value indicates a cash surplus, whereas a negative value (in parentheses) indicates a loan requirement. Note that the *bottom-line* surplus cash or loan requirement shown is a *cumulative amount*. Thus, Unilate must borrow $9.1 million in July; the firm has a cash shortfall during August of $24.3 million as reported on the Net cash flow line, so its total loan requirement at the end of August is $33.4 million = $9.1 million + 24.3 million, as reported on the bottom line for August. Unilate's arrangement with the bank permits it to increase its outstanding loans on a daily basis, up to a prearranged maximum, just as you could increase the amount you owe on a credit card. Unilate will use any surplus funds it generates to pay off its loans, and because the loan can be paid down at any time, on a daily basis, the firm never will have both a cash surplus and an outstanding loan balance. If Unilate actually does have a cash surplus, these funds will be invested in short-term, temporary investments.

This same procedure is used in the following months. Sales will peak in September, accompanied by increased payments for purchases, wages, and other items. Receipts from sales will also go up, but the firm will still be left with a $37 million net cash outflow during the month. The total loan requirement at the end of September will hit a peak of $70.4 million, the cumulative cash deficits plus the target cash balance.[1] This amount is also equal to the $33.4 million needed at the end of August plus the $37 million cash deficit for September.

Sales, purchases, and payments for past purchases will fall sharply in October, but collections will be the highest of any month because they will reflect the high September sales. As a result, Unilate will generate a healthy $43.7 million net cash gain during October. This net gain can be used to pay off borrowings, so loans outstanding will decline by $43.7 million, to $26.7 million.

Unilate will generate an even larger cash surplus in November, which will permit the firm to pay off all of its loans. In fact, the company is expected to have $29.2 million in surplus cash by the month's end, and another cash surplus in December will swell the excess cash to $52.8 million. With such a large amount of unneeded funds, Unilate's treasurer certainly will want to invest in interest-bearing securities or to put the funds to use in some other way. Various types of investments into which Unilate might put its excess funds are discussed later in the chapter.

Before concluding our discussion of the cash budget, we should make some additional points:

1. For simplicity, our illustrative budget for Unilate omitted many important cash flows that are anticipated for 2006, such as dividends, proceeds from stock and bond sales, and investment in additional fixed assets. Some of these are projected to occur in the first half of the year, but those that are projected for the July through December period could easily be added to the example. The final cash budget should contain all projected cash inflows and outflows.

2. Our cash budget example does not reflect interest on loans or income from investing surplus cash. This refinement could easily be added.

3. If cash inflows and outflows are not uniform during the month, we could seriously understate the firm's peak financing requirements. The data in Table 14–1 show the situation expected on the last day of each month, but on any given day during the month it could be quite different. For example, if all payments had to be made on the fifth of each month, but collections came in uniformly throughout the month, the firm would need to borrow much larger amounts than those shown in the table. In this case, we would have to prepare a cash budget identifying requirements on a daily basis.

4. Because depreciation is a noncash charge, it does not appear on the cash budget other than through its effect on taxable income, hence on taxes paid.

---

[1]This figure is calculated easily as follows:

$$\text{CASH}_{\text{Sept}} = \begin{pmatrix} \text{Beginning cash} \\ \text{balance in July} \end{pmatrix} + \text{Net CF}_{\text{July}} + \text{Net CF}_{\text{Aug}} + \text{Net CF}_{\text{Sept}} - \begin{pmatrix} \text{Target cash} \\ \text{balance} \end{pmatrix}$$

$$= \$8.0 + (-\$12.1) + (-\$24.3) + (-\$37.0) - \$5.0 = \$70.4$$

5. Because the cash budget represents a forecast, all the values in the table are *expected* values. If actual sales, purchases, and so on are different from the forecasted levels, then the projected cash deficits and surpluses will also differ.

6. Computerized spreadsheet programs are particularly well suited for constructing and analyzing cash budgets, especially with respect to the sensitivity of cash flows to changes in sales levels, collection periods, and the like. We could change any assumption—for example, the projected monthly sales or the time that customers pay—and the cash budget would automatically and instantly be recalculated. This would show us exactly how the firm's borrowing requirements would change if various other things changed. Also, with a computer model, it is easy to add features like interest paid on loans, interest earned on marketable securities, and so on.

7. Finally, we should note that the target cash balance will probably be adjusted over time, rising and falling with seasonal patterns and with long-term changes in the scale of the firm's operations. Thus, Unilate probably will plan to maintain larger cash balances during August and September than at other times, and, as the company grows, so will its required cash balance. Also, the firm might even set the target cash balance at zero. This could be done if it carried a portfolio of marketable securities that could be sold to replenish the cash account or if it had an arrangement with its bank that permitted it to borrow any funds needed on a daily basis. In that event, the target cash balance would simply be equal to zero. Note, though, that most firms would find it difficult to operate with a zero-balance bank account, just as you would, and the costs of such an operation would in most instances offset the costs associated with maintaining a positive cash balance. Therefore, most firms do set positive target cash balances.

Self-Test Questions

What is the purpose of a cash budget?

Suppose a firm's cash flows do not occur uniformly throughout the month. What impact might this have on the accuracy of the forecasted borrowing requirements?

How is uncertainty handled in a cash budget?

Is depreciation reflected in a cash budget? Explain.

Cash Management Techniques

Most cash management activities are performed jointly by the firm and its primary bank, but the financial manager ultimately is responsible for the effectiveness of the cash management program. Effective cash management encompasses proper management of both the cash inflows and the cash outflows of a firm, which entails consideration of the factors discussed next.

Cash Flow Synchronization

It would be ideal if the receipt of a cash payment from a customer occurred at exactly the same time a bill needs to be paid; that portion paid out would never be idle and any excess could be invested quickly to reduce the time it is idle. Recognizing this point, companies try to arrange it so that cash inflows and cash outflows are matched

SYNCHRONIZED CASH FLOWS
A situation in which cash inflows coincide with cash outflows, thereby permitting a firm to hold low transactions balances.

as well as possible—customers are billed so their billing cycles coordinate with when the firm pays its own bills. Having **synchronized cash flows** enables a firm to reduce its cash balances, decrease its bank loans, lower interest expenses, and boost profits. *The more predictable the timing of the cash flows, the greater the synchronization that can be attained.* Utilities and credit card companies generally have a high degree of cash flow synchronization.

Check-Clearing Process

CHECK CLEARING
The process of converting a check that has been written and mailed into cash in the payee's (receiver's) account.

When a customer writes and mails a check, this does *not* mean that the funds are immediately available to the receiving firm. Most of us have been told by someone that "the check is in the mail," and we also have deposited a check in an account and then been told that we cannot write checks against the deposit until the **check-clearing process** has been completed. Our bank must first make sure that the deposited check is good and then receive funds itself from the customer's bank before it will give us cash.

As shown on the left side of Figure 14–1, quite a bit of time could be required for a firm to process incoming checks and obtain the use of the money. A check must first be delivered through the mail and then be cleared through the banking system before the money can be put to use. Checks received from customers in distant cities are especially subject to delays because of mail time and also because more parties are involved in the check-clearing process. For example, assume that you receive a check and deposit it in your bank. Your bank must send the check to the bank on which it was drawn. Only when this latter bank transfers funds to your bank are the funds available for you to use. If a check is deposited in the same bank on which it was drawn, that bank merely transfers funds by bookkeeping entries from one of its depositors to another. But most deposited checks are drawn from outside banks, so the verification, or clearing process, generally is handled by a check-clearing system, termed a *clearinghouse*, set up by the Federal Reserve or a network of banks in a particular region. The length of time required for checks to clear is a function of the distance between the payer's (check writer's) bank and the payee's (depositor's) bank. In the case of private clearinghouses, it can range from one to three days. The maximum time required for checks to clear through the Federal Reserve System is two days, but mail delays can slow down things on each end of the Fed's involvement in the process.

In an effort to facilitate the check clearing process, the Check Clearing for the 21st Century Act was signed in October 2003 and became effective one year later. The act, termed Check 21, encourages more efficient processing of payments by allowing financial institutions to convert paper checks into substitutes that can be cleared electronically. The *substitute checks* allow financial intermediaries to clear payments more quickly because they are the electronic and legal equivalents of, and contain the same information as, the original paper checks. As Congress and the Federal Reserve implement more electronically friendly clearing mechanisms, the time it takes financial institutions to clear checks or other payment systems should decrease.

Using Float

FLOAT
The difference between the balance shown in a firm's (or individual's) checkbook and the balance on the bank's records.

Float is defined as the difference between the balance shown in a firm's (or individual's) checkbook and the balance on the bank's records. Suppose a firm writes, on average, checks in the amount of $5,000 each day, and it normally takes six days from the time the check is mailed until it is cleared and deducted from the firm's bank account. This

FIGURE 14–1	Diagram of the Check-Clearing Process

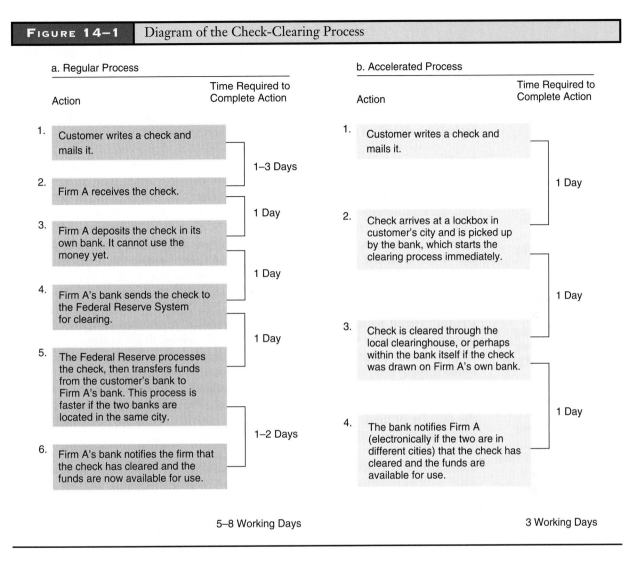

a. Regular Process		b. Accelerated Process	
Action	Time Required to Complete Action	Action	Time Required to Complete Action

a. Regular Process

1. Customer writes a check and mails it.

1–3 Days

2. Firm A receives the check.

1 Day

3. Firm A deposits the check in its own bank. It cannot use the money yet.

1 Day

4. Firm A's bank sends the check to the Federal Reserve System for clearing.

1 Day

5. The Federal Reserve processes the check, then transfers funds from the customer's bank to Firm A's bank. This process is faster if the two banks are located in the same city.

1–2 Days

6. Firm A's bank notifies the firm that the check has cleared and the funds are now available for use.

5–8 Working Days

b. Accelerated Process

1. Customer writes a check and mails it.

1 Day

2. Check arrives at a lockbox in customer's city and is picked up by the bank, which starts the clearing process immediately.

1 Day

3. Check is cleared through the local clearinghouse, or perhaps within the bank itself if the check was drawn on Firm A's own bank.

1 Day

4. The bank notifies Firm A (electronically if the two are in different cities) that the check has cleared and the funds are available for use.

3 Working Days

DISBURSEMENT FLOAT
The value of the checks that have been written and *disbursed* but have not yet fully cleared through the banking system and thus have not been deducted from the account on which they were written.

will cause the firm's own checkbook to show a balance equal to $30,000 = $5,000 × 6 days smaller than the balance on the bank's records; this difference is called **disbursement float.** Now suppose the firm also receives checks in the amount of $5,000 daily, but it loses four days while they are being deposited and cleared. This will result in $20,000 of **collections float.** In total, the firm's **net float**—the difference between $30,000 positive disbursement float and the $20,000 negative collections float—will be $10,000, which means the balance the bank shows in the firm's checking account is $10,000 greater than the balance the firm shows in its own checkbook.

Delays that cause float arise because it takes time for checks (1) to travel through the mail (*mail delay*), (2) to be processed by the receiving firm (*processing delay*), and (3) to clear through the banking system (*clearing, or availability, delay*). Basically, the size of a firm's net float is a function of its ability to speed up collections on checks received and to slow down collections on checks written. Efficient firms go to great lengths to speed up the processing of incoming checks, thus putting the funds to work faster, and they try to delay their own payments as long as possible.

Acceleration of Receipts

COLLECTIONS FLOAT
The amount of checks that have been *received* and deposited but have not yet been made available to the account in which they were deposited.

NET FLOAT
The difference between disbursement float and collections float; the difference between the balance shown in the checkbook and the balance shown on the bank's books.

LOCKBOX ARRANGEMENT
A technique used to reduce float by having payments sent to post office boxes located near the customers.

PREAUTHORIZED DEBIT SYSTEM
A system that allows a customer's bank to periodically transfer funds from its account to a selling firm's bank account for the payment of bills.

CONCENTRATION BANKING
A technique used to move funds from many bank accounts to a more central cash pool to more effectively manage cash.

A firm cannot use customers' payments until they are received *and* converted into a spendable form, such as cash or an increase in a checking account balance. Thus, it would benefit the firm to accelerate the collection of customers' payments and conversion of those payments into cash.

Although some of the delays that cause float cannot be controlled directly, the techniques described next are used to manage collections:

Lockboxes A **lockbox arrangement** requires customers to send their payments to a post office box located in the area near where they live rather than directly to the firm. The firm arranges for a local bank to collect the checks from the post office box, perhaps several times a day, and to immediately deposit them into the company's checking account. By having lockboxes close to the customers, a firm can reduce float because, at the very least, (1) the mail delay is less than if the payment had to travel farther and (2) checks are cleared faster because the banks the checks are written on are in the same Federal Reserve district; thus, fewer parties are involved in the clearing process.

Preauthorized Debits If a firm receives regular, repetitious payments from its customers, it might want to establish a **preauthorized debit system** (sometimes called *preauthorized payments*). With this arrangement, the collecting firm and its customer (paying firm) enter into an agreement whereby the paying firm's bank periodically transfers funds from the paying firm's account to the collecting firm's account, even if that account is located at another bank. Preauthorized debiting accelerates the transfer of funds because mail and check-clearing delays are completely eliminated, and the processing delay is reduced substantially.

Concentration Banking **Concentration banking** is a cash management arrangement used to mobilize funds from decentralized receiving locations, whether they are lockboxes or decentralized company locations, into one or more central cash pools. The cash manager then uses these pools for short-term investing or reallocation among the firm's various bank accounts. By pooling its cash, the firm is able to take maximum advantage of economies of scale in cash management and investment. Often commissions are less per dollar on large investments, and there are instances where investments of larger dollar amounts earn higher returns than smaller investments.

Disbursement Control

Accelerating collections represents one side of cash management, and controlling funds outflows, or disbursements, represents the other side. Three methods commonly used to control disbursements include the following:

Payables Concentration Centralizing the processing of payables permits the financial manager to evaluate the payments coming due for the entire firm and to schedule the availability of funds to meet these needs on a company-wide basis, and it also permits more efficient monitoring of payables and the effects of float. A disadvantage to a centralized disbursement system is that regional offices might not be able to make prompt payment for services rendered, which can create ill will and raise the company's operating costs. But as firms become more electronically

Cash Management—Today versus Yesterday

A recent study completed by Charles E. Maxwell, Lawrence J. Gitman, and Stephanie A. M. Smith (MGS) provides information about cash management techniques used by U.S. and foreign firms.[a] It also gives us an indication as to how the cash management policies followed by U.S. firms today differ from those policies followed by U.S. firms more than two decades ago. To generate their results, MGS surveyed financial executives of large firms in the United States, the European Union, the Pacific Rim, and Mexico. We present the findings of the study here to give you an idea of the cash management policies firms actually follow.

The financial executives were asked how many banks they used for borrowing, checking, and collections services. The responses show that U.S. and foreign firms use about the same number of banks to borrow needed funds—14 or 15 banks. The number of banks has not changed dramatically for U.S. firms since 1979 when the average was nearly 16. On the other hand, the number of banks used by U.S. firms for checking and collections services has decreased considerably since 1979. Large U.S. firms use about nine banks for checking services and about 44 banks for collections services today compared with nearly 32 and 77, respectively, in 1979. The number of banks used by foreign firms for the same services is significantly less than for U.S. firms—about 10 and 11 banks, respectively. This is not a surprising result, given that there are many more individual banks in the United States than other countries.

The differences in banking systems in the United States and in foreign countries might account for the fact that MGS found that foreign firms are much less likely to use lockbox arrangements or concentration banking systems for managing (speed up) cash inflows. Because most foreign countries have few, if any, restrictions on branch banking, there is little need to have concentration banking systems to coordinate cash flows among various accounts at different banks; instead, large firms in other countries can maintain accounts in considerably fewer banks (perhaps just one) than can large firms in the United States. The results also show that although a majority of both U.S. firms and foreign firms centralize their payables systems, U.S. firms are much more likely to use zero-balance accounts and remote (controlled) disbursement accounts to manage (slow) cash outflows.

When asked how they generally pay for the banking services used by their firms, around 80 percent of the financial executives in both U.S. firms and foreign firms indicated they pay for services used directly rather than maintaining compensating balances at their banks. In 1979 the results were reversed—nearly 85 percent of the firms maintained balances at banks to compensate for services used. Thus, in general, firms have reduced the idle balances kept at banks, *perhaps* to take greater advantage of the returns generated by marketable securities.

Finally, the financial executives were asked how their firms managed float, both for collections and for disbursements. The results show that U.S. firms are much more concerned about check-clearing, or availability, float, and mail float than their foreign counterparts both for collections and for disbursements. The explanation for this finding is twofold: (1) we (especially consumers) rely on checks as our means of payment more in the United States than in other countries, and (2) it is a goal of the Federal Reserve to eliminate float that results from check clearing.

[a]Charles E. Maxwell, Lawrence J. Gitman, and Stephanie A. M. Smith, "Working Capital Management and Financial-Service Consumption Preferences of U.S. and Foreign Firms: A Comparison of 1979 and 1996 Preferences," *Financial Education and Practice*, Fall/Winter 1998, 46–52.

proficient, the centralization of disbursements can be coordinated more effectively and such situations should be reduced substantially.

ZERO-BALANCE ACCOUNT (ZBA)

A special checking account used for disbursements that has a balance equal to zero when there is no disbursement activity.

Zero-Balance Accounts A **zero-balance account (ZBA)** is a special disbursement account that has a balance equal to zero when there is no disbursement activity. Typically, a firm establishes several ZBAs in its concentration bank and funds them from a master account. As checks are presented to a ZBA for payment, funds are automatically transferred from the master account.

CONTROLLED DISBURSEMENT ACCOUNTS (CDA)

Checking accounts in which funds are not deposited until checks are presented for payment, usually on a daily basis.

Controlled Disbursement Accounts Whereas ZBAs typically are established at concentration banks, **controlled disbursement accounts (CDA)** can be set up at any bank. Such accounts are not funded until the day's checks are presented against the account. The firm relies on the bank that maintains the CDA to provide information in the morning (before 11 A.M. New York time) concerning the total amount of the checks that will be presented for payment that day. This permits the financial manager (1) to transfer funds to the controlled disbursement account to cover the checks presented for payment or (2) to invest excess cash at midday, when money market trading is at a peak.

Self-Test Questions

What is float? How do firms use float to increase cash management efficiency?

What are some methods firms can use to accelerate receipts?

What are some techniques for controlling disbursements?

Marketable Securities

Realistically, the management of cash and marketable securities cannot be separated. Management of one implies management of the other because the amount of marketable securities held by a firm depends on its short-term cash needs.

Rationale for Holding Marketable Securities

MARKETABLE SECURITIES

Securities that can be sold on short notice without loss of principal or original investment.

Marketable securities, or *near-cash* assets, are extremely liquid, short-term investments that permit the firm to earn positive returns on cash that is not needed to pay bills immediately but will be needed sometime in the near term, perhaps in a few days, weeks, or months. Although such investments typically provide much lower yields than other assets, nearly every large firm has them. The two basic reasons for owning marketable securities are as follows:

1. Marketable securities serve as a *substitute for cash balances*. Firms often hold portfolios of marketable securities, liquidating part of the portfolio to increase the cash account when cash is needed because the *marketable securities offer a place to temporarily put cash balances to work earning a positive return*. In such situations, the marketable securities could be used as a substitute for transactions balances, for precautionary balances, for speculative balances, or for all three.
2. Marketable securities are also used as a *temporary investment* (a) to finance seasonal or cyclical operations and (b) to amass funds to meet financial require-

ments in the near future. For example, if the firm has a conservative financing policy as we discussed in Chapter 13, then its long-term capital will exceed its permanent assets, and marketable securities will be held when inventories and receivables are low.

Characteristics of Marketable Securities

A wide variety of securities is available to firms that choose to hold marketable securities. But the characteristics generally associated with marketable securities are as follows:

1. **Maturity.** Firms hold marketable securities in order to *temporarily* invest cash that otherwise would be idle in the short run. Therefore, marketable securities are short-term investments; often they are held only for a few days or weeks. If the cash budget indicates the funds are not needed in the foreseeable future, then longer-term investments, which generally earn higher returns, should be used.

2. **Risk.** Recall that in Chapter 2 we developed this equation for determining the nominal interest rate:

$$k_{Nom} = k^* + IP + DRP + LP + MRP$$

Here k^* is the real risk-free rate, IP is a premium for expected inflation, DRP is the default risk premium, LP is the liquidity (or marketability) risk premium, and MRP is the maturity (or interest rate) risk premium. Also, remember from Chapter 2 that the risk-free rate, k_{RF}, is equal to $k^* + IP$, and a U.S. Treasury bill comes closest to the risk-free rate. For other instruments considered appropriate as marketable securities, the default and liquidity risks are small, and the interest-rate risk is negligible. These risks are small because marketable securities mature in the short term, and the short run is less uncertain than the long run. Also, recall from Chapter 5 prices of long-term investments, such as bonds, are much more sensitive to changes in interest rates than are prices of short-term investments. In general, then, the total risk associated with a portfolio of marketable securities (short term) is less than the total risk associated with a portfolio of long-term investments.

3. **Liquidity.** We generally judge an asset's *marketability* according to how quickly and easily it can be bought and sold in the financial markets. If an asset can be sold easily on short notice at a fair price that is not substantially lower than its original purchase price, it is said to be *liquid*. Because marketable securities are held as a substitute for cash and as a temporary investment, such instruments should be very liquid.

4. **Return (Yield).** Because the marketable securities portfolio generally is composed of highly liquid, short-term securities with low risks, the returns associated with such investments are relatively low when compared to other investments. But given the purpose of the marketable securities portfolio, treasurers should not sacrifice safety for higher rates of return.

Types of Marketable Securities

Table 14–2 lists the major types of securities available for investment, with an indication of how widely the yields on these securities have fluctuated during the past few decades. Depending on how long they will be held, the financial manager decides upon a suitable set of securities, and a suitable maturity pattern, to hold as *near-cash*

TABLE 14–2	Securities Available for Investment of Surplus Cash

SECURITY	TYPICAL MATURITY AT TIME OF ISSUE	APPROXIMATE YIELDS		
		1/29/77	1/29/82	1/29/04
I. Suitable as Near-Cash Reserves				
U.S. Treasury bills	91 days to 1 year	4.8%	13.4%	1.0%
Commercial Paper	Up to 270 days	4.9	14.5	1.1
Negotiable CDS	Up to 1 year	4.9	14.6	1.2
Money market mutual funds	Instant liquidity	5.0	14.3	0.7
Eurodollar time deposits	Up to 1 year	5.2	15.1	1.1
II. Not Suitable as Near-Cash Reserves				
U.S. Treasury notes	1 to 10 years	6.9	14.5	2.6
U.S. Treasury bonds	10 to 30 years	7.6	14.4	4.8
Corporate bonds (AAA)[a]	Up to 40 years	8.2	16.1	5.1
Municipal bonds (AAA)[a,b]	Up to 30 years	5.2	12.2	4.3
Preferred stocks (AAA)[a,b]	Unlimited	7.5	13.1	6.4
Common stocks[c]	Unlimited	22.6	–4.8	30.6

NOTES:

[a]Rates shown for corporate and municipal bonds and for preferred stock are for longer maturities rated AAA. Lower rated, higher-risk securities have higher yields.

[b]Rates are lower on municipal bonds because the interest they pay is exempt from federal income taxes, and the rate on preferred stocks is low because 70 percent of the dividends paid on them is exempt from federal taxes for corporate owners, who own most preferred stock.

[c]The returns given for common stocks represent the average yield that would have been earned in the stock market during the previous 52-week period. Individual common stock returns vary considerably, even at one point in time.

reserves in the form of marketable securities. As noted in the table, long-term securities are not appropriate investments for marketable securities as we have described in this section. Safety, especially maintenance of principal, should be paramount when putting together a marketable securities portfolio.

Self-Test Questions

What are the characteristics of financial instruments that are considered appropriate marketable securities?

What are some securities commonly held as marketable securities? Why are such securities held by firms?

Credit Management

If you ask financial managers whether they would prefer to sell their products for cash or for credit, you would expect them to respond by saying something like this: "*If sales levels are not affected*, cash sales are preferred because payment is certain and immediate and because the costs of granting credit and maintaining accounts receivable would be eliminated." *Ideally*, then, firms would prefer to sell for cash only. So why do firms sell for credit? The primary reason most firms offer credit sales is because their competitors offer credit. Consider what you would do if you had the opportunity to purchase the same product for the same price from two different firms, but one firm required cash payment at the time of the purchase whereas the other firm allowed you to pay for the product one month after the purchase without any additional cost. From which firm would you purchase? Like you, firms prefer to delay their payments, especially if there are no additional costs associated with the delay.

Effective credit management is extremely important because too much credit is costly in terms of the investment in, and maintenance of, accounts receivables, whereas too little credit could result in the loss of profitable sales. Carrying receivables has both direct and indirect costs, but it also has an important benefit—granting credit should increase profits. Thus, to maximize shareholders' wealth, a financial manager needs to understand how to effectively manage the firm's credit activities.

In this section, we discuss (1) the factors considered important when determining the appropriate credit policy for a firm, (2) procedures for monitoring the credit policy to ensure it is being administered properly, and (3) how to evaluate whether credit policy changes will be beneficial to the firm.

CREDIT POLICY
A set of decisions that includes a firm's credit standards, credit terms, methods used to collect credit accounts, and credit monitoring procedures.

CREDIT STANDARDS
Standards that indicate the minimum financial strength a customer must have to be granted credit.

TERMS OF CREDIT
The payment conditions offered to credit customers; the terms include the length of the credit period and any cash discounts offered.

CREDIT PERIOD
The length of time for which credit is granted; after that time, the credit account is considered delinquent.

Credit Policy

The major controllable variables that affect demand for a company's products are sales prices, product quality, advertising, and the firm's **credit policy.** The firm's credit policy, in turn, includes the factors we discuss next.

1. **Credit standards** refer to the strength and creditworthiness a customer must exhibit in order to qualify for credit. The firm's credit standards are applied to determine which customers qualify for the regular credit terms and how much credit each customer should receive. The major factors that are considered when setting credit standards relate to the likelihood that a given customer will pay slowly or perhaps even end up as a bad debt loss. Determining the credit quality, or creditworthiness, of a customer probably is the most difficult part of credit management. But credit evaluation is a well-established practice and a good credit manager can make reasonably accurate judgments of the probability of default exhibited by different classes of customers by examining a firm's current financial position and evaluating factors that might affect the financial position in the future.

2. **Terms of credit** are the conditions of the credit sale, especially with regard to the payment arrangements. Firms need to determine when the **credit period** begins, how long the customer has to pay for credit purchases before the account is considered delinquent, and whether a cash discount for early payment should be offered. An examination of the credit terms offered by firms in

CASH DISCOUNT
A reduction in the invoice price of goods offered by the seller to encourage early payment.

COLLECTION POLICY
The procedures followed by a firm to collect its accounts receivables.

the United States would show great variety across industries—credit terms range from cash before delivery (CBD) and cash on delivery (COD) to offering **cash discounts** for early payment. For example, a firm that offers terms of 2/10 net 30 gives its customers a 2 percent discount from the purchase price if the bill is paid on or before Day 10 of the billing cycle; otherwise the entire bill (the net amount) is due by Day 30. Due to the competitive nature of trade credit, most financial managers follow the norm of the industry in which they operate when setting credit terms.

3. **Collection policy** refers to the procedures the firm follows to collect its credit accounts. The firm needs to determine when and how notification of the credit sale will be conveyed to the buyer. The quicker a customer receives an invoice, the sooner the bill *can* be paid. In today's world, firms have turned more to the use of electronics to "send" invoices to customers. One of the most important collection policy decisions is how the past-due accounts should be handled. For example, notification might be sent to customers when a bill is 10 days past due; a more severe notice, followed by a telephone call, might be used if payment is not received within 30 days; and the account might be turned over to a collection agency after 90 days.

Receivables Monitoring

RECEIVABLES MONITORING
The process of evaluating the credit policy to determine if a shift in the customers' payment patterns occurs.

Once a firm sets its credit policy, it wants to operate within the policy's limits. Thus, it is important that a firm examine its receivables periodically to determine whether customers' payment patterns have changed such that credit operations are outside the credit policy limits. For instance, if the balance in receivables increases either because the amount of "bad," or uncollectible, sales increases or because the average time it takes to collect existing credit sales increases, the firm should consider making changes in its credit policy. **Receivables monitoring** refers to the process of evaluating the credit policy to determine if a shift in the customers' payment patterns has occurred.

Traditionally, firms have monitored accounts receivables by using methods that measure the amount of time credit remains outstanding. Two such methods are the *days sales outstanding (DSO)* and the *aging schedule:*

DAYS SALES OUTSTANDING (DSO)
The average length of time required to collect accounts receivable; also called the *average collection period.*

Days Sales Outstanding (DSO) **Days sales outstanding (DSO),** which is sometimes called the *average collection period*, represents the average time it takes to collect credit accounts. DSO is computed by dividing *annual* credit sales by *daily* credit sales. For example, in the previous chapter, we found the receivables collection period, or DSO, for Unilate was 43.2 days in 2005. The DSO of 43.2 days can be compared with the credit terms offered by Unilate. If Unilate's credit terms are 2/10 net 30, then we know there are customers that are delinquent when paying their accounts. In fact, if many customers are paying within 10 days to take advantage of the cash discount, the others would, on average, have to be taking much longer than 43.2 days. One way to check this possibility is to use an aging schedule as described next.

AGING SCHEDULE
A report showing how long accounts receivable have been outstanding; the report divides receivables into specified periods, which provides information about the proportion of receivables that is current and the proportion that is past due for given lengths of time.

Aging Schedule An **aging schedule** is a breakdown of a firm's receivables by age of account. Table 14–3 contains the December 31, 2005, aging schedule for Unilate Textiles. The standard format for aging schedules generally includes age categories broken down by month because banks and financial analysts usually want companies to report their receivables' ages in this form. However, more precision, thus better

TABLE 14–3	Unilate Textiles: Receivables Aging Schedule for 2005

AGE OF ACCOUNT (IN DAYS)	NET AMOUNT OUTSTANDING	FRACTION OF TOTAL RECEIVABLES	AVERAGE DAYS
0–30	$ 72,000	40%	18
31–60	90,000	50	55
61–90	10,800	6	77
More than 90	7,200	4	97
	$180,000	100%	

$$DSO = 0.40(18 \text{ days}) + 0.50(55 \text{ days}) + 0.06(77 \text{ days}) + 0.04(97 \text{ days})$$
$$= 43.2 \text{ days}$$

monitoring information, can be attained by using narrower age categories (for example, one or two weeks).

According to Unilate's aging schedule, only 40 percent of its credit sales were collected within the credit period of 30 days; thus, 60 percent of the credit sales collections were delinquent. Some of the payments were delinquent by only a few days, while others were delinquent by three to four times the 30-day credit period.

Management should constantly monitor the days sales outstanding and the aging schedule to detect trends, to see how the firm's collection experience compares with its credit terms, and to see how effectively the credit department is operating in comparison with other firms in the industry. If the DSO starts to lengthen or if the aging schedule begins to show an increasing percentage of past-due accounts, then the firm's credit policy might need to be tightened.

We must be careful when interpreting changes in DSO or the aging schedule, however, because if a firm experiences sharp seasonal variations, or if it is growing rapidly, then both measures could be distorted. For example, recall that Unilate's peak selling season is in the fall. Table 13–1 shows that forecasted receivables are expected to be high, at $251.5 million, at the end of September 2006, while receivables are expected to be much lower, at $198 million, at the end of December 2006. If sales are expected to be $1,650 million in 2006, Unilate's DSO will be $251.5/($1,650/360) = 54.9 days on September 30, but $198/($1,650/360) = 43.2 days on December 31, 2006. This decline in DSO would not indicate that Unilate had tightened its credit policy or more efficiently collected its receivables, only that its sales had fallen due to seasonal factors. Similar problems arise with the aging schedule when sales fluctuate widely. Therefore, *a change in either the DSO or the aging schedule should be taken as a signal to investigate further, but not necessarily as a sign that the firm's credit policy has weakened.* If a firm generally experiences widely fluctuating sales patterns, some type of modified aging schedule should be used to correctly account for these fluctuations.[2] Still, days sales outstanding and the aging schedule are useful tools for reviewing the credit department's performance.

---

[2]See Eugene F. Brigham and Phillip R. Daves, *Intermediate Financial Management*, 8th ed. (Cincinnati, OH: South-Western College Publishing, 2004), Chapter 20, for a more complete discussion of the problems with the DSO and aging schedule and how to correct for them.

Analyzing Proposed Changes in Credit Policy

The key question when deciding on a proposed credit policy change is this: How will the firm's value be affected? Unless the added benefits expected from a credit policy change exceed the added costs on a present value basis, the policy change should *not* be made.

To illustrate how we can evaluate whether a proposed change in a firm's credit policy is appropriate, let's examine what would happen if Unilate Textiles makes changes to reduce its average collection period. Assume that Unilate's financial manager has proposed that this task be accomplished in 2006 by (1) billing customers sooner, and exerting more pressure on delinquent customers to pay their bills on time, and (2) examining the accounts of existing credit customers and suspending the credit of customers who are considered "habitually delinquent." These actions will result in a direct increase in the costs associated with Unilate's credit policy. At the same time, even though Unilate has an extremely loyal customer base, it is expected that some sales will be lost to competitors as the result of some customers having their credit decreased or even eliminated. But because the credit policy changes will have little, if any, effect on the "good" credit customers, the financial manager does not expect there to be a change in the payments of those customers who currently take advantage of the cash discount. If the proposed credit policy changes are approved, the financial manager believes the average collection period, or DSO, for receivables can be reduced from 43.2 days to 35.6 days, which is more in line with the credit terms offered by Unilate (2/10 net 30) and is closer to the industry average of 32.1 days. Also, if the average collection period is reduced, the amount "carried" in accounts receivable is reduced, which means less funds are "tied up" in receivables.

Table 14–4 provides information relating to Unilate's existing credit policy and the financial manager's proposed changes. According to this information, if the company changes its credit policy, its sales will drop by $2 million per year, or by $5,556 per day. Note that only the amount paid by customers who do not take the cash discount will be affected by this decrease, because this group of customers includes the "habitually delinquent" payers, which is the category of customers the credit policy change is intended to affect. As a result, on a daily basis, the amount paid by the *nondiscount* customers will decrease by $5,556, from $3,681,333.3 to $3,675,777.8, if the proposed credit policy is adopted; but the amount paid by the discount customers will remain at $901,944 = ($324.7 million)/360.

To determine whether Unilate should adopt the financial manager's proposal, we need to evaluate the effect the proposed changes will have on the value of the firm. Thus, we must compare the net present values (NPVs) of the two credit policies. To complete the analysis, we make two simplifying assumptions: (1) sales occur evenly throughout the year; and (2) each production/selling cycle is constant such that cash inflows and cash outflows occur at the same point in time relative to the credit sale, no matter what time of the year is examined. These assumptions allow us to evaluate the cash inflows and cash outflows associated with the credit sales for one day to determine whether the proposed credit policy change should be made. Table 14–4 gives specific assumptions concerning the timing of the cash flows, and Figure 14–2 shows the results of the NPV analysis assuming Unilate's required rate of return is 10 percent (annually). According to these results, the NPV for the existing credit policy is $725,800 per day whereas the NPV for the proposed credit policy is $731,400 per day. If the company changes its credit policy, the change in the daily NPV shown in Section III of Figure 14–2 is $5,600. Given the assumptions we have stated here as well as the assumptions given in Table 14–4, we would expect that this

TABLE 14-4	Unilate Textiles: Existing and Proposed Credit Policies—Expected for 2006

	EXISTING POLICY	PROPOSED POLICY
I. General Credit Policy Information		
Credit terms	2/10 net 30	2/10 net 30
Days sales outstanding (DSO) for all customers[a]	43.2 days	35.6 days
DSO for customers who take cash discount (20%)	10.0 days	10.0 days
DSO for customers who forgo cash discount (80%)	51.5 days	42.0 days
II. Annual Credit Sales and Costs ($ millions)		
Gross credit sales	$1,656.6	$1,654.6
Net credit sales[b]	$1,650.0	$1,648.0
Amount paid by discount customers[c]	$ 324.7	$ 324.7
Amount paid by nondiscount customers[c]	$1,325.3	$1,323.3
Variable operating costs (82 percent of net sales)[d]	$1,353.0	$1,351.4
Bad debts	$ 0.0	$ 0.0
Credit evaluation and collection costs[d]	$ 16.0	$ 17.0
III. Daily Credit Sales and Costs ($ thousands)[e]		
Net sales	$4,583.3	$4,577.8
Amount paid by discount customers	$ 901.9	$ 901.9
Amount paid by nondiscount customers	$3,681.4	$3,675.8
Variable operating costs (82 percent of net sales)	$3,758.3	$3,753.9
Bad debts	$ 0.0	$ 0.0
Credit evaluation and collection costs	$ 44.4	$ 47.2

NOTES:

[a]With the existing policy, 20 percent of the customers take the cash discount and pay on Day 10 and the remaining customers (80 percent) pay on average on Day 51.5; thus the DSO for all customers is 43.2 days = 0.20(10 days) + 0.80(51.5 days).

[b]In previous chapters, we determined that Unilate's 2006 *net* forecasted sales is $1,650 million, which represents what the firm expects to collect from credit sales, net of cash discounts. The gross sales, which includes cash discounts, can be computed as follows:

$$\text{Net sales} = 0.80(\text{Gross sales}) + (0.20)(1 - 0.02)(\text{Gross sales})$$

$$= (\text{Gross sales})[0.80 + 0.20(0.98)] = \$1,650 \text{ million}$$

$$\text{Gross sales} = \frac{\$1,650 \text{ million}}{0.996} = \$1,656.6 \text{ million}$$

[c]Twenty percent of Unilate's customers pay on Day 10, taking advantage of the 2 percent cash discount. As a result, the amount paid by this group of customers is $324.7 million = 0.20 × (1.0 − 0.02) × $1,656.6 million. Customers who do not take the discount will pay the full invoice price, or a total of $1,325.3 = 0.80($1,656.6). Because customers who take the discount will not be affected by the credit policy changes that are aimed at delinquent customers, the amount paid by customers who take the discount will be the same under either credit policy—that is, $324.7 million. This means that the $2 million decrease in total sales associated with the proposed credit policy will reduce the amount paid by customers who do not take the discount from $1,325.3 million to $1,323.3 million.

[d]Variable cost of goods sold (CGS) are paid at the time of the credit sale. Fixed operating costs are not included in the analysis because the amount does not change if the credit policy is changed. Expenses related to credit sales (evaluation and collection costs) are also paid at the time of the credit sale. These assumptions are made to simplify the analysis.

[e]Daily figures are required to evaluate whether the proposal should be adopted. See Figure 14–2 for the actual analysis. For consistency, we use a 360-day year to compute the daily figures.

FIGURE 14–2	Unilate Textiles: NPV Analysis of Credit Policies ($ thousands)

I. Existing Credit Policy:

Cash Flow Time Line:

0   k = 10.0%/360 = 0.0278%   10   · · ·   51.5   Days

(3,758.3) = Operating costs   901.9 = Discount   3,681.4 = Nondiscount
(44.4) = Credit costs   customers'   customers'
(3,802.7)   payments   payments

$$NPV_{Existing} = (3,802.7) + \frac{901.9}{(1.000278)^{10}} + \frac{3,681.4}{(1.000278)^{51.5}} = 725.8$$

II. Proposed Credit Policy:

Cash Flow Time Line:

0   k = 10.0%/360 = 0.0278%   10   · · ·   42   Days

(3,753.9) = Operating costs   901.9 = Discount   3,675.8 = Nondiscount
(47.2) = Credit costs   customers'   customers'
(3,801.1)   payments   payments

$$NPV_{Existing} = (3,801.1) + \frac{901.9}{(1.000278)^{10}} + \frac{3,675.8}{(1.000278)^{42}} = 731.4$$

III. Impact on Firm's Value If Proposal Is Adopted

ΔNPV on a daily basis = $731.4 – $725.8 = $5.6

$$\Delta value = \frac{\$5.6}{0.000278} = \$20,143.9$$

---

change has a permanent, or continuing, effect on the firm. Thus, the $5,600 change represents a daily perpetuity, which, according to Section III of Figure 14–2, will increase the value of the firm by $20.1 million. Clearly, then, the proposed changes should be made.

The analysis in Table 14–4 provides Unilate's managers with a vehicle for considering the impact of credit policy changes on the firm's value. However, a great deal of judgment must be applied to the decision because both customers' and competitors' responses to credit policy changes are difficult to estimate. Nevertheless, this type of analysis is essential.

Self-Test Questions

What factors are included in credit policy decisions? Describe how each factor affects sales and profitability.

Define days sales outstanding (DSO). What can be learned from it? How is it affected by sales fluctuations?

What is an aging schedule? What can be learned from it? How is it affected by sales fluctuations?

Describe the procedure used to evaluate a change in credit policy.

Inventory Management

If it could, a firm would prefer to have no inventory at all because while products are in inventory they do not generate returns and they must be financed. However, most firms find it necessary to maintain inventory in some form because (1) demand cannot be predicted with certainty and (2) it takes time to transform a product into a form that is ready for sale. And while excessive inventories are costly to the firm, so are insufficient inventories because customers might purchase from competitors if products are not available when demanded, and future business could be lost.

Although inventory models are covered in depth in production management courses, it is important to understand the basics of inventory management because proper management requires coordination among the sales, purchasing, production, and finance departments. Lack of coordination among these departments, poor sales forecasts, or both, can lead to financial ruin. Therefore, in this section, we describe the concepts of inventory management.

Types of Inventory

An inventory item can be grouped into one of the following categories:

RAW MATERIALS
The inventories purchased from suppliers that ultimately will be transformed into finished goods.

1. **Raw materials** include new inventory items purchased from suppliers; it is the material a firm purchases to transform into finished products for sale. As long as the firm has an inventory of raw materials, delays in ordering and delivery from suppliers do not affect the production process.

WORK-IN-PROCESS
Inventory in various stages of completion; some work-in-process is at the very beginning of the production process while some is at the end of the process.

2. **Work-in-process** refers to inventory items that are at various stages of the production process. If a firm has work-in-process at every stage of the production process, then it will not have to completely shut down production if a problem arises at one of the earlier stages.

FINISHED GOODS
Inventories that have completed the production process and are ready for sale.

3. **Finished goods** inventory represents products that are ready for sale. Firms carry finished goods to ensure that orders can be filled when they are received. If there are no finished goods, the firm has to wait for the completion of the production process before inventory can be sold; thus, demand might not be satisfied when it arrives. When a customer arrives and there is no inventory to satisfy that demand, a **stockout** exists, and the firm might lose the demand to competitors, perhaps permanently.

STOCKOUT
Occurs when a firm runs out of inventory *and* customers arrive to purchase the product.

Optimal Inventory Level

The goal of inventory management is to provide the inventories required to sustain operations at the lowest possible cost. Thus, the first step in determining the optimal inventory level is to identify the costs involved in purchasing and maintaining inventory, and then we need to determine at what point those costs are minimized.

Inventory Costs   We generally classify inventory costs into three categories: those associated with carrying inventory, those associated with ordering and receiving inventory, and those associated with running short of inventory (stockouts). First, let's look at the two costs that are most directly observable—carrying costs and ordering costs.

CARRYING COSTS
The costs associated with having inventory, which include storage costs, insurance, cost of tying up funds, depreciation costs, and so on; these costs generally increase in proportion to the average amount of inventory held.

1. **Carrying costs** include any expenses associated with having inventory, such as rent paid for the warehouse where inventory is stored and insurance on the inventory, and they generally increase in direct proportion to the average amount of inventory carried.
2. **Ordering costs** are those expenses associated with placing and receiving an order for new inventory, which include the costs of generating memos, fax transmissions, and so forth. For the most part, the costs associated with each order are fixed regardless of the order size.[3]

ORDERING COSTS
The costs of placing an order; the cost of *each* order generally is fixed regardless of the average size of the inventory.

If we assume that the firm knows how much total inventory it needs and sales are distributed evenly during each period, then we can combine the total carrying costs (TCC) and the total ordering costs (TOC) to find total inventory costs (TIC) as follows:

$$
\begin{aligned}
\text{Total inventory costs (TIC)} &= \text{Total carrying costs} + \text{Total ordering costs} \\[2mm]
&= \left(\begin{array}{c}\text{Carrying cost} \\ \text{per unit}\end{array}\right) \times \left(\begin{array}{c}\text{Average units} \\ \text{in inventory}\end{array}\right) + \left(\begin{array}{c}\text{Cost per} \\ \text{order}\end{array}\right) \times \left(\begin{array}{c}\text{Number} \\ \text{of orders}\end{array}\right) \\[2mm]
&= (C \times PP) \times \left(\frac{Q}{2}\right) + O \times \left(\frac{T}{Q}\right)
\end{aligned}
$$

14–1

The variables in the equation are defined as follows:

C = Carrying costs as a percent (stated as a decimal) of the purchase price of each inventory item.
PP = Purchase price, or cost, per unit.
Q = Number of units purchased with each order.
T = Total demand, or number of units sold, per period.
O = Fixed costs per order.

According to Equation 14–1, the average investment in inventory depends on how frequently orders are placed and the size of each order. If we order every day, average inventory will be much smaller than if we order once a year and inventory carrying costs will be low, but the number of orders will be large and inventory ordering

---

[3]In reality, both carrying and ordering costs can have variable and fixed cost elements, at least over certain ranges of average inventory. For example, security and utilities charges probably are fixed in the short run over a wide range of inventory levels. Similarly, labor costs in receiving inventory could be tied to the quantity received and hence could be variable. To simplify matters, we treat all carrying costs as variable and all ordering costs as fixed.

FIGURE 14-3 Determination of the Optimal Order Quantity

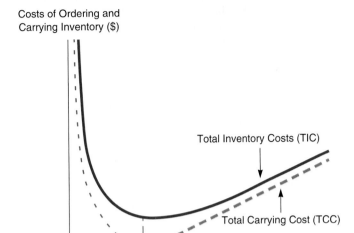

ECONOMIC (OPTIMUM) ORDERING QUANTITY (EOQ)
The optimal quantity that should be ordered; it is this quantity that will minimize the *total inventory costs.*

costs will be high. We can reduce ordering costs by ordering greater amounts less often, but then average inventory, thus the total carrying cost, will be high. This trade-off between carrying costs and ordering costs is shown in Figure 14–3. Note from the figure that there is a point where the total inventory cost (TIC) is *minimized*; this is called the **economic (optimum) ordering quantity (EOQ).**

The Economic Ordering Quantity (EOQ) Model The EOQ is determined by using calculus to find the point where the slope of the TIC curve in Figure 14–3 is perfectly horizontal; thus it equals zero. The result is the following equation:

14–2

$$\text{Economic ordering quantity} = \text{EOQ} = \sqrt{\frac{2 \times O \times T}{C \times PP}}$$

EOQ MODEL
A formula for determining the order quantity that will minimize total inventory costs:

$$\text{EOQ} = \sqrt{\frac{2 \times O \times T}{C \times PP}}$$

The primary assumptions of the **EOQ model** given by Equation 14–2 are that (1) sales are evenly distributed throughout the period examined and can be forecasted precisely, (2) orders are received when expected, and (3) the purchase price (PP) of each item in inventory is the same regardless of the quantity ordered.[4]

---

[4]The EQQ model can also be written as follows:

$$\text{EOQ} = \sqrt{\frac{2 \times O \times T}{C^{*}}}$$

where C^{*} is the annual carrying cost per unit expressed in dollars.

To illustrate the EOQ model, consider the following data supplied by Cotton Tops Inc., a distributor of custom-designed T-shirts that supplies concessionaires at Daisy World:

T = 78,000 shirts per year.
C = 25 percent of inventory value.
PP = \$3.84 per shirt. (The shirts sell for \$9, but this is irrelevant for our purposes here.)
O = \$260 per order.

Substituting these data into Equation 14–2, we find an EOQ equal to 6,500 units:

$$EOQ = \sqrt{\frac{2 \times \$260 \times 78,000}{0.25 \times \$3.84}}$$

$$= \sqrt{42,250,000} = 6,500 \text{ units}$$

If Cotton Tops orders 6,500 shirts each time it needs inventory, it will place 78,000/6,500 = 12 orders per year and carry an average inventory of 6,500/2 = 3,250 shirts. Thus, at the EOQ quantity, Cotton Tops' total inventory costs would equal \$6,240:

$$TIC = (C \times PP)\left(\frac{Q}{2}\right) + O\left(\frac{T}{Q}\right)$$

$$= [0.25(\$3.84)]\left(\frac{6,500}{2}\right) + (\$260)\left(\frac{78,000}{6,500}\right)$$

$$= \$3,120 + \$3,120$$

$$= \$6,240$$

Note these two points: (1) Because we assume the purchase price of each inventory item does not depend on the amount ordered, TIC does *not* include the \$299,520 = 78,000(\$3.84) annual cost of purchasing the inventory itself. (2) As we see both in Figure 14–3 and in the numbers here, at the EOQ, total carrying cost (TCC) equals total ordering cost (TOC). This property is not unique to our Cotton Tops illustration; it always holds.

Table 14–5 contains the total inventory costs that Cotton Tops would incur at various order quantities, including the EOQ level. Note that (1) as the amount ordered increases, the total carrying costs increase but the total ordering costs decrease, and vice versa; (2) if less than the EOQ amount is ordered, then the higher ordering costs more than offset the lower carrying costs; and (3) if greater than the EOQ amount is ordered, the higher carrying costs more than offset the lower ordering costs.

EOQ Model Extensions   It should be obvious that some of the assumptions necessary for the basic EOQ to hold are unrealistic. To make the model more useful, we can apply some simple extensions. First, if there is a delay between the time inventory is ordered and when it is received, the firm must reorder before it runs out of inventory. For example, if it normally takes two weeks to receive orders, then Cotton Tops should reorder when two weeks of inventory is left. Cotton Tops sells 78,000/52 = 1,500 shirts per week, so its **reorder point** is when inventory drops to 3,000 shirts. Even if Cotton Tops orders additional inventory at the appropriate

REORDER POINT
The level of inventory at which an order should be placed.

| | TABLE 14-5 | | Cotton Tops, Inc.: Total Inventory Costs for Various Order Quantities | | |

	QUANTITY	NUMBER OF ORDERS	TOTAL ORDERING COSTS	TOTAL CARRYING COSTS	TOTAL INVENTORY COSTS
	3,000	26	$6,760	$ 1,440	$ 8,200
	5,200	15	3,900	2,496	6,396
	6,000	13	3,380	2,880	6,260
EOQ	**6,500**	**12**	**3,120**	**3,120**	**6,240**
	7,800	10	2,600	3,744	6,344
	9,750	8	2,080	4,680	6,760
	13,000	6	1,560	6,240	7,800
	78,000	1	260	37,440	37,700

T = Annual sales = 78,000 shirts

C = Carrying cost = 25 percent

PP = Purchase price = $3.84/shirt

O = Ordering cost = $260/order

SAFETY STOCKS
Additional inventory carried to guard against unexpected changes in sales rates or production/ shipping delays.

reorder point, unexpected demand might cause it to run out of inventory before the new inventory is delivered. To avoid this, the firm could carry **safety stocks,** which represent additional inventory that helps guard against stockouts. The amount of safety stock a firm holds generally *increases* with (1) the uncertainty of demand forecasts, (2) the costs (in terms of lost sales and lost goodwill) that result from stockouts, and (3) the chances that delays will occur in receiving shipments. The amount of safety stock *decreases* as the cost of carrying this additional inventory increases.

Another factor a firm might need to consider when determining appropriate inventory levels is whether its suppliers offer discounts to purchase large quantities. For example, if Cotton Tops' supplier offered a 1 percent discount for purchases equal to 13,000 units or more, the total reduction in the annual cost of purchasing inventory would be [0.01($3.84)] × 78,000 = $2,995.20. Looking in Table 14–5, we see that the total inventory cost (excluding purchase price) at 13,000 units is $7,800, which is $1,560 = $7,800 – $6,240 greater than the cost at the EOQ level of 6,500 units. But the net benefit of taking advantage of the **quantity discount** is $1,435.20 = $2,995.20 – $1,560.00. Therefore, under these conditions, each time Cotton Tops orders inventory it will be more beneficial to order 13,000 units rather than the 6,500 units prescribed by the basic EOQ model.

QUANTITY DISCOUNT
A discount from the purchase price offered for inventory ordered in large quantities.

In cases in which it is unrealistic to assume that the demand for the inventory is uniform throughout the year, the EOQ should not be applied on an annual basis. Rather, it would be more appropriate to divide the year into the seasons within which sales are relatively constant, say, the summer, the spring and fall, and the winter; then the EOQ model can be applied separately to each period.

Although we did not explicitly incorporate the extensions we mentioned here into the basic EOQ, our discussion should give you an idea of how the EOQ amount should be adjusted to determine the optimal inventory level if any of the conditions exist.

RED-LINE METHOD
An inventory control procedure where a *red line* is drawn around the inside of an inventory-stocked bin to indicate the reorder point level.

COMPUTERIZED INVENTORY CONTROL SYSTEM
A system of inventory control in which a computer is used to determine reorder points and to adjust inventory balances.

JUST-IN-TIME SYSTEM
A system of inventory control in which a manufacturer coordinates production with suppliers so that raw materials of components arrive just as they are needed in the production process.

OUTSOURCING
The practice of purchasing components rather than making them in-house.

Inventory Control Systems

The EOQ model can be used to help establish the proper inventory level, but inventory management also involves the establishment of an *inventory control system*. Inventory control systems run the gamut from very simple to extremely complex, depending on the size of the firm and the nature of its inventories. For example, one simple control procedure is the **red-line method:** Inventory items are stocked in a bin, a red line is drawn around the inside of the bin at the level of the reorder point, and the inventory clerk places an order when the red line shows. This procedure works well for parts such as bolts in a manufacturing process or for many items in retail businesses.

Most firms employ some type of **computerized inventory control systems.** Large companies often have fully integrated computerized inventory control systems in which the computer adjusts inventory levels as sales are made, orders inventory when the reorder point is reached, and records the receipt of an order. The computer records also can be used to determine if the usage rates of inventory items change, and thus adjustments to reorder amounts can be made. Another approach to inventory control that requires a coordinated effort between the supplier and the buyer is called the **just-in-time system,** which was refined by Japanese firms many years ago. With this system, materials are delivered to the company at about the same time they are needed, perhaps a few hours before they are used. Still another important development related to inventories is **outsourcing,** which is the practice of purchasing components rather than making them in-house. Outsourcing often is combined with just-in-time systems to reduce inventory levels.

Inventory control systems require coordination of inventory policy with manufacturing/procurement policies. Companies try to minimize *total production and distribution costs*, and inventory costs are just one part of total costs. Still, they are an important cost, and financial managers should be aware of the determinants of inventory costs and how they can be minimized.

Self-Test Questions

What are the types of inventory?

What are the three categories of inventory costs?

What is the purpose of the EOQ model?

What are safety stocks, and why are they required?

Describe some inventory control systems used in practice.

Multinational Working Capital Management

As we mentioned in the previous chapter, the methods used to manage short-term assets in multinational corporations are essentially the same as those used in purely domestic corporations. But there are some differences, which we discuss in this section.

Cash Management

Like a purely domestic company, a multinational corporation wants (1) to speed up collections and to slow down disbursements where possible, (2) to shift cash as rapidly as possible to those areas where it is needed, and (3) to try to put temporary cash balances to work earning positive returns. Multinational companies use the same general procedures for achieving these goals as domestic firms, but because of longer distances and more serious mail delays, lockbox systems and electronic funds transfers are even more important.

One potential problem a multinational company faces that a purely domestic company does not is the chance that a foreign government will restrict transfers of funds out of the country. Foreign governments often limit the amount of cash that can be taken out of their countries because they want to encourage investment domestically. Even if funds can be transferred without limitation, deteriorating exchange rates might make it unattractive for a multinational firm to move funds to its operations in other countries.

Once it has been determined what funds can be transferred out of the various nations in which a multinational corporation operates, it is important to get those funds to locations where they will earn the highest returns. Whereas domestic corporations tend to think in terms of domestic securities, multinationals are more likely to be aware of investment opportunities all around the world. Most multinational corporations use one or more global concentration banks, located in money centers such as London, New York, Tokyo, Zurich, or Singapore; and their staffs in those cities, working with international bankers, are able to take advantage of the best rates available anywhere in the world.

Credit Management

Credit policy generally is more important for a multinational corporation than for a purely domestic firm for two reasons. First, much U.S. trade is with poorer, less-developed nations, and in such situations granting credit generally is a necessary condition for doing business. Second, and in large part as a result of the first point, developed nations whose economic health depends on exports often help their manufacturing firms compete internationally by granting credit to foreign countries. In Japan, for example, government agencies help firms identify potential export markets and also help potential customers arrange credit for purchases from Japanese firms. The U.S. government has programs that help domestic firms to export products, but it does not provide the degree of financial assistance that other governments offer many multinationals based in other countries.

When granting credit, the multinational firm faces a riskier situation than purely domestic firms because, in addition to the normal risks of default, (1) political and legal environments often make it more difficult to collect defaulted accounts and (2) the multinational corporations must worry about exchange rate changes between the time a sale is made and the time a receivable is collected. We know, however, that hedging can reduce this type of risk, but at a cost.

By pointing out the risks in granting credit internationally, we are not suggesting that such credit is bad. Quite the contrary—the potential gains from international operations far outweigh the risks, at least for companies (and banks) that have the necessary expertise.

Inventory Management

Inventory management in a multinational setting is more complex than in a purely domestic setting because of logistical problems that arise with handling inventories. For example, should a firm concentrate its inventories in a few strategic centers located worldwide? Such a strategy might minimize the total amount of, thus the investment in, inventories needed to operate the global business; but it also might

* ETHICAL DILEMMA

Money Back Guarantee, No Questions Asked

TradeSmart Inc. operates 1,200 discount electronics stores throughout the United States. TradeSmart has been quite successful in a highly competitive industry primarily because it has been able to offer brand name products at prices lower than can be found at other discount outlets. Because of its size, TradeSmart can purchase bulk inventory directly from manufacturers, and the economies of scale it derives from such purchases can be passed on to consumers in the form of lower prices. In addition to low prices, TradeSmart offers an extremely liberal product return policy. Customers are permitted to return products for virtually any reason, and with little regard to the time period covered by manufacturers' warranties. In fact, just a few days ago, a customer returned a digital pager that was more than two years old. TradeSmart gave the customer a full refund even though the pager appeared to have been run over by a car, which, if true, clearly would have voided the manufacturer's warranty. In another instance, a customer was given a refund when he returned the camcorder he had purchased three days earlier to record his daughter's wedding festivities. The customer could not describe the camcorder's malfunction—he said "it just didn't work right." The customer refused an offer to replace the camcorder; instead, he insisted on a full refund, which he was given. The manager of the customer relations department suspected that the customer had "purchased" the camcorder intending all along to return it after his daughter's wedding. But TradeSmart's return policy does not dissuade customers from this practice. According to Ed Davidson, vice president of customer relations, TradeSmart is willing to stand behind every product it sells, regardless of the problem, because the company believes such a policy is needed to attract and keep loyal customers in such a competitive industry. The company's motto—"Customer Satisfaction Is Our Business"—is displayed prominently throughout TradeSmart stores.

With such a liberal return policy, how does TradeSmart keep its prices so low? Actually, TradeSmart ships the returned products back to the manufacturers as defective products, so the return costs are passed on to the manufacturers. According to manufacturers, only one out of every six products returned by TradeSmart actually is defective. But when the manufacturers complain about such returns as used products or products that have no mechanical problems, TradeSmart reminds them that the company does not have a service department, so its personnel are not knowledgeable concerning the technical circuitry of the products—the products are returned to the manufacturers with the customers' complaints attached. TradeSmart's inventory manager would contend that the company does not intentionally deceive or take advantage of the manufacturers' return policies and warranties. Do you agree with TradeSmart's return policy? Is it ethical? What action would you take if you were one of TradeSmart's suppliers?

cause delays in getting goods from central storage locations to user locations all around the world. It is clear, however, that both working stocks and safety stocks will have to be maintained at each user location, as well as at the strategic storage centers.

Exchange rates can significantly influence inventory policy. For example, if a local currency was expected to increase in value against the dollar, a U.S. company operating in that country would want to increase stocks of local products before the rise in the currency, and vice versa. Another factor that must be considered is the possibility of import or export quotas or tariffs. Quotas restrict the quantities of products firms can bring into a country, while tariffs, like taxes, increase the prices of products that are allowed to be imported. Both quotas and tariffs are designed to restrict the ability of foreign corporations to compete with domestic companies; at the extreme, foreign products are excluded altogether.

Another danger in certain countries is the threat of expropriation, or government takeover of the firm's local operations. If the threat of expropriation is large, inventory holdings will be minimized, and goods will be brought in only as needed. Similarly, if the operation involves extraction of raw material, processing plants might be moved offshore rather than located close to the production site.

Taxes also must be considered, and they have two effects on multinational inventory management. First, countries often impose property taxes on assets, including inventories, and when this is done, the tax is based on holdings as of a specific date, say, January 1 or March 1. Such rules make it advantageous for a multinational firm (1) to schedule production so that inventories are low on the assessment date and (2) if assessment dates vary among countries in a region, to hold safety stocks in different countries at different times during the year.

In general, then, multinational firms use techniques similar to those described in this chapter to manage current assets, but their job is more complex because business, legal, and economic environments can differ significantly from one country to another.

Self-Test Questions

What are some factors that make cash management especially complicated in a multinational corporation?

Why is granting credit especially risky in an international context?

What are some factors that make inventory management in multinational firms more complex than in purely domestic firms?

Summary

In this chapter we examine methods used to manage and evaluate current assets. In addition, we provide an indication of the complexities faced by multinational firms when managing these accounts around the world. The key concepts covered in this chapter are listed here:

- The **primary goal of cash management** is to reduce the amount of cash held to the minimum necessary to conduct business.
- The **transactions balance** is the cash necessary to conduct day-to-day business, whereas the **precautionary balance** is a cash reserve held to meet random, unforeseen needs. A **compensating balance** is a minimum checking account balance that a bank requires as compensation either for services provided or as part of a loan agreement. Firms also hold **speculative balances**, which allow them to take advantage of bargain purchases.
- **Effective cash management** encompasses the proper management of cash inflows and outflows, which entails (1) synchronizing cash flows, (2) using float, (3) accelerating collections, (4) determining where and when funds will be needed and ensuring that they are available at the right place at the right time, and (5) controlling disbursements.
- **Disbursement float** is the amount of funds associated with checks written by a firm that are still in process and hence have not yet been deducted by the bank from the firm's account. **Collections float** is the amount of funds associated with checks written to the firm that have not been cleared and hence are not yet available for its use. **Net float** is the difference between disbursement float and collections float, and it also is equal to the difference between the balance in the firm's checkbook and the balance on the bank's records. The larger the net float, the smaller the cash balances the firm must maintain; so net float is good.

- Two techniques that can be used to speed up collections are (1) **lockboxes** and (2) **preauthorized debits.** Also, a **concentration banking system** consolidates cash into a centralized pool that can be managed more efficiently than a large number of individual accounts.
- Three techniques for controlling disbursements are (1) **payables centralization,** (2) **zero-balance accounts,** and (3) **controlled disbursement accounts.**
- Firms can reduce cash balances by holding **marketable securities,** which can be sold easily on short notice at a fair price close to their original market values. Marketable securities serve both as a substitute for cash and as a temporary investment for funds that will be needed in the near future. Safety is the primary consideration when selecting marketable securities.
- When a firm sells goods to a customer on credit, an **account receivable** is created.
- Firms can use an **aging schedule** and the **days sales outstanding (DSO)** to help keep track of their receivables position and to help avoid an increase in bad debts.
- A firm's **credit policy** consists of four elements: (1) credit standards, (2) credit terms, (3) collection policy, and (4) monitoring receivables.
- A firm should change its credit policy only if the **costs** of doing so will be more than offset by the **benefits.**
- **Inventory management** involves determining how much inventory to hold, when to place orders, and how many units to order.
- **Inventory** can be grouped into three categories: (1) **raw materials,** (2) **work-in-process,** and (3) **finished goods.**
- The **economic ordering quantity (EOQ)** model is a formula for determining the order quantity that will minimize total inventory costs:

$$\text{EOQ} = \sqrt{\frac{2 \times O \times T}{C \times PP}}$$

  Here O is the fixed cost per order, T is sales in units, C is the percentage cost of carrying inventory, and PP is the purchase price per unit.
- The **reorder point** is the inventory level at which new items must be ordered. **Safety stocks** are held to avoid shortages (1) if demand increases or (2) if shipping delays are encountered. If suppliers offer **quantity discounts** to purchase materials, it might be beneficial for the firm to order more than the EOQ amount.
- Firms use inventory control systems such as the **red-line method,** as well as **computerized inventory control systems,** to help them keep track of actual inventory levels and to ensure that inventory levels are adjusted as sales change. **Just-in-time (JIT) systems** and **outsourcing** are also used to hold down inventory costs and, simultaneously, to improve the production process.
- **Multinational firms** use techniques similar to purely domestic firms to manage short-term assets, but they face more complex situations due to differences in the business, economic, and legal environments of various countries.

Questions

14–1 What are principal reasons for holding cash? Can a firm estimate its target cash balance by summing the cash held to satisfy each of the reasons?

14–2 Explain how each of the following factors probably would affect a firm's target cash balance if all other factors are held constant.

    a. The firm institutes a new billing procedure that better synchronizes its cash inflows and outflows.

    b. The firm develops a new sales forecasting technique that improves its forecasts.

    c. The firm reduces its portfolio of U.S. Treasury bills.

    d. The firm arranges to use an overdraft system for its checking account.

    e. The firm borrows a large amount of money from its bank and also begins to write far more checks than it did in the past.

    f. Interest rates on Treasury bills rise from 3 percent to 6 percent.

14–3 What is a cash budget? For what purposes should cash budgets be created?

14–4 Why is a cash budget important even when there is plenty of cash in the bank?

14–5 Discuss why it is important for a financial manager to understand the concept of float to effectively manage the firm's cash.

14–6 Why would a lockbox plan make more sense for a firm that makes sales all over the United States than for a firm with the same volume of business that is concentrated where the corporate headquarters are located?

14–7 In general, does a firm wish to speed up or slow down collections of payments made by its customers? Why? How does the same firm wish to manage its disbursements? Why?

14–8 What does the term *liquidity* mean? Which would be more important to a firm that held a portfolio of marketable securities as precautionary balances against the possibility of losing a major lawsuit—liquidity or rate of return? Explain.

14–9 Firm A's management is very conservative whereas Firm B's is more aggressive. Is it true that, other things the same, Firm B would probably have larger holdings of marketable securities? Explain.

14–10 What are the elements of a firm's credit policy? To what extent can firms set their own credit policies as opposed to having to accept policies that are dictated by the competition?

14–11 What are aging schedules, and how can they be used to help the credit manager more effectively manage accounts receivable?

14–12 Indicate by a (+), (–), or (0) whether each of the following events would probably cause accounts receivable (A/R), sales, and profits to increase, decrease, or be affected in an indeterminate manner:

	A/R	Sales	Profits
a. The firm tightens its credit standards	_____	_____	_____
b. The credit terms are changed from 2/10, net 30 to 3/10, net 30	_____	_____	_____
c. The credit manager gets tough with past-due accounts	_____	_____	_____

14–13 Describe the three classifications of inventory and indicate the purpose for holding each type.

14–14 Indicate by a (+), (–), or (0) whether each of the following events would probably cause average annual inventories (the sum of the inventories held at the end of each month of the year divided by 12) to rise, fall, or be affected in an indeterminate manner:

    a. Our suppliers switch from delivering by train to air freight. _____

    b. We change from producing just in time to meet seasonal sales to steady, year-round production. (Sales peak at Christmas.) _____

    c. Competition in the markets in which we sell increases. _____

d. The rate of general inflation increases.   _____

e. Interest rates rise; other things are constant.   _____

14–15 "Every firm should use the EOQ model to determine the optimal level of inventory to maintain." Discuss the accuracy of this statement with respect to the form of the EOQ model presented in this chapter.

Self-Test Problems

(Solutions appear in Appendix B)

key terms **ST-1** Define each of the following terms:

a. Transactions balance; compensating balance; precautionary balance; speculative balance

b. Cash budget; target cash balance

c. Synchronized cash flows

d. Net float; disbursement float; collections float

e. Mail delay; processing delay; clearing (availability) delay

f. Lockbox arrangement; preauthorized debit; concentration banking

g. Zero-balance account (ZBA); controlled disbursement account (CDA)

h. Marketable securities; near-cash reserves

i. Credit policy; credit terms; collection policy

j. Days sales outstanding (DSO); aging schedule

k. Carrying costs; ordering costs; total inventory costs

l. Economic ordering quantity (EOQ); EOQ model

m. Reorder point; safety stock; quantity discount

n. Just-in-time system; outsourcing

float **ST-2** The Upton Company is setting up a new checking account with Howe National Bank. Upton plans to issue checks in the amount of $1 million each day and to deduct them from its own records at the close of business on the day they are written. On average, the bank will receive and clear the checks at 5 P.M. the third day after they are written; for example, a check written on Monday will be cleared on Thursday afternoon. The firm's agreement with the bank requires it to maintain a $500,000 average compensating balance; this is $250,000 greater than the cash balance the firm would otherwise have on deposit. It makes a $500,000 deposit at the time it opens the account.

a. Assuming that the firm makes deposits at 4 P.M. each day (and the bank includes them in that day's transactions), how much must it deposit daily to maintain a sufficient balance once it reaches a steady state? (To do this, set up a table that shows the daily balance recorded on the company's books and the daily balance at the bank until a steady state is reached.) Indicate the required deposit on Day 1, Day 2, Day 3, if any, and each day thereafter, assuming that the company will write checks for $1 million on Day 1 and each day thereafter.

b. How many days of float does Upton have?

c. What ending daily balance should the firm try to maintain (1) on the bank's records and (2) on its own records?

change in credit policy **ST-3** The Boca Grande Company expects to have sales of $10 million this year under its current operating policies. Its variable cost ratio is 80 percent, and its cost of short-term funds is 16 percent. Currently, Boca Grande's credit policy is net 25 (no discount for early payment), but its customers pay on average in

30 days. Boca Grande spends $50,000 per year to collect its credit accounts. It collects all receivables (no bad debts), and its marginal tax rate is 40 percent. All costs associated with the manufacture of the product and with the credit department's operations are paid when the product is sold.

The credit manager is considering two alternative proposals for changing Boca Grande's credit policy. Should a change in credit policy be made?

Proposal 1: Lengthen the credit period by going from net 25 to net 30. Collection expenditures will remain constant. Under this proposal, sales are expected to increase by $1 million annually, and the the DSO is expected to increase from 30 to 45 days on all sales.

Proposal 2: Shorten the credit period by going from net 25 to net 20. Again, collection expenses will remain constant. But sales are expected to decrease by $1 million per year, and the DSO is expected to decline from 30 to 22 days.

EOQ and total inventory costs **ST-4** The Homemade Bread Company buys and then sells (as bread) 2.6 million bushels of wheat annually. The wheat must be purchased in multiples of 2,000 bushels. Ordering costs are $5,000 per order. Annual carrying costs are 2 percent of the purchase price of $5 per bushel. The delivery time is six weeks.

a. What is the EOQ?

b. At what inventory level should an order be placed?

c. What are the total inventory costs?

Problems

disbursement float **14–1** The Garvin Company is setting up a new checking account with Barngrover National Bank. Garvin plans to issue checks in the amount of $1.6 million each day and to deduct them from its own records at the close of business on the day they are written. On average, the bank will receive and clear (that is, deduct from the firm's bank balance) the checks at 5 P.M. the fourth day after they are written; for example, a check written on Monday will be cleared on Friday afternoon. The firm's agreement with the bank requires it to maintain a $1.2 million average compensating balance; this is $400,000 greater than the cash balance the firm would otherwise have on deposit. Garvin will make a $1.2 million cash deposit at the time it opens the account.

a. Assuming that the firm makes cash deposits at 2 P.M. each day (and the bank includes them in that day's transactions), how much must it deposit daily to maintain a sufficient balance once it reaches a steady state? (To find the answer, set up a table that shows the daily balance recorded on the company's books and the daily balance at the bank until a steady state is reached.) Indicate the required deposit on Day 1, Day 2, Day 3, Day 4, if any, and each day thereafter, assuming that the company will write checks for $1.6 million on Day 1 and each day thereafter.

b. How many days of float does Garvin carry?

c. What ending daily balance should the firm try to maintain (1) on the bank's records and (2) on its own records?

d. Explain how net float can help increase the value of the firm's common stock.

cash budgeting **14–2** Patricia Smith recently leased space in the Southside Mall and opened a new business, Smith's Coin Shop. Business has been good, but Smith has frequently run out of cash. This has necessitated late payment on certain orders, which in turn is beginning to cause a problem with suppliers. Smith plans to borrow from the bank to have cash ready as needed, but first she needs a forecast of just how much she must borrow. Accordingly, she has asked you to prepare a cash budget for the critical period around Christmas, when needs will be especially high.

Sales are made on a cash basis only. Smith's purchases must be paid for during the month following the purchase. Smith pays herself a salary of $4,800 per month, and the rent is $2,000 per month. In addition, she must make a tax payment of $12,000 in December. The current cash on hand (on December 1) is $400, but Smith has agreed to maintain an average bank balance of $6,000—this is her target cash balance. (Disregard till cash, which is insignificant because Smith keeps only a small amount on hand to lessen the chances of robbery.)

The estimated sales and purchases for December, January, and February are shown here. Purchases during November amounted to $140,000.

	SALES	PURCHASES
December	$160,000	$40,000
January	40,000	40,000
February	60,000	40,000

a. Prepare a cash budget for December, January, and February.
b. Now suppose Smith started selling on a credit basis on December 1, giving customers 30 days to pay. All customers accept these terms and pay on time, and all other facts in the problem are unchanged. What would the company's loan requirements be at the end of December in this case? (*Hint:* The calculations required to answer this question are minimal.)

cash budgeting **14–3** Carol Moerdyk, owner of Carol's Fashion Designs Inc., is planning to request a line of credit from her bank. She has estimated the following sales forecasts for the firm for parts of 2006 and 2007;

May 2006	$180,000
June	180,000
July	360,000
August	540,000
September	720,000
October	360,000
November	360,000
December	90,000
January 2007	180,000

Collection estimates obtained from the credit and collection department are as follows: collections within the month of sale, 10 percent; collections the month following the sale, 75 percent; collections the second month following the sale, 15 percent. Payments for labor and raw materials are typically made during the month following the one in which these costs are incurred. Total labor and raw materials costs are estimated for each month as follows:

May 2006	$ 90,000
June	90,000
July	126,000
August	882,000
September	306,000
October	234,000
November	162,000
December	90,000

General and administrative salaries will amount to approximately $27,000 a month; lease payments under long-term lease contracts will be $9,000 a month; depreciation charges will be $36,000 a month; miscellaneous expenses will be $2,700 a month; income tax payments of $63,000 will be due in both September and December; and a progress payment of $180,000 on a new design studio must be paid in October. Cash on hand on July 1 will amount to $132,000, and a minimum cash balance of $90,000 will be maintained throughout the cash budget period.

a. Prepare a monthly cash budget for the last six months of 2006.

b. Prepare an estimate of the required financing (or excess funds)—that is, the amount of money Carol's Fashion Designs will need to borrow (or will have available to invest)—for each month during that period.

c. Assume that receipts from sales come in uniformly during the month (that is, cash receipts come in at the rate of 1/30 each day), but all outflows are paid on the fifth of the month. Will this have an effect on the cash budget—in other words, would the cash budget you have prepared be valid under these assumptions? If not, what can be done to make a valid estimate of peak financing requirements? No calculations are required, although calculations can be used to illustrate the effects.

d. Carol's Fashion Designs produces on a seasonal basis, just ahead of sales. Without making any calculations, discuss how the company's current ratio and debt ratio would vary during the year assuming all financial requirements were met by short-term bank loans. Could changes in these ratios affect the firm's ability to obtain bank credit?

lockbox system **14–4** Durst Corporation began operations five years ago as a small firm serving customers in the Denver area. However, its reputation and market area grew quickly so that today Durst has customers throughout the entire United States. Despite its broad customer base, Durst has maintained its headquarters in Denver and keeps its central billing system there. Durst's management is considering an alternative collection procedure to reduce its mail time and processing float. On average, it takes five days from the time customers mail payments until Durst is able to receive, process, and deposit them. Durst would like to set up a lockbox collection system, which it estimates would reduce the time lag from customer mailing to deposit by three days—bringing it down to two days. Durst receives an average of $1,400,000 in payments per day.

a. How many days of collection float now exist (Durst's customers' disbursement float) and what would it be under the lockbox system? What reduction in cash balances could Durst achieve by initiating the lockbox system?

b. If Durst has an opportunity cost of 10 percent, how much is the lockbox system worth on an annual basis?

c. What is the maximum monthly charge Durst should pay for the lockbox system?

relaxing collection efforts **14–5** The Pettit Corporation has annual credit sales of $2 million. Current expenses for the collection department are $30,000, bad debt losses are 2 percent, and the days sales outstanding is 30 days. Pettit is considering easing its collection efforts so that collection expenses will be reduced to $22,000 per year. The change is expected to increase bad debt losses to 3 percent and to increase the days sales outstanding to 45 days. In addition, sales are expected to increase to $2.2 million per year.

Should Pettit relax collection efforts if the opportunity cost of funds is 12 percent, the variable cost ratio is 75 percent, and its marginal tax rate is 40 percent? All costs associated with production and credit sales are paid on the day of the sale.

easing credit terms **14–6** Bey Technologies is considering changing its credit terms from 2/15, net 30 to 3/10, net 30 to speed collections. At present, 40 percent of Bey's paying customers take the 2 percent discount. Under the new terms, discount customers are expected to rise to 50 percent. Regardless of the credit terms, half of the customers *who do not take the discount* are expected to pay on time, whereas the remainder will pay 10 days late. The change does not involve a relaxation of credit standards; therefore, bad debt losses are not expected to rise above their present 2 percent level. However, the more generous cash discount terms are expected to increase sales from $2 million to $2.6 million per year. Bey's variable cost ratio is 75 percent, the interest rate on funds invested in accounts receivable is 9 percent, and the firm's marginal tax rate is 40 percent. All costs associated with production and credit sales are paid on the day of the sale.

  a. What is the days sales outstanding before and after the change?
  b. Calculate the costs of the discounts taken before and after the change.
  c. Calculate the bad debt losses before and after the change.

inventory cost   **d.** Should Bey change its credit terms?

14–7 Computer Supplies Inc. must order diskettes from its supplier in lots of one dozen boxes. Given the information provided here, complete the following table and determine the economic ordering quantity of diskettes for Computer Supplies Inc.

Annual demand: 26,000 dozen
Cost per order placed: $30.00
Carrying cost: 20%
Price per dozen: $7.80

ORDER SIZE (DOZENS)	250	500	1,000	2,000	13,000	26,000
Number of orders	——	——	——	——	——	——
Average inventory	——	——	——	——	——	——
Carrying cost	——	——	——	——	——	——
Order cost	——	——	——	——	——	——
Total cost	——	——	——	——	——	——

EOQ and inventory costs **14–8** The following inventory data have been established for the Thompson Company:

  (1) Orders must be placed in multiples of 100 units.
  (2) Annual sales are 338,000 units.
  (3) The purchase price per unit is $6.
  (4) Carrying cost is 20 percent of the purchase price of goods.
  (5) Fixed order cost is $48.
  (6) Three days are required for delivery.

  a. What is the EOQ?
  b. How many orders should Thompson place each year?
  c. At what inventory level should an order be made?
  d. Calculate the total cost of ordering and carrying inventories if the order quantity is (1) 4,000 units, (2) 4,800 units, or (3) 6,000 units. (4) What are the total costs if the order quantity is the EOQ?

Exam-Type Problems

The problems included in this section are set up in such a way that they could be used as multiple-choice exam problems.

computation of float   **14–9** Clearwater Glass Company examined its cash management policy and found that it takes an average of five days for checks that the company writes to reach its bank and thus be deducted from its checking account balance (that is, disbursement delay, or float, is five days). On the other hand, it is an average of four days from the time Clearwater Glass receives payments from its customers until the funds are available for use at the bank (that is, collection delay, or float, is four days). On an average day, Clearwater Glass writes checks that total $70,000, and it receives checks from customers that total $80,000.

a. Compute the disbursement float, collection float, and net float in dollars.

b. If Clearwater Glass has an opportunity cost equal to 10 percent, how much would it be willing to spend each year to reduce collection delay (float) by two days? (*Hint:* Assume any funds that are freed up are invested at 10 percent annually.)

receivables balance and DSO   **14–10** Morrissey Industries sells on terms of 3/10, net 30. Total sales for the year are $900,000. Forty percent of the customers pay on Day 10 and take discounts; the other 60 percent pay, on average, 40 days after their purchases.

a. What is the days sales outstanding?

b. What is the average amount of receivables?

c. What would happen to average receivables if Morrissey tightened its collection policy with the result that all nondiscount customers paid on Day 30?

tightening credit terms   **14–11** Helen Bowers, the new credit manager of the Muscarella Corporation, was alarmed to find that Muscarella sells on credit terms of net 50 days whereas industry-wide credit terms have recently been lowered to net 30 days. On annual credit sales of $3 million, Muscarella currently averages 60 days' sales in accounts receivable. Bowers estimates that tightening the credit terms to 30 days would reduce annual sales to $2.6 million, but accounts receivable would drop to 35 days of sales, and the savings on investment in them should more than overcome any loss in profit.

Muscarella's variable cost ratio is 70 percent, and its marginal tax rate is 40 percent. If the interest rate on funds invested in receivables is 11 percent, should the change in credit terms be made? All operating costs are paid when inventory is sold.

credit policy change   **14–12** The McCollough Company has a variable operating cost ratio of 70 percent, its cost of capital is 10 percent, and current sales are $10,000. All of its sales are on credit, and it currently sells on terms of net 30. Its accounts receivable balance is $1,500. McCollough is considering a new credit policy with terms of net 45. Under the new policy, sales will increase to $12,000, and accounts receivable will rise to $2,500. Compute the days sales outstanding (DSO) under the existing policy and the proposed policy.

EOQ   **14–13** Green Thumb Garden Centers sells 240,000 bags of lawn fertilizer annually. The optimal safety stock (which is on hand initially) is 1,200 bags. Each bag costs Green Thumb $4, inventory carrying costs are 20 percent, and the cost of placing an order with its supplier is $25.

a. What is the economic ordering quantity?

b. What is the maximum inventory of fertilizer?

c. What will Green Thumb's average inventory be?

d. How often must the company order?

Integrative Problems

cash management **14–14** Ray Smith, a retired librarian, recently opened a sportsman's shop called Smitty's Sports Paradise (SSP). Smith decided at age 62 that he wasn't quite ready to stay at home, living the life of leisure. It had always been his dream to open an outdoor sportsman's shop, so his friends convinced him to go ahead. Because Smith's educational background was in literature and not in business, he hired you, a finance expert, to help him with the store's cash management. Smith is very eager to learn, so he asked you to develop a set of questions to help him understand cash management. Now answer the following questions:

a. What is the goal of cash management?

b. For what reasons do firms hold cash?

c. What is meant by the terms *precautionary* and *speculative* balances?

d. What are some specific advantages for a firm holding adequate cash balances?

e. How can a firm synchronize its cash flows, and what good would this do?

f. You have been going through the store's checkbook and bank balances. In the process, you discovered that SSP, on average, writes checks in the amount of $10,000 each day and that it takes about five days for these checks to clear. Also, the firm receives checks in the amount of $10,000 daily, but loses four days while they are being deposited and cleared. What is the firm's *disbursement float, collections float,* and *net float?*

g. How can a firm speed up collections and slow down disbursements?

h. Why would a firm hold marketable securities?

i. What factors should a firm consider in building its marketable securities portfolio? What are some securities that should and should not be held?

credit policy **14–15** Ray Smith also wants you to examine his company's credit policy to determine if changes are needed because one of his employees, who graduated recently with a finance major, has recommended that the credit terms be changed from 2/10, net 30 to 3/20, net 45 and that both the credit standards and the collection policy be relaxed. According to the employee, such a change would cause sales to increase from $3.6 million to $4.0 million.

Currently, 62.5 percent of SSP's customers pay on Day 10 of the billing cycle and take the discount, 32 percent pay on Day 30, and 5.5 percent pay (on average) on Day 60. If the new credit policy is adopted, Smith estimated that 72.5 percent of customers would take the discount, 10 percent would pay on Day 45, and 17.5 percent would pay late, on Day 90. Bad debt losses for both policies are expected to be trivial.

Variable operating costs are currently 75 percent of sales, the cost of funds used to carry receivables is 10 percent, and its marginal tax rate is 40 percent. None of these factors would change as a result of a credit policy change.

To help decide whether to adopt the new policy, Smith has asked you to answer the following questions:

a. What variables make up a firm's credit policy? In what direction would each be changed if the credit policy is relaxed? How would each variable tend to affect sales, the level of receivables, and bad debt losses?

b. How are the days sales outstanding (DSO) and the average collection period (ACP) related to one another? What would the DSO be if the current credit policy is maintained? If the proposed policy is adopted?

c. What is the dollar amount of discounts granted under the current and the proposed credit policies?

d. Should SSP make the change? Assume that operating and credit costs are paid on the day of the sale.

e. Suppose the company makes the proposed change, but its competitors react by making changes in their own credit terms, with the net result being that gross sales remain at the $3.6 million level. What would be the effect on the company's value?

f. (1) What does the term *monitoring accounts receivable* mean?

(2) Why would a firm want to monitor its receivables?

(3) How might the DSO and the aging schedule be used in this process?

EOQ model **14–16** Now Ray Smith wants you to take a look at the company's inventory position because he thinks that inventories might be too high as a result of the manager's tendency to order in large quantities. Smith has decided to examine the situation for one key product—fly rods, which cost $320 each to purchase and prepare for sale. Annual sales of the product are 2,500 units (rods), and the annual carrying cost is 10 percent of inventory value. The company has been buying 500 rods per order and placing another order when the stock on hand falls to 100 rods. Each time SSP orders, it incurs a cost equal to $64. Sales are uniform throughout the year.

a. Smith believes that the EOQ model should be used to help determine the optimal inventory situation for this product. What is the EOQ formula, and what are the key assumptions underlying this model?

b. What is the formula for total inventory costs?

c. What is the EOQ for the fly rods? What will the total inventory costs be for this product if the EOQ is produced?

d. What is SSP's added cost if it orders 500 rods rather than the EOQ quantity? What if it orders 750 rods each time?

e. Suppose it takes three days for SSP to receive its orders and package the rods before they are ready for sale. Assuming certainty in production time and usage, at what inventory level should SSP order? (Assume a 360-day year, that SSP is open every day, and that SSP orders the EOQ amount.)

f. Of course, there is uncertainty in SSP's usage rate, as well as in order delays, so the company must carry a safety stock to avoid running out of the fly rods and having to lose sales. If a safety stock of 50 rods is carried, what effect would this have on total inventory costs?

g. For most of SSP's products, inventory usage is not uniform throughout the year; rather, it follows some seasonal pattern. Could the EOQ model be used in this situation? If so, how?

h. How would these factors affect the use of the EOQ model?

(1) Just-in-time (JIT) procedures.

(2) The use of air freight for deliveries.

(3) Computerized inventory control systems.

Computer-Related Problems

Work the problem in this section only if you are using the computer problem diskette.

cash budget **14–17** Use the model in File C14 to solve this problem.

a. Refer back to Problem 14–3. Suppose that by offering a 2 percent cash discount for paying within the month of sale, the credit manager of Carol's Fashion Designs Inc. has revised the collection percentages to

50 percent, 35 percent, and 15 percent, respectively. How will this affect the loan requirements?

b. Return the payment percentages to their base case values—10 percent, 75 percent, and 15 percent, respectively—and the discount to zero percent. Now suppose sales fall to only 70 percent of the forecasted level. Production is maintained, so cash outflows are unchanged. How does this affect Carol's Fashion Designs' financial requirements?

c. Return sales to the forecasted level (100%), and suppose collections slow down to 3 percent, 10 percent, and 87 percent for the three months, respectively. How does this affect financial requirements? If Carol's Fashion Designs went to a cash-only sales policy, how would that affect requirements, other things held constant?

tightening credit terms **14–18** Use the model in File C14 to solve this problem.

a. Refer to Problem 14–11. When Bowers analyzed her proposed credit policy changes, she found that they would reduce Muscarella's value and, therefore, should not be enacted. Bowers has reevaluated her sales estimates because all other firms in the industry have recently tightened their credit policies. She now estimates that sales would decline to only $2.8 million if she tightens the credit policy to 30 days. Would the credit policy change be profitable under these circumstances?

b. On the other hand, Bowers believes that she could tighten the credit policy to net 45 days and pick up some sales from her competitors. She estimates that sales would increase to $3.3 million and that the days sales outstanding (DSO) would fall to 50 days under this policy. Should Bowers enact this change?

c. Bowers also believes that if she leaves the credit policy as it is, sales will increase to $3.4 million and the DSO will remain at 60 days. Should Bowers leave the credit policy alone or tighten it as described in either part a or part b? Which credit policy produces the highest value for Muscarella Corporation?

GET REAL with Thomson ONE

14–19 Kimberly-Clark [KMB] is a consumer and business-to-business products manufacturing firm. Analyze Kimberly-Clark's credit policy as compared to peers in its industry. Answer the following questions:

a. What has been the trend of Kimberly-Clark's receivables turnover during the past five years? [*Hint:* Click on Financials/More/SEC Reports and Charts/Receivables Turnover Ratio]

b. Find the peers of Kimberly-Clark based on its industry group. Pick two of Kimberly-Clark's peers and determine the trend of these firms' receivables turnovers during the past five years.

c. What conclusions can you make about Kimberly-Clark's credit policy as compared to other firms in its industry? Explain your answer.

CHAPTER 15

Managing Short-Term Liabilities (Financing)

At the end of 1998, the pilots of Federal Express had threatened to strike if their labor demands were not met. To ensure the company could operate without interruption in the event of a strike, Federal Express made arrangements to increase its *line of credit* by $1 billion, which doubled its existing credit line. The purpose of the additional financing was to support the alternative shipping arrangements the company had made with other airlines and trucking companies. In the end, Federal Express did not need the additional credit line; but the company prepared, just in case.

Also at the end of 1998, Netplex Group Inc., an information services company, arranged with First Union National Bank to increase its line of credit from $2 million to $6 million. The line of credit, which was secured *(pledged)* by the company's accounts receivable, was to be used to help finance working capital needs. Similarly, at about the same time, Integrated Packaging Assembly, which provides assembly and packaging services to the semiconductor industry, replaced its line of credit by selling *(factoring)* accounts receivables to its bank. The arrangement provided the company with about $2.8 million working capital financing during 1999, which was about $700,000 more than its regular line of credit. In another instance, Today's Man Inc., which operates men's clothing stores, increased its *revolving line of credit* from $30 million to $45 million by switching banks. The switch allowed the company to refinance some of its existing loans, reducing the financing costs by about 3 percent.

More recently, in 2002, Schlotzsky's Inc. received a $10 million secured financing arrangement. The loan allowed the company to pay off the $7.3 million it had outstanding on its $40 million *secured line of credit* at Wells Fargo Bank, Frost Bank, and Texas Capital Bank. And, to improve its financial position and to better negotiate with bankers, Xerox made a $2.8 billion payment on its revolving line of credit in an effort to improve its liquidity position.

As you read this chapter, think about the various sources available to companies for financing day-to-day operations, some of which are mentioned here (highlighted in italics). As you will see, the costs and availability of short-term funds can vary widely, both over time and from alternative sources. ■

In Chapter 13 we discussed the decisions the financial manager must make concerning alternative current asset financing policies. We also showed how debt maturities can affect both risk and expected returns: While short-term debt generally is riskier than long-term debt, it generally is also less expensive, and it can be obtained faster and under more flexible terms. The primary purpose of this chapter is to examine the different types of short-term credit that are available to the financial manager. We also examine the types of issues the financial manager must consider when selecting among the various types of short-term credit—that is, short-term, or current, liabilities.

Sources of Short-Term Financing

SHORT-TERM CREDIT
Any liability originally scheduled for repayment within one year.

Statements about the flexibility, cost, and riskiness of short-term debt versus long-term debt depend, to a large extent, on the type of short-term credit that actually is used. **Short-term credit** is defined as any liability *originally* scheduled for payment within one year. There are numerous sources of short-term funds, and in the following sections we describe four major types: (1) accruals, (2) accounts payable (trade credit), (3) bank loans, and (4) commercial paper. In addition, we discuss the costs of short-term funds and the factors that influence a firm's choice of a bank.

Self-Test Question

What types of liabilities are included in short-term credit?

Accruals

Firms generally pay employees on a weekly, biweekly, or monthly basis, so the balance sheet typically will show some accrued wages. Similarly, the firm's own estimated income taxes, the Social Security and income taxes withheld from employee payrolls, and the sales taxes collected generally are paid on a weekly, monthly, or quarterly basis, so the balance sheet typically will show some accrued taxes along with accrued wages.

ACCRUALS
Continually recurring short-term liabilities; liabilities such as wages and taxes that increase spontaneously with operations.

As we showed in Chapter 13, **accruals** increase automatically, or spontaneously, as a firm's operations expand. Further, this type of debt generally is considered "free" in the sense that no explicit interest is paid on funds generated by accruals. However, a firm ordinarily cannot control its accruals: The timing of wage payments is set by economic forces and industry custom, while tax payment dates are established by law. Thus, firms use all the accruals they can, but they have little control over the levels of these accounts.

Self-Test Questions

What types of short-term credits are classified as accruals?

What is the *explicit* cost of accruals?

How much control do financial managers have over the dollar amount of accruals?

Accounts Payable (Trade Credit)

TRADE CREDIT

The credit created when one firm buys on credit from another firm.

Firms generally make purchases from other firms on credit, recording the debt as an *account payable.* This type of financing, which is called **trade credit,** is the largest single category of short-term debt, representing about 40 percent of the current liabilities for the average nonfinancial corporation. The percentage is somewhat larger for smaller firms: Because small companies often do not qualify for financing from other sources, they rely especially heavily on trade credit.[1]

Trade credit is a *spontaneous* source of financing in the sense that it arises from ordinary business transactions. For example, suppose a firm makes average purchases of $2,000 per day on terms of net 30, meaning that it must pay for goods 30 days after the invoice date. As we saw in Chapter 13, on average, the firm will owe 30 times $2,000, or $60,000, to its suppliers. If its sales, and consequently its purchases, were to double, then the firm's accounts payable also would double, to $120,000. So simply by growing, the firm would have spontaneously generated an additional $60,000 of financing. Similarly, if the terms under which it purchases from suppliers are extended from 30 to 40 days, its accounts payable would expand from $60,000 to $80,000. Thus, lengthening the credit period, as well as expanding sales and purchases, generates additional financing.

The Cost of Trade Credit

As we discussed in Chapter 14, firms that sell on credit have a *credit policy* that includes certain *terms of credit.* For example, Microchip Electronics sells on credit with terms of 2/10, net 30, which means that Microchip gives its customers a 2 percent discount from the invoice price if payment is made within 10 days of the billing date; otherwise, if the discount is not taken, the full invoice amount is due and must be paid within 30 days of the billing date.

Note that the *true* price of the products Microchip offers is the net price, which is 98 percent of the list price, because any customer can purchase an item at a 2 percent "discount" as long as payment is made within 10 days. Consider Personal Computer Company (PCC), which buys its memory chips from Microchip. One commonly used memory chip is listed at $100, so the true cost to PCC is $98. If PCC wants an additional 20 days of credit beyond the 10 day discount period, it will effectively incur a finance charge of $2 per chip for that credit. Thus, the $100 list price can be thought of as follows:

$$\text{List price} = \$98 \text{ true price} + \$2 \text{ finance charge}$$

The question that PCC must ask before it takes the additional 20 days of credit from Microchip is whether the firm could obtain similar credit with better terms from some other lender, say, a bank. In other words, could 20 days of credit be obtained for less than $2 per item?

---

[1] In a credit sale, the seller records the transaction as a receivable; the buyer, as a payable. We examined accounts receivable as an assest investment in Chapter 14. Our focus in this chapter is on accounts payable, a liability item. We should also note that if a firm's accounts payable exceed its receivables, it is said to be *receiving net trade credit,* whereas if its receivables exceed its payables, it is *extending net trade credit.* Smaller firms frequently receive net credit; larger firms generally extend it.

To answer the question as to whether PCC should take the cash discount, we must compute the cost of using trade credit to finance the firm. The cost of short-term credit is discussed later in this chapter.

Components of Trade Credit: Free versus Costly

"FREE" TRADE CREDIT
Credit received during the discount period.

On the basis of the preceding discussion, trade credit can be divided into two components: (1) **"free" trade credit,** which involves credit received during the discount period and (2) **costly trade credit,** which involves credit in excess of the free trade credit and whose cost is an implicit one based on the forgone discounts.[2] *Financial managers always should use the free component, but they should use the costly component only after analyzing the cost of this source of financing to make sure that it is less than the cost of funds that could be obtained from other sources.* Under the terms of trade found in most industries, the costly component will involve a relatively high percentage cost (usually greater than 25 percent), so stronger firms will take the cash discounts offered and avoid using trade credit as a source of additional financing.

COSTLY TRADE CREDIT
Credit taken in excess of "free" trade credit, whose cost is equal to the discount lost.

Firms sometimes can and do deviate from the stated credit terms, thus altering the percentage cost figures cited. For example, a California manufacturing firm that buys on terms of 2/10, net 30, makes a practice of paying in 15 days (rather than 10 days), but it still takes discounts. Its treasurer simply waits until 15 days after receipt of the goods to pay and then writes a check for the invoiced amount less the 2 percent discount. The company's suppliers want its business, so they tolerate this practice. Similarly, a Wisconsin firm that also buys on terms of 2/10, net 30, does not take discounts, but it pays in 60 days rather than in 30 days, thus **stretching** its **accounts payable.** Both practices reduce the cost of trade credit. Neither of these firms is "loved" by its suppliers, and neither could continue these practices in times when suppliers operate at full capacity and have order backlogs, but these practices can and do reduce the costs of trade credit to customers during times when suppliers have excess capacity.

STRETCHING ACCOUNTS PAYABLE
The practice of deliberately paying accounts payable late.

Self-Test Questions

What is trade credit?

What is the difference between free trade credit and costly trade credit?

How does the cost of costly trade credit generally compare with the cost of other short-term sources of funds?

Short-Term Bank Loans

Commercial banks, whose loans generally appear on firms' balance sheets as notes payable, are second in importance to trade credit as a source of short-term financing.[3] The influence of banks actually is greater than it appears from the dollar amounts they lend because banks provide *nonspontaneous* funds. As a firm's financing

---

[2]There is some question as to whether any credit is really "free," because the supplier will have a cost of carrying receivables, which must be passed on to the customer in the form of higher prices. Still, if suppliers sell on standard credit terms such as 2/10, net 30, and if the base price cannot be negotiated downward for early payment, then for all intents and purposes the 10 days of trade credit are indeed "free."

[3]Although commercial banks remain the primary source of short-term loans, other sources are available. For example, in 2004 GE Capital Corporation (GECC) had several billion dollars in commercial loans outstanding. Firms such as GECC, which was initially established to finance consumers' purchases of GE's durable goods, often find business loans to be more profitable than consumer loans.

needs increase, it specifically requests additional funds from its bank. If the request is denied, the firm might be forced to abandon attractive growth opportunities. The key features of bank loans are discussed in the following paragraphs.

Maturity

Although banks do make longer-term loans, the *bulk of their lending is on a short-term basis.* Bank loans to businesses frequently are written as 90-day notes, so the loan must be repaid or renewed at the end of 90 days. Of course, if a borrower's financial position has deteriorated, the bank might refuse to renew the loan. This can mean serious trouble for the borrower.

Promissory Note

PROMISSORY NOTE
A document specifying the terms and conditions of a loan, including the amount, interest rate, and repayment schedule.

When a bank loan is approved, the agreement is executed by signing a **promissory note.** The note specifies (1) the amount borrowed; (2) the interest rate; (3) the repayment schedule, which can call for payment either as a lump sum or as a series of installments; (4) any collateral that has to be put up as security for the loan; and (5) any other terms and conditions to which the bank and the borrower have agreed. When the note is signed, the bank credits the borrower's checking account with the amount of the loan, so on the borrower's balance sheet both cash and notes payable increase equally. (See Chapter 13 for an example.)

Compensating Balances

COMPENSATING BALANCE (CB)
A minimum checking account balance that a firm must maintain with a bank to borrow funds—generally 10 to 20 percent of the amount of loans outstanding.

Banks sometimes require borrowers to maintain an average demand deposit (checking account) balance equal to from 10 percent to 20 percent of the amount borrowed. This is called a **compensating balance (CB).** In effect, the bank charges borrowers for servicing the loans (bookkeeping, maintaining a line of credit, and so on) by requiring compensating balances, and such balances might increase the effective interest rate on the loans.[4] Calculating the cost of a bank loan is discussed in the next section.

Line of Credit

LINE OF CREDIT
An arrangement in which a bank agrees to lend up to a specified maximum amount of funds during a designated period.

A **line of credit** is an agreement between a bank and a borrower indicating the maximum credit the bank will extend to the borrower. For example, on December 31 a bank loan officer might indicate to a financial manager that the bank regards the firm as being "good" for up to $200,000 during the forthcoming year. If on January 10 the financial manager signs a 90-day promissory note for $60,000, this would be called "drawing, or taking, down" $60,000 of the total line of credit. This amount would be credited to the firm's checking account at the bank, and before repayment of the $60,000, the firm could borrow additional amounts up to a *total* of $200,000 outstanding at any one time.

REVOLVING (GUARANTEED) LINE OF CREDIT
A formal, committed line of credit extended by a bank or other lending institution.

When a line of credit is *guaranteed,* it is called a **revolving credit agreement.** A revolving credit agreement is similar to a regular, or general, line of credit, except

---

[4]Note, however, that the compensating balance might be set as a minimum monthly *average,* and if the firm generally maintains this average anyway, the compensating balance requirement might not raise the effective interest rate. Also, note that these *loan* compensating balances often are added to any compensating balances that the firm's bank might require for *services performed,* such as clearing checks.

COMMITMENT FEE

A fee charged on the *unused* balance of a revolving credit agreement to compensate the bank for guaranteeing that the funds will be available when needed by the borrower; the fee normally is about 1/4 percent of the unused balance.

the bank has a *legal obligation* to provide the funds when requested by the borrower. The bank generally charges a **commitment fee** on the unused balance (sometimes on the total credit commitment) of the credit line for guaranteeing the availability of the funds. To illustrate, in 2004 Wyoming Paper Company (WPC) negotiated a revolving credit agreement for $100 million with a group of banks. The banks were formally committed for four years to lend the firm up to $100 million *if the funds were needed*. WPC, in turn, paid an annual *commitment fee* of 1/4 percent on the unused balance of the guaranteed line of credit. Thus, if WPC did not draw down any of the $100 million commitment during a year, it would still be required to pay a $250,000 annual fee (1/4 percent of the $100 million credit agreement), normally in monthly installments of $20,833. If WPC borrowed $60 million on the first day of the agreement, the unused portion of the line of credit would fall to $40 million, and the annual commitment fee would fall to $100,000 = 0.0025 × $40 million. Of course, interest also would have to be paid on the money WPC actually borrowed. As a general rule, the rate of interest on "revolvers" is pegged to the prime rate, so the cost of the loan varies over time as interest rates change.[5] WPC's rate was set at prime plus 1/2 percentage point.

Note that an important feature distinguishes a revolving credit agreement from a general line of credit: The bank has a *legal obligation* to honor a revolving credit agreement, and it receives a commitment fee for guaranteeing the funds will be available when requested by the borrower. Neither the legal obligation nor the fee exists under the general line of credit.

The Cost of Bank Loans

The cost of bank loans varies for different types of borrowers at any given point in time and for all borrowers over time. Interest rates are higher for riskier borrowers, and rates also are higher on smaller loans because of the fixed costs involved in making and servicing loans. If a firm can qualify as a "prime credit" because of its size and financial strength, it might be able to borrow at the **prime rate**, which traditionally has been the lowest rate banks charge. Rates on other loans generally are scaled up from the prime rate.[6]

PRIME RATE

A published rate of interest charged by banks to short-term borrowers (usually large, financially secure corporations) with the best credit; rates on short-term loans generally are "pegged" to the prime rate.

Bank rates vary widely over time depending on economic conditions and Federal Reserve policy. When the economy is weak, then (1) loan demand usually is slack; (2) inflation is low; and (3) the Fed also makes plenty of money available to the system. As a result, rates on all types of loans are relatively low. Conversely, when the economy is booming, loan demand typically is strong and the Fed restricts the money supply; the result is high interest rates. As an indication of the kinds of fluctuations that can occur, during 1980, the prime rate exhibited a roller-coaster pattern—it declined from 20 percent in April to 11 percent in July and then rose again to more than 21 percent by the end of the year. In more recent times, the

---

[5]Each bank sets its own prime rate, but because of competitive forces, most banks' prime rates are identical. Further, most banks follow the rate set by the large New York City banks.

[6]In recent years many banks have been lending to the strongest companies at rates below the prime rate. As we discuss later in this chapter, larger firms have ready access to the commercial paper market, and if banks want to do business with these larger companies, they must match or at least come close to the commercial paper rate. As competition in financial markets increases, as it has been doing because of the deregulation of banks and other financial institutions, "administered" rates such as the prime rate are giving way to flexible, negotiated rates based on market conditions.

prime rate was about 6 percent throughout 1993 and 1994, but 4 percent in 2004. Interest rates on other bank loans also vary, generally moving with the prime rate.

Self-Test Questions

Explain how a firm that expects to need funds during the coming year might make sure the needed funds will be available.

How does a revolving line of credit differ from a regular line of credit?

Explain how a compensating balance requirement differs from a commitment fee.

What is the prime rate, and how does this rate influence the costs of bank loans?

Choosing a Bank

Individuals whose only contact with their bank is through the use of its checking services generally choose a bank for the convenience of its location and the competitive cost of its services. However, a business that borrows from banks must look at other criteria, and a potential borrower seeking banking relations should recognize that important differences exist among banks. Some of these differences are considered here.

Willingness to Assume Risks

Banks have different basic policies toward risk. Some banks are inclined to follow relatively conservative lending practices, whereas others engage in what are properly termed "creative banking practices." These policies reflect partly the personalities of officers of the bank and partly the characteristics of the bank's deposit liabilities. Thus, a bank with fluctuating deposit liabilities in a static community will tend to be a conservative lender, whereas a bank whose deposits are growing with little interruption might follow more liberal credit policies. Similarly, a large bank with broad diversification over geographic regions or across industries can obtain the benefit of combining and averaging risks. Thus, marginal credit risks that might be unacceptable to a small bank or a specialized bank can be pooled by a large branch banking system to reduce the overall risk of a group of marginal accounts.

Advice and Counsel

Some bank loan officers are active in providing counsel and in stimulating development loans to firms in their early and formative years. Certain banks have specialized departments that make loans to firms expected to grow and thus to become more important customers. The personnel of these departments can provide valuable counseling to customers.

Loyalty to Customers

Banks differ in the extent to which they will support the activities of borrowers in bad times. This characteristic is referred to as the degree of *loyalty* of the bank. Some banks might put great pressure on a business to liquidate its loans when the firm's outlook becomes clouded, whereas others will stand by the firm and work diligently to help it get back on its feet.

Specialization

Banks differ greatly in their degrees of loan specialization. Larger banks have separate departments that specialize in different kinds of loans—for example, real estate loans, farm loans, and commercial loans. Within these broad categories, there might be a specialization by line of business, such as steel, machinery, cattle, or textiles. The strengths of banks also are likely to reflect the nature of the business and the economic environment in which the banks operate. For example, some California banks have become specialists in lending to technology companies, while many Midwestern banks are agricultural specialists. A sound firm can obtain more creative cooperation and more active support by going to a bank that has experience and familiarity with its particular type of business. Therefore, a bank that is excellent for one firm might be unsatisfactory for another.

Maximum Loan Size

The size of a bank can be an important factor. Because the maximum loan a bank can make to any one customer is limited to 15 percent of the bank's capital accounts (capital stock plus retained earnings), it generally is not appropriate for large firms to develop borrowing relationships with small banks.

Merchant Banking

The term *merchant bank* originally was applied to banks that not only loaned depositors' money but also provided customers with equity capital and financial advice. Prior to 1933, U.S. commercial banks performed all types of merchant banking functions. However, about one-third of the U.S. banks failed during the Great Depression, in part because of these activities, so in 1933 the Glass-Steagall Act was passed in an effort to reduce banks' exposure to risk. Recent legislation has allowed commercial banks to get back into merchant banking, in part because their foreign competitors offer such services, and U.S. banks need to be able to compete with their foreign counterparts for multinational corporations' business. Currently, the larger banks, often through holding companies, do offer merchant banking. This trend should continue, and, if it does, corporations will need to consider a bank's ability to provide a full range of commercial and merchant banking services when choosing a bank.

Other Services

Many banks also provide cash management services, such as those described in Chapter 14, assist with electronic funds transfers, help firms obtain foreign exchange, and the like; and the availability of such services should be taken into account when selecting a bank. Also, if the firm is a small business whose manager owns most of its stock, the bank's willingness and ability to provide trust and estate services also should be considered.

Self-Test Question

What are some of the factors that should be considered when choosing a bank?

Commercial Paper

Commercial paper is a type of unsecured promissory note issued by large, financially strong firms, and it is sold primarily to other businesses, insurance companies, pension funds, money market mutual funds, and banks. This form of financing has grown rapidly in recent years—in 2004, the amount of commercial paper outstanding was about the same as the amount of regular business loans.

Use of Commercial Paper

The use of commercial paper is restricted to a comparatively small number of firms that are *exceptionally* good credit risks. Dealers prefer to handle the "paper" of firms whose net worth is $100 million or more and whose annual borrowing exceeds $10 million. One potential problem with commercial paper is that a debtor who is in temporary financial difficulty might receive little help because commercial paper dealings generally are less personal than are bank relationships. Thus, banks generally are more able and willing to help a good customer weather a temporary storm than is a commercial paper dealer. On the other hand, using commercial paper permits a corporation to tap a wider range of credit sources, including financial institutions outside its own area and industrial corporations across the country, and this can reduce interest costs.

Maturity and Cost

Generally, commercial paper is issued in denominations of $100,000 or greater, so few individuals can afford to invest *directly* in the commercial paper market. Maturities of commercial paper vary from one to nine months, with an average of about five months.[7] The rate on commercial paper fluctuates with supply and demand conditions—it is determined in the marketplace, varying daily as conditions change. Generally, the rates on commercial paper are lower than the stated prime rate of interest. For example, in January 2004, the average rate on 90-day commercial paper was about 1.1 percent, which was 2.9 percent less than the prime rate but nearly 0.3 percent greater than 90-day Treasury bill rates.

Commercial paper is called a discount instrument because it is sold at a price below its face, or maturity, value. The cost of using commercial paper as a source of financing is computed the same as for a discount interest loan, which is discussed in the next section.

Self-Test Questions

What is commercial paper?

What types of companies can use commercial paper to meet their short-term financing needs?

How does the cost of commercial paper compare to the cost of short-term bank loans? To the cost of Treasury bills?

---

[7]The maximum maturity without SEC registration is 270 days. Also, commercial paper can only be sold to "sophisticated" investors; otherwise, SEC registration would be required even for maturities of 270 days or less.

Computing the Cost of Short-Term Credit

For short-term financing, the percentage cost of using the funds for a given period, k_{PER}, can be computed as:

$$\text{15–1} \qquad \frac{\text{Percentage cost}}{\text{per period}} = k_{PER} = \frac{\text{Dollar cost of borrowing}}{\text{Amount of usable funds}}$$

In this equation, the numerator represents the dollar amount that must be paid for using the borrowed funds. This cost includes the interest paid on the loan, application fees, charges for commitment fees, and so forth. The denominator represents the amount of the loan that actually can be used (spent) by the borrower. This amount is not necessarily the same as the principal amount of the loan because discounts, compensating balances, or other costs might reduce the amount of the loan proceeds that the firm can actually use. We show that *when loan restrictions prevent the borrower from using the entire amount of the loan, the effective annual rate paid for the loan is higher than the stated interest rate.*

Using Equation 15–1 and the concepts described in Chapter 3, the effective annual rate (EAR) and the annual percentage rate (APR) for short-term financing can be computed as follows:

$$\text{15–2} \qquad \frac{\text{Effective annual}}{\text{rate (EAR)}} = (1 + k_{PER})^m - 1.0$$

$$\text{15–3} \qquad \frac{\text{Annual percentage}}{\text{rate (APR)}} = k_{PER} \times m = k_{SIMPLE}$$

where m is the number of borrowing (interest) periods in one year—that is, if the loan is for one month, m = 12. Recall from our discussion in Chapter 3 that the EAR incorporates interest compounding in the computation, but the APR does not. Both computations adjust the percentage cost per period so that it is stated on an annual basis. We annualize the cost to make it easier to compare short-term credit instruments with different maturities. Next we illustrate the application of these equations for computing the cost of three short-term financing alternatives: (1) trade credit, (2) bank loans, and (3) commercial paper.

Computing the Cost of Trade Credit (Accounts Payable)

Consider Microchip's credit terms of 2/10, net 30, which allows its customers, such as Personal Computer Company (PCC), to take a 2 percent discount from the purchase price if payment is made on or before Day 10 of the billing cycle; otherwise, the entire bill is due by Day 30. If the invoice price is $100 and the firm does not take the discount, it effectively pays $2 to borrow $98 for a 20-day period, so the cost of using the funds for the additional 20 days is:

$$\text{Periodic rate} = k_{PER} = \frac{\$2}{\$98} = 0.020408 \approx 2.041\%$$

Because there are $18 = 360/20$ 20-day periods in a 360-day year, the APR, or simple interest rate, associated with the trade credit is:

$$APR = 0.02041 \times 18 = 0.367 = 36.7\%$$

The effective annual cost (rate), EAR, of using trade credit with these terms as a source of short-term financing is:

$$EAR = (1 + 0.02041)^{18} - 1.0 = 0.439 = 43.9\%$$

According to this computation, if PCC chooses to pay its bill on Day 30, then it will "forgo" the 2 percent cash discount, which is equivalent to borrowing funds at a rate of nearly 44 percent per year.[8] PCC should forgo the cash discount to pay on Day 30 only if alternative financing, such as bank loans, has a cost greater than 43.9 percent.

Computing the Cost of Bank Loans

A bank loan can take the form of a *simple interest loan*, a *discount loan*, or an *installment loan*. Factors such as a compensating balance or application fees can affect the cost of borrowing for each of these types of loans. Here we give some examples as to how to compute the cost for each of these loans.

SIMPLE INTEREST LOAN

Both the amount borrowed and the interest charged on that amount are paid at the maturity of the loan; there are no payments made before maturity.

FACE VALUE

The amount of the loan, or the amount borrowed; also called the *principal amount* of the loan.

QUOTED, OR SIMPLE, INTEREST RATE

The annual percentage rate (APR) that is used to compute the interest rate per period (k_{PER}).

Simple Interest Loan   With a **simple interest loan,** the borrower receives the **face value** of the loan (amount borrowed, or principal) and repays both the principal and the interest at maturity. For example, with a simple interest loan of $10,000 at 12 percent interest for nine months, the borrower receives the $10,000 upon approval of the loan and pays back the $10,000 principal plus $900 = $10,000[0.12 × (9/12)] in interest at maturity. Note that interest is paid only for the portion of the year the loan is outstanding, which is nine months in this case. The 12 percent is the **quoted, or simple, interest rate.**

The nine-month interest rate for this loan is:

$$k_{PER} = \frac{\text{Nine-month}}{\text{interest rate}} = \frac{\$10,000 \times \left[0.12 \times \left(\dfrac{9}{12}\right)\right]}{\$10,000} = 0.09 = 9.0\%$$

The APR for this loan is:

$$APR = 9.0\% \times \left(\frac{12}{9}\right) = 12.0\%$$

The EAR is

$$EAR = (1.09)^{\left(\frac{12}{9}\right)} - 1.0 = 0.1218 = 12.18\%$$

---

[8]We assume that the firm pays its supplier on the last day possible. That is, if it takes the discount, payment is made on Day 10; if it doesn't take the discount, payment is made on Day 30. This is rational business behavior. If, however, the firm does not take the discount, but pays on Day 20 (or any other time before the final due date), then the cost associated with using this source of financing is higher than computed here. The funds cost more because the firm uses them for a shorter period.

EAR > APR because this is a nine-month loan, which means interest compounding is assumed to occur every nine months.

DISCOUNT INTEREST LOAN
A loan in which the interest, which is calculated on the amount borrowed (principal), is paid at the beginning of the loan period; interest is paid in advance.

Discount Interest Loan   With a **discount interest loan,** the interest due is deducted "up front" so that the borrower receives less than the principal amount, or face value, of the loan. Assume Unilate Textiles receives a $10,000 discount interest loan with a 12 percent quoted (simple) interest rate to be used for a period of nine months. The interest payment on this loan is $900 = $10,000[0.12 × (9/12)]. Because the interest is paid in advance, the Unilate has only $9,100 = $10,000 − $900 available for use. Thus, the nine-month interest rate paid for the loan is

$$k_{PER} = \frac{\text{Nine-month}}{\text{interest rate}} = \frac{\$10,000\left[0.12 \times \left(\frac{9}{12}\right)\right]}{\$10,000 - \left\{\$10,000\left[0.12 \times \left(\frac{9}{12}\right)\right]\right\}}$$

$$= \frac{\$900}{\$9,100}$$

$$= 0.0989 = 9.89\%$$

The APR for the loan is

$$APR = 9.89\% \times \left(\frac{12}{9}\right) = 13.19\%$$

And, the EAR is

$$EAR = (1.0989)^{\left(\frac{12}{9}\right)} - 1.0 = 0.1340 = 13.40\%$$

What do you think the cost of the loan described here would be if Unilate's bank charged a $50 fee to cover the cost of processing the loan? To answer this question, first take a look at Equation 15–1 and determine whether the payment affects the numerator (that is, the dollar cost of borrowing), the denominator (that is, the amount of usable funds), or both. The general rule is that the numerator is affected by any expense associated with the loan, and the denominator is affected if funds must be put aside (for example, to satisfy a compensating balance requirement) or costs are paid out of the proceeds at the beginning of the loan period. Thus, if Unilate uses the proceeds from the loan to pay the $50 fee, both the numerator and the denominator are affected, and the nine-month interest rate is

$$k_{PER} = \frac{\text{Nine-month}}{\text{interest rate}} = \frac{\$900 + \$50}{\$9,100 - \$50} = \frac{\$950}{\$9,050} = 0.1050 = 10.50\%$$

Check to see that the APR and the EAR are now 14.0 percent and 14.2 percent, respectively.

ADD-ON INTEREST
Interest that is calculated and then added to the amount borrowed to obtain the total dollar amount to be paid back in equal installments.

Installment Loan: Add-On Interest   Lenders often charge **add-on interest** on various types of installment loans. The term *add-on* means that the interest is calculated and then added to the amount borrowed to obtain the total dollar amount to be paid back in equal installments. To illustrate, suppose Unilate borrows $10,000 on an add-on basis at a simple rate of 12 percent, with the loan to be repaid in nine monthly installments. At a 12 percent add-on rate, Unilate will pay a total interest charge of $900 as computed earlier, and a total of $10,900 in nine equal payments.

The monthly payments would be $1,211.11 = $10,900/9. Therefore, each month Unilate would pay $100 interest (1/9 of the total interest) and $1,111.11 principal repayment (1/9) of the $10,000 borrowed). Because the loan is paid off in monthly installments, Unilate will have use of the full $10,000 only for the first month, and the outstanding balance declines by $1,111.11 each month such that the remaining principal due at the beginning of the last month of the loan is $1,111.11. As a result, the percent cost of the loan varies each month.

Unilate would pay $900 for the use of approximately 50 percent of the loan's face amount because the average outstanding balance of the loan is only about $5,000 = ($10,000 + $0)/2. (The $10,000 is paid down evenly over the life of the loan.) With this information we can *approximate* the rate for the nine-month period as follows:

$$\frac{\text{Approximate rate}}{\text{per period}} = \frac{\$900}{\$5,000} = 0.18 = 18.0\%$$

The *approximate* APR would be 24.0% = 18.0% × (12/9).

To determine the EAR, recognize that the $1,211.11 payment Unilate makes each month represents an annuity. The cash flow time line for the loan would be:

0 k_{PER} = ?	1	2	3	4	5	6	7	8	9
($10,000)	$1,211.11	$1,211.11	$1,211.11	$1,211.11	$1,211.11	$1,211.11	$1,211.11	$1,211.11	$1,211.11

Using a financial calculator, enter N = 9, PV = –10,000, PMT = 1,211.11, and then solve for I. The *monthly* rate equals 1.759. In this case we assume monthly compounding, because the installment payments are made each month. When we annualize the monthly rate, the EAR is

$$\text{EAR} = (1.01759)^{12} - 1.0 = 0.2327 = 23.27\%$$

Computing the Cost of Commercial Paper

Suppose Unilate issues 270-day commercial paper with a face value equal to $10,000. The simple annual interest rate on the commercial paper is 12 percent, and the total transactions fee, which includes the cost of a backup line of credit, is 1/2 percent of the amount of the issue. Because commercial paper is a discount instrument similar to a discount loan, Unilate will not be able to use the total $10,000 face value. Instead, investors will purchase the commercial paper issue for $9,100 = $10,000 – $10,000[0.10 × (9/12)], and then receive $10,000 at maturity. The transaction fee, which equals $50 = 0.005 × $10,000, is "taken off the top," so Unilate actually would receive only $9,050 = $9,100 –$50 to use from the commercial paper issue. The total dollar cost of borrowing using commercial paper would be $950, which includes interest equal to $900 and the $50 transaction fee. As a result, the nine-month cost of the commercial paper would be:

$$k_{PER} = \frac{\text{Nine-month}}{\text{interest rate}} = \frac{\$10,000\left[0.12 \times \left(\frac{9}{12}\right)\right] + (0.005 \times \$10,000)}{\$10,000 - \left\{\$10,000\left[0.12 \times \left(\frac{9}{12}\right)\right]\right\} - (0.005 \times \$10,000)}$$

$$= \frac{\$900 + \$50}{\$9,050}$$

$$= 0.1050 = 10.50\%$$

The APR for this financing is:

$$\text{APR} = 10.50\% \times \left(\frac{12}{9}\right) = 14.00\%$$

And, the EAR is

$$\text{EAR} = (1.1050)^{\left(\frac{12}{9}\right)} - 1.0 = 0.1424 = 14.24\%$$

Borrowed (Principal) Amount versus Required (Needed) Amount

Compensating balances can raise the effective rate on a loan. To illustrate, suppose Unilate *needs* $10,000 to pay for some equipment it recently purchased. Atlantic/Pacific Bank offers to lend Unilate the money for nine months at a 12 percent simple rate, but the company must maintain a *compensating balance (CB)* equal to 20 percent of the loan amount (principal, or face value). First, note that Unilate needs to be able to use $10,000 to pay for the equipment. If the firm's checking account balance is not sufficient to cover the compensating balance requirement, then the principal amount of the loan must be greater than $10,000 because some of the amount borrowed must be put aside to satisfy the compensating balance requirement. In this case, the question is: How much must be borrowed so the firm will have $10,000 available for use? To answer this question, first we must determine the *usable funds* from a loan:

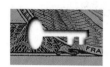

15–4

$$\text{Usable funds} = \left(\begin{array}{c}\text{Face (principal)}\\\text{amount of the loan}\end{array}\right) - \left(\begin{array}{c}\text{Dollar reductions}\\\text{from the face value}\end{array}\right)$$

If the dollar reductions from the face value of the loan are stated as percentages—for example, compensating balances—Equation 15–4 can be written as follows:

15–4a

$$\text{Usable funds} = \left(\begin{array}{c}\text{Face (principal)}\\\text{amount of the loan}\end{array}\right) \times \left[1 - \left(\begin{array}{c}\text{Reductions from the face}\\\text{value stated as a decimal}\end{array}\right)\right]$$

If we know how much of the amount borrowed actually is needed as usable funds, Equation 15–4a can be rearranged to solve for the amount that must be borrowed (principal amount) to provide these needed funds. The computation is:

15–5

$$\begin{array}{c}\text{Required loan}\\\text{(principal) amount}\end{array} = \dfrac{\text{Amount of usable funds needed}}{1 - \left(\begin{array}{c}\text{Reductions from the principal}\\\text{amount (face) stated as a decimal}\end{array}\right)}$$

If it does not have a checking account at Atlantic/Pacific Bank, then Unilate will have to borrow $12,500 to be able to satisfy the 20 percent compensating balance requirement and have $10,000 available to pay for the equipment. The computation follows:

$$\begin{array}{c}\text{Required loan}\\\text{(principal) amount}\end{array} = \frac{\$10,000}{1 - 0.20} = \$12,500$$

In this case, the nine-month rate for this loan would be:

$$k_{\text{PER}} = \begin{array}{c}\text{Nine-month}\\\text{interest rate}\end{array} = \frac{\$12,500\left[0.12\left(\frac{9}{12}\right)\right]}{\$12,500 - \$12,500(0.20)} = \frac{\$1,125}{\$10,000} = 0.1125 = 11.25\%$$

The APR and EAR are:

$$\text{APR} = 11.25\% \times \left(\frac{12}{9}\right) = 0.15 = 15.0\%$$

$$\text{EAR} = (1.1125)^{\left(\frac{12}{9}\right)} - 1.0 = 0.1527 = 15.27\%$$

If a firm normally keeps a positive checking account balance at the lending bank, then (1) it needs to borrow less to have a specific amount of funds available for use, and (2) the effective cost of the loan will be lower.

From the examples presented here, you should recognize that the percentage cost of short-term financing is higher when the dollar expenses, such as those associated with interest, clerical efforts, and loan processing, are higher or when the net proceeds from the loan are less than the principal amount. In most cases, then, the effective interest rate (cost) of short-term financing is greater than its stated (quoted) interest rate. *The effective interest rate of a loan is equal to the quoted (simple) rate only if (1) the entire principal amount borrowed can be used by the borrower for one full year, and (2) the only dollar cost associated with the loan is interest charged on the outstanding balance.*

Self-Test Questions

What is the difference between APR and EAR?

All else equal, what causes the APR and EAR to increase?

How does a discount loan differ from an installment loan?

For what reasons would the amount of a loan that a borrower can actually use be less than the principal amount borrowed?

Everything else equal, how does the effective cost of a loan compare to its simple interest rate if (1) the usable amount is less than the principal amount, or (2) the loan period is less than one year?

Use of Security in Short-Term Financing

Thus far we have not addressed the question of whether loans should be secured. Commercial paper is not secured, but all other types of loans can be secured if this is deemed necessary or desirable. Given a choice, it ordinarily is better to borrow on an unsecured basis because the bookkeeping costs of **secured loans** often are high.

SECURED LOAN

A loan backed by collateral; for short-term loans, the collateral often is inventory, receivables, or both.

However, weak firms might find that they can borrow only if they put up some type of security or that by using security they can borrow at a lower rate.

Several different kinds of security, or collateral, can be employed, including marketable securities, land or buildings, equipment, inventory, and accounts receivable. Marketable securities make excellent collateral, but few firms that need loans also hold such portfolios. Similarly, real property (land and buildings) and equipment are good forms of collateral, but they generally are used as security for long-term loans rather than for working capital loans. Therefore, most secured short-term business borrowing involves the use of accounts receivables and inventories as collateral.

To understand the use of security, consider the case of a Chicago hardware dealer who wanted to modernize and expand his store. He requested a $200,000 bank loan. After examining his firm's financial statements, the bank indicated that it would lend him a maximum of $100,000 and that the interest rate would be 12 percent, discount interest, for an effective rate of 13.6 percent. The owner had a substantial personal portfolio of stocks, and he offered to put up $300,000 of high-quality stocks to support the $200,000 loan. The bank then granted the full $200,000 loan, and at a rate of only 11 percent, simple interest. The store owner also might have used his inventories or receivables as security for the loan, but processing costs would have been high.[9]

UNIFORM COMMERCIAL CODE

A system of standards that simplifies procedures for establishing loan security.

In the past, state laws have varied greatly with regard to the use of security in financing. Today, however, nearly every secured loan is established under the **Uniform Commercial Code,** which has standardized and simplified the procedures for establishing loan security. The heart of the Uniform Commercial Code is the *Security Agreement*, a standardized document on which the specific pledged assets are listed. The assets can be items of equipment, accounts receivable, or inventories. Procedures under the Uniform Commercial Code for using accounts receivable and inventories as security for short-term credit are described in the following sections.

Accounts Receivable Financing

Accounts receivable financing involves either the pledging of receivables or the selling of receivables (called *factoring*). The **pledging** of accounts receivable is characterized by the fact that the lender not only has a claim against the receivables but also has **recourse** to the borrower: If the person or firm that bought the goods does not pay, the selling firm (borrower) rather than the lender must take the loss. Therefore, the risk of default on the pledged accounts receivable remains with the borrowing firm. The customer of the borrowing firm ordinarily is not notified about the pledging of the receivables, and the financial institution that lends on the security of accounts receivable generally is either a commercial bank or one of the large industrial finance companies.

PLEDGING RECEIVABLES

Using accounts receivable as collateral for a loan.

RECOURSE

The lender can seek payment from the borrowing firm when receivables' accounts used to secure a loan are uncollectible.

FACTORING

The outright sale of receivables.

Factoring, or *selling accounts receivable*, involves the purchase of accounts receivable by the lender (called a factor), generally without recourse to the borrower, which means that if a receivable account that is factored cannot be collected, the lender rather than the seller of the goods (borrower) takes the loss. Under factoring, the borrowing firm's customers generally are notified of the transfer and are asked to

---

[9]The term *asset-based financing* is often used as a synonym for *secured financing*. In recent years accounts receivable have been used as security for long-term bonds, and this permits corporations to borrow from lenders such as pension funds rather than being restricted to banks and other traditional short-term lenders.

make payments directly to the lending institution (factor). Because the factor assumes the risk of default on bad accounts, it generally carries out the credit investigation. Accordingly, factors provide not only money but also a credit department for the borrower. Incidentally, the same financial institutions that make loans against pledged receivables also serve as factors. Thus, depending on the circumstances and the wishes of the borrower, a financial institution will provide either type of receivables financing.

Procedure for Pledging Accounts Receivable The financing of accounts receivable is initiated by a legally binding agreement between the seller of the goods (borrower) and the financing institution (lender). The agreement sets forth in detail the procedures to be followed and the legal obligations of both parties. Once the working relationship has been established, the seller periodically takes a batch of invoices to the financing institution. The lender reviews the invoices and makes credit appraisals of the buyers. Invoices of companies that do not meet the lender's credit standards are not accepted for pledging.

The financial institution seeks to protect itself at every phase of the operation. First, selection of sound invoices is one way the lender safeguards itself. Second, if the buyer of the goods does not pay the invoice, the lender still has recourse against the seller (the borrowing firm). Third, additional protection is afforded the lender because the loan generally will be less than 100 percent of the pledged receivables; for example, the lender might advance the selling firm only 85 percent of the amount of the pledged invoices. The percent advanced depends on the quality of the accounts pledged.

Procedure for Factoring Accounts Receivable The procedures used in factoring are somewhat different from those for pledging. Again, an agreement between the seller and the factor specifies legal obligations and procedural arrangements. When the seller receives an order from a customer, a credit approval slip is written and immediately sent to the factoring company for a credit check. If the factor approves the credit, shipment is made and the invoice is stamped to notify the customer to make payment directly to the factoring company. If the factor does not approve the sale, the seller generally refuses to fill the order; if the sale is made anyway, the factor will not buy the account.

The factor normally performs three functions: (1) credit checking, (2) lending, and (3) risk bearing. Consider a typical factoring situation: The goods are shipped, and even though payment is not due for 30 days, the factor immediately makes funds available to the borrower (the firm selling the goods). Suppose $10,000 worth of goods are shipped. Further, assume that the factoring commission for credit checking and risk bearing is 2½ percent of the invoice price, or $250, and that the interest expense is computed at a 9 percent annual rate on the invoice balance, or $75 = $10,000 \times (0.09/360) \times 30$ days. The selling firm would have the following:

Cash	$ 9,175
Interest Expense	75
Factoring Commission	250
Reserve due from factor in collection account	500
Accounts receivable	$10,000

The $500 due from the factor upon collection of the account is a reserve established by the factor to cover disputes between the selling firm and customers over

"Factoring"—A Dirty Word or a Competitive Tool?

Traditionally, the word *factoring* has projected a negative connotation in the business world because it was felt that a firm should sell receivables only when it was financially distressed. And companies that purchased other firms' receivables (called factors) were generally viewed with disdain because the rates they charged ranged from 20 percent and 35 percent or more, which seemed exorbitant. Most large, reputable banks shunned factoring because they favored the more traditional, less risky commercial lending process and because they wanted to avoid the stigma that was associated with factoring. More recently, however, banks have become more interested in factoring and have begun to offer factoring services themselves or have formed close alliances with established factoring organizations. This newfound interest has emerged for two reasons. First, there is a great deal of profit to be made in the factoring business; in the past few years, the volume of factored receivables has grown by more than 10 percent per year. Second, and probably more important, banks now view factoring as a means to establish business relationships with young, upstart companies that have substantial growth potentials. Such firms generally lack either suitable credit reputations or sufficient collateral to allow them to obtain traditional bank financing. But banks now view alternative financing arrangements, such as factoring, as a means to attract customers that might use the more traditional banking services in the future. Thus, banks have begun to establish business relationships with firms that need support for critical growth needs, hoping the firms that survive and establish themselves might later begin using some of the other services that are offered. More banks now view factoring as a way to reach future business today rather than competing for it tomorrow.

Marshall Associates, a satellite-based telecommunications and networking technology company that was founded in 1991, provides an example of how factoring can be used to establish banking relationships. After participating in government projects with major defense companies in 1993 and 1994, Marshall's cash inflows dwindled in 1995 as the government contracts ended. To generate the cash needed to keep the firm going, Marshall took the advice of its bank and sold its receivables to a factoring company (not its bank), which advanced Marshall between 75 percent and 80 percent of the face value of the factored receivables. The cash it received for its receivables helped Marshall keep its head above water. As Marshall's business picked up and it began generating more cash, the factor was used less frequently. And, at the end of 1997, Marshall effectively returned to its bank for financing, establishing a $250,000 line of credit to provide future working capital needs. Had the bank turned its back on Marshall when the company was cash poor, either Marshall would no longer be in business or it might have taken its business to another bank.

Sources: Adam Weintraub, "Factoring on the Rise as Finance Option," *City Business-Minneapolis MNCB* January 1, 1999, and Marlon Millner, "A Matter of Factoring Money: Sterling Businessman Turned to Receivables Financing When the Bank Wouldn't Loan Him Money," *Washington Business Journal*, April 3, 1998. Both articles are from American City Business Journals Inc. and were retrieved using the USF Virtual Library Business and Economics search.

damaged goods, goods returned by customers to the selling firm, and the failure to make an outright sale of goods. The reserve is paid to the selling firm when the factor collects on the account.

Factoring normally is a continuous process instead of the single cycle just described. The firm that sells the goods receives an order; it transmits this order to the factor for approval; upon approval, the firm ships the goods; the factor advances the invoice amount minus withholdings to the selling firm, the buyer (customer) pays the factor when payment is due; and the factor periodically remits any excess in the reserve to the selling firm. Once a routine has been established, a continuous circular flow of goods and funds takes place between the selling firm, the buyers of the goods, and the factor. Thus, once the factoring agreement is in force, funds from this source are *spontaneous* in the sense that an increase in sales automatically generates additional credit.

Visa and MasterCard represent a prime example of nonrecourse factoring. When you purchase from a retailer such as Wal-Mart using Visa or MasterCard, the retailer is paid only 95 to 97 percent of the invoice by these credit companies. The reason the 3 to 5 percent discount is charged by Visa and MasterCard is because they provide credit checking services and suffer any losses due to customer nonpayment—the retailer does not incur these costs.

Cost of Receivables Financing   Both accounts receivable pledging and factoring are convenient and advantageous, but they can be costly. The credit-checking and risk-bearing fee is 1 percent to 5 percent of the amount of invoices accepted by the factor, and it could be even more if the buyers are poor credit risks. The cost of money is reflected in the interest rate (usually 2 to 3 percentage points over the prime rate) charged on the unpaid balance of the funds advanced by the factor.

Evaluation of Receivables Financing   It cannot be said categorically that accounts receivable financing is either a good or a bad way to raise funds. Among the advantages is, first, the flexibility of this source of financing: As the firm's sales expand, more financing is needed, but a larger volume of invoices, and hence a larger amount of receivables financing, is generated automatically. Second, receivables can be used as security for loans that otherwise would not be granted. Third, factoring can provide the services of a credit department that otherwise might be available only at a higher cost.

Accounts receivable financing also has disadvantages. First, when invoices are numerous and relatively small in dollar amount, the administrative costs involved might be excessive. Second, because receivables represent the firm's most liquid non-cash assets, some trade creditors might refuse to sell on credit to a firm that factors or pledges its receivables on the grounds that this practice weakens the firm's financial strength.

Future Use of Receivables Financing   It is easy to make a prediction at this point: In the future, accounts receivable financing will increase in relative importance. Computer technology has advanced to the point where credit records of individuals and firms can be kept on electronic media. For example, one device used by retailers consists of a box which, when an individual's magnetic credit card is inserted, gives a signal that the credit is "good" and that a bank is willing to "buy" the receivable created as soon as the store completes the sale. The cost of handling invoices will be reduced greatly over present-day costs because the new systems will be so highly automated. This will make it possible to use accounts receivable financing for very small sales, and it will reduce the cost of all receivables financing. The net result will be a marked expansion of accounts receivable financing. In fact, when consumers use credit cards such as MasterCard or Visa, the seller is in effect factoring receivables. The seller receives the amount of the purchase, minus a percentage fee, the next working day. The credit card user (buyer) receives 30 days' (or so) credit, at which time he or she remits payment directly to the credit card company or sponsoring bank.

Inventory Financing

A substantial amount of credit is secured by business inventories. If a firm is a relatively good credit risk, the mere existence of the inventory might be a sufficient basis for receiving an unsecured loan. However, if the firm is a relatively poor risk, the lending institution might insist on security in the form of a *lien*, or legal claim, against the inventory. Methods for using inventories as security are discussed in this section.

Blanket Liens   The *inventory blanket lien* gives the lending institution a lien against all of the borrower's inventories. However, the borrower is free to sell inventories, and thus the value of the collateral can be reduced below the level that existed when the loan was granted. A blanket lien generally is used when the inventory put up as collateral is relatively low priced, fast moving, and difficult to identify individually.

Trust Receipts   Because of the inherent weakness of the blanket lien, another procedure for inventory financing has been developed—the *trust receipt*, which is an instrument acknowledging that the goods are held in trust for the lender. Under this method, the borrowing firm, as a condition for receiving funds from the lender, signs and delivers a trust receipt for the goods. The goods can be stored in a public warehouse or held on the premises of the borrower. The trust receipt states that the goods are held in trust for the lender or are segregated on the borrower's premises on the lender's behalf and that any proceeds from the sale of the goods must be transmitted to the lender at the end of each day. Automobile dealer financing is one of the best examples of trust receipt financing.

One defect of trust receipt financing is the requirement that a trust receipt be issued for specific goods. For example, if the security is automobiles in a dealer's inventory, the trust receipts must indicate the cars by registration number. To validate its trust receipts, the lending institution must send someone to the borrower's premises periodically to see that the auto numbers are listed correctly, because auto dealers who are in financial difficulty have been known to sell cars backing trust receipts and then use the funds for other operations rather than to repay the bank. Problems are compounded if the borrower has a number of different locations, especially if they are separated geographically from the lender. To offset these inconveniences, *warehousing* has come into wide use as a method of securing loans with inventory.

Warehouse Receipts   Warehouse receipt financing is another way to use inventory as security. A *public warehouse* is an independent third-party operation engaged in the business of storing goods. Items that require aging, such as tobacco and liquor, are often financed and stored in public warehouses. When the inventory products used as collateral are moved to public warehouses, the financing arrangement is termed *terminal warehousing*. Sometimes terminal warehousing is not practical because of the bulkiness of goods and the expense of transporting them to and from the borrower's premises. In such cases, a *field warehouse* might be established on the borrower's grounds. To provide inventory supervision, the lending institution employs a third party in the arrangement, the field warehousing company, which acts as its agent.

Field warehousing can be illustrated by a simple example. Suppose a firm that has iron stacked in an open yard on its premises needs a loan. A field warehousing concern can place a temporary fence around the iron, erecting a sign stating, "This is a field warehouse supervised by the Smith Field Warehousing Corporation," and then assign an employee to supervise and control the fenced-in inventory.

This example illustrates the three essential elements for the establishment of a field warehouse: (1) public notification; (2) physical control of the inventory; and (3) supervision by a custodian of the field warehousing concern. When the field warehousing operation is relatively small, the third condition is sometimes violated by hiring an employee of the borrower to supervise the inventory. This practice is viewed as undesirable by most lenders because there is no control over the collateral by a person independent of the borrowing firm.[10]

Acceptable Products   Canned foods account for nearly 20 percent of all field warehouse loans. In addition, many other types of products provide a basis for field warehouse financing. Some of these are miscellaneous groceries, which represent nearly 15 percent; lumber products, about 10 percent; and coal and coke, about 5 percent. These products are relatively nonperishable and are sold in well-developed, organized markets. Nonperishability protects the lender if it should have to take over the security. For this reason, a bank would not make a field warehousing loan on perishables such as fresh fish; but frozen fish, which can be stored for a long time, can be field warehoused.

Cost of Financing   The fixed costs of a field warehousing arrangement are relatively high; such financing therefore is not suitable for a very small firm. If a field warehousing company sets up a field warehouse, it typically will set a minimum charge of about $25,000 per year, plus about 1 to 2 percent of the amount of credit extended to the borrower. Furthermore, the financing institution will charge an interest rate of 2 to 3 percentage points over the prime rate. An efficient field warehousing operation requires an inventory of at least $1 million.

Evaluation of Inventory Financing   The use of inventory financing, especially field warehouse financing, as a source of funds has many advantages. First, the amount of funds available is flexible because the financing is tied to the growth of inventories, which in turn is related directly to financing needs. Second, the field warehousing arrangement increases the acceptability of inventories as loan collateral; some inventories simply would not be accepted by a bank as security without such an arrangement. Third, the necessity for inventory control and safekeeping as well as the use of specialists in warehousing often results in improved warehouse practices, which in turn save handling costs, insurance charges, theft losses, and so forth. Thus, field warehousing companies often save money for firms despite the costs of financing that we have discussed. The major disadvantage of field warehousing include the paperwork, physical separation requirements, and, for small firms, the fixed-cost element.

---

[10]The absence of independent control was the main cause of a breakdown that resulted in more than $200 million of losses on loans to the Allied Crude Vegetable Oil Company by Bank of America and other banks. American Express Field Warehousing Company was handling the operation, but it hired men from Allied's own staff as custodians. Their dishonesty was not discovered because of another breakdown—the fact that the American Express touring inspector did not actually take a physical inventory of the warehouses. As a consequence, the swindle was not discovered until losses running into the hundreds of millions of dollars had been suffered.

Self-Test Questions

What is a secured loan?

What two types of current assets are pledged as security for short-term loans?

Differentiate between pledging accounts receivable and factoring accounts receivable.

Identify the services a factor normally provides.

List the advantages and disadvantages of accounts receivable financing.

Describe three methods of inventory financing.

What are some advantages and disadvantages of inventory financing?

Summary

This chapter examined (1) the different types of short-term credit available to firms, (2) the decisions financial managers make when selecting among types of short-term credit, and (3) decisions regarding the use of security to obtain credit. The key concepts covered are listed here:

- **Short-term credit** is defined as any liability originally scheduled for payment within one year. The four major sources of short-term credit are (1) *accruals*, (2) *accounts payable*, (3) *bank loans*, and (4) *commercial paper*.
- **Accruals,** which are continually recurring short-term liabilities, represent free, spontaneous credit.
- **Accounts payable,** or **trade credit,** is the largest category of short-term debt. This credit arises spontaneously as a result of purchases on credit. Firms should use all the **free trade credit** they can obtain, but they should use **costly trade credit** only if it is less expensive than other forms of short-term debt. Suppliers often offer discounts to customers who pay within a stated discount period.
- **Bank loans** are an important source of short-term credit. Interest on bank loans might be quoted as **simple interest, discount interest,** or **add-on interest.**
- When a bank loan is approved, a **promissory note** is signed. It specifies (1) the amount borrowed, (2) the percentage interest rate, (3) the repayment schedule, (4) the collateral, and (5) any other conditions to which the parties have agreed.
- Banks sometimes require borrowers to maintain **compensating balances,** which are deposit requirements set at between 10 percent and 20 percent of the loan amount. Compensating balances generally increase the effective cost of bank loans.
- A **line of credit** is an understanding between the bank and the borrower indicating the maximum amount of credit the bank will extend to the borrower.
- A **revolving credit** agreement is a formal, guaranteed line of credit that involves a **commitment fee.**
- **Commercial paper** is unsecured short-term debt issued by a large, financially strong corporation. Although the cost of commercial paper is lower than the cost of bank loans, commercial paper's maturity is limited to 270 days, and it can be used only by large firms with exceptionally strong credit ratings.
- In a **simple interest loan,** both the amount borrowed and the interest charged on that amount are paid at the maturity of the loan; there are no payments made before maturity.

- **Face value** is the amount of the loan, or the amount borrowed; also called the *principal amount* of the loan.
- The **quoted, or simple, interest rate** is the annual percentage rate (APR) that is used to compute the interest rate per period (k_{PER}).
- A **discount interest loan** is a loan in which the interest, which is calculated on the amount borrowed (principal), is paid at the beginning of the loan period; interest is paid in advance.
- **Add-on interest** is interest that is calculated and then added to the amount borrowed to obtain the total dollar amount to be paid back in equal installments.
- Sometimes a borrower will find it necessary to borrow on a **secured basis,** in which case the borrower pledges assets such as real estate, securities, equipment, inventories, or accounts receivable as collateral for the loan.
- Accounts receivable financing involves either *pledging* or *factoring* receivables. Under a **pledging** arrangement, the lender not only gets a claim against the receivables but also has recourse to the borrower. **Factoring** involves the purchase of accounts receivable by the lender, generally without recourse to the borrower.
- There are three primary methods of inventory financing: (1) An **inventory blanket lien** gives the lender a lien against all of the borrower's inventories. (2) A **trust receipt** is an instrument that acknowledges that goods are held in trust for the lender. (3) **Warehouse receipt** financing is an arrangement under which the lender employs a third party to exercise control over the borrower's inventory and to act as the lender's agent.

Questions

15-1 "Firms can control their accruals within fairly wide limits; depending on the cost of accruals, financing from this source will be increased or decreased." Discuss.

15-2 Is it true that both trade credit and accruals represent a spontaneous source of capital for financing growth? Explain.

15-3 Is it true that most firms are able to obtain some free trade credit and that additional trade credit often is available, but at a cost? Explain.

15-4 The availability of bank credit often is more important to a small firm than to a large one. Why?

15-5 What kinds of firms use commercial paper? Could Mama and Papa Gus's Corner Grocery borrow using this form of credit?

15-6 Suppose a firm can obtain funds by borrowing at the prime rate or by selling commercial paper.
   a. If the prime rate is 5½ percent, what is a reasonable estimate for the cost of commercial paper?
   b. If a substantial cost differential exists, why might a firm like this one actually borrow some of its funds in each market?

15-7 Can you think of some firms that might allow you to purchase on credit, but probably would factor your receivables account?

15-8 On average, which group of borrowers would have to pay a higher effective rate for its short-term loans, those who are required to put up collateral or those who are not? Explain.

Self-Test Problems

(Solutions appear in Appendix B)

key terms **ST-1** Define each of the following terms:
   a. Accruals
   b. Trade credit; stretching accounts payable; free trade credit; costly trade credit
   c. Promissory note; line of credit; revolving credit agreement
   d. Prime rate
   e. Simple interest; discount interest; add-on interest
   f. Compensating balance (CB); commitment fee
   g. Commercial paper
   h. Secured loan
   i. Uniform Commercial Code
   j. Pledging receivables; factoring
   k. Recourse; without recourse
   l. Inventory blanket lien; trust receipt; warehouse receipt financing; field warehouse

receivables financing **ST-2** The Naylor Corporation is considering two methods of raising working capital: (1) a commercial bank loan secured by accounts receivable and (2) factoring accounts receivable. Naylor's bank has agreed to lend the firm 75 percent of its average monthly accounts receivable balance of $250,000 at an annual interest rate of 9 percent. The bank loan is in the form of a series of 30-day loans. The loan would be discounted, and a 20 percent compensating balance would also be required.

A factor has agreed to purchase Naylor's accounts receivable and to advance 85 percent of the balance to the firm. The 15 percent of receivables not loaned to the firm under the factoring arrangement is held in a reserve account. The factor would charge a 3.5 percent factoring commission and annual interest of 9 percent on the invoice price, less both the factoring commission and the reserve account. The monthly interest payment would be deducted from the advance. If Naylor chooses the factoring arrangement, it can eliminate its credit department and reduce operating expenses by $4,000 per month. In addition, bad debt losses of 2 percent of the monthly receivables will be avoided.
   a. What is the annual cost associated with each financing arrangement?
   b. Discuss some considerations other than cost that might influence management's decision between factoring and a commercial bank loan.

Problems

cash discounts **15–1** Suppose a firm makes purchases of $3.6 million per year under terms of 2/10, net 30 and *takes discounts*.
   a. What is the average amount of accounts payable net of discounts? (Assume that the $3.6 million of purchases is net of discounts—that is, gross purchases are $3,673,469 and discounts are $73,469. Also, use 360 days in a year.)
   b. Is there a cost of the trade credit the firm uses?
   c. If the firm did not take discounts and it paid on time, what would be its average payables and the APR and EAR of this non-free trade credit? Assume the firm records accounts payable net of discounts.
   d. What would be the APR and EAR of not taking discounts if the firm can stretch its payments to 40 days?

trade credit versus bank credit

15–2 Gallinger Corporation projects an increase in sales from $1.5 million to $2 million, but it needs an additional $300,000 of current assets to support this expansion. The money can be obtained from the bank at an interest rate of 13 percent, discount interest; no compensating balance is required. Alternatively, Gallinger can finance the expansion by no longer taking discounts, thus increasing accounts payable. Gallinger purchases under terms of 2/10, net 30, but it can delay payment for an *additional* 35 days—paying in 65 days and thus becoming 35 days past due—without a penalty because of its suppliers' current excess capacity problems.
a. Based strictly on effective annual interest rate comparisons, how should Gallinger finance its expansion?
b. What additional qualitative factors should Gallinger consider before reaching a decision?

cost of bank loans

15–3 The UFSU Corporation intends to borrow $450,000 to support its short-term financing requirements during the next year. The company is evaluating its financing options at the bank where it maintains its checking account. UFSU's checking account balance, which averages $50,000, can be used to help satisfy any compensating balance requirements the bank might impose. The financing alternatives offered by the bank include the following:

Alternative 1:   A discount interest loan with a simple interest of 9¼ percent and no compensating balance requirement.
Alternative 2:   A 10 percent simple interest loan that has a 15 percent compensating balance requirement.
Alternative 3:   A $1 million revolving line of credit with simple interest of 9¼ percent paid on the amount borrowed and a ¼ percent commitment fee on the unused balance. No compensating balance is required.

a. Compute the effective cost (rate) of each financing alternative assuming UFSU *borrows* $450,000. Which alternative should UFSU use?
b. For each alternative, how much would UFSU have to borrow to have $450,000 available for use (to pay the firms bills)?

cost of bank loans

15–4 Gifts Galore Inc. borrowed $1.5 million from National City Bank (NCB). The loan was made at a simple annual interest rate of 9 percent a year for three months. A 20 percent compensating balance requirement raised the effective interest rate because the company does not maintain a checking balance at NCB.
a. The APR on the loan was 11.25 percent. What was the EAR?
b. What would be the EAR of the loan if the note required discount interest?
c. What would be the approximate annual interest rate on the loan if National City Bank required Gifts Galore to repay the loan and interest in three equal monthly installments?

short-term financing analysis

15–5 Bankston Feed and Supply Company buys on terms of 1/10, net 30, but it has not been taking discounts and has actually been paying in 60 days rather than 30 days. Bankston's balance sheet follows (thousands of dollars):

Cash	$ 50	Accounts payable[a]	$ 500
Accounts receivable	450	Notes payable	50
Inventories	750	Accruals	50
Current assets	$1,250	Current liabilities	$ 600
		Long-term debt	150
Fixed assets	750	Common equity	1,250
Total assets	$2,000	Total liabilities and equity	$2,000

[a]Stated net of discounts.

Now Bankston's suppliers are threatening to stop shipments unless the company begins making prompt payments (that is, paying in 30 days or less). The firm can borrow on a one-year note (call this a current liability) from its bank at a rate of 15 percent, discount interest, with a 20 percent compensating balance required. (Bankston's $50,000 of cash is needed for transactions; it cannot be used as part of the compensating balance.)

a. Determine what action Bankston should take by calculating (1) the cost of nonfree trade credit and (2) the cost of the bank loan.

b. Assume that Bankston forgoes discounts and then borrows the amount needed to become current on its payables from the bank. How large will the bank loan be?

c. Based on your conclusion in part a, construct a pro forma balance sheet. (*Hint:* Remember that the interest for a discount loan is paid "up front"; therefore, you will need to include an account titled "prepaid interest" under current assets.)

alternative financing arrangements
15–6 Suntime Boats Limited estimates that because of the seasonal nature of its business, it will require an additional $2 million of cash for the month of July. Suntime Boats has the following four options available for raising the needed funds:

(1) Establish a one-year line of credit for $2 million with a commercial bank. The commitment fee will be ½ percent per year on the unused portion, and the interest charge on the used funds will be 11 percent per annum. Assume that the funds are needed only in July and that there are 30 days in July and 360 days in the year.

(2) Forgo the cash discount of 2/10, net 40 on $2 million of purchases during July.

(3) Issue $2 million of 30-day commercial paper at a 9½ percent simple annual interest rate. The total transactions fee, including the cost of a backup credit line, on using commercial paper is ½ percent of the amount of the issue.

(4) Issue $2 million of 60-day commercial paper at a 9 percent per annum interest rate, plus a transactions fee of ½ percent. Because the funds are required for only 30 days, the excess funds ($2 million) can be invested in 9.4 percent per annum marketable securities for the month of August. The total transactions cost of purchasing and selling the marketable securities is 0.4 percent of the amount of the issue.

a. What is the *dollar* cost of each financing arrangement?

b. Is the source with the lowest expected cost necessarily the one to select? Why or why not?

factoring receivables
15–7 Cooley Industries needs an additional $500,000, which it plans to obtain through a factoring arrangement. The factor would purchase Cooley's accounts receivable and advance the invoice amount, minus a 2 percent commission, on the invoices purchased each month. Cooley sells on terms of net 30 days. In addition, the factor charges a 12 percent annual interest rate on the total invoice amount, to be deducted in advance.

a. What amount of accounts receivable must be factored to net $500,000?

b. If Cooley can reduce credit expenses by $3,500 per month and avoid bad debt losses of 2.5 percent on the factored amount, what is the total dollar cost of the factoring arrangement?

c. What would be the total cost of the factoring arrangement if Cooley's funding needs rose to $750,000? Would the factoring arrangement be profitable under these circumstances?

field warehousing   **15-8** Because of crop failures last year, the San Joaquin Packing Company has no funds available to finance its canning operations during the next six months. It estimates that it will require $1,200,000 from inventory financing during the period. One alternative is to establish a six-month, $1,500,000 line of credit with terms of 9 percent annual interest on the used portion, a 1 percent commitment fee on the unused portion, and a $300,000 compensating balance at all times. The other alternative is to use field warehouse financing. The costs of the field warehouse arrangement in this case would be a flat fee of $2,000, plus 8 percent annual interest on all outstanding credit, plus 1 percent of the maximum amount of credit extended.

Expected inventory levels to be financed are as follows:

MONTH	AMOUNT
July	$ 250,000
August	1,000,000
September	1,200,000
October	950,000
November	600,000
December	0

a. Calculate the cost of funds from using the line of credit. Be sure to include interest charges and commitment fees. Note that each month's borrowings will be $300,000 greater than the inventory level to be financed because of the compensating balance requirement.

b. Calculate the total cost of the field warehousing operation.

c. Compare the cost of the field warehousing arrangement to the cost of the line of credit. Which alternative should San Joaquin choose?

Exam-Type Problems

The problems included in this section are set up in such a way that they could be used as multiple-choice exam problems.

cost of trade credit   **15-9** Calculate the APR of nonfree trade credit under each of following terms. Assume payment is made either on the last due date or on the discount date.
   a. 1/15, net 20.
   b. 2/10, net 60.
   c. 3/10, net 45.
   d. 2/10, net 45.
   e. 2/15, net 40.

cost of credit   **15-10** a. If a firm buys under terms of 3/15, net 45, but actually pays on the 20th day and still takes the discount, what is the APR of its nonfree trade credit?

   b. Does the firm receive more or less credit than it would if it paid within 15 days?

cost of bank credit   **15-11** Susan Visscher, owner of Visscher's Hardware, is negotiating with First Merchant's Bank for a $50,000, one-year loan. First Merchant's has offered Visscher the following alternatives. Calculate the effective interest rate (EAR) for each alternative. Which alternative has the lowest EAR?

   a. A 12 percent annual rate on a simple interest loan with no compensating balance required and interest due at the end of the year.

   b. A 9 percent annual rate on a simple interest loan with a 20 percent compensating balance required and interest again due at the end of the year.

    c. An 8.75 percent annual rate on a discounted loan with a 15 percent compensating balance.

    d. Interest is figured as 8 percent of the $50,000 amount, payable at the end of the year, but the $50,000 is repayable in monthly installments during the year.

cost of trade credit   **15–12** Howe Industries sells on terms of 2/10, net 40. Gross sales last year were $4.5 million, and accounts receivable averaged $437,500. Half of Howe's customers paid on Day 10 and took discounts. What is the cost of trade credit to Howe's nondiscount customers? (*Hint:* Calculate sales per day based on a 360-day year, get the average receivables of discount customers, and then find the DSO for the nondiscount customers.)

cost of credit   **15–13** Boles Corporation needs to raise $500,000 for one year to supply capital to a new store. Boles buys from its suppliers on terms of 3/10, net 90, and it currently pays on Day 10 and takes discounts, but it could forgo discounts, pay on Day 90, and get the needed $500,000 in the form of costly trade credit. Alternatively, Boles could borrow from its bank on a 12 percent discount interest rate basis. What is the EAR of the lower cost source?

effective cost of short-term credit   **15–14** The Meyer Company must arrange financing for its working capital requirements for the coming year. Meyer can (a) borrow from its bank on a simple interest basis (interest payable at the end of the loan) for one year at a 12 percent simple rate; (b) borrow on a three-month, renewable loan at an 11.5 percent simple rate; (c) borrow on an installment loan basis at a 6.0 percent add-on rate with 12 end-of-month payments; or (d) obtain the needed funds by no longer taking discounts and thus increasing its accounts payable. Meyer buys on terms of 1/15, net 60. What is the EAR of the least expensive type of credit, assuming 360 days per year?

Integrative Problem

short-term financing   **15–15** C. Charles Smith recently was hired as president of Dellvoe Office Equipment Inc., a small manufacturer of metal office equipment. As his assistant, you have been asked to review the company's short-term financing policies and to prepare a report for Smith and the board of directors. To help you get started, Smith has prepared some questions that, when answered, will give him a better idea of the company's short-term financing policies.

    a. What is short-term credit, and what are the four major sources of this credit?

    b. Is there a cost to accruals, and do firms have much control over them?

    c. What is trade credit?

    d. Like most small companies, Dellvoe has two primary sources of short-term debt: trade credit and bank loans. One supplier, which supplies Dellvoe with $50,000 of materials a year, offers Dellvoe terms of 2/10, net 50.

       (1) What are Dellvoe's net daily purchases from this supplier?

       (2) What is the average level of Dellvoe's accounts payable to this supplier if the discount is taken? What is the average level if the discount is not taken? What are the amounts of free credit and costly credit under both discount policies?

       (3) What is the APR of the costly trade credit? What is its EAR?

    e. In discussing a possible loan with the firm's banker, Smith found that the bank is willing to lend Dellvoe up to $800,000 for one year at a 9 percent simple, or quoted, rate. However, he forgot to ask what the specific terms would be.

(1) Assume the firm will borrow $800,000. What would be the effective interest rate if the loan were based on simple interest? If the loan had been an 8 percent simple interest loan for six months rather than for a year, would that have affected the EAR?

(2) What would be the EAR if the loan were a discount interest loan? What would be the face amount of a loan large enough to net the firm $800,000 of usable funds?

(3) Assume now that the terms call for an installment (or add-on) loan with equal monthly payments. The add-on loan is for a period of one year. What would be Dellvoe's monthly payment? What would be the approximate cost of the loan? What would be the EAR?

(4) Now assume that the bank charges simple interest, but it requires the firm to maintain a 20 percent compensating balance. How much must Dellvoe borrow to obtain its needed $800,000 and to meet the compensating balance requirement? What is the EAR on the loan?

(5) Now assume that the bank charges discount interest of 9 percent and also requires a compensating balance of 20 percent. How much must Dellvoe borrow, and what is the EAR under these terms?

(6) Now assume all the conditions in part 4- that is, a 20 percent compensating balance and a 9 percent simple interest loan- but assume also that Dellvoe has $100,000 of cash balances that it normally holds for transactions purposes, which can be used as part of the required compensating balance. How does this affect (i) the size of the required loan and (ii) the EAR of the loan?

f. Dellvoe is considering using secured short-term financing. What is a secured loan? What two types of current assets can be used to secure loans?

g. What are the differences between pledging receivables and factoring receivables? Is one type generally considered better?

h. What are the differences among the three forms of inventory financing? Is one type generally considered best?

i. Dellvoe had expected a really strong market for office equipment for the year just ended, and in anticipation of strong sales, the firm increased its inventory purchases. However, sales for the last quarter of the year did not meet its expectations, and now Dellvoe finds itself short on cash. The firm expects that its cash shortage will be temporary, only lasting three months. (The inventory has been paid for and cannot be returned to suppliers.) Dellvoe has decided to use inventory financing to meet its short-term cash needs. It estimates that it will require $800,000 for inventory financing during this three-month period. Dellvoe has negotiated with the bank for a three-month, $1,000,000 line of credit with terms of 10 percent annual interest on the used portion, a 1 percent commitment fee on the unused portion, and a $125,000 compensating balance at all times.

Expected inventory levels to be financed are as follows:

Month	Amount
January	$800,000
February	500,000
March	300,000

Calculate the cost of funds from this source, including interest charges and commitment fees. (*Hint:* Each month's borrowings will be $125,000 greater than the inventory level to be financed because of the compensating balance requirement.)

Computer-Related Problem

Work the problem in this section only if you are using the computer problem diskette.

factoring receivables **15–16** Use the model in File C15 to work this problem. Refer back to Problem 15–7.
   a. Would it be to Cooley's advantage to offer to pay the factor a commission of 2.5 percent if it would lower the interest rate to 10.5 percent annually?
   b. Assume a commission of 2 percent and an interest rate of 12 percent. What would be the total cost of the factoring arrangement if Cooley's funding needs rose to $650,000? Would the factoring arrangement be profitable under these circumstances?

GET REAL with Thomson ONE

15–17 One way to measure whether a firm can meet its short-term debt obligations is to analyze the firm's liquidity. Firms that are growing rapidly often find themselves in a liquidity crisis. Cisco Systems, Inc. [CSCO] is a technology firm that manufactures and sells networking and communication products. Answer the following questions:
   a. What have been Cisco's current and quick ratios during the past three years? [*Hint:* Click on Growth Rates/SEC Growth Rates/Annual Ratios]
   b. What has been the trend in Cisco's liquidity position during the three-year time period?
   c. Why is there a difference between the current ratio and the quick ratio?
   d. How has Cisco compared to peer firms in its industry group with regard to liquidity as measured by the quick and current ratios? Be specific in your answer.
   e. Compare the current and quick ratios of Cisco to those of Boeing Company [BA], a more mature defense company. [*Hint:* Click on Peers/Performance/Liquidity Comparison]. What conclusions can you make about the ability of young technology firms like Cisco to meet their short-term debt obligations as compared to more mature firms like those in the defense industry?

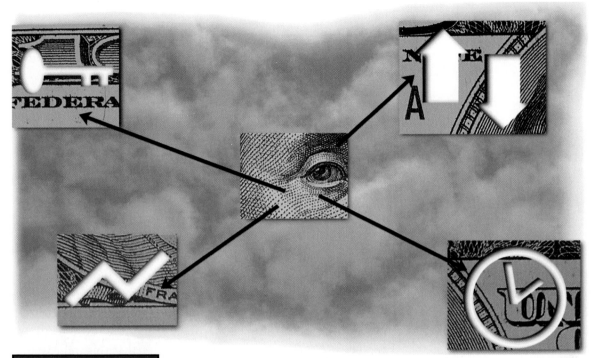

PART VII

Strategic Long-Term Financing Decisions

CHAPTER 16

Common Stock and the Investment Banking Process

The initial public offering (IPO) market is intriguing to investors, many of whom dream about "striking gold" with an IPO such as Microsoft. One share of Microsoft that was first sold to the public in March 1986 for $21 per share was worth more than $8,000 at the beginning of 2004. Even though Microsoft was selling for about $28 per share in January 2004, the company had split the stock nine times since the IPO so that one original share was the equivalent of 288 post-split shares. Thus, if you purchased 100 shares of stock when Microsoft originally went public, your $2,100 investment would have grown to more than $806,000 in 2004. As investors, we all would like to find such success. But it is difficult to find gold mines like Microsoft. Even so, IPOs have been, and will continue to be, one of the more fascinating topics in investments.

The 1990s might be best described as the era of IPOs. In 1996, IPOs hit a record amount, $49.5 billion; while in 1993 a record number of companies went public, 707. More recently, the IPO market has waned somewhat. Although, the IPO market reached record levels, it shifted in 2000 through 2002 when a slump in the economy kept companies from going public. In fact, in 2002 the number of IPOs was the lowest in two decades, when just 83 issues went to the market. As the economy picked up in 2003, so

did the IPO market. Although only 84 companies went public in 2003, experts forecasted that the number of IPOs in 2004 would increase substantially because the stock markets appeared to be much healthier than during the previous two years, and expectations were that this improved health would be sustained for a while.

Which IPOs have been the hottest? In the first half of the 1990s, the most popular IPOs were those associated with technologically innovative companies, especially those that developed software and produced peripheral equipment for computers. During the latter half of the 1990s, the most sought after IPOs were still connected with information technology, with much of the emphasis on Internet-based companies.

Certainly much of the appeal of the IPO market is the potential for huge gains that new issues offer. But even though IPOs offer the potential to earn significant returns, they are not the panacea many investors think. Obviously, many IPOs do well when they are introduced to the market, but most of the profits are earned by company insiders and institutional investors like pension funds, not the average investor. Evidence shows that during the first five years, IPO values decline by about 40 percent, and it is the average investor who generally gets hurt. For example, in 2003, Inter Video and Integrated Alarm Systems went public about the same time (July 16 and 23, respectively), and by the end of the year the value of each firm's stock had dropped more that 15 percent from its original offering price.

As you read this chapter, keep in mind that investment in common stock, whether an IPO or the stock from a "blue chip" company like IBM, is risky. Understanding the concepts presented in this chapter will help you avoid some of the pitfalls commonly made by naive investors, especially when investing in IPOs. Also, read the Industry Practice box for an interesting perspective into IPO trading by an individual investor. ∎

When we discussed capital structure decisions in Chapter 9, we did not spend much time on the specific characteristics of common stock or debt, nor did we discuss the process through which such securities are issued. However, these details actually are quite important. Therefore, in this and the following two chapters we will examine some of the characteristics of different equities (stock) and of the many different types of debt, and we will discuss how firms actually raise long-term capital. The focus in this chapter is on common stock.

Balance Sheet Accounts and Definitions

COMMON EQUITY
The sum of the firm's common stock, paid-in capital, and retained earnings, which equals the common stockholders' total investment in the firm stated at book value.

PAR VALUE
The nominal or face value of a stock or bond.

RETAINED EARNINGS
The balance sheet account that indicates the total amount of earnings the firm has not paid out as dividends throughout its history; these earnings have been reinvested in the firm.

An understanding of legal and accounting terminology is vital to both investors and financial managers if they are to avoid misinterpretations and possibly costly mistakes. Therefore, we begin our analysis of common stock with a discussion of accounting and legal issues. Consider first Table 16–1, which shows the **common equity** section of Unilate Textiles' balance sheet. Unilate's owners—its stockholders—have authorized management to issue a total of 40 million shares, and management has thus far actually issued (or sold) 25 million shares. Each share has a **par value** of $1; this is the minimum amount for which new shares can be issued.[1] During 2005 Unilate earned $54 million, paid $29 million in dividends, and retained $25 million. The $25 million was added to the $260 million accumulated **retained earnings** shown on the year-end 2004 balance sheet to produce the $285 million retained earnings at year-end 2005. Thus, since its inception, Unilate has retained, or plowed back, a total of $285 million of income. This is money that belongs to the stockholders that they could have received in the form of dividends. Instead, the stockholders chose to let management reinvest the $285 million in the business so growth could be achieved.

---

[1]A stock's par value is an arbitrary figure that originally indicated the minimum amount of money stockholders had put up. Today, firms generally are not required to establish a par value for their stock. Thus, Unilate Textiles could have elected to use *no-par* stock, in which case the common stock and additional paid-in capital accounts would have been consolidated under one account called *common stock*, which would show a 2005 balance of $130 million. For simplicity, in Chapter 11 we did not show the detailed breakdown of Unilate's common equity accounts. For purposes of the present discussion it is necessary to show the detail as given in Table 16–1. We should note that a stock's par value is not related to—that is, does not determine—its market value. Recall that the value of a stock is based on its future expected cash flows, not what the firm sets as its par value.

TABLE 16–1	Unilate Textiles: Common Equity Accounts as of December 31 ($ millions, except per share data)	
	2005	**2004**
Common stock (40 million shares authorized, 25 million shares outstanding, $1 par)	$ 25.0	$ 25.0
Additional paid-in capital	105.0	105.0
Retained earnings	285.0	260.0
Total common stockholders' equity (net worth)	$415.0	$390.0
Book value per share = (net worth)/shares	$16.60	$15.60

ADDITIONAL PAID-IN CAPITAL
Funds received in excess of par value when a firm issues new stock.

Now consider the $105 million **additional paid-in capital.** This account shows the difference between the stock's par value and what new stockholders paid when they bought newly issued shares. For example, in 1980, when Unilate was formed, 15 million shares were issued at par value; thus, the first balance sheet showed a zero for paid-in capital and $15 million for the common stock account. However, in 1983, to raise funds for expansion projects, Unilate issued 10 million shares at a market price of $11.50 per share—the total value of the issue was $115 million. At that time, the common stock account was increased by $10 million ($1 par value for the 10 million shares issued), and the remainder of the $115 million issue value— $105 million—was added to additional paid-in capital. Unilate has not issued any more stock since 1983, so the only change in the common equity section since that time has been in retained earnings.

BOOK VALUE PER SHARE
The accounting value of a share of common stock; equal to common equity (common stock plus additional paid-in capital plus retained earnings) divided by the number of shares outstanding.

The **book value per share** shown in Table 16–1 is computed by dividing the amount of total stockholders' equity, which also is called net worth, by the number of shares outstanding. Unilate's book value per share increased in 2005 to $16.60, from $15.60 in 2004. Whenever stock is sold at a price above book value or the change in retained earnings is positive, book value will increase, and vice versa. Because book value is a historical cost amount, investors prefer that the market value of stock be greater than its book value; a stock that is selling below its book value might suggest the company is experiencing financial difficulty.

Self-Test Questions

How is book value per share calculated, and is it generally equal to the par and market values?

What differences would there be in the stockholders' equity accounts of a firm that has par value stock and one that has no-par stock?

How does the amount of earnings retained by a firm affect its common equity accounts?

Legal Rights and Privileges of Common Stockholders

The common stockholders are the owners of a corporation, and as such they have certain rights and privileges. The most important rights are discussed in this section.

Control of the Firm

The stockholders have the right to elect the firm's directors, who in turn elect the officers who manage the business. In a *small* privately owned firm, the major stockholder typically assumes the positions of president and chairperson of the board of directors. In a *large, publicly owned firm*, the managers typically have some stock, but their personal holdings are insufficient to provide voting control. Thus, the managements of most publicly owned firms can be removed by stockholders who might decide a management team is not effective.

Various state and federal laws stipulate how stockholder control is to be exercised. First, corporations must hold an election of directors periodically, usually once a year, with the vote taken at the annual meeting. Frequently, one-third of the directors are elected each year for three-year terms. Each share of stock normally has one vote; thus, the owner of 1,000 shares has 1,000 votes. Stockholders can appear at the annual meeting and vote in person, but typically they either vote via the Internet or mail, or transfer their right to vote to a second party by means of an instrument known as a **proxy**. Management always solicits stockholders' proxies and usually gets them. However, if earnings are poor and stockholders are dissatisfied, an outside group might solicit the proxies in an effort to overthrow management and take control of the business. This is known as a **proxy fight.**

The question of control has become a central issue in finance in recent years. The frequency of proxy fights has increased, as have attempts by one corporation to take over another by purchasing a majority of the outstanding stock. This action is called a **takeover.** Some well-known examples of past takeover battles include Kohlberg Kravis Roberts & Co.'s (KKR) acquisition of RJR Nabisco, Chevron's acquisition of Gulf Oil, and AT&T's takeover of NCR; and, more recently, GE's acquisition of Vivendi Universal and Oracle's takeover of PeopleSoft.

Managers who do not have majority control (more than 50 percent of their firms' stock) are very much concerned about proxy fights and takeovers, and many attempt to get stockholder approval for changes in their corporate charters that would make takeovers more difficult. For example, a number of companies have gotten their stockholders to agree (1) to elect only one-third of the directors each year (rather than electing all directors each year); (2) to require 75 percent of the stockholders (rather than 50 percent) to approve a merger; and (3) to vote in a "poison pill" provision that would allow the stockholders of a firm that is taken over by another firm to buy shares in the second firm at a reduced price. The third provision makes the acquisition unattractive and, thus, wards off hostile takeover attempts. Managements seeking such changes generally cite a fear that the firm will be picked up at a bargain price, but it often appears that managers' concerns about their own positions might be an even more immediate consideration.

The Preemptive Right

Common stockholders sometimes have the right, called the **preemptive right,** to purchase on a pro rata basis any additional shares sold by the firm. The purpose of the preemptive right is twofold. First, it protects the power of control of current stockholders. If it were not for this safeguard, the management of a corporation under criticism from stockholders could prevent stockholders from removing it from office by issuing a large number of additional shares and purchasing these shares itself. Management could thereby secure control of the corporation and frustrate the will of the current stockholders.

PROXY
A document giving one person the authority to act for another, typically the power to vote shares of common stock.

PROXY FIGHT
An attempt by a person or group of people to gain control of a firm by getting its stockholders to grant that person or group the authority to vote their shares in order to elect a new management team.

TAKEOVER
An action whereby a person or group succeeds in ousting a firm's management and taking control of the company.

PREEMPTIVE RIGHT
A provision in the corporate charter or bylaws that gives common stockholders the right to purchase on a *pro rata* basis new issues of common stock (or convertible securities).

The second, and more important, reason for the preemptive right is that it protects stockholders against a dilution of value. For example, suppose 1,000 shares of common stock, each with a price of $100, were outstanding, making the total market value of the firm $100,000. If an additional 1,000 shares were sold at $50 a share, or for $50,000, this would raise the total market value of the firm to $150,000. When the total market value is divided by the new total shares outstanding, a value of $75 per share is obtained. The old stockholders thus lose $25 per share, and the new stockholders have an "instant profit" of $25 per share. Thus, selling common stock at a price below the market value would dilute its price and would transfer wealth from the present stockholders to those who were allowed to purchase the new shares. The preemptive right helps to prevent such occurrences.

Self-Test Questions

Identify some actions that companies have taken to make takeovers more difficult.

What are the two primary reasons for the existence of the preemptive right?

Types of Common Stock

CLASSIFIED STOCK
Common stock that is given a special designation, such as Class A, Class B, and so forth, to meet special needs of the company.

Although most firms have only one type of common stock, in some instances **classified stock** is used to meet the special needs of the company. Generally, when special classifications of stock are used, one type is designated Class A, another Class B, and so on. Small, new companies seeking to obtain funds from outside sources frequently use different types of common stock. For example, when Genetic Concepts went public, its Class A stock was sold to the public and paid a dividend, but this stock did not have voting rights until five years after its issue. Its Class B stock, which was retained by the organizers of the company, had full voting rights for five years, but the legal terms stated that dividends could not be paid on the Class B stock until the company had established its earning power by building up retained earnings to a designated level. The use of classified stock thus enabled the public to take a position in a conservatively financed growth company without sacrificing income, while the founders retained absolute control during the crucial early stages of the firm's development. At the same time, outside investors were protected against excessive withdrawals of funds by the original owners. As is often the case in such situations, the Class B stock was called **founders' shares.**

FOUNDERS' SHARES
Stock owned by the firm's founders who have sole voting rights; this type of stock generally has restricted dividends for a specified number of years.

Note that "Class A," "Class B," and so on, have no standard meanings—one firm could designate its Class B shares as founders' shares and its Class A shares as those sold to the public, whereas another firm could reverse these designations. Still other firms could use stock classifications for entirely different purposes. For example, when General Motors acquired Hughes Aircraft for $5 billion, it paid in part with a new Class H common, GMH, which had limited voting rights and whose dividends were tied to Hughes's performance as a GM subsidiary. The reasons for the new stock were reported to be that (1) GM wanted to limit voting privileges on the new classified stock because of management's concern about a possible takeover and (2) Hughes employees wanted to be rewarded more directly on Hughes's own performance than would have been possible through regular GM stock.[2]

Self-Test Question

What are some reasons a company might use classified stock?

Evaluation of Common Stock as a Source of Funds

Thus far the chapter has covered the main characteristics of common stock. Now we will appraise stock financing both from the viewpoint of the corporation and from a social perspective.

From the Corporation's Viewpoint

The advantages and disadvantages of using common stock as a financing source are listed in this section.

Advantages   Common stock offers several advantages to the corporation:

1. Common stock does not legally obligate the firm to make payments to stockholders: Only if the company generates earnings and has no pressing internal needs for the funds will it pay dividends.
2. Common stock carries no fixed maturity date—it never has to be "repaid" as would a debt issue.
3. Because common stock cushions creditors against losses, the sale of common stock generally increases the creditworthiness of the firm. This in turn raises its bond rating, lowers its cost of debt, and increases its future ability to use debt.
4. If a company's prospects look bright, then common stock often can be sold on better terms than debt. Stock appeals to certain groups of investors because (a) it typically carries a higher expected total return (dividends plus capital gains) than does preferred stock or debt and (b) as a representation of the ownership of the firm, stock provides the investor with a better hedge against unanticipated inflation because common dividends tend to rise during inflationary periods.[3]

---

[2]GM's deal posed a problem for the New York Stock Exchange (NYSE), which had a rule against listing any company's common stock if the company had any nonvoting common stock outstanding. GM made it clear that it was willing to delist if the NYSE did not change its rules. The NYSE concluded that such arrangements as GM had made were logical and were likely to be made by other companies in the future, so it changed its rules to accommodate GM.

[3]For common stock in general, the average rate of increase in dividends has slightly exceeded the rate of inflation since 1970.

Disadvantages   Disadvantages associated with issuing common stock include the following:

1. The sale of common stock gives some voting rights, and perhaps even control, to new stockholders. For this reason, additional equity financing often is avoided by managers who are concerned about maintaining control. The use of founders' shares and other classes of common stock can mitigate this problem.

2. Common stock gives new owners the right to share in the income of the firm; if profits soar, then new stockholders will share in this bonanza, whereas if debt had been used, new investors (creditors in this case) would have received only a fixed return, no matter how profitable the company had been, and existing stockholders would have received the rest.[4]

3. As we shall see, the costs of underwriting and distributing common stock usually are higher than those for debt or preferred stock. Flotation costs for common stock characteristically are higher because (a) the costs of investigating an equity security investment are higher than those for a comparable debt security and (b) stocks are riskier than debt, meaning that investors must diversify their equity holdings, so a given dollar amount of new stock must be sold to a larger number of purchasers than the same amount of debt.

4. As we saw in Chapter 9, if the firm has more equity than is called for in its optimal capital structure, the average cost of capital will be higher than necessary. Therefore, a firm would not want to sell stock if the sale causes its equity ratio (1.0 minus the debt ratio) to exceed the optimal level.

5. Under current tax laws, common stock dividends are not deductible as an expense for tax purposes, but bond interest is deductible. As we saw in Chapter 8, the fact that interest is tax deductible lowers the relative cost of debt as compared with equity.

From a Social Viewpoint

From a social viewpoint, common stock is a desirable form of financing because it makes businesses less vulnerable to the consequences of declines in sales and earnings. Common stock financing involves no fixed charge payments that might force a faltering firm into bankruptcy. From the standpoint of the economy as a whole, if too many firms used too much debt, business fluctuations would be amplified as a result of the leverage, and minor recessions could turn into major ones. Not long ago, when the level of leveraged mergers and buyouts was raising the aggregate debt ratio (the average debt ratio of all firms), the Federal Reserve and other authorities voiced concern over the possible dangers created by the situation, and congressional leaders debated the wisdom of social controls over corporations' use of debt. Like most important issues, this one is debatable, and the debate centers around who can better determine "appropriate" capital structures—corporate managers or government officials.[5]

---

[4]This point has given rise to an important theory: "If a firm sells a large issue of bonds, this is a signal that management expects the company to earn high profits on investments financed by the new capital and that it does not wish to share these profits with new stockholders. On the other hand, if the firm issues stock, this is a signal that its prospects are not so bright." This issue was discussed earlier in Chapters 9 and 10.

[5]When business executives hear someone say, "I'm from Washington and I'm here to help you," they generally cringe and often with good reason. On the other hand, a stable national economy does require sound businesses, and too much debt can lead to corporate instability.

Self-Test Questions

What are the major advantages and disadvantages of common stock financing?

From a social viewpoint, why is common stock a desirable form of financing?

The Market for Common Stock

CLOSELY HELD CORPORATION

A corporation that is owned by a few individuals who are typically associated with the firm's management.

PUBLICLY OWNED CORPORATION

A corporation that is owned by a relatively large number of individuals who are not actively involved in its management.

OVER-THE-COUNTER (OTC) MARKET

The network of dealers that provides for trading securities not listed on organized exchanges.

ORGANIZED SECURITY EXCHANGE

A formal organization, with a tangible physical location, that facilitates trading in designated ("listed") securities.

SECONDARY MARKET

The market in which "used" stocks are traded after they have been issued by corporations.

PRIMARY MARKET

The market in which firms issue new securities to raise corporate capital.

Some companies are so small that their common stocks are not actively traded; they are owned by only a few people, usually the companies' managers. Such firms are said to be *privately owned*, or **closely held, corporations,** and their stock is called *closely held stock.* In contrast, the stocks of most larger companies are owned by a large number of investors, most of whom are not active in management. Such companies are said to be **publicly owned corporations,** and their stock is called *publicly held stock.*

As we saw in Chapter 2, the stocks of smaller publicly owned firms are not listed on an exchange; they trade in the **over-the-counter (OTC) market,** and the companies and their stocks are said to be *unlisted.* However, larger publicly owned companies generally apply for listing on an **organized security exchange** or the NASDAQ market, and they and their stocks are said to be *listed.* As a rule, companies are first listed on a regional exchange, such as the Chicago or Midwest Exchange. As they grow, they move up to the American Stock Exchange (AMEX) and the New York Stock Exchange (NYSE). Most companies are traded in the OTC market (there are 5,000 to 8,000 actively traded stocks), but in terms of market value of both outstanding shares and daily transactions, the NYSE generates about 60 percent of the business with its listing of approximately 2,800 companies.

Institutional investors such as pension trusts, insurance companies, and mutual funds own 45 to 50 percent of all common stocks. These institutions buy and sell fairly actively, however, so they account for more than 75 percent of all transactions. Thus, the institutional investors have a heavy influence on the prices of individual stocks.

Types of Stock Market Transactions

We can classify stock market transactions into three distinct types:

1. **Trading in the outstanding shares of established, publicly owned companies: the secondary market.** Unilate Textiles has 25 million shares of stock outstanding. If the owner of 100 shares sells his or her stock, the trade is said to have occurred in the **secondary market.** Thus, the market for outstanding shares, or used shares, is the secondary market. The company receives no new money when sales occur in this market.

2. **Additional shares sold by established, publicly owned companies: the primary market.** If Unilate decides to sell (or issue) an additional one million shares to raise new equity capital, this transaction is said to occur in the **primary market.**[6]

---

[6]Recall that Unilate has 40 million shares authorized but only 25 million outstanding; thus, it has 15 million authorized but unissued shares. If it had no authorized but unissued shares, management could increase the authorized shares by obtaining stockholders' approval, which would generally be granted without any arguments.

3. **New public offerings by privately held firms: the primary market.** When Coors Brewing Company, which was owned by the Coors family at the time, decided to sell some stock to raise capital needed for a major expansion program, it took its stock public. Whenever stock in a closely held corporation is offered to the public for the first time, the company is said to be **going public.**[7] The market for stock that has recently gone public normally is called the **initial public offering (IPO) market.**

Firms can go public without raising any additional capital. For example, the Ford Motor Company was once owned exclusively by the Ford family. When Henry Ford died, he left a substantial part of his stock to the Ford Foundation. When the foundation later sold some of this stock to the general public, the Ford Motor Company went public, even though the company raised no capital in the transaction.

A firm generally goes *public* when growth opportunities no longer can be financed solely with debt and the existing stockholder base, which generally consists of the original owners and current managers of the corporation and a few investors not actively involved in the company's management. The purpose of going public is to increase the ownership base and the funding sources available to the company so that growth opportunities can be better financed and the firm's value can be increased more than otherwise would be possible. Thus, as a firm experiences greater and greater growth and its size expands significantly, there generally is pressure to go public. Unfortunately, when a firm does go public, the red tape increases, because financial reporting and disclosure guidelines and security regulations are more restrictive for public firms than for private firms.

The Decision to List the Stock

To have its stock listed, a company must apply to an exchange, pay a relatively small fee, and meet the exchange's minimum requirements. These requirements relate to the size of the company's net income as well as to the number of shares outstanding and in the hands of outsiders (as opposed to the number held by insiders, who generally do not trade their stock very actively). The company also must agree to disclose certain information to the exchange; this information is designed to help the exchange track trading patterns and thus try to prevent manipulation of the stock's price.[8] The size qualifications increase as one moves from the regional exchanges to

GOING PUBLIC
The act of selling stock to the public at large by a closely held corporation or its principal stockholders.

INITIAL PUBLIC OFFERING (IPO) MARKET
The market consisting of stocks of companies that have just gone public.

---

[7]The stock Coors offered to the public was designated Class B, and it was nonvoting. The Coors family retained the founders' shares, called Class A stock, which carried full voting privileges. The company was large enough to obtain an NYSE listing, but at that time the NYSE had a requirement that listed common stocks must have full voting rights, which precluded Coors from obtaining an NYSE listing. But in March 1999, Coors began trading on the NYSE.

[8]It is illegal for anyone to attempt to manipulate the price of a stock. Prior to the creation of the Securities and Exchange Commission (SEC) in the 1930s, syndicates would buy and sell stock back and forth at rigged prices for the purpose of deceiving the public into thinking that a particular stock was worth more or less than its true value. The exchanges, with the encouragement and support of the SEC, use sophisticated computer programs to help spot any irregularities that suggest manipulation. They can identify the exact day and time of each trade and the broker who executed it, and they can require the broker to disclose the name of the person for whom the trade was made. Such a system can obviously help identify manipulators. This same system also helps to identify illegal insider trading, as discussed in the next section.

	NYSE	AMEX AND REGIONAL EXCHANGES[a]	NASDAQ
Round lot (100 shares) shareholders	2,000	800	400
Number of public shares (million)	1.1	0.5	1.1
Market value of public shares ($ million)	$ 100	$3	$8
Pre-tax income ($ million)	$2.50	$0.75	$1.00

TABLE 16–2   Listing Requirements for Exchanges and NASDAQ

[a]These numbers are indicative of the listing requirements for larger regional stock exchanges, including the Chicago Stock Exchange, the Pacific Exchange, and the Philadelphia Stock Exchange. The listing requirements for smaller regional exchanges generally are not as restrictive.

the AMEX and on to the NYSE. Table 16–2 shows some examples of the listing requirements for stock markets in the United States.

Assuming that a company qualifies, many people believe that listing is beneficial both to the company and to its stockholders. Listed companies receive a certain amount of free advertising and publicity, and the status as a listed company enhances their prestige and reputation. This might have a beneficial effect on the sales of the firm's products, and it probably is advantageous in terms of lowering the required rate of return on its common stock. Investors respond favorably to increased information, increased liquidity, and confidence that the quoted price is not being manipulated. By providing investors with these benefits in the form of listing their companies' stock, financial managers might lower their firms' costs of capital and increase the value of their stocks.

Regulation of Securities Markets

Sales of new securities, as well as operations in the secondary markets, are regulated by the **Securities and Exchange Commission (SEC)** and, to a lesser extent, by each of the 50 states. For the most part, the SEC regulations are intended to (1) ensure investors receive fair financial disclosure from publicly traded companies and (2) discourage fraudulent and misleading behavior by firms' investors, owners, and employees to manipulate stock prices. The primary elements of SEC regulation are as follows:

1. The SEC has jurisdiction over all interstate offerings of new securities to the general public in amounts of $1.5 million or more. A company wishing to issue new stock must file a **registration statement** that provides financial, legal, and technical information about the company. A **prospectus** that summarizes the information in the registration statement generally is provided to prospective investors for use in selling the securities. SEC lawyers and accountants analyze both the registration statement and the prospectus; if the information is inadequate or misleading, the SEC will delay or stop the public offering.
2. The SEC also regulates all national securities exchanges, and companies whose securities are listed on an exchange must file annual reports similar to the registration statement with both the SEC and the exchange.
3. The SEC has control over stock trades by corporate **insiders.** Officers, directors, and major stockholders must file periodic reports of changes in their

SECURITIES AND EXCHANGE COMMISSION (SEC)
The U.S. government agency that regulates the issuance and trading of stocks and bonds.

REGISTRATION STATEMENT
A statement of facts filed with the SEC about a company that plans to issue securities.

PROSPECTUS
A document describing a new security issue and the issuing company.

INSIDERS
Officers, directors, major stockholders, or others who might have inside, or privileged, information about a company's operations.

holdings of the corporation's stock. Any *short-term* profits from such transactions must be handed over to the corporation.

4. The SEC has the power to prohibit manipulation by such devices as pools (aggregations of funds used to affect prices artificially) or wash sales (sales between members of the same group to record artificial transaction prices).

5. The SEC has control over the form of the proxy and the way the company uses it to solicit votes.

Control over the flow of credit into securities transactions is exercised by the Board of Governors of the Federal Reserve System. The Fed exercises this control through **margin requirements,** which represent the percentage of the purchase price that must be deposited (invested) by investors—the percentage that can be borrowed is equal to 100 percent less the margin requirement set by the Fed. If a great deal of margin borrowing has been going on, a decline in stock prices can result in inadequate loan coverages, which would force stock brokers to issue **margin calls,** which in turn would require investors either to put up more money or to have their margined stock sold to pay off their loans. Such forced sales would further depress the stock market and could set off a downward spiral, such as the events that took place in October 1987. The margin requirement currently is 50 percent.

States also have some control over the issuance of new securities within their boundaries. This control usually is exercised by a "corporation commissioner" or someone with a similar title. State laws relating to securities sales are called **blue sky laws** because they were put into effect to keep unscrupulous promoters from selling securities that offered the "blue sky" but that actually had little or no asset backing.

The securities industry itself realizes the importance of stable markets, sound brokerage firms, and no perception of stock manipulation. Therefore, the various exchanges work closely with the SEC to police transactions on the exchanges and to maintain the integrity and credibility of the system. Similarly, the National Association of Securities Dealers (NASD) cooperates with the SEC to police trading in the OTC market. These industry groups also cooperate with regulatory authorities to set net worth and other standards for securities firms, to develop insurance programs to protect the customers of brokerage houses, and the like.

In general, government regulation of securities trading, as well as industry self-regulation, is designed to ensure that investors receive information that is as accurate as possible, that no one artificially manipulates the market price of a given stock, and that corporate insiders do not take advantage of their position to profit in their companies' stocks at the expense of other stockholders. Neither the SEC, the state regulators, nor the industry itself can prevent investors from making foolish decisions or from having bad luck, but regulators can and do help investors obtain the best data possible for making sound investment decisions.

Margin definitions

MARGIN REQUIREMENTS
The percentage of a security's purchase price that must be deposited by investors.

MARGIN CALL
A call from a broker asking for more money to support a stock purchase loan.

BLUE SKY LAWS
State laws that prevent the sale of securities that have little or no asset backing.

Self-Test Questions

Differentiate between a closely held corporation and a publicly owned corporation.

Differentiate between a listed stock and an unlisted stock.

Differentiate between the primary and secondary markets.

Differentiate between a registration statement and a prospectus.

What is the primary purpose of regulating securities trading, whether it is imposed by law or self-imposed?

✳ **INDUSTRY PRACTICE**

So You Think You Want to Buy an IPO?

We have all heard the stories about initial public offerings (IPOs) that have increased threefold, fourfold, or even more when they first reached the market. In January 1999, for example, MarketWatch.com, a company that provides business news, went public at $17 per share. But its price was pushed up to nearly $120 before the market decided that a price around $97 per share was more appropriate. Think about the one-day return you could have made if you were able to buy MarketWatch.com at the exact time it first went public. Many individual investors do think about such extraordinary returns, and they dream about finding and being able to purchase IPOs like Market-Watch.com. But consider the experience of one individual before you "play the IPO game."

At the end of 1998, Bear Stearns Companies, an investment banker, helped take public theglobe.com, an Internet company that provided Web sites for other companies. The initial price of the IPO was set at $9 per share. The night before the offering, institutional investors subscribed (promised) to purchase 13 times the number of shares available through the IPO—purchase orders totaled more than 40 million shares even though only 3.1 million shares were scheduled to be sold. Clearly, such a large demand would force the price of the IPO to rise significantly once trading started. It did—when the IPO hit the market, the first trade was nearly $90 per share, 10 times the offering price.

After the institutional investors placed their orders to buy large numbers of shares (most were in blocks of more than 10,000 shares), many individual investors placed smaller orders (most were for a few hundred shares). Many of the trades that were placed by the individuals were market buy orders, which instructed brokers to buy at the best possible prices *when the trades reached the stock market*. Unfortunately, most of the individuals placed their orders after the institutional investors; thus, their trades were not executed until after the price of theglobe.com had risen to above $90 per share. One investor, who had placed a market buy order for 500 shares, ended up paying $92 per share, or $46,000, for stock he had hoped to get for a little more than $9 per share, or $4,500. After his order was filled,

the investor saw the price of the stock drop to $63.50, and by the time he was able to sell his 500 shares he had lost $20,000. In the end, this investor lost a substantial amount because he acted impulsively. He knew nothing about the company because he had not evaluated its viability as an investment. It seems he had ignored earlier advice from his broker to buy Dell Computer, which later more than tripled in value, so he was anxious to buy a high-tech stock and not "miss the boat" this time. This investor learned a valuable but expensive lesson, which can be summed up with an old cliche: "Look before you leap."

By the way, at the end of August 1999, theglobe .com, which went public November 13, 1998, was selling for about $11.50 per share. Its high price on opening day was $97; thus, the stock price dropped about 88 percent in a little more than nine months. Much of the loss in value of the company's stock during this period can be attributed to the beginning of the collapse of dot.com companies during the summer of 1999. It was about this time that investors began to see through the "smoke and mirrors" that such companies created in their attempts to manifest future, unsubstantiated value. As a result, theglobe.com's bubble burst, and it burst quickly. By the summer of 2002, the company was nearly out of business. It had fewer than 10 employees who worked out of makeshift offices. Later in 2002 the theglobe.com began to change direction when it purchased technology to make phone calls using the Internet. After raising additional capital, the company introduced its Internet phone product in August 2003 through a subsidiary named voiceglo. At the beginning of 2004, theglobe.com's stock was selling for $1.30, a far cry from the $97 it sold for the day of its IPO a little more than five years earlier.

The performance of theglobe.com IPO was not unique: most of the companies that went public in 1998 either went bankrupt or were selling for less than their initial offering prices in 2004.

Source: Aaron Lucchetti, "Web Tide: Initial Public Offerings Aren't the Same in Era of Internet-Stock Mania," *The Wall Street Journal*, January 19, 1999, A1.

Financial Instruments in International Markets

For the most part, the financial securities of companies and institutions in other countries are similar to those in the United States. There are some differences, however, which we discuss in this section. Also, financial securities exist that have been created to permit investors easier access to international investments, such as *American Depository Receipts.*

American Depository Receipts

AMERICAN DEPOSITORY RECEIPTS (ADRS)

Certificates representing ownership in stocks of foreign companies, which are held in trust by a bank located in the country the stock is traded.

Foreign companies can be traded internationally through *depository receipts,* which represent shares of the underlying stocks of foreign companies. In the United States, most foreign stock is traded through **American Depository Receipts (ADRs).** ADRs are not foreign stocks; rather they are certificates created by such organizations as banks. The certificates represent ownership in stocks of foreign companies that are held in trust by a bank located in the country where the stock is traded. ADRs provide Americans the ability to invest in foreign companies with less complexity and difficulty than might otherwise be possible. Each ADR certificate represents a certain number of shares of stock of a foreign company, and it entitles the owner to receive any dividends paid by the company in U.S. dollars. In addition, ADRs are traded in the stock markets in the United States, which often are more liquid than foreign markets. All financial information, including values, is denominated in dollars and stated in English; thus, there are no problems with exchange rates and language translations.

In many cases, investors can purchase foreign securities directly. But such investments might be complicated by legal issues, the ability to take funds such as dividends out of the country, and interpretation into domestic terms. Thus, ADRs provide investors the ability to participate in the international financial markets without having to bear risks greater than those associated with the corporations in which the investments are made. The market values of ADRs move in tandem with the market values of the underlying stocks that are held in trust.

Foreign Equity Instruments

The equities of foreign companies are like those of U.S. corporations. The primary difference between stocks of foreign companies and those of American companies is that U.S. regulations provide greater protection of stockholders' rights than those of most other countries. In the international markets, equity generally is referred to as *Euro stock* or *Yankee stock.*

1. *Euro stock* refers to stock that is traded in countries other than the home country of the company, not including the United States. Thus, if the stock of a Japanese company is sold in Germany, it would be considered a Euro stock.
2. *Yankee stock* is stock issued by foreign companies that is traded in the United States. If a Japanese company sold its stock in the United States, it would be called Yankee stock in the international markets.

As the financial markets become more global and more sophisticated, the financial instruments offered both domestically and internationally will change. Already, foreign companies and governments have discovered that financial markets in the United States provide excellent sources of funds because a great variety of financial outlets exist. As technology improves and regulations that bar or discourage foreign investing are repealed, the financial markets of other developed countries will become more prominent and new, innovative financial products will emerge.

Self-Test Questions

What is a Yankee stock? A Euro Stock?

What changes do you think will occur in the international markets during the next couple of decades?

The Investment Banking Process

INVESTMENT BANKER

An organization that underwrites and distributes new issues of securities; helps businesses and other entities obtain needed financing.

When a business (or government unit) needs to raise funds in the financial markets, it generally enlists the services of an **investment banker** (see Panel 2 in Figure 2–1). Merrill Lynch, J. P. Morgan, and Goldman Sachs are examples of companies that offer investment banking services. Such organizations (1) help corporations design securities with the features that are most attractive to investors given existing market conditions, (2) buy these securities from the corporations, and (3) then resell them to investors (savers). Although the securities are sold twice, this process really is one primary market transaction, with the investment banker acting as an intermediary (agent) as funds are transferred from savers to businesses.

We should note that investment banking has nothing to do with the traditional banking process as we know it: Investment banking deals with the issuance of new securities, not deposits and loans. The major investment banking houses often are divisions of large financial service corporations engaged in a wide range of activities. For example, Merrill Lynch has a brokerage department that operates thousands of offices worldwide, as well as an investment banking department that helps companies issue securities, take over other companies, and the like. Merrill Lynch's brokers sell previously issued stocks as well as stocks that are issued through their investment banking departments. Thus, financial service organizations such as Merrill Lynch sell securities in both the secondary markets and the primary markets.

In this section we describe how securities are issued in the financial markets, and we explain the role of investment bankers in this process.

Raising Capital: Stage I Decisions

The firm itself makes some preliminary decisions on its own, including the following:

1. **Dollars to be raised.** How much new capital do we need?
2. **Type of securities used.** Should stock, bonds, or a combination be used? Further, if stock is to be issued, should it be offered to existing stockholders or sold directly to the general public?
3. **Competitive bid versus negotiated deal.** Should the company simply offer a block of its securities for sale to the highest bidder, or should it sit down with an investment banker and negotiate a deal? These two procedures are called *competitive bids* and *negotiated deals*. Only a handful of the largest firms on the NYSE, whose securities are already well known to the investment banking

| TABLE 16–3 | Largest Underwriters of Debt and Equity in the United States in 2003 ($ billions) | | | |

RANK	INVESTMENT BANKER	AMOUNT ISSUED	MARKET SHARE	NUMBER OF ISSUES
1	Citigroup	$ 542.7	10.2%	1,872
2	Morgan Stanley	394.8	7.4	1,365
3	Merrill Lynch	380.3	7.1	1,914
4	Lehman Brothers	354.1	6.7	1,264
5	J. P. Morgan	353.9	6.6	1,417
6	Credit Suisse First Boston	338.7	6.4	1,248
7	Deutsche Bank	317.4	6.0	1,256
8	UBS	293.8	5.5	1,147
9	Goldman Sachs	293.3	5.5	807
10	Banc of America Securities	206.4	3.9	737
	Others	1,850.6	34.7	6,558
	Total	$5,326.0	100.0%	19,585

NOTE: Rankings are based on the dollar volume of underwritings by U.S. firms managed during 2003.

SOURCE: Randall Smith, "Securities Underwriters Log Busiest Year," *The Wall Street Journal*, January 2, 2004, R17.

community, are in a position to use the competitive bid process. The investment banks would have to do a large amount of investigative work to bid on an issue unless they were already quite familiar with the firm, and the costs involved would be too high to make it worthwhile unless the investment bank was sure of getting the deal. Therefore, the vast majority of offerings of stocks or bonds are made on a negotiated basis.

4. **Selection of an investment banker.** Assuming the issue is to be negotiated, which investment banker should the firm use? Older firms that have "been to market" before will already have established a relationship with an investment banker, although it is easy enough to change investment bankers if the firm is dissatisfied. However, a firm that is just going public will have to choose an investment bank, and different investment banking houses are better suited for different companies. The older, larger "establishment houses" like J. P. Morgan deal mainly with large companies like AT&T, IBM, and G.E. Other investment bankers specialize in more speculative issues like initial public offerings. Table 16–3 lists in ranked order the top 10 investment bankers in 2003, as measured by the dollar amount of securities underwritten.

Raising Capital: Stage II Decisions

Stage II decisions, which are made jointly by the firm and its selected investment banker, include the following:

1. **Reevaluating the initial decisions.** The firm and its investment banker will reevaluate the initial decisions about the size of the issue and the type of securities to use. For example, the firm initially might have decided to raise $50 million by selling common stock, but the investment banker might convince management that it would be better off, in view of current market conditions, to limit the stock issue to $25 million and to raise the other $25 million as debt.

2. **Best efforts or underwritten issues.** The firm and its investment banker must decide whether the investment banker will work on a best efforts basis or underwrite the issue. In an **underwritten arrangement,** the investment banker generally assures the company that the entire issue will be sold, so the investment banker bears significant risks in such an offering. With this type of arrangement, the investment banking firm typically buys the securities from the issuing firm and then sells the securities in the primary markets, hoping to make a profit. In a **best efforts arrangement,** the investment banker does not guarantee that the securities will be sold or that the company will get the cash it needs. With this type of arrangement, the investment banker does not buy the securities from the issuing firm; rather the securities are handled on a contingency basis, and the investment banker is paid a commission based on the amount of the issue that is sold. The investment banker essentially promises to exert its *best efforts* when selling the securities. With a *best efforts arrangement*, the issuing firm takes the chance the entire issue will not be sold and that all the needed funds will not be raised. For example, the very day IBM signed an *underwritten* agreement to sell $1 billion of bonds in 1979, interest rates rose sharply, and bond prices fell. IBM's investment bankers lost somewhere between $10 million and $20 million. Had the offering been on a best efforts basis, IBM would have been the loser.

3. **Issuance costs.** The investment banker's fee must be negotiated, and the firm also must estimate the other expenses it will incur in connection with the issue, including lawyers' fees, accountants' costs, and printing and engraving. Usually, the investment banker will buy the issue from the company at a discount below the price at which the securities are to be offered to the public, and this **underwriter's spread** covers the investment banker's costs and provides a profit.

    Table 16–4 gives an indication of the **flotation costs** associated with public issues of bonds and common stock. As the table shows, costs as a percentage of the proceeds are higher for stocks than for bonds, and costs are also higher for small issues than for large issues. The relationship between size of issue and flotation costs is primarily due to the existence of fixed costs: certain costs must be incurred regardless of the size of the issue, so the percentage flotation cost is quite high for small issues.

4. **Setting the offering price.** If the company already is publicly owned, the **offering price** will be based on the existing market price of the stock or the yield on the bonds. For common stock, the most typical arrangement calls for the investment banker to buy the securities at a prescribed number of points below the closing price on the last day of registration. For example, on July 1, 2005, the stock of Unilate Textiles had a current price of $23, and it had traded between $20 and $25 a share during the previous three months. Unilate and its underwriter agreed that the investment banker would buy 5 million new shares at $1 below the closing price on the last day of registration, which was expected to be in early October. The stock actually closed at $20.50 on the day the SEC released the issue, so the company received $19.50 a share. The shares then

---

UNDERWRITTEN ARRANGEMENT

Agreement for the sale of securities in which the investment bank guarantees the sale by purchasing the securities from the issuer, thus agreeing to bear any risks involved in the transaction.

BEST EFFORTS ARRANGEMENT

Agreement for the sale of securities in which the investment bank handling the transaction gives no guarantee that the securities will be sold.

UNDERWRITER'S SPREAD

The difference between the price at which the investment banking firm buys an issue from a company and the price at which the securities are sold in the primary market; it represents the investment banker's gross profit on the issue.

FLOTATION COSTS

The costs associated with issuing new stocks or bonds.

OFFERING PRICE

The price at which common stock is sold to the public.

TABLE 16-4	Flotation (Issuance) Costs for Issuing Debt and Equity[a]			
SIZE OF ISSUE ($ MILLIONS)	**BONDS[b]**		**EQUITY[c]**	
	STRAIGHT	**CONVERTIBLE**	**SEASONED ISSUES**	**IPOs**
Under 10.0	4.4%	8.8%	13.3%	17.0%
10.0–19.9	2.8	8.7	8.7	11.6
20.0–39.9	2.4	6.1	6.9	9.7
40.0–59.9	1.3	4.3	5.9	8.7
60.0–79.9	2.3	3.2	5.2	8.2
80.0–99.9	2.2	3.0	4.7	7.9
100.0–199.9	2.3	2.8	4.2	7.1
200.0–499.9	2.2	2.2	3.5	6.5
500.0 and above	1.6	2.1	3.2	5.7

[a]The results provided in this table represent the direct costs as a percent of the size of the issue. Direct costs include underwriting fees, registration fees, legal costs, auditing costs, and other costs directly related to the issue. The numbers presented in this table are intended to provide an indication of the costs associated with issuing debt and equity. Such costs rise somewhat when interest rates are cyclically high, because when money is in relatively tight supply, investment bankers have a more difficult time placing issues. Thus, actual flotation costs vary somewhat over time.

[b]A straight bond is the traditional type of bond we discuss in Chapter 17 in which interest is paid periodically, perhaps every six months, and the principal amount is repaid at maturity. A convertible bond is like a straight bond but can be converted into shares of common stock by the bondholder.

[c]Seasoned equity issues are issues of stock of publicly traded corporations. IPOs, or intial public offerings, are equity issues of privately held companies that are "going public" by offering shares of stock to the general public for the first time.

SOURCE: Lee, Inmoo, Scott Lochhead, and Jay Ritter, 1996, "The Costs of Raising Capital," *The Journal of Financial Research, 21* (Spring), 59–74.

were sold to the public at a price of $20.50. As is typical, Unilate's agreement had an escape clause that provided for the contract to be voided if the price of the stock had fallen below a predetermined figure. In the illustrative case, this "upset" price was set at $18.50 a share. Thus, if the closing price of the shares on the last day of registration had been $18, Unilate would have had the option of withdrawing from the agreement.

Investment bankers have an easier job if an issue is priced relatively low, but the issuer of the securities naturally wants as high a price as possible. Therefore, an inherent conflict of interest on price exists between the investment banker and the issuer. However, if the issuer is financially sophisticated and makes comparisons with similar security issues, the investment banker will be forced to price close to the market.

It is important to note that *if pressure from the new shares drives down the price of the stock, all shares outstanding, not just the new shares, will be affected.* Thus, if Unilate's stock fell from $23 to $20.50 as a result of the financing, and if the price remained at that new level, the company would incur a loss of $2.50 on each of the 25 million shares previously outstanding, or a total market value loss of $62.5 million. In a sense, that loss would be a *flotation cost* because it would be a cost associated with the new issue. However, if the company's prospects really were poorer than investors had thought, then most of the price decline eventually would have occurred anyway. On the other hand, if the company's prospects are not really all that bad (if the signal was incorrect), then over time Unilate's stock price would increase, and the company would not suffer a permanent loss of $62.5 million.

If the company is going public for the first time, it will have no established price (or demand curve), so the investment bankers will have to estimate the equilibrium price at which the stock will sell after issue. If the offering price is set below the true equilibrium price, the stock will rise sharply after issue, and the company and its original stockholders will have given away too many shares to raise the required capital. If the offering price is set above the true equilibrium price, either the issue will fail or, if the investment bankers succeed in selling the stock, their investment clients will be unhappy when the stock subsequently falls to its equilibrium level. Therefore, it is important that the equilibrium price be approximated as closely as possible.

Selling Procedures

Once the company and its investment bankers have decided how much money to raise, the type of securities to issue, and the basis for pricing the issue, they will prepare and file a registration statement and prospectus with the SEC. It generally takes 20 days to six months for the issue to be approved by the SEC. The final price of the stock (or the interest rate on a bond issue) is set at the close of business the day the issue clears the SEC, and the securities are then offered to the public the following day.

Investment bankers must pay the issuing firm within a few days of the time the offering officially begins, so, typically, the investment bankers sell the stock within a day or two after the offering begins. But, on occasion investment bankers miscalculate, set the offering price too high, and are unable to move the issue. Similarly, the market might decline during the offering period, which again would force investment bankers to reduce the price of the stock. In either instance, on an underwritten offering the firm would still receive the price that was agreed upon, and the investment bankers would have to absorb any losses that were incurred.

Because they are exposed to large potential losses, investment bankers typically do not handle the purchase and distribution of an issue single-handedly unless it is a small one. If the amount of money involved is large and the risk of price fluctuations substantial, an investment banker forms an **underwriting syndicate** in an effort to minimize the amount of risk each one carries. The investment banking house that sets up the deal is called the **lead,** or **managing, underwriter.**

In addition to the underwriting syndicate, on larger offerings still more investment bankers are included in a **selling group,** which handles the distribution of securities to individual investors. The selling group includes all members of the underwriting syndicate plus additional dealers who take relatively small participations (or shares of the total issue) from the syndicate members. Members of the selling group act as selling agents and receive commissions for their efforts—they do not purchase the securities, so they do not bear the same risks the underwriting syndicate does. Thus, the underwriters act as wholesalers and bear the risks associated with the issue, whereas members of the selling group act as retailers. The number of investment banking houses in a selling group depends partly on the size of the issue; for

UNDERWRITING SYNDICATE
A syndicate of investment firms formed to spread the risk associated with the purchase and distribution of a new issue of securities.

LEAD, OR MANAGING, UNDERWRITER
The member of an underwriting syndicate that actually *manages* the distribution and sale of a new security offering.

SELLING GROUP
A group (network) of brokerage firms formed for the purpose of distributing a new issue of securities.

✳ **ETHICAL DILEMMA**

It's a "Painful" Decision—By George!

George Anderson works as an analyst for Roberts, Stephens, and Kilmer (RSK), one of the largest investment banking firms in the United States. His primary job is to analyze initial public offerings (IPOs) planned by firms that want to go public to determine the viability of such stock issues. RSK relies on Anderson's evaluations when negotiating with companies that want to enter the markets with IPOs, which can be risky propositions for investment bankers.

RSK currently is handling the IPO of BioPharm, a pharmaceutical company based in Oregon. Created by a brilliant biochemist named Henry Scott, the company has developed and marketed a number of new drugs since its start in 1985. George Anderson's evaluation of BioPharm indicates that the potential for the company is tremendous, especially if its newest drug, which offers a cure for arthritis, is approved by the Food and Drug Administration (FDA). According to Anderson's report, BioPharm has a bright future even if the FDA does not approve the arthritis drug. BioPharm's IPO is scheduled to go to the market tomorrow at a price of $20 per share.

This morning, when he got to work and turned on his computer, Anderson discovered he had a number of e-mail messages marked urgent. The messages were sent by Rachel Raymond, a newspaper reporter from Washington, D.C., who specializes in articles about medical issues, including physician care, surgical practices, and pharmaceutical research and development. In essence, the messages indicated that an unidentified source told Raymond that within the next few days the FDA will announce BioPharm's arthritis treatment has been rejected. Anderson's repeated attempts to contact Raymond about her e-mail messages have been unsuccessful.

Because he could not get in touch with Raymond, Anderson has made inquiries throughout the day to determine the validity of Raymond's messages. The only information he has been able to verify is that William Mezina, CEO of BioPharm, has sold a significant portion of his stock holdings in the company during the past few days. Attempts to corroborate the content of Raymond's messages proved futile. Sources at the FDA will not comment, and a flash fire at BioPharm has temporarily interrupted its communications systems.

At this point Anderson is beside himself because the BioPharm IPO is supposed to be distributed when the markets open tomorrow. RSK has invested considerable funds to get the IPO ready for its introduction tomorrow, and withholding the issue would cost the firm a substantial amount. But if RSK goes ahead with the issue as planned and, within a few days or weeks, the FDA announces the arthritis drug has been rejected, the per price of BioPharm's IPO certainly will plunge. Even worse, if later it can be proven that RSK knew about the FDA's rejection of the arthritis drug, there could be future legal ramifications because withholding such information from stockholders might be considered fraud. What should Anderson do? Should he try to delay the IPO, even though the content of Raymond's messages is unfounded at this time?

example, the one set up when Communications Satellite Corporation (Comsat) went public consisted of 385 members.

Shelf Registrations

The selling procedures described previously, including the 20-day minimum waiting period between registration with the SEC and sale of the issue, apply to most security sales. However, large, well-known public companies that issue securities frequently might file a master registration statement with the SEC and then update it with a short-form statement just prior to each individual offering. In such a case, a company could decide at 10 A.M. to sell registered securities and have the sale com-

SHELF REGISTRATION
Securities are registered with the SEC for sale at a later date; the securities are held "on the shelf" until the sale.

pleted before noon. This procedure is known as **shelf registration** because in effect the company puts its new securities "on the shelf" and then sells them to investors when it thinks the market is right.

Maintenance of the Secondary Market

In the case of a large, established firm like General Motors, the investment banking firm's job is finished once it has disposed of the stock and turned the net proceeds over to the company. However, when a company is going public for the first time, the investment banker is under an obligation to maintain a market for the shares after the issue has been completed. Such stocks typically are traded in the over-the-counter market, and the lead underwriter generally agrees to "make a market" in the stock and to keep it reasonably liquid. The company wants a good market to exist for its stock, as do its stockholders. Therefore, if the investment banking house wants to do business with the company in the future, keep its own brokerage customers happy, and have future referral business, it will hold an inventory of the shares and help to maintain an active secondary market in the stock.

Self-Test Questions

What is the sequence of events when a firm decides to issue new securities?

What type of firm would use a shelf registration? Explain.

What is an underwriting syndicate, and why is it important in the investment banking process?

Summary

This chapter is more descriptive than analytical, but a knowledge of the issues discussed here is essential to an understanding of finance. The key concepts covered are listed here:

- **Stockholders' equity** consists of the firm's **common stock, paid-in capital** (funds received in excess of the par value), and **retained earnings** (earnings not paid out as dividends).
- **Book value per share** is equal to stockholders' equity divided by the number of shares of stock outstanding. A stock's book value often is different from its par value and its market value.
- A **proxy** is a document that gives one person the power to act for another person, typically the power to vote shares of common stock. A **proxy fight** occurs when an outside group solicits stockholders' proxies in order to vote a new management team into office.
- Stockholders often have the right to purchase any additional shares sold by the firm. This right, called the **preemptive right,** protects the control of the present stockholders and prevents dilution of the value of their stock.
- The major **advantages of common stock financing** are as follows: (1) there is no obligation to make fixed payments; (2) common stock never matures; (3) the use of common stock increases the creditworthiness of the firm; and (4) stock often can be sold on better terms than debt.

- The major **disadvantages of common stock financing** are (1) it extends voting privileges to new stockholders; (2) new stockholders share in the firm's profits; (3) the costs of stock financing are high; (4) using stock can raise the firm's cost of capital; and (5) dividends paid on common stock are not tax deductible.
- A **closely held corporation** is one that is owned by a few individuals who typically are associated with the firm's management. A **publicly owned corporation** is one that is owned by a relatively large number of individuals who are not actively involved in its management.
- **Going public** facilitates stockholder diversification, increases liquidity of the firm's stock, makes it easier for the firm to raise capital, and establishes a value for the firm. However, reporting costs are high, operating data must be disclosed, and public ownership might make it harder for management to maintain control of the firm.
- Security markets are regulated by the **Securities and Exchange Commission (SEC).**
- Financial instruments available in the international markets are similar to those issued in the United States. But most Americans invest in foreign companies through **American Depository Receipts (ADRs),** which are certificates that represent foreign stocks held in trust, generally by a bank, in the country where the company is located.
- Stock traded internationally generally is referred to as either *Euro stock* or *Yankee Stock*. **Euro stock** is traded in countries other than the country where the company is located, except the United States, where such stock is called **Yankee stock.**
- An **investment banker** assists in the issuing of securities by helping the firm determine the size of the issue and the type of securities to be used, by establishing the selling price, by selling the issue, and, in some cases, by maintaining an after-market for the stock.

Questions

16-1 Examine Table 16-1. Suppose Unilate Textiles sold 2 million shares, with the company netting $25 per share. Construct a statement of the equity accounts to reflect this sale.

16-2 The SEC attempts to protect investors who are purchasing newly issued securities by requiring issuers to provide relevant financial information to prospective investors. However, the SEC does not provide an opinion about the real value of the securities; hence, an investor might pay too much for some stock and consequently lose heavily. Do you think the SEC should, as a part of every new stock or bond offering, render an opinion to investors on the proper value of the securities being offered? Explain.

16-3 How do you think each of the following items would affect a company's ability to attract new capital and the flotation (issuing) costs involved in doing so?
  a. A decision to list a company's stock; the stock currently trades in the over-the-counter market.
  b. A decision of a privately held company to go public.
  c. The increasing importance of institutions in the stock and bond markets.
  d. The trend toward financial conglomerates as opposed to stand-alone investment banking houses.

    e. Elimination of the preemptive right.

    f. The introduction of shelf registrations.

16–4 Before entering a formal agreement, investment bankers carefully investigate the companies whose securities they underwrite; this is especially true of the issues of firms going public for the first time. Because the bankers do not themselves plan to hold the securities but intend to sell them to others as soon as possible, why are they so concerned about making careful investigations?

16–5 It frequently is stated that the primary purpose of the preemptive right is to allow individuals to maintain their proportionate share of the ownership and control of a corporation.

    a. How important do you suppose this consideration is for the average stockholder of a firm whose shares are traded on the New York or American Stock Exchanges?

    b. Is the preemptive right likely to be of more importance to stockholders of publicly owned or closely held firms? Explain.

16–6 Why would management be interested in getting a wider distribution of its shares?

Self-Test Problem

key terms   **ST-1** Define each of the following terms:

    a. Common equity; paid-in capital; retained earnings

    b. Par value; book value per share; market value per share

    c. Proxy; proxy fight; takeover

    d. Preemptive right

    e. Classified stock; founders' shares

    f. Closely held corporation; publicly owned corporation

    g. Over-the-counter (OTC) market; organized security exchange

    h. Primary market; secondary market

    i. Going public; new issue market; initial public offering (IPO)

    j. Securities and Exchange Commission (SEC); registration statement; shelf registration; blue sky laws; margin requirements; margin call; insiders

    k. Prospectus

    l. Best efforts arrangement; underwritten arrangement

    m. Underwriters' spread; flotation costs; offering price

    n. Underwriting syndicate; lead, or managing, underwriter; selling group

Problems

profit (loss) on a new stock issue   **16–1** Security Brokers Inc. specializes in underwriting new issues by small firms. On a recent offering of Barenbaum Inc., the terms were as follows:

Price to public	$7.50 per share
Number of shares	3 million
Proceeds to Barenbaum	$21,000,000

    The out-of-pocket expenses incurred by Security Brokers in the design and distribution of the issue were $450,000. What profit or loss would Security Brokers incur if the issue were sold to the public at an average price of

    a. $7.50 per share?

    b. $9.00 per share?

    c. $6.00 per share?

16–2 U-Fix-It, a small home improvement building supplier, has been successful and has enjoyed a good growth trend. Now U-Fix-It is planning to go public with an issue of common stock, and it faces the problem of setting an appropriate price on the stock. The company's management and its investment bankers believe that the proper procedure is to select several similar firms with publicly traded common stock and to make relevant comparisons.

Several home improvement building suppliers are reasonably similar to U-Fix-It with respect to product mix, size, asset composition, and debt/equity proportions. Of these companies, Home Headquarters and Loware are most similar. When analyzing the following data, assume that 2000 and 2005 were reasonably normal years for all three companies—that is, these years were neither especially good nor especially bad in terms of sales, earnings, and dividends. At the time of the analysis, the risk-free rate, k_{RF}, was 10 percent and the market rate, k_M, was 15 percent. Home Headquarters is listed on the AMEX and Loware on the NYSE, while U-Fix-It will be traded in the OTC market.

	HOME HEADQUARTERS	LOWARE	U-FIX-IT (TOTALS)
Earnings per share			
2005	$ 3.60	$ 6.00	$ 960,000
2000	2.40	4.40	652,800
Price per share			
2005	$28.80	$52.00	—
Dividends per share			
2005	$ 1.80	$ 3.00	$ 480,000
2000	1.20	2.20	336,000
Book value per share, 2005	$24.00	$44.00	$7,200,000
Market/book ratio, 2005	120%	118%	—
Total assets, 2005	$22.4 million	$ 65.6 million	$16.0 million
Total debt, 2005	$ 9.6 million	$ 24.0 million	$ 8.8 million
Sales, 2005	$32.8 million	$112.0 million	$29.6 million

a. Assume that U-Fix-It has 100 shares of stock outstanding. Use this information to calculate earnings per share (EPS), dividends per share (DPS), and book value per share for U-Fix-It. (*Hint:* U-Fix-It's 2005 EPS = $9,600.)

b. Calculate earnings and dividend growth rates for the three companies. (*Hint:* U-Fix-It's EPS g is 8 percent.)

c. On the basis of your answer to part a, do you think U-Fix-It's stock would sell at a price in the same ballpark as that of Home Headquarters and Loware—that is, in the range of $25 to $100 per share?

d. Assuming that U-Fix-It's management can split the stock so that the 100 shares could be changed to 1,000 shares, 100,000 shares, or any other number, would such an action make sense in this case? Why?

e. Now assume that U-Fix-It did split its stock and has 400,000 shares. Calculate new values for EPS, DPS, and book value per share. (*Hint:* U-Fix-It's new 2005 EPS is $2.40.)

f. Return on equity (ROE) can be measured as EPS/book value per share or as total earnings/total equity. Calculate ROEs for the three companies for 2005. (*Hint:* U-Fix-It's 2000 ROE = 13.3%.)

g. Calculate dividend payout ratios for the three companies. (*Hint:* U-Fix-It's 2005 payout ratio is 50 percent.)

h. Calculate debt/total assets ratios for the three companies. (*Hint:* U-Fix-It's 2005 debt ratio is 55 percent.)

i. Calculate the P/E ratios for Home Headquarters and Loware based on 2005 data. Are these P/E ratios reasonable in view of relative growth, payout, and ROE data? If not, what other factors might explain them? (*Hint:* Home Headquarters' P/E = 8×.)

j. Now determine a range of values for U-Fix-It's stock price, with 400,000 shares outstanding, by applying Home Headquarters' and Loware's P/E ratios, price/dividends ratios, and price/book value ratios to your data for U-Fix-It. For example, one possible price for U-Fix-It's stock is (P/E Home Headquarters) × (EPS U-Fix-It) = 8 × $2.40 = $19.20 per share. Similar calculations would produce a range of prices based on both Home Headquarters' and Loware's data. (*Hint:* Our range was $19.20 to $21.60.)

k. Using the equation $k_s = \hat{D}_1/P_0 + g$, find approximate k_s values for Home Headquarters and Loware. Then use these values in the constant growth stock price model to find a price for U-Fix-It's stock. (*Hint:* We averaged the EPS and DPS g's for U-Fix-It.)

l. At what price do you think U-Fix-It's shares should be offered to the public? You will want to select a price that will be low enough to induce investors to buy the stock but not so low that it will rise too sharply immediately after it is issued. Think about relative growth rates, ROEs, dividend yields, and total returns ($k_s = \hat{D}_1/P_0 + g$).

Exam-Type Problems

The problems included in this section are set up in such a way that they could be used as multiple-choice exam problems.

book value per share **16–3** Atlantic Coast Resources Company had the following balance sheet at the end of 2005:

ATLANTIC COAST RESOURCES COMPANY:
BALANCE SHEET DECEMBER 31, 2005

		Accounts payable	$ 64,400
		Notes payable	71,400
		Long-term debt	151,200
		Common stock	
		(30,000 authorized	
		20,000 shares outstanding)	364,000
		Retained earnings	336,000
Total assets	$987,000	Total liabilities and equity	$987,000

a. What is the book value per share of Atlantic's common stock?

b. Suppose the firm sold the remaining authorized shares and netted $32.55 per share. What would be the new book value per share?

underwriting and **16–4** The Taussig Company, whose stock price now is $30, needs to raise $15 mil-
flotation expenses lion in common stock. Underwriters have informed Taussig's management that it must price the new issue to the public at $27.53 per share to ensure the shares will be sold. The underwriters' compensation will be 7 percent of the issue price, so Taussig will net $25.60 per share. Taussig will also incur

expenses in the amount of $360,000. How many shares must Taussig sell to net $15 million after underwriting and flotation expenses?

Integrative Problem

investment banking process **16–5** Gonzales Food Stores, a family-owned grocery store chain headquartered in El Paso, is considering a major expansion. The proposed expansion would require Gonzales to raise $10 million in additional capital. Because Gonzales currently has a debt ratio of 50 percent, and because the family members already have all their funds tied up in the business, the owners cannot supply any additional equity, so the company will have to sell stock to the public. However, the family wants to ensure that they retain control of the company. This would be Gonzales's first stock sale, and the owners are not sure just what would be involved. Therefore, they have asked you to research the process and to help them decide exactly how to raise the needed capital. In doing so, you should answer the following questions:

a. What are the advantages to Gonzales of financing with stock rather than bonds? What are the disadvantages of using stock?

b. Is the stock of Gonzales Food Stores currently publicly held or privately owned? Would this situation change if the stock sale were made?

c. What is classified stock? Would there be any advantage to Gonzales of designating the stock currently outstanding as "founders' shares"? What type of common stock should Gonzales sell to the public to allow the family to retain control of the business?

d. What does the term *going public* mean? What would be the advantages to the Gonzales family of having the firm go public? What would be the disadvantages?

e. What does the term *listed stock* mean? Do you think that Gonzales's stock would be listed shortly after the company goes public? If not, where would the stock trade?

f. Suppose the firm has decided to issue $10 million of Class B nonvoting stock. Now Gonzales must select an investment banker. Do you think it should select an investment banker on the basis of a competitive bid or do a negotiated deal? Explain.

g. Without doing any calculations, briefly describe of the procedures by which Gonzales and its investment banker will determine the price at which the stock will be offered to the public.

h. What is a prospectus? Why does the SEC require all firms to file registration statements and distribute prospectuses to potential stockholders before selling stock?

i. If Gonzales goes public and sells shares that the public buys at a price of $10 per share, what will be the approximate percentage cost, including both underwriting costs and other costs? Assume the company sells 1.5 million shares. Would the cost be higher or lower if the company were already publicly owned?

j. Would you recommend that Gonzales have the issue underwritten or sold on a best efforts basis? Why? What would be the difference in costs between the two procedures?

k. If some of the Gonzales family members wanted to sell some of their own shares in order to diversify at the same time the company was selling new shares to raise expansion capital, would this be feasible?

GET REAL with Thomson ONE

16–6 J. P. Morgan [JPM], an investment banking firm, experiences variations (swings) in sales based on the state of the economy. A portion of sales comes from initial public offerings (IPOs). Because firms go public and issue IPOs most often during growing economies, sales for investment bankers depend on the economy. Answer the following questions:

   a. What were J. P. Morgan's total annual sales and percentage sales growth during the past five years? [*Hint:* Click on Fundamental Ratios/Worldscope Ratios/Annual Growth Report]

   b. What was the pattern of J. P. Morgan's stock price during the same time period? [*Hint:* Click on Price/Overviews/Datastream Market Data/Actual Value Price History Report]

   c. What conclusions can you draw from the answers to questions a and b?

   d. Pick one of J. P. Morgan's Peers by industry group. Did the peer firm you chose exhibit a similar pattern in total annual sales, percentage sales growth, and stock price history? Explain your answer.

CHAPTER 17

Long-Term Debt

During the past couple of decades, the use of debt has increased significantly in all sectors of the economy—households, businesses, and governments. The increase in business debt has been attributed primarily to the merger and acquisition frenzy that occurred in the 1980s, especially prior to 1989. Much of the merger activity was financed with debt, and some firms even "leveraged up" to make themselves less attractive takeover targets. Consequently, the average debt ratio of companies increased significantly during this era. In 1980, the average firm was financed with about 43 percent debt; by 1989, the debt ratio was more than 57 percent. Significant relative increases in the issuance of corporate debt occurred from 1984 through 1988, which was also the period when there was an unprecedented number of mergers and acquisitions. Debt financing was attractive during this period because, compared to the period from 1979 to 1983, interest rates had decreased considerably and then remained relatively stable.

As a result of the leveraging activity that occurred in the 1980s, more stock was taken out of the capital market than was put back in through new issues. From 1984 to 1990, a net $640 billion of stock was replaced by debt; nearly $200 billion, 7.5 percent of the outstanding equity at the time, was retired in the fourth quarter of 1988.

In the latter part of 1989, economic growth started to slow and firms began to "deleverage."

The burden of servicing high amounts of debt motivated many firms to improve their cash flow positions. Stock repurchases slowed, while new stock issues increased. In 1991 and 1992 new stock issues exceeded repurchases by an average of more than $20 billion per year. Unfortunately, at this pace, it would take almost 30 years to recover the amount of equity that was converted into debt in the 1980s.

Debt ratios of companies decreased somewhat during the 1990s, but the deleveraging effort did not significantly change the overall debt position of the business sector. Many firms found that lower interest rates in the 1990s, especially in 1993, helped them to reduce interest payments substantially through refinancing, which obviates the need to replace debt entirely. Experts estimate that refinancing with cheaper debt reduced annual interest on all business debt by as much as $35 billion per year. And in 1994, stocks performed poorly, making them less attractive for raising funds and more attractive for firms to repurchase. In fact, 1994 stock buybacks were the highest since the record-setting activity of the late 1980s. This record has since been broken because both average stock prices and general interest rates decreased from 2000–2002. As a result, new corporate bond issues increased substantially during this period. In 2001, for example, corporations issued a record $879.2 billion worth of new bonds, which was 31 percent higher than in 2000. New issues of corporate bonds declined to $594.4 billion in 2002 because the economy was slumping. But, with the lowest interest rates in decades, the new issues market rebounded to $743.6 billion in 2003. During this same period, the stock markets performed poorly, which resulted in many bargain-priced stocks. For this reason, many firms used the funds raised in the debt markets to repurchase their stocks. At the beginning of 2004, expectations were that interest rates would increase, which would cause firms to decrease the amount of debt they issue. Thus, we would expect stock repurchases to decline.

In general, businesses in the United States have "releveraged" in recent years. It is unclear which direction firms will go in the future, but merger and acquisition activity is on the increase once again, and this will help sustain the current releveraging movement. In any event, it appears that many companies will experience increasing debt ratios and be saddled with servicing large amounts of debt for some time in the future. As you read this chapter, consider the positive and negative effects of debt on both businesses and our economy. ■

FUNDED DEBT
"Funding" means replacing short-term debt with securities of longer maturity.

Different groups of investors prefer different types of securities, and investors' tastes change over time. Thus, astute financial managers offer a variety of securities, and they package their new security offerings at each point in time to appeal to the greatest possible number of potential investors. In this chapter, we consider the various types of long-term debt available to financial managers.

Long-term debt is often called **funded debt.** When a firm "funds" its short-term debt, this means that it replaces short-term debt with securities of longer maturity. Funding does not imply that the firm places money with a trustee or other repository; it is simply part of the jargon of finance, and it means that the firm replaces short-term debt with permanent capital. Pacific Gas & Electric Company (PG&E) provides a good example of funding. PG&E has a construction program where it typically uses short-term debt to finance construction expenditures. However, once short-term debt has built up to about $100 million, the company sells a stock or bond issue, uses the proceeds to pay off (or fund) its bank loans, and starts the cycle again. There is a fixed cost involved in selling stocks or bonds that makes it quite expensive to issue small amounts of these securities. Therefore, the process used by PG&E and other companies is quite logical.

Traditional Debt Instruments

There are many types of long-term debt instruments: term loans, bonds, secured and unsecured notes, marketable and nonmarketable debt, and so on. In this section, we briefly discuss the traditional long-term debt instruments, after which we examine some important features of debt contracts and some innovations in long-term debt financing.

TERM LOAN
A loan, generally obtained from a bank or insurance company, on which the borrower agrees to make a series of payments consisting of interest and principal on specific dates.

Term Loans

A **term loan** is a contract under which a borrower agrees to make a series of interest and principal payments on specific dates to the lender. Term loans usually are negotiated directly between the borrowing firm and a financial institution—generally a bank, an insurance company, or a pension fund. Although term loans' maturities vary from two to 30 years, most are for periods in the three-year to 15-year range.[1]

Term loans have three major advantages over public offerings—*speed*, *flexibility*, and *low issuance costs*. Because they are negotiated directly between the lender and the borrower, formal documentation is minimized. The key provisions of a term loan can be worked out much more quickly than those for a public issue, and it is not necessary for the loan to go through the Securities and Exchange Commission registration process. A further advantage of term loans has to do with future flexibility. If a bond issue is held by many different bondholders, it is virtually impossible to obtain permission to alter the terms of the agreement, even though new economic conditions might make such changes desirable. With a term loan, the borrower generally can sit down with the lender and work out mutually agreeable modifications to the contract.

The interest rate on a term loan can be either fixed for the life of the loan or variable. If a fixed rate is used, generally it will be set close to the rate on bonds of equivalent maturity and risk. If the rate is variable, it usually will be set at a certain number of percentage points over the prime rate, the commercial paper rate, rates on Treasury securities, or the London Inter-Bank Offered Rate (LIBOR), which is the rate of interest offered by the largest and strongest London banks on deposits of other large banks of the highest credit standing. Then, when the index rate goes up or down, so does the rate charged on the outstanding balance of the term loan. Rates might be adjusted annually, semiannually, quarterly, monthly, or on some other basis, depending on what the contract specifies. Today, many term loans made by banks have floating rates; in 1970, there were few floating-rate term notes. With the increased volatility of interest rates in recent years, banks and other lenders have become increasingly reluctant to make long-term, fixed-rate loans.

Bonds

BOND

A long-term debt
instrument.

A **bond** is a long-term contract under which a borrower agrees to make payments of interest and principal on specific dates to the holder of the bond. Although bonds traditionally have been issued with maturities of between 20 and 30 years, during the past few decade shorter maturities, such as seven to 10 years, have been used to an increasing extent. Bonds are similar to term loans, but a bond issue generally is advertised, offered to the public, and actually sold to many different investors. Indeed, thousands of individual and institutional investors might purchase bonds when a firm sells a bond issue, whereas there usually is only one lender in the case of a term loan.[2] With bonds the interest rate generally is fixed, although in recent years there has been an increase in the use of various types of floating rate bonds. There also are a number of different types of bonds, the more important of which are discussed next.

---

[1]Most term loans are amortized, which means they are paid off in equal installments over the life of the loan. Amortization protects the lender against the possibility that the borrower will not make adequate provisions for the loan's retirement during the life of the loan. See Chapter 3 for a review of amortization. Also, if the interest and principal payments required under a term loan agreement are not met on schedule, the borrowing firm is said to have defaulted, and it can then be forced into bankruptcy.

[2]However, for very large term loans, 20 or more financial institutions might form a syndicate to grant the credit. Also, it should be noted that a bond issue can be sold to one lender (or to just a few); in this case, the issue is said to be "privately placed." Companies that place bonds privately do so for the same reasons that they use term loans—speed, flexibility, and low issuance costs.

MORTGAGE BOND
A bond backed by fixed assets. First mortgage bonds are senior in priority to claims of second mortgage bonds.

Mortgage Bonds   With a **mortgage bond,** the corporation pledges certain assets as security for the bond. To illustrate, in 2005 Scobes Corporation needed $10 million to build a major regional distribution center. Bonds in the amount of $4 million, secured by a mortgage on the property, were issued. (The remaining $6 million was financed with equity capital.) If Scobes defaults on the bonds, the bondholders can foreclose on the property and sell it to satisfy their claims.

If Scobes chooses to, it can issue *second mortgage bonds* secured by the same $10 million plant. In the event of liquidation, the holders of these second mortgage bonds would have a claim against the property, but only after the first mortgage bondholders had been paid off in full. Thus, second mortgages are sometimes called *junior mortgages* (debt) because they are junior in priority to the claims of *senior mortgages* (debt), or *first mortgage bonds.*

All mortgage bonds are written subject to an *indenture*, which is a legal document that spells out in detail the rights of both the bondholders and the corporation (bond issuer). Indentures generally are "open ended," meaning that new bonds might be issued from time to time under the existing indenture. However, the amount of new bonds that can be issued almost always is limited to a specified percentage of the firm's total "bondable property," which generally includes all plant and equipment. For example, Bartow Electric Company can issue first mortgage bonds totaling up to 60 percent of its fixed assets. If its fixed assets totaled $1 billion, and if it had $500 million of first mortgage bonds outstanding, it could, by the property test, issue another $100 million of bonds (60 percent of $1 billion = $600 million).

DEBENTURE
A long-term bond that is not secured by a mortgage on specific property.

Debentures   A **debenture** is an unsecured bond, and as such it provides no lien against specific property as security for the obligation. Therefore, debenture holders are general creditors whose claims are protected by property not otherwise pledged as collateral. In practice, the use of debentures depends both on the nature of the firm's assets and on its general credit strength. An extremely strong company, such as IBM, will tend to use debentures; it simply does not need to put up property as security for its debt. Debentures also are issued by companies in industries in which it would not be practical to provide security through a mortgage on fixed assets. Examples of such industries are the large mail-order houses and commercial banks, which characteristically hold most of their assets in the form of inventory or loans, neither of which is satisfactory security for a mortgage bond.

SUBORDINATED DEBENTURE
A bond having a claim on assets only after the senior debt has been paid off in the event of liquidation.

Subordinated Debentures   The term *subordinate* means "below" or "inferior to," and, in the event of bankruptcy, subordinated debt has claims on assets only after senior debt has been paid off. **Subordinated debentures** might be subordinated either to designated notes payable (usually bank loans) or to all other debt. In the event of liquidation or reorganization, holders of subordinated debentures cannot be paid until all senior debt, as named in the debentures' indenture, has been paid.

CONVERTIBLE BOND
A bond that is exchangeable, at the option of the holder, for common stock of the issuing firm.

WARRANT
A long-term option to buy a stated number of shares of common stock at a specified price.

INCOME BOND
A bond that pays interest to the holder only if the interest is earned by the firm.

Other Types of Bonds   Several other types of bonds are used sufficiently often to warrant mention. First, **convertible bonds** are securities that are convertible into shares of common stock, at a fixed price, at the option of the bondholder. Convertibles have a lower coupon rate than nonconvertible debt, but they offer investors a chance for capital gains in exchange for the lower coupon rate. Bonds issued with **warrants** are similar to convertibles. Warrants are options that permit the holder to buy stock for a stated price, thereby providing a capital gain if the price of the stock rises. Bonds that are issued with warrants, like convertibles, carry lower coupon rates

PUTABLE BOND
A bond that can be redeemed at the bondholder's option.

INDEXED (PURCHASING POWER) BOND
A bond that has interest payments based on an inflation index to protect the holder from inflation.

than straight bonds. **Income bonds** pay interest only when the firm has sufficient income to cover the interest payments. Thus, these securities cannot bankrupt a company, but from an investor's standpoint they are riskier than "regular" bonds. **Putable bonds** are bonds that can be turned in and exchanged for cash at the bondholder's option; generally, the option to turn in the bond can be exercised only if the firm takes some specified action, such as being acquired by a weaker company or increasing its outstanding debt by a large amount. With an **indexed,** or **purchasing power, bond,** which is popular in countries plagued by high rates of inflation, the interest rate payment is based on an inflation index such as the consumer price index; so the interest paid rises automatically when the inflation rate rises, thus protecting the bondholders against inflation.

Self-Test Questions

What are the three major advantages that term loans have over public offerings?

Differentiate between term loans and bonds.

Differentiate between mortgage bonds and debentures.

Define convertible bonds, bonds with warrants, income bonds, putable bonds, and indexed bonds.

Why do bonds with warrants and convertible bonds have lower coupons than bonds that do not have these features?

Specific Debt Contract Features

A firm's managers are concerned with both the effective cost of debt and any restrictions in debt contracts that might limit the firm's future actions. In this section, we discuss features that could affect either the cost of the firm's debt or the firm's future flexibility.

Bond Indentures

In Chapter 1 we discussed *agency problems*, which relate to conflicts of interest among corporate stakeholders—stockholders, bondholders, and managers. Bondholders have a legitimate fear that once they lend money to a company and are "locked in" for up to 30 years, the company will take some action that is designed to benefit stockholders but that harms bondholders. For example, RJR Nabisco, when it was highly rated, sold 30-year bonds with a low coupon rate, and investors bought those bonds in spite of the low yield because of their low risk. Then, after the bonds had been sold, the company announced plans to issue a great deal more debt, increasing the expected rate of return to stockholders but also increasing the riskiness of the bonds. RJR's bonds fell 20 percent the week the announcement was made. Safeway Stores and a number of other companies have done the same thing, and their bondholders also lost heavily as the market yield on the bonds rose and drove the prices of the bonds down.

INDENTURE
A formal agreement (contract) between the issuer of a bond and the bondholders.

TRUSTEE
An official who ensures that the bondholders' interests are protected and that the terms of the indenture are carried out.

Investors attempt to reduce agency problems by use of legal restrictions designed to ensure, insofar as possible, that the company does nothing to cause the quality of its bonds to deteriorate after they are issued. The **indenture** is the legal document that spells out the rights of the bondholders and the corporation. A **trustee,** usually a bank, is assigned to represent the bondholders and to make sure that the terms of the indenture are carried out. The indenture might be several hundred pages in length, and it will include **restrictive covenants** that cover such points as the conditions under which the issuer can pay off the bonds prior to maturity, the level at which the issuer's times-interest-earned ratio must be maintained if the company is to sell additional bonds, and restrictions against the payment of dividends when earnings do not meet certain specifications.

RESTRICTIVE COVENANTS
Provisions in a debt contract that constrain the actions of the borrower.

The trustee is responsible both for making sure the covenants are not violated and for taking appropriate action if they are. What constitutes "appropriate action" varies with the circumstances. It might be that to insist on immediate compliance would result in bankruptcy, which in turn might lead to large losses on the bonds. In such a case, the trustee might decide that the bondholders would be better served by giving the company a chance to work out its problems rather than by forcing it into bankruptcy.

The Securities and Exchange Commission approves indentures for publicly traded bonds and makes sure that all indenture provisions are met before allowing a company to sell new securities to the public. The indentures of many larger corporations were written back in the 1930s or 1940s, and many issues of new bonds, all covered by the same indenture, have been sold down through the years. The interest rates on the bonds, and perhaps also the maturities, change from issue to issue, but bondholders' protection as spelled out in the indenture are the same for all bonds of a given type.[3]

Call Provisions

CALL PROVISION
A provision in a bond contract that gives the issuer the right to redeem the bonds under specified terms prior to the normal maturity date.

Most bonds contain a **call provision,** which gives the issuing corporation the right to call the bonds for redemption. The call provision generally states that the company must pay the bondholders an amount greater than the par value for the bonds when they are called. The additional sum, which is termed a *call premium*, typically is set equal to one year's interest if the bonds are called during the first year possible, and the premium declines at a constant rate of INT/N each year thereafter, where INT = annual interest and N = original maturity in years. For example, the call premium on a $1,000 par value, 10-year, 10 percent bond would generally be $100 if it were called during the first year, $90 during the second year (calculated by reducing the $100, or 10 percent, premium by one-tenth), and so on. However, bonds usually are not callable until several years (generally five to 10) after they are issued; bonds with these *deferred calls* are said to have *call protection.*

Suppose a company sold bonds when interest rates were relatively high. Provided the issue is callable, the company could sell a new issue of low-yielding bonds if and when interest rates drop. It could then use the proceeds to retire the high-rate issue and thus reduce its interest expense. This process is called **refunding.**

REFUNDING
Retiring an existing bond issue with the proceeds of a newly issued bond.

Sinking Funds

SINKING FUND
A required annual payment designed to amortize a bond or preferred stock issue.

A **sinking fund** is a provision that facilitates the orderly retirement of a bond issue. Typically, the sinking fund provision requires the firm to retire a portion of the bond issue each year. On rare occasions the firm might be required to deposit money with a trustee, which invests the funds and then uses the accumulated sum to retire the

---

[3]A firm will have different indentures for each major type of bond it issues, including its first mortgage bonds, its debentures, its convertibles, and so on.

bonds when they mature. A failure to meet the sinking fund requirement causes the bond issue to be thrown into default, which might force the company into bankruptcy. Obviously, a sinking fund can constitute a dangerous cash drain on the firm.

In most cases, the firm is given the right to handle the sinking fund in either of two ways:

1. The company can call in for redemption (at par value) a certain percentage of the bonds each year. For example, it might be able to call 2 percent of the total original amount of the issue at a price of $1,000 per bond. The bonds are numbered serially, and those called for redemption are determined by a lottery administered by the trustee.
2. The company might buy the required amount of bonds on the open market.

The firm will choose the least-cost method. If interest rates have risen, causing bond prices to fall, it will buy bonds in the open market at a discount; if interest rates have fallen, it will call the bonds. Note that a call for sinking fund purposes is quite different from a refunding call as discussed previously. A sinking fund call requires no call premium, but only a small percentage of the issue normally is callable in any one year.

Self-Test Questions

How do trustees and indentures reduce agency problems for bondholders?

What are the two ways a sinking fund can be handled? Which method will be chosen by the firm if interest rates have risen? If interest rates have fallen?

What is the difference between a call for sinking fund purposes and a refunding call?

Are securities that provide for a sinking fund regarded as being riskier than those without this type of provision? Explain.

Why is a call provision so advantageous to a bond issuer? When will the issuer initiate a refunding call? Why?

Bond Innovations in the Past Few Decades

Zero (or Very Low) Coupon Bonds

ZERO COUPON BOND

A bond that pays no annual interest but is sold at a discount below par, thus providing compensation to investors in the form of capital appreciation.

Some bonds pay no interest but are offered at a substantial discount below their par values and hence provide capital appreciation rather than interest income. These securities are called **zero coupon bonds** ("*zeros*"), or *original issue discount bonds (OIDs)*. Corporations first used zeros in a major way in 1981. In the past, many large companies like IBM and JC Penney have used them to raise billions of dollars. Municipal governments also sell "zero munis," and investment bankers have in effect created zero coupon Treasury bonds by "stripping" the interest payments and selling only the right to receive principal repayment at maturity.

Not all original issue discount bonds (OIDs) have zero coupons. For example, a company might sell an issue of five-year bonds with a 3 percent coupon at a time when other bonds with similar ratings and maturities are yielding 9 percent. If an investor purchases these bonds at a price of $762.62, the yield to maturity would be 9 percent. The discount of $1,000 – $762.62 = $237.38 represents the capital appreciation the bondholder receives for holding the bond for five years. Thus, zero coupon bonds are just one type of original issue discount bond. Any nonconvertible bond whose coupon rate is set below the going market rate at the time of its issue will sell at a discount, and it will be classified as an OID bond.

OID bonds are not favored by most individual investors. The primary reason is because the interest income that must be reported each year for tax purposes includes the dollar amount of interest actually received, which is $0 for zero coupons, plus the annual *prorated* capital appreciation. For example, the purchaser of the 3 percent coupon bond just mentioned actually would receive $30 interest each year. But the interest income reported for tax purposes would be $30 + ($237.38/5) = $77.48. Thus, taxes would have to be paid on prorated capital gains that would not be received for five years ($47.48 each year). For this reason, most OID bonds currently are held by institutional investors, such as insurance companies and pension funds, rather than individual investors.

Shortly after corporations began to issue zeros, investment bankers figured out a way to create zeros from U.S. Treasury bonds, which are issued only in coupon form. In 1982 Salomon Brothers (now Salomon Smith Barney) bought $1 billion of 12 percent, 30-year Treasuries. Each bond had 60 coupons worth $60 each, which represented the interest payments due every six months. Salomon then in effect clipped the coupons and placed them in 60 piles; the last pile also contained the now "stripped" bond itself, which represented a promise of $1,000 in the year 2012. These 60 piles of U.S. Treasury promises were then placed with the trust department of a bank and used as collateral for "zero coupon U.S. Treasury Trust Certificates," which are, in essence, zero coupon Treasury bonds. A pension fund that expected to need money in 2007 could have bought 25-year certificates backed by the interest the Treasury will pay in 2007. Treasury zeros are, of course, safer than corporate zeros, so they are very popular with pension fund managers.

Corporate (and municipal) zeros generally are callable at the option of the issuer, just like coupon bonds, after some stated call protection period. The call price is set at a premium over the accrued value at the time of the call. Stripped U.S. Treasury bonds (Treasury zeros) generally are not callable because the Treasury normally sells non-callable bonds. As a result, Treasury zeros are completely protected against reinvestment risk (the risk of having to invest cash flows from a bond at a lower rate because of a decline in interest rates).

Floating Rate Debt

In the early 1980s, inflation pushed interest rates up to unprecedented levels, causing sharp declines in the prices of long-term bonds. Even some supposedly "risk-free" U.S. Treasury bonds lost fully half their value, and a similar situation occurred with corporate bonds, mortgages, and other fixed-rate, long-term securities. As a result, many lenders became reluctant to lend money at fixed rates on a long-term basis, and they would do so only at extraordinarily high rates.

There normally is a *maturity risk premium* embodied in long-term interest rates; this premium is designed to offset the risk of declining bond prices if interest rates rise. Prior to the 1970s, the maturity risk premium on 30-year bonds was about 1 percentage point, meaning that under normal conditions, a firm might expect to pay about 1 percentage point more to borrow on a long-term than on a short-term basis. However, in the early 1980s, the maturity risk premium is estimated to have jumped to about 3 percentage points, which made long-term debt very expensive relative to short-term debt. Lenders were able and willing to lend on a short-term basis, but corporations were correctly reluctant to borrow on a short-term basis to finance long-term assets—such action is extremely dangerous. Therefore, there was a situation in which lenders did not want to lend on a long-term basis, but corporations needed long-term money. The problem was solved by the introduction of long-term, *floating rate debt.*

FLOATING RATE BOND

A bond whose interest rate fluctuates with shifts in the general level of interest rates.

A typical **floating rate bond** works as follows. The coupon rate is set for, say, the initial six-month period, after which it is adjusted every six months based on some market rate. Some corporate issues have been tied to the Treasury bond rate, while other issues have been tied to short-term rates. Many additional provisions can be included in floating rate issues; for example, some are convertible to fixed rate debt, whereas others have upper and lower limits ("caps" and "collars") on how high or low the yield can go.

Floating rate debt is advantageous to investors because the interest rate moves up if market rates rise. This causes the market value of the debt to be stabilized, and it also provides lenders such as banks with income that is better geared to their own obligations. Moreover, floating rate debt is advantageous to corporations because by using it, firms can issue debt with a long maturity without committing themselves to paying a historically high rate of interest for the entire life of the loan. Of course, if interest rates were to move even higher after a floating rate note had been signed, the borrower would have been better off issuing conventional, fixed rate debt.

Junk Bonds

JUNK BOND

A high-risk, high-yield bond used to finance mergers, leveraged buyouts, and troubled companies.

Prior to the 1980s, fixed income investors such as pension funds and insurance companies generally were unwilling to buy risky bonds, so it was almost impossible for risky companies to raise capital in the public bond markets. These companies, if they could raise debt capital at all, had to do so in the term loan market, where the loan could be tailored to satisfy the lender. Then, in the late 1970s, Michael Milken of the investment banking firm Drexel Burnham Lambert, relying on historical studies that showed risky bonds yielded more than enough to compensate for their risk, began to convince certain institutional investors of the merits of purchasing risky debt. Thus was born the **junk bond,** a high-risk, high-yield bond issued to finance a leveraged buyout, a merger, or a troubled company. For example, when Ted Turner attempted to buy CBS, he planned to finance the acquisition by issuing junk bonds to CBS's stockholders in exchange for their shares. Similarly, Public Service of New Hampshire financed construction of its troubled Seabrook nuclear plant with junk bonds, and junk bonds were used in the RJR Nabisco leveraged buyout (LBOs are discussed in the next chapter). In junk bond deals, the debt ratio generally is extremely high, so the bondholders must bear as much risk as stockholders normally would. The bonds' yields reflect this fact—a coupon rate of 25 percent per annum was required to sell the Public Service of New Hampshire bonds.

The emergence of junk bonds as an important type of debt is another example of how the investment banking industry adjusts to and facilitates new developments in capital markets. In the 1980s, mergers and takeovers increased dramatically. People like T. Boone Pickens and Ted Turner thought that certain old-line, established companies were run inefficiently and were financed too conservatively, and they wanted to take these companies over and restructure them. Michael Milken and his staff at Drexel Burnham Lambert began an active campaign to persuade certain institutions (often S&Ls) to purchase high-yield bonds. Milken developed expertise in

✴ **INDUSTRY PRACTICE**

Junk Bonds—Which Way Will the Market Go Next?

It has been more than a decade since Michael Milken, who at the time was considered the "junk bond king," was sent to jail for his role in misleading investors in the junk bond market, and the investment banking firm for which he worked, Drexel Burnham Lambert (DBL), was forced into bankruptcy as a result of its junk bond activities. When DBL dominated the junk-bond industry at the end of the 1980s, it had grown to a $200 billion business. In 1999, the junk bond market exceeded $600 billion. New issues of junk bonds decreased in 2000 to their lowest since the early 1900s, primarily due to investors' concerns about the creditworthiness of the issuers. During the next two years the values of junk bond issues increased and then decreased. But, in 2003 and 2004, the junk bond market experienced a resurgence when nearly $125 billion of new junk bonds were issued in each of these years. This amount was below the record-setting $138 billion that was issued in 1998. Even so, it was estimated that the size of the junk bond market was between $575 billion and $600 billion in 2004, which was near the record level of 1999. Expectations were that the junk bond market would continue to expand as more small, young firms raised additional capital to fund growth. Clearly, then, interest in the high-yield, high-risk debt instruments that are called junk bonds has not diminished.

Donaldson Lufkin & Jenrette Incorporated (DLJ), which was purchased by Credit Suisse in 2000, is now considered the leader in junk bonds—the company underwrites more than 20 percent of all junk-bond issues. It is not surprising that the telecommunications industry has led all issues, with between 25 and 30 percent of the total, because there has been substantial merger activity in the industry in recent years, most of which has been financed by high-yield debt.

One reason the junk bond market has grown so much during the past decade is because the financial markets in general have performed well. When the markets show a propensity to increase, investors

who have not experienced significant market declines become more confident that they will gain rather than lose with their investments; thus they are more inclined to invest in riskier instruments than they normally would in an effort to reap greater rewards. One of the investments to which investors turn is the junk bond, which promises higher yields than bonds that are rated investment grade or better. But with the promise of higher returns comes higher risk.

There are signs that the higher risk associated with junk bonds will "rear its ugly head" some time soon. Even though we are now in 2004 with an expanding economy, it appears that companies and individuals in the United States have overextended themselves with respect to borrowing such that they are having difficulty making debt payments. The problem has been manifested by increases in defaults that have occurred recently. More than 5 percent of companies with junk bonds defaulted on interest payments from the middle of 1998 to the middle of 1999—only about 4 percent defaulted in all of 1998 and a little more than 2 percent defaulted in 1997. When all corporate debt was considered, a little more than 2 percent of companies defaulted during the same period, which was up from 1.3 percent in 1998 and 0.7 percent in 1997. In fact, there was $60 billion of defaulted debt in 1999, which was a record and was much greater than the $11 billion of defaults that occurred in 1998.

Many believe that the record defaults can be traced to the fact that the junk bond market has been somewhat lax with respect to the types of firms that have been allowed to raise funds using these financial instruments. Many of the issuing companies have shown little history of generating profits; thus, they are struggling to repay their debts as they mature. In addition, it appears that bankruptcy is no longer considered the disgrace it once was, so some firms are not as concerned about the ramifications of defaults.

continues

To bring greater structure to the junk bond market, the Securities and Exchange Commission (SEC) recently increased its oversight of junk bond issues. Because nearly all junk bond issues are purchased by such institutional investors as mutual funds and pension funds, which are knowledgeable professionals, many issues consist of unregistered securities for which companies are not required to file the same financial information as are companies that issue registered securities. While the SEC believes that closing the registration loophole will enhance the ability of investors to make informed decisions about junk bonds, critics believe that the rules changes are detrimental to a market that pri-marily caters to start-up companies, which generally are relatively small with fewer outlets for raising funds than their larger counterparts. The future of the junk bond market could depend on which side ultimately prevails: Greater regulation might curtail some junk bond issues, but it might also improve the overall quality of the junk bond market.

Sources: Gregory Zuckerman, "Under Boom Economy, Strain over Debt," *The Wall Street Journal*, August 8, 1999, C1; Pallavi Gogoi, "Four Men Hold Sway Over Junk-Bond World," *The Wall Street Journal*, June 15, 1999; and Michael Schroeder, "SEC Aims for Increased Junk-Bond Oversight," *The Wall Street Journal*, May 21, 1999, C19.

putting together deals that were attractive to the institutions yet apparently feasible in the sense that projected cash flows were sufficient to meet the required interest payments. The fact that interest on the bonds was tax deductible, combined with the much higher debt ratios of the restructured firms, also increased after-tax cash flows and helped make the deals appear feasible.

The development of junk bond financing has done as much as any single factor to reshape the U.S. financial scene. The existence of these securities led directly to the loss of independence of Gulf Oil and hundreds of other companies, and it led to major shakeups in such companies as CBS, Union Carbide, and USX (formerly U.S. Steel). It also caused Drexel Burnham Lambert to leap from essentially nowhere in the 1970s to become the most profitable investment banking firm during the 1980s.

The phenomenal growth of the junk bond market was impressive but controversial. Significant risk, combined with unscrupulous dealings, created significant losses for investors. In early 1989, Drexel Burnham Lambert was forced into bankruptcy, and the so-called junk bond king, Michael Milken, eventually was sent to jail for his role in misleading investors in the junk bond market. (See the Industry Practice box.) These events badly tarnished the junk bond market, which also came under severe criticism for fueling takeover fires and adding to the cost of the S&L bailout that took place in the 1980s. Additionally, the realization that high leverage can spell trouble—as when Campeau, with $3 billion in junk financing, filed for bankruptcy in early 1990—has slowed the growth in the junk bond market. Recently, however, the junk bond market has begun to grow once again.

Self-Test Questions

Explain how the cash flows related to an issue of zero coupon bonds are determined.

What problem was solved by the introduction of long-term floating rate debt, and how is the rate on such bonds actually set?

For what purposes have junk bonds typically been used?

TABLE 17–1	Moody's and S&P Bond Ratings							
	HIGH QUALITY		**INVESTMENT GRADE**		**SUBSTANDARD**	**SPECULATIVE**		
					JUNK BONDS			
Moody's	Aaa	Aa	A	Baa	Ba	B	Caa	C
S&P	AAA	AA	A	BBB	BB	B	CCC	D

NOTE: Both Moody's and S&P use "modifiers" for bonds rated below triple A. S&P uses a plus and minus system; thus, A+ designates the strongest A-rated bonds and A– the weakest. Moody's uses a 1, 2, or 3 designation, with 1 denoting the strongest and 3 the weakest; thus, within the double-A category, Aa1 is the best, Aa2 is average, and Aa3 is the weakest.

Bond Ratings

Since the early 1900s, bonds have been assigned quality ratings that reflect their probability of going into default. The two major rating agencies are Moody's Investors Service (Moody's) and Standard & Poor's Corporation (S&P). These agencies' rating designations are shown in Table 17–1.[4] The triple- and double-A bonds are extremely safe. Single-A and triple-B bonds are strong enough to be called **investment grade bonds,** and they are the lowest-rated bonds that many banks and other institutional investors are permitted by law to hold. Double-B and lower bonds are speculative, or junk bonds; they have a significant probability of going into default, and many financial institutions are prohibited from buying them.

INVESTMENT GRADE BONDS
Bonds rated triple B or better; many banks and other institutional investors are permitted by law to hold only investment-grade or better bonds.

Bond Rating Criteria

Bond ratings are based on both qualitative and quantitative factors. Some of the factors considered by the bond rating agencies include the financial strength of the company as measured by various ratios, collateral provisions, seniority of the debt, restrictive covenants, provisions such as a sinking fund or a deferred call, litigation possibilities, regulation, and so on. Representatives of the rating agencies have consistently stated that no precise formula is used to set a firm's rating; all the factors listed, plus others, are taken into account, but not in a mathematically precise manner. Statistical studies have borne out this contention—researchers who have tried to predict bond ratings on the basis of quantitative data have had only limited success, indicating that the agencies use subjective judgment when establishing a firm's rating.[5]

Importance of Bond Ratings

Bond ratings are important both to firms and to investors. First, because a bond's rating is an indicator of its default risk, the rating has a direct, measurable influence on the bond's interest rate and the firm's cost of debt. Second, most bonds are purchased by institutional investors rather than individuals, and many institutions are

[4]In the following discussion, reference to the S&P code is intended to imply the Moody's code as well. Thus, triple-B bonds mean both BBB and Baa bonds; double-B bonds mean both BB and Ba bonds; and so on.

[5]See Ahmed Belkaoui, *Industrial Bonds and the Rating Process* (London: Quorum Books, 1983).

FIGURE 17–1 Yields on Selected Long-Term Bonds, 1965–2003

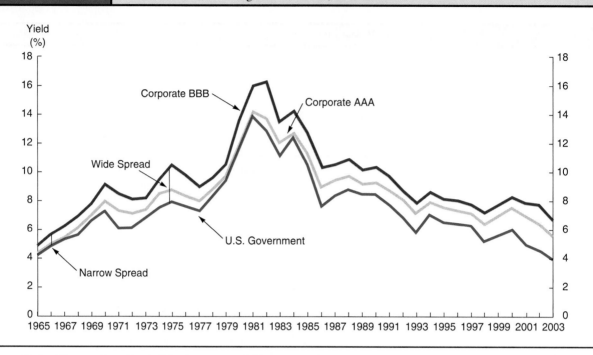

Source: Federal Reserve; http://www.federalreserve.gov.releases.

Note: The yields are based on the averages of monthly yields to maturity. The yields for the government bonds are based on securities with a 10-year maturity.

restricted to securities rated investment-grade or better. Thus, if a firm's bonds fall below BBB, it will have a difficult time selling new bonds because many potential purchasers will not be allowed to buy them.

As a result of their higher risk and more restricted market, lower-grade bonds have higher required rates of return, k_d, than high-grade bonds. Figure 17–1 illustrates this point. In each of the years shown on the graph, U.S. government bonds have had the lowest yields, corporate AAA have been next, and corporate BBB bonds have had the highest yields. The figure also shows that the gaps between yields on the three types of bonds vary over time, indicating that the cost differentials, or risk premiums, fluctuate from year to year. This point is highlighted in Figure 17–2, which gives the average yields on the three types of bonds and the risk premiums for AAA bonds and BBB bonds at three different time periods—December 1965, December 1982, and December 2003.[6] Note first that the risk-

---

[6]The term "risk premium" should reflect only the difference in expected (and required) returns between two securities that results from differences in their risk. However, the differences between yields to maturity on different types of bonds consist of (1) a true risk premium; (2) a liquidity premium, which reflects the fact that U.S. Treasury bonds are more readily marketable than most corporate bonds; (3) a call premium, because most Treasury bonds are not callable whereas corporate bonds are; and (4) an expected loss differential, which reflects the probability of loss on the corporate bonds. As an example of the last point, suppose the yield to maturity on a BBB bond was 10 percent versus 7 percent on government bonds, but there was a 5 percent probability of total default loss on the corporate bond. In this case, the expected return on the BBB bond would be $0.95(10\%) + 0.05(0\%) = 9.5\%$, and the risk premium would be 2.5 percent, not the full three percentage point difference in "promised" yields to maturity. Because of all these points, the risk premiums given in Figure 17–2 overstate somewhat the true (but unmeasurable) risk premiums.

FIGURE 17–2	Relationship between Bond Ratings and Bond Yield for Selected Dates

Percent

	Government BONDS (DEFAULT-FREE) (1)	AAA CORPORATE BONDS (2)	BBB CORPORATE BONDS (3)	Risk Premiums	
				AAA (2)–(1)	BBB (3)–(1)
December 1965	4.45%	4.60%	4.95%	0.15%	0.50%
December 1982	10.55%	11.68%	14.30%	1.13%	3.75%
December 2003	4.30%	5.65%	6.66%	1.35%	2.36%

Source: Federal Reserve; http://www.federalreserve.gov/releases.

free rate, or vertical axis intercept, rose 6.1 percentage points from 1965 to 1982, primarily reflecting the increase in realized and anticipated inflation; the rate was approximately the same in 2003 and in 1965, which indicates inflation expectations were the same during these periods. Second, the slopes of the lines also have increased since 1965, indicating increases in investors' risk aversion. Thus, the penalty for having a low credit rating varies over time. Occasionally, as in 1965, the penalty is relatively small, but at other times, as in 1982, it is extremely large. These slope differences reflect investors' risk aversion. In December 2003, there was uncertainty as to the future of the economy and thus inflation, and at such times there is a "flight to quality," Treasuries are in great demand, and the premium on low-quality over high-quality bonds increases.

Changes in Ratings

Changes in a firm's bond rating affect both its ability to borrow long-term capital and the cost of that capital. Rating agencies review outstanding bonds on a periodic basis, occasionally upgrading or downgrading a bond as a result of its issuer's changed circumstances. For example, in January 2004, Moody's Investors Services upgraded from Ba2 to Ba1 the rating on XTO Energy's unsecured senior debt due in 2012 and 2013. The upgrade was based on a positive outlook for the company that resulted because the firm had a solid capital base and it had recently purchased reserves in Texas and Louisiana that efficiently replaced the company's depleting reserves. At the same time, Moody's was considering downgrading the ratings assigned to TECO Energy debt because of concerns about the company's existing financial difficulties and future problems that might result from write-offs associated with inefficient power plants.

Self-Test Questions

Name the two major rating agencies and some factors that affect bond ratings.

Why are bond ratings important both to firms and to investors?

Rationale for Using Different Types of Securities

Why are there so many different types of long-term securities? At least a partial answer to this question might be seen in Figure 17–3, which depicts the now familiar risk/return trade-off function drawn to show the risk and the expected after-personal-tax returns for the various securities of Allied Air Products.[7] First, U.S. Treasury bills, which represent the risk-free rate, are shown for reference. The lowest-risk long-term securities offered by Allied are its floating rate notes; these securities are free of interest rate risk, but they are exposed to some risk of default. The first mortgage bonds are somewhat riskier than the notes (because the bonds are exposed to interest rate risk), and they sell at a somewhat higher required and expected after-tax return. The second mortgage bonds are even riskier, so they have a still higher expected return. Subordinated debentures, income bonds, and preferred stocks are all increasingly risky, and their expected returns increase accordingly.

Why does Allied issue so many different classes of securities? Why not offer just one type of bond, plus common stock? The answer lies in the fact that different investors have different risk/return trade-off preferences, so to appeal to the broadest possible market, Allied must offer securities that attract as many different types of investors as possible. Also, different securities are more popular at different points in time, and firms tend to issue whatever is popular at the time they need money. Used

---

[7]The yields in Figure 17–3 are shown on an after-tax basis to the recipient. If yields were on a before-tax basis, those on preferred stocks would lie below those on bonds because of the tax treatment of preferreds. In essence, 70 percent of preferred dividends are tax exempt to corporations owning preferred shares, so a preferred stock with a 10 percent pre-tax yield will have a higher after-tax return to a corporation in the 34 percent tax bracket than will a bond with a 12 percent yield.

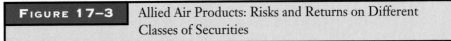

| **FIGURE 17-3** | Allied Air Products: Risks and Returns on Different Classes of Securities |

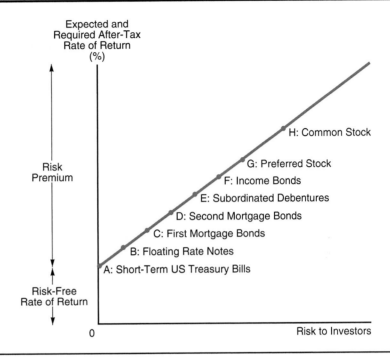

wisely, a policy of selling differentiated securities to take advantage of market conditions can lower a firm's overall cost of capital below what it would be if the firm used only one class of debt.

Self-Test Questions

List the different types of securities in order of highest to lowest risk.

Why do corporations issue so many different classes of securities?

Factors Influencing Long-Term Financing Decisions

As we show in this section, many factors influence a firm's long-term financing decisions. Each factor's relative importance varies among firms at any point in time and for any given firm over time, but any company planning to raise new long-term capital should consider each of these points.

Target Capital Structure

As we discussed in Chapter 9, firms typically establish target capital structures, and one of the most important considerations in any financing decision is how the firm's actual capital structure compares to its target structure. However, few firms finance each year exactly in accordance with their target capital structures, primarily because exact adherence would increase their flotation costs. Because smaller issues of new securities have proportionally larger flotation costs, firms tend to use debt one year and stock the next.

Making fewer but larger security offerings would cause a firm's capital structure to fluctuate above and below its optimal level rather than stay right on target. However, as we discussed in Chapter 9, small fluctuations around the optimal capital structure have little effect either on a firm's cost of debt and equity or on its overall cost of capital. Also, investors would recognize that its actions were prudent and that the firm would save substantial amounts of flotation costs by financing in this manner. Therefore, even though firms do tend to finance over the long haul in accordance with their target capital structures, flotation costs have a definite influence on the specific financing decisions in any given year.

Maturity Matching

Assume that Unilate Textiles decides to float a single $13.5 million nonconvertible bond issue with a sinking fund. It must next choose a maturity for the issue, taking into consideration the shape of the yield curve, management's own expectations about future interest rates, and the maturity of the assets being financed. In the case at hand, Unilate's capital projects during the next two years consist primarily of new, automated manufacturing equipment. This equipment has an expected economic life of 10 years (even though it falls into the MACRS 5-year class life). Should Unilate finance the debt portion of the capital raised for this equipment with one-year, 10-year, 20-year, or 30-year debt, or with debt of some other maturity? *One approach is to match the maturity of the liabilities with the maturity of the assets being financed.*

Note that some of the new capital for the machinery will come from common stock, which generally is considered to be a perpetual security with an infinite maturity. Of course, common stock can always be repurchased on the open market or by other means, so its effective maturity can be reduced significantly, but generally it has no maturity.

Debt maturities, however, are specified at the time of issue. If Unilate financed its capital budgets over the next two years with 10-year sinking fund bonds, it would be matching its asset and liability maturities. The cash flows resulting from the new machinery should be sufficient to make the interest and sinking fund payments on the issue, and the bonds would be retired as the machinery wore out. If Unilate used one-year debt, it would have to pay off the loan with cash flows derived from assets other than the machinery in question. If its operations were stable, the company probably could roll over the one-year debt, but if interest rates rose, then it would have to pay a higher rate. If Unilate subsequently experienced difficulties, its lenders might be hesitant to extend the loan, and the company might be unable to obtain new short-term debt at any reasonable rate. At the other extreme, if it used 20-year or 30-year debt, Unilate would still have to service the debt long after the assets purchased with the debt had been scrapped and had ceased providing cash flows, and this would worry potential lenders.

For all these reasons, one commonly used financing strategy is to match debt maturities with asset maturities. In recognition of this fact, firms do consider maturity relationships, and this factor has a major influence on the type of debt securities used.

Interest Rate Levels

Financial managers also consider interest rate levels, both absolute and relative, when making financing decisions. For example, long-term interest rates were high by historic standards in 1981 and 1982, so many managers were reluctant to issue long-term debt and thus lock in those high costs for long periods. We already know that one solution to this problem is to use long-term debt with a call provision. Callability permits the company to refund the issue should interest rates drop, as they did in 1993 and again in 2001 and 2002. But there is a cost, because firms must pay more if they make their debt callable. Alternatively, a firm might finance with short-term debt whenever long-term rates are historically high, and then, assuming that interest rates subsequently fall, sell a long-term issue to replace the short-term debt. Of course, this strategy has its risks. If interest rates climb even higher, the firm will be forced to renew the short-term debt at higher and higher rates, or to replace the short-term debt with a long-term bond that costs more than it would have cost earlier.

Forecasted Interest Rates

At a time when the interest rate on AAA corporate bonds was over 12 percent, which was high by historical standards, Exxon's (now Exxon Mobil) investment bankers advised the company to tap the Eurodollar bond market for relatively cheap fixed rate financing.[8] At the time, Exxon could have issued its bonds in London at 0.4 percentage points *below* comparable-maturity Treasury bonds. However, one Exxon officer was quoted as cautioning, "I say so what. The absolute level of rates is too high. We would rather wait." The managers of Exxon, as well as those of many other companies, were betting that the next move in interest rates would be down.

This example illustrates that firms do base their financing decisions on expectations about future interest rates. In Exxon's case, the financial staff turned out to be correct. However, the success of such a strategy requires interest rate forecasts to be correct more often than they are wrong, and it is difficult to find someone with a long-term forecasting record better than 50–50.

The Firm's Current and Forecasted Conditions

If a firm's current financial condition is poor, its managers might be reluctant to issue new long-term debt because (1) a new bond issue probably would trigger a review by the rating agencies and (2) long-term debt issued when a firm is in poor financial condition costs more and is subject to more severe restrictive covenants than debt issued from a strong position. Thus, a firm that is in a weakened condition but that is forecasting an improvement would be inclined to delay permanent financing until things improved. Conversely, a firm that is strong now but whose forecasts indicate a potentially bad time just ahead would be motivated to finance long term now rather than to wait. These scenarios imply that the capital markets are inefficient in the sense that investors do not have as much information about the firm's future as does its management. This situation undoubtedly is true at times.

---

[8]A *Eurodollar bond* is a bond sold outside of the United States but denominated in U.S. dollars. We discuss foreign debt later in this chapter.

The firm's earnings outlook, and the extent to which forecasted higher earnings per share are reflected in stock prices, also has an effect on the choice of securities. If a successful research and development program has just been concluded, and, consequently, management forecasts higher earnings than do most investors, the firm would not want to issue common stock. It would use debt, and then, after earnings had risen and pushed up the stock price, it would sell common stock to restore the capital structure to its target level.

Restrictions in Existing Debt Contracts

Earlier we discussed the fact that Bartow Electric has at times been restricted from issuing new first mortgage bonds by its indenture coverage requirements. This is just one example of how indenture covenants can influence a firm's financing decisions. Restrictions on the current ratio, the debt ratio, and so on, can also restrict a firm's ability to use different types of financing at a given time.

Availability of Collateral

Generally, for a particular firm, secured long-term debt will be less costly than unsecured debt. Thus, firms with large amounts of general-purpose (as opposed to specialized) fixed assets are likely to use a relatively large amount of debt, especially mortgage bonds. Additionally, each year's financing decision will be influenced by the amount of newly acquired assets that are available as security for new bonds.

Self-Test Questions

Do most firms finance each year exactly in accordance with their target capital structures? Why or why not?

Why is the matching of debt maturities with asset maturities a commonly used financing strategy?

If a firm's current financial condition is expected to improve shortly, why might its managers be reluctant to issue new long-term debt?

Which type of firm is more likely to use a relatively large amount of debt, a firm with general-purpose fixed assets or one with specialized fixed assets? Explain.

Bankruptcy and Reorganization

During recessions bankruptcies normally rise, and the recessions of 1991–1992 and 2001 were no exceptions. The 1991–1992 casualties included Pan Am, Continental Airlines, and R. H. Macy & Company; the 2001 casualties included Kmart, UAL, and Pacific Gas and Electric. Because of its importance, at least a brief discussion of bankruptcy is warranted within the chapter.

When a business becomes *insolvent*, it does not have enough cash to meet scheduled interest and principal payments—that is, the firm cannot service its debt. A decision must then be made whether to dissolve the firm through *liquidation* or to permit it to *reorganize* and thus stay alive. These issues are addressed in Chapters 7 and 11 of the federal bankruptcy statutes, and the final decision is made by a federal bankruptcy court judge.

The decision to force a firm to liquidate or to permit it to reorganize depends on whether the value of the reorganized firm is likely to be greater than the value of the firm's assets if they were sold off piecemeal. In a reorganization (Chapter 11 bankruptcy), a committee of unsecured creditors is appointed by the court to negotiate with management on the terms of a potential reorganization. The reorganization plan might call for a *restructuring* of the firm's debt, in which case the interest rate might be reduced, the term to maturity lengthened, or some of the debt might be exchanged for equity. The point of the restructuring is to reduce the financial charges to a level that the firm's cash flows can support. Of course, the common stockholders also have to give up something—they normally see their position eroded as a result of additional shares being given to debtholders in exchange for accepting a reduced amount of debt principal and interest. A trustee might be appointed by the court to oversee the reorganization, or the existing management might be allowed to retain control.

Liquidation occurs if the company is deemed to be too far gone to be saved—if it is worth more dead than alive. If the bankruptcy court orders a liquidation, assets are distributed as specified in Chapter 7 of the Bankruptcy Act. As a rule, proceeds are distributed to secured creditors first, then wages and taxes are paid; the remaining proceeds are distributed in order to unsecured creditors, to preferred stockholders, and finally to common stockholders, if anything is left. The priority of claims established by federal bankruptcy statutes *must* be followed when distributing the proceeds from a liquidated firm.

Self-Test Questions

When a business becomes insolvent, what two alternatives are available?

Differentiate between a liquidation and a reorganization.

In the case of liquidation, who gets paid first and who gets paid last?

Refunding Operations

A great deal of long-term debt was issued at high interest rates during the late 1970s and early 1980s. Since then, interest rates have fallen, and the call protection periods of many bonds have expired. As a result, corporations and government units have retired old bonds and have replaced them with lower-interest rate new bonds. In fact, most long-term debt that exists today was issued in 2003 when interest rates were at historically low levels—many older debt issues were refinanced (refunded) at that time.

Bond refunding analysis is similar to capital budgeting analysis, as discussed in Chapters 6 and 7. Also, bond refunding can be compared to the process individuals go through to refinance a house: An existing debt (mortgage) with a high interest rate is replaced by a new debt (mortgage) with a lower interest rate.

The refunding decision actually involves two separate questions: (1) Would it be profitable to call an outstanding issue now and to replace it with a new issue? (2) Even if refunding currently is profitable, would it be better to call now or to postpone the refunding to a later date?

As we noted, refunding decisions are similar to capital budgeting decisions, and the net present value method is the primary tool. In essence, the costs of undertaking the refunding operation (the investment outlay) are compared to the present value of the interest that will be saved if the high-interest rate bond is called and replaced with a new, low-interest rate bond. If the net present value of refunding is positive, then the refunding should take place. The costs of the refunding operation consist primarily of the call premium on the old bond issue and the flotation costs associated with selling the new issue. The cash flow benefits consist primarily of the interest expenses that will be saved if the company replaces high-cost debt with low-cost debt. The discount rate used to find the present value of the interest savings is the after-tax cost of new debt: The interest saved is the difference between two relatively certain cash flow streams, so the difference essentially is riskless. Therefore, a low discount rate should be used, and that rate is today's after-tax cost of new debt in the market.

To illustrate the refunding decision, consider the Strasburg Communications Corporation, which has a $100 million, 13 percent, semiannual coupon bond outstanding with 10 years remaining to maturity. The bond has a call provision that permits the company to retire the issue by calling in the bonds at an 8 percent call premium. Investment bankers have assured Strasburg that it could issue an additional $100 million of new 10 percent coupon, 10-year bonds that pay interest semiannually. Flotation costs on the new refunding issue will amount to $4 million. Predictions are that long-term interest rates are unlikely to fall below 10 percent. Strasburg's marginal tax rate is 40 percent. Should the company refund the $100 million of 13 percent semiannual coupon bonds?

Strasburg's refunding analysis is presented in Table 17–2. Because the marginal tax rate is 40 percent, the company's after-tax cost of new debt is equal to 6 percent, or 3 percent per six-month period. And because the bonds have semiannual coupons, there will be 20 semiannual periods in the analysis.

The net present value of refunding is positive, so Strasburg should refund the old bond issue—the firm's value will be increased by $1,389,727 if the old bond is retired.

Self-Test Questions

How is bond refunding analysis similar to capital budgeting analysis?

What two questions are involved in the bond refunding decision?

What are the primary costs and the primary benefits in a bond refunding analysis?

Why is the after-tax cost of debt used as the discount rate in a bond refunding analysis?

Foreign Debt Instruments

Like the U.S. debt markets, the international debt markets offer a variety of instruments with many different features. In this section, we discuss a few of the more familiar types of debt that are traded internationally.

Any debt sold outside the country of the borrower is called an international debt. However, there are two important types of international debt: foreign debt and Eurodebt. **Foreign debt** is debt sold by a foreign borrower but denominated in the currency of the country in which the issue is sold. For instance, Bell Canada might need U.S. dollars to finance the operations of its subsidiaries in the United States. If it decides to raise the needed capital in the domestic U.S. bond market, the bond will be underwritten by a syndicate of U.S. investment bankers, denominated in U.S. dollars, and sold to U.S. investors in accordance with SEC and applicable state regulations. Except for the foreign origin of the borrower (Canada), this bond will be indistinguishable from those issued by equivalent U.S. corporations. Because Bell Canada

FOREIGN DEBT
A debt instrument sold by a foreign borrower but denominated in the currency of the country in which it is sold.

TABLE 17-2	NPV Refunding Analysis

Cost of Refunding at t = 0

Call premium on old bond (0.08 × $100 million)	$(8,000,000)
Flotation costs on new issue	(4,000,000)
Total initial outlay	$(12,000,000)

Semiannual Interest Savings Due to Refunding: t = 1 to 20
(10 years of payments twice a year)

Interest on old bond (0.065 × $100 million)	$ 6,500,000
Interest on new bond (0.050 × $100 million)	(5,000,000)
Interest savings per period	$ 1,500,000
Increased taxes due to lower interest payment[a] (0.40 × $1,500,000)	$(600,000)
Net interest savings	$ 900,000

Refunding Cash Flow Time Line

Interest period	0		1	2		1 10 Year 20 Interest payments
		$k = 3\%$				
Initial outlay	(12,000,000)					
Interest savings	0		900,000	900,000	. . .	900,000
Net cash flow	(12,000,000)		900,000	900,000	. . .	900,000

NPV of refunding at $k_{dT}/2 = 3\%$ is $1,389,727

---

[a]Strasburg's interest expense will decrease by $1,500,000, thus taxable income will increase by $1,500,000, if the new bond is issued. Strasburg will have to pay 0.40 × $1,500,000 = $600,000 additional taxes on this increased taxable income.

is a foreign corporation, however, the bond will be called a *foreign bond*. Foreign bonds generally are labeled according to the country in which they are issued. For example, if foreign bonds are issued in the United States they are called *Yankee bonds*, if they are issued in Japan they are called *Samurai bonds*, and if they are issued in England they are called *Bulldog bonds*.

EURODEBT

Debt sold in a country other than the one in whose currency the debt is denominated.

The term **Eurodebt** is used to designate any debt sold in a country other than the one in whose currency the debt is denominated. Examples include *Eurobonds*, such as a British firm's issue of pound bonds sold in France or a Ford Motor Company issue denominated in dollars and sold in Germany. The institutional arrangements by which Eurobonds are marketed are different than those for most other bond issues, with the most important distinction being a far lower level of required disclosure than normally is found for bonds issued in domestic markets, particularly in the United States. Governments tend to be less strict when regulating securities denominated in foreign currencies than they are on home-currency securities because the bonds' purchasers generally are more "sophisticated." The lower disclosure requirements result in lower total transaction costs for Eurobonds.

Eurobonds appeal to investors for several reasons. Generally, they are issued in bearer form rather than as registered bonds, so the names and nationalities of investors are not recorded. Individuals who desire anonymity, whether for privacy reasons or for tax avoidance, find Eurobonds to their liking. Similarly, most governments do not withhold taxes on interest payments associated with Eurobonds.

Most Eurobonds are denominated in dollars; Japanese yen, German marks, and the Euro (called Euro-denominated, Eurobonds, or EEBs). Although centered in Europe, Eurobonds truly are international. Their underwriting syndicates include investment bankers from all parts of the world, and the bonds are sold to investors not only in Europe but also in such faraway places as Bahrain and Singapore. Until recently, Eurobonds were issued solely by multinational firms, by international financial institutions, or by national governments. Today, however, the Eurobond market also is being tapped by purely domestic U.S. firms such as electric utilities, which find that by borrowing overseas they can lower their debt costs.

Some other types of Eurodebt include the following:

LIBOR

The London Interbank Offer Rate, which represents the interest rate offered by the best London banks on deposits of other large, very creditworthy banks.

1. **Eurocredits.** Eurocredits are bank loans that are denominated in the currency of a country other than where the lending bank is located. Many of these loans are large, so the lending bank often forms a loan syndicate to help raise the needed funds and to spread out some of the risks associated with the loan.

   Interest rates on Eurocredits, as well as other short-term Eurodebt, typically are tied to a standard rate known by the acronym **LIBOR**, which stands for *London InterBank Offer Rate.* LIBOR is the rate of interest offered by the largest and strongest London banks on deposits of other large banks of the highest credit standing. In January 2004, because interest rates were low universally, LIBOR rates were only about 0.06 percentage point above domestic U.S. bank rates on time deposits of the same maturity—1.09 percent for three-month CDs versus 1.15 percent for three-month LIBOR CDs.

2. **Euro-commercial paper (Euro-CP).** Euro-CP is similar to commercial paper issued in the United States. It is a short-term debt instrument issued by corporations, and it has typical maturities of one, three, and six months. The principal difference between Euro-CP and U.S. commercial paper is that there is not as much concern about the credit quality of Euro-CP issuers.

3. **Euronotes.** Euronotes, which represent medium-term debt, typically have maturities from one year to 10 years. The general features of Euronotes are much like those of longer-term debt instruments like bonds. The principal amount is repaid at maturity and interest often is paid semiannually. Most foreign companies use Euronotes as they would a line of credit, continuously issuing notes to finance medium-term needs.

Self-Test Questions

Differentiate between foreign debt and Eurodebt.

Why do Eurobonds appeal to investors?

What are Eurocredits, Euro-commercial paper, and Euronotes?

Summary

This chapter described the characteristics, advantages, and disadvantages of the major types of long-term debt securities. The key concepts covered are listed here:

- **Term loans** and **bonds** are long-term debt contracts under which a borrower agrees to make a series of interest and principal payments on specific dates to the lender. A term loan is generally sold to one lender (or a few), whereas a bond typically is offered to the public and sold to many different investors.
- There are many different types of bonds. They include **mortgage bonds, debentures, convertibles, bonds with warrants, income bonds, putable bonds,** and **purchasing power (indexed) bonds.** The return required on each type of bond is determined by the bond's riskiness.
- A bond's **indenture** is a legal document that spells out the rights of the bondholders and of the issuing corporation. A **trustee** is assigned to make sure that the terms of the indenture are carried out.
- A **call provision** gives the issuing corporation the right to redeem the bonds prior to maturity under specified terms, usually at a price greater than the maturity value (the difference is a **call premium**). A firm typically will call a bond and refund it if interest rates fall substantially.
- A **sinking fund** is a provision that requires the corporation to retire a portion of the bond issue each year. The purpose of the sinking fund is to provide for the orderly retirement of the issue.
- Some innovations in long-term financing that have occurred in the past few decades include **zero coupon bonds,** which pay no annual interest but are issued at a discount; **floating rate debt,** whose interest payments fluctuate with changes in the general level of interest rates; and **junk bonds,** which are high-risk, high-yield instruments issued by firms that use a great deal of financial leverage.
- Bonds are assigned **ratings** that reflect the probability of their going into default. The higher a bond's rating, the less risky it is considered, so the lower its interest rate.
- A firm's long-term financing decisions are influenced by its **target capital structure,** the **maturity of its assets,** current and forecasted **interest rate levels,** the firm's current and forecasted **financial condition, restrictions** in its existing debt contracts, and the suitability of its assets for use as collateral.
- **Bankruptcy** is an important consideration both to companies that issue debt and to investors, for it has a profound effect on all parties. **Refunding,** or paying off high-interest rate debt with new, lower-cost debt, also is an important consideration, because many firms that issued long-term debt in the early 1980s at rates of 12 percent or more now have an opportunity to refund this debt at a cost of about 6 percent or less.
- The **Eurodebt** market includes any debt sold in a country other than the one in whose currency the debt is denominated. Examples of Eurodebt are **Eurobonds, Eurocredits, Euro-commercial paper,** and **Euronotes.**

Questions

17–1 What effect would each of the following items have on the interest rate a firm must pay on a new issue of long-term debt? Indicate whether each factor would tend to raise, lower, or have an indeterminate effect on the interest rate, and then explain why.

    a. The firm uses bonds rather than a term loan.

    b. The firm uses debentures rather than first mortgage bonds.

    c. The firm makes its bonds convertible into common stock.

    d. If the firm makes its debentures subordinate to its bank debt, what will the effect be on the
       (1) cost of the debentures?
       (2) cost of the bank debt?
       (3) average cost of total debt?
    e. The firm sells income bonds rather than debentures.
    f. The firm must raise $100 million, all of which will be used to construct a new plant, and it is debating the sale of first mortgage bonds or debentures. If it decides to issue $50 million of each type, as opposed to $75 million of first mortgage bonds and $25 million of debentures, how will this affect
       (1) The cost of debentures?
       (2) The cost of mortgage bonds?
       (3) The weighted average cost of the $100 million?
    g. The firm puts a call provision on its new issue of bonds.
    h. The firm includes a sinking fund on its new issue of bonds.
    i. The firm's bonds are downgraded from A to BBB.

17–2 Rank the following securities from lowest (1) to highest (9) in terms of their riskiness for an investor. All securities (except the Treasury bond) are for a given firm. If you think two or more securities are equally risky, indicate so.
    a. Income bond
    b. Subordinated debentures–noncallable   _____
    c. First mortgage bond–no sinking fund   _____
    d. Common stock   _____
    e. U.S. Treasury bond   _____
    f. First mortgage bond–with sinking fund   _____
    g. Subordinated debentures–callable   _____
    h. Term loan   _____

17–3 A sinking fund can be set up in one of two ways:
    (1) The corporation makes annual payments to the trustee, who invests the proceeds in securities (frequently government bonds) and uses the accumulated total to retire the bond issue at maturity.
    (2) The trustee uses the annual payments to retire a portion of the issue each year, either calling a given percentage of the issue by a lottery and paying a specified price per bond or buying bonds on the open market, whichever is cheaper.
    Discuss the advantages and disadvantages of each procedure from the viewpoint of both the firm and its bondholders.

17–4 Draw a Security Market Line (SML) graph. Put a dot on the graph to show (approximately) where you think a particular company's bonds would lie. Now put on a dot to represent a riskier company's bonds.

Self-Test Problems

(Solutions appear in Appendix B)

key terms   **ST-1** Define each of the following terms:
    a. Funded debt
    b. Term loan; bond
    c. Mortgage bond
    d. Debenture; subordinated debenture

e. Convertible bond; warrant; income bond; putable bond; indexed, or purchasing power, bond

f. Indenture; restrictive covenant

g. Trustee

h. Call provision; sinking fund

i. Zero coupon bond; original issue discount bond (OID)

j. Floating rate bond

k. Junk bond

l. Investment grade bonds

m. Foreign debt; Eurodebt

sinking fund   **ST-2** The Vancouver Development Company has just sold a $100 million, 10-year, 12 percent bond issue. A sinking fund will retire the issue over its life. Sinking fund payments are of equal amounts and will be made *semiannually*, and the proceeds will be used to retire bonds as the payments are made. Bonds can be called at par for sinking fund purposes, or the funds paid into the sinking fund can be used to buy bonds in the open market.

a. How large must each semiannual sinking fund payment be?

b. What will happen, under the conditions of the problem thus far, to the company's debt service requirements per year for this issue over time?

c. Now suppose Vancouver Development sets up its sinking fund so that equal annual amounts, payable at the end of each year, are paid into a sinking fund trust held by a bank, with the proceeds being used to buy government bonds that pay 9 percent interest. The payments, plus accumulated interest, must total $100 million at the end of 10 years, and the proceeds will be used to retire the bonds at that time. How large must the annual sinking fund payment be now?

d. What are the annual cash requirements for covering bond service costs under the trusteeship arrangement described in part c? (*Note:* Interest must be paid on Vancouver's outstanding bonds but not on bonds that have been retired.)

e. What would have to happen to interest rates to cause the company to buy bonds on the open market rather than call them under the original sinking fund plan?

Problems

perpetual bond analysis   **17–1** In 1936 the Canadian government raised $55 million by issuing bonds at a 3 percent annual rate of interest. Unlike most bonds issued today, which have a specific maturity date, these bonds can remain outstanding forever; they are, in fact, perpetuities.

At the time of issue, the Canadian government stated in the bond indenture that cash redemption was possible at face value ($100) on or after September 1966; in other words, the bonds were callable at par after September 1966. Believing that the bonds would, in fact, be called, many investors purchased these bonds in 1965 with expectations of receiving $100 in 1966 for each perpetual bond they had. In 1965 the bonds sold for $55, but a rush of buyers drove the price to just below the $100 par value by 1966. Prices fell dramatically, however, when the Canadian government announced that these perpetual bonds were indeed perpetual and would not be paid off.

The bonds' market price declined to $42 in December 1966. Because of their severe losses, hundreds of Canadian bondholders formed the Perpetual Bond Association to lobby for face value redemption of the bonds, claiming that the government had reneged on an implied promise to redeem the bonds. Government officials in Ottawa insisted that claims for face value payment were nonsense because the bonds were and always had been clearly identified as perpetuals. One Ottawa official stated, "Our job is to protect the taxpayer. Why should we pay $55 million for less than $25 million worth of bonds?"

Here are some questions relating to the Canadian issue that will test your understanding of bonds in general:

a. Would it make sense for a business firm to issue bonds like the Canadian government bonds described here? Would it matter whether the firm was a proprietorship or a corporation?

b. Suppose the U.S. government today sold $100 million each of these four types of bonds: five-year bonds, 50-year bonds, "regular" perpetuities, and Canadian-type perpetuities. Rank the bonds from the one with the lowest to the one with the highest expected interest rate. Explain your answer.

c. (1) Suppose that because of pressure by the Perpetual Bond Association, you believe that the Canadian government will redeem this particular perpetual bond issue in four years. Which course of action would be more advantageous to you if you owned the bonds: (i) sell your bonds today at $55.99 or (ii) wait four years and have them redeemed? Assume that similar-risk bonds earn 9 percent today and that interest rates are expected to remain at this level for the next four years.

  (2) If you had the opportunity to invest your money in bonds of similar risk, at what rate of return would you be indifferent to the choice of selling your perpetuals today or having them redeemed in four years—that is, what is the expected yield to maturity on the Canadian bonds?

d. Show mathematically the perpetuities' value if they yield 6.1 percent, pay $3 interest annually, and are considered *regular* perpetuities. Show what would happen to the price of the bonds if the going interest rate fell to 2 percent.

e. Are the Canadian bonds more likely to be valued as *regular* perpetuities if the going rate of interest is above or below 3 percent? Why?

f. Do you think the Canadian government would have taken the same action with regard to retiring the bonds if the interest rate had fallen rather than risen after they were issued?

g. Do you think the Canadian government was fair or unfair in its actions? Give the pros and cons and justify your reason for thinking that one out-weighs the other. Would it matter if the bonds had been sold to "sophisti-cated" as opposed to "naive" investors ?

zero coupon bond **17–2** Filkins Farm Equipment needs to raise $4.5 million for expansion, and its invest-ment bankers have indicated that five-year zero coupon bonds could be sold at a price of $567.44 for each $1,000 bond. Filkins's marginal tax rate is 40 percent.

a. How many $1,000 par value zero coupon bonds would Filkins have to sell to raise the needed $4.5 million?

b. What would be the after-tax yield on the zeros (1) to an investor who is tax exempt and (2) to a taxpayer in the 28 percent marginal tax bracket?

c. What would be the after-tax cost of debt to Filkins if it decides to issue the zeros?

Exam-Type Problems

The problems included in this section are set up in such a way that they could be used as multiple-choice exam problems.

loan payment computation

17-3 Suppose a firm is setting up a term loan. What are the annual payments for a $10 million loan under the following terms:
  a. 8 percent, five years?
  b. 8 percent, 10 years?
  c. 14 percent, five years?
  d. 14 percent, 10 years?

yield to call

17-4 Six years ago The Parrish Company sold a 19-year bond issue with a 14 percent annual coupon rate and a 9 percent call premium. Today Parrish called the bonds. The bonds originally were sold at their face value of $1,000. Compute the realized rate of return for investors who purchased the bonds when they were issued and who surrender them today in exchange for the call price.

EAR on zero coupon bonds

17-5 Assume that the city of Tampa sold an issue of $1,000 maturity value, tax-exempt (muni), zero coupon bonds five years ago. The bonds had a 25-year maturity when they were issued and the interest rate built into the issue was a nominal 10 percent, but with semiannual compounding. The bonds are now callable at a premium of 10 percent over the accrued value. What effective annual rate of return would an investor who bought the bonds when they were issued and who still owns them earn if they are called today?

NPV of refunding

17-6 The city of Gainesville issued $1,000,000 of 14 percent coupon, 30-year, semiannual payment, tax-exempt muni bonds 10 years ago. The bonds had 10 years of call protection, but now Gainesville can call the bonds if it chooses to do so. The call premium would be 10 percent of the face amount. New 19-year, 12 percent, semiannual payment bonds can be sold at par, but flotation costs on this issue would be 2 percent, or $20,000. What is the net present value of the refunding? (*Hint:* Approach this problem just like the capital budgeting problems in Chapters 6 and 7.)

Integrative Problem

long-term debt financing

17-7 Hospital Development Corporation (HDC) needs $10 million to build a regional testing laboratory in Birmingham. Once the lab is completed and fully operational, which should take about five years, HDC will sell it to a health maintenance organization (HMO). HDC tentatively plans to raise the $10 million by selling five-year bonds, and its investment bankers have indicated that either regular or zero coupon bonds can be used. Regular coupon bonds would sell at par and would have annual payment coupons of 12 percent, and zero coupon bonds would also be priced to yield 12 percent annually. Either bond would be callable after three years, on the anniversary date of the issue, at a premium of six months' interest for the regular bonds or 5 percent over the accrued value on the call date for zero coupon bonds. HDC's marginal tax rate is 40 percent. As assistant to HDC's treasurer, you have been assigned the task of making a recommendation as to which type of bonds to issue. As part of your analysis, you have been asked to answer the following questions:
  a. What is the difference between a bond and a term loan? What are the advantages of a term loan over a bond?

b. Suppose HDC issues bonds and uses the medical center (land and buildings) as collateral to secure the issue. What type of bond would this be? Suppose that instead of using secured bonds HDC had decided to sell debentures. How would this affect the interest rate that HDC would have to pay on the $10 million of debt?

c. What is a bond indenture? What are some typical provisions the bondholders would require HDC to include in its indenture?

d. HDC's bonds will be callable after three years. If the bonds were not callable, would the required interest rate be higher or lower than 12 percent? What would be the effect on the rate if the bonds were callable immediately? What are the advantages to HDC of making the bonds callable?

e. (1) Suppose HDC's indenture included a sinking fund provision that required the company to retire one-fifth of the bonds each year. Would this provision raise or lower the interest rate required on the bonds?

    (2) How would the sinking fund operate?

    (3) Why might HDC's investors require it to use a sinking fund?

    (4) For this particular issue, would it make sense to include a sinking fund?

f. If HDC were to issue zero coupon bonds, what initial price would cause the zeros to have an annual return (EAR) of 12 percent? How many $1,000 par value zeros would HDC have to sell to raise the needed $10 million? How many regular 12 percent coupon bonds would HDC have to sell?

g. Set up a cash flow time line that shows the accrued value of the zeros at the end of Years 1 through 5, along with the annual after-tax cash flows from the zeros (1) to an investor in the 28 percent tax bracket and (2) to HDC. (*Hint:* The investor has to pay taxes on the annual accrued value increase of the bonds.)

h. What would be the after-tax yield to maturity on each type of bond to an investor in the 28 percent tax bracket? What would be the after-tax cost of debt to HDC?

i. If interest rates were to fall, causing HDC to call the bonds (either the zero or the coupon) at the end of Year 3, what would be the after-tax yield to call on each type of bond to an investor in the 28 percent tax bracket?

j. HDC is an A-rated firm. Suppose HDC's bond rating was (1) lowered to triple-B or (2) raised to double-A. Who would make these changes, and what would the changes mean? What would be the effect of these changes on the interest rate required on HDC's new long-term debt and on the market value of HDC's outstanding debt?

k. What are some of the factors a firm like HDC should consider when deciding whether to issue long-term debt, short-term debt, or equity? Why might long-term debt be HDC's best choice for this project?

l. What is meant by the terms *default, insolvent, liquidation, reorganization, bankruptcy, Chapter 11,* and *Chapter 7?*

m. In what sense is a bond refunding decision similar to a capital budgeting decision?

GET REAL with Thomson ONE

17–8 Companies in the U.S. rely on long-term debt as one way to finance their operations. Since the early 1990s the use of long-term debt has grown. Delta Air Lines, Inc. [DAL], an air transportation company, General Electric Company [GE], a large conglomerate, and Intel Corporation [INTC], a computer, networking, and communication firm, are three large U.S. firms in different industry sectors. Answer the following questions about these firms:

a. Analyze the financial statements of each firm and calculate both the debt-to-assets ratio and the debt-to-equity ratio for each of the last five years. [*Hint:* Click on Financials for each firm]

b. How have the long-term debt positions of the firms changed during the past five years?

c. With regard to long-term debt, how does each firm compare to peers in its respective industry sector? [*Hint:* Click on Peers/Click to Change Peer Set/Industry Group]

d. Which industry seems to have the highest relative amount of long-term debt? Which has the lowest relative amount of long-term debt?

e. Discuss why you think there exist differences in the long-term debt position of the three firms and their industries.

CHAPTER 18

Alternative Financing Arrangements and Corporate Restructuring

The growth of convertible securities, which are debt or preferred stock issues that can be exchanged for companies' common stocks, has been extraordinary recently. For example, during the past decade, the amount of convertibles in the financial markets has grown more than 200 percent. In addition, the number of issuers and the average size of each issue has grown at a similar pace.

Many firms use convertibles because they feel that funds can be raised more cheaply than with "straight" debt or preferred stock. For example, in 1989 MCI Corporation (now MCI WorldCom) issued $1.3 billion of convertible bonds at rates that were significantly lower than nonconvertible debt. The price of MCI's stock never reached the point where it was attractive for investors to convert, so the bonds were called by the company in 1993 after market interest rates had dropped to historically low levels. In 1999 Amazon.com issued $1.25 billion in convertible notes that had a 4.75 percent coupon rate, which was below the rate on many Treasury notes. The debt, which matures in 2009, allowed investors to convert each $1,000 bond into 12.816 shares of common stock; thus, as long as the price of the stock was above $78.0275 per share (its *conversion price*), it would be worthwhile to convert the bonds into common stock. The convertible also included a call provision that allows Amazon.com to recall the bonds at a price of $1,080.75 for each $1,000 bond. Although bondholders would get 8.075 percent more than the face value of the bonds at call, they would lose the opportunity to convert their bonds into stock. By the end of April 1999, Amazon.com was selling for more than the conversion price; thus, analysts speculated that it wouldn't be long before the bonds were called by the company. A few months later, however, Amazon.com announced earnings that were lower (more negative) than expected; thus, the stock price dropped substantially. On the day of the announcement, the stock lost about 14.6 percent of its value, while the convertible notes lost 17.8 percent during the week. As we write this book, the value of Amazon.com's stock has dropped even further: At the beginning of 2004, the market value was approximately $55 per share which is well below the conversion price of the notes. Therefore, it seems unlikely that the company will call the bonds any time soon.

Convertibles are attractive to investors because they offer the opportunity to earn the substantial returns available with stocks, but they also offer the stability associated with debt or preferred stock. For the past decade, convertibles have generated a return equal to more than 11 percent compared to the 16 percent return provided by large stocks and the 7 percent to 12 percent return associated with small stocks.

As the financial markets strengthen, convertibles gain popularity; but when the financial markets weaken, selling pressure results and convertibles lose favor with investors. Like other financial assets, convertibles are risky—most experts would caution investors not to put large portions of their investments in convertible securities but to diversify instead. Once you have read this chapter and understand the concepts presented, you should be able to make informed decisions regarding convertibles, as well as preferred stock and other hybrid securities. ∎

In the two preceding chapters, we examined the use of common stock and various types of debt. In this chapter, we examine some other types of long-term financing arrangements used by financial managers. We give only fundamental descriptions of these alternative sources of financing to enlighten you about the variety of means by which a firm can raise funds. The fact is many variations and combinations of financial assets exist today, and it would take multiple volumes to describe them all. Firms often engage in "creative financing" when seeking different ways to attract investors, so you should not be surprised to see new forms of financing emerge on a continuous basis. In addition, because firms have become extremely "creative" when determining how to finance mergers and acquisitions, we briefly discuss mergers and merger activity at the end of the chapter.

The purpose of this chapter is to provide you with a basic understanding of (1) some financing techniques we have not discussed in previous chapters and (2) corporate restructuring through mergers and leveraged buyouts. If you want more in-depth discussions, you should look in either an upper-level corporate finance text or an investments text.

Preferred Stock

Preferred stock is a *hybrid* security—similar to bonds in some respects and to common stock in others. The hybrid nature of preferred stock becomes apparent when we try to classify it in relation to bonds and common stock. Like bonds, preferred stock has a par value. Preferred dividends also are similar to interest payments in that they generally are fixed in amount and must be paid before common stock dividends can be paid. However, if the preferred dividend is not earned, the directors can omit (or "pass") it without throwing the company into bankruptcy. So although preferred stock has a fixed payment like bonds, a failure to make this payment will not lead to bankruptcy.

Accountants classify preferred stock as equity and report it in the equity portion of the balance sheet under "preferred stock" or "preferred equity." However, financial analysts sometimes treat preferred stock as debt and sometimes as equity, depending on the type of analysis being made. If the analysis is being made by a common stockholder, the key consideration is the fact that the preferred dividend is a fixed charge that reduces the amount that can be distributed to common shareholders, so from the common stockholder's point of view preferred stock is similar to debt. Suppose, however, that the analysis is being made by a bondholder studying the firm's vulnerability to failure in the event of a decline in sales and income. If the firm's income declines, the debt holders have a prior claim to the available income ahead of preferred stockholders, and if the firm fails, debt holders have a prior claim to assets when the firm is liquidated. Thus, to a bondholder, preferred stock is similar to common equity.

From management's perspective, preferred stock lies between debt and common equity. Because failure to pay dividends on preferred stock will not force the firm into bankruptcy, preferred stock is safer to use than debt. At the same time, if the firm is highly successful, the common stockholders will not have to share that success with the preferred stockholders because preferred dividends are fixed. Remember, however, that the preferred stockholders do have a higher priority claim than the common stockholders. We see, then, that preferred stock has some of the characteristics of debt and some of the characteristics of common stock, and it is used in situations in which conditions are such that neither debt nor common stock is entirely appropriate.

Major Provisions of Preferred Stock Issues

Preferred stock has a number of features, the most important of which are discussed in the following sections. As you will see, some of the features we discuss here are also features included in debt instruments, which we discussed in the previous chapter.

Priority to Assets and Earnings   Preferred stockholders have priority over common stockholders with regard to earnings and assets. As a result, dividends must be paid on preferred stock before they can be paid on the common stock, and, in the event of bankruptcy, the claims of the preferred shareholders must be satisfied before the common stockholders receive anything. To reinforce these features, most preferred stocks have coverage requirements similar to those on bonds. These restrictions limit the amount of preferred stock a company can use, and they also require a minimum level of retained earnings before common dividends can be paid.

Par Value   Unlike common stock, preferred stock always has a par value (or its equivalent under some other name), and this value is important. First, the par value establishes the amount due the preferred stockholders in the event of liquidation. Second, the preferred dividend frequently is stated as a percentage of the par value. For example, an issue of Duke Power's preferred stock has a par value of $100 and a stated dividend of 7.8 percent of par. The same results would, of course, be produced if this issue of Duke's preferred stock simply called for an annual dividend of $7.80.

CUMULATIVE DIVIDENDS

A protective feature on preferred stock that requires preferred dividends previously not paid to be paid before any common dividends can be paid.

Cumulative Dividends   Most preferred stock provides for **cumulative dividends;** that is, any preferred dividends not paid in previous periods must be paid before common dividends can be paid. The cumulative feature is a protective device because if the preferred stock dividends were not cumulative, a firm could avoid paying preferred and common stock dividends for, say, 10 years, plowing back all its earnings, and then pay a huge common stock dividend but pay only the stipulated annual dividend to the preferred stockholders. Obviously, such an action effectively would void the preferred position the preferred stockholders are supposed to have. The cumulative feature helps prevent such abuses.[1]

---

[1]Note, however, that compounding is absent in most cumulative plans—in other words, the unpaid preferred dividends themselves earn no return. Also, many preferred issues have a limited cumulative feature; for example, unpaid preferred dividends might accumulate for only three years.

Convertibility   More than 40 percent of the preferred stock that has been issued in recent years is convertible into common stock. For example, on March 25, 1999, Global Maintech issued 1,600 shares of Series C convertible preferred that can be converted into a minimum of 400 shares of common stock at the option of the preferred shareholder.

Other Provisions   Some other provisions occasionally found in preferred stocks include the following:

1. **Voting rights.** Although preferred stock is not voting stock, preferred stockholders generally are given the right to vote for directors if the company has not paid the preferred dividend for a specified period, such as 10 quarters. This feature motivates management to make every effort to pay preferred dividends.
2. **Participating.** A rare type of preferred stock is one that participates with the common stock in sharing the firm's earnings. Participating preferred stocks generally work as follows: (a) the stated preferred dividend is paid—for example, $5 a share; (b) the common stock is then entitled to a dividend in an amount up to the preferred dividend; (c) if the common dividend is raised, say to $5.50, the preferred dividend must likewise be raised to $5.50.
3. **Sinking fund.** In the past (before the mid–1970s), few preferred issues had sinking funds. Today, however, most newly issued preferred stocks have sinking funds that call for the purchase and retirement of a given percentage of the preferred stock each year. If the amount is 2 percent, which frequently is used, the preferred issue will have an average life of 25 years and a maximum life of 50 years.
4. **Call provision.** A call provision gives the issuing corporation the right to call in the preferred stock for redemption. As in the case of bonds, call provisions generally state that the company must pay an amount greater than the par value of the preferred stock, the additional sum being termed a **call premium.** For example, Bangor Hydro-Electric Company has various issues of preferred stock outstanding, two of which are callable. The call prices on the two issues are $100 and $110. Before it was called in December 1997, Bangor had another callable preferred issue that included a sinking fund provision.
5. **Maturity.** Before the mid–1970s, most preferred stock was perpetual—it had no maturity and never needed to be paid off. Today, however, most new preferred stock has a sinking fund and thus an effective maturity date.

CALL PREMIUM
The amount in excess of par value that a company must pay when it calls a security.

Pros and Cons of Preferred Stock

As noted here, there are both advantages and disadvantages to financing with preferred stock.

Issuer's (Firm's) Viewpoint   By using preferred stock, a firm can fix its financial costs and thus keep more of the potential future profits for its existing set of common stockholders, yet still avoid the danger of bankruptcy if earnings are too low to meet these fixed charges. Also, by selling preferred stock rather than common stock, the firm avoids sharing control with new investors.

However, preferred stock does have a major disadvantage from the issuer's standpoint: It has a higher after-tax cost of capital than debt. The major reason for this higher cost is taxes: Preferred dividends are not deductible as a tax expense, whereas interest expense is deductible.[2] This makes the component cost of preferred stock much greater than that of bonds—the after-tax cost of debt is approximately two-thirds of the stated coupon rate for profitable firms, whereas the cost of preferred stock is the full percentage amount of the preferred dividend. Of course, the deductibility differential is most important for issuers that are in relatively high tax brackets. If a company pays little or no taxes because it is unprofitable or because it has a great deal of accelerated depreciation, the deductibility of interest does not make much difference. Thus, the lower a company's tax bracket, the more likely it is to issue preferred stock.

Preferred Stockholder's (Investor's) Viewpoint   In designing securities, the financial manager must consider the investor's point of view. It is sometimes asserted that preferred stock has so many disadvantages to both the issuer and the investor that it should never be issued. Nevertheless, preferred stock has been issued in substantial amounts. It provides investors with a steadier and more assured income than common stock, and it has a preference over common stock in the event of liquidation. In addition, 70 percent of the preferred dividends received by corporations are not taxable. For this reason, most preferred stock is owned by corporations.

   The principal disadvantage of preferred stock from an investor's standpoint is that although preferred stockholders bear some of the ownership risks, their returns are limited. Other disadvantages are that (1) preferred stockholders have no legally enforceable right to dividends, even if a company earns a profit and (2) *for individual as opposed to corporate investors*, after-tax bond yields generally are higher than those on preferred stock, even though the preferred is riskier.

Self-Test Questions

Explain the following statement: "Preferred stock is a hybrid."

Identify and briefly explain some of the key features of preferred stock.

What are the advantages and disadvantages of preferred stock from an issuer's viewpoint?

What are the advantages and disadvantages of preferred stock from an investor's viewpoint?

Leasing

Firms generally own fixed assets and report them on their balance sheets, but it is the *use* of buildings and equipment that is important, not their ownership per se. One way of obtaining the use of assets is to buy them, but an alternative is to lease them. Prior to the 1950s, leasing generally was associated with real estate—land and buildings. Today, however, it is possible to lease virtually any kind of fixed asset, and in

---

[2]One would think that a given firm's preferred stock would carry a higher coupon rate than its bonds because of the preferred's greater risk from the holder's viewpoint. However, 70 percent of preferred dividends received by corporate owners are exempt from income taxes, and this has made preferred stock attractive to corporate investors. Therefore, most preferred stock is owned by corporations, and in recent years high-grade preferreds, on average, have sold on a lower-yield basis, before taxes, than high-grade bonds. On an after-tax basis, however, the yield on preferred stock generally is greater than the yield on high-grade corporate bonds.

2004 more than 25 percent of all new capital equipment acquired by businesses was leased. In fact, it is estimated that 70 percent of firms listed in the *Fortune 1000* lease some equipment.

Types of Leases

Leasing takes three different forms: (1) sale-and-leaseback arrangements, (2) operating leases, and (3) straight financial, or capital, leases.

SALE AND LEASEBACK

Situation whereby a firm sells land, buildings, or equipment and simultaneously leases the property back for a specified period under specific terms.

LESSEE

The party that uses, rather than the one who owns, the leased property.

LESSOR

The owner of leased property.

OPERATING LEASE

A lease under which the lessor maintains and finances the property; also called a *service lease.*

FINANCIAL LEASE

A lease that does not provide for maintenance services, is not cancelable, and is fully amortized over its life; also called a *capital lease.*

Sale and Leaseback   Under a **sale and leaseback,** a firm that owns land, buildings, or equipment sells the property and simultaneously executes an agreement to lease the property back for a particular period under specific terms. The purchaser could be an insurance company, a commercial bank, a specialized leasing company, or even an individual investor. The sale-and-leaseback plan is an alternative to taking out a mortgage loan. The firm that sells the property, or the **lessee,** immediately receives the purchase price from the buyer, or the **lessor.**[3] At the same time, the seller-lessee firm retains the use of the property just as if it had borrowed and mortgaged the property to secure the loan. Note that under a mortgage loan arrangement, the financial institution normally would receive a series of equal payments just sufficient to amortize the loan while providing a specified rate of return to the lender on the outstanding balance. Under a sale-and-leaseback arrangement, the lease payments are set up in exactly the same way; the payments are set so the investor-lessor recoups the purchase price and earns a specified rate of return on the investment.

Operating Leases   Operating leases, sometimes called *service leases,* provide for both *financing* and *maintenance.* IBM is one of the pioneers of the operating lease contract, and computers and office copying machines, together with automobiles and trucks, are the primary types of equipment involved. Ordinarily, these leases call for the lessor to maintain and service the leased equipment, and the cost of providing maintenance is built into the lease payments.

Another important characteristic of operating leases is the fact that they frequently are *not fully amortized;* in other words, the payments required under the lease contract are not sufficient to recover the full cost of the equipment. However, the lease contract is written for a period considerably shorter than the expected economic life of the leased equipment, and the lessor expects to recover all investment costs through subsequent renewal payments, through subsequent leases to other companies (lessees), or by selling the leased equipment.

A final feature of operating leases is that they frequently contain a *cancellation clause,* which gives the lessee the right to cancel the lease before the expiration of the basic agreement. This is an important consideration for the lessee, because it means that the equipment can be returned if it is rendered obsolete by technological developments or if it no longer is needed because of a decline in the lessee's business.

Financial, or Capital, Leases   **Financial leases,** sometimes called *capital leases,* are differentiated from operating leases in three respects: (1) they do *not* provide for maintenance services; (2) they are *not* cancelable; and (3) they are *fully amortized*—that is, the lessor receives rental payments that are equal to the full price of the leased equipment

---

[3]The term *lessee* is pronounced "less-ee," and *lessor* is pronounced "less-or."

plus a return on the investment. In a typical financial lease arrangement, the firm that will use the equipment (the lessee) selects the specific items it requires and negotiates the price and delivery terms with the manufacturer. The user firm then negotiates terms with a leasing company and, once the lease terms are set, arranges to have the lessor buy the equipment from the manufacturer or the distributor. When the equipment is purchased, the user firm simultaneously executes the lease agreement.

Financial leases are similar to sale-and-leaseback arrangements, except that the leased equipment is new and the lessor buys it from a manufacturer or a distributor instead of from the user-lessee. A sale and leaseback might thus be thought of as a special type of financial lease, and both sale-and-leaseback leases and financial leases are analyzed in the same manner.[4]

Financial Statement Effects

OFF-BALANCE-SHEET FINANCING

Financing in which the assets and liabilities involved do not appear on the firm's balance sheet.

Lease payments are shown as operating expenses on a firm's income statement, but under certain conditions, neither the leased assets nor the liabilities under the lease contract appear on the firm's balance sheet. For this reason, leasing is often called **off-balance-sheet financing.** This point is illustrated in Table 18–1 by the balance sheets of two hypothetical firms, B (for Buy) and L (for Lease). Initially, the balance sheets of both firms are identical, and both have debt ratios of 50 percent. Each firm then decides to acquire fixed assets that cost $100. Firm B borrows $100 to make the purchase, so both an asset and a liability are recorded on its balance sheet, and its debt ratio is increased to 75 percent. Firm L leases the equipment, so its balance sheet is unchanged. The lease might call for fixed charges as high as or even higher than those on the loan, and the obligations assumed under the lease might be equally or more dangerous from the standpoint of financial safety, but the firm's debt ratio remains at 50 percent.

FASB #13

The statement of the Financial Accounting Standards Board (FASB) that details the conditions and procedures for capitalizing leases.

To correct this problem, the Financial Accounting Standards Board (FASB) issued **FASB #13,** which requires that for an unqualified audit report, firms that enter into financial (or capital) leases must restate their balance sheets to report leased assets as fixed assets and the present value of future lease payments as a debt. This process is called *capitalizing the lease,* and its net effect is to cause Firms B and L to have similar balance sheets, both of which will resemble the one shown for Firm B after the asset increase.[5]

The logic behind FASB #13 is as follows. If a firm signs a lease contract, its obligation to make lease payments is just as binding as if it had signed a loan agreement. The failure to make lease payments can bankrupt a firm just as surely as can the failure to make principal and interest payments on a loan. Therefore, for all intents and purposes, a financial lease is identical to a loan.[6] This being the case, when a firm

---

[4]For a lease transaction to qualify as a lease for *tax purposes,* and thus for the lessee to be able to deduct the lease payments, the life of the lease must not exceed 80 percent of the expected life of the asset, and the lessee cannot be permitted to buy the asset at a nominal value. These conditions are IRS requirements, and they should not be confused with the FASB requirements discussed in the next section concerning the capitalization of leases. It is important to consult lawyers and accountants to ascertain whether a prospective lease meets current IRS regulations.

[5]FASB #13, "Accounting for Leases," November 1976, spells out in detail the conditions under which leases must be capitalized and the procedures for doing so.

[6]There are, however, certain legal differences between loans and leases. For example, in a bankruptcy liquidation, the lessor is entitled to take possession of the leased asset, and, if the value of the asset is less than the required payments under the lease, the lessor can enter a claim (as a general creditor) for one year's lease payments. In a bankruptcy reorganization, the lessor receives the asset plus three years' lease payments if needed to bring the value of the asset up to the remaining investment in the lease.

TABLE 18-1	Balance Sheet Effects of Leasing

BEFORE ASSET INCREASE				AFTER ASSET INCREASE							
FIRMS B AND L				FIRM B—PURCHASES ASSET				FIRM L—LEASES ASSET			
Current assets	$ 50	Debt	$ 50	Current assets	$ 50	Debt	$150	Current assets	$ 50	Debt	$ 50
Fixed assets	50	Equity	50	Fixed assets	150	Equity	50	Fixed assets	50	Equity	50
Total	$100		$100	Total	$200		$200	Total	$100		$100
	Debt ratio = 50%				Debt ratio = 75%				Debt ratio = 50%		

signs a lease agreement, it has, in effect, raised its "true" debt ratio and thereby changed its "true" capital structure. Accordingly, if the firm previously had established a target capital structure, and if there is no reason to think that the optimal capital structure has changed, then using lease financing requires additional equity backing in exactly the same manner as does the use of debt financing.

If a disclosure of the lease in the Table 18–1 example were not made, then investors could be deceived into thinking that Firm L's financial position is stronger than it actually is. Even if the lease were disclosed in a footnote, investors might not fully recognize its impact and might not see that Firms B and L essentially are in the same financial position. If this were the case, Firm L would have increased its true amount of debt through a lease arrangement, but its required return on debt, k_d, its required return on equity, k_s, and consequently its weighted average cost of capital would have increased less than those of Firm B, which borrowed directly. Thus, investors would be willing to accept a lower return from Firm L because they would view it as being in a stronger financial position than Firm B. These benefits of leasing would accrue to stockholders at the expense of new investors, who were, in effect, being deceived by the fact that the firm's balance sheet did not fully reflect its true liability situation. This is why FASB #13 was issued.

A lease will be classified as a capital lease, and hence be capitalized and shown directly on the balance sheet, if any one of the following conditions exists:

1. Under the terms of the lease, ownership of the property effectively is transferred from the lessor to the lessee.
2. The lessee can purchase the property or renew the lease at less than a fair market price when the lease expires.
3. The lease runs for a period equal to or greater than 75 percent of the asset's life. Thus, if an asset has a 10-year life and if the lease is written for more than 7½ years, the lease must be capitalized.
4. The present value of the lease payments is equal to or greater than 90 percent of the initial value of the asset.[7]

These rules, together with strong footnote disclosures for operating leases, are sufficient to ensure that no one will be fooled by lease financing. Thus, leases are

---

[7]The discount rate used to calculate the present value of the lease payments must be the lower of (1) the rate used by the lessor to establish the lease payments or (2) the rate of interest that the lessee would have paid for new debt with a maturity equal to that of the lease.

recognized to be essentially the same as debt, and they have the same effects as debt on the firm's required rate of return. Therefore, leasing generally will not permit a firm to use more financial leverage than could be obtained with conventional debt.

Evaluation by the Lessee

Any prospective lease must be evaluated by both the lessee and the lessor. The lessee must determine whether leasing an asset will be less costly than buying it, and the lessor must decide whether the lease will provide a reasonable rate of return. Because our focus in this text primarily is on managerial finance as opposed to investments, we restrict our analysis to that conducted by the lessee.[8]

In the typical case, the events leading to a lease arrangement follow the sequence described in the following list. We should note that a great deal of theoretical literature exists about the correct way to evaluate lease-versus-purchase decisions, and some complex decision models have been developed to aid in the analysis. The analysis given next, however, leads to the correct decision in every case we have encountered.

1. The firm decides to acquire a particular building or piece of equipment. This decision is based on regular capital budgeting procedures, and it is not an issue in the typical lease analysis. In a lease analysis, we are concerned simply with whether to finance the machine by a lease or by a loan.

2. Once the firm has decided to acquire the asset, the next question is how to finance it. Well-run businesses do not have large amounts of excess cash, so new assets must be financed in some manner.

3. Funds to purchase the asset could be obtained by borrowing, by retaining earnings, or by issuing new stock. Alternatively, the asset could be leased. Because of the FASB #13 capitalization/disclosure provision for leases, we assume that a lease would have the same capital structure effect as a loan.

As indicated earlier, a lease is comparable to a loan in the sense that the firm is required to make a specified series of payments, and a failure to make these payments can result in bankruptcy. Thus, it is most appropriate to compare the cost of lease financing with that of debt financing.[9] The lease-versus-borrow-and-purchase analysis is illustrated with data on the Richards Electronics Company. The following conditions are assumed:

1. Richards plans to acquire equipment with a four-year life that has a cost of $10,000 delivered and installed.

---

[8]The lessee typically is offered a set of lease terms by the lessor, which generally is a bank, a finance company such as General Electric Capital (the largest U.S. lessor), or some other institutional lender. The lessee can accept or reject the lease, or shop around for a better deal. In this chapter, we take the lease terms as given for purposes of our analysis. See Chapter 18 of Eugene F. Brigham and Phillip R. Daves, *Intermediate Financial Management*, 8th ed. (Cincinnati, OH: South-Western College Publishing, 2004), for a discussion of lease analysis from the lessor's standpoint, including a discussion of how a potential lessee can use such an analysis in bargaining for better terms.

[9]The analysis should compare the cost of leasing to the cost of debt financing regardless of how the asset is actually financed. The asset might be purchased with available cash if it is not leased, but because leasing is a substitute for debt financing, a comparison between the two is still appropriate.

2. Richards can either purchase the equipment using a four-year, 10 percent loan or lease the equipment for four years at a rental charge of $3,000 per year, payable at the end of each year. If Richards leases the equipment, the lessor will own it upon the expiration of the lease.[10]

3. The equipment definitely will be used for four years, at which time its estimated net salvage value will be $600. Richards plans to continue using the equipment, so (a) if it purchases the equipment, the company will keep it, and (b) if it leases the equipment, the company will exercise an option to buy it at its estimated salvage (residual) value, $600.

4. The lease contract stipulates that the lessor will maintain the equipment. However, if Richards borrows and buys, it will have to bear the cost of maintenance, which will be performed by the equipment manufacturer at a fixed contract rate of $400 per year, payable at the end of each year.

5. The equipment falls in the MACRS 3-year class life, and for this analysis we assume that Richards' effective marginal tax rate is 40 percent.

Net Present Value (NPV) Analysis   Table 18–2 shows the cash flows that would be incurred each year under the two financing plans. All cash flows occur at the end of the year, and the CF_t values are shown on Lines 5 and 10 of Table 18–2 for buying and leasing, respectively.

The top section of the table (Lines 1–6) is devoted to the cost of owning (borrowing and buying). Lines 1–4 show the individual cash flow items. Line 5 summarizes the annual net cash flows that Richards will incur if it finances the equipment with a loan. The present values of these cash flows are summed to find the present value of the cost of owning, which is shown on Line 6 in the Year 0 column. Section II of the table calculates the present value cost of leasing. The cash flows associated with the lease are shown on Lines 7–9, and Line 10 gives the annual net cash flow. The present value of the cash flows is shown on Line 11. Finally, the net advantage to leasing, which is the difference between the present value of purchasing and the present value of leasing, is shown on Line 12. The result of the analysis shown in Table 18–2 indicates that Richards should lease rather than purchase the equipment because the net advantage to leasing is positive.

The rate used to discount the cash flows is a critical issue. In Chapter 4, we saw that the riskier a cash flow, the higher the required return associated with a series of cash flows. This same principle was observed in our discussion of capital budgeting, and it also applies in lease analysis. Just how risky are the cash flows under consideration here? Most of them are relatively certain, at least when compared with the types of cash flow estimates that were developed in capital budgeting. For example, the loan payment schedule is set by contract, as is the lease payment schedule. The depreciation expenses are established by law and generally are not subject to change, and, in many cases, the annual maintenance cost is fixed by contract as well. The tax savings are somewhat uncertain because tax rates can change, although tax rates do not change significantly very often. The residual, or salvage, value is the least certain of the cash flows, but even here Richards' management is fairly confident that it will

---

[10]Lease payments can occur at the beginning of the year or at the end of the year. In this example, we assume end-of-year payments, but we demonstrate beginning-of-year payments in Self-Test Problem ST-2.

TABLE 18–2	Richards Electronics Company: NPV Lease Analysis

	YEAR				
	0	**1**	**2**	**3**	**4**
I. Cost of Owning					
1. Net purchase price	$(10,000)				
2. Maintenance cost		$(400)	$(400)	$(400)	$(400)
3. Maintenance cost tax savings		160	160	160	160
4. Depreciation tax savings		1,320	1,800	600	280
5. Net cash flow	$(10,000)	$ 1,080	$ 1,560	$ 360	$ 40
6. Present value of owning (k = 6%)	$(7,258.8)				
II. Cost of Leasing					
7. Lease payment		$(3,000)	$(3,000)	$(3,000)	$(3,000)
8. Lease payment tax savings		1,200	1,200	1,200	1,200
9. Purchase option price					(600)
10. Net cash flow	$ 0	$(1,800)	$(1,800)	$(1,800)	$(2,400)
11. Present value of leasing (k = 6%)	$(6,712.4)				
III. Cost Comparison					
12. Net advantage to leasing	$ 546.4 = $7,258.8 – $6,712.4				

NOTE: A line-by-line explanation of the table follows:

1. If Richards buys the equipment, it will have to spend $10,000 on the purchase. Alternatively, we could show all the financing flows associated with a $10,000 loan, net of taxes, but the result would be the same because the PV of those flows would be exactly $10,000.

2. If the equipment is owned, Richards must pay $400 at the end of each year for maintenance.

3. The $400 maintenance expense is tax deductible, so it will produce a tax savings of $160 = 0.4($400) each year.

4. If Richards buys the equipment, it can depreciate the equipment for tax purposes and thus lower the taxes paid through lower taxable income. The tax savings in each year is equal to Tax rate × (Depreciation expense) = 0.4(Depreciation expense). As shown in Appendix 7A, the MACRS rates for 3-year class property are 0.33, 0.45, 0.15, and 0.07 in Years 1 through 4, respectively. To illustrate the calculation of the depreciation tax savings, consider Year 2. The depreciation expense is 0.45($10,000) = $4,500, and the tax savings is 0.4($4,500) = $1,800.

5. Sum Lines 1 through 4 to find the net cash flows associated with owning the equipment.

6. The PV of the Line 5 cash flows, discounted at 6 percent, is –$7,258.8.

7. The annual end-of-year lease payment is $3,000.

8. Because the lease payment is tax deductible, a tax savings of $1,200 = 0.4($3,000) results for each year.

9. Because Richards plans to continue to use the equipment after the lease expires, it must purchase the equipment for $600 at the end of Year 4 if it leases.

10. Sum Lines 7 through 9 to find the net cash flows associated with leasing.

11. The PV of the Line 10 cash flows, discounted at 6 percent, is –$6,712.4.

12. The net advantage to leasing is the difference between the PV cost of owning and the PV cost of leasing = $7,258.8 – $6,712.4 = $546.4. Because the NAL is positive, leasing is favored over borrowing and buying.

want to acquire the property and also that the cost of doing so will be close to $600. Because the cash flows under both the lease and the borrow-and-purchase alternatives are reasonably certain, they should be discounted at a relatively low rate. Most analysts recommend that the company's cost of debt be used, and this rate seems reasonable in our example. Further, because all the net cash flows are on an after-tax basis, *the after-tax cost of debt, which is 6 percent, should be used.*

Factors That Affect Leasing Decisions

The basic method of analysis set forth in Table 18–2 is sufficient to handle most situations. However, certain factors warrant additional comments.

RESIDUAL VALUE
The value of leased property at the end of the lease term.

Estimated Residual Value   It is important to note that the lessor will own the property upon the expiration of the lease. The estimated end-of-lease value of the property is called the **residual value.** Superficially, it would appear that if residual value is expected to be large, owning would have an advantage over leasing. However, if the expected residual value is large—as it might be under inflation for certain types of equipment as well as if real property is involved—then competition among leasing companies will force leasing rates down to the point where potential residual value will be fully recognized in the lease contract rate. Thus, the existence of a large residual value on equipment is not likely to bias the decision against leasing.

Increased Credit Availability   As noted earlier, leasing sometimes is said to have an advantage for firms that are seeking the maximum degree of financial leverage. First, it sometimes is argued that a firm can obtain more money, and for a longer period, under a lease arrangement than under a loan secured by the asset. Second, because some leases do not appear on the balance sheet, lease financing has been said to give the firm a stronger appearance in a superficial credit analysis, thus permitting it to use more leverage than it could if it did not lease. There might be some truth to these claims for smaller firms. However, because larger firms are required to capitalize major leases and to report them on their balance sheets, this point is of questionable validity.

Self-Test Questions

Define each of these terms: (1) sale-and-leaseback arrangements, (2) operating leases, and (3) financial, or capital, leases.

What is off-balance-sheet financing? What is FASB #13? How are the two related?

List the sequence of events, for the lessee, leading to a lease arrangement.

Why is it appropriate to compare the cost of lease financing with that of debt financing?

Options

OPTION
A contract that gives the option holder the right to buy (or sell) an asset at some predetermined price within a specified period of time.

An **option** is a contract that gives its holder the right to buy (or sell) an asset at some predetermined price within a specified period of time. "Pure options" are instruments that are created by outsiders (generally investment banking firms) rather than by the firm itself; they are bought and sold primarily by investors (or speculators). However, financial managers should understand the nature of options because this will help them structure warrant and convertible financings, both of which have similar characteristics.

Option Types and Markets

There are many types of options and option markets. To understand how options work, suppose you owned 100 shares of IBM stock that, on January 15, 2004, sold for $90 per share. You could sell to someone else the right to buy your 100 shares at any time during the next seven months at a price of, say, $95 per share. The $95 is called the **striking,** or **exercise, price.** Such options exist, and they are traded on a number of exchanges, with the Chicago Board of Options Exchange (CBOE) being the oldest and largest. This type of option is known as a **call option** because the option holder can "call" in 100 shares of stock for purchase any time during the option period. The seller of a call option is known as an option writer. An investor who writes a call option against stock held in his or her portfolio is said to be selling *covered options;* options sold without the stock to back them up are called *naked options.*

On January 15, 2004, IBM's seven-month, 95 call options sold on the CBOE for $3.10 each. Thus, for ($3.10)(100) = $310, you could buy an option contract that would give you the right to purchase 100 shares of IBM at a price of $95 per share at any time during the following seven months. If the stock stayed below $95 during that period, you would lose your $310, but if the stock's price rose to $100, your $310 investment would be worth ($100 - $95)(100) = $500. That translates into a healthy rate of return on your $310 investment. Incidentally, if the stock price did go up, you probably would not actually exercise your options to buy the stock; rather, you would sell the options to another option buyer, at a price greater than or equal to $5 per option—you originally paid only $3.10.

You also can buy an option that gives you the right to sell a stock at a specified price during some period in the future. This is called a **put option.** For example, suppose you expect IBM's stock price to decline from its current level sometime during the next five months. For $180 = $1.80 × 100 you could buy a five-month put option giving you the right to sell 100 shares (which you would not necessarily own) at a price of $80 per share ($80 is the put option striking price). If you bought a 100-share put contract for $180 and IBM's stock price actually fell to $75, you would make ($80 – $75)(100) = $500 minus the $180 you paid for the put option, for a net profit (before taxes and commissions) of $320.

Options trading is one of the hottest financial activities in the United States today. The leverage involved makes it possible for speculators with just a few dollars to make a fortune almost overnight. Also, investors with sizable portfolios can sell options against their stocks and earn the value of the options (minus brokerage commissions) even if the stocks' prices remain constant. Still, those who have profited most from the development of options trading are security firms, which earn very healthy commissions on such trades.

The corporations on whose stocks options are written, such as IBM, have nothing to do with the options market. They neither raise money in that market nor have any direct transactions in it, and option holders neither receive dividends nor vote for corporate directors (unless they exercise their options to purchase the stock, which few actually do). There have been studies by the Securities and Exchange Commission (SEC) and others as to whether options trading stabilizes or destabilizes the stock market and whether it helps or hinders corporations seeking to raise new capital. The studies have not been conclusive, but options trading is here to stay, and many regard it as the most exciting game in town.

STRIKING (EXERCISE) PRICE
The price that must be paid (buying or selling) for a share of common stock when an option is exercised.

CALL OPTION
An option to buy, or "call," a share of stock at a certain price within a specified period.

PUT OPTION
The option to sell a specified number of shares of stock at a prespecified price during a particular period.

Option Values

The value of an option is closely related to the value of the *underlying* stock, which is the stock on which the option is written, and the striking price. For example, an investor who purchases call options hopes that the value of the underlying stock goes above the striking price during the option period, because then the option could be exercised at a gross profit equal to the market value of the stock less the striking price. In this case, the investor is said to have an **in-the-money option** because he or she can exercise the call option by purchasing the stock at the striking price and then can immediately sell the stock for its market value, which is greater than the striking price. For example, if IBM's stock sells for $100 at the beginning of 2004, call options with a striking price of $95 would be in the money because the option holder could exercise the options by paying the option seller $9,500 for 100 shares of IBM stock, and then the stock could be sold on the NYSE for $10,000—the financial benefit of exercising to the option holder would be $500 before commissions and taxes. If the market value of IBM's stock is $90, or any other amount below the striking price, the call is said to be an **out-of-the-money option** because it would not be favorable for the option holder to exercise the call. If the investor were to exercise the call option, there would be a financial loss because the stock would be purchased at a value (the $95 striking price) greater than it could be sold (the $90 market value). The opposite relationship holds for put options because the striking price represents the price at which an investor can *sell* the stock to the put option writer (seller). To be able to sell to the put option writer, the investor first must *buy* the stock in the market (for example, on the NYSE). Thus, for a put option to be in-the-money, the striking price must be above the market value of the underlying stock.

As you can see, both the value of the underlying stock and the striking price of the option are important in determining whether an option is in-the-money or out-of-the-money. If an option is out-of-the-money on its expiration date, it is worthless. Therefore, the stock price and the striking price are important for determining the market value of an option. In fact, options are called *derivative securities* because their values are dependent on, or derived from, the value of the underlying asset and the striking price.

In addition to the stock price and the striking price, the value of an option also depends on (1) the option's time to maturity and (2) the variability of the underlying stock's price, as explained here:

1. The longer an option has to run, the greater its value. If a call option expires at 4 P.M. today, there is not much chance that the stock price will go way up. Therefore, the option will sell at close to the difference between the stock price and the striking price (P_s – striking price), or zero if this difference is negative. On the other hand, if it has a year to go, the stock price could rise sharply, pulling the option's value up with it.
2. An option on an extremely volatile stock will be worth more than one on a stable stock. We know that an option on a stock whose price rarely moves will not offer much chance for a large gain. On the other hand, an option on a stock that is highly volatile could provide a large gain, so such an option will be valuable. Note also that because losses on options are limited, large declines in a stock's price do not have a corresponding bad effect on call

IN-THE-MONEY OPTION
When it is beneficial financially for the option holder to exercise the option.

OUT-OF-THE-MONEY OPTION
When it is *not* beneficial financially for the option holder to exercise the option—a loss would be incurred if the option is exercised.

option holders. Therefore, stock price volatility can only enhance the value of an option.[11]

If everything else were held constant, then the longer an option's life, the higher its market price would be, no matter the type of option. Also, the more volatile the price of the underlying stock, the higher the option's market price, regardless of the option type.

Self-Test Questions

Differentiate between a call option and a put option.

Do the corporations on whose stocks options are written raise money in the options market? Explain.

Explain how these factors affect the value of an option: (1) the time remaining before the option expires and (2) the volatility of the underlying stock.

How is the value of a call option affected by the value of the underlying stock and the striking price? How is the value of a put option affected by these factors?

Warrants

WARRANT
A long-term option issued by a corporation to buy a stated number of shares of common stock at a specified price.

A **warrant** is an option *issued by a company* that gives the holder the right to buy a stated number of shares of the company's stock at a specified price. Generally, warrants are distributed along with debt, and they are used to induce investors to buy a firm's long-term debt at a lower interest rate than otherwise would be required. For example, when Pac-Atlantic Air (PAA) wanted to sell $100 million of 20-year bonds in 1998, the company's investment bankers informed the financial vice president that straight bonds would be difficult to sell and that an interest rate of 11 percent would be required. However, the investment bankers suggested as an alternative that investors would be willing to buy bonds with an annual coupon rate as low as 8 percent if the company would offer 30 warrants with each $1,000 bond, each warrant entitling the holder to buy one share of common stock at a price of $12 per share.

---

[11]To illustrate this point, suppose that for $2 you could buy a call option on a stock now selling for $20. The striking price is also $20. Now suppose the stock is highly volatile, and you think it has a 50 percent probability of selling for either $10 or $30 when the option expires in one month. What is the expected value of the option? If the stock sells for $30, the option will be worth $30 – $20 = $10; but, if the stock sells for $10, the option will be worthless. Because there is a 50-50 chance that the stock will be worth $10 or $30, the expected value of the option is $5:

$$\text{Expected value of option} = 0.5(0) + 0.5(\$10) = \$5$$

To be exactly correct, we would have to discount the $5 back for one month.

Now suppose the stock was more volatile, with a 50-50 chance of the option being worth zero or $20 (the stock value might be $0 or $40). Here the option would be worth

$$\text{Expected value of option} = 0.5(0) + 0.5(\$20) = \$10$$

This demonstrates that the greater the volatility of the stock, the greater the value of the option. The reason this result occurs is because the large loss on the stock ($20) had no more of an adverse effect on the option holder than the small loss ($10). Thus, option holders benefit greatly if a stock goes way up, but they do not lose too badly if it drops all the way to zero. These concepts have been used to develop formulas for pricing options, with the most widely used formula being the Black-Scholes model, which is discussed in most investments texts.

The stock was selling for $10 per share at the time, and the warrants would expire in 2005 if they had not been exercised previously.

Why would investors be willing to buy Pac-Atlantic's bonds at a yield of only 8 percent in an 11 percent market just because warrants were offered as part of the package? The answer is that warrants are long-term options, and they have a value for the reasons set forth in the previous section. In the PPA case, this value offset the low interest rate on the bonds and made the entire package of low interest bonds plus warrants attractive to investors.

Use of Warrants in Financing

DETACHABLE WARRANT

A warrant that can be detached from a bond and traded independently of it.

Warrants generally are used by small, rapidly growing firms as "sweeteners" to help sell either debt or preferred stock. Such firms frequently are regarded as being very risky, and their bonds can be sold only if the firms are willing to pay extremely high rates of interest and to accept very restrictive indenture provisions. To avoid this, firms such as Pac-Atlantic often offer warrants along with their bonds. However, some strong firms also have used warrants. In one of the largest financings of any type ever undertaken by a business firm at the time, AT&T raised $1.57 billion by selling bonds with warrants. This marked the first use ever of warrants by a large, strong corporation.

Getting warrants along with bonds enables investors to share in a company's growth if that firm does in fact grow and prosper; therefore, investors are willing to accept a lower bond interest rate and less restrictive indenture provisions. A bond with warrants has some characteristics of debt and some of equity. It is a hybrid security that provides the financial manager with an opportunity to expand the firm's mix of securities and to appeal to a broader group of investors, thus lowering the firm's cost of capital. Virtually all warrants today are **detachable warrants,** meaning that after a bond with attached warrants has been sold, the warrants can be detached and traded separately from the bond. Further, when these warrants are exercised, the bonds themselves (with their low coupon rate) will remain outstanding. Thus, the warrants will bring in additional equity capital while leaving low interest rate debt on the books.

The warrants' exercise price generally is set at from 10 percent to 30 percent above the market price of the stock on the date the bond is issued. For example, if the stock sells for $10, the exercise price will probably be set in the $11 to $13 range. If the firm does grow and prosper, and if its stock price rises above the exercise price at which shares can be purchased, warrant holders will turn in their warrants, along with cash equal to the stated exercise price, in exchange for stock. Without some incentive, however, many warrants would never be exercised until just before expiration. Their value in the market would be greater than their exercise value; thus holders would sell warrants rather than exercise them.

Three conditions encourage holders to exercise their warrants:

1. Warrant holders surely will exercise warrants and buy stock if the warrants are about to expire with the market price of the stock above the exercise price. This means that if a firm wants its warrants exercised soon to raise capital, it should set a relatively short expiration date.
2. Warrant holders will tend to exercise voluntarily and buy stock if the company raises the dividend on the common stock by a sufficient amount. Because no dividend is paid on the warrant, it provides no current income. However, if the

common stock pays a high dividend, it provides an attractive dividend yield. Therefore, the higher the stock's dividend, the greater the opportunity cost of holding the warrant rather than exercising it. Thus, if a firm wants its warrants exercised, it can raise the common stock's dividend.

STEPPED-UP EXERCISE PRICE
An exercise price that is specified to be higher if a warrant is exercised after a designated date.

3. Warrants sometimes have **stepped-up exercise prices,** which prod owners into exercising them. For example, the Mills Agricorp has warrants outstanding with an exercise price of $25 until December 31, 2012, at which time the exercise price will rise to $30. If the price of the common stock is over $25 just before December 31, 2012, many warrant holders will exercise their options before the stepped-up price takes effect.

Another useful feature of warrants is that they generally bring in funds only if such funds are needed. If the company grows, it probably will need new equity capital. At the same time, this growth will cause the price of the stock to rise and the warrants to be exercised, thereby allowing the firm to obtain additional cash. If the company is not successful and cannot profitably employ additional money, the price of its stock probably will not rise sufficiently to induce exercise of the options.

Self-Test Questions

What three conditions would encourage holders to exercise their warrants?

Do warrants bring in additional funds to the firm when exercised? Explain.

Explain how a firm can use warrants to issue debt with a lower cost than similar debt without warrants.

Convertibles

CONVERTIBLE SECURITY
A security, usually a bond or preferred stock, that is exchangeable at the option of the holder for the common stock of the issuing firm.

Convertible securities are bonds or preferred stocks that can be exchanged for common stock at the option of the holder (investor). Unlike the exercise of warrants, which provides the firm with additional funds, conversion does not bring in additional capital—debt or preferred stock simply is replaced by common stock. Of course, this reduction of debt or preferred stock will strengthen the firm's balance sheet and make it easier to raise additional capital, but this is a separate action.

Conversion Ratio and Conversion Price

CONVERSION RATIO, CR
The number of shares of common stock that can be obtained by converting a convertible bond or a share of convertible preferred stock.

One of the most important provisions of a convertible security is the **conversion ratio, CR,** defined as the number of shares of stock the convertible holder receives upon conversion. Related to the conversion ratio is the conversion price, P_c, which is the effective price paid for the common stock obtained by converting a convertible security. The relationship between the conversion ratio and the conversion price can be illustrated by the convertible debentures issued at par value by Bee TV Inc. in 2004. At any time prior to maturity on July 1, 2025, a debenture holder can exchange a bond for 20 shares of common stock; therefore, CR = 20. The bond has a par value of $1,000, so the holder would be relinquishing this amount upon conversion. Dividing the $1,000 par value by the 20 shares received gives a conversion price of P_c = $50 a share:

| 18–1 | $$\text{Conversion price} = \frac{\text{Par value of bond}}{\text{Conversion ratio}}$$ |

$$= \frac{\$1,000}{20} = \$50$$

Like a warrant's exercise price, the conversion price usually is set at from 10 percent to 30 percent above the prevailing market price of the common stock at the time the convertible issue is sold. Generally, the conversion price and ratio are fixed for the life of the bond, although sometimes a stepped-up conversion price is used.

Another factor that might cause a change in the conversion price and ratio is a standard feature of almost all convertibles—the clause protecting the convertible against dilution from stock splits, stock dividends, and the sale of common stock at prices below the conversion price. The typical provision states that if common stock is sold at a price below the conversion price, the conversion price must be lowered (and the conversion ratio raised) to the price at which the new stock was issued. Also, if the stock is split (or if a stock dividend is declared), the conversion price must be lowered by the percentage of the stock split (or stock dividend). If this protection were not contained in the contract, a company could completely thwart conversion by the use of stock splits. Warrants are similarly protected against such dilution.

Use of Convertibles in Financing

Convertibles offer three important advantages from the *issuer's* standpoint. First, convertibles, like bonds with warrants, permit a company to sell debt with a lower interest rate and with less restrictive covenants than straight bonds. Second, convertibles generally are subordinated to mortgage bonds, bank loans, and other senior debt, so financing with convertibles leaves the company's access to "regular" debt unimpaired. Third, convertibles provide a way of selling common stock at prices higher than those that currently prevail. Many companies actually want to sell common stock and not debt, but they believe that the price of their stock is temporarily depressed. The financial manager might know, for example, that earnings are depressed because of start-up costs associated with a new project, but he or she might expect earnings to rise sharply during the next year or so, pulling the price of the stock along. In this case, if the company sold stock now it would be giving up too many shares to raise a given amount of money. However, if the firm sets the conversion price at 20 percent to 30 percent above the present market price of its stock, then 20 percent to 30 percent fewer shares must be given up when the bonds are converted. Notice, however, that management is counting on the stock's price rising sufficiently above the conversion price to make the bonds attractive in conversion. If earnings do not rise and pull the stock price up, and hence if conversion does not occur, the company could be saddled with debt in the face of low earnings, which could be disastrous.

How can the company be sure that conversion will occur if the price of the stock rises above the conversion price? Typically, convertibles contain a call provision that enables the issuing firm to force bondholders to convert. Suppose the conversion price is $50, the conversion ratio is 20, the market price of the common stock has risen to $60, and the call price on the convertible bond is $1,050. If the company calls the bond, bondholders could either convert into common stock with a market value of $1,200 or allow the company to redeem the bond for $1,050. Naturally, bondholders prefer $1,200 to $1,050, so conversion will occur. The call provision therefore gives the company a means of *forcing* conversion, but only if the market price of the stock is greater than the conversion price.

Convertibles are useful, but they do have three important disadvantages:

1. The use of a convertible security might in effect give the issuer the opportunity to sell common stock at a price higher than it could sell stock otherwise. However, if the common stock increases greatly in price, the company probably would have been better off if it had used straight debt in spite of its higher interest rate and then later sold common stock to refund the debt.
2. If the company truly wants to raise equity capital, and if the price of the stock does not rise sufficiently after the bond is issued, then the firm will be stuck with debt.
3. Convertibles typically have a low coupon interest rate, an advantage that will be lost when conversion occurs. Warrant financings, on the other hand, permit the company to continue to use the low-coupon debt for a longer period.

Self-Test Questions

Does the exchange of convertible securities for common stock bring in additional funds to the firm? Explain.

How do you calculate the conversion price?

What are the key advantages and disadvantages of convertibles?

Reporting Earnings When Warrants or Convertibles Are Outstanding

If warrants or convertibles are outstanding, a firm theoretically can report earnings per share (EPS) in one of three ways:

1. **Simple EPS.** The earnings available to common stockholders are divided by the average number of shares *actually* outstanding during the period.
2. **Primary EPS.** The earnings available are divided by the average number of shares that would have been outstanding if warrants and convertibles *likely to be converted* in the near future had actually been exercised or converted.
3. **Fully diluted EPS.** This is similar to primary EPS except that all warrants and convertibles are *assumed to be exercised or converted*, regardless of the likelihood of either occurring.

Simple EPS is virtually never reported by firms that have warrants or convertibles likely to be exercised or converted; the SEC prohibits use of this figure, and it requires that primary and fully diluted earnings be shown on the income statement.

Self-Test Question

Differentiate between simple EPS, primary EPS, and fully diluted EPS.

Leveraged Buyouts (LBOs)

LEVERAGED BUYOUT (LBO)

A transaction in which a firm's publicly owned stock is bought up in a mostly debt-financed tender offer, and a privately owned, highly leveraged firm results.

With the extraordinary merger activity that took place in the 1980s, we witnessed a huge increase in the popularity of **leveraged buyouts,** or **LBOs.** The number and size of LBOs jumped significantly during this period. This development occurred for the same reasons that mergers and divestitures occurred—the existence of potential bargains, situations in which companies were using insufficient leverage, and the development of the junk bond market, which facilitated the use of leverage in takeovers.

LBOs can be initiated in one of two ways: (1) The firm's own managers can set up a new company whose equity comes from the managers themselves, plus some equity from pension funds and other institutions. This new company then arranges to borrow a large amount of money by selling junk bonds through an investment banking firm. With the financing arranged, the management group then makes an offer to purchase all the publicly owned shares through a tender offer. (2) A specialized LBO firm, with Kohlberg Kravis Roberts (KKR) being one of the best known, will identify a potential target company, go to the management, and suggest that an LBO deal be done. KKR and other LBO firms have billions of dollars of equity, most put up by pension funds and other large investors, available for the equity portion of the deals, and they arrange junk bond financing just as would a management-led group. Generally, the newly formed company will have at least 80 percent debt, and sometimes the debt ratio is as high as 98 percent. Thus, the term *leveraged* is most appropriate.

To illustrate an LBO, consider the $25 billion leveraged buyout of RJR Nabisco by KKR in 1989. RJR, a leading producer of tobacco and food products with such brands as Winston, Camel, Planters, Ritz, and Oreo, was trading at about $55 a share. Then F. Ross Johnson, RJR Nabisco's president and CEO at the time, announced a $75 per share, or $17.6 billion, offer to take the firm private. The day after the announcement, RJR's stock soared to $77.25, which indicated that investors thought that the final price would be even higher than Johnson's opening bid. A few days later, KKR offered $90 per share, or $20.6 billion, for the firm. The battle between the two bidders continued until late November, when RJR's board accepted a revised KKR bid of cash and securities worth about $109 per share, for a total value of about $25.1 billion.

Was RJR worth $25 billion, or did Henry Kravis and his partners let their egos govern their judgment? At the time the LBO was initiated, analysts believed that the deal was workable, but barely. Six years after the deal, KKR had disposed of all its interest in RJR Nabisco, and many experts called the biggest LBO of its time the biggest financial flop in history. More information about the history of KKR's ownership of RJR Nabisco is provided in the Industry Practice box in this chapter.

It is not clear if LBOs are, on balance, a good or a bad idea. Some government officials and others have stated a belief that the leverage involved might destabilize the economy. On the other hand, LBOs certainly have stimulated some lethargic managements, and that is good. Good or bad, however, LBOs have helped reshape the face of corporate America.

Self-Test Questions

Identify and briefly explain the two ways in which an LBO can be initiated.

How has the development of the junk bond market affected the use of LBOs?

Déjà Vu All Over Again?

One of the largest leveraged buyouts (LBO) was finalized February 1989 when Kohlberg Kravis Roberts & Co. (KKR), a large and powerful LBO firm, acquired RJR Nabisco for just over $25 billion. The deal evolved in October 1988, when a group headed by F. Ross Johnson, chairman of RJR Nabisco at the time, offered stockholders $75 per share in an attempt to purchase the company and take it private; the total offer was equal to nearly $18 billion. Within days, Henry Kravis and George Roberts, KKR's leaders, started a bidding war by offering $90 per share for RJR Nabisco. Ultimately KKR won the war and paid $109 per share, which was nearly twice the per share market price at the time the first buyout offer was made by Johnson. Of the $25 billion paid, only $1.35 billion represented equity invested by KKR; the rest was financed by debt and was raised primarily in the junk bond market. At the time the RJR Nabisco LBO was finalized, there was a great deal of skepticism about whether the deal would be successful. Some experts speculated that the phenomenal price paid for the RJR Nabisco LBO was the result of a battle of egos between two powerful individuals; others believed the LBO was a good deal. In any event, the degree of financial leverage, thus the risk, associated with the LBO was substantial.

Several years after the RJR Nabisco LBO, experts dubbed the "deal of the century" the "turkey of the century." The average annual return earned by KKR on its investment in the LBO was only in the single digits range, quite a contrast to the 25 percent to 30 percent returns KKR normally sees, and well below expectations given the risk involved. According to analysts, KKR made two fundamental mistakes with the RJR Nabisco deal: (1) too much was paid for the buyout, and (2) the investment was made in the wrong industry (tobacco).

Not long after KKR put together the LBO, the junk bond market tumbled. To save RJR from insolvency, in July 1990, KKR refinanced some of the debt by infusing another $1.7 billion of equity; this increased KKR's equity position to about $3.1 billion. Then in 1991, KKR took RJR Nabisco public with an initial public offering (IPO) of 100 million shares at a price of $11.25 per share. The stock sold by KKR represented 60 percent equity ownership in RJR Nabisco. KKR believed the funds raised through the IPO could be used to better stabilize the financial position of RJR. Unfortunately, legal and competitive battles in the tobacco industry resulted in lackluster operating performances by RJR in the 1990s. In 1993, RJR's primary competitor, Philip Morris, started an aggressive campaign to increase its market share in the tobacco industry by significantly cutting cigarette prices and increasing advertising expenses. These actions surprised RJR, so it missed the boat and was left behind by Philip Morris. RJR's profit decreased by 50 percent in 1993. At the same time, increases in both regulation and litigation contributed to a heightened social awareness and a degree of negativism with respect to investing in tobacco companies. Consequently, tobacco stocks were shunned by many investors in the early 1990s. In the middle of 1994, RJR Nabisco stock sold for about $5 per share, less than one half its IPO price two years earlier.

On September 12, 1994, KKR made a bid to acquire Borden Inc., a large food processor, for approximately $14.25 per share. To pay for the $2 billion buyout, KKR exchanged 275 million shares of RJR Nabisco stock for Borden's stock. This move reduced KKR's ownership of RJR from 40 percent to 17.5 percent. Then, in February and March of 1995, KKR sold its remaining stake in RJR through Borden. Six years after it consummated the "deal of the century," KKR had dumped RJR Nabisco and totally removed itself from the situation. During the same period, RJR Nabisco Holdings Corporation sold to the public nearly 20 percent of Nabisco Brands, the food division of RJR Nabisco, which was a big hit in the financial markets.

During the late 1990s, Nabisco Holdings Corporation (NHC) divested itself of the tobacco products divisions in the RJR Nabisco organization. In June 1999, NHC completed the process, and R. J. Reynolds Tobacco Holdings Inc. began trading as a separate company. Thus, RJR and Nabisco are back where they were in 1985 before RJR purchased Nabisco Brands; RJR is an independent tobacco company and Nabisco is an independent food company, and both are independent of KKR. After nearly 15 years, RJR and Nabisco Brands have come full circle—starting with a merger, proceeding through the biggest LBO of its time (there have been larger LBOs in more recent years), and ultimately splitting into two companies that are publicly owned once again.

Mergers

MERGER
The combination of two or more firms to form a single firm.

Mergers have taken place at a feverish pace during the past couple of decades. The brief discussion in this section will help you understand the motivations behind all this activity.[12]

Rationale for Mergers

Two or more firms are merged to form a single firm for five principal reasons.

1. **Synergy.** The primary motivation for most mergers is to increase the value of the combined enterprise—the hope is that *synergy* exists so that the value of the company formed by the merger is greater than the sum of the values of the individual companies taken separately. Synergistic effects can arise from four sources: (a) *operating economies of scale* occur when cost reductions result from the combination of the companies; (b) *financial economies* might include a higher price/earnings ratio, a lower cost of debt, or a greater debt capacity; (c) *differential management efficiency* generally results when one firm is relatively inefficient, so the merger improves the profitability of the acquired assets; and (d) *increased market power* occurs if reduced competition exists after the merger. Operating and financial economies are socially desirable, as are mergers that increase managerial efficiency; but mergers that reduce competition are both undesirable and often illegal.[13]

2. **Tax considerations.** Tax considerations have stimulated a number of mergers. For example, a firm that is highly profitable and in the highest corporate tax bracket could acquire a company with large accumulated tax losses, then use those losses to shelter its own income.[14] Similarly, a company with large losses could acquire a profitable firm. Also, tax considerations could cause mergers to be a desirable use for excess cash. For example, if a firm has a shortage of internal investment opportunities compared to its cash flows, it will have excess cash, and its options for disposing of this excess cash are to (a) pay an extra dividend, (b) invest in marketable securities, (c) repurchase its own stock, or (d) purchase another firm. If the

---

[12]The purpose of this section is to provide you with a general understanding of mergers, the motivations for mergers, and merger activity in the United States. Merger analysis, which is the evaluation of the attractiveness of a merger, should be conducted in the same manner as capital budgeting analysis (if the present value of the cash flows expected to result from the merger exceeds the price that must be paid for the company being acquired, then the merger has a positive net present value and the acquiring firm should proceed with the acquisition). Because the very nature of the merger process is complex, we choose not to discuss the specifics of merger analysis in this section. For a detailed discussion of mergers analysis, see Chapter 25 of Eugene F. Brigham and Philip R. Daves, *Intermediate Financial Management*, 8th ed. (Cincinnati, OH: South-Western College Publishing 2004).

[13]In the 1880s and 1890s, many mergers occurred in the United States, and some of them clearly were directed toward gaining market power at the expense of competition rather than increasing operating efficiency. As a result, Congress passed a series of acts designed to ensure that mergers are not used as a method of reducing competition. Today, the principal acts include the Sherman Act (1890), the Clayton Act (1914), and the Celler Act (1950). These acts make it illegal for firms to combine in any manner if the combination will lessen competition. They are administered by the antitrust division of the Justice Department and by the Federal Trade Commission.

[14]Mergers undertaken only to use accumulated tax losses probably would be challenged by the IRS. However, because many factors are present in any given merger, it is hard to prove that a merger was motivated only, or even primarily, by tax considerations

firm pays an extra dividend, its stockholders will have to pay taxes on the distribution. Marketable securities such as Treasury bonds provide a good temporary parking place for money, but the rate of return on such securities is less than that required by stockholders. A stock repurchase might result in a capital gain for the remaining stockholders, but it could be disadvantageous if the company has to pay a high price to acquire the stock, and, if the repurchase is designed solely to avoid paying dividends, it might be challenged by the IRS. However, using surplus cash to acquire another firm has no immediate tax consequences for either the acquiring firm or its stockholders, and this fact has motivated a number of mergers.

3. **Purchase of assets below their replacement cost.** Sometimes a firm will become an acquisition candidate because the replacement value of its assets is considerably higher than its market value. For example, in the 1980s oil companies could acquire reserves more cheaply by buying out other oil companies than by exploratory drilling. This factor was a motive in Chevron's acquisition of Gulf Oil. The acquisition of Republic Steel (the sixth largest steel company) by LTV (the fourth largest) provides another example of a firm being purchased because its purchase price was less than the replacement value of its assets. LTV found that it was less costly to purchase Republic Steel for $700 million than it would have been to construct a new steel mill. At the time, Republic's stock was selling for less than one-third of its book value. However, the merger did not help LTV's inefficient operations—ultimately, the company filed for bankruptcy.

4. **Diversification.** Managers often claim that diversification helps to stabilize the firm's earnings and thus reduces corporate risk. Therefore, diversification often is given as a reason for mergers. Stabilization of earnings certainly is beneficial to a firm's employees, suppliers, and customers, but its value to stockholders and debt holders is less clear. If an investor is worried about earnings variability, he or she probably could diversify through stock purchases (investment portfolio adjustment) more easily than the firm could through acquisitions.

5. **Maintaining control.** Some mergers and takeovers are considered *hostile* because the management of the acquired firm opposes the merger. One reason for the hostility is that the managers of the acquired companies generally lose their jobs, or at least their autonomy. Therefore, managers who own less than 50 percent plus one share of the stock in their firms look to devices that will lessen the chances of their firms' being taken over. Mergers can serve as such a device. For example, in 1985, when InterNorth of Omaha was under attack, it arranged to merge with Houston Natural Gas Company, paying for Houston primarily with debt. That merger made the combined company, which was renamed Enron in 1986, much larger and hence harder for any potential acquirer to "digest." Also, the much higher debt level resulting from the merger made it hard for any acquiring company to use debt to buy Enron. Such **defensive mergers** are difficult to defend on economic grounds. The managers involved invariably argue that synergy, not a desire to protect their own jobs, motivated the acquisition, but there can be no question that many mergers have been designed more for the benefit of managers than for stockholders.

DEFENSIVE MERGER

A merger designed to make a company less vulnerable to a takeover.

HORIZONTAL MERGER

A combination of two firms that produce the same type of good or service.

Types of Mergers

Economists classify mergers into four groups: (1) horizontal, (2) vertical, (3) congeneric, and (4) conglomerate. A **horizontal merger** occurs when one firm combines with another in its same line of business. For example, the acquisition of Chrysler by Daimler-Benz AG in 1998 was a horizontal merger because both firms

VERTICAL MERGER
A merger between a firm and one of its suppliers or customers.

CONGENERIC MERGER
A merger of firms in the same general industry, but for which no customer or supplier relationship exists.

CONGLOMERATE MERGER
A merger of companies in totally different industries.

are automobile manufacturers. An example of a **vertical merger** is a steel producer's acquisition of one of its own suppliers, such as an iron or coal mining firm. The 1993 merger of Merck & Co., a manufacturer of health care products, and Medco Containment, the largest mail-order pharmacy service, is an example of a vertical merger. Congeneric means "allied in nature or action"; hence, a **congeneric merger** involves related enterprises but not producers of the same product (horizontal) or firms in a producer-supplier relationship (vertical). Examples of congeneric mergers include Viacom's acquisitions of Paramount Communications and Blockbuster Entertainment in 1994. Viacom owns several television stations and cable systems and distributes television programming, while Paramount produces movies and other entertainment shown both on television and in theaters, and Blockbuster's principal business is the rental of movies, most of which previously have been shown in theaters. A **conglomerate merger** occurs when unrelated enterprises combine, as illustrated by Sears, Roebuck & Company acquisitions of Dean Witter Reynolds Organization Inc., a securities broker and investment banker, and Coldwell Banker & Company, a real estate firm, in 1981. (Sears has since divested itself of both firms.)

Operating economies (and also anticompetitive effects) are dependent on the type of merger involved. Vertical and horizontal mergers generally provide the greatest synergistic operating benefits, but they also are the ones most likely to be attacked by the U.S. Department of Justice. In any event, it is useful to think of these economic classifications when analyzing the feasibility of a prospective merger.

Merger Activity

Four major "merger waves" have occurred in the United States. The first was in the late 1800s, when consolidations occurred in the oil, steel, tobacco, and other basic industries. The second was in the 1920s, when the stock market boom helped financial promoters consolidate firms in a number of industries, including utilities, communications, and autos. The third was in the 1960s, when conglomerate mergers were the rage, while the fourth began in the early 1980s, and it is still going strong. Many of the recent mergers have been horizontal mergers.

The current "merger mania" has been sparked by several factors: (1) at times, the depressed level of the dollar relative to Japanese and European currencies have made U.S. companies look cheap to foreign buyers; (2) the unprecedented level of inflation that existed during the 1970s and early 1980s, which increased the replacement value of firms' assets even while a weak stock market reduced their market values; (3) the general belief among the major natural resource companies that it is cheaper to "buy reserves on Wall Street" through mergers than to explore and find them in the field; (4) attempts to ward off raiders by use of defensive mergers; (5) the development of the junk bond market, which has made it possible to use far more debt in acquisitions than had been possible earlier; and (6) the increased globalization of business, which has led to increased economies of scale and to the formation of worldwide corporations.

For the past decade, the pace of merger activity can best be described as furious. Each year from 1995 through 2000 a new record was set for the values of announced mergers, with the peak of $3.4 trillion occurring in 2000. An economic slump decreased merger activity by 53 percent in 2001 and another 25 percent in 2002, but a positive economic outlook in 2003 resulted in a reversal, and merger activity started a new upward trend.

During the current merger frenzy, many of the largest mergers have been in financial services (for example, BankAmerica and NationsBank and J. P. Morgan

Chase & Company and Bank One), telecommunications (for example, WorldCom and MCI Communications and AT&T and Tele-Communications), and technology (for example, Oracle and PeopleSoft). As mergers in these industries continue, the companies' and industries' infrastructures will be reshaped.

Often, large, well-publicized mergers fail because the combination of the two companies is counterproductive. For example, two of the most celebrated and costly mergers—RJR Nabisco and AOL Time Warner—ultimately ended in divorce, and those involved in the mergers ended up losing large amounts of wealth.

Many of the mergers in the 1990s resulted either because the acquired firms were considered undervalued or because it was felt economies of scale could produce less costly combined operations. Increased global competition and governmental reforms were the major reasons for merger activities in the telecommunications and financial services industries, which accounted for the nearly 50 percent of the mergers in 1998. Experts expect these industries and other industries, such as defense, consumer products, and natural resources, to become significantly reshaped as merger activity continues in the future.

Self-Test Questions

What are the four primary motives behind most mergers?

From what sources do synergistic effects arise?

How have tax considerations stimulated mergers?

Is diversification to reduce stockholder risk a valid motive for mergers? Explain.

Explain briefly the four economic classifications of mergers.

What factors have sparked the most recent *merger mania?*

Summary

This chapter discussed three hybrid forms of long-term financing: (1) preferred stock, (2) leasing, and (3) option securities. We also discussed corporate restructuring. The key concepts covered are listed here:

- **Preferred stock** is a **hybrid security** having some characteristics of debt and some of equity. Equity holders view preferred stock as being similar to debt because it has a claim on the firm's earnings ahead of the claim of the common stockholders. Bondholders, however, view preferred stock as equity because debt holders have a prior claim on the firm's income and assets.
- The primary **advantages of preferred stock to the issuer** are (1) preferred dividends are limited and (2) failure to pay them will not bankrupt the firm. The primary disadvantage to the issuer is that the cost of preferred stock is higher than that of debt because preferred dividend payments are not tax deductible.
- To the **investor,** preferred stock offers the advantage of **more dependable income** than common stock, and to a corporate investor, **70 percent of such dividends are not taxable.** The principal disadvantages to the investor are that the returns are limited and the investor has no legally enforceable right to a dividend.
- **Leasing** is a means of obtaining the use of an asset without purchasing that asset. The three most important forms of leasing are (1) **sale-and-leaseback**

arrangements, under which a firm sells an asset to another party and leases the asset back for a specified period under specific terms; (2) **operating leases,** under which the lessor both maintains and finances the asset; and (3) **financial leases,** under which the asset is fully amortized over the life of the lease, the lessor does not normally provide maintenance, and the lease is not cancelable.

■ The **decision to lease or buy an asset** is made by comparing the financing costs of the two alternatives and choosing the financing method with the lower cost. All cash flows should be discounted at the after-tax cost of debt because lease analysis cash flows are relatively certain and are on an after-tax basis.

■ An **option** is a contract that gives its holder the right to buy (or sell) an asset at some predetermined price within a specified period of time. Options features are used by firms to "sweeten" debt offerings.

■ A **warrant** is an **option issued by a firm** that gives the holder the right to purchase a stated number of shares of stock at a specified price within a given period. A warrant will be exercised if it is about to expire and the stock price is above the exercise price.

■ A **convertible security** is a bond or preferred stock that can be exchanged for common stock. When conversion occurs, debt or preferred stock is replaced with common stock, but no money changes hands.

■ The **conversion** of bonds or preferred stock by their holders **does not provide additional funds** to the company, but it does result in a lower debt ratio. The **exercise of warrants does provide additional funds,** which strengthens the firm's equity position, but it still leaves the debt or preferred stock on the balance sheet. Thus, low interest rate debt remains outstanding when warrants are exercised, but the firm loses this advantage when convertibles are converted.

■ A **leveraged buyout (LBO)** is a transaction in which a firm's publicly owned stock is bought up in a mostly debt-financed tender offer, and a privately owned, highly leveraged firm results. Often, the firm's own management initiates the LBO.

■ The reasons **mergers** take place include (1) *synergy,* (2) *tax considerations,* (3) low *asset values,* (4) *diversification,* and (5) ownership *control.* Mergers can be classified as **horizontal, vertical, congeneric,** or **conglomerate.**

Questions

18–1 For purposes of measuring a firm's leverage, should preferred stock be classified as debt or equity? Does it matter if the classification is being made by (a) the firm's management, (b) creditors, or (c) equity investors?

18–2 You are told that one corporation just issued $100 million of preferred stock and another purchased $100 million of preferred stock as an investment. You are also told that one firm has an effective tax rate of 20 percent whereas the other is in the 34 percent bracket. Which firm is more likely to have bought the preferred? Explain.

18–3 One often finds that a company's bonds have a higher before-tax yield than its preferred stock, even though the bonds are considered to be less risky than the preferred to an investor. What causes this yield differential?

18–4 Distinguish between operating leases and financial leases. Would a firm be more likely to finance a fleet of trucks or a manufacturing plant with an operating lease?

18–5 One alleged advantage of leasing voiced in the past was that it kept liabilities off the balance sheet, thus making it possible for a firm to obtain more leverage than it otherwise could have. This raised the question of whether both the lease obligation and the asset involved should be capitalized and shown on the balance sheet. Discuss the pros and cons of capitalizing leases and related assets.

18–6 Suppose there were no IRS restrictions on what constitutes a valid lease. Explain in a manner that a legislator might understand why some restrictions should be imposed.

18–7 Suppose Congress changed the tax laws in a way that (a) permitted equipment to be depreciated over a shorter period, (b) lowered corporate tax rates, and (c) reinstated the investment tax credit. Discuss how each of these changes would affect the relative use of leasing versus conventional debt in the U.S. economy.

18–8 What effect does the expected growth rate of a firm's stock price (subsequent to issue) have on its ability to raise additional funds through (a) convertibles and (b) warrants?

18–9 a. How would a firm's decision to pay out a higher percentage of its earnings as dividends affect each of the following?
  (1) The value of its long-term warrants.
  (2) The likelihood that its convertible bonds will be converted.
  (3) The likelihood that its warrants will be exercised.
 b. If you owned the warrants or convertibles of a company, would you be pleased or displeased if it raised its payout rate from 20 percent to 80 percent? Why?

18–10 Suppose a company simultaneously issues $50 million of convertible bonds with a coupon rate of 9 percent and $50 million of pure bonds with a coupon rate of 12 percent. Both bonds have the same maturity. Does the fact that the convertible issue has the lower coupon rate suggest that it is less risky than the pure bond? Would you regard its cost of capital as being lower on the convertible than on the pure bond? Explain. (*Hint:* Although it might appear at first glance that the convertible's cost of capital is lower, this is not necessarily the case because the interest rate on the convertible understates its cost. Think about this.)

18–11 Describe how LBOs are used to finance mergers.

Self-Test Problems

(Solutions appear in Appendix B)

key terms ST-1 Define each of the following terms:
  a. Cumulative dividends
  b. Lessee; lessor
  c. Sale and leaseback; operating lease; financial lease
  d. Off-balance-sheet financing
  e. FASB #13
  f. Residual value
  g. Option; striking, or exercise, price; call option; put option
  h. Warrant; detachable warrant; stepped-up exercise price
  i. Convertible security; conversion ratio, CR

j. Simple EPS; primary EPS; fully diluted EPS

k. Leveraged buyout (LBO)

l. Merger; synergy

lease analysis **ST-2** The Olsen Company has decided to acquire a new truck. One alternative is to lease the truck on a four-year contract for a lease payment of $10,000 per year, with payments to be made at the beginning of each year. The lease would include maintenance. Alternatively, Olsen could purchase the truck outright for $40,000, financing with a bank loan for the net purchase price, amortized over a four-year period at an interest rate of 10 percent per year, payments to be made at the end of each year. Under the borrow-to-purchase arrangement, Olsen would have to maintain the truck at a cost of $1,000 per year, payable at year-end. The truck falls into the MACRS 3-year class. It has a salvage value of $10,000, which is the expected market value after four years, at which time Olsen plans to replace the truck irrespective of whether it leases or buys. Olsen has a marginal tax rate of 40 percent.

a. What is Olsen's PV cost of leasing?

b. What is Olsen's PV cost of owning? Should the truck be leased or purchased?

c. The appropriate discount rate for use in Olsen's analysis is the firm's after-tax cost of debt. Why?

d. The salvage value is the least certain cash flow in the analysis. How might Olsen incorporate the higher riskiness of this cash flow into the analysis?

Problems

balance sheet effects of leasing **18–1** Two textile companies, Grimm Manufacturing and Wright Mills, began operations with identical balance sheets. A year later, both required additional manufacturing capacity at a cost of $200,000. Grimm obtained a five-year, $200,000 loan at an 8 percent interest rate from its bank. Wright, on the other hand, decided to lease the required $200,000 capacity from American Leasing for five years; an 8 percent return was built into the lease. The balance sheet for each company, before the asset increases, is as follows:

		Debt	$200,000
		Equity	200,000
Total assets	$400,000	Total liabilities and equity	$400,000

a. Show the balance sheet of each firm after the asset increase, and calculate each firm's new debt ratio. (Assume Wright's lease is kept off the balance sheet.)

b. Show how Wright's balance sheet would have looked immediately after the financing if it had capitalized the lease.

c. Would the rate of return (i) on assets and (ii) on equity be affected by the choice of financing? How?

lease analysis **18–2** As part of its overall plant modernization and cost reduction program, the management of Teweles Textile Mills has decided to install a new automated weaving loom. In the capital budgeting analysis of this equipment, the IRR of the project was found to be 20 percent versus a project required return of 12 percent.

The loom has an invoice price of $250,000, including delivery and installation charges. The funds needed could be borrowed from the bank through a four-year amortized loan at a 10 percent interest rate, with payments to be made at the *end* of each year. In the event that the loom is purchased, the manufacturer will contract to maintain and service it for a fee of $20,000 per year paid at the end of each year. The loom falls in the MACRS 5-year class, and Teweles's marginal tax rate is 40 percent.

Apilado Automation Inc., maker of the loom, has offered to lease the loom to Teweles for $70,000 upon delivery and installation (at t = 0) plus four additional annual lease payments of $70,000 to be made at the ends of Years 1 through 4. (Note that there are five lease payments in total.) The lease agreement includes maintenance and servicing. Actually, the loom has an expected life of eight years, at which time its expected salvage value is zero; however, after four years, its market value is expected to equal its book value of $42,500. Teweles plans to build an entirely new plant in four years, so it has no interest in either leasing or owning the proposed loom for more than that period.

a. Should the loom be leased or purchased?

b. The salvage value clearly is the most uncertain cash flow in the analysis. Assume that the appropriate salvage value pretax discount rate is 15 percent. What would be the effect of a salvage value risk adjustment on the decision?

c. The original analysis assumed that Teweles would not need the loom after four years. Now assume that the firm will continue to use it after the lease expires. Thus, if it leased, Teweles would have to buy the asset after four years at the then existing market value, which is assumed to equal the book value. What effect would this requirement have on the basic analysis? (No numerical analysis is required; just verbalize.)

convertible bond   **18–3** The Swift Company was planning to finance an expansion in the summer of 2005. The principal executives of the company agreed that an industrial company like theirs should finance growth by means of common stock rather than by debt. However, they believed that the price of the company's common stock did not reflect its true worth, so they decided to sell a convertible bond.

a. What conversion price should be set by the issuer? The conversion rate will be 5.0; that is, each $1,000 face-value convertible bond can be converted into five shares of common.

b. Do you think the convertible bond should include a call provision? Why or why not?

financing alternatives   **18–4** The Cox Computer Company has grown rapidly during the past five years. Recently its commercial bank urged the company to consider increasing its permanent financing. Its bank loan under a line of credit has risen to $150,000, carrying a 10 percent interest rate, and Cox has been 30 to 60 days late in paying trade creditors.

Discussions with an investment banker have resulted in the decision to raise $250,000 at this time. Investment bankers have assured Cox that the following alternatives are feasible (flotation costs will be ignored):

Alternative 1: Sell common stock at $10 per share.

Alternative 2: Sell convertible bonds at a 10 percent coupon, convertible into 80 shares of common stock for each $1,000 bond (that is, the conversion price is $12.50 per share).

Alternative 3: Sell debentures with a 10 percent coupon; each $1,000 bond will have 80 warrants to buy one share of common stock at $12.50.

Charles Cox, the president, owns 80 percent of Cox's common stock and wishes to maintain control of the company; 50,000 shares are outstanding. The following are summaries of Cox's latest financial statements:

BALANCE SHEET

	Current liabilities	$200,000
	Common stock, $1 par	50,000
	Retained earnings	25,000
Total assets $275,000	Total liabilities and equity	$275,000

INCOME STATEMENT

Sales	$550,000
All costs except interest	(495,000)
EBIT	$ 55,000
Interest	(15,000)
EBT	$ 40,000
Taxes at 40%	(16,000)
Net income	$ 24,000
Shares outstanding	50,000
Earnings per share	$0.48
Price/earnings ratio	18×
Market price of stock	$8.64

a. Show the new balance sheet under each alternative. For Alternatives 2 and 3, show the balance sheet after conversion of the debentures or exercise of the warrants. Assume that $150,000 of the funds raised will be used to pay off the bank loan and the rest to increase total assets.

b. Show Charles Cox's control position under each alternative, assuming that he does not purchase additional shares.

c. What is the effect on earnings per share of each alternative if it is assumed that earnings before interest and taxes will be 20 percent of total assets?

d. What will be the debt ratio under each alternative?

e. Which of the three alternatives would you recommend to Charles Cox and why?

Exam-Type Problem

The problem included in this section is set up in such a way that it could be used as a multiple-choice exam problem.

lease versus buy

18–5 Maltese Mining Company must install $1.5 million of new machinery in its Nevada mine. It can obtain a bank loan for 100 percent of the required amount. Alternatively, a Nevada investment banking firm that represents a group of investors believes that it can arrange for a lease financing plan. Assume that the following facts apply:

(1) The equipment falls in the MACRS 3-year class.

(2) Estimated maintenance expenses are $75,000 per year.

(3) Maltese's marginal tax rate is 40 percent.

(4) If the money is borrowed, the bank loan will be at a rate of 15 percent, amortized in four equal installments to be paid at the end of each year.

(5) The tentative lease terms call for end-of-year payments of $400,000 per year for four years.

(6) Under the proposed lease terms, the lessee must pay for insurance, property taxes, and maintenance.

(7) Maltese must use the equipment if it is to continue in business, so it will almost certainly want to acquire the property at the end of the lease. If it does, then under the lease terms it can purchase the machinery at its fair market value at that time. The best estimate of this market value is the $250,000 salvage value, but it could be much higher or lower under certain circumstances.

To assist management in making the proper lease-versus-buy decision, you are asked to answer the following questions.

a. Assuming that the lease can be arranged, should Maltese lease or should it borrow to buy the equipment? Explain.

b. Consider the $250,000 estimated salvage value. Is it appropriate to discount it at the same rate as the other cash flows? What about the other cash flows—are they all equally risky? (*Hint:* Riskier cash flows are normally discounted at higher rates, but when the cash flows are *costs* rather than *inflows*, the normal procedure must be reversed.)

Integrative Problem

lease analysis

18–6 Kris Crawford, capital acquisitions manager for Heath Financial Services Inc., has been asked to perform a lease-versus-buy analysis on a new stock price quotation system for Heath's Sarasota branch office. The system would receive current prices, record the information for retrieval by the branch's brokers, and display current prices in the lobby.

The equipment costs $1,200,000, and, if it is purchased, Heath could obtain a term loan for the full amount at a 10 percent cost. The loan would be amortized over the four-year life of the equipment, with payments made at the end of each year. The equipment is classified as special purpose, and hence it falls into the MACRS 3-year class. If the equipment is purchased, a maintenance contract must be obtained at a cost of $25,000, payable at the beginning of each year.

After four years the equipment will be sold, and Crawford's best estimate of its residual value at that time is $125,000. Because technology is changing rapidly in real-time display systems, however, the residual value is uncertain.

As an alternative, National Leasing is willing to write a four-year lease on the equipment, including maintenance, for payments of $340,000 at the *begin-*

ning of each year. Heath's marginal tax rate is 40 percent. Help Crawford conduct her analysis by answering the following questions:

a. (1) Why is leasing sometimes referred to as *off-balance-sheet* financing?

(2) What is the difference between a capital lease and an operating lease?

(3) What effect does leasing have on a firm's capital structure?

b. (1) What is Heath's present value cost of owning the equipment? (*Hint:* Set up a table whose bottom line is a time line that shows the net cash flows over the period t = 0 to t = 4, and then find the PV of these net cash flows, or the PV cost of owning.)

(2) Explain the rationale for the discount rate you used to find the present value.

c. (1) What is Heath's present value cost of leasing the equipment? (*Hint:* Again, construct a cash flow time line.)

(2) What is the net advantage to leasing? Does your analysis indicate that Heath should buy or lease the equipment? Explain.

d. Now assume that Crawford believes the equipment's residual value could be as low as $0 or as high as $250,000, but she stands by $125,000 as her expected value. She concludes that the residual value is riskier than the other cash flows in the analysis, and she wants to incorporate this differential risk into her analysis. Describe how this could be accomplished. What effect would it have on Heath's lease decision?

e. Crawford knows that her firm has been considering moving to a new downtown location for some time, and she is concerned that these plans might come to fruition prior to the expiration of the lease. If the move occurs, the company would obtain completely new equipment, and hence Crawford would like to include a cancellation clause in the lease contract. What effect would a cancellation clause have on the riskiness of the lease?

Computer-Related Problem

Work the problem in this section only if you are using the computer problem diskette.

lease versus buy   **18–7** Use the model in File C18 to work this problem.

a. Refer to Problem 18-5. Determine the lease payment at which Maltese would be indifferent to buying or leasing—that is, find the lease payment that equates the NPV of leasing to that of buying. (*Hint:* Use trial and error.)

b. Using the $400,000 lease payment, what would be the effect if Maltese's tax rate fell to 20 percent? What would be the effect if the tax rate fell to zero percent? What do these results suggest?

GET REAL with Thomson ONE

18–8 Issuing preferred stock is one method that firms use to finance their operations. But, not all firms issue preferred stock. Allstate Corporation [ALL], an insurance and investments firm, does have preferred stock in its capital structure. Answer the following questions about Allstate:

a. Has the amount of preferred stock Allstate has outstanding increased or decreased during the past three years? [*Hint:* Click on Financials/Financial Statements]

b. Compare the relative amount of preferred stock Allstate uses with the relative amount used by its peers. [*Hint:* Click on Peers/Market Sector]

c. In general, did the use of preferred stock in this market sector increase or decrease during the three-year time period?

d. What are the advantages and disadvantages of using preferred stock financing?

e. Explain why companies in this market sector use preferred stock as a method of financial whereas companies in other industries do not?

Mathematical Tables

TABLE A–1	Present Value of $1 Due at the End of n Periods:

EQUATION:

$$PVIF_{k,n} = \frac{1}{(1 + k)^n}$$

FINANCIAL CALCULATOR KEYS:

n   k   0   1.0

N   **I**   **PV**   **PMT**   **FV**

Table
Value

PERIOD	1%	2%	3%	4%	5%	6%	7%	8%	9%	10%
1	.9901	.9804	.9709	.9615	.9524	.9434	.9346	.9259	.9174	.9091
2	.9803	.9612	.9426	.9246	.9070	.8900	.8734	.8573	.8417	.8264
3	.9706	.9423	.9151	.8890	.8638	.8396	.8163	.7938	.7722	.7513
4	.9610	.9238	.8885	.8548	.8227	.7921	.7629	.7350	.7084	.6830
5	.9515	.9057	.8626	.8219	.7835	.7473	.7130	.6806	.6499	.6209
6	.9420	.8880	.8375	.7903	.7462	.7050	.6663	.6302	.5963	.5645
7	.9327	.8706	.8131	.7599	.7107	.6651	.6227	.5835	.5470	.5132
8	.9235	.8535	.7894	.7307	.6768	.6274	.5820	.5403	.5019	.4665
9	.9143	.8368	.7664	.7026	.6446	.5919	.5439	.5002	.4604	.4241
10	.9053	.8203	.7441	.6756	.6139	.5584	.5083	.4632	.4224	.3855
11	.8963	.8043	.7224	.6496	.5847	.5268	.4751	.4289	.3875	.3505
12	.8874	.7885	.7014	.6246	.5568	.4970	.4440	.3971	.3555	.3186
13	.8787	.7730	.6810	.6006	.5303	.4688	.4150	.3677	.3262	.2897
14	.8700	.7579	.6611	.5775	.5051	.4423	.3878	.3405	.2992	.2633
15	.8613	.7430	.6419	.5553	.4810	.4173	.3624	.3152	.2745	.2394
16	.8528	.7284	.6232	.5339	.4581	.3936	.3387	.2919	.2519	.2176
17	.8444	.7142	.6050	.5134	.4363	.3714	.3166	.2703	.2311	.1978
18	.8360	.7002	.5874	.4936	.4155	.3503	.2959	.2502	.2120	.1799
19	.8277	.6864	.5703	.4746	.3957	.3305	.2765	.2317	.1945	.1635
20	.8195	.6730	.5537	.4564	.3769	.3118	.2584	.2145	.1784	.1486
21	.8114	.6598	.5375	.4388	.3589	.2942	.2415	.1987	.1637	.1351
22	.8034	.6468	.5219	.4220	.3418	.2775	.2257	.1839	.1502	.1228
23	.7954	.6342	.5067	.4057	.3256	.2618	.2109	.1703	.1378	.1117
24	.7876	.6217	.4919	.3901	.3101	.2470	.1971	.1577	.1264	.1015
25	.7798	.6095	.4776	.3751	.2953	.2330	.1842	.1460	.1160	.0923
26	.7720	.5976	.4637	.3607	.2812	.2198	.1722	.1352	.1064	.0839
27	.7644	.5859	.4502	.3468	.2678	.2074	.1609	.1252	.0976	.0763
28	.7568	.5744	.4371	.3335	.2551	.1956	.1504	.1159	.0895	.0693
29	.7493	.5631	.4243	.3207	.2429	.1846	.1406	.1073	.0822	.0630
30	.7419	.5521	.4120	.3083	.2314	.1741	.1314	.0994	.0754	.0573
35	.7059	.5000	.3554	.2534	.1813	.1301	.0937	.0676	.0490	.0356
40	.6717	.4529	.3066	.2083	.1420	.0972	.0668	.0460	.0318	.0221
45	.6391	.4102	.2644	.1712	.1113	.0727	.0476	.0313	.0207	.0137
50	.6080	.3715	.2281	.1407	.0872	.0543	.0339	.0213	.0134	.0085
55	.5785	.3365	.1968	.1157	.0683	.0406	.0242	.0145	.0087	.0053

| TABLE A–1 | Continued |

PERIOD	12%	14%	15%	16%	18%	20%	24%	28%	32%	36%
1	.8929	.8772	.8696	.8621	.8475	.8333	.8065	.7813	.7576	.7353
2	.7972	.7695	.7561	.7432	.7182	.6944	.6504	.6104	.5739	.5407
3	.7118	.6750	.6575	.6407	.6086	.5787	.5245	.4768	.4348	.3975
4	.6355	.5921	.5718	.5523	.5158	.4823	.4230	.3725	.3294	.2923
5	.5674	.5194	.4972	.4761	.4371	.4019	.3411	.2910	.2495	.2149
6	.5066	.4556	.4323	.4104	.3704	.3349	.2751	.2274	.1890	.1580
7	.4523	.3996	.3759	.3538	.3139	.2791	.2218	.1776	.1432	.1162
8	.4039	.3506	.3269	.3050	.2660	.2326	.1789	.1388	.1085	.0854
9	.3606	.3075	.2843	.2630	.2255	.1938	.1443	.1084	.0822	.0628
10	.3220	.2697	.2472	.2267	.1911	.1615	.1164	.0847	.0623	.0462
11	.2875	.2366	.2149	.1954	.1619	.1346	.0938	.0662	.0472	.0340
12	.2567	.2076	.1869	.1685	.1372	.1122	.0757	.0517	.0357	.0250
13	.2292	.1821	.1625	.1452	.1163	.0935	.0610	.0404	.0271	.0184
14	.2046	.1597	.1413	.1252	.0985	.0779	.0492	.0316	.0205	.0135
15	.1827	.1401	.1229	.1079	.0835	.0649	.0397	.0247	.0155	.0099
16	.1631	.1229	.1069	.0930	.0708	.0541	.0320	.0193	.0118	.0073
17	.1456	.1078	.0929	.0802	.0600	.0451	.0258	.0150	.0089	.0054
18	.1300	.0946	.0808	.0691	.0508	.0376	.0208	.0118	.0068	.0039
19	.1161	.0829	.0703	.0596	.0431	.0313	.0168	.0092	.0051	.0029
20	.1037	.0728	.0611	.0514	.0365	.0261	.0135	.0072	.0039	.0021
21	.0926	.0638	.0531	.0443	.0309	.0217	.0109	.0056	.0029	.0016
22	.0826	.0560	.0462	.0382	.0262	.0181	.0088	.0044	.0022	.0012
23	.0738	.0491	.0402	.0329	.0222	.0151	.0071	.0034	.0017	.0008
24	.0659	.0431	.0349	.0284	.0188	.0126	.0057	.0027	.0013	.0006
25	.0588	.0378	.0304	.0245	.0160	.0105	.0046	.0021	.0010	.0005
26	.0525	.0331	.0264	.0211	.0135	.0087	.0037	.0016	.0007	.0003
27	.0469	.0291	.0230	.0182	.0115	.0073	.0030	.0013	.0006	.0002
28	.0419	.0255	.0200	.0157	.0097	.0061	.0024	.0010	.0004	.0002
29	.0374	.0224	.0174	.0135	.0082	.0051	.0020	.0008	.0003	.0001
30	.0334	.0196	.0151	.0116	.0070	.0042	.0016	.0006	.0002	.0001
35	.0189	.0102	.0075	.0055	.0030	.0017	.0005	.0002	.0001	*
40	.0107	.0053	.0037	.0026	.0013	.0007	.0002	.0001	*	*
45	.0061	.0027	.0019	.0013	.0006	.0003	.0001	*	*	*
50	.0035	.0014	.0009	.0006	.0003	.0001	*	*	*	*
55	.0020	.0007	.0005	.0003	.0001	*	*	*	*	*

*The factor is zero to four decimal places.

TABLE A–2	Present Value of an Annuity of $1 per Period for n Periods:

EQUATION:

$$\text{PVIFA}_{k,n} = \sum_{t=1}^{N} \frac{1}{(1+k)^n} = \frac{1 - \dfrac{1}{(1+k)^n}}{k} = \frac{1}{i} - \frac{1}{i(1+i)^n}$$

FINANCIAL CALCULATOR KEYS:

n	k		1.0	0
N	**I**	**PV**	**PMT**	**FV**
		Table Value		

NUMBER OF PERIODS	1%	2%	3%	4%	5%	6%	7%	8%	9%
1	0.9901	0.9804	0.9709	0.9615	0.9524	0.9434	0.9346	0.9259	0.9174
2	1.9704	1.9416	1.9135	1.8861	1.8594	1.8334	1.8080	1.7833	1.7591
3	2.9410	2.8839	2.8286	2.7751	2.7232	2.6730	2.6243	2.5771	2.5313
4	3.9020	3.8077	3.7171	3.6299	3.5460	3.4651	3.3872	3.3121	3.2397
5	4.8534	4.7135	4.5797	4.4518	4.3295	4.2124	4.1002	3.9927	3.8897
6	5.7955	5.6014	5.4172	5.2421	5.0757	4.9173	4.7665	4.6229	4.4859
7	6.7282	6.4720	6.2303	6.0021	5.7864	5.5824	5.3893	5.2064	5.0330
8	7.6517	7.3255	7.0197	6.7327	6.4632	6.2098	5.9713	5.7466	5.5348
9	8.5660	8.1622	7.7861	7.4353	7.1078	6.8017	6.5152	6.2469	5.9952
10	9.4713	8.9826	8.5302	8.1109	7.7217	7.3601	7.0236	6.7101	6.4177
11	10.3676	9.7868	9.2526	8.7605	8.3064	7.8869	7.4987	7.1390	6.8052
12	11.2551	10.5753	9.9540	9.3851	8.8633	8.3838	7.9427	7.5361	7.1607
13	12.1337	11.3484	10.6350	9.9856	9.3936	8.8527	8.3577	7.9038	7.4869
14	13.0037	12.1062	11.2961	10.5631	9.8986	9.2950	8.7455	8.2442	7.7862
15	13.8651	12.8493	11.9379	11.1184	10.3797	9.7122	9.1079	8.5595	8.0607
16	14.7179	13.5777	12.5611	11.6523	10.8378	10.1059	9.4466	8.8514	8.3126
17	15.5623	14.2919	13.1661	12.1657	11.2741	10.4773	9.7632	9.1216	8.5436
18	16.3983	14.9920	13.7535	12.6593	11.6896	10.8276	10.0591	9.3719	8.7556
19	17.2260	15.6785	14.3238	13.1339	12.0853	11.1581	10.3356	9.6036	8.9501
20	18.0456	16.3514	14.8775	13.5903	12.4622	11.4699	10.5940	9.8181	9.1285
21	18.8570	17.0112	15.4150	14.0292	12.8212	11.7641	10.8355	10.0168	9.2922
22	19.6604	17.6580	15.9369	14.4511	13.1630	12.0416	11.0612	10.2007	9.4424
23	20.4558	18.2922	16.4436	14.8568	13.4886	12.3034	11.2722	10.3711	9.5802
24	21.2434	18.9139	16.9355	15.2470	13.7986	12.5504	11.4693	10.5288	9.7066
25	22.0232	19.5235	17.4131	15.6221	14.0939	12.7834	11.6536	10.6748	9.8226
26	22.7952	20.1210	17.8768	15.9828	14.3752	13.0032	11.8258	10.8100	9.9290
27	23.5596	20.7069	18.3270	16.3296	14.6430	13.2105	11.9867	10.9352	10.0266
28	24.3164	21.2813	18.7641	16.6631	14.8981	13.4062	12.1371	11.0511	10.1161
29	25.0658	21.8444	19.1885	16.9837	15.1411	13.5907	12.2777	11.1584	10.1983
30	25.8077	22.3965	19.6004	17.2920	15.3725	13.7648	12.4090	11.2578	10.2737
35	29.4086	24.9986	21.4872	18.6646	16.3742	14.4982	12.9477	11.6546	10.5668
40	32.8347	27.3555	23.1148	19.7928	17.1591	15.0463	13.3317	11.9246	10.7574
45	36.0945	29.4902	24.5187	20.7200	17.7741	15.4558	13.6055	12.1084	10.8812
50	39.1961	31.4236	25.7298	21.4822	18.2559	15.7619	13.8007	12.2335	10.9617
55	42.1472	33.1748	26.7744	22.1086	18.6335	15.9905	13.9399	12.3186	11.0140

TABLE A-2 Continued

NUMBER OF PERIODS	10%	12%	14%	15%	16%	18%	20%	24%	28%	32%
1	0.9091	0.8929	0.8772	0.8696	0.8621	0.8475	0.8333	0.8065	0.7813	0.7576
2	1.7355	1.6901	1.6467	1.6257	1.6052	1.5656	1.5278	1.4568	1.3916	1.3315
3	2.4869	2.4018	2.3216	2.2832	2.2459	2.1743	2.1065	1.9813	1.8684	1.7663
4	3.1699	3.0373	2.9137	2.8550	2.7982	2.6901	2.5887	2.4043	2.2410	2.0957
5	3.7908	3.6048	3.4331	3.3522	3.2743	3.1272	2.9906	2.7454	2.5320	2.3452
6	4.3553	4.1114	3.8887	3.7845	3.6847	3.4976	3.3255	3.0205	2.7594	2.5342
7	4.8684	4.5638	4.2883	4.1604	4.0386	3.8115	3.6046	3.2423	2.9370	2.6775
8	5.3349	4.9676	4.6389	4.4873	4.3436	4.0776	3.8372	3.4212	3.0758	2.7860
9	5.7590	5.3282	4.9464	4.7716	4.6065	4.3030	4.0310	3.5655	3.1842	2.8681
10	6.1446	5.6502	5.2161	5.0188	4.8332	4.4941	4.1925	3.6819	3.2689	2.9304
11	6.4951	5.9377	5.4527	5.2337	5.0286	4.6560	4.3271	3.7757	3.3351	2.9776
12	6.8137	6.1944	5.6603	5.4206	5.1971	4.7932	4.4392	3.8514	3.3868	3.0133
13	7.1034	6.4235	5.8424	5.5831	5.3423	4.9095	4.5327	3.9124	3.4272	3.0404
14	7.3667	6.6282	6.0021	5.7245	5.4675	5.0081	4.6106	3.9616	3.4587	3.0609
15	7.6061	6.8109	6.1422	5.8474	5.5755	5.0916	4.6755	4.0013	3.4834	3.0764
16	7.8237	6.9740	6.2651	5.9542	5.6685	5.1624	4.7296	4.0333	3.5026	3.0882
17	8.0216	7.1196	6.3729	6.0472	5.7487	5.2223	4.7746	4.0591	3.5177	3.0971
18	8.2014	7.2497	6.4674	6.1280	5.8178	5.2732	4.8122	4.0799	3.5294	3.1039
19	8.3649	7.3658	6.5504	6.1982	5.8775	5.3162	4.8435	4.0967	3.5386	3.1090
20	8.5136	7.4694	6.6231	6.2593	5.9288	5.3527	4.8696	4.1103	3.5458	3.1129
21	8.6487	7.5620	6.6870	6.3125	5.9731	5.3837	4.8913	4.1212	3.5514	3.1158
22	8.7715	7.6446	6.7429	6.3587	6.0113	5.4099	4.9094	4.1300	3.5558	3.1180
23	8.8832	7.7184	6.7921	6.3988	6.0442	5.4321	4.9245	4.1371	3.5592	3.1197
24	8.9847	7.7843	6.8351	6.4338	6.0726	5.4509	4.9371	4.1428	3.5619	3.1210
25	9.0770	7.8431	6.8729	6.4641	6.0971	5.4669	4.9476	4.1474	3.5640	3.1220
26	9.1609	7.8957	6.9061	6.4906	6.1182	5.4804	4.9563	4.1511	3.5656	3.1227
27	9.2372	7.9426	6.9352	6.5135	6.1364	5.4919	4.9636	4.1542	3.5669	3.1233
28	9.3066	7.9844	6.9607	6.5335	6.1520	5.5016	4.9697	4.1566	3.5679	3.1237
29	9.3696	8.0218	6.9830	6.5509	6.1656	5.5098	4.9747	4.1585	3.5687	3.1240
30	9.4269	8.0552	7.0027	6.5660	6.1772	5.5168	4.9789	4.1601	3.5693	3.1242
35	9.6442	8.1755	7.0700	6.6166	6.2153	5.5386	4.9915	4.1644	3.5708	3.1248
40	9.7791	8.2438	7.1050	6.6418	6.2335	5.5482	4.9966	4.1659	3.5712	3.1250
45	9.8628	8.2825	7.1232	6.6543	6.2421	5.5523	4.9986	4.1664	3.5714	3.1250
50	9.9148	8.3045	7.1327	6.6605	6.2463	5.5541	4.9995	4.1666	3.5714	3.1250
55	9.9471	8.3170	7.1376	6.6636	6.2482	5.5549	4.9998	4.1666	3.5714	3.1250

| TABLE A–3 | Future Value of $1 at the End of n Periods: |

EQUATION:

$$FVIF_{k,n} = (1 + k)^n$$

FINANCIAL CALCULATOR KEYS:

n	k	1.0	0	
N	**I**	**PV**	**PMT**	**FV**
				Table Value

PERIOD	1%	2%	3%	4%	5%	6%	7%	8%	9%	10%
1	1.0100	1.0200	1.0300	1.0400	1.0500	1.0600	1.0700	1.0800	1.0900	1.1000
2	1.0201	1.0404	1.0609	1.0816	1.1025	1.1236	1.1449	1.1664	1.1881	1.2100
3	1.0303	1.0612	1.0927	1.1249	1.1576	1.1910	1.2250	1.2597	1.2950	1.3310
4	1.0406	1.0824	1.1255	1.1699	1.2155	1.2625	1.3108	1.3605	1.4116	1.4641
5	1.0510	1.1041	1.1593	1.2167	1.2763	1.3382	1.4026	1.4693	1.5386	1.6105
6	1.0615	1.1262	1.1941	1.2653	1.3401	1.4185	1.5007	1.5869	1.6771	1.7716
7	1.0721	1.1487	1.2299	1.3159	1.4071	1.5036	1.6058	1.7138	1.8280	1.9487
8	1.0829	1.1717	1.2668	1.3686	1.4775	1.5938	1.7182	1.8509	1.9926	2.1436
9	1.0937	1.1951	1.3048	1.4233	1.5513	1.6895	1.8385	1.9990	2.1719	2.3579
10	1.1046	1.2190	1.3439	1.4802	1.6289	1.7908	1.9672	2.1589	2.3674	2.5937
11	1.1157	1.2434	1.3842	1.5395	1.7103	1.8983	2.1049	2.3316	2.5804	2.8531
12	1.1268	1.2682	1.4258	1.6010	1.7959	2.0122	2.2522	2.5182	2.8127	3.1384
13	1.1381	1.2936	1.4685	1.6651	1.8856	2.1329	2.4098	2.7196	3.0658	3.4523
14	1.1495	1.3195	1.5126	1.7317	1.9799	2.2609	2.5785	2.9372	3.3417	3.7975
15	1.1610	1.3459	1.5580	1.8009	2.0789	2.3966	2.7590	3.1722	3.6425	4.1772
16	1.1726	1.3728	1.6047	1.8730	2.1829	2.5404	2.9522	3.4259	3.9703	4.5950
17	1.1843	1.4002	1.6528	1.9479	2.2920	2.6928	3.1588	3.7000	4.3276	5.0545
18	1.1961	1.4282	1.7024	2.0258	2.4066	2.8543	3.3799	3.9960	4.7171	5.5599
19	1.2081	1.4568	1.7535	2.1068	2.5270	3.0256	3.6165	4.3157	5.1417	6.1159
20	1.2202	1.4859	1.8061	2.1911	2.6533	3.2071	3.8697	4.6610	5.6044	6.7275
21	1.2324	1.5157	1.8603	2.2788	2.7860	3.3996	4.1406	5.0338	6.1088	7.4002
22	1.2447	1.5460	1.9161	2.3699	2.9253	3.6035	4.4304	5.4365	6.6586	8.1403
23	1.2572	1.5769	1.9736	2.4647	3.0715	3.8197	4.7405	5.8715	7.2579	8.9543
24	1.2697	1.6084	2.0328	2.5633	3.2251	4.0489	5.0724	6.3412	7.9111	9.8497
25	1.2824	1.6406	2.0938	2.6658	3.3864	4.2919	5.4274	6.8485	8.6231	10.835
26	1.2953	1.6734	2.1566	2.7725	3.5557	4.5494	5.8074	7.3964	9.3992	11.918
27	1.3082	1.7069	2.2213	2.8834	3.7335	4.8223	6.2139	7.9881	10.245	13.110
28	1.3213	1.7410	2.2879	2.9987	3.9201	5.1117	6.6488	8.6271	11.167	14.421
29	1.3345	1.7758	2.3566	3.1187	4.1161	5.4184	7.1143	9.3173	12.172	15.863
30	1.3478	1.8114	2.4273	3.2434	4.3219	5.7435	7.6123	10.063	13.268	17.449
40	1.4889	2.2080	3.2620	4.8010	7.0400	10.286	14.974	21.725	31.409	45.259
50	1.6446	2.6916	4.3839	7.1067	11.467	18.420	29.457	46.902	74.358	117.39
60	1.8167	3.2810	5.8916	10.520	18.679	32.988	57.946	101.26	176.03	304.48

TABLE A–3	Continued

PERIOD	12%	14%	15%	16%	18%	20%	24%	28%	32%	36%
1	1.1200	1.1400	1.1500	1.1600	1.1800	1.2000	1.2400	1.2800	1.3200	1.3600
2	1.2544	1.2996	1.3225	1.3456	1.3924	1.4400	1.5376	1.6384	1.7424	1.8496
3	1.4049	1.4815	1.5209	1.5609	1.6430	1.7280	1.9066	2.0972	2.3000	2.5155
4	1.5735	1.6890	1.7490	1.8106	1.9388	2.0736	2.3642	2.6844	3.0360	3.4210
5	1.7623	1.9254	2.0114	2.1003	2.2878	2.4883	2.9316	3.4360	4.0075	4.6526
6	1.9738	2.1950	2.3131	2.4364	2.6996	2.9860	3.6352	4.3980	5.2899	6.3275
7	2.2107	2.5023	2.6600	2.8262	3.1855	3.5832	4.5077	5.6295	6.9826	8.6054
8	2.4760	2.8526	3.0590	3.2784	3.7589	4.2998	5.5895	7.2058	9.2170	11.703
9	2.7731	3.2519	3.5179	3.8030	4.4355	5.1598	6.9310	9.2234	12.166	15.917
10	3.1058	3.7072	4.0456	4.4114	5.2338	6.1917	8.5944	11.806	16.060	21.647
11	3.4785	4.2262	4.6524	5.1173	6.1759	7.4301	10.657	15.112	21.199	29.439
12	3.8960	4.8179	5.3503	5.9360	7.2876	8.9161	13.215	19.343	27.983	40.037
13	4.3635	5.4924	6.1528	6.8858	8.5994	10.699	16.386	24.759	36.937	54.451
14	4.8871	6.2613	7.0757	7.9875	10.147	12.839	20.319	31.691	48.757	74.053
15	5.4736	7.1379	8.1371	9.2655	11.974	15.407	25.196	40.565	64.359	100.71
16	6.1304	8.1372	9.3576	10.748	14.129	18.488	31.243	51.923	84.954	136.97
17	6.8660	9.2765	10.761	12.468	16.672	22.186	38.741	66.461	112.14	186.28
18	7.6900	10.575	12.375	14.463	19.673	26.623	48.039	85.071	148.02	253.34
19	8.6128	12.056	14.232	16.777	23.214	31.948	59.568	108.89	195.39	344.54
20	9.6463	13.743	16.367	19.461	27.393	38.338	73.864	139.38	257.92	468.57
21	10.804	15.668	18.822	22.574	32.324	46.005	91.592	178.41	340.45	637.26
22	12.100	17.861	21.645	26.186	38.142	55.206	113.57	228.36	449.39	866.67
23	13.552	20.362	24.891	30.376	45.008	66.247	140.83	292.30	593.20	1178.7
24	15.179	23.212	28.625	35.236	53.109	79.497	174.63	374.14	783.02	1603.0
25	17.000	26.462	32.919	40.874	62.669	95.396	216.54	478.90	1033.6	2180.1
26	19.040	30.167	37.857	47.414	73.949	114.48	268.51	613.00	1364.3	2964.9
27	21.325	34.390	43.535	55.000	87.260	137.37	332.95	784.64	1800.9	4032.3
28	23.884	39.204	50.066	63.800	102.97	164.84	412.86	1004.3	2377.2	5483.9
29	26.750	44.693	57.575	74.009	121.50	197.81	511.95	1285.6	3137.9	7458.1
30	29.960	50.950	66.212	85.850	143.37	237.38	634.82	1645.5	4142.1	10143.
40	93.051	188.88	267.86	378.72	750.38	1469.8	5455.9	19427.	66521.	*
50	289.00	700.23	1083.7	1670.7	3927.4	9100.4	46890.	*	*	*
60	897.60	2595.9	4384.0	7370.2	20555.	56348.	*	*	*	*

*FVIF > 99,999.

TABLE A–4	Future Value of an Annuity of $1 per Period for n Periods:

EQUATION:

$$FVIFA_{k,n} = \sum_{t=1}^{n} (1 + k)^{n-t} = \frac{(1 + k)^n - 1}{i}$$

FINANCIAL CALCULATOR KEYS:

n	k	0	1.0	
N	**I**	**PV**	**PMT**	**FV**
				Table Value

NUMBER OF PERIODS	1%	2%	3%	4%	5%	6%	7%	8%	9%	10%
1	1.0000	1.0000	1.0000	1.0000	1.0000	1.0000	1.0000	1.0000	1.0000	1.0000
2	2.0100	2.0200	2.0300	2.0400	2.0500	2.0600	2.0700	2.0800	2.0900	2.1000
3	3.0301	3.0604	3.0909	3.1216	3.1525	3.1836	3.2149	3.2464	3.2781	3.3100
4	4.0604	4.1216	4.1836	4.2465	4.3101	4.3746	4.4399	4.5061	4.5731	4.6410
5	5.1010	5.2040	5.3091	5.4163	5.5256	5.6371	5.7507	5.8666	5.9847	6.1051
6	6.1520	6.3081	6.4684	6.6330	6.8019	6.9753	7.1533	7.3359	7.5233	7.7156
7	7.2135	7.4343	7.6625	7.8983	8.1420	8.3938	8.6540	8.9228	9.2004	9.4872
8	8.2857	8.5830	8.8923	9.2142	9.5491	9.8975	10.260	10.637	11.028	11.436
9	9.3685	9.7546	10.159	10.583	11.027	11.491	11.978	12.488	13.021	13.579
10	10.462	10.950	11.464	12.006	12.578	13.181	13.816	14.487	15.193	15.937
11	11.567	12.169	12.808	13.486	14.207	14.972	15.784	16.645	17.560	18.531
12	12.683	13.412	14.192	15.026	15.917	16.870	17.888	18.977	20.141	21.384
13	13.809	14.680	15.618	16.627	17.713	18.882	20.141	21.495	22.953	24.523
14	14.947	15.974	17.086	18.292	19.599	21.015	22.550	24.215	26.019	27.975
15	16.097	17.293	18.599	20.024	21.579	23.276	25.129	27.152	29.361	31.772
16	17.258	18.639	20.157	21.825	23.657	25.673	27.888	30.324	33.003	35.950
17	18.430	20.012	21.762	23.698	25.840	28.213	30.840	33.750	36.974	40.545
18	19.615	21.412	23.414	25.645	28.132	30.906	33.999	37.450	41.301	45.599
19	20.811	22.841	25.117	27.671	30.539	33.760	37.379	41.446	46.018	51.159
20	22.019	24.297	26.870	29.778	33.066	36.786	40.995	45.762	51.160	57.275
21	23.239	25.783	28.676	31.969	35.719	39.993	44.865	50.423	56.765	64.002
22	24.472	27.299	30.537	34.248	38.505	43.392	49.006	55.457	62.873	71.403
23	25.716	28.845	32.453	36.618	41.430	46.996	53.436	60.893	69.532	79.543
24	26.973	30.422	34.426	39.083	44.502	50.816	58.177	66.765	76.790	88.497
25	28.243	32.030	36.459	41.646	47.727	54.865	63.249	73.106	84.701	98.347
26	29.526	33.671	38.553	44.312	51.113	59.156	68.676	79.954	93.324	109.18
27	30.821	35.344	40.710	47.084	54.669	63.706	74.484	87.351	102.72	121.10
28	32.129	37.051	42.931	49.968	58.403	68.528	80.698	95.339	112.97	134.21
29	33.450	38.792	45.219	52.966	62.323	73.640	87.347	103.97	124.14	148.63
30	34.785	40.568	47.575	56.085	66.439	79.058	94.461	113.28	136.31	164.49
40	48.886	60.402	75.401	95.026	120.80	154.76	199.64	259.06	337.88	442.59
50	64.463	84.579	112.80	152.67	209.35	290.34	406.53	573.77	815.08	1163.9
60	81.670	114.05	163.05	237.99	353.58	533.13	813.52	1253.2	1944.8	3034.8

TABLE A-4 Continued

NUMBER OF PERIODS	12%	14%	15%	16%	18%	20%	24%	28%	32%	36%
1	1.0000	1.0000	1.0000	1.0000	1.0000	1.0000	1.0000	1.0000	1.0000	1.0000
2	2.1200	2.1400	2.1500	2.1600	2.1800	2.2000	2.2400	2.2800	2.3200	2.3600
3	3.3744	3.4396	3.4725	3.5056	3.5724	3.6400	3.7776	3.9184	4.0624	4.2096
4	4.7793	4.9211	4.9934	5.0665	5.2154	5.3680	5.6842	6.0156	6.3624	6.7251
5	6.3528	6.6101	6.7424	6.8771	7.1542	7.4416	8.0484	8.6999	9.3983	10.146
6	8.1152	8.5355	8.7537	8.9775	9.4420	9.9299	10.980	12.136	13.406	14.799
7	10.089	10.730	11.067	11.414	12.142	12.916	14.615	16.534	18.696	21.126
8	12.300	13.233	13.727	14.240	15.327	16.499	19.123	22.163	25.678	29.732
9	14.776	16.085	16.786	17.519	19.086	20.799	24.712	29.369	34.895	41.435
10	17.549	19.337	20.304	21.321	23.521	25.959	31.643	38.593	47.062	57.352
11	20.655	23.045	24.349	25.733	28.755	32.150	40.238	50.398	63.122	78.998
12	24.133	27.271	29.002	30.850	34.931	39.581	50.895	65.510	84.320	108.44
13	28.029	32.089	34.352	36.786	42.219	48.497	64.110	84.853	112.30	148.47
14	32.393	37.581	40.505	43.672	50.818	59.196	80.496	109.61	149.24	202.93
15	37.280	43.842	47.580	51.660	60.965	72.035	100.82	141.30	198.00	276.98
16	42.753	50.980	55.717	60.925	72.939	87.442	126.01	181.87	262.36	377.69
17	48.884	59.118	65.075	71.673	87.068	105.93	157.25	233.79	347.31	514.66
18	55.750	68.394	75.836	84.141	103.74	128.12	195.99	300.25	459.45	700.94
19	63.440	78.969	88.212	98.603	123.41	154.74	244.03	385.32	607.47	954.28
20	72.052	91.025	102.44	115.38	146.63	186.69	303.60	494.21	802.86	1298.8
21	81.699	104.77	118.81	134.84	174.02	225.03	377.46	633.59	1060.8	1767.4
22	92.503	120.44	137.63	157.41	206.34	271.03	469.06	812.00	1401.2	2404.7
23	104.60	138.30	159.28	183.60	244.49	326.24	582.63	1040.4	1850.6	3271.3
24	118.16	158.66	184.17	213.98	289.49	392.48	723.46	1332.7	2443.8	4450.0
25	133.33	181.87	212.79	249.21	342.60	471.98	898.09	1706.8	3226.8	6053.0
26	150.33	208.33	245.71	290.09	405.27	567.38	1114.6	2185.7	4260.4	8233.1
27	169.37	238.50	283.57	337.50	479.22	681.85	1383.1	2798.7	5624.8	11198.0
28	190.70	272.89	327.10	392.50	566.48	819.22	1716.1	3583.3	7425.7	15230.3
29	214.58	312.09	377.17	456.30	669.45	984.07	2129.0	4587.7	9802.9	20714.2
30	241.33	356.79	434.75	530.31	790.95	1181.9	2640.9	5873.2	12941.	28172.3
40	767.09	1342.0	1779.1	2360.8	4163.2	7343.9	22729.	69377.	*	*
50	2400.0	4994.5	7217.7	10436.	21813.	45497.	*	*	*	*
60	7471.6	18535.	29220.	46058.	*	*	*	*	*	*

*FVIFA > 99,999.

Solutions to Self-Test Problems

Note: Except for Chapter 1, we do not show an answer for ST-1 problems because they are verbal rather than quantitative in nature.

Chapter 1

ST-1 Refer to the marginal glossary definitions or relevant chapter sections to check your responses.

Chapter 2

ST-2 **a.** Average = (2% + 3% + 5% + 6%)/4 = 16%/4 = 4.0%.
  b. $k_{T\text{-bond}} = k^* + IP = 3.0\% + 4.0\% = 7.0\%$.
  c. If the five-year T-bond rate is 8 percent, the inflation rate is expected to average approximately 8% − 3% = 5% during the next five years. Thus, the implied Year 5 inflation rate is 9 percent:

$$5\% = (2\% + 3\% + 5\% + 6\% + I_5)/5$$

$$25\% = 16\% + I_5$$

$$Infl_5 = 9\%.$$

ST–3 YTM = average of the one-year rates for each of the next three years:

$$YTM_{3\text{-year}} = (5\% + 9\% + 4\%)/3 = 6\%$$

Chapter 3

ST-2 a. (1)

$$FV_n = PV(1 + k)^n$$

$$\$7,020 = \$5,500(1 + k)^5$$

$$(1 + k)^5 = \frac{\$7,020}{\$5,500} = 1.2764$$

To solve for the rate, use your calculator or solve algebraically. Using your calculator, enter N = 5, FV = 7,020, PV = −5,500, and then press the I key—you should find the result is 5.001. To solve algebraically, recognize that, according to the above computations, $(1 + k)^5 = 1.276364$ (carried to 6 places). Therefore,

$$(1 + k)^5 = 1.276364$$

$$k = (1.276364)^{1/5} = 0.05001 = 5.001\%$$

(2)

0	k = ?	1	2	3	4	5	6	7	8

−5,500   8,126

$$FV_n = PV(1 + k)^n$$

$$\$8,126 = \$5,500(1 + k)^8$$

$$(1 + k)^8 = \frac{\$8,126}{\$5,500} = 1.4775$$

$$k = (1.4775)^{1/8} - 1 = 0.05 = 5.0\%$$

Using your calculator or solving algebraically will yield the same result. Because both investments yield the same return, you should be indifferent between them.

b. If you believe there is greater uncertainty about whether the eight-year investment will pay the amount expected ($8,126) than about whether the five-year investment will pay the amount expected ($7,020), then you should prefer the shorter-term investment. We discuss the effects of risk on value in Chapter 5.

ST-3 a.

1/1/05	8%	1/1/06	1/1/07	1/1/08	1/1/09

                                    −1,000   FV = ?

$1,000 is being compounded for three years, so your balance on January 1, 2009, is $1,259.71:

$$FV_n = PV(1 + k)^n = \$1,000(1 + 0.08)^3 = \$1,259.71.$$

Alternatively, using a financial calculator, input N = 3, I = 8, PV = −1,000, PMT = 0, and FV = ?; FV = $1,259.71.

b.

1/1/05	1/1/06	1/1/07	1/1/08	1/1/09

2%

                        −1,000   FV = ?

$$FV = PV\left(1 + \frac{k}{m}\right)^{n \times m}$$

$$= \$1,000\left(1 + \frac{0.08}{4}\right)^{4 \times 3}$$

$$= \$1,000(1.26824) = \$1,268.24$$

Alternatively, using a financial calculator, input N = 12, I = 2, PV = −1000, PMT = 0, and FV = ?; FV = $1,268.24.

c.

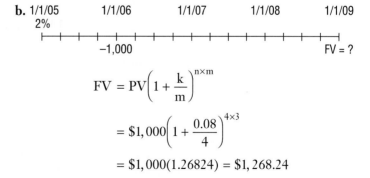

1/1/05	8%	1/1/06	1/1/07	1/1/08	1/1/09

                                    250   250   250   250
                                                                    FV = ?

Using a financial calculator, input N = 4, I = 8, PV = 0, PMT = −250, and FV = ?; FV = $1,126.53

d.

1/1/05	8%	1/1/06	1/1/07	1/1/08	1/1/09
		PMT	PMT	PMT	PMT
					FV = 1,259.71

N = 4; I = 8%; PV = 0; FV = $1,259.71; PMT = ?; PMT = $279.56.

Therefore, you would have to make 4 payments of $279.56 each to have a balance of $1,259.71 on January 1, 2009.

ST-4 a. Set up a time line like the one in the preceding problem:

1/1/05	8%	1/1/06	1/1/07	1/1/08	1/1/09
		PV = ?			1,000

Note that your deposit will grow for three years at 8 percent. The fact that it is now January 1, 2005, is irrelevant. The deposit on January 1, 2006, is the PV, and the FV is $1,000. Here is the solution:

N = 3; I = 8%; PMT = 0; FV = $1,000; PV = ?; PV = $793.83.

$$PV = \$1,000 \left[\frac{1}{(1.08)^3} \right] = \$1,000(0.79383) = \$793.83$$

= Initial deposit to accumulate $1,000.

b.

1/1/05	8%	1/1/06	1/1/07	1/1/08	1/1/09
		PMT	PMT	PMT	PMT
					FV = 1,000

Here we are dealing with a four-year annuity whose first payment occurs one year from today, on 1/1/06, and whose future value must equal $1,000. You should modify the time line to help visualize the situation. Here is the solution:

N = 4; I = 8%; PV = 0; FV = $1,000; PMT = ?; PMT = $221.92.

$$FVA_4 = PMT \left[\frac{(1.08)^4 - 1}{0.08} \right] = \$1,000$$

$$PMT = \frac{\$1,000}{4.50611}$$

$$= \frac{\$1,000}{4.50611} = \$221.92 = \begin{matrix} \text{Payment necessary to} \\ \text{accumulate } \$1,000. \end{matrix}$$

c. This problem can be approached in several ways. Perhaps the simplest is to ask this question: "If I received $750 on 1/1/06 and deposited it to earn 8 percent, would I have acquired $1,000 on 1/1/09?" The answer is no:

1/1/05	8%	1/1/06	1/1/07	1/1/08	1/1/09
		−750			FV = ?

$$FV_3 = \$750(1.08)^3 = \$944.78.$$

This indicates that you should let your father make the payments rather than accept the lump sum of $750.

You could also compare the $750 with the PV of the payments:

1/1/05	8%	1/1/06	1/1/07	1/1/08	1/1/09
PV = ?		221.92	221.92	221.92	221.92

$$N = 4; \ I = 8\%; \ PMT = -\$221.92; \ FV = 0; \ PV = ?; \ PV = \$735.03$$

$$PVA_4 = \$735.03 = \$221.92 \left[\frac{1 - \dfrac{1}{(1.08)^4}}{0.08} \right]$$

$$\$221.92(3.31212) = \$735.03 = \begin{array}{l} \text{Present value at } 1/1/01 \text{ of} \\ \text{the required payments.} \end{array}$$

This is less than the $750 lump sum offer, so your initial reaction might be to accept the lump sum of $750. However, this would be a mistake. The problem is that when you found the $735.03 PV of the annuity, you were finding the value of the annuity *today*, on January 1, 2005. You were comparing $735.03 today with the lump sum of $750 one year from now. This is, of course, invalid. What you should have done was take the $735.03, recognize that this is the PV of an annuity as of January 1, 2005, multiply $735.03 by 1.08 to get $793.83, and compare $793.83 with the lump sum of $750. You would then take your father's offer to make the payments rather than take the lump sum on January 1, 2006. If you solved the PV for an annuity due, you would find the same answer.

d.

1/1/05	k = ?	1/1/06	1/1/07	1/1/08	1/1/09
		−750			1,000

$$N = 3; \ PV = -\$750; \ PMT = 0; \ FV = \$1,000; \ I = ?; \ I = 10.0642\%.$$

e.

1/1/05	k = ?	1/1/06	1/1/07	1/1/08	1/1/09
		186.29	186.29	186.29	186.29
					FV = 1,000

$$N = 4; \ PV = 0; \ PMT = -\$186.29; \ FV = \$1,000: \ I = ?; \ I = 19.9997\%.$$

You might be able to find a borrower willing to offer you a 20 percent interest rate, but there would be some risk involved—he or she might not actually pay you your $1,000 on January 1, 2009.

f.

1/1/05	8%/2	1/1/06	1/1/07	1/1/08	1/1/09
		400 PMT	PMT PMT	PMT PMT	PMT
					FV = 1,000

Find the future value of the original $400 deposit:

$$FV_6 = 400(1.04)^6 = \$400(1.26532) = \$506.13.$$

This means that on January 1, 2009, you need an additional sum of $493.87:

$$\$1,000.00 - \$506.13 = \$493.87.$$

This will be accumulated by making six equal payments that earn 8 percent compounded semiannually, or 4 percent each six months:

$$N = 6; \ I = 4\%; \ PV = 0; \ FV = \$493.87; \ PMT = ?; \ PMT = 74.46.$$

g.   Effective annual rate $= \left(1 + \dfrac{k_{SIMPL:E}}{m}\right)^m - 1.0$

$$= \left(1 + \dfrac{0.08}{2}\right)^2 - 1 = (1.04)^2 - 1$$

$$= 1.0816 - 1 = 0.0816 = 8.16\%.$$

ST-5 Bank A's effective annual rate is 8.24 percent:

Effective annual rate $= \left(1 + \dfrac{0.08}{4}\right)^4 - 1.0$

$$= (1.02)^4 - 1 = 1.0824 - 1$$

$$= 0.0824 = 8.24\%.$$

Now Bank B must have the same effective annual rate:

$$\left(1 + \dfrac{k}{12}\right)^{12} - 1.0 = 0.0824$$

$$\left(1 + \dfrac{k}{12}\right)^{12} = 1.0824$$

$$1 + \dfrac{k}{12} = (1.0824)^{1/12}$$

$$1 + \dfrac{k}{12} = 1.00662$$

$$\dfrac{k}{12} = 0.00662$$

$$k = 0.07944 = 7.94\%.$$

Thus, the two banks have different quoted rates—Bank A's quoted rate is 8 percent, while Bank B's quoted rate is 7.94 percent; however, both banks have the same effective annual rate of 8.24 percent. The difference in their quoted rates is due to the difference in compounding frequency.

Chapter 4

ST-2 a. $\hat{k}_R = 0.5\,(-2\%) + 0.1\,(10\%) + 0.4\,(15) = 6.0\%$
$\hat{k}_S = 0.5\,(20\%) + 0.1\,(12\%) + 0.4\,(2\%) = 12.0\%$

b. $\hat{k}_p = w_R\,\hat{k}_R + w_S\,\hat{k}_S$
$\hat{k}_p = 0.5(6.0\%) + 0.5\,(12.0\%) = 9.0\%$

Alternative computation: Compute the portfolio return for each possible stock outcome.

		RETURNS	
PROBABILITY	**STOCK R**	**STOCK S**	**50/50 PORTFOLIO**
0.5	–2%	20%	9% = 0.5 (–2%) + 0.5 (20%)
0.1	10	12	11.0 = 0.5 (10%) + 0.5 (12%)
0.4	15	2	8.5 = 0.5 (15%) + 0.5 (2%)

Then compute the expected return based on the probability of the outcome.

$$\hat{k}_p = 0.5(9.0\%) + 0.1(11.0\%) + (0.4)(8.5\%)$$

$$= 9.0\%$$

c. Standard deviation $= \sigma = \sqrt{\sigma^2} = \sqrt{\sum_{i=1}^{n}(k_i - \hat{k})^2 Pr_i}$

$$\sigma_R = \sqrt{\sigma_R^2} = \sqrt{0.5(-2\% - 6\%)^2 + 0.1(10\% - 6\%)^2 + 0.4(15\% - 6\%)^2}$$

$$= \sqrt{32 + 1.6 + 32.4} = \sqrt{66} = 8.12\%$$

$$\sigma_S = \sqrt{\sigma_S^2} = \sqrt{0.5(20\% - 12\%)^2 + 0.1(12\% - 12\%)^2 + 0.4(2\% - 12\%)^2}$$

$$= \sqrt{32 + 0 + 40} = \sqrt{72} = 8.49\%$$

$$\sigma_P = \sqrt{\sigma_P^2} = \sqrt{0.5(9.0\% - 9\%)^2 + 0.1(11.0\% - 9\%)^2 + 0.4(8.5\% - 9\%)^2}$$

$$= \sqrt{0 + 0.4 + 0.1} = \sqrt{0.5} = 0.71\%$$

Stock S is riskier because its standard deviation is higher than that of Stock R. Clearly, however, the portfolio, or combination of the two stocks, has the lowest risk.

d. Coefficient of variation $= CV = \dfrac{\text{Risk}}{\text{Return}} = \dfrac{\sigma}{\hat{k}}$

$CV_R = 8.12\%/6\% = 1.35$

$CV_S = 8.49\%/12\% = 0.71$

According to the coefficient of variations computed here, Stock R is riskier than Stock S. Although Stock S has a higher amount of total risk, it also has a much highter expected return than Stock R. The coefficient of variation for the portfolio is 0.08 = 0.71%/9%, which is much lower than for either stock.

e. Because the risk reduction from diversification is large—that is, σ_P is close to zero—it is more likely that the correlation coefficient is –0.9 rather than 0.9. If the correlation coefficient were 0.9, the risk reduction would be much smaller.

f. In this case, because the standard deviation for the two-stock portfolio is close to zero, we would expect that initially there would be little change in the riskiness of the portfolio as additional stocks are added. But, as the number of stocks in the portfolio increases substantially, we would expect that the risk associated with the portfolio should approach the standard deviation of the market, or average, portfolio, which is near 15 percent. See Figure 4–8.

Chapter 5

ST-2 a. This is not necessarily true. Because G plows back two-thirds of its earnings, its growth rate should exceed that of D, but D pays higher dividends ($6 versus $2). We cannot say which stock should have the higher price.

b. Again, we just do not know which price would be higher.

c. This is false. The changes in k_d and k_s would have a greater effect on G— its price would decline more.

d. The total expected return for D is $\hat{k}_D = \hat{D}_1/P_0 + g = 15\% + 0\% = 15\%$. The total expected return for G will have $\hat{D}_1/P_0$ less than 15 percent and g greater than 0 percent, but $\hat{k}_G$ should be neither greater nor smaller than D's total expected return, 15 percent, because the two stocks are stated to be equally risky.

e. We have eliminated a, b, c, and d, so e should be correct. On the basis of the available information, D and G should sell at about the same price, $40; thus, $\hat{k}_s = 15\%$ for both D and G. G's current dividend yield is $2/$40 = 5\%. Therefore, g = 15\% – 5\% = 10\%.

ST-3 a. Pennington's bonds were sold at par; therefore, the original YTM equaled the coupon rate of 12%.

b.

$$V_d = \sum_{t=1}^{50} \frac{\$120/2}{\left(1 + \dfrac{0.10}{2}\right)^t} + \frac{\$1,000}{\left(1 + \dfrac{0.10}{2}\right)^{50}}$$

$$= \$60\left[\frac{1 - \dfrac{1}{(1.05)^{50}}}{0.05}\right] + \$1,000\left[\frac{1}{(1.05)^{50}}\right]$$

$$= \$60(18.25593) + \$1,000(0.08720)$$

$$= \$1,095.36 + \$87.20 = \$1,182.56$$

Alternatively, with a financial calculator, input the following: N = 50, I = 5, PMT = 60, FV = 1000, and PV = ? PV = $1,182.56.

c.

$$\text{Current yield} = \text{Annual coupon payment/Price}$$

$$= \$120/\$1,182.56$$

$$= 0.1015 = 10.15\%.$$

$$\text{Capital gains yield} = \text{Total yield} - \text{Current yield}$$

$$= 10\% - 10.15\% = -0.15\%.$$

d.
$$\$891.64 = \sum_{t=1}^{19} \frac{\$60}{(1 + k_d/2)^t} + \frac{\$1,000}{(1 + k_d/2)^{21}}$$

Using Equation 5–3, the approximate YTM is:

$$YTM \approx \frac{\$60 + \left(\dfrac{\$1,000 - \$891.64}{19}\right)}{\left[\dfrac{2(\$891.64) + \$1,000}{3}\right]}$$

$$= 7.08\%$$

Alternatively, with a financial calculator, input the following: N = 19, PV = – 891.64, PMT = 60, FV = 1,000, and $k_{d/2}$ = I = ? Calculator solution = $k_{d/2}$ = 7.05%; therefore, k_d = 14.1%.

e.   Current yield = \$120/\$891.64 = 13.46%.
Capital gains yield = 14.1% – 13.46% = 0.64%

ST-4 The first step is to solve for g, the unknown variable, in the constant growth equation. Because $\hat{D}_1$ is unknown but D_0 is known, substitute $D_0(1 + g)$ as follows:

$$\hat{P}_0 = P_0 = \frac{\hat{D}_1}{k_s - g} = \frac{D_0(1 + g)}{k_s - g}$$

$$\$36 = \frac{\$2.40(1 + g)}{0.12 - g}$$

Solving for g, we find the growth rate to be 5 percent:

$$\$4.32 - \$36g = \$2.40 + \$2.40g$$

$$\$38.4g = \$1.92$$

$$g = 0.05 = 5\%.$$

The next step is to use the growth rate to project the stock price five years hence:

$$\hat{P}_5 = \frac{D_0(1 + g)^6}{k_s - g}$$

$$= \frac{\$2.40(1.05)^6}{0.12 - 0.05}$$

$$= \$45.95.$$

[Alternatively, $\hat{P}_5$ = \$36(1.05)^5 = \$45.95.]

Therefore, Ewald Company's expected stock price five years from now, $\hat{P}_5$, is \$45.95.

ST-5 a. (1) Calculate the PV of the dividends paid during the supernormal growth period:

$$\hat{D}_1 = \$1.1500(1.15) = \$1.3225.$$

$$\hat{D}_2 = \$1.3225(1.15) = \$1.5209.$$

$$\hat{D}_3 = \$1.5209(1.13) = \$1.7186.$$

$$PV\hat{D} = \$1.3225(0.89286) + \$1.5209(0.79719) + \$1.7186(0.71178)$$

$$= \$1.1809 + \$1.2124 + \$1.2233$$

$$= \$3.6167 \approx \$3.62.$$

(2) Find the PV of Snyder's stock price at the end of Year 3:

$$\hat{P}_3 = \frac{\hat{D}_4}{k_s - g} = \frac{\hat{D}_3(1 + g)}{k_s - g}$$

$$= \frac{\$1.7186(1.06)}{0.12 - 0.06}$$

$$= \$30.36.$$

$$PV \ \hat{P}_3 = \$30.36(0.71178) = \$21.61.$$

(3) Sum the two components to find the value of the stock today:

$$\hat{P}_0 = \$3.62 + \$21.61 \approx \$25.23.$$

Alternatively, the cash flows can be placed on a time line as follows:

$$\hat{P}_3 = \frac{30.3617}{32.0803} = \frac{\$1.8217}{0.12 - 0.06}$$

Enter the cash flows into the cash flow register, I = 12, and press the NPV key to obtain $P_0 = \$25.23$.

b.
$$\hat{P}_1 = \$1.5209(0.89286) + \$1.7186(0.79719) + \$30.36(0.79719)$$

$$= \$1.3580 + \$1.3701 + \$24.2027$$

$$= \$26.9308 \approx \$26.93.$$

(Calculator solution: $26.93.)

$$\hat{P}_2 = \$1.7186(0.89286) + \$30.36(0.89286)$$

$$= \$1.5345 + \$27.1072$$

$$= \$28.6418 \approx \$28.64.$$

(Calculator solution: $28.64.)

c.

YEAR	DIVIDEND YIELD	+	CAPITAL GAINS YIELD		TOTAL = RETURN
1	$\dfrac{\$1.3225}{\$25.23} \approx 5.24\%$		$\dfrac{\$26.93 - \$25.23}{\$25.23} \approx 6.74\%$		$\approx 12\%$
2	$\dfrac{\$1.5209}{\$26.93} \approx 5.65\%$		$\dfrac{\$28.64 - \$26.93}{\$26.93} \approx 6.35\%$		$\approx 12\%$
3	$\dfrac{\$1.7186}{\$28.64} \approx 6.00\%$		$\dfrac{\$30.36 - \$28.64}{\$28.64} \approx 6.00\%$		$\approx 12\%$

Chapter 6

ST-2 a. *Payback:*

To determine the payback, construct the cumulative cash flows for each project:

	CUMULATIVE CASH FLOWS	
YEAR	PROJECT X	PROJECT Y
0	($10,000)	($10,000)
1	(3,500)	(6,500)
2	(500)	(3,000)
3	2,500	500
4	3,500	4,000

$$\text{Payback}_X = 2 + \frac{500}{\$3,000} = 2.17 \text{ years.}$$

$$\text{Payback}_Y = 2 + \frac{\$3,000}{\$3,500} = 2.86 \text{ years.}$$

Net present value (NPV):

$$NPV_X = -\$10,000 + \frac{\$6,500}{(1.12)^1} + \frac{\$3,000}{(1.12)^2} + \frac{\$3,000}{(1.12)^3} + \frac{\$1,000}{(1.12)^4}$$

$$= \$966.01.$$

$$NPV_Y = -\$10,000 + \frac{\$3,500}{(1.12)^1} + \frac{\$3,500}{(1.12)^2} + \frac{\$3,500}{(1.12)^3} + \frac{\$3,500}{(1.12)^4}$$

$$= \$630.72.$$

Alternatively, using a financial calculator, input the cash flows into the cash flow register, enter I = 12, and then press the NPV key to obtain $NPV_X = \$966.01$ and $NPV_Y = \$630.72$.

Internal rate of return (IRR):

To solve for each project's IRR, find the discount rates which equate each NPV to zero:

$$IRR_X = 18.0\%.$$

$$IRR_Y = 15.0\%.$$

b. The following table summarizes the project rankings by each method:

	PROJECT THAT RANKS HIGHER
Payback	X
NPV	X
IRR	X

Note that all methods rank Project X over Project Y. In addition, both projects are acceptable under the NPV and IRR criteria. Thus, both projects should be accepted if they are independent.

c. In this case, we would choose the project with the higher NPV at k = 12%, or Project X.

d. To determine the effects of changing the cost of capital, plot the NPV profiles of each project. The crossover rate occurs at about 6 to 7 percent (6.2%).

   If the firm's required rate of return is less than 6 percent, a conflict exists because $NPV_Y > NPV_X$, but $IRR_X > IRR_Y$. Therefore, if k were 5 percent, a conflict would exist.

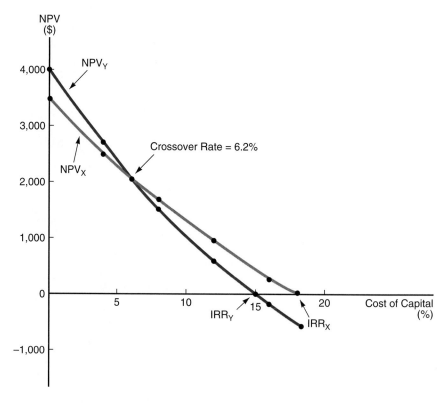

Required Rate of Return	NPV_X	NPV_Y
0%	$3,500	$4,000
4	2,545	2,705
8	1,707	1,592
12	966	631
16	307	(206)
18	5	(585)

e. The basic cause of the conflict is differing reinvestment rate assumptions between NPV and IRR. NPV assumes that cash flows can be reinvested at the cost of capital, whereas IRR assumes reinvestment at the (generally) higher IRR. The high reinvestment rate assumption under IRR makes early cash flows especially valuable, and hence short-term projects look better under IRR.

Chapter 7

ST-2 a. *Estimated investment outlay:*

Price	($50,000)
Modification	(10,000)
Change in net working capital	(2,000)
Total investment outlay	($62,000)

b. *Incremental operating cash flows:*

	YEAR 1	YEAR 2	YEAR 3
1. After-tax cost savings[a]	$12,000	$12,000	$12,000
2. Depreciation[b]	19,800	27,000	9,000
3. Depreciation tax savings[c]	7,920	10,800	3,600
Net cash flow (1 + 3)	$19,920	$22,800	$15,600

[a]$20,000 (1 − T).

[b]Depreciable basis = $60,000; the MACRS percentage allowances are 0.33, 0.45, and 0.15 in Years 1, 2, and 3, respectively; hence, depreciation in Year 1 = 0.33($60,000) = $19,800, and so on. There will remain $4,200, or 7 percent, undepreciated after Year 3; it would normally be taken in Year 4.

[c]Depreciation tax savings = T(Depreciation) = 0.4($19,800) = $7,920 in Year 1, and so on.

c. *Terminal cash flow:*

Salvage value	$20,000
Tax on salvage value[a]	(6,320)
Net working capital recovery	2,000
	$15,680

[a]Sales price	$20,000
Less book value	(4,200)
Taxable income	$15,800
Tax at 40%	$ 6,320

Book value = Depreciable basis − Accumulated depreciation
= $60,000 − ($19,800 + $27,000 + $9,000) = $4,200.

d. *Project NPV:*

```
 0    10%    1        2        3
 ├──────────┼────────┼────────┤
(62,000)   19,920   22,800   31,280
```

$$NPV = -\$62,000 + \frac{\$19,920}{(1.10)^1} + \frac{\$22,800}{(1.10)^2} + \frac{\$31,280}{(1.10)^3}$$

$$= -\$1,547.$$

Alternatively, using a financial calculator, input the cash flows into the cash flow register, enter I = 10, and then press the NPV key to obtain NPV = –$1,547. Because the earthmover has a negative NPV, it should not be purchased.

ST-3 *First determine the initial investment outlay:*

Purchase price	($8,000)
Sale of old machine	3,000
Tax on sale of old machine	(160)[a]
Change in net working capital	(1,500)
Total investment	($6,660)

[a]The market value is $3,000 – $2,600 = $400 above the book value. Thus, there is a $400 recapture of depreciation, and Dauten would have to pay 0.40($400) = $160 in taxes.

Now, examine the operating cash inflows:

Sales increase	$1,000
Cost decrease	1,500
Increase in pretax operating revenues	$2,500

After-tax operating revenue increase:
$$2,500(1 - T) = \$2,500(0.60) = \$1,500$$
Depreciation:

YEAR	1	2	3	4	5	6
New[a]	$1,600	$2,560	$1,520	$ 960	$ 880	$ 480
Old	350	350	350	350	350	350
Change	$1,250	$2,210	$1,170	$ 610	$ 530	$ 130
Depreciation Tax savings[b]	$ 500	$ 884	$ 468	$ 244	$ 212	$ 52

[a]Depreciable basis = $8,000. Depreciation expense in each year equals depreciable basis times the MACRS percentage allowances of 0.20, 0.32, 0.19, 0.12, 0.11, and 0.06 in Years 1–6, respectively.

[b]Depreciation tax savings = T(ΔDepreciation) = 0.4(ΔDepreciation).

Now recognize that at the end of Year 6 Dauten would recover its net working capital investment of $1,500, and it would also receive $800 from the sale of the replacement machine. However, because the machine would be fully depreciated, the firm must pay 0.40($800) = $320 in taxes on the sale. Also, by undertaking the replacement now, the firm forgoes the right to sell the old machine for $500 in Year 6; thus, this $500 in Year 6 must be considered an opportunity cost in that year. No tax would be due because the $500 salvage value would equal the old machine's Year 6 book value.

Finally, place all the cash flows on a time line:

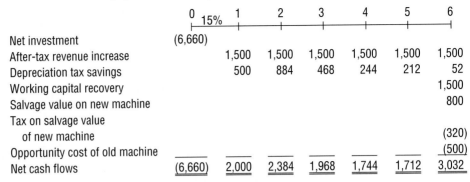

	0 15%	1	2	3	4	5	6
Net investment	(6,660)						
After-tax revenue increase		1,500	1,500	1,500	1,500	1,500	1,500
Depreciation tax savings		500	884	468	244	212	52
Working capital recovery							1,500
Salvage value on new machine							800
Tax on salvage value of new machine							(320)
Opportunity cost of old machine							(500)
Net cash flows	(6,660)	2,000	2,384	1,968	1,744	1,712	3,032

The net present value of this incremental cash flow stream, when discounted at 15 percent, is $1,335. Thus, the replacement should be made.

ST-4 a. First, find the expected cash flows:

YEAR	EXPECTED CASH FLOWS
0	$0.2(-\$100,000) + 0.6(-\$100,000) + 0.2(-\$100,000) = (\$100,000)$
1	$0.2(\$20,000) + \quad 0.6(\$30,000) + \quad 0.2(\$40,000) = \ \$\ 30,000$
2	$\$\ 30,000$
3	$\$\ 30,000$
4	$\$\ 30,000$
5	$\$\ 30,000$
5*	$0.2(\$0) + \quad 0.6(\$20,000) + \quad 0.2(\$30,000) = \ \$\ 18,000$

	0	10%	1	2	3	4	5
	(100,000)		30,000	30,000	30,000	30,000	48,000

Next, determine the NPV based on the expected cash flows:

$$NPV = -\$100,000 + \frac{\$30,000}{(1.10)^1} + \frac{\$30,000}{(1.10)^2} + \frac{\$30,000}{(1.10)^3}$$

$$+ \frac{\$30,000}{(1.10)^4} + \frac{\$48,000}{(1.10)^5} = \$24,900.$$

Using a financial calculator, input the cash flows in the cash flow register, enter I = 10, and then press the NPV key to obtain NPV = $24,900.

b. For the worst case, the cash flow values from the cash flow column farthest on the left are used to calculate NPV:

	0	10%	1	2	3	4	5
	−100,000		20,000	20,000	20,000	20,000	20,000

$$NPV = -\$100,000 + \frac{\$20,000}{(1.10)^1} + \frac{\$20,000}{(1.10)^2} + \frac{\$20,000}{(1.10)^3}$$

$$+ \frac{\$20,000}{(1.10)^4} + \frac{\$20,000}{(1.10)^5} = \$24,184.$$

Similarly, for the best case, use the values from the column farthest on the right. Here the NPV is $70,259.

If the cash flows are perfectly dependent, then the low cash flow in the first year will mean a low cash flow in every year. Thus, the probability of the worst case occurring is the probability of getting the $20,000 net cash flow in Year 1, or 20 percent. If the cash flows are independent, the cash flow in each year can be low, high, or average, and the probability of getting all low cash flows will be

$$0.2(0.2)(0.2)(0.2)(0.2) = 0.2^5 = 0.00032 = 0.032\%.$$

c. The base case NPV is found using the most likely cash flows and is equal to $26,142. This value differs from the expected NPV of $24,900 because the Year 5 cash flows are not symmetric. Under these conditions, the NPV distribution is as follows:

P_R	NPV
0.2	($24,184)
0.6	26,142
0.2	70,259

Thus, the expected NPV is 0.2(–$24,184) + 0.6($26,142) + 0.2($70,259) = $24,900. As is generally the case, the expected NPV is the same as the NPV of the expected cash flows found in part a. The standard deviation is $29,904:

$$\sigma^2_{NPV} = 0.2(-\$24,184 - \$24,900)^2 + 0.6(\$26,142 - \$24,900)^2$$

$$+ 0.2(\$70,259 - \$24,900)^2$$

$$= \$894,261,126.$$

$$\sigma_{NPV} = \sqrt{\$894,261,126} = \$29,904.$$

The coefficient of variation, CV, is $29,904/$24,900 = 1.20.

d. Because the project's coefficient of variation is 1.20, the project is riskier than average, and hence the project's risk-adjusted required rate of return is 10% + 2% = 12%. The project now should be evaluated by finding the NPV of the expected cash flows, as in part a, but using a 12 percent discount rate. The risk-adjusted NPV is $18,357, and therefore the project should be accepted.

Chapter 8

ST-2 a. A break point will occur each time a low-cost type of capital is used up. We establish the break points as follows, after first noting that LEI has $24,000 of retained earnings:

$$\text{Retained earnings} = (\text{Total earnings})(1.0 - \text{Payout})$$

$$= \$34,285.72(0.7)$$

$$= \$24,000.$$

$$\text{Break point} = \frac{\text{Total amount of low-cost capital of a given type}}{\text{Proportion of this type of capital in the capital structure}}.$$

CAPITAL USED UP	BREAK POINT CALCULATION		BREAK NUMBER
Retained earnings	$BP_{RE} = \dfrac{\$24,000}{0.60}$	$= \$40,000$	2
10% flotation common equity	$BP_{10\%E} = \dfrac{\$24,000 + \$12,000}{0.60} = \$60,000$		4
5% flotation preferred stock	$BP_{5\%P} = \dfrac{\$7,500}{0.15}$	$= \$50,000$	3
12% debt	$BP_{12\%D} = \dfrac{\$5,000}{0.25}$	$= \$20,000$	1
14% debt	$BP_{14\%D} = \dfrac{\$10,000}{0.25}$	$= \$40,000$	2

Summary of break points

(1) There are three common equity costs and hence two changes and, therefore, two equity-induced breaks in the MCC. There are two preferred costs and hence one preferred break. There are three debt costs and hence two debt breaks.

(2) The numbers in the third column of the table designate the sequential order of the breaks, determined after all the break points were calculated. Note that the second debt break and the break for retained earnings both occur at $40,000.

(3) The first break point occurs at $20,000, when the 12 percent debt is used up. The second break point, $40,000, results from using up both retained earnings and the 14 percent debt. The MCC curve also rises at $50,000 and $60,000, as preferred stock with a 5 percent flotation cost and common stock with a 10 percent flotation cost, respectively, are used up.

b. Component costs within indicated total capital intervals are as follows:

Retained earnings (used in interval $0 to $40,000):

$$k_s = \frac{\hat{D}_1}{P_0} + g = \frac{D_0(1 + g)}{P_0} + g$$

$$= \frac{\$3.60(1.09)}{\$60} + 0.09$$

$$= 0.0654 + 0.09 \qquad\qquad = 15.54\%.$$

Common with F = 10% ($40,001 to $60,000):

$$k_e = \frac{\hat{D}_1}{P_0(1.0 - F)} + g = \frac{\$3.924}{\$60(0.9)} + 0.09 \qquad = 16.27\%.$$

Common with F = 20% (over $60,000):

$$k_e = \frac{\$3.924}{\$60(0.8)} + 0.09 \qquad\qquad = 17.18\%.$$

Preferred with F = 5% ($0 to $50,000):

$$k_p = \frac{D_p}{P_0 - \text{Flotation costs}} = \frac{\$11}{\$100 - \$5} = 11.58\%.$$

Preferred with F = 10% (over $50,000):

$$k_p = \frac{\$11}{\$100(0.9)} = 12.22\%.$$

Debt at k_d = 12% ($0 to $20,000):

$$k_{dT} = k_d(1 - T) = 12\%(0.6) = 7.20\%.$$

Debt at k_d = 14% ($20,001 to $40,000):

$$k_{dT} = 14\%(0.6) = 8.40\%.$$

Debt at k_d = 16% (over $40,000):

$$k_{dT} = 16\%(0.6) = 9.60\%.$$

c. WACC calculations within indicated total capital intervals:

(1) $0 to $20,000 (debt = 7.2%, preferred = 11.58%, and retained earnings [RE] = 15.54%):

$$WACC_1 = w_d k_{dT} + w_p k_p + w_s k_s$$
$$= 0.25(7.2\%) + 0.15(11.58\%) + 0.60(15.54\%) = 12.86\%.$$

(2) $20,001 to $40,000 (debt = 8.4%, preferred = 11.58%, and RE = 15.54%):

$$WACC_2 = 0.25(8.4\%) + 0.15(11.58\%) + 0.60(15.54\%) = 13.16\%.$$

(3) $40,001 to $50,000 (debt = 9.6%, preferred = 11.58%, and equity = 16.27%):

$$WACC_3 = 0.25(9.6\%) + 0.15(11.58\%) + 0.60(16.27\%) = 13.90\%.$$

(4) $50,001 to $60,000 (debt = 9.6%, preferred = 12.22%, and equity = 16.27%):

$$WACC_4 = 0.25(9.6\%) + 0.15(12.22\%) + 0.60(16.27\%) = 14.00\%.$$

(5) Over $60,000 (debt = 9.6%, preferred = 12.22%, and equity = 17.18%):

$$WACC_5 = 0.25(9.6\%) + 0.15(12.22\%) + 0.60(17.18\%) = 14.54\%.$$

d. IRR calculation for Project E using a financial calculator:
N = 6, PV = –20,000, PMT = 5,427.84, and I = ? I = 16.00%.

e. See the graph of the MCC and IOS schedules for LEI.

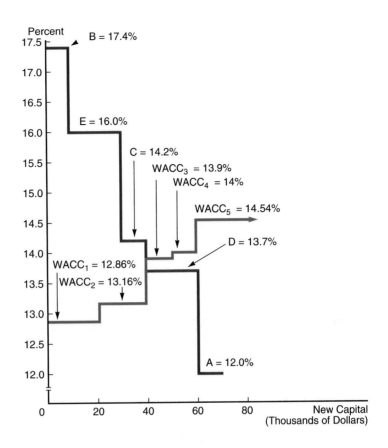

f. LEI should accept Projects B, E, and C. It should reject Projects A and D because their IRRs do not exceed the marginal costs of funds needed to finance them. The firm's capital budget would total $40,000.

Chapter 9

ST-2 a.

EBIT	$4,000,000
Interest ($2,000,000 × 0.10)	(200,000)
Earnings before taxes (EBT)	$3,800,000
Taxes (35%)	(1,330,000)
Net income	$2,470,000

$$\text{EPS} = \$2,470,000/600,000 = \$4.12.$$

$$P_0 = \$4.12/0.15 = \$27.47.$$

b.
$$\text{Equity} = 600,000 \times (\$10) = \$6,000,000.$$

$$\text{Debt} = \$2,000,000.$$

$$\text{Total capital} = \$8,000,000.$$

$$\text{WACC} = w_d[k_d(1 - T)] + w_s k_s$$
$$= (2/8)[(10\%)(1 - 0.35)] + (6/8)(15\%)$$
$$= 1.63\% + 11.25\%$$
$$= 12.88\%.$$

c.

EBIT	$4,000,000
Interest ($10,000,000 × 0.12)	(1,200,000)
Earnings before taxes (EBT)	$2,800,000
Taxes (35%)	(980,000)
Net income	$1,820,000

Shares bought and retired:

$$\Delta \text{Shares} = \Delta \text{Debt}/P_0 = \$8,000,000/\$27.47 = 291,227.$$

New outstanding shares:

$$\text{Shares}_1 = \text{Shares}_0 - \Delta \text{Shares} = 600,000 - 291,227 = 308,773.$$

New EPS:

$$\text{EPS} = \$1,820,000/308,773 = \$5.89.$$

New price per share:

$$P_0 = \$5.89/0.17 = \$34.65 \text{ versus } \$27.47.$$

Therefore, Gentry should change its capital structure.

d. In this case, the company's net income would be higher by $(0.12 - 0.10)$ $(\$2,000,000)(1 - 0.35) = \$26,000$ because its interest charges would be lower. The new price would be

$$P_0 = \frac{(\$1,820,000 + \$26,000)/308,773}{0.17} = \$35.17.$$

In the first case, in which debt had to be refunded, the bondholders were compensated for the increased risk of the higher debt position. In the second case, the old bondholders were not compensated; their 10 percent coupon perpetual bonds would now be worth

$$\$100/0.12 = \$833.33,$$

or $1,666,667 in total, down from the old $2 million, or a loss of $333,333. The stockholders would have a gain of

$$(\$35.17 - \$34.65)(308,773) = \$160,562.$$

This gain would, of course, be at the expense of the old bondholders. (There is no reason to think that bondholders' losses would exactly offset stockholders' gains.)

e.

$$\text{TIE} = \frac{\text{EBIT}}{\text{I}}.$$

$$\text{Original TIE} = \frac{\$4,000,000}{\$200,000} = 20 \times.$$

$$\text{New TIE} = \frac{\$4,000,000}{\$1,200,000} = 3.33 \times.$$

Chapter 10

ST-2 a.

Projected net income	$2,000,000
Less projected capital investments	(800,000)
Available residual	$ 1,200,000
Shares outstanding	200,000

DPS = $1,200,000/200,000 shares = $6 = $\hat{D}_1$.

b. EPS = $2,000,000/200,000 shares = $10.

Payout ratio = DPS/EPS = $6/$10 = 60%, or

Total dividends/NI = $1,200,000/$2,000,000 = 60%.

c. Currently, $P_0 = \dfrac{\hat{D}_1}{k_s - g} = \dfrac{\$6}{0.14 - 0.05} = \dfrac{\$6}{0.09} = \$66.67.$

Under the former circumstances, $\hat{D}_1$ would be based on a 20 percent payout on $10 EPS, or $2. With k_s = 14% and g = 12%, we solve for P_0:

$$P_0 = \frac{\hat{D}_1}{k_s - g} = \frac{\$2}{0.14 - 0.12} = \frac{\$2}{0.02} = \$100.$$

Although CMC has suffered a severe setback, its existing assets will continue to provide a good income stream. More of these earnings should now be passed on to the shareholders, as the slowed internal growth has reduced the need for funds. However, the net result is a 33 percent decrease in the value of the shares.

d. If the payout ratio were continued at 20 percent, even after internal investment opportunities had declined, the price of the stock would drop to $2/(0.14 − 0.06) = $25 rather than to $66.67. Thus, an increase in the dividend payout is consistent with maximizing shareholder wealth.

Because of the downward-sloping IOS curve, the greater the firm's level of investment, the lower the average ROE. Thus, the more money CMC retains and invests, the lower its average ROE will be. We can determine the average ROE under different conditions as follows:

Old situation (with founder active and 20 percent payout):

$$g = (1.0 - \text{Payout ratio})(\text{Average ROE})$$

$$12\% = (1.0 - 0.2)(\text{Average ROE})$$

$$\text{Average ROE} = 12\%/0.8 = 15\% > k_s = 14\%.$$

Note that the *average* ROE is 15 percent, whereas the *marginal* ROE is presumably equal to 14 percent.

New situation (with founder retired and a 60 percent payout):

$$g = 6\% = (1.0 - 0.6)(\text{ROE})$$

$$\text{ROE} = 6\%/0.4 = 15\% > k_s = 14\%.$$

This suggests that the new payout is appropriate and that the firm is taking on investments down to the point at which marginal returns are equal to the cost of capital.

Chapter 11

ST-2 Billingsworth paid $2 in dividends and retained $2 per share. Because total retained earnings rose by $12 million, there must be 6 million shares outstanding. With a book value of $40 per share, total common equity must be $40(6 million) = $240 million. Because Billingsworth has $120 million of debt, its debt ratio must be 33.3 percent:

$$\frac{\text{Debt}}{\text{Assets}} = \frac{\text{Debt}}{\text{Debt} + \text{Equity}} = \frac{\$120 \text{ million}}{\$120 \text{ million} + \$240 \text{ million}}$$

$$= 0.333 = 33.3\%$$

ST-3 a. In answering questions such as this, always begin by writing down the relevant definitional equations, then start filling in numbers. Note that the extra zeros indicating millions have been deleted in the calculations below. The results are not rounded until the final answer.

(1)
$$\text{DSO} = \frac{\text{Accounts receivable}}{\text{Sales}/360}$$

$$40 = \frac{\text{A/R}}{\$1,000/360}$$

$$\text{A/R} = 40(\$2.778) = \$111.1 \text{ million.}$$

(2)
$$\text{Quick ratio} = \frac{\text{Current assets} - \text{Inventories}}{\text{Current liabilities}} = 2.0$$

$$= \frac{\text{Cash and marketable securities} + \text{A/R}}{\text{Current liabilities}} = 2.0$$

$$2.0 = \frac{\$100 + \$111.1}{\text{Current liabilities}}$$

Current liabilities = ($100 + $111.1)/2 = $105.6 million.

(3)
$$\text{Current ratio} = \frac{\text{Current assets}}{\text{Current liabilities}} = 3.0$$

$$= \frac{\text{Current assets}}{\$105.6} = 3.0$$

Current assets = 3.0($105.6) = $316.7 million.

(4)
$$\text{Total assets} = \text{Current assets} + \text{Fixed assets}$$

$$= \$316.7 + \$283.5 = \$600.1 \text{ million.}$$

(5)
$$\text{ROA} = \text{Profit margin} \times \text{Total assets turnover}$$

$$= \frac{\text{Net income}}{\text{Sales}} \times \frac{\text{Sales}}{\text{Total assets}}$$

$$= \frac{\$50}{\$1,000} \times \frac{\$1,000}{\$600.1}$$

$$= 0.05 \times 1.667 = 0.0833 = 8.33\%.$$

(6)
$$\text{ROE} = \frac{\text{NI}}{\text{Equity}}$$

$$12.0\% = \frac{\$50}{\text{Equity}}$$

$$\text{Equity} = \frac{\$50}{0.12}$$

$$= \$416.7 \text{ million.}$$

(7)   Total assets = Total claims = $600.1 million

Current liabilities + Long-term debt + Equity = $600.1 million

$105.6 + Long-term debt + $416.7 = $600.1 million

Long-term debt = $600.1 − $105.6 − $416.7 = $77.8 million.

b. Kaiser's average sales per day were $1,000/360 = $2.778 million. Its DSO was 40, so A/R = 40($2.778) = $111.1 million. Its new DSO of 30 would cause A/R = 30($2.778) = $83.3 million. The reduction in receivables would be $111.1 − $83.3 = $27.8 million, which would equal the amount of cash generated.

(1)   New equity = Old equity − Stock bought back

$$= \$416.7 - \$27.8$$

$$= \$388.9 \text{ million.}$$

Thus,

$$\text{New ROE} = \frac{\text{Net income}}{\text{New equity}}$$

$$= \frac{\$50}{\$388.9}$$

$$= 12.86\% \text{ (versus old ROE of 12.0\%).}$$

(2) $$\text{New ROA} = \frac{\text{Net income}}{\text{Total assets} - \text{Reduction in A/R}}$$

$$= \frac{\$50}{\$600.1 - \$27.8}$$

$$= 8.74\% \text{ (versus old ROA of 8.33\%).}$$

(3) The old debt is the same as the new debt:

$$\text{Debt} = \text{Total claims} - \text{Equity}$$

$$= \$600.1 - \$416.7 = \$183.4 \text{ million.}$$

Old total assets = $600.1 million.

$$\text{New total assets} = \text{Old total assets} - \text{Reduction in A/R}$$

$$= \$600.1 - \$27.8$$

$$= \$572.3 \text{ million.}$$

Therefore,

$$\frac{\text{Debt}}{\text{Old total assets}} = \frac{\$183.4}{\$600.1} = 30.6\%,$$

while

$$\frac{\text{New debt}}{\text{New total assets}} = \frac{\$183.4}{\$572.3} = 32.0\%.$$

ST-4

	2005	2006	2007
Thompson's Taxes as a Corporation			
Income before salary and taxes	$60,000	$90,000	$110,000
Less: salary	(40,000)	(40,000)	(40,000)
Taxable income, corporate	$20,000	$50,000	$ 70,000
Total corporate tax	3,000[a]	7,500	12,500
Salary	$40,000	$40,000	$ 40,000
Less exemptions and deductions	(20,300)	(20,300)	(20,300)
= (3 × $3,100) + $11,000			
Taxable personal income	$19,700	$19,700	$ 19,700
Total personal tax	2,240[b]	2,240	2,240
Combined corporate and personal tax:	$ 5,240	$9,740	$ 14,740
Thompson's Taxes as a Proprietorship			
Total income	$60,000	$90,000	$110,000
Less: exemptions and deductions	(20,300)	(20,300)	(20,300)
Taxable personal income	$39,700	$69,700	$ 89,700
Tax liability of proprietorship	$ 5,240[c]	$10,900	$ 15,900
Advantage to being a corporation:	$ 0	$ 1,160	$ 1,160

[a]Corporate tax in 2005 = (0.15)($20,000) = $3,000.
[b]Personal tax (if Thompson incorporates) in 2005 = $1,430 + ($19,700 − $14,300) 0.15 = $ 2,240
[c]Proprietorship tax in 2005 = $1,430 + ($39,700 − $14,300) 0.15 = $5,240
Proprietorship tax in 2007 = $8,000 + ($89,700 − $58,100) 0.25 = $15,900

The corporate form of organization allows Thompson to pay the lowest taxes in each year; therefore, on the basis of taxes over the three-year period, Thompson should incorporate his business. However, note that to get money out of the corporation so he can spend it, Thompson will have to have the corporation pay dividends, which will be taxed to Thompson, and thus he will, sometime in the future, have to pay additional taxes.

Chapter 12

ST-2 a. (1) Determine the variable cost per unit at present, using the following definitions and equations:

$$Q = \text{units of output (sales)} = 5,000.$$
$$P = \text{average sales price per unit of output} = \$100.$$
$$F = \text{fixed operating costs} = \$200,000.$$
$$V = \text{variable costs per unit.}$$
$$\text{EBIT} = P(Q) - F - V(Q)$$
$$\$50,000 = \$100(5,000) - \$200,000 - V(5,000)$$
$$5,000V = \$250,000$$
$$V = \$50.$$

(2) Determine the new EBIT level if the change is made:

$$\begin{aligned} \text{New EBIT} &= P_2(Q_2) - F_2 - V_2(Q_2) \\ &= \$95(7,000) - \$250,000 - \$40(7,000) \\ &= \$135,000. \end{aligned}$$

(3) Determine the incremental EBIT:

$$\Delta \text{EBIT} = \$135,000 - \$50,000 = \$85,000.$$

(4) Estimate the approximate rate of return on the new investment:

$$\Delta \text{ROA} = \frac{\Delta \text{EBIT}}{\text{Investment}} = \frac{\$85,000}{\$400,000} = 21.25\%.$$

Because the ROA exceeds Olinde's average cost of capital, this analysis suggests that Olinde should go ahead and make the investment.

b.
$$\text{DOL} = \frac{Q(P - V)}{Q(P - V) - F}$$

$$\text{DOL}_{\text{Old}} = \frac{5,000(\$100 - \$50)}{5,000(\$100 - \$50) - \$200,000} = 5.00.$$

$$\text{DOL}_{\text{New}} = \frac{7,000(\$95 - \$40)}{7,000(\$95 - \$40) - \$250,000} = 2.85.$$

This indicates that operating income will be less sensitive to changes in sales if the production process is changed; thus the change would reduce risks. However, the change would increase the breakeven point. Still, with a lower sales price, it might be easier to achieve the higher new breakeven volume.

$$\textit{Old: } Q_{\text{OpBE}} = \frac{F}{P - V} = \frac{\$200,000}{\$100 - \$50} = 4,000 \text{ units.}$$

$$\textit{New: } Q_{\text{OpBE}} = \frac{F}{P_2 - V_2} = \frac{\$250,000}{\$95 - \$40} = 4,545 \text{ units.}$$

c. The incremental ROA is:

$$\Delta ROA = \frac{\Delta Profit}{\Delta Sales} \times \frac{\Delta Sales}{\Delta Assets}$$

Using debt financing, the incremental profit associated with the investment is equal to the incremental profit found in part a minus the interest expense incurred as a result of the investment:

$$\Delta Profit = New\ profit - Old\ profit - Interest$$
$$= \$135,000 - \$50,000 - 0.08(\$400,000)$$
$$= \$53,000.$$

The incremental sales is calculated as:

$$\Delta Sales = P_2Q_2 - P_1Q_1$$
$$= \$95(7,000) - \$100(5,000)$$
$$= \$665,000 - \$500,000$$
$$= \$165,000$$

$$ROA = \frac{\$53,000}{\$165,000} \times \frac{\$165,000}{\$400,000} = 13.25\%$$

The return on the new equity investment still exceeds the average cost of funds, so Olinde should make the investment.

d.
$$DFL = \frac{EBIT}{EBIT - 1}$$

$$DFL_{New} = \frac{\$135,000}{\$135,000 - \$32,000}$$

$$= 1.31.$$

$$EBIT_{FinBE} = \$32,000$$

Chapter 13

ST-2 a. and b.

**Income Statements for Year Ended December 31, 2005
($ Thousands)**

	VANDERHEIDEN PRESS		HERRENHOUSE PUBLISHING	
	a	b	a	b
EBIT	$ 30,000	$ 30,000	$ 30,000	$ 30,000
Interest	(12,400)	(14,400)	(10,600)	(18,600)*
Taxable income	$ 17,600	$ 15,600	$ 19,400	$ 11,400
Taxes (40%)	(7,040)	(6,240)	(7,760)	(4,560)
Net income	$ 10,560	$ 9,360	$ 11,640	$ 6,840
Equity	$100,000	$100,000	$100,000	$100,000
Return on equity	10.56%	9.36%	11.64%	6.84%

* Interest = $80,000(0.20) + $20,000(0.13) = $18,600

The Vanderheiden Press has a higher ROE when short-term interest rates are high, whereas Herrenhouse Publishing does better when rates are lower.

c. Herrenhouse's position is riskier. First, its profits and return on equity are much more volatile than Vanderheiden's. Second, Herrenhouse must renew its large short-term loan every year, and if the renewal comes up at a time when money is very tight, when its business is depressed, or both, then Herrenhouse could be denied credit, which could put it out of business.

ST-3 The Calgary Company: Alternative Balance Sheets

	RESTRICTED (40%)	MODERATE (50%)	RELAXED (60%)
Current assets	$1,200,000	$1,500,000	$1,800,000
Fixed assets	600,000	600,000	600,000
Total assets	$1,800,000	$2,100,000	$2,400,000
Debt	$ 900,000	$1,050,000	$1,200,000
Equity	900,000	1,050,000	1,200,000
Total liabilities and equity	$1,800,000	$2,100,000	$2,400,000

The Calgary Company: Alternative Income Statements

	RESTRICTED	MODERATE	RELAXED
Sales	$3,000,000	$3,000,000	$3,000,000
EBIT (15% of sales)	450,000	450,000	450,000
Interest (10%)	(90,000)	(105,000)	(120,000)
Earnings before taxes (EBT)	$ 360,000	$ 345,000	$ 330,000
Taxes (40%)	(144,000)	(138,000)	(132,000)
Net income	$ 216,000	$ 207,000	$ 198,000
ROE	24.0%	19.7%	16.5%

Chapter 14

ST-2 a. First determine the balance on the firm's checkbook and the bank's records as follows:

	FIRM'S CHECKBOOK	BANK'S RECORDS
Day 1: Deposit $500,000; write check for $1,000,000	($ 500,000)	$500,000
Day 2: Write check for $1,000,000	($1,500,000)	$500,000
Day 3: Write check for $1,000,000	($2,500,000)	$500,000
Day 4: Write check for $1,000,000; deposit $1,000,000	($2,500,000)	$500,000

After Upton has reached a steady state, it must deposit $1,000,000 each day to cover the checks written three days earlier.

b. The firm has three days of float; not until Day 4 does the firm have to make any additional deposits.

c. As shown above, Upton should try to maintain a balance on the bank's records of $500,000. On its own books it will have a balance of *minus* –$2,500,000.

ST-3 Analysis of change:

	CURRENT	PROPOSAL 1	PROPOSAL 2
Annual amounts:			
Sales	$10,000,000	$11,000,000	$9,000,000
Operating expenses (80%)	($ 8,000,000)	($ 8,800,000)	($7,200,000)
Collection expense*	($ 50,000)	($ 50,000)	($ 50,000)
Bad debt losses*	($ 0)	($ 0)	($ 0)
Days sales outstanding (DSO)	30 days	45 days	22 days
Required return, k	16%	16%	16%
Daily amounts:			
Sales = (Annual sales)/360	$ 27,778	$ 30,556	$ 25,000
Operating costs (80%)	($ 22,222)	($ 24,444)	($ 20,000)
Required return = 12%/360	0.0444%	0.0444%	0.0444%

*Because bad debt losses and collection expenses do not change, they are not considered in the analysis.

Current Policy:

```
         0        k = 0.0444%              30
         |——————————————————————————————————|
Production costs  (22,222)                27,778
```

$$NPV_{current} = (\$22,222) + \frac{\$27,778}{\left(1 + \dfrac{0.16}{360}\right)^{30}} = \$5,188$$

Proposal 1:

```
         0        k = 0.0444%                        45
         |————————————————————————————————————————————|
Prodcution costs  (24,444)                          30,556
```

$$NPV_{Proposal1} = (\$24,444) + \frac{\$30,556}{\left(1 + \dfrac{0.16}{360}\right)^{45}} = \$5,507$$

Proposal 2:

```
         0        k = 0.0444%        22
         |——————————————————————————|
Production costs  (20,000)         25,000
```

$$NPV_{Current} = (\$20,000) + \frac{\$25,000}{\left(1 + \dfrac{0.16}{360}\right)^{45}} = \$4,757$$

The NPV is greatest with Proposal 1, so the firm should change its term of credit form net 25 to net 30.

ST-2 a.
$$EOQ = \sqrt{\frac{2 \times O \times T}{C \times PP}}$$

$$= \sqrt{\frac{(2)(\$5,000)(2,600,000)}{(0.02)(\$5.00)}}$$

$$= 509,902 \text{ bushels.}$$

Because the firm must order in multiples of 2,000 bushels, it should order in quantities of 510,000 bushels.

b.
$$\text{Average weekly sales} = 2,600,000/52$$
$$= 50,000 \text{ bushels.}$$
$$\text{Reorder point} = 6 \text{ weeks' sales}$$
$$= 6(50,000)$$
$$= 300,000 \text{ bushels}$$

c. Total inventory costs:

$$TIC = (C)PP\left(\frac{Q}{2}\right) + O\left(\frac{T}{Q}\right)$$

$$= (0.02)(\$5)\left(\frac{510,000}{2}\right) + (\$5,000)\left(\frac{2,600,000}{510,000}\right)$$

$$= \$25,500 + \$25,490.20$$

$$= \$50,990.20$$

Chapter 15

ST-2 a. *Commercial bank loan*

Amount loaned	= (0.75)($250,000)	= $ 187,500
Discount	= (0.09/12)($187,500)	= (1,406)
Compensating balance	= (0.20)($187,500)	= (37,500)
Amount received		= $ 148,594
Interest expense	= (0.09)($187,500)	= $(16,875)
Credit department*	= ($4,000)(12)	= (48,000)
Bad debts*	= (0.02)($250,000)(12)	= (60,000)
Total annual costs		= $(124,875)

*The costs of the credit department and bad debts are expenses that will be incurred if a bank loan is used, but these costs will be avoided if the firm accepts the factoring arrangement.

Factoring

Amount loaned	= (0.85)($250,000)	= $ 212,500
Commission for period	= (0.035)($250,000)	= (8,750)
Prepaid interest	= (0.09/12)($203,750)	= (1,528)
Amount received		= $ 202,222
Annual commission	= ($8,750)(12)	= $(105,000)
Annual interest	= (0.09)($203,750)	= (18,338)
Total annual costs		= $(123,338)

b. The factoring costs are slightly lower than the cost of the bank loan, and the factor is willing to advance a significantly greater amount. On the other hand, the elimination of the credit department could reduce the firm's options in the future.

Chapter 16

Look up the *key terms* in the chapter.

Chapter 17

ST-2 a. $100,000,000/10 = $10,000,000 per year, or $5 million each 6 months. Because the $5 million will be used to retire bonds immediately, no interest will be earned on it.

b. The debt service requirements will decline. As the amount of bonds outstanding declines, so will the interest requirements (amounts given in millions of dollars):

SEMIANNUAL PAYMENT PERIOD (1)	SINKING FUND PAYMENT (2)	OUTSTANDING BONDS ON WHICH INTEREST IS PAID (3)	INTEREST PAYMENT[A] (4)	TOTAL BOND SERVICE (2) + (4) = (5)
1	$5	$100	$6.0	$11.0
2	5	95	5.7	10.7
3	5	90	5.4	10.4
⋮	⋮	⋮	⋮	⋮
20	5	5	0.3	5.3

Interest is calculated as $[(0.12)/2]$(Column 3); for example: interest in Period 2 = $(0.06)($95) = 5.7.

The company's total cash bond service requirement will be $21.7 million for the first year. The requirement will decline by $0.12($10,000,000) = $1,200,000$ per year for the remaining years.

c. Here we have a 10-year, 9 percent annuity whose compound value is $100 million, and we are seeking the annual payment, PMT. The solution can be obtained with a financial calculator. Input N = 10, I = 9, PV = 0, and FV = 100,000,000, and press the PMT key to obtain $6,582,009.
   We could also find the solution using this equation:

$$\$100,000,000 = \sum_{t=1}^{10} PMT(1+k)^t$$

$$= PMT\left[\frac{(1.09)^{10} - 1}{0.09}\right]$$

$$= PMT(15.19293)$$

$$PMT = \frac{\$100,000,000}{15.19293}$$

$$PMT = \$6,582,009 = \text{sinking fund payment.}$$

d. Annual debt service costs will be $100,000,000(0.12) + $6,582,009 = $18,582,009.

e. If interest rates rose, causing the bond's price to fall, the company would use open market purchases. This would reduce its debt service requirements.

Chapter 18

ST-2 a. *Cost of leasing:*

| | **Beginning of Year** | | | |
	0	1	2	3
Lease payment (AT)[a]	($ 6,000)	($6,000)	($6,000)	($6,000)
PV of leasing @ 6%	($ 6,000)	($5,660)	($5,340)	($5,038)
Total PV cost of leasing =	($22,038)			

[a]After-tax payment = $10,000(1 − T) = $10,000(0.60) $6,000.
[b]This is the after-tax cost of debt: 10%(1 − T) = 10%(0.60) = 6.0%.

Alternatively, using a financial calculator, input the following data after switching your calculator to "BEG" mode: N = 4, I = 6, PMT = −6000, and FV = 0. Then press the PV key to arrive at the answer of ($22,038). Now switch your calculator back to "END" mode.

b. *Cost of owning:*

Depreciable basis = $40,000.

Here are the cash flows under the borrow-and-buy alternative:

	END OF YEAR				
	0	**1**	**2**	**3**	**4**
1. Depreciation schedule					
(a) Depreciable basis		$40,000	$40,000	$40,000	$40,000
(b) Allowance		0.33	0.45	0.15	0.07
(c) Depreciation		13,200	18,000	6,000	2,800
2. Cash outflows					
(d) Net purchase price	($40,000)				
(e) Depreciation tax savings[a]		5,280[a]	7,200	2,400	1,120
(f) Maintenance (AT)[b]		(600)	(600)	(600)	(600)
(g) Salvage value (AT)[c]					6,000
(h) Total cash outflows	($40,000)	$ 4,680	$ 6,600	$ 1,800	$ 6,520
PVIFs	1.000	0.9434	0.8900	0.8396	0.7921
PV of owning	($40,000)	$ 4,415	$ 5,874	$ 1,511	$ 5,164
Total PV cost of owning =($23,036)					

[a]Depreciation(T) = $13,200(0.40) = $5,280.

[b]After-tax cost = $1,000(1–0.4) = $600

[c]Because the asset will be fully depreciated, the after tax salvage = $10,000(1–0.4) = $6,000.

Alternatively, input the cash flows for the individual years in the cash flow register and input I = 6, then press the NPV button to arrive at the answer of ($23,035). Because the present value of the cost of leasing is less than that of owning, the truck should be leased: $23,035 – $22,038 = $997, net advantage to leasing.

c. The discount rate is based on the cost of debt because most cash flows are fixed by contract and, consequently, are relatively certain. Thus, the lease cash flows have about the same risk as the firm's debt. Also, leasing is considered to be a substitute for debt. We use an after-tax cost rate because the cash flows are stated net of taxes.

d. Olsen could increase the discount rate on the salvage value cash flow. This would increase the PV cost of owning and make leasing even more advantageous.

Answers to End-of-Chapter Problems

We present here some answers to selected end-of-chapter problems. Please note that your answer might differ slightly from ours due to rounding differences. Also, although we hope not, some of the problems may have more than one correct solution, depending upon what assumptions are made in working the problem. Finally, many of the problems involve some verbal discussion as well as numerical calculations; this verbal material is not presented here.

2–1 a. $k_1 = 9.2\%$; $k_5 = 7.2\%$.

2–3 a. 4.8%.
 b. 6.8%
 c. 5-yr bond = 7.3%

2–4 a. $Infl_5 = 4.6\%$
 b. $MRP_5 = 0.8\%$
 c. $k_5 = 8.4\%$
 d. $k_{10} = 8.4\%$

2–5 a. 0.3%
 c. $k^* = 1.5\%$

2–6 $Infl_2 = 3.4\%$

2–7 a. k_1 in Year 2 = 13%

2–8 k_1 in Year 2 = 15%; Year 2 inflation = 11%

2–9 6.0%

2–10 $k_{2009} = 5.4\%$

2–11 k_1 in Year 3 = 7.0%

3–1 $561.80

3–2 $747.26.

3–3 (1) $499.99.
 (2) $867.13.

3–4 a. ≈ 10 years.

3–5 a. $6,374.97.
 c. (1) $7,012.47.

3–6 a. $2,457.83.
 b. $865.90.
 c. (1) $2,703.61.

3–7 a. Stream A: $1,251.25.

3–8 b. 7%.
 c. 9%.
 d. 15%.

3–9 a. $881.17.
 b. $895.42.
 c. $903.06.
 d. $908.35.

3–10 b. $279.20.
 c. $276.84.
 d. $443.72.

3–11 a. $5,272.32.
 b. $5,374.07.

3–12 a. 1st City = 7%; 2nd City = 6.66%.

3–13 a. PMT = $6,594.94.
 b. $13,189.87.

3–14 a. Z = 9%; B = 8%.
 b. Z = $558.39; $135.98; 32.2%;
 B = $548.33; $48.33; 9.7%.

3–15 a. $61,204.
 b. $11,020.
 c. $6,841.

3–16 a. $176,792.
 b. $150,259.

3–17 $1,901.

3–18 $4,971.

3–19 $1,000 today is worth more.

3–20 a. 14.87%.

3–21 APR = 8.0%; EAR = 8.24%.

3–22 12%.

3–23 9%.

3–24 a. $33,872.11.
 b. $26,243.16 and $0.

3–24 $1,205.55.

3–26 ≈ 15 years.

3–27 5 years; $1,885.09.

3–28 $PV_{7\%}$ = $1,428.57; $PV_{14\%}$ = $714.29.

3–29 $984.88

3–30 a. $260.73.
    b. $263.34.

3–31 k_{SIMPLE} = 15.19%.

3–32 PMT with CU financing = $493.19

4–1 a. $0.5 million.
    d. (2) 15%

4–2 a. 13.5%.
    b. 1.8.
    c. k_F = 8% + 5.5%β_F.
    d. 17.9%.

4–3 a. $\hat{k}_A$ = 13.30%.
    b. $\hat{k}_P$ = 10.65%.
    c. σ_A = 10.1%.
    d. CV_B = 3.1%.

4–4 a. k_A = 11.3%
    c. s_A = 20.8%
    d. CV_A = 1.84

4–5 CV_F = 0.83, which is riskiest

4–6 a. $\hat{k}_M$ = 13.5%; $\hat{k}_S$ = 11.6%.
    b. σ_M = 3.85%; σ_S = 6.22%.
    c. CV_M = 0.29; CV_S = 0.54.

4–7 a. $\hat{k}_Y$ = 14%.
    b. σ_X = 12.20%.

4–8 a. β_B = 2.
    b. k_B = 12.5%.

4–9 a. k_X = 15.5%.
    b. (1) k_X = 16.5%.
    c. (1) k_X = 18.1%.

4–10 β_{New} = 1.16.

4–11 β_p = 0.7625; k_p = 12.1%.

4–12 4.5%.

4–13 β_p = 1.7

5–1 a. $1,251.22.
    b. $898.94.

5–2 a. $1,250.
    b. $833.33.
    d. At 8%, V_d = $1,196.36.

5–3 b. PV = $5.29.
    d. $30.01.

5–4 a. 7%.
    b. 5%.
    c. 12%.

5–5 a. (1) $9.50.
      (2) $13.33.
    b. (1) Undefined.

5–6 a. $7.20.
    b. $41.60.
    c. $35.28.

5–7 a. $1,000.
    b. IBM = $812.59; GM = $711.89.
    d. 5.0%.
    e. IBM return = –13.75%.

5–8 a. Dividend 2007 = $2.66.
    b. P_0 = $39.43.
    c. Dividend yield 2005 = 5.10%; 2009 = 7.00%.

5–9 a. P_0 = $54.11.

5–10 b. P_0 = $21.43.
    c. P_0 = $26.47.
    e. P_0 = $40.54.

5–11 a. New price = $31.34.
    b. beta = 0.49865.

5–12 a. V_L at 5 percent = $1,518.99;
      V_L at 8 percent = $1,171.19;
      V_L at 12 = percent = $863.79.

5–13 a. 8.02%.

5–14 a. YTM at $829 ≈ 15%.

5–15 a. 13.3%.
    b. 10%.
    c. 8%.
    d. 5.3%.

5–16 $23.75.

5–17 a. k_C = 10.6%; k_D = 7%.

5–18 $25.03.

5–19 IBM bond = 9.33%.

5–20 10.2%.

5–21 P_0 = $19.89.

5–22 a. $53,410.26.

6–1 b. NPV = $7,486.68.
    d. PB_{DISC} = 6.51 yrs.

6–2 b. IRR_A = 17.8%; IRR_B = 24.0%.

6–3 a. IRR_A = 20%; IRR_B = 16.7%; Crossover rate ≈16%.

6–4 a. NPV_A = $14,486,808; NPV_B = $11,156,893; IRR_A = 15.03%; IRR_B = 22.26%.

6–5 NPV_P = $409; IRR_P = 15%; Accept; NPV_T = $3,318; IRR_T = 20%; Accept.

6–6 NPV_E = $3,861; IRR_E = 18%; NPV_G = $3,057; IRR_G = 18%; Purchase electric-powered forklift; it has a higher NPV.

6–7 NPV_S = $448.86; NPV_L = $607.20; IRR_S = 15.24%; IRR_L = 14.67%.

6–8 a. PV_C = –$556,717; PV_F = –$493,407; Forklift should be chosen.

6–9 NPV_C = $1,256; IRR_C = 17.3%; NPV_R = $1,459.

6–10 IRR_Q = 15.6%.

6–11 Accept Project Y.

6A-1 d. MIRR = 22.87%.

7–1 a. ($178,000).
  b. $52,440; $60,600; $40,200.
  c. $48,760.
  d. NPV = –$19,549; Do not purchase.

7–2 a. ($126,000).
  b. $42,560; $47,477; $35,186.
  c. $51,268.
  d. NPV = $11,385; Purchase.

7–3 a. ($52,000).
  b. $18,560; $22,400; $12,800; $10,240.
  c. $1,500.
  d. NPV = $1,021; Replace the old machine.

7–4 a. ($776,000).
  c. $199,000; $255,400; $194,300; $161,400; $156,700.
  d. $115,200.
  e. NPV = $436.77; Purchase the new machine.

7–5 a. Expected CF_A = $6,750; Expected CF_B = $7,650; CV_A = 0.0703.
  b. NPV_A = $10,036; NPV_B = $11,624.

7–6 a. 11%.

7–7 NPV_5 = $2,211; NPV_4 = $2,081; NPV_8 = $13,329.

7–8 NPV = 15,301; Buy the new machine.

7–9 NPV = $22,329; Replace the old machine.

7–10 a. 10.6%.
  b. NPV = $1,100; Accept.

7–11 a. 15%.
  b. 1.48; 15.4%; 17%.

7A-1 PV = $1,273,389.

7B-1 a. $NPV_{190–3}$ = $20,070; $NPV_{360–6}$ = $22,256.

7B-2 NPV_A = $12.76 million

8–1 a. 16.3%.
  b. 15.4%.
  c. 16%.

8–2 a. 8%.
  b. $2.81.
  c. 15.8%.

8–3 a. $18 million.
  b. BP = $45 million.
  c. BP_1 = $20 million; BP_2 = $40 million.

8–4 a. g = 3%.
  b. EPS = $5.562.

8–5 a. $67,500,000.
  c. k_s = 12%; k_e = 12.4%.
  d. $27,000,000.
  e. $WACC_1$ = 9%; $WACC_2$ = 9.2%.

8–6 a. k_{dT} = 5.4%; k_s = 15.1%.
  b. WACC = 11.22%.
  d. WACC = 11.70%.

8–7 a. 3 breaks; BP_{D1} = $1,111,111; BP_{RE} = $1,818,182; BP_{D2} = $2,000,000.
  b. $WACC_1$ = 10.96%; $WACC_2$ = 11.50%; $WACC_3$ = 12.14%; $WACC_4$ = 12.68%.
  c. IRR_1 = 16%; IRR_3 = 14%.

8–8 a. 13%.
  b. 10.4%.
  c. 8.58%.

8–9 7.92%.

8–10 11.94%.

8–11 a. F = 10%.
  b. k_e = 15.8%.

8–12 WACC = 12.72%.

8–13 $10 million.

8–14 $42,000.

8–15 $62,000.

8–16 a. 14.40%.
  b. 10.62%.

8–17 7.2%.

8–18 k_e = 16.5%.

9–1 a. $5.10.

9–2 a. DOL_A = 2.80; DOL_B = 2.15; Method A.
  b. DFL_A = 1.32; DFL_B = 1.35; Method B.
  d. Debt = $129,310; D/A = 5.75%.

9–3 a. EPS_{Old} = $2.04; New: EPS_D = $4.74; EPS_S = $3.27.
  b. DOL_{Old} = 2.30; DOL_{New} = 1.60; DFL_{Old} = 1.47; $DFL_{New,Stock}$ = 1.15; $DTL_{New,Debt}$ = 2.53.
  c. 33,975 units.
  d. $Q_{New,Debt}$ = 27,225 units.

9–4 Debt used: E(EPS) = $5.78; σ_{EPS} = $1.05; E(TIE) = 3.49×.
  Stock used: E(EPS) = $5.51; σ_{EPS} = $0.85; E(TIE) = 6.00×.

9–5 a. ROE_{LL} = 14.6%; ROE_{HL} = 16.8%.
  b. ROE_{LL} = 16.5%.

9–6 No leverage: $\widehat{ROE}$ = 10.5%; σ = 5.4%; CV = 0.51; 60% leverage: $\widehat{ROE}$ = 13.7%; σ = 13.5%; CV = 0.99.

10-1 CS = $79.50; PIC = $464.25; RE = $956.25.

10-2 a. (1) $3,960,000.
     (2) $4,800,000.
     (3) $9,360,000.
     (4) Regular = $3,960,000; Extra = $5,400,000.
  c. 15%
  d. 15%.

10-3 a. Payout = 63.16%; BP = $9.55 million; $WACC_1$ = 10.67%; $WACC_2$ = 10.96%.
  b. $15 million.
10-4 $3,250,000.
10-5 Payout = 52%.
10-6 D_0 = $3.44.
10-7 Payout = 31.39%.
11-2 a. Current ratio = 1.98×; DSO = 75 days; Total assets turnover = 1.7×; Debt ratio = 61.9%.
11-3 A/P = $90,000; Inv = $67,500; FA = $160,500.
11-5 a. Quick ratio = 0.85×; DSO = 37 days; ROE = 13.1%; Debt ratio = 54.8%.
11-6 Tax_{2004} = $0; Initial tax_{2006} = $4,500; Initial tax_{2007} = $15,450; Final tax_{2007} = $0.
11-7 a. 2005 advantage as a corporation = $0; 2006 advantage = $350; 2007 advantage = $1,350.
11-9 a. Personal tax = $15,662.50
  c. IBM yield = 8.25%; choose FLA bonds.
  d. 18.18%.
11-10 a. $10,737.50
  b. $4,775
11-11 Net profit margin = 2%; Debt/Assets = 40%
11-12 $262,500; 1.19×.
11-13 Sales = $2,511,628; DSO = 37 days.
11-14 TIE = 3.5.
11-15 ROE = 24.5%; ROA = 9.8%.
11-16 a. +5.54%.
  b. (2) +3.21%.
11-17 Total sources = $102; Net increase in cash and marketable securities = $19.
11-18 a. NOI = $900,000; CF = $2,400,000.
  b. CF = $3,000,000.
11-19 a. Tax = $107,855; NI = $222,145;
  b. Marginal tax rate = 39%; Average tax rate = 33.8%.
11-20 a. $30
  c. $70
11-21 Tax = $32,156; NI = $98,844; Average tax rate = 25.6%
11-22 AT&T bonds = 8.8%; AT&T PS = 8.5%.
12-1 a. Notes payable = $31.44 million.
  b. Current ratio = 2.0×; ROE = 14.2%.
  c. (1) –$14.28 million.
    (2) Total assets = $147 million; Notes payable = $3.72 million.
    (3) Current ratio = 4.25×; ROE = 10.84%.

12-2 a. Total assets = $33,534; AFN = $2,128.
  b. Notes payable = $4,228; AFN = $70; ∆Interest = $213.
12-3 a. DOL = 2.5×; DFL = 3.0×.
12-4 a. First pass AFN = $667.
  b. Increase in notes payable = $51; Increase in CS = $368.
12-5 a. (1) –$60,000.
  b. Q_{OpBE} = 14,000.
  c. (1) –1.33.
12-6 a. (2) $125,000.
  b. Q_{OpBE} = 7,000.
12-7 a. $2,000.
  b. DFL = 1.8.
  c. $3,000.
12-8 a. (1) –$75,000.
    (2) $175,000.
  b. Q_{OpBE} = 140,000.
  c. (1) –8.3.
    (2) 15.0.
    (3) 5.0.
12-9 a. FC_A = $80,000; VC_A = $4.80/unit; P_A = $8.00/unit.
12-10 a. $480,000.
  b. $18,750.
12-11 AFN = $360.
12-12 a. 40,000.
  b. ($0.30).
  c. 48,000.
  d. DOL = 3.0; DFL = 1.7.
13-1 b. 20 days.
13-2 a. (1) 109 days.
    (2) 79 days.
  d. (1) 140 days.
    (2) 113 days.
13-3 a. 32.
  b. $288,000.
  c. $45,000.
  d. (1) 30.
    (2) $378,000.
13-4 a. ROE_T = 11.75%; ROE_M = 10.80%; ROE_R = 9.16%.
13-5 a. 72.
  b. $396,000.
  d. Decrease to 57.
13-6 a. 51.
  b. (1) 2.33.
    (2) 11.67%.

c. (1) 42.
  (2) 2.46.
  (3) 12.3%.
14–1 a. $1,600,000.
  c. Bank = $1,200,000; Books = –$5,200,000.
14–2 b. $164,400.
14–3 b. Oct. loan = $22,800.
14–4 b. $420,000.
  c. $35,000.
14–5 NPV_O = $1,141, NPV_N = $1,196
14–6 a. DSO_O = 27 days; DSO_N = 22.5 days.
  b. D_O = $15,680; D_N = $38,220.
  c. BD_O = $40,000; BD_N = $52,000.
  e. NPV_O = $1,198, NPV_N = $1,515.
14–7 EOQ = 1000.
14–8 a. EOQ = 5,200.
  b. 65.
  c. Every 5.5 days.
  d. (3)   TIC = $6,304.
14–9 a. Net float = $30,000.
  b. $16,000.
14–10 a. DSO = 28 days.
  b. $70,000.
14–11 NPV_O = $2,349, NPV_N = $2,089.
14–12 DSO_O = 54 days, DSO_N = 75 days.
14–13 a. EOQ = 3,873.
  b. 5,073 bags.
  c. 3,137 bags.
  d. Every 6 days.
15–1 a. $100,000.
  c. (1) $300,000.
    (2) Approximate cost = 36.73%; EAR = 43.86%.
15–2 a. $EAR_{DISC.}$ = 14.9%.
15–3 a. Alternative 3 EAR = 9.56%.
  b. Alternative 2 $470,588.
15–4 a. 11.73%.
  b. 12.09%.
  c. 18%.
15–5 b. $384,615.
  c. Cash = $126.9; NP = $434.6.
15–6 a. (1) $27,500.
    (3) $25,833.
15–7 a. $515,464.
15–8 a. $46,167.
  b. $40,667.
15–9 b. 14.69%.
  d. 20.99%.

15–10 a. 44.54%.
15–11 a. 12%; **b.** 11.25%; **c.** 11.48%; **d.** 16%.
15–12 Approximate cost = 14.69%; EAR = 15.65%
15–13 N/P = 13.64%.
15–14 d. 8.37%.
16–1 a. $1,050,000.
  b. $5,550,000.
  c. ($3,450,000).
16–2 a. EPS_{2005} = $9,600; DPS_{2005} = $4,800; BV_{2005} = $72,000/share.
  b. g_{EPS}: HH = 8.4%; L = 6.4%; U = 8%; g_{DPS}: HH = 8.4%; L = 6.4%; U = 7.4%.
  e. EPS_{2005} = $2.40; DPS_{2005} = $1.20; BV_{2005} = $18/share.
  f. ROE_{HH} = 15.00%; ROE_L = 13.64%; ROE_U = 13.33%.
  i. P/E_{HH} = 8×; P/E_L = 8.67×.
  k. k_{HH} = 15.2%; k_L = 12.5%; U-Fix-It's price: $P_0(HH)$ = $17.23; $P_0(L)$ = $26.93.
16–3 a. $35.00.
  b. $34.18.
16–4 600,000 shares.
17–1 c. (2) 20%
  d. at k_d = 6.1%, V = $49.18; at k_d = 2%, V = $150.
17–2 a. 7,930 bonds.
  b. (1) 12%.
    (2) 8.64%.
  c. 7.2%.
17–3 a. $2,504,565.
  b. $1,490,295.
  c. $2,912,835.
  d. $1,917,135.
17–4 15.03%.
17–5 12.37%.
17–6 $30,463.
18–1 a. D/A_W = 50%; D/A_G = 67%.
18–2 a. PV cost of owning = –$185,112; PV cost of leasing = –$187,534; Purchase loom.
18–3 a. $200
18–4 b. Percent ownership: Original = 80%; Plan 1 = 53%; Plans 2 and 3 = 57%.
  c. EPS_0 = $0.48; EPS_1 = $0.60; EPS_2 = $0.64; EPS_3 = $0.86.
  d. D/A_1 = 13%; D/A_2 = 13%; D/A_3 = 48%.
18–5 a. PV cost of owning = ($991,845); PV cost of leasing = ($954,639); Lease equipment.

Selected Equations

Chapter 1

$$\text{Value} = \frac{\hat{CF_1}}{(1+k)^1} + \frac{\hat{CF_2}}{(1+k)^2} + \cdots + \frac{\hat{CF_n}}{(1+k)^n} = \sum_{t=1}^{n} \frac{\hat{CF_t}}{(1+k)^t}.$$

Chapter 2

Rate of return (interest) = k = Risk-free rate + Risk premium.

$k = k^* + IP + DRP + LP + MRP = k_{RF} + DRP + LP + MRP.$

$k_{RF} = k^* + IP.$

$$IP_n = \frac{Infl_1 + Infl_2 + \ldots Infl_n}{n}.$$

Chapter 3

$FV_n = PV(1+k)^n.$

$$PV = FV_n \left[\frac{1}{(1+k)^n} \right].$$

$$FVA_n = PMT \left[\frac{(1+i)^n - 1}{i} \right].$$

$$FVA(DUE)_n = PMT \left\{ \left[\frac{(1+k)^n - 1}{k} \right] \times (1+k) \right\}.$$

$$PVA_n = PMT \left[\frac{1 - \dfrac{1}{(1+i)^n}}{i} \right].$$

$$PVA(DUE)_n = PMT \left\{ \left[\frac{1 - \frac{1}{(1 + k)^n}}{k} \right] \times (1 + k) \right\}.$$

$$PVP = \frac{Payment}{Interest\ rate} = \frac{PMT}{k}.$$

$$PV_{Uneven\ stream} = \sum_{t=1}^{n} CF_t \left[\frac{1}{(1 + k)^t} \right].$$

$$FV_{Uneven\ stream} = \sum_{t=1}^{n} CF_t (1 + k)^{n-t}.$$

$$FV_n = PV \left(1 + \frac{k_{SIMPLE}}{m} \right)^{m \times n}.$$

$$EAR = Effective\ annual\ rate = \left(1 + \frac{k_{SIMPLE}}{m} \right)^m - 1.0.$$

$$Periodic\ rate = k_{per} = \frac{k_{SIMPLE}}{m}.$$

$$k_{SIMPLE} = k_{per} \times m = APR.$$

Chapter 4

$$Expected\ rate\ of\ return = \hat{k} = \sum_{i=1}^{n} Pr_i k_i.$$

$$Variance = \sigma^2 = \sum_{i=1}^{n} (k_i - \hat{k})^2 Pr_i.$$

$$Standard\ deviation = \sigma = \sqrt{\sum_{i=1}^{n} (k_i - \hat{k})^2 Pr_i} = Total\ risk.$$

$$Total\ risk = Systematic\ risk + Unsystematic\ risk.$$

$$CV = \frac{\sigma}{\hat{k}}.$$

$$\hat{k}_P = \sum_{j=1}^{N} w_j \hat{k}_j.$$

$$\beta_P = \sum_{j=1}^{N} w_j \beta_j.$$

$$SML = k_j = k_{RF} + (k_M - k_{RF})\beta_j = k_{RF} + (RP_M)\beta_j.$$

$$\beta = \frac{Y_2 - Y_1}{X_2 - X_1} = slope\ coefficient\ in\ \overline{k}_{jt} = \alpha + \beta\ \overline{k}_{Mt} + \epsilon_t.$$

Chapter 5

Asset value $= V = \sum_{t=1}^{n} \dfrac{\hat{CF}_t}{(1+k)^t}$.

$\begin{matrix}\text{Bond}\\\text{value}\end{matrix} = V_d = \sum_{t=1}^{n} \dfrac{INT}{(1+k_d)^t} + \dfrac{M}{(1+k_d)^n} = INT\left[\dfrac{1 - \dfrac{1}{(1+k_d)^N}}{k_d}\right] + M\left[\dfrac{1}{(1+k_d)^N}\right]$.

$V_d = \sum_{t=1}^{2N} \dfrac{INT/2}{(1+k_d/2)^t} + \dfrac{M}{(1+k_d/2)^{2N}}$.

$\begin{matrix}\text{Approx. yield}\\\text{to maturity}\end{matrix} = \dfrac{\left(INT + \dfrac{M - V_d}{N}\right)}{\left[\dfrac{2(V_d) + M}{3}\right]}$.

Price of callable bond $= \sum_{t=1}^{N} \dfrac{INT}{(1+k_d)^t} + \dfrac{\text{Call price}}{(1+k_d)^{Nc}}$.

Value of stock $= V_s = \sum_{t=1}^{\infty} \dfrac{\hat{D}_t}{(1+k_s)^t} = P_0$.

Zero growth: $g = 0$; $P_0 = \dfrac{D}{k_s}$.

Constant growth: $g_1 = g_2 = \ldots = g_\infty$; $P_0 = \dfrac{\hat{D}_1}{k - g} = \dfrac{D_0(1 + g)}{k - g}$.

$\hat{k}_s = \dfrac{\hat{D}_1}{P_0} + g$.

Capital gains yield $= \dfrac{(\text{Ending value}) - (\text{Beginning value})}{(\text{Beginning value})} = g$.

$\begin{matrix}\text{Current}\\\text{yield}\end{matrix} = \dfrac{INT}{V_d}$.

$\begin{matrix}\text{Dividend}\\\text{yield}\end{matrix} = \dfrac{\hat{D}_1}{P_0}$.

Chapter 6

$PB = \text{Payback} = \left(\begin{matrix}\text{Number of years}\\\text{before full recovery of}\\\text{original investment}\end{matrix}\right) + \left(\dfrac{\begin{matrix}\text{Unrecovered cost at start}\\\text{of full-recovery year}\end{matrix}}{\begin{matrix}\text{Total cash flow during}\\\text{full-recovery year}\end{matrix}}\right)$.

$$NPV = \hat{CF}_0 + \frac{\hat{CF}_1}{(1 + k)^1} + \frac{\hat{CF}_2}{(1 + k)^2} + \ldots + \frac{\hat{CF}_n}{(1 + k)^n} = \sum_{t=0}^{n} \frac{\hat{CF}_t}{(1 + k)^t}.$$

$$IRR: \hat{CF}_0 + \frac{\hat{CF}_1}{(1 + IRR)^1} + \frac{\hat{CF}_2}{(1 + IRR)^2} + \ldots + \frac{\hat{CF}_n}{(1 + IRR)^n} = 0$$

$$\sum_{t=0}^{n} \frac{\hat{CF}_t}{(1 + IRR)^t} = 0.$$

MIRR: PV costs = PV terminal value.

$$= \sum_{t=0}^{n} \frac{COF_t}{(1 + k)^t} = \frac{\sum_{t=0}^{n} CIF_t(1 + k)^{n-t}}{(1 + MIRR)^n} = \frac{TV}{(1 + MIRR)^n}.$$

Chapter 7

Net cash flow = Net income + Depreciation.

Incremental operating $CF_t = \Delta NOI_t (1-T) + \Delta Depr_t = (\Delta S_t - \Delta OC_t)(1 - T) + T(\Delta Depr_t)$.

$$E(NPV) = \sqrt{\sum_{i=1}^{n} Pr_i(NPV_i)}.$$

$$\sigma_{NPV} = \sqrt{\sum_{i=1}^{n} Pr_i[NPV_i = E(NPV)]^2}.$$

$$CV_{NPV} = \frac{\sigma_{NPV}}{E(NPV)}.$$

$$k_{proj} = k_{RF} + (k_M - k_{RF})\beta_{proj}.$$

Chapter 8

After-tax component cost of debt = $k_{dT} = k_d(1 - T)$.

Component cost of preferred stock = $k_{ps} = \dfrac{D_{ps}}{NP} = \dfrac{D_{ps}}{P_0 - \text{Flotation costs}}$.

$$k_s = k_{RF} + RP = \frac{\hat{D}_1}{P_0} + g = \hat{k}_s.$$

$$k_s = k_{RF} + (k_M - k_{RF})\beta_s.$$

$$k_s = \text{Bond yield} + \text{Risk premium} = k_d + RP.$$

$$k_e = \frac{\hat{D}_1}{P_0(1 - F)} + g = \frac{\hat{D}_1}{NP} + g.$$

$$WACC = w_d k_{dT} + w_p k_p + w_s(k_s \text{ or } k_e).$$

$$BP = \frac{\text{Total amount of lower-cost capital of a given type}}{\text{Proportion of this type of capital in the capital structure}}.$$

Chapter 9

$$EPS = \frac{(S - F - VC - I)(1 - T)}{\text{Shares outstanding}} = \frac{(EBIT - I)(1 - T)}{\text{Shares outstanding}}.$$

$$DOL = \frac{Q(P - V)}{Q(P - V) - F} = \frac{S - VC}{S - VC - F} = \frac{\text{Gross profit}}{EBIT}.$$

$$DFL = \frac{EBIT}{EBIT - I}.$$

$$DTL = \frac{Q(P - V)}{Q(P - V) - F - I} = \frac{S - VC}{S - VC - F - I} = \frac{\text{Gross profit}}{EBIT - I} = DOL \times DFL.$$

$$EPS_1 = EPS_0[1 + (DTL)(\%\Delta Sales)].$$

Chapter 10

$$\begin{array}{l}\text{Dollars transferred from} \\ \text{retained earnings due to} \\ \text{stock dividend}\end{array} = \left(\begin{array}{c}\text{Number of} \\ \text{shares} \\ \text{outstanding}\end{array}\right)\left(\begin{array}{c}\text{Stock} \\ \text{dividend as} \\ \text{a percent}\end{array}\right)\left(\begin{array}{c}\text{Market} \\ \text{price of} \\ \text{the stock}\end{array}\right).$$

Chapter 11

$$\begin{array}{l}\text{Equivalent \textbf{pretax} yield} \\ \text{on taxable investment}\end{array} = \frac{\text{Yield on tax-free investment}}{1 - T}.$$

$$\text{Current ratio} = \frac{\text{Current assets}}{\text{Current liabilities}}.$$

$$\text{Quick, or acid test, ratio} = \frac{\text{Current assets} - \text{Inventories}}{\text{Current liabilities}}.$$

$$\text{Inventory turnover ratio} = \frac{\text{Cost of goods sold}}{\text{Inventories}}.$$

$$DSO = \frac{\text{Days sales}}{\text{outstanding}} = \frac{\text{Receivables}}{\text{Average sales per day}} = \frac{\text{Receivables}}{\text{Annual sales/360}}.$$

$$\text{Fixed assets turnover ratio} = \frac{\text{Sales}}{\text{Net fixed assets}}.$$

$$\text{Total assets turnover ratio} = \frac{\text{Sales}}{\text{Total assets}}.$$

$$\text{Debt ratio} = \frac{\text{Total debt}}{\text{Total assets}}.$$

$$\text{Times-interest-earned (TIE) ratio} = \frac{EBIT}{\text{Interest charges}}.$$

$$\begin{array}{l}\text{Fixed charge} \\ \text{coverage ratio}\end{array} = \frac{EBIT + \text{Lease payments}}{\text{Interest charges} + \text{Lease payments} + \left[\dfrac{\text{Sinking fund payments}}{(1 - \text{Tax rate})}\right]}.$$

$$\text{Profit margin on sales} = \frac{\text{Net income}}{\text{Sales}}.$$

$$\text{Return on total assets (ROA)} = \frac{\text{Net income}}{\text{Total assets}}.$$

$$\text{ROA} = \left(\begin{array}{c}\text{Profit}\\\text{margin}\end{array}\right)\left(\begin{array}{c}\text{Total assets}\\\text{turnover}\end{array}\right) = \left(\frac{\text{Net income}}{\text{Sales}}\right)\left(\frac{\text{Sales}}{\text{Total assets}}\right).$$

$$\begin{array}{c}\text{Return on common}\\\text{equity (ROE)}\end{array} = \frac{\text{Net income available to common stockholders}}{\text{Common equity}}.$$

$$\text{ROE} = \text{ROA} \times \text{Equity multiplier}$$

$$= \frac{\text{Net income}}{\text{Total assets}} \times \frac{\text{Total assets}}{\text{Common equity}}$$

$$= \frac{\text{NI}}{\text{Sales}} \times \frac{\text{Sales}}{\text{TA}} \times \frac{\text{TA}}{\text{CE}}$$

$$\text{Price/earnings (P/E) ratio} = \frac{\text{Market price per share}}{\text{Earnings per share}}.$$

$$\text{Earnings per share} = \frac{\text{Net income available to common stockholders}}{\text{Number of common shares outstanding}}.$$

$$\text{Book value per share} = \frac{\text{Common equity}}{\text{Shares outstanding}}.$$

$$\text{Market/book (M/B) ratio} = \frac{\text{Market price per share}}{\text{Book value per share}}.$$

Chapter 12

$$\text{Full capacity sales} = \frac{\text{Sales level}}{\text{Percentage of capacity used to generate sales level}}.$$

$$\text{TC} = \text{F} + (\text{V} \times \text{Q}).$$

$$Q_{\text{OpBE}} = \frac{\text{F}}{\text{P} - \text{V}} = \frac{\text{F}}{\text{Contribution margin}}.$$

$$S_{\text{OpBE}} = \frac{\text{FC}}{1 - \left(\dfrac{\text{V}}{\text{P}}\right)} = \frac{\text{F}}{\text{Gross profit margin}}.$$

$$\text{DOL} = \frac{\left(\dfrac{\Delta\text{EBIT}}{\text{EBIT}}\right)}{\left(\dfrac{\Delta\text{Q}}{\text{Q}}\right)}.$$

$$DOL_Q = \frac{Q(P - V)}{Q(P - V) - F}.$$

$$DOL_S = \frac{S - VC}{S - VC - F} = \frac{\text{Gross profit}}{\text{EBIT}}.$$

$$EBIT = (P \times Q) - (V \times Q) - F = Q(P - V) - F.$$

$$EBIT_{FinBE} = I + \frac{D_{ps}}{(1 - T)}.$$

$$DFL = \frac{\left(\dfrac{\Delta EPS}{EPS}\right)}{\left(\dfrac{\Delta EBIT}{EBIT}\right)}.$$

$$DFL = \frac{EBIT}{EBIT - I}; \text{ if preferred stock} = 0.$$

$$DFL = \frac{EBIT}{EBIT - [\text{Financial BEP}]}.$$

$$DTL = DOL \times DFL = \frac{S - VC}{EBIT - I}; \text{ if preferred stock} = 0.$$

$$DTL = \frac{\text{Gross profit}}{EBIT - [\text{Financial BEP}]}.$$

Chapter 13

$$\frac{\text{Account}}{\text{balance}} = \left(\begin{array}{c}\text{Amount of} \\ \text{daily activity}\end{array}\right) \times \left(\begin{array}{c}\text{Average life} \\ \text{of the account}\end{array}\right).$$

$$\frac{\text{Inventory}}{\text{conversion period}} = \frac{\text{Inventory}}{\text{CGS}/360}.$$

$$\frac{\text{Receivables}}{\text{collection period}} = DSO = \frac{\text{Receivables}}{\text{Sales}/360}.$$

$$\frac{\text{Payables}}{\text{deferral period}} = DPO = \frac{\text{Accounts payable}}{\text{CGS}/360}.$$

$$\frac{\text{Cash conversion}}{\text{cycle}} = \left(\begin{array}{c}\text{Inventory} \\ \text{conversion period}\end{array}\right) + \left(\begin{array}{c}\text{Receivables} \\ \text{collection period}\end{array}\right) - \left(\begin{array}{c}\text{Payables} \\ \text{deferral period}\end{array}\right).$$

Chapter 14

$$\text{Average inventory} = A = \frac{\text{Units per order}}{2} = \frac{Q}{2}.$$

$$\text{Total carrying cost} = TCC = (C)(PP)(A) = (C)(PP)\left(\frac{Q}{2}\right).$$

Total ordering cost $= \text{TOC} = \text{O}\left(\dfrac{T}{Q}\right).$

Total inventory cost $= \text{TIC} = \text{TCC} + \text{TOC}$
$$= (\text{C})(\text{PP})\left(\frac{Q}{2}\right) + \text{O}\left(\frac{T}{Q}\right).$$

Economic ordering quantity $= \text{EOQ} = \sqrt{\dfrac{2(\text{O})(\text{T})}{(\text{C})(\text{PP})}}.$

Reorder point $= (\text{Lead time in days} \times \text{Daily usage}).$

Chapter 15

Percentage cost per period $= k_{per} = \dfrac{\text{Dollar cost of borrowing}}{\text{Amount of usable funds}}.$

Effective annual rate $= \left[1 + \dfrac{k_{SIMPLE}}{m}\right]^{m} - 1.0 = [1 + k_{per}]^{m} - 1.0.$

Annual percentage rate $= \text{APR} = (k_{per}) \times (m) = k_{SIMPLE}.$

$\begin{array}{c}\text{Compensating} \\ \text{balance requirement}\end{array} = \text{CB} = \begin{array}{c}\text{Principal} \\ \text{amount}\end{array} \times \begin{array}{c}\text{Compensating} \\ \text{balance as a decimal}\end{array}$

$\text{Usable funds} = \left(\begin{array}{c}\text{Face (principal)} \\ \text{amount of the loan}\end{array}\right) - \left(\begin{array}{c}\text{Dollar reductions} \\ \text{from the face value}\end{array}\right)$

$\qquad = \left(\begin{array}{c}\text{Face (principal)} \\ \text{amount of the loan}\end{array}\right) \times \left[1 - \left(\begin{array}{c}\text{Reductions from the face} \\ \text{value stated as a decimal}\end{array}\right)\right]$

$\text{Required loan amount} = \dfrac{\text{Amount of usable funds needed}}{1 - \left(\begin{array}{c}\text{Reductions from the principal} \\ \text{amount stated as a decimal}\end{array}\right)}.$

Chapter 18

Conversion price $= P_c = \dfrac{\text{Par value of bond}}{\text{Conversion ratio}}.$

Index

Page numbers in italics indicate tables and figures.

A

B

Frequently Used Symbols

APR	Annual percentage rate
A/R	Accounts receivable
BP	Break point in MCC schedule
β	Beta coefficient, a measure of an asset's riskiness
b	the fraction of a firm's earnings retained rather than paid out as dividends (in percent)
CAPM	Capital Asset Pricing Model
CF	Cash flow; CF_t is the cash flow in Period t
CR	Conversion ratio
CV	Coefficient of variation
D	Dividend per share of stock (DPS); $\hat{D}_t$ is the dividend expected in Period t
DCF	Discounted cash flow
DFL	Degree of financial leverage
DOL	Degree of operating leverage
DPS	Dividends per share
DSO	Days sales outstanding
DTL	Degree of total leverage
EAR	Effective annual rate
EBIT	Earnings before interest and taxes = net operating income = NOI
EOQ	Economic ordering quantity
EPS	Earnings per share
F	(1) Fixed operating costs
	(2) Percentage flotation cost
FV_n	Future value in n years
FVA_n	Future value of an annuity for n years
g	Growth rate in earnings, dividends, and stock prices
I	Interest rate key on some calculators
INT	Interest payment in dollars
IOS	Investment opportunity schedule
IRR	Internal rate of return
k	(1) A percentage discount rate, or cost of capital; also referred to as i
	(2) Required rate of return
k	historic or realized rate of return
$\bar{k}$	"k bar," historic, or realized, average rate of return
$\hat{k}$	"k hat," an expected rate of return
k^*	Real risk-free rate of interest
k_d	Cost of debt
k_{dT}	After-tax cost of debt = $k_d(1 - T)$
k_e	Cost of new common stock (equity)
k_j	Cost of capital for an individual firm or security
k_M	Cost of capital for "the market," or an "average" stock
k_{SIMPLE}	Nominal risk-free rate of interest
k_{ps}	Cost of preferred stock
k_{RF}	Rate of return on a risk-free security
k_s	(1) Cost of retained earnings
	(2) Required return on a stock